AF814176

All in One®

Recommended by Teachers Trusted by Toppers

CHEMISTRY

Class 11

EVERYTHING YOU NEED TO SCORE

- Simplified NCERT Theory
- In-text & Chapter Exercises
- All Types of Exam Pattern Questions
- CBQs; MCQs, A-R, Case Based
- Sample Question Papers

CBSE Exams 2026

All in One®

Recommended by Teachers Trusted by Toppers

CHEMISTRY

Class 11

EVERYTHING YOU NEED TO SCORE

- Simplified NCERT Theory
- In-text & Chapter Exercises
- All Types of Exam Pattern Questions
- CBQs; MCQs, A-R, Case Based
- Sample Question Papers

CBSE Exams 2026

Authors
Tarnija Midha
Saleha Pervez

arihant
SUCCESS AND NOTHING LESS

arihant
SUCCESS AND NOTHING LESS

ARIHANT PRAKASHAN
(School Division Series)

卐 ADMINISTRATIVE & PRODUCTION OFFICES

Regd. Office

'Ramchhaya' 4577/15, Agarwal Road, Darya Ganj, New Delhi -110002
Tele: 011- 47630600, 43518550; Fax: 011- 23280316

卐 *Head Office*

Kalindi, TP Nagar, Meerut (UP) - 250002, Tel: 0121-7156203, 7156204

卐 SALES & SUPPORT OFFICES

Agra, Ahmedabad, Bengaluru, Bareilly, Chennai, Delhi, Guwahati, Hyderabad, Jaipur, Jhansi, Kolkata, Lucknow, Nagpur & Pune.

PO No : TXT-XX-XXXXXXX-X-XX

Published By Arihant Publications (India) Ltd.

For further information about the books published by Arihant, log on to www.arihantbooks.com or e-mail at info@arihantbooks.com

Follow us on

卐 PRICE ₹500.00

PRODUCTION TEAM

Publishing Managers Mahendra Singh Rawat & Keshav Mohan	*Cover Designer* Salman Shaikh	*Inner Designer* Ankit Tyagi
Project Head Akansha Tomar	*Page Layouting* Sanjay Yadav	*Proof Reader* Nisha, Sarthak

Index *cum* Study Planner

One Book- Endless Features
to Help you Succeed

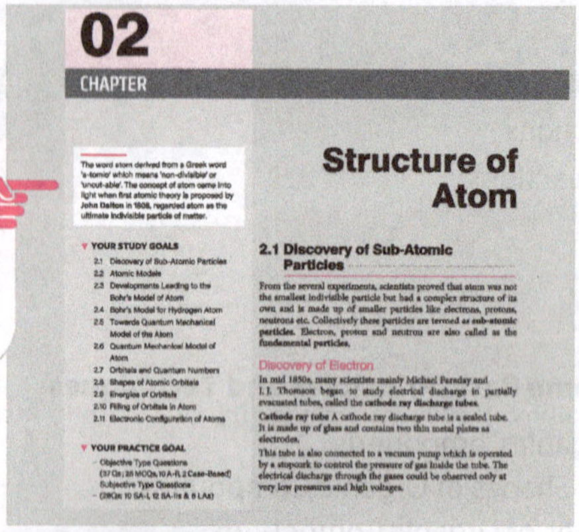
02
CHAPTER

The word atom derived from a Greek word 'a-tomio' which means 'non-divisible' or 'uncut-able'. The concept of atom came into light when first atomic theory is proposed by John Dalton in 1808, regarded atom as the ultimate indivisible particle of matter.

YOUR STUDY GOALS
- 2.1 Discovery of Sub-Atomic Particles
- 2.2 Atomic Models
- 2.3 Developments Leading to the Bohr's Model of Atom
- 2.4 Bohr's Model for Hydrogen Atom
- 2.5 Towards Quantum Mechanical Model of the Atom
- 2.6 Quantum Mechanical Model of Atom
- 2.7 Orbitals and Quantum Numbers
- 2.8 Shapes of Atomic Orbitals
- 2.9 Energies of Orbitals
- 2.10 Filling of Orbitals in Atom
- 2.11 Electronic Configuration of Atoms

YOUR PRACTICE GOAL
- Objective Type Questions (37 Qs; 25 MCQs, 10 A-R, 2 Case-Based) Subjective Type Questions
- (28Qs: 10 SA-I, 12 SA-IIs & 6 LAs)

Structure of Atom

2.1 Discovery of Sub-Atomic Particles

From the several experiments, scientists proved that atom was not the smallest indivisible particle but had a complex structure of its own and is made up of smaller particles like electrons, protons, neutrons etc. Collectively these particles are termed as **sub-atomic particles**. Electron, proton and neutron are also called as the **fundamental particles**.

Discovery of Electron

In mid 1850s, many scientists mainly Michael Faraday and J. J. Thomson began to study electrical discharge in partially evacuated tubes, called the **cathode ray discharge tubes**.

Cathode ray tube A cathode ray discharge tube is a sealed tube. It is made up of glass and contains two thin metal plates as electrodes.

This tube is also connected to a vacuum pump which is operated by a stopcork to control the pressure of gas inside the tube. The electrical discharge through the gases could be observed only at very low pressures and high voltages.

Chapter Intro

A quick information about the coverage of the chapter to explain students about what they are going to study.

2.1 Discovery of Sub-Atomic Particles

From the several experiments, scientists proved that atom was not the smallest indivisible particle but had a complex structure of its own and is made up of smaller particles like electrons, protons, neutrons etc. Collectively these particles are termed as **sub-atomic particles**. Electron, proton and neutron are also called as the **fundamental particles**.

Discovery of Electron

In mid 1850s, many scientists mainly Michael Faraday and J. J. Thomson began to study electrical discharge in partially evacuated tubes, called the **cathode ray discharge tubes**.

Cathode ray tube A cathode ray discharge tube is a sealed tube. It is made up of glass and contains two thin metal plates as electrodes.

This tube is also connected to a vacuum pump which is operated by a stopcork to control the pressure of gas inside the tube. The electrical discharge through the gases could be observed only at very low pressures and high voltages.

TEACHER'S TIP

The energy possessed by one mole of quanta (or photons), i.e. Avogadro's number (N_0) of quanta is called one **Einstein of energy**.

$$(E) = N_0 h\nu = N_0 h\frac{c}{\lambda}.$$

Teacher Tips

Important Points related to given concept to bring students focus on important points.

Simplified Theory

It contains the necessary study material well supported by Definitions, Facts, Figures, Flowcharts, etc.

Quick Test 1

Conceptual Questions

1. Why does the charge to mass ratio of positive rays depend on the residual gas in the discharge tube? Why is the charge to mass ratio of all cathode rays are same?
2. (i) Which of the following will not show deflection from the path on passing through an electric field? Proton, cathode rays, electron, neutron. *NCERT Exemplar*
   (ii) Arrange the following in the increasing order of their e/m values : electron, proton and neutron.
3. In Rutherford's experiment, generally the thin foil of heavy atoms, like gold, platinum etc., have been used to be bombarded by the α-particles.
   If the thin foil of light atoms like aluminium etc., is used, what difference would be observed from the above results?

Numerical Questions

4. In Millikan's experiment, static electric charge on the oil drops has been obtained by shining X-rays. If the static electric charge on the oil drop is -1.282×10^{-18} C, calculate the number of electrons present on it. *NCERT*
5. Find the number and mass of neutrons in 32 mg of O_2 at STP (mass of a neutron $= 1.675\times 10^{-27}$ kg).
6. 2×10^8 atoms of carbon are arranged side by side. Calculate the radius of carbon atom if the length of this arrangement is 2.4 cm. *NCERT*
   Hint : Radius depends upon diameter d as $r = d/2$, so first calculate the diameter by dividing total length with number of carbon atoms present and then calculate radius.
7. (i) Calculate the number of protons, neutrons and electrons in ${}^{80}_{35}Br$.
   (ii) Name the element whose isotope has mass number 14 and 8 neutrons. *NCERT*

Answers

4. 8.0 electrons 5. $1.9270\times 10^{22}, 3.228\times 10^{-5}$ kg 6. 0.060 nm
7. (i) No. of protons = No. of electrons = 35, No. of neutrons = 45 (ii) Carbon

For Solutions, See QR Code on Pg. 82

Quick Tests

To make students understand the chapter in a smooth part-by-part manner, Quick Tests have been given in each chapter. These Exercises help students to assess the understanding of related concepts at regular interval.

One Book- Endless Features

to Help you Succeed

Illustrative Figures

To make the concepts completely visible, illustrative diagrams have been given at various place.

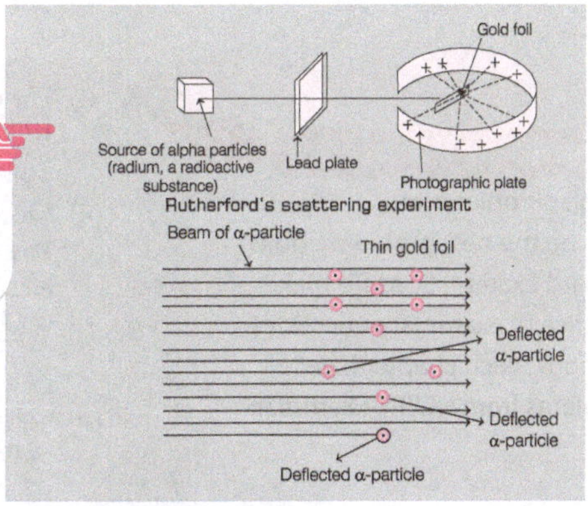

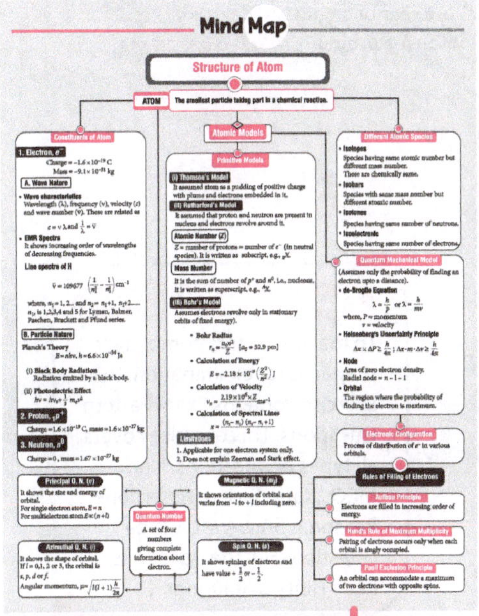

Mind Map

A quick revision visual tool for the complete chapter.

NCERT Questions

To make students completely understand NCERT books, solutions of selected NCERT questions have been given in each chapter.

Example 3 **The wavelength range of the visible spectrum extends from violet (400 nm) to red (750 nm). Express these wavelengths in frequencies (Hz). (1 nm = 10^{-9} m)** **NCERT**

Sol. Given, wavelength of violet light

$$= 400 \text{ nm} = 400 \times 10^{-9} \text{ m}$$

$$\nu = \frac{c}{\lambda} = \frac{3.00 \times 10^{8} \text{ ms}^{-1}}{400 \times 10^{-9} \text{ m}}$$

$$= 7.50 \times 10^{14} \text{ Hz}$$

wavelength of red light = 750 nm

$$= 750 \times 10^{-9} \text{ m}$$

$$\nu = \frac{c}{\lambda} = \frac{3.00 \times 10^{8} \text{ m s}^{-1}}{750 \times 10^{-9} \text{m}}$$

$$= 4.00 \times 10^{14} \text{Hz}$$

The range of visible spectrum is from 4.0×10^{14} to 7.5×10^{14} Hz in terms of frequency units.

One Book- Endless Features

to Help you Succeed

NCERT Exemplar Problems

NCERT Exemplar Problems are considered to be the best problem books for School/Board Examinations. To make students practice of exemplary questions given in this book, each chapter has selected problems from NCERT Exemplar.

9. (i) The electronic configuration of valence shell of Cu is $3d^{10}4s^1$ and not $3d^9 4s^2$. How is this configuration explained?

(ii) Nickel atom can lose two electrons and form Ni^{2+} ion. The atomic number of Ni is 28. From which orbital will nickel lose two electrons? *NCERT Exemplar*

5. (i) Which of the following orbitals are degenerate?

$3d_{xy}, 4d_{xy}, 3d_{z^2}, 3d_{yz}, 4d_{yz}\ 4d_{z^2}$

(ii) Calculate the total number of angular nodes and radial nodes present in 3 p-orbital. *NCERT Exemplar*

SAMPLE QUESTION PAPER 1

A Highly Simulated Sample Question Paper for CBSE Class XI Examination

CHEMISTRY [Fully Solved]

Time : 3 Hours | Max. Marks : 70

General Instructions

Read the following instructions carefully.

1. There are 33 questions in this question paper with internal choice.
2. **SECTION A** consists of 16 Multiple-Choice questions carrying 1 mark each.
3. **SECTION B** consists of 5 Short Answer questions carrying 2 marks each.
4. **SECTION C** consists of 7 Short Answer questions carrying 3 marks each.
5. **SECTION D** consists of 2 Case-Based questions carrying 4 marks each.
6. **SECTION E** consists of 3 Long Answer questions carrying 5 marks each.
7. All questions are compulsory.
8. Use of log tables and calculators is not allowed.

Section-A

The following questions are multiple choice questions with one correct answer. Each question carries 1 mark. There is no internal choice in this section.

1. What will be the K_p for the reaction
$2NOCl(g) \rightleftharpoons 2NO(g) + Cl_2(g)$ at 1000 K?
Given, that K_C at 1000 K is 3.75×10^{-6}.
(a) 3.11×10^{-4}
(b) 0.311×10^{-4}
(c) 31.1×10^{-4}
(d) 0.0311×10^{-4}

2. Why do the deviations occur from idealised shape of H_2O and NH_3 molecules?
(a) Same hybridisation
(b) Different hybridisation
(c) Repulsive effect
(d) None of the above

3. At 363 K, pure water has $[H_3O^+] = 10^{-6}$ M. The value of K_w at this temperature will be
(a) 10^{-6}
(b) 10^{-12}
(c) 10^{-13}
(d) 10^{-14}

4. Two students performed the same experiment separately and each one of them recorded two readings of mass which are given below. Correct reading of mass is 3.0 g.

Students	Readings	
	(i)	(ii)
A	3.01	2.99
B	3.05	2.95

On the basis of given data, mark the correct option out of the following statements.
(a) Results of both the students are neither accurate nor precise.
(b) Results of student A are both precise and accurate.
(c) Results of student B are neither precise nor accurate.
(d) Results of student B are both precise and accurate.

5. Which of the following represents correct increasing order of the boiling point of the given compounds?
(a) $HF < H_2O < NH_3$ (b) $H_2O < HF < NH_3$
(c) $NH_3 < HF < H_2O$ (d) $NH_3 < H_2O < HF$

Sample Question Papers

To make students practice of examination in real sense, there are 5 Sample Question Papers at the end. All these Sample Questions Papers are exactly prepared on the latest syllabus & pattern of examination.

Exam Pattern Exercise

To make students completely prepared for examination, this Exercise contains Exam Pattern Questions. This exercise covers all types of questions, like; MCQs, Case Based, Assertion-Reason, VSA, SA & LA Type Questions. All the questions have Hints & Solutions. .

EXAM PATTERN QUESTIONS

Part I Objective Type Questions

Multiple Choice Questions (MCQs) [1 Mark]

1. Which of the following statements is/are correct regarding Rutherford scattering experiment?
(a) Most of the α-particles passed through the gold foil remain undeflected.
(b) A small fraction of the α-particles was deflected by small angles.
(c) A very few α-particles (~ 1 in 20000) bounced back, i.e. were deflected by nearly 180°.
(d) All of the above

2. Major development(s) responsible for the formulation of Bohr's model of atom were
(a) dual character of the electromagnetic radiation.
(b) experimental results regarding atomic spectra which can be explained only by assuming quantised electronic energy levels in atoms.
(c) Both (a) and (b)
(d) None of the above

D. A black body is a not a perfect radiator of radiant energy.

Choose the correct answer from the options given below.
(a) A, D and C (b) B and C
(c) C and D (d) A, B and C

7. According to Bohr's theory, the radius of electron in an orbit described by principle quantum number (n) and atomic number (Z) is proportional to
(a) Z^2n^2 (b) $\frac{Z^2}{n^2}$ (c) $\frac{Z^2}{n}$ (d) $\frac{n^2}{Z}$

8. The correct mathematical expression of Heisenberg's uncertainty principle is
(a) $\frac{\Delta x}{\Delta v_x} > \frac{h}{4\pi m}$ (b) $\Delta x \times \Delta v_x > \frac{h}{4\pi m}$
(c) $\Delta x \times \Delta v_x = \frac{h}{4\pi m}$ (d) $\Delta x \times \Delta v_x \geq \frac{h}{4\pi m}$

Latest Course Structure

Time: 3 Hrs **Total Marks : 70**

Units	Title	Marks
I	Some Basic Concepts of Chemistry	7
II	Structure of Atom	9
III	Classification of Elements and Periodicity in Properties	6
IV	Chemical Bonding and Molecular Structure	7
V	Chemical Thermodynamics	9
VI	Equilibrium	7
VII	Redox Reactions	4
VIII	Organic Chemistry: Some basic Principles and Techniques	11
IX	Hydrocarbons	10
	Total	70

UNIT I Some Basic Concepts of Chemistry

General Introduction: Importance and scope of chemistry. Nature of matter, laws of chemical combination, Dalton's atomic theory: concept of elements, atoms and molecules. Atomic and molecular masses, mole concept and molar mass, percentage composition, empirical and molecular formula, chemical reactions, stoichiometry and calculations based on stoichiometry.

UNIT II Structure of Atom

Discovery of Electron, Proton and Neutron, atomic number, isotopes and isobars. Thomson's model and its limitations. Rutherford's model and its limitations. Bohr's model and its limitations, concept of shells and subshells, dual nature of matter and light, de-Broglie's relationship, Heisenberg uncertainty principle, concept of orbitals, quantum numbers, shapes of *s*, *p* and *d*-orbitals, rules for filling electrons in orbitals - Aufbau principle, Pauli's exclusion principle and Hund's rule, electronic configuration of atoms, stability of half-filled and completely filled orbitals.

UNIT III Classification of Elements and Periodicity in Properties

Significance of classification, brief history of the development of periodic table, modern periodic law and the present form of periodic table, periodic trends in properties of elements -atomic radii, ionic radii, inert gas radii, Ionisation enthalpy, electron gain enthalpy, electronegativity, valency. Nomenclature of elements with atomic number greater than 100.

UNIT IV : Chemical Bonding and Molecular Structure

Valence electrons, ionic bond, covalent bond, bond parameters, Lewis structure, polar character of covalent bond, covalent character of ionic bond, valence bond theory, resonance, geometry of covalent molecules, VSEPR theory, concept of hybridisation, involving *s*, *p* and *d*-orbitals and shapes of some simple molecules, molecular orbital theory of homonuclear diatomic molecules(qualitative idea only), Hydrogen bond.

UNIT V Chemical Thermodynamics

Concepts of System and types of systems, surroundings, work, heat, energy, extensive and intensive properties, state functions. First law of thermodynamics -internal energy and enthalpy, heat capacity and specific heat, measurement of ΔU and ΔH, Hess's law of constant heat summation, enthalpy of bond dissociation, combustion, formation, atomisation, sublimation, phase transition, ionisation, solution and dilution. Second law of Thermodynamics (brief introduction) Introduction of entropy as a state function, Gibb's energy change for spontaneous and non-spontaneous processes, criteria for equilibrium. Third law of thermodynamics (brief introduction).

UNIT VI Equilibrium

Equilibrium in physical and chemical processes, dynamic nature of equilibrium, law of mass action, equilibrium constant, factors affecting equilibrium - Le-Chatelier's principle, ionic equilibrium- ionisation of acids and bases, strong and weak electrolytes, degree of ionisation, ionisation of polybasic acids, acid strength, concept of pH, hydrolysis of salts (elementary idea), buffer solution, Henderson Equation, solubility product, common ion effect (with illustrative examples).

UNIT VII Redox Reactions

Concept of oxidation and reduction, redox reactions, oxidation number, balancing redox reactions, in terms of loss and gain of electrons and change in oxidation number, applications of redox reactions.

UNIT VIII Organic Chemistry -Some Basic Principles and Techniques

General introduction, methods of purification, qualitative and quantitative analysis, classification and IUPAC nomenclature of organic compounds. Electronic displacements in a covalent bond: inductive effect, electromeric effect, resonance and hyperconjugation. Homolytic and heterolytic fission of a covalent bond: free radicals, carbocations, carbanions, electrophiles and nucleophiles, types of organic reactions.

UNIT IX Hydrocarbons

Aliphatic Hydrocarbons:

Alkanes - Nomenclature, isomerism, conformation (ethane only), physical properties, chemical reactions including free radical mechanism of halogenation, combustion and pyrolysis.

Alkenes - Nomenclature, structure of double bond (ethene), geometrical isomerism, physical properties, methods of preparation, chemical reactions: addition of hydrogen, halogen, water, hydrogen halides (Markownikov's addition and peroxide effect), ozonolysis, oxidation, mechanism of electrophilic addition.

Alkynes - Nomenclature, structure of triple bond (ethyne), physical properties, methods of preparation, chemical reactions: acidic character of alkynes, addition reaction of - hydrogen, halogens, hydrogen halides and water.

Aromatic Hydrocarbons: Introduction, IUPAC nomenclature, benzene: resonance, aromaticity, chemical properties: mechanism of electrophilic substitution. Nitration, sulphonation, halogenation, Friedel Craft's alkylation and acylation, directive influence of functional group in monosubstituted benzene. Carcinogenicity and toxicity.

Note: The following topics are included in the syllabus but will be assessed only formatively to reinforce understanding without adding to summative assessments. This reduces academic stress while ensuring meaningful learning. Schools can integrate these with existing chapters as they align well. Relevant NCERT textual material is enclosed for reference.

1. *s* & *p* Block Elements

Electronic configuration, Atomic & Ionic radii, Ionization Enthalpy, Hydration Enthalpy and general trends in physical and chemical properties of s and p-block elements across the periods and down the groups; unique behavior of the first element in each group.

2. The Gaseous State

Qualitative treatment of Gas laws, Ideal gas equation and deviations from it.

Practicals

Practicals should be conducted alongside the concepts taught in theory classes

LIST OF EXPERIMENTS

Evaluation Scheme for Examination	Marks
Volumetric Analysis	08
Salt Analysis	08
Content Based Experiment	06
Project Work	04
Class Record and Viva	04
Total	**30**

PRACTICAL SYLLABUS

Micro-chemical methods are available for several of the practical experiments. Wherever possible, such techniques should be used.

A. Basic Laboratory Techniques

1. Cutting glass tube and glass rod
2. Bending a glass tube
3. Drawing out a glass jet
4. Boring a cork

B. Characterisation and Purification of Chemical Substances

1. Determination of melting point of an organic compound.
2. Determination of boiling point of an organic compound.
3. Crystallisation of impure sample of any one of the following: Alum, Copper Sulphate, Benzoic Acid.

C. Experiments based on pH

(a) Any one of the following experiments:

- Determination of pH of some solutions obtained from fruit juices, solution of known and varied concentrations of acids, bases and salts using pH paper or universal indicator.
- Comparing the pH of solutions of strong and weak acids of same concentration. Study the pH change in the titration of a strong base using universal indicator.

(b) Study the pH change by common-ion in case of weak acids and weak bases.

D. Chemical Equilibrium

One of the following experiments:

(a) Study the shift in equilibrium between ferric ions and thiocyanate ions by increasing/ decreasing the concentration of either of the ions.

(b) Study the shift in equilibrium between $[Co(H_2O)_6]^{2+}$ and chloride ions by changing the concentration of either of the ions.

E. Quantitative Estimation

(i) Using a mechanical balance/electronic balance.

(ii) Preparation of standard solution of oxalic acid.

(iii) Determination of strength of a given solution of sodium hydroxide by titrating it against standard solution of oxalic acid.

(iv) Preparation of standard solution of Sodium carbonate.

(v) Determination of strength of a given solution of hydrochloric acid by titrating it against standard sodium carbonate solution.

F. Qualitative Analysis

(a) Determination of one anion and one cation in a given salt

Cations- Pb^{2+}, Cu^{2+}, As^{3+}, Al^{3+}, Fe^{3+}, Mn^{2+}, Ni^{2+}, Zn^{2+}, Co^{2+}, Ca^{2+}, Sr^{2+}, Ba^{2+}, Mg^{2+}, NH_4^+

Anions – CO_3^{2-} , S^{2-}, SO_3^{2-} , NO_2^- , SO_4^{2-} , NO_3^- , Cl^- , Br^-, I^-, PO_4^{3-} , CH_3COO^-
(Note: Insoluble salts excluded)

(b) Detection of NH_4^+ nitrogen, sulphur, chlorine in organic compounds.

(c) PROJECTS

Scientific investigations involving laboratory testing and collecting information from other sources.

A few suggested Projects

- Checking the bacterial contamination in drinking water by testing sulphide ion.
- Study of the methods of purification of water.
- Testing the hardness, presence of iron, fluoride, chloride, etc., depending upon the regional variation in drinking water and study of causes of presence of these ions above permissible limit (if any).
- Investigation of the foaming capacity of different washing soaps and the effect of addition of sodium carbonate on it.
- Study the acidity of different samples of tea leaves.
- Determination of the rate of evaporation of different liquids. Study the effect of acids and bases on the tensile strength of fibers.
- Study of acidity of fruit and vegetable juices.

Note: Any other investigatory project, which involves about 10 periods of work, can be chosen with the approval of the teacher.

01

CHAPTER

Some Basic Concepts of Chemistry

Chemistry is the branch of science that studies the preparation, properties, structure and reactions of matter. The basic constituents of matter are atoms and molecules. So, chemistry is called the science of atoms and molecules.

YOUR STUDY GOALS

YOUR PRACTICE GOAL

- Objective Type Questions (32 Qs ; 19 MCQs, 11 A-R & 2 Case Study)
- Subjective Type Questions (31 Qs; 11 SA-I, 12 SA-II & 08 LA)

1.1 Importance and Scope of Chemistry

Chemistry plays an improtant role in daily life. Some of its applications are listed below

- Principles of chemistry are applicable in diverse areas like weather patterns, functioning of brain and operations of a computer, production in chemical industries, manufacturing fertilizers, alkalis, acids, salts, dyes, polymers, drugs, soaps, detergents, metals alloys, etc., including new materials.
- Chemistry helps in the synthesis of many life saving drugs such as ***cis*-platin** and **taxol** (effective in cancer therapy), AZT or azidothymidine [effective for **AIDS** (Acquired Immuno Deficiency Syndrome) patients].
- Better understanding of the chemical principles and properties leads to the production of optical fibres, conducting polymers, etc.
- Several advances in automotive and aerospace engineering rely on improved materials such as ceramics, which are synthesised and engineered in chemistry.
- Safer alternatives to environmentally hazardous substances such as CFCs (chlorofluorocarbons, responsible for ozone layer depletion), have been successfully synthesised.

1.2 Nature of Matter

Matter is anything that has mass and occupies space, e.g. book, pen, pencil, etc.

States of Matter

Depending upon their physical characteristics, matter is generally classified as

(i) **Solids** They have definite shape and definite volume. e.g. ice, pencil, wood, etc.

(ii) **Liquids** They have definite volume but not a definite shape. They usually take the shape of the container in which they are kept. e.g. water, milk, etc.

(iii) **Gases** They have no definite shape or volume. They completely occupy the space in the container in which they are placed. e.g. water vapour, air, etc.

Note The two other states i.e. plasma and Bose-Einstein condensate is also known. These forms exist only in extreme conditions of temperature and pressure.

The three states of matter are interconvertible under different conditions of temperature and pressure.

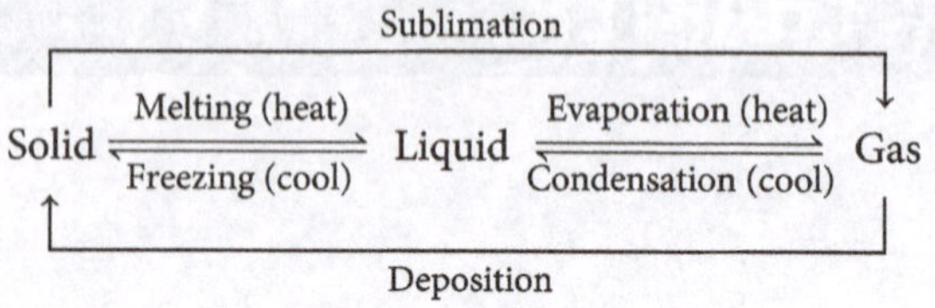

The characteristic properties of the three states are explained in the table given below.

Differentiating the Properties of Solids, Liquids and Gases

Characteristics	Solids	Liquids	Gases
Arrangement of particles	Particles are held very close to each other in an ordered manner.	Particles are close to each other but not so ordered as solids.	Particles are far apart as compared to that of solids and liquids.
Movement of particles	Particles are not free to move.	Particles can move around.	The movement of particles is easy and fast.
Compressibility and hardness	Hard and incompressible due to close packed structure.	More compressible due to more empty space.	Most compressible due to large interparticle empty space.
Volume	Definite	Definite	Not definite
Shape	Definite	Not definite, takes the shape of the container in which they are kept.	Not definite, completely occupy the container in which they are placed.
Diffusion	They do not diffuse.	They show slow diffusion.	They show fast diffusion.

Classification of Matter

Depending upon the chemical composition, at the macroscopic or bulk level, matter is classified as

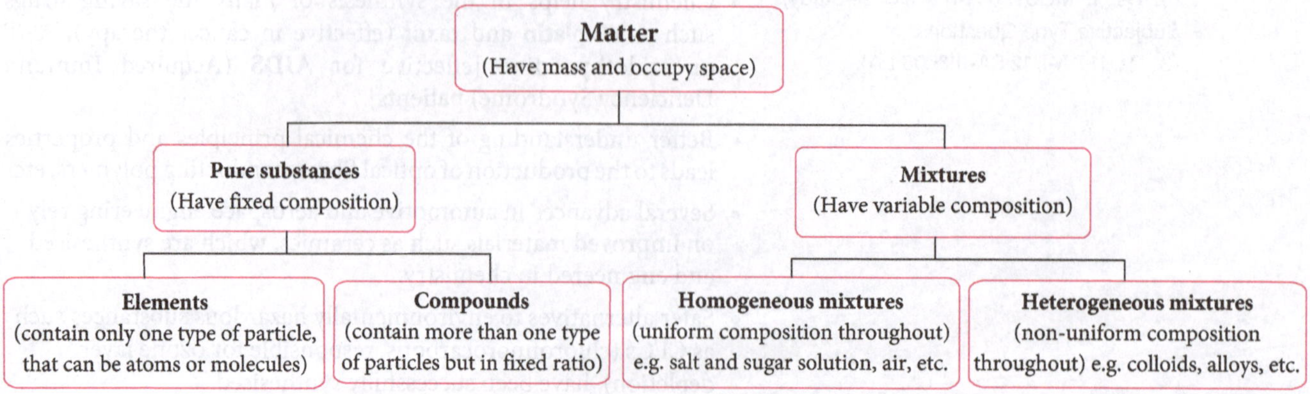

A brief description for classification of matter is given below.

1. Pure Substances

They have a fixed composition and their constituent particles cannot be separated by physical methods, e.g. gold, silver, water, glucose, etc.

A pure substance can be classified as an element or a compound.

(i) **Element** An element is defined as a pure substance that contains only one kind of particle which may be an atom or a molecule. e.g. sodium, copper, silver, gold, aluminium, etc.

Depending upon the physical and chemical properties, the elements are classified as metals, non-metals and metalloids.

(ii) **Compound** A molecule of a compound is formed by the combination of two or more atoms of different elements in a fixed ratio by mass. e.g. water, ammonia, carbon dioxide, gypsum, sugar, etc.

The properties of a compound are different from those of its constituent elements. e.g. H_2 and O_2 are gases, whereas the compound formed by their combination, i.e. water is a liquid.

2. Mixtures

Two or more substances mix together in any ratio to form **mixture**, e.g. air, milk, tea, etc. Pure substances forming mixtures are called its **components**. The components of a mixture can be separated by using physical methods.

Mixture may be categorised into two types

(i) **Homogeneous mixture** The particles of components of this mixture are uniformly distributed (mixed) throughout the bulk of the mixture which cannot be seen separately and its composition is uniform throughout. e.g. salt solution, air, etc.

(ii) **Heterogeneous mixture** The particles of components of this mixture are not uniformly distributed (mixed) throughout the bulk of the mixture and different components can be visible, e.g. mixture of salt and sugar, gunpowder, smoke, etc.

1.3 Properties of Matter and their Measurement

Each substance is associated with some unique set of characteristics, which are collectively called as the **properties of matter**.

The properties of matter are categorised into two types :

(i) Physical Properties

Those properties which can be measured or observed without changing the identity or the composition of the substance are called **physical properties**, e.g. colour, odour, melting point, boiling point, density, etc.

(ii) Chemical Properties

Those properties which requires a chemical change to occur for their measurement or observation are known as **chemical properties**, e.g. characteristic reactions of different substances like acidity, basicity, combustibility, etc.

Unit of Measurement

Several properties of matter like length, area, volume, etc., are quantitative in nature and are called **physical quantities.** These quantities are measured by the help of units.

Thus, a unit is defined as *"the standard of reference chosen to measure a physical quantity"*.

Each physical quantity is represented by a number followed by units in which it is measured. e.g. The length of a pen is 10 cm, here 10 is a number and cm denotes centimetre the unit in which the length is measured.

There are two different systems of measurement, called the **English system** and **Metric system**. Now a days, SI system is widely accepted.

The International System of Units (SI Units)

This system was established by the 11th General Conference on Weights and Measurements. The SI system has 7 base units. These 7 base units are called the **fundamental units,** which are independent and cannot be derived from any other units. These units alongwith their symbols are tabulated.

Base Physical Quantities and their Units

Base physical quantity	Symbol for quantity	Name of SI unit	Symbol for SI unit
Length	l	metre	m
Mass	m	kilogram	kg
Time	t	second	s
Electric current	I	ampere	A
Thermodynamic temperature	T	kelvin	K
Amount of substance	n	mole	mol
Luminous intensity	I_v	candela	cd

The definitions of the SI base units are given in the following table.

Definitions of SI Base Units

Unit of length	metre	• It is defined by taking a fixed numerical value of speed of light in vacuum (c) to be 299792458 when expressed in the unit ms^{-1}. • The second here is defined in terms of the caesium frequency (ΔV_{Cs}).
Unit of mass	kilogram	• It is defined by taking the fixed numerical value of the Planck constant (h) to be 6.62607015 $\times 10^{-34}$ when expressed in the unit Js (or kgm^2s^{-1}). • Here, the metre and the second are defined in terms of c and ΔV_{Cs}.
Unit of time	second	• It is defined by taking the fixed numerical value of the caesium frequency (ν_{Cs}), the unperturbed ground state hyperfine transition frequency of the caesium-133 atom, to be 9192631770 when expressed in the unit Hz, which is equal to s^{-1}.
Unit of electric current	ampere	• It is defined by taking the fixed numerical value of the elementary charge (e) to be 1.602176634 $\times 10^{-19}$, when expressed in the unit C which is equal to As. • Here, the second is defined in terms of ΔV_{Cs}.
Unit of thermodynamic temperature	Kelvin	• It is defined by taking the fixed numerical value of the Boltzmann constant (k) to be 1.380649×10^{-23} when expressed in the unit JK^{-1} (or $kg\,m^2\,s^{-2}\,K^{-1}$). • Here, the kilogram, metre and second are defined in terms of h, c and ΔV_{Cs}.
Unit of amount of substance	mole	• One mole of a substance contains exactly $6.02214076 \times 10^{23}$ elementary entities. • This number is the fixed numerical value of the Avogadro constant (N_A) when expressed in the unit mol^{-1} and is called as the Avogadro number. • The amount of substance (n) of a system is a measure of the number of specified elementary entities, which may be an atom, a molecule, an ion, an electron, any other particle or specified group of particles.
Unit of luminous intensity	Candela	• It is defined by taking the fixed numerical value of the luminous efficiency of monochromatic radiation of frequency 540×10^{12} Hz (K_{cd}) to be 683 when expressed in the unit lm. W^{-1} (or cd. sr. W^{-1} or cd. sr. Kg^{-1} $m^{-2}s^3$). • Here, the kilogram, metre and second are defined in terms of h, c and ΔV_{Cs}.

Prefixes

Some physical quantities are either too small or too large.

To change the order of magnitude, these are expressed by using prefixes before the name of the base units. These standard prefixes allow us to reduce or enlarge the base units.

The various prefixes are listed in the following table

Prefixes Used in SI System

Multiple	Prefix	Symbol	Multiple	Prefix	Symbol
10^{-1}	deci	d	10^{1}	deca	da
10^{-2}	centi	c	10^{2}	hecto	h
10^{-3}	milli	m	10^{3}	kilo	k
10^{-6}	micro	μ	10^{6}	mega	M
10^{-9}	nano	n	10^{9}	giga	G
10^{-12}	pico	p	10^{12}	tera	T
10^{-15}	femto	f	10^{15}	peta	P
10^{-18}	atto	a	10^{18}	exa	E
10^{-21}	zepto	z	10^{21}	zeta	Z
10^{-24}	yocto	y	10^{24}	yotta	Y

Some Physical Quantities

Some major physical quantities are discussed below :

(i) Mass and Weight

- **Mass** (m) is the amount of matter present in a substance. It remains constant for a substance at all the places. **Its unit** (SI unit) **is kilogram** (kg) **but in laboratories usually gram** (1 kg = 1000 g) **is used.** Analytical balance or electrical balance is used to measure the mass of a substance.
- **Weight** (w) is the force exerted by gravity on an object. It varies from place to place due to change in gravity. Its unit is Newton (N).

$$w = m \times g$$

where, m = mass and g = gravity.

(ii) Volume

The space occupied by matter is called its **volume.**

$$\text{Volume} = (\text{length})^3 = m^3$$

Thus, SI unit of volume is m^3. However, in laboratory, smaller volumes like cm^3 (or mL, i.e. millilitre) or dm^3 (or L, i.e. litre) are used.

A common unit, **litre** (L) is used for the measurement of volume of liquids. (L is not a SI unit).

These terms are correlated as

$$\mathbf{1\ L = 1000\ mL = 1000\ cm^3 = 1 dm^3}$$

$$\mathbf{1\ m^3 = 10^6\ cm^3 = 10^3\ dm^3 = 10^3\ L}$$

Example 1 **Convert the following into basic units.**
(i) 28.7 pm (ii) 15.15 μs (iii) 25365 mg

Hint The basic units for length is meter (m), for time is second (s) and for mass is kilogram (kg).

Sol. (i) $28.7\ \text{pm} \times \dfrac{10^{-12}\text{m}}{1\ \text{pm}} = 2.87 \times 10^{-11}\text{m}$

(ii) $15.15\mu\text{s} \times \dfrac{10^{-6}\text{s}}{1\mu\text{s}} = 1.515 \times 10^{-5}\ \text{s}$

(iii) $25365\ \text{mg} \times \dfrac{1\text{g}}{1000\ \text{mg}} \times \dfrac{1\text{kg}}{1000\ \text{g}} = 2.5365 \times 10^{-2}\ \text{kg}$

(iii) Density

It is defined as the amount of mass per unit volume.

Density = Mass/Volume

Its units are $kg\ m^{-3}$ or $g\ cm^{-3}$. (Here, kg or g represents mass and m^3 or cm^3 represents volume).

Density of a substance tells about how closely its particles are packed.

Example 2 **A liquid has a volume of 49.0 cm^3 and a mass of 57.642 g. Find out the density of this liquid in SI unit.**

Sol. $\text{Density} = \dfrac{\text{Mass (kg)}}{\text{Volume (m}^3)}$

$\text{Mass} = 57.642\ \text{g} = 57.642 \times 10^{-3}\ \text{kg}$

$\text{Volume} = 49.0\ \text{cm}^3 = 49.0 \times (10^{-2})^3\ \text{m}^3 = 49.0 \times 10^{-6}\text{m}^3$

$\therefore \text{Density} = \dfrac{57.642 \times 10^{-3}}{49.0 \times 10^{-6}} = 1.176 \times 10^3\ \text{kg/m}^3$

(iv) Temperature

It is defined as the degree of hotness or coldness. Several scales are used to measure temperature, three common scales are **°C** (degree celsius), **K** (kelvin) and **°F** (degree Fahrenheit). **K is the SI unit of temperature.**

The relationship between kelvin and celsius scale is

$$°\text{C} = \text{K} - 273.15$$

or

$$\text{K} = °\text{C} + 273.15$$

The lowest temperature permitted in nature is − 273.15 °C (0 K). This temperature is known as **absolute zero.**

Similarly, the celsius and Fahrenheit scales are related as

$$°\text{C} = \frac{5}{9}(°\text{F} - 32) \text{ or } °\text{F} = \frac{9}{5}(°\text{C}) + 32$$

Note The temperature below 0°C, having negative values are possible in Celsius scale but in Kelvin scale, negative temperature is not possible.

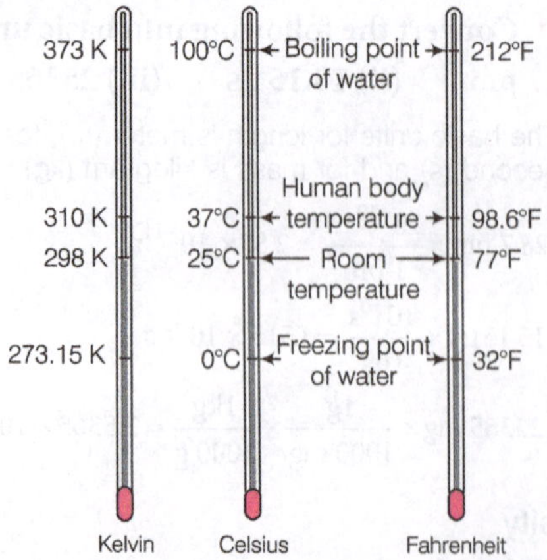

Thermometers using different temperature scales

Example 3 **Convert the following temperatures into degree Fahrenheit.**

(i) 25°C, the room temperature.

(ii) 35°C, physiological (human body) temperature.

Sol. (i) Given, °C = 25°C

$$°F = \frac{9}{5}°C + 32$$

$$= \frac{9}{5} \times 25 + 32 = 45 + 32 = 77°F$$

(ii) Given, °C = 35°C

$$°F = \frac{9}{5}°C + 32$$

$$= \frac{9}{5} \times 35 + 32 = 63 + 32 = 95°F$$

Example 4 **At what temperature will both the Celsius and Fahrenheit scales read the same value?**

Sol. Suppose both read the same value as x.

Then as $°C = \frac{5}{9}(°F - 32)$

$\therefore \quad x = 5/9\,(x - 32)$ or $9x = 5x - 160$

or $\quad 4x = -160$ or $x = -40°$

Example 5 **A measured temperature on Fahrenheit scale is 200°F. What will be this reading on Celsius scale?** **NCERT Exemplar**

Sol. The temperatures on two scales are related to each other by the following relationship, $°F = \frac{9}{5}(°C) + 32$

Putting the values in above equation,

$$200 - 32 = \frac{9}{5}(°C)$$

$$\Rightarrow \quad \frac{9}{5}(°C) = 168$$

$$\Rightarrow \quad t°C = \frac{168 \times 5}{9} = 93.3°C$$

(v) Length

Though the SI unit of length is **metre**, yet it is very common to express length in Angstrom (Å) or nanometre (nm) or picometre (pm).

These are related to SI unit as follows

$$1\,Å = 10^{-10}\ m,\ 1 nm = 10^{-9}\ m,\ 1\ pm = 10^{-12} m$$

Uncertainty in Measurement

In the study of chemistry, there are several ways by which the numbers are handled conveniently and the data is presented realistically with certainty to the possible extent. These ways are scientific notation, significant figures and dimensional analysis.

Scientific Notation

In scientific notation, any number can be represented in the form $N \times 10^n$ where n is an exponent having positive or negative values and N is a number (called digit term) which varies between 1.000... and 9.999....

e.g. 943.876 is written as 9.43876×10^2 in scientific notation, i.e. decimal is moved two places towards left so that only one non-zero digit is left and the number of places moved (2) is the exponent of 10 in scientific notation.

While performing mathematical operations on numbers expressed in scientific notations, following points should be kept in mind.

(i) **Calculations involving multiplication and division** These two operations follow the same rule which are there for exponential numbers, i.e. in multiplication, the number N before the factor 10^n in scientific notation are multiplied and the exponents of 10 are added up. While, in division, the N are divided and the exponents (n) are subtracted.

Let the two numbers be $N_1 \times 10^n$ and $N_2 \times 10^n$, then

Multiplication $(N_1 \times 10^n) \times (N_2 \times 10^n)$

$$= (N_1 + N_2) \times 10^n$$

Division $(N_1 \times 10^n) \div (N_2 \times 10^n) = \frac{N_1}{N_2} \times 10^{(n_1 - n_2)}$

(ii) **Calculations involving addition and subtraction** For these two operations, first the numbers are written in such a way that they have same exponent. After that, 10^n is taken out as common and the coefficients are added or subtracted as the case may be.

Let the two numbers be $N_1 \times 10^n$ and $N_2 \times 10^n$, then

Addition $(N_1 \times 10^n)+(N_2 \times 10^n)=(N_1+N_2)\times 10^n$

Subtraction $(N_1 \times 10^n)-(N_2 \times 10^n)=(N_1-N_2)\times 10^n$

Example 6 Express the following in the scientific notation.

(i) 0.000968 (ii) 157428

(iii) 90,000 (iv) $(5.7\times 10^6)\times(4.2\times 10^{-2})$

(v) $(6.8\times 10^{-9})\div(1.4\times 10^{-6})$

(vi) $(4.56\times 10^3+2.62\times 10^2)$

(vii) $(9.87\times 10^{-3}-2.26\times 10^{-4})$

Sol. (i) $0.000968 = 9.68\times 10^{-4}$

(ii) $157428 = 1.57428\times 10^5$

(iii) $90,000 = 9\times 10^4$

(iv) $(5.7\times 10^6)\times(4.2\times 10^{-2}) = (5.7\times 4.2)(10^{6+(-2)})$
$= 23.94\times 10^4 = 2.394\times 10^5$

(v) $(6.8\times 10^{-9})\div(1.4\times 10^{-6}) = \left(\frac{6.8}{1.4}\right)\times(10^{-9-(-6)})$
$= 4.857\times 10^{-3}$

(vi) $(4.56\times 10^3+2.62\times 10^2)$
$= 45.6\times 10^2+2.62\times 10^2 = (45.6+2.62)\times 10^2$
$= 48.22\times 10^2 = 4.822\times 10^3$

(vii) $(9.87\times 10^{-3}-2.26\times 10^{-4})$
$= 9.87\times 10^{-3}-0.226\times 10^{-3} = (9.87-0.226)\times 10^{-3}$
$= 9.644\times 10^{-3}$

Accuracy and Precision

- **Accuracy** is the agreement of a particular value to the true value of the result or it is a measure of the difference between the experimental value or the mean value of a set of measurements and the true value.

  Accuracy = Mean value − True value

  Smaller the difference between the mean value and the true value, the larger is the accuracy. Accuracy also expresses the correctness of measurement.

- **Precision** refers to the closeness of various measurements for the same quantity or it is expressed as the difference between a measured value or the individual value and the arithmetic mean value for a series of measurements.

  Precision = Individual value − Arithmetic mean value

Smaller the difference between the individual values of repeated measurements, the greater is the precision.

Example 7 Two students performed the same experiment separately and each one of them recorded two readings of mass which are given below. Correct reading of mass is 4.0 g. On the basis of given data, what would you infer about the accuracy and precision in the readings of students *A* and *B*?

Students	Readings	
	(i)	(ii)
A	4.01	3.99
B	4.05	3.95

Sol. Average readings of student, $A = \frac{4.01+3.99}{2} = 4.00$

Average readings of student, $B = \frac{4.05+3.95}{2} = 4.00$

Correct reading = 4.00. For both the students, average value is same as the correct value. Hence, readings of both are accurate.

Readings of student *A* are close to each other (differ only by 0.02) and also close to the correct reading, hence, readings of *A* are precise also. But readings of *B* are not close to each other (differ by 0.1) and hence are not precise.

Significant Figures

These are meaningful digits which are known with certainty plus one which is estimated or uncertain. e.g. If we write a measurement as 49.6 g, we say that 49 is certain and 6 is uncertain and the uncertainty would be ±1 in the last digit.

Note The number of certain digits depends upon the precision of the instrument used for the purpose.

Rules for Counting the Number of Significant Figures

The following rules are followed to count the number of significant figures in a particular number.

- All non-zero digits are significant, e.g. In 285 cm, there are three significant figures and in 0.35 mL, there are two significant figures.
- Zeros between two non-zero digits are significant. e.g. There are four significant figures in 1007.
- Trailing zeros are significant only if the digit contains a decimal point. e.g. 1.560 have 4 significant numbers whereas 450 has 2 significant figures. Such numbers are better represented in scientific notation.

- Leading zeros are not significant because their purpose is simply to place the decimal point.
  e.g. In 0.05, there is only one significant figure whereas 0.0060500 have five significant figures.
- Defined values or counting numbers have infinite number of significant figures, as these are exact numbers and can be represented by writing infinite number of zeros after placing a decimal.
  i.e. $2 = 2.000000$
  or $20 = 20.000000$
- In numbers written in scientific notation, all digits are significant. e.g. 4.01×10^2 has three significant figures, and 8.256×10^{-3} has four significant figures.

Significant Figures in Operational Calculations

(i) In Case of Addition and Subtraction

When the two or more digits are added or subtracted the result cannot have more digits to the right of the decimal point than either of the original numbers. e.g.

1.	6.611	Each number has three decimal places, so the answer has to be reported up to three decimal places. The significant figures in each of the terms is 4 but the result has 5 significant figures.
	5.234	
	+ 2.021	
Actual sum	13.866	
Reported sum	13.866	
2.	19.26	The first number has 2 decimal places and the second has 5 decimal places, so the answer is reported up to 2 decimal place only.
	− 11.02534	
Actual difference	8.23466	
Reported difference	8.23	

(ii) In Case of Multiplication and Division

In these operations, the result must be reported with no more significant figures than there are in the measurement with the least significant figures. e.g.

	41.012	The first term has 5 significant figures, while the second term has 3 significant figures, so the result can have only 3 significant figures.
	× 1.21	
Actual product	49.62452	
Reported product	49.6	

The presence of exact numbers in an expression does not affect the number of significant figures in the answer because exact numbers have infinite number of significant figures.

e.g. $$\frac{4.28 \times 0.146 \times 3}{0.0418} = 44.84784$$

Correct answer is 44.8.

Example 8 **How many significant figures should be present in the answer of the following calculations?**

(i) $$\frac{0.02856 \times 298.15 \times 0.112}{0.5785}$$

(ii) 5×5.364

(iii) $0.8125 + 0.7864 + 0.8215$

Sol. (i) Least precise number of the calculation is 0.112.
Number of significant figures in the answer = Number of significant figures in the least precise number = 3.

(ii) Least precise number of calculation = 5.364.
Number of significant figures in the answer = Number of significant figures in 5.364 = 4.

(iii) Since, the least number of decimal places in each term is four, the number of significant figures in the answer is also 4.

Rounding off the Numbers

The numbers are rounded off to limit the result of a mathematical operation to required number of significant figures. While rounding off the numbers, keep following points in the mind.

- If the rightmost digit to be removed is more than 5, the preceding number is increased by one.
  e.g. in case of 1.386, if we have to remove 6, we have to round off it to 1.39.
- If the rightmost digit to be removed is less than 5, the preceding number is not changed. e.g. In case of 4.334, if 4 is to be removed, the result is rounded off to 4.33.
- If the rightmost digit to be removed is 5, then the preceding number is not changed in case of an even number but it is increased by one in case of an odd number. e.g. If 6.35 is to be rounded by removing 5, we have to increase 3 to 4 giving 6.4 as the result. However, if 6.25 is to be rounded off, it is rounded off to 6.2.

TEACHER'S TIP
In multiple step calculations, do not round off until the end, however keep significant figure in mind.

Example 9 **Round off the following, upto three significant figures.**

(i) 34.216 (ii) 10.4107
(iii) 0.04597 (iv) 2808

Sol. (i) 34.216

The digit to be removed is less than 5, therefore the preceding digit is not changed.

∴ 34.216 rounded upto three significant figures =34.2

(ii) 10.4107

The digit to be removed is less than 5, therefore the preceding digit is not changed.

∴ 10.4107 rounded up to three significant figures =10.4

(iii) 0.04597

The digit to be removed is more than 5, therefore the preceding digit is increased by one.

∴0.04597 is rounded up to three significant figures =0.0460

(iv) 2808

This number can be written as 2.808×10^3.

The digit to be removed is more than 5, therefore the preceding digit is increased by one.

∴ 2.808×10^3 is rounded up to three significant figures $= 2.81 \times 10^3$

Example 10 **Express the result of the given calculation to the appropriate number of significant figures.**

$$\frac{3.24 \times 0.08666}{5.006}$$

Sol. $\frac{3.24 \times 0.08666}{5.006} = 0.0560883$ (Actual result)

As 3.24 has least number of significant figures, i.e. 3, the result should contain 3 significant figures only. Hence, the result will be reported as 0.0561 (after rounding off).

Dimensional Analysis

In calculations, many of the times it become necessary to convert units from one system to another. This is achieved by **factor label method** or **unit factor method** or **dimensional analysis.**

Dimensional analysis involves calculations based on the fact that if two quantities have to be equated, they must have the same dimensions or the same units.

For the application of this method, conversion factors are required which are mentioned in the given table.

Important Conversion Factors

1 ft = 12 inch	$1 \text{ Å} = 10^{-10}$ m
1 yd = 3 ft	$1 \text{ m}^3 = 10^3$ L
1 mile = 5280 ft	$1 \text{ dm}^3 = 1$ L
1 inch = 2.54 cm	$1 \text{ cm}^3 = 10^{-3}$ L
1 m = 39.37 inch	$1 \text{ ft}^3 = 28.32$ L
1 mile = 1.609 km	$1 \text{ kg} = 10^3$ g
1 cal = 4.186 J	$1 \text{ kHz} = 10^3$ Hz $1 \text{ MHz} = 10^6$ Hz
1 minute = 60 s	$1 \text{ erg} = 10^{-7}$ J
1 h = 60 minute	$1 \text{ eV} = 1.6022 \times 10^{-19}$ J
1 day = 24 × 60 × 60 s	$1 \text{ amu} = 1.66053 \times 10^{-27}$ kg = 931.48 MeV
$1 \text{ mg} = 10^{-3}$ g	1 atm = 760 mm Hg
$1 \text{ metric ton} = 10^3$ kg	= 76 cm Hg
1 lb = 453.6 g	= 760 torr
1 HP = 746 W	$1 \text{ bar} = 10^5$ Pa
$1 \text{ dyne} = 10^{-5}$ N	1 atm = 101.325 kPa
1 kg = 2.2 pound (lb)	1 L atm = 101.325 J
1 g = 0.0353 ounce (o)	

Example 11 **How many seconds are there in 2 days?**

Sol. ***Step I*** Here, we know 1 day = 24 hours (h)

or $\frac{1 \text{ day}}{24 \text{ h}} = 1 = \frac{24 \text{ h}}{1 \text{ day}}$ then 1 h = 60 min

or $\frac{1 \text{ h}}{60 \text{ min}} = 1 = \frac{60 \text{ min}}{1 \text{ h}}$

so, for converting 2 days to seconds. i.e. 2 days = ... seconds

Step II The unit factors can be multiplied in series in one step only as follows.

$$2 \text{ day} \times \frac{24 \text{ h}}{1 \text{ day}} \times \frac{60 \text{ min}}{1 \text{ h}} \times \frac{60 \text{ s}}{1 \text{ min}} = 2 \times 24 \times 60 \times 60 \text{ s} = 172800 \text{ s}$$

Example 12 **What is the mass (in grams) of a copper block whose dimensions are 5.0 inch × 6.0 inch × 4.0 inch and whose density is 8.96 g/cm^3? Given that 1 inch = 2.54 cm.**

Sol. Here, unit conversion factors are $1 = \frac{2.54 \text{ cm}}{1 \text{ inch}} = \frac{1 \text{ inch}}{2.54 \text{ cm}}$

Hence, required mass (in g) = 5.0 inch × 6.0 inch × 4.0

$$\text{inch} \times \frac{2.54 \text{ cm}}{1 \text{ inch}} \times \frac{2.54 \text{ cm}}{1 \text{ inch}} \times \frac{2.54 \text{ cm}}{1 \text{ inch}} \times \frac{8.96 \text{ g}}{1 \text{ cm}^3} = 1.76 \times 10^4 \text{ g}$$

1.4 Laws of Chemical Combinations

Elements combine to form compounds in accordance to the following five basic laws, called the **laws of chemical combinations**.

1. Law of Conservation of Mass

This law was put forth by **Antoine Lavoisier** in 1789. According to this law, *"matter can neither be created nor be destroyed but one form of matter can be converted into other"*. This law is also known as **law of indestructibility of matter.**

The other statement for this law is "in all physical and chemical changes, the total mass of the reactants is equal to that of the products." i.e.

Sum of masses of reactants = Sum of masses of products.

Example 13 **If 6.3 g of $NaHCO_3$ are added to 15.0 g of CH_3COOH solution, the residue is found to weigh 18.0 g. What is the mass of CO_2 released in the reaction?**

Sol. $$NaHCO_3 + CH_3COOH \longrightarrow \underbrace{H_2O + CH_3CO\bar{O}\overset{+}{N}a}_{\text{Residue}} + CO_2$$

Sum of the masses of reactants = 6.3 + 15 = 21.3 g

Sum of the masses of products = $x + 18$

$21.3 = x + 18; x = 21.3 - 18 = 3.3$ g

Thus, the mass of the CO_2 released is 3.3 g.

2. Law of Definite Proportions

This law was given by a French chemist, **Joseph Proust** in 1799. According to this law, *"a given compound always contains exactly the same proportion of elements by weight"*. It is sometimes also referred to as **law of definite composition.**

e.g. Pure water obtained from any source (well, river, lake or sea) or any country (India, Russia, America etc.) will always be made up of only hydrogen and oxygen elements combined together in the same fixed ratio of 1 : 8 by mass.

Example 14 **Copper oxide was prepared by the following methods.**

(i) In one case, 1.75 g of the metal was dissolved in nitric acid and igniting the residual copper nitrate yielded 2.19 g of copper oxide.

(ii) In the second case, 1.14 g of metal dissolved in nitric acid were precipitated as copper hydroxide by adding caustic alkali solution. The precipitated copper hydroxide after washing, drying and heating yielded 1.43 g of copper oxide.

(iii) In the third case, 1.46 g of copper when strongly heated in a current of air yielded 1.83 g of copper oxide.

Show that the given data illustrate the law of definite composition.

Sol. **Step I** **In the first experiment,**

2.19 g of copper oxide contained 1.75 g of Cu.

∴ 100 g of copper oxide contained

$$Cu = \frac{1.75}{2.19} \times 100 = 79.91 \text{ g},$$

i.e. % of Cu = 79.91

In the second experiment,

1.43 g of copper oxide contained 1.14 g of copper.

∴ 100 g of copper oxide contained

$$Cu = \frac{1.14}{1.43} \times 100 = 79.72 \text{ g},$$

i.e. % of Cu = 79.72

In the third experiment,

1.83 g of copper oxide contained 1.46 g of copper

∴ 100 g of copper oxide contained

$$Cu = \frac{1.46}{1.83} \times 100 = 79.78 \text{ g},$$

i.e % of Cu = 79.78

Step II The percentage of copper in copper oxide derived from all the three experiments is nearly the same. Hence, the above data illustrate the law of definite composition.

3. Law of Multiple Proportions

This law was proposed by **Dalton** in 1803. It states that *"if two elements can combine to form more than one compound, the masses of one element that combine with a fixed mass of the other element, are in the ratio of small whole numbers"*.

e.g. Two compounds, water and hydrogen peroxide are formed when hydrogen combines with oxygen.

$$\underset{2\text{ g}}{\text{Hydrogen}} + \underset{16\text{ g}}{\text{Oxygen}} \longrightarrow \underset{18\text{ g}}{\text{Water}}$$

$$\underset{2\text{ g}}{\text{Hydrogen}} + \underset{32\text{ g}}{\text{Oxygen}} \longrightarrow \underset{34\text{ g}}{\text{Hydrogen peroxide}}$$

Here, the masses of oxygen (i.e. 16 g and 32 g) that combine with a fixed mass of hydrogen (i.e. 2 g) bear a simple ratio, i.e. 16 : 32 or 1 : 2.

Example 15 **Three oxides of nitrogen contained 63.6%, 46.7% and 30.4% nitrogen respectively. Show that these figures illustrate the law of multiple proportions.**

Sol. **In case first,**

Step I The oxide of nitrogen contains 63.6% N, i.e. 63.6 g of N reacts with (100 – 63.6) g of O = 36.4 g of O.

Step II $\therefore$ 1 g of N will react with $\frac{36.4}{63.6}$ g of O = 0.57g of O.

In case second,

Step I The oxide of nitrogen contains 46.7% N i.e. 46.7g of N reacts with (100 – 46.7) g of O = 53.3 g of O.

Step II $\therefore$ 1g of N will react with $\frac{53.3}{46.7}$ g of O = 1.14 g of O.

In case third,

Step I The oxide of nitrogen contains 30.4% N, i.e. 30.4 g of N reacts with (100 – 30.4) g of O = 69.6 g of O.

Step II $\therefore$ 1g of N will react with $\frac{69.6}{30.4}$ g of O = 2.29 g of O

Step III This means the ratio of the masses of oxygen which combine with 1 g of nitrogen is 0.57 : 1.14 : 2.29, i.e. 1 : 2 : 4. is obviously in accordance with the law of multiple proportions.

Law of Reciprocal Proportions

This law was given by **Richter** in 1792. It states that, "the ratio of the masses of two elements *A* and *B* which combine separately with a fixed mass of the third element *C* is either the same or some simple multiple of the ratio of the masses in which *A* and *B* combine directly with each other".

For instance, in case of H_2S and SO_2, the masses of H and O which combine with the fixed mass of S, i.e. 32 parts are 2 and 32. So, they are in the ratio 2 :32 or 1:16. Now, when H and O combine directly to form H_2O, the ratio of their combining masses are 2:16 or 1:8 These ratios are simple multiple of each other.

4. Gay Lussac's Law of Gaseous Volumes

As the name implies that, this law was given by **Gay Lussac** in 1808. He stated that "*when gases combine or are produced in a chemical reaction they do so in a simple ratio by volume provided all the gases are at same temperature and pressure*".

e.g. One volume of hydrogen and one volume of chlorine always combine to form two volumes of hydrogen chloride gas.

$$\underset{1\text{ vol}}{H_2} + \underset{1\text{ vol}}{Cl_2} \longrightarrow \underset{2\text{ vol}}{2\,HCl}$$

The ratio between the volumes of the reactants and the product in this reaction is simple, i.e. 1 : 1 : 2.

Hence, it illustrates the law of combining volumes.

Example 16 **N_2 reacts with H_2 to form NH_3. If 10 L N_2 reacts with 30 L H_2 to form 20 L NH_3 under same conditions of pressure and temperature. Show that the data is in accordance with law of gaseous volumes.**

Sol. The reaction taking place is

$$N_2 + 3H_2 \longrightarrow 2NH_3$$

The ratio of $N_2 : H_2 : NH_3$ :: 10 : 30 : 20, i.e. 1 : 3 : 2.

Since, the ratio is simple and whole number, thus law of gaseous volume is proved.

5. Avogadro's Law

Avogadro found that the smallest particle of a gas which can exist independently is the molecule, not the atom, therefore, the volume of a gas must be related to the number of molecules (rather than atoms) present in it.

He thus put forward the hypothesis known as **Avogadro's hypothesis**, which states that "*equal volumes of gases at the same temperature and pressure should contain equal number of molecules*".

Applications of Avogadro's law are

(i) Calculation of Atomicity of Elementary Gases

Atomicity of an elementary substance is defined as 'the number of atoms of the element present in one molecule of that substance".

e.g. Atomicity of oxygen (O_2) is two (diatomic) while that of ozone (O_3) is three (triatomic).

(ii) Finding the Relationship between Mass and Volume of a Gas

Molecular mass = 2 × vapour density

$$= 2\times\frac{\text{mass of certain volume of the gas at STP}}{\text{mass of same volume of } H_2 \text{ at STP}}$$

$$= 2\times\frac{\text{mass of 1L of the gas at STP}}{\text{mass of 1L of } H_2 \text{ at STP}}$$

$$= 2\times\frac{\text{mass of 1L of the gas at STP}}{0.089\text{ g}}$$

$$= 22.4\times \text{mass of 1L of the gas at STP}$$

$$= \text{mass of 22.4 L of the gas at STP}$$

Thus, the weight of 22.4 L of any gas at STP is equal to the molecular mass of the gas expressed in gram. This is called **Gram-Molecular Volume** (GMV) law. Vapour density is also known as **relative density of the gas**.

1.5 Dalton's Atomic Theory

The word 'atom' has been derived from the Greek word '*atomos*' meaning **indivisible**. The old ideas were put on a scientific scale by **John Dalton** in the form of a theory, known as Dalton's atomic theory.

Main postulates of this theory are as follows

- Matter consists of minute, indivisible, indestructible particles, called **atoms**.
- Atoms of the same element are identical to each other. They have the same mass.
- Atoms of different elements differ in properties and have different masses.
- **Compounds** are formed when atoms of different elements combine with each other in simple numerical ratios and the relative numbers and kind of atoms are always the same in a given compound.
- Chemical reactions involve reorganisation of atoms. These are neither be created nor destroyed in a chemical reaction.

Dalton's theory could explain the laws of chemical combination. However, it had certain limitations and could not account for some observations which are discussed further.

Limitations of Dalton's Atomic Theory

The main drawbacks of Dalton's atomic theory are

- It could explain the laws of chemical combination by mass but failed to explain the law of gaseous volumes.
- It could not explain why atoms of different elements have different masses, sizes, valencies etc.
- It failed to explain the nature of forces that bind together atoms in a molecule.
- It could not explain how and why atoms of different elements combine with each other to form **compound** or **molecules**.

Quick Test 1

Conceptual Questions

1. Two substances *X* and *Y* combine to give a substance *Z*. The process is exothermic and *Z* has properties different from those of *X* and *Y*. Is the substance *Z*, an element, a mixture or a compound? Give explanation to support your answer.

2. What is the difference between 5.0 g and 5.00 g?

3. Suppose the length of a cardboard has been reported to be 31.24 cm. What is the minimum uncertainty implied in this measurement ?

4. (i) Differentiate between solids, liquids and gases in terms of diffusion, compressibility and hardness.

(ii) State the law of reciprocal proportions

5. 10 mL of H_2 combine with 5 mL of O_2 to form water. When 200 mL of H_2 at STP is passed over heated CuO, the CuO loses 0.144 g of its weight. Does the above data correspond to the law of constant composition?

6. 5.975 g of the higher oxide of metal gave 5.575 g of lower oxide on heating. The quantity of the lower oxide gave 5.175 g of metal on reduction. Prove that these results are in accordance with the law of multiple proportions.

For Solutions, See QR Code on Pg. 37

7. If ten volumes of dihydrogen gas react with five volumes of dioxygen gas, how many volumes of water vapour would be produced? *NCERT*

8. One of the statements of Dalton's atomic theory is given below "compounds are formed when atoms of different elements combine in a fixed ratio".

Which laws of chemical combination is not related to this statement? *NCERT Exemplar*

Numerical Questions

9. Perform the following calculations and express the results to proper number of significant figures.

(i) $144.3\ m^2 + (2.54\ m \times 8.4\ m)$

(ii) $(4.05 \times 10^2\ mL) - (0.0225 \times 10^2 mL)$

10. What mass of silver nitrate will react with 5.85 g of sodium chloride to produce 14.35 g of silver chloride and 8.5 g of sodium nitrate, if the law of conservation of mass is true?

Answers

9. (i) $165.3\ m^2$ (ii) 4.03×10^2 mL

10. 17 g

1.6 Atomic and Molecular Masses

After understanding the basic terms of atoms and molecules, it is important to explore the concept of atomic and molecular masses.

Atomic Mass

Atomic mass is defined as a number that expresses as to how many times an atom of the element is heavier than 1/12th of the mass of carbon atom (^{12}C).

Therefore,

$$\text{Atomic mass} = \frac{\text{mass of an atom}}{(1/12)\times \text{mass of a carbon atom } (^{12}C)}$$

The scale of relative masses of atoms is termed as **atomic mass unit scale** (amu). However, the new symbol used is **u** (known as unified mass) in place of amu. In this system, ^{12}C is assigned a mass of exactly 12 atomic mass unit and masses of all other atoms are given relative to this standard.

Hence, one atomic mass unit is defined as *the mass exactly equal to 1/12th of the mass of an atom of carbon* (^{12}C).

$$1 \text{ amu} = 1.66056\times 10^{-24} \text{ g}$$

Mass of an atom of hydrogen $= 1.6736\times 10^{-24}$ g

Thus, in terms of amu, the mass of hydrogen atom

$$= \frac{1.6736\times 10^{-24} \text{ g}}{1.66056\times 10^{-24} \text{ g}}$$

$$= 1.0078 \text{ u} = 1.0080 \text{ u}$$

Similarly, the mass of oxygen 16 (^{16}O) atom would be 15.995 u.

Note
- Since, the atomic mass is the ratio of the masses, so it has no units. However, we express it as **amu**.
- C-12 is chosen as standard because in such case the masses of most of the elements are **whole number** or nearest to the whole number.

Average Atomic Mass

Average atomic mass is defined as "the average relative mass of atoms of an element as compared with an atom of carbon-12 taken as 12". It is determined with the help of mass spectrometer. If we have the percentage abundances of all the isotopes, the average atomic mass is calculated by the expression.

$$\text{Average atomic mass} = \frac{\Sigma p_i A_i}{100} = \frac{p_1A_1 + p_2A_2 + \ldots}{100}$$

where, p_i is the percentage abundance of isotope having atomic mass A_i. Fractional abundances, f_i can also be used to obtain the atomic mass of an element. **Fractional abundance** is the total number of atoms that is comprised of that particular isotope.

Thus, average atomic mass $= \Sigma f_iA_i = f_1A_1 + f_2A_2 + \ldots$

e.g. Nitrogen has the following two isotopes with relative abundance and atomic masses as shown against each of them

Isotope	Relative abundance %	Atomic mass (amu)
^{14}N	99.33%	14
^{15}N	0.67%	15

From the above data, the average atomic mass of nitrogen can be calculated as

$$= \frac{\Sigma \text{ (Isotopic mass} \times \text{Relative abundance)}}{\Sigma \text{ (Relative abundance)}}$$

$$= \frac{(0.9933\times 14) + (0.0067\times 15)}{0.9933 + 0.0067} = 14.00674 \text{ u}$$

Example 17 **Boron occurs in nature in the form of two isotopes having atomic mass 10 and 11. What are the percentage abundances of two isotopes in a sample of boron having average atomic mass 10.8 u?**

Sol. Let the % abundance of ^{10}B isotope $= x$

Then % abundance of ^{11}B isotope $= 100 - x$

The average atomic mass $= \dfrac{x\times 10 + (100 - x)\times 11}{100}$

But, average atomic mass $= 10.8$ (Given)

$$\therefore \quad \frac{x\times 10 + (100 - x)\times 11}{100} = 10.8$$

or $\quad 10x + 1100 - 11x = 10.8\times 100$

or $\quad -x = -1100 + 1080$

or $\quad x = 20$

Thus, percentage abundance, $^{10}B = 20\%$, $^{11}B = 80\%$

TEACHER'S TIP

In the periodic table of elements, the atomic masses mentioned for different elements actually represented their average **atomic masses.**

Molecular Mass

It is the sum of atomic masses of the elements present in a molecule. Thus, it is obtained by multiplying the atomic mass of each element by the number of its atoms and then adding them together. e.g. Molecular mass of methane (CH_4) can be calculated as

$= 1 \times$ atomic mass of C + 4 × atomic mass of H

$= (12.011\text{u}) + 4\,(1.008\text{ u}) = 16.043\text{ u}$

Example 18 **Calculate molecular mass of glucose ($C_6H_{12}O_6$) molecule.** NCERT

Sol. Molecular mass of glucose ($C_6H_{12}O_6$)

$= 6\,(12.011\text{u}) + 12\,(1.008\text{u}) + 6\,(16.00\text{u})$

$= (72.066\text{u}) + (12.096\text{u}) + (96.00\text{u})$

$= 180.162\text{u}$

Formula Mass

Ionic compounds do not contain discrete molecules as their constituent units. In these compounds, positive and negative ions are arranged in a three-dimensional structure.

Thus, the formula of such compounds is used to calculate the formula mass instead of the molecular mass.

Formula mass of an ionic compound = number of cations × its atomic mass + number of anions × its atomic mass

e.g. Formula mass of sodium chloride

= atomic mass of sodium + atomic mass of chlorine

$= 23.0\text{ u} + 35.5\text{ u} = 58.5\text{ u}$

Formula mass expressed in grams is called **gram formula mass.**

1.7 Mole Concept and Molar Masses

Mole is defined as "the amount of a substance that contains as many particles or entities as there are atoms in exactly 12 g (or 0.012 kg) of the ^{12}C isotope".

The mole of a substance always contain the same number of entities independent of the nature of the substance taken.

The number of atoms in 12 g of ^{12}C is calculated as

Mass of a carbon atom $= 1.992648 \times 10^{-23}$ g

(Determined by mass spectrometer)

1 mole of carbon = 12 g

∴ The number of atoms in 12 g C

$$= \frac{12\text{ g / mol } ^{12}C}{1.992648 \times 10^{-23}\text{ g}/^{12}C\text{ atom}}$$

$$= 6.0221367 \times 10^{23}\text{ atom / mol}$$

This number of entities in 1 mole is known as **Avogadro constant,** denoted by N_A in honour of **Amedeo Avogadro.**

In other words, we can say that, a mole is a collection of 6.022×10^{23} particles which could be atoms, molecules, ions or formula units, depending on the type of substance.

The mass of one mole of a substance in grams is called its **molar mass.** The molar mass in grams is numerically equal to atomic/molecular/formula mass in '*u*'. Its units are g mol^{-1} or kg mol^{-1}.

e.g. Molar mass of water = 18.02 g mol^{-1} and it contains 6.022×10^{23} H_2O molecules.

The following flowchart illustrates the relationship between 1 mole of various substances and their corresponding masses in grams.

6.022×10^{23} atoms of C ←	1 Mole of Carbon atoms	→ 1 mole of carbon atom weighs 12 grams [molar mass of carbon]
6.022×10^{23} atoms of H ←	1 Mole of Hydrogen atoms	→ 1 mole of hydrogen atom weighs 1 gram (molar mass of hydrogen)
6.022×10^{23} particles ←	1 Mole of any particle (atoms, molecules, ions, etc.)	→ 1 mole of these particles equals to their relative atomic or molecular mass in grams
6.022×10^{23} molecules ←	1 Mole of molecules	→ Molecular mass in grams of the molecule (e.g. 18 g for water molecules)
6.022×10^{23} molecules ←	1 Mole of gas at STP	→ Occupies 22.4 L (Molar volume)
6.022×10^{23} formula units ←	1 Mole of an Ionic Compound	→ Molar mass equals to the sum of atomic masses of ions (e.g. 58.5 g for NaCl (Gram formula mass)

Calculation of Mole

Based upon above given relations, number of moles of a substance can be calculated in the following ways

- Number of moles of substance $= \dfrac{\text{Given mass}}{\text{Molar mass}}$

$$n = \frac{w}{M}$$

- Number of moles (when number of particles are given) $= \dfrac{\text{Given number of particles}}{\text{Avogadro's number}}$

$$n = \frac{N}{N_A}$$

(Here $N_A = 6.022 \times 10^{23}$)

- Number of moles of gas

$$= \frac{\text{Volume of the gas (at STP)}}{22.4\ \text{L}}$$

- Number of molecules $= \dfrac{\text{Given mass in grams}}{\text{Molar mass}} \times \text{Avogadro number } (N_A)$

$= \text{Number of moles} \times N_A$

- Number of atoms = Number of molecules × Atomicity

TEACHER'S TIP

To understand the mole concept, the easy method is to apply the given formula:

$$\text{Number of moles} = \frac{w}{M} = \frac{N}{N_A} = \frac{V}{22.4\ \text{L}}$$

[where, w = weight, M = molar mass, N = number of entities, N_A = Avogadro constant, V = Volume of gas (at STP)]

Example 19 Calculate the number of moles in the following.

(i) 7.85 g of iron

(ii) 4.68 mg of silicon

(iii) 65.6 µg of carbon NCERT

Sol. (i) Moles of iron $= \dfrac{\text{Mass of iron}}{\text{Atomic mass of iron}} = \dfrac{7.85\ \text{g}}{55.9\ \text{g/mol}}$

$= 0.140$ moles

(ii) Moles of silicon $= \dfrac{\text{Mass of silicon}}{\text{Atomic mass of silicon}}$

$= \dfrac{4.68 \times 10^{-3}\ \text{g}}{28.1\ \text{g/mol}} = 1.67 \times 10^{-4}$ moles

(iii) Moles of carbon $= \dfrac{\text{Mass of carbon}}{\text{Atomic mass of carbon}}$

$= \dfrac{65.6 \times 10^{-6}\ \text{g}}{12\ \text{g/mol}} = 5.47 \times 10^{-6}$ moles

Example 20 Calculate the number of atoms in each of the following.

(i) 52 moles of Ar **(ii) 52 u of He**

(iii) 52 g of He NCERT

Sol. (i) ∵ 1 mole of Ar contains 6.022×10^{23} atoms

∴ 52 moles of Ar will contain $= 6.022 \times 10^{23} \times 52$

$= 3.13 \times 10^{25}$ atoms

(ii) ∵ 4 u of He = 1 atom

∴ 52 u of He $= \dfrac{1}{4} \times 52 = 13$ atoms

(iii) 4 g of He contains 6.022×10^{23} atoms

52 g of He will contain $= \dfrac{6.022 \times 10^{23} \times 52}{4}$

$= 7.83 \times 10^{24}$ atoms

Example 21 The cost of table salt (NaCl) and table sugar ($C_{12}H_{22}O_{11}$) is ₹ 2 per kg and ₹ 6 per kg, respectively. Calculate their costs per mol.

Sol. One mole of NaCl = 58.5 g

Cost of NaCl per mol $= \dfrac{2}{1000} \times 58.5 =$ ₹ 0.117

= 11.7 paise or 12 paise

One mole of sugar ($C_{12}H_{22}O_{11}$) = 342 g

Cost of sugar per mol $= \dfrac{6}{1000} \times 342 =$ ₹ 2.05

Example 22

(i) Assuming the density of water to be 1g/cm^3, calculate the volume occupied by one molecule of water.

(ii) Assuming the water molecule to be spherical, calculate the diameter of the water molecule.

(iii) Assuming that oxygen atom occupies half of the volume occupied by the water molecule, calculate approximately the diameter of the oxygen atom.

Sol. (i) 1 mole of H_2O = 18g = 18cm^3

(∵ density of H_2O = 1g / cm^3)

$= 6.022 \times 10^{23}$ molecules of H_2O

Thus, 6.022×10^{23} molecules of H_2O have volume

$= 18\ \text{cm}^3$

∴ 1 molecule of H_2O will have volume

$$= \frac{18}{6.022 \times 10^{23}}\ \text{cm}^3 = 2.989 \times 10^{-23}\ \text{cm}^3$$

(ii) As water molecule is assumed to be spherical, if R is its radius, then its volume will be

$$\frac{4}{3}\pi R^3 = 2.989 \times 10^{-23}\ \text{cm}^3$$

or $R^3 = 7.133 \times 10^{-24}$

or $R = (7.133)^{1/3} \times 10^{-8} = 1.925 \times 10^{-8}$ cm

∴ Diameter of water molecule

$= 2 \times 1.925 \times 10^{-8}$ cm

$= 3.85 \times 10^{-8}$ cm

(iii) As oxygen atom occupies half of the volume occupied by water molecule, hence if r is the radius of oxygen atom, then $\frac{4}{3}\pi r^3 = \frac{1}{2} \times 2.989 \times 10^{-23}$

or $r^3 = 3.566 \times 10^{-24}$

$\therefore$ Radius, $r = 1.528 \times 10^{-8}$ cm

$\therefore$ Diameter of oxygen atom

$= 2 \times 1.528 \times 10^{-8}$ cm

$= 3.056 \times 10^{-8}$ cm

1.8 Percentage Composition

The percentage of any element or constituent in a compound is the number of parts by mass of that element or constituent present in 100 parts by mass of the compound.

Percentage or mass % of an element or constituent

$$= \frac{\text{Mass of that element in the compound}}{\text{Molar mass of the compound}} \times 100$$

Percentage composition helps in determining the molecular formula of a compound. Moreover, it is also helpful to check the purity of a given sample.

Example 23 **Calculate the mass percentage of each element of water.**

Sol. Molar mass of water (H_2O) $= 2 \times$ atomic mass of H $+ 1 \times$ atomic mass of O

$= 2 \times 1.008 \text{ g} + 1 \times 16.00 \text{ g} = 18.02 \text{ g}$

$\therefore$ Mass % of hydrogen $= \frac{2 \times 1.008}{18.02} \times 100 = 11.19\%$

and Mass % of oxygen $= \frac{16.00}{18.02} \times 100 = 88.79\%$

Empirical Formula

An empirical formula of a compound represents the simplest whole number ratio of various atoms present in one molecule of the compound.

Method to find Empirical Formula of a Compound

Following are the steps to find the empirical formula of a compound.

Step I **Conversion of mass per cent into gram** by taking 100 g of the compound as the starting material. e.g. 40.7% means 0.407 g if we take 100 g as the starting material.

Usually no direct method is used for finding the percentage of oxygen in a compound. It is calculated by finding the percentages of all elements except oxygen.

Thus, percentage of oxygen = 100 – (sum of percentages of all other elements present in the compound).

Step II **Convert mass (in grams) into number of moles for each element.** Convert mass obtained above into number of moles by dividing them with respective atomic masses of various elements.

Step III Divide the mole values obtained above with the smallest mole value to get the simplest ratio.

Step IV Write empirical formula by mentioning the numbers after writing the symbols of respective elements.

Molecular Formula

The molecular formula shows the exact number of different types of atoms present in the molecule of a compound.

Method to determine the Molecular Formula of a Compound

Following steps are taken to determine the molecular formula of a compound.

Step I Determine the empirical formula as described above.

Step II Calculate the empirical formula mass by adding the atomic masses of the atoms in the empirical formula.

Step III Determine the molecular mass by suitable method.

Step IV Determine the value of n as

$$n = \frac{\text{Molecular mass}}{\text{Empirical formula mass}}.$$

Change n to the nearest whole number.

Step V Multiply empirical formula by n to get the molecular formula.

Molecular formula $= n \times$ Empirical formula

Example 24 **An organic substance containing carbon, hydrogen and oxygen gave the percentage composition as $C = 40.687\%$, $H = 5.085\%$. The vapour density of the compound is 59. Calculate the molecular formula of the compound.**

Sol. *Step* I **To calculate empirical formula of the compound**. Here, % of $O = 100 - (40.687 + 5.085) = 54.228\%$

Element	Symbol	Percentage of element	Atomic mass of element	Moles of the element = $\frac{\text{Percentage}}{\text{Atomic mass}}$ (Relative number of moles)	Simplest molar ratio	Simplest whole number molar ratio
Carbon	C	40.687	12	$\frac{40.687}{12} = 3.390$	$\frac{3.390}{3.389} = 1$	2
Hydrogen	H	5.085	1	$\frac{5.085}{1} = 5.085$	$\frac{5.085}{3.389} = 1.5$	3
Oxygen	O	54.228	16	$\frac{54.228}{16} = 3.389$	$\frac{3.389}{3.389} = 1$	2

Thus, empirical formula is $C_2H_3O_2$.

Step II **To calculate the empirical formula mass of** $C_2H_3O_2 = (2 \times 12) + (3 \times 1) + (2 \times 16) = 59\text{ g}$.

Step III **To calculate the molecular mass of the compound**. The vapour density of the compound = 59 (Given)

Using the relation between vapour density and molecular mass.

We have molecular mass $= 2 \times$ vapour density $= 2 \times 59 = 118\text{ g}$

Step IV **To calculate the value of** $n = \frac{\text{molecular mass}}{\text{empirical formula mass}} = \frac{118\text{ g}}{59\text{ g}} = 2$

Step V **To calculate the molecular formula of the compound,**

Molecular formula $= n \times$ Empirical formula $= 2 \times C_2H_3O_2 = C_4H_6O_4$. Thus, the molecular formula is $C_4H_6O_4$.

TEACHER'S TIP

Follow this map to find molecular formula of compound

Mass% $\rightarrow$ Mass (in g) $\rightarrow$ Number of moles $\rightarrow$ Simplest ratio of mole values $\rightarrow$ Empirical formula $\rightarrow$ Empirical formula mass $\rightarrow$ Molecular mass $\rightarrow n = \frac{\text{molecular mass}}{\text{empirical formula mass}} \rightarrow$ Molecular formula $= n \times$ empirical formula.

Quick Test 2

1. (i) Calculate the number of gram molecules of water in a beaker containing 576 g of water.

(ii) How much copper can be obtained from 100 g of copper sulphate ($CuSO_4$)?

2. A flask *P* contains 0.5 moles of oxygen gas. Another flask *Q* contains 0.4 moles of ozone gas. Which of the two flasks contain greater number of oxygen atoms?

3. Which one of the following will have the largest number of atoms? *NCERT*

(i) 1g Au (s) (ii) 1g Na (s)

(iii) 1g Li (s) (iv) 1g of $Cl_2(g)$

4. One mole of any substance contains 6.022×10^{23} atoms/molecules. What will be the number of molecules of H_2SO_4 present in 100 mL of 0.02 M H_2SO_4. *NCERT Exemplar*

5. In an experiment to determine sulphur content using the Carius method, 0.468 g of an organic sulphur compound is analysed. The reaction yields 0.668 g of barium sulphate. Calculate the percentage of sulphur present in the compound. *Competency Based Que.*

6. The empirical formula and molecular mass of a compound are CH_2O and 180 g/mol respectively. What will be the molecular formula of the compound? *NCERT Exemplar*

7 A compound on analysis was found to contain $C = 34.6\%$, $H = 3.85\%$, and $O = 61.55\%$. Calculate its empirical formula.

Answers

1. (i) 32 gram molecule (ii) 39.81 g Cu
2. Flask *Q* (no. of atoms) > Flask (*P*) (no. of atoms)
3. (iii) 1 g Li(s) **4.** 12.044×10^{20} molecules
5. 19.6% **6.** $C_6H_{12}O_6$ **7.** $C_3H_4O_4$

For Solutions, See QR Code on Pg. 37

1.9 Stoichiometry and Stoichiometric Calculations

The word 'stoichiometry' is derived from the combination of two Greek words, i.e. ***stoicheion*** (means element) and ***metron*** (means measure).

Stoichiometry, thus, deals with the calculation of masses (sometimes volumes also) of the reactants and the products involved in a chemical reaction or in other words, the relationship between the amounts of reactants and products is called as stoichiometry.

The number before the formula unit or molecules used to balance the equation are called as **stoichiometric coefficients.** They show the number of moles/molecules of that particular substance taking part in the reaction or formed in the reaction. Calculations based on chemical equations are termed as **stoichiometric calculations.**

Balancing a Chemical Equation

A chemical equation must be in accordance with the law of conservation of mass which states that the *"total mass of the reactants must be equal to the total mass of the products"*.

A chemical equation having an equal number of atoms of each element in the reactant and the product sides is called the **balanced chemical equation.**

e.g. $4Fe(s) + 3O_2(g) \longrightarrow 2Fe_2O_3(s)$

is a balanced equation.

whereas, $P_4(s) + O_2(g) \longrightarrow P_4O_{10}(s)$

is an unbalanced equation.

There are several methods to balance a chemical equation. These methods are

(a) hit and trial method or trial and error method.

(b) partial equation method.

(c) oxidation number method.

(d) ion-electron method.

The first two methods have already been discussed in class 10th, while the other methods will be taken up in chapter 7 (Redox reactions).

Steps Involved in Stoichiometric Calculations

Step I Write the balanced chemical equation.

Step II Write the stoichiometric coefficient that shows the moles of the respective substance.

Step III Convert moles into required quantity such as mass or volume. (if needed).

Step IV Calculate the required information by unitary method.

These are the general steps involved in all types of stoichiometric calculations.

These calculations are of the following types

(i) Calculations Involving Mole-Mole Relationship

In such problems, the moles of one of the reactant/product is to be calculated, if the moles of others are given.

Example 25 How many moles of CO_2 will be obtained when 0.274 moles of C_2H_5OH is burnt?

Sol. Follow the following steps to solve such problems

Step I Write down the balanced equation for the given reaction and then write the stoichiometric coefficient and after that given moles.

$$C_2H_5OH + 3O_2 \longrightarrow \underset{x}{2CO_2} + 3H_2O$$

Stoichiometric coefficient of $C_2H_5OH = 1$ mole

Given moles $= 0.274$ moles

Step II Calculate the amount of the CO_2 by unitary method.

1 mole of C_2H_5OH produces 2 moles of CO_2

$\therefore$ 0.274 mole of C_2H_5OH will produce CO_2

$$= \frac{2}{1} \times 0.274 = 2 \times 0.274 = 0.548 \text{ moles}$$

Thus, 0.548 moles of CO_2 is obtained from 0.274 moles of C_2H_5OH.

(ii) Calculations Involving Mass-Mass Relationship

In such problems, the mass of one of the reactant/product is to be calculated if we have the mass of others.

Example 26 Calculate the amount of water (g) produced by the combustion of 16 g of methane. NCERT

Sol. Solution of such problems involve following steps

Step I Write the balanced chemical equation.

$$CH_4(g) + 2O_2(g) \longrightarrow CO_2(g) + 2H_2O(g)$$

Step II Write the stoichiometric coefficients of each substance. These represent mole of that particular substance.

$$\underset{1\text{ mol}}{CH_4(g)} + \underset{2\text{ moles}}{2O_2(g)} \longrightarrow \underset{1\text{ mol}}{CO_2(g)} + \underset{2\text{ moles}}{2H_2O(s)}$$

Step III Convert moles into mass by multiplying them with molar mass.

$$\underset{\substack{1\times 16\text{ g}\\ =16\text{ g}}}{CH_4(g)} + \underset{\substack{2\times 32\text{ g}\\ =64\text{ g}}}{2O_2(g)} \longrightarrow \underset{\substack{1\times 44\text{ g}\\ =44\text{ g}}}{CO_2(g)} + \underset{\substack{2\times 18\text{ g}\\ =36\text{ g}}}{2H_2O(g)}$$

Step IV Write the given mass below the respective substance.

$$\underset{16\text{ g}}{CH_4(g)} + \underset{64\text{ g}}{2O_2(g)} \longrightarrow \underset{44\text{ g}}{CO_2(g)} + \underset{36\text{ g}}{2H_2O(g)}$$

Step V Calculate the mass of unknown substance by unitary method.

From the equation, it is already clear that 16 g of methane produces 36 g of water.

(iii) Calculations Involving Mass-Mole or Mole-Mass Relationship

In such problems, the mass or mole of one of the reactant/product is to be calculated if we have the mole or mass of others.

Example 27 Oxygen is prepared by the catalytic decomposition of potassium chlorate ($KClO_3$). Decomposition of potassium chlorate gives potassium chloride (KCl) and oxygen (O_2). If 2.4 moles of oxygen is needed for an experiment, how many grams of potassium chlorate must be decomposed?

Sol. The balanced equation is

$$\underset{\substack{2\text{ moles}\\ 2\times(39+35.5+3\times16)\text{ g}=245\text{ g}\quad x}}{2KClO_3(s)} \longrightarrow 2KCl(s) + \underset{\substack{3\text{ moles}\\ 2.4\text{ moles}}}{3O_2(g)}$$

$\because$ 3 moles of O_2 is produced by decomposition of 245 g $KClO_3$.

$\therefore$ 2.4 moles of O_2 will be produced by the decomposition of

$$KClO_3 = \frac{245 \times 2.4}{3} = 196.0\text{ g}$$

Example 28 How many moles of methane are required to produce 22 g $CO_2(g)$ after combustion? NCERT

Sol. According to the chemical equation,

$$CH_4(g) + 2O_2(g) \longrightarrow CO_2(g) + 2H_2O(g)$$

44 g $CO_2(g)$ is obtained from 16 g $CH_4(g)$.

[$\therefore$ 1 mol $CO_2(g)$ is obtained from 1 mol of $CH_4(g)$]

$$\text{Moles of } CO_2(g) = 22\text{g } CO_2(g) \times \frac{1\text{ mol } CO_2(g)}{44\text{g } CO_2(g)}$$

$$= 0.5\text{ moles } CO_2(g)$$

Hence, 0.5 moles $CO_2(g)$ would be obtained from 0.5 moles $CH_4(g)$ or 0.5 moles of $CH_4(g)$ would be required to produce 22 g $CO_2(g)$.

(iv) Calculations Involving Mass-Volume Relationship

In these problems, mass or volume of one of the reactant or product is calculated from the mass or volume of other substances.

Example 29 Calculate the amount of $KClO_3$ needed to supply sufficient oxygen for burning 112 L of CO gas at NTP.

Sol. Calculation of O_2 gas required to burn 112 L of CO.

$$\underset{\substack{1\text{ mol}\\=22.4\text{ L}}}{CO} + \underset{0.5\text{ moles}}{\frac{1}{2}O_2} \longrightarrow \underset{1\text{ mol}}{CO_2}$$

22.4 L of CO at NTP require O_2 = 0.5 moles

112 L of CO at NTP will require O_2

$$= \frac{0.5}{22.4} \times 112 = 2.5\text{ moles}$$

This O_2 will to be obtained by heating $KClO_3$.

$$\underset{\substack{2\text{ moles}\\2(39+35.5+3\times16)=245\text{ g}}}{2KClO_3} \longrightarrow 2KCl + \underset{3\text{ moles}}{3O_2}$$

3 moles of O_2 is produced from $KClO_3$ = 245 g

2.5 moles of O_2 will be produced from $KClO_3$

$$= \frac{245 \times 2.5}{3} = 204.167\text{ g}$$

Example 30 Hydrogen gas is prepared in the laboratory by reacting dilute HCl with granulated zinc. Following reaction takes place.

$$Zn + 2HCl \longrightarrow ZnCl_2 + H_2$$

Calculate the volume of hydrogen gas liberated at STP when 32.65 g of zinc reacts with HCl. 1 mole of a gas occupies 22.7 L volume at STP; atomic mass of Zn = 65.3u. NCERT Exemplar

Sol. Given that, mass of Zn = 32.65 g

1 mole of gas occupies = 22.7 L volume at STP

Atomic mass of Zn = 65.3 u

The given equation is

$$\underset{65.3\text{ g}}{Zn} + 2HCl \longrightarrow ZnCl_2 + \underset{\substack{1\text{ mol}\\=22.7\text{ L at STP}}}{H_2}$$

From the above equation, it is clear that

65.3 g Zn, when reacts with HCl, produces

= 22.7 L of H_2 at STP

$\therefore$ 32.65 g Zn, when reacts with HCl, will produce

$$= \frac{22.7 \times 32.65}{65.3} = 11.35\text{ L of } H_2 \text{ at STP.}$$

(v) Calculations Involving Volume-Volume Relationship

In these problems, the volume of one of the reactant/product is given and that of the other is to be calculated.

Example 31 What volume of oxygen at STP is required to effect complete combustion of 200 cm^3 of acetylene and what would be the volume of carbon dioxide formed?

Sol. The balanced chemical equation is

$$\underset{\substack{2\text{ moles}\\2\times22400\text{ cm}^3}}{2C_2H_2} + \underset{\substack{5\text{ moles}\\5\times22400\text{ cm}^3}}{5O_2} \longrightarrow \underset{\substack{4\text{ moles}\\4\times22400\text{ cm}^3}}{4CO_2} + 2H_2O$$

$\because$ 2 × 22400 cm^3 of acetylene require O_2 for complete combustion = 5 × 22400 cm^3

$200\ cm^3$ of acetylene will require O_2 for complete combustion $= \frac{5\times 22400}{2\times 22400}\times 200 = 500\ cm^3$ at STP

Further $2\times 22400\ cm^3$ of acetylene produce CO_2
$= 4\times 22400\ cm^3$

$\therefore$ $200\ cm^3$ of acetylene will produce CO_2
$= \frac{4\times 22400}{2\times 22400}\times 200 = 400\ cm^3$ at STP

Limiting Reagents

- In many chemical reactions, one reactant is present in more amount than the amount required by balanced chemical reaction. So, the reactant which is present in the lesser amount gets consumed after sometime, i.e. which limits the amount of product formed is called the **limiting reagent**.
- The reactant other than the limiting reagent, which is present in somewhat excess amount is called the **excess reagent**.
- The remaining amount of excess reagent is calculated by subtracting the available amount of limiting reagent from the amount of the excess reagent.
- The limiting reagent decides the amount of the product obtained.

> - **Theoretical yield** The amount of product obtained from given amounts of reactants (by stoichiometry).
> - **Actual yield** The amount of products obtained by carrying out a chemical reaction in lab.
> - Actual yield is always less than the theoretical yield.
> - **Percentage yield** $= \frac{\text{Actual yield}}{\text{Theoretical yield}}\times 100\%$

Example 33 **50.0 kg of $N_2(g)$ and 10.0 kg of $H_2(g)$ are mixed to produce $NH_3(g)$. Calculate the $NH_3(g)$ formed. Identify the limiting reagent in the production of NH_3 in this situation.** NCERT

Sol. *Step* I **A balanced equation for the above reaction is written as follows**

$$N_2(g) + 3H_2(g) \rightleftharpoons 2NH_3(g)$$

Step II **Calculation of moles.**

$$\text{Moles of } N_2 = 50.0\ \text{kg } N_2 \times \frac{1000\ \text{g } N_2}{1\ \text{kg } N_2}\times\frac{1\ \text{mol } N_2}{28.0\ \text{g } N_2}$$
$$= 17.86\times 10^2 \text{ moles}$$

$$\text{Moles of } H_2 = 10.00\ \text{kg } H_2 \times \frac{1000\ \text{g } H_2}{1\ \text{kg } H_2}\times\frac{1\text{mol } H_2}{2.016\ \text{g } H_2}$$
$$= 4.96\times 10^3 \text{ moles}$$

Step III Then, **find out the limiting reagent.**

$$17.86\times 10^2\ \text{mol } N_2 \times \frac{3\ \text{mol } H_2(g)}{1\ \text{mol } N_2(g)} = 5.36\times 10^3\ \text{mol } H_2$$

But we have only 4.96×10^3 mol H_2. **Hence, dihydrogen is the limiting reagent in this case.** So, $NH_3(g)$ would be formed only from that amount of available dihydrogen, i.e. 4.96×10^3 moles.

Step IV After that, **find out the amount of ammonia.**

Since, 3 mol $H_2(g)$ gives 2 mol $NH_3(g)$

$\therefore$ 4.96×10^3 mol $H_2(g)$ give

$$= 4.96\times 10^3\ \text{mol } H_2(g)\times\frac{2\text{mol } NH_3(g)}{3\ \text{mol } H_2(g)}$$
$$= 3.30\times 10^3\ \text{mol } NH_3(g)$$

3.30×10^3 mol $NH_3(g)$ is obtained from 4.96×10^3 mol $H_2(g)$.

If they are to be converted to grams, it is done as follows

$1\ \text{mol } NH_3(g) = 17.0\ \text{g } NH_3(g)$

$3.30\times 10^3\times 17\text{g } NH_3(g) = 56.1\times 10^3\text{g } NH_3$
$= 56.1\ \text{kg } NH_3$

Example 32 **In a reaction, $A + B_2 \longrightarrow AB_2$ identify the limiting reagent. If any, in the following reaction mixtures.**

(i) 300 atoms of A + 200 molecules of B
(ii) 2 moles of A + 3 moles of B
(iii) 100 atoms of A + 100 molecules of B
(iv) 5 moles of A + 2.5 moles of B
(v) 2.5 moles of A + 5 moles of B NCERT

Sol. The given equation shows that 1 mole of A reacts with 1 mole of B_2 and 1 atom of A reacts with 1 molecule of B_2

(i) B is the limiting reagent because 200 molecules of B_2 will react with 200 atoms of A and 100 atoms of A will be left in excess.

(ii) A is the limiting reagent because 2 moles of A will react with 2 moles of B and 1 mole of B will be left in excess.

(iii) Both will react completely because it is stoichiometric mixture. No limiting reagent.

(iv) 2.5 moles of B will react with 2.5 moles of A. Hence, B is the limiting reagent.

(v) 2.5 moles of A will react with 2.5 moles of B. Hence, A is the limiting reagent.

> **TEACHER'S TIP**
> To find the amount of product formed from the reactants of a balanced chemical equation, first find the limiting reagent out of the reactants and then with the help of limiting reagent find the amount of product formed.

Reactions in Solutions

Most of the reactions occurring in the laboratories are carried out in solutions. In solutions, generally two components are present. The one which is present in lesser amount is called the **solute** and the other one which is present in higher amount is called the **solvent.** The amount of solute present in a given quantity of solvent or solution is expressed in terms of **concentration.**

Terms Expressing Concentration of Solutions

There are several methods by which we can describe the concentration of the solution quantitatively. Some of these are as follows

Concentration Terms	Definition	Formula	Examples
Mass Per cent	It is the mass of a component per 100 g of the solution.	Mass per cent $= \frac{\text{mass of solute}}{\text{mass of solution}} \times 100$	e.g. 10% (w/W) solution of sodium chloride means that 10 g of sodium chloride is present in 90 g of water so that the total mass of the solution is 100 g.
Volume Per cent	It is defined as the volume of the component per 100 parts by volume of the solution.	Volume per cent of A $= \frac{\text{Volume of } A}{\text{Volume of } A + \text{volume of } B} \times 100$	e.g. A 10% solution of sodium chloride (w/V) means that 10 g of sodium chloride is dissolved in 100 mL of solution.
Parts Per million	It is defined as the parts of a component per million parts of the solution.	ppm of $A = \frac{\text{mass of component } A}{\text{total mass of solution}} \times 10^6$	e.g. Suppose a litre of public supply water contains about 3×10^{-3} g of chlorine. $\therefore$ ppm of chlorine $= \frac{3 \times 10^{-3} \times 10^6}{1000} = 3$ ppm
Mole Fraction (χ)	It is the ratio of number of moles of a particular component to the total number of moles of the solution.	In a binary solution, if the number of moles of A and B are n_A and n_B respectively, then mole fraction of A will be $\chi_A = \frac{n_A}{n_A + n_B}$ Similarly, mole fraction of B, $\chi_B = \frac{n_B}{n_A + n_B} \Rightarrow \chi_A + \chi_B = 1$	e.g. Suppose in a solution, where there are 2 moles of solute A and 8 moles of solvent B, then the mole fraction of A, χ_A, is $\chi_A = \frac{2}{2+8} = 0.2$
Molarity (M)	It is defined as the number of moles of the solute in 1 L of the solution.	Molarity $(M) = \frac{\text{number of moles of solute}}{\text{volume of solution in litres}}$ Its unit is mol L^{-1}	e.g. 0.25 mol L^{-1} (or 0.25 M) solution of NaOH means that 0.25 moles (or 10 g) of NaOH has been dissolved in one litre (or one cubic decimetre).
Molality (m)	It is defined as the number of moles of solute present in 1 kg of solvent.	Molality $(m) = \frac{\text{number of moles of solute}}{\text{mass of solvent in kg}}$ Its unit is mol kg^{-1}	e.g. 1.00 mol kg^{-1} (or 1.00 m) solution of KCl means that 1 mole (74.5 g) of KCl is dissolved in 1 kg of water.
Normality (N)	It is defined as the number of gram equivalents of solute present in per litre of solution.	Normality $(N) = \frac{\text{number of gram equivalents of solute}}{\text{volume of solution in litres}}$ Number of gram equivalent of solute $= \frac{\text{Mass of solute}}{\text{Equivalent mass}}$ Its unit is g eq/L	e.g. 1.0 g eq/L of HCl solution means that 1 gram equivalent of HCl is dissolved in 1 litre of solution.

Note Molality is considered better for expressing the concentration as compared to molarity because molarity changes with temperature due to the expansion or contraction of the liquid volume of solution changes but, molality does not change with temperature as the mass of the solvent does not change with change in temperature.

However, molarity is widely used because it is easier to measure the volume of a solution.

Example 34 **A solution is prepared by adding 2 g of substance *A* to 18 g of water. Calculate the mass per cent of the solute.** NCERT

Sol. Mass per cent of $A = \dfrac{\text{Mass of } A}{\text{Mass of solution}} \times 100$

$= \dfrac{2\text{ g}}{2\text{ g of } A + 18\text{ g of water}} \times 100$

$= \dfrac{2\text{g}}{20\text{g}} \times 100 = 10\%$

Example 35 **A solution contains 25% water, 25% ethanol and 50% acetic acid by mass. Calculate the mole fraction of each component.**

Sol. Let the total mass of solution = 100 g

Mass of water = 25 g, Mass of ethanol = 25 g

Mass of acetic acid = 50 g

Moles of water $= \dfrac{25\text{ g}}{18\text{ g/mol}} = 1.388$ moles

($\because$ Molar mass of $H_2O = 18\text{ g/mol}$)

Moles of ethanol = 25 g / 46 g / mol = 0.543 moles

($\because$ Molar mass of $C_2H_5OH = 46\text{ g / mol}$)

Moles of acetic acid = 50 g / 60 g/mol = 0.833 moles

($\because$ Molar mass of $CH_3COOH = 60\text{ g / mol}$)

Total number of moles = (1.388 + 0.543 + 0.833) moles

= 2.764 moles

Mole fraction of water $= \dfrac{1.388}{2.764} = 0.502$

Mole fraction of ethanol $= \dfrac{0.543}{2.764} = 0.196$

Mole fraction of acetic acid $= \dfrac{0.833}{2.764} = 0.302$

Example 36 **Calculate the molarity of NaOH in the solution prepared by dissolving its 4 g in water to form 250 mL of the solution.**

Sol. Since, molarity $(M) = \dfrac{\text{number of moles of solute}}{\text{volume of solution in litres}}$

$= \dfrac{\text{Mass of NaOH / Molar mass of NaOH}}{0.250\text{ L}}$

$= \dfrac{4\text{ g / 40 g}}{0.250\text{ L}} = \dfrac{0.1\text{ mol}}{0.250\text{ L}}$

$= 0.4\text{ mol L}^{-1} = 0.4\text{ M}$

Example 37. **What volume of 10 M HCl and 3 M HCl should be mixed to get 1L of 6 M HCl solution?**

Sol. Suppose volume of 10 M HCl required to prepare 1L of 6 M HCl = x L

Volume of 3 M HCl required = $(1 - x)$ L

Using formula $\underbrace{M_1V_1}_{10\text{ M HCl}} + \underbrace{M_2V_2}_{3\text{ M HCl}} = \underbrace{M_3V_3}_{6\text{ M HCl}}$

$10 \times x + 3(1 - x) = 6 \times 1$

$\Rightarrow \quad 10x + 3 - 3x = 6$

$\Rightarrow \quad 7x = 3$

or $\quad x = \dfrac{3}{7} = 0.428\text{ L}$

$\therefore$ Volume of 10 M HCl required = 0.428 L = 428 mL

Volume of 3 M HCl required = 1 − 0.428

= 0.572 L = 572 mL

Example 38 **Calculate the molality of a solution containing 20.7 g potassium carbonate dissolved in 500 mL of solution (assume density of solution = 1 g mL^{-1}).**

Sol. Mass of $K_2CO_3 = 20.7$ g (Given)

Molar mass of $K_2CO_3 = 2 \times 39\text{ g} + 12\text{ g} + 3 \times 16\text{ g}$

= 138 g

Moles of $K_2CO_3 = \dfrac{20.7}{138} = 0.15$ moles

Mass of solution = (500 mL) × (1 g mL^{-1}) = 500 g

Amount of water = 500 g − 20.7 g = 479.3 g

Molality $= \dfrac{\text{moles of solute}}{\text{mass of solvent in gram}} \times 1000$

$= \dfrac{0.15\text{ moles}}{479.3\text{ g}} \times 1000 = 0.313\text{ m}$

Example 39 **The density of 3 M solution of NaCl is 1.25 g mL^{-1}. Calculate molality of the solution.** NCERT

Sol. $M = 3\text{ mol L}^{-1}$ (Given)

Mass of NaCl in 1 L solution = 3 moles × 58.5 g/mol

= 175.5 g

Mass of 1 L solution = 1000 × 1.25

= 1250 g

(since density = 1.25 g mL^{-1})

Mass of water solution = 1250 − 175.5

= 1074.5 g

= 1.0745 kg

Molality $= \dfrac{\text{number of moles of solute}}{\text{mass of solvent in kg}}$

$= \dfrac{3\text{ moles}}{1.0745\text{ kg}} = 2.79\text{ m}$

Example 40 **Calculate the normality of solution containing 62.3 g of hydrated copper sulphate ($CuSO_4 \cdot 5H_2O$) in 500 mL of solution.**

Sol. Mass of solute = 62.3 g

Equivalent mass of oxalic acid $= \dfrac{249.5}{2} = 124.75$ g

Gram equivalents of oxalic acid $= \dfrac{62.3}{124.75} = 0.5$

Volume of solution = 500 mL

$\because$ Normality $= \dfrac{\text{Number of gram equivalents of solute}}{\text{Volume of solution in litres}}$

$\therefore$ Normality $= \dfrac{0.5}{500} \times 1000 = 1\text{ N}$

Quick Test 3

1. 5.8 g of butane burns in the presence of oxygen gas to produce carbon dioxide and water vapour. Calculate the mass of carbon dioxide produced and the mass of oxygen required. *Diksha*

2. (i) How many moles of iron can be made from Fe_2O_3 by using 16 moles of carbon monoxide in the following reaction?

$$Fe_2O_3 + 3CO \longrightarrow 2Fe + 3CO_2$$

(ii) If 2 L of N_2 is mixed with 2 L of H_2 at a constant temperature and pressure, then what will be the volume of NH_3 formed ?

3. The reactant which is entirely consumed in reaction is known as limiting reagent. In the reaction $2A + 4B \rightarrow 3C + 4D$, when 5 moles of *A* react with 6 moles of *B*, then

(i) which is the limiting reagent?

(ii) calculate the amount of *C* formed? *NCERT Exemplar*

4. How much carbon disulphide will be formed if 4 g of carbon was heated with 8 g of sulphur. Also identify the limiting reagent. *Diksha*

5. Calculate the concentration of nitric acid in mol per litre in a sample which has a density 1.41 g mL^{-1} and the mass percent of nitric acid in it being 69%.

6. How are 0.50 mole Na_2CO_3 and 0.50 M Na_2CO_3 different? *NCERT*

7. Calculate the mass of sodium acetate, CH_3COONa required to make 500 mL of 0.375 molar aqueous solution. Molar mass of sodium acetate is 82.0245 g mol^{-1}. *NCERT*

8. If the density of methanol is 0.793 kg L^{-1}, what is its volume needed for making 2.5 L of its 0.25 M solution? *NCERT*

9. What will be the molality of the solution containing 18.25 g of HCl gas in 500 g of water? *NCERT Exemplar*

For Solutions, See QR Code on Pg. 37

Answers

1. 17.6 g, 20.8s g
2. (i) 10.67 moles (ii) 1.33 L of NH_3
3. (ii) 4.5 moles of C
4. 9.5 g of CS_2
5. 15.44 M
7. 15.38 g
8. 25.22 mL
9. 1 m

Mind Map

Some Basic Concepts of Chemistry

MATTER Anything having mass and occupying space.

Types of Matter

I. Pure Substance

Substance having fixed composition

Types of Pure Substances

- **Elements** They contain only one kind of particles.
- **Compounds** They have particles of more than one kind but in fixed ratio.

II. Mixture

Composition is not fixed.

Types of Mixture

- **Homogeneous** Composition of homogeneous mixture is uniform throughout. They cannot be separated by ordinary methods. e.g. True solutions.
- **Heterogeneous** Composition of heterogeneous mixture is not uniform throughout. They can be separated by physical methods. e.g. Colloids, suspension, etc.

Dalton's Atomic Theory

- Matter is made up of tiny indivisible particles, called **atoms**.
- Atoms of same element are alike.
- Compounds have different atoms but combine in fixed proportion.

Masses

1. Atomic Mass

It is the mass of an atom relative to the 1/12th of the mass of carbon atom (^{12}C).

- **Amu** (Atomic Mass Unit)
  It is the mass exactly equal to one twelfth the mass of one C-12 atom.
  1 amu or $u = 1.66056 \times 10^{-24}$ g.
- **Average Atomic Mass**
  For isotopes, atomic mass is called average atomic mass and given as

$$\text{Av. at. mass} = \frac{\sum x_i A_i}{\sum x_i}$$

where, x_i = % abundance

A_i = atomic mass

2. Molecular Mass

It is the sum of atomic masses of all the elements present in a molecule.

3. Formula Mass

In case of ions, molecular mass is called formula mass.

Mole Concept

- 1 mole of particles = 6.022×10^{23} particles or 1 mole = 22.4 L (for gases)
- $\text{Number of moles} = \frac{\text{Mass}}{\text{Atomic or molar mass}}$
- Number of molecules $= N_A \times$ Number of moles
- Number of atoms = Number of molecules × atomicity.

Percentage Composition

It shows parts by mass of a constituent in 100 parts by mass of compound.

- **Molecular Formula**
  Formula showing exact number of atoms present in a molecule of a compound.
  Molecular formula = $(\text{empirical formula})_n$
- **Empirical Formula**
  It shows simplest whole number ratio of different atoms present in one molecule of the compound.
  It is obtained by following steps
  - Divide mass of all elements by atomic mass.
  - Divide all the obtained values with lowest obtained value.
  - Make the obtained number a whole number if not.
  - Write the obtained number below the symbol of the element.

Stoichiometric Calculations

These are the calculations based on chemical equations.

- **Reactions in Solutions** Reactions occurring in aqueous medium.
- **Limiting Reagent** The reagent which limits the amount of product formed.

(i) **Mass Per cent** It is the mass of substance per 100 g of the solution.

(ii) **Mole Fraction** It is the ratio of moles of a substance to the total number of moles present in the solution.

$$\text{Mole fraction of } A = \frac{\text{Number of moles of } A}{\text{Total number of moles of solution}}$$

(iii) **Molarity (M)** It is moles present per litre of solution. It depends on temperature.

$$M = \frac{w \times 1000}{m' \times V}$$

(iv) **Molality (m)** It is moles present per kg of solvent. It does not vary with temperature.

$$m = \frac{w \times 1000}{m' \times W}$$

Uncertainty in Measurement

- **Scientific notation** (representation of a number as $N \times 10^n$). To get scientific notation if decimal is moved to right, n is –ve and if it is moved towards left, n is +ve.
- **Significant figures** (all certain digits with last digit uncertain.)
- **Dimensional Analysis**
  Required unit = given value × conversion factor

Laws of Chemical Combinations

- Law of conservation of mass (mass of reactants = mass of products).
- Law of definite proportions.
- Law of multiple proportions.
- Gay Lussac's law of gaseous volumes.
- Avogadro's law.

EXAM PATTERN QUESTIONS

Objective Type Questions

Multiple Choice Questions (MCQs) [1 Mark]

1. Which of the following statements is/are incorrect?

(a) The weight of a substance can be determined very accurately by using an analytical balance.

(b) Volume is denoted in dm^3 units.

(c) Density of a substance is its amount present per unit volume.

(d) Candela is the luminous intensity, that emits monochromatic radiation of frequency, 540×10^{12} Hz.

2. Which of the following statements is/are correct regarding significant figures?

(a) All non-zero digits are significant.

(b) Significant figures are meaningful digits which are known with certainty.

(c) Zero between two non-zero digits are significant.

(d) All of the above.

3. 18.72 g of a substance X occupies 1.81 cm^3. What will be its density measured in correct significant figures?

(a) 10.3 g/cm^3

(b) 10.34 g/cm^3

(c) 10.4 g/cm^3

(d) 10.3425 g/cm^3

4. Consider the following table,

Number	Rounding upto 3 significant figures
1.386	X
4.334	Y
2.808	Z

X, Y and Z in the above table are

(a) $X = 1.39, Y = 4.34, Z = 2.809$

(b) $X = 1.39, Y = 4.33, Z = 2.81$

(c) $X = 1.38, Y = 4.34, Z = 2.800$

(d) $X = 1.39, Y = 4.34, Z = 2.80$

5. If the density of a solution is 3.12 g mL^{-1}, the mass of 1.5 mL solution in significant figures is .... **NCERT Exemplar**

(a) 4.7 g (b) 4680×10^{-3} g

(c) 4.680 g (d) 46.80 g

6. Two students performed the same experiment separately and each one of them recorded two readings of mass which are given below. Correct reading of mass is 3.0 g. On the basis of given data, mark the correct option out of the following statements. **NCERT Exemplar**

Students	Readings (i)	Readings (ii)
A	3.01	2.99
B	3.05	2.95

(a) Results of both the students are neither accurate nor precise.

(b) Results of student A are both precise and accurate.

(c) Results of student B are neither precise nor accurate.

(d) Results of student B are both precise and accurate.

7. Which of the following reactions is not correct according to the law of conservation of mass? **NCERT Exemplar**

(a) $2Mg(s) + O_2(g) \longrightarrow 2MgO(s)$

(b) $C_3H_8(g) + O_2(g) \longrightarrow CO_2(g) + H_2O(g)$

(c) $P_4(s) + 5O_2(g) \longrightarrow P_4O_{10}(s)$

(d) $CH_4(g) + 2O_2(g) \longrightarrow CO_2(g) + 2H_2O(g)$

8. Which law states that if two elements can combine to form more than one compound, the masses of one element that combine with a fixed mass of other element, are in the ratio of simple whole numbers?

(a) Avogadro's law

(b) Law of definite composition

(c) Law of multiple proportions

(d) Gay Lussac's law of gaseous volumes

9. Zinc sulphate contains 22.65% zinc and 43.9% water of crystallisation. If the law of constant proportions is true then the weight of zinc required to produce 20 g of the zinc sulphate crystals will be **Competency Based Que.**

(a) 45.3 g (b) 4.53 g

(c) 0.453 g (d) 453 g

10. If 1 mL of water contains 20 drops then number of molecules in a drop of water is

(a) 6.023×10^{23} molecules (b) 1.376×10^{26} molecules

(c) 1.672×10^{21} molecules (d) 4.346×10^{20} molecules

11. **Match the Column I with Column II and choose the correct option using the codes given below**

Column I	Column II
A. Mass of H_2 produced when 0.5 mole of zinc reacts with excess of HCl	(i) 3.01×10^{23}
B. Mass of all atoms of a compound with formula $C_{70}H_{22}$	(ii) 6.023×10^{23}
C. Number of molecules in 35.5 g of Cl_2	(iii) 1.43×10^{-21}
D. Number of molecules in 64 g of SO_2	(iv) 1

Codes **Competency Based Que.**

	A	B	C	D
(a)	(ii)	(i)	(iv)	(ii)
(b)	(i)	(ii)	(iii)	(iv)
(c)	(iv)	(iii)	(i)	(ii)
(d)	(iv)	(iii)	(ii)	(i)

12. **Arrange the following in the order of increasing mass (Atomic mass of O = 16, Cu = 63 and N = 14).**

I. One atom of oxygen
II. One atom of nitrogen
III. 1×10^{-10} mole of oxygen
IV. 1×10^{-10} mole of copper

(a) II < I < III < IV (b) I < II < III < IV
(c) III < II < IV < I (d) IV < II < III < I

13. **A cylinder of compressed gas contains nitrogen and oxygen in the ratio 3 : 1 by mole. If the cylinder is known to contain 2.5×10^4 g of oxygen, then the total mass of the gas mixture will be** **Competency Based Que.**

(a) 7.8125×10^4
(b) 6.5625×10^4
(c) 9.0625×10^4
(d) 6.023×10^5

14. **Which of the following statements regarding the molecular mass is not correct?**

(a) Molecular formula represents the simple whole number ratio of various atoms present in a compound.
(b) Percentage composition of a compound can be calculated from its molecular formula.
(c) Molecular formula can be obtained from empirical formula if molar mass is known.
(d) Molecular formula shows the exact number of different types of atoms present in a molecule.

15. **0.242 g sample of potassium is heated in oxygen, 0.440g of a crystalline compound is obtained. What is the formula of this compound?**

(a) KO (b) K_2O
(c) KO_2 (d) KO_3

16. **A compound contains 69.5% oxygen, 30.5% nitrogen and its molecular weight is 92. The formula of compound is**

(a) N_2O (b) NO_2
(c) N_2O_4 (d) N_2O_5

17. ***x* g of Ag was dissolved in HNO_3 and the solution was treated with excess of NaCl, when 2.87 g of AgCl was precipitated. The value of *x* is**

(a) 1.08 g (b) 2.16 g
(c) 2.70 g (d) 1..62 g

18. **A solution of sugar is obtained by mixing 200g of its 25% solution and 500g of its 40% solution (both by mass). The mass percentage of the resulting sugar solution will be**

(a) 48 (b) 36 (c) 59 (d) 72

19. **What will be the molarity of pure water?**

(a) 18 M (b) 50.0 M
(c) 55.6 M (d) 100 M

Assertion-Reason [1 Mark]

■ Directions (Q. Nos. 20-30) In the following questions, a statement of Assertion is followed by a corresponding statements of Reason of the following statements, choose the correct one.

(a) Both (A) and (R) are correct and (R) is the correct explanation of (A).
(b) Both (A) and (R) are correct but (R) is not the correct explanation of (A).
(c) (A) is correct but (R) is incorrect.
(d) (A) is incorrect but (R) is correct.

20. Assertion (A) A number 138.42 can be written as 1.3842×10^2 in scientific notation.

Reason (R) In scientific notation, a number is generally expressed in the form of $N \times 10^n$.

21. Assertion (A) Significant figures for 0.200 is 3 whereas for 200 it is 1.

Reason (R) Zeros at the end or right of a number are significant provided they are not on the right side of the decimal point.

22. Assertion (A) 1.231 has four significant figures.

Reason (R) All non-zero digits right to the decimal points are significant.

23. Assertion (A) One atomic mass unit is defined as one twelfth of the mass of one carbon-12 atom.

Reason (R) Carbon-12 isotope is the most abundant isotope of carbon and has been chosen as standard.

Competency Based Que.

24. Assertion (A) Combustion of 16 g of methane gives 18 g of water.

Reason (R) In the combustion of methane, water is one of the product.

25. Assertion (A) Equal moles of different substances contain same number of constituent particles.

Reason (R) Equal weights of different substances contains the same number of constituent particles.

Competency Based Que.

26. Assertion (A) Atomicity of oxygen is 2.

Reason (R) 1 mole of an element contains 6.023×10^{23} atoms.

27. Assertion (A) The empirical mass of C_2H_4 is CH_2.

Reason (R) The empirical formula represent the simplest whole number ratio of various atoms present in a compound.

28. Assertion (A) A reactant that is entirely consumed when a reaction goes to completion is known as limiting reaction.

Reason (R) The amount of limiting reactant limits the amount of product formed.

29. Assertion (A) Molarity of a solution does not represents its concentration.

Reason (R) Molarity is the number of moles of solute per litre of solution.

30. Assertion (A) Molality of a solution does not change with temperature.

Reason (R) Mass is affected by temperature.

Case-Study [4 Marks]

31. Read the given case and answer the following questions.

The accurate determination and control of solution concentration play a crucial role in both fundamental and applied chemistry. Concentration units such as molarity, molality, mole fraction, and normality offer chemists the flexibility to tailor measurements to specific experimental needs. Molarity, the moles of solute per litre of solution, is widely used due to its simplicity in preparation; however, its dependence on temperature can limit its use in temperature-sensitive studies. Conversely, molality, defined as moles of solute per kilogram of solvent, remains unaffected by temperature fluctuations, rendering it particularly useful in high-precision experimental setups where stability is paramount.

Mole fraction, a dimensionless ratio, is indispensable in mixtures where the relative proportion of components is critical, such as in the study of gas mixtures. It provides insight into the composition without relying on volume or mass measurements, making it a versatile tool for both theoretical and applied research. Normality, by accounting for reactive units, proves invaluable in titrations and redox reactions, where the exact number of reactive species directly influences reaction outcomes.

These concentration units collectively contribute to a comprehensive understanding of solution behaviour, supporting advancements across analytical, industrial, and environmental chemistry. Their correct application enhances the reliability and accuracy of chemical processes, underscoring their foundational importance in the scientific investigation and industrial innovation.

(i) (a) Calculate the molality of a solution prepared by dissolving 12 grams of KCl (molar mass = 74.5 g/mol) in 250 grams of water.

(b) How does the concept of mole fraction help in understanding the composition of solutions without relying on units like litres or kilograms?

(ii) If a gas mixture contains 5 moles of nitrogen (N_2) and 3 moles of oxygen (O_2), then the mole fraction of nitrogen in the mixture will be

(a) 0.489 (b) 0.625

(c) 0.858 (d) 0.297

(iii) The normality of an oxalic acid ($H_2C_2O_4$) solution when 6.3 g of oxalic acid is dissolved in 500mL of solution will be [equivalent weight of oxalic acid = 63 g/equiv]

(a) 0.15 N (b) 0.05 N

(c) 0.2 N (d) 0.4 N

Or What volume of water is to be added to 100 cm^3 of 0.5 M NaOH solution to make it 0.1 M solution?

(a) 100 cm^3 (b) 400 cm^3

(c) 500 cm^3 (d) 200 cm^3

32. Read the given case and answer the following questions.

The behaviour of elements during reactions is remarkably consistent, governed by a set of fundamental principles known as the laws of chemical combination. Observing these laws reveals an inherent order in chemical processes, where elements come together in predictable ways. In every reaction, the matter remains unchanged in quantity, a striking fact that hints at the delicate balanced maintained even as substances transform.

Chemists have long noted that compounds form with a specific identity, each composition unwavering, no matter the source or scale of synthesis. The ratios in which elements combine reflect an intrinsic simplicity, a natural inclination toward whole-number relationships that underscores the structure of matter itself.

These laws do more than explain chemical behaviour; they act as a guiding framework for discovery. In practice, they allow chemists to anticipate the results of reactions, ensuring precision whether in a laboratory experiment or industrial production.

Understanding these patterns enables scientists to innovate within clear boundaries, transforming elements into the complex compounds that fuel technology and advance scientific knowledge. These enduring principles continue to shape the course of chemistry, offering a glimpse into the elegant logic that drives the combination and transformation of all substances.

(i) A sample of carbon monoxide (CO) contains 12 grams of carbon and 16 grams of oxygen. According to the law of definite proportions, what would be the masses of carbon and oxygen in a 70-gram sample of carbon monoxide?

(ii) Two compounds are formed by combining element *X* with oxygen. In the first compound, 8 grams of *X* combine with 16 grams of oxygen. In the second compound, 8 grams of *X* combine with 32 grams of oxygen. Show that this observation is in agreement with the law of multiple proportions.

(iii) How does the law of definite proportions help chemists to determine whether a sample is a pure compound?

Or Explain why the law of conservation of mass is essential in balancing chemical equations.

Subjective Type Questions

Short Answer Type I Questions [2 Marks]

1. Express each of the following in SI units.

(i) 14 pound per square inch (atmospheric pressure)
(ii) 100 mile per hour
(iii) 6 feet 2 inch
(iv) 150 pound

2. Match the following with their multiples. **NCERT**

	Prefixes	Multiples
(i)	micro	10^6
(ii)	deca	10^9
(iii)	mega	10^{-6}
(iv)	giga	10^{-15}
(v)	femto	10

3. For precious stone, carat is used for specifying its mass. If 1 carat = 3.08647 grains (a unit of mass) and 1 gram = 15.4324 grains. Find the total mass in kilogram of a ring that contains 0.700 carat diamond and 5.00 gram gold. **Competency Based Que.**

4. Pressure is determined as force per unit area of the surface. The SI unit of pressure, pascal is as shown below 1 Pa = 1 Nm^{-2} If the mass of air at sea level is 1034 g cm^{-2}, calculate the pressure in pascal. **NCERT**

Hint :
- The SI unit of mass is kilogram and of length is metre so convert gram to kilogram and cm^2 to m^2 as pressure is to be calculated in SI units.
- Write 1 kg ms^{-2} = 1N and 1 N m^{-2} = 1Pa to obtain pressure in pascal.

5. The water level in a metric measuring cup is 0.75 L before the addition of a pebble weighing 150 g. The water level after submerging the pebble is 0.82 L. Determine the density of the pebble. **Competency Based Que.**

6. If the density of a solution is 3.12 g mL^{-1}, then calculate the mass of 1.5 mL solution in significant figures.

7. Answer the following questions.

(i) Why is the law of Gay Lussac's not obeyed if any reactant or product is not a gas?

(ii) How can you prove that red oxide of copper is not an element?

8. Air contains 20% oxygen by volume. Calculate the theoretical volume of air which will be required for burning completely 500 m^3 of acetylene gas.

All volumes are measured under the same conditions of temperature and pressure. **Competency Based Que.**

9. The atomic mass of most of the elements is fractional. Why?

10. What do you understand by stoichiometric coefficients in a chemical equation?

11. (i) Volume of a solution changes with change in temperature, then, will the molality of the solution be affected by temperature? Give reason for your answer. **NCERT Exemplar**

(ii) If vitamin C is known to contain 1.29×10^{24} hydrogen atoms, then calculate the number of moles of hydrogen atoms.

Short Answer Type II Questions [3 Marks]

12. 1.375 g of cupric oxide was reduced by heating in a current of hydrogen and the weight of copper that remained was 1.098 g. In another experiment, 1.179 g of copper was dissolved in the nitric acid and the resulting copper nitrate was converted into cupric oxide by ignition. The weight of cupric oxide formed was 1.476 g. Show that these results illustrate the law of constant composition.

13. 45.4 L of dinitrogen reacted with 22.7 L of dioxygen and 45.4 L nitrous oxide was formed. The reaction is given below.

$$2\,N_2(g)+O_2(g)\longrightarrow 2\,N_2O(g)$$

Which law is being obeyed in this experiment? Write the statement of the law. **NCERT Exemplar**

14. Calculate the atomic mass (average) of chlorine using the following data. **NCERT**

Isotope	% natural abundance	Molar mass
^{35}Cl	75.77	34.9689
^{37}Cl	24.23	36.9659

15. Calculate the average atomic mass of hydrogen using the following data. **NCERT Exemplar**

Isotope	% Natural abundance	Molar mass
^{1}H	99.985	1
^{2}H	0.015	2

16. Calculate the molar mass of the following:
(i) H_2O (ii) CO_2 (iii) CH_4 **NCERT**

17. Calculate the number of moles in the following masses
(i) 1.46 metric ton of Al (1 metric ton $=10^3$ kg)
(ii) 7.9 mg of Ca

18. Calculate the amount of carbon dioxide that could be produced when
(i) 1 mole of carbon is burnt in air.
(ii) 1 mole of carbon is burnt in 16 g of dioxygen.
(iii) 2 moles of carbon are burnt in 16 g of dioxygen.

Hint : **NCERT**
- In order to find the moles of different elements/ compounds taking part in the reaction, write a balanced chemical equation for combustion of carbon in dioxygen (air).
- Calculate the amount of CO_2 produced with the help of information available from the balanced chemical equation.

19. Chlorine is prepared in the laboratory by treating manganese dioxide (MnO_2) with aqueous hydrochloric acid according to the reaction,

$$4HCl\,(aq)+MnO_2(s)\longrightarrow 2H_2O\,(l)+MnCl_2(aq)+Cl_2(g)$$

How many gram of HCl reacts with 5.0 g of manganese dioxide? **NCERT**

20. (i) What is the mass per cent of carbon in carbon dioxide? **NCERT Exemplar**
(ii) How many molecules are there in one drop of water if its volume is 0.1 cc ? [Given, density of water at room temperature is 1.0 g/cc.]

21. Calculate the mass per cent of different elements present in sodium sulphate, Na_2SO_4. **NCERT**

22. If 4 g of NaOH dissolves in 36 g of H_2O, calculate the mole fraction of each component in the solution. Also, determine the molarity of solution (specific gravity of solution is 1 g mL^{-1}). **NCERT Exemplar**

Hint :
- To proceed the calculation, first calculate the number of moles of NaOH and H_2O.
- Then, find mole fraction of NaOH and H_2O by using the formula,

$$\chi_{NaOH}=\frac{n_{NaOH}}{n_{NaOH}+n_{H_2O}}\left(\text{or } \chi_{H_2O}=\frac{n_{H_2O}}{n_{NaOH}+n_{H_2O}}\right)$$

- Then, calculate molarity $=\dfrac{w\times 1000}{m\times V}$, so in order to calculate molarity we require volume of solution which is, $V=\dfrac{m}{\text{specific gravity}}$, where $m=$ mass of solution.

23. Answer the following questions.
(i) If the concentration of glucose ($C_6H_{12}O_6$) in blood is 0.9 g L^{-1}, what will be the molarity of glucose in blood?
(ii) Write main postulates of Dalton's atomic theory.
(iii) Calculate the number of atoms present in 52 u of He ? **NCERT Exemplar**

Long Answer Type Questions [5 Marks]

24. The following data are obtained when dinitrogen and dioxygen react together to form different compounds.

	Mass of dinitrogen	Mass of dioxygen
(i)	14 g	16 g
(ii)	14 g	32 g
(iii)	28 g	32 g
(iv)	28 g	80 g

(i) Which law of chemical combination is obeyed by the above experimental data? Give statement.

(ii) Fill in the blanks in the following conversion

(a) 1 km = ...mm = ...pm

(b) 1 mg = ...kg = ...ng

(c) 1 mL = ...L = ...dm^3 **NCERT**

25. Define the law of multiple proportions. Explain it with two examples. How does this law point to the existence of atoms? **NCERT Exemplar**

26. Arrange the following in order of their increasing masses in gram (i) One atom of silver, (ii) one gram-atom of nitrogen, (iii) one mole of calcium, (iv) one mole of oxygen molecules, (v) 10^{23} atoms of carbon and (vi) one gram of iron.

27. (i) A mixture of oxalic acid and formic acid is heated with concentrated H_2SO_4 and the gas evolved is collected. On treating the solution with KOH, the volume of the solution decreases by 1/6th. Calculate the molar ratios of two acids in the original mixture.

(ii) If chlorophyll, the green colouring matter of plants, contains 3.64% of magnesium by mass, then determine the number of magnesium atoms in 400 g chlorophyll. [Given atomic mass of magnesium = 24.3 g]

28. (i) The density of the water at room temperature is 0.1 g/mL. How many molecules are there in a drop of water if its volume is 0.05 mL?

(ii) An alloy of iron (53.6%), nickel (45.8%) and manganese (0.6%) has a density of 8.17 g cm^{-3}. Calculate the number of Ni atoms present in the alloy of dimensions 10.0 cm × 20.0 cm × 15.0 cm. **Competency Based Que.**

29. Determine the molecular formula of an oxide of iron in which the mass per cent of iron and oxygen are 69.9 and 30.1 respectively. Given that molar mass of the oxide is 159. 898 g mol^{-1}. **NCERT**

30. A compound made up of two elements *A* and *B* has $A = 70\%$, $B = 30\%$. Their relative number of moles in the compound are 1.25 and 1.88. Calculate

(i) atomic masses of the elements *A* and *B*.

(ii) molecular formula of the compound, if its molecular mass is found to be 160. **Competency Based Que.**

31. A welding fuel gas contains carbon and hydrogen only. Burning a small sample of it in oxygen gives 3.38 g carbon dioxide, 0.690 g of water and no other products. A volume 10.0 L (measured at STP) of this welding gas is found to weigh 11.6 g. Calculate (i) empirical formula (ii) molar mass of the gas and (iii) molecular formula. **NCERT**

Hints & Solutions

Objective Type Questions

1. (*a*) Option (a) is the incorrect statement because weight of the substance cannot be determined very accurately by using an analytical balance.
2. (*d*) All of the above statements are correct.
3. (*a*) The density will be measured as 10.3 g/cm^3. It is because 1.81 has 3 significant figures only while 18.72 has 4 significant figures. So, the result will have only 3 significant figures.
4. (*b*) The set of figures obtained after rounding upto three significant figures are 1.39, 4.33, 2.81.
5. (*a*) Mass = Density × Volume

$$\text{Mass} = 3.12\ g/mL \times 1.5\ mL$$
$$\text{Mass} = 4.68\ g$$
$$= 4.7\ g$$

The mass of the solution will be reported as 4.7 g, i.e. upto two significant figures.

6. (*b*) Results of student *A* are both precise and accurate while the result of student *B* is accurate but not precise.
7. (*b*) The chemical equation given in option (b) is not according to law of conservation of mass. It is because mass of reactants and mass of products are not equal.

$$\underset{44\,g}{C_3H_8(g)} + \underset{32\,g}{O_2(g)} \longrightarrow \underset{44\,g}{CO_2(g)} + \underset{18\,g}{H_2O(g)}$$

8. (*c*) The given statement is law of multiple proportions.
9. (*b*) 100 g of $ZnSO_4$ crystals are obtained from

$$= 22.65\ g\ Zn$$

So, 1 g of $ZnSO_4$ crystals will be obtained from

$$= \frac{22.65}{100}\ g\ Zn$$

∴ 20 g of $ZnSO_4$ crystals will be obtained from

$$= \frac{22.65}{100} \times 20 = 4.53\ g$$

10. (*c*) 1 mL of water = 1 g of water

So, 18 g of water contains 6.023×10^{23} molecules

$\Rightarrow$ 1 mL of water or $\frac{6.022 \times 10^{23}}{18}$ molecules contains

$$= 20\ \text{drops}$$

∴ 1 drop of water will contain $= \frac{6.022 \times 10^{23}}{18 \times 20}$

$$= 1.672 \times 10^{21}\ \text{molecules}$$

11. (*c*)

A. $Zn + 2HCl \longrightarrow ZnCl_2 + H_2$

1 mole of Zn produces 2g of H_2

0.5 mole of Zn will produce 1 g of H_2

B. Molar mass of $C_{70}H_{22} = 862\ g/mol$

Mass of atoms $= \frac{862}{6.023 \times 10^{23}} = 1.43 \times 10^{-21}\ g$

C. 70 g of $Cl_2 = 6.023 \times 10^{23}$ molecules

35.5 g of $Cl_2 = 3.01 \times 10^{23}$ molecules

D. Molar mass of $SO_2 = 64\ g = 1$ mole

64 g or 1 mole of $SO_2 = 6.023 \times 10^{23}$ molecules

Thus, the correct match is

A → (iv), B → (iii), C → (i) and D → (ii)

12. (*a*)

I. Mass of 1 atom of oxygen $= \frac{16}{6.022 \times 10^{23}}$
$$= 2.66 \times 10^{-23}\ g$$

II. Mass of 1 atom of nitrogen $= \frac{14}{6.022 \times 10^{23}}$
$$= 2.32 \times 10^{-23}\ g$$

III Mass of 1×10^{-10} mole of oxygen $= 1 \times 10^{-10} \times 32$
$$= 3.2 \times 10^{-9}\ g$$

IV. Mass of 1×10^{-10} of copper $= 63 \times 1 \times 10^{-10}$
$$= 6.3 \times 10^{-9}\ g$$

So, the correct increasing order is II < I < III < IV.

13. (*c*) Number of moles of oxygen in the cylinder

$$= \frac{\text{Mass (in g)}}{\text{Molecular mass (in g/mol)}}$$

$$= \frac{2.5 \times 10^4}{32} = 781.25\ mol$$

∴ Number of moles of $N_2 = 3 \times 781.25$ mol
$$= 2343.75\ mol$$

Mass of nitrogen in the cylinder

$$= 2343.75\ mol \times 28\ g/mol$$
$$= 65625\ g = 6.5625 \times 10^4\ g$$

Total mass of the gas in the cylinder

$$= 2.5 \times 10^4 + 6.5625 \times 10^4 = 9.0625 \times 10^4\ g$$

14. (*a*) The incorrect statement is (a). Its correct from is, empirical formula represents the simplest whole number ratio of various atoms present in a compound.
15. (*c*) Mass of K = 0.242 g

Mass of compound = 0.440 g

Mass of oxygen = 0.440 − 0.242 = 0.198 g

Relative molar ratio of K $= \frac{0.242}{39} = 0.006$

Relative molar ratio of O $= \frac{0.198}{16} = 0.012$

Simple ratio of K:O = 1:2

So, the formula is KO_2.

16. (c) Moles of oxygen $= \dfrac{69.5\text{ g}}{16\text{ g/mol}} = 4.34$ mol

Moles of nitrogen $= \dfrac{30.5\text{ g}}{14\text{ g/mol}} = 2.18$ moles

Ratio of moles of N and O = 2.18:4.34

=1 : 2

So, the empirical formula is NO_2.

Molecular formula $= (NO_2)_n$

where, $n = \dfrac{\text{molecular mass}}{\text{empirical mass}} = \dfrac{92}{46} = 2$

∴The formula of the compound is N_2O_4.

17. (b) The reaction involved is as follows

$$Ag + Cl \longrightarrow AgCl$$

Atomic mass of Ag = 108 u

Atomic mass of Cl = 35.5 u

Molecular mass of AgCl = 143.5 g/mol. So, 143.5 g AgCl is obtained from 108 g Ag

⇒ 2.87 g of AgCl is obtained from $= \dfrac{108 \times 2.87}{143.5} = 2.16$ g

18. (b) Total mass of sugar in the given mixture is

$= 0.25 \times 200\text{ g} + 0.40 \times 500\text{ g} = 250$ g

Now, total mass of solution = 200 g + 500 g = 700 g

∴ Mass % of sugar solution $= \dfrac{250}{700} \times 100 = 35.7\% \approx 36\%$

19. (c) Molarity $= \dfrac{\text{No. of moles of solute}}{\text{Volume of solution (in L)}}$

No. of moles $= \dfrac{1000\text{g}}{18\text{g/mol}} = 55.55$ moles

So, molarity $= \dfrac{55.55}{1\text{L}} = 55.55$ M or 55.6 M

20. (a) Both (A) and (R) are correct and (R) is the correct explanation of (A).

21. (c) (A) is correct but (R) is incorrect.

Correct Reason Zeros at the end or right of a number are significant provided they are on the right side of the decimal point.

22. (c) (A) is correct but (R) is incorrect.

Correct Reason All the non-zero digits are significant. Hence, 1.231 has four significant figures.

23. (a) Both (A) and (R) are correct and (R) is the correct explanation of (A).

24. (d) (A) is incorrect but (R) is correct.

Correct Assertion The reaction involved in the combustion of methane is as follows

$$CH_4(g) + 2O_2(g) \longrightarrow CO_2(g) + 2H_2O(g)$$

So, 16 g of CH_4 on complete combustion will give 36 g (2 moles) of water.

25. (c) (A) is correct but (R) is incorrect.

Correct Reason Equal moles of different substances contain same number of constituent particles but equal weights of different substances do not contain the same number of constituent particles.

26. (b) Both (A) and (R) are correct but (R) is not the correct explanation of (A). The correct explanation is oxygen exists as diatomic molecule in its common molecular form (O_2).

27. (a) Both (A) and (R) are correct and (R) is the correct explanation of (A).

28. (a) Both (A) and (R) are correct and (R) is the correct explanation of (A).

29. (d) (A) is incorrect but (R) is correct.

Correct Assertion Molarity of a solution represents its concentration.

30. (c) Molality of a solution does not change with temperature, since mass remains unaffected with temperature. Hence, (A) is correct but (R) is incorrect.

31. (i) (a) Given, mass of KCl = 12 g

Molar mass of KCl = 74.5 g/mol

Mass of water = 250 g = 0.25 kg

Molality = Moles of KCl/Mass of water in kg

Therefore, Molality = 0.161/0.25 = 0.644 m **(1)**

(b) Mole fraction is useful for understanding solution composition as it provides a unitless ratio, allowing comparison of components without depending on volume or mass measurement. **(1)**

(ii) (b) Total moles = moles of N_2 + moles of O_2

= 5 moles + 3 moles = 8 moles

Therefore, Mole fraction of N_2 = 5 moles/8 moles

= 0.625 **(1)**

(iii) (c) Given, weight of oxalic acid = 6.3 g

Volume of solution = 500 mL = 0.5 L

Equivalent weight of oxalic acid = 63 g/equiv

Normality $= \dfrac{\text{Given weight}}{\text{Equivalent weight} \times \text{Volume (in L)}}$

$= \dfrac{6.3\text{ g}}{63\text{g/ equiv.} \times 0.5\text{ L}}$

Normality = 0.2N

Or

(b) Since, $M_1V_1 = M_2V_2$

∴ $0.5\ M \times 100\text{ cm}^3 = 0.1\ M \times V_2$

∴ $V_2 = 500\text{ cm}^3$

Thus, volume of water to be added to 100 cm^3 of solution = 500 − 100 = 400 cm^3. **(1)**

32. (i) Given, mass of carbon $=12$ g

Mass of oxygen $=16$ g

$\therefore$ Total mass of initial CO sample $=12\text{ g}+16\text{ g}=28$ g

Now, mass ratio of carbon and oxygen respectively are;

Mass ratio of carbon $=\frac{12\text{ g}}{28\text{ g}}=\frac{3}{7}$

and Mass ration of oxygen $=\frac{16\text{ g}}{28\text{ g}}=\frac{4}{7}$

Thus, mass of carbon in 70 g sample of CO

$=70\times\frac{3}{7}=30$ g

Similarly, mass of oxygen in 70 g sample of CO

$=70\times\frac{4}{7}=40$ g **(2)**

(ii) In the first compound ;

Mass of $X=8$ g and Mass of $O=16$ g

$\therefore$ Ratio of O to $X=\frac{16}{8}=2:1$

Similarly, in the second compound;

Mass of $X=8$ g and Mass of $O=32$ g

$\therefore$ Ratio of O to $X=\frac{32}{8}=4:1$

Thus, the observation is consistent with the law of multiple proportion as the mass of oxygen that combiner with a fixed mass of X is in a simple whole number ratio (2 : 1). **(1)**

(iii) This law helps to identify purity by ensuring that a compound has a consistent element ratio, distinguishing it from impure or mixed samples. **(1)**

Or

This law ensures that the mass of reactants equals the mass of products, making it essential for achieving balanced equations in chemical reactions. **(1)**

Subjective Type Questions

1. (i) 1 pound per square inch = 6894.76 Nm^{-2}

$\therefore$ 14 pound per square inch

$=14\times 6894.76=96526.64\ Nm^{-2}$ **(½)**

(ii) 1 mile/h $=\frac{1.6\times 10^3\text{ m}}{3600\text{ s}}=0.444\text{ ms}^{-1}$

$\therefore$ 100 mile/h = 44.4 m/s **(½)**

(iii) 6 feet 2 inch = 1.8796 m

[$\therefore$ 1 feet = 12 inch, 1m = 39.37 inch] **(½)**

(iv) 1 pound = 0.454 kg

$\therefore$ 150 pound = 68.1 kg **(½)**

2. Micro $=10^{-6}$, deca $=10$, mega $=10^6$, giga $=10^9$ and femto $=10^{-15}$. **(2)**

3. Finding mass of diamond in kg.

1 carat = 3.08647 grains

$\therefore$ 0.700 carat $=0.700\times 3.08647$ grains $=2.16$ grains

Also, 1 gram = 15.4324 grains

$\therefore$ 1 grain $=\frac{1}{15.4324}=0.064799$ grams **(1)**

and 2.16 grains $=2.16\times 0.064799=0.1399$ grams

1 gram $=10^{-3}$ kg $\Rightarrow 0.1399\text{ g}=1.399\times 10^{-4}$ kg

Total mass of the ring in kg

$=1.399\times 10^{-4}\text{ kg}+5\times 10^{-3}\text{ kg}=5.1399\times 10^{-3}$ kg **(1)**

4. Pressure is the force or weight per unit area.

Pressure $=\frac{1034\text{ g}\times 9.8\text{ ms}^{-2}}{1\text{ cm}^2}$ [$\because F=ma$] **(1)**

$=\frac{1034\text{ kg}\times 100\times 100\times 9.8\text{ m s}^{-2}}{1000\text{ m}^2}$

$=101332.0\text{ N m}^{-2}$ ($\because$ 1N = 1 kg m s^{-2})

$=1.01332\times 10^5$ Pa **(1)**

5. The volume displaced by the pebble

$=0.82-0.75=0.07$ L = 70 mL **(1)**

Mass of the pebble = 150 g

Therefore, density of the pebble is

Density $=\frac{\text{Mass}}{\text{Volume}}=\frac{150\text{ g}}{70\text{ mL}}=2.14\text{ g mL}^{-1}$ **(1)**

Mistake Alert *While calculating the volume, one can make a mistake by not taking the volume displaced by the pebble.*

6. Given that, density of solution $=3.12\text{ g mL}^{-1}$

Volume of solution = 1.5 mL

For a solution,

Mass = Volume × Density

$=1.5\text{ mL}\times 3.12\text{ g mL}^{-1}=4.68$ g **(1)**

The digit 1.5 has only two significant figures, so the answer must also be limited to two significant figures. So, it is rounded off to reduce the number of significant figures. Hence, the answer is reported as 4.7 g. **(1)**

7. (i) If any reactant or product is a liquid or solid, the volume occupied by them is extremely small as compared to the gas and hence, the law is not obeyed. **(1)**

(ii) On heating red oxide of copper in the presence of hydrogen, its mass decreases and it forms shining metallic copper which is chemically different from the original compound. The reaction involved is

$$Cu_2O+H_2 \longrightarrow 2Cu+H_2O$$

Hence, red oxide of copper is not an element. **(1)**

8.

$2C_2H_2$ +	$5O_2$	$\longrightarrow 4CO_2$	$+ 2H_2O(g)$
2 vol	5 vol	4 vol	2 vol (Gay-Lussac's Law)
or 1 vol	5/2 vol	4/2 vol	2/2 vol
500 m^3	5/2 ×500 m^3	4/2 ×500 m^3	2/2 ×500 m^3
500 m^3	1250 m^3	1000 m^3	500 m^3

Thus, 1250 m^3 oxygen is required for burning 500 m^3 of acetylene. But the percentage of oxygen in air is 20%

$\therefore$ Volume of air required $= 1250 \times 100 / 20 = 6250 \text{ m}^3$ (2)

9. Atomic mass of most of the elements is fractional because most of the elements occur in nature as a mixture of isotopes and their atomic masses are the average relative atomic masses of the isotopes depending on their abundance. (2)

10. The coefficients of reactants and products involved in a chemical equation represented by the balanced form, are known as stoichiometric coefficients.

e.g. $N_2(g) + 3H_2(g) \longrightarrow 2NH_3(g)$

The stoichiometric coefficients are 1, 3 and 2 respectively. (2)

11. (i) No, molality of solution does not change with temperature since mass remains unaffected with temperature. (1)

Mistake Alert *One can make a mistake of understanding molarity instead of molality.*

(ii) As we know that, no. of moles of hydrogen

$$= \frac{\text{No. of atoms of hydrogen}}{6.022 \times 10^{23}}$$

$\therefore$ No. of moles of hydrogen $= \dfrac{1.29 \times 10^{24}}{6.022 \times 10^{23}} = 2.14$ moles (1)

12. Refer to Example 14 on page 10. (3)

13.
$$\underset{\substack{2V\\45.4\text{ L}\\\frac{45.4}{22.7}=2}}{2N_2(g)} + \underset{\substack{1V\\22.7\text{ L}\\\frac{22.7}{22.7}=1}}{O_2(g)} \longrightarrow \underset{\substack{2V\\45.4\text{ L}\\\frac{45.4}{22.7}=2}}{2N_2O(g)}$$ (1)

Hence, the ratio between the volume of the reactants and the product in the given question is simple i.e. 2 : 1 : 2. It proves the Gay Lussac's law of gaseous volumes. (1)

For Gay Lussac's law of gaseous volumes : Refer to text on page 11. (1)

14. Average atomic mass is the sum of the products of fractional abundances (f_i) of the isotopes and their corresponding mass number (A_i).

Average atomic mass,

$$\overline{A} = \Sigma f_i \cdot A_i = f_1 \times A_1 + f_2 \times A_2 + \ldots\ldots$$ (1)

Average Atomic mass,

$$\overline{A} = 0.7577 \times 34.9689\text{u} + 0.2423 \times 36.9659\text{u}$$
$$= 26.4959 \text{ u} + 8.9568\text{u} = 35.4527 \text{ u}$$ (2)

15. Average atomic mass can be calculated by using the formula,

Average atomic mass

$$= \frac{\{(\text{Natural abundance of } ^1\text{H} \times \text{molar mass of } ^1\text{H}) + (\text{Natural abundance of } ^2\text{H} \times \text{molar mass of } ^2\text{H})\}}{100}$$ (1)

$$= \frac{99.985 \times 1\text{u} + 0.015 \times 2\text{u}}{100} = \frac{99.985\text{u} + 0.030\text{u}}{100}$$
$$= \frac{100.015\text{u}}{100} = 1.00015 \text{ u}$$ (2)

16. (i) Molar mass of H_2O = 2× atomic mass of hydrogen + 1× atomic mass of oxygen

$= 2 \times 1.0079 \text{ u} + 1 \times 16.00 \text{ u} = 18.0158 \text{ u}$ (1)

(ii) Molar mass of CO_2 = 1× atomic mass of carbon + 2× atomic mass of oxygen

$= 1 \times 12.01 \text{ u} + 2 \times 16.00 \text{ u} = 44.01 \text{ u}$ (1)

(iii) Molar mass of CH_4 = 1× atomic mass of carbon + 4× atomic mass of hydrogen

$= 1 \times 12.01 \text{ u} + 4 \times 1.0079 \text{ u} = 16.0416 \text{ u}$ (1)

17. (i) 1.46 metric ton of Al $= 1.46 \times 10^3 \times 10^3$ g of Al

$= 1.46 \times 10^6$ g

Atomic mass of Al = 27u

$\therefore$ Moles of Al $= \dfrac{\text{mass of Al}}{\text{atomic mass}} = \dfrac{1.46 \times 10^6}{27}$ (1½)

$= 5.41 \times 10^4$ moles

(ii) 7.9 mg of Ca $= 7.9 \times 10^{-3}$ g of Ca

Atomic mass of Ca = 40.1u

$\therefore$ Moles of Ca $= \dfrac{\text{mass of Ca}}{\text{atomic mass}} = \dfrac{7.9 \times 10^{-3}}{40.1}$

$= 1.97 \times 10^{-4}$ moles (1½)

18.
$$\underset{1\text{ mol}}{C(s)} + \underset{\substack{1\text{ mol}\\32\text{ g}}}{O_2(g)} \longrightarrow \underset{\substack{1\text{ mol}\\44\text{ g}}}{CO_2(g)}$$

(i) According to the equation when 1 mol of carbon is burnt completely, CO_2 produced is 44 g. (1)

(ii) 1 mol of carbon requires 32 g dioxygen from the reaction. But we have only 16 g dioxygen. Hence, dioxygen is the limiting reagent. So, the amount of CO_2 produced by 16 g dioxygen is 22 g. (1)

(iii) In this case again, dioxygen is the limiting reagent. 16 g dioxygen can react only with 0.5 moles of carbon and produce 22 g CO_2. (1)

19.
$$\underset{4 \times 36.5\text{ g}}{4HCl(aq)} + \underset{87\text{ g}}{MnO_2(s)} \longrightarrow 2H_2O(l) + MnCl_2(aq) + Cl_2(g)$$ (1)

According to the balanced chemical equation, 87 g of MnO_2 reacts with 4× 36.5 g HCl

$\therefore$ 5 g of MnO_2 will react with $\dfrac{4 \times 36.5 \times 5}{87} = 8.39$ g HCl (2)

20. (i) Molecular mass of $CO_2 = 1 \times 12 + 2 \times 16 = 44$g

1 g molecule of CO_2 contains 1g atoms of carbon

$\because$ 44 g of CO_2 contain C = 12 g atoms of carbon

$\therefore$ % of C in $CO_2 = \dfrac{12}{44} \times 100 = 27.27\%$

Hence, the mass per cent of carbon in CO_2 is 27.27%. (1)

(ii) Given, volume = 0.1 cc

Density = 1.0 g/cc

$\because$ Density $= \frac{\text{Mass}}{\text{Volume}}$

$\therefore$ Mass of 0.1 cc water = 1.0 g/cc × 0.1 cc = 0.1 g **(1)**

Now, number of molecules in one drop of water

$= \frac{0.1}{18} \times 6.023 \times 10^{23} = 0.033 \times 10^{23}$ molecules

or $= 0.33 \times 10^{22}$ molecules **(1)**

21. As we know that, Mass per cent of an element

$= \frac{\text{Mass of that element in the compound}}{\text{Molar mass of the compound}} \times 100$

Molar mass of Na_2SO_4

$= (2 \times 22.99\ g) + 32.06\ g + (4 \times 16.00\ g) = 142.04\ g$

Mass per cent of sodium $= \frac{45.98}{142.04} \times 100 = 32.37\%$ **(1)**

Mass per cent of sulphur $= \frac{32.06}{142.04} \times 100 = 22.57\ \%$ **(1)**

Mass per cent of oxygen $= \frac{64}{142.04} \times 100 = 45.06\ \%$ **(1)**

22. Number of moles of NaOH,

$n_{NaOH} = \frac{4}{40} = 0.1$ moles $\left\{\because n = \frac{\text{Mass (g)}}{\text{Molar mass (g mol}^{-1})}\right\}$

Similarly, $n_{H_2O} = \frac{36}{18} = 2$ moles

Now, mole fraction of NaOH,

$\chi_{NaOH} = \frac{\text{moles of NaOH}}{\text{moles of NaOH} + \text{moles of } H_2O}$

$\chi_{NaOH} = \frac{0.1 \text{ moles}}{0.1 + 2 \text{ moles}} = 0.0476$ moles

Similarly, $\chi_{H_2O} = \frac{n_{H_2O}}{n_{NaOH} + n_{H_2O}}$

$= \frac{2 \text{ moles}}{0.1 \text{ moles} + 2 \text{ moles}}$

$= 0.9524$ moles **(2)**

Total mass of solution = mass of solute + mass of solvent

$= 4 + 36 = 40$ g

Volume of solution $= \frac{\text{mass of solution}}{\text{specific gravity}}$

$= \frac{40\ g}{1\ g\ mL^{-1}} = 40$ mL

$\therefore$ Molarity $= \frac{\text{moles of solute} \times 1000}{\text{volume of solution (mL)}}$

$= \frac{0.1 \times 1000}{40} = 2.5$ M **(1)**

23. (i) In the given question, 0.9 g L^{-1} means that 1000 mL (or 1L) solution contains 0.9 g of glucose.

$\therefore$ Number of moles

$= \frac{0.9\ g}{180 g/mol} = 5 \times 10^{-3}$ mol glucose

(where, molecular mass of glucose $(C_6H_{12}O_6) = 12u \times 6 + 12 \times 1u + 6 \times 16u = 180$ u)

i.e. 1L solution contains 0.005 moles of glucose or the molarity of glucose is 0.005 M. **(1)**

(ii) Refer to text on page 12. **(1)**

(iii) 4 u of He = 1 atom of He

$\therefore$ 52 u of He $= \frac{1}{4} \times 52 = 13$ atoms of He. **(1)**

24. (i) On fixing the mass of dinitrogen as 28 g, the masses of dioxygen combined are 32g, 64g, 32g and 80 g in the given four oxides. These are in the simple whole number ratio, i.e. 2 : 4 : 2 : 5. Hence, the given data obey the law of multiple proportions.

Law of multiple proportions Refer to text on page 10. **(2)**

(ii) (a) $1\text{km} = 1\text{ km} \times \frac{1000\text{ m}}{1\text{ km}} \times \frac{100\text{ cm}}{1\text{ m}} \times \frac{10\text{ mm}}{1\text{cm}} = 10^6\text{mm}$

$1\text{ km} = 1\text{ km} \times \frac{1000\text{ m}}{1\text{ km}} \times \frac{1\text{pm}}{10^{-12}\text{ m}} = 10^{15}\text{ pm}$

$\therefore 1\text{ km} = 10^6\text{ mm} = 10^{15}\text{ pm}$ **(1)**

(b) $1\text{ mg} = 1\text{ mg} \times \frac{1\text{g}}{1000\text{ mg}} \times \frac{1\text{ kg}}{1000\text{ g}} = 10^{-6}\text{kg}$

$1\text{ mg} = 1\text{ mg} \times \frac{1\text{ g}}{1000\text{ mg}} \times \frac{1\text{ ng}}{10^{-9}\text{ g}} = 10^6\text{ng}$

$\therefore 1\text{ mg} = 10^{-6}\text{ kg} = 10^6\text{ng}$ **(1)**

(c) $1\text{ mL} = 1\text{ mL} \times \frac{1\text{ L}}{1000\text{ mL}} = 10^{-3}\text{L}$

$1\text{ mL} = 1\text{ cm}^3 = 1\text{ cm}^3 \times \frac{1\text{ dm} \times 1\text{ dm} \times 1\text{ dm}}{10\text{ cm} \times 10\text{ cm} \times 10\text{ cm}}$

$= 10^{-3}\text{ dm}^3$

$\therefore\ 1\text{ mL} = 10^{-3}\text{L} = 10^{-3}\text{dm}^3$ **(1)**

25. Refer to the text on page 10. **(2)**

Understanding regarding how law of multiple proportions points to existence of atoms

The law of multiple proportions is based on an observation of Dalton's atomic theory.

According to this law, when two elements combine to form more than one compound, the mass of one element that combines with a fixed mass of the other element is always a simple whole number ratio.

This law shows that there are constituents which combine in a definite proportion.

Thus, the law of multiple proportions shows the existence of atoms which combine to form molecules. **(3)**

26. (i) 1 mole of Ag atom = 108 g = 6.022×10^{23} atoms.

Mass of 6.022×10^{23} atoms of Ag = 108 g

$$\text{Mass of 1 atom of Ag} = \left(\frac{108}{6.022\times 10^{23}}\right)$$
$$= 1.793\times 10^{-22}\ \text{g} \quad (½)$$

(ii) Mass of gram atom of N = atomic mass of N in gram = 14.0 g **(½)**

(iii) Mass of one mole of Ca = atomic mass of Ca in gram = 40.0 g **(½)**

(iv) Mass of one mole of oxygen molecules = molar mass of oxygen in gram = 32.0 g **(½)**

(v) Mass of one mole of C-atom = 12 g = 6.023×10^{23} atoms

Mass of 6.023×10^{23} atoms of C = 12 g

$$\text{Mass of 1 atom of C} = \left(\frac{12}{6.023\times 10^{23}}\right)\text{g}$$

$$\text{Mass of } 10^{23} \text{ atoms of C} = \left(\frac{12}{6.023\times 10^{23}}\right)\times 10^{23}$$
$$= 1.992\ \text{g} \quad (½)$$

(vi) Mass of iron = 1.0 g **(½)**

Hence, the required order of increasing masses is one atom of silver < one gram of iron < 10^{23} atoms of C < one-gram atom of nitrogen < one mole of oxygen molecules < one mole of calcium **(2)**

27. (i) Let x moles of oxalic acid and y moles of formic acid be heated with conc. H_2SO_4 according to the following equations.

$$\underset{x \text{ mol}}{\begin{matrix}COOH\\ |\\ COOH\end{matrix}} \xrightarrow{H_2SO_4/\text{heat}} \underset{x\text{ mol}}{CO(g)} + \underset{x\text{ mol}}{CO_2(g)} + H_2O(l)$$

$$\underset{y\text{ mol}}{HCOOH} \xrightarrow{H_2SO_4/\text{heat}} \underset{y\text{ mol}}{CO(g)} + H_2O(l) \quad (1)$$

Total moles of gaseous mixture = Moles of CO + Moles of CO_2 = $(x + y)$ moles + x moles = $(2x + y)$ moles

Now, KOH absorbs only CO_2, i.e. x moles and the volume of the solution decreases by 1/6th of its volume. Since equal volume of gases have equal number of moles according to Avogadro's law,

$$\therefore \quad \frac{\text{moles of } CO_2}{\text{moles of } (CO + CO_2)} = \frac{x}{(2x+y)} = \frac{1}{6}$$

or $6x = 2x + y$

or $4x = y$

or $\frac{y}{x} = 4$

∴ Molar ratio of formic acid : oxalic acid = 4 : 1 **(2)**

(ii) Given, mass of Mg in 100 g of chlorophyll = 3.64 g

$$\therefore \text{Mass of Mg in 4.00 g of chlorophyll} = \frac{3.64\times 4.00}{100} = 0.146\ \text{g}$$

∵ 24.3 g of Mg contains number of atoms $= 6.022\times 10^{23}$ atoms.

∴ 0.146 g of Mg contains number of atoms

$$= \frac{6.022\times 10^{23}\times 0.146}{24.3} = 3.62\times 10^{21} \text{ atoms.} \quad (2)$$

28. (i) Volume of a drop of water = 0.05 mL

Mass of a drop of water = volume × density = (0.05 mL) × (1.0 g / mL) = 0.05 g

Gram molecular mass of water (H_2O) = 2 × 1 + 16 = 18 g; 18 g of water = 1 mol **(1)**

$$\therefore \ 0.05 \text{ g of water} = \frac{1\text{ mol}}{(18\text{ g})}\times (0.05\text{ g}) = 0.0028 \text{ moles}$$

∵ 1 mole of water contains molecules $= 6.022\times 10^{23}$

∴ 0.0028 mole of water will contain molecules

$$= 6.022\times 10^{23}\times 0.0028$$
$$= 1.68\times 10^{21} \text{ molecules} \quad (1½)$$

(ii) Volume of the alloy = (10.0 cm) × (20.0 cm) × (15.0 cm) = 3000 cm^3

Mass of the alloy = density × volume = $(8.17\ g\ cm^{-3})\times(3000\ cm^3)$ = 24510 g

$$\text{Mass of Ni in the alloy} = (24510\text{ g})\times\frac{45.8}{100} = 11225.6\text{ g} \quad (1)$$

∵ 59 g Ni have atoms $= 6.022\times 10^{23}$

Gram atomic mass of Ni = 59 g

11225.6 g of Ni have atoms

$$= 6.022\times 10^{23}\times\frac{(11225.6\text{ g})}{(59.0\text{ g})}$$
$$= 1.15\times 10^{26} \text{ atoms} \quad (1½)$$

29. Refer to Example 24 on page 17. **(5)**

30. (i) Relative number of moles of an element

$$= \frac{\%\text{ of the element}}{\text{atomic mass}}$$

$$\text{or atomic mass} = \frac{\%\text{ of element}}{\text{relative number of moles}}$$

$$\therefore \quad \text{Atomic mass of } A = \frac{70}{1.25} = 56\text{ u} \quad (1)$$

$$\text{and Atomic mass of } B = \frac{30}{1.88} = 16\text{ u} \quad (1)$$

(ii) **Calculation of Empirical Formula**

Element	Relative number of moles	Simplest molar ratio	Simplest whole number molar ratio
A	1.25	$\frac{1.25}{1.25}=1$	2
B	1.88	$\frac{1.88}{1.25}=1.5$	3

$\therefore$ Empirical formula = A_2B_3 **(1)**

Calculation of molecular formula

Empirical formula mass = $2\times 56\text{u} + 3\times 16\text{ u} = 160\text{u}$

$$n=\frac{\text{molecular mass}}{\text{empirical formula mass}}=\frac{160}{160}=1$$

$\therefore$ Molecular formula = A_2B_3 **(2)**

31. (i) 44 g CO_2 = 12 g carbon

$$3.38\text{ g } CO_2=\frac{12}{44}\times 3.38\text{ g}=0.9218\text{ g carbon}$$

18 g H_2O = 2 g hydrogen

$$0.690\text{ g } H_2O=\frac{2}{18}\times 0.690\text{ g}=0.0767\text{ g hydrogen}$$

Total mass of compound = 0.9218g + 0.0767 g = 0.9985 g (because compound contains only carbon and hydrogen)

$$\%\text{ of C in the compound}=\frac{0.9218}{0.9985}\times 100=92.32$$

$$\%\text{ of H in the compound}=\frac{0.0767}{0.9985}\times 100=7.68$$ **(1)**

Calculation for Empirical Formula

Element	Per cent by mass	Atomic mass	Relative number of moles of elements	Simplest molar ratio
C	92.32	12	$\frac{92.32}{12}=7.69$	$\frac{7.69}{7.68}=1$
H	7.68	1	$\frac{7.68}{1}=7.68$	$\frac{7.68}{7.68}=1$

Hence, empirical formula = CH **(1)**

(ii) **Calculation for molar mass of the gas**

10.0 L of the given gas at STP weigh = 11.6 g

$\therefore$ 22.4 L of the given gas at STP will weigh

$$=\frac{11.6\times 22.4}{10}$$

$$= 25.984\text{ g}$$

Molar mass = 25.984 ≈ 26 g mol^{-1}. **(1)**

(iii) Empirical formula mass (CH) = 12 + 1 = 13 u

$$\therefore\quad n=\frac{\text{molecular mass}}{\text{empirical formula mass}}$$

$$=\frac{26\text{u}}{13\text{u}}=2$$

Hence, molecular formula

$= n\times CH$

$= 2\times CH = C_2H_2$ **(2)**

QR Code for Quick Test 1

QR Code for Quick Test 2

QR Code for Quick Test 3

SELF ASSESSMENT TEST

Objective Type Questions [1 Mark]

1. Which of the following is true regarding the law of definite proportions?
   (a) It states that a compound contains the same elements in the same proportions by mass, regardless of its source or how it was prepared.
   (b) It states that the mass of the reactants equals the mass of the products in a chemical reaction.
   (c) It states that the ratio of the masses of two elements in a compound is always different.
   (d) It states that elements combine in different ratios to form different compounds.

2. How many atoms are there in 2 moles of carbon dioxide (CO_2)?
   (a) $2 \times 6.022 \times 10^{23}$ (b) $2 \times 3 \times 6.022 \times 10^{23}$
   (c) $2 \times 2 \times 6.022 \times 10^{23}$ (d) $2 \times 4 \times 6.022 \times 10^{23}$

3. Which of the following quantities can be expressed in moles?
   (a) Mass of an element
   (b) Volume of a gas at STP
   (c) Number of molecules in a substance
   (d) All of the above

4. What is the empirical formula of a compound that has a molecular formula of $C_6H_{12}O_6$?
   (a) $C_3H_6O_3$ (b) $C_6H_{12}O_6$
   (c) CH_2O (d) $C_{12}H_{24}O_{12}$

5. What is the number of moles of solute present in 500 mL of a 0.2 M solution'?
   (a) 0.1 moles (b) 0.5 moles
   (c) 0.2 moles (d) 1.0 mole

Assertion-Reason [1 Mark]

■ **Directions** (Q. Nos. 6-8) In the following questions. an Assertion (A) is followed by a corresponding Reason (R). Use the following keys to choose the appropriate answer.

(a) Both (A) and (R) are true and (R) is the correct explanation of (A).
(b) Both (A) and (R) are true and (R) is not the correct explanation of (A).
(c) (A) is true but (R) is false.
(d) (A) is false but (R) is true.

6. **Assertion** (A) The empirical formula of a compound represents the simplest whole number ratio of the elements in the compound.
   Reason (R) The molecular formula of a compound is always the same as its empirical formula.

7. **Assertion** (A) The mole fraction of a component in a solution is always greater than 1.
   Reason (R) Mole fraction is calculated as the ratio of the number of moles of a component to the total number of moles of all components in the solution.

8. **Assertion** (A) The molarity of a solution is defined as the number of moles of solute per litre of solution.
   Reason (R) Molarity can change with temperature because it depends on the volume of the solution, which can expand or contract as temperature changes.

Short Answer Type I Questions [2 Marks]

9. Classify the following substances as elements, compounds, homogeneous mixtures, or heterogeneous mixtures: air, gold, salt, oil and water.

10. Explain the Law of Conservation of Mass and provide an example in a chemical reaction.

11. (i) Define "mole" in terms of quantity.
    (ii) What is the formula to calculate the number of moles from mass?

Short Answer Type II Questions [3 Marks]

12. Differentiate between a homogeneous mixture and a heterogeneous mixture with examples. How would you classify air as a mixture?

13. Answer the following questions:
    (i) A piece of fabric measures 24 inches in length. What is its length in centimeters?
    (ii) A solution has a volume of 500 mL. Convert this volume into L.
    (iii) Convert 25°C to Fahrenheit.

14. A compound has the following elemental composition: 40% Carbon, 6.7% Hydrogen, and 53.3% Oxygen by mass. What is its empirical formula?

Case Study [4 Marks]

15. Read the given case and answer the questions that follow.

A chemical reaction is a change in which one or more substance(s) react(s) to form new substance(s) with entirely different properties. A chemical equation is a brief representation of a chemical reaction in terms of symbols and formulae of substances involved in it, e.g. the reaction of silver nitrate with sodium chloride to give silver chloride and sodium nitrate can be represented as

$$\underset{\text{Reactants}}{AgNO_3 + NaCl} \longrightarrow \underset{\text{Products}}{AgCl + NaNO_3}$$

The substances which react among themselves to bring about the chemical changes are known as **reactants** whereas, the substances which are produced as a result of the chemical change, are known as **products**.

Reactants and products of a chemical equation are separated by arrow pointing towards the products.

Quantitative information conveyed by a chemical equation is as follows

- The relative number of reactant and product species (atoms or molecules) taking part in the reaction.
- The relative number of moles of the reactants and products.
- The relative masses of the reactants and products.
- The relative volumes of gaseous reactants and products.

The reactant which is present in the lesser amount and gets consumed after sometime, i.e. which limits the amount of product formed is called the **limiting reagent.**

The reactant other than the limiting reagent, which is in somewhat excess is called the excess reagent. The remaining amount of excess reagent is calculated by subtracting the available amount of limiting reagent from the amount of the excess reagent.

Remember that in stoichiometric calculations, it is very important to choose the limiting reagent.

(i) For the formation of 3.65 g hydrogen chloride gas, what volume of hydrogen gas and chlorine gas are required at NTP conditions?

(ii) What will be the volume of the mixture after the reaction?

$$\underset{1\,L}{NH_3(g)} + \underset{1.5\,L}{HCl(g)} \longrightarrow NH_4Cl(s)$$

(iii) A gas mixture contains 50% He and 50% CH_4 by volume. What is the percentage by weight of methane in the mixture?

Or

A 15 g sample of calcium carbonate ($CaCO_3$) is heated strongly, causing it decompose completely according to the reaction:

$$CaCO_3(s) \longrightarrow CaO(s) + CO_2(g)$$

Calculate the mass of calcium oxide (CaO) formed.

Long Answer Type Questions [5 Marks]

16. Explain the different states of matter and the changes that occur during phase transitions. Discuss the physical and chemical properties of solids, liquids, and gases, and how these properties are affected by intermolecular forces.

17. A chemist needs to prepare 1 L of a solution with a mass percent of 8% sodium nitrate ($NaNO_3$). If the density of the solution is 1.2 g/mL, calculate the mass of sodium nitrate required and the molarity of the solution. (Molar mass of $NaNO_3$ = 85.00 g/mol)

Answers

1. (a)	2. (b)	3. (d)	4. (c)	5. (a)	6. (c)	7. (d)	8. (b)

13. (i) 60.96 cm (ii) 0.5 L (iii) 77°F 14. CH_2O empirical formula

15. (i) 1.12 L (ii) 0.5 L HCl (iii) 80% or (iii) 8.4 g 17. 1.129 M

02

CHAPTER

Structure of Atom

The word atom derived from a Greek word 'a-tomio' which means 'non-divisible' or 'uncut-able'. The concept of atom came into light when first atomic theory is proposed by **John Dalton** in 1808, regarded atom as the ultimate indivisible particle of matter.

YOUR STUDY GOALS

YOUR PRACTICE GOAL

- Objective Type Questions (37 Qs ; 25 MCQs, 10 A-R, 2 Case-Based)
  Subjective Type Questions
- (28Qs; 10 SA-I, 12 SA-II & 6 LA)

2.1 Discovery of Sub-Atomic Particles

From the several experiments, scientists proved that atom was not the smallest indivisible particle but had a complex structure of its own and is made up of smaller particles like electrons, protons, neutrons etc. Collectively these particles are termed as **sub-atomic particles**. Electron, proton and neutron are also called as the **fundamental particles.**

Discovery of Electron

In mid 1850s, many scientists mainly Michael Faraday and J. J. Thomson began to study electrical discharge in partially evacuated tubes, called the **cathode ray discharge tubes.**

Cathode ray tube A cathode ray discharge tube is a sealed tube. It is made up of glass and contains two thin metal plates as electrodes.

This tube is also connected to a vacuum pump which is operated by a stopcork to control the pressure of gas inside the tube. The electrical discharge through the gases could be observed only at very low pressures and high voltages.

Observation When a high voltage of about 10000 volts is applied between the electrodes and the pressure is reduced to about 10^{-4} atm (about 0.01 mm), the glow between the electrodes disappear but the current continues to flow.

- If a perforated anode is used, a faint greenish glow is observed on the glass wall behind the anode.
- This indicates emission of some invisible rays from the cathode that passed through the holes of the anode and striked the glass wall (which may be coated with a phosphorescent material like zinc sulphide) and a bright spot is developed as shown in the figure given below.

These rays were named as **cathode rays** because they originate from the cathode.

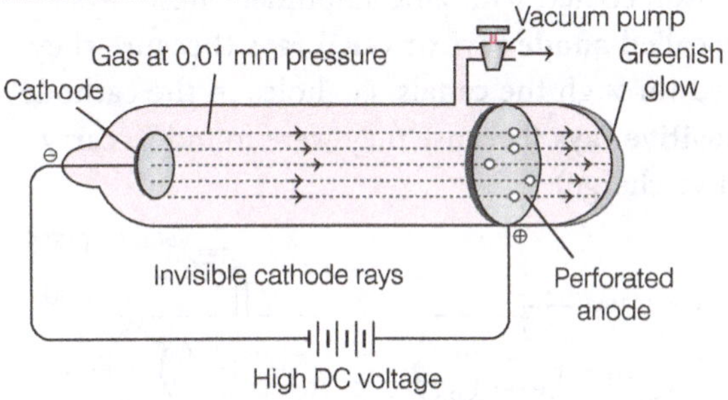

Emission of cathode rays when pressure is reduced to 0.01 mm

Characteristics of Cathode Rays

The cathode rays have been found to show the following characteristics.

- The cathode rays start from cathode and move towards the anode.
- These rays are not visible but their behaviour can be observed with the help of fluorescent or phosphorescent materials which glow when hit by them.

  For instance, television picture tubes are cathode ray tubes. It result due to fluorescence on the television screen coated with certain fluorescent or phosphorescent material.
- Cathode rays travel in straight lines in the absence of electrical or magnetic field.
- When an electric field is applied on the cathode rays, they get deflected towards the positive plate of the electric field, which indicates that cathode rays consist of negatively charged particles, called the **electrons**. Similar, results are obtained in the presence of magnetic field.
- The characteristics of cathode rays (electrons) do not depend upon the material of electrodes and the nature of gas present in the cathode ray tube.

Charge to Mass Ratio of Electron

J.J. Thomson determined the ratio of electrical charge (e) to the mass of electron (m_e) by using cathode ray tube under the influence of electrical and magnetic field. These field are perpendicular to each other as well as to the path followed by electrons as shown below.

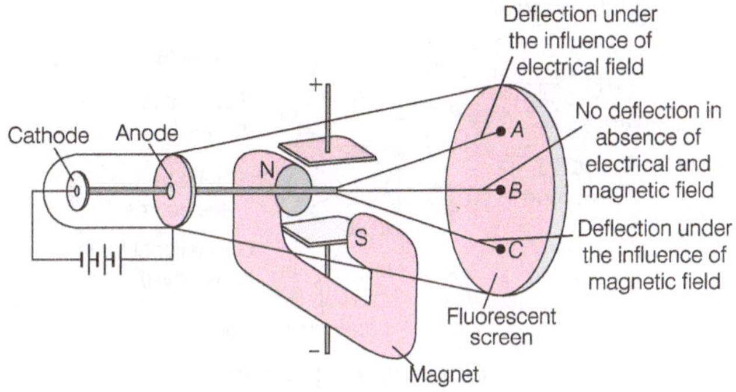

Apparatus to determine the charge to mass ratio of electron

Thomson demonstrate that the amount of deviation of the particles from their path in presence of electrical or magnetic field depends upon following factors.

- Greater the **magnitude of the charge on the particle**, greater is the interaction with electrical or magnetic field thus, greater is the deflection.
- The **mass of the particle** Lighter the particle, greater is the deflection .
- **Strength of the field** The deflection of electrons from its original path increases with increase in the voltage across the electrode or magnetic field strength.

By measuring the amount of deflections observed by the electrons on the electric field strength or magnetic field strength, **Thomson** was able to calculate the value of e / m_e, as

$$\frac{e}{m_e} = 1.758820 \times 10^{11} \text{C kg}^{-1}$$

where, m_e is the mass of the electron in kg and e is the magnitude of the charge on the electron in coulomb (C).

Charge on the Electron : Millikan's Oil Drop Experiment

In order to determine the charge on the electrons, **Robert Andrews Millikan** (1868-1953) devised a method known as **oil drop experiment** (1906-14).

In this experiment, small drops of oil in the form of mist are obtained by an **atomiser** and allowed to fall in between two electrically charged metal plates under the influence of gravitational force. The apparatus used for this experiment is shown in figure given below.

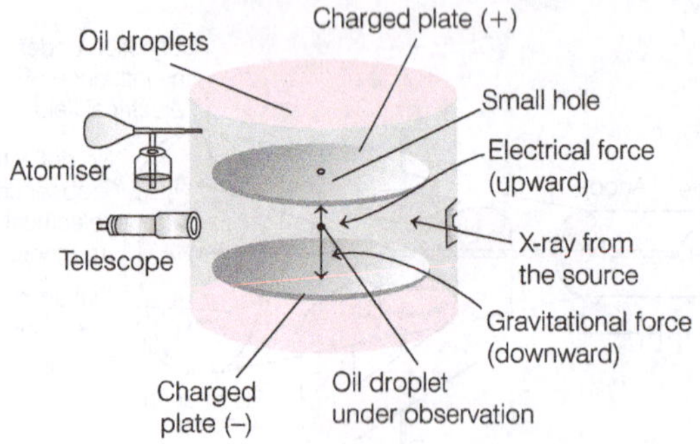

Millikan oil drop apparatus

Millikan measured the rate of fall of these droplets, to measure the mass of oil droplets. He used X-rays beam to ionise the air inside the chamber. The electrical charge on these oil droplets was acquired by collisions with gaseous ions.

By observing the effects of electrical field strength on the motion of oil droplets, Millikan concluded that *"the magnitude of electrical charge (q), on the droplets is always an integral multiple of the electrical charge, (e)", i.e. $q = n e$, where n = integer such as 1, 2, 3...*

The present accepted value of electrical charge is -1.6022×10^{-19} C or 4.8×10^{-10} esu. This is the smallest measurable quantity of charge and is called **one unit.**

Mass of the Electron

The mass of the electron may be calculated from the values of e/m and e as follows

$$m_e = \frac{e}{e/m_e} = \frac{1.6022 \times 10^{-19}\ \text{C}}{1.758820 \times 10^{11}\ \text{C kg}^{-1}}$$
$$= 9.1094 \times 10^{-31}\ \text{kg}$$

The mass, 9.11×10^{-28} g is nearly 1/1837th of that of hydrogen atom.

Hence, the electron may be defined as *"An electron is that fundamental particle which carries one unit negative charge and has a mass nearly equal to 1/1837th of that of hydrogen atom".*

Discovery of Proton : Study of Anode Rays

Goldstein in 1886, performed discharge tube experiments in which he took perforated cathode and a gas at low pressure kept inside the tube, as before.

On passing high voltage between the electrodes, he found that some rays were coming from the side of the anode which passed through the holes in the cathode and produced green fluorescence on the opposite glass wall coated with zinc sulphide. These rays were called **anode rays** or **canal rays** (because they passed through the canals, i.e. holes in the cathode) or **positive rays** (because they were found to carry positive charge).

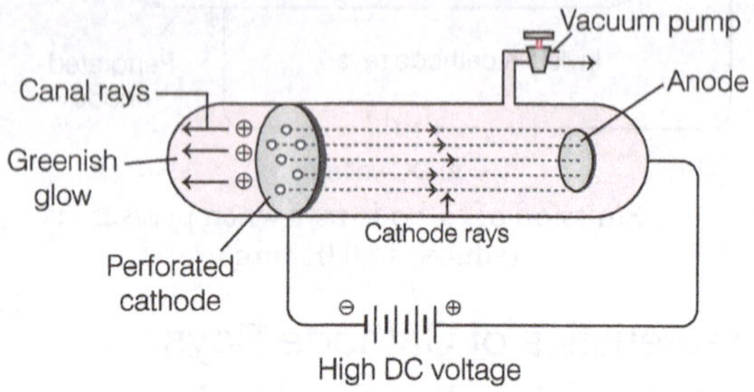

Emission of canal rays at low pressure

Note Anode rays are not emitted from the anode but are produced in the space between the anode and the cathode.

Characteristics of the Anode Rays

The anode rays shown the following characteristics.

- Anode rays travel in a straight line.
- These rays depend upon the nature of gas present in the cathode ray tube. These are simply the positively charged gaseous ions.
- The charge to mass ratio of these particles also depends on the nature of the gas from which these originate.
- Some of the positively charged particles carry a multiple of the fundamental unit of electrical charge.
- The behaviour of these particles in the magnetic or electrical field is opposite to that observed for electron or cathode rays. Therefore, **anode rays consist of positively charged particles.**

Mass of the Proton

The smallest and lightest positive ion was obtained by using hydrogen gas and was called **proton.** Charge on this particle is found to be same as that on the electron, i.e. 1.6×10^{-19} coulomb or one unit. The ratio, charge/mass for each of the particle is 9.58×10^4 coulomb per gram. Hence, the mass of each of this particle,

$$m = \frac{e}{e/m} = \frac{1.6 \times 10^{-19}\,C}{9.58 \times 10^4\,C/g} = 1.67 \times 10^{-24}\ g$$

This mass is nearly the same as that of the hydrogen atom. Hence, a proton may be defined as *"fundamental particle which carries one unit positive charge and has a mass nearly equal to that of hydrogen atom".*

Discovery of Neutron

Chadwick bombarded a thin sheet of beryllium by α-particles and found that electrically neutral particles having a mass slightly greater than that of the protons was emitted. He named these particles as **neutrons.**

$$_4Be^9 + \underset{\alpha\text{- particles}}{_2He^4} \longrightarrow {}_6C^{12} + \underset{\text{Neutron}}{_0n^1}$$

Actual mass of the neutron $= 1.6749 \times 10^{-24}$ g and they are neutral, i.e. charge $= 0$.

Properties of Fundamental Particles

Name	Symbol	Absolute charge/C	Relative charge	Mass/kg	Mass/u	Approx. mass/u	Position
Electron	e or $_{-1}e^0$	-1.6022×10^{-19}	−1	9.10938×10^{-31}	0.00054	0	Outside the nucleus
Proton	p or $_1p^1$	$+1.6022 \times 10^{-19}$	+1	1.67262×10^{-27}	1.00727	1	Inside the nucleus
Neutron	n or $_0n^1$	0	0	1.67493×10^{-27}	1.00867	1	Inside the nucleus

2.2 Atomic Models

To explain the distributions of various sub-atomic particles (i.e. electrons, protons and neutrons) in an atom several models have been proposed. These were called **atomic models.**

Although, some of these models were not able to explain the stability of atoms.

Now, lets discuss these models, one by one.

Thomson's Model of Atom

According to this model, an atom possesses a spherical shape (radius approximately 10^{-10} m) in which the positive charge is uniformly distributed.

The electrons are embedded into it so that the most stable electrostatic arrangement is obtained.

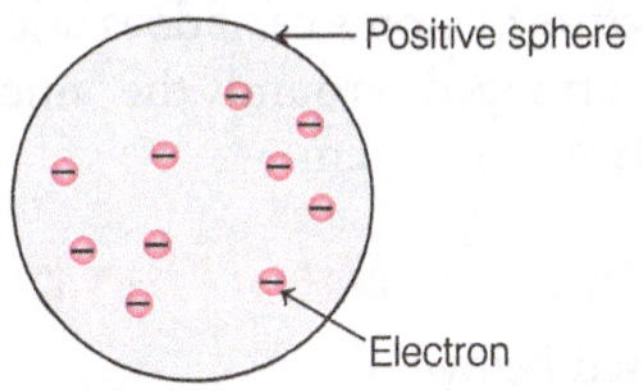

Thomson's model of atom

This model can be visualised as a pudding or watermelon of positive charge with plums or seeds (electrons) embedded into it. Hence, it is also called **plum pudding, raisin pudding** or **watermelon model.**

In this model, the mass of the atom is assumed to be uniformly distributed over the atom.

Limitations of Thomson Model

Although this model was able to explain the overall neutrality of the atom, but was not consistent with the results of later experiments, like α-ray scattering experiment.

> **Radioactivity**
>
> While investigating any possible relation between fluorescence and α-rays, **Henry Becquerel** (1852-1908) observed that there are some specific elements which emit radiation on their own. He named this phenomenon as **radioactivity** and those elements as **radioactive elements.** It was observed that three types of rays are emitted which were α, β and γ-rays.
>
> **Rutherford** found that α-rays consist of high energy particles having 2 units of positive charge and 4 units of atomic mass. (He concluded that α-particles are helium nuclei as when α-particles combined with two electrons yielded helium gas).
>
> β-rays are negatively charged particles like electrons. γ-rays are high energy radiations like X-rays which are neutral in nature and do not consist of particles.

Rutherford's Nuclear Model of Atom

Rutherford along with his students [Hans Geiger and Ernest Marsden] performed alpha scattering experiment. In this experiment they bombarded thin foils (nearly 100 nm thick) of heavy metals like gold, silver, platinum or copper with a beam of fast moving α-particles. The thin gold foil had a circular fluorescent zinc sulphide screen around it. Whenever α-particles struck this screen, a tiny flash of light was produced at that point as shown in figure given below.

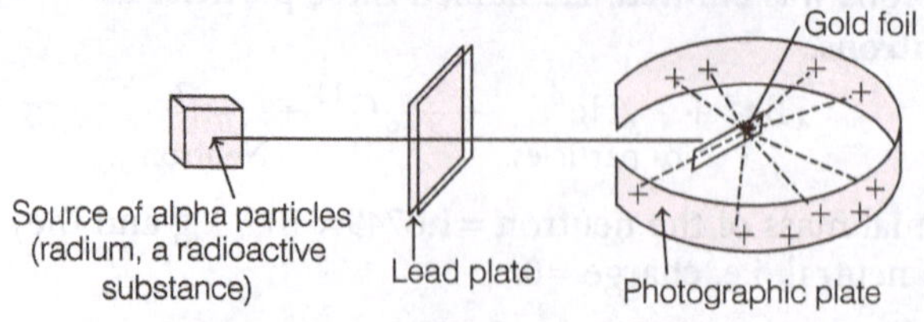

Rutherford's scattering experiment

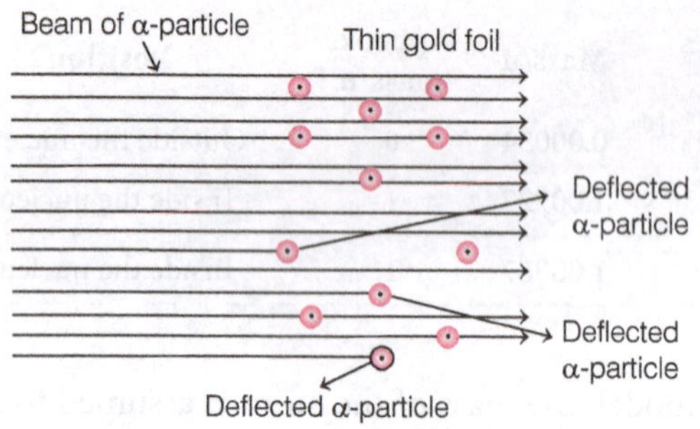

Schematic molecular view of the gold foil

Observations

Following observations was made by this model

- The majority of α-particles passed through the foil without any deflection.
- Some α-particles were deflected by small angles.
- A very few α-particles (about 1 in every 20000) were bounced back, i.e. deflected by nearly 180°.

Conclusions

The main conclusions of this model is as follows

- Most of the space in the atom is empty as most of the α-particles passed through the foil undeflected.
- A few positively charged α-particles were deflected. The deflection must be due to large repulsive force showing that the positive charge of the atom is not spread throughout the atom, as Thomson had presumed. The positive charge has to be concentrated in a very small volume that repelled and deflected the positively charged α-particles.
- Calculations by Rutherford showed that the volume occupied by the nucleus is negligibly small as compared to the total volume of the atom. The radius of the atom is about 10^{-10} m, while that of the nucleus is 10^{-15} m.

Rutherford's Atomic Model

On the basis of above observations and conclusions, Rutherford proposed the nuclear model of atom.

According to this model,

- the positive charge and most of the mass of the atom was densely concentrated in extremely small region of the atom, named as **nucleus** by Rutherford.
- the nucleus is surrounded by electrons that move around the nucleus with a very high speed in circular paths, called **orbits.**
- electrons and the nucleus are held together by electrostatic forces of attraction.

Drawbacks of Rutherford Model

The key issues in this model includes

- According to Rutherford's model, electrons are assumed to move around a nucleus in well defined orbit. However, since these electrons are moving in curved paths, they experience continuous acceleration, even if their speed remains constant.
- According to Maxwell's electromagnetic theory, any accelerated charged particle, like, an electron should emit electromagnetic radiation. As a result, the electron would lose energy, causing its orbit to shrink progressively until it spirals into the nucleus leading to atomic collapse with approx 10^{-8} seconds. But since, atoms are stable in reality, this prediction does not hold true, highlighting Rutherford's model's failure to explain atomic stability.
- If the electrons are considered to be stationary, electrostatic attraction between the dense nucleus and the electrons would pull the electrons toward the nucleus to form a miniature version of Thomson's model of atom.
- This model also does not provide any information on the electronic structure of atoms i.e. it does not explain how electrons are arranged around the nucleus or the energies associated with them.

Atomic Number and Mass Number

These are discussed below :

(i) Atomic Number

The number of protons present in the nucleus of an atom is equal to its atomic number (Z).

Atomic number (Z) = number of protons in the nucleus of an atom
= number of electrons in a neutral atom

(ii) Mass Number

The mass of the nucleus is due to the presence of protons and neutrons, thus, they are collectively called **nucleons.**

The total number of nucleons is termed as **mass number (A) of the atom.**

Mass number (A) = number of protons (Z) + number of neutrons (n)

In other words, the sum of the neutrons and protons is known as mass number.

Representation of an Atom

An atom is generally represented by its symbol for the element. Atomic number (Z) is written as the subscript of the symbol and the mass number (A) is written as the superscript.

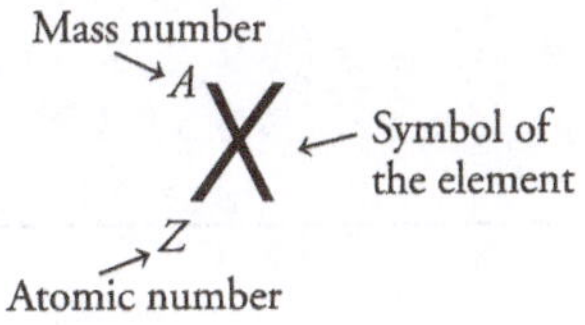

e.g. Lithium with atomic number equal to 3 and mass number equal to 7 may be represented as ${}^{7}_{3}Li$.

Example 1 **How many neutrons and protons are there in the following nuclei?** **NCERT**

$${}^{13}_{6}C,\ {}^{16}_{8}O,\ {}^{24}_{12}Mg,\ {}^{56}_{26}Fe,\ {}^{88}_{38}Sr$$

Sol.

Nucleus	Atomic number (Z)	Mass number (A)	Number of protons $(p) = Z$	Number of neutrons $(n) = A - Z$
${}^{13}_{6}C$	6	13	6	$13 - 6 = 7$
${}^{16}_{8}O$	8	16	8	$16 - 8 = 8$
${}^{24}_{12}Mg$	12	24	12	$24 - 12 = 12$
${}^{56}_{26}Fe$	26	56	26	$56 - 26 = 30$
${}^{88}_{38}Sr$	38	88	38	$88 - 38 = 50$

Example 2 **The number of electrons, protons and neutrons in a species are equal to 18, 16 and 16 respectively. Assign the proper symbol to the species.** **NCERT**

Sol. As, we know that atomic number is equal to number of protons, i.e. 16. Hence, the element is sulphur (S).

Atomic mass number = No. of protons + No. of neutrons
$= 16 + 16 = 32$

The given species is not neutral as the number of protons is not equal to electrons. It is an anion with charge equal to excess electrons $= 18 - 16 = 2$. Therefore, symbol is ${}^{32}_{16}S^{2-}$.

Different Atomic Species

Different atomic species arises due to variations in the number of protons, neutrons or electrons in atoms. These are as follows

(i) **Isotopes** Atoms of the same element having same atomic number (or number of protons) but different mass number (or number neutrons) are called isotopes.

e.g. Protium (${}^{1}_{1}H$), deuterium (${}^{2}_{1}D$) and tritium (${}^{3}_{1}T$) are three isotopes of H. ${}^{12}_{6}C$, ${}^{13}_{6}C$, ${}^{14}_{6}C$ are the isotopes of C and ${}^{35}_{17}Cl$, ${}^{37}_{17}Cl$ are the isotopes of Cl. Number of neutrons present in the nucleus have very little effect on the chemical properties of an element.

Therefore, all isotopes of a given element show same chemical behaviour.

(ii) **Isobars** Atoms of different elements that have same mass number but different atomic number are called isobars. e.g. ${}^{14}_{6}C$ and ${}^{14}_{7}N$.

(iii) **Isotones** These are the species in which number of neutrons are same, e.g. ${}^{14}_{6}C$, ${}^{15}_{7}N$ and ${}^{16}_{8}O$ as each of these contain 8 neutrons. Their atomic number and mass number both are different.

(iv) **Isoelectronic species** The species (atoms or ions) containing the same number of electrons are called isoelectronic species, e.g. O^{2-}, F^{-}, Na^{+}, Mg^{2+}, Al^{3+}, Ne. Each of them contains 10 electrons each and hence, they are isoelectronic.

Quick Test 1

Conceptual Questions

1. Why does the charge to mass ratio of positive rays depend on the residual gas in the discharge tube? Why is the charge to mass ratio of all cathode rays are same?

2. (i) Which of the following will not show deflection from the path on passing through an electric field? Proton, cathode rays, electron, neutron. *NCERT Exemplar*

(ii) Arrange the following in the increasing order of their e/m values : electron, proton and neutron.

3. In Rutherford's experiment, generally the thin foil of heavy atoms, like gold, platinum etc., have been used to be bombarded by the α-particles.
If the thin foil of light atoms like aluminium etc., is used, what difference would be observed from the above results?

Numerical Questions

4. In Millikan's experiment, static electric charge on the oil drops has been obtained by shining X-rays. If the static electric charge on the oil drop is -1.282×10^{-18} C, calculate the number of electrons present on it. *NCERT*

5. Find the number and mass of neutrons in 32 mg of O_2 at STP (mass of a neutron $=1.675\times 10^{-27}$ kg).

6. 2×10^8 atoms of carbon are arranged side by side. Calculate the radius of carbon atom if the length of this arrangement is 2.4 cm. *NCERT*

Hint : Radius depends upon diameter d as $r=d/2$, so first calculate the diameter by dividing total length with number of carbon atoms present and then calculate radius.

7. (i) Calculate the number of protons, neutrons and electrons in $^{80}_{35}Br$.

(ii) Name the element whose isotope has mass number 14 and 8 neutrons. *NCERT*

Answers

4. 8.0 electrons
5. 1.9270×10^{22}, 3.228×10^{-5} kg
6. 0.060 nm
7. (i) No. of protons = No. of electrons = 35, No. of neutrons = 45 (ii) Carbon

For Solutions, See QR Code on Pg. 82

2.3 Developments Leading to the Bohr's Model of Atom

In order to improve Rutherford's atomic model, **Neils Bohr** utilised two concepts which played a major role. These were

- dual nature of electromagnetic radiation: wave as well as particle nature.
- experimental results regarding atomic spectra.

Wave Nature of Electromagnetic Radiations

James Maxwell was the first to give electromagnetic wave theory which gave comprehensive explanation about the interaction between the charged bodies and the behaviour of electrical and magnetic fields on macroscopic level.

When electrically charged particle moves under acceleration, alternating electrical and magnetic fields are generated and transmitted in the forms of waves, called the **electromagnetic waves** or **electromagnetic radiation.**

Characteristics of Waves

The waves are characterised in terms of their wavelength, frequency, velocity and wave number. Thus, different kinds of units are used to represent electromagnetic radiation which are discussed below,

(i) **Wavelength** (λ) The distance between two adjacent crests or troughs is called wavelength. It has the units of length.

Since, different kinds of waves are of much smaller wavelengths, so, smaller units of length are used to describe them.

It is generally expressed in terms of Angstrom units, denoted as Å [$1Å = 10^{-8}$ cm or 10^{-10} m] or 1 nm $=10^{-9}$ m.

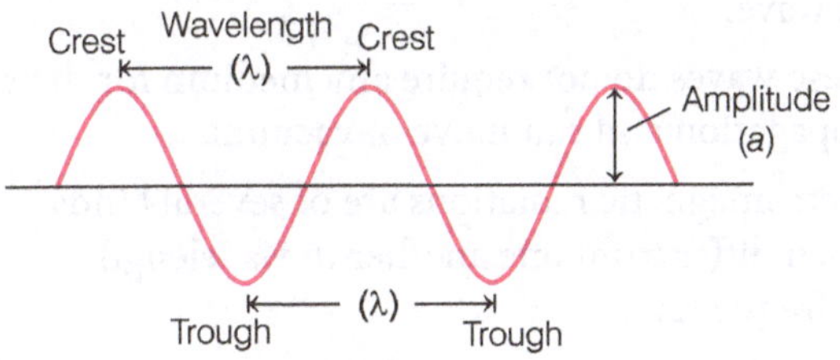

Wave motion

(ii) **Frequency** (ν) It is defined as, the number of waves that pass through a given point in one second. Its units is cycles per second or simply reciprocal of seconds (s^{-1}).

The SI unit of frequency is Hertz (Hz) after the name of **Heinrich Hertz.**

1 Hz = 1 cycle per second

(iii) **Velocity** (c) It is the distance travelled by a wave in one second. It is expressed as ms^{-1}.

In vacuum, all types of electromagnetic radiations, regardless of wavelength, travel with the same speed, i.e. $3.0 \times 10^8 ms^{-1}$ (2.997925×10^8 ms^{-1}, to be precise.) This is called **speed of light** and is given by the symbol c.

(iv) **Wave number** ($\bar{\nu}$) It is defined as, the number of wavelengths per unit length. Its unit is reciprocal of wavelength unit, i.e. m^{-1}.
However, its commonly used unit is cm^{-1} (not SI unit).

Relationship between Wavelength, Wave Number, Frequency and Velocity

These characteristics are related as

$$c = \lambda \times \nu$$

or $\nu = \frac{c}{\lambda}$ and $\frac{1}{\lambda} = \bar{\nu}$

$\therefore$ $\nu = c\bar{\nu}$

Example 3 The wavelength range of the visible spectrum extends from violet (400 nm) to red (750 nm). Express these wavelengths in frequencies (Hz). (1 nm = 10^{-9} m) **NCERT**

Sol. Given, wavelength of violet light

$$= 400 \text{ nm} = 400 \times 10^{-9} \text{ m}$$

$$\nu = \frac{c}{\lambda} = \frac{3.00 \times 10^8 \text{ ms}^{-1}}{400 \times 10^{-9} \text{ m}}$$

$$= 7.50 \times 10^{14} \text{ Hz}$$

wavelength of red light = 750 nm

$$= 750 \times 10^{-9} \text{ m}$$

$$\nu = \frac{c}{\lambda} = \frac{3.00 \times 10^8 \text{ m s}^{-1}}{750 \times 10^{-9} \text{m}}$$

$$= 4.00 \times 10^{14} \text{Hz}$$

The range of visible spectrum is from 4.0×10^{14} to 7.5×10^{14} Hz in terms of frequency units.

Example 4 Calculate (i) wave number and (ii) frequency of yellow radiation having wavelength 5800Å. **NCERT**

Sol. (i) Given, wavelength, $\lambda = 5800$Å

$$= 5800 \times 10^{-8} \text{ cm}$$

$$= 5800 \times 10^{-10} \text{ m}$$

$$\bar{\nu} = \frac{1}{\lambda} = \frac{1}{5800 \times 10^{-10} \text{m}}$$

$$= 1.724 \times 10^6 \text{m}^{-1}$$

$$= 1.724 \times 10^4 \text{ cm}^{-1}$$

(ii) Calculation of the frequency (ν)

$$\nu = \frac{c}{\lambda} = \frac{3 \times 10^8 \text{ms}^{-1}}{5800 \times 10^{-10} \text{m}}$$

$$= 5.172 \times 10^{14} \text{s}^{-1}$$

Example 5 A hypothetical electromagnetic wave is shown in figure. Find out the wavelength of the radiation. **NCERT Exemplar**

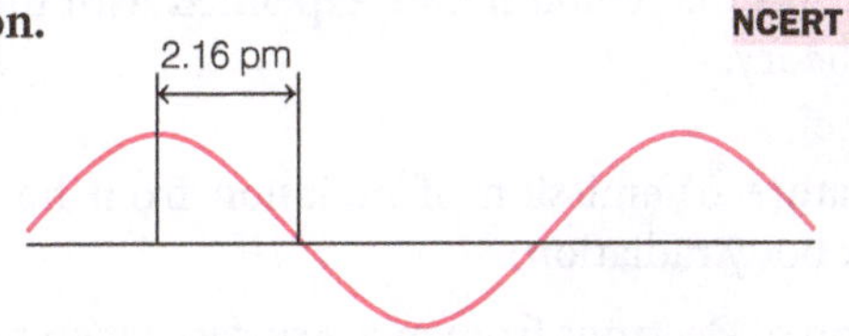

Sol. Wavelength is the distance between two successive crests or two successive troughs of a wave.
Therefore, $\lambda = 4 \times 2.16$ pm $= 8.64$ pm $= 8.64 \times 10^{-12}$ m

Properties of Electromagnetic Waves

Due to the complex nature of electromagnetic wave motion, we will consider only few simple properties on the basis of the given figure.

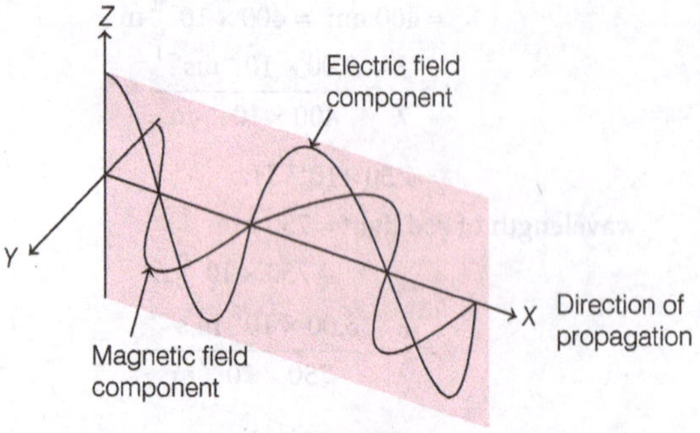

Simplified picture of electromagnetic wave

- The oscillating electric and magnetic fields generated by oscillating charged particles are perpendicular to each other and also to the direction of propagation of the wave.
- These waves do not require any medium for their propagation and can move in vacuum.
- Electromagnetic radiations are of several kinds which differ from one another in wavelength (or frequency).
- When the electromagnetic radiations are arranged in order of their increasing wavelengths or decreasing frequencies, the complete spectrum obtained is called **electromagnetic spectrum** as shown in the figure given below.

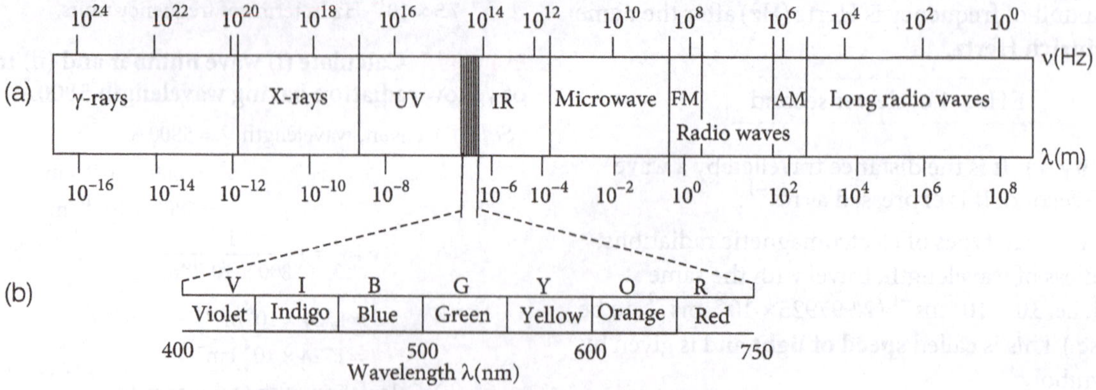

(a) The spectrum of electromagnetic radiation (b) visible spectrum. The visible region is only a small part of entire spectrum.

Limitations of Electromagnetic Wave Theory

The above theory explains the phenomenon like diffraction and interference but, following are some observations that could not be explained with the help of this theory.

These are

- the nature of emission of radiation from hot bodies (black body radiation).
- ejection of electrons from metal surface when radiation strikes it (photoelectric effect).
- variation of heat capacity of solids as a function of temperature.
- line spectra of atoms with special reference to hydrogen.

Note The process of bending of wave around an obstacle is called **diffraction** whereas **interference** is the process of combination of two waves having same or different frequencies to give a wave, distribution of which at each point in space is the algebraic or vector sum of disturbances at that point.

Particle Nature of Electromagnetic Radiation : Planck's Quantum Theory

To explain the phenomena of black body radiation and photoelectric effect, **Max Planck in 1900**, proposed a theory known after his name as Planck's quantum theory. This theory was further extended by **Einstein in 1905**.

The main postulates of this theory are as follows

- The radiant energy is emitted or absorbed not continuously, but discontinuously in the form of small discrete packets of energy, called a **quantum**. In case of light, the quantum of energy is known as **photon**.
- The energy of each quantum is directly proportional to the frequency of the radiation, i.e.

$$E \propto \nu \text{ or } E = h\nu$$

where, h is the proportionality constant, called **Planck's constant.** Its value is approximately equal to 6.626×10^{-27} erg s or 6.626×10^{-34} Joule s.

- The total amount of energy emitted or absorbed by a body will be some whole number of quanta, i.e. **energy is quantised.**

Hence, $E = nh\nu$, where, n is any integer.

It cannot emit or absorb energy in fractional value of $h\nu$.

TEACHER'S TIP

The energy possessed by one mole of quanta (or photons), i.e. Avogadro's number (N_0) of quanta is called one **Einstein of energy**.

$$(E) = N_0 h\nu = N_0 h \frac{c}{\lambda}.$$

(i) Black Body Radiations

- Black body radiation is a term used to describe the relationship between an object's temperature and the wavelength of the electromagnetic radiation it emits.
- When the surface of an object is irradiated with electromagnetic radiation, a part of radiant energy is generally reflected, a part is absorbed and a part of it is transmitted.
- The ideal body, that emits and absorbs radiations of all frequencies uniformly, is called a **black body** and the radiation emitted by such a body is called **black body radiation**. Carbon black fairly closely to black body.
- In particular, the emittance of radiations of different colourations from these bodies was not in accordance with classical wave theory. e.g. If an iron bar is heated, it emites red colour light which changes to yellow and then white as the temperature increases. Finally, it changes to blue at highest temperature.
- The exact wavelength distribution of the emitted radiation (i.e. intensity *versus* frequency curve of the radiation) from a black body depends only on its temperature.
- At a given temperature, intensity of radiation emitted increases with increase of wavelength, reaches a maximum value at a given wavelength and then starts decreasing with further decrease of wavelength, as shown in graph given below.

Also, as the temperature increases ($T_2 > T_1$), maxima of the graph shifts to shorter wavelength.

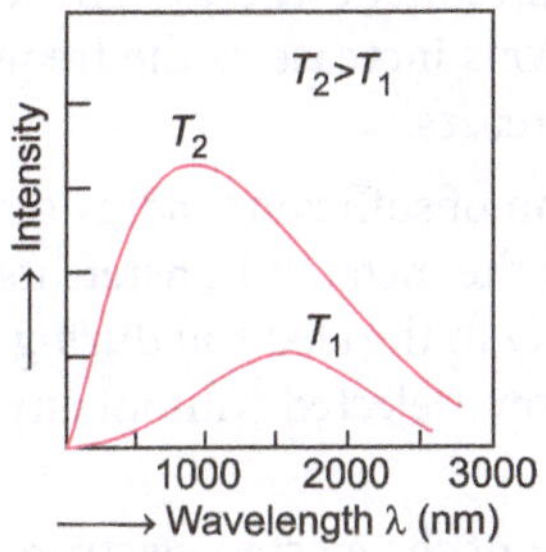

Emission of radiation from a black body at different temperatures (T_2 and T_1).

(ii) Photoelectric Effect

The phenomenon for ejection of electrons from the surface of a metal when light of suitable frequency falls on it, is called the **photoelectric effect** and the emitted electrons are called **photoelectrons.**

In 1887, H. Hertz performed an experiment in which electrons (or electric current) were ejected when certain metals (e.g. potassium, rubidium, caesium etc.) were exposed to a beam of light as shown below in the figure.

The ejected electrons are counted by a detector that measures their kinetic energy .

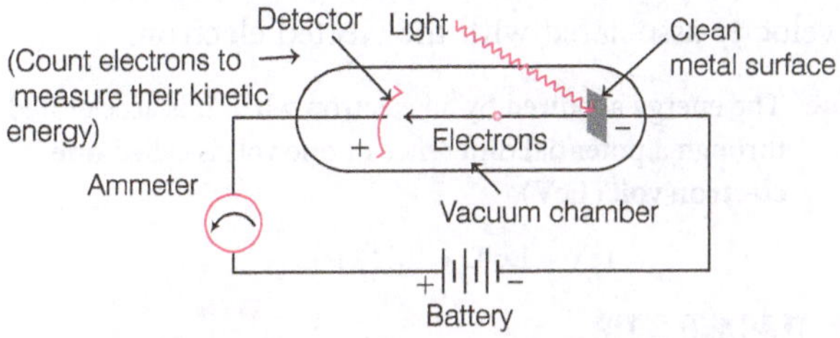

Equipment for studying the photoelectric effect

The results observed in this experiment are as follows

- The electrons are ejected from the metal surface as soon as the beam of light hits the surface, i.e. there is no **time lag**.
- The number of electrons ejected is proportional to the intensity or brightness of light.
- For each metal, there is a characteristic minimum frequency (ν_0) (called the **threshold frequency**) below which this effect is not observed.

  When frequency is $\nu > \nu_0$, the ejected electrons come out with certain kinetic energy. The kinetic energies of these electrons increase as the frequency of the light used increases.
- When a photon of sufficient energy strikes an electron in the atom of the metal, it transfers its energy instantaneously to the electron during the collision and the electron is ejected without any time lag or delay.

  Kinetic energy of the ejected electron is proportional to the frequency of the electromagnetic radiation.

  Energy of striking photon = Threshold energy + Kinetic energy of ejected electron

  Since, the energy of striking photon is $h\nu$ and the minimum energy required to eject the electron is $h\nu_0$ (also called **work function,** W_0), then the difference in energy ($h\nu - h\nu_0$) is transferred as the kinetic energy of the photoelectron.

  Following the law of conservation of energy principle, the kinetic energy of the ejected electron is given by the following equation,

$$h\nu = h\nu_0 + \frac{1}{2} m_e v^2$$

where, m_e is the mass of the electron and v is the velocity associated with the ejected electron.

Note The energy acquired by an electron when it is accelerated through a potential difference of one volt is called **one electron volt** (1 eV).

$$1\text{eV} = 1.602 \times 10^{-19}\text{ J}$$

TEACHER'S TIP

At a given frequency, increase in the intensity of light increases the number of photons, but not the energies of photons. Thus, when the intensity of light is increased, more electrons are ejected. But, the energies of these electrons remains same.

Example 6 The threshold frequency (ν_0) for a metal is $7.0 \times 10^{14}\text{ s}^{-1}$. Calculate the kinetic energy of an electron emitted when radiation of frequency (ν) = $1.0 \times 10^{15}\text{ s}^{-1}$ hits the metal. NCERT

Sol. Given, threshold frequency (ν_0) for metal $= 7 \times 10^{14}\text{ s}^{-1}$

Frequency (ν) $= 1.0 \times 10^{15}\text{s}^{-1}$

According to Einstein's equation,

$$\text{KE} = \frac{1}{2}mv^2 = h(\nu - \nu_0)$$

$$= (6.626 \times 10^{-34}\text{ Js})(1.0 \times 10^{15}\text{s}^{-1} - 7.0 \times 10^{14}\text{s}^{-1})$$

$$= (6.626 \times 10^{-34}\text{ Js})(10.0 \times 10^{14}\text{ s}^{-1} - 7.0 \times 10^{14}\text{s}^{-1})$$

$$= (6.626 \times 10^{-34}\text{ Js}) \times (3.0 \times 10^{14}\text{s}^{-1})$$

$$= 1.988 \times 10^{-19}\text{ J}$$

Limitations of Planck's Quantum Theory

Planck could not explain the **quantisation of energy**.

He was also unable to explain the distribution of intensity in radiation from a black body as a function of frequency at different temperatures with this assumption that energies are quantised.

Dual Nature of Electromagnetic Radiation

To explain the phenomena like reflection, refraction, inteference, diffraction etc., light has been considered as a **wave,** whereas to explain the black body radiation and photoelectric effect, light is considered to be made up of tiny particles (small packets of energy) called **photons.**

In other words, light is a kind of radiation that exhibits dual behaviour, i.e. waves as well as particles behaviour. Such a wave as well as particle like nature of radiation is known as **dual nature of radiation.**

Evidence for the Quantised Electronic Energy Levels : Atomic Spectra

When a ray of light passes from one medium to another, it gets deviated from its original path.

When a ray of light passes through a prism, waves with shorter wavelength bends more than those with longer wavelength, causing the light to split into different colours. This effect is called **dispersion** and the series of coloured bands is known as **spectrum.**

The branch of science dealing with the study of spectra is called **spectroscopy.**

The spectra are broadly classified into following two types

1. Emission Spectra

The spectrum of radiation emitted by a substance that has absorbed energy (either by passing electric discharge through a gas at low pressure or by heating the substance to high temperature) is called an **emission spectrum**.

Atoms, molecules or ions that have absorbed radiation are said to be in **excited state**.

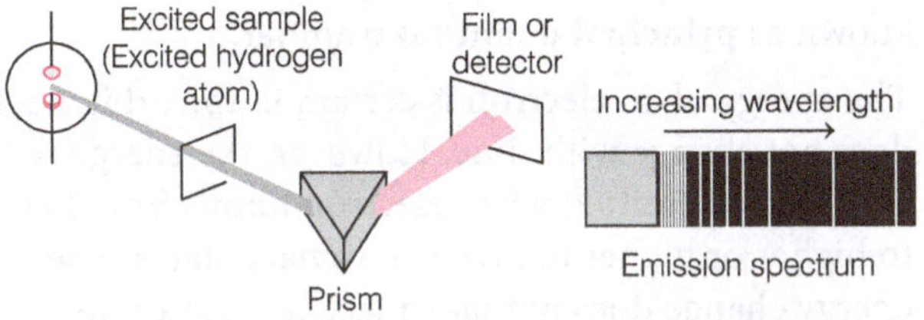

Representation of atomic emission spectrum

Depending upon the source of radiation, the emission spectra are mainly of two types

(i) **Continuous spectrum** Such spectrum have continuity of colours, i.e. one colour merges into the other without any gap or discontinuity. Such spectrum can also be obtained from the light emitted from some susbtances.

e.g. VIBGYOR is a continuous spectra as each and every colour merge simultaneously. It ranges from violet at 7.50×10^{14} Hz to red at 4×10^{14} Hz.

(ii) **Line or atomic spectrum** The emission spectra of atoms in the gas phase, emit light only at certain specific wavelengths with dark spaces between them. Such spectra is called **line** or **atomic spectra** because the emitted radiation is identified by the appearance of bright lines in the spectra.

These dark lines of definite wavelengths are used to identify a substance in the same way as fingerprints are used to identify people, as each element has a unique line emission spectrum.

e.g. The emission spectrum of sodium consists of two important yellow lines at 589 and 589.6 nm.

Robert Bunsen was one of the 1st investigators to use line spectra to identify elements.

2. Absorption Spectra

When a regular amount of radiation is passed through a sample which absorbs radiation of certain wavelengths, an **absorption spectra** is obtained. It is like the photographic negative of an emission spectrum.

The missing wavelength which corresponds to the radiation absorbed by the matter, leaves dark spaces in the bright continuous spectrum.

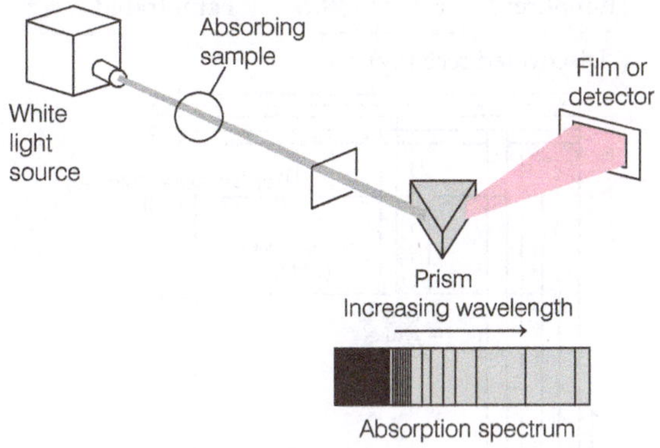

Representation of atomic absorption spectrum

Line Spectrum of Hydrogen

On passing electric discharge through gaseous hydrogen, the H_2 molecules get dissociated to produce energetically excited hydrogen atoms that emit electromagnetic radiation of discrete frequencies.

The hydrogen spectrum consists of several series of lines named after their discoverers on the basis of experiments.

The **Swedish spectroscopist, Johannes Rydberg**, told that all series of lines in the hydrogen spectrum could be described by the following expression.

$$\bar{\nu} = 109{,}677\left(\frac{1}{n_1^2} - \frac{1}{n_2^2}\right)\text{cm}^{-1}$$

where, $n_1 = 1, 2 \ldots,$

$n_2 = n_1 + 1, n_1 + 2 \ldots$

The value 109677 cm^{-1} is called the **Rydberg constant** for hydrogen and is represented by R_H. The first six series of lines that correspond to $n_1 = 1, 2, 3, 4, 5, 6$ are known as Lyman, Balmer, Paschen, Brackett, Pfund and Humphrey series, respectively.

Spectral Lines for Atomic Hydrogen

Series	n_1	n_2	Spectral region
Lyman	1	2, 3...	Ultraviolet
Balmer	2	3, 4...	Visible
Paschen	3	4, 5...	Infrared
Brackett	4	5, 6...	Infrared
Pfund	5	6, 7 ...	Infrared
Humphrey*	6	7, 8...	Far infrared

(*Discovered recently)

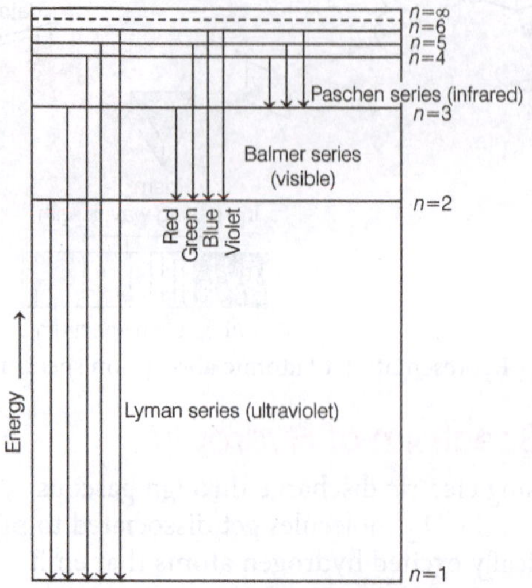

Transitions of the electron in the hydrogen atom (The diagram shows the Lyman, Balmer and Paschen series of transitions)

Note
- **Hydrogen spectrum** has five lines in the visible region of the electromagnetic spectrum-red, green, blue, violet 1 and violet 2. But Balmer could see only four lines and a continuum.
- The limiting line of any spectral series in the hydrogen spectrum is the line when n_2 in the Rydberg's formula is infinity, i.e. $n_2 = \infty$.

2.4 Bohr's Model for Hydrogen Atom

In order to overcome the drawbacks of Rutherford's model of atom and to explain the line spectrum of hydrogen, Neils Bohr, proposed a new model of atom based upon Planck's quantum theory, called **Bohr's atomic model**.

Postulates of Bohr's Atomic Model

The main postulates of this model are as follows

- The electron in the hydrogen atom can move around the nucleus in a circular path of fixed radius and energy (i.e. energy of an electron is quantised). These paths are called **orbits, stationary states** or **allowed energy states.** These orbits are arranged concentrically around the nucleus.

  The stationary states for electron are numbered $n = 1, 2, 3$ or $K, L, M\ldots$. The integral numbers are known as **principal quantum number.**
- The energy of an electron is certain in the orbit, i.e. it does not change with time. However, the energy is absorbed or emitted when electron jumps from lower to higher or higher to lower stationary states. The energy change does not take place in a continuous manner.
- The frequency of radiation absorbed or emitted when transition occurs between two stationary states that differ in energy by ΔE is given by

$$\nu = \frac{\Delta E}{h} = \frac{E_2 - E_1}{h}$$

  where, E_1 and E_2 are the energies of the lower and higher allowed energy states respectively. This expression is commonly known as **Bohr's frequency rule.**
- The angular momentum (mvr) of an electron in a given stationary state can be expressed by the following equation

$$m_e v\, r = n \cdot \frac{h}{2\pi} \qquad (n = 1, 2, 3\ldots)$$

  where, m_e is the mass of electron, v is the velocity and r is the radius of orbit in which electron is moving.

  Thus, an electron can move only in those orbits for which its angular momentum is an integral multiple of $h/2\pi$. This postulate, therefore, introduces the concept of **quantisation of angular momentum.** Radiation is emitted or absorbed only when transition of electron takes place from one quantised value of angular momentum to other.

Significance of Bohr's Model

This model is found useful to explain the following facts

1. Stability of an Atom

Bohr suggested that an electron revolving in a particular orbit cannot radiate energy. Therefore, emission of radiation is not possible as long as the electron remains in one of its energy levels and hence, there is no cause of instability in his model.

2. Calculation of Bohr Radius

According to Bohr's model, radius of nth orbit is given by the expression

$$r_n = \frac{n^2h^2}{4\pi^2me^2Z} \quad \text{[For hydrogen atom, } Z = 1\text{]}$$

$$\boxed{r_n = a_0 n^2}$$

where, $a_0 = 52.9$ pm.

Thus, the radius of first stationary state is called the **Bohr radius** and has value 52.9 pm (or 0.0529 nm or 0.529 Å).

Hence, for H-atom, radius of first orbit is **52.9 pm**.

As n increases the value of r will increase, and the electron will be present away from the nucleus.

Similarly, **for hydrogen like ions,** the radii may be given by the expression,

$$r_n = \frac{a_0 n^2}{Z}$$

or $$r_n(\text{H-like}) = \frac{r_n\ (\text{H-atom})}{Z}$$

or $$\boxed{r_n = \frac{52.9\,n^2}{Z}\ \text{pm}} \quad \text{or} \quad \frac{0.0529\,n^2}{Z}\ \text{nm}$$

where, Z is the nuclear charge. (Radius becomes smaller with increase of Z.)

Example 7 Which state of the triple ionised beryllium (Be^{3+}) has the same orbit radius as that of the ground state of hydrogen atom?

Sol. For H-atom, radius of ground state is

$$r_1 = \frac{h^2}{4\pi^2me^2} \quad \text{...(i)}$$

For hydrogen like atom,

$$r_n' = \frac{n^2h^2}{4\pi^2mZe^2} \quad \text{...(ii)}$$

Dividing Eq. (ii) by Eq. (i)

$$\frac{r_n'}{r_1} = \frac{n^2}{Z}$$

For Be^{3+} ion, $Z = 4$

$$\therefore \quad \frac{r_n'}{r_1} = \frac{n^2}{4}$$

Now, $$r_n' = r_1$$

$$\therefore \quad n^2 = 4 \quad \text{or} \quad n = 2$$

Thus, the second orbit of Be^{3+} has the same radius as the Bohr's radius of hydrogen atom.

3. Calculation of Energy of the Electron

Bohr on the basis of his postulates, derived a mathematical expression to calculate the energy of an electron moving in a particular orbit of hydrogen atom. He considered hydrogen atom as a system having single electron of mass m and negative charge electron, revolving in a circular orbit.

The energy of the electron in the nth orbit has been found to be $E_n = -R_H\left(\frac{1}{n^2}\right)$ $(n = 1, 2, 3 \ldots)$

where, R_H = Rydberg constant $= \frac{2\pi^2me^4}{h^2} = 2.18 \times 10^{-18}$ J

so that $$E_n = -\frac{2\pi^2 me^4}{n^2h^2}$$

Therefore, the energy of the lowest state, also called as the **ground state**, is

$$E_1 = -2.18 \times 10^{-18}\left(\frac{1}{1^2}\right) = -2.18 \times 10^{-18}\ \text{J}$$

Similarly, for nth orbit,

$$\boxed{E_n = -\frac{2.18 \times 10^{-18}}{n^2}\ \text{J per atom}}$$

$$\boxed{E_n = -\frac{13.595\ \text{eV}}{n^2}\ \text{per atom}}$$

$[\because 1\ \text{eV} = 1.6022 \times 10^{-19}\ \text{J}]$

$$E_n = -\frac{1311.8}{n^2}\ \text{kJ mol}^{-1} \approx -\frac{1312}{n^2}\ \text{kJ mol}^{-1}$$

Thus, for each value of n, an energy level exists for the electron. With increase in the value of n the energy difference between successive energy levels decreases.

i.e. $E_2 - E_1 > E_3 - E_2 > E_4 - E_3$ and so on.

The energy of the electron in a hydrogen atom has a negative sign for all possible orbits.

This is because the energy of the electron in the atom is lower than the energy of a free electron at rest. A free electron is infinitely far away from the nucleus (not influenced by it) and has a zero energy.

Mathematically, as $n \rightarrow \infty$, $E_\infty = 0$. In this state hydrogen atom is called **ionised H-atom.** As the electron gets closer to the nucleus (as n decreases), E_n becomes more negative, indicating increased binding to nucleus. The most negative value is at $n = 1$, representing the ground state.

Similary, for hydrogen like species,

$$E_n = -\frac{2\pi^2 me^4 Z^2}{n^2 h^2} = -2.18 \times 10^{-18}\left(\frac{Z^2}{n^2}\right) \text{J}$$

$$= -1311.8\left(\frac{Z^2}{n^2}\right) \text{kJ mol}^{-1}$$

where, Z is the nuclear charge which is equal to atomic number. e.g. For He^+ $Z = 2$, for Li^{2+} $Z = 3$.

As Z increases, energy becomes more negative. This means that electron will be tightly bound to the nucleus.

4. Calculation of Velocity of an Electron

Velocity of the revolving electron in n^{th} orbit is given by the expression,

$$V_n = \frac{2\pi Ze^2 k}{nh} \quad \text{or} \quad \frac{V_H \times Z}{n}$$

where, V_H = velocity of hydrogen atom $= 2.188 \times 10^8$ cm/s.

The magnitude of velocity of an electron increases with increase of positive charge on the nucleus and it decreases with increase in the value of 'n'.

5. Calculation of Frequency and Wave Number for a Transition

The energy gap between the two orbits is given by equation,

$$\Delta E = E_f - E_i \quad \text{...(i)}$$

We know that, $\left(E = -\frac{R_H}{n_1^2}\right)$ ...(ii)

Combining Eqs. (i) and (ii), we get

$$\Delta E = R_H\left(\frac{1}{n_i^2} - \frac{1}{n_f^2}\right) = 2.18 \times 10^{-18} \text{ J}\left(\frac{1}{n_i^2} - \frac{1}{n_f^2}\right)$$

(where, n_i and n_f show initial orbit and final orbit)

The frequency (ν) associated with the absorption and emission of the photon can be evaluated by using equation

$$\nu = \frac{\Delta E}{h} = \frac{E_2 - E_1}{h} = \frac{R_H}{h}\left(\frac{1}{n_i^2} - \frac{1}{n_f^2}\right)$$

$$\boxed{\nu = 3.29 \times 10^{15}\left(\frac{1}{n_i^2} - \frac{1}{n_f^2}\right) \text{Hz}}$$

Now, frequency is related to wavelength as

$$\nu = \frac{c}{\lambda} \quad [\because \nu \times \lambda = c]$$

where, c is the velocity of light.

$\therefore$ In terms of wave numbers ($\bar{\nu}$).

$$\bar{\nu} = \frac{\nu}{c} = \frac{R_H}{hc}\left(\frac{1}{n_i^2} - \frac{1}{n_f^2}\right) \quad \left(\because \bar{\nu} = \frac{1}{\lambda}\right)$$

$$= 1.09667 \times 10^7\left(\frac{1}{n_i^2} - \frac{1}{n_f^2}\right) \text{m}^{-1}$$

$$\therefore \quad \boxed{\bar{\nu} = 109677\left[\frac{1}{n_i^2} - \frac{1}{n_f^2}\right] \text{cm}^{-1}}$$

For absorption spectrum, $n_f > n_i$ and the term in the parenthesis is positive and energy is absorbed. On the other hand, for emission spectrum $n_i > n_f$, ΔE is negative and energy is released.

Example 8 **What are the frequency and wavelength of a photon emitted during a transition from $n = 5$ state to the $n = 2$ state in the hydrogen atom?** NCERT

Sol. Initial state, $n_i = 5$ and final state $n_f = 2$. This transition give rise to a spectral line in the visible region of the Balmer series.

$$\Delta E = 2.18 \times 10^{-18} \text{ J}\left[\frac{1}{n_i^2} - \frac{1}{n_f^2}\right]$$

$$= 2.18 \times 10^{-18} \text{ J}\left[\frac{1}{5^2} - \frac{1}{2^2}\right] = -4.58 \times 10^{-19} \text{ J}$$

It is an emission energy. Frequency of photon is given by

$$\nu = \frac{\Delta E}{h} = \frac{4.58 \times 10^{-19} \text{ J}}{6.626 \times 10^{-34} \text{ Js}}$$

[Taking energy in terms of magnitude]

$$= 6.91 \times 10^{14} \text{ Hz}$$

$$\lambda = \frac{c}{\nu} = \frac{3.0 \times 10^8 \text{ ms}^{-1}}{6.91 \times 10^{14} \text{ Hz}} = 434 \text{ nm}$$

Example 9 **Calculate the wave number for the longest wavelength transition in the Balmer series of atomic hydrogen.** NCERT

Hint • For longest wavelength (λ), wave number ($\bar{v}$) should be minimum, i.e. the difference between n_1 and n_2 is minimum.

• For Balmer series, $n_1 = 2$, and $n_2 = 3$

Sol. Wave number,

$$\bar{v} = R_H\left[\frac{1}{n_1^2} - \frac{1}{n_2^2}\right] = 109677\left(\frac{1}{2^2} - \frac{1}{3^2}\right)\text{cm}^{-1}$$

$$\therefore \bar{v} = 15232.91\text{ cm}^{-1} = 1.523 \times 10^4\text{ cm}^{-1} = 1.523 \times 10^6\text{ m}^{-1}$$

Example 10 **Calculate the wavelength for the emission transition if it starts from the orbit having radius 1.3225 nm and ends at 211.6 pm. Name the series to which this transition belongs and the region of the spectrum.** NCERT

Sol. Radius of nth orbit H-like species, $r_n = \frac{52.9\,(n^2)}{Z}$ pm

$$r_1 = 1.3225\text{ nm} = 1322.5\text{ pm} = \frac{52.9\,n_1^2}{Z}$$

$$r_2 = 211.6\text{ pm} = \frac{52.9\,n_2^2}{Z}$$

$$\frac{r_1}{r_2} = \frac{1322.5}{211.6} = \frac{n_1^2}{n_2^2}$$

$$\Rightarrow \quad \frac{n_1^2}{n_2^2} = 6.25 \text{ or } \frac{n_1}{n_2} = 2.5$$

If $n_1 = 5, n_2 = 2$, then, the transition (emission transition) is from 5th orbit to 2nd orbit and it belongs to Balmer series.

$$\bar{v} = \frac{1}{\lambda} = 1.09677 \times 10^7\left(\frac{1}{n_1^2} - \frac{1}{n_2^2}\right)\text{m}^{-1}$$

$$\frac{1}{\lambda} = 1.09677 \times 10^7\left(\frac{1}{2^2} - \frac{1}{5^2}\right)\text{m}^{-1}$$

$$\frac{1}{\lambda} = 1.09677 \times 10^7 \times \frac{21}{100} = 2.303 \times 10^6\text{m}^{-1}$$

$$\lambda = 0.434 \times 10^{-6}\text{ m} = 434 \times 10^{-9}\text{m} = 434\text{ nm}$$

It belongs to visible region.

6. Explanation of Line Spectrum of Hydrogen

Since a sample of hydrogen gas contains a large number of atoms and when energy is supplied by passing electric discharge, the electrons in different hydrogen atoms absorb different amounts of energies. Therefore, these are raised to different energy states.

The excited electrons can come back from the higher energy levels to the ground state in one or more jumps.

That's why **the number of lines observed in the hydrogen spectrum is very large,** e.g. when the electron jumps from all the energy levels higher than $n = 1$, i.e. $n = 2, 3, 4, 5, \ldots$ to $n = 1$ energy level, the lines obtained, fall in the ultraviolet region. These lines are called **Lyman series.**

In general, the number of emission lines when an electron jumps from n_2 level to n_1 level are given by the expression. $\frac{(n_2 - n_1)(n_2 - n_1 + 1)}{2}$

TEACHER'S TIP

The questions asked in the exams mostly are to find the maximum number of emission lines from n^{th} state to ground state.

So, remember the simple formula of $\frac{n(n-1)}{2}$ to find the same.

Note The brightness or intensity of spectral lines depends upon the number of photons of same wavelengths or frequency absorbed or emitted.

Limitations of Bohr's Model

Bohr's model of the hydrogen atom was an improvement over Rutherford's nuclear model, since it explains the stability and line spectra of hydrogen atom and hydrogen like species (e.g. He^+, Li^{2+}, Be^{3+} and so on).

However, it was too simple to explain the following facts.

- It was unable to explain the spectrum of multi-electron systems different from the hydrogen and hydrogen like species. e.g. He^+, Be^{3+} etc.
- The splitting of spectral lines in the magnetic field is called **Zeeman effect** while the splitting of spectral lines in the electric field is called **Stark effect.** Bohr's atomic model was unable to explain such splitting of spectral lines.
- This model fails to account for the finer details (doublet, that is two closely spaced lines) of the hydrogen atom spectrum observed by using sophisticated spectroscopic techniques.
- It could not explain the ability of atoms to form molecules by chemical bonds.
- Bohr gave a flat model of atom. But now, it is well established that the atom is three-dimensional and not flat, as had been suggested by Bohr.
- Many scientist introduced the concept of dual behaviour of electron and also pointed out that the path of the motion of the electron cannot be well defined. Thus, these over-ruled the Bohr's idea of well defined circular paths.

Quick Test 2

Conceptual Questions

1. (i) How does the intensity of the spectral line vary with wavelength?
(ii) What do you mean by saying that energy of the electron is quantised?

2. What is the experimental evidence in support of the idea that electronic energies in an atom are quantised? *NCERT Exemplar*

3. Arrange the following type of radiations in increasing order of frequency.
(i) Radiation from microwave oven
(ii) Amber light from traffic signal
(iii) Radiation from FM radio
(iv) Cosmic rays from outer space and
(v) X-rays

Numerical Questions

4. Nitrogen laser produces radiation at a wavelength of 337.1 nm. If the number of photons emitted is 5.6×10^{24}, calculate the power of lens. *NCERT*

5. Find energy of each of the photons which
(i) correspond to light of frequency 3×10^{15} Hz.
(ii) have wavelength of 0.50Å. *NCERT*

6. Yellow light emitted from a sodium lamp has a wavelength (λ) of 580 nm. Calculate the frequency (ν) and wave number ($\bar{\nu}$) of the yellow light. *NCERT*

7. (i) The energy associated with the first orbit in the hydrogen atom is -2.18×10^{-18} J atom^{-1}. What is the energy associated with the fifth orbit?
(ii) Calculate the radius of Bohr's fifth orbit for hydrogen atom. *NCERT*

8. Electrons are emitted with zero velocity from a metal surface when it is exposed to radiation of wavelength 6800 Å. Calculate threshold frequency (ν_0) and work function (W_0) of the metal.

9. What transition in the hydrogen spectrum would have the same wavelength as the Balmer transition $n = 4$ to $n = 2$ of He^+ spectrum? *NCERT*

10. (i) An atom has 3 energy levels, how many spectral lines will be possible when it shows emission spectrum?
(ii) Calculate the distance of separation between 3rd and 4th orbit of H-atom.

11. What is the maximum number of emission lines when the excited electron of a H-atom in $n = 6$ drops to the ground state? *NCERT*

Answers

4. 3.3×10^6 J **5.** (i) 1.9878×10^{-18} J (ii) 3.975×10^{-15} J **6.** 5.17×10^{14} s^{-1} and 1.724×10^4 cm^{-1} **7.** (i) -8.72×10^{-20} J (ii) 1.3225 nm
8. 4.41×10^{14} s^{-1}, 2.922×10^{-19} J **9.** $n_1 = 1$ and $n_2 = 2$ **10.** (i) 3 spectral lines (ii) 3.703 Å **11.** 15

For Solutions, See QR Code on Pg. 82

2.5 Towards Quantum Mechanical Model of the Atom

In order to overcome the drawbacks of the Bohr's model, several attempts were made to develop a more suitable and general model for atoms. The development of new model was mainly based on the following concepts.

1. Dual behaviour of matter
2. Heisenberg uncertainty principle

1. Dual Behaviour of Matter

It was the **French physicist, de-Broglie**, who in 1924 proposed that matter, like radiations, should also exhibit dual behaviour, i.e. it should exhibit particle as well as wave like properties.

It means that just like photon, electrons should also have momentum as well as wavelength. The wave associated with a particle is called a **matter wave** or **de-Broglie wave**. de-Broglie suggested that the wavelength associated with a particle of mass m, moving with velocity v can be given as

$$\lambda = \frac{h}{mv} = \frac{\lambda}{p}$$

where, h is Planck's constant, with value 6.626×10^{-34} Js and p $(= mv)$ is momentum of the particles moving with velocity, v. This equation is called **de-Broglie equation**.

Derivation of de-Broglie Equation

de-Broglie equation can be derived by combining the mass-energy relationships proposed by Max Planck and Einstein.

or $$\frac{h}{\lambda} = mc \quad \text{or} \quad \boxed{\lambda = \frac{h}{mc}}$$

This equation is applicable for a photon. de-Broglie suggested that by substituting the mass of the particle (m) and its velocity (v) in place of mass of electron, m and velocity of light (c), the equation can also be used for material particles. Since, h is constant.

$$\therefore \quad \lambda \propto \frac{1}{\text{Momentum}}$$

This means that the wavelength of a particle in motion is inversely proportional to its momentum. It is called the **de-Broglie relationship.**

Significance of de-Broglie Equation

de-Broglie suggested that every object in motion have a wave character. But it is significant for microscopic bodies only. This is because the wavelengths associated with ordinary objects are so short due to their large masses that their wave properties cannot be detected.

Therefore, practically these bodies are said to have no wavelengths, whereas the wavelength associated with electrons and other sub-atomic particles can be detected experimentally.

Example 11 If the velocity of the electron in Bohr's first orbit is 2.19×10^6 ms^{-1}, calculate the de-Broglie wavelength associated with it. NCERT

Sol. We know that, mass of electron $= 9.11 \times 10^{-31}$ kg

$$h = 6.626 \times 10^{-34} \text{ J s}$$

$$\text{Wavelength, } \lambda = \frac{h}{mv} = \frac{6.626 \times 10^{-34} \text{ kg m}^2\text{s}^{-1}}{9.11 \times 10^{-31} \text{ kg} \times 2.19 \times 10^6 \times \text{ms}^{-1}}$$

$$\lambda = 3.32 \times 10^{-10} \text{m} = 332 \text{ pm}$$

Example 12 Show that the circumference of the Bohr orbit for the hydrogen atom is an integral multiple of the de-Broglie wavelength associated with the electron revolving around the orbit. NCERT

Sol. According to Bohr model for H-atom, the angular momentum of an electron in a given stationary state,

$$mvr = \frac{nh}{2\pi} \quad \text{or} \quad 2\pi r = \frac{nh}{mv} \quad \ldots\text{(i)}$$

From de-Broglie equation, wavelength, $\lambda = \frac{h}{mv}$ ...(ii)

From equations (i) and (ii), we get $2\pi r = n\lambda$

Therefore, the circumference ($2\pi r$) of the Bohr orbit for H-atom is an integral multiple of de-Broglie wavelength. (Here, n = number of waves in nth orbit).

2. Heisenberg's Uncertainty Principle

This principle is a result of dual nature of matter and radiation. It is put forward by **W. Heisenberg** a German physicist in 1927.

According to this principle, *"it is impossible to determine simultaneously, the exact position and exact momentum (or velocity) of an electron"*.

Mathematically, it can be given as

$$\Delta x \times \Delta p_x \geq \frac{h}{4\pi} \quad \text{or} \quad \Delta x \times \Delta(mv_x) \geq \frac{h}{4\pi}$$

or $$\Delta x \times \Delta v_x \geq \frac{h}{4\pi m}$$

where, Δx is the uncertainty in position and Δp_x (or Δv_x) is the uncertainty in momentum (or velocity) of the particle. If we know the position of the electron with high degree of accuracy (Δx is small), then the uncertainty in the velocity of the electron (Δv_x) will be large and *vice-versa*.

Significance of Uncertainty Principle

- This principle rules out the existence of definite paths or trajectories of electrons and other similar particles. Since, the position of an object and its velocity fix its trajectory.
- The effect of this principle is significant only in **case of motion of microscopic objects** and is negligible in case of macroscopic object. This is because in dealing with milligram sized or heavier objects, the associated uncertanities are hardly of any real consequences.

  For an object of 10^{-6} kg mass (macroscopic object), $\Delta v \cdot \Delta x$ or uncertainty is

  $$\Delta v \cdot \Delta x = \frac{h}{4\pi m} = \frac{6.626 \times 10^{-34} \text{ Js}}{4 \times 3.1416 \times 10^{-6} \text{ kg}} = 10^{-28} \text{ m}^{-2}\text{s}^{-1}$$

  (Insignificant)

  But, for an electron of 9.11×10^{-31} kg mass (microscopic object) $\Delta v \cdot \Delta x$ obtained is

  $$\Delta v \cdot \Delta x = \frac{h}{4\pi m} = \frac{6.626 \times 10^{-34} \text{ Js}}{4 \times 3.1416 \times 9.11 \times 10^{-31} \text{ kg}}$$

  $$= 10^{-4} \text{ m}^2\text{s}^{-1}$$

  (Significant)
- The precise statement of the position and momentum of electrons have to be replaced by the statements of probability that the electron has at a given position and momentum.

Example 13 A golf ball has a mass of 40 g and a speed of 45 m/s. If the speed can be measured within accuracy of 2%, calculate the uncertainty in the position. NCERT

Sol. Uncertainty in velocity, $\Delta v = \frac{45 \times 2}{100} = 0.9\ \text{ms}^{-1}$

From Heisenberg's principle,

$$\Delta x = \frac{h}{4\pi m \cdot \Delta v} = \frac{6.6 \times 10^{-34}\ \text{kg m}^2\text{s}^{-1}}{4 \times 3.14 \times 40 \times 10^{-3}\ \text{kg} \times 0.9\ \text{ms}^{-1}}$$

$$= 1.46 \times 10^{-33}\ \text{m}$$

Example 14 If the position of the electron is measured within an accuracy of ± 0.002 nm, calculate the uncertainty in the momentum of the electron. Suppose the momentum of the electron is $\frac{h}{4\pi m \times 0.05\ \text{nm}}$, is there any problem in defining this value. NCERT

Sol. Given, $\Delta x = 0.002\ \text{nm} = 2.00 \times 10^{-12}\ \text{m}$

From Heisenberg's uncertainty principle, $\Delta x \times \Delta p \geq \frac{h}{4\pi}$

$$\Delta p = \frac{h}{4\pi \Delta x} = \frac{6.626 \times 10^{-34}\ \text{kg m}^2\text{s}^{-1}}{4 \times 3.14 \times 2.00 \times 10^{-9}\ \text{m}}$$

$$\Delta p = 2.638 \times 10^{-23}\ \text{kg m s}^{-1}$$

$$\text{Actual momentum} = \frac{h}{4\pi \times 0.05\ \text{nm}} = \frac{6.626 \times 10^{-34}\ \text{kg m}^2\text{s}^{-1}}{4 \times 3.14 \times 0.05 \times 10^{-9}\ \text{m}}$$

$$= 1.055 \times 10^{-24}\ \text{kg m s}^{-1}$$

It cannot be defined, as the actual value of momentum is smaller than uncertainty.

Reasons for the Failure of the Bohr Model

Different reasons for failure of the Bohr model are discussed below

- Bohr model considered electron as a charged particle moving in well defined circular orbits about the nucleus. It did not consider the dual behaviour of matter (specially wave character).
- It considered that an orbit is a clearly defined path which can completely be defined only if both the position and the velocity of the electron are known exactly at the same time. But this is against the Heisenberg uncertainty principle.

2.6 Quantum Mechanical Model of the Atom

Classical mechanics is based on Newton's laws of motion and is applicable only to macroscopic objects as it ignores the concept of dual behaviour of matter and the uncertainty principle. However, quantum mechanics deals with the microscopic particles.

The branch of science that deals with the dual behaviour of matter, i.e. wave as well as particle nature is called **quantum mechanics.** When quantum mechanical concept is applied to macroscopic objects (for which wave character is negligible) the results are the same as those from the classical mechanics.

On the basis of quantum mechanics, Schrodinger proposed a **quantum mechanical model** of an atom. This model is the picture of the structure of atom, which emerges from the application of the Schrodinger equation to atoms.

Schrodinger Wave Equation

In 1926, **Erwin Schrodinger** gave following **Schrodinger wave equation** to describe the wave motion of the electron in three dimensional space around the nucleus.

$$\frac{\partial^2 \psi}{\partial x^2} + \frac{\partial^2 \psi}{\partial y^2} + \frac{\partial^2 \psi}{\partial z^2} + \frac{8\pi^2 m}{h^2}(E - V)\psi = 0$$

where, ψ (psi) = a wave function of space coordinates x, y and z and represents the amplitude of the electron wave

h = Planck's constant, (= 6.626×10^{-34} Js)

m = mass of an electron

E = permissible total energy, which the electron can have. The total energy of the system means the kinetic energies of all the sub-atomic particles (electrons, nuclei), attractive potential between the electrons and nuclei and repulsive potential among the electrons and nuclei individually.

V = potential energy of the electron $\frac{Ze^2}{r}$.

When this equation is solved for ψ, three integers, n, l, m were obtained. These integers are called **quantum numbers.** For systems like atoms or molecules, energy of which does not change with time, the Schrodinger wave equation may be written as $\hat{H}\psi = E\psi$.

Here, $\hat{H}$ is a mathematical operator, called **Hamiltonian operator.** (Schrodinger introduced this operator $\hat{H}$ from the expression for the total energy of the system). ψ is the wave function.

Probability Picture of an Electron : Concept of Atomic Orbital

According to quantum mechanical approach, it is not possible to simply locate an electron at a particular point, but there are certain regions in space around the nucleus where the probability (chances) of finding the electron is maximum (90-95%). These most probable regions in space are referred as **orbitals**.

Thus, *"an orbital is a region in space around the nucleus where the probability of finding the electron is maximum".*

Difference Between Orbit and Orbital

Orbit	Orbital
It is a well defined circular path around the nucleus in which the electron revolve.	Its shows the three dimensional space around the nucleus within which the probability of finding an electron is maximum (upto 90%).
The concept of an orbit does not consider the wave character of electrons and uncertainty principle.	The concept of an orbital is in accordance with the wave character of electrons and uncertainty principle.
They do not have any directional characteristics.	Except *s*-orbitals, all orbitals have directional characteristics.
The maximum number of electrons that an orbit can have is given by $2n^2$ where, n is the number of the orbit.	The maximum number of electrons that can be occupied by an orbital is always two.

Significance of ψ and ψ^2

In an atom the wave function ψ for an electron has no physical significance as such. However, its square, i.e. ψ^2 at any point gives the intensity of the electron wave at that point. In view of Heisenberg's uncertainty principle, it shows the probability of finding the electron at that point and therefore, termed as **probability density.** Its value is always positive.

Important Features of the Quantum Mechanical Model of Atom

The following are the important features of this model

- The energy of electrons in atoms is quantised (i.e. can only have certain specific values).
- The existence of quantised electronic energy levels is a direct consequence of the wave like properties of electrons and are allowed solutions of Schrodinger wave equation.
- It is not possible to determine both the exact position and exact velocity of an electron in an atom simultaneously.
- The wave function ψ for an electron in an atom shows the atomic orbital of that electron. In each orbital, the energy of electron is definite and an orbital can occupy a maximum of two electrons. In case of a multi-electron atom, the electrons are filled in various orbitals in increasing order of energy.
- From the value of $|\psi|^2$ at different points within an atom, it is possible to predict the region around the nucleus, where probability of finding the electron is maximum. $|\psi|^2$ is known as probability density and is always positive.

Quick Test 3

Conceptual Questions

1. Out of the electron and proton which one will have, a higher velocity to produce matter waves of the same wavelength? Explain it. *NCERT Exemplar*
2. (i) Why does a car cannot seem to travel in the form of a wave although de-Broglie relation is applicable to it?
   (ii) de-Broglie concept cannot be applied to a moving cricket ball. Explain why?
3. The effect of uncertainty principle is significant only for motion of microscopic particles and is negligible for the macroscopic particles. Justify the statement with the help of a suitable example. *NCERT Exemplar*
4. How does the Bohr theory of the hydrogen atom differ from that of Schrodinger?
5. What kind of information about an electron in an atom is obtained from its wave function?

Numerical Questions

6. Find out the number of waves made by a Bohr electron in one complete revolution in its 3rd orbit.
7. (i) What will be the wavelength of a ball of mass 0.1 kg moving with a velocity of 10 ms^{-1}? *NCERT*
   (ii) Can we apply Heisenberg's uncertainty principle to a stationary electron? Why or why not?
8. (i) Calculate the mass of a photon with wavelength 3.6 Å. *NCERT*
   (ii) Derive an equation to explain the relationship between wavelength, mass and velocity of a particle. *Diksha*
9. A microscope using suitable photons is employed to locate an electron in an atom within a distance of 0.1 Å. What is the uncertainty involved in the measurement of its velocity? *NCERT*

Answers

6. 3 7. (i) 6.626×10^{-34} m 8. (i) 6.135×10^{-29} kg 9. 5.79×10^{6} ms^{-1}

For Solutions, See QR Code on Pg. 82

2.7 Orbitals and Quantum Numbers

The characteristics of an orbital are expressed in terms of three numbers, called **principal** (n), **azimuthal** (l) and **magnetic quantum numbers** (m_l). These numbers are obtained from the solutions of the Schrodinger wave equation.

Further, to represent the spin (rotation) of the electron about its own axis, a fourth quantum number, called **spin quantum number** has been introduced.

Thus, a set of four numbers which give us complete information, i.e. location, energy, the type of orbital occupied, shape and orientation of that orbital, etc., about all the electrons present in an atom, is called the **quantum numbers.**

The various quantum numbers are briefly discussed below

1. Principal Quantum Number (n)

- It determines the size and to a large extent the energy of the orbital.
- It is always a positive integer with value of $n = 1, 2, 3 \ldots$
- This quantum number also identifies as **shell.** The shell with $n = 1$ is called the **first shell.** The shell with $n = 2$ is called the **second shell** and so on. The various shells are represented by the following letters

$$\text{Shell} = K\ L\ M\ N \ldots$$
$$n = 1\ \ 2\ \ 3\ \ 4 \ldots$$

- With the help of this quantum number the average distance of the electron from the nucleus can be determined.
- Distance of the electron from the nucleus and energy and size of orbital increases as the value of principal quantum number 'n' increases.
- Further with the increase in the value of 'n', the number of allowed orbital increases and are given by 'n^2'.

2. Azimuthal Quantum Number (l)

- It determines the angular momentum of the electron and is also known as **orbital angular momentum** or **subsidiary quantum number.**
- Moreover, it shows the three dimensional shape of the orbital.
- For a given value of n, the value of l can vary from 0 to $n-1$, i.e. for a given value of n, the possible value of l are $l = 0, 1, 2, \ldots\ldots(n-1)$.

  e.g. If $n = 1$, value of l is only 0.
- In each shell there are one or more **subshells** or **sub levels.** The number of subshells in a principal shell is equal to the value of principal quantum number, n. For example, in the first shell ($n = 1$), there is one sub-shell ($l = 0$) and in the second shell ($n = 2$), there are two sub-shells ($l = 0, 1$).

  Each subshell is assigned an azimuthal quantum number (l). Subshells corresponding to different values of l are indicated by the following symbols.

  Value for l : 0 1 2 3 4 5...
  Notation for subshell : s p d f g h ...
- **Angular momentum of the electron in an orbital**
$$= \sqrt{l(l+1)}\,\frac{h}{2\pi}$$
- The energies of the different subshells present within the same principal shell are found to be in order $s < p < d < f$.

  The energy of an electron present in the s-subshell is lower than that present in the p-subshell of the same principal shell. It will be proved later in this section that in the **s, p, d and f-subshells, the maximum number of electrons are 2, 6, 10 and 14 respectively.**

3. Magnetic Quantum Number (m_l)

- It shows the behaviour of electron in a magnetic field. It gives information related to the spatial orientation of the orbital with respect to standard set of coordinate axis.
- For a given value of l (subshell), $2l+1$ values are possible for m_l. These values are given by $m_l = -l, -(l-1), -(l-2) \ldots 0, 1 \ldots (l-2), (l-1), l$.

  Thus, the value of m_l varies from $-l$ to $+l$ including zero.
- **For s-subshell** ($l = 0$), $m_l = 0$, i.e. only one orientation is possible which means s-subshell consists of only one orbital.

- **For p-subshell** ($l=1$), $m_l=-1, 0, +1$, i.e. three different orientations (i.e. along x-axis, y-axis and z-axis) are possible in case of p-subshell which means that p-subshell contains three orbitals.
- Likewise ***d*-subshell** contains five orbitals and ***f*-subshell** contains seven orbitals. Thus, it can also be said that the magnetic quantum number gives the number of orbitals present in a given subshell.

The following chart gives the relation between the subshell and the number of orbitals present in it.

Value of l	0	1	2	3	4	5
Subshell notation	s	p	d	f	g	h
Number of orbitals	1	3	5	7	9	11

4. Spin Quantum Number (s)

- A fourth quantum number called the **electron spin quantum number** (m_s) is introduced to explain the line spectra of multi-electron atoms.
- An electron spins around its own axis like earth spins around its own axis while revolving around the sun. Thus, an electron has intrinsic spin angular quantum number, which is a vector quantity and can have two orientations relative to the chosen axis.

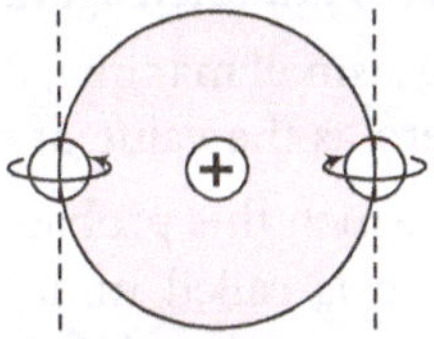

Spinning of electrons

- To distinguish between these two orientations, two values $+1/2$ or $-1/2$ are assigned to the spin quantum number, m_s. These are known as the **two spin states of the electron** and are generally represented by two arrows, ↑ (spin up) and ↓ (spin down).
- Two electrons having different m_s values (one $+1/2$ and the other $-1/2$) are said to have opposite spins. Thus, an orbital can hold a maximum of two electrons with opposite spins.
- The magnitude of spin angular momentum can be calculated from the following formula

$$\text{Spin angular momentum} = \sqrt{s(s+1)}\,\frac{h}{2\pi}$$

TEACHER'S TIP

Some important results to remember are
- Number of subshells in n^{th} shell $= n$
- Number of orbitals in a subshell $= 2l+1$
- Maximum number of electrons in a subshell $= 2(2l+1)$
- Number of orbitals in n^{th} shell $= n^2$
- Maximum number of electrons in n^{th} shell $= 2n^2$

Example 15 **Using s, p, d, f notations describe the orbital with the following quantum numbers.** **NCERT**

(i) $n=2, l=1$, **(ii) $n=4, l=0$,**
(iii) $n=5, l=3$, **(iv) $n=3, l=2$**

Sol.

	n	l	Orbital
(i)	2	1	$2p$
(ii)	4	0	$4s$
(iii)	5	3	$5f$
(iv)	3	2	$3d$

Example 16 **What is the total number of orbitals associated with the principal quantum number $n=3$?** **NCERT**

Sol. For $n=3$, the possible values of l are 0, 1 and 2. Thus, one $3s$-orbital ($n=3, l=0$ and $m_l=0$); three $3p$-orbitals ($n=3, l=1$ and $m_l=-1, 0, +1$); five $3d$-orbitals ($n=3, l=2$ and $m_l=-2, -1, 0, +1, +2$) are present in it.

Therefore, the total number of orbitals is $1+3+5=9$.

Alternatively; Number of orbitals $= n^2 = 3^2 = 9$.

2.8 Shapes of Atomic Orbitals

Schrodinger wave equation helps to find out the probability of finding an electron at any point around the nucleus, i.e. to find out the density of the points.

Radial Wave Functions

- The shapes of orbitals can also be obtained from the variation of wave function ψ as a function of r (distance from the nucleus). It is also called **radial dependence** or radial wave function.

- The graphs of ψ *vs* r for 1s, 2s and 2p-orbitals are shown in the figure given below

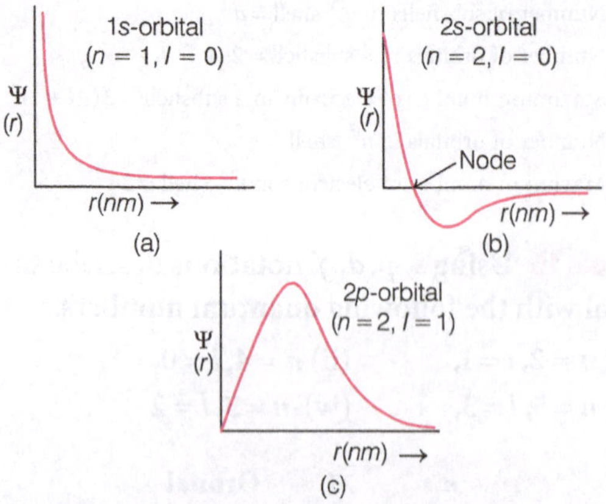

Plots of wave function (ψ) with distance from the nucleus for (a) 1s-orbital (b) 2s-orbital (c) 2p-orbital

- **Figure (a)** clearly reveals that wave function for 1s orbital continuously decreases as the value of r increases.

  However, in case of 2s-orbital **Figure (b)**, the wave function first decreases, becomes zero at a particular distance and then becomes negative.
- The point, at which wave function becomes zero is called **radial nodal surface** or **simply node.** At this point, the value of wave function gets inverted, i.e. becomes negative from positive.
- The wave function in case of 2p-orbital **Figure (c)** first increases to maximum and then decreases.
- In other words, number of nodes increases with increase of principal quantum number (n).
- The value of 2s wave function can be positive or negative depending upon the distance from the nucleus.

  Here, **positive and negative signs refer to the sign of the wave function and are not related with the positive and negative charges.**
- In all cases ψ approaches zero as r approaches infinity.

Probability Density (ψ^2) Graphs

- German physicist, **Max Born** suggested that the probability density of the electron at any point is obtained by the square of the wave function (i.e. ψ^2) at that point.
- The variation of ψ^2 as a function of r for 1s and 2s-orbitals is shown in figure below. Here again, the curves for 1s and 2s-orbitals are different.
- These graphs are known as **probability density graphs.**

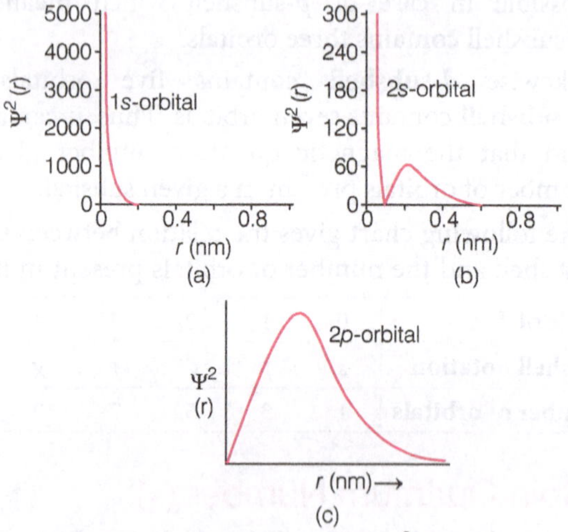

Variation of probability density ψ^2 as a function of distance r of the electron from the nucleus

- From the graph (a), it is obvious that **for 1s-orbital** the probability density is maximum at the nucleus and then decreases sharply as the distance further increases.
- However, in case of **2s-orbital,** it first decreases sharply upto zero and then again starts increasing.

  After reaching a small maxima, it decreases again and approaches zero as the value of r increases further.
- The region at which this probability density function reduced to zero is called **nodal surfaces** or **simply nodes.** Always remember that all the orbitals (except s-orbital) have zero electron density at the nucleus.
- In general, it has been found that there are $(n-1)$ nodes for ns-orbitals, $(n-2)$ nodes for np-orbitals and so on.

Boundary Surface Diagrams

The probability density variation can be visualised in terms of charge cloud diagrams, called the boundary surface diagrams. In these diagrams, the density of the dots in a region shows the electron probability density in that region.

Although several such boundary surface diagrams may be possible but the shape of an orbital is given by only that boundary surface diagram where the probability density $|\psi|^2$ is constant, i.e. which encloses a region or volume of about 90% probability of finding the electron.

In other words, **boundary surface diagrams shows the most probable region to find an electron.**

Note **Probability density** $|\psi|^2$ has always some value, however it may be, small, at any finite distance from the nucleus. It is therefore, not possible to draw a boundary surface diagram of a rigid size where the probability of finding the electron is 100%.

The boundary surface diagrams of some orbitals are discussed below

(i) **Shapes of *s*-orbitals** Boundary surface diagram of a *s*-orbital is actually a sphere centred on the nucleus.
In two dimensions, it looks like a circle which encloses a region where probability of finding the electron is about 90%.

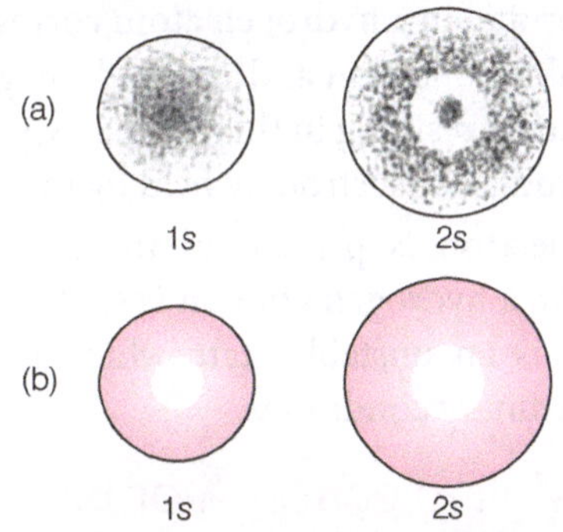

(a) Probability density plots of 1*s* and 2*s* atomic orbitals
(b) Boundary surface diagram for 1*s* and 2*s*- orbitals

Thus, the shape of all the *s*-orbitals are spherical, i.e. there is equal probability of finding the electron at a given distance in all the directions further.
It is also observed that the size of the *s*-orbital increases as the value of *n* increases. Thus, the order of size of *s*-orbital is $4s > 3s > 2s > 1s$.

(ii) **Shapes of *p*-orbitals** Boundary surface diagrams for three 2*p*-orbitals ($l = 1$) are shown in the figure below.
In these diagrams, the nucleus is at the origin. Each *p*-orbital have two sections which are called its **lobes**. These lobes lie on either side of the plane that passes through the nucleus.
The probability density function is zero on the plane where the two lobes touch each other.
These three *p*-orbitals are identical in size, shape and energy but differ in orientation of lobes.
Since, the lobes may be considered to lie along the *x*, *y* or *z*-axis, they are represented by $2p_x$, $2p_y$ and $2p_z$. **The size and energy of *p*-orbitals like *s*-orbitals, increases as the value of principal quantum number *n* increases.**
Thus, the order of the energy and size of various *p*-orbitals is $4p > 3p > 2p$.

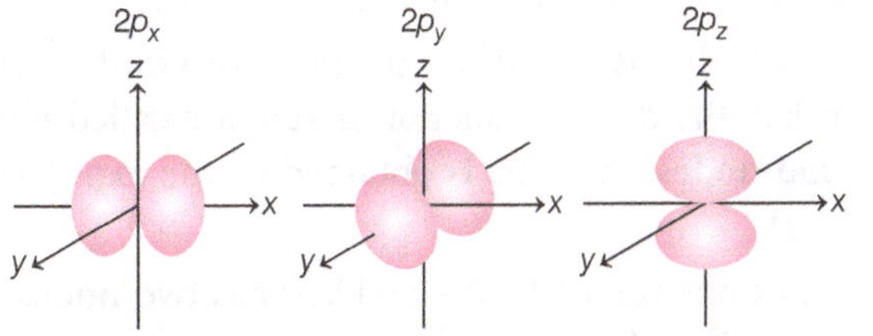

Boundary surface diagrams of the three 2*p*-orbitals

Further, like *s*-orbitals, the probability density functions for *p*-orbital also pass through value zero, besides at zero and infinite distance, as the distance from the nucleus increases.

(iii) **Shapes of *d*-orbitals** $l = 2$ shows *d*-orbital. The minimum value of principal quantum number (n) for which is 3. (This is because the value of l cannot be greater than $n - 1$).
For $l = 2$, m_l have five values ($-2, -1, 0, +1$ and $+2$) thus there are five *d*-orbitals. The boundary surface diagram of these five *d*-orbitals are given below.

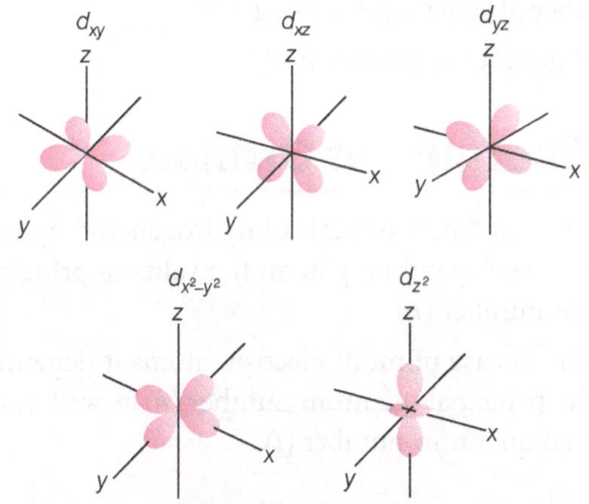

Boundary surface diagrams of the five 3*d*-orbitals

The five *d*-orbitals are designated as d_{xy}, d_{yz}, d_{xz}, $d_{x^2-y^2}$ and d_{z^2} and are of equal energy, i.e. degenerate.

The first four d-orbitals have similar shape but the shape of fifth one, i.e. d_{z^2}, is different from that of the other. d-orbitals having higher value of n, i.e. ($4d$, $5d$ ...) also have shapes similar to $3d$-orbital, but differ in energy and size.

Nodes and Nodal Planes

As we have discussed earlier, the place or point where the probability density function is zero are called **nodes** or **radial nodes**. Its value is obtained by the **expression** $(n - l - 1)$.

e.g. $2s$ has one node $(2 - 0 - 1 = 1)$, $3s$ has two nodes $(3 - 0 - 1 = 2)$ and so on.

In case of np and nd-orbitals, the probability density functions are zero at the plane(s) passing through the nucleus (origin). These nodes are called **angular nodes**. e.g. For p_z-orbital, xy-plane is a nodal plane, for d_{xy}-orbital there are two nodal planes passing through the origin and bisecting the xy-plane containing z-axis. This is at an angle of 45 degree from x and y axis.

The number of angular nodes are equal to 'l', i.e. one angular node for p-orbitals, two angular nodes for d-orbitals and so on.

In general, in an orbital

- Number of angular nodes $= l$
- Number of radial nodes $= n - l - 1$
- Total number of nodes $= n - 1$

2.9 Energies of Orbitals

Energies of different orbitals of hydrogen and hydrogen like particles depend only upon the value of principal quantum number (n).

However, in case of multi-electron atoms it depends upon the principal quantum number (n) as well as on the azimuthal quantum number (l).

1. For H-Atom and H-like Atoms

- The energy of an electron in a hydrogen atom is determined by the principal quantum number.
- Thus, the increasing order of energy of different orbitals is $1s < 2s = 2p < 3s = 3p = 3d < 4s = 4p = 4d = 4f$. It is shown in figure below.

The orbitals of the same subshell having the same energy are called **degenerate orbitals.**

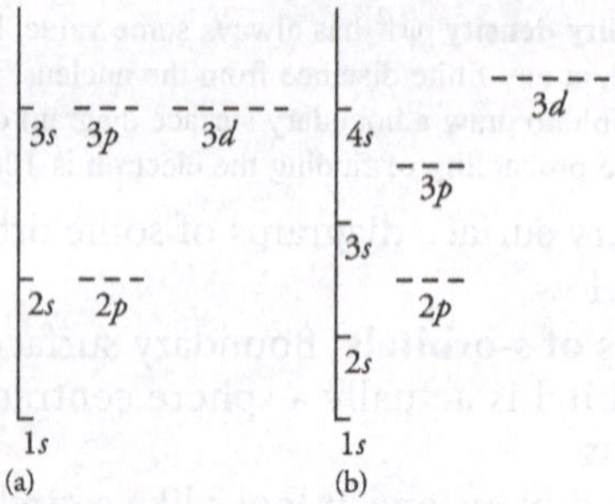

Energy level diagrams for the few electronic shells of (a) hydrogen atom and (b) multi-electronic atoms.

- The $1s$-orbital in a hydrogen atom corresponds to the most stable condition and is called the **ground state.** The electron residing in this orbital experience lowest energy and is most strongly held by the nucleus.
- If the electron is present in the $2s$, $2p$ or higher orbitals in a hydrogen atom, it is said to be in **excited state.** It is an unstable state which is not possible under ordinary conditions.

2. For Multi-electron Atoms

- In these atoms, for different subshells, the energy is different. The main reason for having different energies of the subshells is the mutual repulsion among the electrons.
- In general, the energy of an electron in an orbital is affected by the nuclear charge, principal energy level and the presence of electrons in the inner shells.
- The shielding of the outer shell electrons from the nucleus by the inner shell electrons is called **shielding** or **screening effect** and due to this the outer shell electrons will not experience the full positive charge of the nucleus. This effect is different in different type of orbitals.
- The net positive charge experienced by the electron from the nucleus is called **effective nuclear charge** (Z_{eff}). This decreases with increasing shielding effect.
- The order of shielding (also in case of orbitals of same shell) is $s > p > d > f$. Thus, the electron present in a s-orbital will be more tightly bound to the nucleus as compared to that which is present in p-orbital. Similarly, an electron in p-orbital will be more tightly bound than the d-orbital electron and so on.

- Since, the extent of shielding from the nucleus is different for electrons in different orbitals, so it leads to the splitting of energy levels within the same shell.
- The energy of electrons in different orbitals of the same shell is in order : $s < p < d < f$.

$(n + l)$ Rule

According to this rule "the lower the value of $(n + l)$ for an orbital, the lower is its energy. If for two orbitals, the value of $(n + l)$ is same, the one with lower value of n will have the lower energy". This rule is also helpful to account for the fact that the energy of $3d$-orbital is higher than the $4s$-orbital.

Let us apply this rule to $4s$ and $3d$-orbitals.

For $3d$-orbital, $(n + l)$ value $= 3 + 2 = 5$ while for $4s$-orbital it is $4 + 0 = 4$.

Thus, $4s$-orbital has lesser energy than $3d$-orbital and, therefore, is filled first. Further energies of the orbitals in the same subshell decrease as the atomic number (Z) increases.

e.g. Energy of $2s$-orbital of hydrogen atom is greater than that of $2s$-orbital of lithium and that of lithium is greater than that of sodium and so on, i.e.

$$E_{2s}(\text{H}) > E_{2s}(\text{Li}) > E_{2s}(\text{Na}) > E_{2s}(\text{K}).$$

Arrangement of Orbitals with Increasing Energy on the Basis of $(n + l)$ Rule

Orbital	Value of n	Value of l	Value of $(n+l)$	
$1s$	1	0	$1+0=1$	
$2s$	2	0	$2+0=2$	
$2p$	2	1	$2+1=3$	$2p(n=2)$ has lower energy than
$3s$	3	0	$3+0=3$	$3s(n=3)$
$3p$	3	1	$3+1=4$	$3p(n=3)$ has lower energy than
$4s$	4	0	$4+0=4$	$4s(n=4)$
$3d$	3	2	$3+2=5$	$3d(n=3)$ has lower energy than
$4p$	4	1	$4+1=5$	$4p(n=4)$

Example 17 **Among the following pairs of orbitals, which orbital will experience the larger effective nuclear charge?** **NCERT**

(i) $2s$ and $3s$, (ii) $4d$ and $4f$, (iii) $3d$ and $3p$

As the distance between the nucleus and orbital increases, effective nuclear charge decreases.

Sol. (i) $2s$-orbital experiences larger effective nuclear charge than $3s$ because $2s$ is closer to nucleus than $3s$.

(ii) Similarly, $4d$-orbital experiences larger effective nuclear charge than $4f$-orbital.

(iii) In $3d$ and $3p$-orbitals, $3p$-orbital experiences larger effective nuclear charge.

Example 18 **How many electrons in an atom may have the following quantum numbers?** **NCERT**

(i) $n = 4, m_s = -\frac{1}{2}$ (ii) $n = 3, l = 0$

Sol. (i) Total electrons if $n = 4$ is $2n^2$, $2 \times 4^2 = 32$

half of the total electrons, i.e. 16 electrons have $m_s = -\frac{1}{2}$.

(ii) $n = 3, l = 0$ it is $3s$-orbital and it can have two electrons.

2.10 Filling of Orbitals in Atom

The filling of electrons in different orbitals is governed by the following rules

1. Aufbau Principle

According to this principle, in the ground state of the atoms, the orbitals are filled in increasing order of energies, i.e. electrons first occupy the lowest energy orbital available to them and then enter into higher energy orbitals provided that the lower energy orbitals are completely occupied.

Hence, the order in which the orbitals are filled is $1s, 2s, 2p, 3s, 3p, 4s, 3d, 4p, 5s, 4d, 5p, 6s, 4f, 5d, 6p, 7s \ldots$

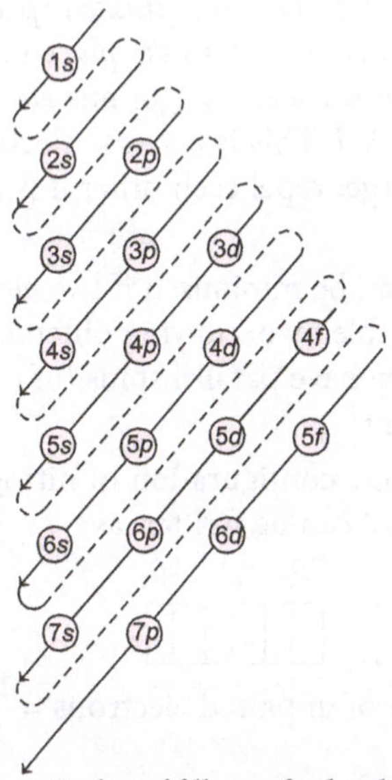

Order of filling of orbitals

2. Pauli's Exclusion Principle

This principle states that, *"No two electrons in an atom can have the same set of four quantum numbers"*.

This principle can also be stated that, *"only two electrons may exist in the same orbital and these electrons must have opposite spin" (or an orbital can accommodate a maximum of two electrons with opposite spins).*

e.g. Two electrons in an orbital can be indicated either by (i) or (ii) but, not by (iii) or (iv).

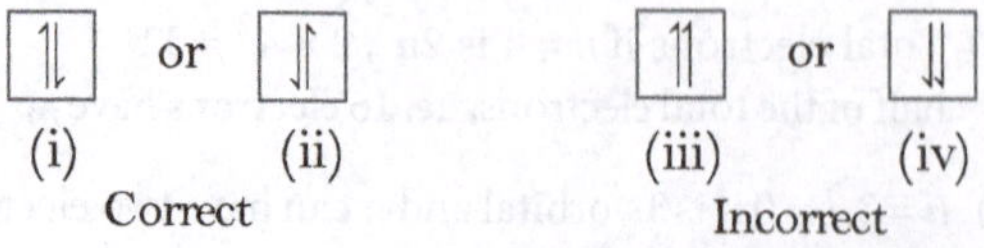

- It means that if for two electrons the three quantum numbers n, l and m_l, have same value, the value of fourth quantum number, i.e. spin quantum number is different, i.e. +1/2 for one and −1/2 for other.
- This restriction in the filling of electrons in an orbital helps in calculating the capacity of electrons to be present in any subshell. e.g. In case of $1s$ subshell, there is only one orbital and hence, the maximum number of electrons present in $1s$ subshell are two.

  Thus, the rule can be summed up as "the maximum number of electrons present in a shell with principal quantum number n is equal to $2n^2$."

3. Hund's Rule of Maximum Multiplicity

According to this rule, *pairing of electrons in the orbitals belonging to the same subshell (p, d or f), i.e. degenerate orbitals, does not take place until each orbital belonging to that subshell has got one electron each, i.e. it is singly occupied.* This is because electrons being identical in charge, repel each other if present in the same orbital.

The repulsion can be minimised if two electrons move as far apart as possible by occupying different degenerate orbitals or if they have parallel spins (of course in different orbitals).

e.g. The electronic configuration of nitrogen having atomic number 7 can be written as

(i) 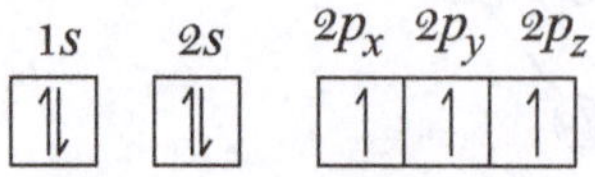

Total spin of unpaired electrons $= \frac{1}{2} + \frac{1}{2} + \frac{1}{2} = 1\frac{1}{2}$

(ii) 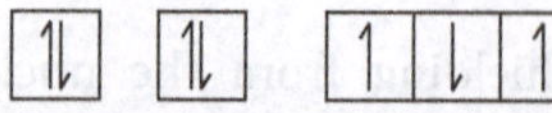

Total spin of unpaired electrons $= +\frac{1}{2} - \frac{1}{2} + \frac{1}{2} = \frac{1}{2}$

(iii) 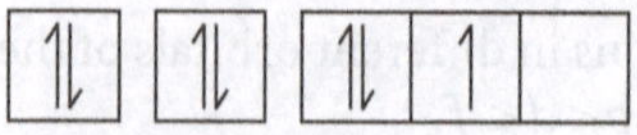

Total spin $= 1/2$

The term maximum multiplicity, means the total spin of unpaired electrons is maximum. e.g. The total spin of the unpaired electrons in configurations (i), (ii), and (iii) are respectively $1\frac{1}{2}, \frac{1}{2}$ and $\frac{1}{2}$.

Thus, configuration (i) with maximum multiplicity of $1\frac{1}{2}$ is correct according to Hund's rule of maximum multiplicity.

Example 19 **Which of the following representations of electronic configuration is excluded by the Aufbau principle, the Pauli's exclusion principle and Hund's rule ? Which is the correct representation? Explain how a principle or rule is violated in the others.**

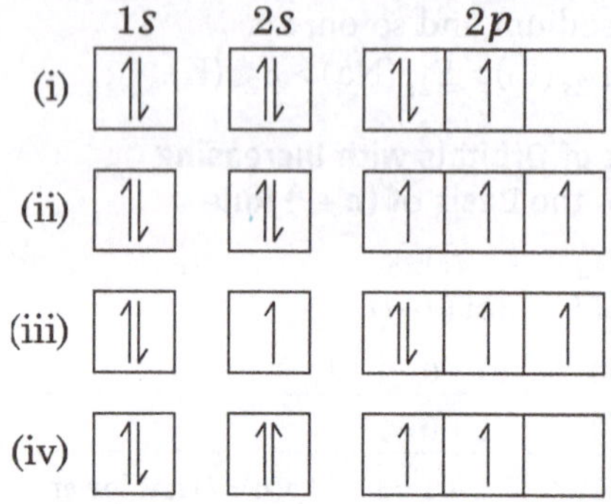

Sol. (i) Representation of electronic configuration is excluded by Hund's rule since electrons are not shown in separate orbitals of the same subshell with parallel spins.

(ii) Representation of electronic configuration is correct.

(iii) Representation of electronic configuration is excluded by the Aufbau principle because the $2s$-subshell fills before the $2p$.

(iv) Representation of electronic configuration is excluded by the Pauli exclusion principle since the two electrons in the $2s$-orbital cannot have the same spin.

2.11 Electronic Configuration of Atoms

The distribution of electrons into orbitals of an atom is called its **electronic configuration**.There are following two ways to assign the electronic configuration of different atoms. These ways are as

(i) $s^a p^b d^c$ ...**notation** In it, the letter symbol shows subshell and the superscript such as *a*, *b*, *c*,... etc., shows, the number of electrons present in the subshell. The similar subshell represented for different shells is differentiated by writing the principal quantum number before the respective subshell.

> **Alternatively,** the electronic configuration of any orbital can be simply represented by the notation nl^x, where, n = principal quantum number or number of the main or principal shell, l = symbol of the subshell or orbital, i.e. *s*, *p*, *d*, *f* and x = number of electrons present in that orbital. Thus, $4p^1$ means that one electron is present in *p*-subshell of the 4th main shell.

(ii) **Orbital diagram** In this notation, box is used to represent each orbital of the subshell and an arrow [with positive (↑) or negative (↓) spins] represents the electron.

e.g.

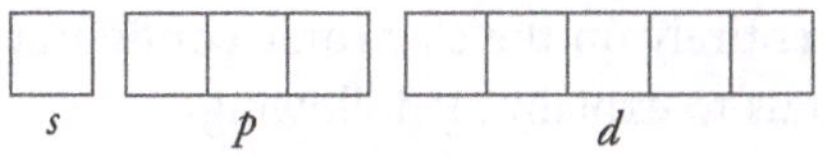

The advantage of this notation over the other is that it shows all the four quantum numbers.

Nitrogen (Atomic number = 7) The seventh electron in case of nitrogen enters in $2p_z$-orbital.

$N (Z = 7)\ 1s^2\ 2s^2\ 2p_x^1\ 2p_y^1\ 2p_z^1$ or

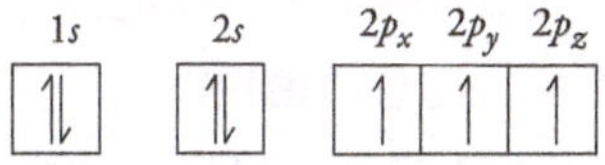

The electrons present in the completely filled shells are called **core electrons** and the electrons that are added to the electronic shell with the highest principal quantum number are called the **valence electrons.**

e.g. $Na = [Ne]3s^1 = 1s^2, 2s^2, 2p^6, 3s^1$

The electrons present in Ne-atom (or $1s^2, 2s^2, 2p^6$) are the core electrons and the electrons present in 3rd shell are the valence electrons.

Electronic Configuration of the Elements

Atomic number	Symbol	Electronic configuration	Atomic number	Symbol	Electronic configuration
1	H	$1s^1$	19	K	$[Ar]4s^1$
2	He	$1s^2$	20	Ca	$[Ar]4s^2$
3	Li	$[He]2s^1$	21	Sc	$[Ar]4s^2 3d^1$
4	Be	$[He]2s^2$	22	Ti	$[Ar]4s^2 3d^2$
5	B	$[He]2s^2 2p^1$	23	V	$[Ar]4s^2 3d^3$
6	C	$[He]2s^2 2p^2$	24	Cr	$[Ar]4s^1 3d^5$
7	N	$[He]2s^2 2p^3$	25	Mn	$[Ar]4s^2 3d^5$
8	O	$[He]2s^2 2p^4$	26	Fe	$[Ar]4s^2 3d^6$
9	F	$[He]2s^2 2p^5$	27	Co	$[Ar]4s^2 3d^7$
10	Ne	$[He]2s^2 2p^6$	28	Ni	$[Ar]4s^2 3d^8$
11	Na	$[Ne]3s^1$	29	Cu	$[Ar]4s^1 3d^{10}$
12	Mg	$[Ne]3s^2$	30	Zn	$[Ar]4s^2 3d^{10}$
13	Al	$[Ne]3s^2 3p^1$	31	Ga	$[Ar]4s^2 3d^{10} 4p^1$
14	Si	$[Ne]3s^2 3p^2$	32	Ge	$[Ar]4s^2 3d^{10} 4p^2$
15	P	$[Ne]3s^2 3p^3$	33	As	$[Ar]4s^2 3d^{10} 4p^3$
16	S	$[Ne]3s^2 3p^4$	34	Se	$[Ar]4s^2 3d^{10} 4p^4$
17	Cl	$[Ne]3s^2 3p^5$	35	Br	$[Ar]4s^2 3d^{10} 4p^5$
18	Ar	$[Ne]3s^2 3p^6$	36	Kr	$[Ar]4s^2 3d^{10} 4p^6$

Significance of Electronic Configuration

The modern approach to the chemistry, depends almost entirely on the electronic configuration.
It helps us to explain the following

- Two or more atoms combine to form molecules.
- Some elements are metals while others are non-metals or metalloids.
- Elements like helium and argon are not reactive but elements like the halogens are reactive.

Stability of Completely Filled and Half-filled Subshells

In certain elements like Cu, or Cr, in which the energy of two subshells (4s and 3d) is only slightly different, an electron shifts from a subshell of lower energy (4s) to a subshells of higher energy (3d), as it results in either completely filled or half-filled orbitals of the subshell of higher energy.

The valence shell electronic configurations of Cr and Cu, therefore, are $3d^5\,4s^1$ and $3d^{10}\,4s^1$ respectively and not $3d^4\,4s^2$ and $3d^9\,4s^1$. It has been found that these configurations are more stable as compared to the former one. The more stability of completely filled and completely half-filled subshells is because of the following reasons.

1. Symmetrical Distribution of Electrons

The completely filled or half-filled subshells because of the symmetrical distribution of electrons in them, and symmetry leads to greater stability.

2. Exchange Energy

The electrons present in the different orbitals of the same subshell can exchange their positions. Each such exchange results in release of energy (called **exchange energy**), which leads to greater stability.

The number of exhanges that can take place is maximum in the half-filled or completely filled orbitals (as shown in the figure given below). Therefore, exchange energy is maximum and so is the stability.

In other words, it can be said that the extra stability of half-filled and completely filled subshell is because of (i) relatively small shielding, (ii) smaller coulombic repulsion energy and (iii) larger exchange energy. [More details about the exchange energy you will read in higher classes].

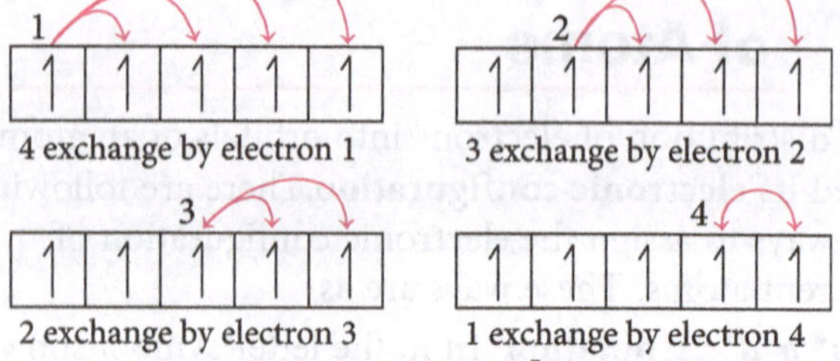

Possible exchange for a d^5-configuration

Example 20. **Iron pieces are attracted towards a magnet but zinc pieces are not. Why ?**

Sol. Electronic configuration of iron suggests that it contains unpaired electrons.

$_{26}Fe = [Ar]^{18} 3d^6 4s^2 =$ [⇅][↑][↑][↑][↑] [⇅] and hence, it is paramagnetic whereas zinc has no unpaired electron ($_{30}Zn = [Ar]^{18} 3d^{10}\,4s^2$) and hence, it is diamagnetic. It is rather repelled by the magnet.

Electronic Configuration of Ions

The electronic configuration of the ions may also be written almost in the same manner as that for atoms. However, in case of negatively charged ions, the extra electrons equal to the charge are added to the outermost orbital after writing the electronic configuration of atom.

e.g. $Cl\,(Z=17)\ :\ 1s^2\ 2s^2\ 2p^6\ 3s^2\ 3p_x^2\ 3p_y^2\ 3p_z^1$

$Cl^-(Z=17+1=18) : 1s^2\ 2s^2\ 2p^6\ 3s^2\ 3p_x^2\ 3p_y^2\ 3p_z^2$

In case of positively charged ions, the electrons equal to the charge on the ion are removed from the configuration of neutral atom.

Here, remember that always remove the electrons having the highest value of n first.

If there are more than one subshell of the valence shell, the one with the highest value of l loses the electron first.

e.g. $Mg\,(Z=12)\ :\ 1s^2 2s^2 2p^6 3s^2$

$Mg^{2+}\,(Z=12) :\ 1s^2 2s^2 2p^6$

$Fe\,(Z=26)\ :\ 1s^2\ 2s^2 2p^6 3s^2 3p^6 3d^6 4s^2$

$Fe^{2+}\ (Z=26) : 1s^2 2s^2 2p^6 3s^2 3p^6 3d^6$

Thus, in case of Fe^{2+} ion, the electrons are removed from 4s-orbital first (highest value of n) and not from 3d-orbitals.

Quick Test 4

1. (i) Using *s*, *p*, *d* notations, describe the orbital with the following quantum numbers.

(a) $n=1, l=0$ (b) $n=3, l=1$

(c) $n=4, l=2$ (d) $n=4, l=3$. *NCERT*

Hint: *n* represents the main shell and 0, 1, 2, 3, ... values of *l* represent the *s*, *p*, *d*, *f* ... orbitals respectively.

(ii) How many quantum numbers are required to describe an orbital? Name them. *Diksha*

2. (i) How many subshells are associated with $n=4$?

(ii) How many electrons will be present in the subshell having m_s value of $-1/2$ for $n=4$? *NCERT*

3. Which of the following sets of orbitals are degenerate and why?

(i) 1*s*, 2*s* and 3*s* in Mg-atom.

(ii) $2p_x$, $2p_y$ and $2p_z$ in C-atom.

(iii) 3*s*, $3p_x$ and 3*d*-orbitals in H-atom.

4. (i) What is the common between d_{xy} and $d_{x^2-y^2}$ orbitals?

(ii) What is the difference between them?

(iii) What is the angle between the lobes of the above two orbitals?

5. (i) Which of the following orbitals are degenerate?

$3d_{xy}, 4d_{xy}, 3d_{z^2}, 3d_{yz}, 4d_{yz}\ 4d_{z^2}$

(ii) Calculate the total number of angular nodes and radial nodes present in 3*p*-orbital. *NCERT Exemplar*

6. (i) Arrange *s*, *p* and *d*-subshells of a shell in the increasing order of effective nuclear charge (Z_{eff}) experienced by the electron present in the nucleus. *NCERT Exemplar*

(ii) In which element, the outermost electron can have the following set of quantum numbers?

$$n=3, l=0, m_l=0, m_s=-1/2$$

7. (i) The bromine atom possesses 35 electrons. It contains 6 electrons in 2*p*-orbital, 6 electrons in 3*p*-orbital and 5 electrons in 4*p*-orbital. Which of these electron experiences the lowest effective nuclear charge?

(ii) The unpaired electrons in Al and Si are present in 3*p*-orbital. Which electrons will experience more effective nuclear charge from the nucleus? *NCERT Exemplar*

8. Explain the rule of filling of electrons in degenerate orbital. *Diksha*

9. (i) The electronic configuration of valence shell of Cu is $3d^{10}4s^1$ and not $3d^9 4s^2$. How is this configuration explained?

(ii) Nickel atom can lose two electrons and form Ni^{2+} ion. The atomic number of Ni is 28. From which orbital will nickel lose two electrons? *NCERT Exemplar*

Answers

2. (i) 4

(ii) 16 electrons

5. (ii) Radial nodes $=1$, Angular nodes $(l)=1$

For Solutions, See QR Code on Pg. 82

Mind Map

Structure of Atom

ATOM — The smallest particle taking part in a chemical reaction.

Constituents of Atom

1. Electron, e^-

Charge $= -1.6 \times 10^{-19}$ C

Mass $= -9.1 \times 10^{-31}$ kg

A. Wave Nature

- **Wave characteristics**
  Wavelength (λ), frequency (ν), velocity (c) and wave number ($\bar{\nu}$). These are related as
  $$c = \nu\lambda \text{ and } \frac{1}{\lambda} = \bar{\nu}$$
- **EMR Spectra**
  It shows increasing order of wavelengths of decreasing frequencies.

Line spectra of H

$$\bar{\nu} = 109677 \left(\frac{1}{n_1^2} - \frac{1}{n_2^2}\right) \text{cm}^{-1}$$

where, $n_1 = 1, 2...$ and $n_2 = n_1+1, n_1+2......$

n_1, is 1,2,3,4 and 5 for Lyman, Balmer, Paschen, Brackett and Pfund series.

B. Particle Nature

Planck's Theory

$$E = nh\nu, h = 6.6 \times 10^{-34} \text{ Js}$$

(i) **Black Body Radiation**
Radiation emitted by a black body.

(ii) **Photoelectric Effect**
$$h\nu = h\nu_0 + \frac{1}{2} m_e v^2$$

2. Proton, $_1p^+$

Charge $= 1.6 \times 10^{-19}$ C, mass $= 1.6 \times 10^{-27}$ kg

3. Neutron, n^0

Charge $= 0$, mass $= 1.67 \times 10^{-27}$ kg

Atomic Models

Primitive Models

(i) Thomson's Model
It assumed atom as a pudding of positive charge with plums and electrons embedded in it.

(ii) Rutherford's Model
It assumed that proton and neutron are present in nucleus and electrons revolve around it.

Atomic Number (Z)
Z = number of protons = number of e^- (in neutral species). It is written as subscript, e.g. $_ZX$.

Mass Number
It is the sum of number of p^+ and n^0, i.e. nucleons. It is written as superscript, e.g. ^AX.

(iii) Bohr's Model
Assumes electrons revolve only in stationary orbits of fixed energy).

- **Bohr Radius**
  $$r_n = \frac{a_0 n^2}{Z} \quad [a_0 = 52.9 \text{ pm}]$$
- **Calculation of Energy**
  $$E = -2.18 \times 10^{-18}\left(\frac{Z^2}{n^2}\right) \text{J}$$
- **Calculation of Velocity**
  $$v_n = \frac{2.19 \times 10^6 \times Z}{n} \text{ms}^{-1}$$
- **Calculation of Spectral Lines**
  $$x = \frac{(n_2 - n_1)(n_2 - n_1 + 1)}{2}$$

Limitations

1. Applicable for one electron system only.
2. Does not explain Zeeman and Stark effect.

Different Atomic Species

- **Isotopes**
  Species having same atomic number but different mass number.
  These are chemically same.
- **Isobars**
  Species with same mass number but different atomic number.
- **Isotones**
  Species having same number of neutrons.
- **Isoelectronic**
  Species having same number of electrons.

Quantum Mechanical Model

(Assumes only the probability of finding an electron upto a distance).

- **de-Broglie Equation**
  $$\lambda = \frac{h}{P} \text{ or } \lambda = \frac{h}{mv}$$
  where, P = momentum
  v = velocity
- **Heisenberg's Uncertainty Principle**
  $$\Delta x \times \Delta P \geq \frac{h}{4\pi}; \Delta x \cdot m \cdot \Delta v \geq \frac{h}{4\pi}$$
- **Node**
  Area of zero electron density.
  Radial node $= n - l - 1$
- **Orbital**
  The region where the probability of finding the electron is maximum.

Electronic Configuration

Process of distribution of e^- in various orbitals.

Rules of Filling of Electrons

Aufbau Principle
Electrons are filled in increasing order of energy.

Hund's Rule of Maximum Multiplicity
Pairing of electrons occurs only when each orbital is singly occupied.

Pauli Exclusion Principle
An orbital can accommodate a maximum of two electrons with opposite spins.

Quantum Number

A set of four numbers giving complete information about electron.

Principal Q. N. (n)

- It shows the size and energy of orbital.
- For single electron atom, $E \propto n$
- For multielectron atom $E \propto (n+l)$

Magnetic Q. N. (m_l)

It shows orientation of orbital and varies from $-l$ to $+l$ including zero.

Azimuthal Q. N. (l)

- It shows the shape of orbital.
- If $l = 0, 1, 2$ or 3, the orbital is s, p, d or f.
- Angular momentum, $\mu = \sqrt{l(l+1)}\frac{h}{2\pi}$

Spin Q. N. (s)

It shows spining of electrons and have value $+\frac{1}{2}$ or $-\frac{1}{2}$.

EXAM PATTERN QUESTIONS

Objective Type Questions

Multiple Choice Questions (MCQs)

[1 Mark]

1. Which of the following statements is/are correct regarding Rutherford scattering experiment?

(a) Most of the α-particles passed through the gold foil remain undeflected.

(b) A small fraction of the α-particles was deflected by small angles.

(c) A very few α-particles (~ 1 in 20000) bounced back, i.e. were deflected by nearly 180°.

(d) All of the above

2. Major development(s) responsible for the formulation of Bohr's model of atom were

(a) dual character of the electromagnetic radiation.

(b) experimental results regarding atomic spectra which can be explained only by assuming quantised electronic energy levels in atoms.

(c) Both (a) and (b)

(d) None of the above

3. The only series of lines appear in the visible region of the electromagnetic spectrum of hydrogen is

(a) Lyman series (b) Balmer series
(c) Paschen series (d) Pfund series

4. If travelling at same speeds, which of the following matter waves have the shortest wavelength?

NCERT Exemplar

(a) Electron (b) Alpha particle (He^{2+})
(c) Neutron (d) Proton

5. In the line spectrum of hydrogen, the lines described by the formula,

$$\bar{\nu} = 109,677\left(\frac{1}{2^2} - \frac{1}{n^2}\right)\text{cm}^{-1}$$

where, n = integer, $n \geq 3$ constitutes

(a) Balmer series (b) Lyman series
(c) Pfund series (d) Paschen series

6. Which of the following statements are correct about black body?

A. The ideal body, which emits and absorbs all frequencies is called a black body.

B. The exact frequency distribution of the emitted radiation from a black body depends on its temperature.

C. The radiation emitted goes from a lower frequency to a higher frequency as temperature increases.

D. A black body is a not a perfect radiator of radiant energy.

Choose the correct answer from the options given below.

(a) A, D and C (b) B and C
(c) C and D (d) A, B and C

7. According to Bohr's theory, the radius of electron in an orbit described by principle quantum number (n) and atomic number (Z) is proportional to

(a) Z^2n^2 (b) $\frac{Z^2}{n^2}$ (c) $\frac{Z^2}{n}$ (d) $\frac{n^2}{Z}$

8. The correct mathematical expression of Heisenberg's uncertainty principle is

(a) $\frac{\Delta x}{\Delta v_x} > \frac{h}{4\pi m}$ (b) $\Delta x \times \Delta v_x > \frac{h}{4\pi m}$

(c) $\Delta x \times \Delta v_x = \frac{h}{4\pi m}$ (d) $\Delta x \times \Delta v_x \geq \frac{h}{4\pi m}$

9. Calculate the wavelength (in nanometer) associated with a proton moving at 1.0×10^3 ms^{-1} (Mass of proton $= 1.67 \times 10^{-27}$ kg and $h = 6.63 \times 10^{-34}$ Js)

(a) 0.032 nm (b) 0.40 nm
(c) 2.5 nm (d) 14.0 nm

10. In the Schrodinger equation, $\hat{H}$ is

(a) a mathematical operator called Hamiltonian operator.

(b) introduced by Schrodinger from the expression for the total energy of the system.

(c) Both (a) and (b)

(d) None of the above

11. The correct set of four quantum numbers for the valence electrons of rubidium atom ($Z = 37$) is

(a) 5, 0, 0, $+\frac{1}{2}$ (b) 5, 1, 0, $+\frac{1}{2}$

(c) 5, 1, 1, $+\frac{1}{2}$ (d) 5, 0, 1, $+\frac{1}{2}$

12. Which combinations of quantum number n, l, m and s for the electron in an atom does not provide a permissible solution of the wave equation?

Competency Based Que.

(a) 3,2,1, $\frac{1}{2}$ (b) 3,1,1, $-\frac{1}{2}$

(c) 3, 3, 1, $-\frac{1}{2}$ (d) 3, 2, −2, $\frac{1}{2}$

13. Which one of the following sets of quantum numbers represents the highest energy level in an atom?

(a) $n=4, l=0, m=0, s=+\frac{1}{2}$ (b) $n=3, l=1, m=1, s=+\frac{1}{2}$

(c) $n=3, l=2, m=-2, s=+\frac{1}{2}$ (d) $n=3, l=0, m=0, s=+\frac{1}{2}$

14. Match the Column I with Column II.

Column I (Quantum number)	Column II (Information provided)
A. Principal quantum number.	1. Orientation of the orbital.
B. Azimuthal quantum number.	2. Energy and size of orbital.
C. Magnetic quantum number.	3. Spin of electron.
D. Spin quantum number	4. Shape of the orbital.

Choose the correct option.

	A	B	C	D		A	B	C	D
(a)	1	2	3	4	(b)	2	4	1	3
(c)	3	2	1	4	(d)	4	3	2	1

15. Total number of orbitals associated with third shell will be .... NCERT Exemplar

(a) 2 (b) 4 (c) 9 (d) 3

16. The probability density plots of 1s and 2s-orbitals are given in figure.

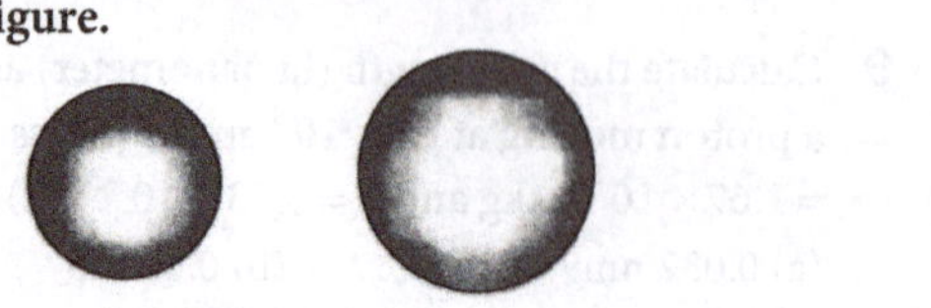

The density of dots in a region represents the probability density of finding electrons in the region.

On the basis of above diagram which of the following statements is incorrect? NCERT Exemplar

(a) 1s and 2s-orbitals are spherical in shape.

(b) The probability of finding the electron is maximum near the nucleus.

(c) The probability of finding the electron at a given distance is equal in all directions.

(d) The probability density of electrons for 2s-orbital decreases uniformly as distance from the nucleus increases.

17. $3d_{xy}$ orbital can be represented as

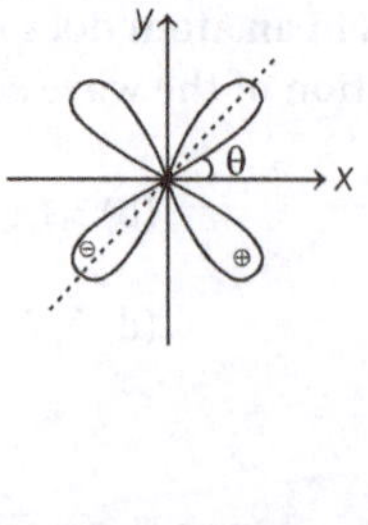

Select incorrect statements about this $3d_{xy}$ orbital.

(a) It is non-axial orbital.

(b) Positive and negative sign represent sign of amplitude of electron wave.

(c) The orbital drawn has two nodal plane *xz* and *yz*.

(d) The minimum probability point lies along $\theta = 45°$.

18. The plot of the radial wave function *R* as a function of distance (*r*) of the electron from the nucleus for 2*p*-orbital is Competency Based Que.

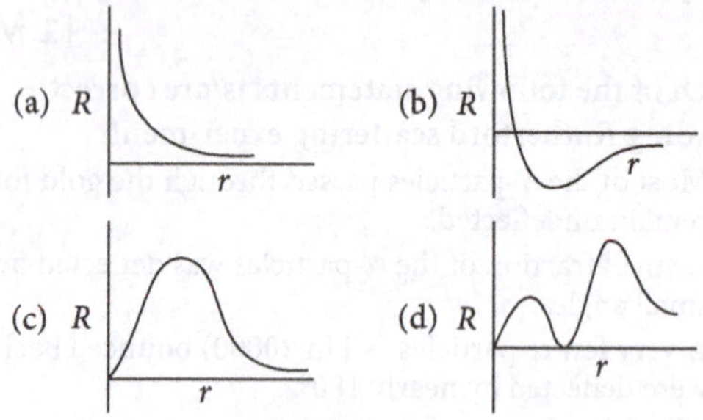

19. Consider the following table.

Column I (Orbitals)	Column II (Radial nodes)	Column III (Angular nodes)
2*s*	1	0
4*p*	2	*X*
7*f*	*Y*	3
6*d*	3	2

***X* and *Y* are**

(a) $X=2, Y=1$ (b) $X=1, Y=2$

(c) $X=1, Y=3$ (d) $X=1, Y=1$

20. For the electrons of oxygen atom, which of the following statement is correct?

(a) The two electrons present in the 2*s*-orbital have spin quantum number m_s with opposite sign.

(b) Z_{eff} for an electron in 1*s*-orbital is the same as Z_{eff} for an electron in a 2*s*-orbital.

(c) Z_{eff} for an electron in a 2*s*-orbital is the same as Z_{eff} for an electron in a 2*p*-orbital.

(d) An electron in a 2*s*-orbital has the same energy as an electron in a 2*p*-orbital.

21. The atomic numbers of elements *X*, *Y* and *Z* are 19, 21 and 25 respectively. The number of electrons present in the *M*-shell of these elements follow the order

(a) $Z > X > Y$ (b) $X > Y > Z$

(c) $Z > Y > X$ (d) $Y > Z > X$

22. Which of the following is responsible to rule out the existence of definite paths or trajectories of electrons?

(a) Pauli's exclusion principle

(b) Heisenberg's uncertainty principle

(c) Hund's rule of maximum multiplicity

(d) Aufbau principle

23. **Electronic configuration of five elements I, II, III, IV and V is mentioned below.**

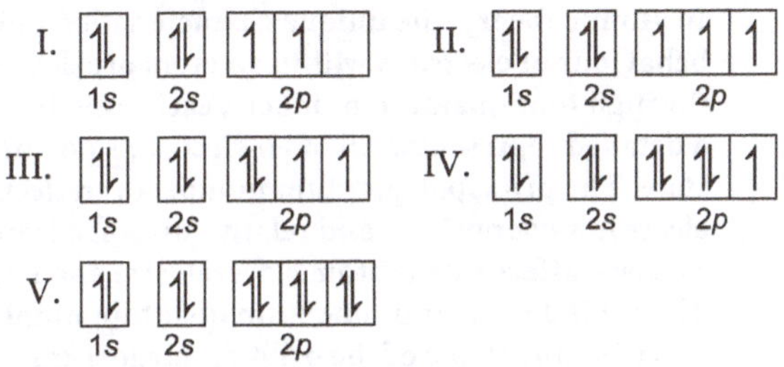

In the above configuration element I, II, III, IV and V represent as **Competency Based Que.**

(a) C, N, O, F, Ne (b) Ne, F, O, N, C
(c) C, O, N, Ne, F (d) O, C, F, Ne, V

24. **The pair of ions having same electronic configuration is ....** **NCERT Exemplar**

(a) Cr^{3+}, Fe^{3+} (b) Fe^{3+}, Mn^{2+}
(c) Fe^{3+}, Co^{3+} (d) Sc^{3+}, Cr^{3+}

25. **Which of the following options does not represent ground state electronic configuration of an atom?**

(a) $1s^2 2s^2 2p^6 3s^2 3p^6 3d^8 4s^2$
(b) $1s^2 2s^2 2p^6 3s^2 3p^6 3d^9 4s^2$
(c) $1s^2 2s^2 2p^6 3s^2 3p^6 3d^{10} 4s^1$
(d) $1s^2 2s^2 2p^6 3s^2 3p^6 3d^5 4s^1$

Assertion-Reason [1 Mark]

Directions (Q. Nos. 26-35) In the following questions, an Assertion (A) is followed by a corresponding Reason (R) Use the following keys to choose the appropriate answer.

(a) Both (A) and (R) are correct and (R) is the correct explanation of (A).
(b) Both (A) and (R) are correct but (R) is not the correct explanation of (A).
(c) (A) is correct but (R) is incorrect.
(d) (A) is incorrect but (R) is correct.

26. **Assertion** (A) Cathode rays consist of negatively charged particles, called electrons.

Reason (R) In the presence of electrical/ magnetic field, the behaviour of cathode rays is similar to the negatively charged particles.

27. **Assertion** (A) All isotopes of a given element show the same type of chemical behaviour.

Reason (R) The chemical properties of an atom are controlled by the number of electrons in the atom.

28. **Assertion** (A) Black body is an ideal body that emits and absorbs radiations of all frequencies.

Reason (R) The frequency of radiation emitted by a body goes from a lower frequency to higher frequency with an increase in temperature. **NCERT Exemplar**

29. **Assertion** (A) Threshold frequency is a characteristic for a metal.

Reason (R) Threshold frequency is the maximum frequency required for the ejection of electrons from the metal surface.

30. **Assertion** (A) Energy or radiation is large if its wavelength is large.

Reason (R) Energy $= h\nu$ (where, $\nu =$ frequency).

31. **Assertion** (A) The radius of first orbit of hydrogen atom is 0.529 Å.

Reason (R) Radius for each circular orbital

$$(r_n) = 0.529\left(\frac{n^2}{Z}\right)$$

where, $n = 1, 2, 3$ and $Z =$ atomic number.

Competency Based Que.

32. **Assertion** (A) It is impossible to determine the exact position and exact momentum of an electron simultaneously.

Reason (R) The path of an electron in an atom is clearly defined. **NCERT Exemplar**

33. **Assertion** (A) For a given principal quantum number, *s, p, d, f* ...., subshells, all have different energies.

Reason (R) Mutual repulsion exists among the electrons in a multielectron atoms.

34. **Assertion** (A) For $n = 3, l$ may be 0, 1 and 2 and m may be $0, \pm 1$ and ± 2.

Reason (R) For each value of n, there are 0 to $(n-1)$ possible values of l, and for each value of l, there are 0 to $\pm l$ values of m. **Competency Based Que.**

35. **Assertion** (A) *s*-orbital electron will be more tightly bound to the nucleus than *p*-orbital electron.

Reason (R) Z_{eff} experienced by the electron decreases with increase of azimuthal quantum number (l).

Case Study [4 Marks]

36. **Read the case given below and answer the questions that follow**

When an electric discharge passes through gaseous hydrogen, the H_2 molecules break apart into individual hydrogen atoms in an excited state. These energised atoms emit light at specific frequencies, creating a distinctive hydrogen emission spectrum. This spectrum, essential to atomic theory, consists of several series of lines, each associated with a particular energy transition. The lines are named after scientists who discovered them through extensive experimental work, contributing greatly to our understanding of atomic structure.

Among these researchers was the Swedish spectroscopist Johannes Rydberg, who found that all series of lines in the hydrogen spectrum could be described by a single mathematical formula. This formula, known as the Rydberg formula, precisely calculates the wave number $\bar{\nu}$ for each spectral line, represented as :

$$\bar{\nu} = 109{,}677\left(\frac{1}{n_1^2} - \frac{1}{n_2^2}\right)\text{cm}^{-1}$$

In this equation, n_1 and n_2 are whole numbers corresponding to the electron's energy levels, with n_2 being greater than n_1. The constant 109,677cm^{-1} is the Rydberg's constant, a fundamental value that applies universally to hydrogen.

Rydberg's formula plays a vital role in understanding atomic transitions, as each spectral line represents an electron moving from a higher energy level to a lower one. This mathematical description of the hydrogen spectrum is foundational in fields like atomic physics and quantum mechanics, where it helps scientists to decode the structure of atoms and their behaviour.

Competency Based Que.

(i) An electron in an excited hydrogen atom falls from sixth energy level to fourth energy level. In which region, the spectrum line will be observed and is part of which series of the atomic spectrum?

(ii) What is the maximum number of emission lines when the excited electron of a hydrogen atom is $n = 5$ drops to ground state?

(a) 12 (b) 20 (c) 6 (d) 10

(iii) Calculate the wavelength of light emitted when the electron in a hydrogen atom undergoes transition from $n = 4$ to $n = 2$.

(a) 486×10^{-7} m (b) 486×10^{-7} cm
(c) 486×10^{-11} cm (d) 4.86×10^{-9} m

Or

Which series of hydrogen spectrum do not appears in infrared region?

(a) Bracket (b) Balmer (c) Paschen (d) Pfund

37. Read the case given below and answer the questions that follows

In atomic theory, the unique characteristics and behaviour of electrons within an atom are described through four quantum numbers, each contributing to a detailed representation of an electron's position and state. The principal quantum number (n) reflects the electron's energy level and relative distance from the nucleus, affecting the atom's overall size and energy. The orbital angular momentum quantum number (l) describes the shape of the orbital, categorising it into types such as s, p, d and f, which influence the spatial distribution where the electron is most likely found. The magnetic quantum number (m_l) further refines this spatial understanding by indicating the orientation of the orbital in three-dimensional space, while the spin quantum number (s) specifies the electron's intrinsic angular momentum, or spin, which can adopt one of two opposing states. Together, these quantum numbers provide a unique identity to each electron, adhering to Pauli's exclusion principle that prevents any two electrons in an atom from sharing the same set of quantum numbers.

This framework of quantum numbers not only explains the arrangement of electrons within orbitals but also support essential principles of atomic behaviour, such as electron configuration, bonding patterns, and atomic stability. By defining an electron's unique quantum state, these numbers offer insights into how atoms interact and form the foundation of molecular structure and chemical reactions.

(i) Discuss the use of principal quantum numbers to determine electronic configuration of an atom.

(ii) s-orbital electrons will be more tightly bound to the nucleus than p-orbital electrons. Give reason?

(iii) What is the difference between orbit and orbitals?

Or Spin quantum number depends on the value of principal quantum number or not?

Subjective Type Questions

Short Answer Type I Questions [2 Marks]

1. Answer the following questions.

(i) An atom having atomic mass number 13 and contain 7 neutrons. What is the atomic number of the atom?

(ii) Which two discoveries put strong challenge to the Bohr model?

2. (i) A certain particle carries 2.5×10^{-16} C of the static electric charge. Calculate the number of electrons present in it. **NCERT**

(ii) If the diameter of a carbon atom is 0.15 nm, Calculate the number of carbon atoms which can be placed side by side in a straight line across a length of scale of length 20 cm long. **NCERT**

3. Symbols $^{79}_{35}Br$ and ^{79}Br can be written, whereas symbols $^{35}_{79}Br$ and ^{35}Br are not acceptable. Answer briefly. **NCERT**

4. Calculate the energy associated with the first orbit of He^+. What is the radius of this orbit? **NCERT**

5. What is the number of photons of light with a wavelength of 4000 pm that provide 1 J of energy? **NCERT**

Hint : • Number of photons is calculated by dividing total energy by energy of 1 photon, so first calculate the energy of 1 photon by applying, $E = hc/\lambda$

• Then, calculate the number of photons by using the formula; $N = \frac{\text{total energy}}{\text{energy of one photon}}$

Wavelength, $\lambda = 4000$ pm $= 4000 \times 10^{-12}$ m

6. Show that ground state energy of electrons in hydrogen atom is equal to the first excited state energy of electron in He^+ ion, assuming that their Rydberg's constants are equal.

7. Two particles *A* and *B* are in motion. The momentum of particle *B* is the half of *A*. If the wavelength associated with the particle *A* is 5×10^{-8} m, calculate the wavelength associated with the particle *B*. **Competency Based Que.**

8. List the values of *n* and *l* for the following orbitals.

(i) 3*s* (ii) 4*p* (iii) 4*f* (iv) 3*d*

9. What is the angular momentum of an electron in (i) 2*s*-orbital (ii) 4*f*-orbital?

10. (i) Why is the electronic configuration of oxygen written as $1s^2\ 2s^2\ 2p_x^2\ 2p_y^1\ 2p_z^1$ and not as $1s^2\ 2s^2\ 2p_x^2\ 2p_y^2$?

(ii) Write electronic configurations of chromium and copper.

Short Answer Type II Questions [3 Marks]

11. The figure given below shows Thomson's "plum pudding model", where negatively charged electrons are embedded within a positively charged sphere. **Competency Based Que.**

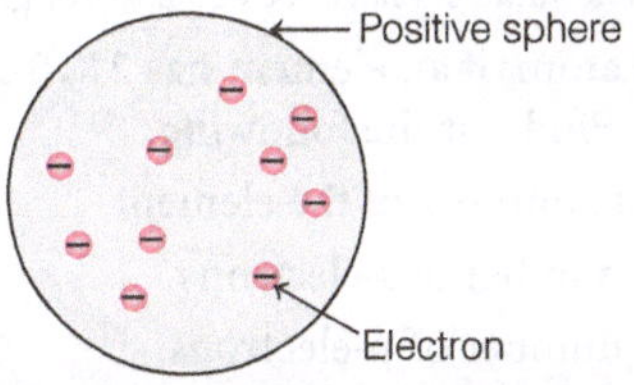

Based on the given figure, answer the following questions

(i) In Thomson's model, what does the positively charged sphere represent, and why is it necessary?

(ii) Where are the electrons located in Thomson's model, and how does this arrangement contribute to the structure of atom?

(iii) How does Thomson's model explain why the atom has no overall charge?

12. According to Rutherford's model of the atom, where is the positive charge concentrated? What does it predict about the relative size of the nucleus and the radius of the atom? What is the nucleus composed of according to his model? **Competency Based Que.**

13. Neon gas is generally used in sign boards. If it emits strongly at 616 nm, calculate

(i) the frequency of emission.

(ii) distance travelled by this radiation is 30 s.

(iii) energy of quantum.

(iv) number of quanta present if it produces 2 J of energy. **NCERT**

14. A photon of wavelength 4×10^{-7} m strikes on metal surface, the work function of the metal being 2.13 eV. Calculate

(i) the energy of the photon (eV).

(ii) the kinetic energy of the emission.

(iii) the velocity of the photoelectron (1 eV $= 1.6020 \times 10^{-19}$ J).

Hint : Direct formula based question.

(i) Calculate the energy of a photon by using, $E = \frac{hc}{\lambda}$ in Joule and convert it in eV.

(ii) Calculate the kinetic energy of ejected electron, KE $= h\nu - h\nu_0$ where, $E = h\nu$ and $h\nu_0 =$ work function.

(iii) Calculate the velocity of electron by using the formula, $KE = \frac{1}{2}mv^2$. **NCERT**

15. How much energy is required to ionise a H-atom if the electron occupies $n = 5$ orbit? Compare your answer with the ionisation enthalpy of H-atom (energy required to remove the electron from $n = 1$ orbit). **NCERT**

Hint : • Find ΔE when, $n_i = 5$ and $n_f = \infty$.

• Find $\Delta E'$ when $n_i = 1$ and $n_f = \infty$ and compare them.

16. Emission transitions in the Paschen series end at orbit $n = 3$ and start from orbit *n* and can be represented as $\nu = 3.29 \times 10^{15}\ (\text{Hz}) \left[\frac{1}{3^2} - \frac{1}{n^2}\right]$. Calculate the value of *n* if the transition is observed at 1285 nm. Find the region of the spectrum. **NCERT**

17. What is the energy in joules, required to shift the electron of the hydrogen atom from the first Bohr orbit to the fifth Bohr orbit and what is the wavelength of the light emitted when the electron returns to the ground state? The ground state electron energy is -2.18×10^{-11} ergs. **NCERT**

18. According to de-Broglie, matter should exhibit dual behaviour, that is both particle and wave like properties. However, a cricket ball of mass 100 g does not move like a wave when it is thrown by a bowler at a speed of 100 km/h. Calculate the wavelength of the ball and explain why it does not show wave nature? **NCERT Exemplar**

19. (i) A beam of helium atoms move with a velocity of 2.0×10^3 ms^{-1}. Find the wavelength of the particle constituting the beam ($h = 6.626 \times 10^{-34}$ Js).

(ii) An electron is moving with a kinetic energy of 2.275×10^{-25} J. Calculate its de-Broglie wavelength. (Mass of electron $= 9.1 \times 10^{-31}$ kg, $h = 6.6 \times 10^{-34}$ Js) **Competency Based Que.**

20. (i) Calculate the wavelength of an electron moving with a velocity of 2.05×10^7 ms^{-1}. Also calculate the wave number of the electron.

(ii) In atom, an electron is moving with a speed of 600 m/s with an accuracy of 0.005%. Certainty with which the position of the electron can be located is ($h = 6.6 \times 10^{-34}$ kg m^2 s^{-1}, mass of electron, $e_m = 6.6 \times 10^{-31}$ kg) **Competency Based Que.**

21. (i) State the principle that suggests the presence of only two electrons in an orbital.

(ii) Account for the following.

(a) Chromium has configuration $3d^5\ 4s^1$ and not $3d^4\ 4s^2$.

(b) Bohr's orbits are called stationary orbits or states.

22. (i) Write the electronic configurations of the following ions.

(a) H^- (b) Na^+ (c) O^{2-} (d) F^-

(ii) What are the atomic numbers of elements whose outermost electrons are represented by?

(a) $3s^2$ (b) $2p^3$ (c) $3p^5$

(iii) Which atoms are indicated by the following configuration?

(a) $[He]2s^1$

(b) $[Ne]3s^2 3p^3$

(c) $[Ar]4s^2 3d^1$ **NCERT**

Long Answer Type Questions [5 Marks]

23. What observations in scattering experiment led Rutherford to make the following conclusions?

(i) The most of the space in an atom is empty.

(ii) The whole of the mass of the atom is present in the centre of the nucleus.

(iii) Nucleus has positive charge. On the basis of scattering of α-particles by a thin metal foil, describe the Rutherford model of an atom. What are the drawbacks of this model? **Competency Based Que.**

24. When an electric discharge is passed through hydrogen gas, the hydrogen molecules dissociated to produce excited hydrogen atoms. These excited atoms emit electromagnetic radiation of discrete frequencies which can be given by the general formula

$$\bar{v} = 109677\left[\frac{1}{n_i^2} - \frac{1}{n_f^2}\right] cm^{-1}$$

What points of Bohr's model of an atom can be used to arrive at this formula? Based on these points derive the above formula giving description of each step and each term. **NCERT Exemplar**

25. (i) Why was a change in the Bohr model of atom is required, due to which important development(s), concept of movement of an electron in an orbit was replaced by the concept of probability of finding electron in an orbital? What is the name given to the changed model of atom? **NCERT Exemplar**

(ii) A molecule of O_2 and that of SO_2 travel with the same velocity. What is the ratio of their wavelengths?

26. (i) Enumerate the main postulates of Planck's quantum theory.

(ii) How is 1s-orbital different from 2s orbital. **Diksha**

27. (i) An atomic orbital has $n = 3$. What are the possible values of l and m_l?

(ii) List the quantum numbers (m_l and l) of electrons for 3d-orbital.

(iii) Which of the following orbitals are possible? 1p, 2s, 2p and 3f. **NCERT**

Hint :
- l has the values 0 to $(n-1)$.
- m has the values $-l$ to $+l$.
- The value of l never be equal to n or greater than it.

28. A neutral atom of an element has $2K$, $8L$ and $5M$ electrons. Find out the following.

(i) Atomic number of the element

(ii) Total number of s-electrons

(iii) Total number of p-electrons

(iv) Number of protons in the nucleus

(v) Valency of the element **Competency Based Que.**

Hints & Solutions

Objective Type Questions

1. (*d*) All of the above
2. (*c*) Both (a) and (b)
3. (*b*) All the wavelengths in the Balmer series are in the visible region of the spectrum.
4. (*b*) From de-Broglie equation, $\lambda \propto \frac{1}{m}$

   Greater the mass of matter waves, lesser is wavelength and *vice-versa*. In the given matter waves, alpha particle (He^{2+}) has the higher mass and therefore, shortest wavelength.
5. (*a*) $\bar{v} = 109,677\left[\frac{1}{(2)^2} - \frac{1}{n^2}\right] \text{cm}^{-1}$; $n \geq 3$

   this equation represents the spectral lines of Balmer series.
6. (*d*) Among the given statements, only A, B and C are correct while D is incorrect.

   Its corrected form is :

   A black body is a perfect radiator of radiant energy.
7. (*d*) $r_n = \frac{52.9(n^2)}{Z}$ pm
8. (*d*) Expression of Heisenberg's uncertainty principle is

$$\Delta x.\Delta p \geq \frac{h}{4\pi}$$

$$\Delta x.m\Delta v_x \geq \frac{h}{4\pi}$$

$$\Delta x.\Delta v_x \geq \frac{h}{4\pi m}$$

9. (*b*) $\lambda = \frac{h}{mv} = \frac{6.63 \times 10^{-34}}{1.67 \times 10^{-27} \times 1 \times 10^3}$

   $= 3.97 \times 10^{-10}$ m ~ 0.40 nm
10. (c) In Schrodinger equation, $\hat{H}$ is a mathematical operator called Hamiltonian. It was introduced by Schrodinger from the expression for the total energy of the system.
11. (*a*) Given, atomic number of Rb, $Z = 37$

    Thus, its electronic configuration is $[Kr]5s^1$. Since, the last electron or valence electron enter in 5*s* subshell.

    So, the quantum numbers are $n = 5$, $l = 0$, (for *s*-orbital) $m = 0 (\because m = +l \text{ to } -l), s = +1/2 \text{ or } -1/2$.
12. (*c*) When $n = 3$, number of values of l are 0 to $(n-1)$ i.e. 0,1, 2. hence, when $n = 3$, then $l = 3$ does not exist.
13. (*c*) (a) $n = 4, l = 0, m = 0, s = +\frac{1}{2} \rightarrow 4s$ energy level.

    (b) $n = 3, l = 1, m = -1, s = +\frac{1}{2} \rightarrow 3p$ energy level.

    (c) $n = 3, l = 2, m = -2, s = +\frac{1}{2} \rightarrow 3d$ energy level.

    (d) $n = 3, l = 0, m = 0, s = +\frac{1}{2} \rightarrow 3s$ energy level.

    According to Aufbau principle, the energy of orbitals (other than H-atom) depend upon $n + l$ value. $n + l$ for $3d = 3 + 2 = 5$. So, it is highest energy level.
14. (*b*) The correct match is A-2, B-4, C-1, D-3.
15. (*c*) Total number of orbitals associated with n^{th} shell $= n^2$

    ∴Total number of orbitals associated with third shell $= (3)^2 = 9$
16. (*d*) The probability density of electrons in 2*s*-orbital first increases then decreases and after that it begins to increase again as distance increases from the nucleus.
17. (*d*) The incorrect statement is given in option (d).
18. (*c*) Among the given plot, option (c) represent the plot of the radial wave function *R* as a function of distance, *r* of the electron from the nucleus for 2*p*-orbital.
19. (*c*) The correct value of $X = 1$ and $Y = 3$.
20. (*a*) Among the given statement, (a) is correct while other statements are incorrect. Their correct form are as follows :
    - Z_{eff} of 1*s*-orbital ≠ Z_{eff} of 2*s*-orbital
    - Electrons in 2*s* and 2*p*-orbitals have different screening effect. Hence, Z_{eff} is different.

      Z_{eff} of 2*s*-orbital > Z_{eff} of 2*p*-orbital
    - Energy of 2*s*-orbital < Energy of 2*p*-orbital
21. (*c*) The total electrons in *K*-shell is 2, in *L*-shell is 8, in *M*-shell is 18.

	K	*L*	*M*
Atomic no. 19	2	8	9
Atomic no. 21	2	8	11
Atomic no. 25	2	8	15

The order of electrons in *M*-shell is $Z > Y > X$.

22. (*b*) Werner Heisenberg, a German physicist in 1927, gave uncertainty principle which states that it is impossible to determine simultaneously, the exact position and exact momentum of an electron.

    Mathematically, $\Delta x \times \Delta p \geq h/4\pi$

    The important implications of the Heisenberg uncertainty principle is that it rules out existence of definite paths or trajectories of electrons and other similar particles.

23. (*a*)

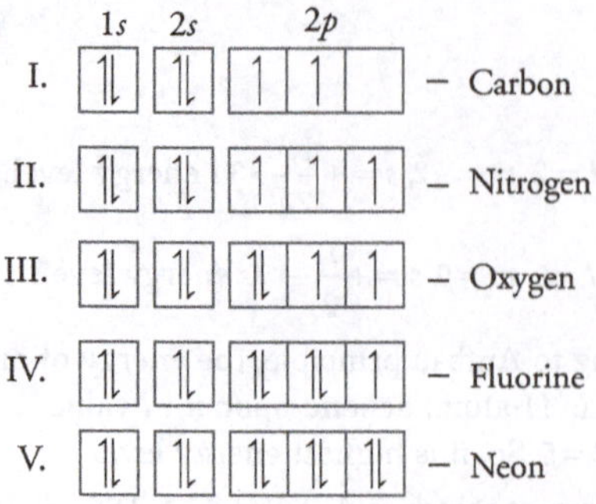

24. (*b*) $_{26}Fe = [Ar]3d^6, 4s^2$ $\quad _{26}Fe^{3+} = [Ar]3d^5$

$_{25}Mn = [Ar]3d^5, 4s^2$ $\quad _{25}Mn^{2+} = [Ar]3d^5$

25. (*b*) Correct configuration should be $1s^2 2s^2 2p^6 3s^2 3p^6 3d^{10} 4s^1$ for the copper which has atomic number 29 ($_{29}Cu$). Due to extra stability of fully-filled orbital of *d*-subshell, the last electron enter into *d*-orbital instead of *s*-orbital.

Mistake Alert *One can make a mistake of writing the configuration of* Cu *as* $[Ar]3d^9 4s^2$ *instead of* $[Ar]3d^{10} 4s^1$.

26. (*a*) Both (A) and (R) are correct and (R) is the correct explanation of (A).

27. (*a*) Both (A) and (R) are correct and (R) is the correct explanation of (A). Isotopes have the same atomic number, i.e. same number of electrons which are responsible for their chemical behaviour.

Hence, these exhibit similar chemical properties.

28. (b) Both (A) and (R) are correct but (R) is not the correct explanation of (A).

A black body is called ideal becuase it absorbs all light and energy at all frequencies when heated depending only on its temperature.

29. (c) (A) is the correct but (R) is incorrect. The correct Reason is ;

Threshold frequency is the minimum frequency required for the ejection of electrons from metal surface.

30. (*d*) (A) is incorrect but (R) is correct. The correct Assertion is;

The amount of energy is inversely proportional to the wavelength. Energy is large if its wavelength is small.

31. (*a*) Both (A) and (R) are correct and (R) is the correct explanation of (A).

32. (*c*) (A) is correct but (R) is incorrect.

We cannot determine the exact position and momentum of an electron simultaneously. As the electrons in an atom are always in motion.

So, it has come uncertainty in its momentum and from which it led to uncertainty in position. Hence, the path of electrons in an atom is not clearly known.

33. (*b*) Both (A) and (R) are correct but (R) is not the correct explanation of (A).

The correct explanation is ;

Energy of an orbital depends upon $n+l$ value.

34. (*a*) Both (A) and (R) are correct and (R) is the correct explanation of (A).

35. (*a*) Both (A) and (R) are correct and (R) is the correct explanation of (A).

36. (i) The brackett series corresponds to transitions where electron falls to the fourth energy level producing spectral lines in the infrared region of the spectrum. Therefore, this spectral line will be observed in the infrared region. **(2)**

(ii) (*d*) Maximum number of emission lines from n^{th} energy state to ground state $= \frac{n(n-1)}{2}$

Given, $n = 5$

$$\therefore \frac{n(n-1)}{2} = \frac{5(5-1)}{2} = \frac{5 \times 4}{2} = 10 \text{ lines}$$ **(1)**

(iii) (*b*) According to formula, $\bar{v} = R_H \left[\frac{1}{n_1^2} - \frac{1}{n_2^2}\right]$

$$n_1 = 2, n_2 = 4, R_H = 109677$$

$$\bar{v} = 109677 \left[\frac{1}{(2)^2} - \frac{1}{(4)^2}\right]$$

$$= 109677 \left[\frac{1}{4} - \frac{1}{16}\right] = 20564 \text{ cm}^{-1}$$

$$\lambda = \frac{1}{\bar{v}} = \frac{1}{20564} = 4.86 \times 10^{-5} = 486 \times 10^{-7} \text{cm}$$ **(1)**

Or (*b*) Balmer series fall in the visible region of the electromagnetic spectrum. **(1)**

37. (i) The principal quantum number (n) is used to determine the electronic configuration of an atom by indicating the main energy level or shell in which electron resides. The principal quantum number also helps in determining the number of subshells within each energy level.

For example, if $n = 3$, this means the electron is in the third energy level, which can contain three subshells (3*s*, 3*p* and 3*d*).

Therefore, the total number of electrons that can be accommodated in the third energy level is 18 (2 in 3*s*, 6 in 3*p* and 10 in 3*d*). This arrangement helps in understanding the structured placement of electrons in an atom. **(2)**

(ii) *s*-orbital electrons will be more tightly bound to the nucleus because there is very low distance between electrons and the nucleus. **(1)**

(iii) Orbit represents the circular path along which the electron moves but orbtial represents the three dimensional space around the nucleus within which the probability of finding the electron is maximum. **(1)**

Or

The value of spin quantum number can be either +1/2 or −1/2 and it is independent of value of principal quantum number. (1)

Subjective Type Questions

1. (i) Mass number $(A) = n + p$

$\therefore \quad p = A - n = 13 - 7 = 6$

Hence, atomic number, $Z = p = 6$ (1)

(ii) Heisenberg's uncertainty principle and de-Broglie's concept of dual nature of matter are the two discoveries that put strong challenge to the Bohr model. (1)

2. (i) As, charge on 1 electron $(e) = 1.6022\times 10^{-19}$ C

Total charge $(q) = 2.5\times 10^{-16}$ C

$\therefore$ Number of electrons present in particle,

$$n = \frac{2.5\times 10^{-16}}{1.6022\times 10^{-19}} = 1560.4 \text{ electrons}$$

$n \simeq 1560$ electrons (1)

(ii) Given, diameter of a carbon atom

$= 0.15 \text{ nm} = 0.15\times 10^{-9}$ m

Length along which atoms are to be placed

$= 20$ cm $= 0.2$ m

Number of carbon atom which can be placed in the given length $= \dfrac{0.2\text{m}}{0.15\times 10^{-9}\text{m}} = \dfrac{0.2\times 10^{9}\text{ m}}{0.15 \text{ m}}$

$= 1.33\times 10^{9}$ atoms (1)

3. The composition of any atom can be represented by using the normal element symbol X with superscript on the left hand side as the mass number A and subscript Z on the left hand side as the atomic number, i.e. ${}^{A}_{Z}X$.

Hence, the symbols ${}^{35}_{79}\text{Br}$ and ${}^{35}\text{Br}$ are not acceptable. (2)

4. As we know that, $E_n = \dfrac{(-2.18\times 10^{-18}\text{ J})Z^2}{n^2}$ atom^{-1}

For He^{+}, $n = 1$, $Z = 2$

$$E_1 = \frac{(-2.18\times 10^{-18}\text{ J})(2^2)}{(1)^2} = -8.72\times 10^{-18}\text{ J}$$ (1)

Now, the radius of the orbit is given by $r_n = \dfrac{(0.0529\text{ nm})n^2}{Z}$

Since, $n = 1$ and $Z = 2$

$$r_n = \frac{(0.0529\text{ nm})1^2}{2} = 0.02645\text{ nm}$$ (1)

5. Energy of one photon,

$$E = \frac{hc}{\lambda} = \frac{6.626\times 10^{-34}\text{ Js}\times 3.0\times 10^{8}\text{ m s}^{-1}}{4000\times 10^{-12}\text{m}}$$

$[\because 1\text{ pm} = 10^{-12}\text{ m}]$

$= 4.9695\times 10^{-17}$ J (1)

Now, number of photons,

$$N = \frac{1\text{ J}}{4.9695\times 10^{-17}\text{ J}} = 2.0122\times 10^{16}\text{ photons}$$ (1)

6. As we know that, $E_n = -R_n\dfrac{Z^2}{n^2}$

For H-atom, $Z = 1$,

For ground state, $n = 1$ (1)

$\therefore \quad E_1 = -R_H$

Similarly for He^{2+} ion, $Z = 2$,

For first exicted state, $n = 2$

$$\therefore \quad E_2 = -R_H\frac{(2)^2}{(2)^2} = -R_H$$

Thus, $\quad E_1 = E_2 = -R_H$ (1)

7. According to de-Broglie's equation : $\lambda = \dfrac{h}{p}$

where, h = Planck's constant

p = momentum

$\because \lambda_A = 5\times 10^{-8}$m and momentum of B is half of A.

So, $\quad \lambda_B = 2\times\lambda_A$

$\lambda_B = 10\times 10^{-8}$ m

$\lambda_B = 1000$Å (2)

8. The value of n and l for following orbitals.

(i) 3s ; $n = 3$, $l = 0$ (ii) 4p ; $n = 4$, $l = 1$ (1)

(iii) 4f ; $n = 4$, $l = 3$ (iv) 3d ; $n = 3$, $l = 2$ (1)

9. Angular momentum of an atom in any orbital

$$= \sqrt{l(l+1)}\,h/2\pi$$

(i) For 2s-orbital,

$$l = 0$$

$$\sqrt{l(l+1)}\,h/2\pi = \sqrt{0(0+1)}\,h/2\pi$$

For 2s-orbital, angular momentum in 0. (1)

(ii) For 4f-orbital, $l = 3$

Angular momentum $= \sqrt{3(3+1)}\dfrac{h}{2\pi} = \sqrt{12}\dfrac{h}{2\pi}$ (1)

10. (i) The electronic configuration of oxygen is written as $1s^2, 2s^2, 2p_x^2, 2p_y^1, 2p_z^1$. According to Hund's rule, electrons occupy degenerate orbitals single first, with parallel spins, before pairing begins. (1)

(ii) (a) Electronic configuration of Cr$(Z = 24)$

$= 1s^2 2s^2 2p^6 3s^2 3p^6\, 3d^5 4s^1$.

(b) Electronic configuration of copper $(Z = 29)$

$= 1s^2 2s^2 2p^6 3s^2 3p^6 3d^{10} 4s^1$. (1)

11. (i) The positively charged sphere represents a diffuse positive charge that holds the negatively charged electrons in place. It is necessary to balance the electrons negative charges, making the atom electrically neutral. (1)

(ii) In Thomson's model, electrons are spread out within the positively charged sphere. This arrangement creates a stable structure by embedding electrons uniformly throughout the atom. (1)

(iii) Thomson's model explains that the atom is neutral because the positive charge of the sphere exactly balances the negative charge of the electrons, resulting in no overall charge. (1)

12. According to Rutherford's model of atom, the positive charge is concentrated at the centre, that is, at the nucleus.

Since, a small fraction of α-particles were deflected through small angle and also a few of them bounced back, it proved that the nucleus occupies a very small volume in the atom. (2)

Further, the radius of the atom is about 10^{-10}m while of nucleus is 10^{-15}m.

The nucleus is composed of protons and neutrons and is surrounded by revolving electrons. (1)

13. Given, wavelength (λ) of neon gas = 616 nm

$$= 616 \times 10^{-9} \text{ m}$$

(i) Frequency, $\nu = \frac{c}{\lambda}$

$$\nu = \frac{3.0\times 10^8 \text{ ms}^{-1}}{616\times 10^{-9} \text{ m}} = 4.870\times 10^{14} \text{ s}^{-1}$$ (1/2)

(ii) Distance travelled = speed × time

$$= 3.0\times10^8 \text{ ms}^{-1} \times 30 \text{ s} = 9.0\times10^9 \text{ m}$$ (1/2)

(iii) Energy of quantum (or photon),

$$E = h\nu = 6.626\times 10^{-34} \text{ J s} \times 4.870\times 10^{14}\text{s}^{-1}$$

$$= 32.269\times 10^{-20} \text{ J}$$ (1)

(iv) Number of quanta present

$$= \frac{\text{Total energy produced}}{\text{Energy of 1 quanta}} = \frac{2 \text{ J}}{32.27\times 10^{-20} \text{ J}}$$

$$\approx 6.2\times 10^{18} \text{quanta}$$ (1)

14. (i) Energy of a photon,

$$E = \frac{hc}{\lambda}$$

$$= \frac{6.626\times 10^{-34} \text{ Js}\times 3.0\times 10^8 \text{ ms}^{-1}}{4\times 10^{-7} \text{ m}}$$

$$E = 4.969\times 10^{-19} \text{ J}$$

Or $$4.969\times 10^{-19} \text{ J} = \frac{4.969\times 10^{-19}}{1.602\times 10^{-19}} = 3.10 \text{ eV}$$

$(\because 1.602\times 10^{-19} \text{ J} = 1 \text{ eV})$ (1)

(ii) Kinetic energy of an ejected electron, KE $= h\nu - h\nu_0$

$h\nu = 3.10$ eV (energy of striking photon)

$h\nu_0 = W_0 = 2.13$ eV (work function of the metal)

$$\text{KE} = \frac{1}{2} mv^2 = 3.10 - 2.13 = 0.97 \text{ eV}$$ (1)

(iii) $\because \text{KE} = \frac{1}{2} mv^2 = 0.97$ eV

$$\therefore \frac{1}{2} mv^2 = 0.97\times 1.602\times 10^{-19} \text{ J}$$

$(1 \text{ eV} = 1.602\times 10^{-19} \text{ J})$

$$\frac{1}{2}\times 9.11\times10^{-31} \text{ kg}\times v^2 = 0.97\times 1.602\times 10^{-19} \text{ J}$$

$(\because \text{Mass of } 1\, e^- = 9.11\times 10^{-31} \text{ kg})$

$$v^2 = \frac{0.97\times 1.602\times 10^{-19}\times 2 \text{ J}}{9.11\times 10^{-31} \text{ kg}} = 0.341\times 10^{12}$$

$$v^2 = 0.341\times 10^{12} \text{ (ms}^{-1})^2$$

$$v = 0.584\times 10^6 = 5.84\times 10^5 \text{ ms}^{-1}$$ (1)

Note Minimum energy required to eject the electron is $h\nu_0$. It is also called work function, W_0.

15. Energy change, $\Delta E = E_f - E_i$

$$\Delta E = 2.18\times 10^{18} \text{ J}\left(\frac{1}{n_i^2} - \frac{1}{n_f^2}\right)$$

When $n_i = 5$ and $n_f = \infty$,

$$\Delta E = 2.18\times 10^{-18} \text{ J}\left(\frac{1}{5^2} - \frac{1}{\infty}\right) = 0.0872\times 10^{-18} \text{ J}$$ (1)

When $n_i = 1$ and $n_f = \infty$,

$$\Delta E' = 2.18\times 10^{-18} \text{ J}\left(\frac{1}{1^2} - \frac{1}{\infty}\right)$$

$$\Delta E' = 2.18\times 10^{-18} \text{ J}$$

$$\frac{\Delta E'}{\Delta E} = \frac{2.18\times 10^{-18} \text{ J}}{0.0872\times 10^{-18} \text{ J}} = 25$$ (1)

Hence, energy required to remove an electron from first orbit is 25 times greater than that required to remove an electron from fifth orbit. (1)

16. Given, frequency, $\nu = \frac{c}{\lambda} = 3.29\times 10^{15} \text{ Hz}\left(\frac{1}{3^2} - \frac{1}{n^2}\right)$

$$\nu = \frac{3.0\times 10^8 \text{ ms}^{-1}}{1285\times 10^{-9} \text{ m}} = 3.29\times 10^{15} \text{ Hz}\left(\frac{1}{9} - \frac{1}{n^2}\right)$$ (1)

$[\because \text{Given } \lambda = 1285 \text{ nm}]$

$$\frac{3.0\times 10^8 \text{ ms}^{-1}}{1285\times 10^{-9} \text{ m}\times 3.29\times 10^{15} \text{ Hz}} = \left(\frac{1}{9} - \frac{1}{n^2}\right)$$

$$\Rightarrow \quad 7.096\times 10^{-4}\times 10^2 = \left[0.111 - \frac{1}{n^2}\right]$$

$$\Rightarrow \quad 7.096\times10^{-2} = \left[0.111 - \frac{1}{n^2}\right]$$

$$\Rightarrow \quad 0.0709 = \left[0.111 - \frac{1}{n^2}\right]$$

$$\Rightarrow \quad \frac{1}{n^2} = 0.1111 - 0.0709$$

$$\Rightarrow \quad n^2 = 25 \text{ or } n = 5$$ (1)

∴ The electrons jump from $n=5$ to $n=3$, i.e. the transitions occurs in Paschen series and lies in infrared region. Moreover, the radiation 1285 nm lies in the infrared region. (1)

17. $\Delta E = E_5 - E_1 = 2.18\times 10^{-11}\left(\frac{1}{n_i^2}-\frac{1}{n_f^2}\right)$ erg

$[n_i = 1 \text{ and } n_f = 5]$

$\Delta E = 2.18\times 10^{-11}\left(\frac{1}{1^2}-\frac{1}{5^2}\right)$ erg

$\Delta E = 2.18\times 10^{-11}\times\frac{24}{25}$

$= 2.0928\times 10^{-11}$ erg

$= 2.0928\times 10^{-18}$ J $\quad [\because 1 \text{ erg} = 10^{-7} \text{ J}]$ (2)

When electron returns to ground state, it emits energy equals to ΔE hence,

$$\Delta E = \frac{hc}{\lambda}$$

or $\lambda = \frac{hc}{\Delta E} = \frac{6.626\times 10^{-34} \text{ Js}\times 3.0\times 10^{8} \text{ ms}^{-1}}{2.0928\times 10^{-18} \text{ J}}$

$= 9.498\times 10^{-8}$ m $= 949.8\times 10^{-10}$ m $= 949.8$ Å (1)

18. Given, $m = 100$ g $= 0.1$ kg

$v = 100$ km/h $= \frac{100\times 1000}{60\times 60} = \frac{1000}{36}$ ms^{-1} (1)

From de-Broglie equation, wavelength,

$\lambda = \frac{h}{mv} = \frac{6.626\times 10^{-34} \text{ kg m}^2\text{s}^{-1}}{0.1 \text{ kg}\times \frac{1000}{36} \text{ ms}^{-1}} = 238.5\times 10^{-36}$ m (1)

As the wavelength is very small so wave nature cannot be detected. (1)

19. (i) Given, velocity of beam of helium atoms $= 2.0\times 10^3$ ms^{-1}

Mass of helium atom $= \frac{4 \text{ g}}{6.022\times 10^{23}}$

$= 6.64\times 10^{-24}$ g

$= 6.64\times 10^{-27}$ kg (1/2)

According to de-Broglie equation, $\lambda = \frac{h}{mv}$

$= \frac{6.626\times 10^{-34} \text{ kg m}^2\text{s}^{-1}}{(6.64\times 10^{-27} \text{ kg})\times(2.0\times 10^3 \text{ ms}^{-1})}$

$= 4.99\times 10^{-11}$ m

$= 49.9$ pm (1)

(ii) Kinetic energy of electron, $\frac{1}{2}mv^2 = 2.275\times 10^{-25}$ J

or $v^2 = \frac{2\times 2.275\times 10^{-25} \text{ J}}{9.1\times 10^{-31} \text{ kg}}$

$= \frac{2\times 2.275\times 10^{-25} \text{ Kg m}^2\text{s}^{-2}}{9.1\times 10^{-31} \text{ Kg}} = 0.5\times 10^{6} \text{ m}^2\text{s}^{-2}$

$v = 0.707\times 10^3$ ms^{-1} (1/2)

Now, $\lambda = \frac{h}{mv}$

$= \frac{6.6\times 10^{-34} \text{ kg m}^2\text{s}^{-1}}{(9.1\times 10^{-31} \text{ kg})\times(0.707\times 10^3 \text{ m s}^{-1})}$

$= 1.026\times 10^{-6}$ m

$= 1026$ nm (1)

20. (i) $v = 2.05\times 10^7$ m/s

We know, de-Broglie's equation

$\lambda = \frac{h}{mv}$

$\lambda = \frac{6.626\times 10^{-34} \text{ Js}}{(9.10939\times 10^{-31} \text{ kg})(2.05\times 10^7 \text{ ms}^{-1})}$

$\lambda = 3.548\times 10^{-11}$ m (1½)

$\therefore \quad \bar{v} = \frac{1}{\lambda} = \frac{1}{3.548\times 10^{-11}} = 0.282\times 10^{11}$ m^{-1}

(ii) By Heisenberg's uncertainty principle,

$\Delta x\cdot m\Delta v = \frac{h}{4\pi}$

$\Delta v = 0.005\%$ of 600 m/s

$= \frac{600\times 0.005}{100} = 0.03$

$\Delta x\times 9.1\times 10^{-31}\times 0.03 = \frac{6.6\times 10^{-34}}{4\times 3.14}$

Hence, $\Delta x = \frac{6.6\times 10^{-34}}{4\times 3.14\times 0.03\times 9.1\times 10^{-31}}$

$= 1.92\times 10^{-3}$ m (1½)

21. (i) Only two electrons exist in the same orbital and these electrons must have opposite spin. This principle is known as Pauli's exclusion principle. (1)

(ii) (a) Chromiun has configuration $3d^5 4s^1$ because of stability of d-orbitals as half and fully-filled orbitals are more stable.

(b) Refer to text on page 52. (2)

22. (i) (a) ${}_1$H $= 1s^1$, $H^- = 1s^2$

(b) ${}_{11}$Na $= 1s^2 2s^2, 2p^6, 3s^1$, $Na^+ = 1s^2 2s^2 2p^6$

(c) ${}_8$O $= 1s^2 2s^2, 2p^4$, $O^{2-} = 1s^2 2s^2 2p^6$

(d) ${}_9$F $= 1s^2 2s^2, 2p^5$, $F^- = 1s^2 2s^2 2p^6$ (2)

(ii) To obtain atomic number of an element fill the orbitals in order of their increasing energies up to the given outer orbital configuration.

(a) $1s^2 2s^2, 2p^6, 3s^2 (Z=12)$

(b) $1s^2 2s^2, 2p^3 (Z=7)$

(c) $1s^2 2s^2, 2p^6, 3s^2, 3p^5 (Z=17)$ (1½)

(iii) (a) [He] $2s^1$ represents ${}_3$Li (lithium)

(b) [Ne] $3s^2, 3p^3$ represents ${}_{15}$P (phosphorus)

(c) [Ar] $4s^2, 3d^1$ represents ${}_{21}$Sc (scandium) (1½)

23. Refer to text on pages 43 and 44. **(5)**

24. The two important points of Bohr's model can be used to derive the given formula are as follows

(i) Electrons revolve around the nucleus in a circular path of fixed radius and energy. These paths are called orbits, stationary states or allowed energy states. **(1)**

(ii) Energy is emitted or absorbed when an electron moves from higher stationary state to lower stationary state or from lower stationary state to higher stationary state respectively. **(1)**

Derivation Refer to text on page 54 (Under the heading calculation of frequency and wave number for a transition). **(3)**

25. (i) In Bohr model, an electron is regarded as a charged particle moving in well defined circular orbits about the nucleus. An orbit can completely be defined only if both the position and the velocity of the electron are known exactly at the same time. This is not possible according to the Heisenberg uncertainty principle. Furthermore, the wave character of the electron is not considered in Bohr model. **(1)**

Therefore, concept of movement of an electron in an orbit was replaced by the concept of probability of finding electron in an orbital due to de-Broglie concept of dual nature of electron and Heisenberg's uncertainty principle. **(1)**

The changed model is called quantum mechanical model of the atom. **(1)**

(ii) $\lambda_{O_2}/\lambda_{SO_2} = 2$ (because $\lambda = \frac{h}{mv}$, i.e. $\lambda \propto \frac{1}{m}$ and mass of SO_2 molecule *viz.* 64 u, is double than that of O_2 molecule *viz.* 32 u). **(2)**

26. (i) Refer to text on page 49. **(4)**

(ii) 2*s*-orbital is larger than 1*s* orbital and 2*s*-orbital has one node whereas, 1*s*-orbital has no nodes. **(1)**

27. (i) For $n = 3$, $l = 0, 1$ and 2

$l = 0$, $m_l = 0$

$l = 1$, $m_l = -1, 0, +1$

$l = 2$, $m_l = -2, -1, 0, +1, +2$ **(1)**

(ii) For 3*d*-orbital, $n = 3$, $l = 2$, $m_l = -2, -1, 0, +1, +2$ **(1)**

(iii) $1p$ is not possible because if $n = 1$ then $l = 0$ only and for p, $l = 1$.

2*s* is possible because if $n = 2$ then $l = 0$, 1 and for s, $l = 0$.

2*p* is possible because if $n = 2$ then $l = 0$, 1 and for p, $l = 1$.

3*f* is not possible because if $n = 3$ then $l = 0$, 1 and 2 for f, $l = 3$. **(3)**

28. The electronic configuration of the element with 2*K*, 8*L* and 5*M* electrons will be

$$1s^2 2s^2 2p_x^2 2p_y^2 2p_z^2 3s^2 3p_x^1 3p_y^1 3p_z^1$$

(i) Total number of electrons $= 2 + 8 + 5 = 15$

$\therefore$ Atomic number of the element $= 15$ **(1)**

(ii) Total number of s-electrons $= 2 + 2 + 2 = 6$ **(1)**

(iii) Total number of p-electrons $= 6 + 3 = 9$ **(1)**

(iv) Since, the atom is neutral.

$\therefore$ Number of protons = Number of electrons = Atomic number $= 15$ **(1)**

(v) The valence electrons (outermost shell) are in the *M*-shell and are equal to 5. To acheive a stable octet, the atom needs 3 more electrons, so its valency is 3. **(1)**

QR Code for Quick Test 1

QR Code for Quick Test 2

QR Code for Quick Test 3

QR Code for Quick Test 4

SELF ASSESSMENT TEST

Objective Type Questions [1 Mark]

1. Which of the following is not an electromagnetic radiation?
   (a) Infrared rays (b) X-rays
   (c) Cathode rays (d) γ-rays

2. If λ_1 and λ_2 are the wavelength of characteristic X-rays and gamma rays respectively, then the relation between them is
   (a) $\lambda_1 = \frac{1}{\lambda_2}$ (b) $\lambda_1 = \lambda_2$
   (c) $\lambda_1 > \lambda_2$ (d) $\lambda_1 < \lambda_2$

3. The relationship between the energy E_1 of the radiation with a wavelength 8000 Å and the energy E_2 of the radiation with a wavelength 16000Å is
   (a) $E_1 = 6E_2$ (b) $E_1 = 2E_2$
   (c) $E_1 = 4E_2$ (d) $E_1 = \frac{1}{2E_2}$

4. Which of the following electron transition in hydrogen atom will require largest amount of energy?
   (a) From $n = 2$ to $n = 1$ (b) From $n = 3$ to $n = 2$
   (c) From $n = \infty$ to $n = 1$ (d) From $n = 5$ to $n = 3$

5. Uncertainty in position of a particle of 25 g in space is 10^{-5} m. Hence, uncertainty in velocity (ms^{-1}) is (Planck's constant $h = 6.6 \times 10^{-34}$ Js)
   (a) 2.1×10^{-28} (b) 2.1×10^{-34}
   (c) 0.5×10^{-34} (d) 5.0×10^{-24}

Assertion-Reason [1 Mark]

■ **Directions** (Q. Nos. 6-8) In the following questions, an Assertion (A) is followed by a corresponding Reason (R). Use the following keys to choose the appropriate answer.

(a) Both (A) and (R) are true and (R) is the correct explanation of (A).
(b) Both (A) and (R) are true and (R) is not the correct explanation of (A).
(c) (A) is true but (R) is false.
(d) (A) is false but (R) is true.

6. **Assertion** (A) The nucleus of an atom contains protons and neutrons.
   Reason (R) Protons are positively charged particles, while neutrons have no charge.

7. **Assertion** (A) The photoelectric effect demonstrates the particle nature of light.
   Reason (R) Electrons are emitted from a metal surface when it is exposed to light of sufficient frequency.

8. **Assertion** (A) The magnetic quantum number determines the shape of an orbital.
   Reason (R) It describes the orientation of orbitals within a given sub-shell.

Short Answer Type I Questions [2 Marks]

9. Wavelengths of different radiations are given below.
   $\lambda(A) = 300$ nm, $\lambda(B) = 300$ µm, $\lambda(C) = 3$ nm, $\lambda(D) = 30$ Å
   Arrange these radiations in the increasing order of their energies.

10. A certain radio station broadcasts on a frequency of 980 kHz (kilohertz). What is the wavelength of electromagnetic radiation broadcast by the radio station?

11. A microscope using suitable photons is employed to locate an electron in an atom within a distance of 0.1 Å. What is the uncertainty involved in the measurement of its velocity?

12. Write the values of the quantum number n, l, m and s for electron filling 21st place in the atom of element with atomic number 24.

Short Answer Type II Questions [3 Marks]

13. (i) Calculate the number of electrons which will together weigh one gram.
    (ii) Calculate the mass and charge of one mole of electrons.

14. An ion with mass number 56 contains 3 units of positive charge and 30.4 % more neutron than the electrons. Assign the symbol to this ion.

15. The ejection of the photoelectron from the silver metal in the photoelectric effect experiment can be stopped by applying the voltage of 0.35 V when the radiation of 256.7 nm is used. Calculate the work function for silver metal.

Case Study [4 Marks]

16. Read the case given below and answer the questions that follow

In the study of atomic structure, orbitals are essential regions around the nucleus where electrons are likely to be found, each with a unique shape and orientation. The shape of an orbital is primarily defined by the azimuthal quantum number (l), which classifies orbitals into types : s, p, d and f. s-orbitals, where $l = 0$, are spherical and symmetrical around the nucleus, allowing electrons to be close to the nucleus in a low-energy, stable state. This spherical shape simplifies electron distribution within s-orbitals, which only have a single orientation.

p-orbitals, associated with $l = 1$, have a distinct dumbbell shape and exist in three orientations : p_x, p_y and p_z each aligned along a different spatial axis. This three-dimensional arrangement provides electrons with more spatial freedom within the same energy level, influencing bonding and chemical reactivity. The d-orbitals ($l = 2$) are even more complex, with five orientations and varied shapes that play a significant role in the chemical properties of elements, especially transition metals. These-orientations allow atoms to accommodate more electrons and interact with other atoms in unique ways.

The complex shapes and orientations of these orbitals determine how electrons are distributed in atoms and affect atomic stability, bonding patterns, and reactivity. By understanding these orbital shapes, chemists can predict electron configuration and the types of bonds an atom might form. This spatial organization lays the groundwork for comprehending how atoms interact within molecules and participate in chemical reactions, helping to explain the diverse behaviours of elements across the periodic table.

(i) For a given principal quantum number, s, p, d, f, ..., subshells, all have different energies. Why?

(ii) Calculate the number of nodes present in 2s-orbital.

(iii) In case of 2p-orbitals, spherical nodes are present or not?

Or

Why do half-filled and fully-filled sets of degenerate orbitals (like p, d or f) exhibit extra stability?

Long Answer Type Questions [5 Marks]

17. (i) Following results are observed when sodium metal is irradiated with different wavelength. Calculate

(a) threshold wavelength

(b) Planck's constant

λ (nm)	500	450	400
$v \times 10^5$ (ms^{-1})	2.55	4.35	5.20

(ii) If the photon of the wavelength 150 pm strikes an atom and one of its inner bound electrons is ejected out with a velocity of 1.5×10^7 ms^{-1}, calculate the energy with which it is bound to the nucleus.

18. (i) The arrangement of orbitals on the basis of energy is based upon their $(n + l)$ value. Lower the value of $(n + l)$, lower is the energy. For orbitals having same values of $(n + l)$, the orbitals with lower value of n will have lower energy.

(a) Based upon the above information, arrange the following orbitals in the increasing order of energy.

I. 1s 2s 3s 2p II. 4s 3s 3p 4d

III. 5p 4d 5d 4f 6s IV. 5f 6d 7s 6p

(b) Based upon the above information, solve the questions given below.

I. Which of the following orbitals has the lowest energy?

4d 4f 5s 5p

II. Which of the following orbitals has the highest energy?

5p 5d 5f 6s 6p

(ii) The first shell may contain upto 2 electrons, the second shell upto 8, the third shell upto 18, and the fourth shell upto 32. Explain this arrangement in terms of quantum number.

Answers

1. (c) *2.* (c) *3.* (b) *4.* (a) *5.* (a)

6. (a) *7.* (a) *8.* (d)

9. B < A < C = D *10.* 306 m *11.* 5.79×10^6 ms^{-1}

12. $n = 3$, $l = 2$, $s = +\frac{1}{2}$ or $-\frac{1}{2}$, m can have any value out of $-2, -1, 0, +1, +2$.

13. (i) 1.0976×10^{27} electrons

(ii) 5.486×10^{-7} kg and 9.65×10^4 C

14. $^{56}_{26}Fe^{3+}$ *15.* 4.48 eV

17. (i) (a) 5.31×10^{-7} m (b) 6.6539×10^{-34} Js

(ii) 7.63×10^3 eV

03 CHAPTER

In this chapter, we will study the historical developments of the periodic table, consequence of the electronic configuration of atoms on the periodic classification of elements and some of the important periodic trends in the physical and chemical properties of elements.

YOUR STUDY GOALS

YOUR PRACTICE GOAL

- Objective Type Questions (36 Qs ; 24 MCQs, 10 A-R, 2 Case Study)
- Subjective Type Questions (32 Qs; 11 SA-I, 12 SA-II, 9 LA)

Classification of Elements and Periodicity in Properties

Need of Classification

Till now 118 elements have been discovered. With such a large number of elements, scientists felt the need of some simple methods to systematise the study of properties of different elements and their compounds. This need gave rise to the classification of elements into various groups having similar properties and led to the formulation of periodic table.

Thus, *"periodic table is an arrangement of elements with similar properties placed together."*

3.1 Genesis of Periodic Classification

We will discuss here first some earlier attempts made to classify elements and then, the long form of periodic table.

Dobereiner's Triads

On the basis of similarity in properties, German chemist, **Johann Dobereiner** in 1817, classified certain elements into group of three, called **triad**. *If elements of a triad were arranged in increasing order of their atomic weights, the atomic weight of the middle element was approximately the arithmetic mean (average) of other two elements.* e.g.

Dobereiner's Triads

Element	Atomic weight	Element	Atomic weight	Element	Atomic weight
Li	7	Ca	40	Cl	35.5
Na	23	Sr	88	Br	80
K	39	Ba	137	I	127

Also, the properties of the middle element were in between those of the other two members. Thus, Dobereiner's relationship was also referred as **law of triads**.

Limitation

This law worked good only for a few elements, so it was discarded.

de-Chancourtois Classification

A.E.B. de-Chancourtois in 1862, arranged the elements in increasing order of their atomic weights and develop a cylindrical table of elements to show periodic reccurrence of properties.

Limitation

This classification fails to receive much attention.

Newlands' Law of Octaves

The english chemist, **John Alexander Newlands'** suggested that *when elements are arranged in increasing order of their atomic weights, every eighth element resembles its properties with the first one.* The relationship was just like the eighth note of a musical scale. This generalisation was named as **Newlands' law of octaves.** A few octaves based on the Newlands' generalisation are tabulated below.

Newlands' Octaves

Element	Li	Be	B	C	N	O	F
Atomic weight	7	9	11	12	14	16	19
Element	Na	Mg	Al	Si	P	S	Cl
Atomic weight	23	24	27	29	31	32	35.5
Element	K	Ca					
Atomic weight	39	40					

This law was the greatest discovery as it relates for the first time, the properties of elements with their atomic weights. Moreover, it also revealed the periodicity in the properties of elements.

Limitations

This law was discarded because of the following limitations.

- This law failed when applied to heavier elements beyond calcium (Ca).
- Further after the discovery of noble gases, it was the ninth element that show resemblance in properties with the first one.
- No space was left for the unknown elements at that time.

Note Although in the beginning, the **Newlands' law** was not widely accepted. However, later, Royal society of London recognised his work and awarded him Davy Medal in 1887.

Lothar Meyer's Classification

Lothar Meyer after studying the physical properties of elements proposed the periodic law which states that, *"when elements are arranged in increasing order of their atomic weights, similarities in physical and chemical properties appear at regular intervals or the physical properties of the elements are the periodic function of their atomic weights".*

Lothar Meyer also plotted the physical properties such as atomic volume, melting point, boiling point etc., with atomic weight and observed a periodic repetition in their properties. He also observed that the length of the repeating pattern changed continuously.

He had developed a table of the elements that closely resembles the Modern Periodic Table. However, his work was not published until after the work of Mendeleev.

Limitations

This classification has the following limitations.

- It does not consider the chemical properties of elements.
- It was incomplete when compared with Mendeleev's periodic table.

Mendeleev's Periodic Table

The Russian chemist, **Dmitri Mendeleev (1869)** proposed that when elements are arranged in increasing order of their atomic weights, element having similar properties, reoccurs at regular intervals.

On this basis, he gave a law called the Mendeleev's periodic law. He states that, *"the physical and chemical properties of the element are the periodic function of their atomic weights".*

The repetition of properties of elements after certain regular intervals is called **periodicity of properties.**

S. No.	GROUPS OF ELEMENTS								
	0	I	II	III	IV	V	VI	VII	VIII
1		Hydrogen H 1.008							
2	Helium He 4.0	Lithium Li 7.03	Beryllium Be 9.1	Boron B 11.0	Carbon C 12.0	Nitrogen N 14.04	Oxygen O 16.00	Fluorine F 19.0	
3	Neon Ne 19.9	Sodium Na 23.5	Magnesium Mg 24.3	Aluminium Al 27.0	Silicon Si 28.4	Phosphorus P 31.0	Sulphur S 32.06	Chlorine Cl 35.45	
4	Argon Ar 38	Potassium K 39.1	Calcium Ca 40.1	Scandium Sc 44.1	Titanium Ti 48.1	Vanadium V 51.4	Chromium Cr 52.1	Manganese Mn 55.0	Iron Fe 55.9; Cobalt Co 59; Nickel Ni (Cu) 59
5		Copper Cu 63.6	Zinc Zn 65.4	Gallium Ga 70.0	Germanium Ge 72.3	Arsenic As 75	Selenium Se 79	Bromine Br 79.95	
6	Krypton Kr 81.8	Rubidium Rb 85.4	Strontium Sr 87.6	Yttrium Y 89.0	Zirconium Zr 90.6	Niobium Nb 94.0	Molybdenum Mo 96.0	—	Ruthenium Ru 101.7; Rhodium Rh 103.0; Palladium Pd (Ag) 106.5
7		Silver Ag 107.9	Cadmium Cd 112.4	Indium In 114.0	Tin Sn 119.0	Antimony Sb 120.0	Tellurium Te 127.6	Iodine I 126.9	
8	Xenon Xe 128	Caesium Cs 132.9	Barium Ba 137.4	Lanthanum La 139	Cerium Ce 140	—	—	—	
9		—	—	—	—	—	—	—	
10	—	—	—	Ytterbium Yb 173	—	Tantalum Ta 183	Tungsten W 184	—	Osmium Os 191; Iridium Ir 193; Platinum Pt (Au) 194.9
11		Gold Au 197.2	Mercury Hg 200.0	Thallium T 204.1	Lead Pb 206.9	Bismuth Bi 208	—	—	
12	—	—	Radium Ra 224	—	Thorium Th 232	—	Uranium U 239	— —	
HIGHER SALINE OXIDES	*R*	*R_2O*	*RO*	*R_2O_3*	*RO_2*	*R_2O_5*	*RO_3*	*R_2O_7*	*RO_4*
HIGHER GASEOUS HYDROGEN COMPOUNDS					*RH_4*	*RH_3*	*RH_2*	*RH*	

Mendeleev's Periodic Table Published Earlier

- Among chemical properties, Mendeleev considered mainly the properties of compound of elements with **oxygen** and **hydrogen** (i.e. properties of their oxides and hydrides).
- **Reason for the selection of these compounds** as the basis of classification are the high reactivity of hydrogen and oxygen and formation of large number of compounds by these elements.
- Mendeleev arranged the elements then known in horizontal rows and vertical columns in order of their increasing atomic weights and generated a table called **periodic table.**
- The elements with similar properties occupied the same **vertical column** or **group.**
- At some place of periodic table, he occasionally ignored the strict order of atomic weights, prioritising the grouping of elements with similar properties.

  e.g. Iodine with lower atomic weight than that of tellurium (Group VI) was placed in Group VII along with fluorine, chlorine, bromine because of similarities in properties.
- At the same time, keeping his primary aim of arranging the elements of similar properties in the same group, he proposed that some of the elements were still undiscovered and hence left several gaps in the table. e.g. Both **gallium** and **germanium** were unknown at the time Mendeleev published his periodic table. He left the gap under aluminium and a gap under silicon, and called these elements **Eka-Aluminium** and **Eka-Silicon**. These elements were discovered later.

Characteristics of Mendeleev's Periodic Table

The periodic table, generated by Mendeleev had the following features.

- In this periodic table, there were eight vertical columns, named as **groups**. These were represented by Roman numerals I to VIII. Each group is divided into sub-groups *A* and *B* except the VIII group which had nine elements arranged in three rows as triads, i.e. in the group of three.
- In this table, there were six horizontal rows, named as **periods** which were further divided into 12 series.

Limitations

Some limitations of Mendeleev's periodic table are as follows

- **Position of hydrogen** Hydrogen resembles both, the alkali metals and the halogens in properties, so Mendeleev could not decide where to place it.
- **Position of isotopes** As atomic weight of isotopes differs, they should have placed in different position in Mendeleev's periodic table. But, no separate place for isotopes is given.
- **Anomalous pairs of elements** There were some pair of elements which do not follow the increasing order of atomic weight. e.g. Ar (40) and Co (63.5) were placed before K(39) and Ni (58.7), respectively.
- **Similar elements placed in different groups** There were some elements like, Platinum (Pt) and gold (Au) which have similar properties were placed in different groups.
- **Position of lanthanides and actinides** The fourteen elements each of lanthanides and actinides were assigned a single place in the table despite having different atomic weights.
- **Unlike elements were placed in one group** Cu, Ag and Au were placed in 1st group along with Na, K etc., while differ in their properties (only similar in having ns^1 electronic configuration).

3.2 Modern Periodic Law and the Present Form of the Periodic Table

Henry Moseley observed regularities in the characteristic X-ray spectra of the elements. A plot of $\sqrt{v}$ (where, v is frequency of X-rays emitted) against atomic number (Z) gave a straight line and not the plot of $\sqrt{v}$ *vs* atomic mass. He modified the Mendeleev's periodic law and gave **modern periodic law**, which states that, *"the physical and chemical properties of the elements are the periodic functions of their atomic numbers,"*

Long Form of Periodic Table

Several periodic tables have been proposed from time to time. Some were based on chemical reactions and valence electrons while the others were focused on the electronic configuration of elements. The most convenient and widely used version among them is called the **long form of periodic table.**

Representative elements (s-block elements) | Transition elements (d-block elements) | Representative elements (p-block elements) | Noble gases

Period number	GROUP NUMBER 1 IA	2 IIA	3 IIIB	4 IVB	5 VB	6 VIB	7 VIIB	8 ←	9 VIII	10 →	11 IB	12 IIB	13 IIIA	14 IVA	15 VA	16 VIA	17 VIIA	18 0
1	1 H $1s^1$																	2 He $1s^2$
2	3 Li $2s^1$	4 Be $2s^2$											5 B $2s^2 2p^1$	6 C $2s^2 2p^2$	7 N $2s^2 2p^3$	8 O $2s^2 2p^4$	9 F $2s^2 2p^5$	10 Ne $2s^2 2p^6$
3	11 Na $3s^1$	12 Mg $3s^2$											13 Al $3s^2 3p^1$	14 Si $3s^2 3p^2$	15 P $3s^2 3p^3$	16 S $3s^2 3p^4$	17 Cl $3s^2 3p^5$	18 Ar $3s^2 3p^6$
4	19 K $4s^1$	20 Ca $4s^2$	21 Sc $3d^1 4s^2$	22 Ti $3d^2 4s^2$	23 V $3d^3 4s^2$	24 Cr $3d^5 4s^1$	25 Mn $3d^5 4s^2$	26 Fe $3d^6 4s^2$	27 Co $3d^7 4s^2$	28 Ni $3d^8 4s^2$	29 Cu $3d^{10} 4s^1$	30 Zn $3d^{10} 4s^2$	31 Ga $4s^2 4p^1$	32 Ge $4s^2 4p^2$	33 As $4s^2 4p^3$	34 Se $4s^2 4p^4$	35 Br $4s^2 4p^5$	36 Kr $4s^2 4p^6$
5	37 Rb $5s^1$	38 Sr $5s^2$	39 Y $4d^1 5s^2$	40 Zr $4d^2 5s^2$	41 Nb $4d^4 5s^1$	42 Mo $4d^5 5s^1$	43 Tc $4d^5 5s^2$	44 Ru $4d^7 5s^1$	45 Rh $4d^8 5s^1$	46 Pd $4d^{10}$	47 Ag $4d^{10} 5s^1$	48 Cd $4d^{10} 5s^2$	49 In $5s^2 5p^1$	50 Sn $5s^2 5p^2$	51 Sb $5s^2 5p^3$	52 Te $5s^2 5p^4$	53 I $5s^2 5p^5$	54 Xe $5s^2 5p^6$
6	55 Cs $6s^1$	56 Ba $6s^2$	57 La* $5d^1 6s^2$	72 Hf $4f^{14} 5d^2 6s^2$	73 Ta $5d^3 6s^2$	74 W $5d^4 6s^2$	75 Re $5d^5 6s^2$	76 Os $5d^6 6s^2$	77 Ir $5d^7 6s^2$	78 Pt $5d^9 6s^1$	79 Au $5d^{10} 6s^1$	80 Hg $5d^{10} 6s^2$	81 Tl $6s^2 6p^1$	82 Pb $6s^2 6p^2$	83 Bi $6s^2 6p^3$	84 Po $6s^2 6p^4$	85 At $6s^2 6p^5$	86 Rn $6s^2 6p^6$
7	87 Fr $7s^1$	88 Ra $7s^2$	89 Ac** $6d^1 7s^2$	104 Rf	105 Db	106 Sg	107 Bh	108 Hs	109 Mt	110 Ds	111 Rg	112 Cn	113 Nh	114 Fl	115 Mc	116 Lv	117 Ts	118 Og

Inner-transition elements (f-block elements)

*Lanthanoids $4f^n 5d^{0-1} 6s^2$	58 Ce $4f^2 5d^0 6s^2$	59 Pr $4f^3 5d^0 6s^2$	60 Nd $4f^4 5d^0 6s^2$	61 Pm $4f^5 5d^0 6s^2$	62 Sm $4f^6 5d^0 6s^2$	63 Eu $4f^7 5d^0 6s^2$	64 Gd $4f^7 5d^1 6s^2$	65 Tb $4f^9 5d^0 6s^2$	66 Dy $4f^{10} 5d^1 6s^2$	67 Ho $4f^{11} 5d^0 6s^2$	68 Er $4f^{12} 5d^0 6s^2$	69 Tm $4f^{13} 5d^0 6s^2$	70 Yb $4f^{14} 5d^0 6s^2$	71 Lu $4f^{14} 5d^1 6s^2$
**Actinoids $5f^n 6d^{0-2} 7s^2$	90 Th $5f^0 6d^2 7s^2$	91 Pa $5f^2 6d^1 7s^2$	92 U $5f^3 6d^1 7s^2$	93 Np $5f^4 6d^1 7s^2$	94 Pu $5f^6 6d^0 7s^2$	95 Am $5f^7 6d^0 7s^2$	96 Cm $5f^7 6d^1 7s^2$	97 Bk $5f^9 6d^0 7s^2$	98 Cf $5f^{10} 6d^0 7s^2$	99 Es $5f^{11} 6d^0 7s^2$	100 Fm $5f^{12} 6d^0 7s^2$	101 Md $5f^{13} 6d^0 7s^2$	102 No $5f^{14} 6d^0 7s^2$	103 Lr $5f^{14} 6d^1 7s^2$

Long form of the Periodic Table

Features of Long Form of Periodic Table

This table is based on the electronic configuration of the elements and is also called the **Bohr's table** as it follows the Bohr's scheme to arrange various electrons around the nucleus.

Salient features of this table are as follows

- In this table, there are 18 vertical columns, called the **groups** or **families**. These groups are numbered from 1 to 18 (according to IUPAC, replacing the older notations of groups IA......VIIA, VIII, IB, ...VIIB and 0).

  Each group or family contains a number of elements with same electronic configuration of valence shell (i.e. the outermost shell).
- Elements of 1, 2 and 13 to 17 are called the **main group** or **typical** or **representative elements.**

  Elements of group 1 and 2 are also called **alkali metals** and **alkaline earth metals** respectively.
- Elements of group 3 to 12 are called **transition elements.**
- Elements with atomic number 58 to 71 are called **lanthanoids** and elements with atomic number 90 to 103 are called **actinoids.** Lanthanoids and actinoids are placed in two separate rows below the periodic table in order to avoid the unnecessary side-wise expansion of the periodic table.

Note The work of **Glenn T. Seaborg** in 20th century starting with the discovery of **plutonium** (in 1940), followed by those of all the transuranium elements from 94-102 led to the placement of the actinoids below lanthanoids. He was also awarded the Nobel Prize in chemistry for his work and element 106, seaborgium was named in his honour.

- This periodic table has seven horizontal rows, called the **periods,** which are numbered as 1, 2, 3, 4, 5, 6, 7 from top to bottom. *The period number represents the highest principal quantum number (n) of the elements in the period.*

- There are two elements, in the first period and 8, 8, 18, 18 and 32 elements, respectively in the subsequent periods. Thus, first period is known as the **shortest period**, second and third are **short periods**, fourth and fifth as **long periods** and sixth as the **longest period**.
- Each period begins with an element having one electron in a new energy level (or new shell).

  Thus, the first element of each period is an **alkali metal** (with an exception of hydrogen) and the last element of each period is a **noble gas**.

TEACHER'S TIP

The numbers 2, 8, 8, 18, 18, 32 are sometimes referred as magic numbers as the repetition in properties is observed after these number of elements in successive periods.

Merits of Long Form of Periodic Table

This table is based on the atomic number which is the basic fundamental property of an atom and hence, it is found helpful in removing most of the anomalies of Mendeleev's periodic table.

Some of its important merits are as follows

- This table removed the anomalies of inversions that existed in the Mendeleev's periodic table, e.g. potassium with atomic number 19 is placed after argon with atomic number 18.

  Similarly, cobalt with atomic number 27 is placed before nickel with atomic number 28.
- In this table same position is allotted to each isotope of an element as all the isotopes of an element have same atomic number.
- Other anomalies of Mendeleev's periodic table like grouping of dissimilar elements together and similar elements separately has also been removed by this table.
- It also explains the cause of periodicity on the basis of electronic configuration. Further it relates the position of an element in the periodic table with its electronic configuration, which indeed determines the physical and chemical properties of elements and their compounds.
- It provides an easier way to remember all the elements and their properties by just knowing their atomic numbers and electronic configurations.

Defects of Long Form of the Periodic Table

Although this periodic table provided a systematic way to study the chemistry of elements and removed most of the anomalies of Mendeleev's and other modern periodic tables, yet it suffers from the following defects.

- In this periodic table also, the position of hydrogen is not clear, although it is placed in a separate box just above the group-I.
- Lanthanoids and actinoids has not been merged within the main body of the periodic table.

Quick Test 1

1. If A, B and C are the three members of a Dobereiner's triad and the atomic mass of A is 7 and that of C is 39, then what will be the atomic mass of B?
2. State any two significant features of the Mendeleev's periodic table.
3. Which important property did Mendeleev use to classify the elements in his periodic table and did he stick to that? NCERT
4. Mendeleev's classification was superior to the other classification. Comment.
5. Which properties of the elements depend on the electronic configuration of the atoms and which do not?
6. (i) What is the basic theme of organisation in the periodic table? NCERT
   (ii) Which element do you think would have been named by
   (a) Lawrence and Berkeley laboratory ?
   (b) Seaborg's group? NCERT
7. What is the basic difference in approach between the Mendeleev's periodic law and the modern periodic law? NCERT, Diksha
8. (i) Write the number designation of a group that has 2 electrons beyond a noble gas configuration.
   (ii) What are magic numbers? Diksha

For Solutions, See QR Code on Pg. 120

3.3 Nomenclature of Elements with Atomic Number Greater than 100

The basic rules to write the name of an element in accordance with the system of nomenclature are

- The name of an element is derived directly from its atomic number using the numerical roots for 0 and numbers 1-9. These roots are tabulated below.

Notation for IUPAC Nomenclature of Elements

Digit	Name	Abbreviation
0	nil	n
1	un	u
2	bi	b
3	tri	t
4	quad	q
5	pent	p
6	hex	h
7	sept	s
8	oct	o
9	enn	e

- To write the name of an element, the roots are put one after the other in the same fashion of digits as in the atomic number and the suffix 'ium' is added at the end. e.g. The element with atomic number 108 is named as **unniloctium** (no spacing between the words).
- To write the symbol of the element, put the first letter of the roots in the same order of digits as in the atomic number. e.g. The symbol for element having atomic number 108 is Uno. (The first letter of the symbol must be in upper case).

IUPAC Nomenclature of Elements with At. no. above 100

Atomic number	Name according to IUPAC nomenclature	Symbol	IUPAC official name	IUPAC symbol
101	Unnilunium	Unu	Mendelevium	Md
102	Unnilbium	Unb	Nobelium	No
103	Unniltrium	Unt	Lawrencium	Lr
104	Unnilquadium	Unq	Rutherfordium	Rf
105	Unnilpentium	Unp	Dubnium	Db
106	Unnilhexium	Unh	Seaborgium	Sg
107	Unnilseptium	Uns	Bohrium	Bh
108	Unniloctium	Uno	Hassium	Hs
109	Unnilennium	Une	Meitnerium	Mt
110	Ununnilium	Uun	Darmstadtium	Ds
111	Unununium	Uuu	Rontgenium	Rg
112	Ununbium	Uub	Copercinium	Cn
113	Ununtrium	Uut	Nihonium	Nh
114	Ununquadium	Uuq	Flerovium	Fl
115	Ununpentium	Uup	Moscovium	Mc
116	Ununhexium	Uuh	Livermorium	Lv
117	Ununseptium	Uus	Tennessine	Ts
118	Ununoctium	Uuo	Oganesson	Og

All these elements are man-made through artificial nuclear reactions. As of now, elements with atomic numbers upto 118 have been discovered. Official names of all elements have been announced by IUPAC.

Example 1 **What would be the IUPAC name and symbol for the element with atomic number 120?** **NCERT**

Sol. As we know that, the roots for 1, 2 and 0 are un, bi and nil respectively. Thus, its IUPAC name is $\underset{1\ \ 2\ \ 0}{\text{unbinilium}}$ and its symbol is Ubn.

3.4 Electronic Configurations of Elements and the Periodic Table

Long form of periodic table is completely based on the electronic configuration and with the help of electronic configuration, it is possible to find out the position (period and group) of an element in the periodic table.

Electronic Configurations in Periods

The period of an element is indicated by its principal quantum number (n) for the outermost or valence shell. The number of elements present in any period is twice the number of atomic orbitals available in that energy level.

(i) **Elements in first period** First period corresponds to $n=1$ (or K shell) starts with the filling of lowest level 1s and therefore, has two elements-hydrogen ($1s^1$) and helium ($1s^2$) when the first shell is completed.

(ii) **Elements in second period** This period corresponds to $n=2$ (or L shell) which contains one 2s and three 2p orbitals with a capacity of 8 electrons. Therefore, eight elements starting from lithium ($1s^2 2s^1$) to neon ($1s^2 2s^2 2p^6$) are present in this period.

(iii) **Elements in third period** This period corresponds to $n=3$ (or M shell). Consequently, this period involves the filling of four orbitals, i.e. one 3s-orbital and three 3p-orbitals. Therefore, eight elements from sodium ($3s^1$) to argon ($3s^2 3p^6$) are included in this period.

(iv) **Elements in fourth period** This period corresponds to $n=4$ (or N shell). This period involves the filling of nine orbitals, i.e. one 4s, three 4p and five 3d orbitals. Therefore, the period contains eighteen elements from potassium ($Z=19$) to krypton ($Z=36$).

(v) **Elements in fifth period** This period corresponds to $n=5$. Just like fourth period, it involves the filling of one $5s$, five $4d$ and three $5p$-orbitals and hence, total 18 electrons can be accommodated in these orbitals. Thus, this period also contains a total of eighteen elements from rubidium ($5s^1$) to xenon ($5s^2 5p^6$).

(vi) **Elements in sixth period** This period corresponds to $n=6$, i.e. sixth shell. Thus, one $6s$, seven $4f$, five $5d$ and three $6p$ orbital, i.e. total 16 orbitals are present. Hence, this period has 32 elements. This period begins with caesium ($6s^1$) and ends at radon ($6s^2 6p^6$).

(vii) **Elements in seventh period** This period corresponds to $n=7$, i.e. seventh shell. Just like sixth period, it involves the filling of $7s, 5f, 6d$ and $7p$ i.e. total 16 orbitals successively. However, most of the elements of this period are synthetic or man-made radioactive elements.

Note Filling of orbitals in each period is according to Aufbau principle.

Groupwise Electronic Configurations

Elements in a group or same vertical column have similar electronic configuration, same number of electrons in valence orbitals and similar properties. e.g. Group 1 elements (alkali metals) have general electronic configuration, ns^1.

3.5 Electronic Configurations and Types of Elements : s, p, d, f-Blocks

Depending upon the nature of atomic orbitals in which the last electron enters, the elements can be classified into four blocks *viz*, *s*-block, *p*-block, *d*-block and *f*-block. There are two exceptions in this categorisation.

- Placing of hydrogen
- Placing of helium

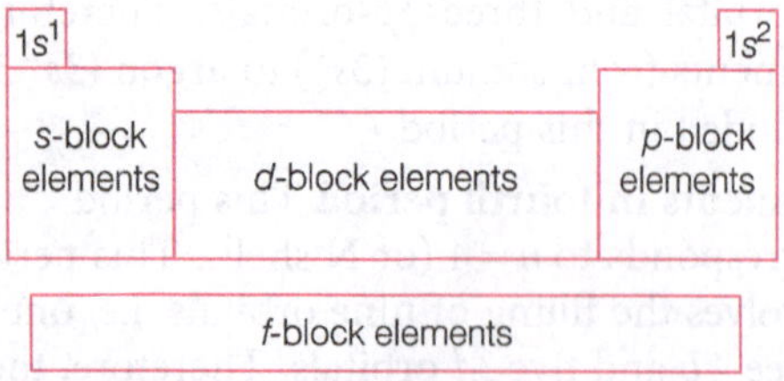

Division of periodic table into *s*, *p*, *d* and *f*-blocks

General characteristics of these blocks are described below.

The s-Block Elements

The elements in which the last electron enters in the *s*-orbital of their respective outermost shell are called the ***s*-block elements.**

Since, *s*-subshell have only one orbital which can accommodate a maximum of two electrons, so only two groups, i.e. **group 1** (alkali metals) and **group 2** (alkaline earth metals) belong to this block. These groups lie on the extreme left of the periodic table.

General characteristics of elements of this block are as follows

- General electronic configuration of elements of this block is ns^{1-2} (where, $n=1, 2, \ldots$). Thus, the valence shell configuration of alkali metals is ns^1 and of alkaline earth metals is ns^2.
- They are soft metals with low melting and boiling points.
- Because of their lower ionisation enthalpy, these metals are highly reactive and hence, never found pure in nature. Reactivity of these metals increases on moving down the group as the distance between the valence electrons and nucleus increases.
- They are electropositive and metallic elements. Their metallic character also increases on moving down the group.
- They are strong reducing agents.
- They show +1 oxidation state (in case of alkali metals) or +2 oxidation state (in case of alkaline earth metals).
- They are predominantly ionic with the exception of those of lithium and beryllium.

Note Alkali metals like K, Rb and Cs are used in photoelectric cells due to their low ionisation enthalpy.

The p-Block Elements

The elements in which the last electron enters in any of the three *p*-orbitals of their respective outermost shell are called the ***p*-block elements.**

Since, a *p*-subshell can accommodate a maximum of 6 electrons, thus, six group, i.e. group 13 to 18 belong to this block.

Elements of group 15, 16, 17 and 18 are respectively known as **pnictogens** (choking producer), **chalcogens, halogens** and **noble gases.** Group 13 to 18 are present on the extreme right of the periodic table.

General characteristics of elements of this block are as follows

- The outermost electronic configurations of these elements varies from $ns^2\ np^1$ to $ns^2\ np^6$ in each period, i.e. the general configuration for these elements can be written as $\boldsymbol{ns^2\ np^{1-6}}$ (where, $n = 1, 2, \ldots$).
- They are generally non-metals but some metals and metalloids are also present. The non-metallic character increases from left to right along a period but metallic character increases on moving down a group of this block.
- They have high electron gain enthalpy (negative) and ionisation energy. Both properties increases along a period from left to right and decreases on moving down the group.
- Their oxidising character increases on moving from left to right along a period and reducing character increases from top to bottom in a group.
- Most of them are electronegative.

The *d*-Block Elements (Transition Elements)

Elements in which the last electron enters in one of the inner *d*-orbital are called ***d*-block elements**.

Since, there can be a maximum of ten electrons in a *d*-subshell, so ten groups, i.e. group 3, 4, 5, 6, 7, 8, 9, 10, 11, 12 belong to this block.

The properties of elements of these groups are midway between those of *s*-block and *p*-block elements, thus, they act as a bridge between the highly reactive metals of *s*-block and the less reactive elements of group 13 and 14, i.e. they show transition (change) in behaviour and hence, known as **transition elements**. General characteristics of elements of this block are as follows

- General electronic configuration of elements of this block is $(n-1)\,d^{1-10}ns^{(0-2)}$.
- They all are metals with very high melting and boiling points.
- Most of them form coloured ions because of the presence of partially filled *d*-orbitals.
- They generally exhibit variable valency (oxidation states) because the 3*d* and 4*s*-orbitals are of comparable energy and hence, take part in bonding.
- They generally show paramagnetism because of the presence of unpaired electrons in the *d*-orbitals. (Higher the number of unpaired electrons, more is the paramagnetic character).
- They are used as catalysts because of their variable valency and partially filled *d*-orbitals.

TEACHER'S TIP

Zn, Cd and Hg because of the presence of completely filled *d*-orbitals (i.e. $(n-1)\,d^{10}\,ns^2$ configuration) do not exhibit most of the properties of transition elements and hence, these are not considered as **typical transition elements**. Typical transition elements have partially filled *d*-orbitals in any of their oxidation states.

The *f*-Block Elements (Inner-Transition Elements)

The elements in which the last electron enters in *f*-orbital of anti-penultimate shells are called the ***f*-block elements**. These are also called **inner-transition elements** because of the filling of inner-penultimate or anti-penultimate shell by last electron.

This block contains two series of elements, called the 4*f* and 5*f* series, each of which contains 14 elements. The elements of 4*f* series [i.e. from atomic number 58 (Ce) to 71(Lu)] are called **lanthanoids** and the elements of 5*f* series [i.e. from atomic number 90 (Th) to 103 (Lr)] are called **actinoids.** These two series of elements are present at the bottom of the periodic table.

General characteristics exhibited by elements of this block are as follows

- General outer electronic configuration for these elements is $(n-2)\,f^{1-14}(n-1)\,d^{0-1}ns^2$. Thus, the outer electronic configuration for lanthanoids and actinoids are $4f^{1-14}\,5d^{0-1}\,6s^2$ and $5f^{1-14}\,6d^{0-1}\,7s^2$, respectively.
- They are all heavy metals with high melting and boiling points.
- Actinoids exhibit a large number of oxidation states because of the comparable energy of 5*f*, 6*d* and 7*s* orbitals and hence, their chemistry is more complicated as compared to the corresponding lanthanoids. However, the most common oxidation state exhibited by *f*-block elements is +3.
- All the actinoids are radioactive in nature. The first three elements, i.e. thorium (Th), protoactinium (Pa) and uranium (U) are natural but the remaining, i.e. from neptunium to copernicium (Cn) are synthetic, i.e. man made by nuclear reactions.
- The elements after uranium are also called **transuranic** or **transuranium elements**.

- Lanthanoids are also known as **rare earth elements** because they occur scarcely in the earth's crust.

Anomalies Associated with *s, p, d, f* Classification

Although the classification is very important and helpful for predicting the properties of an element or a group of elements, yet it is associated with certain anomalies which are as follows

(i) Position of Helium (He)

The electronic configuration of helium is $1s^2$, so it should be kept in *s*-block as the last electron enters in *s*-orbital. But it is placed in *p*-block with elements of group 18, due to the presence of completely filled valence or outermost shell ($1s^2$) and hence, exhibits similarity in properties with other noble gases.

(ii) Position of Hydrogen (H)

The electronic configuration of hydrogen is $1s^1$. Because of the presence of only one electron in *s*-orbital, it can be placed in group 1 with alkali metals. But it can also accept an electron to achieve the electronic configuration of nearest inert gas (which is helium) like halogens (elements of group 17) so it can also be placed alongwith them. Because of its unique behaviour, hydrogen is placed at the top of the periodic table.

Algorithm for Predicting Position of an Element in the Periodic Table

In the prediction of position of an element in the periodic table, following steps are involved.

Step 1 First write the electronic configuration of the element, if not given.

Step 2 Find the principal quantum number of the valence shell, it shows the period of the element.

Step 3 Predict the orbital which receives the last electron. It shows the block of the element.

Step 4 The group of an element is then predicted as

(i) If the element belongs to *s*-block, its group number = Number of valence (or outermost shell) electrons.

(ii) If the element belongs to *p*-block,
Group number = 10 + number of valence electrons
= 10 + *ns*-electrons + *np*-electrons
(here, *n* = outermost shell)

(iii) If the element belongs to *d*-block,
Group number = number of electrons in $(n-1)d$ subshell + number of electrons in *ns*-shell.

(iv) If the element belongs to *f*-block,
Group number = 3.

Example 2 How would you justify the presence of 18 elements in the 5th period of the periodic table? NCERT

Sol. The 5th period begins with the filling of principal quantum number, $n = 5$. When $n = 5, l = 0, 1, 2, 3$. But according to Aufbau principle, in 5th period, electrons can be filled only in 5*s*, 4*d* and 5*p*-subshells whose energies increases in the order $5s < 4d < 5p$.

Thus, the available orbitals are one 5*s*, five 4*d* and three 5*p*-orbitals, i.e. total 9 orbitals which can accommodate a maximum of 18 electrons. Hence, this period contains 18 elements.

Example 3 Write down the outermost electronic configurations of alkali metals. How will you justify their placement in group 1 of the periodic table? NCERT Exemplar

Sol. All the elements of group IA (or I), i.e. alkali metals have the similar outer electronic configuration, i.e. ns^1 where, *n* refers to the number of principal shells.

Their electronic configurations are given below.

Atomic number	Symbol	Electronic configuration
3	Li	$1s^2 2s^1$ (or) $[He]2s^1$
11	Na	$1s^2 2s^2 2p^6 3s^1$ (or) $[Ne]3s^1$
19	K	$1s^2 2s^2 2p^6 3s^2 3p^6 4s^1$ (or) $[Ar]4s^1$
37	Rb	$1s^2 2s^2 2p^6 3s^2 3p^6 4s^2 3d^{10} 4p^6 5s^1$ (or) $[Kr]\ 5s^1$
55	Cs	$1s^2 2s^2 2p^6 3s^2 3p^6 3d^{10} 4s^2 4p^6 4d^{10} 5s^2 5p^6 6s^1$ (or) $[Xe]\ 6s^1$
87	Fr	$[Rn]7s^1$

Hence, placement of all these elements of group 1 of the periodic table because of similarity in electronic configuration and properties. Thus, it is also evident that the physical and chemical properties of the elements depend on their atomic number and not on their atomic mass.

Example 4 The elements $Z = 117$ and 120 have not yet been discovered. In which family/group would you place these elements and also give the electronic configuration in each case? NCERT

Sol.

Step I Electronic configuration of the given elements is

$$Z = 117 = [Rn]\ 5f^{14}\ 6d^{10}\ \underbrace{7s^2\ 7p^5}_{\text{Valence shell}}$$

$$Z = 120 = [Uuo]\ \underbrace{8s^2}_{\text{Valence shell}}$$

Step II (i) Principal quantum number of the valence shell is 7 for $Z = 117$, so it belongs to 7th period.

(ii) Principal quantum number of the valence shell is 8, so element with atomic number 120 belongs to 8th period.

Step III (i) Element with $Z = 117$, belongs to p-block.
(ii) Element with $Z = 120$, belongs to s-block.

Step IV (i) Thus, for element with $Z = 117$
Group number $= 10 + 2 + 5 = 17$
i.e. it belongs to **halogen family.**
(ii) For element with $Z = 120$,
Group number = number of electrons in valence shell = 2
So, it belongs to **alkaline earth metals.**

Example 5 Write the name and atomic number of the following elements.

(i) The third alkali metal
(ii) The fourth alkaline earth metal
(iii) The sixth element of second transition series
(iv) The second inner transition element
(v) The fifth noble gas.

Sol. (i) Potassium, K ($Z = 19$) (ii) Strontium, Sr ($Z = 38$)
(iii) Ruthenium, Ru ($Z = 44$) (iv) Praseodymium, Pr ($Z = 59$)
(v) Xenon, Xe ($Z = 54$)

Example 6

(i) Write the electronic configurations of the elements given below.
A (Atomic number = 11), B (Atomic number = 27), C (Atomic number = 54), D (Atomic number = 58)

(ii) Classify them as representative elements, noble gases, transition and inner transition elements.

Sol. (i) Electronic configurations of the elements A, B, C, D are as follows

Element	Atomic number	Electronic configuration
A	11	$1s^2 2s^2 2p^6 3s^1$
B	27	$1s^2 2s^2 2p^6 3s^2 3p^6 4s^2 3d^7$
C	54	$1s^2 2s^2 2p^6 3s^2 3p^6 3d^{10} 4s^2 4p^6 4d^{10} 5s^2 5p^6$
D	58	$1s^2 2s^2 2p^6 3s^2 3p^6 3d^{10} 4s^2 4p^6 4d^{10} 5s^2 5p^6 6s^2 5d^1 4f^1$

(ii) **Element A** is a representative element since its last electron enters in s-orbital.

Element B is a transition element, since it receives its last electron in the d-orbital.

Element C is a p-block element with completely filled p-orbital of the valence shell. Such type of p-block element is called a noble gas.

Element D is an inner tansition element since it receives its last electron in the f-orbital.

3.6 Metals, Non-metals and Metalloids

In addition to s-, p-, d-and f-block classification, elements can also be classified as metals, non-metals and metalloids.

1. Metals

These comprise more than 78% of all known elements and appear on the left side of the periodic table.

Some important properties of metals are as follows

- They are generally solid at room temperature with an exception of mercury which is liquid at room temperature.
- They have very high melting and boiling point except gallium and caesium (melting point of which are respectively 303 K and 302 K).
- They are good conductors of heat and electricity.
- They are malleable (i.e. can be flattened into thin sheets by hammering) and ductile (i.e. can be drawn into wires).
- They have high densities.

2. Non-Metals

These are present only in p-block and occupy the top right side of the periodic table. (Although p-block also have some metals and metalloids also). Some important properties exhibited by non-metals are as follows

- They can be either solid or gas at room temperature with an exception of bromine (which is in liquid state at room temperature).
- Their melting and boiling points are very low with exception of boron and carbon.
- They are bad conductors of heat (except diamond) and electricity (except graphite).
- They are generally brittle and are neither malleable nor ductile.

3. Metalloids

These are very few in numbers and present in between metals and non-metals. They exhibit the properties of both metals and non-metals. That's why, they are called **semi-metals** or **metalloids.**

e.g. Silicon, germanium, arsenic, antimony, tellurium etc. In the periodic table, these elements form a *zig-zag* line and separates metals from non-metals.

Example 7 **Considering the atomic number and position in the periodic table, arrange the following elements in the increasing order of metallic character : Si, Be, Mg, Na, P.** NCERT

Sol. Metallic character increases down a group and decreases along a period as we move from left to right. The position of these elements in the periodic table is as follow

I	II	III	IV	V
	Be			
Na	Mg		Si	P

Thus, the order of increasing metallic character is

$P < Si < Be < Mg < Na$.

Quick Test 2

1. What would be IUPAC names and symbols for elements with atomic numbers 122, 127, 135, 149 and 150?
2. How many elements can be accommodated in the present set up of the long form of the periodic table? Explain.
3. (i) Why do elements in the same group have similar physical and chemical properties? NCERT, Diksha
   (ii) If each orbital can take maximum of three electrons, what is the number of elements in 2nd period?
4. All transition elements are *d*-block elements, but all *d*-block elements are not transition elements. Explain. NCERT Exemplar
5. Give the name and atomic number of the inert gas atom in which the total number of *d*-electrons is equal to the difference in numbers of total *p* and *s*-electrons.
6. Elements have been classified as *s*, *p*, *d* and *f*-block elements on the basis of the type of orbital which receives the last electron. Are there any exceptions to this generalisation? Comment.
7. Write the atomic number of the element present in the third period and seventeenth group of the periodic table. NCERT
8. (i) Helium has an electronic configuration of $1s^2$ but it is placed in *p*-block in group 18. Explain.
   (ii) In terms of period and group where would you locate the element with $Z = 114$? NCERT
9. What are the major differences between metals and non-metals? NCERT

For Solutions, See QR Code on Pg. 120

3.7 Periodic Trends in Properties of Elements

The repetition of similar properties after regular intervals is called **periodicity**. The cause of periodicity is the periodic repetition of similar electronic configuration of elements as the atomic number increases. The properties which show periodicity are called **periodic properties**.

Here, we will discuss the periodic trends in physical properties as well as in chemical properties.

Periodic Trends in Physical Properties

Let us discuss the periodic trends in the physical properties like atomic and ionic radii, ionisation enthalpy, electron gain enthalpy and electronegativity one by one.

Atomic Radius

The **atomic radius**, is defined as, *"the distance from the centre of the nucleus to the outermost shell containing electrons."*

The determination of exact radius of atom is not possible because of the very small size (~ 1.2 Å) of atom and since the electron cloud surrounding the atom have a non-sharp boundary. Thus, atomic radius is generally estimated by knowing the distance between the atoms in the combined form.

Depending upon the nature of combining atoms, atomic radius can be of following types.

(i) Covalent Radius

If the combining atoms are non-metals (except noble gases), their radius is called the **covalent radius**.

Covalent radius is defined as, *"the one-half of the distance between the centres of nuclei of two covalently bonded atoms of the same element in a molecule."*

i.e. $r_{covalent} = 1/2$ [Internuclear distance between two covalently bonded atoms with a single bond]

For homonuclear diatomic molecule, $r_A = \frac{d_{A-A}}{2}$

For heteronuclear diatomic molecule, $d_{A-B} = r_A + r_B$

where, d_{AB} is the distance between two molecules *A* and *B* bonded covalently (having similar electronegativity).

(ii) Metallic Radius

In case of metals, the atomic radius is called the **metallic radius** and is defined as, *"the one-half of the internuclear distance separating the metal cores in the metallic crystal."*

(iii) van der Waals' Radius (Inert Gas Radius)

In case of noble gases, the atomic radius is called the **van der Waals' radius**, which is defined as *"one-half of the distance between the nuclei of two identical non-bonded isolated atoms".*

Since, the van der Waals' forces are very weak and hence, the internuclear distance between the atoms held by van der Waals' forces is much larger as compared to that between covalently bonded atoms.

Hence, van der Waals' radius is much larger than covalent radius. (In other words, we can also say that the radius of a noble gas is largest in its period as they are mono-atomic and are held by van der waals' forces).

Note The order of different atomic radius is van der Waals' radius > metallic radius >> covalent radius.

The van der Waals' radius is also called the **non-bonded radius** as it is the radius of non-bonded atoms or molecules.

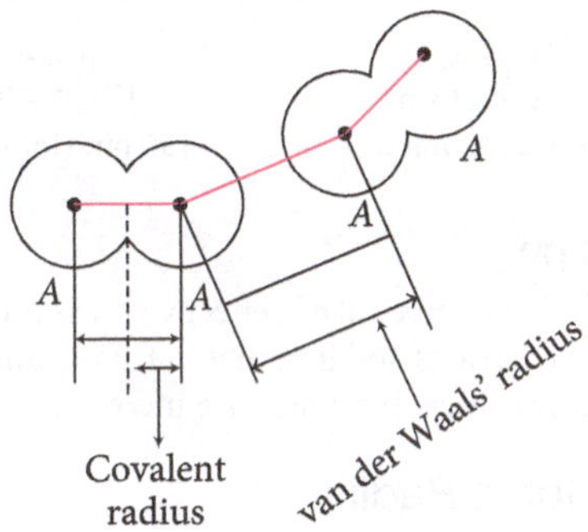

Covalent and van der Waals' radii of A_2 molecules

For the sake of convenience, we will use the term atomic radius for covalent, metallic and van der Waals' radii in this book. X-ray and other spectroscopic methods are used to measure the atomic radii.

Screening Effect and Effective Nuclear Charge

- The electrons of inner shells, also called the core electrons, shield or screen the outermost electron(s) from the attractive pull of the nucleus. This effect is therefore, called the **shielding (or screening) effect**.
- **Effective nuclear charge** (Z^*_{eff}) is defined as the net nuclear attraction towards the valence shell electrons or in other words, the actual nuclear charge whose electrostatic force of attraction is being experienced by the outer electron. Greater the effective nuclear charge, more tightly is the hold with nucleus.

Variation of Atomic Radii in the Periodic Table

The variation of atomic radii along a period and in a group in the periodic table are as follows

(i) Variation Along a Period

The atomic radius generally decreases from left to right along a period, as illustrated in the below graph for the elements of second period. This is because, within a period, the outer electron is added to the same valence shell, due to which the effective nuclear charge increases (as atomic number increases) and hence, the outer electron is held by the nucleus more tightly which results in decreased radii.

Here, it is important to note that the electrons of the same shell do not screen each other, hence the increased nuclear charge is not compensated by the screening effect and thus, results in decreased radii.

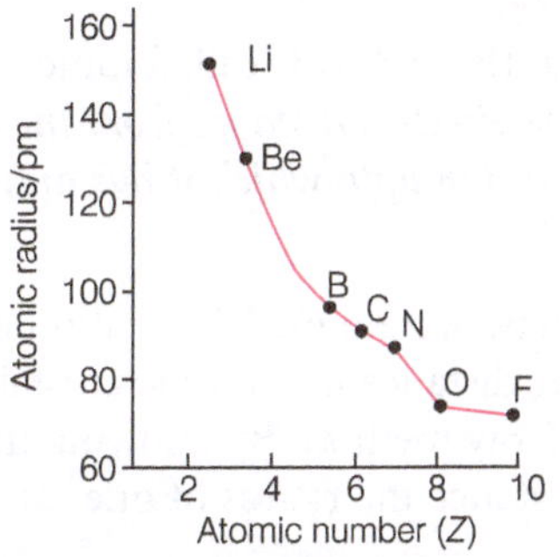

Variation of atomic radius with atomic number across the second period

EXCEPTION

- Transition elements show a little variation in their atomic radii due to poor shielding effect of d-electrons.
- Lanthanoid also exhibit a little variation in their atomic radii due to lanthanoid contraction.

(ii) Variation in a Group

The atomic radius generally increases on moving down a group as illustrated in the below graph for alkali metals and halogens.

This is because the electrons are added in the successive shells, i.e. principal quantum number (n) increases and thus, the electrons of inner shells shield the electrons of principal energy level from the pull of the nucleus.

Due to which the distance between the valence electron and the nucleus increases and hence, the atomic radius increases. Here, note that the shielding effect is more pronounced than the effect of increased nuclear charge.

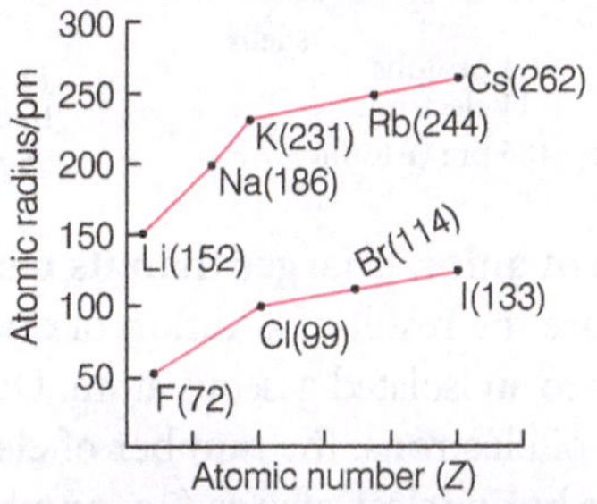

Variation of atomic radius with atomic number for alkali metals and halogens

EXCEPTION

Among *d*-block elements, the radii increases from member of first series to the corresponding member of second but the radius of members of second and third series are almost equal due to lanthanoid contraction.

Ionic Radius

In case of ions, the radius is called ionic radius and is defined as, *"the effective distance from the centre of the nucleus of an ion upto which it has an influence in the ionic bond"*.

The distance between the nuclei of cation and anion, i.e. internuclear distance in an ionic crystals can be measured by X-ray method. By knowing the internuclear distance the radius of one ion can be determined.

Internuclear distance = radii of cation + radii of anion

A **cation** is formed by removal of an electron from an atom and an **anion** is formed by gaining of an electron by an atom.

Comparison of the Ionic Radii with Corresponding Atomic Radii

The study of ionic radii leads to following two generalisation.

(i) **The size of cation is smaller than its parent atom.** A cation is formed by the loss of electron, thus, has fewer electrons while its nuclear charge (i.e. number of protons) is same as that present in parent atom.
Consequently, the nucleus binds the electrons more tightly (i.e. effective nuclear charge increases) and hence, the size of the atom decreases.

e.g.

$$Na \longrightarrow Na^+ + e^-$$

	Na	Na^+
	$1s^2\,2s^2\,2p^6\,3s^1$ } three shells	$1s^2\,2s^2\,2p^6$ } two shells
	11 protons, 11 electrons	11 protons, 10 electrons
Radii	186 pm (Atomic)	95 pm (Ionic)

(ii) **The size of anion is larger than its parent atom.** Anions are the result of addition of one or more electrons to an isolated gaseous atom. Due to addition of electrons, the number of electrons increases but nuclear charge (i.e. number of protons) remains the same.

Thus, more electrons are held by the same nuclear charge, i.e. effective nuclear charge decreases.

Further, addition of electron(s), also leads to the repulsion among the electrons, due to which the electron cloud gets expanded. This results in lesser force of attraction or more distance between the nucleus and the outermost electron(s), which in turn results in increased ionic radius.

e.g.

$$F + e^- \longrightarrow F^-$$

	F	F^-
	Two {$1s^2\,2s^2\,2p^5$ shells	$1s^2\,2s^2\,2p^6$ } Two shells
	9 protons, 9 electrons	9 protons, 10 electrons
Radii	64 pm (Atomic)	136 pm (Ionic)

TEACHER'S TIP

If number of $p^+ >$ number of e^-, effective nuclear charge increases, size decreases and if number of $p^+ <$ number of e^-; effective nuclear charge decreases, size increases.

Variation of Ionic Radii

Ionic radii shows same trend in the periodic table as shown by the atomic radii, i.e. it decreases across a period and increases on moving down the group.

Isoelectronic Species and their Radii

- Species (atoms or ions) having the same number of electrons are called the **isoelectronic species.**
- For these species, the number of valence electrons are same but nuclear charge is different, e.g. O^{2-}, F^-, Na^+ and Mg^{2+}.
- In case of isoelectronic species, as the magnitude of nuclear charge increases, force of attraction by the nucleus on the electrons increases and hence, ionic radius decreases. In short,

$$\text{Ionic radius} \propto \frac{1}{\text{nuclear charge}}$$

- The cation with the greater positive charge will have a smaller radius because of the greater attraction of the electrons.
- Anion with the greater negative charge will have the larger radius because the net repulsion of the electrons will out weigh the nuclear charge and the ion will expand in size.
- In case of O^{2-}, F^-, Na^+ and Mg^{2+} the order of their radii is $Mg^{2+} < Na^+ < F^- < O^{2-}$.

Ionisation Enthalpy (IE)

- The minimum amount of energy required to remove an electron from an isolated gaseous atom (X) in its ground state is called the **ionisation enthalpy**.
$$X(g) \longrightarrow X^+(g) + e^-; \Delta_i H = +\text{ve}$$
$$X(g) + \Delta_i H \longrightarrow X^+(g) + e^-$$
It is actually the quantitative measure of the tendency of an element to lose electron.
- The ionisation enthalpy can be expressed in **kJ mol^{-1}** or **kcal mol^{-1}** or **eV atom^{-1}**.
$$1 \text{ eV/atom} = 96.49 \text{ kJ mol}^{-1}$$
Thus, one electron volt is the energy acquired by an electron when it is moving under a potential difference of one volt.

Successive Ionisation Enthalpies

- The energy required to remove the most loosely bound electron from an isolated gaseous atom is called the **first ionisation enthalpy** and is represented by $\Delta_i H_1$.
e.g. $X(g) \longrightarrow X^+(g) + e^-; \Delta_i H_1 = +\text{ve}$
- Similarly, the energies required to remove the second, third or successive electrons from the positive ion, are called the **second, third** and **successive ionisation energies** respectively.
e.g. $X^+(g) + \Delta_i H_2 \longrightarrow X^{2+}(g) + e^-(g)$
$X^{2+}(g) + \Delta_i H_3 \longrightarrow X^{3+}(g) + e^-(g)$
where, $\Delta_i H_2$ and $\Delta_i H_3$ are the second and third ionisation enthalpies respectively.
- The second ionisation enthalpy is always higher than the first one. Similarly, the third ionisation enthalpy is higher than the second one and so on.
This is because, the positive ion has more effective nuclear charge which holds the remaining electrons more firmly and hence, a large amount of energy is required to remove the electron from it as compared to a neutral atom.
- Thus, the order of successive ionisation enthalpies is $\Delta_i H_3 > \Delta_i H_2 > \Delta_i H_1$.
- It is also interesting to note that the ionisation enthalpies are always positive. This is because energy is always required to remove an electron from an atom/ion.

Factors Affecting Ionisation Enthalpy

Ionisation enthalpy depends upon the several factors, which are discussed below

(i) Screening or Shielding Effect

In general, greater the screening (shielding) effect, easier is the removal of loosely bound electron and lesser is the ionisation enthalpy. Shielding effect is most effective when the orbitals of inner shells are completely filled, as present in case of alkali metals.

(ii) Nuclear Charge

The ionisation enthalpy increases as the nuclear charge increases. This is because nucleus with greater nuclear charge bound the electron more firmly and hence, large amount of energy is required to remove the electron from the atom.
e.g. The ionisation enthalpy increases across a period from left to right due to increased nuclear charge.

(iii) Penetration Effect of the Electrons

In case of a multielectron atoms, the order of penetrating power of different electrons of the same shell (i.e. having same value of n) follows the order $s > p > d > f$.

If penetration power is more, electron will be closer to the nucleus and held more firmly, thus, a large amount of energy is required to remove the electron, i.e. ionisation energy is higher.

(iv) Electronic Configuration

Since, the configuration with half-filled or fully-filled orbitals is more stable, so in case of atoms having such a configuration, ionisation energy is high because a large amount of energy is required to remove the electron.

Noble gases have highest ionisation enthalpies within their respective period because they have (ns^2np^6) configuration.

Variation of Ionisation Enthalpy in the Periodic Table

The variation of ionisation enthalpy along a period and in a group in the periodic table are as follows

(i) Variation Along a Period

On moving along a period from left to right, the successive addition of one electron results in increased nuclear charge but since the electrons are added to the orbitals of same principal quantum level, the shielding effect remains the same and is not enough to compensate for the increased nuclear charge (i.e. increased attraction of the electron to the nucleus).

Thus, increased nuclear charge outweighs the shielding effect across a period. As a result, the outermost electrons are held more and more firmly and hence, ionisation enthalpy increases across a period.

Note Ionisation enthalpy is maximum (highest) for noble gases and lowest for alkali metals in a period.

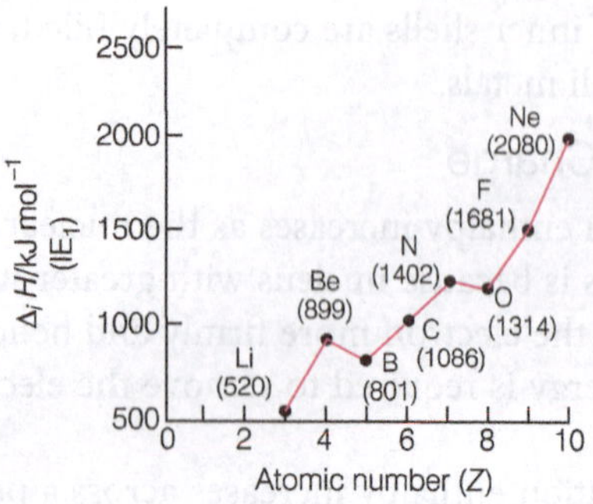

First ionisation enthalpies ($\Delta_i H$) of elements of the second period as a function of atomic number (Z).

EXCEPTION

I. **The first ionisation enthalpy of elements of group-2 is higher than the corresponding elements of group-13,** although the later have the greater nuclear charge.

Explanation The outer configuration of elements of second group is ns^2 (fully-filled) and that of thirteen group is ns^2np^1.

Therefore, it is easier to remove an electron from the *np* orbital as compared to *ns*-orbital (mainly due to penetration effect).

II. **The ionisation enthalpy of elements of group 15 is higher than that of corresponding elements of group 16.**

Explanation The valence shell configuration for group 15 elements is $ns^2\ np^3$ and for group 16 elements is ns^2np^4.

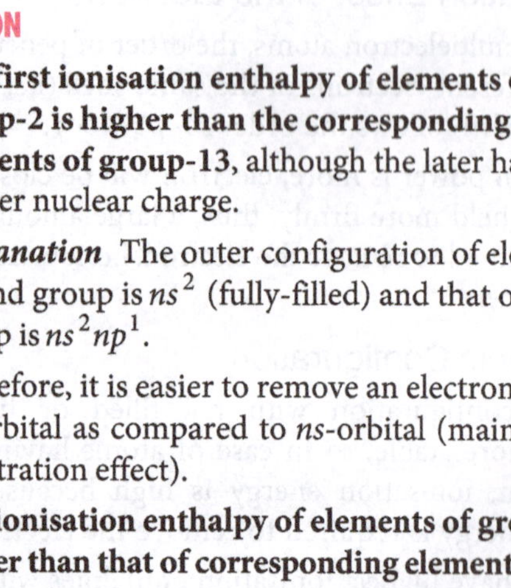

In case of group 16, two of the four *np*-electrons must occupy the same *np*-orbital and results in an increased electron-electron repulsion. This repulsion makes the removal of fourth electron from the *np*-orbital easier as compared to third electron from the same orbital.

Also, due to presence of half-filled *p*-orbitals in case of elements of group 15 than the incomplete *p*-orbitals in case of elements of group 16.

III. **Transition elements show a small variation in their ionisation enthalpy**

Explanation This can be explained on the basis of net effect of increased nuclear charge and shielding effect as shielding power of *d*-electrons is much lesser than the *s*-electrons.

(ii) Variation in a Group

On moving down a group, the ionisation enthalpy decreases. This can be explained as follows

- Increase in atomic size due to progressive addition of new energy level for each element.
- The nuclear charge increases due to addition of electrons but since the electrons are added to the new energy levels, i.e. distance between the valence electron(s) and nucleus increases, the shielding effect on the outermost electron(s) increases due to increase in the number of inner electrons.
- The increased atomic size and shielding effect outweighs the increasing nuclear charge and thus, a less amount of energy is required to remove the outermost electrons.
- Variation of $\Delta_i H_1$ for alkali metal is shown in the figure given below.

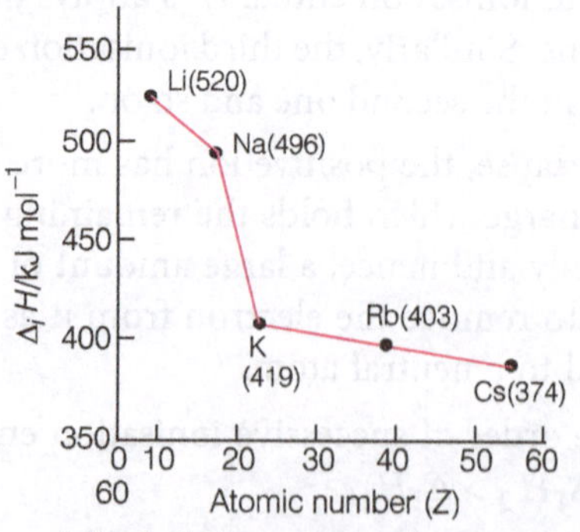

$\Delta_i H$ of alkali metals as a function of Z

Quick Test 3

1. Atomic radii of fluorine is 72 pm whereas atomic radii of neon is 160 pm. Why? *NCERT Exemplar*

2. Explain why cations are smaller and anions are larger in radii than their parent atoms? *NCERT*

3. (i) In group 1 of the periodic table, three elements *X*, *Y* and *Z* have ionic radii 133 pm, 95 pm, 60 pm respectively. Giving a reason, arrange these elements in the order of increasing atomic number in the group.

(ii) Give examples of three cations and three anions which are isoelectronic with neon.

4. Out of Na and Mg, which has higher second ionisation energy?

5. What are the various factors due to which the ionisation enthalpy of the main group elements tends to decrease down a group? *NCERT*

6. Four elements have the following first ionisation enthalpies (in kJ mol^{-1}); 869, 941, 1191 and 1142. The elements, in random order, are Se, Br, Te and I. Which element has an ionisation enthalpy of 869 kJ mol^{-1} and 1142 kJ mol^{-1} respectively?

7. The first ionisation enthalpy values (in kJ mol^{-1}) of group 13 elements are

B	Al	Ga	In	Tl
801	577	579	558	589

How would you explain this deviation from the general trend? *NCERT*

8. Energy of an electron in the ground state of the hydrogen atom is -2.18×10^{-18} J. Calculate the ionisation enthalpy of atomic hydrogen in terms of J mol^{-1}. *NCERT, Diksha*

Answer 8. 13.13×10^{5}

For Solutions, See QR Code on Pg. 120

3.8 Electron Gain Enthalpy ($\Delta_{eg}H$)

- When an electron is added to a gaseous atom (X) in its ground state to convert it into a negative ion, the enthalpy change accompanying the process is called the **electron gain enthalpy** ($\Delta_{eg}H$).
- It is a direct measure of the ease with which an atom attracts an electron to form anion.

  The equation can be represented by

  $$X(g)+e^- \longrightarrow X^-(g);\quad \Delta H=\Delta_{eg}H$$
- The most stable state of an atom is the ground state. If an isolated gaseous atom is in excited state, comparatively lesser energy will be released on adding an electron. So, electron gain enthalpies of gaseous atoms must be determined in their ground states.
- The values of electron gain enthalpy are expressed either in **electron volt per atom or kilo joules per mole of atoms.** e.g. Electron affinity of chlorine is -348 kJ mol^{-1}.
- **Nature of electron gain enthalpy** The electron gain enthalpy can be **positive** (i.e. endothermic process) **or negative** (i.e. exothermic process) depending upon the nature of element to which electron is to be added.

  However, for most of the elements, it is generally negative, i.e. energy is released when an electron is added to an isolated gaseous atom.

  e.g. The general electronic configuration for halogen family is ns^2np^5. Thus, to attain the stable noble gas electronic configuration, they have very high tendency to attract an electron. Hence, their electron gain enthalpy is highly negative.
- On the other hand, noble gases have large positive electron gain enthalpies because the electron has to be enter the next higher principal quantum level leading to a very unstable electronic configuration.

Note The **energy released** when an electron is added to an isolated gaseous atom is called the **electron affinity** (A_e). It is positive when energy is released on adding an electron to an atom (contrary to thermodynamic convention) and is negative if energy is required for adding an electron to an atom.

Successive Electron Gain Enthalpies

Generally, magnitude of first electron gain enthalpy is negative. However, when an electron is added to a negative ion, there is a repulsion between the electron and negative charge. To overcome this repulsion, energy has to be supplied.

Thus, the second and further electron gain enthalpies are generally positive, i.e. the process is endothermic. e.g. Let us study the addition of electrons to oxygen atom.

First electron gain enthalpy of O-atom

$$O(g)+e^- \longrightarrow O^-(g);\ \Delta_{eg}H_1=-141\text{ kJ}$$

(energy is released)

Second electron gain enthalpy of O-atom

$$O^- (g) + e^- \longrightarrow O^{2-} (g); \ \Delta_{e_g} H_2 = +780 \text{ kJ}$$

(energy is absorbed)

Factors Affecting Electron Gain Enthalpies

Electron gain enthalpy depends upon the following factors

(i) Atomic Size

As the atomic size increases, i.e. distance between the nucleus and outermost shell increases, the force of attraction between the two decreases.
Hence, the electron gain enthalpy becomes less negative.

(ii) Nuclear Charge

As the nuclear charge increases, force of attraction between the nucleus and incoming electron increases and hence, the electron gain enthalpy becomes more negative.

(iii) Electronic Configuration

In case of elements having half-filled or fully-filled outer shell, because of their higher stability, energy has to be supplied to add an electron, i.e. the value of electron gain enthalpy is positive, e.g. noble gases, elements of group 15, etc.

Variation of Electron Gain Enthalpy in the Periodic Table

The variation of electron gain enthalpy is not as regular as that of ionisation enthalpy.

The variation of electron gain enthalpy in the periodic table is shown as

(i) Variation Along a Period

On moving from left to right across a period, effective nuclear charge increases and hence size decreases, thus, the added electron on an average would be closer to the positively charged nucleus, i.e. strongly attracted by the nucleus.

Thus, the value of electron gain enthalpy becomes more negative as we move from left to right along a period.

EXCEPTION

Electron gain enthalpies of elements of group 2 and 15 is low because of their stable half-filled configuration but that of elements of group 18 is positive because of their complete valence shell.

(ii) Variation Along a Group

On moving down a group, the size of atom increases and hence, the distance between the nucleus and incoming electron increases or force of attraction between the nucleus and incoming electron decreases. Thus, the value of electron gain enthalpy becomes less negative.

EXCEPTION

The electron gain enthalpy of elements of second period (N, O, F) is less negative than the succeeding elements (P, S, Cl) of third period.

This is because in case of elements of second period, the incoming electron enters in the smaller $n = 2$ quantum level and hence, experience greater force of repulsion by the other electrons present in the level.

Whereas in elements of third period, it enters in larger $n = 3$ quantum level and hence, the force of repulsion is much lesser as compared to that in case of elements of second period.

Example 8 **Which of the following will have the most negative electron gain enthalpy and which is the least negative? (P, S, Cl, F) Explain your answer.** **NCERT**

Sol. As we know the negative value of electron gain enthalpy increases along a period and decreases on moving down the group.

But the elements of second period like F have lesser electron gain enthalpy than the corresponding element of third period. This is because of the smaller size and hence greater repulsion in case of F as compared to Cl.

Thus, the order of electron gain enthalpy is P < S < F < Cl. The electron gain enthalpy is most negative for chlorine and less negative for phosphorus.

3.9 Electronegativity

- A qualitative measure of the ability of an atom in a chemical compound to attract the shared pair of electrons towards itself is called **electronegativity**.
- Other properties such as electron gain enthalpy and ionisation enthalpy are related to the isolated state of atom but electronegativity is related to the combined or bonded state of atom.
- In general, greater the electronegativity, higher is its tendency to attract the shared pair of electron. Since, this tendency is highest in **fluorine**, so it **is the most electronegative element**. Further, noble gases because of their stable outermost electronic arrangement do not exhibit electronegativity.

- Ionisation energy and electron gain enthalpy are always constant but electronegativity is not a constant quantity.
- Electronegativity is not a measurable quantity, so several numerical scales of electronegativity of elements *viz.* Pauling scale, Mulliken-Jaffe scale, Allred-Rochow scale have been developed. The one which is most widely used is the Pauling scale.

Pauling Scale (For Calculating Electronegativity)

- It is the most widely used scale and was proposed by Linus Pauling, an American scientist, in 1922.

  He arbitrarily assigned a value of 4.0 to the most electronegative element, fluorine and calculate the electronegativity of other elements with respect to it by using the formula

  $$X_A - X_B = 0.1017\sqrt{\Delta}$$

  (if bond dissociation enthalpies are in kJ mol^{-1})

  Or

  $$X_A - X_B = 0.208\sqrt{\Delta}$$

  (if bond dissociation enthalpies are in kcal mol^{-1})

  where, $\Delta = E_{A-B} - \sqrt{E_{A-A} \times E_{B-B}}$

  $X_A - X_B$ = electronegativity difference between two atoms A and B.
- E_{A-B}, E_{A-A} and E_{B-B} = bond energies of the molecules AB, A_2 and B_2, respectively.

Factors Affecting the Magnitude of Electronegativity

Various factors which affect the magnitude of electronegativity are as follows

(i) Atomic Radius

As the atomic radius of the elements increases, the electronegativity value decreases, i.e.

$$\text{Electronegativity} \propto \frac{1}{\text{Atomic radius}}$$

(ii) Effective Nuclear Charge

The electronegativity value increases as the effective nuclear charge on the atomic nucleus increases.

$$\text{Electronegativity} \propto \text{Effective nuclear charge } (Z_{\text{eff}})$$

(iii) Oxidation State

The electronegativity increases as the oxidation state (i.e. the number of positive charge) of the atom increases.

(iv) Hybridisation

If the *s*-character in the hybridisation state of the atom increases, electronegativity also increases because *s*-electrons are comparatively close to the nucleus.

Variation of Electronegativity in the Periodic Table

The variation of electronegativity in the periodic table is given as follows

(i) Variation Along a Period

On moving from left to right across a period, as the effective nuclear charge increases and size decreases, the value of electronegativity increases due to increase in the attraction between the outer (or valence) electrons and the nucleus.

(ii) Variation Along a Group

On moving down a group, as the atomic size increases, the force of attraction between the outer (valence) electron and the nucleus decreases and hence, the electronegativity decreases.

Applications of Electronegativity

Some important applications of electronegativity are

(i) Nature of Bond

If the difference between the electronegativities of two atoms (bonded together) is less than 1.9, the bond formed between them is predominantly covalent and if this difference is more than 1.9, the bond is predominantly ionic, but if the difference is 1.9, the bond is 50% ionic and 50% covalent.

(ii) Metallic and Non-metallic Character

Non-metals have strong tendency to attract the electrons, so these are more electronegative. On the other hand, metals, because of their very less tendency to attract the electrons, generally have low electronegativity.

Thus, electronegativity is directly related to the non-metallic character but inversely related to the metallic character.

Hence, as the electronegativity increases across a period, the non-metallic character also increases (but metallic character decreases).

Similarly, the electronegativity decreases down a group, the non-metallic character decreases (but metallic character increases) down a group.

Difference between Electron Gain Enthalpy and Electronegativity

Electron gain enthalpy	Electronegativity
Electron gain enthalpy is the tendency of an isolated gaseous atom to attract an electron.	Electronegativity is the tendency of an atom in a molecule to attract the shared pair of electrons.
It is the absolute electron attracting power of an atom.	It is the relative attracting power of an atom.
It is the property of an isolated atoms.	It is the property of a bonded atom.
It can be experimentally measured.	It is only a relative number, cannot be measured experimentally.
Electron gain enthalpy value for an atom is constant.	Electronegativity of an atom is not constant.

The periodic trends of different periodic properties of elements in the periodic table are shown.

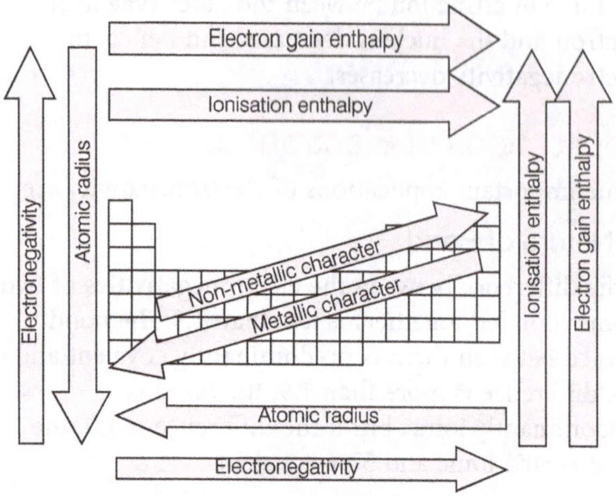

Periodic trends of elements in the periodic table

3.10 Periodic Trends in Chemical Properties

The periodic properties play a key role in the study of chemistry of different elements and their compounds. Moreover, these properties also affect the chemical behaviour of the elements to a larger extent.

However, most of trends in chemical properties of elements like diagonal relationships, inert pair effect, lanthanoid contraction and its effect will be discussed later along with the study of chemistry of different blocks. Here, we will discuss only some of the chemical properties.

Periodicity of Valency or Oxidation States

Valency of an element is defined as, "*the number of hydrogen or halogen atoms or double the number of oxygen atoms that combine(s) with an atom of the element.*"

For representative elements (*s* and *p*-block elements), valency is generally equal to the number of electrons present in the outermost (or valence) shell and or equal to eight minus the number of electrons present in the outermost shell.

Valency of Representative Elements

Group	1	2	13	14	15	16	17	18
Number of valence electron	1	2	3	4	5	6	7	8
Valency	1	2	3	4	3,5	2,6	1,7	0,8
	s-block		*p*-block					

However, now-a-days the term **oxidation state** is more in use as compared to valency. It is defined as, "*the charge acquired by an atom on the basis of electronegativities of other atoms in the molecule.*"

e.g.

- In the two oxygen compounds, OF_2 and Na_2O, the order of electronegativity of the elements is F > O > Na.
- In OF_2, each fluorine atom with outer electronic configuration $2s^2\ 2p^5$ shares its one electron with the oxygen. Being most electronegative, F has an oxidation state of –1.
- Oxygen with outer electronic configuration $2s^2\ 2p^4$, shares two electrons with two fluorine atoms and acquires two positive charge, i.e. its oxidation state in OF_2 is +2.
- Further, in Na_2O, oxygen being more electronegative accepts two electrons from two Na atoms (one from each Na atom) and hence, shows the oxidation state –2. Whereas Na with outer electronic configuration $3s^1$, loses this electrons to oxygen and thus, exhibits an oxidation state +1.
- The above discussion also shows that oxidation state of an element can be zero, positive or negative.
- Higher *p*-block elements show more stability for lower oxidation state because of inert pair effect (i.e. reluctance of *s*-electron of the valence shell to take part in bonding) e.g. Pb^{4+} is less stable than Pb^{2+}.
- For *d*-block elements, maximum oxidation state $=(n-1)\,d$ electron (unpaired) + *ns* electrons.

Variation of Valency in the Periodic Table

On moving from left to right along a period, the number of valence electrons increases from 1 to 8, the valency of the elements with respect to hydrogen and chlorine increases from 1 to 4 and then decreases to zero (in case of group-18 elements). It can be better understood by taking examples of different elements of second period.

Variation of Valency of Elements of Second Period

Group	1	2	13	14	15	16	17
Second period	Li	Be	B	C	N	O	F
Valence with respect to H	LiH (1)	BeH_2 (2)	BH_3 or B_2H_6 (6)	CH_4 (4)	NH_3 (3)	H_2O (2)	HF (1)
Valence with respect to Cl	LiCl (1)	$BeCl_2$ (2)	BCl_3 (3)	CCl_4 (4)	NCl_3 (3)	Cl_2O (2)	ClF (1)

In a group, all the elements have same valency as the number of valence electrons are same in all.

Note Transition elements and actinoids also exhibit variable valency which we shall study later.

Prediction of the Formula of a Compound from Valency

- From the valencies of the elements, it is possible to predict the formula of the compound formed by them. e.g. If we have element beryllium and chlorine and want to know the formula of the compound formed by these elements, then first of all, we have to find their valency.
- Beryllium belongs to group second (2) and has 2 valence electrons, chlorine however, belongs to halogen with the valence of 1. When these two combine, the formula of the compound obtained would be $BeCl_2$.

Anomalous Properties of Second Period Elements

The first member of each group of the representative elements [i.e. group 1 (lithium), 2 (beryllium) and group 13 to 17 (boron to fluorine)] differ from the other members of their respective groups.

This anomalous behaviour is because of (*i*) their small size (*ii*) large charge/radius ratio (*iii*) high electronegativity (*iv*) absence of *d*-orbitals.

Some of the anomalous properties are as follows.

(i) Diagonal Relationship

Some elements of second period like lithium, beryllium and boron resemble in their properties with the corresponding element of third period placed diagonally to them. This similarity in properties of elements placed diagonally to each other is called the **diagonal relationship in the periodic properties.**

e.g.

Group 1		Group 2		Group 13		Group 14
Li	↘	Be	↘	B	↘	C
Na		Mg		Al		Si

(ii) Nature of Compounds

The nature of compounds formed by lithium, beryllium and boron is generally covalent but other members of their respective groups predominantly form ionic compounds.

e.g. LiCl is covalent but NaCl is purely ionic.

(iii) Maximum Covalency

In the first member of each group, only four valence orbitals (i.e. one 2*s* and three 2*p* orbitals) are available for bonding, whereas for the second members, the number of available valence orbitals is nine (i.e. one 3*s*, three 3*p* and five 3*d*).

Thus, the maximum covalency exhibited by first member of each group is 4 (e.g. boron can only form $[BF_4^-]$ but not $[BF_6^-]$) whereas the other members of the group can expand their valence shell to show a covalency of 6. e.g. Aluminium generally form $[AlF_6]^{3-}$. This is because of the presence of *d*-orbital in it.

(iv) $p\pi$-$p\pi$ Multiple Bonding

Because of their smaller size and higher electronegativity, the first member of each group of *p*-block show a higher tendency to form $p\pi$ -$p\pi$ multiple bonds with its own atoms (like C=C, C≡C, N≡N etc.) and with the other elements of second period (like C=O, C=N, C≡N, N=O) as compared to the subsequent members of the same group.

Periodic Trends and Chemical Reactivity

We shall now try to explore relationships between the fundamental properties (like, atomic and ionic radii, ionisation enthalpy, electron gain enthalpy and valence) of elements with their chemical reactivity.

- The ionisation enthalpy of the extreme left element in a period is the least and electron gain enthalpy of the element on the extreme right is the highest negative (except noble gases).
- The chemical reactivity of the alkali metals is maximum (at the extreme left) with their tendency to lose an electron, while at the extreme right, halogens by the gain of an electron have maximum chemical reactivity.
- The centre part of the periodic table has the lowest chemical reactivity.
- The normal oxides of the elements present on extreme left are the most basic (e.g. Na_2O) as they form strong base when dissolved in water and the oxides of the elements present on extreme right are most acidic (e.g. Cl_2O_7) as they give strong acid when dissolved in water.
- The amphoteric oxides show the acidic and basic character. They behave as acidic with bases and basic with acids. On the other hand, the neutral oxides have no acidic or basic properties.
- Oxides of the elements present in the centre are generally neutral (e.g. CO, NO, N_2O, etc) or amphoteric (e.g. Al_2O_3, As_2O_3).

$$\underset{\text{Alumina}}{Al_2O_3(s)} + \underset{\text{Acid}}{6\,HCl(aq)} \longrightarrow 2\,AlCl_3(aq) + 3H_2O(l)$$

$$\underset{\text{Alumina}}{Al_2O_3(s)} + \underset{\text{Base}}{2\,NaOH(aq)} + 3H_2O(l) \longrightarrow 2Na[Al(OH)_4](aq)$$

- Thus, in short, it can be said that across a period from left to right, the acidic character of oxides increases whereas basic character decreases.
- However, on moving down the group, acidic character of oxides decreases (because non-metallic character decreases) whereas basic character of oxides increases (due to increase in metallic character).

Trends of Some Other Chemical Properties

Trends of some other chemical properties are as follows

(i) Electropositive Character or Metallic Character

It is the tendency of an atom to lose its outermost electron to form cation. It generally increases as the ionisation enthalpy decreases. Thus, it is highest for alkali metals and lowest for halogens.

On moving down the group, electropositive character or metallic character increases due to decrease in ionisation enthalpy. Transition elements, however, are less electropositive than group 1 and 2 metals because of their lower ionisation enthalpy.

(ii) Electronegative Character or Non-metallic Character

It is the tendency of an element to accept electrons to form anion. It generally increases along a period from left to right and decreases on moving down a group.

(iii) Oxidising and Reducing Property

Reducing property depends upon the tendency to lose electron, i.e. electropositive or metallic character whereas oxidising property depends upon the tendency to gain electron, i.e. electronegative or non-metallic character. In the periodic table, reducing property increases down the group whereas oxidising property decreases down the group. Alkali metals are strong reducing agents while halogens are strong oxidising agents.

The increasing order of reducing character of alkali metal is Na < K < Rb < Cs. On the other hand, the increasing order of oxidising character of halogens is $I_2 < Br_2 < Cl_2 < F_2$.

Quick Test 4

1. Arrange the following elements in order of decreasing electron gain enthalpy : B, C, N, O.
2. Would you expect the second electron gain enthalpy of O as positive, more negative or less negative than the first? Justify your answer. **NCERT**
3. Nitrogen has positive electron gain enthalpy whereas oxygen has negative. However, oxygen has lower ionisation enthalpy than nitrogen. Explain. **NCERT Exemplar**
4. (i) Are the oxidation state and covalency of Al in $[AlCl(H_2O)_5]^{2+}$ same? **NCERT, Diksha**
   (ii) Among alkali metals which element do you expect to be least electronegative and why? **NCERT Exemplar**
5. First member of each group of representative elements (i.e. *s*-and *p*-block elements) shows anomalous behaviour. Illustrate with two examples. **NCERT Exemplar**
6. Show by a chemical reaction with water that Na_2O is a basic oxide and Cl_2O_7 is an acidic oxide. **NCERT, Diksha**
7. The increasing order of reactivity among group 1 elements is Li < Na < K < Rb < Cs whereas that among group 17 elements is F > Cl > Br > I. Explain. **NCERT**
8. How does the metallic and non-metallic character vary on moving from left to right in a period? **NCERT Exemplar**

For Solutions, See QR Code on Pg. 120

Mind Map

Classification of Elements and Periodicity in Properties

Periodic Table
Arrangement of elements on the basis of similarity and dissimilarity in properties to systematise their study.

Earlier Attempts
(i) Dobereiner's Triads

In the triad of elements, the atomic weight of middle element is the arithmetic mean of other two elements.

(ii) Newland's Law of Octaves

When elements are arranged in increasing order of their weights ,the properties of every eigth element are similar to the first one.

(iii) Lothar Mayer's Classification

When elements are arranged in increasing order of their atomic weights, similarities in physical and chemical properties appear at regular intervals.

(iv) Mendeleev's Periodic Table

- It is based on Mendeleev's periodic law which states that the properties of the elements are the periodic function of their atomic weights.
- This table contains 8 groups and 7 periods.

Long Form of Periodic Table
It is based on modern periodic law which states that the properties of the elements are the periodic functions of their atomic numbers.
This table contains 18 groups and 7 periods.
The elements present in 1,2,3,4,5,6 and 7 periods are respectively 2,8,8,18,18,32 and 32.

Nomenclature of Elements with Atomic Number > 100
Root word for each number + ium
e.g., 112 = ununbium

Position of Elements in the Periodic Table
- Period = Principal quantum number of valence shell.
- Block = Orbital receiving last electron.
- Group = Number of valence electrons (for s and p-block)
  $= (n-1)\ de^- + nse^-$ (for d-block)
  $= 3$ (for f-block)

s, p, d, f-Blocks
- ***s*-Blocks**
  General configuration (GC) : ns^{1-2}
  Includes group 1 and 2
- ***p*-Blocks**
  GC : ns^2, np^{1-6}
  Includes mainly non-metals.
- ***d*-Blocks**
  GC : $(n-1)\ d^{1-10}\ ns^{(0-2)}$
  Also called transition elements.
- ***f*-Blocks**
  GC : $(n-2)\ f^{1-14}(n-1)d^{0-1}ns^2$
  Also called inner transition element.
  Contains lanthanoids and actinoids.

Periodic Properties
Properties showing regular gradation along the period and group.

Physical Properties
1. Atomic Radius
It may be covalent, metallic or van der Waals' radii.
It decreases along a period from left to right but increases on moving down the group.

2. Ionic Radius
It also follows the same trend as atomic radius. A cation is smaller than its parent atom but an anion is larger than its parent atom.

3. Ionisation Energy (IE)
It is the minimum amount of energy required to remove an electron from isolated gaseous atom in its ground state. It decreases in a group and increases along a period.

4. Electron Gain Enthalpy ($\Delta_{eg}H$)
It is the energy change occurring during the conversion of an atom into anion. It also follows the same trend as IE.

5. Electronegativity
It is the electron attracting power of an element in a compound. It also follows the same trend as IE.

Chemical Properties

Metallic and Non-metallic Character
Metallic character increases on moving down a group and decreases along a period. Reverse is true for non-metallic character.

Oxidising and Reducing Property
In s-block, the reducing property increases but oxidising decreases down the group. In case of p-block, the order is reverse.

Valency
It is equal to the number of electrons in the outermost orbitals and/or equal to eight minus the number of outermost electrons.

Nature of Oxides
Acidic nature of oxides increases along a period form left to right but decreases on moving down the group. Opposite is true for basic nature.

EXAM PATTERN QUESTIONS

Objective Type Questions

Multiple Choice Questions (MCQs)

[1 Mark]

1. Upto which element Newland's law of octave is applicable? Diksha

(a) Chromium (b) Calcium
(c) Cerium (d) Caesium

2. Mendeleev's left the gap under aluminium and a gap under silicon having atomic weights 68 and 72 respectively. These elements are respectively

(a) Eka-aluminium and Eka-silicon
(b) aluminium and silicon
(c) Eka-germanium and Eka-silicon
(d) Eka-aluminium and Eka-germanium

3. The horizontal rows and the vertical columns in the periodic table are termed as respectively

(a) periods, groups (b) groups, periods
(c) series, periods (d) family, periods

4. The symbol and name according to the IUPAC system for the element with atomic number 120, respectively are

(a) Ubn and unbinilium
(b) Ubn and unbiunium
(c) Ubn and unnilbium
(d) Ubn and unnilium

5. Which one of the following is not the representative elements?

(a) Fe (b) K
(c) Ba (d) N

6. The elements in which electrons are progressively filled in 4*f*-orbital are called NCERT Exemplar

(a) actinoids (b) transition elements
(c) lanthanoids (d) halogens

7. Which of the following is not an actinoid? NCERT Exemplar

(a) Curium ($Z = 96$)
(b) Californium ($Z = 98$)
(c) Uranium ($Z = 92$)
(d) Terbium ($Z = 65$)

8. An element *A* belongs to third period and fifteenth group of the periodic table. Which one of the following is correct regarding the outer electronic configuration of *A*? NCERT

(a) It has completely filled *s*-orbital and *p*-orbital.
(b) It has partially filled *d*-orbitals and completely filled *s*-orbital.
(c) It has half-filled *d*-orbitals and completely filled *s*-orbitals.
(d) It has completely filled *s*-orbital and half-filled *p*-orbitals.

9. An element has electronic configuration $1s^2 2s^2 2p^6 3s^2 3p^6 3d^1 4s^2$. Predict its period, group and block. Diksha

(a) Period = 4, Group = 3, Block = *s*
(b) Period = 3, Group = 2, Block = *s*
(c) Period = 4, Group = 3, Block = *d*
(d) Period = 3, Group = 12, Block = *d*

10. Match Column I with Column II and select the correct option using given codes.

	Column I (Elements)		Column II (Properties)
A.	He	(i)	Highest electronegativity
B.	F	(ii)	Most electropositive
C.	Rb	(iii)	Strongest reducing agent
D.	Li	(iv)	Highest ionisation energy

Codes

	A	B	C	D
(a)	(iv)	(ii)	(iii)	(i)
(b)	(i)	(iv)	(ii)	(iii)
(c)	(iv)	(i)	(iii)	(ii)
(d)	(iv)	(i)	(ii)	(iii)

11. An element of atomic weight 40 has 2, 8, 8, 2 as the electronic configuration. Which one of the following statements regarding this element is not correct? Competency Based Que.

(a) It belongs to II group of the periodic table.
(b) It has 20 neutrons.
(c) The formula of its oxide is MO_3.
(d) It belongs to 4th period of the periodic table.

12. If the bond distance in chlorine molecule (Cl_2) is 198 pm, then the radius of chlorine is

(a) 198 pm (b) 49.5 pm (c) 99 pm (d) 24.75 pm

13. The order of screening effect of electrons of *s, p, d* and *f*-orbitals of a given shell of an atom on its outer shell electrons is **NCERT Exemplar**

(a) $s > p > d > f$ (b) $f > d > p > s$
(c) $p < d < s > f$ (d) $f > p > s > d$

14. Which of the following is the correct order of size of the given species? **NCERT Exemplar**

(a) $I > I^- > I^+$ (b) $I^+ > I^- > I$
(c) $I > I^+ > I^-$ (d) $I^- > I > I^+$

15. Consider the isoelectronic species, Na^+, Mg^{2+}, F^- and O^{2-}. The correct order of increasing length of their radii is **NCERT Exemplar**

(a) $F^- < O^{2-} < Mg^{2+} < Na^+$
(b) $Mg^{2+} < Na^+ < F^- < O^{2-}$
(c) $O^{2-} < F^- < Na^+ < Mg^{2+}$
(d) $O^{2-} < F^- < Mg^{2+} < Na^+$

16. Consider the following graph.

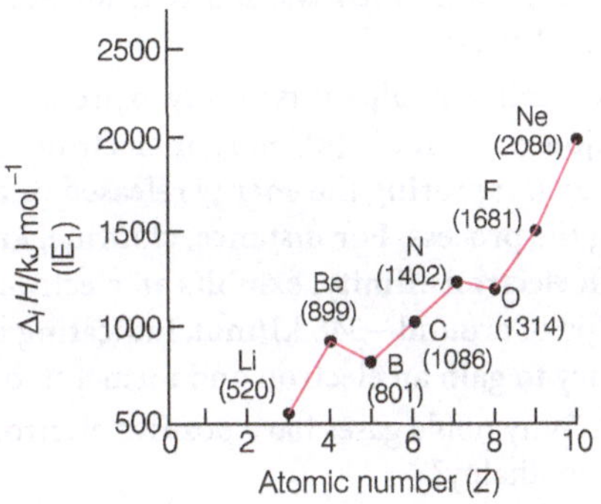

What could be the possible reason for a dip at boron (B) in the above plot? **NCERT**

(a) Size of boron is smaller than Be.
(b) 2*p* electrons are more shielded as compared to 2*s* electrons.
(c) The penetration of a 2*s*-electron is less than that of a 2*p*-electron.
(d) Size of boron is equal to Be.

17. The ionisation energy of nitrogen is more than oxygen because of

(a) more attraction of electrons by the nucleus.
(b) the extra stability of half-filled *p*-orbitals.
(c) the ionic radius of nitrogen atom is smaller.
(d) All of the above are correct.

18. The first ionisation enthalpies of Na, Mg, Al and Si are in the order **NCERT Exemplar**

(a) Na < Mg > Al < Si
(b) Na > Mg > Al > Si
(c) Na < Mg < Al < Si
(d) Na > Mg > Al < Si

19. Among halogens, the correct order of amount of energy released in electron gain (electron gain enthalpy) is **NCERT Exemplar**

(a) F > Cl > Br > I (b) F > Cl < Br < I
(c) F < Cl > Br > I (d) F < Cl < Br < I

20. Consider the following table,

	Column I (Atomic number)	Column II (Position in the periodic table)	Column III (Elements)
A.	52	*s*-block	Te
B.	56	*A*	Ba
C.	57	*d*-block	*B*
D.	60	*C*	Nd

A, *B* and *C* are **Competency Based Que.**

(a) *s*-block, La, *f*-block
(b) *p*-block, Cs, *d*-block
(c) *f*-block, Cs, *p*-block
(d) *p*-block, La, *f*-block

21. What effect is observed, on the size of an atom when an electron is removed and in another case an electron is added to the same atom? **Competency Based Que.**

(a) Size increases and decreases respectively.
(b) Size decreases and increases respectively.
(c) Size increases in both cases.
(d) Size decreases in both cases.

22. In general, the properties that decrease and increase down a group in the periodic table, respectively are **NCERT**

(a) electronegativity and atomic radius
(b) electronegativity and electron gain enthalpy
(c) electron gain enthalpy and electronegativity
(d) atomic radius and electronegativity

23. An element in the third row of the periodic table has atomic number 11. It is .... **Diksha**

(a) a metal with oxidation number +3
(b) a metal with oxidation number +1
(c) a non-metal with oxidation number −3
(d) a non-metal with oxidation number −1

24. The nature of normal oxide formed by the element present on extreme left in the periodic table is

(a) most acidic
(b) most basic
(c) amphoteric
(d) neutral

Assertion-Reason [1 Mark]

Directions (Q. Nos. 25-34) In the following questions an Assertion (A) is followed by a corresponding Reason (R). Use the following keys to choose the appropriate answer.

(a) Both (A) and (R) are correct and (R) is the correct explanation of (A).
(b) Both (A) and (R) are correct but (R) is not the correct explanation of (A).
(c) (A) is correct but (R) is incorrect.
(d) (A) is incorrect but (R) is correct.

25. **Assertion** (A) Element in the same vertical column have similar properties.

Reason (R) Elements have periodic dependence upon the atomic number.

26. **Assertion** (A) Noble gases are highly reactive.

Reason (R) Noble gases have stable closed shell electronic configuration.

27. **Assertion** (A) The atomic and ionic radii generally decreases toward right in a period.

Reason (R) The ionisation enthalpy increases on moving towards left in a period.

28. **Assertion** (A) Na^+ and Al^{3+} are isoelectronic.

Reason (R) Na belongs to *s*-block, while Al belongs to *p*-block.

29. **Assertion** (A) Be and Al show some similar properties.

Reason (R) The metallic radius of Be is less than the metallic radius of Al.

30. **Assertion** (A) Isoelectronic species have same radii.

Reason (R) They contain same number of electrons.

31. **Assertion** (A) The highest IE in a period is shown by noble gases.

Reason (R) Noble gases are at the extreme right of the period.

32. **Assertion** (A) First ionisation enthalpy for nitrogen is lower than that of oxygen.

Reason (R) Across a period, effective nuclear charge increases.

33. **Assertion** (A) Removal of *s*-electron is relatively difficult than removal of *p*-electrons of the same main shell.

Reason (R) *s*-electron are closer to the nucleus than *p*-electron of the same shell and hence are more strongly attracted by nucleus. **Competency Based Que.**

34. **Assertion** (A) The elements having $1s^2, 2s^2, 2p^6, 3s^2$ and $1s^2, 2s^2$ electronic configuration belong to same group.

Reason (R) Both have same outermost electronic configuration. **Competency Based Que.**

Case-Study [4 Marks]

35. **Read the given case and answer the following questions.**

The fundamental stability of an atom is most readily observed in its ground state, the lowest energy state where it naturally resides. When an isolated gaseous atom is excited, the addition of an electron releases comparatively less energy. Therefore, to achieve accurate measurements, electron gain enthalpies are determined exclusively for atoms in their ground state. This is essential because electron gain enthalpy, much like ionisation enthalpy, provides insights into an atom's tendency to attract electrons, a key factor in forming stable anions.

To accurately define electron gain enthalpy, it is essential to specify that the atom must be in an isolated, gaseous state and in its ground energy level. This precision in definition ensures that the measurement reflects the atom's intrinsic ability to attract an additional electron.

Electron gain enthalpy is typically expressed in units of kilojoules per mole (kJ/mol) or electron volts per atom (eV), capturing the energy released or absorbed during the process. For instance, chlorine, known for its high electron affinity, exhibits an electron gain enthalpy of around −348 kJ/mol, indicating a strong tendency to gain an electron and form a stable anion.

(i) (a) Why noble gases have positive electron gain enthalpy?

(b) What is the main factor affecting electron gain enthalpy?

(ii) Why is the electron gain enthalpy of O or F is less than that of S or Cl?

(iii) Give the order of the electron gain enthalpy (in kJ/mol) of fluorine, chlorine, bromine andiodine.

Or Which of the following represents the correct order of increasing electron gain enthalpy with negative sign for the elements O,S, F and Cl?

36. **Read the given case and answer the following questions.**

In the modern periodic table, elements are arranged in order of increasing atomic numbers which is related to the electronic configuration.

Depending upon the type of orbitals receiving the last electron, the elements in the periodic table have been divided into four blocks, *viz, s, p, d* and *f*.

The modern periodic table consists of 7 periods and 18 groups. Each period begins with the filling of a new energy shell. In accordance with the Aufbau principle, the seven periods (1 to 7) have 2, 8, 8, 18, 18, 32, and 32 elements respectively.

The seventh period is still incomplete. To avoid the periodic table being too long, the two series of *f*-block elements, called lanthanoids and actinoids are placed to the bottom of the main body of the periodic table. Competency Based Que.

(i) The element with atomic number 57 belongs to which group. Explain?

(ii) The outermost electronic configuration of last element of *p*-block in 6th period is

(a) $4f^{14}5d^{10}6s^26p^6$
(b) $4f^{14}5d^{10}6s^26p^5$
(c) $5f^{14}6d^{10}7s^27p^5$
(d) $5f^{14}6d^{10}7s^27p^6$

(iii) Among the given electronic configuration of some elements;

I. $1s^22s^22p^2$ II. $1s^22s^22p^63s^2$
III. $1s^22s^22p^63s^23p^3$ IV. $1s^22s^22p^63s^23p^2$

How many of them will belong to the same group in the periodic table?

(a) 3 (b) 4 (c) 2 (d) 1

Or The electronic configuration of element which is just above the element with the atomic number 43 in the same group is

(a) $1s^22s^22p^63s^23p^63d^54s^2$
(b) $1s^22s^22p^63s^23p^63d^54s^1$
(c) $1s^22s^22p^63s^23p^63d^34s^2$
(d) $1s^22s^22p^63s^23p^63d^44s^2$

Subjective Type Questions

Short Answer Type I Questions [2 Marks]

1. (i) An element *X* belongs to the third period of *p*-block. It has 4 electrons in the outermost shell. Name the element.
(ii) What is the most important cause of periodicity?

2. (i) A boy has reported the radii of Cu, Cu^+, Cu^{2+} as 0.096 nm, 0.122 nm and 0.072 nm respectively. However, it has been noticed that he interchanged the values by mistake. Assign the correct values to different species.
(ii) Noble gases have more size than halogens, Explain why? Competency Based Que.

3. Name the species that will be isoelectronic with the following atoms or ions.
(i) Na (ii) Cl^-

4. Would you expect the first ionisation enthalpies for two isotopes of the same element to be the same or different? Justify your answer. NCERT

5. Give reasons for the following statements.
(i) Halogens act as good oxidising agents.
(ii) Electron gain enthalpy of noble gases is almost zero.

6. (i) Among alkali metals which element do you expect to be least electronegative and why? NCERT Exemplar
(ii) Name one metal and one halogen which is liquid at 30°C.

7. Arrange the following elements N, P, O and S in the order of
(i) increasing first ionisation enthalpy.
(ii) increasing non-metallic characters.

8. Arrange the following elements in the increasing order of non-metallic character B, C, Si, N, F.

9. Eka-aluminium and eka-silicon were the names given by Mendeleev for the unknown elements gallium and germanium respectively. A recently discovered element was first named as eka-mercury. What is its atomic number? Write its group number, electronic configuration, IUPAC and official names. Competency Based Que.

10. On the basis of quantum numbers, justify that sixth period of the periodic table should have 32 elements. NCERT

11. Write answers for the following.
(i) Which orbitals are filled with electrons in third period?
(ii) What are transuranium elements?
(iii) Which series comprises of all radioactive elements?

Short Answer Type II Questions [3 Marks]

12. What do you understand by isoelectronic species? Name a species that will be isoelectronic with each of the following atoms or ions. NCERT, Diksha
(i) F^- (ii) Ar (iii) Mg^{2+} (iv) Rb^+

13. Consider the following species N^{3-}, O^{2-}, F^-, Na^+, Mg^{2+} and Al^{3+}.
(i) What is common in them?
(ii) Arrange them in the order of increasing ionic radii. **NCERT**

14. Which of the following species will have the largest and the smallest size? Mg, Mg^{2+}, Al, Al^{3+}. **NCERT**

15. Which of the elements Na, Mg, Si and P would have the greatest difference between the first and second ionisation enthalpies ? Briefly explain your answer.

16. The first ionisation enthalpy ($\Delta_i H$) values of the third period elements, Na, Mg and Si are respectively 496, 737 and 786 kJ mol^{-1}. Predict whether the first $\Delta_i H$ value for Al will be more close to 575 or 760 kJ mol^{-1}? Justify your answer. **NCERT**

17. Answer the following questions.
(i) Which is largest in size Cu^+, Cu^{2+} or Cu and why?
(ii) Which element in periodic table has highest ionisation energy (IE)?
(iii) Which element is more metallic Mg or Al and why?

18. Among the elements B, Al, C and Si,
(i) which element has the highest first ionisation enthalpy?
(ii) which element has the most metallic character?
Justify your answer in each case. **NCERT Exemplar, Diksha**

19. Which of the following pairs of elements would have a more negative electron gain enthalpy?
(i) O or F (ii) F or Cl

20. How would you react to the statement that the electronegativity of N on Pauling scale is 3.0 in all the nitrogen compounds? **NCERT**

21. Explain, why the electronegativity values of noble gases are zero while those of halogens are the highest in each period? **NCERT**

22. Using the periodic table, predict the formulae of compounds which might be formed by the following pairs of elements;
(i) silicon and bromine
(ii) aluminium and sulphur. **NCERT**

23. Match the correct ionisation enthalpies and electron gain enthalpies of the following elements.

	Elements		$\Delta_i H_1$	$\Delta_i H_2$	$\Delta_{eg} H$
(i)	Most reactive non-metal	A.	419	3051	−48
(ii)	Most reactive metal	B.	1681	3374	−328
(iii)	Least reactive element	C.	738	1451	−40
(iv)	Metal forming binary halide	D.	2372	5251	+48

Competency Based Que.

Long Answer Type Questions [5 Marks]

24. Justify the given statement with suitable examples "the properties of the elements are a periodic function of their atomic numbers". **NCERT Exemplar**

25. Name the four blocks into which the elements of the periodic table have been classified. Why are they named so?

List the groups of periodic table belonging to each block. Also give the general characteristics of *p* and *f*-block elements. **Diksha**

26. Which elements have the following electronic configurations? (Use only the periodic table.) **Competency Based Que.**
(i) $1s^2, 2s^2, 2p^5$
(ii) [Ar] $4s^2, 3d^{10}, 4p^1$
(iii) [Xe] $6s^2$
(iv) [Xe] $6s^2, 5d^1, 4f^7$
(v) [Ar] $4s^1, 3d^{10}$ (exception to rules)

27. Use the periodic table to answer the following questions.
(i) Identify an element with five electrons in the outer subshell.
(ii) Identify an element that would tend to lose two electrons.
(iii) Identify an element that would tend to gain two electrons.
(iv) Identify the group having metal, non-metal, liquid as well as gas at the room temperature. **NCERT**

28. Ionisation enthalpies of elements of second period are given below.

Ionisation enthalpy/kcal mol^{-1} : 520, 899, 801, 1086, 1402, 1314, 1681, 2080.

Match the correct enthalpy with the elements and complete the graph given in figure. Also write symbols of elements with their atomic number. **NCERT Exemplar**

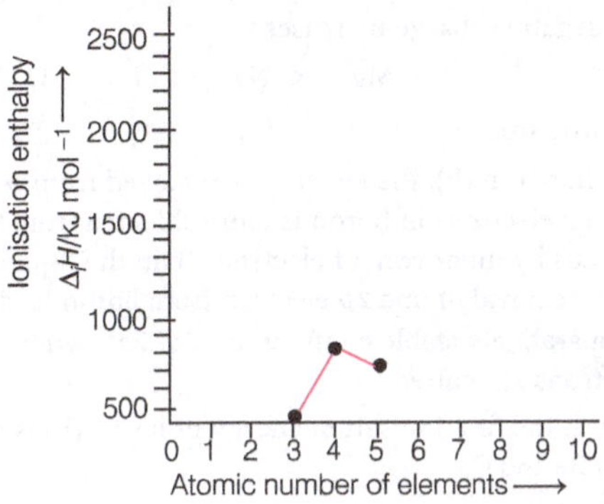

29. (i) Among the second period elements, the actual ionisation enthalpies are in the order.

$$Li < B < Be < C < O < N < F < Ne$$

Explain why?

(a) Be has higher $\Delta_i H$ than B ?

(b) O has lower $\Delta_i H$ than N and F? **NCERT**

(ii) Which one (atom/ion) in the following pairs has higher electron gain enthalpy?

(a) O^-, S (b) O, S^- (c) O^-, S^- (d) N^-, P

30. Discuss the factors affecting electron gain enthalpy and the trend in its variation in the periodic table. **NCERT Exemplar**

31. Predict the formulae of the stable binary compounds that would be formed by the combination of the following pairs of elements.

(i) Lithium and oxygen

(ii) Magnesium and nitrogen

(iii) Aluminium and iodine

(iv) Silicon and oxygen

(v) Phosphorus and fluorine

(vi) Element 71 and fluorine **NCERT**

32. *p*-block elements form acidic, basic and amphoteric oxides. Explain each property by giving two examples and also write the reactions of these oxides with water. **NCERT Exemplar**

Hints & Solutions

Objective Type Questions

1. (b) Newlands' law of octaves is applicable till calcium ($Z = 20$).

2. (a) Mendeleev left the gap under aluminium and a gap under silicon, are called Eka-aluminium and Eka-silicon, respectively.

3. (a) The horizontal rows (which Mendeleev called **series**) are called **periods** and the vertical columns are called **groups**.

4. (a) Atomic number $(Z) = 120$

IUPAC name = Unbinilium

Symbol = Ubn

5. (a) Fe (iron) is not the representative element as it belongs to d-block, so, it is a transition element.

6. (c) The elements in which electrons are progressively filled in $4f$-orbital are called **lanthanoids**. Lanthanoids consist of elements from $Z = 58$ (cerium) to 71 (lutetium).

7. (d) Elements with atomic number, $Z = 90$ to 103 are called actinoids. Thus, terbium ($Z = 65$) is not an actinoid instead terbium belong to lanthanoids.

8. (d) The element A can be phosphorus (P) and its electronic configuration is

$A(\text{P}) = 1s^2, 2s^2 2p^6, 3s^2 3p^3$

So, element 'A' has completely filled s-orbital and half-filled p-orbitals.

9. (c) The maximum value of principal quantum number (n) is 4 so, period = 4. Since, the last electron enters d-orbital and therefore, block = d and the group number = (number of electrons in $3d$) + (number of electrons in $4s$) $= 1 + 2 = 3$.

10. (d) The correct match is A-(iv), B-(i), C-(ii), D-(iii).

Helium (He) $1s^2$	→	Highest ionisation energy due to noble gas in nature.
Fluorine (F) $1s^2 2s^2 2p^5$	→	High electronegativity in nature due to small size and −1 oxidation state.
Rubidium (Rb)	→	Most electropositive element due to large atomic size.
Lithium (Li)	→	Strongest reducing agent due to small size and positive oxidation state (+1).

11. (c) An element of atomic weight 40 has 2, 8, 8, 2 as the electronic configuration then the formula of its oxide will be MO.

12. (c) $$\text{Radius of Cl-atom} = \frac{\text{Bond distance in } Cl_2}{2} = \frac{198}{2} = 99 \text{ pm}$$

13. (a) For the same shell, screening effect decreases in the order $s > p > d > f$.

14. (d) Anion is formed after the gain of electron to the neutral atom whereas, cation is formed after the lose of electron from the outer shell. Hence, cation has smaller size but anion has bigger size than its neutral atom. Thus, $I^- > I > I^+$.

15. (b) In case of isoelectronic species,

$$\text{ionic radii} \propto \frac{1}{\text{atomic number}}$$

The ionic radii increases as the positive charge decreases or the negative charge increases.

Ion	Mg^{2+}	<	Na^+	<	F^-	<	O^{2-}
Atomic number	(12)		(11)		(9)		(8)

16. (b) In boron (B), the electron is removed from p-orbital. The $2p$-electrons of boron is more shielded from the nucleus by inner core of electrons than the $2s$-electrons. Also, removal of one $2p$-electron from boron leads to a comparatively stable configuration of $2s^2$, where the two electrons are paired.

Hence, the first ionisation energy of boron (B) is lower than both Be and C.

17. (b) Ionisation energy of nitrogen is more than oxygen due to half-filled p-orbitals, which gives it extra stability.

18. (a) The IE increases along a period from left to right but IE of Mg is higher than that of Al due to completely filled $3s$ orbital in Mg. Thus, the correct order is

$$\text{Na} < \text{Mg} > \text{Al} < \text{Si}$$

19. (c) As we move from Cl to I, the electron gain enthalpy (i.e. energy released in electron gain) become less and less negative due to a corresponding increase in the atomic size. However, the electron gain enthalpy of F is less negative than that of Cl due to its small size. Thus, the negative electron gain enthalpy follows the order

$$\text{F} < \text{Cl} > \text{Br} > \text{I}$$

20. (a) A = s-block, B = La, C = f-block.

21. (b) When an electron is removed, size of atom decreases and when an electron is added, size of atom increases.

22. (a) Electronegativity decreases and atomic radius increases down a group in the periodic table.

23. (b) An element with $Z = 11$ can lose one electron easily to attain a noble gas configuration (of neon). So, the element with $Z = 11$ (sodium) is a metal (alkali metal) with +1 oxidation number.

24. (b) The normal oxide formed by the element present on the extreme left of periodic table is the most basic, e.g. Na_2O.

25. (a) Both (A) and (R) are correct and (R) is the correct explanation for (A).

26. (d) (A) incorrect but (R) is correct.

Noble gases are very less reactive due to stable closed shell electronic configuration like ns^2np^6 or ns^2. They are reluctant to share electrons from their filled outer electron shells, noble gases are generally considered unreactive.

27. (c) (A) is correct but (R) is incorrect.

The ionisation enthalpy of elements increases on moving towards extreme right in period.

28. (*b*) Both (A) and (R) are correct but (R) is not the correct explanation of (A). The ions or atoms having same number of electrons are called isoelectronic species. Both Na^+ and Al^{3+} are isoelectronic due to presence of 10 electrons.

29. (*b*) Both (A) and (R) are correct but (R) is not the correct explanation of (A) as the metallic radius difference does not explain why Be and Al have similar properties. The similarity arises due to the diagonal relationship in the periodic table.

30. (*d*) (A) is incorrect but (R) is correct.

Isoelectronic species have different radii.

31. (*b*) Both (A) and (R) are correct but (R) is not the correct explanation of (A).

Noble gases have highest IE in a period because they have stable closed shell electronic configuration.

32. (*d*) (A) is incorrect but (R) is correct. The correct (A) is, In a period from left to right, effective nuclear charge increases and size decreases as a result ionisation energy increases. But element of II A and IA group on the account of their half-filled and completely filled orbitals have high IE than the elements of III A and VI A group, respectively. Thus, (A) is incorrect but (R) is correct.

33. (*a*) As *s*-electrons are mostly strongly attracted by nucleus, hence they are difficult to remove. Therefore, both (A) and (R) are correct and (R) is the correct explanation of (A).

34. (*a*) Both (A) and (R) are correct and (R) is the correct explanation of (A).

35. (i) (a) Noble gases have stable configuration and thus they have positive electron gain enthalpy. **(1)**

(b) The main factor affecting electron gain enthalpy is atomic size. **(1)**

(ii) The electron gain enthalpy of O and F is less than that of S and Cl is due to small size of oxygen and fluorine. The interelectronic repulsion in O and F is much more than the repulsion in 3*p*-orbital of S and Cl.

Hence, the incoming new electron feels less attraction in case of O and F. **(1)**

(iii) The correct order is Cl > F > Br > I. **(1)**

Or

In general, electron affinity of group 17 elements is higher (or more negative) than that of group 16 elements. However, electron affinity of the elements of third period is higher than that of the elements of second period.

Thus, on this basis the correct order would be

$$O < S < F < Cl$$ **(1)**

36. (i) The element with atomic number 57 belongs to *d*-block as the last electron enters the 5*d*-orbital against the Aufbau principle. This anomalous behaviour can be explained on the basis of greater stability of the xenon (inert gas) core.

After barium ($Z = 56$), the addition of the next electron (i.e. 57th) should occur in $4f$-orbital in accordance with Aufbau principle. This will however, tend to destabilise the xenon core ($Z = 54$), [Kr] ($4d^{10}\,4f^0\,5s^2\,5p^6\,5d^0$) since the $4f$-orbital lie inside the core.

Therefore, the 57th electron prefers to enter 5*d*-orbital which lies outside the xenon core and energy of which is only slightly higher than that of $4f$-orbital. In doing so, the stability conferred on the atom due to xenon core more than compensates the slight instability caused by the addition of one electron to the higher energy 5*d*-orbital instead of the lower energy $4f$-orbital.

Thus, the outer electronic configuration of La($Z = 57$) is $5d^1\,6s^2$ rather than the expected $4f^1\,6s^2$. **(2)**

(ii) (*a*) Each period starts with the filling of electrons in a new principal energy shell. Therefore, 6th period starts with the filling of 6*s*-orbital and ends when 6*p*-orbitals are completely filled.

In between, $4f$ and 5*d*-orbitals are filled in accordance with Aufbau principle. Thus, the outermost electronic configuration of the last element of the *p*-block in the 6th period is

$$6s^2\,4f^{14}\,5d^{10}\,6p^6 \text{ or } 4f^{14}\,5d^{10}\,6s^2\,6p^6.$$ **(1)**

(iii) (*c*) Among the given electronic configuration of some elements, only two, i.e. (I) and (IV) belong to the same group in the periodic table as they both have same number of valence electrons. **(1)**

Or

(*a*) The fifth period begins with Rb($Z = 37$) and ends at Xe ($Z = 54$). Thus, the element with $Z = 43$ lies in the 5th period. Since, the 4th period has 18 elements, therefore, the atomic number of the element which lies just above the element with atomic number 43 is $43 - 18 = 25$.

Now, the electronic configuration of element with $Z = 25$ is $1s^2\,2s^2\,2p^6\,3s^2\,3p^6\,3d^5\,4s^2$ (i.e. Mn). **(1)**

Subjective Type Questions

1. (i) The outer electronic configuration of the element is $3s^2\,3p^2$ (as it has 4 elements in outermost shell). Thus, the complete configuration is $1s^2\,2s^2\,2p^6\,3s^2\,3p^2$. So, the atomic number is $2 + 8 + 4 = 14$. Hence, the element is silicon. **(1)**

(ii) Similarity in outer electronic configuration and gradual addition of an electron into the successive elements, are the most important cause of periodicity. **(1)**

2. (i) Cu [0.122 nm], Cu^+ [0.096 nm], Cu^{2+} [0.072 nm].

$$\because \quad \text{Size} \propto \frac{1}{\text{Positive charge}}$$ **(1)**

(ii) Noble gases have more size than halogens due to complete filling of electron in the outermost shell. **(1)**

3. Isoelectronic species are those which have same number of electrons.

(i) Na has 10 electrons. Therefore, the species N^{3-}, O^{2-}, F^-, Mg^{2+}, Al^{3+} etc., each of which has also 10 electrons and hence, isoelectronic with it. **(1)**

(ii) Cl^- has 18 electrons. Therefore, the species P^{3-}, S^{2-}, Ar, K^+ and Ca^{2+}, each one of which contains 18 electrons and hence, isoelectronic with it. **(1)**

4. First ionisation enthalpies of two isotopes of the same element are expected to be same because ionisation enthalpy depends upon the electronic configuration and effective nuclear charge. **(1)**

Isotopes of an element have same electronic configuration and thus, have the same nuclear charge.

5. (i) Due to highly negative electron gain enthalpy they act as good oxidising agents as they can gain electrons easily. **(1)**

(ii) Electronic configuration of noble gases is such that all subshells are completely filled. Hence, their electron gain enthalpy is almost zero. **(1)**

6. (i) On moving down the group, electronegativity decreases because atomic size increases. Fr has the largest size, therefore, it is least electronegative. **(1)**

(ii) Metal = Mercury (Hg) and Halogen = Bromine (Br). **(1)**

7.

	Group 15	Group 16
2nd period	N	O
3rd period	P	S

(i) Ionisation enthalpy of nitrogen ($_7N = 1s^2 2s^2 2p^3$) is greater than oxygen ($_8O = 1s^2\ 2s^2\ 2p^4$) due to extra stable half-filled $2p$-orbitals.

Similarly, ionisation enthalpy of phosphorus ($_{15}P = 1s^2\ 2s^2\ 2p^6\ 3s^2\ 3p^3$) is greater than sulphur ($_{16}S = 1s^2\ 2s^2\ 2p^6\ 3s^2\ 3p^4$).

On moving down the group, ionisation enthalpy decreases with increasing atomic size.

So, the increasing order of first ionisation enthalpy is $S < P < O < N$. **(1)**

(ii) Non-metallic character across a period (left to right) increases but on moving down the group it decreases. So, the increasing order of non-metallic character is $P < S < N < O$. **(1)**

8. The given non-metals are arranged in the increasing order of non-metallic character as follows

$$Si < B < C < N < F$$
$$\xrightarrow{\hspace{3cm}}$$
Increasing non-metallic character **(2)**

9. The element which comes after mercury in the periodic table is called eka-mercury.

Its various parameters are

Atomic number $(Z) = 80 + 32 = 112$

IUPAC name : Ununbium (Uub)

Official name : Cn (copernicium)

Electronic configuration = $[Rn]\ 5f^{14}\ 6d^{10}\ 7s^2$ **(2)**

10. In the modern periodic table, each period starts with the filling of a new principal energy level. Sixth period begins with filling of principal quantum number, $n = 6$.

According to Aufbau principle, in the ground state of the atoms, the orbitals are filled in order of their increasing energies. Therefore, in sixth period, electrons enter in $6s$, $4f$, $5d$ and $6p$ subshells, and these have $1 + 7 + 5 + 3 = 16$ orbitals. Number of electrons in each orbital can be 2. So maximum number of elements in 6th period is 32 (16×2). **(2)**

11. (i) In third period, $3s$ and $3p$-orbitals are filled. **(1/2)**

(ii) Transuranium elements are the elements after uranium. **(1)**

(iii) Actinoid series (f-block elements). **(1/2)**

12. Isoelectronic species have the same number of electrons but different nuclear charges.

In case of isoelectronic species, as the nuclear charge increases, their size decreases. **(1)**

(i) F^- has 10 electrons (9 + 1).

(ii) Ar has 18 electrons.

(iii) Mg^{2+} has 10 electrons (12−2) and

(iv) Rb^+ has 36 electrons (37−1). **(1)**

N^{3-}, O^{2-}, Ne, Na^+ and Al^{3+} are some species which are isoelectronic with F^- and Mg^{2+}.

P^{3-}, S^{2-}, Cl^-, K^+ and Ca^{2+} are some species which are isoelectronic with Ar.

Similarly, Br^-, Kr and Sr^{2+} are isoelectronic with Rb^+. **(1)**

13. (i) All the given species have same number of electrons ($10e^-$). Therefore, all are isoelectronic species. **(1)**

(ii) The ionic radii of isoelectronic species decreases with increase in atomic number (as magnitude of the nuclear charge increases with increase in atomic number).

Therefore, their ionic radii increases in the order

$$\begin{matrix} Al^{3+} < & Mg^{2+} < & Na^+ < & F^- < & O^{2-} < & N^{3-} \\ Z = 13 & 12 & 11 & 9 & 8 & 7 \end{matrix}$$ **(2)**

Mistake Alert *While calculating the ionic radii order of isoelectronic species, one can make a mistake of not considering the relation,* $Z \propto \dfrac{1}{\text{ionic radii}}$.

14. Mg and Al belongs to same period (i.e. third period) and along a period, atomic radii decreases. Thus, the order of size of Mg and Al is Al < Mg **(1)**

Further, the size of a cation is always smaller than its parent atom and in case of isoelectronic species, size decreases as the nuclear charge increases.

Thus, the size of $Mg^{2+} > Al^{3+}$ **(1)**

∴ The correct order of size is $Al^{3+} < Al < Mg^{2+} < Mg$.

Hence, Mg is the largest atom and Al^{3+} is the smallest ion. **(1)**

15. Among the given elements, Na being alkali metal has only one electron in the valence shell, therefore has very low $\Delta_i H_1$. However, after the removal of one electron, it acquires nearest inert gas or neon gas configuration, i.e. Na^+ ($1s^2$, $2s^2$, $2p^6$). Therefore, its $\Delta_i H_2$ is expected to be very high. Consequently, the difference in first and second ionisation enthalpies would be greatest in case of Na. **(2)**

On the other hand, it may be noted here that in case of Mg, Si and P, although their $\Delta_i H_1$ will be much higher than that of Na but their $\Delta_i H_2$ will be much lower than that of Na. As a result, the difference in their respectively, $\Delta_i H_1$ and $\Delta_i H_2$ would be much lower than that of Na. **(1)**

16. We know that, the first ionisation enthalpy generally increases from left to right along a period but the ionisation enthalpy of elements of group 2 (i.e. Mg) is higher than that of the corresponding element of group 13 (i.e. Al) due to the more penetrating power and less shielding of *ns*-electron. **(2)**

Thus, the correct order of ionisation enthalpy is

$$\text{Na} < \text{Al} < \text{Mg} < \text{Si}$$

We know $496 < ? < 737 < 786$

Therefore, the ionisation enthalpy of Al must be lower than that of the Mg, so its value will be close to 575 (which is less than 737). **(1)**

17. (i) Cu is largest due to less effective nuclear charge. It has 29 electrons, 29 protons. Whereas, Cu^+ has 28 electrons and 29 protons, Cu^{2+} has 27 electrons and 29 protons. **(1)**

(ii) He (helium) has highest ionisation energy. **(1)**

(iii) On going from left to right along a period in periodic table, metallic character decreases. And hence Mg will be more metallic than Al. Also, Mg has lower ionisation energy than Al. **(1)**

18. The placing of elements are as

Period	Group 13	Group 14
2nd period	Boron (B)	Carbon (C)
3rd period	Aluminium (Al)	Silicon (Si) **(1)**

(i) Ionisation enthalpy increases along a period (as we move from left to right in a period) with decrease in atomic size and decreases down the group with increase in atomic size. Hence, carbon has the highest first ionisation enthalpy. **(1)**

(ii) Metallic character decreases across a period but increases on moving down the group. Hence, aluminium has the most metallic character. **(1)**

19. (i) Oxygen and fluorine both belong to second period. Electron gain enthalpy generally becomes more negative across a period as we move from left to right. On moving from oxygen to fluorine, the effective nuclear charge increases and atomic size decreases with increase in atomic number. **(1)**

Due to this, forces of attraction of the nucleus increases for the incoming electron. That's why electron gain enthalpy becomes more negative for fluorine than that of oxygen.

Furthermore, fluorine attains stable gas configuration by gaining an electron.

$$\underset{2,7}{F(g)} + e^- \longrightarrow \underset{2,8}{F^-(g)}$$

Therefore, electron gain enthalpy of fluorine (F) is much more negative (-328 kJ mol^{-1}) than that of (O) oxygen ($-$ 141 kJ mol^{-1}). **(1)**

(ii) Electron gain enthalpy becomes less negative on moving down a group. But electron gain enthalpy of chlorine is more negative ($-$ 349 kJ mol^{-1}) than that of the fluorine ($-$ 328 kJ mol^{-1}).

This is due to small size of fluorine as the electron-electron repulsions in relatively compact $2p$-orbital is greater than that in the larger $3p$-orbital and hence, the incoming electron feels greater repulsion in fluorine than in the chlorine. That's why chlorine (Cl) have more negative electron gain enthalpy than that of fluorine (F). **(1)**

20. The statement that electronegativity of N on Pauling scale is 3.0 in all the nitrogen compounds is wrong because electronegativity of any given element is not constant. It varies depending on the element to which it is bound. It increases as the oxidation state of the element increases or percentage of *s*-character of hybrid orbital increases. **(3)**

21. Since, noble gases have a stable electronic configuration (ns^2, np^6 and $1s^2$ in case of He), they have no tendency to attract the bond pair to themselves. Therefore, their electronegativity is zero. **(1)**

On the other hand, halogens are only one electron short of noble gas configuration. Hence, they have a very high tendency of attracting electron towards itself. Therefore, their electronegativity values are the highest in the respective periods. **(2)**

22. (i) Silicon (Si) being a member of group 14 have four valence electrons, i.e. its valency is 4. Bromine is a member of halogen family and hence, its valency is 1. When these combine, the formula of the compound formed would be $\overset{4}{Si}\ \overset{1}{Br}$ or $SiBr_4$. **(1½)**

(ii) Aluminium being a member of group 13 contains three valence electrons so its valency is 3. Sulphur, on the other hand, belongs to group 16 and has 6 valence electrons, so its valency is $8 - 6 = 2$. When these combine, the formula of the compound formed would be $\overset{3}{Al}\ \overset{2}{S}$ or Al_2S_3. **(1½)**

23. (i) Most reactive non-metal has high $\Delta_i H_1$ and $\Delta_i H_2$ and most negative $\Delta_{e_g} H$. Therefore, the element is (B).

(ii) Most reactive metal has low $\Delta_i H_1$ and high $\Delta_i H_2$ (because the second electron has to be lost from noble gas configuration) and has small negative $\Delta_{e_g} H$. Therefore, the element is (A).

(iii) Noble gases are the least reactive elements. They have very high $\Delta_i H_1$ and $\Delta_i H_2$ and have positive $\Delta_{e_g} H$ values. Thus, the element is (D).

(iv) Metal forming binary halides are alkaline earth metals. They have moderate $\Delta_i H_1$ and $\Delta_i H_2$ values and have comparatively slightly less negative $\Delta_{eg} H$ values. Thus, the element is (C). **(3)**

24. There are numerous physical properties of elements such as melting points, boiling points, heats of fusion and vaporisation, energy of atomisation, etc., which show periodic variations. **(1)**

The cause of periodicity in properties is the repetition of similar outer electronic configuration after certain regular intervals. e.g. All the elements of 1st group (alkali metals) have similar outer electronic configuration, i.e. ns^1.

$$_3Li = 1s^2, 2s^1$$

$$_{11}Na = 1s^2 2s^2 2p^6 3s^1$$

$$_{19}K = 1s^2 2s^2 2p^6 3s^2 3p^6 4s^1$$ **(2)**

Therefore, due to similar outermost shell electronic configuration, all alkali metals have similar properties. e.g., sodium and potassium both are soft and reactive metals. They all form basic oxides and their basic character increases down the group. They all form unipositive ion by the loss of one electron.

Similarly, all the elements of 17th group (halogens) have similar outermost shell electronic configuration, i.e. $ns^2 np^5$ and thus possess similar properties.

$$_9F = 1s^2 2s^2 2p^5$$

$$_{17}Cl = 1s^2 2s^2 2p^6 3s^2 3p^5$$

$$_{35}Br = 1s^2 2s^2 2p^6 3s^2 3p^6 3d^{10} 4s^2 4p^5$$ **(2)**

25. Refer to text on pages 92 and 93.

26. (i) The outer electronic configuration of $1s^2 2s^2 2p^5$ is $2s^2 2p^5$. Therefore, this element is a *p*-block element and belongs to the second period and group 17. Thus, the element is fluorine, F. **(1)**

(ii) The outer electronic configuration of [Ar] $4s^2 3d^{10} 4p^1$ is $4s^2 4p^1$, therefore, it is a *p*-block element. It belongs to the fourth period and 13 group . Hence, the element is gallium, Ga. **(1)**

(iii) The outer electronic configuration of [Xe] $6s^2$ is $6s^2$, therefore, it is a *s*-block element and belongs to the sixth period and group 2 of the periodic table. Hence, the element is barium, Ba. **(1)**

(iv) In the electronic configuration [Xe] $6s^2, 5d^1, 4f^7$ the outermost electrons are in $4f$ shell, therefore, it is a *f*-block element and belongs to the sixth period and third group.

Hence, the element is gadolinium, Gd. **(1)**

(v) The outer electronic configuration of [Ar] $4s^1, 3d^{10}$ is $4s^1, 3d^{10}$, therefore, it is a *d*-block element and belongs to the fourth period and group 11. Hence, the element is copper, Cu. **(1)**

27. (i) General electronic configuration of elements having five electrons in the outer subshell is $ns^2 np^5$. This configuration belongs to halogen family, i.e. F, Cl, Br, I, At. **(1)**

(ii) Elements of second group are known as alkaline earth metals (Mg, Ca, Sr, Ba, etc.). Their general electronic configuration for valence shell is ns^2. These elements can form dipositive cations by the loss of two electrons easily. **(1)**

(iii) 16th group elements such as O, S, Se etc., have a tendency to accept two electrons because by the gain of two electrons they attain noble gas configuration. Their general electronic configuration for valence shell is $ns^2 np^4$. **(1)**

(iv) Group 1 or 17 of the periodic table contains metal, non-metal, that are liquid as well as gas at the room temperature, e.g. H is a non-metal and present in gaseous state (H_2) at room temperature. **(1)**

All other elements of this group are metals. Cs is a liquid metal. Similarly, Br_2 is a liquid non-metal while other elements of this group are gaseous non-metals. Iodine can form I^+ so it has metallic properties also. **(1)**

28. As on moving from left to right across a period, the ionisation enthalpy keeps on increasing due to increased nuclear charge and simultaneous decrease in atomic radius. However, there are some exceptions also. **(1)**

(i) Inspite of increased nuclear charge, the first ionisation enthalpy of B is lower than that of Be. This is due to the reason that in case of Be, the outermost electron lies in the 2*s*-orbital but in case of B, it is present in a 2*p*-orbital. Since, the electrons in 2*s*-orbital are more tightly held by the nucleus than those present in 2*p*-orbital, therefore, ionisation enthalpy of B is lower than that of Be.

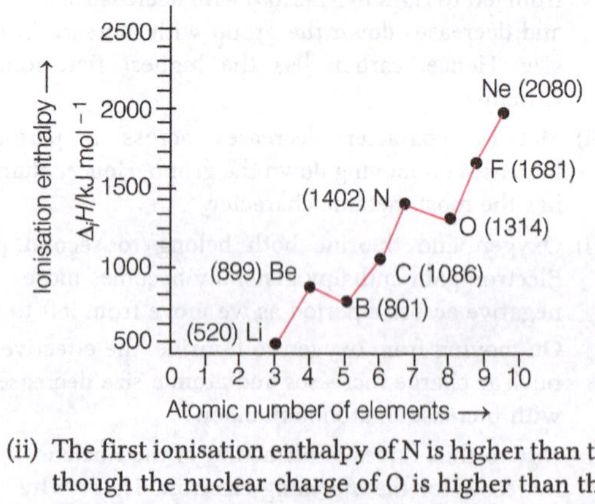

(2)

(ii) The first ionisation enthalpy of N is higher than that of O though the nuclear charge of O is higher than that of N. This is due to the reason that in case of N, ($1s^2\ 2s^2\ 2p_x^1\ 2p_y^1\ 2p_z^1$) the electron is to be removed from a more stable exactly half-filled electronic configuration but in case of O ($1s^2\ 2s^2\ 2p_x^2\ 2p_y^1\ 2p_z^1$), it is not so.

Therefore, the first ionisation enthalpy of N is higher than that of O. The symbols of elements along with their atomic numbers are given in the above graph. **(2)**

29. (i) (a) Be has higher $\Delta_i H$ (ionisation enthalpy) than B. In both the cases, the electron need to be removed belongs to the same principal shell. In ${}_4Be = (1s^2\ 2s^2)$, it is 2s-electron while in boron ${}_5B = (1s^2\ 2s^2\ 2p^1)$ it is 2p-electron. The penetration of a 2s-electron to the nucleus is more than that of a 2p-electron. It means 2s-electrons are more strongly attracted by the nucleus than 2p-electrons.

Therefore, higher amount of energy is required to remove 2s-electron than a 2p-electron. Hence, Be has higher $\Delta_i H$ than B. **(1½)**

(b) O has lower $\Delta_i H$ than N and F.

$${}_7N = 1s^2\ 2s^2\ 2p_x^1\ 2p_y^1\ 2p_z^1$$
$${}_8O = 1s^2\ 2s^2\ 2p_x^2\ 2p_y^1\ 2p_z^1$$
$${}_9F = 1s^2\ 2s^2\ 2p_x^2\ 2p_y^2\ 2p_z^1$$

Across a period, ionisation enthalpy increases as we move from left to right due to decrease in atomic size. But $\Delta_i H$ of nitrogen is greater than oxygen. It is because of the more stable electronic configuration (exactly half-filled orbitals are more stable) of nitrogen, so it is difficult to remove an electron from nitrogen than from oxygen. That's why oxygen has lower ionisation enthalpy than nitrogen and fluorine. **(1½)**

(ii) (a) Due to repulsions between the electrons on O^- and the additional incoming electron, the electron gain enthalpy of O^- is positive while that of S is negative.

(b) On similar grounds, the electron gain enthalpy of S^- is positive while that of O is negative.

(c) Due to small size, repulsions between O^- and the incoming electron is much more than in S^-. Therefore, electron gain enthalpy of O^- is more positive than that of S^-.

(d) Due to repulsions between N^- and the incoming electron, electron gain enthalpy of N^- is positive while that of P is negative. **(2)**

30. Refer to text on page 102. **(5)**

31.
- *In case of s and p-block elements (representative elements), the valency of an atom is generally equal to either the number of valence electrons or equal to 8 minus the number of valence electrons.*
- *In case of lanthanoids (inner-transition elements), there is involvement of d and f-electrons with valence shell electrons in bond formation. Common valency for lanthanoids is 3.*
- *Electronic configuration of* ${}_{71}Lu = [Xe]4f^{14}, 5d^1, 6s^2$; *(Valency = 3).*

S.No.	Element	Group number	Electrons in valence shell	Valency	Formulae of binary compound
(i)	Lithium (Li)	Group 1	1	1	Li_2O
	Oxygen (O)	Group 16	6	8 − 6 = 2	
(ii)	Magnesium (Mg)	Group 2	2	2	Mg_3N_2
	Nitrogen (N)	Group 15	5	8 − 5 = 3	
(iii)	Aluminium (Al)	Group 13	3	3	AlI_3
	Iodine (I)	Group 17	7	8 − 7 = 1	
(iv)	Silicon (Si)	Group 14	4	4	SiO_2
	Oxygen (O)	Group 16	6	8 − 6 = 2	
(v)	Phosphorus (P)	Group 15	5	3 or 5	PF_3 or PF_5
	Fluorine (F)	Group 17	7	8 − 7 = 1	
(vi)	Element 71 (Lutetium) (Lu)	Group 3	3	3	LuF_3
	Fluorine (F)	Group 17	7	8 − 7 = 1	

(5)

32. In *p*-block, when we move from left to right in a period, the acidic character of the oxides increases due to increase in electronegativity.

e.g.

(i) **2nd period**

$B_2O_3 < CO_2 < N_2O_3$ acidic character increases.

(ii) **3rd period**

$Al_2O_3 < SiO_2 < P_4O_{10} < SO_3 < Cl_2O_7$ acidic character increases. **(1)**

On moving down the group, acidic character decreases and basic character increases.

e.g.

(a) **Nature of oxides of 13 group elements**

B_2O_3	Al_2O_3	Ga_2O_3	In_2O_3	Tl_2O
Weakly acidic	Amphoteric	Amphoteric	Basic	Strongly basic

(b) **Nature of oxides of 15 group elements**

N_2O_5	P_4O_{10}	As_4O_{10}	Sb_4O_{10}	Bi_2O_3
Strongly acidic	Moderately acidic	Amphoteric	Amphoteric	Basic

(1)

Among the oxides of same element, higher the oxidation state of the element, stronger is the acid. e.g. SO_3 is a stronger acid than SO_2.

B_2O_3 is weakly acidic and on dissolution in water, it forms orthoboric acid. Orthoboric acid does not act as a protonic acid (it does not ionise) but acts as a weak Lewis acid.

$$\underset{\text{Boron trioxide}}{B_2O_3} + 3H_2O \rightleftharpoons \underset{\text{Orthoboric acid}}{2H_3BO_3}$$

$$B(OH)_3 + H\text{—}OH \longrightarrow [B(OH)_4]^- + H^+$$

Al_2O_3 is amphoteric in nature. It is insoluble in water but dissolves in alkalies and react with acids. **(1)**

$$\underset{\text{Aluminium trioxide}}{Al_2O_3} + 2NaOH \xrightarrow{\Delta} \underset{\text{Sodium meta aluminate}}{2NaAlO_2} + H_2O$$

$$Al_2O_3 + 6HCl \xrightarrow{\Delta} \underset{\text{Aluminium chloride}}{2AlCl_3} + 3H_2O$$ **(1)**

Tl_2O is as basic as NaOH due to its lower oxidation state (+1).

$$Tl_2O + 2HCl \longrightarrow 2TlCl + H_2O$$

P_4O_{10} on reaction with water gives orthophosphoric acid.

$$\underset{\text{Phosphorus pentoxide}}{P_4O_{10}} + 6H_2O \longrightarrow \underset{\text{Orthophosphoric acid}}{4H_3PO_4}$$

Cl_2O_7 is strongly acidic in nature and on dissolution in water, it gives perchloric acid.

$$\underset{\text{Dichlorine heptoxide}}{Cl_2O_7} + H_2O \longrightarrow \underset{\text{Perchloric acid}}{2HClO_4}$$ **(1)**

QR Code for Quick Test 1

QR Code for Quick Test 2

QR Code for Quick Test 3

QR Code for Quick Test 4

SELF ASSESSMENT TEST

Objective Type Questions [1 Mark]

1. Which of the following statements is correct?
   (a) X^- ion is larger in size than X-atom.
   (b) X^+ ion is larger in size than X-atom.
   (c) X^+ ion is larger in size than X^- ion.
   (d) X^+ and X^- ions are equal in size.
2. The first four ionisation energy values of an element are 191, 578, 872 and 5962 kcal. The number of valence electrons in the element is
   (a) 1 (b) 2 (c) 3 (d) 4
3. Which of the following transitions involves maximum amount of energy?
   (a) $M^-(g) \rightarrow M(g)$ (b) $M(g) \rightarrow M^+(g)$
   (c) $M^+(g) \rightarrow M^{2+}(g)$ (d) $M^{2+}(g) \rightarrow M^{3+}(g)$
4. Variable valency is characteristic of
   (a) noble gas
   (b) alkali metals
   (c) transition metals
   (d) non-metallic elements
5. Which one of the following orders presents the correct sequence of the increasing basic nature of the given oxides?
   (a) $Al_2O_3 < MgO < Na_2O < K_2O$
   (b) $MgO < K_2O < Al_2O_3 < Na_2O$
   (c) $Na_2O < K_2O < MgO < Al_2O_3$
   (d) $K_2O < Na_2O < Al_2O_3 < MgO$

Assertion-Reason [1 Mark]

■ **Directions** (Q. Nos. 6-8) In the following questions, a statement of Assertion (A) is followed by a corresponding statements of Reason (R) of the following statements, choose the correct one.

(a) Both (A) and (R) are true and (R) is the correct explanation of (A).
(b) Both A and (R) are true but (R) is not the correct explanation of (A).
(c) (A) is true but (R) is false.
(d) (A) is false but (R) is true.

6. **Assertion** (A) The modern periodic table is based on atomic number rather than atomic mass.
   Reason (R) The atomic number is a more fundamental property that determines the chemical behaviour of elements.
7. **Assertion** (A) Non-metals are generally good conductors of electricity.
   Reason (R) Non-metals have a high electronegativity.
8. **Assertion** (A) The second ionisation energy of an element is always higher than the first.
   Reason (R) Removing an electron from a positively charged ion requires more energy.

Short Answer Type I Questions [2 Marks]

9. Write answers from the following.
   (i) How do the electronic configuration of the elements with $Z = 107$ to 109 differ from one another?
   (ii) Rn is the last noble gas discovered. Predict what will be the atomic number of the next noble gas to be discovered? Write its symbol.
10. Can an element with atomic number 126, if discovered, be accommodated in the present set up of the long form of periodic table?
11. Name the species that will be isoelectronic with the following ions.
    (i) Ca^{2+}
    (ii) Rb^+

Short Answer Type II Questions [3 Marks]

12. Predict the period and block to which each of the following elements belong?
    (i) ${}_{13}Al$ (ii) ${}_{24}Cr$ (iii) ${}_{29}Cu$
13. ${}_{31}Ga$ has slightly higher ionisation enthalpy than ${}_{13}Al$, although it occupies lower position in the group? Explain.

14. The amount of energy released when one million of atoms of iodine in vapour state are converted to I^- ions is 4.9×10^{-13} J according to the reaction:

$$I(g) + e^- \longrightarrow I^-(g)$$

Express the electron gain enthalpy of iodine in terms of kJ mol^{-1} and eV per atom.

Case-Study [4 Marks]

15. Read the case given below and answer the questions that follows

Determining the atomic radius of an atom is challenging because an atom lacks a definite boundary, as electrons are constantly moving around the nucleus with no fixed position. This uncertainty in electron position means there is no precise boundary to measure. Instead, atomic radii are measured based on the distance between the nuclei of bonded atoms, known as internuclear distance.

There are different types of atomic radii, each based on different types of bonds. A covalent radius is half the distance between the nuclei of two identical atoms bonded by a covalent bond. In the case of ionic bonds, the ionic radius is half the distance between the nuclei of a cation and an anion in an ionic compound, adjusted for the size difference between the ions. For metals, the metallic radius is half the distance between the nuclei of adjacent atoms in a crystalline metal structure.

Noble gases are typically excluded from atomic radius trends because their radii are difficult to measured accurately due to weak interatomic interactions.

(i) Expalin why the atomic radius of elements generally increases down a group but decreases across a period from left to right. Illustrate your answer with examples.

(ii) Arrange O^{2-}, O^-, O in decreasing radius.

(iii) Why is the covalent radius generally smaller than the van der Waals radius for the same element?

Or

Among Na^+ and Mg^{2+} which ion is smaller and why?

Long Answer Type Questions [5 Marks]

16. Assign the position of the element having outer electronic configuration.

(i) ns^2np^4 for $n = 3$

(ii) $(n-1)d^2ns^2$ for $n = 4$ and

(iii) $(n-2)f^7(n-1)d^1ns^2$ for $n = 6$, in the periodic table.

17. For each of the following pairs, predict which one has lower first ionisation enthalpy?

(i) N or O (ii) Na or Na^+

(iii) Be^+ or Mg^{2+} (iv) I or I^-

Answers

1. (a) *2.* (c) *3.* (d) *4.* (c)
5. (a) *6.* (a) *7.* (d) *8.* (a)
14. –295 kJ mol^{-1} and –3.06 eV/atom

04

CHAPTER

A molecule is a group of atoms exist together as one species having characteristic properties.
In this chapter, we will study about the attractive forces which holds the constituent atoms in a molecule together.

Chemical Bonding and Molecular Structure

YOUR STUDY GOALS

YOUR PRACTICE GOAL

- Objective Type Questions (39 Qs ; 25 MCQs, 12 A-R, 2 Case Study)
- Descriptive Type Questions (35 Qs; 10 SA-I, 17 SA-II, 8 LA)

4.1 Chemical Bonding

Chemical bond is a kind of force of attraction which holds various constituents (atoms, ions, etc.) together in different chemical species. The process of their combination is called **chemical bonding.**

The chemical bonds can be classified into various categories like the ionic bond, covalent bond, coordinate bond, metallic bond, hydrogen bond and van der Waals' forces.

Several theories have been put forward from time to time to explain the concept of chemical bonding.

Kössel-Lewis Approach to Chemical Bonding

Kössel and Lewis was the first scientist to explain about a chemical bond in terms of electrons.

Kössel and **Lewis** succeeded independently in giving a satisfactory explanation about the cause of combination between atoms which was based upon the understanding of electronic configuration of noble gases. Since, their theory was based on the electronic concept of atom, so it is also referred as **electronic theory of valency**. The main points of this theory are as follows

- Lewis pictured the atom in terms of a positively charged 'Kernel' (the nucleus plus the inner electrons) and the outer shell, which is called the **valence shell**. The electrons present in this shell are called the **valence electrons**. The combining capacity of an element depends upon the number of valence electrons.

- The electronic configurations of the noble gases are stable as (given in the table below) they have 8 electrons in their outermost orbit (except in case of helium which has 2 electrons). These eight electrons occupy all the corners of a cube which surround the 'Kernel'.

Electronic Configurations of the Noble Gases

Noble gas	Atomic number	Electronic configuration
Helium	2	2
Neon	10	2, 8
Argon	18	2, 8, 8
Krypton	36	2, 8, 18, 8
Xenon	54	2, 8, 18, 18, 8
Radon	86	2, 8, 18, 32, 18, 8

- Lewis postulated that atoms achieve the stable octet (or duplet in case of H, He and Li etc.) when they are joined through chemical bonds. Atoms join together by three ways

  I. by losing of electrons II. by gaining of electrons

  III. by sharing of electrons

The above postulates provide a base to develop the modern concept about the ion formation by electron transfer and the formation of ionic crystalline compounds.

Lewis Symbols

In the formation of a molecule, only the outer shell electrons take part in chemical combination and they are known as **valence electrons.**

The simple notations to represent the valence electrons of an atom are called **Lewis symbols.**

In these symbols, the valence electrons are represented by placing dots (·) or crosses (×) around the symbol.

e.g. The Lewis symbols for the atoms of second period are

$$\dot{\text{Li}},\ \dot{\text{B}}\text{e},\ \dot{\text{B}}\cdot,\ \cdot\dot{\underset{\cdot}{\text{C}}}\cdot,\ :\dot{\underset{\cdot}{\text{N}}}\cdot,\ :\ddot{\text{O}}\cdot,\ :\ddot{\text{F}}:,\ :\ddot{\underset{\cdot\cdot}{\text{Ne}}}:$$

Significance of Lewis Symbols

- The Lewis symbols help to calculate the common or group valency of the element.
- The group valency of the elements is generally either equal to the number of dots in Lewis symbols or 8 minus the number of dots or **valence electrons.**

e.g. In case of Na, Mg, Al, the group valency is equal to the number of dots, i.e. 1, 2 and 3 respectively but in case of N, O, F and Ne it is equal to 8 – number of dots in Lewis symbol, i.e.

$(8-5)=3, (8-6)=2, (8-7)=1$ and $(8-8)=0$ respectively.

Octet Rule

According to this, atoms of various elements strive to attain the configuration of eight electrons in their outermost shell to achieve stability. This is known as **octet rule.**

4.2 Ionic or Electrovalent Bond

The bond formed as a result of electrostatic force of attraction between two oppositely charged ions is called **ionic bond** or **electrovalent bond.**

This type of bond is formed by the complete transfer of electrons from one atom to another (generally between a non- metal and a metal) in order to complete their octet resulting in positively and negatively charged ions.

The number of unit charge(s) present on the ion is the **electrovalence** of that ion.

e.g. Formation of sodium chloride.

$$\underset{(2,8,1)}{\text{Na}\cdot} + \underset{(2,8,7)}{\cdot\ddot{\underset{\cdot\cdot}{\text{Cl}}}:} \longrightarrow \underset{(2,8)}{\text{Na}^+}\ \underset{(2,8,8)}{:\ddot{\underset{\cdot\cdot}{\text{Cl}}}:^-}$$

Note The number of oppositely charged ions present as the nearest neighbours around that ion in an ionic crystal is called the **coordination number of that ion.**

Factors Affecting the Formation of Ionic Bond

Formation of ionic bond depends upon the following factors

(i) **Low ionisation energy of metal atom** Ionisation energy is the amount of energy required to remove the most loosely bound electron from an isolated gaseous atom to form a positive ion.

So, lesser the ionisation energy of metal atom, greater is the ease of losing the valence electron and hence greater is the tendency to form ionic bonds.

(ii) **High negative value of electron gain enthalpy of non-metal atom** The electron gain enthalpy is the energy change when an electron is added to an isolated gaseous atom to form a negative ion.

So, higher the value of negative electron gain enthalpy greater will be the ease of formation of anion and hence greater is the tendency to form ionic compounds.

(iii) A qualitative measure of the stability of an ionic compound is provided by its enthalpy of lattice formation and not simply by achieving octet of electrons around the ionic species in gaseous state. Higher the value of lattice energy higher is the ease of formation of ionic compound.

Lattice Enthalpy

The amount of energy required to completely separate one mole of a solid ionic compound into gaseous constituent ions is called **lattice enthalpy** of an ionic solid.

Lattice enthalpy is released in the formation of the crystal lattice by the arrangement of positive and negative ions in the solid.

Factors Affecting Lattice Enthalpy

The value of lattice enthalpy depends upon the following factors

(i) **Charge on the ions** Higher the charge on the ions, greater is the force of attraction and hence larger is the amount of energy released. e.g. Lattice enthalpies of some ionic compounds are in the order

$$\underset{\text{(Uni-univalent)}}{\underset{(-758)}{\overset{+\ -}{NaCl}}} < \underset{\text{(Bi-univalent)}}{\underset{(-2254)}{\overset{+2\ -1}{CaCl_2}}} < \underset{\text{(Bi-bivalent)}}{\underset{(-3932)\ kJ\ mol^{-1}}{\overset{+2\ -2}{MgO}}}$$

(ii) **Size of the ions** Larger is the size of ions, greater is the internuclear distance and lesser will be the force of attraction, i.e. lattice energy.

e.g. Lattice enthalpies of some ionic compounds follow the order

$$\underset{(-758)}{NaCl} > \underset{(-752)}{NaBr} \qquad \underset{(-1033)}{LiF} > \underset{(-140)}{LiI}$$

[Lattice enthalpy is calculated with the help of **Born Haber cycle** which will be discussed in chapter 5.]

Note If Lattice enthalpy + Electron gain enthalpy > Ionisation enthalpy, the net effect will be the release of energy and hence results in the formation of an ionic bond.

Properties of Ionic Compounds

The compounds in which ionic bonds are present, are called **ionic compounds**. The characteristic properties exhibited by these compounds are

1. Physical State

These compounds generally exist as crystalline solids, known as **crystal lattice**, which consist of orderly three dimensional arrangements of cations and anions, held together by coulombic interaction.

2. Melting and Boiling Points

In ionic compounds, the ions are tightly held together by strong electrostatic forces of attraction and hence a huge amount of energy is required to break the crystal lattice, thus they possess high melting and boiling points.

3. Solubility

Ionic compounds are soluble in solvents like water having high polarity and high dielectric constant.

Furthermore, the ions may combine with the solvent to liberate energy called the **hydration enthalpy** which is adequate to overcome the attractive forces between the ions.

TEACHER'S TIP

Ionic compounds are soluble in polar solvents because polar solvent interacts with the ions of the crystals and further the high dielectric constant of the solvent cuts off the force of attraction between these ions.

4. Electrical Conductivity

Ionic compounds are good conductors of electricity in the aqueous solution or in their molten states, because of the presence of free ions in these states.

However, these do not conduct electricity in their solid state because of the absence of free ions as strong electrostatic forces of attraction bind the ions.

5. Ionic Reactions

These compounds split up into oppositely charged ions when dissolved in water.

Thus, the chemical reactions of these compounds are characteristic of their constituent ions and are known as **ionic reactions**. These reactions are almost instantaneous.

e.g. $Na^+Cl^-(aq) + Ag^+NO_3^-(aq) \longrightarrow AgCl(s) + NaNO_3(aq)$

6. Non-Directional Character

The ionic bond is non-directional. This is because, each ion is surrounded by oppositely charged ions uniformly distributed all around the ion.

The formula of an ionic compound can easily be written by knowing the valency of combining atoms or charges of ions.

e.g. The formula of barium is

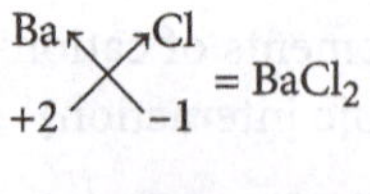

4.3 Covalent Bond

Langmuir improved the Lewis concept by introducing the term covalent bond.

The bond formed by mutual sharing of electrons between the combining atoms of the same or different elements is called the **covalent bond.** This bond is generally formed between two electronegative, i.e. non-metallic elements.

The number of electrons shared by an atom in order to complete its octet is called the **covalency of that atom.** e.g.

- **Formation of chlorine molecule, Cl_2** The electronic configuration of Cl-atom is [Ne] $3s^2 3p^5$. It has one electron less than the stable noble gas configuration. Cl_2 molecule can be formed by sharing two electrons between two chlorine atoms, each chlorine atom contributing one electron to the shared pair so that, both chlorine atom attain the outer shell octet of nearest noble gas (i.e. argon).

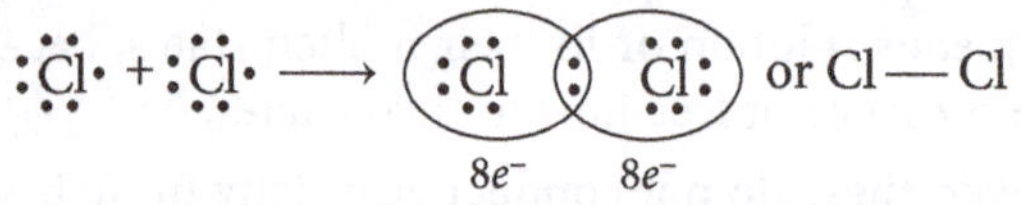

Covalent bond between two Cl atoms

Since, both the Cl-atoms share one electron, the covalency of chlorine atom is 1.

- **Formation of HCl molecule**

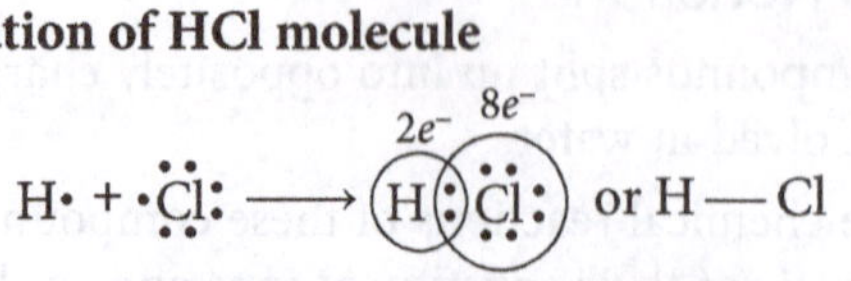

Hydrogen atom attains a duplet of electron and Cl, attains the octet

Conditions for the Formation of a Covalent Chemical Bond

The various conditions for the formation of a covalent chemical bond are as follows

- Bond should be formed by the sharing of an electron pair between the atoms.
- There should be contribution of atleast one electron by each combining atom to the shared pair.
- The sharing of electrons should be in such a way that the combining atoms attain the nearest noble gas configuration.

Types of Covalent Bond Based on Number of Shared Electron Pairs

Depending upon the number of electrons (2, 4 or 6) shared between two atoms, a covalent bond is called single, double or triple bond respectively. e.g.

(i) H : H or H—H (H_2 molecule)
Single bond

(Here, duplets of both the H-atoms are complete.)

(ii) 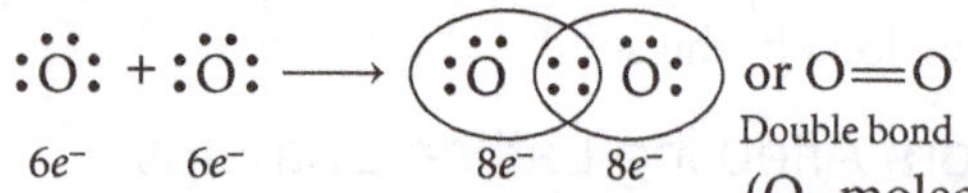

(O_2 molecule)

(Here, octets of both the O-atoms are complete.)

(iii) 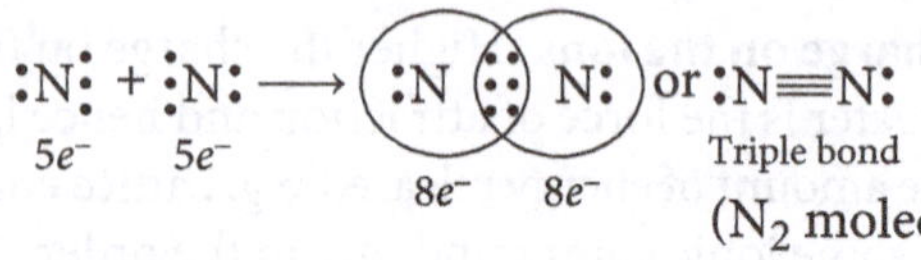

(N_2 molecule)

Types of Covalent Bond Based on Electronegativity of Atoms

Depending upon the electronegative character of combining atoms, the covalent bonds can be of two types.

1. Non-polar Covalent Bond

When a covalent bond is formed between two atoms having almost same electronegativity, then the shared pair of electrons are equally shared by the two atoms and are situated exactly between the two identical nuclei (or in other words the two homonuclear atoms).

This type of covalent bond is called non-polar covalent bonds. e.g. Bond in $H_2, O_2, Cl_2, F_2, Br_2$ etc.

2. Polar Covalent Bond

When a covalent bond is formed between two atoms having significant difference in their electronegativities, then the shared pair of the electrons slightly shift towards the more electronegative atom and the bond thus formed attain partial ionic character.

This type of covalent bond is called polar covalent bond.

This type of bond is usually found between two dissimilar (or heteronuclear) atoms,

e.g. $H^{\delta+}—Cl^{\delta-}$, $H^{\delta+}—F^{\delta-}$, $H^{\delta+}—O^{\delta-}—H^{\delta+}$ etc.

Characteristics of Covalent Compounds

Compounds having covalent bond(s) are called covalent compounds.

(i) **Physical state** The covalent compounds exist in all the three states *viz.*, solid, liquid and gas. They usually contain molecules rather than ions.

(ii) **Low melting and boiling points** These compounds have low melting and boiling points because of the presence of weak forces of attraction between the molecules which are easily overcome at low temperatures.

(iii) **Solubility** Being non-polar these are generally insoluble or less soluble in water and other polar solvents.

However, these are soluble in non-polar solvents such as benzene, carbon tetrachloride, etc. (like dissolves like).

Note Covalent compounds having H-bonding can be dissolved in water.

(iv) **Electrical conductivity** Since, there are no free ions in covalent compounds to conduct electricity, they are bad conductors of electricity. However, graphite is an exception to this fact.

(v) **Molecular reactions** Since, these compounds are molecular in nature, their reactions are molecular and proceed at a much slower rate as compared to the ionic compounds.

(vi) **Directional characteristics** Since, the covalent bond is localised in between the nuclei of atoms, it is directional in nature.

Important Points

- A bond in which the electron pair (lone pair) is donated by one atom but shared by both the atoms so as to complete their octets, is called **coordinate bond** or **dative bond**.
- The bond is represented by an arrow (⟶) pointing towards the acceptor atoms.

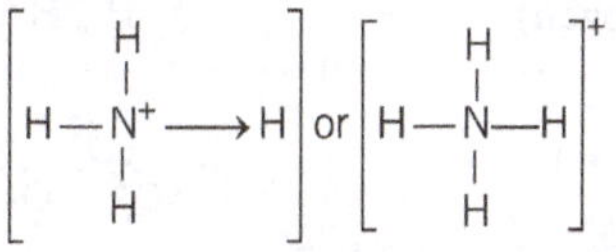

Other examples are, SO_3, SO_2, O_3, H_3O^+, NO_3^-, HNO_3 etc.

- The shared pairs of electrons present between the combining atoms are called the **bond pairs**. As these are responsible for the bonding between the atoms.
- On the other hand, the valence electrons that are not involved in bonding (i.e. in sharing) are called the **non-bonding electrons** or **lone pairs** or **unshared pairs**.

Lewis Representation of Simple Molecules (The Lewis Structures)

The structures that provide a picture of bonding in molecules and ions in terms of the shared pairs of electrons and the octet rule, are called the **Lewis dot structures.**

Although these structures do not explain the bonding and behaviour of a molecule completely, yet they are helpful to understand the properties and formation of molecules to a greater extent.

Steps for Writing Lewis Dot Structure

Step I Count the total number of electrons required for writing the structures by adding the valence electrons of the combining atoms.

Step II In case of anion, add one electron to the total number of valence electrons for each negative charge and for cation, subtract one electron from the total number of valence electrons for each positive charge.

Step III Write the chemical symbols of the combining atoms and skeletal structure of the compound, and try to distribute the total number of electrons as bonding shared pairs between the atoms in proportion to the total bonds.

Step IV Generally, the least electronegative atoms occupies the central position in the molecule/ion and is called the central atom.

Step V After distributing the shared pairs of electrons for single bonds, the remaining electron pairs are either utilised for multiple bonding or remain as such in the form of lone pairs, provided that each combining atoms gets an octet of electrons.

Lewis Representation of Molecules/Ion

Molecule/Ion	Lewis representation	Molecule/Ion	Lewis representation
H_2 (Hydrogen)	H:H or H—H	O_2 (Oxygen)	:O::O: or :O=O:
O_3 (Ozone)	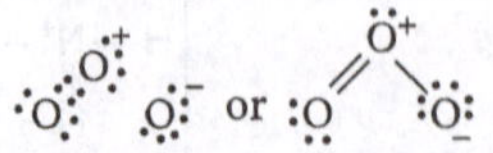	CO_3^{2-} (Carbonate ion)	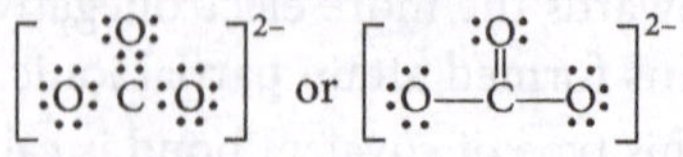
NF_3 (Nitrogen trifluoride)	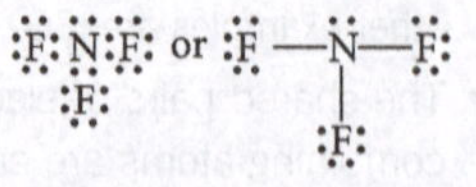	H_3PO_4 (Phosphoric acid)	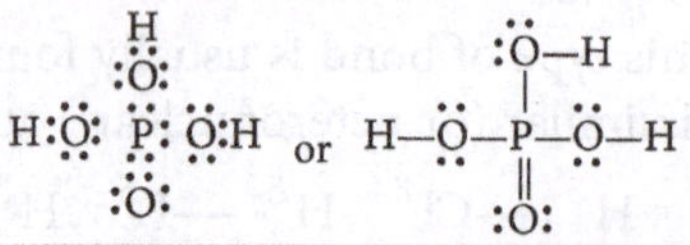
OF_2 (Oxygen difluoride)	:F:O:F: or :F—O—F:	$HClO_4$ (Perchloric acid)	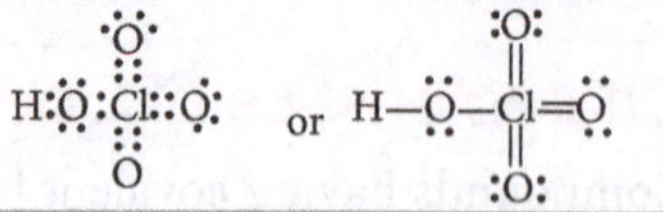
$SiCl_4$ (Silicon tetrachloride)	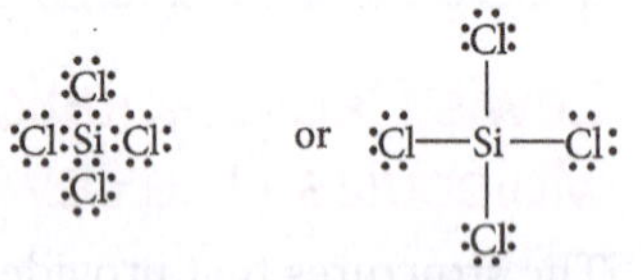	O_2^{2-} (Peroxide ion)	$[:O:O:]^{2-}$ or $[:O—O:]^{2-}$
HNO_2 (Nitrous acid)	H:O:N::O: or H—O—N=O:	CN^- (Cyanide ion)	$[:C:::N:]^-$ or $[:C\equiv N:]^-$
HNO_3 (Nitric acid)	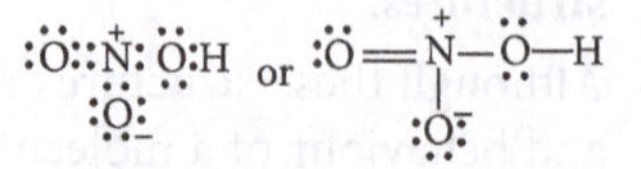	SO_4^{2-} (Sulphate ion)	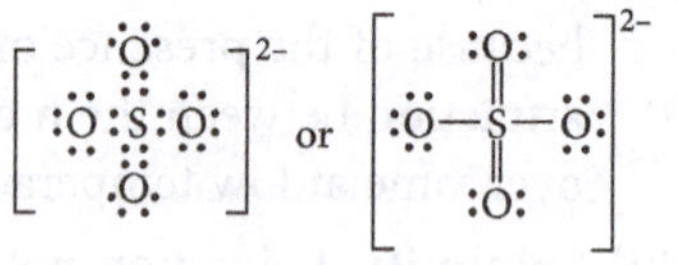

Example 1 **Write the Lewis dot structure of CO molecule.** NCERT

Sol.

Step I The valence shell configurations of carbon and oxygen atoms are $2s^2\,2p^2$ and $2s^2\,2p^4$, respectively. Therefore, the valence electrons available are $4 + 6 = 10$.

Step II The skeletal structure of CO can be written as CO.

Step III Join C and O by a single bond (one shared electron pair) and complete the octet on O, the remaining two electrons are the lone pair of C.

:C:O: or :C—O:

(The molecule contains only 2 atoms, so step 4 is not required, whereas we can consider C as the central atom because of its less electronegativity).

Step IV Still the octet on carbon is incomplete, so we have to resort to multiple bonding (in this case a triple bond) between C and O-atoms which satisfies the octet rule condition for both the atoms.

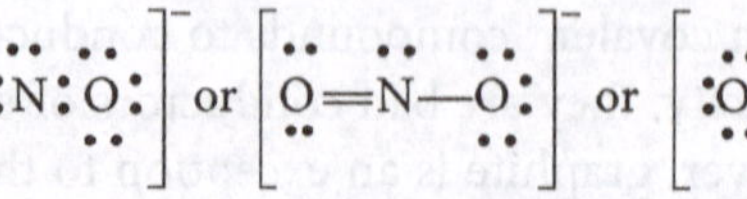

Example 2 **Write the Lewis structure of the nitrite ion, NO_2^-.** NCERT

Sol. Draw the Lewis structure in the same manner discussed in the above example you will get the following Lewis structures.

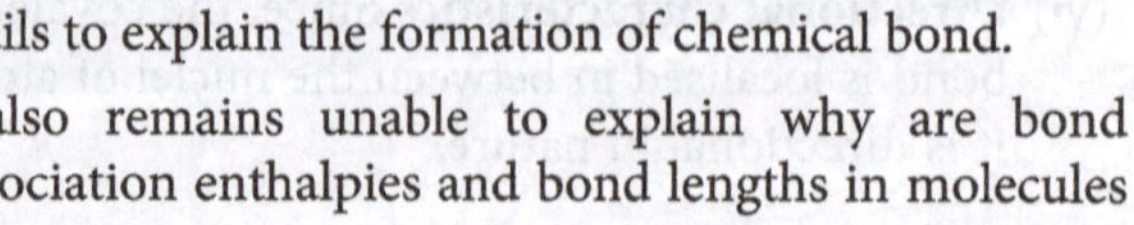

Limitations of Lewis Approach

Although with the help of Lewis approach, structure of several molecules can be explained but there are certain limitations of this approach, which are as follows

- It fails to explain the formation of chemical bond.
- It also remains unable to explain why are bond dissociation enthalpies and bond lengths in molecules

like H_2 (435.8 kJ mol^{-1}, 74 pm) and F_2 (155 kJ mol^{-1}, 144 pm) are different. Although both of them involve the formation of a single covalent bond by sharing of an electron pair between the respective atoms.

- It also does not give any idea about the shapes of polyatomic molecules.

Formal Charge

The **formal charge** of an atom in a polyatomic molecule or ion may be defined as *"the difference between the number of valence electrons of that atom in an isolated or free state and the number of electrons assigned to that atom in the Lewis structure"*. It is represented as

$$FC = V - L - \frac{1}{2}S$$

where, FC = Formal charge on an atom in a Lewis structure

V = Total number of valence electrons in the free atom.

L = Total number of non-bonding (lone pair) electrons.

S = Total number of bonding (shared) electrons.

Significance of Formal Charges

- It is a factor which is based on a pure covalent view of bonding in which electron pairs are shared equally by neighbouring atoms.
- Formal charge do not indicate the real charge separation within the molecule but it only helps in keeping track of the valence electrons in the molecule.
- It also helps to select the lowest energy structures from a number of possible Lewis structures for a given species. Generally, the structure having the smallest formal charges on the atoms is of lowest energy.

TEACHER'S TIP

When several Lewis structures are possible, the one with formal charges closest to zero is the most stable and is preferred.

Example 3 **Calculate formal charge on each O-atom of O_3 molecule.**

Sol. The Lewis structure of O_3 may be drawn as

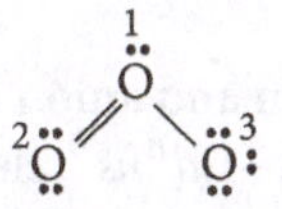

The oxygen atoms have been numbered as 1, 2 and 3. The formal charge on

(i) the central O-atom marked as $1 = V - L - \frac{1}{2}S$

$$= 6 - 2 - \frac{1}{2}(6) = +1$$

(ii) the end O-atom marked as $2 = V - L - \frac{1}{2}S$

$$= 6 - 4 - \frac{1}{2}(4) = 0$$

(iii) the end O-atom marked as $3 = V - L - \frac{1}{2}S$

$$= 6 - 6 - \frac{1}{2}(2) = -1$$

Hence, the O_3 molecule alongwith the formal charges can be represented as follows

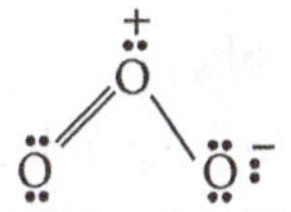

Limitations of Octet Rule

Although octet rule can explain the formation of a large number of compounds but it has few exceptions also, which are discussed below

(i) **Electron deficient molecules** (Incomplete octet of the central atom) There are some molecules in which the central atom is surrounded by less than eight electrons, i.e. their octet is incomplete.

Elements having less than four valence electrons generally form molecules of this category,

e.g. (a) $BeCl_2 \longrightarrow$ Cl :Be: Cl

(b) $BF_3 \longrightarrow$ F:B:F (with F above B)

(c) $BeH_2 \longrightarrow$ H :Be: H

(ii) **Odd electron molecules** Molecules like NO, NO_2 etc., have bonded atoms with odd number of electron(s) (usually 3). That's why these are called **odd electron molecules.**

In case of these molecules, the octet rule is not satisfied for all the atoms. e.g.

(a) Nitric oxide (NO) $\longrightarrow$:N:: O: or N=O

(b) Nitrogen dioxide (NO_2)$\longrightarrow$:O:: N :O: or O=N$^+$—O$^-$

Note Species with one unpaired electron are called **free radicals.** These are paramagnetic and most of them are generally unstable.

(iii) **Electron rich molecules** (The expanded octet) Elements of the third and higher periods of the periodic table can expand their covalency, due to the availability of *d*-orbitals and can accommodate more than eight valence electrons around the central atom. This is called as **expanded octet.**

Here also, the octet rule is not applicable. e.g. PF_5 (10 electrons around P-atom), SF_6 (12 electrons around S-atom), H_2SO_4 (12 electrons around S-atom).

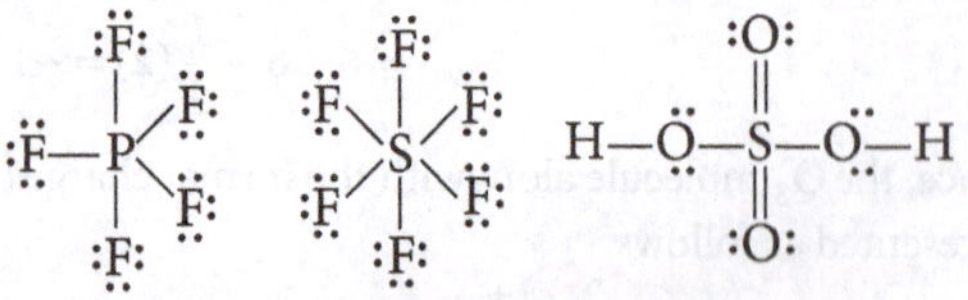

PF_5 SF_6 H_2SO_4

Compounds having expanded octet are also termed as **hypervalent compounds.**

(iv) **Other drawbacks** Some other drawbacks of this theory are as follows

- Octet rule is based on the inertness of noble gases but some noble gases like xenon and krypton form several compounds with oxygen and fluorine like $XeF_2, XeF_4, XeF_6, XeOF_4, XeO_2F_2, KrF_2$ etc.
- It does not tell anything about the shapes of molecules and their relative stabilities.
- It fails to explain the paramagnetic behaviour of oxygen (which should be diamagnetic according to this rule but it is infact paramagnetic in nature).
- Octet theory is totally silent about the energy of a molecule.

4.4 Covalent Character in Ionic Bonds : Fajans' Rule

The existence of a purely ionic or covalent bond is an ideal situation. Just as all the covalent bonds have some partial ionic character, the ionic bonds also have some partial covalent character.

When a cation approaches an anion, the positive ion tends to distort the electron cloud of the negative ion towards itself. This effect is called **polarisation.** The power of cations to cause distortion in the electron cloud of the negative ion is called **polarising power.**

The ability of anion to undergo distortion is called **polarisability.**

The partial covalent character of ionic bonds depends on polarising power of cation, polarisability of anion and extent of distortion of anion which are discussed by Fajans' in terms of the following rules, called the Fajans' rule.

These rules are as follows.

1. Small Size of Cation

The small cations because of their high electron density tend to distort or polarise the electron cloud of the anion to a greater extent.

Hence, the compounds containing **small cations will have more covalent character.** e.g. LiCl is more covalent than NaCl and KCl due to smaller size of Li^+ ion as compared to Na^+ and K^+.

2. Large Size of the Anion

Larger the anion, greater is its polarisability. So, greater will be the covalent character in the bond, e.g. covalent character of lithium halides is in the order LiI > LiBr > LiCl > LiF.

3. High Charge on the Cation or Anion

Higher the charge on the cation, greater is its polarising power (because the cation attracts the electron cloud of the anion more easily and strongly). Hence, covalent character increases. That's why the covalent character of the chlorides follow the order

$$Na^+Cl^- < Mg^{2+}Cl^- < Al^{3+}Cl^-.$$

Similarly, greater the charge on the anion, more easily it gets polarised.

4. Electronic Configuration of the Cation

In case of two cations having the same size and charge, the one with $(n-1)d^n ns^0$, typical of transition metals, is more polarising than the one with noble gas configuration, ns^2np^6, typical of alkali and alkaline earth metals.

Conclusion

According to Fajans' rules, the covalent character will be favoured by

- small size of cation
- large size of anion
- high charge of cation and anion
- the cation having $(n-1)d^n ns^0$ electronic configuration.

Quick Test 1

1. If the electronic configuration of an element is $1s^2\,2s^2\,2p^6\,3s^2\,3p^6\,3d^2\,4s^2$, the four electrons involved in chemical bond formation will be......
2. The skeletal structure of CH_3COOH as shown below is correct, but some of the bonds are shown incorrectly. Write the correct Lewis structure for acetic acid. NCERT

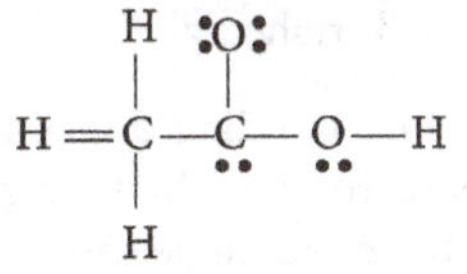

3. Write the Lewis structure for the following atoms and ions: S and S^{2-}; Al and Al^{3+}; H and H^- NCERT
4. Use Lewis symbols to show electron transfer between the following atoms to form cations and anions. NCERT
   (i) K and S (ii) Ca and O (iii) Al and N
5. Calculate the formal charge on each atoms of
   (i) Carbonate ion
   (ii) SO_2 molecule
6. Which of the following has highest lattice energy and why?
   CsF, CsCl, CsBr, CsI
7. Give reasons for the following:
   Covalent bonds are directional bond, while ionic bonds are non-directional.
8. Arrange the bonds in order of increasing ionic character in the molecules; LiF, K_2O, N_2, SO_2 and ClF_3. NCERT

For Solutions, See QR Code on Pg. 172

4.5 Bond Parameters

The various characteristics shown by a bond are called the bond parameters. These are as follows.

1. Bond Length

The equilibrium distance between the nuclei of two bonded atoms in a molecule is called the **bond length**. It is expressed in terms of Angstrom (1Å $= 10^{-10}$ m) or picometer (1 pm $= 10^{-12}$ m).

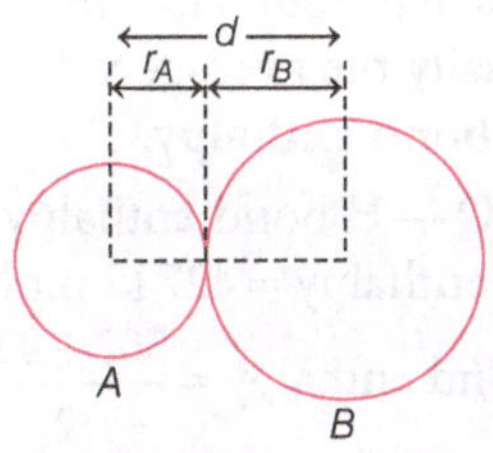

The bond length (d) in a covalent molecule, AB.

In a covalent bond, the contribution from each atom is called **covalent radius.** It is measured as the radius of an atoms core which is in contact with the core of an adjacent atom in a bonded situation. It is equal to half of the distance between two similar atoms combined together by a covalent bond in the same molecule.

Bond length $(d) = r_A + r_B$

Covalent radius $= r_A = r_B = \dfrac{d}{2}$ [if $r_A = r_B$]

Here, r_A and r_B are the covalent radii of two atoms A and B respectively.

van der Waals' radius represents the overall size of the atom, including its valence shell in a non-bonded situation. It is equal to half of the distance between two similar atoms in separate molecules in a solid.

Covalent and van der Waals' radii of chlorine are shown in the below figure.

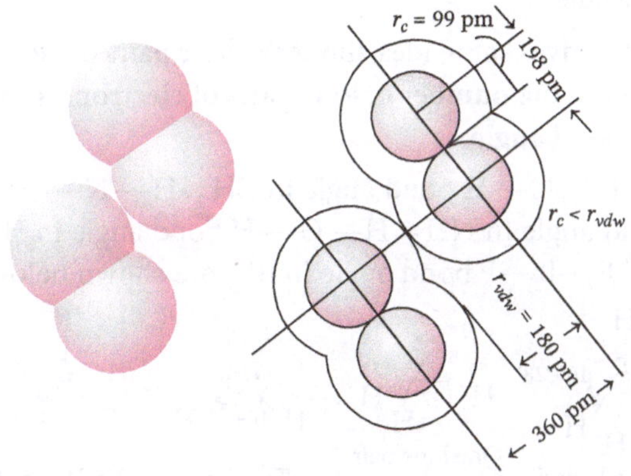

Covalent and van der Waals' radii' in a chlorine molecule

r_c represents the covalent radius and r_{vdw} represents the van der Waals' radius.

Factors Affecting Bond Length

The various factors that affect bond length are as follows

(i) **Size of the atoms** The bond length increases with increase in the size of the atoms.

Thus, **the order of bond length of H—X bond is**

H—F < H—Cl < H—Br < H—I

Similarly, C—C < Si—Si < Ge—Ge

(ii) **Bond multiplicity** The bond length decreases as the multiplicity of the bond increases.

Thus, **the carbon-carbon bond lengths** follow the order

C≡C < C=C < C—C

(iii) **Type of hybridisation** Bond length also increases as the p-character increases or s-character decreases.

i.e. $\underset{\text{more } p\text{-character}}{sp^3} > sp^2 > sp.$

Note About p-character and hybridisation like sp^3, sp^2 etc., you will learn later in this chapter.

2. Bond Angle

The angle between the orbitals containing bonding electron pairs around central atom in a molecule/complex ion is called the **bond angle.** It is expressed in degree which can be experimentally determined by spectroscopic methods.

- Bond angle gives some idea about the distribution of orbitals around the central atom in a molecule and hence, helps in determining the shape of the molecule.
- It also gives some idea about the lone pairs of electrons as **more the number of lone pairs of electrons, lesser is the bond angle.**

  e.g. H—C—H bond angle in CH_4, H—N—H bond angle in NH_3, H—O—H bond angle in H_2O and F—B—F bond angle in BF_3 are shown below.

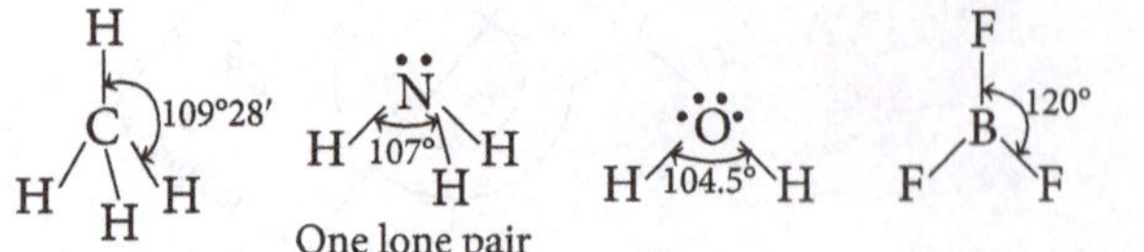

Tetrahedral (no lone pair) | One lone pair so less than tetrahedral | Two lone pairs | No lone pair (trigonal planar)

TEACHER'S TIP

If there are four bonding domains the bond angle is 109°28′ (but if one of the domain is lone pair, bond angle is less than 109°28′), if there are three bonding domains, bond angle is 120° and if there are only two bonding domains, bond angle is 180°(but if there is/are lone pair(s) the angle will be less than 180°).

Factors Affecting Bond Angle

The various factors that affect the bond angle are as follows

- bond angle decreases with decrease in s-character, i.e. $sp > sp^2 > sp^3$.
- Bond angle is affected by the presence of lone pairs, i.e. lp - lp repulsion decreases the bond angle.

Example 4 **Predict all the bond angles in these molecules**

(i) CH_3Cl (ii) CH_2 ═CHCl

Sol. (i) The Lewis structure for CH_3Cl is

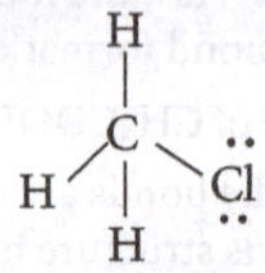

Tetrahedral

Because here four bonding domain are present, i.e. the carbon is surrounded by four groups through single bond, the bond angle should be equal to 109°28′.

(ii) The Lewis structure for CH_2 ═CHCl is

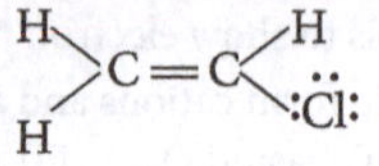

surrounded by three bonding domains. Thus, the bond angle is 120°.

3. Bond Enthalpy

The amount of energy required to break one mole of bonds of a particular type between two atoms in gaseous state is called **bond enthalpy.** The unit of bond enthalpy is kJ mol^{-1}. e.g. The H—H bond enthalpy in hydrogen molecule is 435.8 kJ mol^{-1}.

$$H_2(g) \longrightarrow H(g) + H(g);\ \Delta_a H^\ominus = 435.8 \text{ kJ mol}^{-1}$$

TEACHER'S TIP

Larger the bond dissociation enthalpy, stronger will be the bond in the molecule.

In case of **diatomic molecules** such as H_2, O_2, N_2, HCl etc., the bond enthalpies are equal to their dissociation enthalpies and hence, have fixed values while in case of **polyatomic molecules,** a particular type of bond is present in different molecules (e.g. O—H bond in H—O—H or CH_3O—H etc.) or even in the same molecule (e.g. four C—H bonds in CH_4).

It does not possess the same bond enthalpy (due to different electronic environment), hence, bond enthalpies are usually the average values and are called **mean** or **average bond enthalpy.**

e.g. In H_2O, first O—H bond enthalpy = 502 kJ mol^{-1} and second bond enthalpy = 427 kJ mol^{-1}.

Hence, average bond enthalpy $= \dfrac{502 + 427}{2}$

$= 464.5$ kJ mol^{-1}

(A more detailed study of bond enthalpy will be given in chapter 5).

Factors Affecting Bond Enthalpy

Several factors that affect the bond enthalpy are

(i) **Size of the atoms** Greater the size of the atom, greater is the bond length and hence, lesser is the bond dissociation enthalpy, i.e. lesser is the bond strength.

(ii) **Bond multiplicity** Greater the multiplicity of the bond, greater is the bond dissociation enthalpy. This is because atoms come closer and the number of bonds to be broken is more.

e.g. Bond dissociation enthalpies of H_2, O_2 and N_2 follow the order $H—H < O=O < N\equiv N$.

(iii) **Number of lone pairs of electrons** Greater the number of lone pairs of electrons present on the bonded atoms, greater is the repulsion between the atoms and hence, lesser is the bond dissociation enthalpy.

(iv) **Extent of overlapping** Higher the extent of overlapping, stronger is the bond and higher is the bond strength.

4. Bond Order

In the Lewis description of covalent bond, the number of bonds formed between the two atoms in a molecule is called the **bond order**.

e.g. The bond orders of a few molecules are given below.

Molecule	H—H	O=O	N≡N	C≡O
Bond order	1	2	3	3

In case of **odd electron molecules**, the three electron bonds are considered as equivalent to half covalent bond thus, bond order can be **fractional** also. e.g.

Lewis structure of NO is $:\dot{N}=\ddot{O}:$

Therefore, the bond order $= 2\frac{1}{2}$.

In case of **isoelectronic molecules** and ions, the bond orders may be identical. e.g. F_2 and O_2^{2-} have bond order 1. N_2, CO and NO^+ have bond order 3.

> **TEACHER'S TIP**
> With increase in bond order, bond enthalpy increases and bond length decreases.
> i.e. **Bond order $\propto$ Bond enthalpy $\propto \frac{1}{\text{Bond length}}$.**

5. Resonance

According to the concept of resonance whenever, a single Lewis structure cannot describe all the properties of a molecule, then a number of structures with similar energy, positions of nuclei, bonding and non-bonding pairs of electrons are written to describe all the properties.

- The actual structure is in between of all these contributing structures and is known as the **resonance hybrid** and the different individual structures are termed as **resonating structures** or **canonical forms**. This phenomenon is called **resonance**. Double headed arrows are used in between canonical structures to separate them as shown below.
- Experimentally determined oxygen-oxygen bond lengths in the O_3 molecule are same (128 pm) which is not represented by either structure 'a' or 'b'. Thus, the oxygen-oxygen bond in O_3 molecule are intermediate between a double and a single bond and is represented by resonance hybrid (structure 'c').

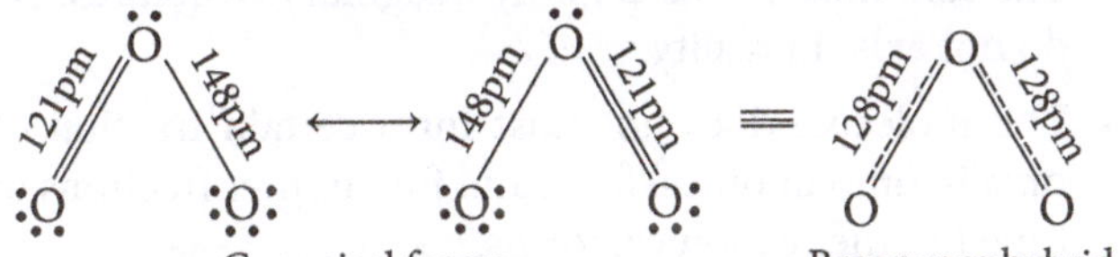

Resonance in O_3 molecule

Conditions for Writing Resonating Structures

Only those canonical or contributing structures contribute towards resonance which obey the following rules.

- In all the contributing structures, position of atoms should be the same. They should differ only in the positions of electrons.
- Number of unpaired electrons must also be the same in all the contributing structures.
- The energy of contributing structures should be nearly the same.

Stability of a Resonance Hybrid

In order to find the most stable hybrid form, follow the following rules

- Non-polar molecules are always more stable as compared to polar (charged) molecules.
- Canonical form having more number of covalent bonds is more stable.
- Canonical form having negative charge on electronegative atom and positive charge on electropositive or less electronegative atom is more stable.

Resonance Energy

The difference in the energy of the resonance hybrid and the most stable contributing structure (having least energy) is called **resonance energy**.

Note **Resonance stabilizes the molecule** as the energy of the resonance hybrid is less than the energy of any single canonical structure.

Clarification of Some Misconceptions Associated with Resonance

Several misconceptions are associated with resonance and there is a need to dispel them. One should remember that :

- The canonical forms are only imaginary structures, i.e. do not exist in reality.
- The molecule does not exist for a certain fraction of time in one canonical form and for another fractions of time in other canonical forms.
- Unlike tautomeric forms (keto and enol forms), canonical forms are not in the state of equilibrium.
- The molecule as such has a single structure which is the resonance hybrid of the canonical forms and cannot be depicted by a single Lewis structure.

Example 6 **All the chlorine-oxygen bond distance in ClO_4^- are 144 pm. What explanation can be given for this?**

Sol. ClO_4^- ion is a resonance hybrid of the following structures I, II, III and IV.

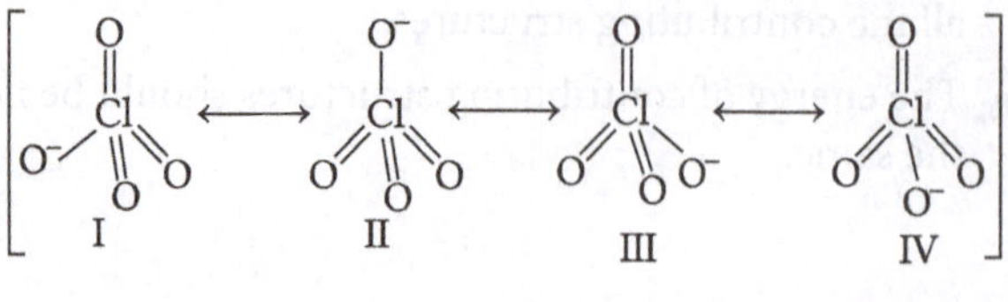

The probable hybrid structure is

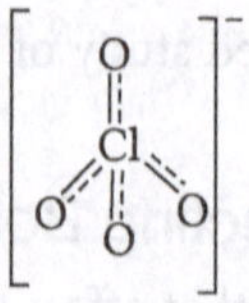

Thus, all the Cl—O bonds are equivalent having bond order = 1.75.

6. Polarity of Bonds : Dipole Moment

The magnitude of ionic character in a polar covalent bond is measured through a quantity called **dipole moment**. It is the measure of degree of polarity and is defined as *"the product of the magnitude of the charge and the distance between the centres of positive and negative charge"*. It is usually represented by a Greek **letter** μ (mu).

Mathematically, it is expressed as

Dipole moment (μ) = charge (Q) × distance of separation (r)

It is usually expressed in Debye units (D).

$$1\text{ D} = 3.33564 \times 10^{-30}\text{ C m}$$

where, C is coulomb and m is metre.

or $$1\text{ D} = 1 \times 10^{-18}\text{ esu (or, stat C cm)}$$

Here, esu = electrostatic unit

stat C cm = static coulomb centimeter

It is a vector quantity and is represented by the crossed arrow (⟶ with a cross) pointing towards the more electronegative atom.

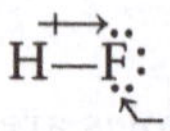

More electronegative atom

Dipole Moment of Molecular Structures

Dipole moment of different types of molecules are as follows

(i) **Dipole moment in case of diatomic molecules** In **diatomic polar molecules,** the dipole moment of the molecule is equal to the dipole moment of the polar bond. e.g. The dipole moment of HCl molecule is the same as that of H—Cl bond (μ = 1.07 D).

The degree of polarity of such molecules is also affected by the magnitude of electronegativity difference. *Greater the difference in the electronegativites of the combining atoms, greater will be the charge separation and hence, greater will be the polarity of the molecule.*

(ii) **Dipole moment of polyatomic molecules** In polyatomic molecules, the dipole moment not only depend upon the dipole moment of individual bonds (i.e. bond dipoles) but also upon the spatial arrangement of various bonds present in the molecule.

In such molecules, the net dipole moment is the vector sum of the dipole moments of various bonds.

In case of symmetrical tetra and polyatomic molecules like BF_3, CH_4 and CCl_4, without lone pair of electron will have dipole moment (μ) equal to zero as their μ cancels out that lies in opposite direction.

Bond dipoles in BeF_2

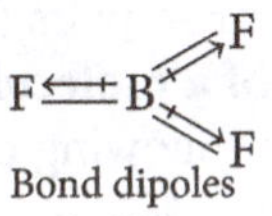

Bond dipoles in BF_3

- However, if all the bonds are not identical, the molecule may have a net dipole moment. e.g. $CHCl_3$ is also tetrahedral but has a dipole moment of 1.04 D.
- Lone pair of electrons also posseses some dipole moment and thus, its magnitude and direction also reflect the net dipole moment of the molecule.

  e.g. NH_3 and NF_3 (nitrogen trifluoride) both are trigonal pyramidal molecule with one lone pair but the dipole moment of NH_3 is greater than that of NF_3. This is because, in case of NH_3 the orbital dipole of lone pair is in the same direction as the resultant dipole moment of the N—H bonds, whereas in NF_3, the orbital dipole is in the direction opposite to the resultant dipole moment of the three N—F bonds.
- The orbital dipole because of lone pair reduces the effect of the resultant N—F bond moments, which results in the low dipole moment of NF_3.

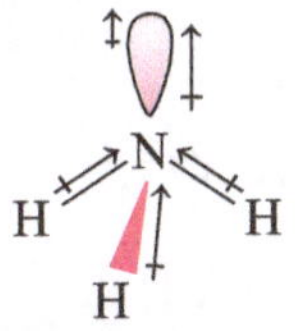

Resultant dipole moment in $NH_3 = 4.90 \times 10^{-30}$ C m

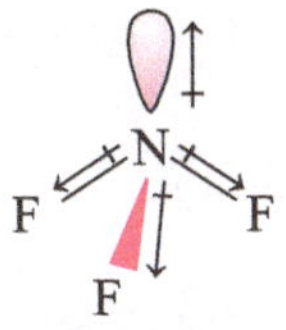

Resultant dipole moment in $NF_3 = 0.80 \times 10^{-30}$ C m

Dipole Moments of Some of the Molecules

Type of molecule	Example	Dipole moment, μ(D)	Geometry
Molecule (AB)	H_2	0	linear
	HF	1.78	linear
	HCl	1.07	linear
	HBr	0.79	linear
	HI	0.38	linear
Molecule (AB_2)	CO_2	0	linear
	H_2O	1.85	bent
	H_2S	0.95	bent
Molecule (AB_3)	BF_3	0	trigonal-planar
	NH_3	1.47	trigonal-pyramidal
	NF_3	0.23	trigonal-pyramidal
Molecule (AB_4)	CH_4	0	tetrahedral
	CCl_4	0	tetrahedral
	$CHCl_3$	1.04	tetrahedral

Ionic Character in a Molecule

The percentage of ionic character can be calculated from the ratio of the observed dipole moment to the dipole moment for the complete electron transfer (100% ionic character) by using the formula.

$$\%\text{ ionic character} = \frac{\mu_{\text{observed}}}{\mu_{\text{calculated for 100\% ionic}}} \times 100$$

4.6 Valence Shell Electron Pair Repulsion (VSEPR) Theory

Lewis concept is unable to explain the shapes of molecules in many cases.

In order to explain the shapes of these molecules adequately, a theory was proposed by Sidgwick and Powell which was further developed by Nyholm and Gillespie. It was based on the repulsive interaction of the electron pairs in the valence shell of the atoms called VSEPR theory.

Postulates

The main postulates of this theory are as follows

- The number of valence shell electron pairs (bonded or non-bonded) present around the central atom decides the shape of the molecules. (The shared electron pairs are called bond pairs and unshared or non-bonding electrons are called lone pairs).
- Electron pairs of valence shell repel one another because their electron clouds are negatively charged.
- These electron pairs arrange themselves in such a way so that there is minimum repulsion and maximum distance in between them.
- The valence shell is considered as a sphere in which the electron pairs are localised on the spherical surface at maximum distance from one another.
- A multiple bond is treated as, if it is a single electron pair and the two or three electron pairs of a multiple bond are treated as a single super pair.
- If a molecule has several resonating structures, the VSEPR model is applicable to any such structure.
- A lone pair occupies more space than a bonding pair, since it lies closer to the central atom.

  This means that the **repulsion between the different electron pairs** follow the order

  Lone pair-lone pair > lone pair-bond pair > bond pair-bond pair

  The effects of these repulsions are deviations from idealised shapes and alterations in bond angles in molecules.

Geometrical Shapes of Molecules on the Basis of VSEPR Theory

The geometry of a molecule depends upon the total number of electron pairs (*lps* + *bps*) **present around the central atom of a molecule.** It is convenient to divide molecules into following categories as

(i) **Geometry of molecules in which the central atom has no lone pair of electrons.** e.g. If there are only two bond pairs and no lone pairs around the central atom, the only way to keep them as far apart as possible is to arrange them at an angle of 180° to each other. The molecule in such a case will adopt **linear** geometry.

Geometry and Arrangement of Electron Pairs of few Compounds

Number of electron pairs	Arrangement of electron pairs	Molecular geometry	Examples
2	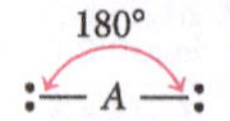 Linear	*B*—*A*—*B* Linear	$BeCl_2$, $HgCl_2$, $ZnCl_2$
3	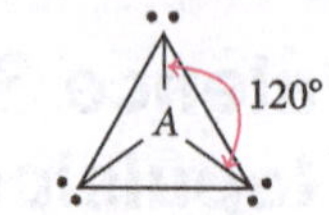 Trigonal planar	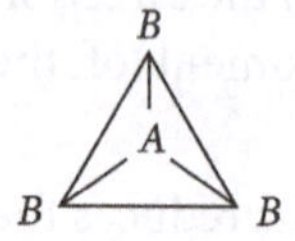 Trigonal planar	BF_3 , AlF_3
4	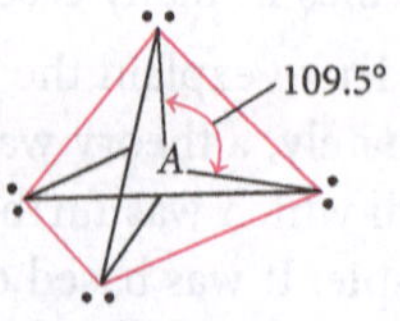 Tetrahedral	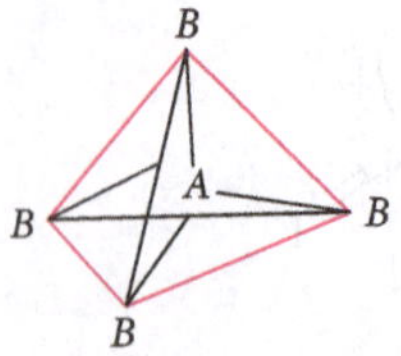 Tetrahedral	CH_4, NH_4^+, CCl_4

Number of electron pairs	Arrangement of electron pairs	Molecular geometry	Examples
5	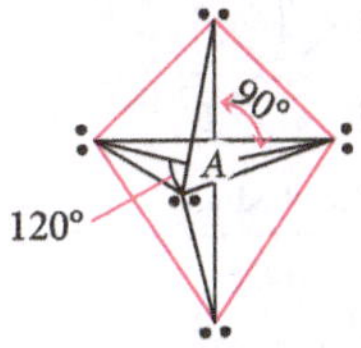 Trigonal bipyramidal	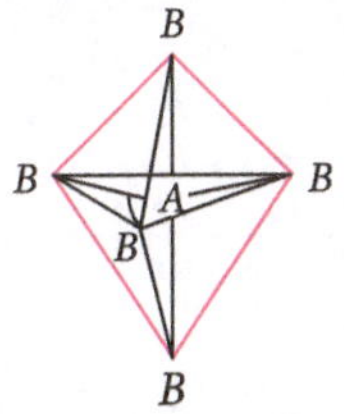 Trigonal bipyramidal	PCl_5
6	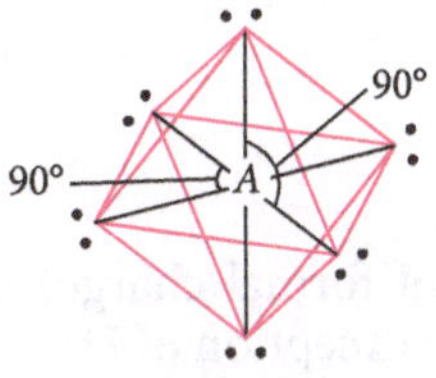 Octahedral	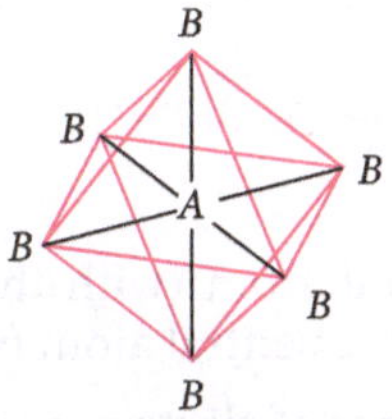 Octahedral	SF_6

(ii) **Geometry (Shape) of some simple molecules/ions with central ions having one or more lone pairs of electrons (*e*).** In the molecule type given below, '*A*' is the central atom '*B*' the side atom and '*E*' is the lone pair of electrons.

Molecule type	No. of bonding pairs	No. of lone pairs	Arrangement of electron pairs	Shape	Examples
AB_2E	2	1	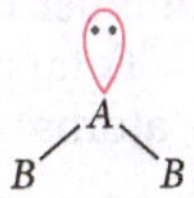 Trigonal planar	Bent	SO_2, O_3
AB_3E	3	1	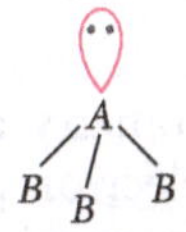 Tetrahedral	Trigonal pyramidal	NH_3, PCl_3
AB_2E_2	2	2	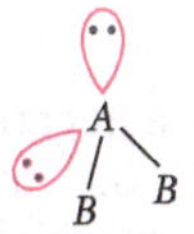 Tetrahedral	Bent	H_2O
AB_4E	4	1	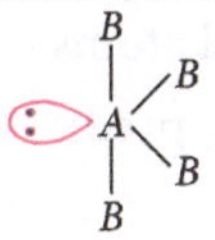 Trigonal bipyramidal	*See-saw*	SF_4
AB_3E_2	3	2	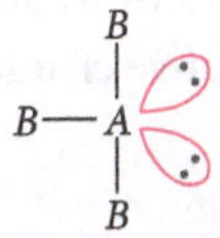 Trigonal bipyramidal	T-shape	ClF_3

Molecule type	No. of bonding pairs	No. of lone pairs	Arrangement of electron pairs	Shape	Examples
AB_5E	5	1	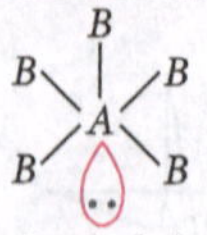 Octahedral	Square pyramidal	BrF_5
AB_4E_2	4	2	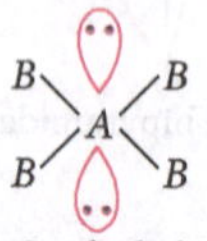 Octahedral	Square planar	XeF_4

Steps for Predicting the Shape of Molecules

It involves the following steps

Step I First of all identify the central atom (with the help of formal charge). Also remember that mostly, less electronegative atom acts as the central atom (with the exception of H).

Step II Now calculate the total number of electron pair around central atom as given below.

Total number of electron pairs around central atom

$$= \frac{\text{Number of valence } e^- \text{ of central atom} + \text{Number of atoms linked to central atom by single bond.}}{2}$$

Number of bond pairs (shared pairs) = Number of atoms attached to central atom

Number of lone pairs = Total number of electron pairs − number of shared pairs = Total number of electron pairs − number of atoms linked to central atom.

Step III Multiple bond, if present, are considered as equivalent to single bond.

Step IV Now find the structure or geometry associated with the obtained number of electron pairs with the help of table 1 and 2. When working out the shape of an ion, you also need to include the charge in the calculation.

Step V In case the central atom carries a negative charge or positive charge, add 1 or subtract 1 respectively from the number of valence e^- of central atoms and then calculate the total number of electron pair around central atoms.

Example 7 **On the basis of VSEPR theory, predict the shapes of the following**

(i) NH_2^- **(ii) O_3**

Sol. (i) **Shape of NH_2^-** Number of valence electrons on central N atom = 5 + 1 (due to one unit negative charge) = 6

Number of atoms linked to it = 2

∴ Total number of electron pairs around

$$N = \frac{6+2}{2} = 4 \text{ and number of bond pairs} = 2$$

∴ Number of lone pairs = 4 − 2 = 2.

Thus, the ion is of the type AB_2E_2.

Hence, it has **bent** shape (V-shape).

(ii) **Shape of O_3** While predicting geometry, molecules containing the double (or multiple) bond is considered as one electron pair.

e.g. In case of ozone, its two resonating structures are

Thus, the central O-atom is considered to have two bond pairs and one lone pair, i.e. it is of the type AB_2E.

Hence, it is a **bent molecule**. Thus, the two resonating structures will be

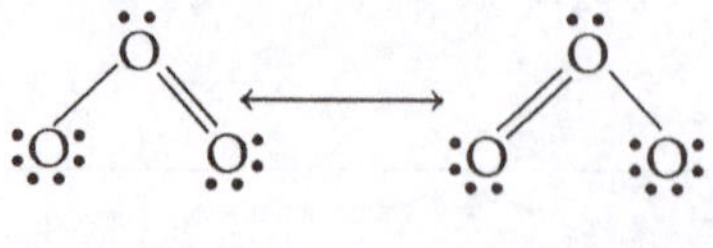

Shape (Geometry) of Molecules having Lone Pair and Bond Pair

1. Shape of SO_2 Molecule (AB_2E Type)

In SO_2, S is the central atom ($1s^2\ 2s^2\ 2p^6\ 3s^2\ 3p^4$) with six valence electrons. There are two O-atoms each of which form double bond with S-atom and therefore the molecule contains 2 bond pairs (a double bond and triple bond are considered to be equivalent to single bond).

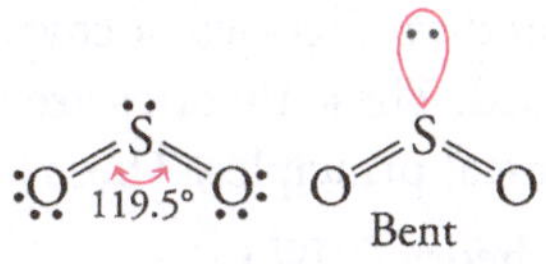

Theoretically the shape of the molecule should have been triangular planar but actually it is found to be bent or V-shaped. This is because the lone pair-bond pair repulsion is much more as compared to the bond pair-bond pair repulsion. Thus, the angle is also reduced to 119.5° from 120°.

2. Shape of NH_3 Molecule (AB_3E Type)

In NH_3, N is the central atom ($1s^2 2s^2 2p^3$) with five valence electrons. The three hydrogen atoms from single bond with N-atom and therefore the molecule contains 3 bond pairs.

The two electrons remain localise as non-bonded pair on nitrogen atom.

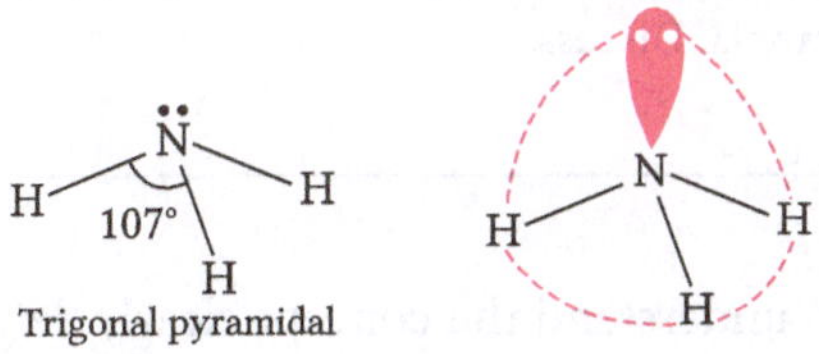

If there is a *bp* in place of *lp*, the shape would have been tetrahedral but one lone pair is present and due to the repulsion between *lp-bp* (which is more than *bp-bp* repulsion) the angle between bond pairs is reduced to 107° from 109.5°.

3. Shape of H_2O Molecule (AB_2E_2 Type)

In H_2O, O is the central atom ($1s^2\ 2s^2\ 2p^4$) with six valence electrons. The two hydrogen atoms from single bond with O-atom and therefore the molecule contains 2 bond pairs.

The four electrons remain localised as two lone pairs on oxygen atom.

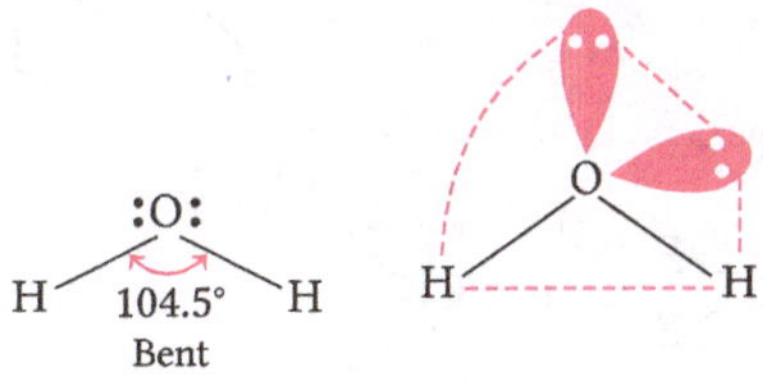

The shape should have been tetrahedral if there were all *bp* but two *lp* are present so the shape is distorted tetrahedral or angular.

The reason is *lp-lp* repulsion is more than *lp-bp* repulsion which is more than *bp-bp* repulsion. Thus, the angle is reduced to 104.5° from 109.5°.

4. Shape of Sulphur Tetrafluoride (SF_4) Molecule (AB_4E Type)

In this molecule, S is the central atom with six valence electrons. Out of which four are involved in bonding with four F-atoms and the remaining two behave as a lone pair.

The possible arrangement of these pairs are as follows

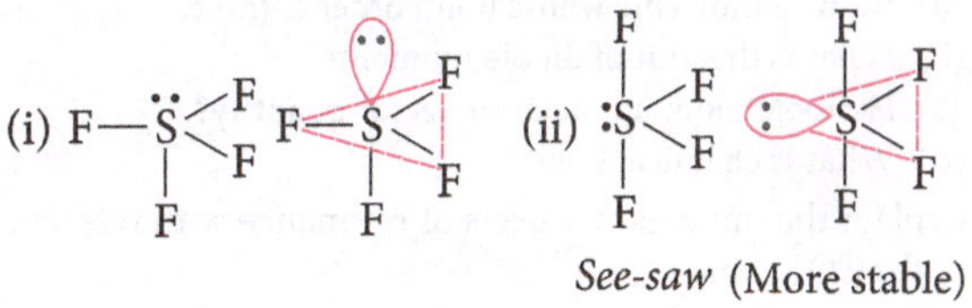

In (i) the *lp* occupy axial position so there are three *lp-bp* repulsions at 90°. In (ii) the *lp* occupy an equatorial position, and hence there are two *lp-bp* repulsions.

Hence, arrangement (ii) is more stable. The shape shown in structure (ii) is a distorted tetrahedron, a folded square or a *see-saw*.

5. Shape of Chlorine Trifluoride (ClF_3) Molecule (AB_3E_2 Type)

Here, Cl is the central atom with 7 valence electrons, out of which three are involved in bonding with three F atoms and the remaining four act as two lone pairs. These 5 electron pairs (3*bp* + 2*lp*) arrange them in trigonal bipyramidal geometry in the following manner.

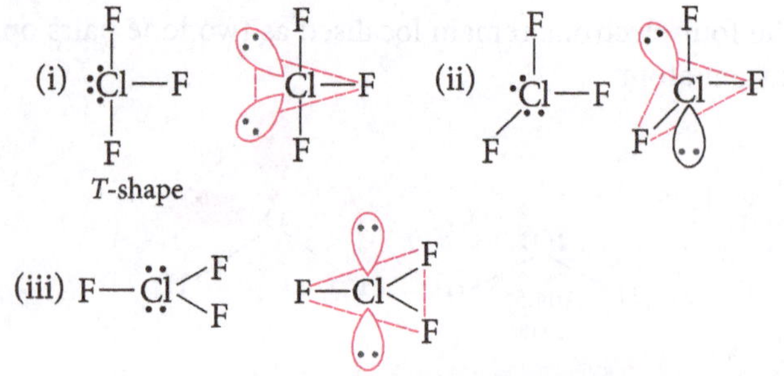

In structure (i) the lone pairs occupy equitoral positions so there are less *lp-bp* repulsions as compared to others in which the lone pairs occupy axial positions. So, structure (i) T-shape is most stable.

Limitations of VSEPR Theory

The VSEPR theory is useful for predicting the geometry of a large number of molecules, especially the compounds of *p*-block elements. This theory is also successful in determining the geometry quite accurately even when the energy difference between possible structures is very small.

However, it fails to explain the theoretical basis of this theory regarding the effects of electron pair repulsions on molecular shapes. Lewis approach helps to write the structure of molecule, but it fails to explain the chemical bond formation.

To overcome the above limitations, two important theories, called modern theories of covalent bonding have been proposed. These theories are based on quantum mechanical principles. These are

- Valence bond theory (VBT)
- Molecular orbital theory (MOT)

Quick Test 2

1. How do you express the bond strength in terms of bond order? NCERT
2. Although both CO_2 and H_2O are triatomic molecules, the shape of the H_2O molecule is bent, while that of CO_2 linear. Explain this on the basis of dipole moment. NCERT
3. (a) Name a molecule whose bond order is three.
   (b) What is the unit of dipole moment?
   (c) Is dipole moment scalar or vector quantity?
   (d) What is chemical bond? Diksha
4. Explain the important aspects of resonance with reference to the CO_3^{2-} ion. NCERT Exemplar
5. Explain giving reasons whether BH_4^- and H_3O^+ will have same or different geometry.
6. Calculate the number of bond pairs and lone pairs in IF_5 molecule.
7. Why NF_3 is pyramidal but BF_3 is triangular planar?
8. What do you understand by bond pairs and lone pairs of electrons? Illustrate by giving one example of each type. NCERT
9. Explain the shape of BrF_5. NCERT Exemplar
10. Arrange the following in order of decreasing bond angle, give reason also.
    NO_2, NO_2^+, NO_2^-
11. Although geometries of NH_3 and H_2O molecules are distorted tetrahedral, bond angle in water is less than that of ammonia. Discuss. NCERT

For Solutions, See QR Code on Pg. 172

4.7 Valence Bond Theory (VBT)

This theory was introduced by **Heitler** and **London**. The VBT came into picture because VSEPR theory was unable to explain the geometry of simple molecules and has limited applications.

It is based on the knowledge of atomic orbitals, electronic configurations of elements, the criteria of overlapping of atomic orbitals, the hybridisation of atomic orbitals and the principles of variation and superposition.

In order to understand the concept clearly, let us consider the formation of H_2 molecule.

Structure of H_2 Molecule as Per VBT

Consider two hydrogen atoms *A* and *B* approaching each other. Their nuclei are N_A and N_B and electrons present in them are represented by e_A and e_B.

When the two atoms are far apart, there is no interaction between them but as they approach each other, some new attractive and repulsive forces begin to operate.

- Attractive forces arise between
  - nucleus of one atom and its own electron, i.e. $N_A - e_A$ and $N_B - e_B$.
  - nucleus of one atom and electron of other atom i.e. $N_A - e_B$ and $N_B - e_A$.
- Similarly, repulsive forces arise between
  - electrons of two atoms, i.e. $e_A - e_B$.
  - nuclei of two atoms, $N_A - N_B$.

Attractive forces tend to bring the combining atoms close to each other, whereas repulsive forces tend to push them apart as shown in the figure.

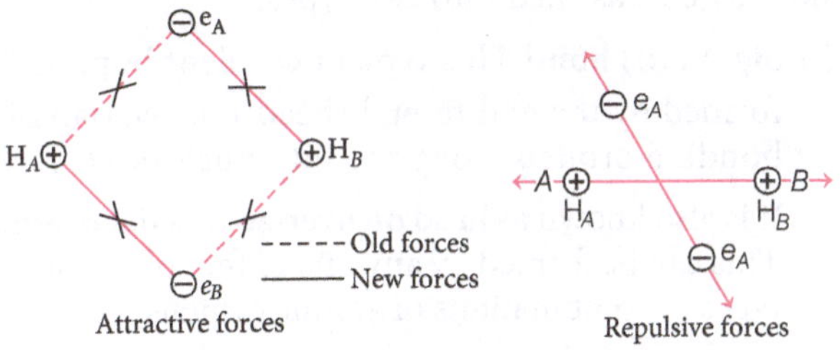

Forces of attraction and repulsion during the formation of H_2 molecule

Experiment also revealed that the magnitude of new attractive force is more than the new repulsive forces. As a result, potential energy decreases due to approaching of two atoms towards each other.

Ultimately a stage is reached when the net force of attraction balances the force of repulsion and system acquires minimum energy.

This is the state when two hydrogen atoms are bonded together to form a stable molecule with H—H bond length of 74 pm.

The energy liberated is 435.8 kJ/mol which is known as **bond energy**.

- If the distance between the two atoms is decreased further, repulsive forces exceed the attractive forces and the potential energy of the system shoots up.
- If the atoms containing electrons with parallel spins approach each other, the potential energy of the two hydrogen atoms goes on increasing, the bond formation doesn't take place.

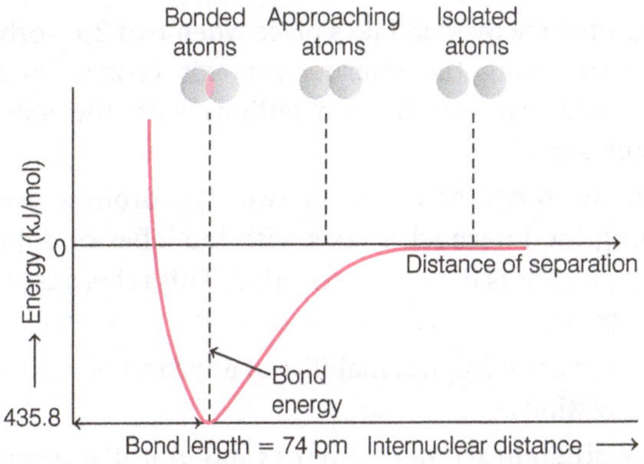

The potential energy curve for the formation of H_2 molecule as a function of internuclear distance of the H-atoms. The minimum in the curve corresponds to

Orbital Overlap Concept

According to this concept, a covalent bond is formed by the overlapping of two half-filled atomic orbitals, of valence shell having electrons with opposite spins. This results in the pairing of electrons. The extent of overlap decides the strength of a covalent bond. Greater the overlapping of atomic orbitals, stronger is the bond formed between two atoms.

Directional Properties of Bonds

The valence bond theory explains the formation and directional properties of bonds in polyatomic molecules like CH_4, NH_3 and H_2O etc., in terms of overlap and hybridisation of atomic orbitals. Hence, it also account for the geometry of the resulting molecules.

Since, the strength of the bond depends upon the extent of overlapping, orbitals (apart from *s*-orbitals) form bond only in certain directions to give maximum overlap.

Overlapping of Atomic Orbitals

- When orbitals of two atoms overlap to form bond, their overlap may be positive, negative or zero. It depends upon the sign (phase) and direction of orientation of amplitude of orbital wave functions of atomic orbitals. (It is not related to charge)

e.g. Positive overlap takes place when two $2p_z$-orbitals overlap along the internuclear axis (z-axis is taken as molecular axis by convention) with the lobes of same sign.

- On the other hand, when two $2p_z$-orbitals overlap along the internuclear axis with the lobes of opposite sign, it results in negative overlap. This is because lobes of opposite sign cannot combine.
- Zero overlap implies inability of any kind of interactions.
- The different arrangements of s and p-orbitals resulting in positive, negative and zero overlaps are given below.

Positive or in phase overlap Negative or out of phase overlap

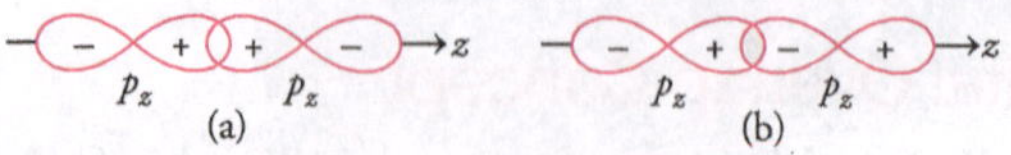

Combination of $2p_z$ atomic orbitals

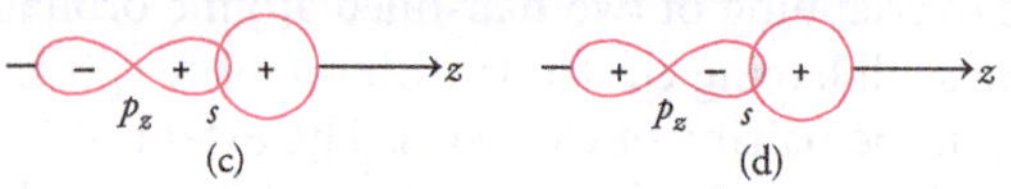

Combination of $2p_z$ and 2 s atomic orbitals

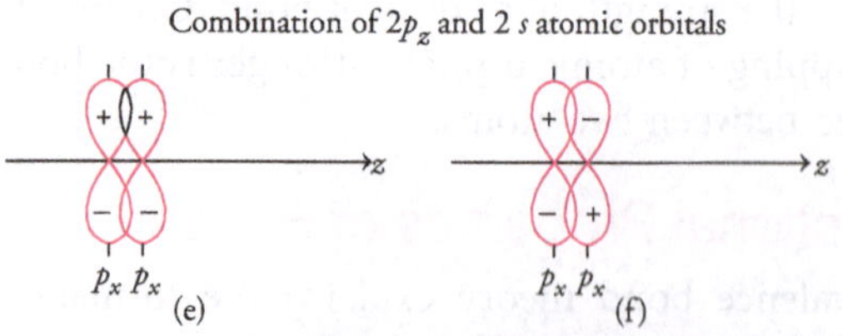

Combination of $2p_x$ atomic orbitals

Zero overlap (out of phase due to different orientation direction of approach)

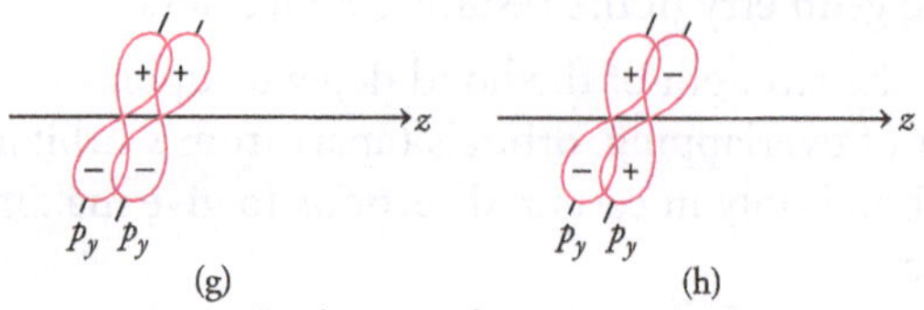

Combination of $2p_y$ atomic orbitals

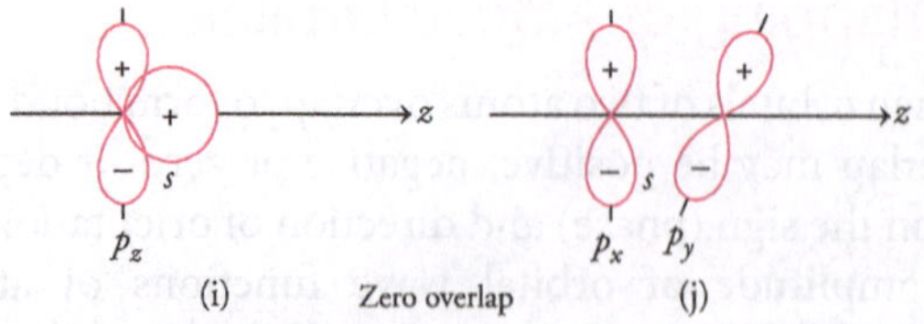

Positive, negative and zero overlaps of s and p atomic orbitals

- The criterion of overlap of atomic orbitals of combining atoms is the main factor for the formation of covalent bonds both in homonuclear as well as in heteronuclear diatomic molecules and polyatomic molecules.
- In case of polyatomic molecules like, CH_4, NH_3 and H_2O, the VBT should be taken into consideration for their characteristics shapes.
- As we know, the shapes of CH_4, NH_3 and H_2O molecules are tetrahedral, pyramidal and bent, respectively. Their shapes can be described in terms of the orbital overlaps.

Types of Overlapping and Nature of Covalent Bonds

Depending upon the types of overlapping, the covalent bond may be classified into two types.

(i) **Sigma (σ) bond** This type of covalent bond is formed by the end to end (head-on) overlap of bonding orbitals along the internuclear axis.

It is also known as **head on overlap** or **axial overlap.** This can be formed by any one of the following types of combinations of atomic orbitals.

- ***s-s* overlapping** In it, there is overlap of two half-filled s-orbitals along the internuclear axis as shown below.

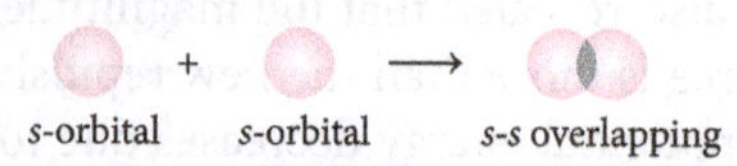

- ***s-p* overlapping** This type of overlap takes place between half-filled s-orbitals of one atom and half-filled p-orbitals of another atom.

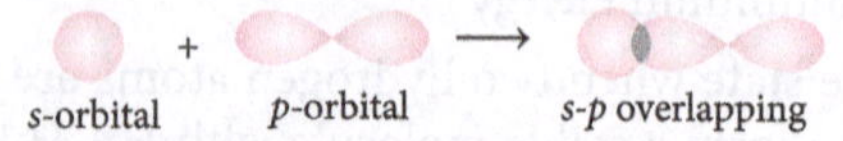

- ***p-p* overlapping** It occurs between half-filled p-orbitals of the two approaching atoms.

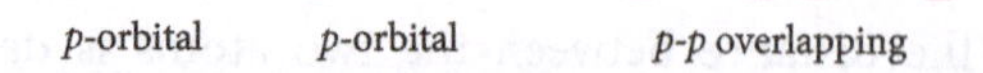

Note If z-axis is chosen as the internuclear axis, no overlapping can take place between s and p_x or p_y-orbital, or p_x and p_y-orbitals, i.e. there is zero overlap.

(ii) **pi (π) bond** When the atomic orbitals overlap in such a way that their axis remain parallel to each other and perpendicular to the internuclear axis, the bond formed is called **π-bond.**

The orbitals formed as a result of sidewise overlapping contains two saucer type charged clouds above and below the plane of the participating atoms.

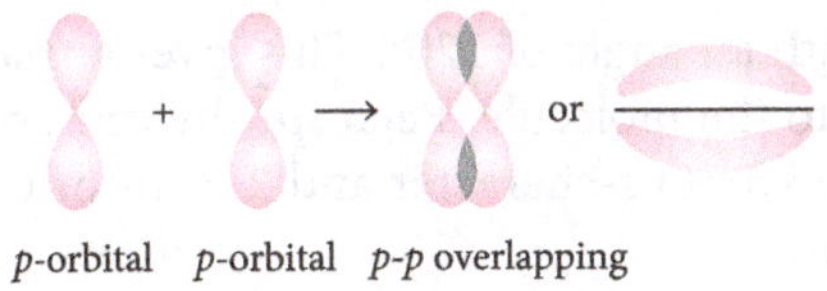

Note π-**bond** is a weaker bond as compared to σ-**bond** due to smaller extent of overlapping. In the formation of multiple bonds (double or triple bonds) between two atoms of a molecule, π-bond(s) is formed in addition to a sigma bond.

e.g. A double bond contains one σ and one π-bond, whereas a triple bond contains one σ and two π-bonds.

Comparison of Sigma and Pi-Bonds

Sigma (σ) bond	Pi (π) bond
This bond is formed by end to end overlap of s - s, s - p and p - p orbitals along their internuclear axis.	This bond is formed by sideways overlapping of p - p orbitals.
As overlapping takes place to a greater extent hence, σ- bond is a strong bond.	As overlapping takes place to a smaller extent hence, π-bond is a weak bond.
Free rotation around a σ-bond is possible.	Free rotation around a π-bond is not possible because on rotation overlapping diminishes and thus, the bond breaks.
In this case, the electron cloud is symmetrical about the line joining the two nuclei.	Electron cloud of π-bond is unsymmetrical.

4.8 Hybridisation

This concept was put forward by **Pauling**. He suggested that the atomic orbitals mix together to generate a new set of equivalent orbitals, called the **hybrid orbitals** or **hybridised orbitals**. These orbitals are used in bond formation. The phenomenon is called **hybridisation**.

It can be defined as *"the process of intermixing of the orbitals of slightly different energies so as to redistribute their energies, to generate a new set of orbitals of equivalent energies and shape"*.

e.g. When one $2s$ and three $2p$-orbitals of carbon hybridise, they result in the formation of four new sp^3-hybrid orbitals.

Salient Features of Hybridisation

The main features of hybridisation are as follows

- The number of hybrid orbitals generated and the number of the atomic orbitals that are hybridised are equal in number.
- The hybridised orbitals have equivalent energies and identical shapes.
- The hybrid orbitals are more effective in forming stable bonds than the pure atomic orbitals.
- These hybrid orbitals arrange themselves in space in such a direction so that there is minimum repulsion between electron pairs and thus a stable arrangement is obtained. Therefore, the type of hybridisation indicates the geometry of the molecules.

Important Conditions for Hybridisation

There are some necessary conditions which are required for hybridisation. These are as follows :

- Only valence shell orbitals of an atom take part in hybridisation.
- The orbitals undergoing hybridisation should have almost equal energy.
- Promotion of electron prior to hybridisation is not necessary.
- It is not necessary that only half-filled orbitals involve in the hybridisation. In some cases, even filled orbitals of valence shell can also involve in hybridisation.

Types of Hybridisation

There are many types of hybridisation involving s, p and d-orbitals. The different types of hybridisations are as follows :

1. *sp*-hybridisation

It occurs when one s and one p-orbital mix together and result in the formation of two equivalent sp-hybrid orbitals. Each sp-hybrid orbitals is associated with 50% s-character and 50% p-character.

Such a molecule in which the central atom is sp-hybridised and linked directly to two other central atoms have linear geometry. This hybridisation is also known as **diagonal hybridisation.**

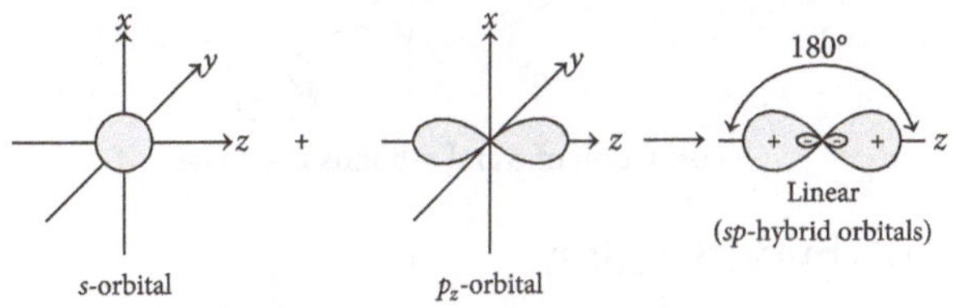

Formation of sp-hybrids from s and p-orbitals

e.g.

(i) $BeCl_2$ The ground state electronic configuration of Be is $1s^2 2s^2$. In the excited state, one electron from $2s$ orbital is promoted to vacant $2p$ orbital to make it bivalent.

One $2s$ and one $2p$ orbital gets hybridised to form two *sp* hybridised orbitals oriented at an angle of 180°. Each of the *sp* hybridised orbital overlaps with the $2p$-orbital of chlorine axially and forms two Be—Cl sigma bonds.

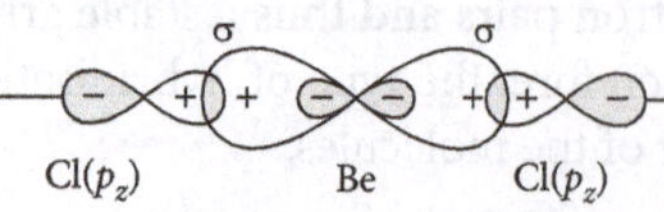

$BeCl_2$ molecule (Linear shape)

(ii) C_2H_2 (ethyne) **molecule** An ethyne molecule is formed when both the carbon atoms undergo *sp*-hybridisation. It has two unhybridised orbital, i.e. $2p_y$ and $2p_x$. One *sp*-hybrid orbital of one carbon atom overlaps axially with *sp*-hybrid orbital of the other C-atom to form C—C σ-bond.

While the other hybridised orbital of each C-atom overlaps axially with the half-filled *s*-orbital of hydrogen atoms to form C—H σ-bonds.

The remaining two unhybridised *p*-orbitals of both the C-atoms overlaps sidewise to form two π bonds between the C-atoms.

Thus, the triple bond present between the two C-atoms in a ethyne molecule is made up of one σ and two π-bonds as shown in the following figure

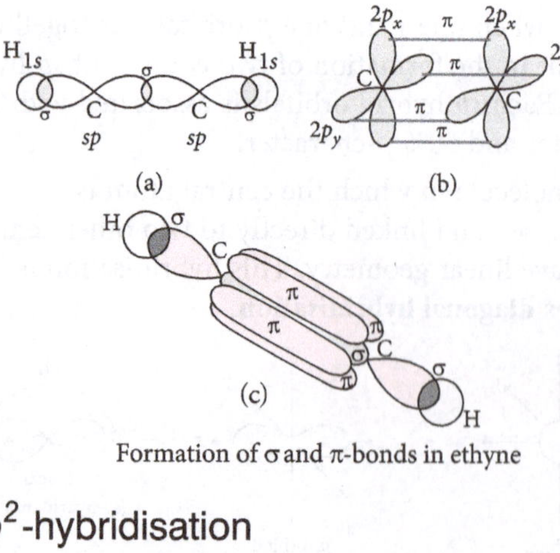

Formation of σ and π-bonds in ethyne

2. sp^2-hybridisation

When one *s* and two *p*-orbitals mix together, they result in the formation of three equivalent sp^2-hybridised orbitals. These three sp^2-hybrid orbitals are directed towards the three corners of an equilateral triangle with an angle of 120°. This gives a triangular geometry to the molecule. Each sp^2-hybrid orbital has 1/3rd (or 33.33%) *s*-character and 2/3 rd (or 66.7%) *p*-character.

e.g.

(i) BCl_3 The ground state electronic configuration of central boron atom is $1s^2 2s^2 2p^1$. In the excited state, one of the $2s$ electrons is promoted to vacant $2p$-orbital so that boron has three unpaired electrons.

These three orbitals (one $2s$ and two $2p$) undergo hybridisation to give three sp^2-hybrid orbitals oriented in a trigonal planar arrangement. Three sp^2 hybrid orbitals overlap with $2p$-orbitals of chlorine to form three B—Cl bonds. Therefore, the geometry of BCl_3 is trigonal planar with Cl—B—Cl bond angle of 120°.

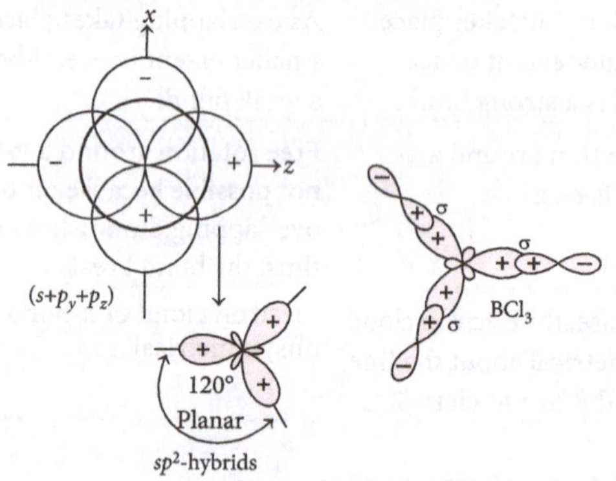

Formation of sp^2 hybrids and the BCl_3 molecule

(ii) C_2H_4 (ethene) **molecule** In the formation of ethene molecule, one of the sp^2-hybrid orbitals of one C-atom overlaps axially with sp^2-hybridised orbital of another C-atom to form a C—C sigma bond. The remaining two sp^2-hybrid orbitals of each C-atom form sp^2-*s* sigma bond with *s*-orbital of two hydrogen atoms.

The unhybridised orbital ($2p_x$ or $2p_y$) of one C-atom overlaps sidewise with the similar orbital of the other carbon atom to form a weak π-bond, which consists of two equal electron clouds distributed above and below the plane of C and H-atoms.

Thus, in ethene, the C—C bond contains one sp^2-sp^2 σ bond and one π-bond. The C—C bond length is 134 pm. The C—H bond is sp^2-*s* σ with bond length 108 pm. The H—C—H bond angle is 117.6°, while the H—C—C angle is 121°.

The formation of sigma and pi-bonds in ethene can be shown as

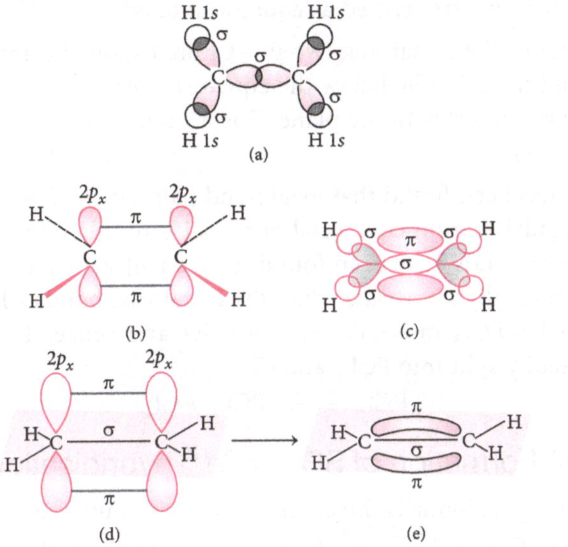

Formation of σ and π-bonds in ethene

3. sp^3-hybridisation

In this hybridisation, one *s* and three *p*-orbitals of the valence shell intermix to form four sp^3-hybrid orbitals of equivalent energies and shape. Each sp^3-hybrid orbital contains 25% *s*-character and 75% *p*-character.

The four sp^3-hybrid orbitals so obtained are directed towards the four corners of a regular tetrahedron.

The angle between sp^3-hybrid orbitals is 109.5°.

e.g.

(i) **Formation of methane** (CH_4) In this, one 2*s* and three 2*p*-orbitals of carbon intermix to form four sp^3-hybrid orbitals, that overlaps with 1*s*-orbital of four H-atoms to form four C—H bonds.

Since, the orbitals are directed towards the corners of a tetrahedron, the shape of methane is tetrahedral with H—C—H bond angle 109° 28′(~ 109.5°).

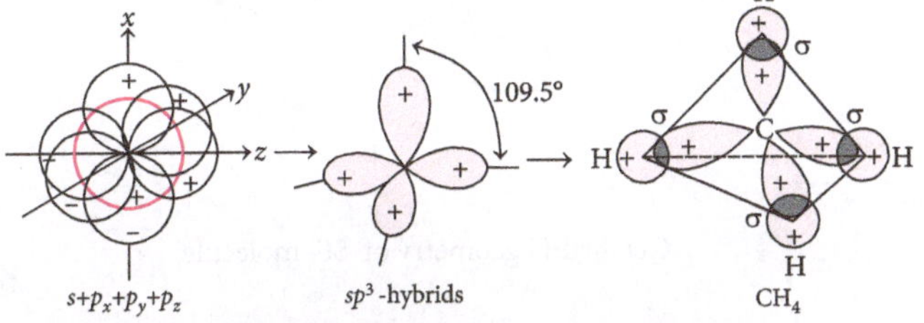

Formation of sp^3-hybrids by the combination of *s*, p_x, p_y and p_z atomic orbitals of carbon and the formation of CH_4 molecule

(ii) **Formation of ammonia** (NH_3) In NH_3, nitrogen is the central atom with the valence shell (outer) electronic configuration (ground state) $2s^2\,2p_x^1\,2p_y^1\,2p_z^1$ and its one *s* and three *p*-orbitals give four sp^3-hybridised orbital of equal energy. Three sp^3-hybrid orbitals contains three unpaired electrons, whereas the fourth have a lone pair of electrons. These hybrid orbitals having unpaired electron overlap with 1*s*-orbitals of hydrogen atoms to form three N—H σ bonds.

As *lp-bp* repulsions are greater than *bp-bp* repulsions, the molecule thus gets distorted and the bond angle is reduced to 107° from 109.5°.

The geometry of such a molecule will be pyramidal as shown below

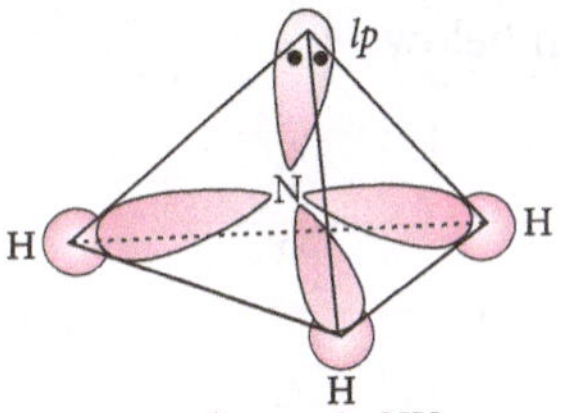

Ammonia, NH_3

(iii) **Formation of ethane (C_2H_6) molecule** In ethane molecule, both the carbons are assumed to be sp^3 hybridised. One of the four sp^3 hybrid orbitals of one carbon atom overlaps axially with similar orbitals of the other carbon atom to form sp^3 - sp^3 sigma bond.

The other three sp^3 hybrid orbitals of each carbon atom are used to form sp^3-*s* sigma bond with hydrogen atoms. Therefore, in ethane C—C bond length is 154 pm and each C—H bond length is 109 pm.

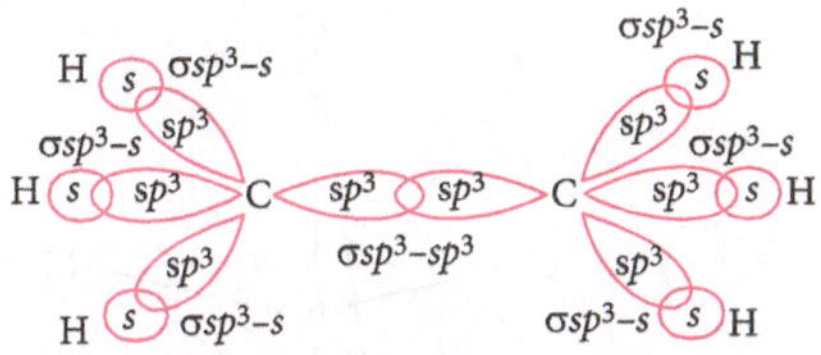

Formation of ethane molecule

Hybridisation of Elements Involving *d*-Orbitals

Elements of third period have *d*-orbitals alongwith *s* and *p*-orbitals, which are also involved in hybridisation. This is because the energy of the 3*d*-orbitals are comparable to the energy of the 3*s* and 3*p*-orbitals.

The energy of 3*d*-orbitals are also comparable to those of 4*s* and 4*p*-orbitals, consequently the hybridisation involving either 3*s*, 3*p* and 3*d* or 3*d*, 4*s* and 4*p* is possible.

TEACHER'S TIP

Due to the significant difference in the energies of 3*p* and 4*s*-orbital, no hybridisation involving 3*p*,3*d* and 4*s*-orbitals is possible.

The most common examples involving hybridisation of *d*-orbitals are

(i) Formation of PCl_5 (sp^3d-hybridisation)

The ground state and the excited state outer electronic configurations of the central atom, i.e. phosphorus ($Z = 15$) are given below.

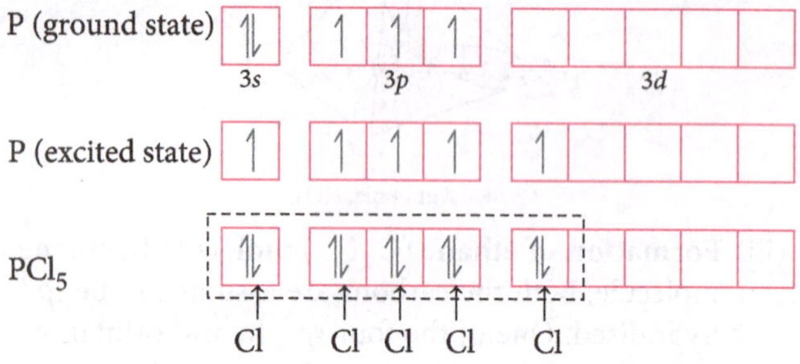

sp^3d-hybridisation

Thus, the five orbitals (i.e. one *s*, three *p* and one *d*-orbitals) undergo hybridisation and give a set of five sp^3d-hybrid orbitals which are directed towards the five corners of a trigonal bipyramidal as shown in the figure.

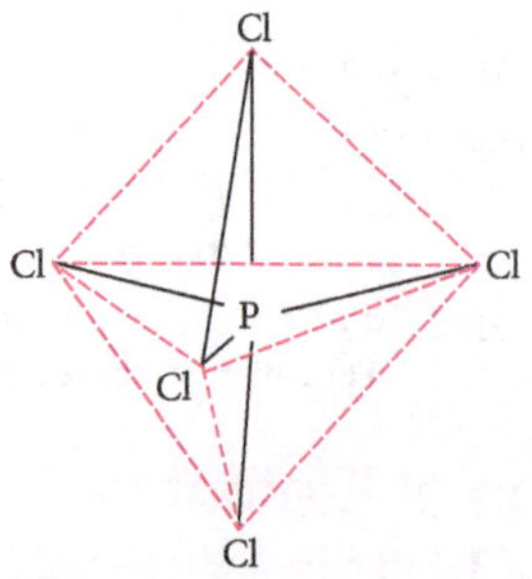

Trigonal bipyramidal geometry of PCl_5 molecule

In PCl_5, the five sp^3d-orbitals of phosphorus overlap with the singly occupied *p*-orbitals of chlorine atoms to form five P—Cl σ-bonds out of which three P—Cl bonds lie in one plane at an angle of 120° with each other and are termed as **equatorial bond.**

Out of the remaining two P—Cl bonds, one lie above and the other lie below the equatorial plane, making an angle of 90° with the plane. These bonds are called **axial bonds.**

It has been found that axial bond pair suffer greater repulsion from equatorial bond pairs and therefore, the axial bonds have been found to be slightly longer and hence, slightly weaker than the equatorial bonds which makes PCl_5 molecule more reactive and hence, it readily split into PCl_3 and Cl_2.

$$PCl_5 \longrightarrow PCl_3 + Cl_2$$

(ii) Formation of SF_6 (sp^3d^2-hybridisation)

In SF_6, sulphur is the central atom with outer electronic configuration $3s^2 3p^4$. In the excited state, the available six orbitals, i.e. one *s*, three *p* and two *d* are singly occupied by electrons and hybridise to form six new sp^3d^2-hybrid orbitals, that are projected towards the six corners of a regular octahedron in SF_6.

These six sp^3d^2-hybrid orbitals overlap with singly occupied orbitals of fluorine atoms to form six S—F σ-bonds.

Thus, SF_6 molecule has a regular octahedral geometry.

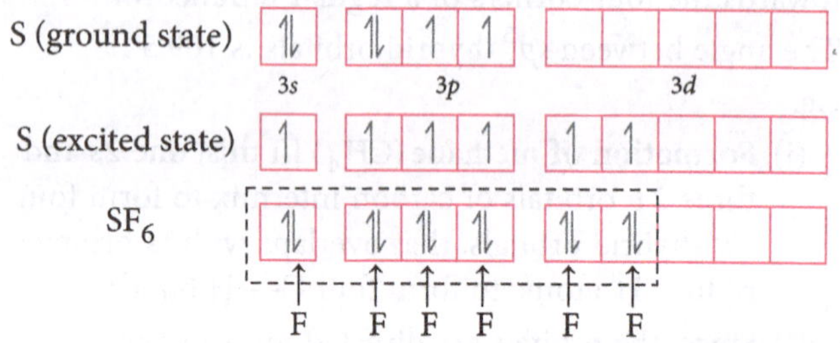

sp^3d^2-hybridisation

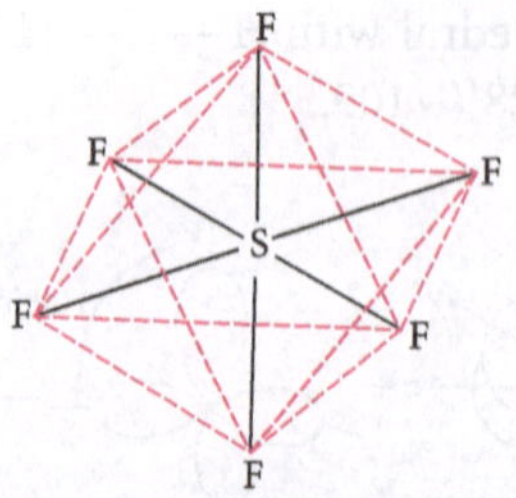

Octahedral geometry of SF_6 molecule

Hybrid Orbitals and Molecular Shapes of Molecules Involving *s*, *p* and *d*-orbitals

No. of electron pairs ($lp + bp$)	Type of hybridisation	Atomic orbitals	Shape	Bond angle	Examples
2	sp	$s+p$	Linear	180°	$HgCl_2$, $BeCl_2$, C_2H_2
3	sp^2	$s+2(p)$	Trigonal planar	120°	BF_3, $AlCl_3$, C_2H_4, CO_3^{2-}, NO_3^-
4	sp^3	$s+3(p)$	Tetrahedral	109.5°	CH_4, $SiCl_4$, NH_4^+, ClO_4^-
4	dsp^2	$d+s+2(p)$	Square planar	90°	$[Ni(CN)_4]^{2-}$, $[PtCl_4]^{2-}$
5	sp^3d	$s+3(p)+d$	Trigonal bipyramidal	90°, 120°	PF_5, PCl_5
6	sp^3d^2 or d^2sp^3 or sp^3d^2	$s+3(p)+2(d)$ or $2(d)+s+3(p)$ $s+3(p)+2(d)$	Octahedral Square pyramidal	90° 90°	SF_6, CrF_6^{3-} $[Co(NH_3)_6]^{3+}$ BrF_5
7	sp^3d^3 (d are d_{xy}, d_{yz}, d_{zx})	$s+3(p)+3(d)$	Pentagonal bipyramidal	90° 72°	IF_7

Note Molecules having same shape (and hybridisation) are called *iso*-structural. e.g. NH_4^+ and BH_4^-, NO_3^- and BF_3, etc.

Method for Predicting the Hybridisation and Shapes of Molecules

Predicting Hybridisation

Hybridisation of central atom can be calculated by using the formula, $H = \frac{1}{2}[V + M - C + A]$

where, V = no. of valence e^- of central atom.

M = monovalent atom surrounding central atom.

C = charge on cation.

H = no. of orbitals involved in hybridisation.

A = charge on anion

The hybridisation with different values of H are

Value of H	2	3	4	5	6	7
Type of hybridisation	sp	sp^2	sp^3	sp^3d	sp^3d^2	sp^3d^3

Predicting Shape

If number of hybrid orbitals is equal to the number of surrounding atoms/groups (monovalent or divalent etc.) the molecule/ion has a regular geometry and the shape is same as that predicted by hybridisation.

However, if number of surrounding atoms/groups is less than the number of hybrid orbitals, the difference gives the number of lone pairs present on the central atom and the species is said to have irregular geometry and the shape is predicted by leaving the hybrid orbitals containing the lone pairs.

Hybridisation of Some Important Molecules

S.No.	Molecule/Ion	$H=\frac{1}{2}[V+M-C+A]$	Hybridisation	Hybrid orbitals containing lone pairs	Shape
(i)	CO_2 ($_6C = 2, 4$)	$H=\frac{1}{2}[4+0-0+0]=2$	sp	0	Linear
(ii)	BF_3 ($_5B = 2, 3$)	$H=\frac{1}{2}[3+3-0+0]=3$ ($M = 3$ as three F's are monovalent)	sp^2	0	Trigonal planar
(iii)	SiF_4 ($_{14}Si = 2, 8, 4$)	$H=\frac{1}{2}[4+4-0+0]=4$	sp^3	0	Tetrahedral
(iv)	NH_3 ($_7N = 2, 8$)	$H=\frac{1}{2}[5+3-0+0]=4$ ($M=3$ as three H's are monovalent)	sp^3	1	Pyramidal
(v)	IF_7	$H=\frac{1}{2}[7+7-0+0]=7$	sp^3d^3	0	Pentagonal bipyramidal
(vi)	H_2O ($_8O = 2, 6$)	$H=\frac{1}{2}[6+2-0+0]=4$	sp^3	2	Bent (V-shaped)
(vii)	NH_4^+ ($_7N = 2, 5$)	$H=\frac{1}{2}[5+4-1+0]=4$ ($C=1$ as charge on cation $=1$)	sp^3	0	Tetrahedral
(viii)	H_3O^+ ($_8O = 2, 6$)	$H=\frac{1}{2}[6+3-1+0]=4$	sp^3	1	Pyramidal
(ix)	CH_3^+ (Carbocation)	$H=\frac{1}{2}[4+3-1+0]=3$	sp^2	0	Trigonal planar
(x)	NO_3^- ($_7N = 2, 5$)	$H=\frac{1}{2}[5+0-0+1]=3$ ($A=1$ as charge on anion $=1$)	sp^2	0	Trigonal planar
(xi)	CO_3^{2-} ($_6C = 2, 4$)	$H=\frac{1}{2}[4+0-0+2]=3$ ($A=2$ as charge on anion $=2$)	sp^2	0	Trigonal planar
(xii)	SO_4^{2-} ($_{16}S = 2, 8, 6$)	$H=\frac{1}{2}[6+0-0+2]=4$ ($M = 0$ as oxygen is divalent)	sp^3	0	Tetrahedral
(xiii)	ClO_4^- (Perchlorate ion)	$H=\frac{1}{2}[7+0-0+1]=4$	sp^3	0	Tetrahedral

Quick Test 3

1. Why does the type of overlap given in the following figure not result in bond formation? *NCERT Exemplar*

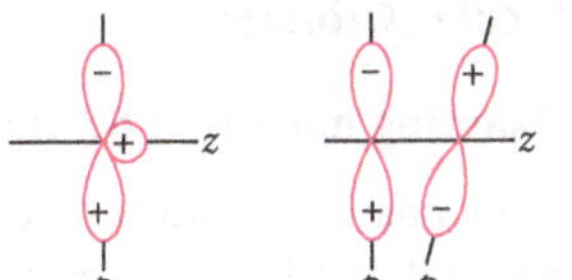

p_x (I) p_x p_y (II)

2. (a) Out of σ and π-bonds, which one is stronger and why?
(b) Why is free rotation about a π-bond not possible?

3. Out of *p*-orbital and *sp*-hybrid orbital which has greater directional character and why?

4. Why axial bonds of PCl_5 are longer than equitorial bonds?

5. Arrange the following in order of decreasing bond angles.
(i) $CH_4, NH_3, H_2O, BF_3, C_2H_2$
(ii) NH_3, NH_2^-, NH_4^+

6. Explain how the strength of a bond is related to extent of overlapping.

7. Draw diagram to show the formation of a double bond and a triple bond between the C-atoms in C_2H_4 and C_2H_2. *NCERT*

8. BH_4^- and NH_4^+ are isostructural. Explain.

9. Apart from tetrahedral geometry, another possible geometry for CH_4 is square planar with the four H-atoms at the corners of the square and the C-atom at its centre. Explain, why CH_4 is not square planar? *NCERT*

10. Define hybridisation. What type of hybridisation is involved in SF_6? *Diksha*

11. Predict the hybridisation of each carbon in the molecule of organic compound given below. Also indicate the total number of σ and π-bonds in this molecule. *NCERT Exemplar*

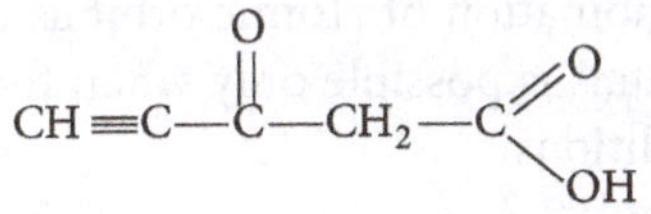

12. Is there any change in the hybridisation of B and N-atoms as a result of the reaction?

$$BF_3 + NH_3 \longrightarrow F_3B \cdot NH_3$$ *NCERT*

For Solutions, See QR Code on Pg. 172

4.9 Molecular Orbital Theory (MOT)

This theory was given by **F. Hund** and **R.S. Mulliken** in 1932, in order to explain the characteristics of molecules like their relative bond strengths, magnetic nature etc.

Salient Features of MOT

The main features of this theory are as follows

- The electrons in a molecule occupy various molecular orbitals just like the electrons of atoms are present in various atomic orbitals.
- Molecular orbitals are obtained when atomic orbitals of comparable energies and proper symmetry combine together.
- While an electron in an atomic orbital is under the influence of one nucleus, in a molecular orbital it is under the influence of two or more nuclei depending upon the number of atoms in the molecule. Thus, an atomic orbital is called **monocentric,** while a molecular orbital is termed as **polycentric.**
- The number of molecular orbital obtained is always equal to the number of combining atomic orbitals. When two atomic orbitals combine, two types of molecular orbitals are obtained. One is known as **bonding molecular orbital,** while the other is known as **antibonding molecular orbital.**
- The bonding molecular orbital because of their lower energy have greater stability than the corresponding antibonding molecular orbital.
- A molecular orbital shows the electron probability distribution around a group of nuclei in a molecule.
- Just like atomic orbitals, the molecular orbitals are filled in accordance with the Aufbau principle obeying the Pauli's exclusion principle and the Hund's rule.
- The bonding molecular orbitals are represented by σ, π, δ, etc., while antibonding molecular orbitals are represented by σ*, π*, δ*, etc.

Formation of Molecular Orbitals : Linear Combination of Atomic Orbitals (LCAO)

According to this method, the molecular orbitals are formed by the linear combination of atomic orbitals that can takes place by addition and by subtraction of wave functions of individual atomic orbitals.

Consider two hydrogen atoms *A* and *B* in a hydrogen molecule, each of which in its ground state contains one electron in 1*s*-orbital.

The atomic orbitals of these atoms are represented by the wave functions ψ_A and ψ_B respectively.

Then, these atomic orbitals combine by the addition and subtraction of wave functions of individual atomic orbitals as shown below.

$$\psi_{MO} = \psi_A \pm \psi_B$$

Differences Between Bonding and Antibonding Molecular Orbitals

Bonding molecular orbitals	Antibonding molecular orbitals
It is formed by linear combination of two atomic orbitals when their wave functions are added, i.e., $\psi_b = \psi_A + \psi_B$.	It is formed by linear combination of two atomic orbitals when their wave functions are subtracted, i.e., $\psi_{ab} = \psi_A - \psi_B$.
These are represented by σ, π, δ, etc.	These are represented by σ^*, π^*, δ^*, etc.
In the formation of these orbitals, two electron waves of the bonding atoms reinforce each other due to constructive interference. 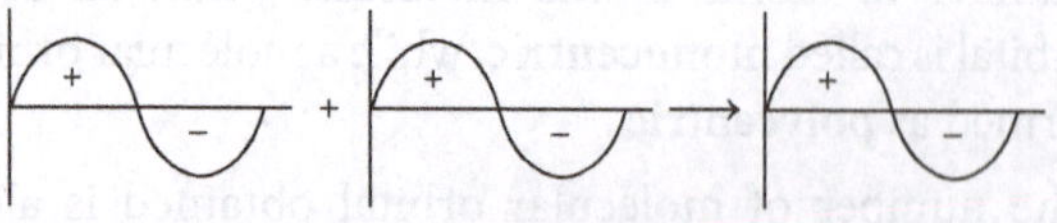 Constructive interference; amplitude are added up.	In the formation of these orbitals, two electron waves cancel each other due to destructive interference. 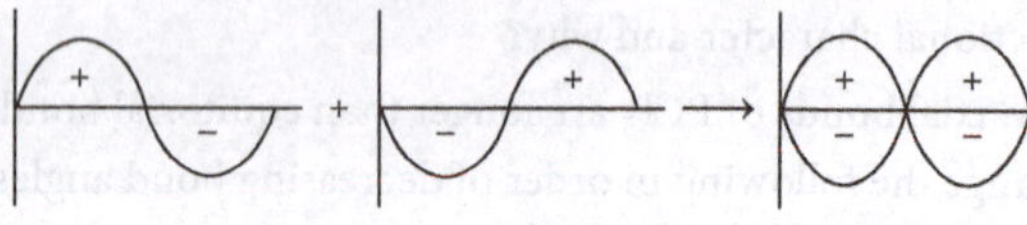 Destructive interference; amplitude are subtracted.
It is formed when the lobes of combining orbitals have the same sign.	It is formed when the lobes of combining orbitals have the opposite sign.
Electron density is located between the nuclei of bonded atoms, because of which repulsion between the nuclei is very less.	Electron density is located away from the space in between the nuclei.
The electrons present in these orbitals tends to hold the nuclei together (by attraction) and thus, stabilizes a molecule.	The electron present in these orbitals destabilize the molecule due to inter-electronic repulsion, which is more than the attractive forces between the electrons and the nuclei.
Its energy is less than the combining atomic orbitals.	Its energy is more than the combining atomic orbitals.
It has no nodal plane where electron density is zero.	It has a nodal plane.

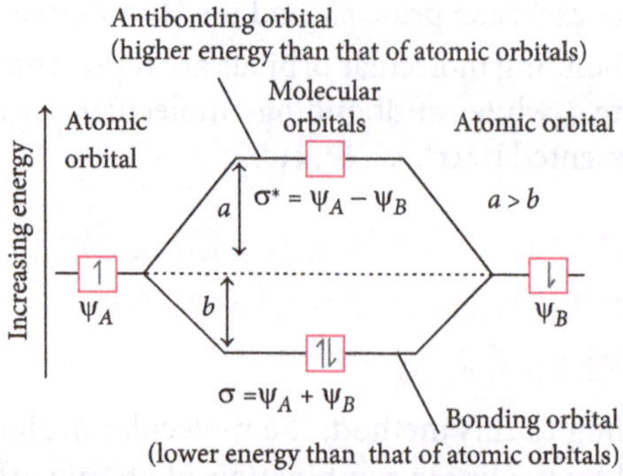

Formation of bonding (σ) and antibonding (σ^*) molecular orbitals

TEACHER'S TIP
The energy of the **antibonding orbitals** is more than the energy of combined atomic orbitals, whereas the energy of the bonding orbitals is lower than the parent orbitals. However, the total energy of two molecular orbitals remains same as that of two original atomic orbitals.

Conditions for the Combination of Atomic Orbitals

The linear combination of atomic orbitals to form molecular orbitals is possible only when they satisfy the following conditions

(i) **Similar energy of combining atomic orbitals** The combining atomic orbitals must possess the same or nearly the same energy.

e.g. 1*s*-orbital can combine with another 1*s*-orbital but not with 2*s*-orbital because 2*s*-orbital is appreciably higher than that of 1*s*-orbital. However, it is not true in case of very different atoms.

(ii) **Similar symmetry of combining atomic orbitals** The combining atomic orbitals must possess the same symmetry about the molecular axis alongwith the same energy.

e.g. $2p_z$-orbital of one atom can combine with $2p_z$-orbital or $2s$-orbital of the other atom but not with the $2p_x$ or $2p_y$-orbitals as their symmetries are different.

(iii) **Maximum overlap** The combining atomic orbitals must overlap to the maximum extent. Higher the extent of overlapping, more will be the electron-density between the nuclei of a molecular orbital.

Types of Molecular Orbitals

In case of diatomic molecules, molecular orbitals are designated as σ (sigma), π (pi), δ (delta), etc. If the molecular orbital is symmetrical about the internuclear axis (or bond axis) it is called **σ-molecular orbital** and if it is not symmetrical about the internuclear axis, it is called π **molecular orbital.**

(i) **Combination of *s*-atomic orbitals** The linear combination of 1*s*-orbitals centered on two nuclei gives two molecular orbitals that are symmetrical around the bond-axis.

Such molecular orbitals are of the σ type and are designated as σ 1*s* and $\overset{*}{\sigma}$ 1*s*.

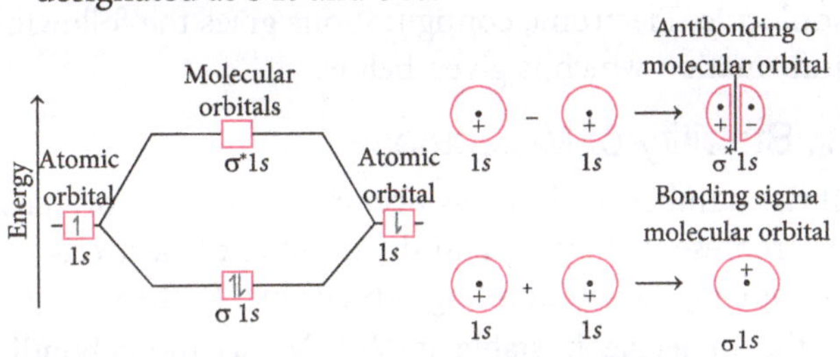

Similarly, 2*s* atomic orbitals combine to give σ 2*s* and $\overset{*}{\sigma}$ 2*s* orbitals.

(ii) **Combination of 2*p*-atomic orbitals** The three *p*-orbitals namely $2p_x$, $2p_y$ and $2p_z$ are directed in space along the *x*, *y* and *z* coordinate axes respectively. If *z*-axis is the internuclear axis, the *x* and *y*-axis would then be perpendicular to it. The combination of 2*p*-orbitals results in two types of MOs, *viz.*, sigma (σ) MOs and pi (π) MOs.

(a) **Formation of σ-molecular orbitals** It is the result of head on overlapping of two $2p_z$ orbitals, along the internuclear axis. Thus, two $2p_z$ atomic orbitals combine to give two molecular orbitals, i.e. bonding MO ($\sigma 2p_z$) and antibonding MO ($\sigma^* 2p_z$).

(b) **Formation of π-molecular orbitals** These are obtained by sidewise overlap of $2p_x$ and $2p_y$ orbitals which are not symmetrical around the bond axis because of the presence of positive lobes above and negative lobes below the molecular plane.

The molecular orbitals obtained are designated π and π*. A π-bonding MO has larger electron density above and below the internuclear axis. The π*-antibonding MO has a node between the nuclei.

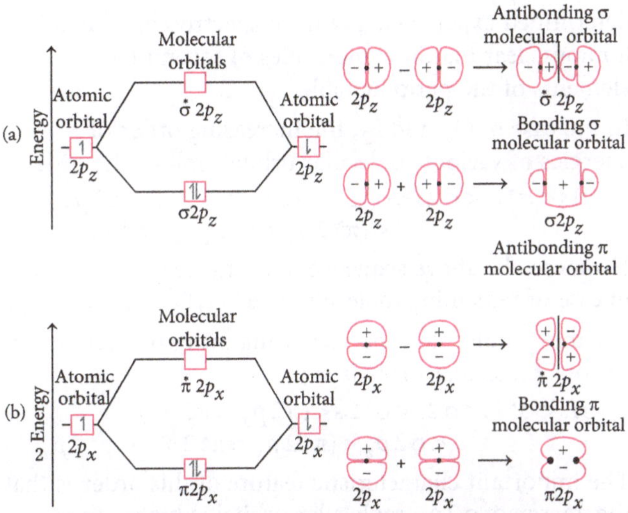

Contours and energies of bonding and antibonding molecular orbitals formed through combinations of (a) $2p_z$ atomic orbitals and (b) $2p_x$ atomic orbitals

Note $\pi 2p_x$ or $\pi 2p_y$ contains one nodal plane, whereas $\overset{*}{\pi} 2p_x$ or $\overset{*}{\pi} 2p_y$ contains two nodal planes.

Example 8 **Label the molecular orbitals formed by the following combinations of atomic orbitals (assume *z*-axis as internuclear axis).**

(i) $2s + 2s$ **(ii)** $2p_x - 2p_x$
(iii) $2p_z + 2p_z$ **(iv)** $1s - 1s$
(v) $2p_y + 2p_y$

Sol. The MOs formed are

(i) $2s + 2s = \sigma 2s$ and $\sigma^* 2s$

(ii) $2p_x - 2p_x = \pi^* 2p_x$ and $\pi^* 2p_x$

(iii) $2p_z + 2p_z = \sigma 2p_z$ and $\sigma^* 1p_z$

(iv) $1s - 1s = \sigma 1s$ and $\sigma^* 1s$

(v) $2p_y + 2p_y = \pi 2p_y$ and $\pi^* 2p_y$

Energy Level Diagram for Molecular Orbitals

You have studied that $1s$ atomic orbitals form two molecular orbitals designated as $\sigma 1s$ and $\overset{*}{\sigma}1s$. Similarly, $2s$ and $2p$ atomic orbitals (eight atomic orbitals on two atoms) combine to give following eight molecular orbitals.

Antibonding	MOs	$\overset{*}{\sigma}2s$	$\overset{*}{\sigma}2p_z$	$\overset{*}{\pi}2p_x$	$\overset{*}{\pi}2p_y$
Bonding	MOs	$\sigma 2s$	$\sigma 2p_z$	$\pi 2p_x$	$\pi 2p_y$

The energy levels of these orbitals have been determined experimentally from spectroscopic data for homonuclear diatomic molecules of second row elements of the periodic table.

In the case of O_2 and F_2, the increasing order of energies of various molecular orbitals follow the order

$$\sigma 1s < \sigma^* 1s < \sigma 2s < \sigma^* 2s < \sigma 2p_z < (\pi 2p_x \approx \pi 2p_y) < (\pi^* 2p_x \approx \pi^* 2p_y) < \sigma^* 2p_z$$

However, the above sequence of energy levels is not true in case of remaining molecules like $Li_2, Be_2, B_2, C_2, N_2$.

For these molecules, the increasing order of energies of various molecular orbitals is

$$\sigma 1s < \sigma^* 1s < \sigma 2s < \sigma^* 2s < (\pi 2p_x \approx \pi 2p_y) < \sigma 2p_z < (\pi^* 2p_x \approx \pi^* 2p_y) < \sigma^* 2p_z$$

The important characteristic feature of this order is that the energy of $\sigma 2p_z$ molecular orbital is higher than that of $\pi 2p_x$ and $\pi 2p_y$ molecular orbitals.

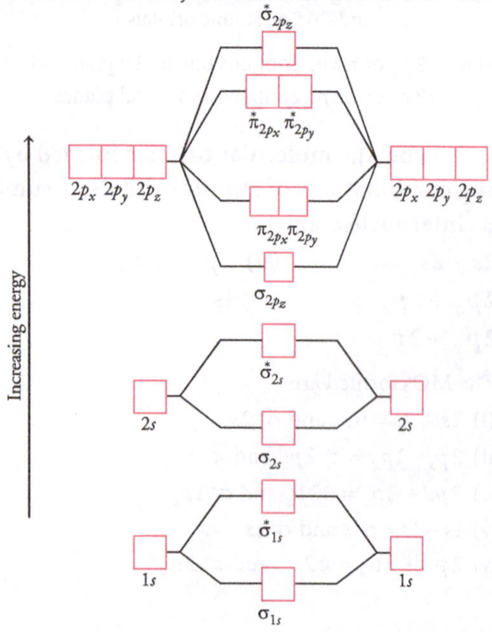

Molecular orbitals energy level diagram for O_2 and F_2

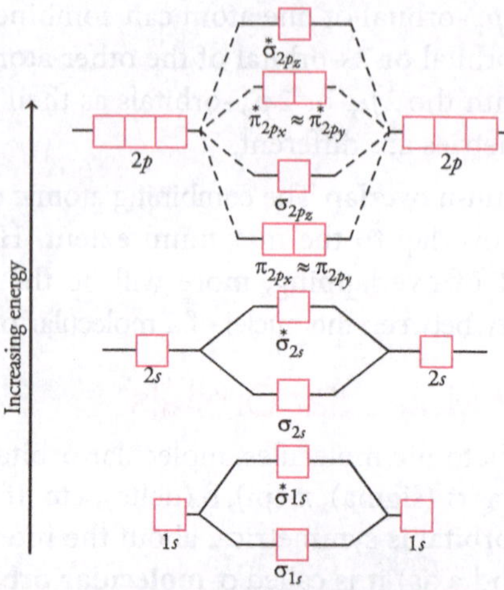

(For Li_2, Be_2, B_2, C_2, N_2 molecules)

Molecular orbital energy level diagram for Li_2, Be_2, B_2, C_2 and N_2 molecules

Electronic Configuration and Molecular Behaviour

The distribution of electrons in various molecular orbitals is called **the electronic configuration of the molecule.** Electronic configurations gives the following information which is given below.

1. Stability of Molecules

If the number of electrons occupying bonding orbitals are represented by N_b and the number of electrons occupying the antibonding orbitals by N_a then

- the molecule is stable if $N_b > N_a$ as more bonding orbitals are occupied and the bonding influence is stronger and
- the molecule is unstable if $N_b < N_a$ as antibonding influence is stronger.

2. Bond Order

Bond order is one half of the difference between the number of electrons present in the bonding and the antibonding orbitals. i.e.

$$\boxed{\text{Bond order (BO)} = 1/2(N_b - N_a)}$$

If $N_b > N_a$ (positive bond order) $\Rightarrow$ molecule is stable.
If $N_b < N_a$ (negative bond order)
$N_b = N_a$ (zero bond order) $\Rightarrow$ molecule is unstable.

3. Nature of the Bond

If bond order is 1, 2 or 3, it shows the presence of single, double or triple bonds, respectively.

4. Bond-Length

It is measured with the help of bond order.

The bond length decreases as the bond order increases.

5. Magnetic Nature

If all the molecular orbitals in a molecule are doubly occupied i.e. contains two electrons, the substance is diamagnetic (repelled by magnetic field).

However, if one or more molecular orbitals are singly occupied, the molecule is paramagnetic (attracted by magnetic field). e.g. O_2 molecule.

Bonding in Some Homonuclear Diatomic Molecules

Here the term homonuclear means that there is only one type of nucleus, i.e. one element is present and diatomic means that the molecule is composed of two atoms.

Example of some such molecules are given below.

1. Hydrogen Molecule (H_2)

It is formed when two hydrogen atoms combine together. Number of electrons in one H-atom =1. ($1s^1$).

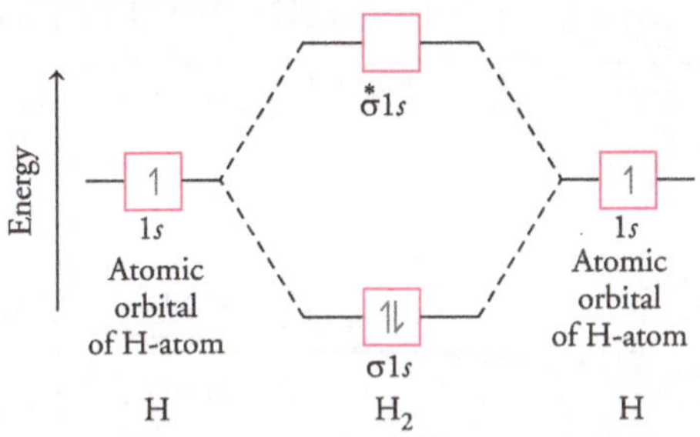

Molecular orbital energy level diagram for H_2 molecule

∴ Number of electrons in H_2 molecule $=1+1=2$.

MO configuration of $H_2 = \sigma 1s^2$

Here, $N_b = 2$ and $N_a = 0$

∴ The bond order $= \dfrac{N_b - N_a}{2}$

$= \dfrac{2-0}{2} = 1$

Bond order =1 means that the two hydrogen atoms are bonded together by a single covalent bond. The bond dissociation energy of hydrogen molecule has been found to be 438 kJ mol^{-1} and bond length equal to 74 pm.

Since, there is no unpaired electron in the hydrogen molecule, so it is diamagnetic. Its molecular orbital energy level diagram is given above.

2. Helium Molecule (He_2)

It is formed when two helium atoms combine together. Number of electrons in one He atom = 2 ($1s^2$).

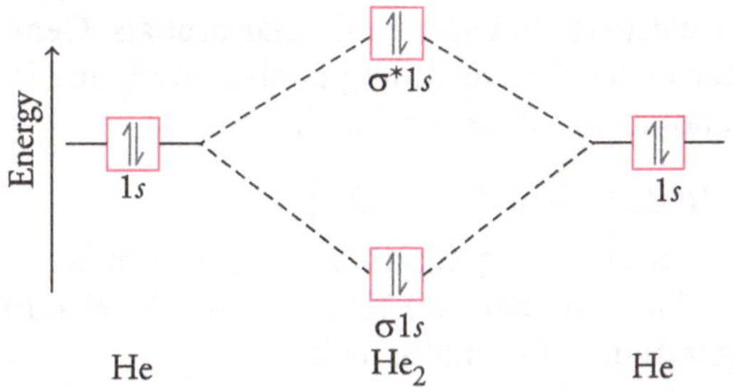

Molecular orbital energy level diagram for He_2 molecule

∴ Number of electrons in He_2 molecule $= 2+2=4$

M.O. configuration of $He_2 = \sigma 1s^2\ \sigma^*1s^2$

Here, $N_b = 2$ and $N_a = 2$

∴ The bond order $= \dfrac{N_b - N_a}{2} = \dfrac{2-2}{2} = 0$

Bond order zero means that He_2 molecule is unstable and does not exist. Similarly, it can be shown that Be_2 molecule $\sigma 1s^2\ \sigma^*1s^2\ \sigma 2s^2\ \sigma^*2s^2$ does not exist.

3. Lithium Molecule (Li_2)

It is formed when two lithium atoms combine together. Number of electron in one Li atom is 3 ($1s^2 2s^1$). So, there are six electrons in Li_2. The electronic configuration of Li_2 molecule is

$$Li_2 : \sigma 1s^2\ \sigma^*1s^2\ \sigma 2s^2$$

From the electronic configuration, we can see that $4e^-$ are present in bonding orbital and $2e^-$ are present in antibonding orbital.

So, B.O $= \dfrac{N_b - N_a}{2} = \dfrac{4-2}{2} = 1$

B.O =1 means that Li_2 molecule is stable and contains no unpaired electrons. Hence, it is diamagnetic.

4. Carbon Molecule (C_2)

The electronic configuration of carbon is $1s^2 2s^2 2p^2$. So, there are twelve electrons in C_2. The electronic configuration of C_2 molecule is

$$C_2 : \sigma 1s^2\ \sigma^*1s^2\ \sigma 2s^2 \sigma^* 2s^2\ (\pi 2p_x^2 = \pi 2p_y^2)$$

From the electronic configuration we can see that 8 electrons are present in bonding orbital and $4e^-$ are present in antibonding orbital.

So, $\text{B.O.} = \dfrac{N_b - N_a}{2} = \dfrac{8-4}{2} = 2$

It is diamagnetic in nature. It is important to note that in C_2 both π-bonds are present because of the presence of four electrons in two π-molecular orbtials. Generally, in other molecules containing double bond, one is sigma bond and other is π-bond.

5. Oxygen Molecule (O_2)

The electronic configuration of oxygen atom is $1s^2\ 2s^2\ 2p^4$. So, there are 16 electrons. The electronic configuration of O_2 molecule is

$$O_2 : = \sigma 1s^2\ \sigma 1s^2\ \sigma 2s^2\ \sigma^* 2s^2\ \sigma 2p_z^2\ (\pi 2p_x^2 \equiv \pi 2p_y^2)\ (\pi^* 2p_x^1 \equiv \pi^* 2p_y^1)$$

From the electronic configuration of O_2, it is clear that 10 electrons are present in bonding molecular orbital and $6e^-$ are present in antibonding molecular orbital.

$\therefore$ Bond order $= \dfrac{1}{2}[N_b - N_a] = \dfrac{1}{2}[10-6] = 2$

Bond order 2, indicates that atoms are held by a double bond. Further, two unpaired e^- are present in $\pi^* 2p_x$ and $\pi^* 2p_y$ molecular orbital. So, O_2 is paramagnetic in nature. Similarly, the electronic configuration of some homonuclear and heteronuclear molecules and their ions can be found out, which is given in the table.

Bond Order and Magnetic Property of Some Homonuclear and Heteronuclear Molecules and their Ions

S.No.	Molecule/ Ion	No. of electrons	Electronic configuration	Bond order $1/2(N_b - N_a)$	Magnetic property
1.	H_2	2	$\sigma 1s^2$	$\frac{1}{2}(2-0)=1$	Diamagnetic
2.	H_2^+	1	$\sigma 1s^1$	$\frac{1}{2}(1-0)=1/2$	Paramagnetic
3.	H_2^-	3	$\sigma 1s^2\ \sigma^* 1s^1$	$\frac{1}{2}(2-1)=1/2$	Paramagnetic
4.	He_2	4	$\sigma 1s^2\ \sigma^* 1s^2$	$\frac{1}{2}(2-2)=0$	Does not exist
5.	He_2^+	3	$\sigma 1s^2\ \sigma^* 1s^1$	$\frac{1}{2}(2-1)=1/2$	Paramagnetic
6.	Li_2	6	$\sigma 1s^2\ \sigma^* 1s^2\ \sigma 2s^2$	$\frac{1}{2}(4-2)=1$	Diamagnetic
7.	Li_2^+	5	$\sigma 1s^2\ \sigma^* 1s^2\ \sigma 2s^1$	$\frac{1}{2}(3-2)=1/2$	Paramagnetic
8.	Be_2	8	$\sigma 1s^2\ \sigma^* 1s^2\ \sigma 2s^2\ \sigma^* 2s^2$	$\frac{1}{2}(4-4)=0$	Does not exist
9.	B_2	10	$\sigma 1s^2\ \sigma^* 1s^2\ \sigma 2s^2\ \sigma^* 2s^2\ \pi 2p_x^1 \approx \pi 2p_y^1$	$\frac{1}{2}(6-4)=1$	Paramagnetic
10.	C_2	12	$\sigma 1s^2\ \sigma^* 1s^2\ \sigma 2s^2\ \sigma^* 2s^2\ \pi 2p_x^2 \approx \pi 2p_y^2$	$\frac{1}{2}(8-4)=2$	Diamagnetic
11.	C_2^+	11	$\sigma 1s^2 \sigma^* 1s^2\ \sigma 2s^2\ \sigma^* 2s^2\ \pi 2p_x^2 \pi \approx 2p_y^1$	$\frac{1}{2}(7-4)=3/2$	Paramagnetic
12.	C_2^-	13	$\sigma 1s^2\ \sigma^* 1s^2\ \sigma 2s^2 \sigma^* 2s^2\ \pi\ 2p_x^2 \approx \pi\ 2p_y^2 \sigma\ 2p_z^1$	$\frac{1}{2}(9-4)=5/2$	Paramagnetic
13.	N_2	14	$\sigma 1s^2\ \sigma^* 1s^2\ \sigma 2s^2\ \sigma^* 2s^2\ \pi\ 2p_x^2 \approx \pi\ 2p_y^2\ \sigma\ 2p_z^2$	$\frac{1}{2}(10-4)=3$	Diamagnetic
14.	N_2^+	13	$\sigma 1s^2\ \sigma^* 1s^2\ \sigma 2s^2\ \sigma^* 2s^2\ \pi\ 2p_x^2 \approx \pi\ 2p_y^2\ \sigma\ 2p_z^1$	$\frac{1}{2}(9-4)=5/2$	Paramagnetic
15.	O_2	16	$\sigma 1s^2\ \sigma^* 1s^2\ \sigma 2s^2\ \sigma^* 2s^2\ \sigma 2p_z{}^2\ \pi 2p_x^2 \approx \pi 2p_y^2\ \pi^* 2p_x^1 \approx \pi^* 2p_y^1$	$\frac{1}{2}(10-6)=2$	Paramagnetic

S.No.	Molecule/ Ion	No. of electrons	Electronic configuration	Bond order $1/2(N_b - N_a)$	Magnetic property
16.	O_2^+	15	$\sigma 1s^2\, \sigma^* 1s^2\, \sigma 2s^2\, \sigma^* 2s^2\, \sigma 2p_z{}^2\, \pi 2p_x^2 \approx \pi 2p_y^2\, \pi^* 2p_x^1 \approx \pi^* 2p_y^0$	$\frac{1}{2}(10-5)=5/2$	Paramagnetic
17.	O_2^-	17	$\sigma 1s^2\, \sigma^* 1s^2\, \sigma 2s^2\, \sigma^* 2s^2\, \sigma 2p_z{}^2\, \pi 2p_x^2 \approx \pi 2p_y^2\, \pi^* 2p_x^2 \approx \pi^* 2p_y^1$	$\frac{1}{2}(10-7)=3/2$	Paramagnetic
18.	O_2^{2-}	18	$\sigma 1s^2\, \sigma^* 1s^2\, \sigma 2s^2\, \sigma^* 2s^2\, \sigma 2p_z{}^2\, \pi 2p_x^2 \approx \pi 2p_y^2\, \pi^* 2p_x^2 \approx \pi^* 2p_y^2$	$\frac{1}{2}(10-8)=1$	Diamagnetic
19.	F_2	18	$\sigma 1s^2\, \sigma^* 1s^2\, \sigma 2s^2\, \sigma^* 2s^2\, \sigma 2p_z{}^2\, \pi 2p_x^2 \approx \pi 2p_y^2\, \pi^* 2p_x^2 \approx \pi^* 2p_y^2$	$\frac{1}{2}(10-8)=1$	Diamagnetic
20.	F_2^+	17	$\sigma 1s^2\, \sigma^* 1s^2\, \sigma 2s^2\, \sigma^* 2s^2\, \sigma 2p_z{}^2\, \pi 2p_x^2 \approx \pi 2p_y^2\, \pi^* 2p_x^2 \approx \pi^* 2p_y^1$	$\frac{1}{2}(10-7)=3/2$	Paramagnetic
21.	F_2^-	19	$\sigma 1s^2\, \sigma^* 1s^2\, \sigma 2s^2\, \sigma^* 2s^2\, \sigma 2p_z{}^2\, \pi 2p_x^2 \approx \pi 2p_y^2\, \pi^* 2p_x^2 \approx \pi^* 2p_y^2\, \sigma^* 2p_z^1$	$\frac{1}{2}(10-9)=1/2$	Paramagnetic
22.	Ne_2	20	$\sigma 1s^2\, \sigma^* 1s^2\, \sigma 2s^2\, \sigma^* 2s^2\, \sigma 2p_z{}^2\, \pi 2p_x^2 \approx \pi 2p_y^2\, \pi^* 2p_x^2 \approx \pi^* 2p_y^2\, \sigma^* 2p_z^2$	$\frac{1}{2}(10-10)=0$	Does not exist
23.	Ne_2^+	19	$\sigma 1s^2\, \sigma^* 1s^2\, \sigma 2s^2\, \sigma^* 2s^2\, \sigma 2p_z{}^2\, \pi 2p_x^2 \approx \pi 2p_y^2\, \pi^* 2p_x^2 \approx \pi^* 2p_y^2\, \sigma^* 2p_z^1$	$\frac{1}{2}(10-9)=1/2$	Paramagnetic
24.	NO	15	$\sigma 1s^2\, \sigma^* 1s^2\, \sigma 2s^2\, \sigma^* 2s^2\, \sigma 2p_z^2\, \pi 2p_x^2 \approx \pi 2p_y^2\, \pi^* 2p_x^1 \approx \pi^* 2p_y^0$	$\frac{1}{2}(10-5)=5/2$	Paramagnetic
25.	$(NO)^+$	14	$\sigma 1s^2\, \sigma^* 1s^2\, \sigma 2s^2\, \sigma^* 2s^2\, \sigma 2p_z^2\, \pi 2p_x^2 \approx \pi 2p_y^2$	$\frac{1}{2}(10-4)=3$	Diamagnetic
26.	CO	14	$\sigma 1s^2\, \sigma^* 1s^2\, \sigma 2s^2\, \sigma^* 2s^2\, \sigma 2p_z{}^2\, \pi 2p_x^2 \approx \pi 2p_y^2$	$\frac{1}{2}(10-4)=3$	Diamagnetic

4.10 Hydrogen Bonding

The attractive force which binds hydrogen atom of one molecule with the highly electronegative atom (F, O or N) of the same or another molecule is called **hydrogen bonding.** It is represented by a dotted line (------). It is weaker than covalent bond.

e.g. In case of HF molecule, the hydrogen bond exists between hydrogen atom of one molecule and fluorine atom of another molecule as shown below.

$$\ldots H^{\delta+}—F^{\delta-}\ldots\ldots H^{\delta+}—F^{\delta-}\ldots\ldots\ldots H^{\delta-}—F^{\delta-}$$

Here, hydrogen bond behaves like a bridge between two atoms that holds one atom by covalent bond and the other by hydrogen bond.

Cause of Formation of Hydrogen Bond

If hydrogen is bonded to a highly electronegative element X, the shared pair of electrons moves far away from hydrogen atom.

Consequently, the hydrogen atom becomes highly electropositive with respect to the other atom X.

Since, there is displacement of electrons towards X, the hydrogen acquires partial positive charge (δ^+), while X gains partial negative charge (δ^-). It results in the formation of a polar molecule with electrostatic force of attraction as shown below.

$$H^{\delta+}—X^{\delta-}\ldots H^{\delta+}—X^{\delta-}\ldots H^{\delta+}—X^{\delta-}$$

The magnitude of H-bonding also depends on the physical state of the compound. In case of solid, it is maximum and for gases, it is minimum.

Thus, the hydrogen bonds have great influence on the structure and physical properties of the compounds.

Types of H-Bonds

There are two types of H-bonds.

1. Intermolecular Hydrogen Bond

Such bond exists between two different molecules of the same or different compounds, e.g. H-bond in case of HF molecule, alcohol or water molecules, etc.

It results in association of two molecules and hence results in increased melting point, boiling points and solubility.

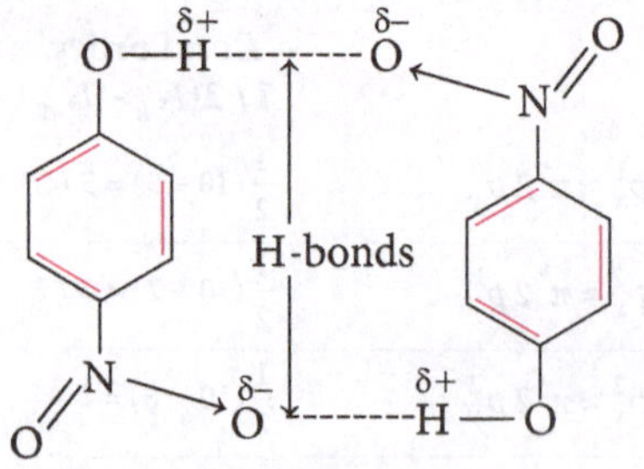

Intermolecular hydrogen bonding in *p*-nitrophenol

2. Intramolecular Hydrogen Bond

Such bond exists when hydrogen atom is in between the two highly electronegative (F, O, N) atoms present within the same molecule. e.g. In *o*-nitrophenol, the hydrogen is in between the two oxygen atoms.

This bonding prevents the association of molecules and hence, it decreases melting point, boiling point, and solubility. e.g. *o*-nitrophenol has lower boiling point that *p*-nitrophenol.

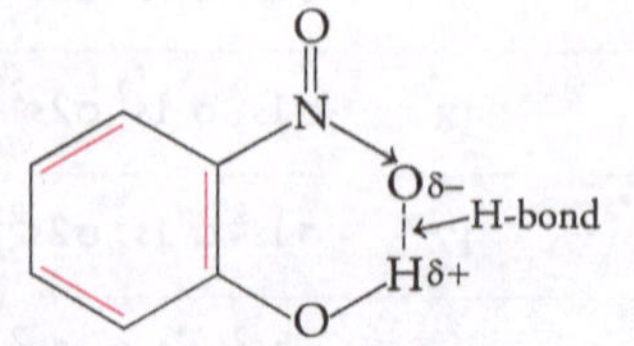

Intramolecular hydrogen bonding in *o*-nitrophenol molecule

Quick Test 4

1. Write the significance of a plus and a minus sign shown in representing the orbitals. NCERT

2. Write the important conditions required for the linear combination of atomic orbitals to form molecular orbitals. NCERT

3. Can we have a diatomic molecule with its ground state molecular orbitals full with electrons? Give a reason for your answer. Competency Based Que.

4. Why is the energy of $\pi 2p_x$ and $\pi 2p_y$ molecular orbital are lower than $\sigma 2p_z$ molecular orbital in N_2 molecule?

5. Is it correct to say that bond order always increases when an electron is lost? Competency Based Que.

6. Why KHF_2 exists but $KHCl_2$ does not? Competency Based Que

7. Out of H and H_2, the latter has higher first ionisation energy while out of O and O_2, the former has higher first ionisation energy. Explain why?

8. Compare the relative stabilities of the following species.

$$O_2, O_2^+, O_2^-, O_2^{2-}$$

9. What is the effect of following process on the bond order in N_2 and O_2?

(i) $N_2 \longrightarrow N_2^+ + e^-$

(ii) $O_2 \longrightarrow O_2^+ + e^-$

10. A molecule of H_2 exists while that of He_2 does not exist. Explain. Diksha

11. Explain why HF is less viscous than H_2O.

For Solutions, See QR Code on Pg. 172.

Mind Map

Chemical Bonding and Molecular Structure

CHEMICAL BOND: Force of attraction holding various constituents together in different chemical species.

Kössel-Lewis Approach
Atoms try to complete their octet (except H which completes its duplet).

Lewis Symbols
Notation to represent the valence electrons of an atom.

Bond and Its Types

Lattice Enthalpy
Amount of energy required to completely separate one mole of a solid ionic compound into gaseous constituent ions.

Covalent Character in Ionic Bond
According to Fajan's rule, the covalent character will be favoured by small size of cation, large size of anion, high charge of cation and anion, the cation having $(n-1)\ d^n\ ns^0$ electronic configuration.

Hydrogen Bond
Attractive force that binds H-atom attached directly with electronegative atom.

Ionic Bond
Formed by complete transfer of electrons.

Covalent Bond
Formed by sharing of electrons.

Formal Charge

Formal charge on an atom in a Lewis structure = (Total number of valence electrons in the free atom) – (Total number of non-bonding (lone pair electrons) –1/2 (Total numbers of bonding (shared) electrons.

Bond Parameters

1. Bond Length

Distance between nuclei of two nearest atoms.

Bond length $\propto$ size of atom$\propto$ 1/Bond multiplicity

2. Bond Angle

Angle between the orbitals containing bonding electron pairs around central atom.

3. Bond Enthalpy

Amount of energy required to break one mole of bonds in gaseous phase.

4. Bond Order

Number of bonds formed between two atoms in a covalent compound.

Bond order $\propto$ bond enthalpy.

5. Dipole Moment

Dipole moment (μ) = Charge × Distance of separation

$$\%\text{ ionic character} = \frac{\mu_{\text{observed}}}{\mu_{\text{calculated for 100\% ionic}}} \times 100$$

6. Resonance

When all the properties cannot be shown by a single structure, a number of resonating structures are used to describe all the properties and phenomenon is called resonance.

Theories of Covalent Bonding

VSEPR Theory
Number of valence shell electron pairs (bonded or non-bonded) present around the central atom decides the shape of the molecule.

Molecular Orbital Theory
Molecular orbitals (bonding and anti-bonding) are combination of atomic orbitals of comparable energies and proper symmetry.

Stability of Molecules

If $N_b > N_a \Rightarrow$ molecule is stable

If $N_b < N_a \Rightarrow$ molecule is unstable.

Bond Order

BO = ½($N_b - N_a$)

If BO is 1, 2 or 3, it shows the presence of single, double or triple bonds, respectively.

Bond length decreases or BO increases.

Magnetic Nature

All molecular orbitals are doubly occupied $\Rightarrow$ diamagnetic substance

Atleast one molecular orbital is singly occupied $\Rightarrow$ paramagnetic substance.

Valence Bond Theory
Between two interactive nuclei force of attraction and repulsion applied. At bonding stage, both of these are equal.

Orbital overlapping

This leads to the formation of σ and π bonds.

Hybridisation

Phenomenon of intermixing of orbitals of slightly different energies and shapes to generate orbitals of same energy and shape.

EXAM PATTERN QUESTIONS

Objective Type Questions

Multiple Choice Questions [1 Mark]

1. According to Lewis and Kössel approach, which of the following molecule has complete octet of the central atom?

(a) LiCl (b) BeH_2 (c) BCl_3 (d) CO_2

2. The group valency of the element is generally equal to the

(a) number of dots in Lewis symbol
(b) eight minus the number of dots
(c) valence electrons
(d) any of the above may possible

3. Ionic bonds will be formed more easily between elements with comparatively

(a) low ionisation enthalpy and high electron affinity
(b) high ionisation enthalpy and high electron affinity
(c) low ionisation enthalpy and low electron affinity
(d) high ionisation enthalpy and low electron affinity

4. The formal charges of oxygen labelled 3, 2, 1 in ozone respectively are

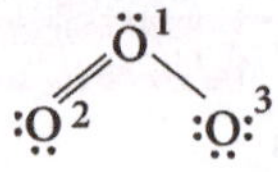

(a) −1, +1, 0 (b) 0, 0, −1
(c) −1, 0, +1 (d) 0, +1, −1

5. Select the incorrect statements from the following about resonance.

A. Resonance structures should have equal energy.
B. In resonance structure, the constituent atoms should be in the same position.
C. In resonance structure, there should not be the same number of electron pairs.
D. In resonance, the position of atoms are not fixed.

Choose the correct option.

(a) B and D (b) A, B and C
(c) A and C (d) C and D

6. Lewis dot structure of CO, NO_2^- and CO_3^{2-} are I, II and III respectively

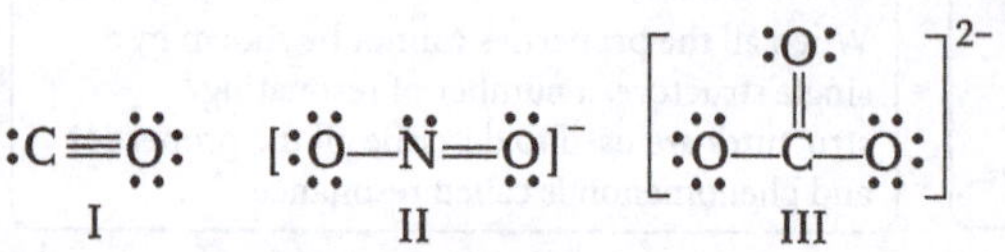

Which of the above structure(s) is/are wrong? **Competency Based Que.**

(a) Only I (b) Only II
(c) Only III (d) None of these

7. Which of the following molecules has a triple bond?

(a) CH_4 (b) C_2H_4 (c) C_2H_2 (d) O_3

8. Which one of the following species has trigonal planar shape?

(a) $BeCl_2$ (b) NO_3^- (c) NO_2^- (d) CO_2

9. Number of π-bonds and σ-bonds in the following structure is

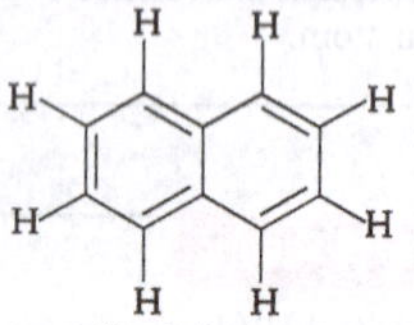

Naphthalene

(a) 6, 19 (b) 4, 20 (c) 5, 19 (d) 5, 20

10. Bond length of a multiple (double or triple) bond is always .... than the corresponding single bond. **Diksha**

(a) shorter (b) longer
(c) equal to (d) None of the above

11. The table shown below gives the bond dissociation energies (E_{diss}) for single covalent bonds of carbon (C) atoms with element 'A', 'B', 'C' and 'D'. Which element has the smallest atoms? **Competency Based Que.**

Bond	E_{diss} (kJ mol^{-1})
C-*A*	240
C-*B*	328
C-*C*	276
C-*D*	485

Choose the correct option among the given options.

(a) *A* (b) *B* (c) *C* (d) *D*

12. Which of the following is correct?

(a) Bond order $\propto \dfrac{1}{\text{bond length}} \propto \dfrac{1}{\text{bond enthalpy}} \propto$ stability

(b) Stability $\propto \dfrac{1}{\text{bond order}} \propto \dfrac{1}{\text{bond length}} \propto \dfrac{1}{\text{bond enthalpy}}$

(c) Stability ∝ bond order ∝ bond length ∝ bond enthalpy

(d) Stability ∝ bond order ∝ bond enthalpy $\propto \dfrac{1}{\text{bond length}}$

13. **The molecule of hydrogen atom is formed due to the overlapping of orbitals of two hydrogen atoms. Which of the following types of overlapping takes place in the formation of H_2 molecule?** **Competency Based Que.**

(a) 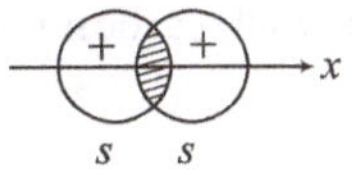

(b) 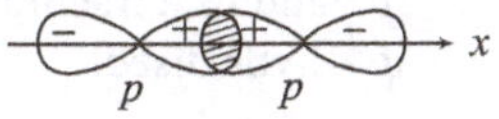

(c) 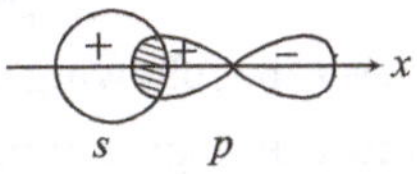

(d) All of these

14. **Which of the following does not represent positive overlap?**

(a) 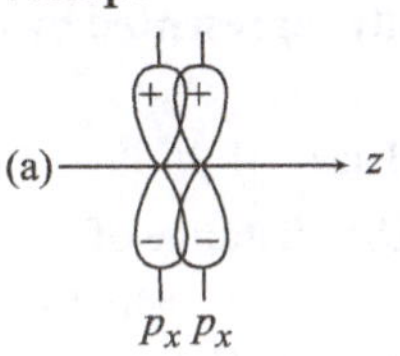

(b) 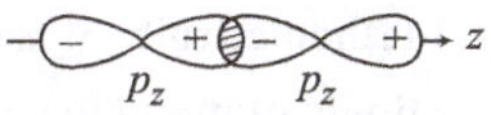

(c) 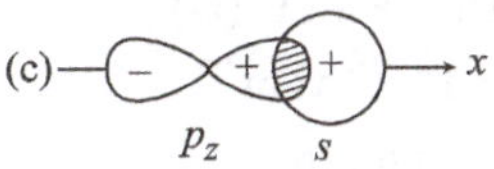

(d) 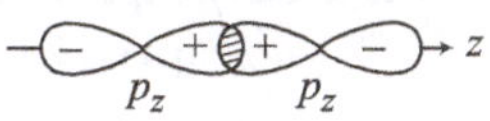

15. **Diagonal hybridisation is the another name of**

(a) sp^3- hybridisation (b) sp^2- hybridisation
(c) sp- hybridisation (d) All of these

16. **Which of the following angle corresponds to sp^2-hybridisation?** **NCERT Exemplar**

(a) 90° (b) 120° (c) 180° (d) 109°

17. **Number of bonding pairs (X) and lone pairs (Y) around the central atom in the I_3^- ion are**

	X	Y		X	Y
(a)	2	2	(b)	2	3
(c)	3	2	(d)	4	3

18. **The decreasing order of the repulsive interaction of electron pairs is (Here, *lp* = lone pair, *bp* = bond pair)**

(a) *lp-lp* > *lp-bp* > *bp-bp* (b) *lp-bp* > *lp-lp* > *bp-bp*
(c) *lp-lp* > *bp-bp* > *lp-bp* (d) *bp-bp* > *lp-lp* > *lp-bp*

19. **Which of the following is responsible for the deviations occur from idealised shape of H_2O and NH_3 molecules?**

(a) Same hybridisation
(b) Different hybridisation
(c) Repulsive effect
(d) None of the above

20. **Polarity in a molecule and hence the dipole moment depends primarily on electronegativity of the constituent atoms and shape of a molecule. Which of the following has the highest dipole moment?** **NCERT Exemplar**

(a) CO_2 (b) HI
(c) H_2O (d) BF_3

21. **The correct decreasing order of the boiling points of given compounds is** **NCERT Exemplar**

(a) $HF > H_2O > NH_3$ (b) $H_2O > HF > NH_3$
(c) $NH_3 > HF > H_2O$ (d) $NH_3 > H_2O > HF$

22. **If N_b is the number of electrons occupying bonding orbitals and N_a is the number of electrons occupying the antibonding orbitals, then the molecule will be stable if**

(a) $N_b > N_a$ (b) $N_b < N_a$
(c) $N_b = N_a$ (d) $N_b \le N_a$

23. **Which of the following geometry and angle corresponds to dsp^2 hybridisation?** **Diksha**

(a) Square planar, 90° (b) Tetrahedral, 109°28'
(c) Octahedral, 90° (d) Trigonal planar, 120°

24. **The shape of the XeF_4 molecule is .... as it has .... bond pair and .... lone pair of electrons.** **Diksha**

(a) square pyramidal, 5, 1 (b) T-shaped, 3, 2
(c) square planar, 4, 2 (d) octahedral, 4, 2

25. **Match the compounds in Column I with the structures in Column II.**

Column I	Column II
A. $(CH_3)_3B$	1. Square planar
B. NH_4Cl	2. Trigonal bipyramidal
C. $[ICl_4]^-$	3. Tetrahedral
D. PCl_5	4. Trigonal planar

Choose the correct option among the given options.

	A	B	C	D		A	B	C	D
(a)	4	3	1	2	(b)	4	1	2	3
(c)	3	4	1	2	(d)	3	4	2	1

Assertion-Reason [1 Mark]

■ **Directions** (Q. Nos. 26-37) In the following questions. an Assertion (A) is followed by a corresponding Reason (R) Use the following keys to choose the appropriate answer.

(a) Both (A) and (R) are correct and (R) is the correct explanation of (A).
(b) Both (A) and (R) are correct but (R) is not the correct explanation of (A).
(c) (A) is correct and (R) is incorrect.
(d) (A) is incorrect and (R) is correct.

26. **Assertion** (A) The electronic structure of O_3

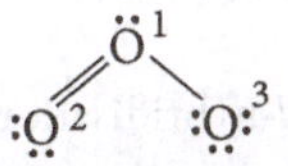

is not allowed.

Reason (R) In structure, 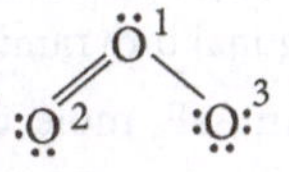

octet around O cannot be expanded.

27. **Assertion** (A) SF_4 molecule has two types of structure,

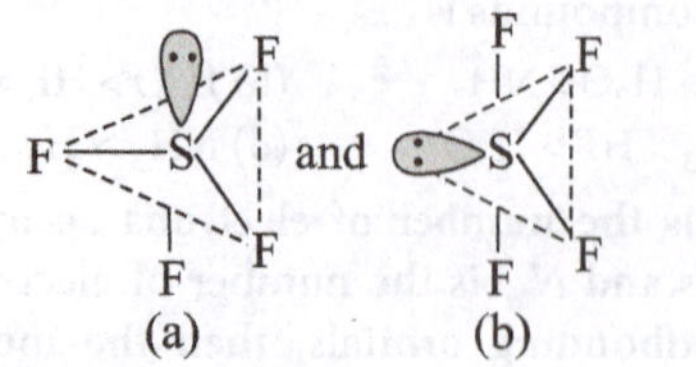

where structure (b) is more stable than (a).

Reason (R) *lp-bp* repulsions decide the greater stability of structure (b). **Competency Based Que.**

28. **Assertion** (A) Oxygen does not possess *d*-orbitals in their valence shell.

Reason (R) The covalency of oxygen is two.

29. **Assertion** (A) PCl_5 molecule has trigonal bipyramidal shape.

Reason (R) PCl_5 contains 5 electron pairs and its hybridisation is sp^3d.

30. **Assertion** (A) BrF_5 and SF_6 both have same hybridisation.

Reason (R) BrF_5 is square pyramidal, while SF_6 molecule is octahedral.

31. **Assertion** (A) The values of dipole moment of CO_2 molecule is zero.

Reason (R) CO_2 molecule is linear.

32. **Assertion** (A) NO^+ and CN^- both have same bond order and magnetism.

Reason (R) NO^+ and CN^- are isoelectronic species.

33. **Assertion** (A) Among the two O—H bonds in H_2O molecule the energy required to break the first O—H bond and the other O—H bond is not the same.

Reason (R) This is because the electronic environment around oxygen is the same even after breakage of one O—H bond. **Competency Based Que.**

34. **Assertion** (A) Ionic bond is non-directional.

Reason (R) Each ion is surrounded by a uniformly distributed electric field.

35. **Assertion** (A) In NH_3, N is sp^3-hybridised, but angle is found to be 107°

Reason (R) The decrease in bond angle is due to repulsion between the lone pair on nitrogen and bond pair between N and H.

36. **Assertion** (A) AsF_5 molecule has sp^3d-hybridisation and have trigonal bipyramidal geometry.

Reason (R) In AsF_5 molecule, the *d*-orbital involved in sp^3d-hybridisation is $d_{x^2-y^2}$.

37. **Assertion** (A) The Cl—C—Cl angle in 1, 1, 2, 2-tetrachloroethene and tetrachloromethane is 120° and 109.5°

Reason (R) In 1, 1, 2, 2-tetrachloroethene each carbon is sp^3 and in tetrachloromethane each carbon is sp^2-hybridised.

Case-Study [4 Marks]

38. **Read the given case and answer the following questions.**

Dipole moment is the measure of degree of polarity and is defined as the product of the magnitude of the charge and the distance between the centres of positive and negative charge. It is usually represented by a Greek letter μ (mu).

Mathematically, it is expressed as :

Dipole moment (μ) = charge (Q) × distance of separation (*r*)

It is usually expressed in Debye units (D).

$$1\ D = 3.33564 \times 10^{-30}\ C\ m$$

where, C is coulomb and m is metre.

or $1\ D = 1 \times 10^{-18}$ **esu (or, stat C m)**

Here, esu = electrostatic unit

stat C cm = static coulomb centimeter

It is a vector quantity and is represented by the crossed arrow (⟼) pointing towards the more electronegative atom. **Competency Based Que.**

$\overset{+\!\!\longrightarrow}{H—\ddot{F}:}$ → More electronegative atom

(i) What is the relation between resultant dipole moment of NH_3 and NF_3?

(ii) CO_2 molecule is non-polar. Why?

Or

Give the expression of dipole moment and its unit.

(iii) In a diatomic molecule the bond distance is 1×10^{-8} cm. Its dipole moment is 1.2 D. What is the charge on each atom in coulomb?

39. **Read the given case and answer the following questions.**

Chemical bonding, involves interactions that account for the association of atoms into molecules, ions, crystals, and other stable species that make up the familiar substances of the everyday world. When atoms approach one another, their nuclei and electrons interact and tend to distribute themselves in space in such a way that the total energy is lower than it would be in any alternative arrangement. If the total energy of a group of atoms is lower than the sum of the energies of the components atoms, then bond together and the energy lowering is the bonding energy.

The ideas that helped to establish the nature of chemical bonding came during early 20th century, after the electron had been discovered and quantum mechanics had provided a language for the description of the behaviour of electrons in atoms. However, even though chemists need quantum mechanics to attain a detailed quantitative understanding of bond formation, much of their pragmatic understanding of bonds is expressed in simple intuitive models. These models treat bonds as primarily of two kinds-namely, ionic and covalent.

The type of bond that is most likely to occur between two atoms can be predicted on the basis of the location of the elements in the periodic table, and to some extent the properties of the substances so formed can be related to the type of bonding.

A key concept in a discussion of chemical bonding is that of the molecule. Molecules are the smallest unit of compounds that can exist. One feature of molecules that can be predicted with reasonable success is their shape. Molecular shapes are of considerable importance for understanding the reactions that compounds can undergo, and so the link between chemical bonding and chemical reactivity is discussed briefly here. **Competency Based Que.**

(i) Why Li_2^+ molecule is more stable than Li_2^-?

(ii) Which of the following compound contains both covalent and ionic bonds?

(a) CCl_4 (b) $CaCl_2$
(c) NH_4Cl (d) NaCl

Or

In PO_4^{3-}, the formal charge on each O-atom and the P−O bond order respectively are

(a) −0.75, 0.6 (b) −0.75, 1.0
(c) −0.75, 1.25 (d) −3, 1.25

(iii) The number of nodal planes present in a σ^* anti-bonding orbital is

(a) 0 (b) 3 (c) 1 (d) 2

Subjective Type Questions

Short Answer Type I Questions [2 Marks]

1. Give reason for the following.

(i) Ionic compounds are soluble in water whereas covalent compounds are mostly insoluble in water.

(ii) Ionic compounds have higher melting points than the covalent compounds.

2. Aluminium forms the ion Al^{3+} but not Al^{4+}. Why?

3. Which is more polar : CO_2 or N_2O? Give reason.

4. In each of the following pairs of compounds, which one is more covalent and why?

(i) AgCl, AgI (ii) $BeCl_2$, $MgCl_2$

5. Why does formic acid exist as dimer? What is its one consequence?

6. With the help of molecular orbital theory, predict which of the following species is diamagnetic, H_2^+, O_2, O_2^{2+}? **Competency Based Que.**

7. Draw the shape of the following hybrid orbitals sp, sp^2 and sp^3.

8. Using valence bond theory, draw the molecular structures of OSF_4 and XeF_4 indicating the location of lone pair(s) of electrons and hybridisation of central atoms.

9. What is the magnetic nature of the anion of KO_2?

10. Explain why HCl is a covalent compound but it ionises in the solution.

Short Answer Type II Questions [3 Marks]

11. Explain why PCl_5 is trigonal bipyramidal, whereas IF_5 is square pyramidal?

12. Explain why carbon has a valency of four and not two. Also, why the four C—H bonds in methane are identical.

13. What is the total number of sigma and pi bond in the following molecules?

(i) C_2H_3Cl (ii) $C_4H_4Cl_2$

(iii) 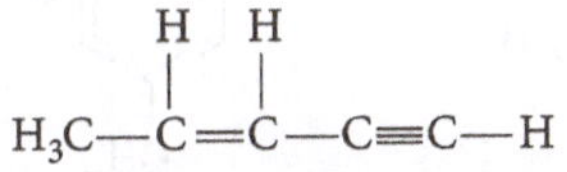

14. Which of the species have linear shape and why? NO_2^-, NO_2^+, CO_2, O_3

15. Arrange the following sets of molecules in the decreasing order of bond angle.

(i) SF_6, CCl_4, H_2O, NH_3 (ii) CH_4, NH_3, H_2O, BF_3

16. Define octet rule. Write its significance and limitations. **NCERT**

17. Draw the Lewis structures for the following molecule and ions. **NCERT**

H_2S, $SiCl_4$, BeF_2, CO_3^{2-}, HCOOH

18. What is meant by term bond order? Calculate the bond order of N_2, O_2, O_2^+ and O_2^-. **NCERT**

19. (i) What factors favour the formation of ionic bond. Explain with examples.
(ii) Arrange the following in increasing order of ionic character and also give the reason.
$NaCl, CaCl_2, MgCl_2, MgO$.

20. (i) What are polar covalent bonds?
(ii) Define the characteristics of covalent compounds.

21. What is an ionic bond? With two suitable examples explain the difference between an ionic and a covalent bond? **NCERT Exemplar**

22. (i) Discuss the significance/applications of dipole moment.
(ii) Represent diagrammatically the bond moments and the resultant dipole moment in CO_2, NF_3 and $CHCl_3$. **NCERT Exemplar**

23. What are the main postulates of valence shell electron pair repulsion (VSEPR) theory?

24. Discuss the shape of the following molecules using VSEPR model. **NCERT**
$BeCl_2, BCl_3, SiCl_4, AsF_5, H_2S, PH_3$

25. (i) Draw the structure of following molecular shapes and give the various bond angles in the following: linear, trigonal planar, tetrahedral and octahedral.
(ii) What are the shapes of PCl_5, NH_3, BCl_3, SF_6, H_2O, CCl_4, SF_4, ClF_3, XeF_4, XeF_2? **Competency Based Que.**

26. Define hydrogen bond. Is it weaker or stronger than the van der Waals' forces? **NCERT**

27. Structures of molecules of two compounds are given below.

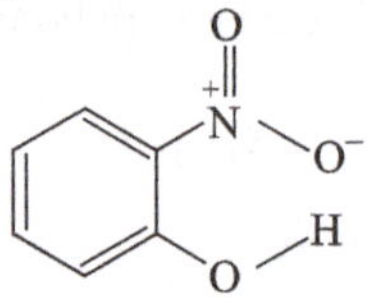
(I)

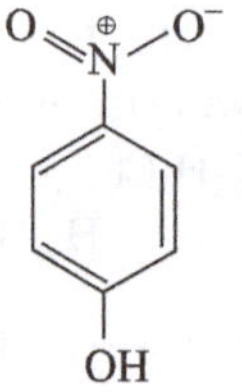
(II)

(a) Which of the two compounds will have intermolecular hydrogen bonding and which compound is expected to show intramolecular hydrogen bonding ?
(b) The melting point of a compound depends on, among other things, the extent of hydrogen bonding. On this basis explain which of the above two compounds will show higher melting point ?
(c) Solubility of compounds in water depends on power to form hydrogen bonds with water. Which of the above compounds will form hydrogen bond with water easily and be more soluble in it ? **NCERT**

Long Answer Type Questions [5 Marks]

28. Explain the formation of H_2 molecule on the basis of valence bond theory. **NCERT**

29. What is meant by hybridisation of atomic orbitals. Describe the shapes of sp, sp^2 and sp^3 hybrid orbitals. **NCERT**

30. Which hybrid orbitals are used by C-atoms in the following molecules?
(i) CH_3-CH_3 (ii) $CH_3CH=CH_2$
(iii) CH_3CH_2OH (iv) CH_3CHO
(v) CH_3COOH **NCERT**

31. The energy of $\sigma 2p_z$ molecular orbital is greater than $\pi 2p_x$ and $\pi 2p_y$ molecular orbitals in nitrogen molecule. Write the complete sequence of energy levels in the increasing order of energy in the molecule. Compare the relative stability and the magnetic behaviour of the following species.
$N_2, N_2^+, N_2^-, N_2^{2+}$ **NCERT Exemplar**

32. Describe hybridisation in the case of PCl_5 and SF_6. The axial bonds are longer as compared to equatorial bonds in PCl_5 whereas in SF_6 both axial bonds and equatorial bonds have the same bond length. Explain. **NCERT Exemplar**

33. Use the molecular orbital energy level diagram to show that N_2 would be expected to have a triple bond; F_2 a single bond and Ne_2, no bond. **NCERT**

34. How is bonding molecular orbitals different from antibonding molecular orbitals? Give electronic configuration of
(i) H_2^+ (ii) Li_2, (iii) B_2 and (iv) C_2. Calculate their bond order and predict their paramagnetic behaviour. **Competency Based Que.**

35. (i) Discuss the concept of hybridisation. What are its different types in a C-atom? **NCERT**
(ii) What is the type of hybridisation of carbon atoms marked with star?
(a) $\overset{*}{C}H_2=CH-\overset{*}{C}(=O)-O-H$
(b) $CH_3-\overset{*}{C}H_2-OH$
(c) $CH_3-CH_2-\overset{*}{C}(=O)-H$
(d) $\overset{*}{C}H_3-CH=CH-CH_3$
(e) $CH_3-\overset{*}{C}\equiv CH$ **NCERT Exemplar**

Hints & Solutions

Objective Type Questions

1. (*d*) Lewis structure of CO_2 can be represented as

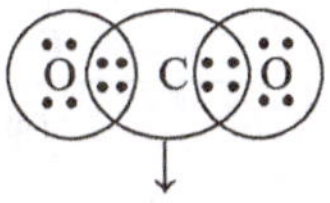

Complete octet

2. (*d*) The group valence of the elements is generally equal to either the number of dots in Lewis symbols or eight minus the number of dots or valence electrons.

3. (*a*) Ionic bonds will be formed more easily between elements with comparatively low ionisation enthalpy and high negative value of electron gain enthalpy.

4. (*c*) The formal charge of oxygen labelled (3, 2, 1) in ozone is −1, 0, +1.

5. (*d*) Among the given statements C and D are incorrect while other are correct.

   Their corrected forms are
   - In resonance structure there should be the same number of electron pairs.
   - In resonance, the position of atoms remains fixed.

6. (*a*) I may be correctly represented as

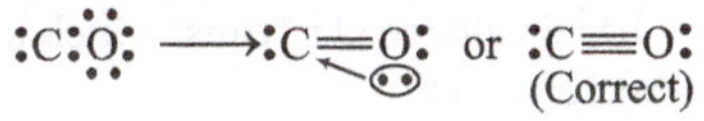

7. (*c*) (i) $CH_4 \longrightarrow$

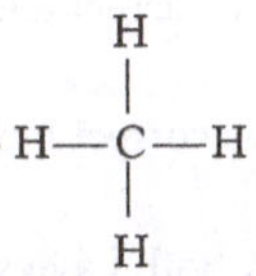

   (ii) $C_2H_4 \longrightarrow$

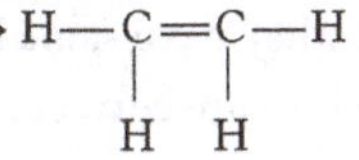

   (iii) $C_2H_2 \longrightarrow H{-}C{\equiv}C{-}H$

   (iv) $O_3 \longrightarrow O{=}O^+{-}O^-$

   Thus, C_2H_2 has triple bond.

8. (*b*) Among the given options, NO_3^- has trigonal planar shape and is sp^2-hybridised.

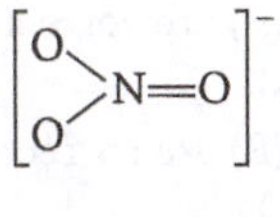

9. (*c*) Double bonds consists of one σ and one π-bond, while single bond consists of σ-bond only.

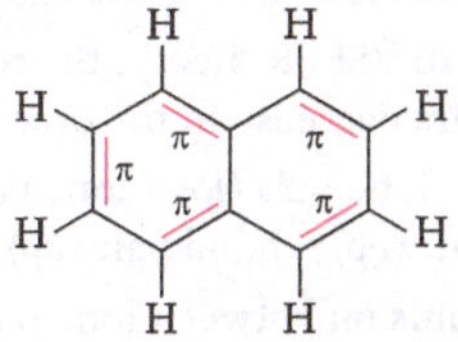

   Thus, napthalene has 5π-bonds and 19σ-bonds.

10. (*a*) Multiple bonds are stronger, having high bond dissociation energy, so they are shorter. More the bond order, the more will be bond dissociation energy and shorter will be the bond length. So, order of bond length is :

    Triple bond < Double bond < Single bond.

11. (*d*) Smallest the atom, larger the overlapping hence, higher will be the bond dissociation energy.

12. (*d*) A general correlation useful for understanding the stabilities of molecules is that, with increase in bond order, bond enthalpy increases and bond length decreases. Stability increases with increase in bond order and bond enthalpy.

    Therefore, stability ∝ bond order ∝ bond enthalpy.
    Stability increases with decrease in bond length.

    Therefore, stability $\propto \frac{1}{\text{bond length}}$

13. (*a*) H-atom has only *s*-orbital. Therefore, *s*-*s* overlapping takes place in the formation of H_2 molecule.

14. (*b*) Out of phase overlap occurs in

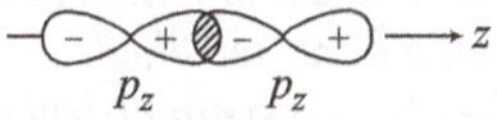

    Thus, it shows negative overlap.

15. (*c*) The *sp*-hybridisation is also called diagonal hybridisation.

16. (*b*) For sp^2-hybridisation, the geometry is generally trigonal planar.

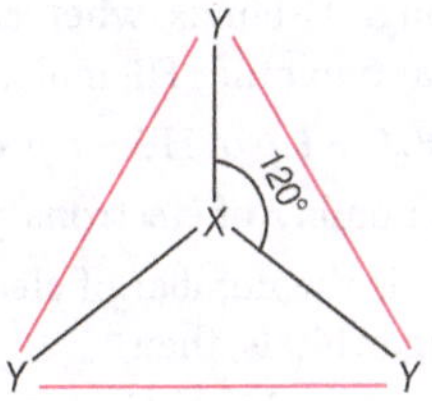

    Thus, bond angle is 120°.

17. (*b*)

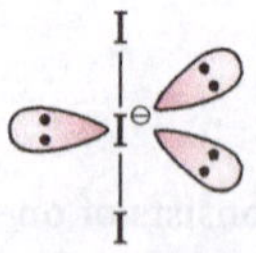

Three lone pairs on central atom and two bonding pairs.

18. (*a*) According to VSEPR theory, the repulsive interaction of electron pairs decrease in the order.
Lone pair (*lp*)– lone pair (*lp*) > lone pair (*lp*) – bond pair (*bp*) > bond pair (*bp*) – bond pair (*bp*).

19. (*c*) Greater repulsion between lone pairs of electrons as compared to the lone pair- bond pair and bond pair-bond pair repulsions.
These repulsive effects result in deviations from idealised shapes and alterations in bond angles in the molecules.

20. (*c*) CO_2 and BF_3 being symmetrical have zero dipole moment.

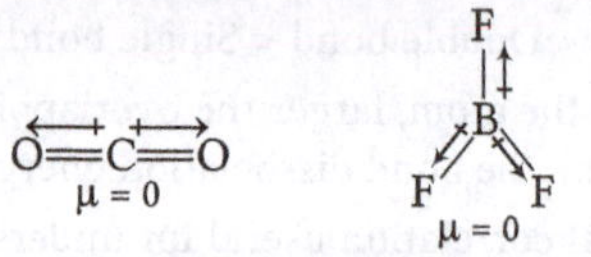

Among HI and H_2O, dipole moment is highest for H_2O. As in it, the central atom contains 2 bond pairs. So, the dipole moment adds up.

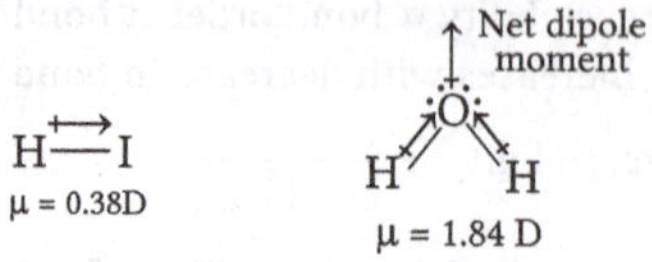

> **Mistake Alert** *One can make a mistake while calculating the dipole moment of molecules having linear, trigonal planar, tetrahedral and octahedral geometry. They have a symmetrical shape, so their dipole moment (μ) is zero.*

21. (*b*) Strength of H-bond is in the order

H....F > H.....O > H.....N.

But each H_2O molecule is linked to four other H_2O molecules through H-bonds, whereas each HF molecule is linked only to two other HF molecules.
Hence, *b.p* of H_2O > *b.p* of HF > *b.p.* of NH_3.

22. (*a*) If N_b is the number of electrons occupying bonding orbitals and N_a is the number of electrons occupying the antibonding orbitals, then
(i) the molecule is stable if N_b is greater than N_a.
(ii) the molecule is unstable if N_b is less than N_a.

23. (*a*) A molecule with dsp^2 hybridisation forms four dsp^2 orbital which orient themselves at 90° to give square planar geometry to the molecule.

24. (*c*) Xe $(Z = 54) = [Kr]4d^{10}5s^2 5p^6$

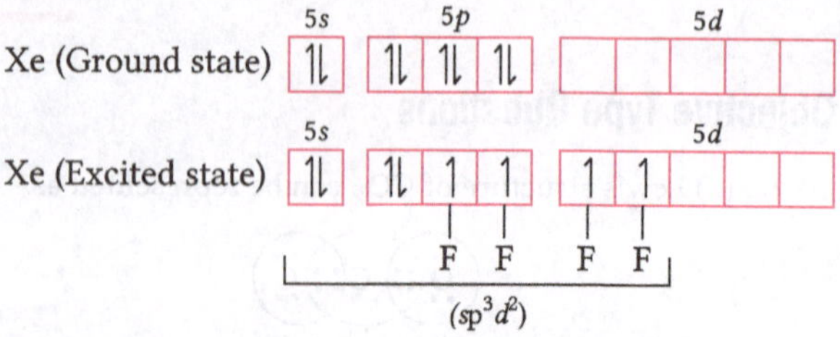

XeF_4 has 4 bond pairs and two lone pairs. The 2 lone pairs orients themselves in such a way that lone pair-lone pair repulsion is minimized. So, the shape of XeF_4 molecule is square planar.

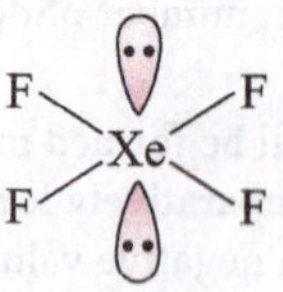

(Square planar)
(sp^3d^2)

25. (*a*) The correct match is A-4, B-3, C-1, D-2.

26. (*a*) Both A and R are true and R is the correct explanation of A.

27. (*a*) Both (A) and (R) are correct and (R) is the correct explanation of (A).

28. (*b*) Both (A) and (R) are correct but (R) is not the correct explanation of (A).
Correct Reason Oxygen does not have *d*-orbitals because it has 6 valence electrons, which are distributed in its 2*s* and 2*p* orbital.

29. (*a*) Both (A) and (R) are correct and (R) is the correct explanation of (A).

30. (*b*) Both (A) and (R) are correct but (R) is not the correct explanation of (A).
Correct Explanation Both have same no. of hybrid orbitals. Hence, they have same hybridisation.

31. (*a*) Both (A) and (R) are correct and (R) is the correct explanation of (A).

32. (*a*) Both (A) and (R) are correct and (R) is the correct explanation of (A).

33. (*c*) (A) is correct and (R) is incorrect.
Correct Reason The electronic charge on oxygen atom is different after breaking of one of the O—H bond.

34. (*a*) Both (A) and (R) are correct and (R) is the correct explanation of (A).

35. (*a*) Both (A) and (R) are correct and (R) is the correct explanation of (A).

36. (*c*) A is true but R is false. The correct form of R is
In AsF_5 molecule, the *d*-orbital involved in sp^3d-hybridisation is d_{z^2}.

37. (c) A is true but R is false. The correct form of R is In 1, 1, 2, 2-tetrachloroethene, each carbon is sp^2 and in tetrachloromethane, carbon is sp^3-hybridised.

38. (i)

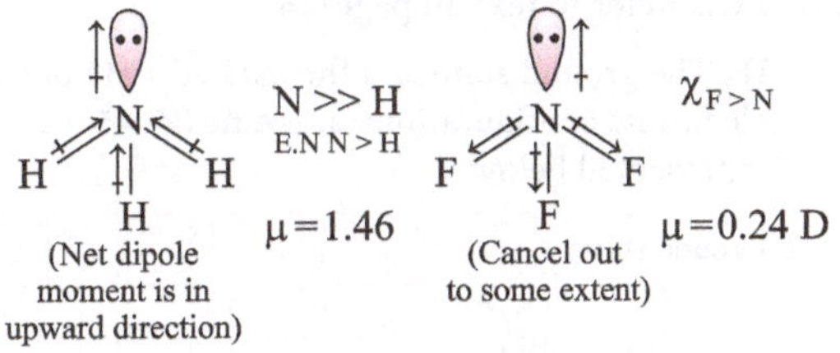

Hence, $\mu_{NH_3} > \mu_{NF_3}$. **(1)**

(ii) CO_2 molecule is a non-polar linear molecule.

$$\overleftarrow{O{=}}C\overrightarrow{{=}O}$$

Linear

$\mu = 0$ (non-polar) **(1)**

Or

Dipole moment, $\mu = q \times d$.

Dipole moment is expressed in Debye unit (D). **(1)**

(iii) (μ) Dipole moment $= q \times d$

$$\mu = 1.2\text{ D} = 1.2 \times 3.33564 \times 10^{-30}\text{ cm}$$

$$d = 1 \times 10^{-8}\text{ cm} = 1 \times 10^{-10}\text{ m}$$

$$q = \frac{\mu}{d} = \frac{1.2 \times 3.33564 \times 10^{-30}\text{ cm}}{1 \times 10^{-10}\text{ m}}$$

$$q = 4.003 \times 10^{-20}\text{ C}$$ **(2)**

39. (i) **According to MOT**

The electronic configuration of $Li_2^+ (Z = 5)$ is $\sigma 1s^2\, \sigma^* 1s^2\, \sigma 2s^1$.

$$\text{So, its B.O.} = \frac{N_b - N_a}{2}$$

$$= \frac{3-2}{2} = \frac{1}{2}$$

Now, the electronic configuration of $Li_2^- (Z = 7)$ $= \sigma 1s^2\, \sigma^* 1s^2\, \sigma 2s^2\, \sigma^* 2s^1$.

$$\text{Bond order (B.O.)} = \frac{N_b - N_a}{2} = \frac{4-3}{2} = \frac{1}{2}$$

For the species having the same value of B.O, the species having lesser number of antibonding electrons $[N_a]$ will be more stable.

Here, N_a of $Li_2^+(2) < N_a$ of $Li_2^-(3)$. So, their order of stability is $Li_2^+ > Li_2^-$. **(2)**

(ii) (c) NH_4Cl contains four covalent bonds between nitrogen and four hydrogen atoms formed by sharing of electrons just like ammonia.

The molecule has two ions, cation ammonium and anions chloride. Thus, there exists an ionic bond between NH_4Cl. **(1)**

Or

(c) 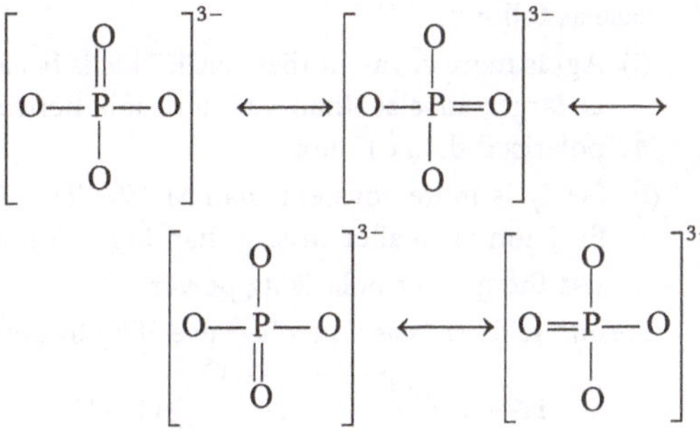

Formal charge on each O-atom

$$= \frac{\text{Total Charge}}{\text{No.of O-atoms}} = \frac{-3}{4} = -0.75$$

(P – O) Bond order

$$= \frac{\text{Total no.of bonds}}{\text{Total no. of resonating structures}}$$

$$= \frac{5}{4} = 1.25$$ **(1)**

(iii) (c) The molecular orbital σ^*s formed by the overlapping of two s–orbitals.

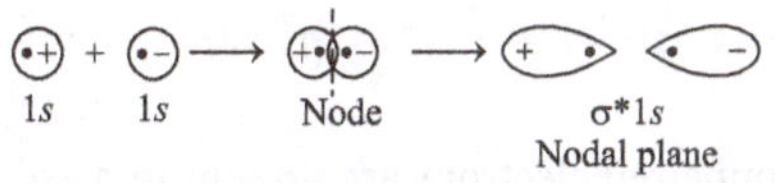

The σ^* anti-bonding orbital has one nodal plane. **(1)**

Subjective Type Questions

1. (i) Being polar in nature ionic compounds are soluble in water but covalent compounds are generally non-polar so they are insoluble in water (it forms the principle, like dissolves like). **(1)**

(ii) Because of the presence of strong electrostatic forces of attraction melting points of ionic compounds are higher than that of covalent compounds. **(1)**

2. Aluminium ([Ne] $3s^2 3p^1$ can achieve the electronic configuration of the nearest noble gas (Ne) by losing only three electrons. : $Al^{3+} = 1s^2\, 2s^2\, 2p^6$. Aluminium will not form the Al^{4+} ion because an extremely high amount of energy would be required to remove an electron from the stable noble gas configuration. **(2)**

3. N_2O is more polar than CO_2. This is because CO_2 is linear and symmetrical. Its net dipole moment is zero ($O \overset{\leftarrow}{=} C \overset{\rightarrow}{=} O$). N_2O on the other hand, is linear but unsymmetrical. It is considered as a resonance hybrid of the following two structures

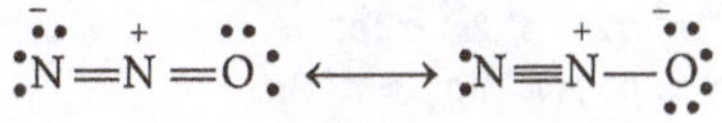

It has a net dipole moment of 0.116 D. **(2)**

4. Applying Fajans' rules the result can be obtained in each case as follows

(i) AgI is more covalent that AgCl. This is because I^- ion is larger in size than Cl^- ion and hence, is more polarised than Cl^- ion. **(1)**

(ii) $BeCl_2$ is more covalent than $MgCl_2$. This is because Be^{2+} ion is smaller in size than Mg^{2+} ion and hence has the greater polarising power. **(1)**

5. Formic acid exists as dimer because of hydrogen bonding.

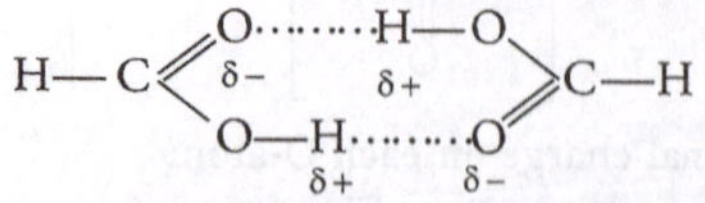

Because of hydrogen bonding, it has larger size and molecular mass. **(2)**

6. The diamagnetic species are those which contain only paired electrons. This can be predicted from the molecular orbital electronic configurations as given below.

$H_2^+ : \sigma 1s^1$

One unpaired electron is present in $\sigma 1s^2$ orbital. So, it is paramagnetic.

$O_2 : \sigma 1s^2\ \overset{*}{\sigma} 1s^2\ \sigma 2s^2\ \overset{*}{\sigma} 2s^2\ \sigma 2p_z^2\ \pi 2p_x^2 \approx \pi 2p_y^2$

$\pi^* 2p_x^1 \approx \pi^* 2p_y^1$ **(1)**

Two unpaired electrons are present in $\pi^* 2p_x^1$ and $\pi^* 2p_y^1$ orbital. So, it is also paramagnetic.

$O_2^{2+} : \sigma 1s^2\ \overset{*}{\sigma} 1s^2\ \sigma 2s^2\ \overset{*}{\sigma} 2s^2\ \sigma 2p_z^2\ \pi 2p_x^2 = \pi 2p_y^2$

Since, O_2^{2+} contains all paired electrons, it will be diamagnetic. **(1)**

7.

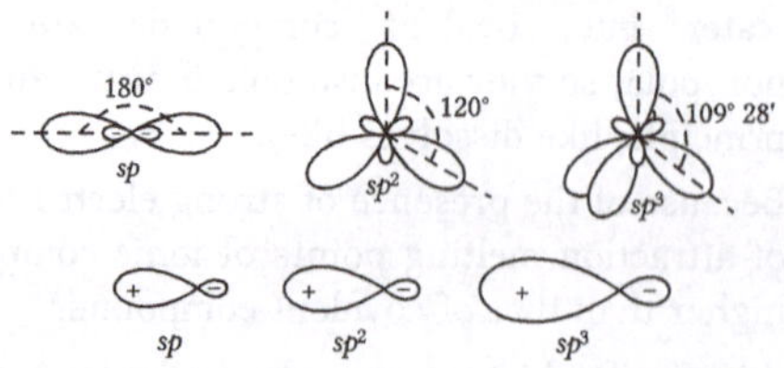

(1)

All the hybrid orbitals have same shape. However, their sizes are in the order : $sp < sp^2 < sp^3$. **(1)**

8.

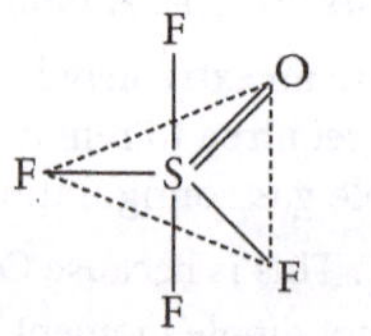

Trigonal bipyramidal
(sp^3d-hybridisation)

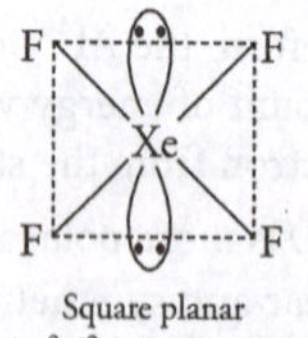

Square planar
(sp^3d^2-hybridisation) **(2)**

9. Anion of KO_2 is O_2^- (super oxide ion) which has 17 electrons and electronic configuration of

$\sigma 1s^2\ \sigma^* 1s^2\ \sigma 2s^2\ \sigma^* 2s^2\ \sigma 2p_z^2$
$(\pi 2p_x^2 \approx \pi 2p_y^2)(\pi^* 2p_x^2 \approx \pi^* 2p_y)$

It has one unpaired electron and hence, it is paramagnetic. **(2)**

10. This is because of large difference in the electronegativity of H and Cl-atoms. Due to which polarity is generated which is responsible for separation of ions.
Hence, HCl ionises in the solution. **(2)**

11. PCl_5 Refer to text on page146. **(1)**

IF_5 The ground state and the excited state outer electronic configurations of iodine (Z = 53) are represented below

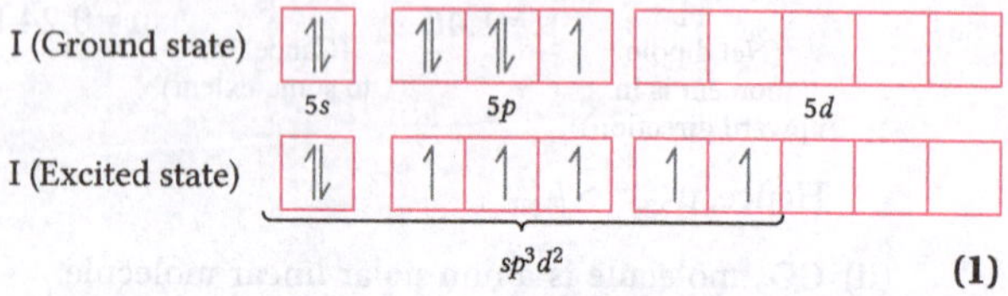

(1)

In IF_5, I is sp^3d^2-hybridised therefore, shape of IF_5 is square pyramidal as it contains one lone pair of electrons.

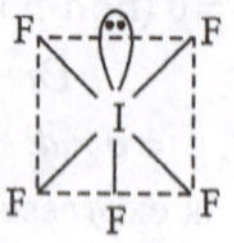

(1)

12. The ground state electronic configuration of carbon is $1s^2\ 2s^2\ 2p^2$. But carbon forms bond with other atoms in excited state.

The electronic configuration in excited state is $1s^2\ 2s^1\ 2p_x^1\ 2p_y^1\ 2p_z^1$. **(1)**

The 1s-orbital and 3p-orbitals of the valence shell intermix to form four sp^3-hybrid orbitals of equivalent energies and shape. These hybrid orbitals are arranged tetrahedrally at an angle of 109° 28′ to each other. The four sp^3-hybrid orbitals overlap with the half-filled. **(1)**

1s-orbitals of four H-atoms to form CH_4 as shown below.

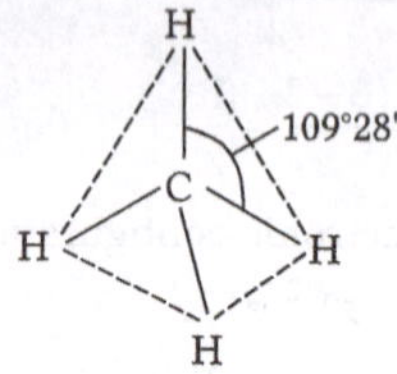

(1)

13. (i) 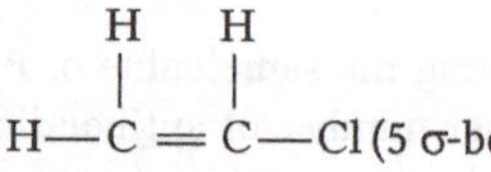

(5 σ-bonds, one π-bonds) **(1)**

(ii) 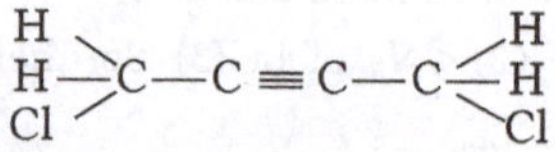

(9 σ-bonds, 2π-bonds) **(1)**

(iii) 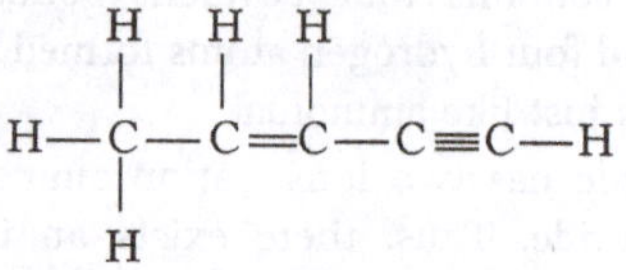

(10 σ-bonds, 3 π-bonds) **(1)**

14. NO_2^+ and CO_2 are *sp*-hybridised, therefore, they have linear shape.

$O=\overset{+}{N}=O$, $O=C=O$

Linear   Linear (1)

NO_2^- and O_3 are sp^2-hybridised. Both have lone pair of electrons. (1)

Thus, their shape is angular.

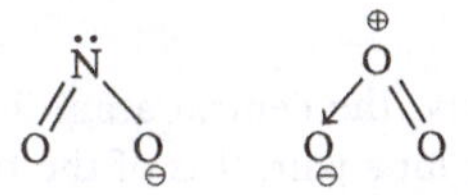

Angular   Angular (1)

Mistake Alert *One can make a mistake of not considering the coordinate bond in O_3. O_3 can also be written as*

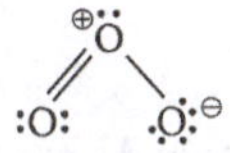

(1)

15. (i) $CCl_4(109.5°) > NH_3(107°) > H_2O(104.5°) > SF_6(90°)$ (1½)

Tetrahedral   Pyramidal   Angular   Octahedral

(ii) $BF_3(120°) > CH_4(109.5°) > NH_3(107°) > H_2O(104.5°)$ (1½)

Planar   Tetrahedral   Pyramidal   Angular

16. **Octet rule** Atoms can combine either by transfer of valence electrons from one atom to another (gaining or losing) or by sharing of valence electrons in order to have an octet in their valence shell. (1)

Significance of octet rule It helps to explain why different atoms combine with each other to form ionic or covalent compounds. (1)

Limitations of octet rule Refer to text on page 129. (1)

17. In Lewis structures, all the elements (except H) have 8 electrons in their outer shell. H has only 2 electrons.

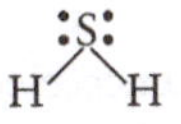

H_2S

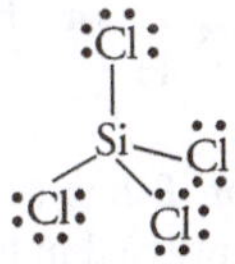

$SiCl_4$

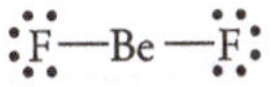

BeF_2

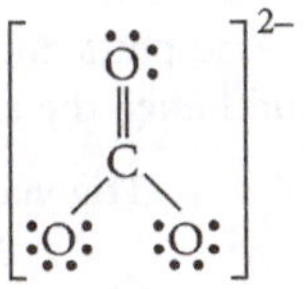

CO_3^{2-}

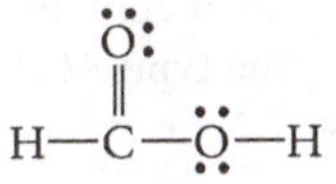

HCOOH

(3)

18. **Bond order** is defined as one half of the difference between the number of electrons present in the bonding and antibonding orbitals, i.e.

$$\text{Bond order (B.O.)} = \frac{1}{2}(N_b - N_A)$$

A positive bond order means a stable molecule while a negative or zero bond order means an unstable molecule.

Stability of a molecule ∝ bond order

$$\text{Bond length} \propto \frac{1}{\text{bond order}}$$

Bond order values 1,2 or 3 correspond to single, double or triple bonds, respectively. (1)

Calculation of the bond order of N_2, O_2, O_2^+ and O_2^-

Electronic configuration of N_2 (14 electrons)

$\sigma 1s^2\ \overset{*}{\sigma} 1s^2\ \sigma 2s^2\ \overset{*}{\sigma} 2s^2\ (\pi\ 2p_x^2 \approx \pi\ 2p_y^2)\ \sigma 2p_z^2$

$$\text{Bond order} = \frac{1}{2}[N_b - N_a] = \frac{1}{2} \times (10-4) = 3 \quad (½)$$

E.C. of O_2 (16 electrons)

$= \sigma 1s^2\ \overset{*}{\sigma} 1s^2 \sigma 2s^2\ \overset{*}{\sigma} 2s^2 \sigma 2p_z^2\ (\pi\ 2p_x^2 \approx \pi\ 2p_y^2)$
$(\overset{*}{\pi} 2p_x^1 \approx \overset{*}{\pi} 2p_y^1)$

$$\text{Bond order} = \frac{1}{2}(N_b - N_a) = \frac{1}{2}(10-6) = 2 \quad (½)$$

E.C. of O_2^+ (15 electrons)

$= \sigma 1s^2\ \overset{*}{\sigma} 1s^2 \sigma 2s^2\ \overset{*}{\sigma} 2s^2 \sigma 2p_z^2\ (\pi\ 2p_x^2 \approx \pi 2p_y^2)$
$(\overset{*}{\pi} 2p_x^1 \approx \overset{*}{\pi} 2p_y^0)$

$$\text{Bond order} = \frac{1}{2}(N_b - N_a) = \frac{1}{2}(10-5) = 2.5 \quad (½)$$

E.C. of O_2^- (17 electrons)

$= \sigma 1s^2\ \overset{*}{\sigma} 1s^2 \sigma 2s^2\ \overset{*}{\sigma} 2s^2 \sigma 2p_z^2\ (\pi\ 2p_x^2 \approx \pi\ 2p_y^2)$
$(\overset{*}{\pi} 2p_x^2 \approx \overset{*}{\pi} 2p_y^1)$

$$\text{Bond order} = \frac{1}{2}(N_b - N_a) = \frac{1}{2}(10-7) = 1.5 \quad (½)$$

19. (i) Refer to text on page 124-125. (1½)

(ii) Ionic character ∝ Lattice enthalpy and lattice enthalpy ∝ 1/size of cation.

Thus, the order of ionic character is

$CaCl_2 < MgCl_2 < NaCl < MgO$. (1½)

20. (i) Refer to text on page 127. (1)

(ii) Refer to text on page 127. (2)

21. **Ionic bond** The bond formed as a result of the electrostatic attraction between the positive and negative ions is termed as the electrovalent bond or ionic bond. (1)

e.g. The formation of NaCl from sodium and chlorine can be explained as

$$\underset{[Ne]\,3s^1}{Na} \longrightarrow \underset{[Ne]}{Na^+} + e^-$$

$$\underset{[Ne]\,3s^2 3p^5}{Cl} + e^- \longrightarrow \underset{[Ne]\,3s^2 3p^6 \text{ or } [Ar]}{Cl^-}$$

$$Na^+ + Cl^- \longrightarrow NaCl \text{ or } Na^+Cl^-$$

Similarly, the formation of CaF_2 may be shown as

$$\underset{[Ar]4s^2}{Ca} \longrightarrow \underset{[Ar]}{Ca^{2+}} + 2e^-$$

$$\underset{[He]\ 2s^2 2p^5}{F} + e^- \longrightarrow \underset{[He]\ 2s^2 2p^6 \text{ or } [Ne]}{F^-}$$

$$Ca^{2+} + 2F^- \longrightarrow CaF_2 \text{ or } Ca^{2+}F^-$$ **(1)**

Covalent bond The bond formed between the two atoms by mutual sharing of electrons between them is called covalent bond. e.g. The formation of chlorine molecule can be explained as

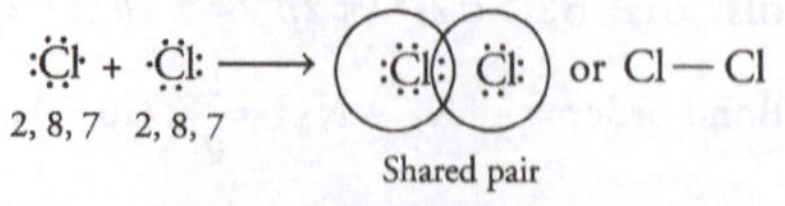

Similarly, in the formation of HCl

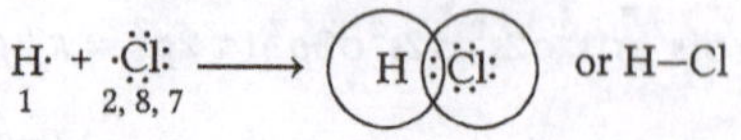

(1)

22. (i) Applications of dipole moment are

(a) The dipole moment helps to predict whether a molecule is polar or non-polar. As $\mu = q \times d$, greater is the magnitude of dipole moment, higher will be the polarity of the bond. For non-polar molecules, the dipole moment is zero.

(b) The percentage of ionic character can be calculated as

$$\text{Percentage of ionic character} = \frac{\mu_{\text{observed}}}{\mu_{\text{ionic}}} \times 100$$

(c) Symmetrical molecules have zero dipole moment although they have two or more polar bonds. (In determination of symmetry). **(2)**

(ii)

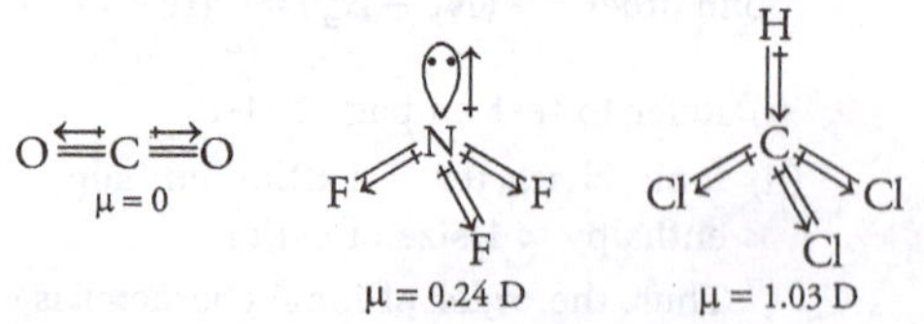

(1)

23. Refer to text on page 136. **(3)**

24. According to VSEPR theory, the shape of a molecule depends upon the number of valence shell electron pairs (bonded or non-bonded) around the central atom. Pairs of electrons in the valence shell repel each other. The order of their repulsions is as follows

$$lp\text{-}lp > lp\text{-}bp > bp\text{-}bp$$

(i) **$BeCl_2$** Cl — Be — Cl or Cl $\times\!\!\bullet$ Be $\bullet\!\!\times$ Cl

The central atom Be has only 2 valence electrons which are bonded to Cl, so there are only 2 bond pairs and no lone pairs. It is of the type AB_2 and hence, the shape is linear. **(½)**

(ii) **BCl_3**

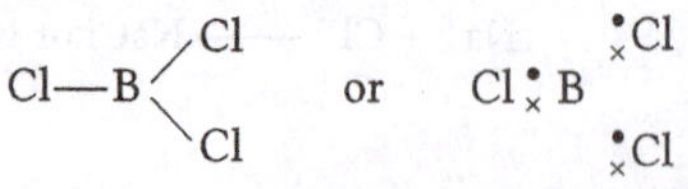

The central atom B has only 3 valence electrons which are bonded with three Cl-atoms, so it contains only 3 bond pairs and no lone pair. It is of the type AB_3 and hence, the shape is trigonal planar. **(½)**

(iii) **$SiCl_4$**

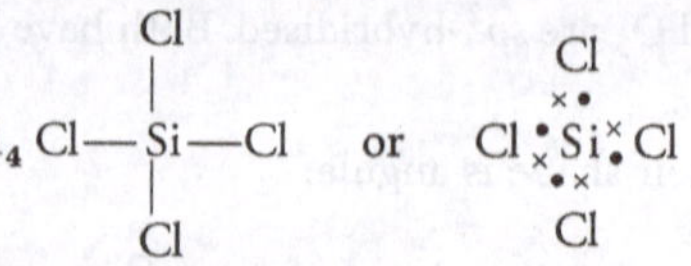

Similarly, the central atom Si has only 4 bond pairs and no lone pair. It is of the type AB_4 and hence, the shape is tetrahedral. **(½)**

(iv) **AsF_5**

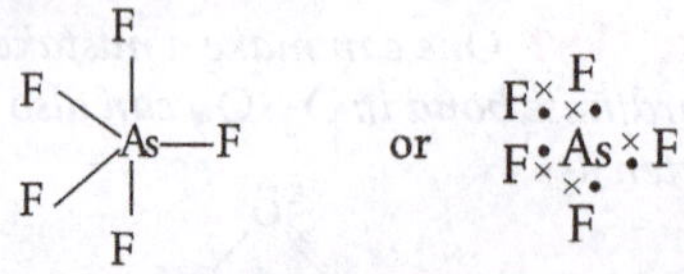

The central atom As has only 5 bond pairs and no lone pair. It is of the type AB_5 and hence, the shape is trigonal bipyramidal. **(½)**

(v) **H_2S**

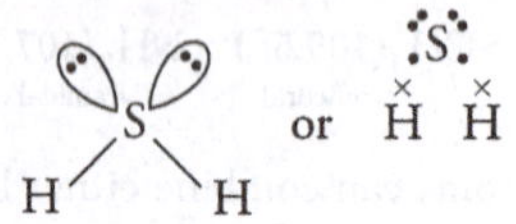

The central atom S has 6 valence electrons. Out of these only two are used in bond formation with two H-atoms while four (two pairs) remains as non-bonding electrons (i.e. lone pairs).

So, it contains 2 bond pairs and 2 lone pairs. It is of the type AB_2E_2 and hence, the shape is bent or V-shaped. **(½)**

(vi) **PH_3**

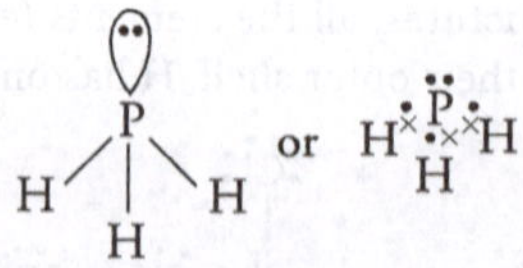

The central atom P has 5 valence electrons. Out of which three are utilised in bonding with H-atoms and one pair remains as lone pair.

So, it contains 3 bond pairs and one lone pair. It is of the type AB_3E and hence the shape is pyramidal. **(½)**

25. (i)

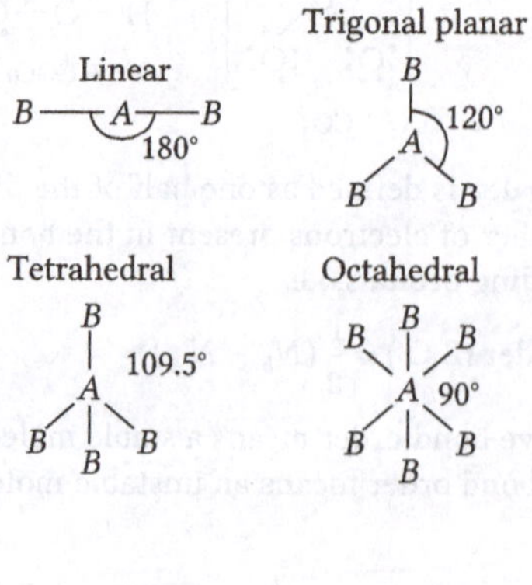

(1)

(ii) The shape of the molecules are given below.

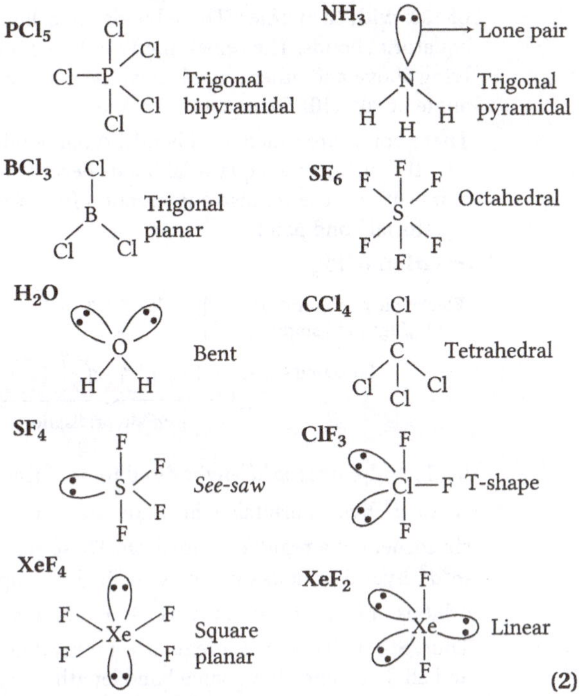

(2)

26. Whenever in a molecule H-atom is linked with an atom of electronegative element like F, O or N, the shared pair electrons of the covalent bond are shifted towards the more electronegative atom. Due to this H-atom acquires partial positive charge and more electronegative atom acquires partial negative charge. This partially positively charged hydrogen of one molecule forms a bond with the other partially negatively charged more electronegative atom. This bond is known as **hydrogen bond**, e.g. In HF molecule hydrogen acquires partial positive charge and F acquires partial negative charge due to the shifting of shared pair of electrons towards F. This partial positive charged H-atom of one molecule forms a hydrogen bond with partial negative charged F atom of another molecule.

$$\cdots \overset{\delta+}{H} - \overset{\delta-}{F} \cdots \overset{\delta+}{H} - \overset{\delta-}{F} \cdots \overset{\delta+}{H} - \overset{\delta-}{F}$$

Hydrogen bond (2)

Thus, **H-bond** can be defined as the attractive force which binds H-atom of one molecule with the electronegative atom like F, O or N of another molecule.

Hydrogen bond is stronger than van der Waals' forces. (1)

27. (a) Compound (I) will form intramolecular H-bonding. Intramolecular H-bonding is formed when H-atom, in between the two highly electronegative atoms, is present within the same molecule. In *ortho*-nitrophenol (compound I), H-atom is in between the two oxygen atoms.

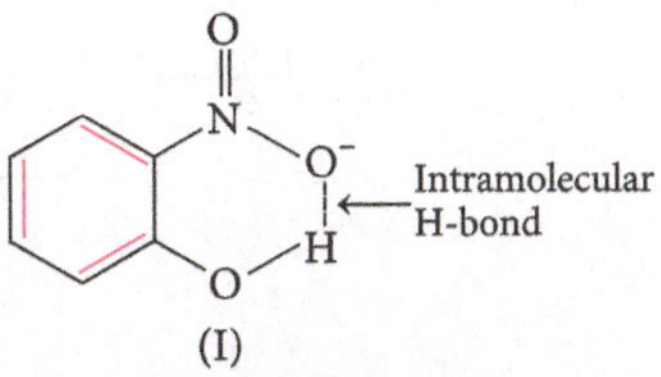

(I)

Compound (II) forms intermolecular H-bonding. In *para*- nitrophenol (II) there is a gap between —NO$_2$ and —OH group. So, H-bond exists between H-atom of one molecule and O-atom of another molecule as depicted below.

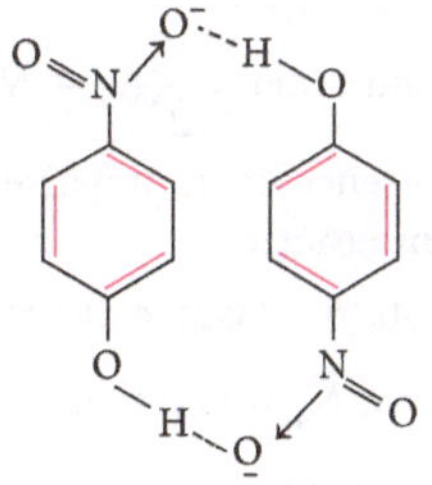

(II)

(1)

(b) Compound (II) will have higher melting point because large number of molecules are joined together by H-bonds. (1)

(c) Due to intramolecular H-bonding compound (I) is not able to form H-bond with water, so it is less soluble in water. While molecules of compound II form H-bonding with H$_2$O easily, so it is soluble in water. (1)

28. Refer to text on page 140-141. (5)

29. Refer to text on pages 143 to 145. (5)

30.

(i) 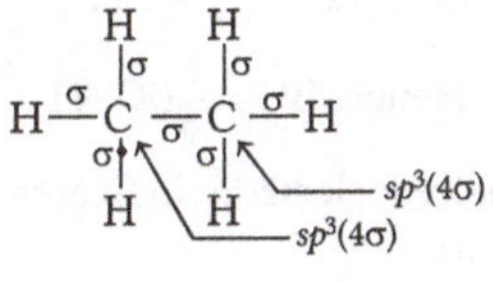

(C_2H_6) (4σ) or CH_3—CH_3

(ii) 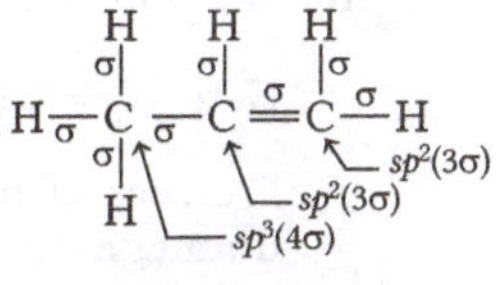

(CH_3CH=CH_2)

(iii) 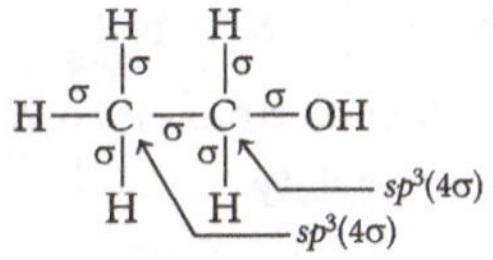

(CH_3CH_2OH)

(iv) 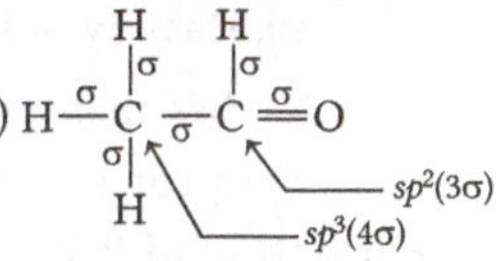

(CH_3CHO)

(v) 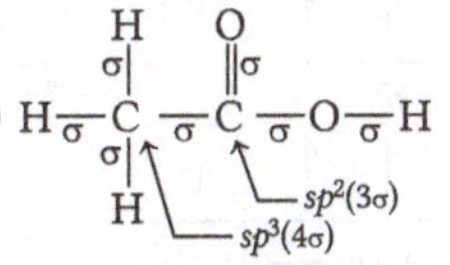

(CH_3COOH)

If a C-atom is bonded by only single bonds, it is sp^3-hybridised and if it is bonded by a double bond, it is sp^2-hybridised and if it is bonded by one triple bond, it is *sp*-hybridised. (5)

31. Electronic configuration of N-atom ($Z = 7$) is $1s^2 2s^2 2p_x^1 2p_y^1 2p_z^1$. Total number of electrons present in N_2 molecule is 14, 7 from each N-atom. From the view of various rules for filling of molecular orbitals, the electronic configuration of N_2 molecule will be

$$\sigma 1s^2 \sigma^* 1s^2 \sigma 2s^2 \sigma^* 2s^2 \pi 2p_x^2 \approx \pi 2p_y^2 \sigma 2p_z^2$$ (1)

Comparative study of the relative stability and the magnetic behaviour of the following species

(i) **N_2 molecule**

$\sigma 1s^2 \sigma^* 1s^2 \sigma 2s^2 \sigma^* 2s^2 \pi 2p_x^2 \approx \pi 2p_y^2 \sigma 2p_z^2$

Here, $N_b = 10$, $N_a = 4$.

Hence, Bond order $= \frac{1}{2}(N_b - N_a) = \frac{1}{2}(10-4) = 3$

Hence, presence of no unpaired electron indicates it to be **diamagnetic**. **(1)**

(ii) **N_2^+ ions** $\sigma 1s^2 \sigma^* 1s^2 \sigma 2s^2 \sigma^* 2s^2 \pi 2p_x^2 \approx \pi 2p_y^2 \sigma 2p_z^1$

Here, $N_b = 9$, $N_a = 4$ so that

Bond order $= \frac{1}{2}(9-4) = \frac{5}{2} = 2.5$

Further, as N_2^+ ion has one unpaired electron in the $\sigma(2p_z)$ orbital, therefore, it is **paramagnetic** in nature. **(1)**

(iii) **N_2^- ions**

$\sigma 1s^2 \sigma^* 1s^2 \sigma 2s^2 \sigma^* 2s^2 \pi 2p_x^2 \approx \pi 2p_y^2 \sigma 2p_z^2 \pi^* 2p_x^1$

Here, $N_b = 10$, $N_a = 5$ so that

$BO = \frac{1}{2}(10-5) = \frac{5}{2} = 2.5$

Again, as it has one unpaired electron in the $\pi^*(2p_x)$ orbital, therefore, it is **paramagnetic**. **(1)**

(iv) **N_2^{2+} ions** $\sigma 1s^2 \sigma^* 1s^2 \sigma 2s^2 \sigma^* 2s^2 \pi 2p_x^2 \approx \pi 2p_y^2$

Here, $N_b = 8$, $N_a = 4$. Hence, $BO = \frac{1}{2}(8-4) = 2$

Presence of no unpaired electron indicates it to be **diamagnetic** in nature. **(1)**

Since, BO $\propto$ stability of a molecule.

So, stability order : $N_2 > N_2^+ > N_2^- > N_2^{2+}$

N_2^- has more antibonding electrons than N_2^+ which contributes to its lower stability.

32. Formation of PCl_5

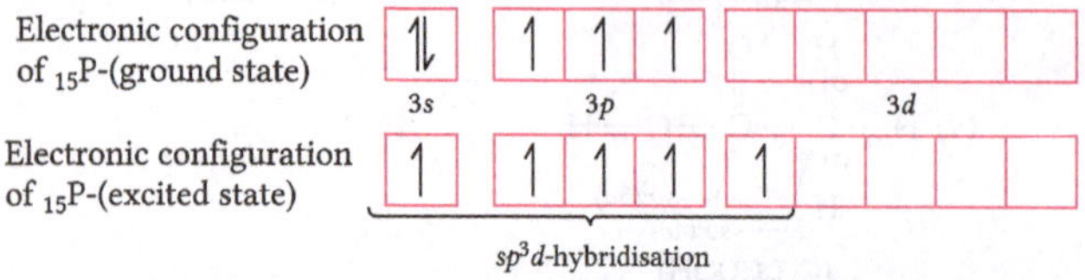

In PCl_5, phosphorus is sp^3d-hybridised to produce a set of five sp^3d-hybrid orbitals which are directed towards the five corners of a trigonal bipyramidal. These five sp^3d-hybrid orbitals overlap with singly occupied p-orbitals of Cl-atoms to form five P—Cl σ-bonds.

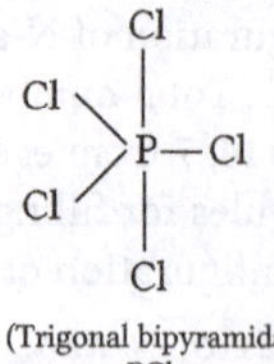

(Trigonal bipyramidal)
PCl_5

Three P—Cl bonds lie in one plane and make an angle of 120° with each other. These bonds are called equatorial bonds. The remaining two P—Cl bonds one lying above and other lying below, the plane make an angle of 90° with the equatorial plane.

These bonds are called axial bonds. Axial bonds are slightly longer than equatorial bonds because axial bond pairs suffer more repulsive interaction from the equatorial bond pairs. **(2½)**

Formation of SF_6

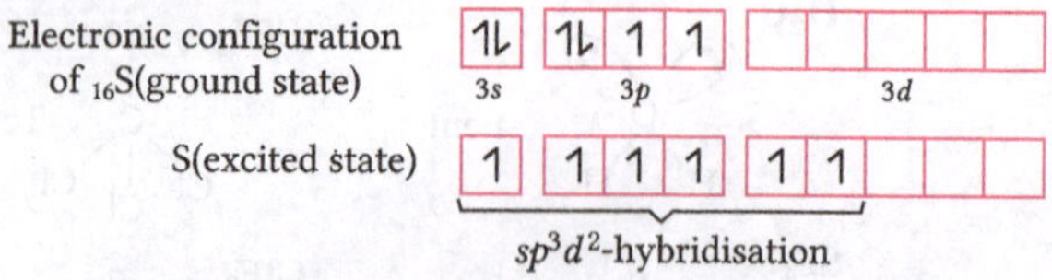

In SF_6, sulphur is sp^3d^2-hybridised to produce a set of six sp^3d^2-hybrid orbitals which are directed towards the six corners of a regular octahedron. These six sp^3d^2-hybrid orbitals overlap with singly occupied orbitals of F - atoms to form six S—F σ-bonds.

Thus, SF_6 molecule has a regular octahedral geometry and all S–F bonds have same bond length. **(2½)**

Mistake Alert *One can make a mistake of considering the bond lengths in octahedral geometry to be unequal as present in trigonal bipyramidal geometry.*

33. Formation of N_2 molecule

$_7N = 1s^2 2s^2 2p_x^1 2p_y^1 2p_z^1$

$N_2 = \sigma 1s^2 \overset{*}{\sigma} 1s^2 \sigma 2s^2 \overset{*}{\sigma} 2s^2 \pi 2p_x^2 \approx \pi 2p_y^2 \sigma 2p_z^2$

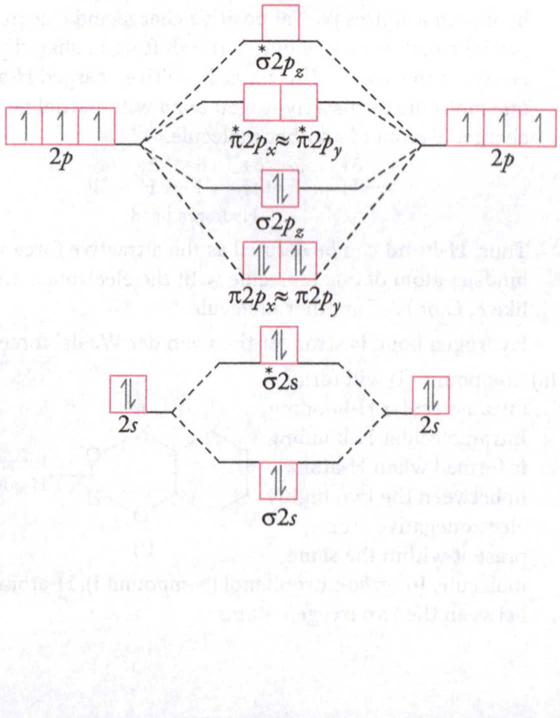

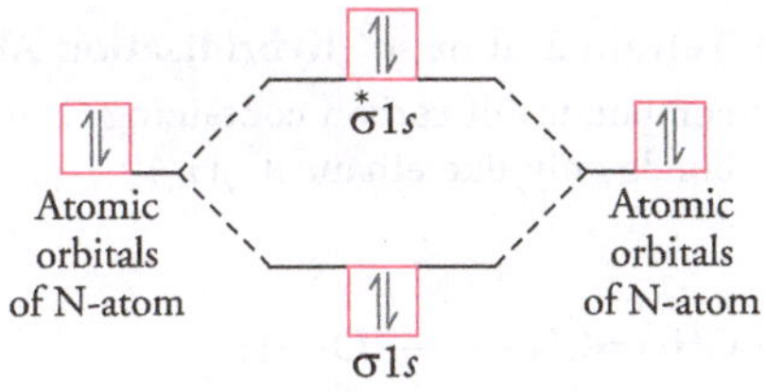

Molecular orbitals of N_2 molecule

$$\text{Bond order} = \frac{1}{2}[N_b - N_a]$$

$$= \frac{1}{2}(10-4) = 3$$

Bond order value of 3 means that N_2 contains a triple bond. **(1½)**

Formation of F_2 molecule

$_9F = 1s^2 2s^2 2p_x^2 2p_y^2 2p_z^1$

$F_2 = \sigma 1s^2 \overset{*}{\sigma}1s^2 \sigma 2s^2 \overset{*}{\sigma}2s^2 \sigma 2p_z^2 \pi 2p_x^2 \approx \pi 2p_y^2 \, \overset{*}{\pi}2p_x^2 \approx \overset{*}{\pi}2p_y^2$

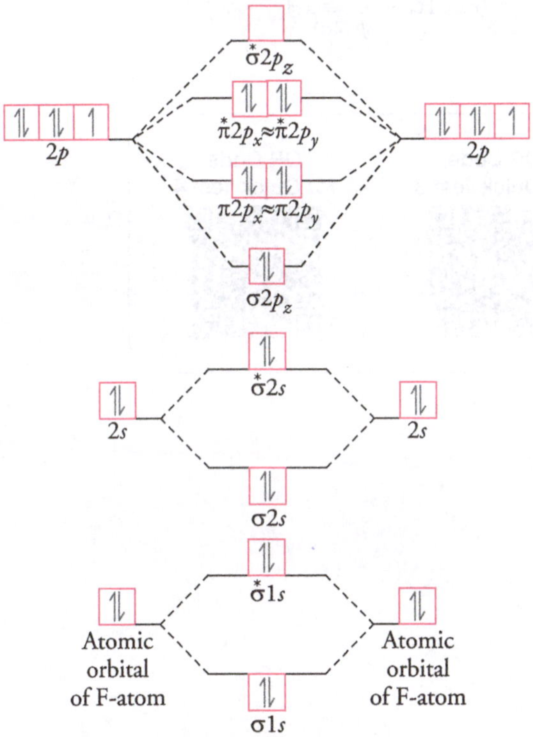

Molecular orbitals of F_2 molecule

$$\text{Bond order} = \frac{1}{2}[N_b - N_a] = \frac{1}{2}(10-8) = 1$$

Bond order value 1 means that F_2 contains single bond. **(1½)**

Formation of Ne_2 molecule

$_{10}Ne = 1s^2 2s^2 2p_x^2 2p_y^2 2p_z^2$

$Ne_2 = \sigma 1s^2 \overset{*}{\sigma}1s^2 \sigma 2s^2 \overset{*}{\sigma}2s^2 \sigma 2p_z^2 \pi 2p_x^2 \approx \pi 2p_y^2$

$\overset{*}{\pi}2p_x^2 \approx \overset{*}{\pi}2p_y^2 \, \overset{*}{\sigma}2p_z^2$

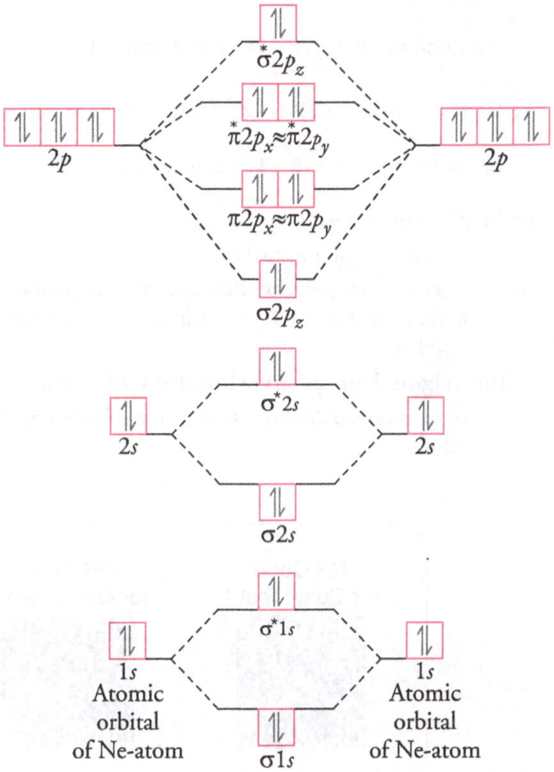

Molecular orbital of Ne_2 molecule

$$\text{Bond order} = \frac{1}{2}[N_b - N_a]$$

$$= \frac{1}{2}(10-10) = 0$$

Bond order value zero means that there is no formation of bond between two Ne atoms.

Hence, Ne_2 molecule does not exist. **(2)**

Mistake Alert *While writing the MO diagram for N_2 and F_2 (or Ne_2) one can make a mistake of writing the order of energy levels of the MOs, as they have different orders.*

34. Difference between molecular and atomic orbitals.
Refer to text on page 150 **(3)**

(i) $H_2^+ (1) = (\sigma 1s)^1$

$\Rightarrow$ Bond order $= 1/2(1-0) = 1/2$, paramagnetic **(½)**

(ii) $Li_2\ (6) = (\sigma 1s)^2\ (\overset{*}{\sigma} 1s)^2\ (\sigma 2s)^2$

$\Rightarrow$ Bond order $= \frac{1}{2}(4-2) = \frac{2}{2} = 1$, diamagnetic **(½)**

(iii) $B_2(10) = (\sigma 1s)^2\ (\overset{*}{\sigma} 1s)^2\ (\sigma 2s)^2\ (\overset{*}{\sigma} 2s)^2\ (\pi 2p_x^1 \approx \pi 2p_y^1)$

$\Rightarrow$ Bond order $= \frac{1}{2}(6-4) = 1$, paramagnetic **(½)**

(iv) $C_2\ (12) = (\sigma 1s)^2\ (\overset{*}{\sigma} 1s)^2\ (\sigma 2s)^2\ (\overset{*}{\sigma} 2s)^2\ (\pi 2p_x^2 \approx \pi 2p_y^2)$

$\Rightarrow$ Bond order $= \frac{1}{2}(8-4) = 2$, diamagnetic **(½)**

35. **Hybridisation** Refer to text on page 143.

Types of hybridisation in carbon atom.

(i) (a) **Digonal or *sp*-hybridisation** All compounds of carbon containing C≡C triple bond like ethyne (C_2H_2).

(b) **Trigonal or sp^2-hybridisation** All compounds of carbon containing C=C (double bond) like ethene (C_2H_4).

(c) **Tetrahedral or sp^3-hybridisation** All compounds of carbon containing C—C single bonds only like ethane (C_2H_6). **(2½)**

(ii) (a) $\overset{*}{C}H_2=CH-\overset{*}{C}(=O)-O-H$ — sp^2 (3σ), sp^2 (3σ)

(b) $CH_3-\overset{*}{C}H_2-OH$ — sp^3 (4σ)

(c) $CH_3-CH_2-\overset{*}{C}(=O)-H$ — sp^2 (3σ)

(d) $\overset{*}{C}H_3-CH=CH-CH_3$ — sp^3 (4σ)

(e) $CH_3-\overset{*}{C}\equiv CH$ — sp (2σ) **(2½)**

QR Code for Quick Test 1

QR Code for Quick Test 2

QR Code for Quick Test 3

QR Code for Quick Test 4

SELF ASSESSMENT TEST

Objective Type Questions [1 Mark]

1. Which of the following statements is incorrect?
   (a) He_2 does not exist because its bond order is zero.
   (b) O_2, O_2^- and O_2^+ are all paramagnetic.
   (c) Any two atomic orbitals can combine to form two molecular orbitals.
   (d) $\pi(2p_x)$ and $\pi(2p_y)$ are degenerate molecular orbitals.
2. Which of the following pairs will form the most stable ionic bond?
   (a) Na and Cl (b) Mg and F
   (c) Li and F (d) Na and F
3. The planar structure of BF_3 can be explained by the fact that BF_3 is
   (a) *sp*-hybridised (b) sp^2-hybridised
   (c) sp^3-hybridised (d) sp^3d-hybridised
4. Intramolecular hydrogen bond is present in
   (a) water (b) *o*-nitrophenol
   (c) *p*-nitrophenol (d) ethanol
5. NH_3 has a net dipole moment, but boron trifluoride (BF_3) has zero dipole moment, because
   (a) B is less electronegative than N
   (b) F is more electronegative than H
   (c) BF_3 is a pyramidal while NH_3 is planar
   (d) NH_3 is pyramidal while BF_3 is trigonal planar

Assertion - Reason [1 Mark]

■ **Directions** (Q. Nos. 6-8) In the following questions. an Assertion (A) is followed by a corresponding Reason (R). Use the following keys to choose the appropriate answer.
   (a) Both (A) and (R) are true and (R) is the correct explanation of (A).
   (b) Both (A) and (R) are true but (R) is not the correct explanation of (A).
   (c) (A) is true but (R) is false.
   (d) (A) is false but (R) is true.

6. **Assertion** (A): The shape of a molecule can be predicted using the VSEPR theory.
   Reason (R) VSEPR theory considers both bonding and non-bonding electron pairs.
7. **Assertion** (A) Covalent bonds are formed by the sharing of electrons between atoms.
   Reason (R) Atoms in covalent bonds always have the same electronegativity.
8. **Assertion** (A) Lewis structures are used to visualize how atoms achieve an octet in molecules.
   Reason (R) Lewis structures represent the arrangement of both bonding and non-bonding electrons.

Short Answer Type I Questions [2 Marks]

9. Explain why BeH_2 molecule has a zero dipole moment, although the Be—H bonds are polar?
10. H_3PO_3 can be represented by structures I and II shown below. Can these two structures be taken as the canonical forms of the resonance hybrid representing H_3PO_3? If not give reasons for the same.

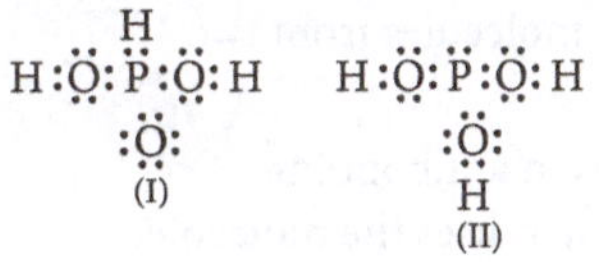

11. Use molecular orbital theory to explain why the Be_2 molecule does not exist?

Short Answer Type II Questions [3 Marks]

12. (i) *X*, *Y* and *Z* elements have 4, 5 and 7 valence electrons. Draw the structure of XH_4, YH_5, YH_3 and H—*Z*.
    (ii) Which of the above compounds has the highest dipole moment?
13. In both water and dimethyl ether $\left(CH_3-\ddot{\underset{\cdot\cdot}{O}}-CH_3\right)$, oxygen atom is central atom and has the same hybridisation, yet they have different bond angles. Which one has the greater bond angle? Give reason.
14. Describe the change in hybridisation (if any) of the Al-atom in the following reaction.
    $$AlCl_3 + Cl^- \longrightarrow AlCl_4^-$$

Case Study [4 Marks]

15. Molecular orbital theory is a theory on chemical bonding, developed by F. Hund and R.S Mulliken to describe the structure and properties of different molecules. The valence bond theory failed to explain how certain molecules contains two or more equivalent bonds whose bond orders lie between that of a single bond and double bond, such as the bonds in resonance stabilised molecules. This is where the molecular orbital theory proved to be more powerful.

In simple terms, the molecular orbital theory states that each atom tends to combine together and form molecular orbitals. As a result of such arrangement electrons are found in various atomic orbitals and they are usually associated with different nuclei.

(i) According to MOT, H_2^{2-} molecule does not exist why?

(ii) Acetophenone has higher dipole moment than ethanol. Explain?

Or

On the basis of valence bond theory, explain the formation of H_2 molecules from two H-atoms.

(iii) Addition of electrons in antibonding molecular orbital destabilises the molecule. Why?

Long Answer Type Questions [5 Marks]

16. (a) Write Lewis structure of the following compounds and show formal charge an each atom.

HNO_3, NO_2, H_2SO_4

(b) Predict the dipole moment of

(i) a molecule of the type AX_2 having a linear geometry.

(ii) a molecule of the type AX_4 having tetrahedral geometry.

(iii) a molecule of the type AX_2 having angular geometry.

(iv) a molecule of the type AX_4 having square planar geometry.

17. (a) Explain the following on the basis of valence bond theory.

(i) BF_3 is planar but NH_3 is not.

(ii) CCl_4 and $SiCl_4$ are tetrahedral.

(iii) The HSH bond angle in H_2S is closer to 90° than HOH bond angle in H_2O.

(b) (i) How bond energy varies from N_2^- to N_2^+ and why?

(ii) On the basis of molecular orbital theory what is the similarity between

(a) F_2, O_2^{2-}? (b) CO, N_2, NO^+?

Answers

1. (c)	2. (b)	3. (b)	4. (b)	5. (d)
6. (a)	7. (c)	8. (a)		

05

CHAPTER

Thermodynamics

The word "thermodynamics" is derived from two Greek words, i.e. therme (heat) and dynamics (flow or motion). Thus, collective meaning of the word "thermodynamics" is "science associated with heat" and its transformation.

Thermodynamics is mainly based on four fundamental laws, called the zeroth, first, second and third laws of thermodynamics.

YOUR STUDY GOALS

5.1 Thermodynamic Terms
5.2 Work
5.3 Heat
5.4 First Law of Thermodynamics
5.5 Enthalpy
5.6 Measurement of ΔU and ΔH : Calorimetry
5.7 Enthalpies for Different Types of Reactions
5.8 Spontaneity
5.9 Gibbs Free Energy
5.10 Absolute Entropy : Third Law of Thermodynamics

YOUR PRACTICE GOAL

- Objective Type Questions (33 Qs ; 23 MCQs, 8 A-R, 2 Case Study)
- Subjective Type Questions (25 Qs; 11 SA-I, 9 SA-II, 5 LA)

5.1 Thermodynamic Terms

It is essential to know the terms used in thermodynamics before learning more about it. These terms are as follows.

The System, Surroundings and Boundary

The part of the universe that is under thermodynamic observations is called the **system**, while the remaining part of the universe that can interact with the system is called **surroundings**.

System and surroundings together constitute the **universe**, i.e.

$$\boxed{\text{Universe} = \text{System} + \text{Surroundings}}$$

The real or imaginary surface or lines separating two or more systems or a system from its surroundings is called the **boundary**. It helps us to control and keep track of all movements of matter and energy in or out of the system.

e.g. When two substances let X and Y kept in a beaker, the beaker containing the reaction mixture is the system, whereas, the room where the beaker is kept is the surrounding.

The physical boundary, i.e. beaker which define system is boundary.

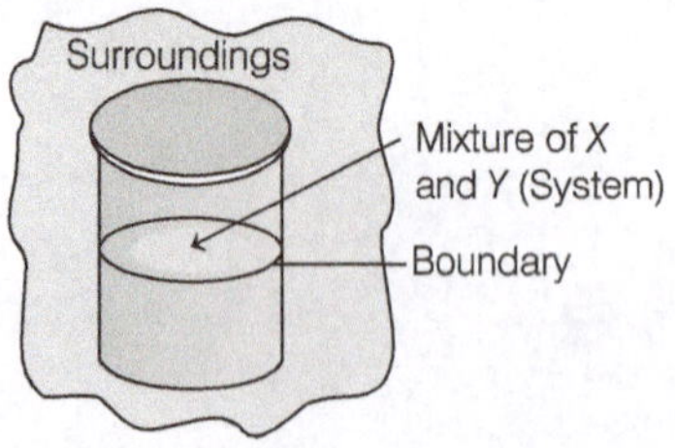

System, surroundings and boundary

Types of the System

Depending upon the movement of matter or energy in or out of the systems, the systems can be of following types

1. Open System

An open system can exchange matter as well as energy with its surroundings. The boundary here is not sealed and non-insulated thermally, i.e. it is generally imaginary.

e.g. Presence of reactants in an open beaker, reactions occurring in all living systems, car engines, etc. For such system, $\Delta m \neq 0$, $\Delta E \neq 0$, i.e. change in mass and energy is not zero.

2. Closed System

A closed system does not exchange matter with its surroundings but can exchange energy in the form of heat, work or radiations, i.e. here the boundary is sealed but not insulated.

e.g. Presence of substance (like hot water) in a closed vessel made of conducting material (like copper or steel). For such a system, $\Delta m = 0$, $\Delta E \neq 0$.

3. Isolated System

An isolated system neither exchanges matter nor energy with its surroundings, i.e. here the boundary is sealed as well as insulated.

e.g. Presence of substance in a thermos flask or closed insulated vessel.

For such a system, $\Delta m = 0$, $\Delta E = 0$

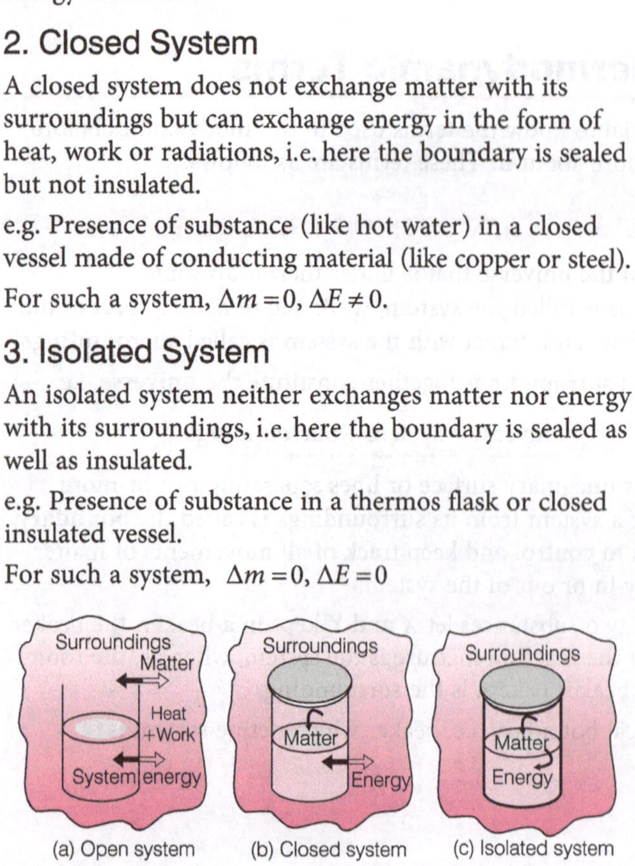

Open, closed and isolated systems

Macroscopic Properties

The properties of a system which arise from the collective behaviour of large number of species are called macroscopic properties or **bulk properties of a system,** These properties are further divided into two types :

1. Intensive Properties

The properties which do not depend on the quantity or size of matter are called **intensive properties.**

e.g. pressure, temperature, density, concentration, surface tension, viscosity, refractive index etc.

2. Extensive Properties

The properties which depend on the quantity or size of matter are called **extensive properties.**

e.g. Volume, Gibbs energy (G), number of moles (n), enthalpy (H), entropy (S), mass, work, internal energy (E or U), heat capacity (C_p or C_V), etc. It may be noted that the "ratio of the two extensive properties becomes intensive in nature".

If χ is any extensive property of n moles of system, the molar property of the system χ_m is intensive because it refers to the property of 1 mole of the system and is independent of the quantity of matter.

$$\chi_m = \chi / n$$

Similarly, molar volume (V_m) and molar heat capacity (C_m) are intensive properties.

State of the System

If the values of macroscopic properties are definite, then the existence of system is said to be in a definite state.

The state of a system is a complete description of a system at a given time, including its temperature and pressure, the amount of matter it contains, its chemical compositions and the physical state of the matter.

State Functions and Path Functions

The variables depending only upon the initial and final states of a system but not on the path followed are called state functions or **state variables,** e.g. pressure, volume, internal energy (U), enthalpy (H), entropy (S), Gibbs free energy (G), temperature (T), etc.

However, the variables, values of which are also affected by the path followed, are called **path functions,** e.g. work (W), heat (q) etc.

Note The state of the surroundings are generally incompletely specified, as there is no need to specify its state.

Types of Thermodynamic Processes

The state of system can be changed depending upon the conditions in which these changes occur *via* thermodynamic process.

These processes are of the following types

(i) **Adiabatic process** In adiabatic process, the system does not exchange heat (q) with its surroundings, i.e. no heat can flow in or out of the system. i.e. $dq = 0$.

In this process, the wall separating the system and the surroundings is called the **adiabatic wall.**

(ii) **Isothermal process** The isothermal process is carried out at constant temperature, i.e. it is the process in which temperature remains fixed. i.e. $dT = 0$ **and thus,** $dU = 0$

(iii) **Isobaric process** In isobaric process, change of state is brought about at constant pressure, i.e. $dp = 0$.

(iv) **Isochoric process** In an isochoric process, volumes of the system remains constant, i.e. $dV = 0$.

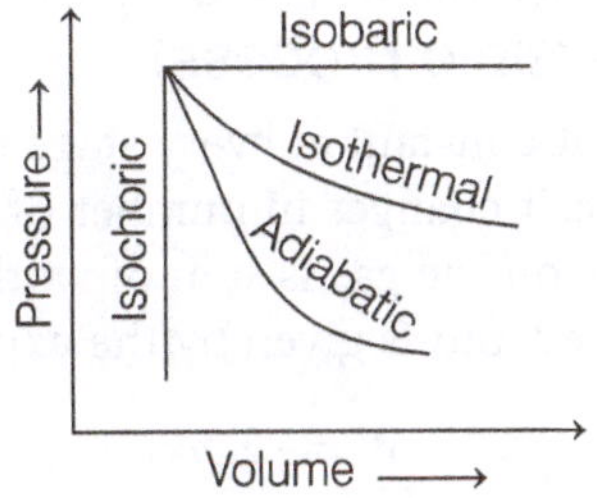

pV-plot for thermodynamic processes

(v) **Reversible process** A reversible process is defined as a process in which the direction of process may be reversed at any stage by a small change in a variable like temperature, pressure, etc. It occurs infinitesimally slowly.

Reversible process is an ideal process. It proceeds by a series of equilibrium states such that system and the surroundings are always in near equilibrium with each other.

(vi) **Irreversible process** An irreversible process is one, the direction of which cannot be reversed by small change in variables. All natural processes are generally irreversible and the net work done in an irreversible process is somewhat less than that in reversible process, i.e. $W_{irr} < W_{rev}$. (This will be proved later in this chapter).

Internal Energy as a State Function

Every system is associated with a definite amount of energy, in thermodynamics it is known as the **internal energy (U or E) of the system.** It is the sum of chemical, electrical, mechanical or any other form of energy. However, gravitational energy is generally neglected.

It is a state function, i.e. independent on the path followed. It may change when,

- heat flows into or out of the system,
- work is done on or by the system,
- matter enters or leaves the system.

It is an **extensive property**, i.e. depends upon the mass of the substance.

The absolute value of internal energy possessed by a substance cannot be calculated because it is not possible to predict the exact values of different forms of energy. Thus, **we can just calculate the change in internal energy (ΔU) which is achieved by changing the state of a system.**

$$\Delta U = U_2 - U_1$$

where, U_1 and U_2 are the internal energies of system 1 and 2.

5.2 Work

It is defined as, *"a mode of transfer of energy to and from the system with reference to the surroundings".*

If an object is displaced through a distance dx by a force F, the amount of work done (W) is given by

$$W = F \times dx$$

Work done is a path function, not a state function, as it depends upon the path followed. **Work done on the system** increases the energy of the system and is taken as positive while **work done by the system** is taken as negative. i.e.

Work done by the system	= – ve
Work done on the system	= + ve

Or

In other words, if a system loses energy, work is done by the system and if it gains energy, work is done on the system.

Note In physics, negative sign was assigned when the work is done on the system and positive sign when the work is done by the system.

Mechanical or Pressure Volume (pV) Work Done by a System

Consider a cylinder, having one mole of an ideal gas fitted with a frictionless piston. Let the total volume and pressure of the gas are respectively V_t and p.

If p_{ex} is the external pressure and if $p_{ex} > p$, the piston moves inward till the pressure of the gas becomes equal to external pressure (i.e. $p = p_{ex}$).

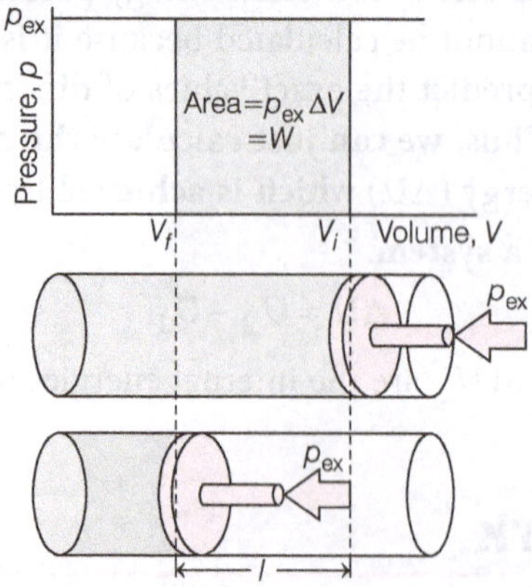

Work done on an ideal gas in a cylinder when it is compressed by a constant external pressure, p_{ex} (in single step).

The condition of $p = p_{ex}$ can be achieved by following two ways

(i) If it is Achieved in a Single Step (i.e. Irreversible Process)

Let final volume of the gas is V_f if the change is carried out in a single step. Suppose during compression, the piston moves a distance l and the area of cross-section of the piston is A.

Then, volume change $= l \times A = \Delta V = (V_f - V_i)$

As we know,

$$\text{Pressure} = \frac{\text{Force}}{\text{Area}}$$

$\therefore$ Force on the piston $= p_{ex} \cdot A$

If W is the work done on the system by movement of the piston then, $W = \text{force} \times \text{distance} = p_{ex} \cdot A \cdot l$

$$= p_{ex} \cdot (-\Delta V) = -p_{ex}\Delta V$$

$$\boxed{W = -p_{ex}(V_f - V_i)}$$

Significance of negative sign in the expression of work

The negative sign in the expression of work is required to obtain conventional sign for W, which will be positive. It represents that in case of compression, work is done on the system, so the sign of W should be positive. It is achieved by multiplying the negative value of $(V_f - V_i)$ with negative sign.

Example 1 **Two litres of an ideal gas at a pressure of 10 atm expands isothermally against a constant external pressure of 1 atm, until its total volume is 10 L. How much work is done during the expansion?** **NCERT**

Sol. $W = -p_{ex}(\Delta V) = -1(10-2) = -1(8) = -8$ L atm

(ii) If it is Achieved in a Number of Steps (i.e. Reversible Process)

If pressure is not constant at every stage of compression, i.e. it changes in number of finite steps, then work done on the gas is sum of work done in all the steps involved and is given by the expression.

$$\boxed{W = -\Sigma p \Delta V}$$

This work in the p *vs* V plot can be represented by the shaded area as shown below.

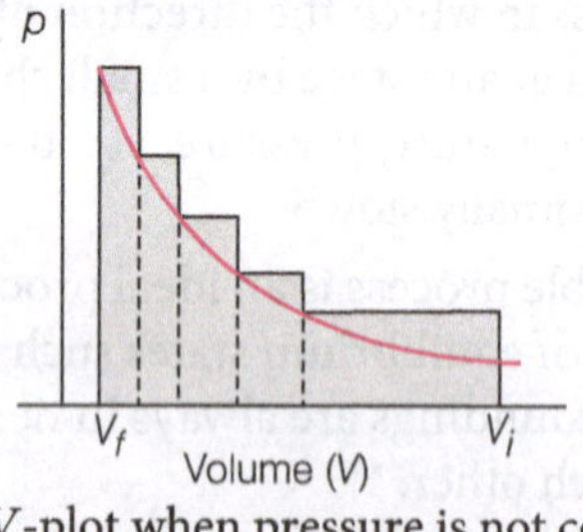

pV-plot when pressure is not constant and changes in finite steps

If pressure is not constant at each stage of compression and changes such that it is always infinitesimally greater than the pressure of the gas then the volume during the process decreases by an infinitesimal amount dV, and work done is given by the expression

$$\boxed{W = -\int_{V_i}^{V_f} p_{ex} dV}$$

In case of compression, $p_{ex} = p_{in} + dp$ (i.e. external pressure is greater than the pressure of the gas) and in case of expansion, $p_{ex} = p_{in} - dp$ (i.e. external pressure is less than the pressure of the gas).

In general, $p_{ex} = (p_{in} \pm dp)$

$$\therefore \quad W_{rev} = -\int_{V_i}^{V_f} (p_{in} \pm dp) dV$$

The above expression shows that work is done during reversible conditions.

Since, $dp \times dV$ is the product of extremely small quantities and its product is very small in comparison to $p_{in} dV$, so it can be neglected. Thus, the equation becomes

$$W_{rev} = -\int_{V_i}^{V_f} p_{in} dV$$

In terms of volume, from ideal gas equation ($pV = nRT$) for n moles of an ideal gas.

or $\quad p_{in} \quad$ or $\quad p = nRT/V$

$\therefore$ At constant temperature (isothermal process),

$$W_{rev} = -\int_{V_i}^{V_f} nRT \frac{dV}{V}$$

$$= -nRT \ln \frac{V_f}{V_i}$$

$$\boxed{W_{rev} = -2.303\, nRT \log \frac{V_f}{V_i}}$$

[where, V_i = initial volume, V_f = final volume, n = number of moles , R = gas constant and T = absolute temperature (in K)].

If variable given is p then $W_{rev} = -2.303\, nRT \log \frac{p_i}{p_f}$

In case of infinitesimal changes in pressure, the pressure in the p *vs* V plot is shown by the area of the plot (as shown in the following figure.)

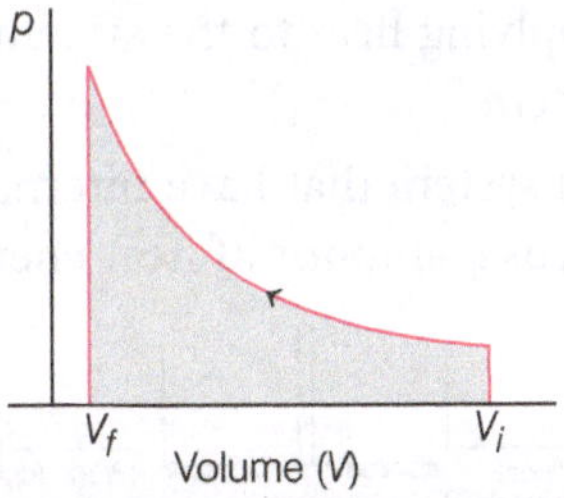

pV-plot when pressure is not constant and changes in infinite steps (reversible conditions)

Work in Case of Free Expansion

When a gas expands under vacuum, i.e. no external pressure works on it ($p_{ex} = 0$), its expansion is called **free expansion.**

Since, $p_{ex} = 0$, W is also 0 in case of free expansion of an ideal gas, i.e. no work is done for a free expansion of an ideal gas, whether the process is reversible or irreversible.

Example 2

(i) 5.2 moles of ideal gas at 3 atm and 25° C expands isothermally to 3 times of its original volume against the external pressure of 1 atm. Calculate work done.

(ii) If the same gas expands isothermally in a reversible manner, then what will be the value of work done?

Sol. (i) Given, moles of ideal gas (n) = 5.2 mol

Pressure (p) = 3 atm

Temperature (T) = 25°C

$$W = -p_{ex}(V_2 - V_1)$$

Now, initial volume $(V_1) = \frac{nRT}{p}$

$$= \frac{5.2 \text{ mol} \times 0.082 \text{ L atm mol}^{-1}\text{K}^{-1} \times 298 \text{ K}}{3 \text{ atm}} = 42.35 \text{L}$$

Final volume $(V_2) = 42.35 \times 3 = 127.05$ L

Now, $W = -1(127.05 - 42.35) = -84.7$ L atm

$= -84.7 \times 101.325$ J $= -8582.22$ J

(ii) For isothermal reversible expansion of ideal gas,

$$W_{rev} = -2.303\, nRT \log \frac{V_2}{V_1}$$

$$= -2.303 \times 5.2 \text{ mol} \times 8.314 \text{ J mol}^{-1}\text{K}^{-1} \times 298 \text{ K} \log\left(\frac{127.05 \text{ V}}{42.35 \text{ V}}\right)$$

$$= -14156.38 \text{ J}$$

5.3 Heat

- Temperature is the measure of degree of hotness or coldness. Moreover, the quantity of energy which flows between system and surroundings on account of temperature difference is called heat, q.
- It is also a path function, i.e. depends upon the path followed.

This process of transference is continued till system and surrounding will achieve same energy level.

- The value of **q is positive**, when heat is transferred from the surroundings to the system and the internal energy of the system increases.
 Whereas, the value of **q is negative** when heat is transferred from system to the surroundings resulting in decrease in the internal energy of the system.
 If change in temperature is ΔT, then heat transferred, $q = \text{coefficient} \times \Delta T$. The magnitude of the coefficient depends upon the size, composition and nature of the system.

Note Zeroth law of thermodynamics was put forward much after the establishment of the first and second law of thermodynamics and states that, "if each of the two objects is in thermal equilibrium with a third object then they are also in thermal equilibrium with each other." It is also called **law of temperature** or **law of thermal equilibrium.**

Heat Capacity

In the expression of heat, i.e. $q = \text{coefficient} \times \Delta T$
if coefficient is C, then $q = C\,\Delta T$.

This coefficient, i.e. C is called the heat capacity and is defined as *"the quantity of heat required to raise the temperature of a system by* 1° C or 1 K".

If the magnitude of heat capacity is large, there is only a small rise in temperature by a given amount of heat as it depends on the size, composition and nature of the system. e.g. Heat capacity of H_2O is large, thus a large amount of heat is required to raise its temperature.

Specific Heat Capacity and Molar Heat Capacity

In chemical calculations we often use specific heat capacity (or specific heat) and molar heat capacities. Specific heat capacity is defined as *"the heat required to raise the temperature of one unit mass of a substance by 1 degree Celsius or 1 Kelvin".*

The specific heat capacity is denoted by c and can be calculated with the help of following formula.

$$q = c \times m \times \Delta T = C\Delta T$$

where, q = heat required to raise the temperature by 1°C
c = specific heat capacity, m = mass
ΔT = temperature change (in °C)

If C is the heat capacity of n mole of the system, then its molar heat capacity C_m is given by $C_m = C/n$. Thus, the molar heat capacity can be defined as *the quantity of heat needed to raise the temperature of one mole of substance by one degree Celsius (or one Kelvin)".*

Heat Capacity at Constant Volume (C_V)

It is defined as the amount of heat required to raise the temperature of one mole of a gas by one degree Celsius or one Kelvin, when volume of the gas is kept constant.

$$q_V = C_V \Delta T$$

Heat Capacity at Constant Pressure (C_p)

It is defined as the amount of heat required to raise the temperature of one mole of a gas by one degree Celsius or one Kelvin when pressure of the gas is kept constant.

$$q_p = C_p \Delta T$$

Heat capacity at constant pressure (C_p) is always greater than heat capacity at constant volume (C_V).

C_p/C_V Ratio

The ratio of molar heat capacities at constant pressure and constant volume is represented by γ. The value of γ gives information about the atomicity of gases. The value of γ is 1.67, 1.40 and 1.33 for monoatomic, diatomic and triatomic gases, respectively.

5.4 First Law of Thermodynamics

It was proposed by Helmholtz and Robert Mayer who stated that the energy of an isolated system is constant, i.e. energy can neither be created nor be destroyed but can be converted from one form to another. That's why it is also called **law of conservation of energy.**

Mathematical Formulation of First Law of Thermodynamics

The internal energy of a system can be increased in two ways, i.e. by supplying heat to the system and by doing work on the system.

Let, us assume a system that have internal energy as U_1 and which absorbs q amount of heat energy.

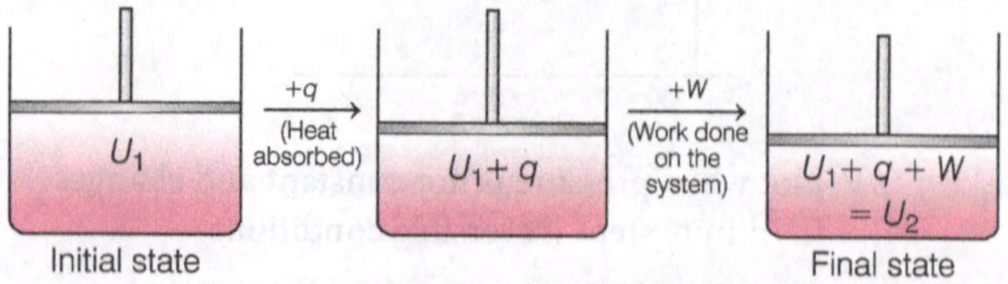

Increasing internal energy by absorption of heat and by doing work on the system

Therefore, the internal energy will become $U_1 + q$. Again, let, W amount of work done on it, then the internal energy will further increase and become equal to U_2.

Now, $$U_2 = U_1 + q + W$$

$$U_2 - U_1 = q + W$$

$$\boxed{\Delta U = q + W}$$

i.e. (Change in internal energy) = (Heat absorbed) + (Work done on the system)

This equation is **the mathematical formulation of the first law of thermodynamics.**

Depending upon the conditions the equation of first law of thermodynamics can be represented as

- If work done is the work of expansion, then
$$W = -p\Delta V$$
$$\Delta U = q - p\Delta V$$
or $$q = \Delta U + p\Delta V$$
Here, ΔV = change in volume and p = external pressure.
- When a system undergoes isothermal change $\Delta U = 0$, i.e. there is no increase or decrease in the internal energy of the system then the first law of thermodynamics reduces to $0 = q + W$ or $q = -W$
  - In case of **isothermal reversible** change.
$$W_{rev} = nRT \ln \frac{V_f}{V_i}$$
$$q = -W = 2.303\, nRT \log \frac{V_f}{V_i}$$
  - In case of **isothermal irreversible** change.
$$q = -W = p_{ex}(V_f - V_i)$$
  - In case the **process is carried out at constant volume** (i.e. $\Delta V = 0$). So, work done will be zero, the first law reduces to
$$\boxed{\Delta U = q_V}$$
i.e. increase in internal energy of the system is equal to the heat absorbed by the system or decrease in internal energy of the system is equal to heat lost by the system. Here, subscript V in q_v indicates that heat is given at constant volume.
- When a system undergoes adiabatic change $q = 0$, i.e. there is no exchange of heat between system and surroundings the first law reduces to
$$\boxed{\Delta U = W_{ad.}}$$
i.e. work is done at the expense of internal energy.
- **In case of gaseous system**, if a gas expands against the constant external pressure, p, let the volume change be ΔV, the mechanical work done by the gas is equal to $-p \times \Delta V$.
Substituting this value in $\Delta U = q + W$
$$\Delta U = q - p\Delta V$$
- For an isolated system, $W = 0$ and $q = 0$, therefore $\Delta U = 0$.

Limitations of First Law of Thermodynamics

This law fails to explain

- the extent and direction of the convertibility of one form of energy into another.
- how much heat energy would be transferred from one system to another.

Example 3 **Two litres of an ideal gas at a pressure of 10 atm expands isothermally into a vacuum until its total volume is 10 L.**

(i) How much heat is absorbed and how much work is done in the expansion?

(ii) Consider the same expansion, to a final volume of 10 L conducted reversibly. In such condition how much heat is absorbed? **NCERT**

Sol. (i) For isothermal process, $\Delta U = 0$, so from first law of thermodynamics $0 = q + W$

or $$q = -W = p_{ex}\,(10 - 2)$$
$$= 0(8) = 0 \quad [\text{in vacuum } p_{ex} = 0]$$

Thus, no work is done; and hence, no heat is absorbed.

(ii) We have $q = -W = 2.303 \times 2 \times 10 \log\left(\frac{10}{2}\right)$

$$\left[q = -W = 2.303 \times pV \log \frac{V_f}{V_i}\right]$$
$$(\because pV = nRT)$$
$$= 32.2 \text{ L atm}$$

Example 4 **In a process, 701 J of heat is absorbed by a system and 394 J of work is done by the system. What is the change in internal energy for the process?** **NCERT**

Sol. Given, $q = +701$ J (heat is absorbed, hence q is positive).

$W = -394$ J (work is done by the system, hence W is negative). By first law of thermodynamics;

Internal energy change, $\Delta U = q + W$
$$= +701 \text{ J} + (-394 \text{ J}) = +307 \text{ J}$$

Hence, internal energy of the system increases by 307 J.

5.5 Enthalpy

The total heat content of a system at constant pressure is called the **enthalpy of the system**. Indeed, it is the sum of internal energy and the product of work done (i.e. product of pressure and change in volume) by the system.

It is an **extensive** quantity and represented by the symbol *H*. Like internal energy, it is also a **state function**.

$\therefore \quad H = U + p\Delta V \quad$ ...(i)

Its units are kcal/mol or kJ/mol.

Suppose a system absorbs heat, q_p at constant pressure and its volume changes from V_1 to V_2. The work done by the system,

$$W = -p(V_2 - V_1) = -p\Delta V$$

Now applying the first law of thermodynamics,

$$\Delta U = q_p - p(V_2 - V_1)$$

$$(U_2 - U_1) = q_p - p(V_2 - V_1)$$

or $\quad (U_2 + pV_2) - (U_1 + pV_1) = q_p \quad$ ...(ii)

We know that, $U + pV = H$ (i.e. enthalpy of the system)

Thus, $(U_2 + pV_2) = H_2$ and $(U_1 + pV_1) = H_1$

By putting these values in Eq. (ii), we get

$$H_2 - H_1 = q_p$$

or $\quad \Delta H = q_p$

Now in the equation

$$\boxed{\Delta U + p\Delta V = \Delta H}$$

ΔH is negative for exothermic reaction which evolve heat during the reaction and ΔH is positive for endothermic reactions which absorb heat from the surroundings.

If change in volume is constant.

i.e. $\Delta V = 0$, $\Delta H = \Delta U$ and as $\Delta H = q_p$

Hence, $\quad \Delta U = q_V$

Here, q_V = heat supplied at constant volume

Thus, we can say that *"heat supplied at constant pressure is the measure of enthalpy change, while the heat supplied at constant volume is the measure of internal energy change."*

Note *q* is a path dependent function but q_p is independent of path.

Relationship Between ΔH and ΔU

The difference in ΔH and ΔU is insignificant in case of solids and liquids. They do not suffer significant volume changes upon heating. However, the differences becomes significant for gases , if pressure and temperature remain constant and V_A be the total volume of the gaseous reactants, V_B is the total volume of the gaseous products, n_A is the total number of moles of gaseous reactants and n_B is the total number of moles of gaseous products then from ideal gas equation.

For reactants, $\quad pV_A = n_A RT$

and for products, $\quad pV_B = n_B RT$

Thus, $\quad pV_B - pV_A = n_B RT - n_A RT$

or $\quad p(V_B - V_A) = (n_B - n_A)RT$

or $\quad p\Delta V = \Delta n_g RT$

Here, Δn_g refers to the total number of moles of gaseous products minus the total number of moles of gaseous reactants.

i.e. $\quad \Delta n_g = n_P - n_R$

Substituting the value of $p\Delta V$ in the expression of enthalpy change, (i.e. $\Delta H = \Delta U + p\Delta V$), we get

$$\Delta H = \Delta U + \Delta n_g RT$$

This equation is helpful for calculating ΔH from ΔU and *vice-versa*.

If, ***Case* I** $\Delta n_g = 0$ then $\Delta H = \Delta U$

***Case* II** $\Delta n_g < 0$ then $\Delta H < \Delta U$

***Case* III** $\Delta n_g > 0$ then $\Delta H > \Delta U$

Relationship between C_p and C_v from the Expression of Enthalpy Change

If *q* is the amount of heat involved in a system then

- at constant volume

$$q = q_V = C_V \Delta T = \Delta U \text{ (Internal energy)}$$

- at constant pressure

$$q = q_P = C_P \Delta T = \Delta H \text{ (Enthalpy)}$$

For a mole ($n = 1$) of an ideal gas, enthalpy change

$$\Delta H = \Delta U + \Delta(pV) = \Delta U + \Delta(RT) = \Delta U + R\Delta T$$

$$\therefore \quad \Delta H = \Delta U + R\Delta T$$

On substituting the values of ΔH and ΔU, we get

$$C_p\Delta T = C_V\Delta T + R\Delta T \text{ or } C_p = C_V + R \text{ or } \boxed{C_p - C_V = R}$$

If number of moles is n, then

$$\boxed{C_p - C_V = nR}$$

TEACHER'S TIP

- Since, $q_v = C_v\Delta T$ and $q_v = \Delta U$, thus, $\Delta U = C_v\Delta T$. At constant temperature, $\Delta T = 0$ (isothermal process), so $\Delta U = 0$.
- Since, $q_p = C_p\Delta T$ and $q_p = \Delta H$, thus, $\Delta H = C_p\Delta T$.

Example 5 **The reaction of cyanamide, $NH_2CN(s)$, with dioxygen was carried out in a bomb calorimeter, and ΔU was found to be -742.7 kJ mol^{-1} at 298 K. Calculate the enthalpy change for the reaction at 298 K ($R = 8.314 \times 10^{-3}$ kJ K^{-1} mol^{-1}).**

$$NH_2CN(s) + \frac{3}{2}O_2(g) \longrightarrow N_2(g) + CO_2(g) + H_2O(l)$$

NCERT

Sol. Use the following steps to solve out such problems.

Step I **Write the balanced equation**

$$NH_2CN(s) + \frac{3}{2}O_2(g) \longrightarrow N_2(g) + CO_2(g) + H_2O(l)$$

Step II **Calculate Δn_g**

Difference of moles of gaseous products and reactants, $\Delta n_g = n_p - n_r = 2 - \frac{3}{2} = \frac{1}{2} = 0.5$ mol

Step III **Calculate ΔH by using the formula**

$$\Delta H = \Delta U + \Delta n_g RT$$

$$\Delta H = -742.7 \text{ kJ mol}^{-1} + (0.5 \text{ mol} \times 8.314 \times 10^{-3} \text{ kJ K}^{-1}\text{mol}^{-1} \times 298 \text{ K})$$

$$= -741.46 \text{ kJ mol}^{-1}$$

During calculation always remember the units of different quantities, i.e. ΔH, ΔU and R must be the same.

Note In a laboratory most of the reactions are carried out at constant pressure, so ΔH is more significant than ΔU.

Example 6 **If water vapour is assumed to be a perfect gas, molar enthalpy change for vaporisation of 1 mole of water at 1 bar and 100°C is 41 kJ mol^{-1}. Calculate the internal energy change, when**

(i) 1 mole of water is vaporised at 1 bar pressure and 100°C.

(ii) 1 mole of water is converted into ice. **NCERT**

Sol. (i) For the change $H_2O(l) \longrightarrow H_2O(g)$

$$\Delta H = \Delta U + \Delta n_g RT$$

or $$\Delta U = \Delta H - \Delta n_g RT$$

$$\Delta U = 41.000 \text{ kJ mol}^{-1} - 8.3 \text{ J mol}^{-1}\text{ K}^{-1} \times 373 \text{ K}$$

$$= 41.00 \text{ kJ mol}^{-1} - 3.096 \text{ kJ mol}^{-1}$$

$$= 37.904 \text{ kJ mol}^{-1}$$

(ii) In the conversion, $H_2O(l) \longrightarrow H_2O(s)$

There is negligible change in the volume.

So, we can put $p\Delta V = \Delta n_g RT \approx 0$ in this case,

$$\Delta H \simeq \Delta U.$$

So, $\Delta U = 41.00$ kJ mol^{-1}

5.6 Measurement of ΔU and ΔH : Calorimetry

The experimental technique with the help of which, we can measure the energy changes occurring during various physical or chemical processes is called **calorimetry.**

The vessel used to carry out the process is called the **calorimeter.**

The calorimeter is immersed in a known volume of a liquid. By knowing the heat capacity of the liquid in which calorimeter is immersed and the heat capacity of calorimeter, it is easy to determine the heat evolved in the process by measuring temperature changes.

Measurements are made under two different conditions.

(i) At constant volume, q_V

(ii) At constant pressure, q_p

1. ΔU Measurements

Heat change occurring at constant volume is measured by using bomb calorimeter, in which a steel vessel, called the **bomb**, is immersed in a water bath. The whole device is called calorimeter.

The water bath is used for ensuring no heat loses to the surroundings during the process.

When the combustible substance placed in the steel bomb is burnt in pure dioxygen, the evolved heat is transferred to the water present around the bomb.

The temperature of the water is measured. Since, the bomb calorimeter is sealed, its volume remains the same, (i.e. $\Delta V = 0$) and the energy changes associated with reactions are measured at constant volume and hence, no work is done on or by the system.

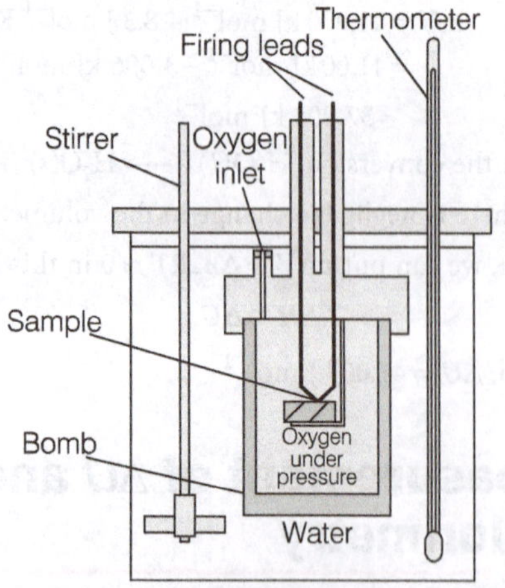

Bomb calorimeter

From the temperature change, the heat (i.e. q_V or U) is calculated by the expression

$$q_V = C \cdot m \cdot \Delta T \ (C = \text{heat capacity of calorimeter}) = C \cdot \Delta T$$

$$\Delta U = \frac{C \cdot \Delta T \cdot M}{m_i} \ (M = \text{molar mass}, m_i = \text{mass})$$

2. ΔH Measurements

Heat change occurring at constant pressure (generally under atmospheric pressure) are measured by using the calorimeter shown below.

We know that at constant pressure, $\Delta H = q_p$

Thus, at constant pressure heat absorbed or evolved, i.e. q_p is also called the heat of reaction or enthalpy of reaction, $\Delta_r H$.

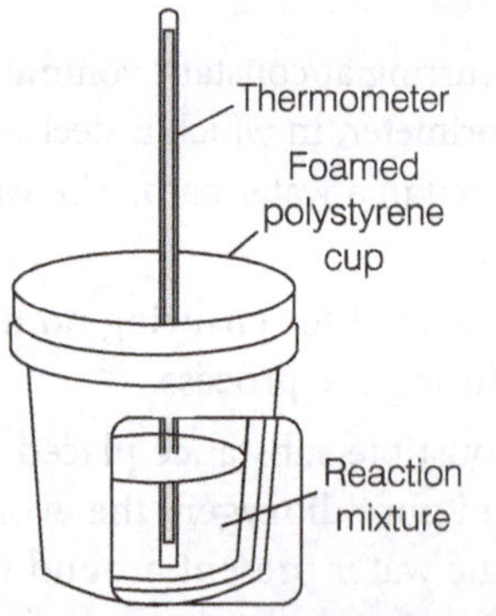

Calorimeter for measuring heat changes at constant pressure (atmospheric pressure)

In case of **exothermic reaction,** i.e. reactions in which heat is evolved, the system loses heat to the surroundings, thus q_p and $\Delta_r H$ will be negative. Further, the endothermic reactions are accompanied with the absorption of heat, thus q_p and $\Delta_r H$ will be positive.

Example 7 1g of graphite is burnt in a bomb calorimeter in excess of oxygen at 298 K and 1 atmospheric pressure according to the equation

$$C\,(\text{graphite}) + O_2(g) \longrightarrow CO_2(g)$$

During the reaction, temperature rises from 298 K to 299 K. If the heat capacity of the bomb calorimeter is 20.7 kJ/K, what is the enthalpy change for the above reaction at 298 K and 1 atm? NCERT

Sol. In bomb calorimeter, volume remains constant, thus, the heat involved is internal energy, i.e. ΔU. We know that, $\Delta U = q_V = C_V \Delta T$. Since, heat is lost by the system,

$$\therefore q_V = -C_V \Delta T = -20.7\ \text{kJ/K} \times (299 - 298)\ \text{K} = -20.7\ \text{kJ}$$

(Here, negative sign indicates the exothermic nature of the reaction.)

Thus, ΔU for the combustion of the 1 g of graphite

$$= -20.7\ \text{kJ K}^{-1}$$

For combustion of 1 mole (12.0 g) of graphite

$$= \frac{12.0\ \text{g mol}^{-1} \times (-20.7\ \text{kJ})}{1\ \text{g}}$$

$$= -2.48 \times 10^2\ \text{kJ mol}^{-1}$$

Since, $\Delta n_g = 0, \Delta H = \Delta U = -2.48 \times 10^2\ \text{kJ mol}^{-1}$

Quick Test 1

Conceptual Questions

1. Identify the state functions and path functions out of the following. Enthalpy, entropy, heat, temperature, work, free energy. *NCERT Exemplar*
2. For the same increase in volume, why work done is more if the gas is allowed to expand reversibly at higher temperature?
3. How will you calculate the work done on an ideal gas in a compression, when change in pressure is carried out in infinite steps? *NCERT Exemplar*
4. Although heat is path function but heat absorbed by the system under certain specific conditions is independent of path. What are those conditions? Explain. *NCERT Exemplar*
5. Express the change in internal energy of a system when
   (i) no heat is absorbed by the system from the surroundings, but work (W) is done on the system. What type of wall does the system have?
   (ii) no work is done on the system, but q amount of heat is taken out from the system and given to the surroundings. What type of wall does the system have?
   (iii) W amount of work is done by the system and q amount of heat is supplied to the system. What type of system would it be? *NCERT*

Numerical Questions

6. An ideal gas is allowed to expand against a constant pressure of 2 bar from 10 L to 50 L in one step. Calculate the amount of work done by the gas. If the same expansion were carried out reversibly, will the work done be higher or lower than the earlier case (given that 1 L bar = 100 J)? *NCERT Exemplar*

7. Expansion of a gas in vacuum is called free expansion. Calculate the work done and the change in internal energy when 1 L of ideal gas expands isothermally into vacuum until its total volume is 5 L? *NCERT Exemplar*

8. 1.0 mole of a monoatomic ideal gas is expanded from state (1) to state (2) as shown in figure. Calculate the work done for the expansion of gas from state (1) to state (2) at 298 K. *NCERT Exemplar*

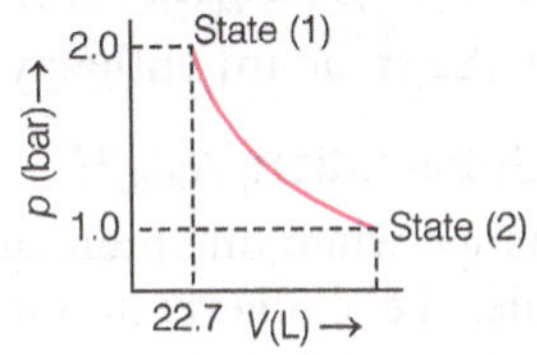

9. 10 g of argon is compressed isothermally and reversibly at a temperature of 27°C from 10 L to 5 L. Calculate $q, W, \Delta U$ and ΔH for this process. $R = 2.0$ cal $K^{-1} mol^{-1}$, log 2 = 0.30, atomic weight, of Ar = 40.

10. The enthalpy change for the reaction,
$Zn(s) + 2H^+(aq) \longrightarrow Zn^{2+}(aq) + H_2(g)$, is -154.40 kJ mol^{-1}. The formation of 2 g of hydrogen expands the system by 22.4 L at 1 atm pressure. What is the internal energy change of the reaction?

11. Calculate the number of kJ of heat necessary to raise the temperature of 60.0 g of aluminium from 35°C to 55°C. Molar heat capacity of Al is 24 J mol^{-1} K^{-1}. Molar mass of Al = 27 g mol^{-1} *NCERT*

Answers

6. −8 kJ 7. 0 8. $W = -1717.63$ kJ
9. +103.635 cal, −103.635 cal 0, 0 10. −156.67 kJ
11. 1.067 kJ

For Solutions, See QR Code on Pg. 209

Thermochemical Equations

A balanced chemical equation in which the value of enthalpy of reaction ($\Delta_r H^\ominus$) is also mentioned, is called a thermochemical equation.

In such equation, physical states (alongwith allotropic state) of the substances are also mentioned, as enthalpy change depends upon the physical states of the substance.

e.g. The thermochemical equation for the combustion of ethanol at constant temperature and pressure is written as :

$$C_2H_5OH(l) + 3O_2(g) \longrightarrow 2CO_2(g) + 3H_2O(l) + 1367 \text{ kJ mol}^{-1}$$

or $$C_2H_5OH(l) + 3O_2(g) \longrightarrow 2CO_2(g) + 3H_2O(l); \quad \Delta_r H^\ominus = -1367 \text{ kJ mol}^{-1}$$

Conventions about Thermochemical Equations

Some conventions related to thermochemical equations are as follows

- Negative $\Delta_r H^\ominus$ means the reactions is exothermic and positive $\Delta_r H^\ominus$ means the reaction is endothermic.
- The coefficients of different substances in a balanced thermochemical equation show only their number of moles (never molecules) involved in that reaction. These coefficients are infact equal to the stoichiometric coefficients of different substances in the balanced equation.
- The unit of enthalpy change is kJ mol^{-1}, i.e. it shows the heat change per mole of the reaction.
- On reversing a reaction, the sign of ΔH is also reversed but its magnitude remain the same.

Enthalpy Change, $\Delta_r H$ of a Reaction or Reaction Enthalpy

Enthalpy change of a reaction is the enthalpy change accompanying a chemical reaction or it may also be defined as the enthalpy change when the quantities (moles) of reactants have reacted completely as indicated by balanced chemical equation.

e.g. $2H_2(g) + O_2(g) \longrightarrow 2H_2O(l); \ \Delta H = -572$ kJ

It can be calculated by the following expression.

$\Delta_r H$ = sum of enthalpies of products − sum of enthalpies of reactants

$$\Delta_r H = \sum_i x_i H_P - \sum_i y_i H_R$$

where, x_i and y_i = stoichiometric coefficients of products and reactants respectively in a balanced equation.

Σ = sigma, used for summation.

H_P = enthalpy of formation of products.

H_R = enthalpy of formation of reactants.

e.g. For the reaction,

$$CH_4(g) + 2O_2(g) \longrightarrow CO_2(g) + 2H_2O(l)$$

$\Delta_r H$ is written as

$$\Delta_r H = [H_{(CO_2,g)} + 2 \times H_{(H_2O,l)}] - [H_{(CH_4,g)} + 2 \times H_{(O_2,g)}]$$

Enthalpy of a reaction depends on the conditions under which a reaction is carried out. Thus, it is necessary that we must specify some standard condition.

TEACHER'S TIP

- If H_P is lesser than H_R, the reaction occur with the evolution of heat, i.e. the reaction is exothermic and ΔH is negative.
- If H_R is lesser than H_P, the reaction occur with the absorption of heat, i.e. the reaction is endothermic and ΔH is positive.

Standard Enthalpy of Reaction, $\Delta_r H^\ominus$

The enthalpy change occurring during a reaction when all the involved substances are in their standard states, is called the **standard enthalpy of the reaction.**

The purest and most stable form of a substance at 1 bar and at a specified temperature is called its **standard state.**

e.g. The standard state of solid iron at 500 K is pure iron at 1 bar. **The standard enthalpy change is represented by writing the superscript ⊖ to the symbol ΔH, i.e. by $\Delta H^\ominus$.**

Enthalpy Change During Phase Transformations

We know that energy is required to convert a substance from one phase (say solid) to another phase (say liquid).

The process of conversion of solid into liquid is called **melting** whereas the process of conversion of liquid into gas is called **vaporisation** and the process of conversion of solid directly into gases is called **sublimation.** These processes are collectively known as **phase transformations** and they involve energy changes.

During phase change, temperature remains constant.

Depending upon the type of process, enthalpy change further can be of following types

1. Enthalpy of Fusion, $\Delta_{fus} H^\ominus$

The enthalpy change occurring when 1 mole of a solid substance in its standard state melts completely into its liquid form is called **standard or molar enthalpy of fusion, $\Delta_{fus} H^\ominus$**. This takes place at constant temperature.

e.g. $H_2O(s) \longrightarrow H_2O(l); \Delta_{fus} H^\ominus = 6.00 \text{ kJ mol}^{-1}$ (at 273 K)

Melting of solid is endothermic so all enthalpies of fusion are positive.

If water freezes, i.e. the above process is reversed, equal amount of heat is given off to the surroundings. So, $\Delta_{freezing} H$ is negative, i.e. the process is exothermic.

2. Enthalpy of Vaporisation, $\Delta_{vap} H^\ominus$

The enthalpy change when one mole of a liquid is converted into vapours at its constant boiling temperature and under standard pressure (1 bar) is called **enthalpy of vaporisation** or **molar enthalpy of vaporisation ($\Delta_{vap} H$).**

e.g. $H_2O(l) \longrightarrow H_2O(g); \Delta_{vap} H^\ominus = +40.79 \text{ kJ mol}^{-1}$

Here, $\Delta_{vap} H^\ominus$ is the standard enthalpy of vaporisation.

3. Enthalpy of Sublimation, $\Delta_{sub} H^\ominus$

The enthalpy change when one mole of a solid substance sublimes, i.e. converts into its vapours without melting at a constant temperature below its melting point and at 1 bar (constant) pressure is called the **enthalpy of sublimation or molar enthalpy of sublimation, $\Delta_{sub} H^\ominus$.**

e.g. $I_2(s) \xrightarrow{\Delta} I_2(g); \Delta_{sub} H^\ominus (I_2) = 62.4 \text{ kJ mol}^{-1}$

$\underset{\text{Dry ice}}{CO_2(s)} \xrightarrow[195 \text{ K}]{\Delta} CO_2(g); \Delta_{sub} H^\ominus = 25.2 \text{ kJ mol}^{-1}$

Factors Affecting Enthalpy of Phase Transformation

- The magnitude of enthalpy change depends upon the strength of intermolecular forces working on the substances that undergo phase transformations. e.g. In between water molecules, strong hydrogen bonds exist which are strong enough for keeping water in liquid phase.
- Further, the organic liquids like acetone have weak intermolecular forces (i.e. dipole-dipole interactions) so less amount of heat is required to vapourise 1 mole of acetone as compared to that required for the vaporisation of 1 mole of water.
- In general, the order of enthalpy of vaporisation is ionic liquid > > polar liquids > non-polar liquids.

Note As sublimation is, infact a combination of both fusion and vaporisation, so we can write as

$$\Delta_{sub} H^\ominus = \Delta_{fus} H^\ominus + \Delta_{vap} H^\ominus$$

Example 8 **When 1g of liquid naphthalene ($C_{10}H_8$) solidifies, – 149 J of heat is evolved. Calculate the heat of fusion of naphthalene.**

Sol. Molecular mass of naphthalene,

$$C_{10}H_8 = 10\times 12 + 8\times 1 = 128 \text{ g mol}^{-1}$$

For the solidification reaction $C_{10}H_8(l) \longrightarrow C_{10}H_8(s)$

Heat evolved when 1 g of naphthalene solidifies = 149 J

Heat evolved when 128 g of naphthalene solidify

$$= -149 \times 128 = -19072 \text{ J}$$

As solidification is reverse of fusion, therefore enthalpy of fusion will have same magnitude as that of enthalpy of solidification but with opposite sign.

i.e. $C_{10}H_8(s) \longrightarrow C_{10}H_8(l);\ \Delta_{fus}H^\ominus = +19072 \text{ J}$

Standard Molar Enthalpy of Formation, $\Delta_f H^\ominus$

- The enthalpy change accompanying the formation of one mole of a compound from its constituent elements, when they are in their most stable states of aggregation or reference states, is called standard molar enthalpy of formation, $\Delta_f H^\ominus$.
- The subscript '*f*' indicates that one mole of the compound in question has been formed in its standard state from its elements in their most stable state of aggregation.

e.g. $H_2(g) + \frac{1}{2}O_2(g) \longrightarrow H_2O(l);$

$$\Delta_f H^\ominus = -285.8 \text{ kJ mol}^{-1}$$

$C(\text{graphite}, s) + 2H_2(g) \longrightarrow CH_4(g);$

$$\Delta_f H^\ominus = -74.81 \text{ kJ mol}^{-1}$$

$2C(\text{graphite}, s) + 3H_2(g) + \frac{1}{2}O_2(g) \longrightarrow C_2H_5OH(l);$

$$\Delta_f H^\ominus = -277.7 \text{ kJ mol}^{-1}$$

- The most stable state of aggregation of an element at 25°C and 1 bar pressure is called its **reference state.** e.g. H_2 gas is the reference state of dihydrogen.
- It should be noted that enthalpy changes for all reactions are not enthalpy of formation. e.g. The following reaction shows the formation of calcium carbonate from calcium oxide and carbon dioxide.

$CaO(s) + CO_2(g) \longrightarrow CaCO_3(s);$

$$\Delta_r H^\circ = -178.3 \text{ kJmol}^{-1}.$$

Here, the $\Delta_r H^\circ$ is not equal to enthalpy of formation $\Delta_f H^\ominus$ of calcium carbonate because calcium carbonate has been formed from other compounds and not from its constituent elements.

The following general equation can be used for the calculation of enthalpy change for the reaction using standard enthalpy of formation.

$$\Delta_r H^\ominus = \sum_i x_i \Delta_f H^\ominus_{\text{products}} - \sum_i y_i \Delta_f H^\ominus_{\text{reactions}}$$

where, x and y represent the coefficients of the products and reactants in the balanced equation.

Hess's Law of Constant Heat Summation

The enthalpy is a state function (is same whether it occurs in one step or in a series of steps), thus the change in enthalpy is independent of the path between initial state (reactants) and final state (products). Thus, according to Hess's law,

"If a reaction takes place in several steps, then its standard reaction enthalpy is the sum of the standard enthalpies of the intermediate reactions into which the overall reaction may be divided at the same temperature".

Suppose, enthalpy change for direct conversion $A \longrightarrow B$ is ΔH, B can also be prepared from A through intermediates C and D, for which enthalpy changes are ΔH_1, ΔH_2 and ΔH_3 respectively as shown in the figure.

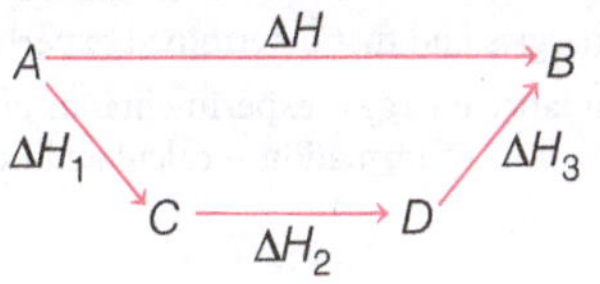

Then according to Hess's law, $\Delta H = \Delta H_1 + \Delta H_2 + \Delta H_3$

It clearly indicates that when chemical equations are added, subtracted or multiplied, the heat changes can also be added, substracted or multiplied accordingly.

Example 9 **Given,**

$$NH_3(g) + 3Cl_2(g) \rightleftharpoons NCl_3(g) + 3HCl(g); -\Delta H_1$$
$$N_2(g) + 3H_2(g) \rightleftharpoons 2NH_3(g); -\Delta H_2$$
$$H_2(g) + Cl_2(g) \rightleftharpoons 2HCl(g); \Delta H_3$$

What is the heat of formation of $NCl_3(g)$ in terms of ΔH_1, ΔH_2 and ΔH_3?

Sol. I. $NH_3(g) + 3Cl_2(g) \rightleftharpoons NCl_3(g) + 3HCl(g), -\Delta H_1$ ...(i)

II. $N_2(g) + 3H_2(g) \rightleftharpoons 2NH_3(g), -\Delta H_2$ ...(ii)

III. $H_2(g) + Cl_2(g) \rightleftharpoons 2HCl(g), \Delta H_3$ ...(iii)

On multiplying Eq. (iii) by 3, we get

$$3H_2(g) + 3Cl_2(g) \rightleftharpoons 6HCl(g); 3\times \Delta H_3 \quad \text{...(iv)}$$

On inverting Eq. (iv), we get

$$6HCl(g) \rightleftharpoons 3H_2(g) + 3Cl_2(g); -3\times \Delta H_3 \quad \text{...(v)}$$

On multiplying Eq. (i) with 2, we get

$$2NH_3 + 6Cl_2 \rightleftharpoons 2NCl_3 + 6HCl; \; -2 \times \Delta H_1 \quad ...(vi)$$

On adding Eqs. (ii), (v) and (iv), we get

$$N_2 + 3Cl_2 \rightleftharpoons 2NCl_3; \Delta H_r = -\Delta H_2 - 3\Delta H_3 - 2 \times \Delta H_1$$

$$\therefore \Delta H_f = \frac{\Delta H_r}{2} = -\frac{\Delta H_2}{2} - \frac{3}{2}\Delta H_3 - \Delta H_1$$

Applications of Hess's Law

- For the determination of enthalpies of formation of compounds.
- For the determination of enthalpies of extremely slow reactions.
- For the determination of enthalpies of transformation of one allotropic form into another.
- For the determination of bond energies (which have been given later in the chapter).

$$\Delta H_{\text{reaction}} = \Sigma_{\text{bond energies of reactants}} - \Sigma_{\text{bond energies of products}}$$

- For the determination of resonance energy.

Note • In case of atomic species, bond energy is replaced by enthalpy of atomisation.

• When a compound shows resonance, there is considerable difference between the heat of formation as calculated from bond energies and that determined experimentally.

∴ Resonance energy = experimental or actual heat of formation − calculated heat of formation.

5.7 Enthalpies for Different Types of Reactions

Depending upon the type of reactions, the enthalpies can be of following types

Standard Enthalpy of Combustion, $\Delta_c H^\ominus$

The amount of heat evolved when one mole of the substance is burnt completely in oxygen or air and all the reactants and products are in their standard states at the specified temperature, is called the **standard enthalpy of combustion.**

e.g. $C_4H_{10}(g) + \frac{13}{2}O_2(g) \longrightarrow 4CO_2(g) + 5H_2O(l);$

$$\Delta_c H^\ominus = -2658.0 \text{ kJ mol}^{-1}$$

$$C_6H_{12}O_6(g) + 6O_2(g) \longrightarrow 6CO_2(g) + 6H_2O(l);$$

$$\Delta_c H^\ominus = -2802.0 \text{ kJ mol}^{-1}$$

Combustion is an exothermic process, so enthalpy of combustion is always negative.

Calorific Value

The grading of food articles and various fuels can be done on the basis of the values of enthalpies of combustion. If enthalpy of combustion is measured in K cal/g or kJ/g (i.e. calculated for one gram of a substance), it is called the calorific value.

In other words, the amount of heat produced in calorie or joule when one gram of a substance (food or fuel) is completely burnt or oxidised is called calorific value.

Mathematically, Calorific value $= \frac{\Delta_c H}{\text{mass}}$

Example 10 The combustion of one mole of benzene takes place at 298 K and 1 atm. After combustion, $CO_2(g)$ and $H_2O(l)$ are produced and 3267.0 kJ of heat is liberated. Calculate the standard enthalpy of formation, $\Delta_f H^\ominus$ of benzene. Standard enthalpies of formation of $CO_2(g)$ and $H_2O(l)$ are − 393.5 kJ mol^{-1} and − 285.83 kJ mol^{-1} respectively. NCERT

Sol. The reaction for the formation of benzene is given by

$$6C\,(\text{graphite}) + 3H_2(g) \longrightarrow C_6H_6(l); \Delta_f H^\ominus = ? \quad ...(i)$$

The enthalpy of combustion of 1 mole of benzene is

$$C_6H_6(l) + \frac{15}{2}O_2(g) \longrightarrow 6CO_2(g) + 3H_2O(l);$$

$$\Delta_c H^\ominus = -3265 \text{ kJ mol}^{-1} \quad ...(ii)$$

The enthalpy of formation of 1 mole of CO_2 (g) is

$$C\,(\text{graphite}) + O_2(g) \longrightarrow CO_2(g);$$

$$\Delta_f H^\ominus = -393.5 \text{ kJ mol}^{-1} \quad ...(iii)$$

The enthalpy of formation of 1 mole of $H_2O(l)$ is

$$H_2(g) + \frac{1}{2}O_2(g) \longrightarrow H_2O(l);$$

$$\Delta_f H^\ominus = -285.83 \text{ kJ mol}^{-1} \quad ...(iv)$$

On multiplying Eq. (iii) by 6 and Eq. (iv) by 3 we get

$$6C\,(\text{graphite}) + 6O_2(g) \longrightarrow 6CO_2(g);$$

$$\Delta_f H^\ominus = -2361 \text{ kJ mol}^{-1} \quad ...(v)$$

$$3H_2(g) + \frac{3}{2}O_2(g) \longrightarrow 3H_2O(l);$$

$$\Delta_f H^\ominus = -857.49 \text{ kJ mol}^{-1} \quad ...(vi)$$

On adding Eqs. (v) and (vi), we get

$$6C\,(\text{graphite}) + 3H_2(g) + \frac{15}{2}O_2(g) \rightarrow 6CO_2(g) + 3H_2O(l)$$

$$\Delta_f H^\ominus = -3218.49 \text{ kJ mol}^{-1} \quad ...(vii)$$

On reversing Eqs (ii);

$$6CO_2(g) + 3H_2O\,(l) \longrightarrow C_6H_6(l) + \frac{15}{2}O_2(g);$$

$$\Delta_f H^\ominus = 3267.0 \text{kJ mol}^{-1} \quad ...(viii)$$

Adding Eqs. (vii) and (viii), we get

$$6C\,(\text{graphite}) + 3H_2(g) \longrightarrow C_6H_6(l);$$

$$\Delta_f H^\ominus = 48.51 \text{ kJ mol}^{-1}$$

Alternative The reaction of combustion of benzene is

$$C_6H_6(l) + \frac{15}{2} O_2(g) \longrightarrow 6CO_2(g) + 3H_2O(l);$$
$$\Delta_c H^\ominus = -3267 \text{ kJ mol}^{-1}$$

For this reaction, $\Delta_r H = (6 \times \Delta H_{CO_2} + 3 \times \Delta H_{H_2O})$
$$-(\Delta H_{C_6H_6} + \frac{15}{2} \Delta H_{O_2}) - 3267 \text{ kJ}$$
$$= [6 \times (-393.5) + 3(-285.83) - (\Delta H_{C_6H_6} + 0)]$$

or $\Delta H_{C_6H_6} = -3218.49 + 3267 = 48.51$ kJ mol^{-1}

Enthalpy of Atomisation, $\Delta_a H^\ominus$

The enthalpy change on breaking one mole of bonds completely to obtain atoms in the gas phase is called the enthalpy of atomisation. e.g.

(i) $CH_4(g) \longrightarrow C(g) + 4H(g); \Delta_a H = 1665 \text{ kJ mol}^{-1}$

(ii) $Na(s) \longrightarrow Na(g); \Delta_a H = 108.4 \text{ kJ mol}^{-1}$

(In this case, enthalpy of atomisation is same as that of sublimation.)

(iii) $H_2(g) \longrightarrow 2H(g); \Delta_a H = 435.0 \text{ kJ mol}^{-1}$

(Here, enthalpy of atomisation is same as the bond dissociation enthalpy.)

Bond Enthalpy, $\Delta_{bond} H^\ominus$

In chemical reactions, there is simultaneous making and breaking of bonds.

In bond breaking, energy is required and in bond making, energy is released.

Thus, enthalpy change is related to the types of bonds formed or broken. In general, enthalpy change associated with chemical bonds is defined in two terms.

- In terms of bond dissociation enthalpy (for diatomic molecules).
- In terms of mean bond enthalpy (for polyatomic molecules).

1. Bond Dissociation Enthalpy

The enthalpy change accompanying the breaking of one mole of covalent bonds of a gaseous covalent compound to give products in the gas phase, is called **the bond dissociation enthalpy**. e.g.

$$H_2(g) \longrightarrow 2H(g); \Delta_{H-H} H^\ominus = 435.0 \text{ kJ mol}^{-1}$$

The bond dissociation enthalpy of dihydrogen, i.e. $\Delta_{H-H} H^\ominus$ is the same as its enthalpy of atomisation. This is true for all diatomic molecules.

e.g. $Cl_2(g) \longrightarrow 2Cl(g); \Delta_{Cl-Cl} H^\ominus = 242 \text{ kJ mol}^{-1}$

$O_2(g) \longrightarrow 2O(g); \Delta_{O=O} H^\ominus = 428 \text{ kJ mol}^{-1}$

2. Mean Bond Enthalpy

In case of polyatomic molecules, all the bonds between similar atoms are identical in bond length and energy. However, they differ in their strength, i.e. different amounts of energy is required to break each individual bond.

So, in case of these molecules, the mean of bond dissociation enthalpies of all the bonds present in the compound is taken, and the bond enthalpy is called the **mean bond enthalpy**. e.g. The enthalpy of atomisation for methane is given as

$$CH_4(g) \longrightarrow CH_3(g) + H(g); \Delta_{bond} H^\ominus = +427 \text{ kJ mol}^{-1}$$
$$CH_3(g) \longrightarrow CH_2(g) + H(g); \Delta_{bond} H^\ominus = +439 \text{ kJ mol}^{-1}$$
$$CH_2(g) \longrightarrow CH(g) + H(g); \Delta_{bond} H^\ominus = +452 \text{ kJ mol}^{-1}$$
$$CH(g) \longrightarrow C(g) + H(g); \Delta_{bond} H^\ominus = +347 \text{ kJ mol}^{-1}$$

Therefore, $CH_4(g) \longrightarrow C(g) + 4H(g);$
$$\Delta_a H^\ominus = 1665 \text{ kJ mol}^{-1}$$

Thus, in CH_4, $\Delta_{C-H} H^\ominus$ is calculated as

$$\Delta_{C-H} H^\ominus = \frac{1}{4}(\Delta_a H^\ominus) = \frac{1}{4}(1665 \text{ kJ mol}^{-1})$$
$$= 416 \text{ kJ mol}^{-1}$$

The mean bond enthalpy vary slightly from compound to compound but it does not differ in a great deal.

From the bond enthalpy, it is possible to calculate enthalpy change of a reaction by using the expression,

$$\Delta_r H^\ominus = \Sigma_{\text{bond enthalpies reactants}} - \Sigma_{\text{bond enthalpies products}}$$

or $\Delta_r H^\ominus = \Sigma \Delta_f H^\ominus_{\text{(bonds of products)}}$
$$- \Sigma \Delta_f H^\ominus_{\text{(bonds of reactants)}}$$

i.e. the net enthalpy change of a reaction is the amount of energy required to break all the bonds in the reactant molecules minus the amount of energy required to break all the bonds in the product molecules.

The above relations are valid only when the reactants and products are in gaseous state.

Note
- Bond dissociation enthalpy and mean bond enthalpy have the same symbol.
- As the bond multiplicity increases, bond enthalpy increases.
- C—C < C=C < C≡C (order of bond enthalpy)
  414 611 837

Example 11 **Calculate the enthalpy change (ΔH) of the following reaction.**

$$C_2H_2(g) + \frac{5}{2} O_2(g) \longrightarrow 2\,CO_2(g) + H_2O(g)$$

Given average bond enthalpies of various bonds, i.e. C—H, C≡C, O=O, C=O, O—H as 414, 814, 499, 724 and 460 kJ mol^{-1} respectively.

Sol. The equation representing various substances involved in chemical reaction is

$$(H-C\equiv C-H) + \frac{5}{2}(O=O) \longrightarrow 2(O=C=O) + (H-O-H)$$

The reaction involves the breaking of 2C—H bonds, C≡C bonds, $\frac{5}{2}$ O=O bonds and formation of 4C=O bonds and 2 O—H bonds.

$$\Delta_r H^\ominus = \begin{bmatrix}\text{Sum of bond}\\ \text{enthalpies of reactions}\end{bmatrix} - \begin{bmatrix}\text{Sum of bond}\\ \text{enthalpies of products}\end{bmatrix}$$

$$= [2\Delta_{C-H}H^\ominus + \Delta_{C\equiv C}H^\ominus + \frac{5}{2}\Delta_{O=O}H^\ominus] - [4\Delta_{C=O}H^\ominus + 2\Delta_{O-H}H^\ominus]$$

$$= (2 \times 814 + 814 + \frac{5}{2} \times 499) - (4 \times 724 + 2 \times 460)$$

$$= 2889.5 - 3816 = -926.5 \text{ kJ mol}^{-1}$$

Enthalpy of Hydration, $\Delta_{hyd}H^\ominus$

The enthalpy change can be defined as **enthalpy** or **heat of hydration** when one mole of anhydrous or partially hydrated salt combines with required number of moles of water to form a specific hydrate. Its symbol is $\Delta_{hyd}H$,

e.g. $CuSO_4(s) + 5H_2O(l) \longrightarrow CuSO_4 \cdot 5H_2O(s);$

$$\Delta_{hyd}H^\circ = 78.22 \text{ kJ}$$

In general cases, hydration is an exothermic process but there are some cases also where hydration is an endothermic process.

Enthalpy of Neutralisation $\Delta_n H^\ominus$

The enthalpy of neutralisation is defined as the enthalpy change accompanying the formation of one mole of H_2O by combination of one mol H^+ ions furnished by acid and one mole of $\bar{O}H$ ions furnished by base in dilute solutions at the standard conditions.

It should be noted that, **$\Delta_n H^\ominus$ of strong acid - strong base is constant and is numerically equal to −57.1 kJ.**

$$H^+(aq) + OH^-(aq) \longrightarrow H_2O(l);\ \Delta_n H^\ominus = -57.1 \text{ kJ}$$

The value of enthalpy of neutralisation of weak acid/strong base or strong acid/ weak base is numerically less than 57.1 kJ.

Lattice Enthalpy, $\Delta_{lattice}H^\ominus$

The enthalpy change when one mole of an ionic compound dissociates completely into its constituent ions in gaseous state is called the lattice enthalpy of the ionic compound.

e.g. $Na^+Cl^-(s) \longrightarrow Na^+(g) + Cl^-(g);$

$$\Delta_{lattice}H^\ominus = +788 \text{ kJ mol}^{-1}$$

Higher the lattice enthalpy, lesser the dissolution of an ionic compound in water. It is impossible to determine lattice enthalpies directly by experiment, therefore, lattice enthalpy is calculated, indirectly by using **Born-Haber cycle** (which has also been described in chapter 4).

The steps involved in Born-Haber cycle (in case of NaCl) are as follows

(i) $Na(s) \longrightarrow Na(g)$, sublimation of sodium metal,

$$\Delta_{sub}H^\ominus = 108.4 \text{ kJ mol}^{-1}$$

(ii) $Na(g) \longrightarrow Na^+(g) + e^-(g)$, the ionisation of sodium atoms, ionisation enthalpy.

$$\Delta_i H^\ominus = 496 \text{ kJ mol}^{-1}$$

(iii) $\frac{1}{2}Cl_2(g) \longrightarrow Cl(g)$, the dissociation of chlorine, the reaction enthalpy is half of the bond dissociation enthalpy.

$$\frac{1}{2}\Delta_{bond}H^\ominus = 121 \text{ kJ mol}^{-1}$$

(iv) $Cl(g) + e^-(g) \longrightarrow Cl^-(g)$ electron gained by chlorine atoms.

The electron gain enthalpy, $\Delta_{eg}H^\ominus = -348.6 \text{ kJ mol}^{-1}$

(v) $Na^+(g) + Cl^-(g) \longrightarrow Na^+Cl^-(s); \; \Delta_{lattice}H^\ominus = ?$

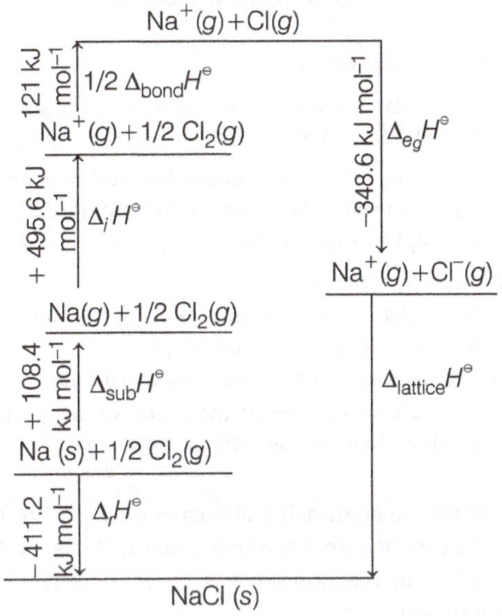

Enthalpy diagram for lattice enthalpy of NaCl

On applying Hess's law, we get

$$\Delta_{lattice}H^\ominus = 411.2 + 108.4 + 121 + 495.6 - 348.6;$$
$$\Delta_{lattice}H^\ominus = +788 \text{ kJ}$$

If $\Delta_{hyd}H^\ominus$ is -784 kJ mol^{-1} for NaCl

As $\Delta_{sol}H^\ominus = \Delta_{lattice}H^\ominus + \Delta_{hyd}H^\ominus$

then $\Delta_{sol}H^\ominus = +788 \text{ kJ mol}^{-1} - 784 \text{ kJ mol}^{-1}$
$= +4 \text{ kJ mol}^{-1}$

Ionisation Energy and Electron Affinity

- Ionisation enthalpy and electron affinity (about which you have read before) are defined at absolute zero. At any other temperature, only heat capacities are considered.
- $\Delta_f H^\ominus(T) = \Delta_r H^\ominus(0) + \int_0^T \Delta_r C_p^\ominus \, dT$

and $\Delta_r C_p^\ominus = +\frac{5}{2}R$ (For ionisation)

$\Delta_r C_p^\ominus = -(5/2)R$ (For electron gain)

Therefore, $\Delta_r H^\ominus$ (Ionisation enthalpy) $= IE + (5/2)RT$

- $\Delta_r H^\ominus$ (Electron gain enthalpy) $= -EA - (5/2)RT$

Enthalpy of Solution, $\Delta_{sol}H^\ominus$

The enthalpy change when one mole of solute is dissolved completely in specified amount of solvent or water is called **enthalpy of solution**.

If solvent is in excess, i.e. the interactions between the ions (or solute molecules) are negligible, the enthalpy change is called **enthalpy of solution at infinite dilution**.

When an ionic compound, like *AB*, dissolves in a solvent, the ions leave their ordered positions on the crystal lattice and move freely in the solution. But solvation of these ions (or hydration in case of water as a solvent) also occurs at the same time. This can be shown as

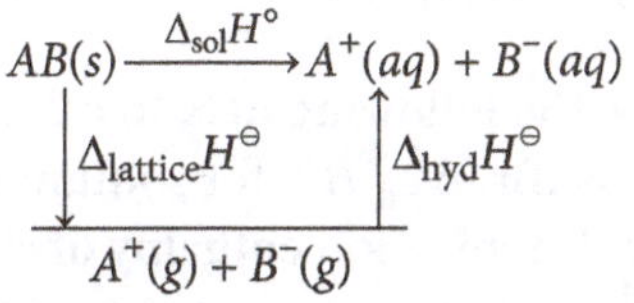

The enthalpy of solution is in water given as

$$\Delta_{sol}H^\ominus = \Delta_{lattice}H^\ominus + \Delta_{hyd}H^\ominus$$

$\Delta_{sol}H^\ominus$ is generally positive for most of the ionic compounds and dissolution is an endothermic process. Therefore, their solubility increases with rise in temperature.

The dissolution of the compound may not take place, if the lattice enthalpy is very high.

Enthalpy of Dilution

The enthalpy change when the solution containing one mole of a substance is diluted from one concentration to another is called **enthalpy** or **heat of dilution.**

e.g. $HCl(g) + 25(aq.) \longrightarrow HCl \cdot 25(aq.)$

$$\Delta H_1 = -72.03 \text{ kJ/mol}$$

$HCl(g) + 40(aq.) \longrightarrow HCl \cdot 40(aq.)$

$$\Delta H_2 = -72.79 \text{ kJ/mol}$$

Now, $\Delta_{dil.}H$, for the reaction

$HCl \cdot 25(aq.) + 15(aq.) \longrightarrow HCl \cdot 40(aq.)$ is,

$$\Delta_{dil.}H = \Delta H_2 - \Delta H_1$$
$$= [-72.79 - (-72.03)] \text{ kJ/mol}$$
$$= -0.76 \text{ kJ/mol}$$

This $\Delta_{dil.}H$ is the enthalpy of dilution and it is the heat withdrawn from the surroundings when additional solvent is added to the solution. The $\Delta_{dil.}H$ is dependent on the original concentration of the solution and the amount of solvent added.

Enthalpy of Ionisation, $\Delta_{ion}H^{\ominus}$

The enthalpy change when one mole of an electrolyte (weak acid or weak base) is completely ionised into its constituents is called **enthalpy of ionisation ($\Delta_{ion}H$)**,

e.g. $CH_3COOH(aq) \rightleftharpoons CH_3COO^-(aq) + H^+(aq)$; $\Delta H = 1.9\ kJ\ mol^{-1}$

Heat of ionisation can be obtained by subtracting the heat of neutralisation of weak acid or a weak base from the heat of neutralisation of strong acid and strong base (– 57.32 kJ or 13.7 kcal).

Example 12 **Use the following data to calculate $\Delta_{lattice}\ H^{\ominus}$ for NaBr. $\Delta_{sub}H^{\ominus}$ for sodium metal = 108.4 kJ mol^{-1}, ionisation enthalpy of sodium = 496 kJ mol^{-1}, electron gain enthalpy of bromine = –325 kJ mol^{-1}, bond dissociation enthalpy of bromine = 192 kJ mol^{-1}, $\Delta_f H^{\ominus}$ for NaBr(s) = –360.1 kJ mol^{-1}**

Hint This question is based upon the concept of Born-Haber cycle as well as Hess's law. Following steps are used to solve this problem.

- $Na(s) \longrightarrow Na(g); \Delta_{sub}H^{\ominus}$
- $Na(g) \longrightarrow Na^+(g) + e^-(g)$; IE
- $\frac{1}{2}Br_2(g) \longrightarrow Br(g); \Delta_{diss}\ H^{\ominus}$
- $Br(g) + e^-(g) \longrightarrow Br^-(g); \Delta_{e_g}H^{\ominus}$
- Applying Hess's law,

$$\Delta_f H^{\ominus} = \Delta_{sub}\ H^{\ominus} + IE + \Delta_{diss}\ H^{\ominus} + \Delta_{e_g}\ H^{\ominus} + U$$

Sol. Given that, $\Delta_{sub}H^{\ominus}$ for Na metal = 108.4 k J mol^{-1}

IE of Na = 496 k J mol^{-1}

$\Delta_{e_g}\ H^{\ominus}$ of Br = – 325 k J mol^{-1}

$\Delta_{diss}\ H^{\ominus}$ of Br = 192 k J mol^{-1}

$\Delta_f\ H^{\ominus}$ for NaBr = – 360.1 kJ mol^{-1}

Born-Haber cycle for the formation of NaBr is as

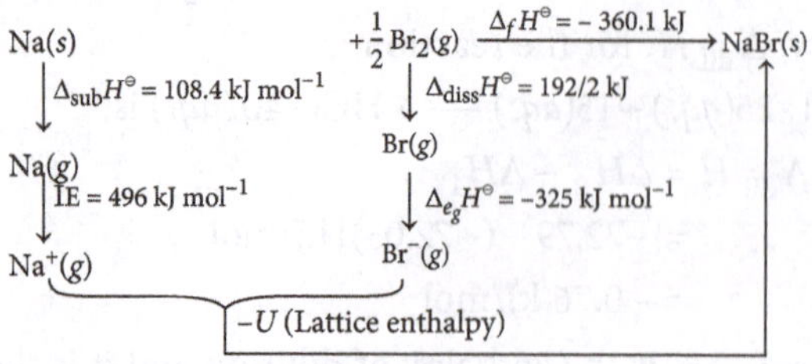

By applying Hess's law,

$$\Delta_f H^{\ominus} = \Delta_{sub}\ H^{\ominus} + IE + \Delta_{diss}\ H^{\ominus} + \Delta_{e_g}H^{\ominus} + U$$

$$-360.\ 1 = 108.\ 4 + 496 + 96 + (-325) - U$$

$$U = +735.5\ kJ\ mol^{-1}$$

Quick Test 2

Conceptual Questions

1. (i) The molar enthalpy of vaporisation of acetone is less than that of water. Why? *NCERT Exemplar*

(ii) One mole of acetone requires less heat to vaporise than 1 mole of water. Which of the two liquids has higher enthalpy of vaporisation? *NCERT Exemplar*

2. Give the appropriate reason.

(i) It is preferable to determine the change in enthalpy rather than the change in internal energy.

(ii) It is necessary to define the 'standard state'.

(iii) It is necessary to specify the phases of the reactants and products in a thermochemical equation. *Competency Based Que.*

3. Standard molar enthalpy of formation, $\Delta_f\ H°$ is just a special case of enthalpy of reaction, $\Delta_r H°$. Is the $\Delta_r H°$ for the following reaction same as $\Delta_f\ H°$? Give reason for your answer.

$CaO(s) + CO_2(g) \longrightarrow CaCO_3(s); \Delta_f\ H° = -178.3\ kJ\ mol^{-1}$ *NCERT Exemplar*

Numerical Questions

4. If enthalpy of fusion and enthalpy of vaporisation of sodium metals are 2.6 and 98.2 kJ mol^{-1} respectively, what is the enthalpy of sublimation of sodium.

5. Standard vaporisation enthalpy of benzene at boiling point is 30.8 kJ mol^{-1}. For how long would 100 W electric heater have to operate in order to vaporise a 100 g sample at that temperature (power= energy/time and 1 W = 1 Js^{-1})?

6. Given,

$N_2(g) + 3H_2(g) \longrightarrow 2NH_3(g); \Delta_r H° = -92.4\ kJ\ mol^{-1}$

What is the standard enthalpy of formation of NH_3 gas ? *NCERT*

Hint: Firstly standard enthalpy of formation means heat released in the formation of 1 mole of substance.

7. Enthalpies of formation of $CO(g), CO_2(g), N_2O(g)$ and $N_2O_4(g)$ are –110, –393, 81 and 9.7 kJ mol^{-1} respectively. Find the value of $\Delta_r H$ for the reaction.

$N_2O_4(g) + 3CO(g) \longrightarrow N_2O(g) + 3CO_2(g)$ *NCERT*

8. Calculate the enthalpy change on freezing of 1.0 mole of water at 10.0°C to ice at – 10.0°C. $\Delta_{fus}H$ = 6.03 kJ mol^{-1} at 0°C. *NCERT*

$C_p[H_2O(l)] = 75.3\ J\ mol^{-1}K^{-1}; C_p[H_2O(s)] = 36.8\ J\ mol^{-1}K^{-1}$

9. The net enthalpy change of a reaction is the energy required to break all the bonds in reactant molecules minus amount of energy required to form all the bonds in the product molecules. What will be the enthalpy change for the following reaction ?

$$H_2(g) + Br_2(g) \longrightarrow 2HBr(g)$$

Given that bond energy of H_2, Br_2 and HBr is 435 kJ mol^{-1}, 192 kJ mol^{-1} and 368 kJ mol^{-1} respectively. *NCERT Exemplar*

10. If the combustion of 1 g of graphite produces 20.7 kJ of heat, what will be molar enthalpy change? Give the significance of sign also. *NCERT Exemplar*

Answers

4. 100.8 kJ mol^{-1} 5. 6.6 min 6. −46.2 kJ mol^{-1}
7. −778 kJ mol^{-1} 8. −7.151 kJ mol^{-1} 9. −109 kJ mol^{-1}
10. -2.48×10^2 kJ mol^{-1}

For Solutions, See QR Code on Pg. 209

5.8 Spontaneity

A physical or chemical change that occurs by its own, i.e. without the assistance of external source, is called **spontaneous process** (spontaneity) or **natural process** or **feasible process** or **probable process.**

Or

A spontaneous process is an **irreversible process** and may only be reversed by some external agency, e.g. rolling ball, heat flow, gas flow etc.

However, it does not tell about the rate of reaction or process and spontaneous reactions cannot reverse their direction on their own.

There are also some processes which require some initiation before they proceed spontaneously. These processes are also considered as spontaneous processes.

Thus, we can say that spontaneous processes are of two types

(i) Spontaneous processes which does not require initiation, e.g. dissolution of sugar in water, evaporation of water from river, ponds etc.

(ii) Spontaneous processes where initiation is required,

e.g. $$2H_2(g) + O_2(g) \xrightarrow[\text{spark}]{\text{Electric}} 2H_2O(l)$$

Here, the reaction is initiated by electric spark and then proceeds spontaneously.

$$CH_4(g) + 2O_2(g) \longrightarrow CO_2(g) + 2H_2O(g)$$

Here, CH_4 burns spontaneously when ignited initially.

Rest of the other processes which require a continuous supply of energy from outside the system are called **non-spontaneous processes.** e.g.

Electrolysis of water In this process external energy is required. As the current flow stops, electrolysis also stops.

$$H_2O(l) \xrightarrow{\text{Electricity}} H_2(g) + \frac{1}{2}O_2(g) \text{ (Non-spontaneous)}$$

Decrease in Enthalpy as a Criterion for Spontaneity

All the spontaneous process have a tendency to acquire the state of minimum energy. Further, in case of exothermic reactions, the enthalpy (energy) of the system (reaction) decreases, thus these reactions are considered as spontaneous processes.

e.g. $$\frac{1}{2}N_2(g) + \frac{3}{2}H_2(g) \longrightarrow NH_3(g); \quad \Delta_r H^\ominus = -46.1 \text{ kJ mol}^{-1}$$

$$\frac{1}{2}H_2(g) + \frac{1}{2}Cl_2(g) \longrightarrow HCl(g); \quad \Delta_r H^\ominus = -92.32 \text{ kJ mol}^{-1}$$

Thus, it can be concluded that a tendency to attain the minimum energy, i.e. decrease in energy is responsible for the spontaneity or feasibility of a reaction.

The enthalpy diagram, for an exothermic reaction, showing the decrease in enthalpy when reactants are converted into products is shown below.

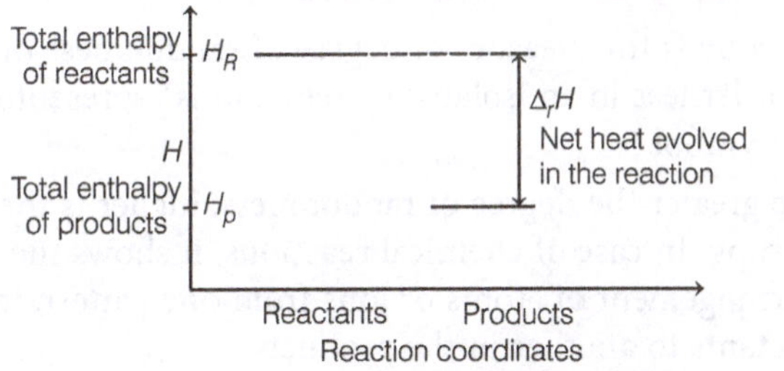

Enthalpy diagram for exothermic reactions

Limitations of the Criterion of Decrease in Energy (Enthalpy)

The above criterion fails to explain the following facts

- In case of endothermic reaction, ΔH is positive, i.e. enthalpy (or energy) of the system increases, but there are several endothermic reactions that are spontaneous.

e.g. $$\frac{1}{2}N_2(g) + O_2(g) \longrightarrow NO_2(g); \quad \Delta_r H^\ominus = +33.2 \text{ kJ mol}^{-1}$$

The enthalpy diagram for such reactions is shown below.

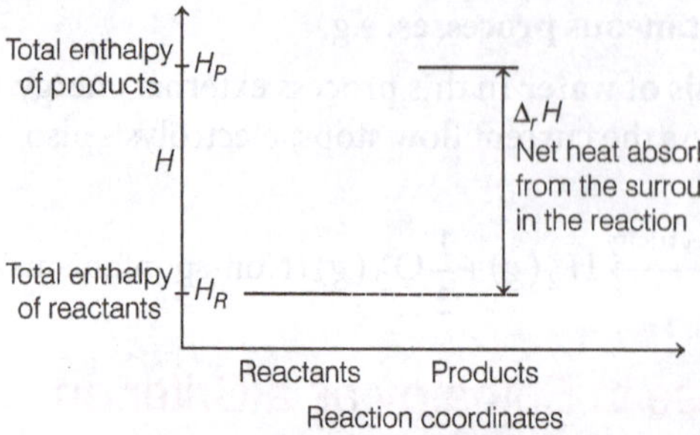

Enthalpy diagram for endothermic reactions

- Several such reactions are also spontaneous for which ΔH is zero.

e.g. $CH_3COOH(l) + C_2H_5OH(l) \longrightarrow CH_3COOC_2H_5(l) + H_2O(l)$
Ethyl acetate

- Even those reactions for which ΔH is negative, rarely proceed to completion even though ΔH remains negative throughout.
- Reversible reaction, e.g. the reactions that occur in forward as well as reverse direction, are also spontaneous in both the directions. From the above discussion, it is obvious that although decrease in enthalpy may be a criteria for spontaneity but it is not true for all the processes.

Entropy and Spontaneity

Entropy is the measure of degree of randomness or disorderness in an isolated system and is represented by the **symbol *S*.**

The greater the degree of randomness, higher is the entropy. In case of chemical reactions, it shows the rearrangement of atoms or ions from one pattern in the reactants to another in the products.

If the structure of products is more disordered as compared to reactants, entropy of the reaction increases and if the structure of reactant is more disordered as compared to products, it results in decreased entropy.

Thus, the change in entropy accompanying a chemical reaction may be estimated qualitatively by consideration of the structures of the species taking part in the reaction.

Some examples in which entropy either increases or decreases are

- For a given substance, the crystalline solid state is most ordered and therefore, has the lowest entropy while gaseous state is most disordered, therefore, has the highest entropy. The liquid state is the intermediate between the two. Thus, **the order of randomness and thus the entropy is**

gas > liquid > solid.

- In case of atoms or molecules belonging to different elements, the one with higher mass have greater entropy, i.e. for inert gases.

$$S_{He} < S_{Ne} < S_{Ar} < S_{Kr} < S_{Xe} < S_{Rn}$$

Similarly, for halogens $S_{F_2} < S_{Cl_2} < S_{Br_2} < S_{I_2}$

- The molecules with more atoms of given type or with greater number of chemical bonds or greater capacity to take up energy means greater thermal disorder thus, have greater entropy. e.g.

$$S_{acetylene} < S_{ethylene} < S_{ethane}$$

- Vaporisation and fusion result in the increase of entropy while crystallisation results in decrease of entropy.
- Stretching of rubber band results in increase in entropy while in case of boiling of egg, entropy decreases.
- If similar amount of heat is given to a system at lower temperature and a system at higher temperature, the randomness is more in the system having lower temperature than the system having higher temperature. It shows that entropy change varies inversely with temperature.

Entropy as State Function

Entropy like any other thermodynamic property such as internal energy (U) and enthalpy (H) is a state function and **independent of path.**

i.e. $\Delta S = S_2 - S_1$

$= \Sigma S_{products} - \Sigma S_{reactants}$

Entropy Change in Reversible Process

Consider an isothermal reversible process. In this process, let the system absorbs q amount of heat from surroundings at temperature, T.

The increase in the entropy of the system will be

$$\Delta S_{system} = +\frac{q_{sys, rev}}{T}$$

On the other hand, surroundings lose the same amount of heat at the same temperature. The decrease in the entropy of the surroundings will be

$$\Delta S_{surroundings} = -\frac{q_{surroundings, rev}}{T}$$

Total change in entropy of the process = entropy change in system + entropy change in surroundings

$$\Delta S_{total} = \Delta S_{system} + \Delta S_{surroundings} = \frac{q}{T} - \frac{q}{T} = 0$$

When the reversible process is adiabatic, there will be no heat exchange between system and surroundings, i.e.

$$q = 0$$

$$\therefore \quad \Delta S_{system} = 0$$

$$\Delta S_{surroundings} = 0$$

$$\Delta S_{total} = \Delta S_{system} + \Delta S_{surroundings} = 0$$

Units of entropy is JK^{-1}.

Entropy Change in Irreversible Processes

Consider a system at higher temperature T_1 and its surroundings at lower temperature T_2. q amount of heat goes irreversibly from system to surroundings.

$$\therefore \quad \Delta S_{system} = -\frac{q}{T_1}; \quad \Delta S_{surroundings} = +\frac{q}{T_2}$$

$$\Delta S_{total} = \Delta S_{system} + \Delta S_{surroundings}$$

$$= -\frac{q}{T_1} + \frac{q}{T_2} = q\left[\frac{T_1 - T_2}{T_1 T_2}\right]$$

But $T_1 > T_2$

$$\therefore \quad T_1 - T_2 = +\text{ve} \text{ or } \Delta S_{total} > 0$$

Hence, entropy increases in an irreversible process, and this is the criteria for a spontaneous change.

Note Most of the natural phenomenon are irreversible in nature as most of the systems have a natural tendency to move towards more randomness.

TEACHER'S TIP

For spontaneous process,

$$\Delta S_{total} = \Delta S_{system} + \Delta S_{surroundings} > 0$$

$$\Delta S_{sys} = \frac{\Delta_r H}{T} \quad \left(\text{as } \Delta S_{sys} = \frac{q}{T}\right)$$

Entropy Change During Phase Transition

The change of matter from one state to another is called **phase transition**. The entropy changes at the time of phase change can be summarised as

$$\Delta S_{melting} = S_{liq} - S_{sol} = \frac{\Delta H_{fusion}}{T_m}$$

where, T_m = melting point of substance, S_{liquid} = molar entropy of the liquid, S_{solid} = molar entropy of the solid

$$\Delta S_{vaporisation} = S_{vap} - S_{liq} = \frac{\Delta H_{vaporisation}}{T_b}$$

where, T_b = boiling point of substance, S_{vap} = molar entropy of the vapour.

Similarly, $\Delta S_{sublimation} = S_{vap} - S_{sol} = \dfrac{\Delta H_{sublimation}}{T_{sub}}$

where, T_{sub} = sublimation temperature.

Example 13 **For oxidation of iron,**

$$4Fe(s) + 3O_2(g) \longrightarrow 2Fe_2O_3(s)$$

entropy change is $-549.4\ JK^{-1}mol^{-1}$ at 298 K. Inspite of negative entropy change of this reaction, why is the reaction spontaneous?

($\Delta_r H^\ominus$ for this reaction is $-1648 \times 10^3 J\ mol^{-1}$) NCERT

Sol The spontaneity of the reaction is decided by considering $\Delta S_{total}(\Delta S_{sys} + \Delta S_{surr})$. At temperature T, entropy change of the surroundings.

$$\Delta S_{surr} = -\frac{\Delta_r H^\ominus}{T} \quad \text{(At constant pressure)}$$

$$= -\frac{(-1648 \times 10^3 Jmol^{-1})}{298\ K} = 5530.20\ JK^{-1}mol^{-1}$$

Thus, total entropy change for this reaction

$$\Delta S_{total} = 5530\ JK^{-1}mol^{-1} + (-549.4\ JK^{-1}mol^{-1})$$

$$= 4980.6\ JK^{-1}mol^{-1} \ [\because \Delta_{sys}S = -549.4\ JK^{-1}\ mol^{-1}]$$

Positive value of ΔS_{total} shows that the above reaction is spontaneous.

5.9 Gibbs Free Energy

Neither decrease in enthalpy nor increase in entropy alone can determine the direction of spontaneous change for a system. For this purpose, a new thermodynamic function is defined which is Gibbs energy or Gibbs function.

The maximum amount of energy available to a system, during a process, that can be converted into useful work is called **free energy** or **Gibbs free energy** or **Gibbs energy**. It was called **Gibbs free energy** in early literature but in accordance with IUPAC recommendations we shall use the term **free energy** for it.

Free energy is denoted by G and mathematically expressed as

$$G = H - TS$$

where, H = enthalpy of system, S = entropy of system
T = absolute temperature

Gibbs function, G is an extensive property and a state function.

The change in Gibbs energy for the system, ΔG_{sys} can be written as,

$$\Delta G_{sys} = \Delta H_{sys} - T\Delta S_{sys} - S_{sys}\Delta T$$

At constant temperature, $\Delta T = 0$

$$\therefore \quad \Delta G_{sys} = \Delta H_{sys} - T\Delta S_{sys}$$

Usually the subscript 'sys' (for system) is dropped and the equation simply can be represented as

$$\boxed{\Delta G = \Delta H - T\Delta S}$$

where, ΔG = change in free energy
ΔH = enthalpy change, ΔS = change in entropy
T = absolute temperature

The above equation is called **Gibbs Helmholtz** equation or **simply Gibbs equation**. In this equation,
The units of ΔG is same as that of units of energy because ΔH and $T\Delta S$ ($\because T\Delta S = \text{K JK}^{-1} = \text{J}$) both are energy terms.

Gibbs Free Energy as a Criterion of Spontaneity

We know that, $\Delta S_{total} = \Delta S_{sys} + \Delta S_{surr}$
At the state of thermal equilibrium, the temperature of the surrounding is same as that of the system. Also, increase in enthalpy of the surroundings = Decrease in the enthalpy of the system.
Thus, entropy change of surroundings.

$$\Delta S_{surr} = \frac{\Delta H_{surr}}{T} = -\frac{\Delta H_{sys}}{T}$$

$$\Delta S_{total} = \Delta S_{sys} + \left(-\frac{\Delta H_{sys}}{T}\right)$$

Rearranging the above equation.

$$T\Delta S_{total} = T\Delta S_{sys} - \Delta H_{sys}$$

For spontaneous process, $\Delta S_{total} > 0$, so

$$T\Delta S_{sys} - \Delta H_{sys} > 0$$

$$\Rightarrow \quad -(\Delta H_{sys} - T\Delta S_{sys}) > 0$$

Using equation, $\Delta G = \Delta H - T\Delta S$, the above equation can be written as

$$-\Delta G > 0 \text{ or } \Delta G = \Delta H - T\Delta S < 0$$

Here, ΔH_{sys} = enthalpy change of the reaction.
$T\Delta S_{sys}$ = energy which is unavailable for doing useful work.
ΔG = net energy available for doing useful work, so, it is the measure of free energy.

At a given temperature and pressure,

- if ΔG is negative, (< 0) the process is spontaneous.
- if ΔG is positive (> 0), the process is non-spontaneous.
- if ΔG is zero, the process is in equilibrium state.

The various conditions in which a reaction occur spontaneously are tabulated below.

Effect of Temperature on Spontaneity of Reactions

$\Delta_r H^\ominus$	$\Delta_r S^\ominus$	$\Delta_r G^\ominus$	Description
−	+	− (at all T)	Reaction spontaneous at all temperatures.
−	−	− (at low T)	Reaction spontaneous at low temperature.
−	−	+ (at high T)	Reaction non-spontaneous at high temperature.
+	+	+ (at low T)	Reaction non-spontaneous at low temperature.
+	+	− (at high T)	Reaction spontaneous at high temperature.
+	−	+ (at all T)	Reaction non-spontaneous at all temperature.

Note The term low temperature and high temperature are relative. For a particular reaction, high temperature could even mean room temperature.

From the given table, it is obvious that an endothermic reaction moves spontaneously towards more randomness at a higher temperature as for this $\Delta H = +\text{ve}$, $\Delta S = +\text{ve}$ and T is high enough so that $T\Delta S > \Delta H$ and hence, $\Delta G = \Delta H - T\Delta S < 0$ and thus, reaction is spontaneous.

Standard Free Energy Change

The free energy change for a process at 298 K and 1 atm pressure in which the reactants in their standard state, are converted into products in their standard state is called **standard free energy change**. It is denoted by $\Delta G^\ominus$.

$$\Delta_r G^\ominus = \begin{bmatrix}\text{Sum of the standard free energy} \\ \text{of formation of products}\end{bmatrix} - \begin{bmatrix}\text{Sum of the standard free energy} \\ \text{formation of reactants}\end{bmatrix}$$

$$= \sum \Delta_f G^\ominus(\text{product}) - \sum \Delta_r G^\ominus(\text{ reactant})$$

Entropy and Second Law of Thermodynamics

The second law of thermodynamics can be stated as

- Whenever a spontaneous process takes place, it is always accompanied by an increase in total entropy of the universe.

  In the above statement, the term universe means the system and the surroundings.

  Thus, $\Delta S_{univ} = \Delta S_{sys} + \Delta S_{surr}$
- For an isolated system, change in energy is constant so, increase in entropy is the cause of a spontaneous change.
- For an exothermic reaction, heat released by the reaction increases the disorderedness of the surroundings and the overall entropy change is positive which makes the reaction spontaneous.

5.10 Absolute Entropy : Third Law of Thermodynamics

According to third law of thermodynamics, *"the entropy of a pure crystalline substance, (which have perfect order in a crystal), approaches zero as the absolute zero of temperature is approached".*

$$\lim_{T \to 0} S = 0$$

This law is applicable for pure crystalline solids. Only as theoretical arguments and practical evidences have shown that entropy of solutions and supercooled liquids is not zero at 0 K. Thus, this law help in calculation of absolute values of entropy of pure substance from thermal data alone.

In case of CO and NO molecules in solid state, there is randomness even at 0 K due to their dipole moment hence entropy in such cases is not zero even at 0 K.

Note The entropy possessed by a substance at absolute zero is called its **residual entropy**.

Gibbs Free Energy and Equilibrium Constant

So far we have considered free energy changes in irreversible reactions. Let us now examine the free energy changes in reversible reactions. This means that the reactions in both the directions should proceed with a decrease in free energy, which seems impossible. It is possible only, if at equilibrium the free energy of the system is minimum. If it is not, the system would spontaneously change to configuration of lower free energy.

Consider the following reaction, $A + B \rightleftharpoons C + D$

Reaction quotient for this reaction, i.e. $Q = \frac{[C][D]}{[A][B]}$

The free energy change and standard free energy change are related as,

$$\Delta G = \Delta G^\ominus + RT \ln Q$$

At equilibrium, $\Delta G = 0$ and $Q = K$

On putting the values, we get

$$0 = \Delta G^\ominus + RT \ln K \text{ or } \Delta G^\ominus = -RT \ln K$$

Thus, the standard free energy $(\Delta G^\ominus)$ is related to equilibrium constant K as

$$\boxed{\Delta G^\ominus = -RT \ln K, \text{ i.e. } \Delta G^\ominus = -2.303RT \log K}$$

$$K = e^{-\Delta G^\circ/RT} \text{ or } K = 10^{-\Delta G^\ominus/2.303\,RT}$$

Also, $\Delta G^\ominus = \Delta H^\ominus - T\Delta S^\ominus = -RT \ln K$

The above equation is helpful in the following ways

- For strongly endothermic reactions, the value of ΔH° may be large and positive. In such a case, value of $K << 1$ and the reaction is unlikely to form much product.
- For exothermic reactions, ΔH° is large and negative and ΔG is also large and negative.

  In such case, $K >> 1$ and hence the reaction can go to near completion.
- It is possible to obtain an estimate of $\Delta G^\ominus$ from the measurement of $\Delta H^\ominus$ and $\Delta S^\ominus$, and then calculate K at any temperature for economic yields of the products.

If K is measured directly in the laboratory, value of ΔG° at any other temperature can be calculated.

Relationship between the Standard Free Energy Change and the Equilibrium Constant

ΔG°	$\log K$	K	Comment
$\Delta G^\circ=0$	$\log K=0$	1	The equilibrium mixture contains comparable amounts of reactants and products (K=1 for 1M concentrations and 1 atm partial pressures).
$\Delta G^\circ<0$	$\log K>0$	$K>1$	The equilibrium mixture is mainly products.
$\Delta G^\circ>0$	$\log K<0$	$K<1$	The equilibrium mixture is mainly reactants.

Gibbs Free Energy and EMF of a cell

The free energy change (ΔG) is related to the electrical work done in the cell as

$$\Delta G = -n\,FE_{cell}$$

where, E_{cell} = emf of the cell

n = number of moles of electrons involved

F = Faraday's constant, i.e. 96500 C

If reactants and products are in their standard state,

$$\Delta G^\ominus = -nFE^\ominus$$

where, $E^\ominus$ = standard cell potential.

Quick Test 3

Conceptual Questions

1. Comment on the thermodynamic stability of NO(g), given

$$\frac{1}{2}N_2(g)+\frac{1}{2}O_2(g)\longrightarrow NO(g);\ \Delta_rH^\circ=90\text{ kJ mol}^{-1}$$

$$NO(g)+\frac{1}{2}O_2(g)\longrightarrow NO_2(g);\ \Delta_rH^\circ=-74\text{ kJ mol}^{-1}$$

NCERT

2. (i) What is entropy and why does entropy of a solid increase on melting?

(ii) State second law of thermodynamics. Diksha

3. For an isolated system, $\Delta U=0$, what will be ΔS? NCERT

4. Represent the potential energy/enthalpy change in the following processes graphically

(i) Throwing a stone from the ground to roof.

(ii) $\frac{1}{2}H_2(g)+\frac{1}{2}Cl_2(g)\rightleftharpoons HCl(g);\Delta_rH^\ominus=-92.32\text{ kJ mol}^{-1}$

In which of the processes potential energy/enthalpy change is contributing factor to the spontaneity?

NCERT Exemplar

5. At 298 K, K_p for the reaction, $N_2O_4(g)\rightleftharpoons 2NO_2(g)$ is 0.98. Predict whether the reaction is spontaneous or not.

NCERT Exemplar

Numerical Questions

6. Calculate the entropy change in surroundings when 1.00 mole of $H_2O(l)$ is formed under standard conditions. $\Delta_f H^\circ=-286\text{ kJ mol}^{-1}$. NCERT

7. The enthalpy of vaporisation of liquid diethyl ether $(C_2H_5)_2O$ is 26.0 kJ mol^{-1} at its boiling point (35.0°C). Calculate ΔS° for the conversion of

(i) liquid to vapour and (ii) vapour to liquid at 35°C.

8. For the reaction at 298 K, $2A+B\rightarrow C$

$\Delta H=400\text{ kJ mol}^{-1}$ and $\Delta S=0.2\text{ kJ K}^{-1}\text{ mol}^{-1}$

At what temperature will the reaction become spontaneous considering ΔH and ΔS to be constant over the temperature range? NCERT

9. Calculate the equilibrium constant for the following reaction at 298 K and 1 atm pressure

$$NO(g)+\frac{1}{2}O_2(g)\rightleftharpoons NO_2(g)$$

Given ΔH_f° at 298 K are $NO(g)=90.4\text{ kJ mol}^{-1}$ and $NO_2(g)\Delta=33.8\text{ kJ mol}^{-1}$, ΔS° at 298 K for the reaction $=-70.0\text{ JK}^{-1}\text{mol}^{-1}$, $R=8.31\text{ JK}^{-1}\text{mol}^{-1}$.

Answers

6. 959.7 $\text{JK}^{-1}\text{mol}^{-1}$ 7. (i) 84.4 $\text{JK}^{-1}\text{ mol}^{-1}$ (ii) –84.4 $\text{JK}^{-1}\text{ mol}^{-1}$ 8. 2000 K 9. 1.85×10^6

For Solutions, See QR Code on Pg. 209

Mind Map

Thermodynamics

It is the branch of science dealing with different forms of energies and their inter-relationships.

Thermodynamics Properties

These are physical quantities used to define the state of a system.

Intensive - do not depend upon quantity

Extensive - depend upon quantity.

Thermodynamics Processes

- If $dq = 0$, process is adiabatic.
- If $dT = 0$ and $dE = 0$, the process is isothermal.
- If $dV = 0$, process is isochoric
- If $dp = 0$, process is isobaric

Heat, q

It is a path function.

$q = C\Delta T$,

C = Heat capacity and $C_p - C_V = nR$

Work, W

It is the mode of transfer of energy

- $W = -p_{ex}(V_f - V_i)$ (for irreversible process)
- $W = -2.303\ nRT \log \frac{V_f}{V_i}$ (for reversible process).
- In vacuum, $p_{ex} = 0$, so $W = 0$
- It is a path function.
- Work done by the system = – ve
- Work done on the system = + ve

Internal Energy, U

It is the total energy of a system's particles, including their kinetic and potential energy and it is a state function.

System

It is the part that is under thermodynamic studies.

Open system - $\Delta m \neq 0, \Delta E \neq 0$

Closed system - $\Delta m = 0, \Delta E \neq 0$

Isolated system - $\Delta m = 0, \Delta E = 0$

State Functions and Path Functions

- State function are the variable that depend only on initial and final states of a system. e.g., pressure, volume, entropy, etc.
- Path function are the variable which does not depend on path. e.g., work, heat.

Enthalpy, H

It is the total heat content of a system at constant pressure.

$\Delta H = \Delta U + \Delta n_g RT,\ \Delta n_g = n_p - n_R$

Enthalpy Change of a Reaction

It is the enthalpy change when a given reactant reacts completely.

$\Delta_r H = \Sigma H_P - \Sigma H_R$

Standard Enthalpy of Formation

It is the enthalpy change occurring during the formation of 1 mole of a substance from its constituents.

Resonance Energy (RE)

RE = Experimental heat of formation – calculated heat of formation.

Hess's law of Constant heat Summation

$\Delta H = \Delta H_1 + \Delta H_2 + \Delta H_3 + \ldots\ldots\ldots$

Enthalpy Change During Phase Transformation

Enthalpy change occurring during the conversion of 1 mole of a substance from one state to another is called enthalpy change during phase transformation.

First Law of Thermodynamics

Change in internal energy,

$\Delta U = q + W$

- For adiabatic process, $q = 0$
  $\Delta U = W_{ad}$
- Similarly for isochoric process, $\Delta V = 0$
  $W = p\Delta V = 0, \Delta U = q_V$

Second Law of Thermodynamics

It states in a spontaneous process, total entropy of the universe increases.

Entropy, S

It is the measure of randomness, $\Delta S = \frac{\Delta H}{T}$

- For reversible process, $\Delta S_{total} = 0$
- For irreversible process, $\Delta S_{total} > 0$

Gibbs Energy, G

- It is the measure of useful work.
  $\Delta G = \Delta H - T\Delta S$
- For a spontaneous process, ΔG must be –ve.
- If $\Delta G = 0$, process is at equilibrium and $\Delta G^\circ = -RT \ln k$
  Also $\Delta G = -nFE_{cell}$

Third Law of Thermodynamics

Entropy of pure crystalline substance approaches zero as the absolute zero of temperature is approached.

Enthalpies for Different Types of Reactions

Standard Enthalpy of Combustion, $\Delta_c H^\ominus$

It is the enthalpy change when one mole of a substance burnt completely in air.

Enthalpy of Atomisation

The amount of energy needed to break all the bonds in a substance and separate its atoms.

Enthalpy of Solution

$\Delta_{sol} H^\ominus = \Delta_{lattice} H^\ominus + \Delta H^\ominus_{hyd}$

where, $\Delta_{lattice} H^\ominus$

$= \Delta_{sub}H^\circ + \Delta_i H^\circ + \frac{1}{2}\Delta_{dis}H^\circ - \Delta_{eg}H + \Delta_f H^\circ$

Bond Enthalpy

It is the enthalpy change accompanying the breaking of one mole of a specific chemical bond in a molecule.

EXAM PATTERN QUESTIONS

Objective Type Questions

Multiple Choice Questions (MCQs) [1 Mark]

1.

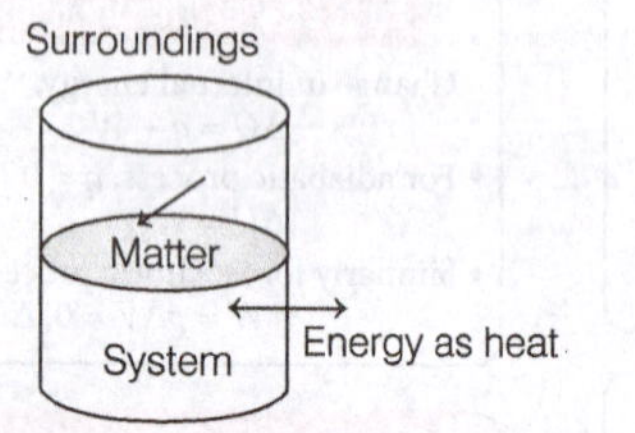

Name the type of wall used in the above figure.

(a) Adiabatic walls

(b) Thermally insulating walls

(c) Thermally conducting walls

(d) None of the above

2. No work is done on the system, but q amount of heat is taken out from the system and given to the surrounding. The change in internal energy of a system is **Competency Based Que.**

(a) $\Delta U = -q$ (b) $\Delta U = +q$

(c) $\Delta U = W_{ad}$ (d) $\Delta U = q - W$

3. Which of the following is an intensive property?

(a) Temperature (b) Viscosity

(c) Surface tension (d) All of these

4. Which of the following is not a state function?

(a) Internal energy (b) Free energy

(c) Work (d) Enthalpy

5. A system that cannot exchange both energy and matter with the surroundings is called

(a) open system (b) Closed system

(c) isolated system (d) None of these

6. Match the following Columns and choose the correct option.

	Column I		Column II
A.	Isothermal process	(i)	$q = \Delta U$
B.	Adiabatic process	(ii)	$W = -p\Delta V$
C.	Isobaric process	(iii)	$W = \Delta U$
D.	Isochoric process	(iv)	$W = nRT \ln\left(\frac{V_2}{V_1}\right)$

(a) A-(iv), B-(ii), C-(iii), D-(i)

(b) A-(iv), B-(iii), C-(ii), D-(i)

(c) A-(i), B-(iii), C-(ii), D-(iv)

(d) A-(iii), B-(i), C-(iv), D-(ii)

7. For an adiabatic process, pressure is related to volume as

(a) $pV = \text{constant}$

(b) $pV^{\gamma} = \text{constant}$

(c) $pV^3 = \text{constant}$

(d) $pV^2 = \text{constant}$

8. Which of the following relations is true if the work is done on an adiabatic wall?

(a) $\Delta U = -W$ (b) $\Delta U = W$

(c) $\Delta U + W = 0$ (d) $\Delta U = -W$

9. The work done in case of isothermal free expansion is

(a) maximum (b) minimum

(c) zero (d) positive

10. Which of the following correctly represents the relation between C_p and C_V for an ideal gas?

(a) $C_V - C_p = R$ (b) $C_V + C_p = R$

(c) $C_p - C_V = RT$ (d) $C_p - C_V = R$

11. The bond dissociation energies of H_2, Cl_2 and HCl are 104, 58 and 103 kcal mol^{-1} respectively. The enthalpy of formation of HCl would be

(a) –22 kcal mol^{-1} (b) – 44 kcal mol^{-1}

(c) +44 kcal mol^{-1} (d) +22 kcal mol^{-1}

12. For the given reaction,

$$CH_4(g) + 2O_2(g) \longrightarrow CO_2(g) + 2H_2O(l)$$

the correct expression for $\Delta_r H$ is **Competency Based Que.**

(a) $[H_m(CO_2, g) + 2H_m(O_2, g)] - [2H_m(H_2O, l) + H_m(CH_4, g)]$

(b) $[2H_m(O_2, g) + H_m(CH_4, g)] - [H_m(CO_2, g) + 2H_m(H_2O, l)]$

(c) $[H_m(CO_2, g) + 2H_m(H_2O, l)] - [H_m(CH_4, g) + 2H_m(O_2, g)]$

(d) $[H_m(CO_2, g) + H_m(H_2O, l)] - [H_m(CH_4, g) + 2H_m(O_2, g)]$

13. If the sublimation energy and enthalpy of fusion of I_2 are 57.3 kJ mol^{-1} and 15.5 kJ mol^{-1}, respectively then, calculate the enthalpy of vaporisation of I_2.

(a) –72.8 kJ mol^{-1} (b) 72.8 kJ mol^{-1}

(c) – 41.8 kJ mol^{-1} (d) +41.8 kJ mol^{-1}

14. **Under which of the following conditions is the relation $\Delta H = \Delta E + p\Delta V$ valid for a closed system?**
(a) Constant pressure
(b) Constant temperature
(c) Constant temperature and pressure
(d) Constant temperature, pressure and composition

15. **Select the incorrect expression from the following.**
(a) $\Delta S_{total} = \Delta S_{system} + \Delta S_{surr}$
(b) $\Delta S_{surr} = \frac{\Delta H_{surr}}{T} = -\frac{\Delta H_{sys}}{T}$
(c) $\Delta S_{total} < 0$ (spontaneous process)
(d) $\Delta G = \Delta H - T\Delta S$

16. **Which of the following expression is correct for a reversible process in a state of equilibrium?**
(a) $\Delta G = -\frac{2.30R}{T}\log K$ (b) $\Delta G = \frac{2.30\,R}{T}\log K$
(c) $\Delta G° = -2.303RT\log K$ (d) $\Delta G° = 2.303RT\log K$

17. **The sign of ΔG for a spontaneous and non-spontaneous process respectively are**
(a) positive and negative (b) negative and positive
(c) zero and positive (d) positive and zero

18. **For both reversible and irreversible expansion of an ideal gas, under isothermal condition,**
Competency Based Que.
(a) $\Delta U = 0, \Delta S_{total} \neq 0$ (b) $\Delta U \neq 0, \Delta S_{total} = 0$
(c) $\Delta U \neq 0, \Delta S_{total} = 0$ (d) $\Delta U \neq 0, \Delta S_{total} \neq 0$

19. **The value of $\Delta_r G°$ is equal to**
(a) $-2.303\,RT\log K$ (b) $+2.303\,RT\log K$
(c) $\Delta_r H° - T\Delta_r S°$ (d) Both (a) and (c)

20. **Free energy change in a reaction and its corresponding equilibrium constant are related as**
(a) $\Delta G = -RT\ln K_C$ (b) $\Delta G° = RT\ln K_C$
(c) $\Delta G° = -RT\ln K_C$ (d) $\Delta G = RT\ln K_C$

21. **Which one of the following reaction has $\Delta S°$ greater than zero?**
(a) $CaO(s) + CO_2(g) \rightleftharpoons CaCO_3(s)$
(b) $NaCl(aq) \rightleftharpoons NaCl(s)$
(c) $NaNO_3(s) \rightleftharpoons Na^+(aq) + NO_3^-(aq)$
(d) $N_2(g) + 3H_2(g) \rightleftharpoons 2NH_3(g)$

22. **The value of entropy in the universe is**
(a) constant (b) decreasing (c) increasing (d) zero

23. **The free energy change for a reversible reaction at equilibrium is**
Diksha
(a) zero (b) positive
(c) negative (d) None of these

Assertion-Reason [1 Mark]

Directions (Q. Nos. 24-31) In the following questions, a statement of Assertion (A) is followed by a corresponding statements of Reason (R) of the following statements, choose the correct one.
(a) Both (A) and (R) are correct and (R) is the correct explanation of (A).
(b) Both (A) and (R) are correct but (R) is not the correct explanation of (A).
(c) (A) is correct and (R) is incorrect.
(d) (A) is incorrect and (R) is correct.

24. **Assertion** (A) In the equation, $H = U + pV$, H is a state function and independent of path.
Reason (R) U, p, V all are state functions.

25. **Assertion** (A) For the combustion of methane $\Delta E < \Delta H$.
Reason (R) ΔH is related to ΔE by the expression.
$$\Delta H = \Delta E + \Delta n_g RT$$

26. **Assertion** (A) The entropy increase when the temperature of a crystalline solid is raised from 0 K to 115 K.
Reason (R) On raising temperature 0 K to 115 K, the constituent particles are more randomly moving.
Competency Based Que.

27. **Assertion** (A) The variables like q, V, T are called state functions.
Reason (R) The values of state function depend only on the state of the system.

28. **Assertion** (A) First law of thermodynamics is identical to the law of conservation of energy.
Reason (R) It states that the total energy of the universe is constant.

29. **Assertion** (A) Enthalpy change for a reaction is same whether it occurs in one step or in a series of steps.
Reason (R) Enthalpy is state function as the change in enthalpy is independent of the path between initial state and final state.

30. **Assertion** (A) For a reaction,
$$2NH_3(g) \longrightarrow N_2(g) + 3H_2(g), \Delta H > \Delta U$$
Reason (R) Enthalpy change is always greater than internal energy change.

31. **Assertion** (A) Internal energy is a state function and extensive property.
Reason (R) Internal energy of a substance depends upon the gravitational force of attraction.

Case-Study [4 Marks]

32. Read the given case and answer the following questions.

Thermodynamics involve energy changes in chemical reactions and other processes. Internal energy is total energy stored in a substance. We can specify absolute value of volume but not the absolute value of internal energy. We can measure only change in internal energy (ΔU). Work done on the system is taken as positive and work done by the system is taken as negative. Heat (q) absorbed by the system +ve and heat given out by system is negative. $\Delta U = q + w$ according to first law of thermodynamics. ΔH (enthalpy change) is measured at constant pressure, ΔU is measured at constant volume. ΔH, ΔS (entropy change), ΔG (free energy change) and temperature help to decide spontaneity of the process.

Competency Based Que.

(i) The heat of combustion of carbon to CO_2 is -393.5 kJ / mol. What is the heat released upon the formation of 35.2 g of CO_2 from carbon and oxygen gas?

(ii) Calculate the enthalpy change for the following reaction.

$$CH_4(g) + 2O_2(g) \longrightarrow CO_2(g) + 2H_2O(l)$$

given enthalpies of formation of CH_4, CO_2 and H_2O are -74.8 kJ mol^{-1}, -393.5 kJ mol^{-1} and -286.2 kJ mol^{-1} respectively.

(a) -890.7 kJ (b) 445.35 kJ
(c) 890 kJ (d) -630 kJ

(iii) $N_2(g) + 3H_2(g) \longrightarrow 2NH_3(g)$. For the above reaction, the relation between ΔH and ΔU is

(a) $\Delta H > \Delta U$
(b) $\Delta H = \Delta U$
(c) $\Delta H < \Delta U$
(d) $\Delta H >> \Delta U$

Or

The standard heat of formation at 298 K for CCl_4 (g), $H_2O(g)$, $CO_2(g)$ and HCl (g) are -25.5, -57.8, -94.1 and -22.1 kcal mol^{-1} respectively. What is $\Delta_r H°$ for the reaction?

$$CCl_4(g) + 2H_2O(g) \longrightarrow CO_2(g) + 4HCl(g)$$

(a) -110 kcal
(b) -41.4 kcal
(c) -520 kcal
(d) 414 kcal

33. Read the given case and answer the following questions.

In a chemical reaction, reactants are converted into products and is represented by, Reactants $\rightarrow$ Products. The enthalpy change accompanying a reaction is called the reaction enthalpy. The enthalpy change of a chemical reaction, is given by the symbol $\Delta_r H$.

$\Delta_r H$ = (sum of enthalpies of products) − (sum of enthalpies of reactants)

$$= \sum_i a_i H_{\text{products}} - \sum_i b_i H_{\text{reactants}}$$

Here symbol Σ (sigma) is used for summation and a_i and b_i are the stoichiometric coefficients of the products and reactants respectively in the balanced chemical equation. For example, for the reaction

$$CH_4(g) + 2O_2(g) \longrightarrow CO_2(g) + 2H_2O(l)$$

$$\Delta_r H = \sum_i a_i H_{\text{products}} - \sum_i b_i H_{\text{reactants}}$$

$$= [H_m(CO_2, g) + 2H_m(H_2O, l)] - [H_m(CH_4, g) + 2H_m(O_2, g)]$$

where H_m is the molar enthalpy. Enthalpy change is a very useful quantity. Knowledge of this quantity is required when one needs to plan the heating or cooling required to maintain an industrial chemical reaction at constant temperature. It is also required to calculate temperature dependence of equilibrium constant.

Standard enthalpy of reactions enthalpy of a reaction depends on the conditions under which a reaction is carried out. It is, therefore necessary that we must specify some standard conditions. The standard enthalpy of reaction is the enthalpy change for a reaction when all the participating substances are in their standard states.

The standard state of a substance at a specified temperature is its pure form at 1 bar. For example, the standard state of liquid ethanol at 298 K is pure liquid ethanol at 1 bar; standard state of solid iron at 500 K is pure iron at 1 bar. Usually data are taken at 298 K. Standard conditions are denoted by adding the superscript 0 to the symbol ΔH, e.g., $\Delta H°$.

Competency Based Que.

(i) Draw enthalpy diagram for endothermic reaction.

(ii) Are all exothermic reaction spontaneous?

Or

Why is molar entropy of vaporisation for water more than ethanol?

(iii) For the reaction, $2Cl(g) \longrightarrow Cl_2(g)$, What are the signs of ΔH and ΔS?

Subjective Type Questions

Short Answer Type I Questions [2 Marks]

1. Show that for an isothermal expansion of an ideal gas (i) $\Delta U = 0$ and (ii) $\Delta H = 0$.

2. Give main differences between a reversible process and an irreversible process.

3. Extensive properties depend on the quantity of matter but intensive properties do not. Explain whether the following properties are extensive or intensive. Mass, internal energy, pressure, heat capacity, molar heat capacity, density, mole fraction, specific heat, temperature and molarity. **NCERT Exemplar**

4. Heat has randomising influence on a system and temperature is the measure of average chaotic motion of particles in the system. Write the mathematical relation which relates these three parameters. **Competency Based Que.**

5. How can you say that universe is going towards chaos?

6. Why for predicting the spontaneity of a reaction, free energy criteria is better than the entropy criteria?

7. Why standard entropy of an elementary substance is not zero whereas standard enthalpy of formation is taken as zero?

8. Why in some reactions heat is evolved while some reactions take place only on absorption of heat?

9. The fact that enthalpy is a state function forms the basis of a very useful law. Name the law.

10. 6.72 dm^3 of an unknown gas at STP requires 113.35 J of heat raise its temperature by 15°C at constant volume. Calculate C_V, C_p and atomicity of the gas.

11. At 60°C, dinitrogen tetraoxide is fifty percent dissociated. Calculate the standard free energy change at this temperature and at one atmosphere. **NCERT Exemplar**

Short Answer Type II Questions [3 Marks]

12. (i) Carbon monoxide is allowed to expand isothermally and reversibly from 10 m^3 to 20 m^3 at 300 K and work obtained is 4.754 kJ. Calculate the number of moles of carbon monoxide.

(ii) 100 mL of a liquid is contained in an insulated container at a pressure of 1 bar. The pressure is steeply increased to 100 bar. The volume of the liquid is decreased by 1 mL at this constant pressure. Find ΔH and ΔU.

13. (i) Enthalpy of combustion of carbon to CO_2 is -393.5 kJ mol^{-1}. Calculate the heat released upon formation of 35.2 g of CO_2 from carbon and dioxygen gas. (Molar mass of CO_2=44 g mol^{-1} **NCERT**

(ii) The value of $\Delta_f H^\ominus$ for NH_3 is –91.8 kJ mol^{-1}. Calculate enthalpy change for the following reaction.

$$2NH_3(g) \longrightarrow N_2(g) + 3H_2(g)$$ **NCERT Exemplar**

14. (i) The enthalpy of formation of carbon monoxide and steam are -110.5 and -243.0 kJ respectively. Calculate the heat of the reaction when steam is passed over coke as

$$C(s) + H_2O(g) \longrightarrow CO(g) + H_2(g)$$

(ii) An average healthy man needs about 10000 kJ of energy per day. How much carbohydrates (in mass) he will have to consume assuming that all this energy needs are met only by carbohydrates in the form of glucose? The enthalpy of combustion of glucose is 2816 kJ mol^{-1}.

15. (i) Find out the value of equilibrium constant for the following reaction at 298 K.

$$2NH_3(g) + CO_2(g) \rightleftharpoons NH_2CONH_2(aq) + H_2O(l)$$

Standard Gibbs energy change, $\Delta G^\ominus$ at the given temperature is -13.6 kJ mol^{-1}. **NCERT**

(ii) Calculate the free energy change when 1 mole of NaCl is dissolved in water at 298 K. (Given, lattice energy of NaCl $= -777.8$ kJ mol^{-1}, hydration energy $= -774.1$ kJ mol^{-1} and $\Delta S = 0.043$ kJ $K^{-1} mol^{-1}$ at 298 K).

16. (i) When 20.0 g of ammonium nitrate (NH_4NO_3) is dissolved in 125 g of water in a coffee cup calorimeter, the temperature falls from 296.5 K to 286.4 K. Find the value of q for the calorimeter. (Treat heat capacity of water as the heat capacity of the calorimeter and its contents).

(ii) A chemist while studying the properties of gaseous CCl_2F_2, a chlorofluorocarbon refrigerant, cooled a 1.25 g sample at constant atmospheric pressure of 1.0 atm from 320 K to 293 K. During cooling, the sample volume decreased from 274 to 248 mL. Calculate ΔH and ΔU for the chlorofluorocarbon for this process. For CCl_2F_2, $C_p = 80.7$ J/(mol K). **Competency Based Que.**

17. The figure given below represents pV diagram of different stages of a thermodynamic process. Calculate the work done in each stage and also the net work done in the complete cyclic process.

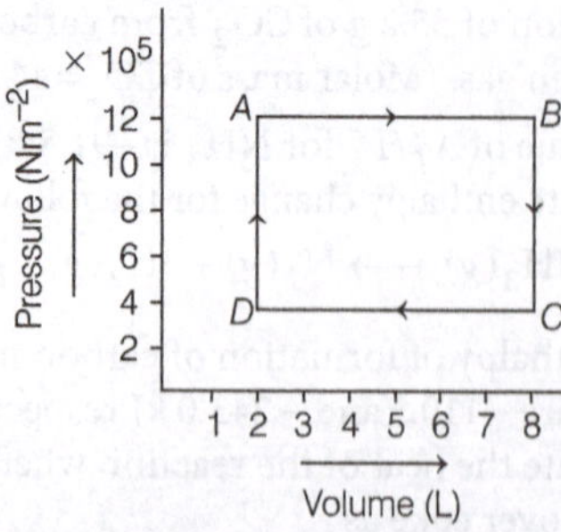

18. (i) An athlete is given 100 g of glucose of energy equivalent to 1560 kJ. He utilises 50% of this gained energy in the event. In order to avoid storage of energy in the body, calculate the weight of water that would need to perspire. The enthalpy of vaporisation of water is 44 kJ mol^{-1}.

(ii) Compound with carbon-carbon double bond, such as ethylene, C_2H_4, add hydrogen in a reaction called hydrogenation,

$$C_2H_4(g) + H_2(g) \longrightarrow C_2H_6(g)$$

Calculate enthalpy change for the reaction, using the following combustion data

$$C_2H_4(g) + 3O_2(g) \longrightarrow 2CO_2(g) + 2H_2O(l);$$
$$\Delta_c H^\circ = -1401 \text{ kJ mol}^{-1} \quad \ldots\text{(i)}$$

$$C_2H_6(g) + \frac{7}{2}O_2(g) \longrightarrow 2CO_2(g) + 3H_2O(l);$$
$$\Delta_c H^\circ = -1550 \text{ kJ mol}^{-1} \quad \ldots\text{(ii)}$$

$$H_2(g) + \frac{1}{2}O_2(g) \longrightarrow H_2O(l);$$
$$\Delta_c H^\circ = -286.0 \text{ kJ mol}^{-1} \quad \ldots\text{(iii)}$$

Competency Based Que.

19. (i) A cylinder of gas supplied by a company is assumed to contain 14 kg of butane. If a normal family requires 20000 kJ of energy per day for cooking, how long will the cylinder last?

(ii) If the air supplied to the burner is insufficient, a portion of gas escapes without combustion. Assuming that 25% of the gas is wasted due to this inefficiency, how long will the cylinder last (Heat of combustion of butane = 2658 kJ/mol)?

20. Sodium carbonate, Na_2CO_3 can be obtained by heating sodium hydrogen carbonate, $NaHCO_3$ as

$$2NaHCO_3(s) \longrightarrow Na_2CO_3(s) + H_2O(g) + CO_2(g).$$

The essential data are

	$NaHCO_3(s)$	$Na_2CO_3(s)$	$CO_2(g)$	$H_2O(g)$
$\Delta_f H^\circ$ (kJ mol^{-1})	−947.7	−1130.9	−393.51	−241.82
S°_m (J mol^{-1})	102.1	136	188.83	213.74

Calculate the temperature above which $NaHCO_3$ decomposes to give products at 1 bar. **Competency Based Que.**

Long Answer Type Questions [5 Marks]

21. Write expression for the work done by 1 mole of the gas in each of the following case.

(i) For irreversible expansion of the gas from volume V_1 to V_2.

(ii) For reversible isothermal expansion of the gas from volume V_1 to V_2.

(iii) For expansion of the gas into an evacuated vessel.

22. ΔG is net energy available to do useful work and is thus a measure of "free energy". Show mathematically that ΔG is a measure of free energy. Find the unit of ΔG. If a reaction has positive enthalpy change and positive entropy change, under what condition will the reaction be spontaneous? **NCERT Exemplar**

23. (i) Comment on the spontaneity of a reaction at constant temperature and pressure in the following cases

(a) $\Delta H < 0$ and $\Delta S > 0$ (b) $\Delta H > 0$ and $\Delta S < 0$

(c) $\Delta H < 0$ and $\Delta S < 0$ (d) $\Delta H > 0$ and $\Delta S > 0$

(ii) Give difference between spontaneous and non-spontaneous processes by giving examples.

24. (i) Establish a relationship between ΔH and ΔU in Haber's process of synthesis of ammonia assuming that gaseous reactants and products are ideal.

(ii) Acetic acid (ethanoic acid) and hydrochloric acid react with KOH solution. The enthalpy of neutralisation of ethanoic acid is −55.8 kJ mol^{-1} while that of hydrochloric acid is −57.3 kJ mol^{-1}. Can you think of why are these different?

25. (i) Air contains about 99% of N_2 and O_2 gases. Why do not they combine to form NO under the standard conditions? Standard Gibbs energy of formation of NO(g) is 86.7 kJ mol^{-1}

(ii) Using the data (all values are in kilocalories per mole at 25°C) given below, calculate the bond energy of C—C and C—H bonds.

ΔH° combustion (ethane) = −372.0

ΔH° combustion (propane) = −530.0

ΔH° for C (graphite) $\longrightarrow$ C(g) = 172.0

Bond energy of H—H = 104.0

$\Delta_f H^\circ$ of $H_2O(l)$ = − 68.0; ΔH° for $CO_2(g)$ = −94.0

Hints & Solutions

Objective Type Questions

1. (c) The wall used in the given diagram is thermally conducting walls.
2. (a) When no work is done on the system, but q amount of heat is taken out from the system and given to the surrounding then for the formula, $\Delta U = q + W$

$$W = 0$$

$$\therefore \quad \Delta U = -q$$

(ΔU is −ve as heat is taken out from the system and given to surroundings).
3. (d) The properties of the system whose value is independent of the amount of substance present in the system are called intensive properties, e.g. viscosity, surface tension, temperature, pressure, etc.
4. (c) Work is a path function i.e. amount of work done depends on the path taken to reach a final state.
5. (c) An isolated system cannot exhange either matter or energy with its surroundings.
6. (b) Isothermal process – $W = nRT \ln\left(\frac{V_2}{V_1}\right)$

Adibatic process – $W = \Delta U$

Isobaric process – $W = -p\Delta V$

Isochoric process – $q = \Delta U$
7. (b) For adiabatic process, $pV^{\gamma} = \text{constant}$
8. (b) For adiabatic process

$W = \Delta U$ or $\Delta U = W$
9. (c) In case of isothermal free expansion, $W = 0$
10. (d) For ideal gas, $C_p - C_V = R$
11. (a) For the reaction,

$$\frac{1}{2}H_2 + \frac{1}{2}Cl_2 \longrightarrow HCl$$

$$\Delta_f H_{(HCl)} = \Delta H_{\text{reactant}} - \Delta H_{\text{product}}$$

$$= \frac{1}{2}(104) + \frac{1}{2}(58) - 103$$

$$= 52 + 29 - 103 = -22 \text{ kcal/mol}$$

Mistake Alert *One can make a mistake in calculating $\Delta_f H°$ using bond dissociation energies, as only in this we subtract product's energy from reactant's energy and not vice-versa.*

12. (c) For the reaction,

$$CH_4(g) + 2O_2(g) \longrightarrow CO_2(g) + 2H_2O(l)$$

The correct expression for $\Delta_r H$ is

$$[H_m(CO_2, g] + 2H_m(H_2O, l)] - [H_m(CH_4, g) + 2H_m(O_2, g)]$$
13. (d) As, $\Delta_{\text{sub}} H_{I_2} = \Delta_{\text{fus}} H_{I_2} + \Delta_{\text{vap}} H_{I_2}$

$$57.3 = 15.5 + \Delta_{\text{vap}} H_{I_2}$$

$$\Delta_{\text{vap}} H_{I_2} = 57.3 - 15.5 = 41.8 \text{ kJ mol}^{-1}$$
14. (a) $H = E + pV$

$\therefore \Delta H = \Delta E + p\Delta V + V\Delta p$

At constant p, $V\Delta p = 0$

and $\Delta H = \Delta E + p\Delta V$
15. (c) Among the given option the incorrect expression is $\Delta S_{\text{total}} < 0$ (spontaneous process). The correct expression is $\Delta S_{\text{total}} > 0$ (spontaneous process).
16. (c) $\Delta G° = -2.303 RT \log K$
17. (b) The sign of ΔG for a spontaneous and non-spontaneous process are negative and positive respectively.
18. (a) $\Delta U = 0$, $\Delta S_{\text{total}} \neq 0$
19. (d) $\Delta_r G° = -2.303 RT \log K$

$$= \Delta_r H° - T\Delta_r S°$$
20. (c) $\Delta G° = -RT \ln K_c$
21. (c) Among the given option the entropy in case of (c) is greater than zero. As in this case, reactant is present in solid form and product is present in aqueous form.
22. (c) The value of entropy in the universe is increasing. (Second law of thermodynamics)
23. (a) At equilibrium, $\Delta G = 0$.
24. (a) Both (A) and (R) are correct and (R) is the correct explanation of (A).
25. (d) Combustion of methane is

$$CH_4(g) + 2O_2(g) \longrightarrow CO_2(g) + 2H_2O(l)$$

The relation between ΔH and ΔE is $\Delta H = \Delta E + \Delta n_g RT$

$$\Delta n_g = n_p - n_r = 1 - 3 = -2$$

$$\Delta H = \Delta E - 2RT$$

$$\Delta H < \Delta E$$

Thus, (A) is incorrect and (R) is correct.
26. (a) Both (A) and (R) are correct and (R) is the correct explanation of (A). The entropy increase when the temperature of a crystalline solid is raised (from 0 K to 115 K) as randomness increases.
27. (d) (A) is incorrect while (R) is correct. Among the given variable functions, q is not the state function, it is the path function.
28. (a) Both the statements are correct and (R) is the correct explanation of (A).
29. (a) Both (A) and (R) are correct and (R) is the correct explanation of (A).
30. (c) (A) is correct and (R) is incorrect.

For the reaction,

$$2NH_3(g) \longrightarrow N_2(g) + 3H_2(g)$$

$$\Delta H = \Delta U + \Delta n_g RT$$

$\Delta n = 4 - 2 = 2$

$\Delta H > \Delta U$

Both enthalpy change is not always greater than internal energy change.

31. (c) (A) is correct and (R) is incorrect. The correct Reason is internal energy depends on the initial and final stages of the substance and not on gravitational force of attraction.

32. (i) $C(s) + O_2(g) \longrightarrow CO_2(g); \Delta H = -393.5$ kJ / mol

Molecular weight of CO_2 = 1 mole of CO_2 = 44 kg

Amount of heat released in formation of 44 g CO_2

$= 393.5$ kJ (1)

$\therefore$ Amount of heat released on formation of 35.2 g CO_2

$= \frac{393.5}{44} \times 35.2 = 314.8 \simeq 315$ kJ (1)

(ii) (a) $\Delta H^\circ = [\Delta H^\circ_{f\,(\text{products})} - \Delta H^\circ_{f\,(\text{reactants})}]$

$= [\Delta H^\circ_{(CO_2)} + 2\Delta H^\circ_{(H_2O)}] - [\Delta H^\circ_{(CH_4)} + 2\Delta H^\circ_{(O_2)}]$

$= [-393.5 + 2 \times (-286.2)] - [-74.8 + 2 \times 0]$

$= -891.1$ kJ (1)

(iii) (c) $\Delta n_g = 2 - 4 = -2$

$\Delta H = \Delta U + \Delta n_g RT = \Delta U - 2RT$

$\Delta H < \Delta U$ (1)

Or

(b) $[\Delta H_{f\,(CO_2)} - \Delta H_{f\,(HCl)}] - [\Delta H_{f\,(CCl_4)} - \Delta H_{f\,(H_2O)}]$

$= [-94.1 + 4 \times (-22.1)] - [-25.5 + 2(-57.8)]$

$= -41.4$ kcal (1)

33. (i) Chemical reactions that absorb energy is endothermic reaction.

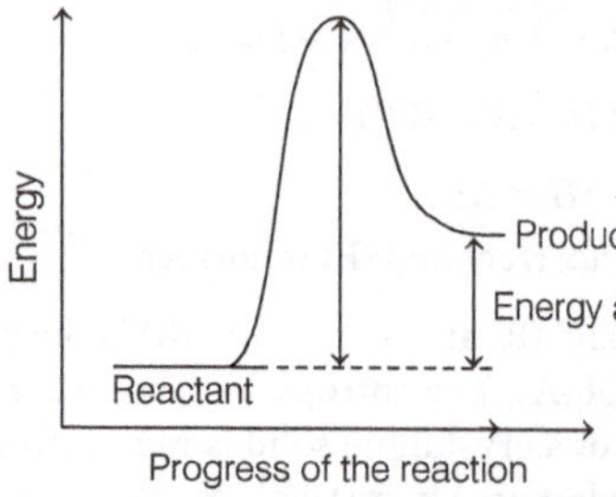

(2)

(ii) Thermodynamically an exothermic reaction is sometimes not spontaneous. (1)

Or

The molar enthalpy of vaporisation for water is more than ethanol. It is due to the pressure of hydrogen bonding present in water molecule. (1)

(iii) For the reaction, $2Cl(g) \longrightarrow Cl_2(g)$

The ΔH value is negative, as there is the formation of chlorine molecule from chlorine atoms. Thus, in this case bond formation takes place.

As, two moles of chlorine atoms have more randomness than one mole of a chlorine molecule.

Thus, in this case the randomness decreases from reactant to product. Thus, ΔS value is negative for the given reaction. (1)

Part-II

1. (i) For one mole of an ideal gas, $C_V = (\Delta U / \Delta T)_V$

or $\Delta U = C_V \Delta T$

For an isothermal process, T is constant so $\Delta T = 0$

$\therefore \Delta U = 0$ (1)

(ii) $\Delta H = \Delta U + \Delta(pV)$

For an ideal gas, $pV = RT$

$\therefore \Delta H = \Delta U + \Delta(RT)$

$= \Delta U + R\Delta T$

Since T is constant, $\Delta T = 0$

$\therefore \Delta H = 0$ $[\because \Delta U = 0]$ (1)

2. Refer to text on page 177.

3. **Extensive properties** Those properties whose value depends on the quantity or size of matter present in the system is known as extensive properties, e.g. **mass, internal energy, heat capacity.** (1)

Intensive properties Those properties which do not depend on the quantity or size of matter present are known as intensive properties, e.g. **pressure, molar heat capacity, density, mole fraction, specific heat, temperature and molarity**. Mole fraction or molarity of a solution is same whether we take a small amount of the solution or large amount of the solution. Ratio of two extensive properties is always intensive.

$$\frac{\text{Extensive}}{\text{Extensive}} = \text{Intensive}$$

So, mole fraction and molarity are intensive properties. (1)

e.g. Mole fraction $= \frac{\text{Moles of the component}}{\text{Total number of moles}} = \frac{\text{Extensive}}{\text{Extensive}}$

and Molarity $= \frac{\text{Mole}}{\text{Volume}} = \frac{\text{Extensive}}{\text{Extensive}}$

Intensive properties cannot be added or subtracted directly. Only extensive properties can be added or subtracted.

4. Heat has randomising influence on a system and temperature is the measure of average chaotic motion of particles in the system.

The mathematical relation which relates these three parameters is $\Delta S = q_{rev}/T$ (1)

Here, ΔS = change in entropy

q_{rev} = heat of reversible reaction

T = temperature (1)

5. Most of the naturally occurring processes are accompanied by increase of randomness. Hence, randomness of the universe is continuously increasing. Thus, we are going towards chaos. (2)

6. Criteria of free energy change is better because it requires free energy change of the system only whereas the entropy change requires the total entropy change of the system and the surroundings. **(2)**

7. A substance has a perfectly ordered arrangement of its constituent particles only at absolute zero. Hence, entropy is zero only at absolute zero. Enthalpy of formation is the heat change involed in the formation of one mole of the substance from its elements. An element formed from itself means no heat change, i.e. $\Delta_f H° = 0$. **(2)**

8. Every substance has energy stored in it in the form of heat content. If heat content of reactants (H_R) is greater than that of products (H_P), heat is evolved. If $H_R < H_P$, heat is absorbed. **(2)**

9. Hess's law of heat summation. **(2)**

10. $22.4\ dm^3$ of a gas at STP = 1 mol

$\therefore 6.72\ dm^3$ of the gas at STP $= \frac{1}{22.4} \times 6.72 = 0.3$ mol

Thus, for 15° rise, 0.3 mol of the gas at constant volume require heat = 113.35 J

$\therefore$ For 1° rise, 1 mole of the gas at constant volume will require heat $= \frac{113.35}{15 \times 0.3}$ J = 25.19 J

$\therefore \quad C_V = 25.19\ JK^{-1} mol^{-1}$ **(1/2)**

Now, $C_p = C_V + R = 25.19\ JK^{-1}\ mol^{-1} + 8.314\ JK^{-1}\ mol^{-1}$
$= 33.5\ JK^{-1}\ mol^{-1}$ **(1/2)**

$\therefore \quad \gamma = \frac{C_p}{C_V} = \frac{33.5}{25.19} = 1.33.$ **(1/2)**

Hence, the gas is triatomic. **(1/2)**

11. $N_2O_4(g) \rightleftharpoons 2\ NO_2(g)$

If N_2O_4 is 50% dissociated,

$$x_{N_2O_4} = \frac{1-0.5}{1+0.5} \Rightarrow x_{NO_2} = \frac{2 \times 0.5}{1+0.5}$$

$$p_{N_2O_4} = \frac{0.5}{1.5} \times 1\,atm,\ p_{NO_2} = \frac{1}{1.5} \times 1\,atm.$$

The equilibrium constant K_p is given by

$$K_p = \frac{(p_{NO_2})^2}{p_{N_2O_4}} = \frac{1.5}{(1.5)^2\ (0.5)} = 1.33\ atm$$ **(1)**

Since, $\Delta_r G^\ominus = -RT \ln K_p$

$\Delta_r G^\ominus = (-8.314\ JK^{-1}\ mol^{-1}) \times (333\ K) \times (2.303) \times (0.1239)$
$= -789.99\ kJ\ mol^{-1}$ **(1)**

12. (i) $W = -2.303\ nRT \log \frac{V_2}{V_1}$

$$-4754 = -2.303 \times n \times 8.314 \times 300 \times \log \frac{20}{10}$$

On solving, $n = 2.75$ mol **(1)**

(ii) $p_1 = 1$ bar, $p_2 = 100$ bar, $V_1 = 100$ mL, $V_2 = 99$ mL

For adiabatic process, $q = 0$, $\Delta U = q + W$

$$\Delta U = W$$

$W = -p\Delta V = -100\,(99 - 100) = 100$ bar mL **(1)**

$\Delta H = \Delta U + \Delta pV = 100 + p_2V_2 - p_1V_1$
$= 100 + (100 \times 99) - (1 \times 100)$
$= 100 + 9900 - 100 = 9900$ bar mL **(1)**

13. (i) The reaction for the combustion of carbon into CO_2 is

$$C(s) + O_2(g) \longrightarrow \underset{44\,g}{CO_2(g)};\ \Delta H = -393.5\ kJ\ mol^{-1}$$

Heat released in the formation of 44 g CO_2 = 393.5 kJ

$\therefore$ Heat released in the formation of 35.2 g CO_2

$$= \frac{393.5\ kJ \times 35.2\ g}{44\ g} = 314.8\ kJ$$ **(1)**

(ii) Given,

$$\frac{1}{2}N_2(g) + \frac{3}{2}H_2(g) \longrightarrow NH_3(g);$$
$$\Delta_f H^\ominus = -91.8\ kJ\ mol^{-1}$$

($\Delta_f H^\ominus$ means enthalpy of formation of 1 mole of NH_3)

$\therefore$ Enthalpy change for the formation of 2 moles of NH_3

$$N_2(g) + 3H_2(g) \longrightarrow 2NH_3(g);$$
$$\Delta_f H^\ominus = 2 \times -91.8 = -183.6\ kJ\ mol^{-1}$$ **(1)**

And for the reverse reaction,

$$2NH_3(g) \longrightarrow N_2(g) + 3H_2(g);$$
$$\Delta_f H^\ominus = +183.6\ kJ\ mol^{-1}$$ **(1)**

14. (i) We are given

(i) $C(s) + \frac{1}{2}O_2(g) \longrightarrow CO(g);\ \Delta H = -110.5$ kJ

(ii) $H_2(g) + \frac{1}{2}O_2(g) \longrightarrow H_2O\,(g);\ \Delta H = -243.0$ kJ

Subtracting Eq. (ii) from Eq. (i), we get

$C(s) + H_2O(g) \longrightarrow CO(g) + H_2(g);\ \Delta H = +132.5$ kJ **(1)**

(ii) Enthalpy of combustion of glucose = 2816 kJ mol^{-1}

Molecular mass of glucose ($C_6H_{12}O_6$)

$= 6 \times 12 + 12 \times 1 + 6 \times 16 = 180\,g\ mol^{-1}$ **(1)**

2816 kJ of energy is evolved from glucose = 180 g

10000 kJ of energy will be evolved from glucose

$$= \frac{180}{2816} \times 10000 = 639.20\ g$$ **(1)**

15. (i) $\log K = \frac{-\Delta_r G^\ominus}{2.303\ RT} = \frac{-(-13.6 \times 10^3)}{2.303 \times 8.314 \times 298} = 2.38$

Hence, K = antilog 2.38 = 2.4×10^2 **(1)**

(ii) ΔH = hydration energy − lattice energy

$\Delta H = -774.1\ kJ\ mol^{-1} - (-777.8\ kJ\ mol^{-1}) = 3.7\ kJ\ mol^{-1}$ **(1)**

$\Delta G = \Delta H - T\Delta S = +3.7 - 298 \times 0.043 = +3.7 - 12.81$

$\Delta G = -9.11\ kJ\ mol^{-1}$ **(1)**

16. (i) As heat capacity of water = heat capacity of calorimeter, the heat gained by water = heat lost by calorimeter

$$= 125 \times (286.4 - 296.5) \times 4.184 \text{ J}$$

$$= -5282 \text{ J} = -5.282 \text{ kJ}$$ **(1)**

(ii) $\Delta H = q_p$ and C_p is heat evolved or absorbed per mole for 1° fall or rise in temperature. Here, fall in temperature (320 − 293) = 27 K.

Molar mass of $CCl_2F_2 = 12 + 2\times 35.5 + 2\times 19 = 121 \text{ g mol}^{-1}$ **(1/2)**

∴ Heat evolved from 1.25 g of the sample on being cooled from 320 K to 293 K at constant pressure

$$= \frac{80.7}{121} \times 1.25 \times 27 \text{ J} = 22.51 \text{ J}$$ **(1/2)**

Further, $\Delta H = \Delta U + p\Delta V = -22.51 \text{ J}$

$$\left[\because p\Delta V = 1 \text{ atm} \times \frac{(248 - 274)}{1000} \text{ L} = -0.026 \text{ L atm}\right]$$

$$= -0.026 \times 101.325 \text{ J} = -2.63 \text{ J}$$

∴ $-22.51 = \Delta U - 2.63 \text{ J}$

or $\Delta U = -22.51 + 2.63 \text{ J} = -19.88 \text{ J}$ **(1)**

17. Process $A \longrightarrow B$ (expansion),

$$p = 12\times 10^5 \text{ Nm}^{-2}, \Delta V = 8 - 2 = 6 \text{ L} = 6\times 10^{-3} \text{ m}^3$$

∴ Work done $= -p\Delta V$

$$= -(12\times 10^5)\times(6\times 10^{-3}) \text{ J} = -7200 \text{ J}$$ **(1/2)**

Process $B \longrightarrow C$. No change in volume, i.e. $\Delta V = 0$.

∴ Work done = 0 **(1/2)**

Process $C \longrightarrow D$ (contraction),

$$\Delta V = 8 - 2 = 6\text{L} = 6\times 10^{-3} \text{ m}^3,$$

$$p = 4\times 10^5 \text{ Nm}^{-2}$$

∴ Work done,

$$p\Delta V = (4\times 10^5)(6\times 10^{-3}) = 2400 \text{ J}$$ **(1/2)**

Process $D \rightarrow A$. No change in volume, i.e. $\Delta V = 0$

∴ Work done = 0 **(1/2)**

∴ Net work done in the complete cyclic process

$$= -7200 + 2400 \text{ J}$$

$$= -4800 \text{ J}$$ **(1)**

Minus sign shows that net work has been done by the system

18. (i) 100 g of glucose is equivalent to 1560 kJ of energy. Energy utilised in the event, i.e. the remaining 50% must be dissipated as heat.

$$= \frac{1560 \times 50}{100} = 780 \text{ kJ}$$

Energy left unutilised = 1560 − 780 = 780 kJ

Enthalpy of vaporisation of water = 44 kJ/mol

1 mole of water absorbs 44 kJ when evaporated moles of water $= \frac{780}{44} = 17.73$ moles.

Mass of water required to perspire

$$= 17.73 \times 18 = 319.14 \simeq 319 \text{ g or } 0.319 \text{ kg.}$$ **(1)**

(ii) Adding Eqs. (i) and (iii) and substract Eq. (ii),

$$C_2H_4(g) + 3\,O_2(g) + H_2(g) + \frac{1}{2}O_2(g) - C_2H_6(g)$$

$$-\frac{7}{2}O_2(g) \longrightarrow 2\,CO_2(g) + 2\,H_2O\,(l) + H_2O(l)$$

$$-2\,CO_2\,(g) - 3\,H_2O(l)$$

and $\Delta_r H° = -1401 \text{ kJ mol}^{-1} - 286.0 \text{ kJ mol}^{-1} - (-1550 \text{ kJ mol}^{-1})$ **(1)**

These equations give,

$$C_2H_2(g) + H_2(g) \longrightarrow C_2H_6(g);$$

$$\Delta_r H° = -137 \text{ kJ mol}^{-1}$$ **(1)**

19. (i) Molecular formula of butane = C_4H_{10}

Molecular mass of butane = $4\times 12 + 10\times 1 = 58$

Heat of combustion of butane = 2658 kJ mol^{-1}

1 mole or 58 g of butane on complete combustion gives heat = 2658 kJ

∴ 14×10^3 g of butane on complete combustion will give heat $= \frac{2658 \times 14 \times 10^3}{58} = 641586$ **(1/2)**

The family needs 20000 kJ of heat per day.

∵ 20000 kJ of heat is used for cooking by a family in 1 day

∴ 641586 kJ of heat will be used for cooking by a family in $= \frac{641586}{20000} = 32$ days **(1)**

The cylinder will last for 32 days.

(ii) 25 per cent of the gas is wasted due to inefficiency. This means that only 75% of butane gets combusted. Therefore, the energy produced by 75% combustion of butane

$$= \frac{641586 \times 75}{100} = 481189.5 \text{ kJ}$$ **(1/2)**

∴ The number of days the cylinder will last.

$$= \frac{481189.50}{20000} = 24 \text{ days}$$ **(1)**

20. $2NaHCO_3(s) \longrightarrow Na_2CO_3(s) + CO_2(g) + H_2O(g)$

$$\Delta_r H° = \Delta_f H°(Na_2CO_3) + \Delta_f H°(CO_2) + \Delta_r H°(H_2O) - 2\Delta_f H°(NaHCO_3)$$

$$= -1130.9 + (-393.51) + (-241.82) - 2\times(-947.7)$$

$$= -1766.23 + 1895.4 = 129.17 \text{ kJ mol}^{-1}$$ **(1)**

$$\Delta_r S° = \Delta_r S°_m(Na_2CO_3) + S°_m(CO_2) + S°_m(H_2O) - 2S°_m(NaHCO_3)$$

$= 136.0 + 188.83 + 213.74 - 2 \times 102.1$

$= 538.57 - 204.2 = 334.37\ \text{J K}^{-1}\text{mol}^{-1}$ **(1)**

From second law of thermodynamics,

$$\Delta_r S^\circ = \frac{\Delta_r H^\circ}{T}$$

$$\therefore \quad T = \frac{\Delta_r H^\circ}{\Delta_r S^\circ} = \frac{129.17}{334.37 \times 10^{-3}} = 386.3\ \text{K}$$

∴ Reaction will be spontaneous above 386.3 K. **(1)**

21. (i) Irreversible expansion takes place when external pressure (p_{ext}) remains constant

$$W_{irrev} = -p_{ext}(V_2 - V_1) = -p_{ext}\Delta V \quad \textbf{(2)}$$

(ii) Reversible expansion takes place when internal pressure is infinitesimally greater than external pressure at every stage.

$$W_{rev} = -nRT \ln \frac{V_2}{V_1} \quad \textbf{(2)}$$

(iii) The expansion is irreversible. Further, as $p_{ext} = 0$, therefore, $W = -p_{ext}\Delta V = 0 \times (\Delta V) = 0$ **(1)**

22. Refer to text on pages 196 and 197.

23. (i) Refer to text on pages 196 and 197.

(ii) Refer to text on pages 196.

24. (i) Haber's process of synthesis for ammonia is

$$N_2(g) + 3H_2(g) \longrightarrow 2NH_3(g)$$

$$\Delta n_g = 2 - (1 + 3) = -2 \quad \textbf{(1)}$$

But $\quad \Delta H = \Delta U + \Delta n_g RT$

$\therefore \quad \Delta H = \Delta U - 2RT$ **(1)**

(ii) The thermochemical equations for the neutralisation of acetic acid and hydrochloric acids are,

$CH_3COOH(aq) + KOH(aq) \longrightarrow CH_3COOK(aq) + H_2O(l);\ \Delta_n H^\circ = -55.8\ \text{kJ mol}^{-1}$

and $HCl\,(aq) + KOH\,(aq) \longrightarrow KCl(aq) + H_2O\,(l);$
$\Delta_n H^\circ = -57.3\ \text{kJ mol}^{-1}$ **(1)**

In dilute solution, HCl is completely ionised into H^+ and Cl^-, whereas CH_3COOH is ionised to very small extent. This difference between the enthalpy of neutralisation of the two acids is due to the endothermic nature of the reaction involving the ionisation of acetic acid, i.e. **(1)**

$$CH_3COOH(aq) \rightleftharpoons CH_3COO^-(aq) + H^+(aq)$$

$\Delta_{ion} H^\circ = -55.8 - (-57.3)\ \text{kJ mol}^{-1} = 1.5\ \text{kJ mol}^{-1}$ **(1)**

25. (i) For the combination of N_2 and O_2 to form NO, the standard Gibbs energy of formation is +ve.

$$\frac{1}{2} N_2(g) + \frac{1}{2} O_2(g) \longrightarrow NO\,(g) \quad \textbf{(1)}$$

$$(\Delta_f G^\circ_{NO} = +86.7\ \text{kJ mol}^{-1})$$

Therefore, this reaction is non-spontaneous under the standard conditions and hence N_2 and O_2 do not combine.

(ii) We are given

(a) $C_2H_6(g) + \frac{7}{2} O_2(g) \longrightarrow 2CO_2(g) + 3H_2O;$
$\Delta H^\circ = -372.0$ kcal

(b) $C_3H_8(g) + 5\,O_2(g) \longrightarrow 3\,CO_2(g) + 4\,H_2O;$
$\Delta H^\circ = -530.0$ kcal

(c) $C\,(s) \longrightarrow C\,(g);\ \Delta H^\circ = 172.0$ kcal

(d) $H_2(g) \longrightarrow 2\,H(g);\ \Delta H^\circ = 104.0$ kcal

(e) $H_2(g) + \frac{1}{2} O_2(g) \longrightarrow H_2O(l);\ \Delta H^\circ = -68.0$ kcal

(f) $C\,(s) + O_2(g) \longrightarrow CO_2(g);\ \Delta H^\circ = -94.0$ kcal

Suppose the bond energy of C—C bond $= x$ kcal mol^{-1} and that of C—H bond $= y$ kcal mol^{-1}. Then for $C_2H_6(g)$,

i.e. 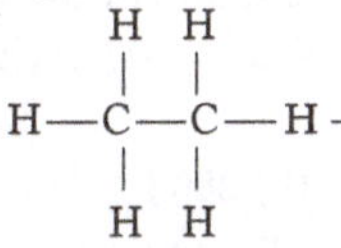 $\longrightarrow 2\,C\,(g) + 6\,H;\ \Delta H = x + 6y$ ...(vii)

and for $C_3H_8(g)$; i.e.

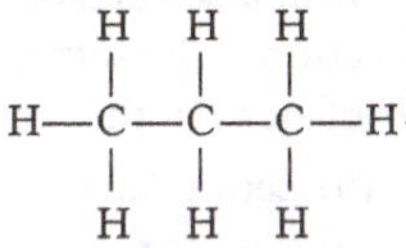 $\longrightarrow 3\,C\,(g) + 8\,H\,(g);$
$\Delta H = 2x + 8y$ ...(viii)

To get Eq. (vii), operate Eq. (i) + 2 × Eq. (iii) + 3 × Eq. (iv) − 3 × Eq. (v) − 2 × Eq. (vi).

It gives $\Delta H = 676$ kcal **(1)**

To get Eq. (viii), operate Eq. (ii) + Eq. (iii) + 4 × Eq (iv) − 4 × Eq. (v) − 3 × Eq. (vi)

It gives $\Delta H = 956$ kcal

Thus, $\quad x + 6y = 676, \quad 2x + 8y = 956$ **(1)**

On solving these equations, we get $x = 82,\ y = 99$ **(1)**

Hence, C—C bond energy = 82 kcal mol^{-1} and C—H bond energy = 99 kcal mol^{-1}. **(1)**

QR Code for Quick Test 1

QR Code for Quick Test 2

QR Code for Quick Test 3

SELF ASSESSMENT TEST

Objective Type Questions [1 Mark]

1. If the enthalpy change for a reaction is negative, the reaction is
   (a) endothermic (b) exothermic
   (c) isothermal (d) adiabatic

2. What is the relationship between the change in internal energy (ΔU), work done (W) and heat exchanged (q) in a system?
   (a) $\Delta U = W + q$ (b) $\Delta U = q - W$
   (c) $\Delta U = q + W$ (d) $\Delta U = W - q$

3. A gas expands against a constant external pressure of 1 atm from 3 L to 8 L. Calculate the work done by the gas. (1 L·atm = 101.3 J)
   (a) 506.5 J (b) 506 J
   (c) – 506.5 J (d) – 506 J

4. If the heat capacity at constant pressure (C_p) of a gas is 29 J/(mol·K) and the temperature of 2 moles of the gas is increased by 10 K, what is the change in enthalpy (ΔH)?
   (a) 580 J (b) 290 J
   (c) 350 J (d) 600 J

5. Which law states that the heat absorbed or released in a chemical reaction is the same, regardless of the number of steps in the reaction?
   (a) Hess's Law (b) Zeroth Law
   (c) First Law (d) Second Law

Assertion-Reason [1 Mark]

■ **Directions** (Q. Nos. 6-8) In the following questions. an Assertion (A) is followed by a corresponding Reason (R). Use the following keys to choose the appropriate answer.

(a) Both (A) and (R) are true and (R) is the correct explanation of (A).
(b) Both (A) and (R) are true and (R) is not the correct explanation of (A).
(c) (A) is true but (R) is false.
(d) (A) is false but (R) is true.

6. **Assertion** (A) In an isothermal process, the temperature of the system remains constant.

   Reason (R) In an isothermal process, heat absorbed by the system is equal to the work done by the system.

7. **Assertion** (A) Addition of Q and W gives ΔU.

   Reason (R) Addition of two path functions cannot give state function.

8. **Assertion** (A) The second law of thermodynamics states that the total entropy of an isolated system always increases.

   Reason (R) Entropy is a measure of the disorder of a system, and natural processes tend to move towards higher disorder.

Short Answer Type I Questions [2 Marks]

9. A sample of 1.0 mole of a monoatomic ideal gas is taken through a cyclic process of expansion and compression as shown in the figure. What will be the value of ΔH for the cycle as a whole?

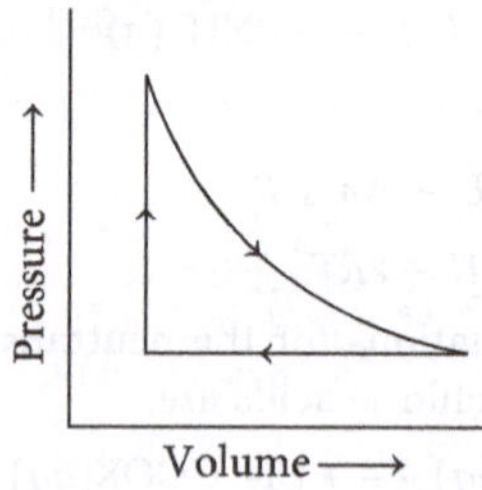

10. (i) Given that $\Delta H = 0$ for mixing of two gases. Explain whether the diffusion of these gases into each other in a closed container is a spontaneous process or not?
    (ii) Water can be lifted into the water tank at the top of the house with the help of a pump. Then why is it not considered to be spontaneous?

11. (i) Under what condition, the heat evolved or absorbed in a reaction is equal to its free energy change?
    (ii) Calculate $\Delta_r G^\circ$ for conversion of oxygen to ozone, $\frac{3}{2}O_2(g) \longrightarrow O_3(g)$ at 298 K, if K_p for this conversion is 2.47×10^{-29}.

Short Answer Type II Questions [3 Marks]

12. Identify the steps involved in the following cyclic process. Temperature at *A*, *B* and *F* is T_1 and at *C*, *D* and *E* is T_2. Given, $T_1 > T_2$.

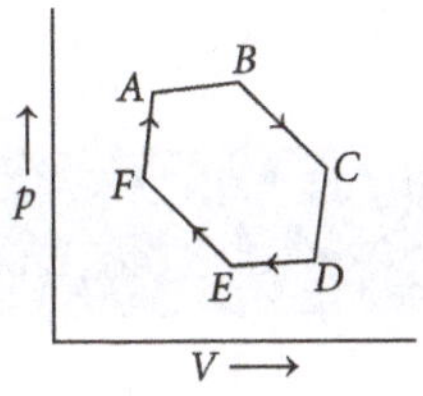

13. Calculate $\Delta_r H°$ for the reaction,

$$\underset{\text{H}\ \ \ \text{H}}{\text{H—C=C—H}} + 3\text{O=O} \longrightarrow 2\text{O=C=O} + 2\text{H—O—H}$$

The average bond enthalpies of various bonds are as follows

Bond	Bond enthalpy (kJ mol^{-1})
C—H	414
O=O	499
C=O	724
O—H	460
C=C	619

14. Calculate the standard enthalpy of formation of $CH_3OH(l)$ from the following data

(i) $CH_3OH(l) + \frac{3}{2}O_2(g) \longrightarrow CO_2(g) + 2H_2O(l);$

$\Delta_r H° = -726$ kJ mol^{-1}

(ii) $C_{(graphite)} + O_2(g) \longrightarrow CO_2(g);$

$\Delta_c H° = -393$ kJ mol^{-1}

(iii) $H_2(g) + \frac{1}{2}O_2(g) \longrightarrow 2H_2O(l);$

$\Delta_f H° = -286$ kJ mol^{-1}

Case Study [4 Marks]

15. Every system is associated with a definite amount of energy, called the **internal energy** (*U* or *E*) of the system. It is the sum of chemical, electrical, mechanical or any other form of energy that **anyone** may think of. However, gravitational energy is generally neglected.

(i) heat flows into or out of the system,
(ii) work is done on or by the system,
(iii) matter enters or leaves the system.

The absolute value of internal energy possessed by a substance cannot be calculated because it is not possible to predict the exact values of different forms of energy. Thus, we can just calculate the change in internal energy, which is achieved by changing the state of a system.

First law of thermodynamics was proposed by Helmholtz and Robert-Mayer who stated that the energy of an isolated system is constant, i.e. energy can neither be created nor be destroyed but can converted from one form to another. That's why also called law of conservation of energy.

(i) Neither *q* nor *w* is a state function but $q + w$ state function. Explain why?

(ii) Out of mass and density, which is an intensive property and why?

Or

Explain thermodynamically how is the heat absorbed by system is used in doing work at constant temperature and pressure.

(iii) What is the change in the energy of system if 500 cal of heat energy are added to a system and system does 350 cal of work on the surroundings?

Long Answer Type Questions [5 Marks]

16. The standard Gibbs energy change for the reaction, $N_2(g) + 3H_2(g) \rightleftharpoons 2NH_3(g)$ is -33.2 kJ mol^{-1} at 298 K.

(i) Calculate the equilibrium constant for the above reaction.

(ii) What would be the equilibrium constant if the reaction is written as

$$\frac{1}{2}H_2(g) + \frac{3}{2}H_2(g) \rightleftharpoons NH_3(g)$$

(iii) What will be the equilibrium constant if the reaction is

$$NH_3(g) \rightleftharpoons \frac{1}{2}N_2(g) + \frac{3}{2}H_2(g)$$

17. (i) Define the following terms :

(a) Molar enthalpy of fusion
(b) Molar enthalpy of vaporisation

(ii) The molar enthalpy of fusion of ice is 6.01 kJ/mol and the molar enthalpy of vaporisation of water is 40.7 kJ/mol. Calculate the total heat required to convert 36g of ice at 0°C to steam at 100°C. Assume no heat is lost to the surrounding. (Molar mass of water=18 g/mol)

Answers

1. (b)	2. (c)	3. (c)	4. (a)	5. (a)
6. (a)	7. (c)	8. (a)	9. zero	

11. (ii) 163 kJ mol^{-1} 13. -964 kJ mol^{-1}

14. -239 kJ mol^{-1}

16. (i) 6.6×10^5 (ii) 8.1×10^2 (iii) 1.23×10^{-3}

17. (ii) 108.47 kJ

06

CHAPTER

Equilibrium

There are certain reactions that proceed in forward as well as in reverse direction and never go to completion. Such, reactions are called reversible reactions. The state of a process/reaction, at which the rates of forward and backward processes/reactions become equal is called the **equilibrium state**.

YOUR STUDY GOALS

YOUR PRACTICE GOAL

- Objective Type Questions (41 Qs ; 29 MCQs, 10 A-R, 2 Case Study)
- Subjective Type Questions (36 Qs; 11 SA-I, 15 SA-II, 10 LA)

Equilibrium can be established for both physical and chemical processes. Chemical equilibria are important in numerous biological and environmental processes.

In this chapter, we will explore how equilibrium shapes the stability of systems in chemical reactions.

6.1 Equilibrium in Physical Processes

The equilibrium developing between different phases or physical properties of a substance is termed as **physical equilibria**.

Examples of Physical Equilibrium

Some examples of equilibrium existing between physical states of a substance (phase transformation processes) are as follows

(i) Solid-Liquid Equilibrium

When ice (solid) and water (liquid) are kept in a perfectly insulated thermos flask at 273 K and 1 atmospheric pressure, they are in a state of equilibrium,

i.e. $$H_2O(s) \rightleftharpoons H_2O(l)$$

At this condition, the mass of ice and water do not change with time and the temperature of the reaction mixture remains constant. However, the equilibrium is not static, because the rates of transfer of ice into water and of water into ice are equal at 273 K and 1 atmospheric pressure.

The temperature at which the solid and liquid phases of a pure substance at atmospheric pressure are at equilibrium is called the **normal melting point** or **normal freezing point of the substance.**

At equilibrium,

Rate of melting of ice = Rate of freezing of water

(ii) Liquid-Vapour Equilibrium

Water and water vapour are in equilibrium position at atmospheric pressure (1.013 bar) and at 100°C or 373 K in a closed vessel. Here, the rate of evaporation becomes equal to the rate of condensation.

$$H_2O(l) \underset{\text{Rate of condensation}}{\overset{\text{Rate of evaporation}}{\rightleftharpoons}} H_2O(vap)$$

At equilibrium,

Rate of evaporation = Rate of condensation

It is observed that different liquids have different equilibrium vapour pressures at same temperature. The liquid which has a higher vapour pressure is more volatile and has a lower boiling point.

Note In an open system, the equilibrium is not set up as the rate of condensation is much less than the rate of evaporation due to availability of large volume for vapours.

The temperature at which the liquid and vapours of a pure liquid at one atmospheric pressure are at equilibrium is called the **normal boiling point of the liquid**. Boiling point of the liquid depends on the atmospheric pressure. It also depends on the altitude of the place, at high altitude, the boiling point decreases.

(iii) Solid-Vapour Equilibrium

Such equilibrium exists only in case of substances which undergo sublimation, i.e. solid directly converts into vapour without liquefaction.

e.g. If a sublimate like solid iodine is placed in a closed vessel, after sometime the vessel gets filled up with violet vapours and the intensity of colour increases with time. After sometime, the intensity of colour becomes constant and at this stage the rate of sublimation of solid iodine to iodine vapours becomes equal to the rate of condensation of iodine vapours into solid iodine.

This stage is referred to the equilibrium state, i.e.

$$I_2(s) \rightleftharpoons I_2(vap)$$

Other examples showing solid-vapour equilibrium are

$$\text{Camphor (solid)} \rightleftharpoons \text{Camphor (vapour)}$$

$$NH_4Cl\ (\text{solid}) \rightleftharpoons NH_4Cl\ (\text{vapour})$$

(iv) Equilibrium Involving Dissolution of Solid or Gases in Liquids

(a) **Solids in liquids** In a saturated solution (the solution in which no more solute can be dissolved in it at a particular temperature, there is an equilibrium between the solid solute and its solution (i.e. solute solution).

e.g. $\quad$ Sugar (solution) $\rightleftharpoons$ Sugar (solid)

At equilibrium,

Rate of dissolution = Rate of crystallisation

(b) **Gases in liquids** When a gas is dissolved in water, an equilibrium is developed between the gaseous molecules and dissolved molecules of the gas in the liquid under pressure.

e.g. Dissolution of CO_2 under pressure in soda water bottle.

$$CO_2(g) \rightleftharpoons CO_2(\text{solution})$$

Such equilibrium is governed by **Henry's law**, according to which, *"the mass of a gas dissolved in a given mass of a solvent at any temperature (i.e. extent of solubility) is directly proportional to the pressure of the gas above the solvent"*,

i.e.

$$m \propto p \quad \text{or} \quad m = K_H p$$

where, K_H is the proportionality constant, called the **Henry's law constant** and depends upon the temperature. Thus, on increasing the temperature or decreasing the pressure, the amount of dissolved gas decreases.

General Characteristics of Equilibria Involving Physical Processes

For the physical processes discussed above, following characteristics are common to the system at equilibrium.

- Equilibrium is possible only in a closed system at a given temperature.
- Both the opposing processes occur at the same rate and there is a dynamic but stable condition.
- All measurable properties of the system remain constant.
- When equilibrium is attained for a physical process, it is characterised by constant value of one of its parameters (such as melting point, concentration of solute, ratio of product to reactant, etc.) at a given temperature.
- The magnitude of such quantities at any stage indicates the extent to which the reaction has proceeded before reaching equilibrium.

6.2 Equilibrium in Chemical Processes : Dynamic Equilibrium

In case of reversible reactions, when the concentration of reactants (i.e. the reacting species) and products (i.e. the obtained species) do not change with time, the reaction is called in a **state of chemical equilibrium** or dynamic equilibrium.

In other words, the stage at which the rate of forward reaction becomes equal to the rate of backward reaction and there is no net change in composition, is called the **chemical equilibrium state.** A mixture of reactants and products in the equilibrium state is called an **equilibrium mixture.**

The variation of concentration of reactants and products in a reversible reaction can be seen as

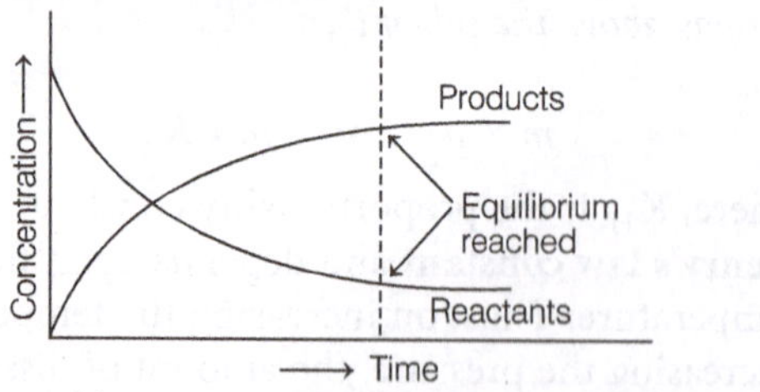

Variation of the concentration of the reactants and products

e.g. Haber's process explain the dynamic nature of equilibrium,

$$N_2(g) + 3H_2(g) \rightleftharpoons 2NH_3(g)$$

In this process, as the reaction proceeds, the concentration of ammonia increases while concentration of dinitrogen and dihydrogen decreases. But after a certain time the concentration of reactants and products become equal. This shows that reaction has reached equilibrium.

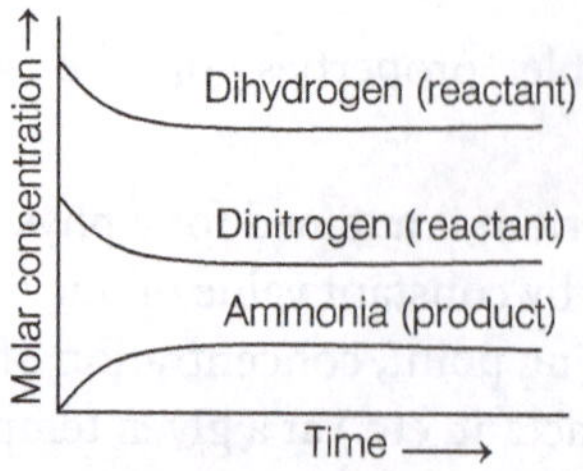

Depiction of equilibrium for the reaction
$N_2(g) + 3H_2(g) \rightleftharpoons 2NH_3(g)$

Similarly, let us consider the reaction,

$$H_2(g) + I_2(g) \rightleftharpoons 2HI(g)$$

From the graph, it can be observed that chemical equilibrium can be attained from either direction of reaction.

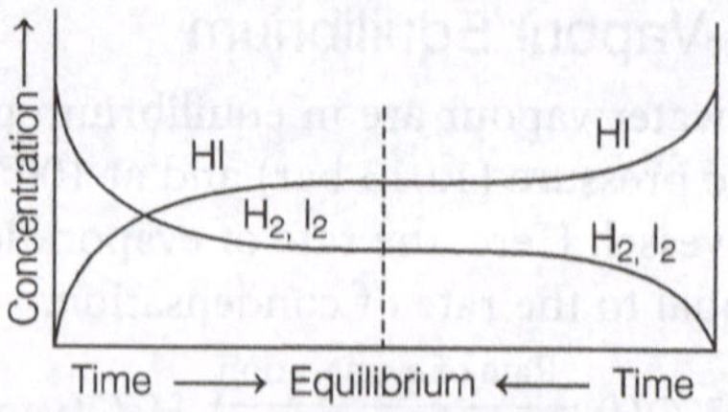

Chemical equilibrium in the reaction, $H_2(g) + I_2(g) \rightleftharpoons 2HI(g)$ can be attained from either direction.

Types of Chemical Equilibrium

Depending upon the number of phases, chemical equilibrium can be of following two types

(i) Homogeneous Equilibrium

If all the reactants and products of an equilibrium reaction are in the same phase.

e.g. $H_2(g) + I_2(g) \rightleftharpoons 2HI(g)$

(ii) Heterogeneous Equilibrium

If all the reactants and products of an equilibrium reaction are present in two or more phases.

e.g. $MgCO_3(s) \rightleftharpoons MgO(s) + CO_2(g)$

6.3 Law of Mass Action

According to this law, *"the rate at which a substance reacts is proportional to its active mass and hence the rate of a chemical reaction is proportional to the product of the active masses of the reactants".*

The term **active mass** means the molar concentration, i.e. number of moles per litre. It is expressed by enclosing the formula of substance in square brackets.

Thus, for the reaction, $aA + bB \longrightarrow$ product

According to law of mass action,

$$\text{Rate} = k[A]^a[B]^b \quad (\text{where, } k \text{ is rate constant.})$$

Note **Active masses** of pure solids and liquids are taken as unity because their concentration (or density) remain same throughout the reaction.

Law of Chemical Equilibrium and Equilibrium Constant

Consider a homogeneous reversible reaction,

$$aA + bB \rightleftharpoons cC + dD$$

According to law of mass action,

Rate of forward reaction,

$$R_f \propto [A]^a[B]^b \text{ or } R_f = k_f[A]^a[B]^b$$

Rate of backward reaction,

$$R_b \propto [C]^c[D]^d \text{ or } R_b = k_b[C]^c[D]^d$$

where, k_f and k_b are the rate constants for forward and backward reactions respectively.

At equilibrium,

rate of forward reaction = rate of backward reaction

i.e. $$k_f[A]^a_{eq}[B]^b_{eq} = k_b[C]^c_{eq}[D]^d_{eq}$$

[Generally the subscript 'eq' which is used to show state of equilibrium is omitted from the concentration terms].

$$\therefore \quad \frac{k_f}{k_b} = \frac{[C]^c[D]^d}{[A]^a[B]^b} \text{ or } \boxed{K_C = \frac{[C]^c[D]^d}{[A]^a[B]^b}}$$

Here subscript 'c' shows that K_C is expressed in concentration of mol L^{-1}. K_C is known as **equilibrium constant.**

Thus, at a given temperature, the value obtained by dividing the product of concentrations of reaction products raised to the respective stoichiometric coefficient in the balanced chemical equation by the product of concentrations of reactants raised to their individual stoichiometric coefficients is constant. This is called **law of chemical equilibrium** or **equilibrium law** and the obtained value is called **equilibrium constant.**

e.g. Equilibrium constant for the reaction,
$4NH_3(g) + 5O_2(g) \rightleftharpoons 4NO(g) + 6H_2O(g)$ is written as

$$K_C = \frac{[NO]^4\,[H_2O]^6}{[NH_3]^4\,[O_2]^5}$$

Example 1 **PCl_5, PCl_3, and Cl_2 are at equilibrium at 500 K in a closed container and their concentrations are 0.8×10^{-3} mol L^{-1}, 1.2×10^{-3} mol L^{-1} and 1.2×10^{-3} mol L^{-1}, respectively. Calculate the value of K_C for the reaction.**

$$PCl_5(g) \rightleftharpoons PCl_3(g) + Cl_2(g)$$ **NCERT Exemplar**

Sol. For the reaction, $PCl_5 \rightleftharpoons PCl_3 + Cl_2$
At 500 K in a closed container,

$[PCl_5] = 0.8 \times 10^{-3}$ mol L^{-1}

$[PCl_3] = 1.2 \times 10^{-3}$ mol L^{-1}

$[Cl_2] = 1.2 \times 10^{-3}$ mol L^{-1}

$$K_C = \frac{[PCl_3]\,[Cl_2]}{[PCl_5]}$$

$$= \frac{(1.2 \times 10^{-3}) \times (1.2 \times 10^{-3})}{(0.8 \times 10^{-3})} = 1.8 \times 10^{-3}$$

Characteristics of Equilibrium Constant

The important characteristics of equilibrium constant are as follows

- The equilibrium constant has a definite value for every chemical reaction at a particular temperature.
- It is independent of initial concentrations of the reacting species or the direction from which the equilibrium is achieved. The value of equilibrium constant, K changes with change in temperature only.
- If an equation is **divided by a factor 'n'** the new equilibrium constant is nth root of the previous value.

$$K' = (K)^{1/n}$$

e.g. $H_2(g) + I_2(g) \rightleftharpoons 2HI(g)$

The value of $K_C = \dfrac{[HI]^2}{[H_2][I_2]}$

If this equation is divided by 2 the new equilibrium constant is $K'_C = \dfrac{[HI]}{[H_2]^{1/2}[I_2]^{1/2}}$

$$K'_C = (K_C)^{1/2}$$
$$= \sqrt{K_C}$$

- If the equation is **multiplied by a factor 'n'**, the new equilibrium constant is nth power of the previous value.

$$K' = (K)^n$$

If an equation is multiplied by 2 the new equilibrium constant becomes

$$K'_C = (K_C)^2$$

- If the equation representing equilibrium constant is reversed, the new equilibrium constant is also inversed.

i.e. $$K' = \frac{1}{K}$$

- If two equations are added their equilibrium constants are multiplied and if they are subtracted, their equilibrium constants are divided.

Note Equilibrium constants are never added or subtracted.

- The value of the equilibrium constant is not affected by the addition of a catalyst to the reaction. This is because the catalyst increases the speed of the forward reaction and the backward reaction to the same extent.

Variation of Equilibrium Constant with Variation of Reaction Equation (K = Equilibrium Constant for Original Reaction)

When the equation is	New equilibrium constant
Multiplied by n	K^n
Divided by n	$K^{1/n}$
Reversed	$\frac{1}{K}$
Added	$K = K_1 \times K_2$
Subtracted	$K = \frac{K_1}{K_2}$

Example 2 **At 500 K, equilibrium constant, K_C, for the following reaction is 5.**

$$\frac{1}{2}H_2(g) + \frac{1}{2}I_2(g) \rightleftharpoons HI(g)$$

What would be the equilibrium constant K_C for the reaction?

$$2HI(g) \rightleftharpoons H_2(g) + I_2(g)$$

Sol. For the reaction,

$$\frac{1}{2}H_2(g) + \frac{1}{2}I_2(g) \rightleftharpoons HI(g)$$

$$K_C = \frac{[HI]}{[H_2]^{1/2}[I_2]^{1/2}} = 5$$

Thus, for the reaction, $2HI(g) \rightleftharpoons H_2(g) + I_2(g)$

$$K_C = \frac{[H_2][I_2]}{[HI]^2} = \left(\frac{1}{K_C}\right)^2 = \left(\frac{1}{5}\right)^2 = \frac{1}{25} = 0.04$$

Example 3 **K_{a_1}, K_{a_2} and K_{a_3} are the respective ionisation constants for the following reactions.**

$$H_2S \rightleftharpoons H^+ + HS^-$$
$$HS^- \rightleftharpoons H^+ + S^{2-}$$
$$H_2S \rightleftharpoons 2H^+ + S^{2-}$$

Write the correct relationship between K_{a_1}, K_{a_2}, K_{a_3}.

TEACHER'S TIP

To find out the correct relationship between three ionisation constants (K_{a_1}, K_{a_2} and K_{a_3}) this must be keep in mind that when two reactions are added, their equilibrium constants are multiplied.

Sol. For the reaction,

$$H_2S \rightleftharpoons H^+ + HS^-$$

$$K_{a_1} = \frac{[H^+][HS^-]}{[H_2S]}$$

For the reaction, $HS^- \rightleftharpoons H^+ + S^{2-}$

$$K_{a_2} = \frac{[H^+][S^{2-}]}{[HS^-]}$$

When, the above two reactions are added, their equilibrium constants are multiplied, thus

$$K_{a_3} = \frac{[H^+]^2[S^{2-}]}{[H_2S]} = K_{a_1} \times K_{a_2}$$

Hence, $K_{a_3} = K_{a_1} \times K_{a_2}$

6.4 Equilibrium Constant in Gaseous Systems

When all the products and reactants of a reaction are in gaseous state, their concentration is expressed in term of partial pressures. If in the following reaction,

$$aA + bB \rightleftharpoons cC + dD$$

The partial pressure of A, B, C and D are p_A, p_B, p_C and p_D respectively, then, the expression of equilibrium constant, K_p is given as

$$K_p = \frac{p_C^c \cdot p_D^d}{p_A^a \cdot p_B^b}$$

Relation between K_p and K_c

Consider a gaseous phase reaction,

$$n_1A + n_2B \rightleftharpoons m_1C + m_2D$$

$$K_p = K_C(RT)^{\Delta n_g}$$

[$\Delta n_g = (m_1 + m_2) - (n_1 + n_2)$ or Δn_g = moles of gaseous products – moles of gaseous reactants]

If, $\Delta n_g = 0$ then $K_p = K_C$

If, $\Delta n_g = +$ve then $K_p > K_C$

If, $\Delta n_g = -$ve then $K_p < K_C$

TEACHER'S TIP

While calculating the value of K_p, pressure should be expressed in bar because standard state for pressure is 1 bar.

- 1 pascal, Pa = 1 Nm^{-2} and • 1 bar = 10^5 Pa

6.5 Equilibrium Constant of Heterogeneous System

Heterogeneous equilibria often involve pure solids or liquids but the concentration of a pure solid or liquid is constant (i.e. independent of the amount present). Therefore, we can simplify equilibrium expression for the heterogeneous equilibria by taking the concentrations of pure solids and liquids as unity.

e.g. Equilibrium constant of the following heterogeneous equilibria is given as

$$CaCO_3(s) \overset{\Delta}{\rightleftharpoons} CaO(s) + CO_2(g);$$

$$K_C = [CO_2], K_p = p_{CO_2}$$

Since, $[CaCO_3(s)]$ and $[CaO(s)]$ are both constant.

Example 4 **Write the expression for the equilibrium constant, K_C for each of the following reactions.**

(i) $2NOCl(g) \rightleftharpoons 2NO(g) + Cl_2(g)$

(ii) $2Cu(NO_3)_2(s) \rightleftharpoons 2CuO(s) + 4NO_2(g) + O_2(g)$

(iii) $CH_3COOC_2H_5(aq) + H_2O(l) \rightleftharpoons CH_3COOH(aq) + C_2H_5OH(aq)$

(iv) $Fe^{3+}(aq) + 3OH^-(aq) \rightleftharpoons Fe(OH)_3(s)$

(v) $I_2(s) + 5F_2(g) \rightleftharpoons 2IF_5(g)$ **NCERT**

Sol. (i) $K_C = \frac{[NO]^2[Cl_2]}{[NOCl]^2}$

(ii) $K_C = [NO_2]^4 [O_2]$

(because molar concentrations of pure solids are constant)

(iii) $K_C = \frac{[CH_3COOH][C_2H_5OH]}{[CH_3COOC_2H_5]}$

(iv) $K_C = \frac{1}{[Fe^{3+}][OH^-]^3}$ because $[Fe(OH)_3(s) = 1]$

(v) $K_C = \frac{[IF_5]^2}{[F_2]^5}$ (because $[I_2(s) = 1]$)

Example 5 **We know that the relationship between K_C and K_p is $K_p = K_C (RT)^{\Delta n_g}$**

What would be the value of Δn_g for the reaction?

$$NH_4Cl(s) \rightleftharpoons NH_3(g) + HI(g)$$

Sol. The relationship between K_p and K_C is

$$K_p = K_C (RT)^{\Delta n_g}$$

where, Δn_g = (number of moles of gaseous products) − (number of moles of gaseous reactants)

For the reaction,

$$NH_4Cl(s) \rightleftharpoons NH_3(g) + HCl(g)$$

$$\Delta n_g = 2 - 0 = 2$$

Example 6 **For the equilibrium**

$$2NOCl(g) \rightleftharpoons 2NO(g) + Cl_2(g)$$

the value of the equilibrium constant, K_C is 3.75×10^{-6} at 1069 K.

Calculate the K_p for the reaction at this temperature? **NCERT**

Sol. We know that, $K_p = K_C (RT)^{\Delta n_g}$

For the above reaction,

$$\Delta n_g = (2 + 1) - 2 = 1$$

$$K_p = 3.75 \times 10^{-6} (0.0831 \times 1069)$$

$$K_p = 0.033 \times 10^{-4}$$

Units of Equilibrium Constant

The units of K_p and K_C also depend upon the value of Δn_g.

- If number of moles of reactants and products are equal (i.e. $\Delta n_g = 0$)

  e.g. $2NO(g) \rightleftharpoons N_2(g) + O_2(g)$

  then, K_p as well as K_C have no units.
- If a reaction proceeds with increase or decrease in number of moles then, unit of K_p is $(\text{atmosphere})^{\Delta n_g}$ and unit of K_C is $(\text{mol per litre})^{\Delta n_g}$.

Applications of Equilibrium Constants

Equilibrium constant is helpful in

- predicting the extent of a reaction on the basis of its magnitude.
- predicting the direction of the reaction, and
- calculating the equilibrium concentrations and pressure.

(i) Predicting the Extent of a Reaction

The numerical values of equilibrium constant for a reaction helps us to predict the extent of a reaction. But it does not give any information about the rate at which the equilibrium is reached.

- If the value of K_C is greater than 10^3, products predominates over reactants, i.e. reaction go to nearly completion.
- If value of K_C is less than 10^{-3}, reactant predominates over products, i.e. the reaction occurs rarely.
- If K_C is in between 10^3 to 10^{-3}, considerable amounts of both reactants and products are present.

The above generalisations are shown in the following figure.

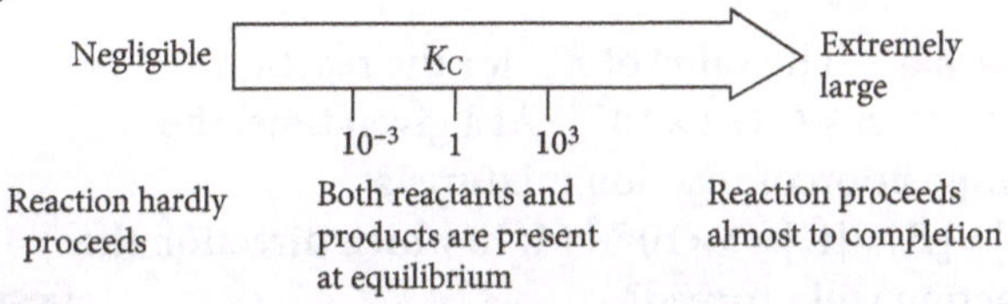

Dependence of extent of reaction on K_C

TEACHER'S TIP

Higher value of K_C shows the reaction will go in the forward direction and products are more stable than the reactants.

(ii) Predicting the Direction of the Reaction

Equilibrium constant is also found useful for predicting the direction in which a reaction will progress at any stage. For this a new term, reaction quotient is introduced.

Reaction quotient (Q) is the ratio of the molar concentration or partial pressure of the product species to that of reactant species at any stage in the reaction, not necessarily at equilibrium.

For a reaction, $aA + bB \rightleftharpoons cC + dD$

$$Q_C = \frac{[C]^c[D]^d}{[A]^a[B]^b}$$

Reaction quotient, Q is denoted as Q_c or Q_p depending upon whether the concentration is taken in terms of moles per litre or partial pressure, respectively.

With the help of reaction quotient we can predict the direction of reaction.

- If $Q_C = K_C$ or $Q_p = K_p$; the reaction is in equilibrium, i.e. no net reaction occurs.
- If $Q_C > K_C$ or $Q_p > K_p$; the reaction moves from right to left, (i.e. in backward direction or in the direction of reactants).
- If $Q_C < K_C$ or $Q_p < K_p$; the reaction moves from left to right (i.e. in forward direction or in the direction of products).

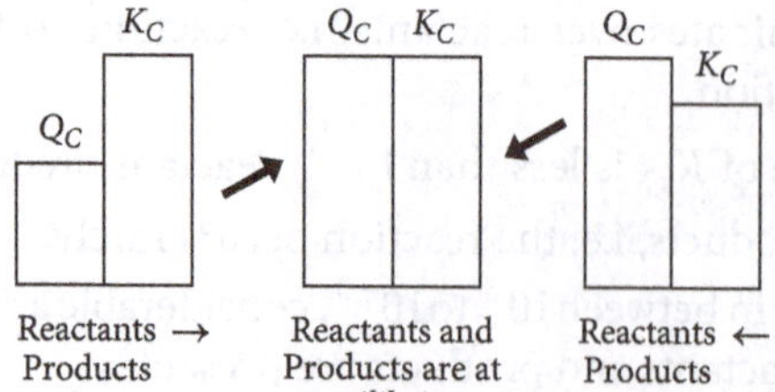

Predicting the direction of the reaction

Example 7 **The value of K_C for the reaction $2A \rightleftharpoons B + C$ is 2×10^{-3}. At a given time, the composition of reaction mixture is $[A]=[B]=[C]=3\times10^{-4}$ M. In which direction the reaction will proceed?** **NCERT**

Sol. For the reaction,

$$Q_C = [B]\,[C]\,/\,[A]^2$$

as $[A] = [B] = [C] = 3\times10^{-4}$ M

$$Q_C = (3\times10^{-4})\ (3\times10^{-4})\,/\,(3\times10^{-4})^2 = 1$$

As $Q_C > K_C$, so the reaction will proceed in the reverse direction.

Example 8 **A mixture of 1.57 moles of N_2, 1.92 moles of H_2 and 8.13 moles of NH_3 is introduced into a 20 L reaction vessel at 500 K. At this temperature, the equilibrium constant, K_C for the reaction, $N_2(g)+3H_2(g) \rightleftharpoons 2NH_3(g)$ is 1.7×10^2. Predict the direction of the reaction.** **NCERT**

Sol. $N_2(g) + 3H_2(g) \rightleftharpoons 2NH_3(g)\,;\ Q_C = \frac{[NH_3]^2}{[N_2][H_2]^3}$

Given, $[NH_3] = \frac{8.13}{20}\ M = 0.4065\ M$

$[N_2] = \frac{1.57}{20}\ M = 0.0785\ M\,;\ [H_2] = \frac{1.92}{20}\ M = 0.096\ M$

$$Q_C = \frac{[0.4065\ M]^2}{[0.0785\ M][0.096\ M]^3} = 2.379\times 10^3\ M^{-2}$$

$Q_C \neq K_C$, so the reaction mixture is not in equilibrium.
$Q_C > K_C$, it indicates that the reaction will proceed in the direction of reactants, i.e. the reverse direction.

(iii) Calculating Equilibrium Concentration

The value of equilibrium constant also helps us in calculating the equilibrium concentration of various substances taking part in a reaction.

Algorithm for Calculating Equilibrium Concentration

Step I Write the balanced equation for the given reaction.

Step II Make a list of the following information for each substance below the balanced equation. (The information related to a substance must be written just below its formula or symbol).

The information required is

- the initial concentration.
- the change in concentration on going to equilibrium.
- the equilibrium concentration.

For making the list, consider the concentration (mol/L) of one of the substance that reacts on going to equilibrium be x. Now determine the concentrations of other substances in terms of x by using the stoichiometry of the reaction.

Step III Substitute the values of equilibrium concentration and equilibrium constant in the expression of equilibrium equation for the given reaction and solve the equation to get the value of x.

[If a quadratic equation of the type $ax^2 + bx + c = 0, a \neq 0$ is formed, solve it by using the formula $x = \frac{-b \pm \sqrt{b^2 - 4ac}}{2a}$]

Step IV From the value of x, calculate the equilibrium concentrations of different substances.

Step V Check your results by substituting the equilibrium concentration into the equilibrium equation.

Example 9 **The value of K_p for the reaction,**

$$CO_2(g) + C(s) \rightleftharpoons 2CO(g)$$

is 3.0 at 1000 K. If initially $p_{CO_2} = 0.48$ bar and $p_{CO} = 0$ bar and pure graphite is present, calculate the equilibrium partial pressures of CO and CO_2. NCERT

Sol. For the reaction, let 'x' be the decrease in pressure of CO_2, then

	$CO_2(g)$ + $C(s)$	$\rightleftharpoons 2CO(g)$
Initial pressure	0.48 bar	0
At equilibrium	$(0.48 - x)$ bar	$2x$ bar

$$K_p = \frac{p^2_{CO}}{p_{CO_2}}$$

$$\Rightarrow \quad K_p = \frac{(2x)^2}{(0.48 - x)} = 3$$

$$4x^2 = 3(0.48 - x) \text{ or } 4x^2 + 3x - 1.44 = 0$$

$$a = 4, b = 3, c = -1.44$$

By applying $x = \frac{(-b \pm \sqrt{b^2 - 4ac})}{2a}$

$$x = 2.66 / 8 = 0.33$$

The equilibrium partial pressures are

$$p_{CO} = 2x = 2 \times 0.33 = 0.66 \text{ bar}$$

$$p_{CO_2} = 0.48 - x = 0.48 - 0.33 = 0.15 \text{ bar}$$

Relationship between Equilibrium Constant (*K*), Reaction Quotient (*Q*) and Gibbs Energy (*G*)

Gibbs free energy change and reaction quotient are related as

$$\Delta G = \Delta G^\circ + RT \ln Q_C$$

where, ΔG° = Standard Gibbs energy

At equilibrium, $\Delta G = 0$ and $Q_C = K_C$

On substituting values, $\Delta G^\circ = -RT \ln K_C$

Similarly, $\Delta G^\circ = -RT \ln K_p$ (for ideal gases)

$$\therefore \quad \ln K = -\frac{\Delta G^\circ}{RT}$$

Taking antilog on both sides, we get

$$\boxed{K = e^{-\Delta G^\circ / RT}}$$

The above equation is helpful in predicting the spontaneity of the reaction. e.g.

- If $\Delta G^\circ < 0$, $-\Delta G^\circ / RT = +$ve and $e^{-\Delta G^\circ / RT} > 1$ and hence, $K > 1$. It means that the reaction occurs spontaneously in the forward direction or products predominate over reactants.
- If $\Delta G^\circ > 0$; $-\Delta G^\circ / RT = -$ve and $e^{-\Delta G^\circ / RT} < 1$ and hence, $K < 1$. It means that the reaction is non-spontaneous in forward direction (i.e. product side) but spontaneous in reverse direction (i.e. reactants predominate over products) or the reaction occurs rarely.

Example 10 **Hydrolysis of sucrose gives,**

$$\textbf{Sucrose} + H_2O \rightleftharpoons \textbf{Glucose} + \textbf{Fructose}$$

Equilibrium constant K_C for the reaction is 2×10^{13} at 300 K. Calculate $\Delta G^\ominus$ at 300 K. NCERT

Sol. $\Delta G^\ominus = -RT \ln K_C$

$$\Delta G^\ominus = -8.314 \text{ J mol}^{-1}\text{K}^{-1} \times 300 \text{ K} \ln (2 \times 10^{13})$$

$$\Delta G^\ominus = -7.64 \times 10^4 \text{ J mol}^{-1}$$

Example 11 **Calculate (i) ΔG° and (ii) the equilibrium constant for the formation of the NO_2 from NO and O_2 at 298 K.** NCERT

$$NO(g) + \frac{1}{2}O_2(g) \rightleftharpoons NO_2(g)$$

where, $\Delta_f G^\circ(NO_2) = 52.0$ kJ/mol,

$\Delta_f G^\circ(NO) = 87.0$ kJ/mol, $\Delta_f G^\circ(O_2) = 0$ kJ/mol

Hints
- Calculate the $\Delta_r G^\circ$ by using the formula $\Delta_r G^\circ = \Sigma \Delta_f G^\circ_p - \Sigma \Delta_f G^\circ_r$ (p = products and r = reactants.)
- Calculate the equilibrium constant, K_C by using the formula, $\Delta G^\circ = -2.303 RT \log K_C$.

Sol. (i) $NO(g) + \frac{1}{2}O_2(g) \rightleftharpoons NO_2(g)$;

$$\Delta_r G^\circ = \Sigma \Delta_f G^\circ_{(\text{products})} - \Sigma \Delta_f G^\circ_{(\text{reactants})}$$

$$\Delta_r G^\circ = \Delta_f G^\circ(NO_2) - \left(\Delta_f G^\circ(NO) + \frac{1}{2}\Delta_f G^\circ(O_2)\right)$$

$$\Delta_r G^\circ = 52.0 - \left(87.0 + \frac{1}{2} \times 0\right) \text{kJ mol}^{-1}$$

$$\Delta_r G^\circ = -35.0 \text{ kJ mol}^{-1}$$

(ii) $\Delta_r G° = -2.303\, RT \log K_C = 35000\ \text{J mol}^{-1}$

$= -2.303 \times 8.314\ \text{J mol}^{-1}\text{K}^{-1} \times 298\ \text{K} \times \log K_C$

$\log K_C = \dfrac{35000}{5705.85} = 6.134$

$K_C = \text{antilog } 6.134$

$K_C = 1.361 \times 10^6$

Example 12 K_p **for the reaction,**

$N_2(g) + 3H_2(g) \rightleftharpoons 2NH_3(g)$ **at 400°C is**

$1.64 \times 10^{-4}\ \text{atm}^{-2}$**. Find** K_C**, also calculate** $\Delta G°$ **using** K_p **and** K_C **values and interpret the difference.**

Sol. $N_2(g) + 3H_2(g) \rightleftharpoons 2NH_3(g)$

$\Delta n = 2 - 4 = -2$

$K_p = K_C (RT)^{\Delta n_g}$

$1.64 \times 10^{-4}\ \text{atm}^{-2} = K_C (0.0821\ \text{L atm mol}^{-1}\text{K}^{-1} \times 673\ \text{K})^{-2}$

$[T = 400 + 273 = 673\ \text{K}]$

Or $K_C = \dfrac{1.64 \times 10^{-4}\ \text{atm}^{-2}}{(0.0821 \times 673\ \text{L atm mol}^{-1})^{-2}}$

$= 0.5006\ \text{mol}^2\text{L}^{-2}\ \text{atm}^{-4}$

Now, $\Delta G° = -2.303\, RT \log K$

If $K = K_p$,

$\Delta G° = -2.303 \times (8.314\ \text{JK}^{-1}\text{mol}^{-1})(673\ \text{K}) \times \log(1.64 \times 10^{-4})$

$= -2.303 \times 8.314 \times 673 \times (-3.7852)\ \text{J mol}^{-1}$

$= 48.78\ \text{kJ mol}^{-1}$

If $K = K_C$

$\Delta G° = -2.303 \times (8.314\ \text{J K}^{-1}\text{mol}^{-1}) \times (673\text{K}) \times \log(0.5006)$

$= -2.303 \times 8.314 \times 673 \times (-0.30)\ \text{J mol}^{-1}$

$= 3865.80\ \text{J mol}^{-1}$

As $\Delta G°$ is positive (> 0) the K will be less than 1 and the reaction will be non-spontaneous in forward direction.

6.6 Factors Affecting Equilibria

The factors from which the state of equilibrium can be affected are

- Change in concentration of reactants or products
- Change in temperature
- Change in pressure
- Addition of inert gas (at constant pressure)
- Addition of catalyst

Effect of change in all the above mentioned factors on an equilibrium, is decided by using **Le-Chatelier's principle** which is described below.

Le-Chatelier's Principle

According to this principle, *'if any of the factors that determine the equilibrium condition of a system (like temperature, pressure, concentration, etc.,) is changed, the system will move in such a direction so that effect of the change is reduced or to counteract the effect of change.'*

This law is true for almost all physical and chemical equilibria.

Thus, the effects of various factors on the state of equilibrium according to Le-Chatelier's principle are as follows.

Effect of Concentration Change

According to Le-Chatelier's principle,

- The concentration stress due to the addition of reactant/product is relieved by shifting of the net reaction in that direction where the added substance is consumed.
- The concentration stress due to the removal of reactant/product is relieved by shifting of the net reaction in that direction where the removed substance is replenished.
- Let us take the reaction,

$$H_2(g) + I_2(g) \rightleftharpoons 2HI(g)$$

If H_2 is added to the reaction mixture at equilibrium, then the equilibrium of the reaction is disturbed. In order to restore it, the reaction proceeds in a direction where in H_2 is consumed, i.e. more H_2 and I_2 react to form HI and finally the equilibrium shifts in right (forward) direction.

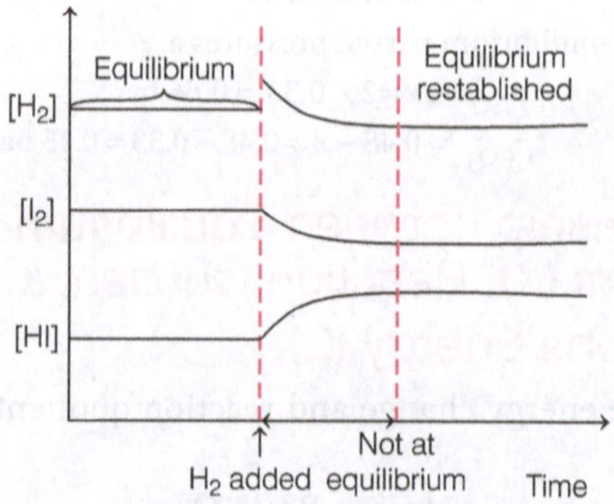

Effect of addition of H_2 on reaction $H_2(g) + I_2(g) \rightleftharpoons 2HI(g)$

An Experiment to Show Effect of Concentration

- This can be demonstrated by the following reaction,

$$\underset{\text{Yellow}}{Fe^{3+}(aq)} + \underset{\text{Colourless}}{SCN^{-}(aq)} \rightleftharpoons \underset{\text{Deep red}}{[Fe(SCN)]^{2+}(aq)}$$

- If we add few drops of potassium sulphocyanide to the above equilibrium, the intensity of the red colour of the solution increases as it shifts the equilibrium to the right.
- The equilibrium can be shifted in opposite direction by adding *aq*. $HgCl_2$ because Hg^{2+} reacts with SCN^- ions to form stable complex ion, $[Hg(SCN)_4]^{2-}$.

  Thus, decreasing the concentration of free SCN^- ions. Hence, the rate of backward reaction increases and intensity of red colour decreases.

Effect of Pressure Change

Pressure change, that is achieved by changing the volume of the system, generally affect the yield of products of gaseous reactions having different number of moles of gaseous reactants and products. It has no effect on solids/liquids as the volume (and concentration) of liquids is nearly independent of pressure.

In general, **increase in pressure shifts the equilibrium in that direction where the number of moles of the gas or pressure decreases and *vice-versa*.**

Effect of Change in Number of Moles

If $\Delta n_g = 0$, pressure change has no effect on the state of equilibrium. If $\Delta n_g < 0$, increased pressure favours forward reaction and if $\Delta n_g > 0$, increased pressure favours backward reaction or decreased pressure favours forward reaction.

e.g. $$\underset{0}{C(s)} + \underset{1}{CO_2(g)} \longrightarrow \underset{2}{2CO(g)}; \Delta n_g = 2 - 1 = 1$$

Since, $\Delta n_g > 0$, increased pressure favours the backward reaction or formation of CO is favoured by low pressure.

Effect of Inert Gas Addition

Inert gas can be added to an equilibrium mixture, under the following two conditions.

(i) At Constant Volume

Since inert gas (e.g. argon) does not take part in the reaction, so the equilibrium remains unaffected if volume is kept constant. This is because at constant volume, the partial pressures or the molar concentrations of the substance involved in the reaction remain unchanged.

(ii) At Constant Pressure

If an inert gas is added to an equilibrium process at constant pressure, the volume of the process will increase. Hence, the equilibrium will shift in a direction in which there is an increase in the number of moles of the gases.

If number of moles on either side of equilibrium are same, there will be no-effects of adding an inert gas on the rate of equilibrium.

Effect of Temperature Change

Temperature directly affects the value of equilibrium constant, K_C and rates of reactions. In general, the temperature dependence of the equilibrium constant depends on the sign of ΔH for the reaction as,

- In case of an **exothermic reaction** ($\Delta H = -$ ve), the equilibrium constant decreases with rise in temperature and hence, to make it constant the reaction proceeds in backward direction.

  e.g. Production of ammonia according to the reaction, $N_2(g) + 3H_2(g) \rightleftharpoons 2NH_3(g)$; $\Delta H = -92.38 \text{ kJ mol}^{-1}$

  is an **exothermic process**. According to Le-Chatelier's principle, raising the temperature shifts the equilibrium to left and decreases the equilibrium concentration of ammonia.

- In case of an **endothermic reaction** ($\Delta H = +$ ve), the equilibrium constant increases with rise in temperature and hence, the reaction moves in forward direction.

  e.g. At room temperature, the equilibrium mixture is blue due to $[CoCl_4]^{2-}$. When cooled in a freezing mixture, the colour of the mixture turns pink due to $[Co(H_2O)_6]^{3+}$.

$$\underset{\text{Pink}}{[Co(H_2O)_6]^{3+}(aq)} + \underset{\text{Colourless}}{4Cl^{-}(aq)} \rightleftharpoons \underset{\text{Blue}}{[CoCl_4]^{2-}(aq)} + 6H_2O(l)$$

Effect of Catalyst

A catalyst alters the rate of a reaction by providing a new pathway of lower activation energy. It affects the rate of forward and backward reactions to the same extent. Hence, have no effect on the state of equilibrium. However, in the presence of a catalyst, the equilibrium is achieved in lesser time.

For example, in the synthesis of ammonia (NH_3) by Haber's process, iron is used as a catalyst.

Similarly, in the manufacturing of SO_3, platinum or V_2O_5 is used as a catalyst.

Note A catalyst has no effect on the equilibrium composition of the mixture. Further, it is not shown in the balanced chemical equation or in the expression of equilibrium constant.

Effect of Varying Conditions of the Equilibrium, $aA + bB \rightleftharpoons cC + dD, \Delta n_g = (c+d)-(a+b)$

S.No.	Change imposed on the system in equilibrium	Equilibrium position moves	Equilibrium constant	Any other points
1.	Conc. of A and/or B increased	To right	No change	No change
2.	Conc. of C and/or D increased	To left	No change	No change
3.	Pressure increased	To right if $(c+d)<(a+b)$, i.e. $\Delta n_g = -ve$ To left if $(c+d)>(a+b)$, i.e. $\Delta n_g = +ve$ No change if $(c+d)=(a+b)$, i.e. $\Delta n_g = 0$	No change No change No change	Very little effect (if any) on reactions in liquid solution
4.	Temperature increased	To left if $\Delta H = -ve$ (exothermic) To right if $\Delta H = +ve$ (endothermic)	Value decreased Value decreased	Equilibrium achieved faster
5.	Addition of catalyst	No change	No change	Equilibrium achieved faster
6.	Addition of inert gas			
	(i) At constant p	To the direction of increasing gaseous moles	No change	No change
	(ii) At constant V	No effect	No change	No change

Applications of Le-Chatelier's Principle

Some of its applications are mentioned below.

(i) Formation of HI

$$H_2(g) + I_2(g) \rightleftharpoons 2HI(g); \Delta H = -12.4 \text{ kcal}$$

The favourable conditions for forward reaction are

- high concentration of H_2 or/and I_2.
- unaffected by pressure change (as $\Delta n_g = 0$).
- low reaction temperature (as the reaction is exothermic).
- no effect of addition of inert gas.

(ii) Haber's Process of Synthesis of Ammonia

$$N_2(g) + 3H_2(g) \rightleftharpoons 2NH_3(g); \Delta H = -22.4 \text{ kcal}$$

The favourable conditions are

- high concentration of N_2 or/and H_2.
- high pressure (as $\Delta n_g = -2$).
- low temperature (as the reaction is exothermic).

Although the low temperature favour the formation of NH_3, yet an optimum temperature is set, as the rate of reaction is very slow at low temperature. A temperature of 500°C is selected and a pressure of 200 atm is applied in practice.

To enhance the rate of reaction, catalyst, finely divided iron containing molybdenum (acts as promoter) is used.

(iii) Manufacture of Sulphuric Acid by Contact Process

The first step of the process is the conversion of SO_2 into SO_3.

$$2SO_2(g) + O_2(g) \rightleftharpoons 2SO_3(g); \Delta H = -196 \text{ kJ mol}$$

But the process is very slow so its speed is increased by using catalyst like platinum or divanadium pentaoxide V_2O_5. Other conditions favouring this process are

- increase in pressure (as $\Delta n_g = -1$).
- high concentration of SO_2 and O_2.
- low concentration of SO_3.
- low temperature as the reaction is exothermic.

(iv) Manufacture of Nitric Acid (Birkeland-Eyde Process)

$$N_2(g) + O_2(g) \rightleftharpoons 2NO(g); \Delta H = +43.2 \text{ kcal}$$

The factors favouring formation of NO are

- increase in concentration of N_2 and O_2.
- unaffected by pressure change (as $\Delta n_g = 0$).
- increase in temperature (as the reaction is endothermic).

Quick Test 1

Conceptual Questions

1. Explain, why pure liquids and solids can be ignored while writing the equilibrium constant expression? NCERT

2. The equilibrium constant expression for a gas reaction is,

$$K_C = \frac{[NH_3]^4\ [O_2]^5}{[NO]^4\ [H_2O]^6}$$

Write the balanced chemical equation corresponding to this expression. NCERT

3. Predict which of the following reaction will have appreciable concentration of reactants and products?

(i) $Cl_2(g) \rightleftharpoons 2Cl(g);\ K_C = 5 \times 10^{-39}$

(ii) $Cl_2(g) + 2NO(g) \rightleftharpoons 2NOCl(g);\ K_C = 3.7 \times 10^{-8}$

(iii) $Cl_2(g) + 2NO_2(g) \rightleftharpoons 2NO_2Cl(g);\ K_C = 1.8$ NCERT

4. For the reaction, $H_2(g) + I_2(g) \rightleftharpoons 2HI(g)$, the standard free energy is $\Delta G^\ominus > 0$. How is the equilibrium constant affected? NCERT Exemplar

Numerical Questions

5. At 450 K, $K_p = 2.0 \times 10^{10}$/bar for the given reaction at equilibrium.

$$2SO_2(g) + O_2(g) \rightleftharpoons 2SO_3(g)$$

What is K_C at this temperature? NCERT

6. At a certain temperature and total pressure of 10^5 Pa, iodine vapour contains 40% by volume of I atoms

$$I_2(g) \rightleftharpoons 2I(g)$$

Calculate K_p for the equilibrium. NCERT

7. What is the equilibrium concentration of each of the substances in the equilibrium when the initial concentration of ICl was 0.78 M ?

$$2ICl(g) \rightleftharpoons I_2(g) + Cl_2(g);\ K_C = 0.14$$ NCERT

8. One of the reaction that takes place in producing steel from iron ore is the reduction of iron(II) oxide by carbon monoxide to give iron metal and CO_2.

$FeO(s) + CO(g) \rightleftharpoons Fe(s) + CO_2(g);K_p = 0.265$ atm at 1050K

What are the equilibrium partial pressures of CO and CO_2 at 1050 K if the initial partial pressures are, $p_{CO} = 1.4$ atm and $p_{CO_2} = 0.80$ atm? NCERT

9. The equilibrium constant for the following reaction is 1.6×10^5 at 1024 K.

$$H_2(g) + Br_2(g) \rightleftharpoons 2HBr(g)$$

Find the equilibrium pressure of all gases if 10.0 bar of HBr is introduced into a sealed container at 1024 K. NCERT

10. At 1127 K and 1 atm pressure, a gaseous mixture of CO and CO_2, in equilibrium with solid carbon has 90.55% CO by mass.

$$C(s) + CO_2(g) \rightleftharpoons 2CO(g)$$

Calculate K_C for this reaction at the above temperature. NCERT

Answers

5. 7.479×10^{11} L mol^{-1} **6.** 0.2666×10^5 Pa $\approx 2.67 \times 10^4$ Pa

7. $[I_2] = [Cl_2] = 0.1668$ M, $[ICl] = 0.45$ M **8.** 1.739 atm, 0.461 atm

9. $p_{H_2} = p_{Br_2} = 2.5 \times 10^{-2}$ bar, $p_{HBr} = 10$ bar, **10.** 0.153

For Solutions, See QR Code on Pg. 254

6.7 Ionic Equilibrium in Solution

Equilibria that involves ions only are called ionic equilibrium. e.g. Following equilibrium established between iron (II) thiocyanate and its constituent ions when it is dissolved in water.

$$[Fe(SCN)]^{2+}(aq) \rightleftharpoons Fe^{3+}(aq) + SCN^-(aq)$$

Such equilibrium reactions are known as ionic equilibrium. The substances which dissociate into their constituent ions, conduct electricity in aqueous or molten state. On this basis, Michael Faraday classified the substances into following two categories.

Non-Electrolytes

A solution of substances like urea, glucose, etc., that does not dissociate into ions when dissolved in water hence are a bad conductor of electricity. Such substances are termed as non-electrolytes.

Electrolytes

The substance that dissociate into ions when dissolved in water are called electrolytes. Such substance conduct electricity in aqueous solution.

Depending upon the extent of ionisation, the electrolytes are further classified into two classes by Faraday.

(i) Strong Electrolytes

These are dissociated largely or almost completely (100 %) in solution and consequently becomes very good conductor of electricity. e.g. Aqueous solution of common salt (NaCl) contains mainly sodium ions and chloride ions. These electrolytes are completely ionised in aqueous ionisation and is represented by putting a single arrow.

e.g. $NaOH(aq) \longrightarrow Na^+(aq) + OH^-(aq)$

Other examples of strong electrolytes are HCl, H_2SO_4, HNO_3, NaOH, KOH, KCl, KNO_3, NH_4Cl etc.

(ii) Weak Electrolytes

These never get completely dissociated. In ordinary conditions, weak electrolytes dissociate in solution to a small extent (~ 5%) and the solution, consequently, is a bad conductor of electricity.

e.g. Aqueous solution of acetic acid contains mainly unionised acetic acid molecules and only some acetate ions and hydronium ions.

These electrolytes are partially ionised, thus their ionisation is represented by putting double arrows ($\rightleftharpoons$) in between.

e.g. $CH_3COOH + H_2O \rightleftharpoons CH_3COO^- + H_3O^+$

Other examples of such electrolytes are H_3PO_4, H_3BO_3, NH_4OH, $(NH_4)_2CO_3$, HCN etc.

Degree of Dissociation/Ionisation

In the solution of weak electrolytes, an equilibrium is established between the ions and unionised electrolytes. Such equilibrium is called **ionic equilibrium**.

e.g. An electrolyte *AB* ionises as

$$AB \rightleftharpoons A^+ + B^-$$

The equilibrium established between *AB* and A^+ and B^- is called ionic equilibrium. The fraction of total number of molecules that undergo ionisation or dissociation is called the **degree of ionisation** or **dissociation** (α).

$$\text{Thus, } \alpha = \frac{\text{number of molecules of electrolyte ionised as ions}}{\text{total number of molecules of electrolyte dissolved}}$$

$$\text{or} \quad \alpha = \frac{\text{amount of electrolyte ionised}}{\text{initial amount}}$$

Degree of ionisation (α) increases with dilution and reaches to maximum limit (unity) at infinite dilution for weak electrolytes.

The extent of ionisation also depends upon the strength of the bond and the extent of solvation of ions obtained.

Acids, bases and salts come under the category of electrolytes and may act as either strong or weak electrolytes.

Note The process of separation of ions that are already present in the solid compound is called **dissociation**, whereas process of splitting of a neutral molecule into charged ions is called **ionisation**. However, both the terms are widely used without any difference.

6.8 Acids, Bases and Salts

The substance that have sour taste, turns blue litmus red, liberates hydrogen with some metals and neutralises base is termed as an **acid**, e.g. hydrochloric acid.

On the other hand, the substance having bitter taste, turns red litmus blue, feel soapy and neutralises acids is termed as a **base**.

e.g. When acid and base react together, they neutralise each other and result in the formation of **salt** alongwith water. e.g. sodium chloride, barium sulphate, sodium nitrate.

Although the above mentioned concepts of acids and bases are not applicable for all the substances. Hence, many scientist have been proposed the revised definitions of acids and bases from time to time.

Arrhenius Concept of Acids and Bases

According to this concept, *"all substances that give hydrogen ions,* H^+ *(aq) in their aqueous solutions are called* ***acids****, while that, which furnish hydroxyl ions,* OH^- *(aq) in water are called* ***bases****".*

e.g. $HA(aq) \longrightarrow H^+(aq) + A^-(aq)$ (Acid)

Or $HA(aq) + H_2O(l) \longrightarrow H_3O^+(aq) + A^-(aq)$ (Acid)

Similarly, $BOH(aq) \longrightarrow B^+(aq) + OH^-(aq)$ (Base)

Number of H^+ ions delivered by an acid in its aqueous solution is called **basicity** or **protocity** of the acid. The acids are referred as monobasic, dibasic, tribasic, etc., according to the number of protons given in aqueous solution as one, two or three.

Similarly, the number of OH^- furnished by the base in its aqueous solution is called its **acidity.** The substance that furnish both H^+ *(aq)* and OH^- *(aq)* are called **amphoteric substance.**

e.g. $\underset{\text{Water}}{H_2O(l)} \rightleftharpoons \underset{\text{Hydrogen ion}}{H^+(aq)} + \underset{\text{Hydroxyl ion}}{OH^-(aq)}$

Note
- A bare proton, H^+ because of its high reactivity, small size and intense electric field, combines with oxygen of water molecule through lone pair and forms **hydronium ion,** $H^+ + H_2O \longrightarrow H_3O^+$ (trigonal pyramidal geometry)
- The obtained hydronium ion further hydrate to give species such as $H_5O_2^+$, $H_7O_3^+$ and $H_9O_4^+$.
- Also, the OH^- ion is hydrated to form ionic species like $H_3O_2^-$, $H_5O_3^-$ and $H_7O_4^-$, etc.

Limitations of Arrhenius Theory

- Free H^+ and OH^- ions because of their high reactivity do not exist in water.
- This concept is limited to aqueous solutions only.
- The acidic character of certain salts like, $AlCl_3$, BF_3 and basic character of NH_3, PH_3 cannot be explained with the help of this concept.
- It is not applicable to the compounds which do not contain free H^+ or OH^- ions.

The Bronsted-Lowry Acids and Bases

According to this concept, *"an acid is a substance (molecule or ion) which can donate* H^+ *to a base and a base is a substance which can accept a proton from an acid".*

Thus, an acid is a proton donor (protogenic) and a base is proton acceptor (protophilic).

The acid-base pair, which differ by a proton are said to form a conjugate acid-base pair.

Adds proton

$$NH_3\,(aq) + H_2O(l) \rightleftharpoons NH_4^+(aq) + OH^-(aq)$$

Base | Acid | Conjugate acid | Conjugate base

Loses proton

Thus, the acid-base pair in the above example are

$$NH_3 \underset{-H^+}{\overset{+H^+}{\rightleftharpoons}} NH_4^+ \text{ and } H_2O(l) \underset{+H^+}{\overset{-H^+}{\rightleftharpoons}} OH^-$$

The general form of such reactions is

Add proton

Acid + Base $\rightleftharpoons$ Conjugate base + Conjugate acid

Loses proton

If Bronsted acid is a strong acid, then its conjugate base is a weak base and *vice-versa*.

It is also interesting to note that some substances exhibit dual behaviour, i.e. they have the tendency of accepting as well as donating the H^+ ion or in other words, they behave as acid and base both.

Such substances are called **amphoteric** or **amphiprotic substances.** e.g. NH_3, H_2O, CH_3COOH, etc.

Acid + Base		Conjugate acid	Conjugate base
$H_2O + H_2O$	$\rightleftharpoons$	H_3O^+	$+ OH^-$
$NH_3 + NH_3$	$\rightleftharpoons$	NH_4^+	$+ NH_2^-$
$CH_3COOH + CH_3COOH$	$\rightleftharpoons$	$CH_3COOH_2^+$	$+ CH_3COO^-$

Limitations of Bronsted-Lowry Concept

- This definition is unable to explain the reactions occurring in the non-protonic solvents such as $COCl_2$, SO_2, N_2O_4, etc.
- It cannot explain the reactions between some acidic oxides (such as CO_2, SO_2, SO_3) and basic oxides (such as CaO, BaO, MgO) which take place even in the absence of the solvent.
  e.g. $CaO + SO_3 \longrightarrow CaSO_4$
- BF_3, $AlCl_3$, etc., do not have any hydrogen and hence, cannot give a proton but are known to behave as acids.

Example 13 Conjugate acid of a weak base is always stronger. What will be the decreasing order of basic strength of the following conjugate bases?

$$OH^-, RO^-\ CH_3COO^-, Cl^-$$

NCERT Exemplar

Sol. Conjugate acid of the given bases are H_2O, ROH, CH_3COOH and HCl. Order of their acidic strength is $HCl > CH_3COOH > H_2O > ROH$.

Hence, order of basic strength of their conjugate bases is $Cl^- < CH_3COO^- < OH^- < RO^-$.

Example 14 The ionisation of hydrochloric acid in water is given below.

$$HCl\,(aq) + H_2O\,(l) \rightleftharpoons H_3O^+\,(aq) + Cl^-\,(aq)$$

Label two conjugate acid-base pairs in this ionisation.

NCERT Exemplar

Adds proton

Sol. $HCl\,(aq) + H_2O(l) \rightleftharpoons H_3O^+(aq) + Cl^-(aq)$

Acid | Base | Conjugate acid | Conjugate base

Loses proton

TEACHER'S TIP

Generally, the conjugate acid has one extra proton and each conjugate base has one less proton.

Lewis Acids and Bases

According to this concept, a **base** is a substance that have a tendency to donate an electron pair to form a coordinate bond and an **acid** is a substance that accepts the electron pair donated by the Lewis base.

Thus, a Lewis acid is an electrophile or electron deficient species. e.g. $AlCl_3$, Co^{3+}, Mg^{2+}, etc., whereas a Lewis base is a nucleophile or electron rich species, e.g. H_2O, NH_3, OH^-, NO, CO etc.

According to Lewis, a general acid-base reaction can be expressed in the following manner.

$$A + :B \longrightarrow A \leftarrow B$$

$$\text{Acid} + \text{Base} \longrightarrow \text{Complex}$$

$$H^+ + :OH^- \longrightarrow H \leftarrow OH$$

$$BF_3 + :NH_3 \longrightarrow H_3N \rightarrow BF_3$$

It is also interesting to notify that **all Bronsted-Lowry bases also act as Lewis bases** because of the presence of lone pairs on all the bases.

But **all Bronsted Lowry acids do not behave as Lewis acids** because of the absence of proton, as in BF_3 which because of its electron deficiency acts as Lewis acid but not as Brönsted acid (due to the absence of proton).

Limitations of Lewis Concept

- The strength of Lewis acids and bases is found to depend on the type of reaction, it is not possible to arrange them in any order of their relative strength.
- It does not explain the behaviour of protonic acids such as HNO_3, HCl, H_2SO_4, etc.
- Catalytic activity of Lewis acid can't be explained because the catalytic activity of many acids is due to their tendency to furnish H^+. Lewis acid does not do so.
- All acid-base reactions do not involve co-ordinate bond formation.

Ionisation of Acids and Bases

Arrhenius concept of acids and bases becomes useful in case of ionisation of acids and bases as mostly ionisation in chemical and biological systems occur in aqueous medium.

Strengths of Acids and Bases

(i) According to Arrhenius Concept

According to this concept the acids that dissociate almost completely into their constituent ions in an aqueous medium and thus, readily provide a proton are called **strong acids.**

e.g. Perchloric acid ($HClO_4$), hydrochloric acid (HCl), hydroiodic acid (HI), nitric acid (HNO_3), sulphuric acid (H_2SO_4), etc.

Similarly, the bases that dissociate almost completely into their constituent ions in an aqueous medium and thus, readily provide a hydroxyl ion, are called **strong bases,** e.g. Alkali metal hydroxides (NaOH, LiOH, KOH, CsOH), barium hydroxide $[Ba(OH)_2]$, etc.

Note Higher the value of ionisation constant, K_a, more is the acidic strength. Similarly, higher the value of K_b more is the basic strength. More about K_a and K_b you will read in next topic.

(ii) According to Bronsted- Lowry Concept

According to this concept, between the two acids, the acid having higher tendency to give a proton is termed as the **stronger acid** and in such a condition, the equilibrium reaction goes in the direction of weaker acid.

e.g. In the reaction,

$$\underset{\text{Acid}}{HA(aq)} + \underset{\text{Base}}{H_2O(l)} \rightleftharpoons \underset{\text{Conjugate acid}}{H_3O^+(aq)} + \underset{\text{Conjugate base}}{A^-(aq)}$$

If HA is a stronger acid than H_3O^+, it readily gives its proton to H_2O and the reaction shifts in the forward direction, i.e. the solution will mainly contain A^- and H_3O^+ ions.

The H_3O^+ and A^- both are weaker as strong acid gives its proton to a strong base.

It means that **the conjugate base obtained from a strong acid is weak and that obtained from a weak acid is strong**, e.g. ClO_4^-, Cl^-, Br^-, I^-, NO_3^-, and HSO_4^- that are the conjugate base of strong acids are much weaker bases than water, whereas, NO_2, F^-, CH_3COO^- the conjugate base of weak acids are stronger than water.

Similarly, **a conjugate acid obtained from a strong base is weak and that obtained from a weak base is strong**, e.g. NH_2^-, O^{2-} and H^- being good acceptor are stronger base as compared to water.

Note Water soluble organic compounds such as phenolphthalein and bromothymol blue are weak acids and have different colour in their acid (H In) and conjugate base (In^-) forms, so these are widely used as indicators in acid- base titrations. They are also used in finding out H^+ ion concentration.

$$\underset{\substack{\text{Acid}\\\text{Indicator}\\(\text{Colour }A)}}{HIn(aq)} + \underset{\text{Base}}{H_2O(l)} \rightleftharpoons \underset{\text{Conjugate acid}}{H_3O^+(aq)} + \underset{\substack{\text{Conjugate base}\\(\text{Colour }B)}}{In^-(aq)}$$

The Ionisation Constant of Water and its Ionic Product

It is well known now that the water acts as both acid and base. In pure water, one water molecule acts as an acid by donating its proton while the other acts as a base by accepting the proton at the same time.

Thus, the following equilibrium exists in the water.

$$\underset{\text{Acid}}{H_2O(l)} + \underset{\text{Base}}{H_2O(l)} \rightleftharpoons \underset{\text{Conjugate acid}}{H_3O^+(aq)} + \underset{\text{Conjugate base}}{OH^-(aq)}$$

Applying law of mass action, the dissociation constant,

$$K = \frac{[H_3O^+][OH^-]}{[H_2O]^2}$$

Since, water is a pure liquid, so its concentration remains constant.

Hence, $[H_2O]^2$ is incorporated with K (equilibrium constant) and a new constant, K_w is used in place of $K[H_2O]^2$. i.e.

$$K_w = [H_3O^+][OH^-]$$

or $$K_w = [H^+][OH^-]$$

$[\because [H_3O^+]$ and $[H^+]$ are same$]$

K_w is called the **ionic product of water.**

From the experiments, it is found that at 298 K,

$$[H^+] = [H_3O^+] = 1.0 \times 10^{-7} \text{ M}$$

Since, water produces $[H_3O^+]$ and $[OH^-]$ in equal numbers, so $[H_3O^+] = [OH^-] = 1.0 \times 10^{-7}$ M

On substituting the values, we get

$$K_w = (1 \times 10^{-7})^2 = 1 \times 10^{-14} \text{ M}^2 \quad \text{(at 298 K)}$$

TEACHER'S TIP

- $K_w = [H^+][OH^-]$ (at 298 K)
- If $[H^+] = [OH^-]$, solution is neutral.
- If $[H^+] > [OH^-]$, solution is acidic.
- If $[H^+] < [OH^-]$, solution is basic.

Note The value of K_w is temperature dependent as it is an equilibrium constant.

Example 15 **At 363 K, pure water has $[H_3O^+] = 10^{-6}$ M. Calculate the value of K_w at this temperature.**

Sol. Given, $[H_3O^+] = [OH^-] = 10^{-6}$ M

$$K_w = [H_3O^+][OH^-] = 10^{-12} \text{ M}$$

Example 16 **Calculate H_3O^+ and OH^- ion concentrations at 25°C in**

(i) 0.02 N HNO_3 solution

(ii) 0.005 N KOH solution

Sol. (i) HNO_3 completely ionises as

$$HNO_3 + H_2O \longrightarrow H_3O^+ + NO_3^-$$

$\therefore [H_3O^+] = [HNO_3] = 0.02$ N (Given)

$= 0.02$ M $\quad (\because HNO_3$ is monobasic)

$= 2 \times 10^{-2}$ M

Now, as $[H_3O^+][OH^-] = K_w = 10^{-14}$

$$\therefore [OH^-] = \frac{K_w}{[H_3O^+]} = \frac{10^{-14}}{2 \times 10^{-2}}$$

$= 5 \times 10^{-13}$ M

(ii) KOH completely ionises as $KOH \longrightarrow K^+ + OH^-$

$\therefore [OH^-] = [KOH] = 0.005$ N (Given)

$= 5 \times 10^{-3}$ M $\quad (\because$KOH is monoacidic)

Now, as $[H_3O^+][OH^-] = K_w = 10^{-14}$s

$$\therefore [H_3O^+] = \frac{K_w}{[OH^-]} = \frac{10^{-14}}{5 \times 10^{-3}} = 2 \times 10^{-12} \text{ M}$$

6.9 pH Scale

In order to represent the hydronium ion concentration expressed in molarity more conveniently. **Sorensen** introduced a logarithmic scale, called the **pH scale**. The pH of a solution is defined as *"the negative logarithm to base 10 of the activity of hydrogen ion (a_{H^+})"*. If the solution is very dilute (i.e.) < 0.01M), the activity of hydrogen ion becomes equal to its molarity, i.e.

$$a_{H^+} = \frac{[H^+]}{\text{mol L}^{-1}}$$

(a_{H^+} is a dimensionless quantity)

From the definition of pH,

$$pH = -\log a_{H^+} = (-\log H^+ / \text{mol L}^{-1})$$

or $$pH = -\log[H^+] = \log\frac{1}{[H^+]}$$

e.g. pH of an acidic solution of HCl of concentration 10^{-2}M is 2 and a basic solution of NaOH having $[OH^-] = 10^{-4}$ M and $[H_3O^+] = 10^{-10}$M is 10.

Also, at 25°C the hydrogen ion concentration of water $= 10^{-7}$ M. Hence, pH of pure water is given as

$$pH = -\log(10^{-7}) = 7$$

Acidic solution has pH < 7 (as $[H^+] > 10^{-7}$M)

Basic solution has pH > 7 (as $[H^+] < 10^{-7}$M)

Neutral solution has pH = 7 (as $[H^+] = 10^{-7}$M)

Since, pH scale is a logarithmic scale, so a decrease of a single pH unit corresponds to ten folds increase in acidic nature.

That's why **change in pH with temperature is often ignored.**

Example 17 **The concentration of hydrogen ion in a sample of soft drink is 3.8×10^{-3} M. What is its pH?**

NCERT Exemplar

Sol. $pH = -\log [H^+] = -\log [3.8 \times 10^{-3}]$

$= \log [3.8] + \log [10^{-3}]$

$= -[(0.58) + (-3.0)] = -[-2.42] = 2.42$

Therefore, the pH of the soft drink is 2.42.

Measurement of pH

pH of a solution is generally measured by using pH paper, which gives different colours with the solutions of different pH. The pH in the range of 1-14 can be determined with an accuracy of ~0.5 by using pH papers.

The pH paper consists of strips which show different colours with different pH value. The pH value can be determined by matching the strip with a reference colour chart provided with it.

pH of some common substances are tabulated below.

The pH of some common substances

Name of the fluid	pH	Name of the fluid	pH
Saturated solution of NaOH	~ 15	Black coffee	5.0
0.1 M NaOH solution	13	Tomato juice	~ 4.2
Lime water	10.5	Soft drinks and vinegar	~ 3.0
Milk of magnesia	10	Lemon juice	~2.2
Egg white, sea water	7.8	Gastric juice	~1.2
Human blood	7.4	1 M HCl solution	~0
Milk	6.8	Concentrated HCl	~1.0
Human saliva	6.4		~-1.0

pOH Value

Just as pH indicates H^+ ion concentration, pOH represents the OH^- ion concentration. i.e.

$$pOH = -\log [OH^-]$$

Relation between pH and pOH

- In case of pure water at 25° C

  $[H^+] = [OH^-] = 1 \times 10^{-7}$, thus $pH = pOH = 7$ represents neutrality.
- In case of acidic solution,

  $[H^+] > [OH^-]$, thus pH < 7 and pOH > 7.
- Also, in case of alkaline solution, $[H^+] < [OH^-]$, thus, pH > 7 and pOH < 7.

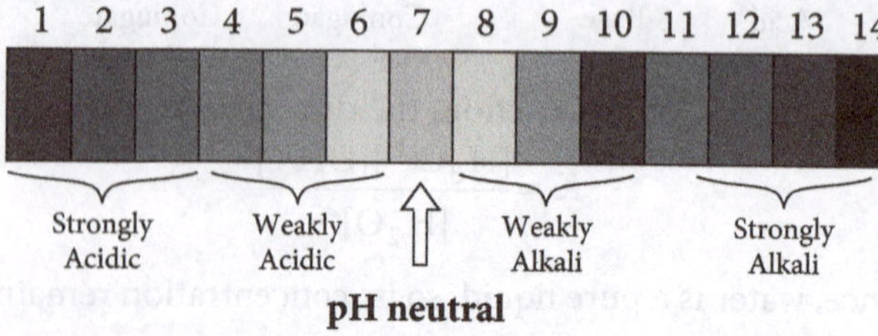

Example 18 **Calculate the pH of *N*/1000 sodium hydroxide solution assuming complete ionisation ($K_w = 1.0 \times 10^{-14}$).**

Sol. NaOH completely ionises as $NaOH \longrightarrow Na^+ + OH^-$

$\therefore [OH^-] = [NaOH] = \frac{N}{1000} = 10^{-3}\ N = 10^{-3}\ M$

[∵ Eq. mass = mass in case of NaOH]

Now, as $[H_3O^+][OH^-] = 10^{-14}$

$\because\ [H_3O^+] = \frac{10^{-14}}{[OH^-]} = \frac{10^{-14}}{[OH^-]} = \frac{10^{-14}}{10^{-3}} = 10^{-11}$

$\therefore\quad pH = -\log [H_3O^+] = -\log 10^{-11} = 11$

Limitations of pH Scale

- pH values of the solutions do not give us immediate idea of the relative strengths of the solutions.
- pH value of 1 N solution of strong acid is obtained zero. But in case the concentration is 2 N, 3N, 10 N, etc., the respective pH values are negative.
- A solution of an acid having very low concentration say 10^{-8} N shows pH value less than 7 and not 8 as shown by pH formula.

Example 19 **Calculate the pH of 10^{-8} M HCl solution.**

Sol. $\because\ pH = -\log [H^+] = -\log 10^{-8} = 8$

But this is not true because an acidic solution cannot have pH greater than 7. In this condition, $[H^+]$ of water cannot be neglected.

Therefore, $[H^+]_{total} = [H^+]_{HCl} + [H^+]_{H_2O} = 10^{-8} + 10^{-7}$

$= 10^{-8}\ (1 + 10) = 11 \times 10^{-8}$

Now from, $pH = -\log [H^+] = -\log (11 \times 10^{-8})$

$= -\log 11 - \log 10^{-8} = 6.958$

6.10 Ionisation Constants of Weak Acids and Bases

Ionisation Constants of Weak Acids

Consider a weak acid HX that ionises only partially and after sometime the following equilibrium is established.

$$H_2O(l) + HX(aq) \longrightarrow H_3O^+(aq) + X^-(aq)$$

Initial conc.	C	0	0
At equilibrium conc.	$C(1-\alpha)$	$C\alpha$	$C\alpha$

where, C (mol/L) be the initial concentration of the weak acid at $t=0$ and α be the degree of dissociation. So, dissociation constant or ionisation constant of acid HX, K_a may be given as

$$K_a = \frac{[H^+][X^-]}{[HX]} = \frac{C\alpha \times C\alpha}{C(1-\alpha)} = \frac{C\alpha^2}{1-\alpha} \quad \ldots(i)$$

At a given temperature T, K_a is a measure of the strength of the acid HX, i.e. larger the value of K_a, the stronger is the acid. K_a is a dimensionless quantity with the understanding that the standard state concentration of all species is 1M.

Since, the standard state concentration of all the species is 1M, so K_a is a dimensionless quantity. If the acid is very weak, $\alpha <<< 1 \Rightarrow (1-\alpha) \approx 1$

$$\therefore \quad K = C\alpha^2 \text{ or } \alpha = \sqrt{\frac{K}{C}}$$

or $$\alpha \propto \frac{1}{\sqrt{C}} \propto \sqrt{V} \quad \left(\because C \propto \frac{1}{V}\right)$$

(where, V = volume of solution)

Thus, "the degree of dissociation is proportional to the square root of dilution for weak electrolytes." This is the statement of **Ostwald law.** Degree of dissociation increases as dilution increases.

Note The approximation $(1-\alpha)=1$ can be applied only if $\alpha < 50\%$. If on solving a problem by applying the approximate formula, α comes out to be $>50\%$, the problems may be solved by applying the exact formula and α may be calculated applying the solution of the quadratic equation.

$$\alpha = \frac{-b \pm \sqrt{b^2 - 4ac}}{2a} \quad (\text{for, } a\alpha^2 + b\alpha + c = 0)$$

Example 20 The ionisation constant of phenol is 1.0×10^{-10}. What is the concentration of phenolate ion in 0.05 M solution of phenol? What will be its degree of ionisation if the solution is also 0.01 M in sodium phenolate? NCERT

Sol. The equation of the dissociation of phenol is

$$C_6H_5OH \longrightarrow C_6H_5O^- + H^+(H_3O^+)$$

By Ostwald dilution law, $[C_6H_5O^-] = [H_3O^+]$

$$= \sqrt{K_a \cdot C} = \sqrt{1.0 \times 10^{-10} \times 0.05} = 2.24 \times 10^{-6} \text{ M}$$

When mixture contains 0.05 M phenol and 0.01 M phenolate ion (from sodium phenolate) then

$$K_a = \frac{[C_6H_5O^-][H_3O^+]}{[C_6H_5OH]}$$

$$1.0 \times 10^{-10} = \frac{[0.01] \times [H_3O^+]}{[0.05]}$$

$$[H_3O^+] = \frac{0.05 \times 1.0 \times 10^{-10}}{0.01} = 5 \times 10^{-10} \text{ M}$$

$$[H_3O^+] = C \cdot \alpha = 5 \times 10^{-10}$$

or $$\alpha = \frac{5 \times 10^{-10}}{C} = \frac{5 \times 10^{-10}}{0.05} = 1 \times 10^{-8}$$

Ionisation Constants of Weak Bases

Consider a weak base, MOH, ionises only partially in the following manner,

$$MOH(aq) \rightleftharpoons M^+(aq) + OH^-(aq)$$

Initial conc.	C	0	0
Conc. at equilibrium	$C - C\alpha = C(1-\alpha)$	$C\alpha$	$C\alpha$

The ionisation constant of the base,

$$K_b = \frac{[M^+][OH^-]}{[MOH]} = \frac{C\alpha \cdot C\alpha}{C(1-\alpha)} = \frac{C\alpha^2}{(1-\alpha)}$$

Base ionisation constant K_b relates directly with hydroxyl ion concentration, so it is a measure of basicity of a base. **Higher the K_b value, more basic is the base.** Like K_a, K_b is also a dimensionless quantity.

Example 21 0.16 g N_2H_4 is dissolved in water and the total volume is made upto 500 mL. Calculate the percentage of N_2H_4 that has reacted with water in this solution. K_b for N_2H_4 is 4.0×10^{-6} M.

Sol. N_2H_4 ionises in the following manner

$$N_2H_4 + H_2O \rightleftharpoons N_2H_5^+ + OH^-$$

Initially	1	0	0
After diss.	$1-\alpha$	α	α

$$K_b = \frac{C\alpha^2}{(1-\alpha)} = C\alpha^2 \quad [\text{if } (1-\alpha) \approx 1]$$

$$C = [N_2H_4] = \frac{0.16 \times 1000}{32 \times 500} = 0.01$$

$$K_b = 4 \times 10^{-6} \text{ M}$$

$$\alpha = \sqrt{\frac{4 \times 10^{-6}}{0.01}} = 0.02 \text{ or } 2\%$$

Relation between K_a and K_b

K_a and K_b represents the strength of an acid and a base, respectively.

The equilibrium constant for a net reaction obtained after adding two or more reactions equal the product of the equilibrium constants for individual reactions.

$$K_{net} = K_1 \times K_2 \times .....$$

Similarly, in case of a conjugate acid-base pair,

$$K_a \times K_b = K_w$$

p*K* Value

p stands for negative logarithm. Thus, p*K* is the negative logarithm of dissociation constant.

$\therefore$ $pK_a = -\log K_a$ and $pK_b = -\log K_b$

Weak acids have higher pK_a values. Similarly weak bases have higher pK_b values.

For any conjugate acid-base pair in aqueous solution, we know that,

$$K_a \times K_b = K_w = 1 \times 10^{-14} \quad \text{(at 298 K)}$$

Taking logarithm on both sides, we have

$$\log (K_a \times K_b) = \log (1 \times 10^{-14})$$

or $\log K_a + \log K_b = -14$

or $(-\log K_a) + (-\log K_b) = 14$

or $pK_a + pK_b = 14$ (at 298 K)

Algorithm for Calculating pH of a solution

In case of weak electrolytes, the calculation of pH involves following steps

- Specify the acids and bases, (Bronsted-Lowry) taking part in the dissociation process.
- Write balanced equations for all possible reactions.
- The reaction with highest value of K_a is the primary reaction and the others are the subsidiary reactions.
- Enlist the following values for each species of the primary reaction.
  - (a) Initial concentration, *C*
  - (b) Change in concentration on proceeding to equilibrium in terms of α
  - (c) Equilibrium concentration
- Write the equilibrium constant expression and substitute the equilibrium concentrations into it and solve for α.
- Calculate the concentration of each species taking part in the reaction.
- Calculate pH by using the expression, $pH = -\log[H^+]$.

Note Strength of a weak acid can also be measured by **"percent dissociation"**.

$$\text{Percent dissociation} = \frac{[HA]_{dissociated}}{[HA]_{initial}} \times 100\%$$

Example 22 The ionisation constant of HF is 3.2×10^{-4}. Calculate the degree of dissociation of HF in its 0.02 M solution. Calculate the concentration of all species present (H_3O^+, F^- and HF) in the solution and its pH. **NCERT**

Sol. **Step I** HF is a Bronsted acid and water is a base here.

Step II The following proton transfer reactions are possible

(i) $HF + H_2O \rightleftharpoons H_3O^+ + F^-; K_a = 3.2 \times 10^{-4}$

(ii) $H_2O + H_2O \rightleftharpoons H_3O^+ + OH^-;$ $K_w = 1.0 \times 10^{-14}$

Step III As $K_a >> K_w$, (i) is the principle reaction.

Step IV $HF + H_2O \rightleftharpoons H_3O^+ + F^-$

	HF	H_3O^+	F^-
Initial conc.	0.02	0	0
Change	$-0.02\,\alpha$	$+0.02$	$+\ 0.02\,\alpha$
Equili. conc.	$0.02 - 0.02\,\alpha$	$0.02\,\alpha$	$0.02\,\alpha$

Step V Equilibrium constant,

$$K_a = \frac{(0.02\,\alpha)^2}{(0.02 - 0.02\alpha)}$$

$$= \frac{0.02\,\alpha^2}{(1-\alpha)} = 3.2 \times 10^{-4}$$

or $\alpha^2 + 1.6 \times 10^{-2}\,\alpha - 1.6 \times 10^{-2} = 0$

using $x = \dfrac{-b \pm \sqrt{b^2 - 4ac}}{2a}$

we get $\alpha = +0.12$ and -0.12

The negative root is not acceptable and hence, $\alpha = 0.12$

Step VI $\therefore [H_3O^+] = [F^-] = C\alpha = 0.02 \times 0.12$

$= 2.4 \times 10^{-3}$ M

$[HF] = C(1-\alpha) = 0.02\,(1 - 0.12)$

$= 17.6 \times 10^{-3}$ M

Step VII $pH = -\log [H^+]$

$= -\log (2.4 \times 10^{-3}) = 2.62$

Example 23 **The pH of 0.1 M monobasic acid is 4.50. Calculate the concentration of species H^+, A^- and HA at equilibrium. Also, determine the value of K_a and pK_a of the monobasic acid.** NCERT

Sol. $\because$ $pH = -\log[H^+]$

$\therefore$ $[H^+] = 1\times 10^{-pH}$

$= 1\times 10^{-4.50} = 3.16\times 10^{-5}$

Since, $[H^+] = [A^-] = 3.16\times 10^{-5}$

and $K_a = [H^+][A^-]/[HA]$

$[HA]_{equilibrium} = 0.1 - (3.16\times 10^{-5}) \approx 0.1$

$$K_a = \frac{(3.16\times 10^{-5})^2}{0.1} / 0.1 = 1.0\times 10^{-8}$$

$pK_a = -\log(10^{-8}) = 8$

Example 24 **Calculate the pH of 0.08 M solution of hypochlorous acid, HOCl. The ionisation constant of the acid is 2.5×10^{-5}. Determine the percent dissociation of HOCl.** NCERT

Sol. The ionisation equation of HOCl is as follows

$$HOCl(aq) + H_2O(l) \rightleftharpoons H_3O^+(aq) + ClO^-(aq)$$

	HOCl		H_3O^+	ClO^-
Initial conc. (M)	0.08		0	0
Change in conc. (M)	$-x$		$+x$	$+x$
To reach equili. conc. (M)	$0.08 - x$		x	x

$$\therefore \quad K_a = \left\{\frac{[H_3O^+][ClO^-]}{[HOCl]}\right\} = \frac{x^2}{(0.08 - x)}$$

$\because$ $x << 0.08$,

$\therefore$ $0.08 - x \simeq 0.08$

$$\therefore \quad \frac{x^2}{0.08} = 2.5\times 10^{-5}$$

$x^2 = 2.0\times 10^{-6}$

or $x = 1.41\times 10^{-3}$

$[H^+] = 1.41\times 10^{-3}$ M

$$\text{Percent dissociation} = \left\{\frac{[HOCl]_{dissociated}}{[HOCl]_{initial}}\right\}\times 100$$

$$= \frac{1.41\times 10^{-3}}{0.08}\times 10^2 = 1.76\%$$

$pH = -\log[H^+] = -\log(1.41\times 10^{-3}) = 2.85$

Example 25 **The pH of 0.004 M hydrazine solution is 9.7. Calculate its ionisation constant K_b and pK_b.** NCERT

Sol. Hydrazine undergoes ionisation in the following manner,

$$NH_2NH_2 + H_2O \rightleftharpoons NH_2NH_3^+ + OH^-$$

$[H^+] = \text{antilog}(-pH) = \text{antilog}(-9.7) = 1.67\times 10^{-10}$

$$[OH^-] = \frac{K_w}{[H^+]} = \frac{1\times 10^{-14}}{1.67\times 10^{-10}} = 5.98\times 10^{-5} = [NH_2NH_3^+]$$

$$K_b = \frac{[NH_2NH_3^+][OH^-]}{[NH_2NH_2]}$$

$$= \frac{(5.98\times 10^{-5})^2}{0.004} = 8.96\times 10^{-7}$$

$pK_b = -\log K_b = -\log(8.96\times 10^{-7}) = 6.04$

Di- and Polybasic Acids and Di- and Polyacidic Bases

Acids having more than one ionisable proton per molecule of acids are known as polybasic or polyprotic acids, e.g. oxalic acid (HOOC—COOH), sulphuric acid (H_2SO_4), phosphoric acid (H_3PO_4), etc.

The ionisation reactions for a dibasic acid, H_2X involve following two steps as shown below.

$$H_2X(aq) \rightleftharpoons H^\oplus(aq) + HX^\ominus(aq)$$

$$HX^\ominus(aq) \rightleftharpoons H^\oplus(aq) + X^{2-}(aq)$$

The equilibrium constants for the above two reactions are as follow

$$K_{a_1} = \frac{[H^\oplus][HX^\ominus]}{[H_2X]}$$

and $$K_{a_2} = \frac{[H^\oplus][X^{2-}]}{[HX^\ominus]}$$

(K_{a_1} and K_{a_2} are the first and second ionisation constants, respectively, of the acid H_2X).

Thus, the solution of a diprotic acid contains H_2X, HX^- and A^{2-}. The H^+ ions are mainly obtained from the first ionisation step. Overall equilibrium

$$H_2X(aq) \rightleftharpoons 2H^+(aq) + X^{2-}(aq)$$

$$K_a = \frac{[H^+]^2[X^{2-}]}{[H_2X]} = K_{a_1}\times K_{a_2}$$

Similarly, in case of a tribasic acids such as H_3PO_4, there are three ionisation constants.

$$H_3PO_4 \rightleftharpoons H^+ + H_2PO_4^-$$

$$H_2PO_4^- \rightleftharpoons H^+ + HPO_4^{2-}$$

$$HPO_4^{2-} \rightleftharpoons H^+ + PO_4^{3-}$$

Overall equilibrium : $H_3PO_4 \rightleftharpoons 3H^+ + PO_4^{3-}$

Equilibrium constant for the above three steps are as follows

$$K_{a_1} = \frac{[H^+][H_2PO_4^-]}{[H_3PO_4]}$$

$$K_{a_2} = \frac{[H^+][HPO_4^{2-}]}{[H_2PO_4^-]}$$

and $$K_{a_3} = \frac{[H^+][PO_4^{3-}]}{[HPO_4^{2-}]}$$

$$K_a = K_{a_1} \times K_{a_2} \times K_{a_3}$$

It is found that K_{a_1} of polyprotic acid is greater than K_{a_2} or K_{a_3} (i.e. $K_{a_1} > K_{a_2} > K_{a_3}$), because it is more difficult to remove a positively charged proton from a negative ion due to electrostatic forces. Similarly, it is more difficult to remove a proton from a doubly charged anion as compared to single charged anion. Similarly, poly acidic bases also ionise in steps with ionisation constants, $K_b = K_{b_1} \times K_{b_2} \times K_{b_3}$ etc.

Example 26 **K_1 and K_2 for dissociation of H_2S are 4×10^{-3} and 1×10^{-5} respectively. Calculate sulphide ion concentration in 0.1 M H_2S solution.**

Sol. The first step of the dissociation of H_2S is

$$H_2S \rightleftharpoons H^{\oplus} + HS^{\ominus}$$

$$K_1 = \frac{[H^{\oplus}][HS^{\ominus}]}{[H_2S]} = 4 \times 10^{-3}$$

$\because$ $[H^{\oplus}] = C\alpha, [HS^{\ominus}] = C\alpha, [H_2S] = C(1-\alpha)$

$\therefore$ $4 \times 10^{-3} = \frac{C\alpha \cdot C\alpha}{C(1-\alpha)} = \frac{C\alpha^2}{(1-\alpha)}$

$4 \times 10^{-3} = \frac{0.1 \times \alpha^2}{(1-\alpha)}$ $(1-\alpha$ should not be neglected)

or $\alpha = 0.18$,

$\therefore$ $[H^{\oplus}] = C\alpha = 0.1 \times 0.18 = 0.018$ M

$[HS^{\ominus}] = C\alpha = 0.1 \times 0.18 = 0.018$ M

$[H_2S] = C(1-\alpha) = 0.1(1-0.18) = 0.082$ M

Now, $HS^{\ominus}$ further dissociates to $H^{\oplus}$ and S^{2-}

$C_1 = [HS^{\ominus}] = 0.018$ M

$$\underset{\substack{1 \\ (1-\alpha_1)}}{HS^{\ominus}} \rightleftharpoons \underset{\substack{0 \\ \alpha_1}}{H^{\oplus}} + \underset{\substack{0 \\ \alpha_1}}{S^{2-}}$$

$\therefore$ $K_2 = 1 \times 10^{-5} = \frac{[H^{\oplus}][S^{2-}]}{[HS^{\ominus}]}$

Because $[H^{\oplus}]$ already in solution $= 0.018$ and thus, dissociation of $HS^{\ominus}$ further suppresses due to common ion effect and $1 - \alpha \approx 1$.

$\therefore$ $1 \times 10^{-5} = \frac{0.018 \times C_1\alpha_1}{C_1(1-\alpha_1)} = 0.018 \times \alpha_1$

$\therefore$ $\alpha_1 = \frac{1 \times 10^{-5}}{0.018} = 5.55 \times 10^{-4}$

$\therefore$ $[S^{2-}] = C_1\alpha_1 = 0.018 \times 5.55 \times 10^{-4} = 0.099 \times 10^{-4}$

Factors Affecting Acid Strength

In general, the strength of an acid is affected by two main factors.

(i) Strength of H—*A* bond.

(ii) Polarity of H—*A* bond (where, *A* = any element except H)

When strength of H—*A* bond decreases, that is, the energy required to break the bond decreases, H*A* becomes a stronger acid. Also, when the H—*A* bond becomes more polar, i.e. the electronegativity difference between the atoms H and *A* increases and there is charge separation, cleavage of the bond becomes easier there by increasing the acidity.

- **In a group** of the periodic table, the acidic strength is decided by the strength of H—*A* bond.

  On moving down the group, as the size of *A* atom increases, H—*A* bond length and hence the tendency to give a proton increases, i.e. acidic strength increases.

  e.g. Size increases →

  HF << HCl << HBr << HI →

  Acid strength increases

  Similarly, $H_2O << H_2S < H_2Se < H_2Te$.

- **Along a period** of the periodic table, the acidic strength is decided by the polarity of the H—*A* bond. In general, as the electronegativity of atom *A* increases, polarity charge separation in H—*A* bond increases. Thus, the bond cleaved readily and hence, the strength of acid increases. e.g.

  Electronegativity of *A* increases →

  $CH_4 < NH_3 < H_2O < HF$

  → Acid strength increases

Common Ion Effect in the Ionisation of Acids and Bases

The degree of dissociation of an electrolyte or weak acid or weak base is suppressed by the addition of another electrolyte containing a common ion. This phenomenon is termed as **common ion effect**. It is based on Le chatelier's principle. e.g. *HAc* is a weak acid and ionises in the following manner.

$$HAc(aq) \rightleftharpoons H^+(aq) + Ac^-(aq); \; K_a = \frac{[H^+][Ac^-]}{[HAc]}$$

If an another electrolyte that furnish either H^+ or Ac^- is added to the above equilibrium, it will increase the concentration of H^+ or Ac^- ions and in order to keep K_a constant, the concentration of HAc must increase, i.e. the equilibrium shifts towards undissociated acid.

Example 27 **Calculate the pH of a 0.10M ammonia solution. Calculate the pH after 50.0 mL of this solution is treated with 25.0 mL of 0.10M HCl. The dissociation constant of ammonia, $K_b = 1.77 \times 10^{-5}$**

Sol. $NH_3 + H_2O \longrightarrow NH_4^+ + OH^-$

$$K_b = [NH_4^+][OH^-]/[NH_3] = 1.77 \times 10^{-5}$$

Before neutralisation.

$$[NH_4^+] = [OH^-] = x$$

$$[NH_3] = 0.10 - x \approx 0.10$$

$$x^2/0.10 = 1.77 \times 10^{-5}$$

Thus, $x = 1.33 \times 10^{-3} = [OH^-]$

Therefore, $[H^+] = K_w / [OH^-]$

$$= 10^{-14}/(1.33 \times 10^{-3}) = 7.51 \times 10^{-12}$$

$$pH = -\log(7.5 \times 10^{-12}) = 11.12$$

On addition of 25 mL of 0.1 M HCl solution (i.e. 2.5 mmol of HCl) to 50 mL of 0.1 M ammonia solution (i.e. 5 mmol of NH_3) 2.5 mmol of ammonia molecules are neutralised.

	NH_3	+ HCl	$\longrightarrow NH_4^+$	$+ Cl^-$
	2.5	2.5	0	0
At equilibrium	0	0	2.5	2.5

The resulting 75 mL of solution contains 2.5 mmol of NH_4^+ ions. (i.e. 0.033 M) and 2.5 mmol (i.e. 0.33 M) of unneutralised NH_3 molecules. This NH_3 exists in the following equilibrium.

$$\underset{0.033\,M - y}{NH_4OH} \rightleftharpoons \underset{y}{NH_4^+} + \underset{y}{OH^-}$$

Where, $y = [OH^-] = [NH_4^+]$

The final 75 mL solution after neutralisation already contains 2.5 m mol NH_4^+ ions (i.e. 0.033 M), thus total concentration of NH_4^+ ions is given as $[NH_4^+]$ $= 0.033\text{ M} + y$

As y is small, $[NH_4OH] \approx 0.033$ M and $[NH_4^+] \approx 0.033$ M.

We know, $K_b = \dfrac{[NH_4^+][OH^-]}{[NH_4OH]} = \dfrac{y\,(0.033)}{(0.033)} = 1.77 \times 10^{-5}$ M

Thus, $y = 1.77 \times 10^{-5} = [OH^-]$

$$[H^+] = \frac{10^{-14}}{1.77 \times 10^{-5}} = 0.56 \times 10^{-9}$$

Hence, $pH = 9.24$

Quick Test 2

Conceptual Questions

1. Why solution of sugar in water does not conduct electricity whereas that of common salt in water does?
2. (i) Write the conjugate acids for the following Bronsted bases NH_2^-, NH_3 and $HCOO^-$. *NCERT*
   (ii) Write the conjugate acid and conjugate base of H_2O. *Diksha*
3. (i) Define Lewis acid and lewis base.
   (ii) Which of the following are Lewis acids?
   H_2O, BF_3, H^+, NH_4^+ *NCERT*
4. Classify the following species into Lewis acids and Lewis bases and show how these act as Lewis acid/base? *NCERT*
   (i) OH^- (ii) F^- (iii) H^+ (iv) BCl_3
5. Ionisation constant of a weak base MOH, is given by the expression $K_b = \dfrac{[M^+][OH^-]}{[MOH]}$
   Values of ionisation constant of some weak bases at a particular temperature are given below.

Base	Dimethyl amine	Urea	Pyridine	Ammonia
K_b	5.4×10^{-4}	1.3×10^{-14}	1.77×10^{-9}	1.77×10^{-5}

   Arrange the bases in decreasing order of the extent of their ionisation at equilibrium. Which of the above base is the strongest? *NCERT Exemplar*

Numerical Questions

6. Calculate the pH of a solution formed by mixing equal volumes of two solutions, A and B of a strong acid having pH = 6 and pH = 4 respectively. *NCERT Exemplar*
7. Calculate the pH of 1×10^{-8} M solution of HCl.
8. Ionic product of water at 310 K is 2.7×10^{-14}. What is the pH of neutral water at this temperature? *NCERT*
9. The average concentration of SO_2 in atmosphere over a city on a certain day is 10 ppm, when the average temperature is 298 K. Given that the solubility of SO_2 in water at 298 K is 1.3653 mol/L and the pK_a of H_2SO_3 is 1.92, estimate the pH of acid rain on that day. *Competency Based Que.*
10. The pH of 0.005 M codeine ($C_{18}H_{21}NO_3$) solution is 9.95. Calculate its ionisation constant and pK_b. *NCERT*

Answers

6. 4.3 7. 6.98 8. 6.7844
9. 4.865 10. 1.588×10^{-6}, 5.80

For Solutions, See QR Code on Pg. 254

6.11 Hydrolysis of Salts and pH of their Solutions

The process of interaction of cation or anion or both provided by salt with water is called **hydrolysis** or **salt hydrolysis**. This process also affects the pH of the solutions.

Depending upon the nature of acid and base from which a salt is obtained, the salts are categorised into four categories.

(i) Salts of Strong Acid and Strong Base

The cations obtained from strong bases (like alkali metal ions and alkaline earth metal ions, i.e. Ba^{2+}, Ca^{2+}) and anions obtained from strong acids (like Cl^-, Br^-, NO_3^-, ClO_4^-, etc.,) do not hydrolyse.

It involves only ionisation of water and no hydrolysis.

Thus, the salt formed by halides, nitrates and sulphates of Na, K, Ca, Ba etc., are not hydrolysed by water and hence, the solutions of such salts remain neutral with pH 7.

e.g. $NaCl + H_2O \longrightarrow NaOH + HCl$

or $Na^+ + Cl^- + H_2O \longrightarrow Na^+ + OH^- + H^+Cl^-$

or $H_2O \longrightarrow H^+ + OH^-$

(ii) Salts of Weak Acids and Strong Bases

Salts of sodium and potassium other than halides, sulphates and nitrates fall in this category. e.g. CH_3COONa.

Such a salt, *BA* in aqueous medium exhibits following equilibrium.

$$BA \longrightarrow B^+ + A^-$$

$$B^+ + A^- + H_2O \rightleftharpoons HA + BOH$$

or $$A^- + H_2O \rightleftharpoons HA + \overset{\ominus}{O}H$$

Thus, this process is called **anionic hydrolysis**. This results in increase in OH^- ion concentration in the solution, thus making it more alkaline. So, solutions of such salts have a pH more than 7. (*BOH* being a strong base remains dissociated completely).

(a) Degree of Hydrolysis

It is defined as the fraction of total salt that has undergone hydrolysis on attainment of equilibrium. It is denoted by *h*. Let *C* be the concentration of salt and *h* be its degree of hydrolysis.

$$\underset{C-Ch}{A^\ominus} + H_2O \rightleftharpoons \underset{Ch}{\overset{\ominus}{O}H} + \underset{Ch}{HA} \text{ (equation of hydrolysis)}$$

$$K_h = \frac{[\overset{\ominus}{O}H][HA]}{[A^\ominus]} = \frac{(Ch)(Ch)}{C-Ch} = \frac{Ch^2}{1-h}$$

$$\therefore \quad K_h = Ch^2 \quad \text{[assuming } h << 1]$$

$$h = \sqrt{\frac{K_h}{C}}$$

Now, considering the dissociations of weak acid *HA* and H_2O.

$$HA \rightleftharpoons H^\oplus + A^\ominus; \quad K_a = \frac{[H^\oplus][A^\ominus]}{[HA]} \quad \ldots(i)$$

$$H_2O \rightleftharpoons H^\oplus + \overset{\ominus}{O}H; \quad K_w = [H^\oplus][\overset{\ominus}{O}H] \quad \ldots(ii)$$

$$K_h = \frac{K_w}{K_a}$$

(where, K_h is called hydrolysis constant)

(Subtracting Eq. (i) from Eq. (ii), we get the above equation of hydrolysis)

Now substituting the value of K_h in expression of *h*.

$$h = \sqrt{\frac{K_w}{K_a C}}$$

> **TEACHER'S TIP**
> Weaker is the acid, greatest is the hydrolysis constant. The degree of hydrolysis increases, when *C* decreases, i.e. with dilution.

(b) pH of Solution

pH of a basic solution is given as

$$pH + pOH = 14 \Rightarrow pH = 14 - pOH$$

$$pH = 14 - (-\log[OH^-])$$

and $$[\overset{\ominus}{O}H] = Ch = \sqrt{K_h C}$$

Substituting for K_h, we get $[\overset{\ominus}{O}H] = \sqrt{\frac{K_w C}{K_a}}$

$$pOH = -\log\sqrt{\frac{K_w C}{K_a}}$$

$$\Rightarrow \quad pH = 14 + \log\sqrt{\frac{K_w C}{K_a}} \quad [\because pH + pOH = 14]$$

$$\Rightarrow \quad pH = pK_w + \frac{1}{2}[\log(K_w) + \log C - \log K_a]$$

$$= pK_w - \frac{1}{2}pK_w + \frac{1}{2}[pK_a + \log C]$$

$$= \frac{1}{2} pK_w + \frac{1}{2}[pK_a + \log C]$$

$$= 7 + \frac{1}{2}(pK_a + \log C) \text{ at } 25°C$$

$$[\because K_w = 1\times10^{-14} \Rightarrow pK_w = 14]$$

Clearly, $pH > 7$

(iii) Salts of Strong Acids and Weak Bases

Halides, sulphates and nitrates of metals other than sodium, potassium fall in this category. e.g. NH_4Cl. The aqueous solution of such a salt BA, exhibits following equilibrium.

$$BA \longrightarrow B^+ + A^-$$

$$B^+ + A^- + H_2O \rightleftharpoons BOH + HA$$

or $$B^+ + H_2O \rightleftharpoons BOH + H^+$$

Since, B^+ ion undergoes hydrolysis, so this process is called **cationic hydrolysis.** Because of the generation of H^+ ions, the solution becomes acidic. [as the acid HA is strong]. Thus pH of salt solution is less than 7.

The hydrolysis constant is given by, $K_h = \frac{[H^+][BOH]}{[B^+]}$

(a) Degree of Hydrolysis

The net reaction of hydrolysis is

$$\underset{C-Ch}{B^{\oplus}} + H_2O \rightleftharpoons \underset{Ch}{BOH(aq)} + \underset{Ch}{H^{\oplus}(aq)}$$

$$K_h = \frac{[BOH][H^{\oplus}]}{[B^{\oplus}]} = \frac{(Ch)(Ch)}{C - Ch}$$

$$= \frac{Ch^2}{1-h} = Ch^2$$

$$(h << 1) \Rightarrow h = \sqrt{\frac{K_h}{C}}$$

Considering ionisation of weak base BOH and H_2O

$$BOH \rightleftharpoons B^{\oplus} + \overset{\ominus}{O}H; \quad K_b = \frac{[B^{\oplus}][\overset{\ominus}{O}H]}{[BOH]} \quad \text{...(i)}$$

$$H_2O \rightleftharpoons H^{\oplus} + \overset{\ominus}{O}H; \quad K_w = [H^{\oplus}][\overset{\ominus}{O}H] \quad \text{...(ii)}$$

Relation between K_w, K_b and K_h can be written as

$$\frac{K_w}{K_b} = K_h$$

Thus, the hydrolysis constant K_h, varies inversely with the dissociation constant, K_b of the weak base.

As in the above case, the degree of dissociation,

$$h = \sqrt{\frac{K_w}{K_b C}}$$

(b) pH of Solution

Now, $$pH = -\log [H^{\oplus}]$$

and $$[H^{\oplus}] = Ch = C\sqrt{\frac{K_h}{C}}$$

$$= \sqrt{K_h C} = \sqrt{\frac{K_w C}{K_b}}$$

$$\Rightarrow \quad pH = -\log\sqrt{\frac{K_w C}{K_b}}$$

$$\Rightarrow \quad pH = \frac{1}{2}(pK_w - pK_b - \log C)$$

$$= 7 - \frac{1}{2}(pK_b + \log C) \text{ at } 25°C$$

Clearly, $pH < 7$

(iv) Salts of Weak Acids and Weak Bases

The salts other than halides, sulphates, nitrates of metals (other than sodium, potassium) fall in this category, e.g. CH_3COONH_4.

In aqueous solution such as salt BA exhibits following equilibrium.

$$B^+ + A^- + H_2O \rightleftharpoons BOH + HA$$

Here cation and anion both undergo hydrolysis.

The hydrolysis constant is given by, $K_h = \frac{[BOH][HA]}{[B^+][A^-]}$

(a) Degree of Hydrolysis

$$B^+ + A^{\ominus} + H_2O \rightleftharpoons \underset{\text{(Weak base)}}{BOH(aq)} + \underset{\text{(Weak acid)}}{HA(aq)}$$

	B^+	$A^{\ominus}$	BOH	HA
Initially	C	C	0	0
At equili.	$C - Ch$	$C - Ch$	Ch	Ch

$$\Rightarrow K_h = \frac{[BOH][HA]}{[B^{\oplus}][A^{\ominus}]} = \frac{(Ch)(Ch)}{(C - Ch)^2}$$

$$\Rightarrow K_h = \frac{h^2}{(1-h)^2}$$; taking square root on both sides to get

$$h = \frac{\sqrt{K_h}}{1 + \sqrt{K_h}} \quad (\text{Here}, 1 - h \neq 1)$$

(**Remember** that the degree of hydrolysis of such salts is independent of the concentration of salt solution).

Now considering the dissociation of both weak base and acid.

$$HA \rightleftharpoons H^{\oplus} + A^{\ominus}; K_a = \frac{[H^{\oplus}][A^{\ominus}]}{[HA]}$$

$$BOH \rightleftharpoons B^{\oplus} + \overset{\ominus}{O}H; K_b = \frac{[B^{\oplus}][\overset{\ominus}{O}H]}{[BOH]}$$

$$H_2O \rightleftharpoons H^{\oplus} + \overset{\ominus}{O}H; K_w = [H^{\oplus}][\overset{\ominus}{O}H]$$

Combining K_h, K_b, K_a and K_w, we have

$$K_h = \frac{K_w}{K_a K_b} \quad \text{and} \quad h = \frac{\sqrt{K_h}}{1+\sqrt{K_h}}$$

It is also called cationic-anionic hydrolysis. (If K_h is small, then $h = \sqrt{K_h}$)

(b) pH of Solution

Consider, $K_a = \dfrac{[H^{\oplus}][A^{\ominus}]}{[HA]}$

$\Rightarrow \quad [H^{\oplus}] = K_a \dfrac{[HA]}{[A^{\ominus}]}$

Since, bases and acids are weaker, hence

$$[BOH] = [HA]$$

$\Rightarrow \quad [B^{\oplus}] = [A^{\ominus}]$

$\Rightarrow \quad K_h = \dfrac{[BOH][HA]}{[B^{\oplus}][A^{\ominus}]} = \dfrac{[HA]^2}{[A^{\ominus}]^2}$

$\Rightarrow \quad [H^{\oplus}] = K_a\sqrt{K_h} = \sqrt{\dfrac{K_w K_a}{K_b}}$

$$pH = -\log [H^{\oplus}] = -\log \sqrt{\frac{K_w K_a}{K_b}}$$

$\Rightarrow \quad pH = \dfrac{1}{2}(pK_w + pK_a - pK_b)$

$$(\text{at } 25°C) = 7 + \frac{1}{2}(pK_a - pK_b)$$

If $pK_a = pK_b$, i.e. the dissociation constants of acid and base are equal, then pH = 7. Thus, the solution will be neutral, despite the fact that hydrolysis has taken place.

***Case* I** If $pK_a > pK_b$ or $K_a < K_b$, i.e. **base** is relatively stronger then, pH > 7.

***Case* II** If $pK_a < pK_b$ or $K_a > K_b$, i.e. **acid** is relatively stronger then, pH < 7.

Summary of Salt Hydrolysis

Salt	Nature	Degree of hydrolysis	pH
NaCl (strong acid + strong base)	Neutral	No hydrolysis	(pH = 7)
CH_3COONa (weak acid + strong base)	Basic	$h = \sqrt{\dfrac{K_w}{CK_a}} = \sqrt{\dfrac{K_b}{C}}$	$pH = \dfrac{1}{2}[pK_w + pK_a + \log C]$
NH_4Cl (strong acid + weak base)	Acidic	$h = \sqrt{\dfrac{K_w}{CK_b}} = \dfrac{K_b}{C}$	$pH = \dfrac{1}{2}[pK_w - pK_b - \log C]$
CH_3COONH_4 (weak acid + weak base)	(Depends on pK_a and pK_b value)	$h = \sqrt{\dfrac{K_w}{K_a \times K_b}} = \sqrt{K_h}$	$pH = \dfrac{1}{2}[pK_w + pK_a - pK_b]$

Example 28 **The pK_a of acetic acid and pK_b of ammonium hydroxide are 4.76 and 4.75 respectively. Calculate the pH of ammonium acetate solution.** **NCERT**

Sol. Ammonium acetate is a salt of weak acid and weak base and for such salts,

$$pH = 7 + \frac{1}{2}[pK_a - pK_b]$$

$$= 7 + \frac{1}{2}[4.76 - 4.75] = 7 + \frac{1}{2}[0.01]$$

$$= 7 + 0.005 = 7.005$$

6.12 Buffer Solutions

The solutions that resist change in their pH on dilution or on addition of small amounts of acids or alkalies are called **buffer solutions** and the ability of a buffer solution to resist changes in pH on adding acids or base is called the **buffer action** of the buffer solution.

Different Types of Buffer Solution

(i) Acidic Buffer

It is a mixture of a weak acid and its conjugate base (or salt with strong base).

e.g. (a) $CH_3COOH + CH_3COONa$ (pH = 4.75)

(b) Boric acid + Borax

(ii) Basic Buffer

It is a mixture of weak base and its conjugate acid (or its salt with strong acid).

e.g. $NH_4OH + NH_4Cl$ (pH = 9.25)

Designing Buffer Solution

To prepare the buffer solution of known pH, knowledge of pK_a, pK_b and equilibrium constant are required.

Preparation of Acidic Buffer

To prepare a buffer of acidic pH we use weak acid and its salt formed with strong base.

For the general case where the weak acid, HA ionises in water.

$$HA + H_2O \rightleftharpoons H_3O^+ + A^-$$

$$\therefore \quad K_a = \frac{[H_3O^+][A^-]}{[HA]}$$

On rearranging the above expression, we get

$$[H_3O^+] = K_a \frac{[HA]}{[A^-]}$$

Taking logarithm on both sides and rearranging the terms, we get

$$pK_a = pH - \log\frac{[A^-]}{[HA]} \quad \text{or,} \quad pH = pK_a + \log\frac{[A^-]}{[HA]}$$

$$\therefore \quad pH = pK_a + \log\frac{[\text{Conjugate base, } A^-]}{[\text{Acid, } HA]}$$

This expression is known as **Henderson- Hasselbach equation.**

$$pH = pK_a + \log\frac{\text{Salt}}{\text{Acid}}$$

If concentration of $[A^-]$ is equal to the concentration of $[HA]$ then $pH = pK_a$. So, for preparing the buffer solution of the required pH we select that acid whose pK_a is close to required pH.

Preparation of Basic Buffer

A similar analysis of a buffer made with a weak base and its conjugate acid leads to the result.

$$pOH = pK_b + \log\frac{[\text{Conjugate acid, } BH^+]}{[\text{Base, } B]}$$

pH of the buffer solution can be calculated by using the equation,

$$pH + pOH = 14$$

We know that, $pH + pOH = pK_w$

and $\quad pK_a + pK_b = pK_w$

On substituting these value of above equation, we get,

$$pK_w - pH = pK_w - pK_a + \log\frac{[\text{Conjugate acid, } BH^+]}{[\text{Base, } B]}$$

$$pH = pK_a + \log\frac{[\text{Conjugate acid, } BH^+]}{[\text{Base, } B]}$$

If molar concentration of base and its conjugate acid is same then pH of the buffer solution will be same as pK_a for the base.

Note pH of the buffer solution is not affected by dilution because ratio under the logarithmic term remains unchanged.

Applications of Buffer Solution

- Normal blood has pH of 7.4. This pH is maintained by buffer action of following two buffers.
  - Buffer of carbonic acid (H_2CO_3 and $NaHCO_3$)
  - Buffer of phosphoric acid ($H_2PO_4^-$, HPO_4^{2-})
- Buffers find numerous applications in industrial processes, like manufacture of paper, drugs, dyes, inks, paints, etc.
- Buffer solutions are applied for digestion process of food.
- These are used as preservatives of foods, fruits, many dairy and agricultural products.

Example 29 A weak acid HA after treatment with 12 mL of 0.1 M strong base has a pH of 5. At the end point, the volume of same base required is 26.6 mL. Calculate the value of K_a.

Sol. For complete neutralisation,

Total millieq. of acid = millieq. of base $= 26.6 \times 0.1 = 2.66$

For partial neutralisation, millieq. of base $= 12 \times 0.1 = 1.2$

	HA	+ BOH ⟶	BA	+ H_2O
Before reaction	2.66	1.2	0	0
After reaction	1.46	0	1.2	1.2

The resultant mixture has HA and BA and thus acts as buffer.

$$pH = -\log K_a + \log\frac{[\text{Salt}]}{[\text{Acid}]}$$

$$\Rightarrow \quad 5 = -\log K_a + \log\frac{1.2}{1.46} \quad \text{or} \quad K_a = 8.31 \times 10^{-6}$$

6.13 Solubility Equilibria of Sparingly Soluble Salts

Lattice enthalpy and solvation enthalpy play a key role in deciding the solubility of the salts in a particular solvent. For a salt to be able to dissolve in a particular solvent, its solvation enthalpy must be higher than its lattice enthalpy, i.e. ion solvent interaction must be higher than the interaction between the ions.

The amount of solvation enthalpy depends on the nature of the solvent.

Non-polar solvent have very small solvation enthalpy which is not sufficient to overcome the lattice enthalpy of the salt. Hence, salts are generally insoluble in non-polar solvents.
Depending upon their solubility, the salts are categories into three groups.

Category I	Soluble	Solubility > 0.1 M
Category II	Slightly soluble	0.01 M < Solubility < 0.1 M
Category III	Sparingly soluble	Solubility < 0.01 M

Solubility Product

The concentration of substance in a saturated solution is defined as its solubility (S). Its value depends upon the nature of solvent and the temperature. Consider saturated solution of sparingly soluble electrolyte, AB.

$$\underset{\text{Solid}}{AB} \rightleftharpoons \underset{\text{Unionised dissolved}}{AB} \rightleftharpoons \underbrace{A^+ + B^-}_{\text{Ions}}$$

Applying the law of mass action, $K = \frac{[A^+][B^-]}{[AB]}$. Since, the solution is saturated, the concentration of unionised molecules of the electrolyte will be constant at a particular temperature, i.e. $[AB] = \text{constant} = K'$ (say).
Hence, $[A^+][B^-] = KK' = K_{sp}$ (constant)
This new constant K_{sp} is called **solubility product** and is defined as the product of the concentration of ions in a saturated solution of an electrolyte at a given temperature. Consider, in general, the electrolyte of the type A_xB_y, which is dissociated as

$$A_xB_y \rightleftharpoons xA^{y+} + yB^{x-};\ K_{sp} = [A^{y+}]^x[B^{x-}]^y$$

Thus, **solubility product** may be defined as the product of concentrations of the ions raised to a power equal to the number of times the ions occur in the equation representing the dissociation of the electrolyte at a given temperature when the solution is saturated.

Finding Relationship Between S and K_{sp}

In order to find the relation between solubility (S) and solubility product (K_{sp}) follow the following steps.

Steps	Example
***Step* I** Dissociate electrolyte into ion as $A_xB_y \rightleftharpoons xA^{y+} + yB^{x-}$	$Ag_2CO_3 \rightleftharpoons 2Ag^+ + CO_3^{2-}$
***Step* II** Write solubility of each ion. (Remember, if solubility of one ion is S, then for x ions, it is xS.) $\underset{S}{A_xB_y} \rightleftharpoons \underset{xS}{xA^{y+}} + \underset{yS}{yB^{x-}}$	$\underset{S}{Ag_2CO_3} \rightleftharpoons \underset{2\times S}{2Ag^+} + \underset{1\times S}{CO_3^{2-}}$
***Step* III** Write the expression of K_{sp} and put the values of solubilities of ions. $K_{sp} = [A^{y+}]^x[B^{x-}]^y = (xS)^x(yS)^y$	$K_{sp} = [Ag^+]^2[CO_3^{2-}] = (2S)^2(S)$
***Step* IV** Solve the equation obtained to get the relation $K_{sp} = x^xy^yS^{x+y}$	$K_{sp} = 4S^2 \cdot S = 4S^3$

> **TEACHER'S TIP**
> If the solubility is asked in gL^{-1}, then use the formula :
> Solubility (in gL^{-1}) = Molarity (mol L^{-1}) × Molar mass (g mol^{-1})

Example 30 **Calculate the solubility of A_2X_3 in pure water, assuming that neither kind of ion reacts with water. The solubility product of A_2X_3 is $K_{sp} = 1.1 \times 10^{-23}$.** **NCERT**

Sol. $A_2X_3 \longrightarrow \underset{2S}{2A^{3+}} + \underset{3S}{3X^{2-}}$;
$\quad S$

$$K_{sp} = [A^{3+}]^2[X^{2-}]^3 = 1.1 \times 10^{-23}$$

$$\therefore \quad K_{sp} = (2S)^2(3S)^3 = 108\,S^5 = 1.1 \times 10^{-23}$$

or $\quad S^5 = 1 \times 10^{-25}$

$\Rightarrow \quad S = 1.0 \times 10^{-5}$ mol / L

Example 31 **The values of K_{sp} of two sparingly soluble salts $Ni(OH)_2$ and AgCN are 2.0×10^{-15} and 6×10^{-17} respectively. Which salt is more soluble? Explain.** NCERT

Sol. $AgCN \longrightarrow Ag^+ + CN^-$

$$K_{sp} = [Ag^+][CN^-] = 6\times10^{-17}$$

$$Ni(OH)_2 \longrightarrow Ni^{2+} + 2OH^-$$

$$K_{sp} = [Ni^{2+}][OH^-]^2 = 2\times10^{-15}$$

Let $[Ag^+] = S_1$, then $[CN^-] = S_1$

Let $[Ni^{2+}] = S_2$ then $[OH^-] = 2S_2$

$$S_1^2 = 6\times10^{-17}, S_1 = 7.8\times10^{-9}$$

$$(S_2)(2S_2)^2 = 2\times10^{-15}, S_2 = 7.9\times10^{-6}$$

Thus, $Ni(OH)_2$ is more soluble than AgCN.

Predicting Precipitate Formation from K_{sp}

At the state of equilibrium, the value of K_{sp} is equal to the value of Q_{sp} but if the concentration of any ion is not in equilibrium, $Q_{sp} \neq K_{sp}$.

In order to make, $Q_{sp} = K_{sp}$, the reaction moves in the required direction.

The value of Q_{sp} (ionic product) and K_{sp} are also helpful for predicting whether a precipitate is formed or not. In general,

- If $Q_{sp} > K_{sp}$, then precipitation will take place.
- If $Q_{sp} < K_{sp}$, then no precipitation will occur.
- If $Q_{sp} = K_{sp}$, the reaction is at equilibrium.

Example 32 **The solubility product of $BaSO_4$ at 25°C is 1.0×10^{-9}. What would be the concentration of H_2SO_4 necessary to precipitate $BaSO_4$ from a solution of 0.01 M Ba^{2+} ions?**

Sol. Precipitation will take place when

Ionic product > Solubility product

$$\underset{0.01}{} BaSO_4 \rightleftharpoons \underset{0.01}{Ba^{2+}} + \underset{S}{SO_4^{2-}}$$

$\because$ $K_{sp} = [Ba^{2+}][SO_4^{2-}]$

$\therefore$ $S = \dfrac{1.0\times10^{-9}}{0.01}$

$= 10^{-7}$ mol/L

So, $[SO_4^{2-}]$ should be more than 10^{-7} M for precipitation to occur.

Common Ion Effect on Solubility of Ionic Salts

Let S is the solubility of silver chromate,

$$Ag_2CrO_4 \rightleftharpoons 2Ag^+ + CrO_4^{2-}$$

The solubility product of Ag_2CrO_4 is

$$K_{sp} = (2S)^2 \times S = 4S^3 \quad \text{...(i)}$$

Now suppose that x mol/L of $AgNO_3$ is added and in this solution, the solubility of Ag_2CrO_4 is S', then

$$[Ag^+] = 2S' + x \text{ and } [CrO_4^{2-}] = S'$$

So, $K_{sp} = (2S' + x)(S')$ ...(ii)

Eqs. (i) and (ii) can be used to find S'. If K_{sp} is very small, we may neglect $2S'$ against x in Eq. (ii) and it becomes

$$K_{sp} = xS'$$

Note The common ion effect is also used for almost complete precipitation of a particular ion as its sparingly soluble salt (with very low value of K_{sp}) for gravimetric estimation.

Example 33 **A sparingly soluble salt gets precipitated only when the product of concentration of its ions in the solution (Q_{sp}) becomes greater than its solubility product. If the solubility of $BaSO_4$ in water is 8×10^{-4} mol dm^{-3}. Calculate its solubility in 0.01 mol dm^{-3} of H_2SO_4.** NCERT Exemplar

Sol. $BaSO_4(s) \rightleftharpoons Ba^{2+}(aq) + SO_4^{2-}(aq)$

K_{sp} for $BaSO_4 = [Ba^{2+}][SO_4^{2-}] = S\times S = S^2$

But $S = 8\times10^{-4}$ mol dm^{-3}

$\therefore$ $K_{sp} = (8\times10^{-4})^2 = 64\times10^{-8}$

In the presence of 0.01 M H_2SO_4, the expression for K_{sp} will be

$K_{sp} = [Ba^{2+}][SO_4^{2-}] \Rightarrow K_{sp} = (S)\cdot(S + 0.01)$

(0.01 M SO_4^{2-} ions from 0.01 M H_2SO_4)

$\Rightarrow$ $64\times10^{-8} = S\cdot(S + 0.01)$

$\Rightarrow$ $S^2 + 0.01S - 64\times10^{-8} = 0$

$$\therefore \quad S = \frac{-0.01 \pm \sqrt{(0.01)^2 + (4\times64\times10^{-8})}}{2}$$

$$= \frac{-0.01 \pm \sqrt{10^{-4} + (256\times10^{-8})}}{2}$$

$$= \frac{-0.01 \pm \sqrt{10^{-4}(1 + 256\times10^{-4})}}{2}$$

$$= \frac{-0.01 \pm 10^{-2}\sqrt{1 + 0.0256}}{2}$$

$$= \frac{10^{-2}(-1 \pm 1.012719)}{2}$$
$$= 5 \times 10^{-3}(-1 + 1.012719)$$
$$= 6.4 \times 10^{-5} \text{ mol dm}^{-3}$$

Note $S <<< 0.01$, so $S + 0.01 \approx 0.01$ and $64 \times 10^{-8} = S \times 0.01$

$$S = \frac{64 \times 10^{-8}}{0.01} = 6.4 \times 10^{-5}$$

Example 34 **Calculate the molar solubility of $Ni(OH)_2$ in 0.10 M NaOH. The ionic product of $Ni(OH)_2$ is 2.0×10^{-15}.** NCERT

Sol.
$$\underset{S\text{ mol/L}}{Ni(OH)_2} \rightleftharpoons \underset{S\text{ mol/L}}{Ni^{2+}} + \underset{2S\text{ mol/L}}{2OH^-}$$

$$\underset{0.10\text{ M}}{NaOH} \longrightarrow \underset{0.10\text{ M}}{Na^+} + \underset{0.10\text{ M}}{OH^-} \qquad [OH^-]_{total} = (2S + 0.10)$$
$$K_{sp} = 2.0 \times 10^{-15} = [Ni^{2+}][OH^-]^2$$
$$= (S)(0.10 + 2S)^2$$

As K_{sp} is small, $2S << 0.10$, thus $(0.10 + 2S) \approx 0.10$

$$\therefore \quad 2.0 \times 10^{-15} = S(0.10)^2$$
$$\Rightarrow \quad S = 2.0 \times 10^{-13} \text{ M} = [Ni^{2+}]$$

Effect of pH on Solubility

The solubility of salts of weak acids such as phosphates increases with decrease in pH as at lower pH, the anion gets protonated and hence, its concentration decreases. So, the solubility of a salt increases with increase in hydrogen ion concentration or decrease in pH.

Quick Test 3

Conceptual Questions

1. Predict if the solutions of the following salts are neutral, acidic or basic

NaCl, KBr, NaCN, NH_4NO_3, $NaNO_2$ and KF NCERT

2. Arrange the following in increasing order of pH. NCERT Exemplar

$KNO_3(aq)$, $CH_3COONa\ (aq)$, $NH_4Cl(aq)$, $C_6H_5COONH_4(aq)$

3. A certain buffer is made by mixing sodium formate and formic acid in water. With the help of equations explain how this buffer neutralises addition of a small amount of an acid or a base? Competency Based Que.

4. The concentration of sulphide ion in 0.1 M HCl solution saturated with hydrogen sulphide is 1.0×10^{-19} M. If 10 mL of this is added to 5 mL of 0.04 M solution of the following $FeSO_4$, $MnCl_2$, $ZnCl_2$ and $CdCl_2$, in which of these solutions precipitation will take place?
(Given, K_{sp} of FeS $= 6.3 \times 10^{-18}$, K_{sp} of MnS $= 2.5 \times 10^{-13}$, K_{sp} of ZnS $= 1.6 \times 10^{-24}$, K_{sp} of CdS $= 8.0 \times 10^{-27}$) NCERT

Numerical Questions

5. A 0.02 M solution of pyridinium hydrochloride has pH = 3.44. Calculate the ionisation constant of pyridine.

6. The ionisation constant of nitrous acid is 4.5×10^{-4}. Calculate the pH of 0.04 M sodium nitrite solution and also its degree of hydrolysis. NCERT

7. The ionisation constant of chloroacetic acid is 1.35×10^{-3}. What will be the pH of 0.1 M acid and its 0.1 M sodium salt solution? NCERT

8. The buffers of *X* and *Y* of pH 4.0 and 6.0 respectively are prepared from acid H*A* and the salt Na*A*. Both the buffers are 0.50 M in H*A*. What would be the pH of the solution obtained by mixing equal volumes of the two buffers? ($K_{HA} = 1.0 \times 10^{-5}$)

9. What is the minimum volume of water required to dissolved 1g of calcium sulphate at 298 K? (For calcium sulphate, K_{sp} is 9.1×10^{-6}). NCERT

10. What is the maximum concentration of equimolar solutions of ferrous sulphate and sodium sulphide so that when mixed in equal volumes, there is no precipitation of iron sulphide? (For iron sulphide, $K_{sp} = 6.3 \times 10^{-18}$) NCERT

11. The solubility of $Sr(OH)_2$ at 298 K is 19.23 g/L of solution. Calculate the concentrations of strontium and hydroxyl ions and the pH of the solution. NCERT

Answers

5. 1.5×10^{-9} **6.** 7.97, 2.36×10^{-5} **7.** 7.94
8. 5.702 **9.** 2.437 L **10.** 5.02×10^{-9} M
11. 13.5

NCERT For Solutions, See QR Code on Pg. 254

Mind Map

Equilibrium

The state at which rate of forward reaction becomes equal to the rate of backward reaction.

Chemical Equilibrium

The equilibrium established between two opposite reactions or processes.

Equilibrium in Physical Processes

It involves
- Solid-liquid equilibria
- Liquid-vapour equilibria
- Solid-vapour equilibria
- Gas-liquid equilibria

Equilibrium in Chemical Processes

When concentration of reactants and products do not change with time dynamic equilibrium.

Types of Chemical Equilibrium

(i) **Homogeneous** All the species of a reaction are in same phase.

(ii) **Heterogeneous** The phases of all the species are not same.

Law of Chemical Equilibrium and Equilibrium Constant, K

$aA \rightarrow bB + cC$

$K_c = \frac{[B]^b [C]^c}{[A]^a}$ and $K_p = K_c (RT)^{\Delta n_g}$

$K_c = (\text{mol/L})^{\Delta n_g}, K_p = (\text{atm})^{\Delta n_g}$

Characteristics

- If a reaction is multiplied by n, $K = k^n$
- If reaction is divided by n, $K = (K)^{1/n}$
- If two reactions are added, $K = K_1 \times K_2$
- If two reactions are subtracted, $K = K_1 / K_2$

Applications

- **Extent of Reaction**
  If $K_c > 10^3$, products predominate
  $K_c < 10^{-3}$, reactants predominate
  $10^{-3} < K_c > 10^3$, both reactant and product are present.
- **Direction of Reaction**
  If $Q = K$, equilibrium
  If $Q > K$, backward reaction
  If $Q < K$, forward reaction

Acids and Bases

Acids are sour and turn blue litmus red while bases are bitter turn red litmus blue.

Definitions

(i) Arrhenius Concept
Acids give $H^+ (aq)$ while bases give $OH^- (aq)$ in water.

(ii) Bronsted-Lowry Concept
Acids are H^+ donor but bases are H^+ acceptor.

Or

Conjugate Acid-Base Pair is the pair that differ by a proton. e.g., NH_3, NH_4^+

(iii) Lewis Concept
Acids are electron pair acceptor while bases are electron pair donor.

Ionisation Constant

It is the ratio of ionised and unionised forms.

Ionisation of Water

$K_W = [H^+] [OH^-] = 10^{-14} M^2$

Ionisation of weak acid/base

K_a or $K_b = C\alpha^2 = K_a \cdot K_b = K_w$

pH Scale

- Introduced by Sorenson.
- $pH = -\log [H^+]$
- $pOH = -\log [OH^-]$
- $pH + pOH = 14$

Common Ion Effect

It is the suppression in the dissociation of weak electrolyte in the presence of common ion.

Le-Chatelier's Principle

(i) If $[P]$ is removed or $[R]$ is added, reaction moves in forward direction.

(ii) If $\Delta n_g = 0$ no effect of pressure, if $n_p > n_R$ high pressure favours reverse reaction.

(iii) For endothermic reaction, high temperature favours forward reaction and for exothermic reaction it favours backward reaction.

Ionic Equilibrium

The equilibrium established between ionised and unionised forms of a substance.

Electrolytes

These are the substance which provide ions when dissolved in water.

Salts

These are the neutralisation product of acid and a base.

Salt Hydrolysis

It is the process of interaction of ions of salt with water. If cation reacts with water, it is called cationic hydrolysis and if anion reacts with water it is called anionic hydrolysis.

1. **Salt of strong acid and strong base**
   e.g., KCl, NaCl, Na_2SO_4 They do not hydrolyse. pH of their solution is always 7.
2. **Salt of weak acid and strong base**
   e.g., CH_3COONa.
   $pH = 7 + 1/2 (pK_a + \log C)$, $h = \sqrt{\frac{K_W}{K_a C}}$
3. **Salt of weak base and strong acid**
   e.g., NH_4Cl,
   $pH = 7 + 1/2 (pK_b + \log C)$, $h = \sqrt{\frac{K_W}{K_b C}}$
4. **Salt of weak acid and weak base**
   $pH = 7 + 1/2 (pK_a - pK_b)$, $h = \sqrt{\frac{K_W}{K_a K_b}}$

Buffer Solutions

These solutions resist their pH.

1. **Acidic buffer**
   It is a mixture of weak acid and its conjugate base.
   $pH = pK_a + \log \frac{[\text{Salt}]}{[\text{Acid}]}$
2. **Basic buffer**
   It is a mixture of weak base and its conjugate acid.
   $pOH = pK_b + \log \frac{[\text{Salt}]}{[\text{Base}]}$

Solubility Product, K_{sp}

$K_{sp} = x^x y^y s^{x+y}$ where s = solubility, x and y = number of ions. Solubility decreases with increase in pH.

Precipitate Formation

If $Q > K_{sp}$, precipitate will form.
If $Q < K_{sp}$, no precipitation will occur.
If $Q_{sp} = K_{sp}$, reaction is at equilibrium.

EXAM PATTERN QUESTIONS

Objective Type Questions

Multiple Choice Questions (MCQs) [1 Mark]

1. **Which of the following is not a general characteristic of equilibria involving physical processes?** NCERT Exemplar

(a) Equilibrium is possible only in a closed system at a given temperature.

(b) All measurable properties of the system remain constant.

(c) All the physical processes stop at equilibrium.

(d) The opposing processes occur at the same rate and there is dynamic but stable condition.

2. **In the equilibrium, $AB \rightleftharpoons A + B$, if the equilibrium concentration of A is double, then equilibrium concentration of B will be**

(a) half (b) twice (c) $\frac{1}{4}$ th (d) $\frac{1}{8}$ th

3. **A reaction is given by $aA + bB \longrightarrow cC + dD$. The equilibrium constant for this reaction is represented by**

(a) $\frac{[A]^a[B]^b}{[C]^c[D]^d}$ (b) $\frac{[C]^c[D]^d}{[A]^a[B]^b}$ (c) $\frac{[A][B]}{[C][D]}$ (d) $\frac{[C][D]}{[A][B]}$

4. **Which of the following is indicated by a higher equilibrium constant?**

(a) Reaction occurs faster

(b) Rate of backward reaction is faster

(c) Both the backward and forward reactions are equal

(d) Reaction may be slower than usual

5. **For the reaction,**

$$H_2(g) + Br_2(g) \rightleftharpoons 2HBr(g)$$

The equilibrium constant is given as 0.04. Now, the equilibrium constant for the reverse reaction will be Competency Based Que.

(a) 0.04 (b) 4

(c) 25 (d) 100

6. **Consider the following reaction :**

$$N_2(g) + O_2(g) \rightleftharpoons 2NO(g)$$

At 800 K, the concentrations are as follows :

$N_2 = 3.0 \times 10^{-3}$ M

$O_2 = 4.2 \times 10^{-3}$ M

$NO = 2.8 \times 10^{-3}$ M

Then the equilibrium constant for the given reaction will be Competency Based Que.

(a) 0.622 (b) 0.6 (c) 0.63 (d) 0.94

7. **If 'K' is the equilibrium constant for the reaction $aA + bB \longrightarrow cC + dD$, then the equilibrium constant for $naA + nbB \longrightarrow ncC + ndD$ is**

(a) K (b) nK

(c) K^n (d) K/n

8. **PCl_5, PCl_3, and Cl_2 are at equilibrium at 500 K in a closed container and their concentrations are 0.8×10^{-3} mol L^{-1}, 1.2×10^{-3} mol L^{-1} and 1.2×10^{-3} mol L^{-1}, respectively. The value of K_C for the reaction,** NCERT Exemplar

$$PCl_5(g) \rightleftharpoons PCl_3(g) + Cl_2(g) \text{ will be}$$

(a) 1.8×10^3 mol L^{-1} (b) 1.8×10^{-3}

(c) 1.8×10^{-3} mol^{-1} L (d) 0.55×10^4

9. **Which of the following options will be correct for the stage of half completion of the reaction $A \rightleftharpoons B$?** NCERT Exemplar

(a) $\Delta G^{\ominus} = 0$ (b) $\Delta G^{\ominus} > 0$

(c) $\Delta G^{\ominus} < 0$ (d) $\Delta G^{\ominus} = -RT \ln K$

10. **Match standard free energy of the reaction (Column I) with the corresponding equilibrium constant (Column II).**

Column I	Column II
(i) $\Delta G^\circ > 0$	(p) $K > 1$
(ii) $\Delta G^\circ < 0$	(q) $K = 1$
(iii) $\Delta G^\circ = 0$	(r) $K = 0$
	(s) $K < 1$

Choose the correct option among the given options.

(a) (i)-(q), (ii)-(p), (iii)-(s) (b) (i)-(s), (ii)-(p), (iii)-(q)

(c) (i)-(q), (ii)-(r), (iii)-(s) (d) (i)-(r), (ii)-(q), (iii)-(p)

11. **What would be the value of Δn for the reaction?** NCERT Exemplar

$$NH_4Cl(s) \rightleftharpoons NH_3(g) + HCl(g)$$

(a) 1 (b) 0.5 (c) 1.5 (d) 2

12. What will be the conjugate bases for the following Bronsted acids?

$$HF, H_2SO_4 \text{ and } HCO_3^-$$

(a) F^-, SO_4^{2-} and CO_3^{2-} (b) F^-, SO_4^{2-} and H_2CO_3
(c) F^-, HSO_4^- and H_2CO_3 (d) F^-, HSO_4^- and CO_3^{2-}

13. Bronsted base is a substance which can
(a) lose pair of electrons (b) donate protons
(c) gain a pair of electrons (d) accept protons

14. The strong conjugate base is
(a) NO_3^{2-} (b) Cl^-
(c) SO_4^{2-} (d) CH_3COO^-

15. Acidity of BF_3 can be explained on the basis of which of the following concepts? **NCERT Exemplar**
(a) Arrhenius concept
(b) Bronsted Lowry concept
(c) Lewis concept
(d) Bronsted Lowry as well as Lewis concept

16. A 0.2 molar solution of formic acid is 3.2% ionised. Its ionisation constant is **Competency Based Que.**
(a) 9.6×10^{-3} (b) 2.1×10^{-4}
(c) 1.25×10^{-6} (d) 4.8×10^{-5}

17. At 363K, pure water has $[H_3O^+] = 10^{-6}$ M. The value of K_w at this temperature will be
(a) 10^{-6} (b) 10^{-12}
(c) 10^{-13} (d) 10^{-14}

18. Which of the following will produce a buffer solution when mixed in equal volumes? **NCERT Exemplar**
(a) 0.1 mol dm^{-3} NH_4OH and 0.1mol dm^{-3} HCl
(b) 0.05 mol dm^{-3} NH_4OH and 0.1mol dm^{-3} HCl
(c) 0.1 mol dm^{-3} NH_4OH and 0.05 mol dm^{-3} HCl
(d) 0.1 mol dm^{-3} CH_3COONa and 0.1mol dm^{-3} NaOH

19. One litre of a buffer solution containing 0.01 M NH_4Cl and 0.1 M NH_4OH having pK_b of 5 has pH of
(a) 9 (b) 10
(c) 6 (d) 7

20. Which of the following pairs constitutes a buffer?
(a) NaOH and HCl (b) HNO_3 and NH_4NO_3
(c) HCl and KCl (d) HNO_2 and $NaNO_2$

21. The addition of NaCl to AgCl decreases the solubility of AgCl because
(a) solubility product decreases
(b) solubility product remains constant
(c) solution becomes unsaturated
(d) solution becomes supersaturated

22. Solubility of calcium phosphate (molecular mass, M) in water is w g per 100 mL at 25°C. Its solubility product at 25°C will be approximately.
(a) $10^7\left(\frac{w}{M}\right)^3$ (b) $10^7\left(\frac{w}{M}\right)^5$
(c) $10^5\left(\frac{w}{M}\right)^5$ (d) $10^3\left(\frac{w}{M}\right)^5$

23. 2 moles of PCl_5 were heated in a closed vessel of 2 litre capacity. At equilibrium, 40% PCl_5 is dissociated into PCl_3 and Cl_2. The equilibrium constant is **Diksha**
(a) 0.267 (b) 0.53
(c) 2.63 (d) 5.3

24. Predict which of the following reaction will have appreciable concentration of reactants and products?
(a) $Cl_2(g) \rightleftharpoons 2Cl(g)$; $K_C = 5 \times 10^{-39}$
(b) $Cl_2(g) + 2NO(g) \rightleftharpoons 2NOCl(g)$; $K_C = 3.7 \times 10^8$
(c) $Cl_2(g) + 2NO_2(g) \rightleftharpoons 2NO_2(g)$; $K_C = 1.8$
(d) All have appreciable concentration of reactants and products

25. In the reaction, $C(s) + CO_2(g) \rightleftharpoons 2CO(g)$, when pressure is increased, the reaction goes in the
(a) forward direction (b) reverse direction
(c) dynamic equilibrium (d) None of these

26. The equilibrium constant in a reversible reaction at a given temperature **Diksha**
(a) depends on the initial concentration of the reactants.
(b) depends on the concentration of products at equilibrium.
(c) It is not characteristic of the reaction.
(d) does not depend on the initial concentration.

27. In the following reaction,

$$\underset{\text{Acid}}{H_2O(l)} + \underset{X}{H_2O(l)} \rightleftharpoons \underset{\text{Conjugate acid}}{H_3O^+(aq)} + \underset{Y}{OH^-(aq)}$$

X and Y respectively are
(a) base and conjugate acid (b) acid and conjugate base
(c) base and conjugate base (d) acid and conjugate acid

28. A solution of an acid has pH = 4.70. Find out the concentration of OH^- ions ($pK_w = 14$).
(a) 5×10^{-10} (b) 6×10^{-10}
(c) 2×10^{-5} (d) 9×10^{-5}

29. The pH of a solution of hydrochloric acid is 4. The molarity of the solution is
(a) 4.0 (b) 0.4
(c) 0.0001 (d) 0.04

Assertion-Reason [1 Mark]

Directions (Q. Nos. 30-39) In the following questions, a statement of assertion is followed by a corresponding statements of reason of the following statements, choose the correct one.

(a) Both (A) and (R) are correct and (R) is the correct explanation of (A).
(b) Both (A) and (R) are correct but (R) is not the correct explanation of (A).
(c) (A) is correct and (R) is incorrect.
(d) (A) is incorrect and (R) is correct.

30. **Assertion** (A) A mixture of the solutions of a weak acid and its sodium salt acts as a good buffer.
Reason (R) The ratio of the salt to the acid in the mixture does not change substantially when small amount of acid and base is added to the buffer.

31. **Assertion** (A) On mixing equal volumes of 1M HCl and 2 M CH_3COONa, an acidic buffer solution is formed.
Reason (R) Resultant mixture contains CH_3COOH and CH_3COONa which are a part of acidic buffer.

Competency Based Que.

32. **Assertion** (A) If pK_a of an acid (HA) is x then pK_b of a conjugate base A^- is $(14-x)$.
Reason (R) At 298K, in aqueous solution,
$$[H_3O^+][OH^-]=1\times10^{-14}=K_w$$

33. **Assertion** (A) When ice and water are kept in a perfectly insulated thermos flask at 273 K and the atmospheric pressure, there is no change in mass of ice and water.
Reason (R) The system is in static equilibrium.

34. **Assertion** (A) For the reaction,
$$N_2(g)+3H_2(g)\rightleftharpoons 2NH_3(g)$$
K_p is not equal to K_C.
Reason (R) Concentration of gaseous reactants and products is taken as unity.

35. **Assertion** (A) K_p can be less than, greater than or equal to K_C.
Reason (R) Relation between K_p and K_C depends on the change in number of moles of gaseous reactants and products (Δn_g).

36. **Assertion** (A) In the dissociation of PCl_5 at constant pressure and temperature, addition of helium at equilibrium increases the dissociation of PCl_5.
Reason (R) Helium reacts with Cl_2 and hence shifts the equilibrium in forward direction.

37. **Assertion** (A) There is an equilibrium between the gaseous molecules and dissolved molecules of the gas under pressure.
Reason (R) Such equilibrium is governed by Henry's law.

38. **Assertion** (A) $N_2O_4(g)\rightleftharpoons 2NO_2(g)$ is the example of homogeneous equilibria.
Reason (R) The reactants and products are present in the same phase.

39. **Assertion** (A) When a catalyst is added to a reaction mixture in equilibrium the amount of the products increases.
Reason (R) The forward reaction becomes faster on adding the catalyst.

Case-Study [4 Marks]

40. Read the given case and answer the following questions.

For the following reaction,
$$N_2(g)+3H_2(g)\rightleftharpoons 2NH_3(g);\quad \Delta H=-22.4\text{ kcal};$$
the favourable conditions are
(i) high concentration of N_2 and H_2.
(ii) high pressure (as $\Delta n_g=-2$).
(iii) low temperature (as the reaction is exothermic).
Although the low temperature favours the formation of NH_3, yet an optimum temperature is set, as the rate of reaction is very slow at low temperature. A temperature of 500°C is selected and a pressure of 200 atm is applied in practice.

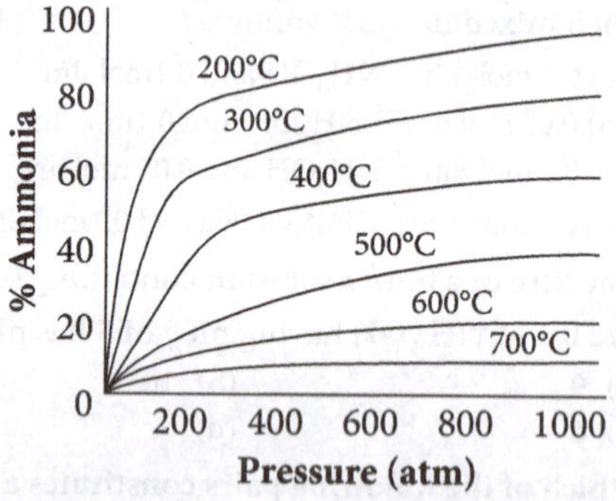

(i) What is the expression of equilibrium constant for synthesis of NH_3?
(ii) Formation of ammonia is a gaseous phase reaction taking place in 1 L flask at 127°C. If starting with 1 mole N_2 and 3 moles H_2, equilibrium mixture requires 500 mL of 1M HCl. What is the value of K_C?
(a) 0.1
(b) 0.01
(c) 0.03
(d) 0.2

(iii) What happens to the yield of ammonia produced when the pressure is increased?
(a) Increases (b) Becomes double
(c) Decreased (d) No effect

Or

Which substance is used as a catalyst promoter in the synthesis of ammonia?
(a) Ni (b) Fe
(c) Ni + Fe (d) Dil. H_2SO_4

41. Read the given case and answer the following questions.

The concentration of a substance in a saturated solution is defined as its solubility (*S*). Its value depends upon the nature of solvent and the temperature.

Consider saturated solution of sparingly soluble electrolyte, *AB*.

$$\underset{\text{Solid}}{AB} \rightleftharpoons \underset{\text{Unionised molecules}}{AB} \rightleftharpoons \underbrace{A^+ + B^-}_{\text{Ions}}$$

Applying the law of mass action, $K = \dfrac{[A^+][B^-]}{[AB]}$.

Since, the solution is saturated, the concentration of unionised molecules of the electrolyte will be constant at a particular temperature, i.e. $[AB]$ = constant = K' **(say).**

Hence, $[A^+][B^-] = KK' = K_{sp}$ **(constant)**

This new constant K_{sp} **is called solubility product and is defined as the product of the concentration of ions in a saturated solution of an electrolyte at a given temperature.**

(i) Why does the solubility of salt of weak acids increases with decrease in pH?

(ii) What will happen if K_{sp} < Ionic product?

Or

Write the K_{sp} expression for $Zr_3(PO_4)_4$ if its solubility is *S* mole/litre.

(iii) If K_{sp} of AgCl is 5×10^{-10} and K_{sp} of AgBr is 5×10^{-13}. Which one will precipitate first?

Subjective Type Questions

Short Answer Type I Questions [2 Marks]

1. A tank is full of water. Water is coming in as well as going out at same rate. What will happen to level of water in a tank ? What is name given to such a state?

2. At 0°C, ice and water are present in equilibrium. What will happen on increasing the pressure?

3. BF_3 does not have proton but still acts as an acid and reacts with NH_3. Why is it so? What type of bond is formed between the two? **NCERT Exemplar**

4. When hydrochloric acid is added to cobalt nitrate solution at room temperature, the following reaction takes place and the reaction mixture becomes blue. On cooling the mixture it becomes pink. On the basis of this information. What would you infer about the enthalpy of the reaction?

$$\underset{\text{(Pink)}}{[Co(H_2O_6)]^{3+}}(aq) + 4Cl^-(aq) \rightleftharpoons \underset{\text{(Blue)}}{[CoCl_4]^{2-}}(aq) + 6H_2O(l)$$

NCERT Exemplar

5. Some processes are given below. What happens to the process if it is subjected to a change given in the brackets?

(i) Ice $\xrightleftharpoons{\text{Melting point}}$ Water (Pressure is increased)

(ii) Dissolution of NaOH in water (Temperature is increased) **Competency Based Que.**

6. K_b for NH_4OH is 1.8×10^{-5} and for CH_3NH_2 is 4.4×10^{-4}. Which of them is strongest base and why?

7. What happens to ionic product of water if some acid is added to it ?

8. pK_a value of acids *A, B, C, D* are 1.5, 3.5, 2.0 and 5.0. Which of them is strongest acid ?

9. The aqueous solution of sugar does not conduct electricity. However, when sodium chloride is added to water, it conducts electricity. How will you explain this statement on the basis of ionisation and how is it affected by concentration of sodium chloride? **NCERT Exemplar**

10. Glycine is an α-amino acid. It exists in the form of Zwitter ion as $^+NH_3CH_2COO^-$.

Write the formula of its
(i) conjugate acid. (ii) conjugate base.

11. The concentration of hydrogen ion in a sample of soft drink is 3.8×10^{-3} M. What is its pH? **NCERT**

Short Answer Type II Questions [3 Marks]

12. Urine has a pH of 6.0. If a patient eliminates 1300 mL of urine per day, how many gram equivalents of the acid he eliminates per day ?

13. What is meant by the conjugate acid-base pair? Find the conjugate acid/base for the following species.
$HNO_2, CN^-, HClO_4, F^-, OH^-, CO_3^{2-}$ and S^{2-}. **NCERT**

14. A sparingly soluble salt having general formula $A_x^{p+} B_y^{q-}$ and molar solubility S is in equilibrium with its saturated solution. Derive a relationship between the solubility and solubility product for such salt.

15. The value of K_C for the reaction,
$3O_2(g) \rightleftharpoons 2O_3(g)$ is 2.0×10^{-50} at 25°C. If the equilibrium concentration of O_2 in air at 25°C is 1.6×10^{-2}, what is the concentration of O_3? **NCERT**

16. A sample of pure PCl_5 was introduced into an evacuated vessel at 473 K. After equilibrium was attained, concentration of PCl_5 was found to be 0.5×10^{-1} mol L^{-1}. If value of K_C is 8.3×10^{-3}, what are the concentration of PCl_3 and Cl_2 at equilibrium? **NCERT**

17. At 700 K, equilibrium constant for the reaction,
$$H_2(g) + I_2(g) \rightleftharpoons 2HI(g) \text{ is } 54.8.$$
If 0.5 mol L^{-1} of HI(g) is present at equilibrium at 700 K, what are the concentration of $H_2(g)$ and $I_2(g)$ assuming that we initially started with HI(g) and allowed it to reach equilibrium 700 K? **NCERT**

18. 50.0 g of $CaCO_3$ are heated to 1073 K in a 5 L vessel. What percent of the $CaCO_3$ would decompose at equilibrium? K_p for the reaction,
$CaCO_3(s) \rightleftharpoons CaO(s) + CO_2(g)$ is 1.15 atm at 1073 K.

19. $K_p = 0.04$ atm at 899 K for the equilibrium shown below.
$$C_2H_6(g) \rightleftharpoons C_2H_4(g) + H_2(g)$$
What is the equilibrium concentration of C_2H_6 when it is placed in a flask at 4.0 atm pressure and allowed to come to equilibrium?

20. (i) One millilitre solution of 0.01 M HCl is added to 1 L of sodium chloride solution. What will be the pH of the resulting solutions?
(ii) Calculate the pH of a solution containing 0.1 M acetic acid and 0.1 M benzoic acid, K_a for CH_3COOH and C_6H_5COOH are 1.8×10^{-5} and 6.5×10^{-5} respectively. **Competency Based Que.**

21. The ionisation constant of HF, HCOOH and HCN at 298 K are 6.8×10^{-4}, 1.8×10^{-4} and 4.8×10^{-9} respectively. Calculate the ionisation constants of the corresponding conjugate base. **NCERT**

22. The pH of milk, black coffee, tomato juice, lemon juice and egg white are 6.8, 5.0, 4.2, 2.2 and 7.8 respectively. Calculate the corresponding hydrogen ion concentration in each. **NCERT**

23. The ionisation constant of propanoic acid is 1.32×10^{-5}. Calculate the degree of ionisation of the acid in its 0.05 M solution and also its pH. What will be its degree of ionisation if the solution is 0.01 M in HCl also? **NCERT**

24. The K_{sp} values of two slightly soluble salts AB and PQ_2 are each equal to 4.0×10^{-18}. Which salt is more soluble?

25. The solubility product of AgCl is 1.5×10^{-10}. Predict whether there will be any precipitation by mixing 50 mL of 0.01 M NaCl and 50 mL of 0.01 M $AgNO_3$ solution.

26. How much volume of 0.1 M CH_3COOH should be added to 50 mL of 0.2 M CH_3COONa solution to prepare a buffer solution of pH 4.91. (pK_a of AcH is 4.76).

Long Answer Type Questions [5 Marks]

27. Write a relation between ΔG and Q and define the meaning of each term and answer the following.
(i) Why a reaction proceeds forward when $Q < K$ and no net reaction occurs when $Q = K$?
(ii) Explain the effect of increase in pressure in terms of reaction quotient Q. **Competency Based Que.**

28. On the basis of Le-Chatelier's principle explain how temperature and pressure can be adjusted to increase the yield of ammonia in the following reaction.
$N_2(g) + 3H_2(g) \rightleftharpoons 2NH_3(g); \Delta H = -92.38$ kJ mol^{-1}
What will be the effect of addition of argon to the above reaction mixture at constant volume? **NCERT Exemplar**

29. (i) Describe the effect of
(a) addition of H_2
(b) addition of CH_3OH
(c) removal of CO
(d) removal of CH_3OH on the equilibrium of the reaction,
$$2H_2(g) + CO(g) \rightleftharpoons CH_3OH(g)$$
(ii) What happens to an equilibrium in a reversible reaction if a catalyst is added to it? **NCERT**

30. Which of the following reactions will get affected by increasing the pressure? Also, mention whether change will cause the reaction to go into forward or backward direction. **NCERT**
(i) $COCl_2(g) \rightleftharpoons CO(g) + Cl_2(g)$
(ii) $CH_4(g) + 2S_2(g) \rightleftharpoons CS_2(g) + 2H_2S(g)$
(iii) $CO_2(g) + C(s) \rightleftharpoons 2CO(g)$
(iv) $2H_2(g) + CO(g) \rightleftharpoons CH_3OH(g)$
(v) $CaCO_3(s) \rightleftharpoons CaO(s) + CO_2(g)$
(vi) $4NH_3(g) + 5O_2(g) \rightleftharpoons 4NO(g) + 6H_2O(g)$

31. Dihydrogen gas is obtained from natural gas by partial oxidation with steam as per following endothermic reaction,

$$CH_4(g) + H_2O(g) \rightleftharpoons CO(g) + 3H_2(g)$$

(i) Write an expression of K_p for the above reaction.

(ii) How will the values of K_p and composition of equilibrium mixture be affected by

(a) increasing the pressure

(b) increasing the temperature

(c) using a catalyst? **NCERT**

32. Show that the degree of dissociation (α) for the dissociation of PCl_5 into PCl_3 and Cl_2 in pressure p is given by $\alpha = \left(\dfrac{K_p}{p + K_p}\right)^{1/2}$. **Competency Based Que.**

33. Calculate the pH of the following solutions.

(i) 2 g of TlOH dissolved in water to give 2 L of solution.

(ii) 0.3 g of $Ca(OH)_2$ dissolved in water to give 500 mL solution.

(iii) 0.3 g of NaOH dissolved in water to give 200 mL of solution.

(iv) 1 mL of 13.6 M HCl is diluted with water to give 1 L of solution. **NCERT**

34. Determine the solubilities of silver chromate, barium chromate, ferric hydroxide, lead chloride and mercurous iodide at 298 K from their solubility product constants.

(i) $K_{sp}(Ag_2CrO_4) = 1.1 \times 10^{-12}$

(ii) $K_{sp}(BaCrO_4) = 1.2 \times 10^{-10}$

(iii) $K_{sp}[Fe(OH)_3] = 1.0 \times 10^{-38}$

Determine also the molarities of individual ions. **NCERT**

35. (i) The solubility product constant of Ag_2CrO_4 and AgBr are 1.1×10^{-12} and 5.0×10^{-13} respectively. Calculate the ratio of the molarities of their saturated solutions.

(ii) For the following equilibrium, $K_C = 6.3 \times 10^{14}$ at 1000 K

$$NO(g) + O_3(g) \rightleftharpoons NO_2(g) + O_2(g)$$

Both the forward and reverse reactions in the equilibrium are elementary bimolecular reactions. What is the K_C for the reverse reaction? **NCERT**

36. (i) (a) Is it possible to get precipitate of $Fe(OH)_3$ at pH = 2? Give reason.

(b) Will AgCl be more soluble in aqueous solution or NaCl solutions and why?

(c) Why pH of our blood remains almost constant at 7.4 though we quite often eat spicy food?

(ii) It has been found that the pH of a 0.01 M solution of an organic acid is 4.15. Calculate the concentration of the anion, the ionisation constant of the acid and its pK_a. **NCERT**

Hints & Solutions

Objective Type Questions

1. (c) At equilibrium both forward and backward reactions occur at same rate. So, the equilibrium is dynamic in nature and all physical processes do not stop at equilibrium.

2. (a) $AB \rightleftharpoons A + B$ or $K = \frac{[A][B]}{[AB]}$

If concentration of A is doubled, the equilibrium concentration of B becomes half to maintain K constant.

3. (b) For $aA + bB \longrightarrow cC + dD$

$$K_C = \frac{[C]^c[D]^d}{[A]^a[B]^b}$$

4. (a) Higher equilibrium constant depict that the reaction in forward direction is occuring faster.

5. (c) Equilibrium constant for reverse reaction $= \frac{1}{K}$

i.e. $\frac{1}{0.04} = 25$

6. (a) $K = \frac{[NO]^2}{[N_2][O_2]}$

$$= \frac{[2.8 \times 10^{-3}\ M]^2}{(3.0 \times 10^{-3}\ M)(4.2 \times 10^{-3}\ M)} = 0.622$$

7. (c) K^n will be the equilibrium constant for the given reaction.

8. (b) For the reaction, $PCl_5 \rightleftharpoons PCl_3 + Cl_2$

$$K_C = \frac{[PCl_3][Cl_2]}{[PCl_5]} = \frac{(1.2 \times 10^{-3}) \times (1.2 \times 10^{-3})}{(0.8 \times 10^{-3})} = 1.8 \times 10^{-3}$$

9. (a) As we know that,

$$\Delta G° = -RT \ln K$$

At the stage of half completion of the reaction,

$$A \rightleftharpoons B, [A] = [B]$$

Therefore, $K = 1$.

Thus, $\Delta G^\ominus = 0$

10. (b)

(i) If $\Delta G° > 0$, $\Delta G°$ is +*ve*, $\ln k = -ve$ i.e. $k < 1$

(ii) If $\Delta G° < 0$, $\Delta G°$ is −*ve*, $\ln k = +ve$ i.e. $k > 1$

(iii) If $\Delta G° = 0$, $\ln k = 0$ i.e. $k = 1$

11. (d) $\Delta n = (n_p - n_r) = (2 - 0) = 2$

where, n_p = moles of gaseous products

n_r = moles of gaseous reactants

12. (d) The conjugate bases should have one proton less in each case and therefore, the corresponding conjugate bases are F^-, HSO_4^- and CO_3^{2-} respectively.

13. (d) A base according to Bronsted concept is a substance which can accept protons.

14. (d) As CH_3COOH is a weak acid, CH_3COO^- is the strongest congugate base.

15. (c) Property of acidic nature of BF_3 can be explained using the Lewis concept. GN Lewis in 1923 defined an acid as a species which accepts an electron pair and base which donates an electron pair. As BF_3 is an electron deficient compound, hence, it is a Lewis acid.

16. (b) $K = C\alpha^2 = 0.2 \times (0.032)^2 = 2.1 \times 10^{-4}$

17. (b) Since water is pure, $[H_3O^+] = [OH^-] = 10^{-6}$ M

$$K_w = [H_3O^+][OH^-] = 10^{-6} \times 10^{-6} = 10^{-12}\ M$$

18. (c) When the concentration of NH_4OH (weak base) is higher than the strong acid (HCl), a mixture of weak base and its conjugate acid is obtained, which acts as basic buffer.

	NH_4OH +	HCl $\longrightarrow$	$NH_4Cl + H_2O$
Initially	0.1 M	0.05M	0
After reaction	0.05 M	0	0.05 M

19. (b) $pOH = pK_b + \log \frac{[salt]}{[base]}$

$$= 5 + \log \frac{0.01}{0.1} = 5 + \log 10^{-1} = 5 - 1 = 4$$

$\therefore$ pH = 14 − 4 = 10

20. (d) HNO_2 and $NaNO_2$ represents a buffer mixture.

21. (b) $[Cl^-]$ increases but $K_{sp} = [Ag^+][Cl^-]$ remains constant. So, $[Ag^+]$ decreases.

22. (b) $S = \frac{10w}{M}$ moL/L

K_{sp} of $Ca_3(PO_4)_2 = 108\ S^5$

$$= 108 \left(\frac{10w}{M}\right)^5 \approx 10^7 \left(\frac{w}{M}\right)^5 \text{ (approximately)}$$

Mistake Alert One can make a mistake in calculating solubility, as the value of solubility in mol L^{-1} has to be calculated from g/100 mL given in the question.

23. (a)

	$PCl_5(g)$	$\rightleftharpoons$	$PCl_3(g) + Cl_2(g)$
Initial conc.	$\frac{2\text{ mole}}{2\text{ L}} = 1\text{ mol L}^{-1}$		
Equilibrium conc.	$1 - 0.4 = 0.6$		0.4 0.4

[as 40% dissociation]

$$K_C = \frac{[PCl_3][Cl_2]}{[PCl_5]}$$

$$= \frac{0.4 \times 0.4}{0.6} = 0.267$$

24. (c) When the value of the equilibrium constant is around one, appreciable quantities of both reactants and products are present.

25. (*b*) In reaction,
$C(s) + 2O_2(g) \rightleftharpoons 2CO_2(g)$, when pressure increases, the reaction goes in decreasing number of moles side that is in reverse direction.
As number of moles of gas increases in the forward direction.

26. (*d*) The equilibrium constant does not depend on the initial concentrations, but depends on the equilibrium concentrations of both reactants and products.

27. (*c*) *X*-base, *Y*-conjugate base
a molecule of water acts as an acid, donating H^+ ion and forming the conjugate base OH^- and an other molecule of water acts as a base, accepting the H^+ ion and forms the conjugate acid, H_3O^+.

28. (*a*) As we know,

$$pH + pOH = 14$$
$$pOH = 14 - pH$$
$$= 14 - 4.70 = 9.30$$
$$pOH = -\log[OH^-]$$
$$[OH^-] = 10^{-9.30} = 5 \times 10^{-10}$$
$$[OH^-] = 5 \times 10^{-10}$$

29. (*c*) $pH = -\log[H^+]$

$$= -\log[10^{-4}] = 0.0001 \text{ M}$$

30. (*a*) Both (A) and (R) are correct and (R) is the correct explanation of (A).

31. (*a*) Both (A) and (R) are correct and (R) is the correct explanation of (A).

32. (*a*) Both (A) and (R) are correct and (R) is the correct explanation of (A).

33. (*c*) (A) is correct and (R) is incorrect.
There is no change in mass of ice and water, because the transfer of molecules from ice into water and reverse transfer from water into ice is equal at atmosphere pressure and 273 K. The system is in dynamic equilibrium.

34. (*c*) (A) is correct, (R) is incorrect.
The concentration of pure solid and liquid are taken as unity.

35. (*a*) Both (A) and (R) are correct, (R) is the correct explanation of (A).

36. (*c*) (A) is correct and (R) is incorrect.

$$PCl_5(g) \rightleftharpoons PCl_3(g) + Cl_2(g)$$

When a noble gas is added to the system in equilibrium at constant pressure and temperature, then the total volume will increase and the number of moles per unit volume of reactants and products will decrease. Hence, the equilibrium will shift towards the direction in which there is increase in number of moles of gases that is forward direction. So, it will increase the dissociation of PCl_5.

37. (*a*) Both (A) and (R) are correct and (R) is the correct explanation of (A).

38. (*a*) Both (A) and (R) are correct and (R) is the correct explanation of (A).

39. (*d*) (A) is incorrect and (R) is correct.
A catalyst increases the rate of reaction by lowering the activation energy. A catalyst increases the rate of reaction in both forward and backward direction. It does not shift equilibrium or increase product amount.

40. (i) Let the equilibrium constant for synthesis of NH_3 is *K*.

$$K = \frac{[NH_3]^2}{[N_2][H_2]^3}$$

(ii) (c) NH_3 produced is equal to the 500 mL of 1 M HCl it means, NH_3 produced = 0.5 mol as volume = 1 Litre
$[NH_3] = 0.5 \text{ mol L}^{-1}$

	N_2	+ $3H_2$	$\rightleftharpoons 2NH_3$
At $t = 0$	1 mol	3 mol	–
At $t = t$	$1 - x$	$3 - 3x$	$2x$

$$2x = 0.5 \text{ (from the above)}$$
$$x = 0.25$$
$$[N_2] = 1 - x = 1 - 0.25 = 0.75 \text{ mol L}^{-1}$$
$$[H_2] = 3 - 3x = 3 - 3 \times 0.25 = 2.25 \text{ mol L}^{-1}$$
$$K_C = \frac{[NH_3]^2}{[N_2][H_2]^3} = \frac{(0.5)^2}{0.75 \times (2.25)^3} = 0.029$$
$$\approx 0.03$$

(iii) (a) If pressure in increased, the equilibrium position moves to the right, So, the yield of ammonia or increases.

Or

(b) The iron (Fe) is used as a catalyst to increase the rate of reaction.

41. (i) The solubility of salt of weak acids increases with decrease in pH as at lower pH, anion of weak acid gets protonated and its concentration decreases, so the solubility of weak acid increases (as equilibrium shifts in forward direction).

(ii) $K_{sp} < K_{ip}$ means that, when we increase the concentration of dissociated ions then equilibrium will shift backward so there will be formation of precipitate.

Or

$$\underset{(S)}{Zr_3(PO_4)_4} \rightleftharpoons \underset{3S}{3Zr^{4+}} + \underset{4S}{4PO_4^{3-}}$$
$$K_{sp} = [Zr^{4+}]^3 [PO_4^{3-}]^4 = (3S)^3(4S)^4$$
$$= 27S^3 . 256S^4 = 6912S^7$$

(iii) The compound having less value of solubility product, precipitate out first from the solution.
Solubility product of Ag Br < Ag Cl.

$$K_{sp} \text{ of AgBr} = 5 \times 10^{-13} \text{ and } K_{sp} \text{ of AgCl} = 5 \times 10^{-10}$$

Subjective Type Questions

1. It will remain the same because rate of inflow is equal to rate of outflow. The state is called state of 'equilibrium'. **(2)**

2. On increasing the pressure, ice melts to form water (because water has lesser volume than ice). **(2)**

3. BF_3 is an electron deficient compound and hence act as Lewis acid. NH_3 has one lone pair which it can donate to BF_3 and form a coordinate bond. **(1)**
Hence, NH_3 acts as a Lewis base.

$$H_3N\!: \longrightarrow BF_3$$ **(1)**

4. In the reaction,

$$\underset{\text{(Pink)}}{[Co(H_2O)_6]^{3+}(aq)} + 4Cl^-(aq) \rightleftharpoons \underset{\text{(Blue)}}{[CoCl_4]^{2-}(aq)} + 6H_2O(l)$$ **(1)**

On cooling, the equilibrium shifts backward direction or on heating, the equilibrium shifts forward direction. Hence, reaction is endothermic, i.e. $\Delta H > 0$. **(1)**

5. (i) Equilibrium will shift in the forward direction, i.e. more of ice will melt. **(1)**
(ii) Solubility will decrease because it is an exothermic process. **(1)**

6. CH_3NH_2 is strongest base because it has high value of base dissociation constant. **(2)**

7. When an acid is added to pure water, ionic product will remain unchanged even though the concentration of hydrogen and hydroxide ions change. **(2)**

8. Acid *A* with $pK_a = 1.5$ is the strongest acid, lower the value of pK_a stronger will be the acid. **(2)**

9. Explanation for the given statement on the basis of ionisation and effect upon the concentration of sodium chloride is given below.
(i) Sugar being a non-electrolyte does not ionise in water whereas NaCl ionises completely in water and produces Na^+ and Cl^- ions which help in the conduction of electricity. **(1)**
(ii) When concentration of NaCl is increased, more Na^+ and Cl^- ions will be produced. Hence, conductance or conductivity of the solution increases. **(1)**

10. Conjugate acid $\overset{+}{N}H_3CH_2COOH$ **(1)**
Conjugate base $NH_2CH_2COO^-$ **(1)**

11. $\because$ $pH = -\log [H^+]$

$$= -\log [3.8 \times 10^{-3}] = 2.4202 \approx 2.42$$ **(2)**

12. $\because$ pH = 6.0

$\therefore$ $[H_3O^+] = 10^{-6}$ M, **(1)**
i.e. $[\text{Acid}] = 10^{-6}\ M = 10^{-6}\ N$ **(1)**
Thus, 1000 mL of the urine contains acid $= 10^{-6}$ g eq.
$\therefore$ 1300 mL of the urine will contain acid $= 1.3 \times 10^{-6}$ g eq. **(1)**

13. An acid-base pair differ by a proton is known as conjugate acid-base pair. **(1)**
Conjugate bases for HNO_2, $HClO_4$ and OH^- are NO_2^-, ClO_4^- and O^{2-} respectively. **(1)**
Conjugate acids for CN^-, F^-, OH^-, CO_3^{2-} and S^{2-} are HCN, HF, H_2O, HCO_3^- and HS^- respectively. **(1)**

14. A sparingly soluble salt having general formula $A_x^{p+} B_y^{q-}$. Its molar solubility is S mol L^{-1}. **(1)**
Then, $A_x^{p+} B_y^{q-} \rightleftharpoons \underset{xS}{xA^{p+}(aq)} + \underset{yS}{yB^{q-}(aq)}$ **(1)**
S moles of A_xB_y dissolve to give x moles of A^{p+} and y moles of B^{q-}. Therefore, solubility product

$$(K_{sp}) = [A^{p+}]^x [B^{q-}]^y$$
$$= [xS]^x [yS]^y = x^x y^y S^{x+y}$$ **(1)**

15. $3O_2(g) \rightleftharpoons 2O_3(g)$ **(1)**

$$K_C = \frac{[O_3]^2}{[O_2]^3}$$ **(1)**

or $O_3 = \sqrt{K_C[O_2]^3} = \sqrt{(2.0 \times 10^{-50})(1.6 \times 10^{-2})^3}$
$[O_3] = 2.86 \times 10^{-28}$ mol L^{-1} **(1)**

16. $$PCl_5(g) \rightleftharpoons PCl_3(g) + Cl_2(g)$$
At equili. 0.5×10^{-1} M $\quad x \quad x$

$\therefore$ $$K_C = \frac{[PCl_3][Cl_2]}{[PCl_5]}$$ **(1)**

$$8.3 \times 10^{-3} = \frac{x^2}{0.05} \text{ (because } [PCl_3] = [Cl_2])$$

or $x^2 = 0.415 \times 10^{-3} = 4.15 \times 10^{-4}$
$x \approx 2.04 \times 10^{-2}$ mol L^{-1} **(1)**
Hence, $[PCl_3] = [Cl_2] = 2.04 \times 10^{-2}$ mol L^{-1} **(1)**

17. $H_2(g) + I_2(g) \rightleftharpoons 2HI(g)$; $K_C = 54.8$

$$2HI(g) \rightleftharpoons H_2(g) + I_2(g);\ K'_C = \frac{1}{K_C} = \frac{1}{54.8}$$

Again, $$K'_C = \frac{[H_2][I_2]}{[HI]^2} = \frac{1}{54.8}$$ **(1)**

Given, [HI] = 0.5 mol L^{-1}
According to equation, $[H_2] = [I_2] = [x]$

$$\frac{x \cdot x}{[0.5]^2} = \frac{1}{54.8} \text{ or } x^2 = \frac{[0.5]^2}{54.8} = 0.00456$$
$x = 0.0675$ M **(1)**
Hence, $[H_2] = [I_2] = x = 0.0675$ M **(1)**

18. $CaCO_3(s) \rightleftharpoons CaO(s) + CO_2(g)$

$$K_p = p_{CO_2} = 1.15 \text{ atm}, pV = nRT$$
$$n_{CO_2} = \frac{p_{CO_2}V}{RT}$$
$$= \frac{115 \times 5}{0.082 \times 1073} = 0.065 \text{ mol}$$ **(1)**

1 mole of CO_2 is obtained by decomposition of 1 mole $CaCO_3$. Therefore, moles of $CaCO_3$ decomposed is equal to the moles of CO_2 = 0.065 mol.

Moles of $CaCO_3$ initially present $= \frac{50}{100} = 0.5$ mol **(1)**
[Molecular mass of $CaCO_3$ = 100]

Per cent of $CaCO_3$ decomposed $= \frac{0.065}{0.5} \times 100 = 13\%$ **(1)**

19. $$C_2H_6(g) \rightleftharpoons C_2H_4(g) + H_2(g) \quad \textbf{(1)}$$

Initial pressure	4.0 atm	0	0
Equili. pressure	$(4.0-p)$ atm	p	p

$$K_p = \frac{p_{C_2H_4} \cdot p_{H_2}}{p_{C_2H_6}} = \frac{p \times p}{4.0 - p}$$

$$0.04 = \frac{p^2}{4.0 - p} \quad \text{or} \quad 0.16 - 0.04p = p^2$$

$$p = -0.04 \pm \frac{\sqrt{0.0016 - 4(-0.16)}}{2}$$

$$p = \frac{-0.04 \pm 0.80}{2} \Rightarrow p = 0.38$$

(1) (by taking positive value)

Hence, $p_{C_2H_6} = 4.0 - 0.38 = 3.62$ atm **(1)**

20. (i) NaCl is neutral, it simply dilutes the HCl solution from 1 mL to 1000 mL so that

$$[H^+] = \frac{0.01}{1000} = 10^{-5} \text{ M}$$

$$pH = -\log(10^{-5}) = 5 \quad \textbf{(1)}$$

(ii) $[H_3O^+] = \sqrt{K_{a_1}C_1 + K_{a_2}C_2}$

$$= \sqrt{(1.8\times 10^{-5})(0.1) + (6.5\times 10^{-5})(0.1)}$$

$$= \sqrt{1.8\times 10^{-6} + 6.5\times 10^{-6}}$$

$$= \sqrt{8.3\times 10^{-6}} = 2.88\times 10^{-3} \text{ M} \quad \textbf{(1)}$$

$$pH = -\log[H_3O^+] = -\log(2.88\times 10^{-3})$$

$$= 3 - 0.4594 = 2.5406 \quad \textbf{(1)}$$

21. If K_a is the ionisation constant of a weak acid (HA) and K_b is the ionisation constant of its conjugate base (A^-), then

$$K_a \cdot K_b = K_w$$

$$K_b(F^-) = \frac{K_w}{K_a(HF)} = \frac{1\times 10^{-14}}{6.8\times 10^{-4}} = 1.47\times 10^{-11} \quad \textbf{(1)}$$

$$K_b(HCOO^-) = \frac{K_w}{K_a(HCOOH)} = \frac{1\times 10^{-14}}{1.8\times 10^{-4}} = 5.56\times 10^{-11} \quad \textbf{(1)}$$

$$K_b(CN^-) = \frac{K_w}{K_a(HCN)} = \frac{1\times 10^{-14}}{4.8\times 10^{-9}} = 2.08\times 10^{-6} \quad \textbf{(1)}$$

22. $pH = -\log[H^+]$ **(1/2)**

(i) pH of milk = 6.8

$\log[H^+] = -6.8$

$[H^+] = 10^{-6.8} = 1.585\times 10^{-7}$ M **(1/2)**

(ii) pH of black coffee = 5.0

$\log[H^+] = -5.0$

$[H^+] = 10^{-5}$ M **(1/2)**

(iii) pH of tomato juice = 4.2

$\log[H^+] = -4.2$

$[H^+] = 10^{-4.2} = 6.310\times 10^{-5}$ M **(1/2)**

(iv) pH of lemon juice = 2.2

$\log[H^+] = -2.2$

$[H^+] = 10^{-2.2} = 6.310\times 10^{-3}$ M **(1/2)**

(v) pH of egg white = 7.8

$\log[H^+] = -7.8$

$[H^+] = 10^{-7.8} = 1.585\times 10^{-8}$ M **(1/2)**

23. $$CH_3CH_2COOH + H_2O \rightleftharpoons CH_3CH_2COO^- + H_3O^+;$$

Propanoic acid $(0.05\text{-}C\alpha)$ $(C\alpha)$ $C\alpha$

From Ostwald's dilution law,

$$\alpha = \sqrt{K_a / C} = \sqrt{\frac{1.32\times 10^{-5}}{0.05}} = 0.016248 \quad \textbf{(1)}$$

$$[H_3O^+] = C\alpha = 0.05\times 0.016248$$

$$= 0.0008124 = 8.124\times 10^{-4}$$

From, $pH = -\log[H_3O^+]$

$$= -\log(8.124\times 10^{-4}) = 3.0902 \approx 3.09 \quad \textbf{(1)}$$

When the solution contains 0.01 M HCl

$$K_a = \frac{[CH_3CH_2COO^-][H_3O^+]}{[CH_3CH_2COOH]}$$

$$1.32\times 10^{-5} = \frac{C\alpha \times 0.01}{(0.05 - C\alpha)}$$

($[H_3O^+] = 0.01$ M from HCl. In the presence of 0.01 M HCl, dissociation of propanoic acid decreases).

$$C\alpha = \frac{1.32\times 10^{-5}\times(0.05 - C\alpha)}{0.01} = \frac{1.32\times 10^{-5}\times 0.05}{0.01}$$

[as $(0.05 - C\alpha) \approx 0.05$]

or $\quad 0.05\times\alpha = 6.60\times 10^{-5}$

$$\alpha = \frac{6.60\times 10^{-5}}{0.05} = 1.32\times 10^{-3} \quad \textbf{(1)}$$

24. For AB salt, $K_{sp} = [A^+][B^-]$. If x is the solubility, then

$$x^2 = 4.0\times 10^{-18} \text{ or } x = 2.0\times 10^{-9} \quad \textbf{(1)}$$

For PQ_2 salt, $K_{sp} = [P^{2+}][Q^-]^2$

If y is the solubility, then

$$K_{sp} = [y][2y]^2 = 4y^3$$

$$4y^3 = K_{sp} = 4.0\times 10^{-18} \text{ or } y = 1.0\times 10^{-6} \quad \textbf{(1)}$$

Since, y is more than x, PQ_2 salt has more solubility. **(1)**

25. On mixing 50 mL of 0.01 M NaCl and 50 mL of 0.01 M $AgNO_3$, the total volume becomes 100 mL. Therefore,

$$\text{Conc. of NaCl in 100 mL} = \frac{0.01\times 50}{100} = 0.005 \text{ M} \quad \textbf{(1)}$$

$$\text{Conc. of } AgNO_3 \text{ in 100 mL} = \frac{0.01\times 50}{100} = 0.005 \text{ M} \quad \textbf{(1)}$$

Now $\quad NaCl(aq) = Na^+(aq) + Cl^-(aq)$

and $AgNO_3(aq) = Ag^+(aq) + NO_3^-(aq)$

$$[Cl^-] = [NaCl] = 0.005 \text{ N}$$

$$[Ag^+] = [AgNO_3] = 0.005 \text{ M}$$

$\therefore$ Ionic product of $[Ag^+][Cl^-] = 0.005\times 0.005 = 2.5\times 10^{-5}$ **(1)**

Since ionic product is greater than its solubility product, precipitation will occur.

26. According to Henderson's equation,

$$pH = pK_a + \log\frac{[Salt]}{[Acid]};\ pH = 4.91,\ pK_a = 4.76 \quad (1)$$

$$4.91 = 4.76 + \log\frac{[Salt]}{[Acid]}$$

$$\log\frac{[NaAc]}{[AcH]} = 4.91 - 4.76 = 0.15$$

$$\frac{[NaAc]}{[AcH]} = \text{antilog}\,(0.15) = 1.41 \quad (1)$$

If V is the volume of 0.1 M AcH required

$$\frac{[NaAc]}{[AcH]} = \frac{\frac{0.2\times 50}{1000}}{\frac{0.1\times V}{1000}} = 1.41 \Rightarrow \frac{0.2\times 50}{0.1\times V} = 1.41$$

or $$V = \frac{0.2\times 50}{0.1\times 1.41} = 70.92\ \text{mL}$$

Volume of 0.1 M acetic acid required = 70.92 mL (1)

27. The relation between ΔG and Q is

$$\Delta G = \Delta G^\ominus + RT \ln Q$$

ΔG = change in free energy as the reaction proceeds

$\Delta G^\ominus$ = standard free energy

Q = reaction quotient

R = gas constant

T = absolute temperature in K (1)

(i) Since, $\Delta G^\ominus = -RT \ln K$

$\therefore \Delta G = -RT\ln K + RT\ln Q;\ \Delta G = RT \ln\frac{Q}{K}$

If $Q < K$, ΔG will be negative and the reaction proceeds in the forward direction. If $Q = K$, $\Delta G = 0$ reaction is in equilibrium and there is no net reaction. (1)

(ii) $CO(g) + 3H_2(g) \rightleftharpoons CH_4(g) + H_2O(g)$

$$K_C = \frac{[CH_4]\,[H_2O]}{[CO]\,[H_2]^3} \quad (1)$$

On increasing pressure, volume decreases. If we double the pressure, volume will be halved but the molar concentrations will be doubled. Then,

$$Q_C = \frac{2[CH_4]\cdot 2[H_2O]}{2[CO]\,\{2[H_2]\}^3} = \frac{1}{4}\frac{[CH_4]\,[H_2O]}{[CO]\,[H_2]^3} = \frac{1}{4}K_C \quad (1)$$

Therefore, Q_C is less than K_C, so Q_C will tend to increase to re-establish equilibrium and the reaction will go in forward direction.

$$CO(g) + 3H_2(g) \rightleftharpoons CH_4(g) + H_2O(g) \quad (1)$$

28. $N_2(g) + 3H_2(g) \rightleftharpoons 2NH_3(g);\ \Delta H = -92.38\ \text{kJ mol}^{-1}$

It is an exothermic process as ΔH is negative. (1/2)

Effect of temperature According to Le-Chatelier's principle, low temperature is favourable for high yield of ammonia, but practically very low temperatures slow down the reaction. So, optimum temperature 700 K is favourable in attainment of equilibrium. (1½)

Effect of pressure Similarly, high pressure about 200 atm is favourable for high yield of ammonia. On increasing pressure, reaction goes in the forward direction because the number of moles decreases in the forward direction. (1½)

Addition of argon At constant volume addition of argon does not affect the equilibrium because it does not change the partial pressures of the reactants or products involved in the reaction and the equilibrium remains undisturbed. (1½)

29. (i) $2H_2(g) + CO(g) \rightleftharpoons CH_3OH(g)$

According to Le-Chatelier's principle,

(a) addition of H_2 (increase in concentration of reactants) shifts the equilibrium in forward direction (more product is formed). (1)

(b) addition of CH_3OH (increase in concentration of product) shifts the equilibrium in backward direction. (1)

(c) removal of CO also shifts the equilibrium in backward direction. (1)

(d) removal of CH_3OH shifts the equilibrium in forward direction. (1)

(ii) When catalyst is added, the state of equilibrium is not disturbed but equilibrium is attained quickly. This is because the catalyst increases the rate of forward and backward reaction to the same extent. (1)

30. (i) $n_p > n_r$, the reaction will go in backward direction. (1)

(ii) $n_p = n_r$, the reaction will not be affected by increasing pressure.

(iii) $n_p > n_r$, the reaction will go in backward direction. (1)

(iv) $n_p < n_r$, the reaction will go in forward direction. (1)

(v) $n_p > n_r$, the reaction will go in backward direction. (1)

(vi) $n_p > n_r$, the reaction will go in backward direction. (1)

31. $CH_4(g) + H_2O(g) \rightleftharpoons CO(g) + 3H_2(g)$ (1)

(i) $$K_p = \frac{p_{CO}\cdot p_{H_2}^3}{p_{CH_4}\cdot p_{H_2O}} \quad (1)$$

(ii) (a) Increase in pressure shifts the equilibrium in the direction where pressure decreases (i.e. number of moles are less). This is backward direction. K_p remains unaffected from pressure change. (1)

(b) Since, ΔH = +ve (endothermic reaction), reaction takes place with absorption of heat. Hence, increase in temperature shifts the equilibrium in the direction where heat is absorbed (i.e. forward). It also increases the value of K_p. (1)

(c) No effect, since catalyst affects rate of both directions equally. (1)

32.

	PCl_5	$\rightleftharpoons$	PCl_3	+	Cl_2	
						(1)
Initial moles	1		0		0	
Moles after diss.	$1-\alpha$		α		α	(Total = $1+\alpha$)

$$\therefore\ p_{PCl_5} = \frac{1-\alpha}{1+\alpha}\times p,\ p_{PCl_3} = \frac{\alpha}{1+\alpha}\times p, \quad (1)$$

$$p_{Cl_2} = \frac{\alpha}{1+\alpha}\times p, \quad (1)$$

$$K_p = \frac{p_{PCl_3} \times p_{Cl_2}}{p_{PCl_5}} = \frac{\left(\frac{\alpha}{1+\alpha}p\right)\left(\frac{\alpha}{1+\alpha}p\right)}{\left(\frac{1-\alpha}{1+\alpha}p\right)} = \frac{\alpha^2 p}{1-\alpha^2}$$ **(1)**

or $(1-\alpha^2)K_p = \alpha^2 p$ or $(p + K_p)\alpha^2 = K_p$

or $$\alpha = \left(\frac{K_p}{p + K_p}\right)^{1/2}$$ **(1)**

33. (i) Molecular mass of TlOH = 204 + 16 + 1 = 221 g mol^{-1}

Conc. in mol L^{-1} (molarity)

$$= \frac{\text{mass of TlOH (g)}}{\text{molar mass of TlOH} \times \text{volume of solution (L)}}$$

$$= \frac{2}{221 \times 2} = 0.00452 = 4.52 \times 10^{-3} \text{ M}$$

$\because$ pOH = − log [OH^-] = − log [4.52×10^{-3}] = 2.344

From, pH + pOH = 14

pH = 14 − 2.334 = 11.656 ≈ 11.66 **(1)**

(ii) Molecular mass of $Ca(OH)_2$

= 40 + [(16 + 1) × 2] = 74 g mol^{-1}

Molarity, M

$$= \frac{\text{mass of } Ca(OH)_2 (g) \times 1000}{\text{molar mass of } Ca(OH)_2 \times \text{volume of solution (mL)}}$$

$$M = \frac{0.3 \times 1000}{74 \times 500} = 0.0081$$ **(1)**

One mole of $Ca(OH)_2$ gives 2 moles of OH^-.

So, [OH^-] = 2 × 0.0081 = 0.0162 M

pOH = − log [OH^-] = − log [0.0162]

= 1.7905 ≈ 1.79

From, pH + pOH = 14

or pH = 14 − 1.79 = 12. 21 **(1)**

(iii) Molecular mass of NaOH = 23 + 16 + 1 = 40

$$M = \frac{\text{mass of NaOH (g)} \times 1000}{\text{molar mass of NaOH} \times \text{volume of solution (mL)}}$$

$$= \frac{0.3 \times 1000}{40 \times 200} = 0.0375$$

pOH = − log [0 .0375] = − log [3.75×10^{-2}]

= 1.426 ≈ 1.43

From, pH + pOH = 14

pH = 14 − 1.43 = 12.57 **(1)**

(iv) In case of dilution, $M_1V_1 = M_2V_2$

$13.6 \times 1 = M_2 \times 1000$

$$M_2 = \frac{13.6 \times 1}{1000} = 0.0136 = 1.36 \times 10^{-2} \text{ M}$$

pH = − log [1.36×10^{-2}]

= − 0.1335 + 2 = 1.8665 pH = 1.87 **(1)**

34. (i) $\underset{S}{Ag_2CrO_4} \rightleftharpoons \underset{2S}{2Ag^+} + \underset{S}{CrO_4^{2-}}$; $K_{sp} = 1.1 \times 10^{-12}$

$K_{sp} = [Ag^+]^2 \cdot [CrO_4^{2-}]$

$K_{sp} = [2S]^2 \cdot [S] = 4S^3$,

$$S^3 = \frac{K_{sp}}{4}$$

or $$S^3 = \frac{1.1 \times 10^{-12}}{4} = 0.275 \times 10^{-12}$$ **(1)**

On solving $S = 6.503 \times 10^{-5}$ M

$[Ag^+] = 2S = 2 \times 6.503 \times 10^{-5}$

$= 13.006 \times 10^{-5} \approx 1.3 \times 10^{-4}$ M

and $[CrO_4^{2-}] = S = 6.503 \times 10^{-5}$ M **(1)**

(ii) $\underset{S}{BaCrO_4} \rightleftharpoons \underset{S}{Ba^{2+}} + \underset{S}{CrO_4^{2-}}$; $K_{sp} = 1.2 \times 10^{-10}$

(Solubility of $BaCrO_4$ is S mol L^{-1})

$K_{sp} = 1.2 \times 10^{-10} = [Ba^{2+}] \cdot [CrO_4^{2-}] = S^2$

$S = \sqrt{1.2 \times 10^{-10}} = 1.1 \times 10^{-5}$ M

$[Ba^{2+}] = [CrO_4^{2-}] = 1.1 \times 10^{-5}$ M **(1)**

(iii) $\underset{S}{Fe(OH)_3} \rightleftharpoons \underset{S}{Fe^{3+}} + \underset{3S}{3\,OH^-}$; $K_{sp} = 1.0 \times 10^{-38}$

(Solubility of $Fe(OH)_3$ is S mol L^{-1})

$K_{sp} = [Fe^{3+}][OH^-]^3$

$K_{sp} = S \cdot (3S)^3 = 27S^4$ or $S^4 = \frac{K_{sp}}{27}$

$$S^4 = \frac{1.0 \times 10^{-38}}{27} = 0.037 \times 10^{-38}$$

$S = 1.387 \times 10^{-10}$, $S \approx 1.39 \times 10^{-10}$ **(1)**

$[Fe^{3+}] = 1.39 \times 10^{-10}$ M

$[OH^-] = 3S = 3 \times 1.39 \times 10^{-10} = 4.17 \times 10^{-10}$ M **(1)**

35. (i) $\underset{S}{Ag_2CrO_4} \rightleftharpoons \underset{2S}{2Ag^+} + \underset{S}{CrO_4^{2-}}$; $K_{sp} = 1.1 \times 10^{-12}$

(Solubility of Ag_2CrO_4 is S mol L^{-1})

$K_{sp} = [Ag^+]^2[CrO_4^{2-}]$; $K_{sp} = (2S)^2 \cdot S = 4S^3$

or $$S^3 = \frac{K_{sp}}{4} = \frac{1.1 \times 10^{-12}}{4} = 0.275 \times 10^{-12}$$

$S^3 = 2.75 \times 10^{-13}$

$S = 6.503 \times 10^{-5}$ M **(1)**

Thus, solubility of $[Ag_2CrO_4] = 6.503 \times 10^{-5}$ M

$\underset{S}{AgBr} \rightleftharpoons \underset{S}{Ag^+} + \underset{S}{Br^-}$; $K_{sp} = 5.0 \times 10^{-13}$

(Solubility of AgBr is S mol L^{-1})

$K_{sp} = [Ag^+][Br^-] = S \cdot S = S^2$

or $S = \sqrt{K_{sp}} = \sqrt{5.0 \times 10^{-13}} = \sqrt{50 \times 10^{-14}}$

$S = 7.07 \times 10^{-7}$ M **(1)**

Ratio of their solubilities

$$\frac{S\,(Ag_2CrO_4)}{S\,(AgBr)} = \frac{6.50 \times 10^{-5} \text{ M}}{7.07 \times 10^{-7} \text{ M}} = 91.93 \approx 92$$

Therefore, Ag_2CrO_4 is 92 times more soluble than AgBr. **(1)**

(ii) For the reaction,

$$NO(g) + O_3(g) \rightleftharpoons NO_2(g) + O_2(g)$$

$K_C = 6.3 \times 10^{14}$ at 1000 K

$$K_C = \frac{[NO_2][O_2]}{[NO][O_3]} = 6.3 \times 10^{14} \quad \text{...(i)}$$ **(1)**

For reverse reaction,

$$NO_2(g) + O_2(g) \rightleftharpoons NO(g) + O_3(g)$$

$$K'_C = \frac{[NO][O_3]}{[NO_2][O_2]} \quad \text{...(ii)}$$

From Eqs. (i) and (ii), we get

$$K'_C = \frac{1}{K_C} = \frac{1}{6.3 \times 10^{14}} = 1.587 \times 10^{-15}$$ **(1)**

36. (i) (a) No, because $Fe(OH)_3$ will dissolve in strongly acidic medium. **(1)**

(b) In NaCl solution, the Cl^- ions will increase. Since solubility product, $K_{sp} = [Ag^+][Cl^-]$ remains constant, $[Ag^+]$ will decrease. Therefore, solubility of AgCl will be less in NaCl solution than in water. **(1)**

(c) Blood is a buffer containing carbonic acid (H_2CO_3) and bicarbonate ions (HCO_3^-). Small amounts of the acid or base produced from the spicy food do not disturb its pH. **(1)**

(ii) $HA \rightleftharpoons H^+ + A^-$

$$pH = -\log [H^+] = 4.15$$

$$\log [H^+] = -4.15$$

$$\log [H^+] = \bar{5}.85 \text{ or } [H^+] = \text{antilog } \bar{5}.85 = 7.079 \times 10^{-5}$$

$$[H^+] = [A^-] = 7.079 \times 10^{-5} \text{ M}$$ **(1)**

Thus,
$$K_a = \frac{[H^+][A^-]}{[HA]}$$

$$= \frac{(7.079 \times 10^{-5})(7.079 \times 10^{-5})}{0.01}$$

$$= 5011.22 \times 10^{-10} = 5.0 \times 10^{-7}$$

From,
$$pK_a = -\log K_a$$

$$= -\log [5.0 \times 10^{-7}]$$

$$= -0.699 + 7 = 6.301$$ **(1)**

QR Code for Quick Test 1

QR Code for Quick Test 2

QR Code for Quick Test 3

SELF ASSESSMENT TEST

Objective Type Questions [1 Mark]

1. If the concentration of OH^- ions in the reaction $Fe(OH)_3(s) \rightleftharpoons Fe^{3+}(aq) + 3OH^-(aq)$, is decreased by $\frac{1}{4}$ times, then equilibrium concentration of Fe^{3+} will increase by

(a) 16 times (b) 64 times
(c) 4 times (d) 8 times

2. $A(g) + 3B(g) \rightleftharpoons 4C(g)$

Initially concentration of A is equal to that of B. The equilibrium concentrations of A and C are equal. K_C is

(a) 0.08 (b) 0.08
(c) 8 (d) 80

3. 50 mL of 0.1 M HCl and 50 mL of 0.2 M NaOH are mixed. The pH of the resulting solution is

(a) 1.30 (b) 4.2
(c) 12.70 (d) 11.70

4. The $[H_3O^+]$ in the rain water of pH $= 4.35$ is

(a) 4.5×10^{-5} M (b) 6.5×10^{-5} M
(c) 9.5×10^{-5} M (d) 12.5×10^{-5} M

5. In which of the following cases, reaction does not go farthest to completion?

(a) $K = 10^3$ (b) $K = 10^{-2}$
(c) $K = 10$ (d) $K = 1$

Assertion-Reason [1 Mark]

■ **Directions** (Q. Nos. 6-8) In the following questions, an Assertion (A) is followed by a corresponding Reason (R). Use the following keys to choose the appropriate answer.

(a) Both (A) and (R) are true and (R) is the correct explanation of (A).
(b) Both (A) and (R) are true but (R) is not the correct explanation of (A).
(c) (A) is true but (R) is false.
(d) (A) is false but (R) is true.

6. Assertion (A) Le-Chatelier's principle can predict the effect of changes in concentration, temperature, and pressure on a system at equilibrium.

Reason (R) Le-Chatelier's principle states that a system at equilibrium will adjust to counteract any change imposed on it.

7. Assertion (A) A catalyst affects the position of equilibrium.

Reason (R) A catalyst speeds up both the forward and reverse reactions equally.

8. Assertion (A) The common ion effect decreases the solubility of a salt in a solution that already contains one of its ions.

Reason (R) According to Le Chatelier's principle, adding a common ion shifts the equilibrium towards the solid state.

Short Answer Type I Questions [2 Marks]

9. (i) For an exothermic reaction, what happens to the equilibrium constant if temperature is increased?

(ii) Ice melts slowly at higher altitudes. Explain why?

10. $2NO(g) + O_2(g) \rightleftharpoons 2NO_2(g); \Delta H = -117$ kJ

(i) Predict the effect of an increase in concentration of NO on the equilibrium concentration of NO_2.

(ii) Predict the effect of pressure decrease as a result of increased volume on the equilibrium concentration of NO_2.

11. (i) Sulphuric acid is a very strong acid, yet it can also act as base in some reactions. Explain how?

(ii) All Brönsted acids are not Lewis acids. Explain.

Short Answer Type II Questions [3 Marks]

12. (i) One mole of H_2O and one mole of CO are taken in 10 L vessel and heated to 725 K. At equilibrium, 40% of water (by mass) reacts with CO according to the equation,

$$H_2O(g) + CO(g) \rightleftharpoons H_2(g) + CO_2(g)$$

Calculate the equilibrium constant for the reaction.

(ii) What is K_C for the following equilibrium when the equilibrium concentration of each substance is

$[SO_2] = 0.60$ M, $[O_2] = 0.82$ M and $[SO_3] = 1.90$ M?

$$2SO_2(g) + O_2(g) \rightleftharpoons 2SO_3(g)$$

13. Following data is given for the reaction,

$$CaCO_3(s) \longrightarrow CaO(s) + CO_2(s)$$

$\Delta_f H^\circ[CaO(s)] = -635.1$ kJ mol^{-1}

$\Delta_f H^\circ[CO_2(g)] = -393.5$ kJ mol^{-1}

$\Delta_f H^\circ[CaCO_3(s)] = -1206.9$ kJ mol^{-1}

Predict the effect of temperature on the equilibrium constant of the above reaction.

14. (i) pH of a solution of a strong acid is 5.0. What will be the pH of the solution obtained after diluting the given solution 100 times?

(ii) Calculate

(a) Dissociation constant of conjugate base of HF, $K_a = 6.8 \times 10^{-4}$.

(b) Dissociation constant of conjugate acid of CO_3^{2-}, $K_b = 2.1 \times 10^{-4}$.

Case Study [4 Marks]

15. Equilibrium represents the state of a process in which properties like temperature, pressure, concentration of a system do not show any change. Any reaction at equilibrium can be represented as

$$aA + bB \rightleftharpoons cC + dD$$

Equilibrium is characterised by equilibrium constant K_C (reactant in solution) or K_p (reactants as gases). This constant is the ratio of concentration of products to reactant raised to the power of their stoichiometric quotient. This same ratio at condition other than equilibrium is known as reaction quotient and their difference shows if the reaction goes forward or backward.

(i) The value of K_C for the reaction, $2A \rightleftharpoons B + C$ is 2×10^{-3}. At a given time, the composition of reaction mixture is $[A] = [B] = [C] = 3 \times 10^{-4}$ M. In which direction the reaction well proceed?

(ii) Write the expression for the equilibrium constant, K_C for the following reactions.

$$2Cu(NO_3)_2(s) \rightleftharpoons 2CuO(s) + 4NO_2(g) + O_2(g)$$

Or What is the unit of K_p and K_C for the reaction

$$2NO(g) \rightleftharpoons N_2(g) + O_2(g)$$

(iii) For the equilibrium,

$$2NOCl(g) \rightleftharpoons 2NO(g) + Cl_2(g)$$

the value of the equilibrium constant, K_C is 3.17×10^{-6} at 1069 K.

Calculate the K_p for the reaction at this temperature.

Long Answer Type Questions [5 Marks]

16. (i) An equilibrium mixture at 300 K contains N_2O_4 and NO_2 at 0.28 and 1.1 atm pressure respectively. If the volume of the container is doubled, calculate the new equilibrium pressure of two gases.

(ii) pH of 0.08 mol dm^{-3} HOCl solution is 2.85. Calculate its ionisation constant.

17. (i) What is the expression for K_{sp} of Ag_2CrO_4?

(ii) The solubility product of $Al(OH)_3$ is 2.7×10^{-11}. Calculate its solubility (in g L^{-1}) and also find out pH of this solution. (Atomic mass of Al = 27 u)

Answers

1. (b) **2.** (c) **3.** (c) **4.** (a) **5.** (b) **6.** (a)

7. (d) **8.** (a) **12.** (i) 0.444 (ii) 12.23 M^{-1}

13. +178.3 kJ mol^{-1}

14. (i) 6.699, (ii) (a) 1.47×10^{-11}, (b) 4.76×10^{-11}

16. (ii) 2.4957×10^{-5}

17. (i) $4s^3$, (ii) 7.8×10^{-2} g L^{-1}, 11.4771

07

CHAPTER

Redox Reactions

Redox reactions are one of the most important category of reactions that play an significant role in our daily life. Some common examples of redox reactions includes burning of cooking gas, coal, wood, rusting of iron, electro-plating, extraction of metals, bleaching and many more.

YOUR STUDY GOALS

- 7.1 Classical Idea of Redox Reactions : Oxidation and Reduction Reactions
- 7.2 Redox Reactions in Terms of Electron Transfer Reactions
- 7.3 Oxidation Number
- 7.4 Types of Redox Reactions
- 7.5 Balancing of Redox Reactions
- 7.6 Applications of Redox Reactions

YOUR PRACTICE GOAL

- Objective Type Questions (32 Qs ; 20 MCQs, 10 A-R, 2 Case-study) Subjective Type Questions
- (27 Qs; 10 SA-I, 7 SA-II, 10 LA)

7.1 Classical Idea of Redox Reactions : Oxidation and Reduction Reactions

To understand the concept of redox reactions, it is essential to become aware of the oxidation and reduction processes.

Oxidation

According to classical concept, oxidation is defined as the process that involves **addition of oxygen/ electronegative** element to a substance or **removal of hydrogen/electropositive** element from a substance.

Reduction

According to classical concept, reduction is defined as a process that involves **removal of oxygen/electronegative** element from a substance or process of **addition of hydrogen/electropositive element** to a substance.

Classical Idea of Oxidation and Reduction Reactions

Oxidation	Reduction
(i) Addition of oxygen $2Mg(s) + O_2(g) \longrightarrow 2MgO(s)$ All combustion processes are examples of it. $CH_4(g) + 2O_2(g) \longrightarrow CO_2(g) + 2H_2O(l)$	Addition of hydrogen $\underset{\text{Ethene}}{CH_2{=}CH_2(g)} + H_2(g) \longrightarrow \underset{\text{Ethane}}{CH_3{-}CH_3(g)}$

Oxidation	Reduction
(ii) Removal of hydrogen $2H_2S(g) + O_2(g) \longrightarrow 2S(s) + 2H_2O(l)$	Removal of oxygen $2HgO(s) \xrightarrow{\Delta} 2Hg(l) + O_2(g)$
(iii) Addition of electronegative elements $Mg(s) + \underset{\text{Electronegative elements}}{Cl_2(g)} \longrightarrow MgCl_2(s)$	Addition of electropositive element $2HgCl_2(aq) + SnCl_2(aq) \longrightarrow Hg_2Cl_2(s) + SnCl_4(aq)$ Addition of Hg as an electropositive element
(iv) Removal of electropositive elements $2K_4[Fe(CN)_6](aq) + H_2O_2(aq) \longrightarrow 2K_3[Fe(CN)_6](aq) + 2KOH(aq)$	Removal of electro-negative element. $2FeCl_3(aq) + H_2(g) \longrightarrow 2FeCl_2(aq) + 2HCl(aq)$

Redox Reactions

The reactions that involve oxidation and reduction as their two half reactions are called redox reactions.

Or

In other words, *redox reactions are the reactions in which oxidation and reduction processes occur simultaneously*. e.g.

Addition of chlorine (an electronegative element)

Oxidation

$$2\,HgCl_2(aq) + SnCl_2(aq) \longrightarrow Hg_2Cl_2(s) + SnCl_4(aq)$$

Addition of Hg (an electropositive element)

Reduction

Since, in the above reaction oxidation and reduction occur simultaneously, so it is an example of redox reaction.

TEACHER'S TIP

The *'red'* of redox comes from **reduction** and *'ox'* from **oxidation**. Always remember, that if in a reaction a substance is oxidised, then another gets reduced at the same time or *vice-versa*.

Thus, it can be said that oxidation and reduction reactions are complementary, i.e. they always go hand in hand or side by side or oxidation occurs at the cost of reduction.

Oxidising and Reducing Agents

In a redox reaction, the substance which oxidises the other or which itself undergoes reduction is called the **oxidising agent**, whereas the substance that reduces the other and itself undergoes oxidation is called the **reducing agent**.

Thus, in the above given example, $HgCl_2$ is an oxidising agent (as it reduces itself) and $SnCl_2$ is a reducing agent (as it oxidises itself).

Common Oxidising/Reducing Agents and their Reduced/Oxidised Forms

Oxidising agent	Reduced form
HNO_3 (conc.)	$NO_2 + H_2O$
HNO_3 (dil.)	$NO + H_2O$
MnO_4^- (in acidic medium)	Mn^{2+}
MnO_4^- (in basic medium)	MnO_2
$Cr_2O_7^{2-}$ or CrO_4^{2-}	$Cr^{3+} + H_2O$
F_2, Cl_2, Br_2, I_2	F^-, Cl^-, Br^-, I^-
Fe^{3+}	Fe^{2+}
Sn^{4+}	Sn^{2+}
Reducing agent	**Oxidised form**
Metals	Respective cations
H_2S	S or SO_2 or SO_4^{2-}
HCl, HBr, HI	Cl_2, Br_2, I_2
Fe^{2+}	Fe^{3+}
Sn^{2+}	Sn^{4+}
$C_2O_4^{2-}$ (oxalate)	$CO_2 + H_2O$

Example 1 **In the reactions given below, identify the species undergoing oxidation and reduction.**

(i) $H_2S(g) + Cl_2(g) \longrightarrow 2HCl(g) + S(s)$

(ii) $3Fe_3O_4(s) + 8\,Al(s) \longrightarrow 9\,Fe(s) + 4Al_2O_3(s)$

NCERT

Sol.

Removal of hydrogen, i.e. oxidation

(i) $H_2S(g) + Cl_2(g) \longrightarrow 2HCl(g) + S(s)$

Addition of hydrogen, i.e. reduction

Thus, here H_2S undergoes oxidation and Cl_2 undergoes reduction.

Removal of O, i.e. reduction

(ii) $3Fe_3O_4(s) + 8Al(s) \longrightarrow 9Fe(s) + 4Al_2O_3(s)$

Addition of O, i.e. oxidation

Thus, here Fe_3O_4 undergoes reduction and Al undergoes oxidation.

Prediction of oxidation and reduction processes in some reaction is a difficult task on the basis of classical concept so there was a need to find a method with the help of which these can be predicted easily. Such a method was given in terms of electron transfer reactions.

Note There are some compounds which can act as an oxidant and reductant both, i.e. HNO_2, SO_2, H_2O_2, O_3, CrO_2, MnO_2, ZnO, CuO, Al_2O_3. They are also called as **amphoteric oxide.**

7.2 Redox Reactions in Terms of Electron Transfer Reactions

Electronic concept is the modern concept used to define redox reactions. It defines oxidation and reduction in terms of transfer of electrons as follows

Oxidation in Terms of Electron Transfer

According to electronic concept, oxidation is the process which involves loss of electron(s).

The species that undergoes oxidation becomes more positive (i.e. acquires more positive charge) or less negative (i.e. negative charge reduces).

e.g. $Na \longrightarrow Na^+ + e^-$ (positive charge increases on Na)

$2Cl^- \longrightarrow Cl_2 + 2e^-$ (negative charge decreases on Cl)

Because of the loss of electrons, the oxidation process can also be named as **de-electronation.**

Reduction in Terms of Electron Transfer

Electronic concept also suggested that reduction is the process that involves gain of electron(s). The species undergoing reduction becomes more negative (i.e. acquires more negative charge) or less positive (i.e. positive charge reduces). e.g.

$Cl_2 + 2e^- \longrightarrow 2Cl^-$ (negative charge increases on Cl)

$Fe^{3+} + e^- \longrightarrow Fe^{2+}$ (positive charge reduces on Fe^{3+})

Because of the gain of electron, reduction process is also called **electronation.**

Redox Reaction in Terms of Electron Transfer

The electron lost in an oxidation reaction is simultaneously gained in a reduction reaction. Because of simultaneous loss and gain of electrons in oxidation reduction processes, the **redox reactions,** (or the oxidation-reduction reactions) are also called **electron transfer reactions.**

e.g. The reaction between sodium and chlorine to give sodium chloride is a redox reaction as shown below.

Loss of $2e^-$ (oxidation half reaction)

$$2Na(s) + Cl_2(g) \longrightarrow 2\overset{+}{Na}\overset{-}{Cl}(s)$$

Gain of $2e^-$ (reduction half reaction)

The two half reactions can be written as

$$2Na(s) \longrightarrow 2Na^+(g) + 2e^-$$

$$Cl_2(g) + 2e^- \longrightarrow 2Cl(g)$$

Similarly, the following two redox reactions can also be illustrated in terms of loss and gain of electrons.

Loss of $2e^-$ (oxidation half reaction)

$$2Na(s) + O_2(g) \longrightarrow (\overset{+}{Na})_2\overset{2-}{O}(s)$$

Gain of $2e^-$ (reduction half reaction)

Loss of $2e^-$ (oxidation half reaction)

$$2Na(s) + S(s) \longrightarrow (\overset{+}{Na})_2 S^{2-}(s)$$

Gain of $2e^-$ (reduction half reaction)

Oxidising and Reducing Agents in Terms of Electron Transfer

The species that gain electron(s) is called **oxidising agent** or **oxidant** and the one that loss or donate the electron(s) to the interacting element is called the **reducing agent** or **reductant.**

e.g.

Increase in positive charge, i.e. oxidation or loss of electron

$$Zn(s) + Cu^{2+}(aq) \longrightarrow Cu(s) + Zn^{2+}(aq)$$

Decrease in positive charge, i.e. reduction or gain of electron

Thus, here Zn acts as reducing agent as it reduces Cu^{2+} by providing it two electrons and Cu^{2+} acts as oxidising agent, as it gains (or accepts) two electrons from Zn.

Example 2 Justify that the reactions.

(i) $2Na(s)+H_2(g) \longrightarrow 2NaH(s)$ and **NCERT**

(ii) $4Na(s)+O_2(g) \longrightarrow 2Na_2O(s)$ are redox reactions.

Sol. (i) Sodium hydride is an ionic compound, so it can be represented as Na^+H^-. Thus, oxidation half reaction (i.e. increase in positive charge) can be given as

$$2Na(s) \longrightarrow 2Na^+(g) + 2e^- \quad ...(i)$$

and the reduction half reaction (i.e. increase in negative charge) can be given as

$$H_2(g) + 2e^- \longrightarrow 2H^-(g) \quad ...(ii)$$

The sum of above two reactions give the overall reaction [while adding two reactions, remember that the number of electron lost must be equal to the number of electrons gained. If these two are not equal, make them equal by multiplying with a suitable integer as done in case of reaction (i).]

Thus, $2Na(s) + H_2(g) \longrightarrow 2Na^+(aq) + 2H^-(aq)$

or $2Na(s) + H_2(g) \longrightarrow 2NaH(s)$

Since, this reaction involves oxidation and reduction as its two half reaction, it is a redox reaction.

(ii) Like NaH, sodium oxide is also an ionic compound and have the formula $(Na^+)_2O^{2-}$. Thus, oxidation and reduction half reactions can be written as

$$2Na(s) \xrightarrow[\text{Loss of } 2e^-]{} 2Na^+(g) + 2e^-$$

(Oxidation half reaction) ...(i)

$$O_2(g) + 4e^- \xrightarrow[\text{Gain of } 4e^-]{} 2O^{2-}(g)$$

(Reduction half reaction) ...(ii)

To equalise number of electrons, equation (i) is multiplied with 2, and hence, we get

$$4Na(s) \longrightarrow 4Na^+(g) + 4e^- \quad ...(iii)$$

On adding equations (ii) and (iii), we get

$$4Na(s) + O_2(g) \longrightarrow 4Na^+ + 2O^{2-}$$

Or $4Na(s) + O_2(g) \longrightarrow 2(Na^+)_2O^{2-}(s)$

Since, the above reaction involve oxidation and reduction as its two half reactions, so it is a redox reaction.

Note NaCl and Na_2S being ionic compounds can also be represented as Na^+Cl^- and Na^+S^{2-}.

Example 3 Identify the oxidant and reductant in each of the following reactions.

(i) $MnO_4^-(aq) + C_2H_5OH(aq) \longrightarrow Mn^{2+}(aq) + CH_3COOH(aq)$

(ii) $Zn(s) + 2H^+(aq) \longrightarrow Zn^{2+}(aq) + H_2(g)$

(iii) $PbO(s) + C(s) \longrightarrow Pb(s) + CO(g)$

Sol. (i) MnO_4^- loses oxygen, therefore it is an oxidant while C_2H_5OH gains oxygen, therefore it is a reductant.

(ii) Zn is reductant while hydrogen (H) is oxidant.

(iii) PbO is oxidant while C is reductant.

Example 4 Write the half reactions for the following redox reactions.

(i) $Al(s) + 3Ag^+(aq) \longrightarrow Al^{3+}(aq) + 3Ag(s)$

(ii) $2K(s) + Cl_2(g) \longrightarrow 2KCl(s)$

Sol. (i) $Al(s) \longrightarrow Al^{3+}(aq) + 3e^-$ (oxidation half reaction)

$3Ag^+(aq) \longrightarrow 3Ag(s)$ (reduction half reaction)

(ii) $K \longrightarrow K^+ + e^-$ (oxidation half reaction)

$\frac{1}{2}Cl_2 + e^- \longrightarrow Cl^-$ (reduction half reaction)

Competitive Electron Transfer Reactions

Different elements and ions differ in their electron gaining or losing tendencies.

If these are arranged in decreasing order of electron losing tendency, or increasing order of electron gaining tendency, a series is obtained which is known as the **metal activity series** or **electrochemical series.** This series is found helpful to decide the feasibility of a reaction. The series is

Li > K > Ba > Sr > Na > Mg > Al > Mn > Zn > Cr > Fe > Co > Ni > Sb > Pb > H > Cu > Hg > Ag > Pd > Pt > Au

[For details see table at page 273] e.g.

- **When a metallic zinc strip is placed into the aqueous solution of copper nitrate (Fig. 7.1) it gets coated with reddish metallic copper and the blue colour of copper nitrate solution disappears.**

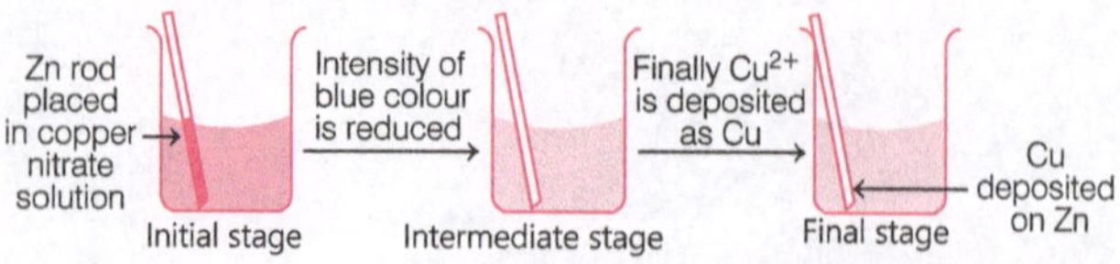

Fig. 7.1 Redox reaction between zinc and aqueous solution of copper nitrate occurring in a beaker

If hydrogen sulphide gas is passed through the colourless solution and the medium is made alkaline by adding ammonia, a white precipitate of zinc sulphide (ZnS) appears, which shows the presence of Zn^{2+} ions in the solution. The net reaction,

Release of $2e^-$

$$Zn(s) + Cu^{2+}(aq) \longrightarrow Zn^{2+}(aq) + Cu(s)$$

Gain of $2e^-$

The state of equilibrium for the above reaction can be represented by placing a strip of metallic copper in a zinc sulphate solution.

No visible reaction is noticed and attempt to detect the presence of Cu^{2+} ions by passing H_2S gas through the solution to produce black colour cupric sulphide (CuS), does not succeed.

Thus, the state of equilibrium for the reaction greatly favours the products over the reactants.

- In another example, if copper strip is placed in silver nitrate solution (Fig. 7.2) the strip gets covered with silver and the colour of solution becomes blue.

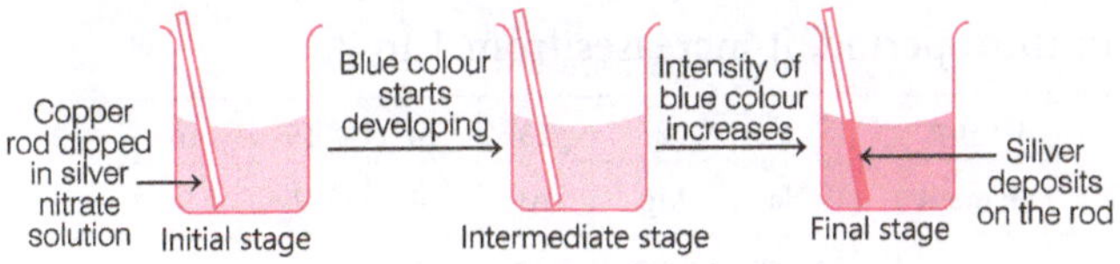

Fig. 7.2 Redox reaction between copper and aqueous solution of silver nitrate occurring in a beaker

The equilibrium greatly favour the products $Cu^{2+}(aq)$ and Ag(*s*) and the net reaction is

Lose of $2e^-$

$$Cu(s) + 2Ag^+(aq) \longrightarrow Cu^{2+}(aq) + 2Ag(s)$$

Gain of $2e^-$

In contrast, when metallic cobalt placed in nickel sulphate solution the following reaction will takes place.

Release of $2e^-$

$$Co(s) + Ni^{2+}(aq) \longrightarrow Co^{2+}(aq) + Ni(s)$$

Gain of $2e^-$

At equilibrium, both $Ni^{2+}(aq)$ and $Co^{2+}(aq)$ are present at moderate concentrations. Hence, neither the reactants [Co(s) and $Ni^{2+}(aq)$] nor the products [$Co^{2+}(aq)$ and Ni(s)] are greatly favoured.

Quick Test 1

1. Identify the substance that get reduced in the following reaction.
$$Fe_2O_3(s) + 3CO(g) \longrightarrow 2Fe(s) + 3CO_2(g)$$

2. The compound AgF_2 is unstable compound. However, if formed, the compound acts as a very strong oxidising agent. Why? *NCERT*

Hint :
- Due to the presence of completely filled configuration Ag^+ is more stable than Ag^{2+}.
- An oxidising agent has a great tendency of accepting electron.

3. In the given reaction which substance is getting oxidised and which substance is getting reduced? Name reducing agent and oxidising agent.
$$2Cu_2S + 3O_2 \longrightarrow 2Cu_2O + 2SO_2$$

4. Why does the following reaction occur?
$$XeO_6^{4-}(aq) + 2F^-(aq) + 6H^+(aq) \longrightarrow XeO_3(g) + F_2(g) + 3H_2O(l)$$
What conclusion about the compound Na_4XeO_6 (of which XeO_6^{4-} is a part) can be drawn from the reaction? *NCERT*

5. Consider the reactions,
$$2S_2O_3^{2-}(aq) + I_2(s) \longrightarrow S_4O_6^{2-}(aq) + 2I^-(aq)$$
$$S_2O_3^{2-}(aq) + 2Br_2(l) + 5H_2O(l) \longrightarrow 2SO_4^{2-}(aq) + 4Br^-(aq) + 10H^+(aq)$$
Why does the same reductant, thiosulphate react differently with iodine and bromine? *NCERT*

6. Decide whether each of the following reaction involves oxidation-reduction reaction or not. If it does, identify which species is oxidised and which gets reduced?

(i) $4\,CH_3\overset{\overset{O}{\|}}{C}CH_3 + LiAlH_4 + 4H_2O \rightleftharpoons 4CH_3\overset{\overset{OH}{|}}{C}HCH_3 + LiOH + Al(OH)_3$

(ii) $CH_3CH_2OH \xrightarrow{H_2SO_4} CH_2 = CH_2 + H_2O$

(iii) $CH_3\overset{\overset{O}{\|}}{C}OH + CH_3NH_2 \rightleftharpoons CH_3\overset{\overset{O}{\|}}{C}O^- + CH_3NH_3^+$

Competency Based Que.

For Solutions, See QR Code on Pg. 290

7.3 Oxidation Number

Oxidation number is defined as the charge that an atom of the element has in its ion or appear to have when present in the combined state with other atoms.

Or

In other words, it is also defined as *"the charge that an atom appear to have in a compound when all other atoms are removed as ions from the compound"*.

e.g. $\overset{0}{H_2}(s)+\overset{0}{Cl_2}(g) \longrightarrow 2\overset{+1\ -1}{HCl}(g)$

$\overset{-4\ +1}{CH_4}+4\overset{0}{Cl_2}(g) \longrightarrow \overset{+4\ -1}{CCl_4}(s)+4\overset{+1\ -1}{HCl}(g)$

Rules for Calculating Oxidation Number

These rules are given below.

	Oxidation number with example	Exception
Rule 1 All elements in free or elementary state or any allotropes.	0 [H in H_2, S in S_8, P in P_4, O in O_2 or O_3, C in diamond]	—
Rule 2 Atomic ions	Charge on the ion [Na^+, Mg^{2+}, Fe^{3+}, Cl^-, O^{2-} have oxidation number of +1, +2, +3, −1, −2, respectively]	—
Rule 3 • Alkali metals • Alkaline earth metals • Aluminium	+1 +2 +3	—
Rule 4. Oxygen, O	−2	• Peroxides (hydrogen peroxide, H_2O_2) = −1, superoxides • Potassium superoxide, $(KO_2) = -\frac{1}{2}$ • Oxygen difluoride $(OF_2) = +2$ Dioxygen difluoride $(O_2F_2 = +1)$
Rule 5 Hydrogen, H	+1	O.S. of metallic hydrides (NaH, CaH_2) = −1
Rule 6 Fluorine, F Chlorine, Cl Bromine, Br Iodine, I	−1	— Cl, Br and I in oxoacids and oxoanions have positive O.S.
Rule 7 Neutral compounds	Sum of oxidation numbers of all atoms = 0 (e.g. sum of O.S. of two H-atoms and one O-atom in H_2O is equal to zero)	—
Rule 8 Polyatomic ions	Sum of oxidation number of all atoms = Charge on the ion (e.g. sum of O.S. of three O-atoms and one C-atoms in the CO_3^{2-} ion must be equal to −2)	—

Note Metals generally exhibit positive oxidation states whereas, the oxidation state in case of non-metals may be positive or negative. Moreover, transition elements exhibit variable oxidation states.

TEACHER'S TIP

Highest oxidation number for first two groups = group number.

Highest oxidation number for other groups = group number − 10

[Here, group number are in accordance with long form of periodic table]

e.g. In SF_6, highest oxidation number of S = 16 − 10 = 6.

The highest oxidation number exhibited by an element generally increases along a period of the periodic table. In third period, it increases from 1 to 7.

Group	1	2	13	14	15	16	17
Element	Na	Mg	Al	Si	P	S	Cl
Compound	NaCl	$MgSO_4$	AlF_3	$SiCl_4$	P_4O_{10}	SF_6	$HClO_4$
Highest oxidation number/State of the group element	+1	+2	+3	+4	+5	+6	+7

A term that is often used interchangeably with the oxidation number is the **oxidation state**.

Steps for Calculation of Oxidation Number (ON)

The following steps are involved while calculating the oxidation number of an atom in a given compound/ion.

Step **I** Write down the formula of given compound/ion leaving some space between the atoms.

Step **II** Write the oxidation number of each element above its atoms. Write down *x* above the atom, oxidation number of which we have to find out.

Step **III** Multiply the oxidation numbers of each element with the number of atoms of that element present in the compound. Enclose the product in a bracket.

Step **IV** Equate the algebraic sum of the oxidation numbers of all the atoms present in a compound to zero or to the charge in case of ionic species.

Step **V** Solve the equation obtained for the value of *x*.

Example 5 **Calculate the oxidation state of (i) Mn in $KMnO_4$ and (ii) N in NO_3^-.**

Sol. (i) Let the oxidation number of Mn in $KMnO_4$ be *x*. Writing the oxidation number of each atom above its symbol.

$$\overset{+1}{K}\overset{x}{Mn}\overset{-2}{O_4}$$

$$[1\times(+1)+(1\times x)+4\times(-2)]=0$$
$$1+x+(-8)=0$$
$$1+x-8=0$$
$$x-7=0$$
$$\therefore \quad x=+7$$

Hence, the oxidation number of Mn in $KMnO_4$ is + 7.

(ii) **N in NO_3^-.**

Let the oxidation number of N in NO_3^- be *x*. Writing the oxidation number of each atom above its symbol.

$$\overset{x}{N}\overset{-2}{O_3^-}$$

$\therefore$ Sum of the oxidation number of all the atoms in
$$NO_3^- = x+3(-2)=x-6$$

But the sum of oxidation numbers of all the atoms in NO_3^- ion is equal to the charge present on it, i.e. −1.

$$\therefore \quad x-6=-1 \text{ or } x=+5$$

Thus, the oxidation number of N in NO_3^- is + 5 .

Paradox of Fractional Oxidation Number

In case of some compounds, oxidation state of a particular element in the compund is found out to be in fraction.

It is indeed the average oxidation state of the element under consideration. This can also be illustrated by the following examples.

(i) **Oxidation state of C in C_3O_2** (carbon suboxide)

The oxidation state of C in $C_3O_2 = 4/3$. But as we know it is only the average oxidation state. Thus, the actual oxidation state of each atom is calculated as follows

The structure of C_3O_2 is as

$$O{=}C{=}C{=}C{=}O$$

The oxidation states of terminal O-atoms is – 2, the oxidation states of C bonded with O is + 2 and the oxidation state of central C-atom is 0.

Thus, $\overset{-2}{O}=\overset{+2}{C}=\overset{0}{C}=\overset{+2}{C}=\overset{-2}{O}$

and the average of oxidation states of 3C- atoms in

$$C_3O_2 = \frac{2+2+0}{3} = \frac{4}{3}$$

(ii) **Oxidation state of Br in Br_3O_8**

(Tribromooctaoxide) The average oxidation state of Br (with the help of rules) in Br_3O_8 is 16/3.

The structure of Br_3O_8 is

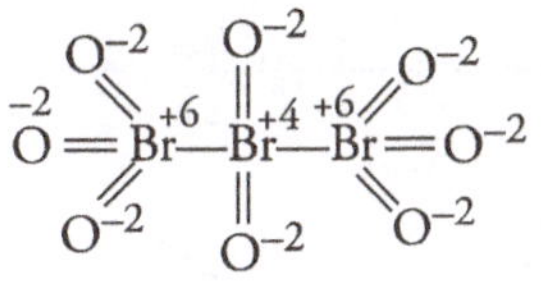

The average O.S. of 3 Br atom in Br_3O_8

$$\frac{6+4+6}{3} = 16/3.$$

(iii) **Oxidation state of S in $S_4O_6^{2-}$** (Tetrathionate ion)

The average oxidation state of S in $S_4O_6^{2-}$ is 2.5.

The structure of $S_4O_6^{2-}$ ion is

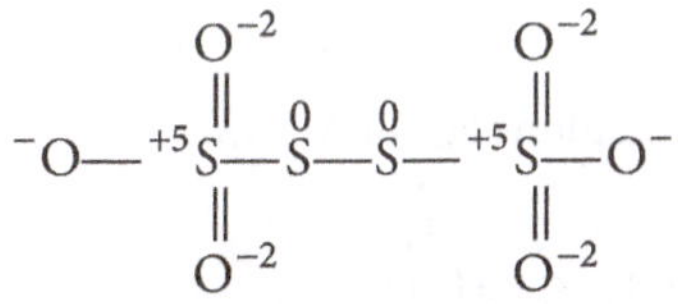

The average O.S of 4 S-atoms in $S_4O_6^{-2}$

$$\frac{5+0+0+5}{4} = 10/4$$

Note The oxidation state of O_2^+ and O_2^- are + 1/2 and – 1/2 respectively, i.e. fractional.

Applications of Oxidation Number

The important applications of oxidation numbers are as follows

(i) Stock Notation

According to this notation, the oxidation number of an element can be expressed as roman numeral in parenthesis ( ) after the symbol of that element in the molecular formula.

With the help of Stock notations, it is possible to predict that whether the species is present in oxidised form or reduced form.

Stock Notation of some Important Compounds

Compound/Formula	Oxidation state of metal	Stock notation
$SnCl_2$ (Stannous chloride)	+2	Sn (II) Cl_2
$SnCl_4$ (Stannic chloride)	+4	Sn(IV) Cl_4
$FeSO_4$ (Ferrous sulphate)	+2	Fe (II) SO_4
V_2O_5 (Vanadium pentoxide)	+5	V_2(V)O_5
Cr_2O_3 (Chromium trioxide)	+3	Cr_2(III)O_3

Note PCl_3 and PCl_5 can never be represented by Stock notations because non-metallic elements shows variable valencies.

Example 6 Using Stock notation, represent the following compounds $HAuCl_4$, Tl_2O, FeO, Fe_2O_3, CuI, CuO, MnO and MnO_2. NCERT

Sol. **$HAuCl_4$**

Let the oxidation state of Au is x.

$$\overset{+1}{H}\ \overset{x}{Au}\ \overset{-1}{Cl_4}$$
$$(+1)\quad x\quad 4(-1)$$

$(+1)+x+4(-1)=0$ or $x-3=0$ or $x=+3$

Thus, the Stock notation for the compound is $HAu(III)Cl_4$.

Find the Stock notations of other compounds in the same manner as shown above. You will get the answer as Tl_2(II) O, Fe_2(II)O, Fe_2(III)O_3, Cu (I)I, Cu(II)O, Mn(II)O, Mn(IV)O_2.

(ii) Prediction of Oxidation-Reduction Reactions

In terms of the concept of oxidation number, oxidation is defined as *"the process in which the oxidation number of an element increases whereas reduction is the processs in which the oxidation number of an element decreases"*. e.g. Consider the following reaction,

Oxidation (Zn → $ZnCl_2$)

$$\overset{0}{Zn} + 2\overset{+1\,-1}{HCl} \longrightarrow \overset{+2\,-1}{ZnCl_2} + \overset{0}{H_2}$$

Reduction (HCl → H_2)

In the above reaction, oxidation number of Zn increases from 0 to +2 but of H decreases from +1 to 0. Thus, here Zn is oxidised, whereas HCl is reduced. Hence, it is a redox reaction.

(iii) Prediction of Oxidising and Reducing Agents

In terms of the concept of oxidation number (ON), an **oxidising agent** or **oxidant** is the substance, oxidation number of which decreases in the chemical reaction. It is the substance that itself undergoes reduction, whereas **reducing agent** or **reductant** is the substance, oxidation number of which increases in the chemical reaction. Thus, it is the substance that itself undergoes oxidation. e.g. Consider the following reaction,

Increase in O.N. (oxidation)

$$\overset{0}{Cl_2}(g) + 2\overset{-1}{Br^-}(aq) \longrightarrow 2\overset{-1}{Cl^-}(aq) + \overset{0}{Br_2}(aq)$$

Oxidant Reductant

Decrease in ON (reduction)

Here, oxidation number of Br increases from −1 to 0, so it behaves as a **reductant** whereas the oxidation number of Cl decreases from 0 to −1, so it behaves as an **oxidant**.

TEACHER'S TIP

- A substance behaves as an oxidant only when any one of its elements is present in its highest oxidation state. e.g. $KMnO_4$.
- A substance behaves as a reductant only, when any one of its element is present in its lowest possible oxidation state. e.g. H_2S.
- Substance having an element in its intermediate oxidation state can behave as oxidant as well as reductant. e.g. H_2O_2.

Example 7 Justify that the reaction,

$$2Cu_2O(s)+Cu_2S(s) \longrightarrow 6Cu(s)+SO_2(g)$$

is a redox reaction. Identify the species oxidised/ reduced, which acts as an oxidant and which acts as a reductant. NCERT

Sol.

Step I Write the oxidation number of each element above it in the given reaction.

e.g. $2\overset{+1\,-2}{Cu_2O}(s)+\overset{+1\,-2}{Cu_2S}(s) \longrightarrow 6\overset{0}{Cu}(s) + \overset{+4\,-2}{SO_2}(g)$

Step II Mark arrow to show the increase and decrease in oxidation number. Also mention it over the arrow.

Increase in oxidation number

$$2\overset{+1\,-2}{Cu_2O}(s) + \overset{+1\,-2}{Cu_2S}(s) \longrightarrow 6\overset{0}{Cu}(s) + \overset{+4}{SO_2}(g)$$

Decrease in oxidation number

Step III Since, in the above reaction oxidation state decreases as well as increases simultaneously, so it is a redox reaction (proved).

Step IV Here, oxidation number of S increases from – 2 to + 4, so Cu_2S is oxidised here. Further, oxidation number of Cu decreases for + 1 to 0, so Cu_2O is reduced.

Thus, here Cu_2S is oxidised and Cu_2O is reduced .

Step V Further predict oxidant and reductant on the basis of the fact that oxidation number in case of oxidant decreases but in case of reductant increases.

Thus, here Cu_2O is oxidant and Cu_2S is reductant.

Limitations of Concept of Oxidation Number

The limitations of concept of oxidation number are as follows

(i) Many times the result of concept of oxidation state does not resemble with that obtained from classical approach.

e.g. Consider the following reaction,

$$\overset{+4}{Si}\,\overset{-1}{Cl_4} + \overset{+1}{Li}\,\overset{+3}{Al}\,\overset{-1}{H_4} \longrightarrow \overset{-4}{Si}\,\overset{+1}{H_4} + \overset{+1}{Li}\,\overset{-1}{Cl} + \overset{+3}{Al}\,\overset{-1}{Cl_3}$$

According to classical approach, here silicon is reduced and lithium as well as aluminium are oxidised. But these results are not supported by concept of oxidation number as none of the species is undergoing any change in oxidation number.

(ii) Many times, it is difficult to classify some reactions as redox reaction on the basis of concept of oxidation number.

$$CH_3NCO + H_2O \longrightarrow CH_3NH_2 + CO_2$$

7.4 Types of Redox Reactions

The redox reactions can be classified into following types

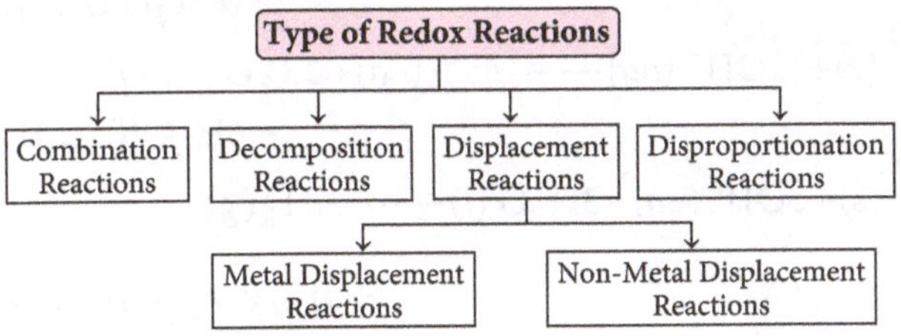

Combination Reactions

The reactions in which two or more atoms or molecules combine together to give only a single compound are called **combination reactions.** All combustion reactions are included in this category.

e.g. $$2\overset{0}{Mg}(s) + \overset{0}{O_2}(g) \longrightarrow 2\overset{+2}{Mg}\overset{-2}{O}(s)$$

For a combination reaction to be a redox reaction atleast one of its reactant must be in its elemental form.

All combustion reactions, which make use of elemental dioxygen, as well as other reactions involving elements other than dioxygen are called redox reactions.

$$\overset{0}{C}(s) + \overset{0}{O_2}(g) \xrightarrow{\Delta} \overset{+4}{C}\overset{-2}{O_2}(g)$$

$$3\overset{0}{Mg}(s) + \overset{0}{N_2}(g) \xrightarrow{\Delta} \overset{+2}{Mg_3}\,\overset{-3}{N_2}(g)$$

Decomposition Reactions

These are just opposite to the combination reaction, i.e., in **decomposition reactions,** one compound split into two or more simpler compounds, atleast one of which must be in elemental form.

e.g. $$2\overset{+1}{Na}\overset{-1}{H}(s) \xrightarrow{\Delta} 2\overset{0}{Na}(s) + \overset{0}{H_2}(g)$$

Note It should be noted that **all the decomposition reactions are not the redox reactions.**

e.g. $$\overset{+2}{Ca}\overset{+4}{C}\overset{-2}{O_3}(s) \xrightarrow{\Delta} \overset{+2}{Ca}\overset{-2}{O}(s) + \overset{+4}{C}\overset{-2}{O_2}(g)$$

Displacement Reactions

The reactions in which an atom (or ion) replaces the ion (or atom) of another element from a compound, are known as **displacement reactions.** These reactions can be represented as

$$X + YZ \longrightarrow XZ + Y$$

Depending upon the nature of element displaced, these reactions can be further classified into two categories.

1. Metal Displacement Reactions

When a more reactive metal displaces less reactive metal from its compounds, the reaction is known as **metal displacement reactions.**

e.g. $$\overset{+2}{Cu}\overset{+6}{S}\overset{-2}{O_4}(aq) + \overset{0}{Zn}(s) \longrightarrow \overset{0}{Cu}(s) + \overset{+2}{Zn}\overset{+6}{S}\overset{-2}{O_4}(aq)$$

$$\overset{+5}{V_2}\overset{-2}{O_5}(s) + 5\overset{0}{Ca}(s) \xrightarrow{\Delta} 2\overset{0}{V}(s) + 5\overset{+2}{Ca}\overset{-2}{O}(s)$$

In the above reactions, the metal which displaces the other from their salt is a good reducing agent, i.e. have more tendency to lose electrons as compared to the one that is displaced or reduced. Above reactions also reveals that the metal displacement reactions are generally redox reactions.

Note An important application of these reactions is in **metallurgical processes** where pure metals are obtained from their compounds in ores.

2. Non-metal Displacement Reactions

When some of the non-metal is displaced by a metallic or a non-metallic element, the reaction is said to be **non-metal displacement reaction.**

In these reactions, generally the hydrogen is displaced but in some reactions, displacement of oxygen or halogen has also been observed.

(i) **Reactions in which hydrogen is displaced**

Examples of these reactions are as follows

(a) Highly reactive metals like alkali metals and some alkaline earth metals (such as Ca, Sr and Ba) being good reductants or reducing agents, displace hydrogen from cold water.

e.g. $$2\overset{0}{Na}(s)+2\overset{+1-2}{H_2O}(l) \longrightarrow 2\overset{+1\,2+1}{NaOH}(aq)+\overset{0}{H_2}(g)$$
(Cold)

$$\overset{0}{Ca}(s)+2\overset{+1-2}{H_2O}(l) \longrightarrow \overset{+2-2+1}{Ca(OH)_2}(aq)+\overset{0}{H_2}(g)$$
(Cold)

(b) Less reactive metals like magnesium and iron produce hydrogen only when they are treated with steam.

e.g. $$\overset{0}{Mg}(s)+2\overset{+1\,-2}{H_2O}(l) \xrightarrow{\Delta} \overset{+2\,-2+1}{Mg(OH)_2}(s)+\overset{0}{H_2}(g)$$
(Steam)

$$2\overset{0}{Fe}(s)+3\overset{+1-2}{H_2O}(l) \xrightarrow{\Delta} \overset{+3\,-2}{Fe_2O_3}(s)+3\overset{0}{H_2}(g)$$
(Steam)

(c) Several metals including those which do not displace hydrogen from cold water can displace hydrogen from mineral acids (i.e. $HCl\,H_2SO_4$, etc.).

e.g. $$\overset{0}{Zn}(s)+2\overset{+1-1}{HCl}(aq) \longrightarrow \overset{+2-1}{ZnCl_2}(aq)+\overset{0}{H_2}(g)$$

Note Highly reactive metals (e.g. Mg) readily lose electrons and get oxidised. These electrons are accepted by the H^+ ions provided by mineral acid. After accepting electrons H^+ ions get converted into hydrogen gas. Thus, hydrogen gas is evolved.

However, least reactive metals because of their less tendency to lose electron, are generally unable to convert H^+ into H_2. Thus, there is no evolution of hydrogen with less reactive metals.

(ii) **Reaction in which oxygen is displaced** Fluorine being the strongest oxidising agent displaces oxygen when treated with water.

e.g. $$2\overset{+1-2}{H_2O}(l)+2\overset{0}{F_2}(g) \longrightarrow 4\overset{+1-1}{HF}(aq)+\overset{0}{O_2}(g)$$

(iii) **Reactions in which halogens are displaced** Fluorine has maximum oxidising power and can oxidise chlorine, bromine and iodine.

However, because of its high reactivity with water, its reaction with chloride, bromide and iodide are not generally carried out in aqueous solution.

Chlorine, however is capable of displacing bromide and iodide ions from their aqueous solution.

Oxidation

$$\overset{0}{Cl_2}(g)+2\overset{+1-1}{KBr}(aq) \longrightarrow 2\overset{+1-1}{KCl}(aq)+\overset{0}{Br_2}(l)$$

$$\overset{0}{Cl_2}(g)+2\overset{+1-1}{KI}(aq) \longrightarrow 2\overset{+1-1}{KCl}(aq)+\overset{0}{I_2}(s)$$

Bromine can displace only iodide ion from its solution.

$$\overset{0}{Br_2}(l)+2\overset{-1}{I^-}(aq) \longrightarrow 2\overset{-1}{Br^-}(aq)+\overset{0}{I_2}(s)$$

The halogen displacement reactions have a direct industrial application.

Disproportionation Reactions

These are a **special kind of redox reactions** in which the same element undergoes oxidation as well as reduction.

In these reaction, one of the reacting substances always contains an element that can exist in at least three oxidation states. The element present in the reacting substance, is in the intermediate oxidation state and both higher and lower oxidation states of that element are formed in the product.

e.g. In hydrogen peroxides, disproportionation reaction occurs as

Reduction

$$2\overset{+1\,-1}{H_2O_2}(aq) \longrightarrow 2\overset{+1\,-2}{H_2O}(l)+\overset{0}{O_2}(g) \quad \ldots(i)$$

Oxidation

Similarly, chlorine, sulphur and phosphorus undergo disproportionation in the alkaline medium as shown below.

$$\overset{0}{Cl_2}(g)+2OH^-(aq) \longrightarrow \overset{+1}{ClO^-}(aq)+\overset{-1}{Cl^-}(aq)+H_2O(l) \quad \ldots(ii)$$

$$\overset{0}{S_8}(s)+12OH^-(aq) \longrightarrow 4S^{2-}(aq)+2\overset{+2}{S_2}O_3^{2-}(aq)+6H_2O(l) \quad \ldots(iii)$$

$$\overset{0}{P_4}(s)+3OH^-(aq)+3H_2O(l) \longrightarrow \overset{-3}{P}H_3(g)+3H_2\overset{+1}{P}O_2^-(aq) \quad \ldots(iv)$$

The (ClO^-) formed in the reaction (ii) oxidises the colour-bearing stains of the substances to coloureless substances. Thus, the reaction (ii) describes the formation of household bleaching agents.

Also, bromine and iodine show same trend as shown by chlorine in reaction (ii).

Whereas fluorine shows deviation from this behaviour when reacts with alkali. The reaction involve in case of fluorine is shown below.

$$2F_2(g)+2OH^-(aq) \longrightarrow 2F^-(aq)+OF_2(g) + H_2O(l) \quad ...(v)$$

Fluorine also react with water to produce some oxygen. This behaviour shown by fluorine is not surprising as we know that fluorine do not exhibit any positive oxidation state. Thus, fluorine does not show a disproportionation tendency.

Example 8 **Suggest a scheme of classification of the following redox reactions.**

(i) $N_2(g)+O_2(g) \longrightarrow 2NO(g)$

(ii) $2Pb(NO_3)_2(s) \longrightarrow 2PbO(s) + 4NO_2(g)+O_2(g)$

(iii) $NaH(s)+H_2O(l) \longrightarrow NaOH(aq) + H_2(g)$

(iv) $2NO_2(g)+2OH^-(aq) \longrightarrow NO_2^-(aq)+NO_3^-(aq) + H_2O(l)$ **NCERT**

Sol. (i) Since, the two molecules are combining to give a single product, so it is an example of **combination redox reaction.**

(ii) Since, the compound splits up into several simpler substances, out of which O_2 is in the elemental form, thus, it is an example of **decomposition redox reaction.**

(iii) $NaH(s) + H_2O(l) \longrightarrow NaOH(aq) + H_2(g)$

The ionic form of the reaction is

$$H^-(s) + H_2O(l) \longrightarrow OH^-(aq) + H_2(g)$$

Here, H^- (hydride ion) displaces hydrogen from water molecule, so it is an example of **displacement redox reaction.**

(iv) Oxidation ($+4 \to +5$); Reduction ($+4 \to +3$)

$$(iv)\ \overset{+4}{2NO_2}(g) + 2OH^-(aq) \longrightarrow \overset{+3}{NO_2^-}(aq) + \overset{+5}{NO_3^-}(aq) + H_2O(l)$$

Since, in the above reaction, the same element undergoes oxidation as well as reduction, so it is an example of **disproportionation redox reaction.**

Example 9 **Which of the following species, do not show disproportionation reaction and why?**

$$ClO^-,\ ClO_2^-,\ ClO_3^- \text{ and } ClO_4^-$$

Also write reaction for each of the species that disproportionates. **NCERT**

Sol. Disproportionation reaction is shown by the species in which the element exhibit intermediate oxidation state.

Among the oxo anions of chlorine listed above, ClO_4^- does not disproportionate because in the oxo anion chlorine is present in its highest oxidation state that is +7. The disproportionation reactions for the other three oxoanions of chlorine are as follows

$$3\overset{+1}{Cl}O^- \longrightarrow 2\overset{-1}{Cl^-} + \overset{+5}{Cl}O_3^-$$

$$6\overset{+3}{Cl}O_2^- \xrightarrow{h\nu} 4\overset{+5}{Cl}O_3^- + 2\overset{-1}{Cl^-}$$

$$4\overset{+5}{Cl}O_3^- \longrightarrow \overset{-1}{Cl^-} + 3\overset{+7}{Cl}O_4^-$$

Quick Test 2

Theoretical Questions

1. MnO_4^{2-} undergoes disproportionation reaction in acidic medium but MnO_4^- does not. Give reason. *NCERT*

2. The reaction

$Cl_2(g) + 2OH^-(aq) \longrightarrow ClO^-(aq) + Cl^-(aq) + H_2O(l)$

represents the process of bleaching. Identify and name the species that bleaches the substances due to its oxidising action. *NCERT Exemplar*

Hint : Write the oxidation number of each element above its symbol and then identify the bleaching reagent by observing the change in oxidation number.

3. Identify the type of redox reaction taking place in the following.

(i) $3\overset{0}{Mg}(s) + \overset{0}{N_2}(g) \longrightarrow \overset{+2\ -3}{Mg_3N_2}(s)$

(ii) $\overset{+5\ -2}{V_2O_5}(s) + 5\overset{0}{Ca}(s) \longrightarrow 2\overset{0}{V}(s) + 5\overset{+2\ -2}{CaO}(s)$

(iii) $2\ \overset{+1\ +5\ -2}{KClO_3}(s) \longrightarrow 2\overset{+1\ -1}{KCl}(s) + 3\overset{0}{O_2}(g)$

Numerical Questions

4. Assign oxidation number to the underlined elements in each of the following species. *NCERT*

(i) $NaH_2\underline{P}O_4$ (ii) $NaH\underline{S}O_4$ (iii) $H_4\underline{P}_2O_7$ (iv) $K_2\underline{Mn}O_4$ (v) $Ca\underline{O}_2$

5. Calculate the oxidation number of each sulphur atom in the following compounds *NCERT Exemplar*

(i) $Na_2S_2O_3$ (ii) $Na_2S_4O_6$ (iii) Na_2SO_3 (iv) Na_2SO_4

6. The compound $YBa_2Cu_3O_7$, which shows superconductivity, has copper in x oxidation state. Assume that the rare earth element yttrium is in its usual +3 oxidation state. Predict the value of x.

Answers

4. (i) +5, (ii) +6, (iii) +5, (iv) +6, (v) −1

5. (i) +2, (ii) $\frac{5}{2}$ (iii) +4 (iv) +6 **6.** $\frac{7}{3}$

For Solutions, See QR Code on Pg. 290

7.5 Balancing of Redox Reactions

In the balanced chemical reactions the number of atoms of each element are equal on both sides of the chemical equation.

Several methods can be used to balance a redox reaction. These methods are as follows

(i) Hit and Trial method

(ii) Partial equation method

(iii) Oxidation number method

(iv) Half equation method or Ion-electron method.

The former two methods have been described in chapter 1. The discussion of the later two methods is given below.

Oxidation Number Method

This method is based on the change in the oxidation number of oxidant and reductant. The common steps involves in this method are as follows

For balancing reaction of $K_2Cr_2O_7$ with Na_2SO_3 in an acid to give chromium ion and the sulphate ion.

Step 1 **Write skeletal ionic equation**

$$Cr_2O_7^{2-}(aq) + SO_3^{2-}(aq) \longrightarrow Cr^{3+}(aq) + SO_4^{2-}(aq)$$

Step 2 **Assign oxidation state to each element and balance atoms other than H and O.**

$$\overset{+6\ -2}{Cr_2O_7^{2-}} + \overset{+4\ -2}{SO_3^{-2}} \longrightarrow \overset{+3}{Cr^{3+}} + \overset{+6\ -2}{SO_4^{2-}}$$

Step 3 **Finding change in oxidation number and equalise it.**

There is decrease of +3 in O.S. of Cr and there is an increase of +2 in O.S. of S.

To make the increase and decrease of O.S. equal, place numeral 2 before Cr ion an right hand side and numeral 3 before sulphate ion on right hand side and balance the Cr and S atoms on both the side of the equation.

Thus, we get

$$Cr_2O_7^{2-} + 3SO_3^{2-} \longrightarrow 2\,Cr^{3+} + 3SO_4^{2-}$$

Step 4 **Balance the ionic charge by adding H^+ or OH^-.**

If medium is acidic, use H^+ ion and if medium is basic use OH^- ions on the appropriate side.

In given reaction, add $8H^+$ on the left to make ionic charges equal.

$$Cr_2O_7^{2-} + 3SO_3^{2-} + 8H^+ \longrightarrow 2Cr^{3+} + 3SO_4^{2-}$$

Step 5 **Balance H and O-atoms**

Finally, count the hydrogen atoms and add appropriate number of water molecules (H_2O).

In given reaction, add 4 water molecules on the right side to achieve balanced redox change.

$$Cr_2O_7^{2-}(aq) + 3SO_3^{2-}(aq) + 8H^+(aq) \longrightarrow 2Cr^{3+}(aq) + 3SO_4^{2-}(aq) + 4H_2O(l)$$

TEACHER'S TIP

If in any equation, you find that all the reactants are only oxidised or reduced then there is something wrong. It may be the formula of reactants or products or the oxidation numbers of the element have not been assigned properly.

Example 10 **Permanganate ion reacts with bromide ion in basic medium to give manganese dioxide and bromate ion. Write the balanced ionic equation for the reaction.** **NCERT**

Sol. *Step* I The skeletal ionic equation is

$$MnO_4^-(aq) + Br^-(aq) \longrightarrow MnO_2(s) + BrO_3^-(aq)$$

Step II Assign oxidation numbers for Mn and Br

$$\overset{+7}{Mn}O_4^-(aq) + \overset{-1}{Br^-}(aq) \longrightarrow \overset{+4}{Mn}O_2(s) + \overset{+5}{Br}O_3^-(aq)$$

This indicates that permanganate ion is the oxidant and bromide ion is the reductant.

Step III Calculate the increase and decrease of oxidation number, and make the increase equal to the decrease.

$$2\overset{+7}{Mn}O_4^-(aq) + \overset{-1}{Br^-}(aq) \longrightarrow 2\overset{+4}{Mn}O_2(s) + \overset{+5}{Br}O_3^-(aq)$$

Step IV As the reaction occurs in the basic medium, and the ionic charges are not equal on both sides, add $2OH^-$ ions on the right to make ionic charges equal.

$$2MnO_4^-(aq) + Br^-(aq) \longrightarrow 2MnO_2(s) + BrO_3^-(aq) + 2OH^-(aq)$$

Step V Finally, count the hydrogen atoms and add appropriate number of water molecules (i.e. one H_2O molecule) on the left side to achieve balanced redox change.

$$2MnO_4^-(aq) + Br^-(aq) + H_2O(l) \longrightarrow 2MnO_2(s) + BrO_3^-(aq) + 2OH^-(aq)$$

Half Reaction Method or Ion Electron Method

This method is based upon the splitting of a redox reaction into two half reactions (one is oxidation half reaction and the other is reduction half reaction).

Suppose we are able to balance the equation showing the oxidation of Fe^{2+} ions to Fe^{3+} ions by dichromate ions $(Cr_2O_7)^{2-}$ in acidic medium, wherein, $Cr_2O_7^{2-}$ ions are reduced to Cr^{3+} ions.

The following steps are involved as

Step 1 Converting unbalanced equation into ionic form

It can be achieved by splitting the ionic compounds into constituent ions and by cancelling spectator ions.

$$Cr_2O_7^{2-}(aq) + Fe^{2+}(aq) + SO_4^{2-}(aq) \longrightarrow Cr^{3+}(aq) + Fe^{3+}(aq) + SO_4^{2-}(aq)$$

Here, SO_4^{2-} is the spectator ion so after leaving it, the reaction becomes

Oxidation

$$\overset{+6}{Cr_2O_7^{2-}}(aq) + Fe^{2+}(aq) \longrightarrow Cr^{3+}(aq) + Fe^{3+}$$

Reduction

Step 2 Splitting the equation into two halves

Separate the equation into oxidation half and reduction half reactions.

- Oxidation half equation, $Fe^{2+}(aq) \longrightarrow Fe^{3+}(aq)$
- Reduction half equation,

$$\overset{+6\ -2}{Cr_2O_7^{2-}}(aq) \longrightarrow Cr^{3+}(aq)$$

Step 3 Balancing all elements other than H and O

Balance all other elements except H and O in each half reaction individually.

Here, oxidation half reaction is already balanced with respect to Fe atoms but to balance reduction half reaction, we have to multiply the Cr^{3+} by 2.

$$Cr_2O_7^{2-}(aq) \longrightarrow 2Cr^{3+}(aq)$$

Step 4 Balancing H and O-atoms by adding H_2O

In oxidation half reaction, there is no need to balance H and O atoms, as in it these are not present. In reduction half reaction, we have to add $7H_2O$ towards product side to balance O-atoms and then add $14H^+$ towards reactant side to balance H-atoms.

$$Cr_2O_7^{2-} + \underset{\text{To balance H-atoms}}{14H^+} \longrightarrow 2Cr^{3+} + \underset{\text{To balance O-atoms}}{7H_2O}$$

Step 5 Balancing of charge

Balance the charge by adding e^- toward the side having more positive charge.

(i) $\underset{+2}{Fe^{2+}}(aq) \longrightarrow \underset{+3}{Fe^{3+}}(aq)$

So, we have to add one electron towards Fe^{3+} side.

Thus, $Fe^{2+}(aq) \longrightarrow Fe^{3+}(aq) + e^-$

Similarly, $Cr_2O_7^{2-}(aq) + 14H^+(aq) \longrightarrow 2Cr^{3+}(aq) + 7H_2O(l)$

Charge on LHS	Charge on RHS
$-2 + 14$	$2 \times (+3)$
$+12$	$+6$

So, we have to add $6e^-$ towards the reactant side.

$$Cr_2O_7^{2-}(aq) + 14H^+(aq) + 6e^- \longrightarrow 2Cr^{3+}(aq) + 7H_2O(l)$$

(ii) $[Fe^{2+}(aq) \longrightarrow Fe^{3+}(aq) + e^-] \times 6$ to equalise number of electrons.

Step 6 Adding the half reactions

On adding the half reaction, we get the overall balanced equation.

$$6Fe^{2+}(aq) + Cr_2O_7^{2-}(aq) + 14H^+(aq) \longrightarrow 6Fe^{3+}(aq) + 2Cr^{3+}(aq) + 7H_2O(l)$$

Step 7 Verification of balanced equation

Since, the number of atoms of each element are equal on both the sides, so it is a balanced chemical equation.

Further; $6Fe^{2+}(aq) + Cr_2O_7^{2-}(aq) + 14H^+(aq) \longrightarrow 6Fe^{3+}(aq) + 2Cr^{3+}(aq) + 7H_2O(l)$

$$6 \times (+2) + (-2) + 14(+1) \equiv 6 \times (+3) + 2 \times (+3)$$

$$12 - 2 + 14 \equiv 18 + 6$$

$$\Rightarrow \quad 24 = 24$$

Thus, the equation is also balanced with respect to charge.

Step 8 Conversion of ionic equation into molecular form

As we know SO_4^{2-} is the spectator ion, and there are $6Fe^{2+}$ (which require $6SO_4^{2-}$ ions) and $14H^+$ ions (that require $7SO_4^{2-}$ ions), so, we have to add $13SO_4^{2-}$ ions on both the sides.

$$6Fe^{2+}(aq) + 6SO_4^{2-}(aq) + Cr_2O_7^{2-}(aq) + 14H^+(aq) + 7SO_4^{2-}(aq) \longrightarrow 6Fe^{3+}(aq) + 9SO_4^{2-}(aq) + 2Cr^{3+} + 3SO_4^{2-}(aq) + 7H_2O + SO_4^{2-}$$

or $6FeSO_4 + Cr_2O_7^{2-}(aq) + 7H_2SO_4 \longrightarrow 3Fe_2(SO_4)_3 + Cr_2(SO_4)_3 + 7H_2O + SO_4^{2-}$

7.6 Applications of Redox Reactions

Redox reactions are widely used in extraction of metals, electrochemical cells, titrations, quantitative analysis. In this section, we will study titrations and electrode processes.

Redox Reactions as the Basis for Titration

Before discussing the role of redox reaction in titrations, it is necessary to became aware from the basic terminology used in titrimetric analysis.

Terminology Used in Titrimetric Analysis

The main terms used in titrimetric analysis are discussed below.

(i) **Titration** It is a common laboratory technique used to calculate the strength of unknown solution quantitatively against a standard solution, using a colour/pH sensitive substance.

(ii) **Standard solution or titrant** It is the solution of known concentration and is taken in the burette during titrimetric analysis.

(iii) **Analyte** This term is used for solution of unknown concentration taken in titration flask.

(iv) **End point or equivalence point** The stage at which the two substance (standard solution and solution of unknown concentration) react completely is called the equivalence point or end point. It is determined with the help of indicator.

(v) **Indicator** It is a colour/pH sensitive substance, used to find the end point of a titration.

Redox Titrations

In redox titrations, the strength of a reductant/oxidant is determined by titrating it with standard solution of oxidant/reductant using a redox sensitive indicator. The indicators used for redox titrations depend upon the nature of redox reaction or reagent and product involved.

Some examples of indicators used in different conditions of redox titrations are given below.

(i) When one of the Reagents is Intensely Coloured

In redox titrations, if one of the reagents is intensely coloured, then it itself behaves as an indicator. Such an indicator is called **self** or **auto-indicator**.

e.g. permanganate ion (MnO_4^-). Reactions involved in these titrations are

$$MnO_4^- + 8H^+ + 5e^- \longrightarrow Mn^{2+} + 4H_2O$$
$$[Fe^{2+} \longrightarrow Fe^{3+} + e^-] \times 5$$
$$\overline{MnO_4^- + 8H^+ + 5Fe^{2+} \longrightarrow 5Fe^{3+} + Mn^{2+} + 4H_2O}$$

The visible end point in this case is achieved after the last of the reductant (Fe^{2+}) is oxidised and the first lasting tinge of pink colour, appears. This ensures a minimal 'over shoot' in colour beyond the equivalence point, the point where the reductant and the oxidant are equal in terms of their mole stoichiometry.

(ii) When one of the Reagents Oxidises the Indicator

Indicators are the substances that get oxidised immediately after the consumption of last drop of reductant is consumed and produce a drastic colour change. It is generally the case of potassium dichromate ($K_2Cr_2O_7$) titrations.

The indicators used in its titrations are of two types

(a) **External indicators** These indicators are not added inside the reaction mixture but after the equivalence point, drops of indicator is placed over few drops of reaction mixture taken in watch glass with the help of glass rod to produce an intense blue colour, thus indicating the end point.

Potassium ferricyanide is an example of such indicator.

(b) **Internal indicators** These are added directly into the solution or titration flask before the process of titration.

Diphenylamine (which produces intense blue colour at the end point) and N-phenylanthranilic acid (which produces violet-red colour at the end point) are the examples of such indicators.

(iii) When the Reagent can Oxidise Iodide Ion into Iodine or Iodine to Iodide Ion

(a) Titration in which the liberated iodine (from an oxidising agent) is titrated with standard solution of sodium thiosulphate is called **iodometric titration.**

e.g. $2Cu^{2+}(aq) + 4I^-(aq) \longrightarrow Cu_2I_2(s) + \underset{\text{In presence of starch twins blue}}{I_2(aq)}$

$$2Na_2S_2O_3(aq) + \underset{\text{Blue colour}}{I_2(aq)} \longrightarrow \underset{\text{Blue colour disappear}}{2NaI} + Na_2S_4O_6(aq)$$

(b) When iodine is titrated directly against a reducing agent such as sodium thiosulphate, the titration is known as **iodimetric titration.**

e.g.

$$\underset{\text{Blue with starch}}{I_2(aq)} + 2S_2O_3^{2-}(aq) \longrightarrow \underset{\text{Blue colour disappear}}{2I^-(aq)} + \underset{\text{Tetrathionate ion}}{S_4O_6^{2-}(aq)}$$

In such reactions, **starch** acts as the indicator as it produces violet or intense blue colour with the molecular iodine, so helps in detection of end point.

TEACHER'S TIP

Although I_2 is insoluble in water, it readily dissolves in aqueous solution of KI due to shift of equilibrium because of the formation of KI_3 which contains I_3^- as a polyhalide ion.

Stoichiometry of Redox Reactions in Solutions

Stoichiometry of redox reactions means the amounts of reductants and oxidants in redox reactions. These calculations are based on **mole concept** or **molarity equation**. (Both of which have been discussed in unit I). For both the methods a balanced redox equation is required.

Recall the molarity equation $\underset{\text{(Oxidant)}}{\dfrac{M_1V_1}{n_1}} = \underset{\text{(Reductant)}}{\dfrac{M_2V_2}{n_2}}$

where, M_1 and V_1 are the molarity and volume of oxidant and M_2 and V_2 are the molarity and volume of reductant n_1 and n_2 are their stoichiometric coefficients.

Redox Reactions and Electrode Processes

The redox reactions in which the oxidation and reduction half reactions occur in the same vessel are called the **direct redox reactions**.

e.g. Placing a zinc strip inside the copper sulphate solution, where Zn is oxidised to Zn^{2+} and copper sulphate is reduced to metallic copper. During this reaction heat is evolved.

The equation of reaction can be represented as shown below.

$$Zn(s)+Cu^{2+}(aq) \longrightarrow Zn^{2+}(aq)+Cu(s)$$

The redox reactions in which the oxidation and reduction half reactions are carried out into separate vessels, are called **indirect redox reactions.**

In these reactions, the reaction occurs in both the vessels as well as at the interface of the metal. These reactions form the basis of **electrochemical cell** where indirect redox reaction is used as a source of energy and **electrolytic cell**, where a non-spontaneous reaction is carried out with the help of energy.

Terminology Used in Electrode Processes

Before discussing the role of redox reactions in the electrode processes, it is essential to become aware from the following terms.

(i) **Electrodes** A metal rod or strip dipped in its own salt solution is called an **electrode.** e.g. When copper rod is dipped in the copper sulphate solution, then term electrode is used for this rod.

(ii) **Anode** The electrode at which oxidation, i.e. loss of electrons from the metal takes place is called the **anode**. It is negative pole in case of an electrochemical cell but a positive pole in case of an electrolytic cell.

(iii) **Cathode** It is the electrode at which reduction, i.e. gain of electron by the metal ion occurs. It is the positive pole in an electrochemical cell whereas negative pole in an electrolytic cell.

(iv) **Redox couple** The combination of the oxidised and reduced forms of a substance taking part in an oxidation or reduction half reaction is called the **redox couple.**

e.g. Zn is the reduced form of Zn^{2+} and Zn^{2+} is the oxidised form of Zn. When these two are present together, they show a redox couple.

A redox couple is represented by separating the oxidised and reduced forms with the help of a vertical line or a slash which shows the interface. e.g. The redox couple of Zn and Zn^{2+} is represented as Zn^{2+} / Zn.

Note It should be noted that in a redox couple the oxidised form is placed before the reduced form. Just like zinc couple, the redox couple for copper is represented as Cu^{2+} / Cu.

(v) **Electrode potential** The potential associated with an electrode is known as the **electrode potential**. It is represented by the symbol E.

(vi) **Standard electrode potential** The potential of an electrode in which the concentration of each species taking part in the electrode reaction is unity (if any gas is involved in the electrode reaction, its pressure is taken as 1 atmosphere) and temperature is maintained at 298 K is called the **standard electrode potential**.

It is represented by $E°$. By convention, the standard electrode potential ($E°$) of hydrogen electrode is 0.00 volts.

The negative value of $E°$ shows that the electrode has a higher tendency to lose electrons, i.e. acts as a **stronger reducing agent** as compared to a H^+/H_2 couple.

Similarly, a positive value of $E°$ shows its higher tendency to gain electrons, i.e. to act as a **stronger oxidising agent** or a weaker reducing agent as compared to H^+/H_2 couple.

Electrochemical Cell

It is a device which is used to convert chemical energy into electrical energy. Daniell or voltaic cell is an important example of this cell.

In order to construct a Daniell cell, zinc rod is placed in 1M solution of zinc sulphate and copper rod is placed in 1M solution of copper sulphate.

The beakers containing these two solutions are put side by side and connected through a **salt-bridge.**

Salt bridge is a U-tube containing a solution of potassium chloride or ammonium nitrate usually solidified by boiling with *agar-agar* and later cooling to a jelly like substance.

The metallic rods are connected through a wire having provision for a switch. The set up is shown in the following figure.

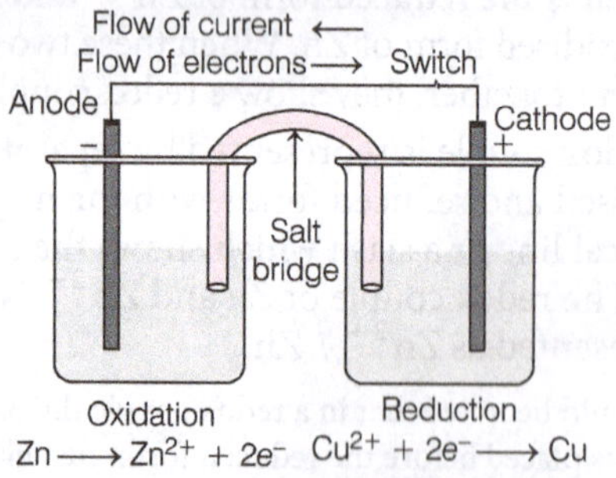

The set up for Daniell cell

When the switch is in off position, there is no reaction in either of the beakers and no current flows through the metallic wire. When switch is turned on,

- the electrons generated at the anode and reach at the cathode.
- deflection in the galvanometer, indicates the flow of electrons through the connecting wires. The direction of deflection indicates the flow of convention current from copper to zinc.
- the electricity flows from the solution of one beaker to the solution of other beaker through the salt bridge.
- the current flows because the potentials of two redox couples are different.
- the difference between the potentials of two redox couple is called the **cell potential.** It is calculated by using the expression,

$$E^\circ_{cell} = E^\circ_{cathode} - E^\circ_{anode} = E^\circ_{reduction} + E^\circ_{oxidation}$$

For a cell reaction to be feasible, the E°_{cell} must be positive.

- The copper rod gains mass whereas the zinc rod loses mass.
- The concentration of copper sulphate solution decreases.
- The solutions in the two beakers remain electrically neutral throughout.
- An electrochemical cell stops working after some time. This is because, as cell works, the concentration of metal ion towards the anode increases which results in increased electrode potential.
- At the same time, the concentration of metal ions towards the cathode decreases which results in decrease of electrode potential. Ultimately, a stage is reached at which the electrode potentials of the two half couples become equal, i.e. the cell potential becomes zero, and the cell stops working.

Functions of Salt-Bridge

The main functions of the salt bridge are as follows

- It completes the cell circuit by connecting the solutions of two half cells, without allowing them to mix with each other.
- It maintains the electrical neutrality of the solutions in the two half cells because of the flow of ions.
- The salt-bridge contains only those electrolytes for which the ionic mobilities of cations and anions are nearly the same.
- If salt-bridge is removed, the cell potential drops to zero, i.e. there is no current flow. This is because of the accumulation of positive ions around the anode and negative ions (that are obtained after the reduction of metal ion) around the cathode, which results in the development of charges in the solution and hence, the current stops flowing.

Representation of an Electrochemical Cell

To represent an electrochemical cell, the anode half reaction (or electrode) is written at the left and cathode half reaction (or electrode) is written at the right. These two are separated by two vertical lines representing the salt bridge.

Thus, a Daniell cell can be represented as

Anode half reaction (oxidation)

$$Zn \longrightarrow Zn^{2+} + 2e^-$$

Cathode half reaction (reduction)

$$Cu^{2+} + 2e^- \longrightarrow Cu$$

Thus, the Daniell cell is $\underset{\text{Anode}}{Zn|Zn^{2+}}\ \underset{\text{Salt-bridge}}{||}\ \underset{\text{Cathode}}{Cu^{2+}|Cu}$

[More details about the representation of cell will be discussed in electrochemistry chapter of Class XII].

Electrochemical Series

When different electrodes or redox couples are arranged in decreasing order of their standard reduction potentials, $E°$ (or standard electrode potentials), the obtained series is called electrochemical series or electromotive series. The series is given below.

The Electrochemical Series ($E°$ values at 298 K)

Reaction (Oxidised form + ne^- ⟶ Reduced form)		$E°$/V
$F_2(g) + 2e^-$	$\rightarrow 2F^-$	2.87
$Co^{3+} + e^-$	$\rightarrow Co^{2+}$	1.81
$H_2O_2 + 2H^+ + 2e^-$s	$\rightarrow 2H_2O$	1.78
$MnO_4^- + 8H^+ + 5e^-$	$\rightarrow Mn^{2+} + 4H_2O$	1.51
$Au^{3+} + 3e^-$	$\rightarrow Au(s)$	1.40
$Cl_2(g) + 2e^-$	$\rightarrow 2Cl^-$	1.36
$Cr_2O_7^{2-} + 14H^+ + 6e^-$	$\rightarrow 2Cr^{3+} + 7H_2O$	1.33
$O_2(g) + 4H^+ + 4e^-$	$\rightarrow 2H_2O$	1.23
$MnO_2(s) + 4H^+ + 2e^-$	$\rightarrow Mn^{2+} + 2H_2O$	1.23
$Br_2 + 2e^-$	$\rightarrow 2Br^-$	1.09
$NO_3^- + 4H^+ + 3e^-$	$\rightarrow NO(g) + 2H_2O$	0.97
$2Hg^{2+} + 2e^-$	$\rightarrow Hg_2^{2+}$	0.92
$Ag^+ + e^-$s	$\rightarrow Ag(s)$	0.80
$Fe^{3+} + e^-$	$\rightarrow Fe^{2+}$	0.77
$O_2(g) + 2H^+ + 2e^-$	$\rightarrow H_2O_2$	0.68
$I_2(s) + 2e^-$	$\rightarrow 2I^-$	0.54
$Cu^+ + e^-$	$\rightarrow Cu(s)$	0.52
$Cu^{2+} + 2e^-$	$\rightarrow Cu(s)$	0.34
$AgCl(s) + e^-$	$\rightarrow Ag(s) + Cl^-$	0.22
$AgBr(s) + e^-$	$\rightarrow Ag(s) + Br^-$	0.10
$2H^+ + 2e^-$	**$\rightarrow H_2(g)$**	**0.00**
$Pb^{2+} + 2e^-$	$\rightarrow Pb(s)$	−0.13
$Sn^{2+} + 2e^-$	$\rightarrow Sn(s)$	−0.14
$Ni^{2+} + 2e^-$	$\rightarrow Ni(s)$	−0.25
$Fe^{2+} + 2e^-$	$\rightarrow Fe(s)$	−0.44
$Cr^{3+} + 3e^-$	$\rightarrow Cr(s)$	−0.74
$Zn^{2+} + 2e^-$	$\rightarrow Zn(s)$	−0.76
$2H_2O + 2e^-$	$\rightarrow H_2(g) + 2OH^-$	−0.83
$Al^{3+} + 3e^-$	$\rightarrow Al(s)$	−1.66
$Mg^{2+} + 2e^-$	$\rightarrow Mg(s)$	−2.36
$Na^+ + e^-$	$\rightarrow Na(s)$	−2.71
$Ca^{2+} + 2e^-$	$\rightarrow Ca(s)$	−2.87
$K^+ + e^-$	$\rightarrow K(s)$	−2.93
$Li^+ + e^-$	$\rightarrow Li(s)$	−3.05

↑ Increasing strength of oxidising agent

↓ Increasing strength of reducing agent

The table of electrochemical series is found to be helpful in the following facts.

(i) Predicting the Strength of Oxidant or Reductant

The tendency of the substance to get reduced decreases on moving downwards.

Thus, it is clear that an element can reduce all the elements placed above it in the series or it can be oxidised by all the elements present above it in the series. Thus,

- a negative E° means that the redox couple is a stronger reducing agent than the H^+/H_2 couple.
- a positive E° means that the redox couple is a weaker reducing agent than the H^+/H_2 couple.

TEACHER'S TIP

In a redox couple, the reduced form is written after oxidised form.

Example 13 **Given the standard electrode potentials, $K^+/K = -2.93V$, $Ag^+/Ag = 0.80V$, $Hg^{2+}/Hg = 0.79V$, $Mg^{2+}/Mg = -2.37\ V$, $Cr^{3+}/Cr = -0.74\ V$ Arrange these metals in their increasing order of reducing power.**

Note Lower the electrode potential (E°_{red}), stronger is the reducing agent.

Sol. The arrangement of metals in their increasing order of reducing power is as follows Ag < Hg < Cr < Mg < K.

(ii) Comparing the Reactivity of Metals

A metal having more negative value of electrode potential can displace the metal having less negative value of electrode potential from their salt solutions. e.g. Zn (with $E^\circ = -0.76$), can displace Cu (with $E^\circ = +0.34$) from $CuSO_4$ solution but opposite is not true.

$$Zn(s) + CuSO_4(aq) \longrightarrow ZnSO_4(aq) + Cu(s)$$

Thus, zinc is more reactive than copper.

(iii) Predicting Feasibility of a Redox or Cell Reaction

The feasibility of a reaction is decided by its cell potential or emf ($E^\circ_{cell} = E^\circ_{cathode} - E^\circ_{anode}$). A positive value of E°_{cell} suggest that the cell reaction is feasible. However, if E°_{cell} is negative or zero, the cell reaction will not exist.

Example 14 **Predict whether the following cell does exist or not?**

$$Zn|Zn^{2+}(1M)||Cd^{2+}(1M)|Cd$$

[Given, $E^\circ_{Zn,\ Zn^{2+}} = 0.76\ V$ and $E^\circ_{Cd,\ Cd^{2+}} = 0.40\ V$]

Sol. Follow the following steps to solve such problems.

***Step* I** Obtain the value of E°_{red} for both the redox couples (if not given).

Since, the given E° values shows the oxidation electrode potential, so invert this value to get E°_{red} (reduction electrode potential) and also reverse its sign i.e.

$$E^\circ_{Zn^{2+}/Zn} = -0.76\ V;$$

$$E^\circ_{Cd^{2+}/Cd} = -0.40\ V$$

***Step* II** Find cathode and anode for the cell.

Here, Zn/Zn^{2+} couple is anode and Cd^{2+}/Cd couple is cathode.

[If cell is not given, the couple having more negative E°_{cell} or E° value, acts as anode and the other one acts as cathode]

***Step* III** Calculate the cell potential or emf using the expression, $E^\circ_{red} = E^\circ_{cathode} - E^\circ_{anode}$

$$E^\circ_{cell} = -0.40 - (-0.76)$$

$$= -0.40 + 0.76 = +0.36\ V$$

***Step* IV** If E°_{cell} is positive the reaction is feasible and the cell exists and if E°_{cell} is negative or zero, the cell does not exist.

Since, we get positive E°_{cell}, so the cell will exist.

(iv) Predicting the Liberation of Hydrogen from an Acid

Highly reactive metals (i.e. metals having negative value of E°) displaces hydrogen from acids.

Thus, metals like Mg, Al, Zn, Fe etc., replace hydrogen from HCl or H_2SO_4. Further, metals with positive value of E° are not capable to replace hydrogen from mineral acids.

(v) Predicting the Product of Electrolysis

If electrolysis is carried out in aqueous solution, along with the cation, H^+ also tries to get reduced.

So, there is a competition between the metal ion and H^+ ions to get reduced.

Similarly, OH^- competes with the negative ion and electrode potential play an important role in deciding the product of electrolysis.

At anode, that species is oxidised, oxidation potential of which is higher or reduction potential of which is lower (i.e. more negative).

Similarly, at cathode that species is reduced, reduction potential of which is higher or oxidation potential of which is lower (i.e. less negative).

TEACHER'S TIP

- In aqueous solution, having metal ions $Li^+, Na^+, K^+, Ba^{2+}, Mg^{2+}$ or Al^{3+}, it is hydrogen ion that get reduced at cathode, thus, metal is not obtained.
- Similarly, if the solution contains SO_4^{2-} or NO_3^- ions, it is the water that get oxidised at anode,
e.g. $2H_2O \longrightarrow O_2 + 4H^+ + 4e^-$

Example 15 **Predict the products of electrolysis in each of the following.**

(i) **An aqueous solution of $AgNO_3$ with silver electrodes.**
(ii) **An aqueous solution of $AgNO_3$ with platinum electrodes.**
(iii) **A dilute solution of H_2SO_4 with platinum electrodes.**
(iv) **An aqueous solution of $CuCl_2$ with platinum electrodes.** NCERT

Hint :

- Higher the oxidation potential of an element, more readily it gets oxidised.
- In case of aqueous solution, H^+ and OH^- ions are also present, so compare the oxidation potential of the elements/ions with that of the H^+ and OH^- to decide the product.

Sol. (i) **An aqueous solution of $AgNO_3$ with silver electrodes.**

Two oxidation and two reduction half reactions must be considered.

Oxidation (at anode)

(a) $Ag(s) \longrightarrow Ag^+(aq) + e^-$; $E° = -0.80$ V

(b) $2H_2O(l) \longrightarrow O_2(g) + 4H^+(aq) + 4e^-$; $E° = -1.23$ V

Reduction (at cathode)

(c) $Ag^+(aq) + e^- \longrightarrow Ag(s)$; $E° = +0.80$ V

(d) $2H_2O(l) + 2e^- \longrightarrow H_2(g) + 2OH^-(aq)$; $E° = -0.83$ V

By $E°$ values of (a) and (b), it appears that **at anode**, silver gets oxidised more readily because oxidation potential of Ag is greater than that of H_2O molecule.

Similarly, by $E°$ values of (c) and (d), it appears that **at cathode**, reduction potential of Ag^+ions higher than that of H_2O molecules.

Therefore, on electrolysis of aqueous $AgNO_3$ solution with silver electrodes, Ag from silver anode dissolves while $Ag^+(aq)$ ions present in the solution gets reduced and deposited at cathode.

(ii) **An aqueous solution of $AgNO_3$ with platinum electrodes.** Platinum is an inert electrode so at anode oxidation of water takes place. As a result of this, O_2 is released at anode according to equation (b) [as in (i)]. At cathode, reduction of Ag^+ ions takes place.

Therefore, on electrolysis of aqueous $AgNO_3$ solution with platinum electrodes, O_2 is released at anode and Ag^+ ions from solution gets deposited at cathode.

(iii) **A dilute solution of H_2SO_4 with platinum electrodes.**

$$H_2SO_4\,(aq) \rightleftharpoons 2H^+ + SO_4^{2-}$$

When current is passed, either H^+ ions or H_2O molecules are reduced at cathode.

$$2H^+(aq) + 2e^- \longrightarrow H_2(g);\ E° = 0.0\text{ V}$$

$$2H_2O(aq) + 2e^- \longrightarrow H_2(g) + 2OH^-(aq);\ E° = -0.83\text{ V}$$

At cathode, H^+ ions gets reduced first because reduction potential of H^+ ions is greater than H_2O molecules.

Similarly, on passing current either SO_4^{2-} ions or H_2O molecules are oxidised at anode.

SO_4^{2-} ions are resistant to oxidation and are not discharged at anode.

So, at anode, H_2O molecules are oxidised to release O_2 gas.

$$2H_2O(l) \longrightarrow O_2(g) + 4H^+(aq) + 4e^-;\ E° = -1.23\text{ V}$$

Therefore, an electrolysis of an aqueous solution of H_2SO_4, only electrolysis of water occurs releasing H_2 at cathode and O_2 at anode.

(iv) **An aqueous solution of $CuCl_2$ with platinum electrodes.**

$$CuCl_2(aq) \rightleftharpoons Cu^{2+} + 2Cl^-(aq);$$
(ionisation of $CuCl_2$ in water)

Two oxidation and two reduction half reactions must be considered.

Oxidation (at anode)

(a) $2Cl^-(aq) \longrightarrow Cl_2(g) + 2e^-$; $E° = -1.36$ V

(b) $2H_2O(l) \longrightarrow O_2(g) + 4H^+(aq) + 4e^-$; $E° = -1.23$ V

Reduction (at cathode)

(c) $Cu^{2+}(aq) + 2e^- \longrightarrow Cu(s)$; $E° = +0.34$ V

(d) $2H_2O(l) + 2e^- \longrightarrow H_2(g) + 2OH^-$; $E° = -0.83$ V

Although oxidation potential of H_2O molecule is greater than that of Cl^- ions, oxidation of Cl^- ions take place in preference to H_2O. It is because of the overvoltage of O_2.

Much lower potential than −1.36 V is required for oxidation of H_2O molecules.

Since, the reduction potential of Cu^{2+} is much higher than the reduction potential of H_2O molecules. therefore, Cu^{2+} ions are reduced at cathode.

Therefore, on electrolysis of an aqueous solution of $CuCl_2$, Cu metal is released at the cathode while Cl_2 gas is evolved at the anode.

Quick Test 3

1. Write balanced chemical equation for the following reactions.
   Permanganate ion (MnO_4^-) reacts with sulphur dioxide gas in acidic medium to produce Mn^{2+} and hydrogen sulphate ion. (Balance by ion electron method) *Competency Based Que.*
2. Can we use KCl as an electrolyte in the salt-bridge of the cell,
   $$Cu(s)|Cu^{2+}(aq) \,||\, Ag^+(aq)\,|Ag(s)$$
3. Write the anode reaction, the cathode reaction and the net cell reaction in the following cells. Which electrode would be positive terminal in each cell ?
   (i) $Zn(s)\,|\,Zn^{2+}\,||\,Br_2\,|\,Br^-\,|\,Pt(s)$
   (ii) $Cr(s)\,|\,Cr^{3+}\,||\,I_2\,|\,I^-\,|\,Pt(s)$
   (iii) $Pt(s)\,|\,H_2(g)\,|\,H^+(aq)\,||\,Cu^{2+}|\,Cu(s)$
4. Represent a galvanic cell in electrode and ions containing Cu electrode dipped in molar solution of copper sulphate and silver electrode dipped in molar solution of silver nitrate.
   [Given: $E^\circ_{Cu^{2+}/Cu\,(s)} = 0.34$ V, $E^\circ_{Ag^+/Ag(s)} = 0.80$ V]
5. Out of aluminium and silver vessel, which one will be more suitable to store 1 M HCl solution and why ?
   $$E^\circ_{Al^{3+}|\,Al} = -1.66 \text{ V}, E^\circ_{Ag^+\,|\,Ag} = +0.80 \text{ V}$$
6. Arrange the following metals in the order in which they displace each other from the solution of their salts.
   Al, Cu, Fe, Mg and Zn *NCERT*
7. What sorts of informations can you draw from the following reaction? *NCERT*
   $$(CN)_2(g) + 2OH^-(aq) \longrightarrow CN^-(aq) + CNO^-(aq) + H_2O(l)$$

For Solutions, See QR Code on Pg. 290

Mind Map

Redox Reactions

Reactions in which oxidation and reduction occurs simultaneously.

Oxidation

It involves

- Addition of oxygen or other electronegative element.
- Removal of H or other electropositive element.
- Loss of electron (s).

Reduction

It is just opposite of oxidation, i.e., it involves

- Addition of H or other electropositive element.
- Removal of oxygen or other electronegative element.
- Gain of electron (s).

Oxidising Agent

It causes oxidation of other substance and itself undergoes reduction.

Reducing Agent

It causes reduction of other substance and itself undergoes oxidation.

Oxidation Number (O.N.)

It is the charge that an atom appear to have in a compound when all other atoms are removed.

- It is zero for free elements. e.g. P_4, O_2, S_8 etc. −2 for O, +1 for H and −1 for F (generally).
- It is equal to group number for elements of group 1 and 2. Algebraic sum of oxidation numbers = Zero (for compound) = charge (for ion)

Paradox of Fractional O.N.

- In C_3O_2, O.N. of two C atoms is +2 and one C atom is zero (0).
- In $S_4O_6^{2-}$, O.N. of two S is 5 and other two S is zero (0).
- In Fe_3O_4, O.N. of two Fe is +3 and one Fe is +2.

Types of Redox Reactions

1. **Combination Reactions**
   These involve combination of two or more atoms to give a single product.
2. **Decomposition Reactions**
   These involve splitting of a compound into two or more simpler products. However, all such reactions are not the decomposition reactions.
3. **Displacement Reactions**
   These involve displacement of one atom (or ion) by other.
4. **Disproportionation Reactions**
   In these reactions, the same element is oxidised as well as reduced simultaneously.

e.g. $\overset{+1\,-1}{2H_2O_2} \longrightarrow \overset{+1\,-2}{2H_2O} + \overset{0}{O_2}$

Redox Reactions and Electrode Processes

- **Electrolytic cell** It converts electric energy into chemical energy.
- **Electrochemical cell** It converts chemical energy into electric energy e.g. Daniell cell, lead storage battery.
- **Salt Bridge** It completes the circuit and maintain electrical neutrality.

Terminology

Electrode It is a metal rod dipped in its own salt solution.

- The electrode at which oxidation takes place is called **anode**.
- The electrode at which reduction takes place is called **cathode**.

Electrode Potential

It is the potential associated with an electrode.

Standard Electrode Potential

It is the electrode potential measured in standard conditions.

Balancing of Redox Reactions

1. **Oxidation Number Method**
   Steps involved in it are
   - Write skeletal ionic equation.
   - Assign O.N. and balance all other atoms except H and O.
   - Finding change in O.N. and equalise it.
   - Balance charge by adding H^+ or OH^-.
   - Balance H and O.
2. **Ion Electron Method**
   Steps involved in it are
   - Write ionic equation.
   - Split it into two halves.
   - Balance all other atoms except H and O.
   - Balance H and O by adding H_2O.
   - Balance charge.
   - Add half equation.
   - Verify balanced equation.
   - Convert ionic equation into molecular form.

Redox Reactions in Titrations

The titration involving redox reactions are called redox titration. e.g., titration of MnO_4^- with Fe^{2+} or $C_2O_4^{2-}$, iodometric titrations, etc.

Electrochemical Series

A series of decreasing E°.
e.g. $F^- > Au > Br^- > Cu > Ag > H_2 > Pb > Sn > Fe > Cr > Zn > Al > Mg > Na > Ca > K > Li$.

Applications

- Element with more negative $E°$ is good reductant.
- Element with less $E°$ can displace the metal with high $E°$ from their salt solution.
- $E°_{cell} = E°_{cathode} - E°_{anode}$. For feasible reaction, $E°_{cell}$ = +ve.

EXAM PATTERN QUESTIONS

Objective Type Questions

Multiple Choice Questions [1 Mark]

1. **From the given species such as Li, K, Ca and Na, which of the following is the strongest reducing agent?**

(a) Na (b) Li (c) Ca (d) K

2. **Consider the given reaction,**

$Cr_2O_7^{2-} + 14H^+ + 6Fe^{2+} \longrightarrow 2Cr^{3+} + 7H_2O + 6Fe^{3+}$

the oxidising agent in the given reaction is

(a) $Cr_2O_7^{2-}$ (b) Fe^{2+}
(c) H^+ (d) H_2O

3. **Which is the best description of behaviour of bromine in the given equation?**

$$H_2O + Br_2 \longrightarrow HBr + HOBr$$

(a) Proton acceptor
(b) Both oxidised and reduced
(c) Only oxidised
(d) Only reduced

4. **In the reaction,**

$2KClO_3 \longrightarrow 2KCl + 3O_2$, the elements which have been oxidised and reduced respectively are

(a) chlorine and oxygen (b) oxygen and chlorine
(c) potassium and oxygen (d) oxygen and potassium

5. **The largest oxidation number exhibited by an element depends on its outer electronic configuration. With which of the following outer electronic configurations the element will exhibit largest oxidation number?** **NCERT Exemplar**

(a) $3d^1 4s^2$ (b) $3d^3 4s^2$
(c) $3d^5 4s^1$ (d) $3d^5 4s^2$

6. **Water molecule is formed by the reaction,**

$$2H_2 + O_2 \longrightarrow 2H_2O,$$

What does happen in this reaction?

(a) Electrons are transferred from H to O-atom
(b) Electrons are transferred from O to H-atom
(c) Electrons are accepted by H from O-atom
(d) Electrons are donated by O to H-atom

7. **What is the oxidation state of sulphur in sodium dithionite ($Na_2S_2O_4$)?**

(a) +3 (b) +4
(c) +5 (d) +2

8. **In which of the following oxidation number of chlorine is +5 ?**

(a) Cl^- (b) ClO^- (c) ClO_2^- (d) ClO_3^-

9. **Which of the following species contain an element in an oxidation state that is not a whole number?**

(a) VO_4^{3-} (b) Mn_2O_3
(c) $S_4O_6^{2-}$ (d) Cl_2O_7

10. **In the redox reaction,**

$MnO_4^- + 8H^+ + 5Br^- \longrightarrow Mn^{2+} + 4H_2O + \frac{5}{2}Br_2$

Which one is the reducing agent? **Competency Based Que.**

(a) H^+ (b) MnO_4^-
(c) Br^- (d) Mn^{2+}

11. **The reaction, $2H_2O(l) \xrightarrow{\Delta} 2H_2(g) + O_2(g)$ is an example of**

(a) addition reaction (b) decomposition reaction
(c) displacement reaction (d) None of these

12. **Which of the following statements about a disproportionation reaction is true?**

(a) Both oxidation and reduction occur to the same species
(b) It requires an external oxidising agent
(c) It always involves a neutral species
(d) The oxidation state of the same element decreases in both products

13. **Identify disproportionation reaction** **NCERT Exemplar**

(a) $CH_4 + 2O_2 \longrightarrow CO_2 + 2H_2O$
(b) $CH_4 + 4Cl_2 \longrightarrow CCl_4 + 4HCl$
(c) $2F_2 + 2OH^- \longrightarrow 2F^- + OF_2 + H_2O$
(d) $2NO_2 + 2OH^- \longrightarrow NO_2^- + NO_3^- + H_2O$

14. **In the reaction, $8Al + 3Fe_3O_4 \longrightarrow 4Al_2O_3 + 9Fe$, the number of electrons transferred from the reductant to the oxidant is**

(a) 8 (b) 4
(c) 16 (d) 24

15. **The value of 'n' in the reaction,**

$Cr_2O_7^{2-} + 14H^+ + nFe^{2+} \longrightarrow 2Cr^{3+} + nFe^{3+} + 7H_2O$

will be

(a) 2 (b) 3
(c) 6 (d) 7

16. **Which of the following reaction is a balanced chemical equation?**

(a) $2MnO_4^- + 3Br^- + H_2O \longrightarrow 2MnO_2 + 3BrO_3^- + 2OH^-$

(b) $MnO_4^- + 5Br^- + H_2O \longrightarrow MnO_2 + 3BrO_3^- + 2OH^-$

(c) $MnO_4^- + 3Br^- + H_2O \longrightarrow MnO_2 + 3BrO_3^- + 2OH^-$

(d) $2MnO_4^- + 3Br^- + H_2O \longrightarrow 2MnO_2 + 3BrO_3^-$

17. **Solution of potassium chloride or ammonium nitrate in salt-bridge usually solidified by boiling with**

(a) *agar-agar* (b) starch (c) cellulose (d) glycogen

18. **Using the standard electrode potential, find out the pair between which redox reaction is not feasible.**

$E^\ominus$ **values:** $Fe^{3+}/Fe^{2+} = +0.77; I_2/I^- = +0.54;$

$Cu^{2+}/Cu = +0.34; Ag^+/Ag = +0.80$ V

NCERT Exemplar

(a) Fe^{3+} and I^- (b) Ag^+ and Cu

(c) Fe^{3+} and Cu (d) Ag and Fe^{3+}

19. **Negative** $E^\ominus$ **indicates that redox couple is**

(a) weaker reducing agent than H^+/H_2 couple

(b) stronger reducing agent than H^+/H_2 couple

(c) stronger oxidising agent than H^+/H_2 couple

(d) None of the above

20. **Consider the given standard electrode potentials.**

I. $K^+/K = -3.02$ V II. $Cu^{2+}/Cu = +0.34$ V

III. $Hg^{2+}/Hg = 0.92$ V IV. $Cr^{3+}/Cr = -0.74$ V

Decreasing order of reducing power of these elements is **Competency Based Que.**

(a) I > II > III > IV (b) I > IV > III > II

(c) I > IV > II > III (d) III > II > IV > I

Assertion-Reason [1 Mark]

Directions (Q. Nos. 21-30) In the following questions. an Assertion (A) is followed by a corresponding Reason (R) Use the following keys to choose the appropriate answer.

(a) Both (A) and (R) are correct and (R) is the correct explanation of (A).

(b) Both (A) and (R) are correct but (R) is not the correct explanation of (A).

(c) (A) is correct and (R) is incorrect.

(d) (A) is incorrect and (R) is correct.

21. **Assertion** (A) Lithium ion is a poor oxidising agent.

Reason (R) Lithium ion has the lowest electrode potential.

22. **Assertion** (A) Bromide ion acts as a reducing agent in given following reaction.

$$2MnO_4^-(aq) + Br^-(aq) + H_2O(l) \longrightarrow MnO_2(aq) + BrO_3^-(aq) + 2OH^-(aq)$$

Reason (R) Oxidation number of Br increases from −1 to +5.

23. **Assertion** (A) In acidic medium, MnO_4^- is reduced to Mn^{2+}

Reason (R) In acidic conditions, MnO_4^- accepts electrons and undergoes reduction.

24. **Assertion** (A) Oxidation and reduction always occur simultaneously in a redox reaction.

Reason (R) Oxidation involves the loss of electrons, whereas reduction involves the gain of electrons.

25. **Assertion** (A) The decomposition of hydrogen peroxide to form water and oxygen is an example of disproportionation reaction. **NCERT Exemplar**

Reason (R) The oxygen of peroxide is in −1 oxidation state and it is converted to zero oxidation state in O_2 and −2 oxidation state in H_2O. **Competency Based Que.**

26. **Assertion** (A) Redox couple is the combination of oxidised and reduced form of a substance involved in an oxidation or reduction half cell. **NCERT Exemplar**

Reason (R) In the representation $E^\ominus_{Fe^{3+}/Fe^{2+}}$ and $E^\ominus_{Cu^{2+}/Cu}$, Fe^{3+}/Fe^{2+} and Cu^{2+}/Cu are redox couples.

27. **Assertion** (A) Among halogens, fluorine is the best oxidant.

Reason (R) Fluorine is the most electronegative atom.

28. **Assertion** (A) Fe reacts with HCl to produce H_2 gas.

Reason (R) Fe is a better oxidising agent than H_2.

29. **Assertion** (A) When Zn rod is dipped in solution, blue colour of solution starts fading.

Reason (R) In this reaction, Zn gets reduced and Cu^{2+} ions gets oxidised.

30. **Assertion** (A) In the reaction,

$$Zn + CuSO_4 \longrightarrow ZnSO_4 + Cu$$

Zinc acts as a reducing agent.

Reason (R) Zinc has a higher standard electrode potential than copper.

Case-Study [4 Marks]

31. **Read the given case and answer the following questions.**

The oxidation state of an individual atom in its free state is 0. The total oxidation state of all atoms in a neutral species is 0 and in an ions is equal to the charge. Group 1 metals have an oxidation state of +1 and group 2 an oxidation state of +2. The oxidation state of fluorine is −1 in compounds. Hydrogen generally has an oxidation state of +1 in compounds. Oxygen generally has an oxidation state of −2 in compounds.

In binary metal compounds, group 17 elements have an oxidation state of –1, group 16 elements of –2, and group 15 element of –3. The sum of the oxidation states is equal to zero for neutral compounds and equal to the charge for polyatomic ion species.

Competency Based Que.

(i) How many moles of I_2 is liberated when one mole of acidified $K_2Cr_2O_7$ is reacted with excess KI?

(ii) What is the change occur in oxidation state during reduction and oxidation ?

Or What is the oxidation state of N in HNO_2?

(iii) How many moles of H_2O_2 are oxidised by mole of ClO_2 when ClO_2 oxidises H_2O_2 to O_2 in alkaline medium?

32. Read the given case and answer the following questions.

The concept of the electron transfer is found unable to explain the redox changes or electron shift in case of covalent compounds.

To explain these changes a new concept, called oxidation number is introduced.

The oxidation state is the simplest attribute of an element in a compound. It is taught early in the chemistry curriculum as convenient electron-counting scheme for redox reactions. Its applications range from descriptive chemistry of elements to nomenclature and electrochemistry, or as an independent variable in plots and databases of bonded-atom properties.

The history of the oxidation state goes back about 200 years when it described the stepwise increase in the amount of oxygen bound by elements that form more than one oxide. In his 1835 textbook Unorganische Chemie, Wöheler speaks of such an "oxydationsstufe". This expression remains in use for oxidation state in several languages. The equivalent term oxidation number is also common; in English this refers more to redox balancing than to the chemical systematics of an element.

Competency Based Que.

(i) Name the compund of Mn in which it shows highest oxidation state.

(ii) What is the change in oxidation number of Mn when manganous salt is fused with a mixture of KNO_3 and solid NaOH?

Or What is the oxidation state of I in IPO_4?

(iii) What is the oxidation state of Fe in brown ring complex?

Subjective Type Questions

Short Answer Type I Questions [2 Marks]

1. Calculate the oxidation number of phosphorus in the following species.

(i) HPO_3^{2-} (ii) PO_4^{3-} **NCERT Exemplar**

2. Why does fluorine not show disproportionation reaction? **NCERT Exemplar**

3. Fluorine reacts with ice and results in the change.

$$H_2O(s)+F_2(g) \longrightarrow HF(g)+HOF(g)$$

Justify that this reaction is a redox reaction. **NCERT**

Hint: Redox reactions involve oxidation and reduction as its two half reactions. So, find the oxidation state of each element given in the equation to find which substance is oxidising and which is reducing, then check, if the given reaction is redox reaction or not.

4. (i) Explain oxidation and reduction in terms of electron transfer with examples.

(ii) What is oxidation number? How is it useful in redox reactions?

5. Nitric acid is an oxidising agent and reacts with PbO but it does not react with PbO_2. Explain why? **NCERT Exemplar**

6. What are the net charges on the left and right side of the following equations? Add electrons as necessary to make each of them balanced half reactions.

(i) $NO_3^- + 10H^+ \longrightarrow NH_4^+ + 3H_2O$

(ii) $Cl_2 + 4H_2O \longrightarrow 2ClO_3^- + 8H^+$

7. The Mn^{3+} ion is unstable in solution and undergoes disproportionation to give Mn^{2+}, MnO_2 and H^+ ions. Write a balanced ionic equation for the reaction.

8. A solution of silver nitrate was stirred with iron rod. Will it cause any change in the concentration of silver and nitrate ions?

9. An iron rod is immersed in solution containing 1.0 M $NiSO_4$ and 1.0 M $ZnSO_4$. Predict giving reasons which of the following reactions is likely to proceed?

(i) Fe reduces Zn^{2+} ions, (ii) Iron reduces Ni^{2+} ions.

Given, $E^\circ_{Zn^{2+}/Zn} = -0.76$ V, $E^\circ_{Fe^{2+}/Fe} = -0.44$ V and $E^\circ_{Ni^{2+}/Ni} = -0.25$ V

10. Which method can be used to find out strength of reductant/oxidant in a solution ? Explain with an example. **NCERT Exemplar**

Short Answer Type II Questions [3 Marks]

11. Write formulae for the following compounds.

(i) Mercury (II) chloride

(ii) Nickel (II) sulphate

(iii) Tin (IV) oxide

(iv) Thallium (I) sulphate

(v) Iron (III) sulphate

(vi) Chromium (III) oxide **NCERT**

Hint:
- While writing the formula of a compound, oxidation state (or valency) of cation is written as the subscript of anion and valency of anion is written as the subscript of cation.
- Valency of chloride (Cl^-), sulphate (SO_4^{2-}) and oxide (O^{2-}) are -1, -2 and -2 respectively. Valencies of metals are given in brackets.

12. Why do the following reactions proceed differently?

$Pb_3O_4 + 8HCl \longrightarrow 3PbCl_2 + Cl_2 + 4H_2O$ and

$Pb_3O_4 + 4HNO_3 \longrightarrow 2Pb(NO_3)_2 + PbO_2 + 2H_2O$

NCERT

13. How does Cu_2O act as both oxidant and reductant? Explain with proper reactions showing the change of oxidation numbers in each example.

14. PbO and PbO_2 react with HCl according to following chemical equations

$$2PbO + 4HCl \longrightarrow 2PbCl_2 + 2H_2O$$
$$PbO_2 + 4HCl \longrightarrow PbCl_2 + Cl_2 + 2H_2O$$

Why do these compounds differ in their reactivity?

NCERT Exemplar

15. Calculate the oxidation number of sulphur, chromium and nitrogen in H_2SO_5, $Cr_2O_7^{2-}$ and NO_3^-. Suggest the structure of these compounds. Count for the fallacy.

NCERT

16. While sulphur dioxide and hydrogen peroxide can act as oxidising as well as reducing agents in their reactions, ozone and nitric acid act only as oxidants. Why? **NCERT**

Hint: An element, in its lowest oxidation state, can behave only as reductant while in its highest oxidation state can behave only as oxidants. In intermediate oxidation states, elements can behave as oxidant as well as reductant.

17. Depict the galvanic cell in which the reaction,

$$Zn(s) + 2Ag^+(aq) \longrightarrow Zn^{2+}(aq) + 2Ag(s)$$

takes place, further show **NCERT**

(i) which of the electrode is negatively charged?
(ii) the carriers of the current in the cell.
(iii) individual reaction at each electrode.

Long Answer Type Questions [5 Marks]

18. What do you understand by oxidation and reduction? Classify the following substances into oxidising and reducing agents.

(i) Carbon
(ii) Ozone
(iii) Nascent hydrogen
(iv) Nitric acid
(v) Chlorine

19. Using electron transfer concept, identify the oxidant and reductant in the following redox reactions.

(i) $Zn(s) + 2H^+(aq) \longrightarrow Zn^{2+}(aq) + H_2(g)$
(ii) $2[Fe(CN)_6]^{4-}(aq) + H_2O_2(aq) + 2H^+(aq) \longrightarrow 2[Fe(CN)_6]^{3-}(aq) + 2H_2O(l)$
(iii) $2[Fe(CN)_6]^{3-}(aq) + 2OH^-(aq) + H_2O_2(aq) \longrightarrow 2[Fe(CN)_6]^{4-}(aq) + O_2(g) + 2H_2O(l)$
(iv) $BrO_3^-(aq) + F_2(g) + 2OH^-(aq) \longrightarrow BrO_4^-(aq) + 2F^-(aq) + H_2O(l)$
(v) $2NaClO_3(aq) + I_2(aq) \longrightarrow 2NaIO_3(aq) + Cl_2(g)$

Competency Based Que.

20. What are the oxidation numbers of the underlined elements in each of the following and how do you rationalise your results?

(i) $K\underline{I}_3$ (ii) $H_2\underline{S}_4O_6$ (iii) $\underline{Fe}_3O_4$ (iv) $\underline{C}H_3\underline{C}H_2OH$
(v) $\underline{C}H_3\underline{C}OOH$ **NCERT**

21. Justify that the following reactions are redox reactions.

(i) $CuO(s) + H_2(g) \longrightarrow Cu(s) + H_2O(g)$ **NCERT**
(ii) $Fe_2O_3(s) + 3CO(g) \longrightarrow 2Fe(s) + 3CO_2(g)$
(iii) $4BCl_3(g) + 3LiAlH_4(s) \longrightarrow 2B_2H_6(g) + 3LiCl(s) + 3AlCl_3(s)$
(iv) $2K(s) + F_2(g) \longrightarrow 2K^+F^-(s)$
(v) $4NH_3(g) + 5O_2(g) \longrightarrow 4NO(g) + 6H_2O(g)$

22. Write correctly the balanced equations for the following redox reactions using half reactions.

(i) $H_2S + Fe^{3+} \longrightarrow Fe^{2+} + S + H^+$
(ii) $I^- + IO_3^- + H^+ \longrightarrow I_2 + H_2O$
(iii) $Bi(s) + NO_3^- + H^+ \longrightarrow NO_2 + Bi^{3+} + H_2O$
(iv) $I^- + O_2(g) + H_2O \longrightarrow I_2 + OH^-$

State what is oxidised to and what is reduced in the reactions expressed by the equations?

23. Balance the following redox reactions by ion-electron method.

(i) $MnO_4^-(aq) + I^-(aq) \longrightarrow MnO_2(s) + I_2(s)$ (in basic medium)
(ii) $MnO_4^-(aq) + SO_2(g) \longrightarrow Mn^{2+}(aq) + HSO_4^-(aq)$ (in acidic solution)
(iii) $H_2O_2(aq) + Fe^{2+}(aq) \longrightarrow Fe^{3+}(aq) + H_2O(l)$ (in acidic solution)
(iv) $Cr_2O_7^{2-}(aq) + SO_2(g) \longrightarrow Cr^{3+}(aq) + SO_4^{2-}(aq)$ (in acidic solution) **NCERT**

24. Write balanced chemical equation for the following reactions. **NCERT Exemplar**

(i) Permanganate ion (MnO_4^-) reacts with sulphur dioxide gas in acidic medium to produce Mn^{2+} and hydrogen sulphate ion. (Balance by ion electron method)

(ii) Reaction of liquid hydrazine (N_2H_4) with chlorate ion (ClO_3^-) in basic medium produces nitric oxide gas and chloride ion in gaseous state.
(Balance by oxidation number method)

(iii) Dichlorine heptaoxide (Cl_2O_7) in gaseous state combines with an aqueous solution of hydrogen peroxide in acidic medium to give chlorite ion (ClO_2^-) and oxygen gas.
(Balance by ion electron method)

25. How do you account for the following observations?

(i) Though alkaline potassium permanganate and acidic potassium permanganate both are used as oxidants, yet in the manufacture of benzoic acid from toluene we use alcoholic potassium permanganate as an oxidant. Why? Write a balance redox equation for the reaction.

(ii) When concentrated sulphuric acid is added to an inorganic mixture containing chloride, we get colourless pungent smelling gas HCl, but if the mixture contains bromide, then we get red vapour of bromine. Why? **NCERT**

Hint: • Like dissolves like, i.e. benzoic acid and toluene being covalent readily dissolve in alcohol and form homogeneous solution.
• HBr is a stronger reducing agent than HCl, so reduces H_2SO_4 to SO_2.

26. (i) Use the following reactions to arrange the elements A, B, C and D in order of their redox reactivity.

(a) $A + B^+ \longrightarrow A^+ + B$

(b) $B + D^+ \longrightarrow B^+ + D$

(c) $C^+ + D \longrightarrow$ No reaction

(d) $B + C^+ \longrightarrow B^+ + C$

(ii) On the basis of above redox activity series, predict which of the following reactions would you expect to occur?

(a) $A^+ + C \longrightarrow A + C^+$

(b) $A^+ + D \longrightarrow A + D^+$ **Competency Based Que.**

27. Which method can be used to find out strength of reductant/oxidant in a solution? Explain with an example. **NCERT Exemplar**

Hints & Solutions

Objective Type Questions

1. (b) Among the given species Li is the strongest reducing agent as its standard electrode reduction potential value is very negative.

2. (a) In the given reaction, $Cr_2O_7^{2-}$ undergoes reduction, where chromium goes from an oxidation state of +6 to +3. It oxidises Fe^{2+} to Fe^{3+}.

3. (b) In reaction, $H_2O + \overset{0}{Br_2} \longrightarrow \overset{+1}{HOBr} + \overset{-1}{HBr}$

The oxidation number of bromine increases from 0 (Br_2) to +1 (HOBr) and decreases from, 0 (Br) to −1 (HBr), hence bromine is both oxidised as well as reduced in given reaction.

4. (b) $\overset{+1\,+5\,-2}{KClO_3} \longrightarrow \overset{+1\,-1}{2KCl} + \overset{0}{3O_2}$

The oxidation number of Cl decreases from +5 ($KClO_3$) to −1 (KCl), while that of oxygen increases from −2 ($KClO_3$) to 0 (O_2).

Thus, chlorine is reduced and oxygen is oxidised.

5. (d) The largest oxidation number is exhibited by $3d^5 4s^2$ as $2+5=7$. The largest oxidation number exhibited by an element depends on its outer electronic configuration.

6. (a) $\overset{0}{2H_2} + \overset{0}{O_2} \longrightarrow \overset{+1\,-2}{2H_2O}$

In the above reaction electrons are transferred from H to O-atom.

7. (a) $2(+1) + 2x + 4(-2) = 0$

$$2 + 2x - 8 = 0$$
$$x = +3$$

8. (d) The oxidation number Cl is +5 in ClO_3^-.

$$x + 3(-2) = -1$$
$$\Rightarrow \quad x = +5$$

9. (c) In $S_4O_6^{2-}$, let 'x' be the oxidation number of S.

$$\therefore \quad 4x - 12 = -2$$
$$x = \frac{10}{4} = \frac{5}{2}$$

10. (c)

$$\overset{+7}{MnO_4^-} + 8H^+ + 5Br^- \longrightarrow Mn^{2+} + 4H_2O + \frac{5}{2}\overset{0}{Br_2}$$

(Oxidation: $Br^- \rightarrow Br_2$; Reduction: $MnO_4^- \rightarrow Mn^{2+}$)

Since, in this reaction Br^- reduces MnO_4^- into Mn^{2+} and itself gets oxidised into Br_2, so here Br^- act as the reducing agent.

11. (b) In reaction, $2H_2O(l) \xrightarrow{\Delta} 2H_2(g) + O_2(g)$, H_2O on heating will split into H_2 and O_2. Thus, it is an example of decomposition reaction.

12. (a) In disproportionation reaction, the same element undergoes both oxidation and reduction.

13. (d) $\overset{+4}{2NO_2} + \overset{-}{2OH} \longrightarrow \overset{+3}{NO_2^-} + \overset{+5}{NO_3^-} + H_2O$

This is an example of disproportionation reaction as oxidation state of N changes from +4 to +3 and +5, respectively.

14. (d) $\overset{0}{8Al} + \overset{8/3}{3Fe_3O_4} \longrightarrow \overset{+3\,-2}{4Al_2O_3} + \overset{0}{9Fe}$

Oxidation half reaction.

$[2Al + 3H_2O \longrightarrow Al_2O_3 + 6e^- + 6H^-] \times 4$

Reduction half reaction.

$[3Fe_3O_4 + 8e^- + 8H^+ \longrightarrow 3Fe + 4H_2O] \times 3$

So, 24 electrons transferred.

15. (c) $Cr_2O_7^{2-} + 14H^+ + nFe^{2+} \longrightarrow 2Cr^{3+} + nFe^{3+} + 7H_2O$

$$Cr_2O_7^{2-} + 14H^+ + 6e^- \longrightarrow 2Cr^{3+} + 7H_2O \quad \text{...(i)}$$
$$Fe^{2+} \longrightarrow Fe^{3+} + e^- \quad \text{...(ii)}$$

Multiply eq. (ii) by 6.

$$6Fe^{2+} \longrightarrow 6Fe^{3+} + 6e^-$$

Thus, balanced equation is

$$Cr_2O_7^{2-} + 14H^+ + 6Fe^{2+} \longrightarrow 2Cr^{3+} + 6Fe^{3+} + 7H_2O$$

$\therefore$ The value of n is 6.

16. (a) In an alkaline medium MnO_4^- is reduced to MnO_2 and Br^- is oxidised to BrO_3^-.

$\therefore \; 2MnO_4^- + 3Br^- + H_2O \longrightarrow 2MnO_2 + 3BrO_3^- + 2OH^-$

17. (a) Salt-bridge is a U-tube containing a solution of potassium chloride or ammonium nitrate usually solidified by boiling with *agar-agar*.

18. (d) Among the given cases, reaction does not occurs between Ag and Fe^{3+}. This is because $E°$ value of this reaction is comes out to be − 0.003 V.

19. (b) The negative $E°$ value indicates that redox couple is stronger reducing agent than H^+/H_2 couple.

20. (c) More negative is the $E°$ value greater is the reducing power. Thus, decreasing order of reducing power is

$$I > IV > II > III.$$

21. (a) Both (A) and (R) are correct and (R) is the correct explanation of (A).

22. (a) Both (A) and (R) are correct and (R) is the correct explanation of (A).

23. (a) Both (A) and (R) are correct and (R) is the correct explanation of (A).

24. (a) Both (A) and (R) are correct and (R) is the correct explanation of (A).

25. (*a*) Both (A) and (R) are true and (R) is the correct explanation of (A).

26. (*a*) Both (A) and (R) are true (R) is the correct explanation of (A).

27. (*b*) Fluorine has the maximum $E°$ value among the halogens, hence it reduces first than other halogen and acts as best oxidant.
Fluorine is most electronegative atom due to its small size.
Thus, both statement are correct but (R) is not the correct explanation of (A).

28. (*c*) (A) is correct while (R) is incorrect. Correct (R) is Fe is a better reducing agent than H_2.

29. (*c*) (A) is correct while (R) is incorrect. When Zn rod is dipped in $Cu(NO_3)_2$ solution, Zn gets oxidised and Cu^{2+} ions gets reduced.

$$\overset{0}{Zn} + \overset{+2}{Cu}(NO_3)_2 \longrightarrow \overset{+2}{Zn}(NO_3)_2 + \overset{0}{Cu}$$

Reduced (Cu: +2 → 0)
Oxidised (Zn: 0 → +2)

30. (*c*) Zinc acts as a reducing agent because it is more electropositive than copper.

31. (i) The balanced chemical equation is

$$K_2Cr_2O_7 + 6KI + 7H_2SO_4 \longrightarrow 4K_2SO_4 + Cr_2(SO_4)_3 + 7H_2O + 3I_2 \text{ (1)}$$

Hence, 3 moles of iodine will be liberated.

(ii) In oxidation → oxidation state increases.
In reduction → oxidation state decreases. **(1)**

Or

HNO_2
Let, the O.S. of N be x.

$$1 + x + 2(-2) = 0$$
$$x - 3 = 0$$
$$x = +3$$

(iii) In alkaline medium balanced equation is

$$2ClO_2 + 5H_2O_2 + 2OH^- \longrightarrow 2Cl^- + 5O_2 + 6H_2O$$

2 moles of ClO_2 oxidise 5 moles of H_2O_2

1 mole of ClO_2 will oxidise $= \frac{5}{2} \times 1 = 2.5$ mol **(2)**

32. (i) $KMnO_4$ is the compound of manganese which has highest oxidation state.

$$KMnO_4 (+1) + x + 4(-2) = 0$$
$$x = +7 \quad \text{(2)}$$

(ii) $\overset{(+2)}{Mn^{2+}} + 2NO_3^- + 2OH^- \longrightarrow \overset{(+6)}{Mn}O_4^{2-} + 2H_2O + 2NO$

The oxidation number of Mn changes from +2 to +6. **(1)**

Or

Let the oxidation state of I in IPO_4 be x.

$x + (-3) = 0$. [PO_4^{3-} ion has charge equal to −3.]

$$x = +3$$

(iii) The brown ring complex is $[Fe(H_2O)_5NO]SO_4$. In this oxidation number of Fe is +1. **(1)**

Subjective Type Questions

1. (i) Suppose that the oxidation number of P in HPO_3^{2-} be x.
Then, $1 + x + 3(-2) = -2$ or $x + 1 - 6 = -2$
or $x = +3$ **(1)**

(ii) Suppose that the oxidation number of P in PO_4^{3-} be x.
Then, $x + 4(-2) = -3$ or $x - 8 = -3$
or $x = +5$ **(1)**

2. In a disproportionation reaction, the same species simultaneously get oxidised as well as reduced. Therefore, for such a redox reaction to occur, the reacting species must contain an element which has atleast three oxidation states.

The element, in reacting species, is present in an intermediate state while lower and higher oxidation states are available for reduction and oxidation, respectively to occur.

Fluorine is the strongest oxidising agent. It does not show positive oxidation state. That's why fluorine does not show disproportionation reaction. **(2)**

3. $\overset{+1\,-2}{H_2O}(s) + \overset{0}{F_2}(g) \longrightarrow \overset{+1\,-1}{HF}(g) + \overset{+1\,-2\,+1}{HOF}(g)$

In the above reaction, as the oxidation state of F decreases from 0 to −1 and increases from 0 to +1. That means, F is both oxidised and reduced. Hence, the given reaction is a redox reaction.

Note It is an exceptional case where fluorine shows positive oxidation state. **(2)**

4. (i) Refer to text on page 259.
(ii) Refer to text on page 261.

5. PbO is a base. It reacts with nitric acid and forms soluble lead nitrate.

$$PbO + 2HNO_3 \longrightarrow \underset{\text{Soluble}}{Pb(NO_3)_2} + H_2O \text{ (acid base reaction)}$$

Nitric acid does not react with PbO_2. Both of them are strong oxidising agents. In HNO_3, nitrogen is in its maximum oxidation state (+5) and in PbO_2, lead is in its maximum oxidation state (+ 4). Therefore, no reaction takes place. **(2)**

6. (i) +9 charge on the left, +1 charge on the right; add 8 electrons to the left side. **(1)**

(ii) 0 charge on the left, +6 charge on the right; add 6 electrons on the right side. **(1)**

7. The skeletal equation is,

$$Mn^{3+}(aq) \longrightarrow Mn^{2+}(aq) + MnO_2(s) + H^+(aq)$$

After balancing above equation we get,

$$2Mn^{3+}(aq) + 2H_2O(l) \longrightarrow Mn^{2+} + MnO_2(s) + 4H^+(aq)$$ **(2)**

8. Since, $E°$ of Fe^{2+} /Fe (– 0.44 V) is lower than that of Ag^+ / Ag (+ 0.80 V) electrode, therefore, Ag^+ gets reduced and Fe gets oxidised. As a result, concentration of Ag^+ ions decreases while that of NO_3^- ions remain unchanged.

$$2\,Ag^+(aq) + Fe(s) \longrightarrow 2\,Ag(s) + Fe^{2+}(aq)$$ **(2)**

9. (i) Since, $E°$ of Zn is more negative than that of Fe, therefore, Zn will be oxidised to Zn^{2+} ions while Fe^{2+} ions will be reduced to Fe. In other words, Fe will not reduce Zn^{2+} ions. **(1)**

(ii) Since, $E°$ of Fe is more negative than that of Ni, therefore, Fe will be oxidised to Fe^{2+} ions while Ni^{2+} ions will be reduced to Ni. Thus, Fe reduces Ni^{2+} ions. **(1)**

10. Measure the electrode potential of the given species by connecting the redox couple of the given species with standard hydrogen electrode.

If it is positive, the electrode of the given species acts as reductant and if it is negative, it acts as an oxidant.

Find the electrode potentials of the other given species in the same way, compare the values and determine their comparative strength or an reductant or oxidant. e.g. Measurement of standard electrode potential of Zn^{2+}/Zn electrode using SHE as a reference electrode. **(2)**

11. (i) $Hg(II)Cl_2$ **(1/2)** (ii) Ni (II) SO_4 **(1/2)**
(iii) $Sn(IV)O_2$ **(1/2)** (iv) $Tl_2(I)\ SO_4$ **(1/2)**
(v) $Fe_2(III)(SO_4)_3$ **(1/2)** (vi) $Cr_2(III)O_3$ **(1/2)**

12. Pb_3O_4 is actually a stoichiometric mixture of 2 moles of PbO and 1 mole of PbO_2, i.e. $(2\,PbO \cdot PbO_2)$. In PbO_2, lead is present in + 4 oxidation state, whereas the stable oxidation state of lead in PbO is +2. PbO_2 thus can act as an oxidant (oxidising agent) and therefore, can oxidise Cl^- ion of HCl into chlorine.

We may also keep in mind that PbO is a basic oxide. Therefore, the reaction

$$Pb_3O_4 + 8HCl \longrightarrow 3PbCl_2 + Cl_2 + 4H_2O$$

can be splitted into two reactions namely

$$2\,PbO + 4\,HCl \longrightarrow 2\,PbCl_2 + 2H_2O \quad \text{(acid-base reaction)}$$

$$\overset{+4}{Pb}O_2 + 4H\overset{-1}{Cl} \longrightarrow \overset{+2}{Pb}Cl_2 + \overset{0}{Cl_2} + 2H_2O \quad \text{(redox reaction)}$$

Since, HNO_3 itself is an oxidising agent, therefore it is unlikely that the reaction may occur between PbO_2 and HNO_3.

However, the acid-base reaction occurs between PbO and HNO_3 as

$$2\,PbO + 4\,HNO_3 \longrightarrow 2Pb(NO_3)_2 + 2H_2O$$

It is the passive nature of PbO_2 against HNO_3 that makes the reaction different from the one that follows with HCl. **(3)**

13. Cu^+ undergoes disproportionation to form Cu^{2+} and Cu.

$$2\,Cu^+(aq) \longrightarrow Cu^{2+}(aq) + Cu(s)$$

Thus, Cu^+ or Cu_2O acts both as an oxidant as well as reductant. **(1)**

(i) When heated in air, Cu_2O is oxidised to CuO.

$$\overset{+1}{Cu_2}\overset{-2}{O} + \frac{1}{2}\overset{0}{O_2} \longrightarrow 2\overset{+2}{Cu}\overset{-2}{O}$$ **(1)**

i.e. Cu_2O acts as a reductant as it reduces O_2 to O^{2-}.

(ii) When heated with Cu_2S, it oxidises S^{2-} to SO_2 and hence, Cu_2O acts as an oxidant.

$$2\overset{+1}{Cu_2}\overset{-2}{O} + \overset{+1}{Cu_2}\overset{-2}{S} \longrightarrow 6\overset{0}{Cu} + \overset{+4}{S}O_2$$ **(1)**

14. **Writing the oxidation number of each element above its symbol in the following reactions**

(a) $$2\overset{+2}{Pb}\overset{-2}{O} + 4\overset{+1}{H}\overset{-1}{Cl} \longrightarrow 2\overset{+2}{Pb}\overset{-1}{Cl_2} + 2\overset{+1}{H_2}\overset{-2}{O}$$
Basic oxide   Acid

In this reaction, oxidation number of each element remains same hence, it is not a redox reaction. In fact, it is an example of **acid-base reaction.** **(1½)**

(b) $$\overset{+4}{Pb}\overset{-2}{O_2} + 4\overset{+1}{H}\overset{-1}{Cl} \longrightarrow \overset{+2}{Pb}\overset{-1}{Cl_2} + \overset{0}{Cl_2} + 2\overset{+1}{H_2}\overset{-2}{O}$$

In PbO_2, Pb is in +4 oxidation state. Due to inert pair effect Pb in +2 oxidation state is more stable.

So, Pb in +4 oxidation state (PbO_2) acts as an oxidising agent.

It oxidises Cl^- to Cl_2 and itself gets reduced to Pb^{2+}.

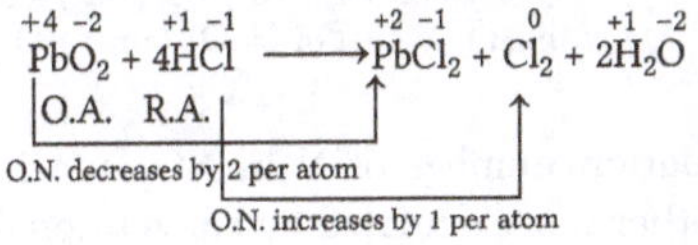

(1½)

15. (i) Oxidation number of S in H_2SO_5 is

$$2(+1) + x + 5(-2) = 0 \text{ or } x = +8$$

But oxidation number of S cannot be more than 6 because S has only 6 valence electrons. This misconception is removed by calculating oxidation number of S by chemical bonding method.

Let us consider the structure of H_2SO_5,

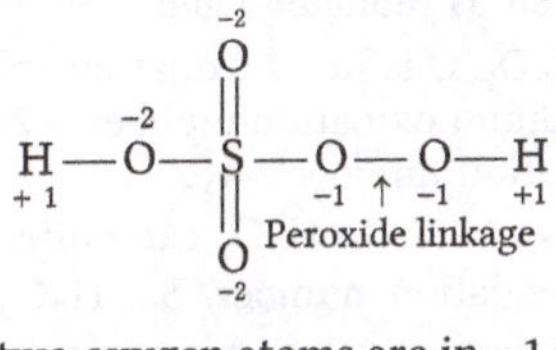

In H_2SO_5, two oxygen atoms are in –1 oxidation state and other three are in –2 oxidation state

Let the oxidation number of S be x.

$$\underset{\text{For H}}{2(+1)} + \underset{\text{For three O}}{3(-2)} + x + \underset{\text{For O—O}}{2(-1)} = 0$$

$$2 + (-6) + x + (-2) = 0$$

$$x = +6$$

Therefore, the oxidation number of S in H_2SO_5 is + 6. **(1)**

(ii) Oxidation number of Cr in $Cr_2O_7^{2-}$ is

$$2x + (-2)7 = -2$$
$$2x = +12$$
$$x = +6$$

Let us consider the structure of $Cr_2O_7^{2-}$ ion

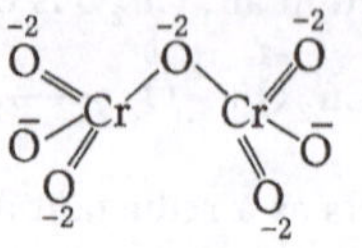

Let the oxidation number of each Cr-atom be x.

$$4(-2) + (-2) + 2(-1) + 2x = 0$$
$$-8 - 2 - 2 + 2x = 0$$
$$2x = +12,\ x = +6$$

Oxidation number of Cr in $Cr_2O_7^{2-}$ is same, i.e. + 6 whether it is calculated by conventional method or by chemical bonding method.

Hence, there is no fallacy. **(1)**

(iii) Oxidation number of N in NO_3^- be x.

$[x + 3(-2) = -1$ or $x = +5]$

Let us consider the structure of NO_3^- ion.

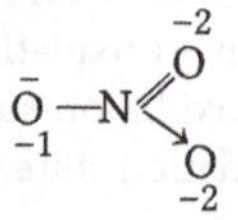

Let the oxidation number of N be x.

$$\underset{\text{For } \bar{O}}{1(-1)} + x + \underset{\text{For } (=O)}{1(-2)} + \underset{\text{For } (\to O)}{1(-2)} = 0$$

$$x = +5$$

Oxidation number of N in NO_2^- ion is same, i.e. + 5 whether it is calculated by conventional method or by chemical bonding method. **(1)**

Hence, there is no fallacy.

16. (i) In SO_2, S is in + 4 oxidation state. It can have minimum oxidation number − 2 and maximum oxidation number is + 6.

Therefore, S in SO_2 can either decrease or increase its oxidation number. So, SO_2 can act both as an oxidising as well as reducing agent.

(ii) In H_2O_2, O is in −1 oxidation state. It can have minimum oxidation number − 2 and maximum oxidation number zero.

Therefore, O in H_2O_2 can either decrease or increase its oxidation number. So, H_2O_2 can act both as an oxidising as well as reducing agent. **(1½)**

(iii) In O_3, O is in zero oxidation state. It cannot increase its oxidation number, it can only decrease its oxidation number from zero to −1 or −2. So, ozone can act only as an oxidising agent.

(iv) In HNO_3, the oxidation number of N is + 5. It is maximum. So, N in HNO_3 can only decrease its oxidation number. So, it can act as an oxidising agent only. **(1½)**

17. The given redox reaction for the galvanic cell is

$$Zn(s) + 2Ag^+(aq) \longrightarrow Zn^{2+}(aq) + 2Ag(s)$$

At anode, Zn is oxidised to Zn^{2+} ions and at cathode, Ag^+ ions are reduced to Ag metal.

Thus, galvanic cell for the above redox reaction may be depicted as $Zn \mid Zn^{2+}(aq) \parallel Ag^+(aq) \mid Ag$

(i) Zn electrode is negatively charged because of the oxidation of Zn to Zn^{2+} ions, electrons are accumulated on zinc electrode. **(1)**

(ii) The ions carry current in the cell. Current flows from Ag electrode to Zn electrode. While electrons flow from Zn electrode to Ag electrode. **(1)**

(iii) Individual reaction at each electrode

At anode, $Zn \longrightarrow Zn^{2+} + 2e^-$

At cathode, $Ag^+(aq) + e^- \longrightarrow Ag(s)$ **(1)**

18. Refer to text on pages 257 and 258. **(2½)**

(i) Carbon has a high affinity towards oxygen so it is generally used as reducing agent. However, in case of highly reactive metals, it cannot be used as a reducing agent. **(1/2)**

(ii) Ozone being a source of oxygen generally behaves as an oxidising agent. **(1/2)**

(iii) As, we know addition of hydrogen is called reduction. So, nascent hydrogen behaves as a reducing agent. **(1/2)**

(iv) Nitric acid is a good oxidant, i.e. oxidising agent as it readily provides oxygen. **(1/2)**

(v) Chlorine can behave as oxidant as well as reductant depending upon the nature of other reactant. **(1/2)**

19. Oxidants (i) H^+ (ii) H_2O_2 (iii) $[Fe(CN)_6]^{3-}$ (iv) F_2 (v) $NaClO_3$ **(2½)**

Reductants (i) Zn (ii) $[Fe(CN)_6]^{4-}$ (iii) H_2O_2 (iv) BrO_3^- (v) I_2 **(2½)**

(For details see electron transfer concept given on page 259).

20. (i) **KI_3**

$$\overset{+1}{K}\overset{x}{I_3}$$

$$1(+1) + 3x = 0 \quad \text{or} \quad x = -1/3$$

Therefore, the average oxidation number of I is $-\frac{1}{3}$.

It is wrong. Let us consider the structure of KI_3.

$\overset{+1}{K}\,(I-I \leftarrow I)^{-1}$, in this structure, coordinate bond is formed between I_2 molecule and I^- ion. Hence, the oxidation number of three I-atoms in KI_3 are 0,0 (in I_2) and −1 respectively. **(1)**

(ii) **$H_2S_4O_6$**

Let the oxidation number of S be x.

$$\overset{+1}{H_2}\overset{x}{S_4}\overset{-2}{O_6}$$

$$2(+1) + 4x + 6(-2) = 0$$
$$4x = +10$$

or $$x = +\frac{10}{4} = +2.5$$

Therefore, the average oxidation state of S be 2.5

Let us consider the structure of $H_2S_4O_6$.

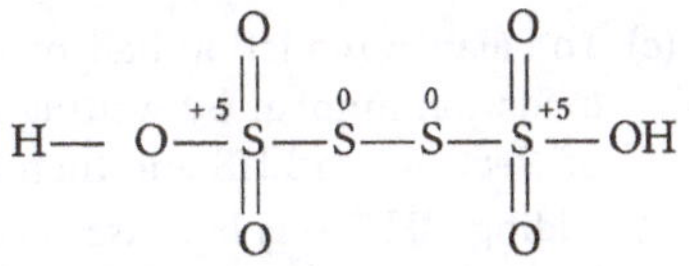

In $H_2S_4O_6$, the oxidation number of each of two S-atoms which are linked with each other by a single bond (in the centre) is zero and each of remaining two S-atoms is + 5.

Hence, the oxidation number of 4 S-atoms in $H_2S_4O_6$ from left to right are + 5, 0, 0 and + 5 respectively. **(1)**

(iii) $\mathbf{Fe_3O_4}$ Let the oxidation number of Fe be x then,

$$x \times 3 + 4(-2) = 0 \Rightarrow x = 8/3$$

Let us consider the structure,

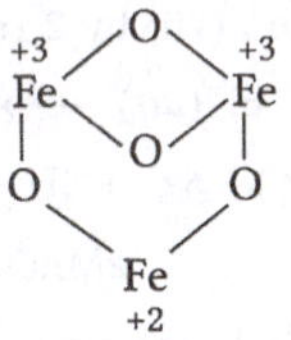

Here, 2 Fe atom have oxidation number of +3 and one Fe atom has oxidation number of +2.

Thus, average O.N of Fe be $(3+3+2)/3$ i.e. 8/3. **(1)**

(iv) $\mathbf{C\underline{H}_3\underline{C}H_2OH}$ $\overset{x}{C_2}\overset{+1}{H_6}\overset{-2}{O}$

$$2x + 6(+1) + 1(-2) = 0$$
$$2x = -4 \text{ or } x = -2$$

Therefore, the average oxidation number of C is – 2.

Let us consider the structure of CH_3CH_2OH.

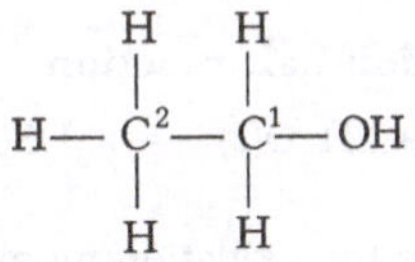

Oxidation number of C_1-atom

$$= 1(+1) + 2(+1) + x + 1(-1) = 0$$

[C_1-atom is attached to one —CH_3 group (oxidation number = + 1), two H-atoms and one — OH group (oxidation number = – 1)]

$$x = -2$$

Oxidation number of C_2-atom $= 3(+1) + x + 1(-1) = 0$

[C_2-atom is attached to three H-atoms and one — CH_2OH group (oxidation number = – 1)]

$$x = -2$$ **(1)**

(v) $\mathbf{\underline{C}H_3\underline{C}OOH}$ $\overset{x}{C_2}\overset{+1}{H_4}\overset{-2}{O_2}$

$$2x + 4(+1) + 2(-2) = 0$$
$$2x + 4 + (-4) = 0 \text{ or } x = 0$$

Therefore, the average oxidation number of C is zero.

Let us consider the structure of CH_3COOH.

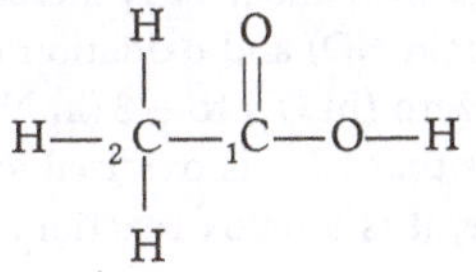

Oxidation number of C_1-atom

$$= 1(+1) + x + 1(-2) + 1(-1) = 0$$

[C_1-atom is attached to one —CH_3 group (oxidation number = + 1), one oxygen atom and one — OH group (oxidation number = – 1)]

$$x = +2$$

Similarly, oxidation number of C_2-atom

$$3(+1) + x + 1(-1) = 0$$
$$\Rightarrow x = -2$$ **(1)**

21. (i) $CuO(s) + H_2(g) \longrightarrow Cu(s) + H_2O(g)$

Assign oxidation numbers of each atom above its symbol.

$$\overset{+2}{Cu}\overset{-2}{O}(s) + \overset{0}{H_2}(g) \longrightarrow \overset{0}{Cu}(s) + \overset{+1}{H_2}\overset{-2}{O}(g)$$

Oxidation number of Cu in CuO is + 2. It decreases from + 2 to zero in Cu.

While oxidation number of hydrogen increases from 0 (in H_2) to + 1 (in H_2O). This shows that CuO is reduced to Cu but H_2 is oxidised to H_2O. Hence, it is an example of redox reaction. **(1)**

(ii) $\overset{+3}{Fe_2}\overset{-2}{O_3}(s) + 3\overset{+2}{C}\overset{-2}{O}(g) \longrightarrow 2\overset{0}{Fe}(s) + 3\overset{+4}{C}\overset{-2}{O_2}(g)$

Oxidation number of Fe decreases from + 3 (in Fe_2O_3) to zero (in Fe) and oxidation number of C increases from + 2 (in CO) to + 4 (in CO_2). This shows that Fe_2O_3 is reduced to Fe and CO is oxidised to CO_2. Hence, it is a redox reaction.

(iii) $4\,\overset{+3}{B}\overset{-1}{Cl_3}(g) + 3\,\overset{+1}{Li}\overset{+3}{Al}\overset{-1}{H_4}(s) \longrightarrow$

$2\,\overset{-3}{B_2}\overset{+1}{H_6}(g) + 3\,\overset{+1}{Li}\overset{-1}{Cl}(s) + 3\,\overset{+3}{Al}\overset{-1}{Cl_3}(s)$ **(1)**

Oxidation number of B decreases from + 3 (in BCl_3) to – 3 (in B_2H_6) and oxidation number of H increases from – 1 (in $LiAlH_4$) to + 1 (in B_2H_6). This shows that BCl_3 is reduced to B_2H_6 and $LiAlH_4$ is oxidised. Hence, it is a redox reaction. **(1)**

(iv) $2\overset{0}{K}(s) + \overset{0}{F_2} \longrightarrow 2\,\overset{+1}{K}\overset{-1}{F}(s)$

Oxidation number of K increases from zero (in K) to + 1 (in KF) and oxidation number of F reduces from zero (in F_2) to – 1 (in KF). This shows that K is oxidised and F_2 is reduced. Hence, it is a redox reaction. **(1)**

(v) $4\overset{-3+1}{NH_3}(g) + 5\overset{0}{O_2}(g) \longrightarrow 4\overset{+2-2}{NO}(g) + 6\overset{+1-2}{H_2O}(g)$

Oxidation number of N increases from -3 (in NH_3) to $+2$ (in NO) and oxidation number of O decreases from zero (in O_2) to -2 (in NO and H_2O). This shows that NH_3 is oxidised and O_2 is reduced. Hence, it is a redox reaction. **(1)**

22. (i) Reduction

$$H_2\overset{-2}{S} + Fe^{3+} \longrightarrow Fe^{2+} + \overset{0}{S} + H^+$$

Oxidation

Here, H_2S is oxidised to sulphur (S), and Fe^{3+} is reduced to Fe^{2+}.

The balanced chemical equation is given as

$$2Fe^{3+} + H_2S \longrightarrow 2Fe^{2+} + S + 2H^+$$

(ii) Reduction

$$I^- + \overset{+5}{IO_3^-} + H^+ \longrightarrow \overset{0}{I_2} + H_2O$$

Oxidation **(2½)**

Here, I^- is oxidised to I_2 and IO_3^- is reduced to I_2.

On solving, we get the following balanced equation

$$2IO_3^- + 10I^- + 12H^+ \longrightarrow 6I_2 + 6H_2O$$

(iii) Reduction

$$\overset{0}{Bi}(s) + \overset{+5}{NO_3^-} + H^+ \longrightarrow \overset{+4}{NO_2} + Bi^{3+} + H_2O$$

Oxidation

Here, $Bi(s)$ is oxidised to Bi^{3+}, while NO_3^- is reduced to NO_2.

The balanced chemical equation is given as

$$Bi(s) + 3NO_3^- + 6H^+ \longrightarrow 3NO_2 + Bi^{3+} + 3H_2O$$

(iv) Reduction

$$I^- + \overset{0}{O_2}(g) + H_2O \longrightarrow \overset{0}{I_2} + \overset{-2}{OH^-}$$

Oxidation

Here, I^- is oxidised to I_2 and $O_2(g)$ is reduced to OH^-.

$$4I^- + O_2(g) + 2H_2O \longrightarrow 4OH^- + 2I_2$$ **(2½)**

23. (i) $\overset{+7}{Mn}O_4^-(aq) + I^-(aq) \longrightarrow \overset{+4}{Mn}O_2(s) + \overset{0}{I_2}(s)$

(in basic medium)

(a) Separate the equation into oxidation half reaction and reduction half reaction.

Oxidation half reaction,

$$I^-(aq) \longrightarrow I_2(s) \quad \text{...(i)}$$

Reduction half reaction,

$$MnO_4^-(aq) \longrightarrow MnO_2(s) \quad \text{...(ii)}$$

(b) To balance I-atoms in the oxidation half reaction, we write it as

$$2I^-(aq) \longrightarrow I_2(s) \quad \text{...(iii)}$$

and to balance oxidation number add $2e^-$ to RHS

$$2I^-(aq) \longrightarrow I_2 + 2e^- \quad \text{...(iv)}$$

There is no need to balance the charge (charge on either side of equation is balanced).

(c) To balance reduction half reaction, first balance oxidation number by writing required number of electrons to LHS and then balance charge by adding OH^- ions because reaction occurs in basic medium.

$$MnO_4^-(aq) + 3e^- \longrightarrow MnO_2(s) \quad \text{...(v)}$$

$$MnO_4^-(aq) + 3e^- \longrightarrow MnO_2 + 4\,OH^- \quad \text{...(vi)}$$

(d) Balance oxygen atoms by adding H_2O

$$MnO_4^- + 3e^- + 2H_2O \longrightarrow MnO_2 + 4\,OH^- \quad \text{...(vii)}$$

By doing so, H atoms are automatically balanced.

(e) Now to equalise number of electrons we multiply oxidation half reaction (iv) by 3 and reduction half reaction (vii) by 2 respectively.

$$6I^-(aq) \longrightarrow 3\,I_2(s) + 6e^- \quad \text{...(viii)}$$

$$2\,MnO_4^-(aq) + 6e^- + 4H_2O(l) \longrightarrow 2MnO_2(s) + 8OH^-(aq) \quad \text{...(ix)}$$

(f) Add two half reactions to obtain net reactions after cancelling electrons on both sides.

$$2\,MnO_4^-(aq) + 6I^-(aq) + 4\,H_2O(l) \longrightarrow 2\,MnO_2(s) + 3\,I_2(s) + 8OH^-(aq)$$

This represents the final balanced redox reaction.

(ii) $MnO_4^-(aq) + SO_2(g) \longrightarrow Mn^{2+}(aq) + HSO_4^-$

(in acidic medium)

Reduction half reaction

$$MnO_4^-(aq) + 8H^+(aq) + 5e^- \longrightarrow Mn^{2+}(aq) + 4H_2O(l) \quad \text{...(i)}$$

Oxidation half reaction

$$SO_2(g) + 2H_2O(l) \longrightarrow HSO_4^-(aq) + 3H^+(aq) + 2e^- \quad \text{...(ii)}$$

(Balance the oxidation number as in (i). After balancing the oxidation number, charge is balanced on either side of equation by adding H^+ ions because the reaction occurs in acidic medium).

Multiply equation (i) by 2 and equation (ii) by 5 and add, we get

$$2MnO_4^-(aq) + H^+(aq) + 5SO_2(g) + 2H_2O(l) \longrightarrow 2Mn^{2+}(aq) + 5HSO_4^-(aq)$$ **(4)**

(iii) By following the steps discussed in (i), we get

$$H_2O_2(aq) + 2\,Fe^{2+}(aq) + 2H^+(aq) \longrightarrow 2\,H_2O(l) + 2\,Fe^{3+}(aq)$$

(iv) By following the steps discussed in (i), we get

$$Cr_2O_7^{2-}(aq) + 2H^+(aq) + 3\,SO_2(g) \longrightarrow 2\,Cr^{3+}(aq) + 3\,SO_4^{2-}(aq) + H_2O(l)$$ **(1)**

24. (i) **Ion electron method** Write the skeleton equation for the given reaction.

$$MnO_4^-(aq) + SO_2(g) \longrightarrow Mn^{2+}(aq) + HSO_4^-(aq)$$

Find out the elements which undergo change in O.N.

O.N. of Mn decreases by 5

$$2\overset{+7}{Mn}O_4^-(aq) + \overset{+4}{S}O_2(g) \longrightarrow \overset{2+}{Mn}(aq) + H\overset{+6}{S}O_4^-(aq)$$

O.N. of S increases by 2

Divide the given skeleton into two half equations.

Reduction half equation : $MnO_4^-(aq) \longrightarrow Mn^{2+}(aq)$

Oxidation half equation : $SO_2(g) \longrightarrow HSO_4^-(aq)$

To balance reduction half equation

In acidic medium, balance H and O-atoms

$$MnO_4^-(aq) + 8H^+(aq) + 5e^- \longrightarrow Mn^{2+}(aq) + H_2O(l)$$

To balance oxidation half equation.

$$SO_2(g) + 2H_2O(l) \longrightarrow HSO_4^-(aq) + 3H^+(aq) + 2e^-$$

To balance the complete reaction.

$$2MnO_4(aq) + 16H^+(aq) + 10e^- \longrightarrow Mn^{2+}(aq) + 8H_2O(l)$$
$$5SO_2(g) + 10H_2O(l) \longrightarrow 5HSO_4^-(aq) + 15H^+(aq) + 10e^-$$

$$2MnO_4^-(aq) + 5SO_2(g) + 2H_2O(l) + H^+(aq) \longrightarrow 2Mn^{2+}(aq) + 5HSO_4^-(aq)$$ (1½)

(ii) **Oxidation number method** Write the skeleton equation for the given reaction.

$$N_2H_4(l) + ClO_3^-(aq) \longrightarrow NO(g) + Cl^-(g)$$

O.N. increases by 4 per N-atom

$$\overset{-2}{N_2}H_4(l) + \overset{+5}{Cl}O_3^-(aq) \longrightarrow \overset{+2}{N}O(g) + \overset{-1}{Cl^-}(aq)$$

O.N. decreases by 6 per Cl-atom

Multiply NO by 2 because in N_2H_4 there are 2N atoms

$$N_2H_4(l) + ClO_3^-(aq) \longrightarrow 2NO(g) + Cl^-(aq)$$

Total increase in O.N. of N = $2 \times 4 = 8$ ($8e^-$ lost)

Total decrease in O.N. of Cl = $1 \times 6 = 6$ ($6e^-$ gain)

Therefore, to balance increase or decrease in O.N. multiply N_2H_4 by 3, 2NO by 3 and ClO_3^-, Cl^- by 4

$$3N_2H_4(l) + 4ClO_3^-(aq) \longrightarrow 6NO(g) + 4Cl^-(aq)$$

Balance O and H-atoms by adding 6 H_2O to RHS

$$3N_2H_4(l) + 4ClO_3^-(aq) \longrightarrow 6NO(g) + 4Cl^-(aq) + 6H_2O(l)$$ (2)

(iii) **Ion electron method** Write the skeleton equation for the given reaction.

$$Cl_2O_7(g) + H_2O_2(aq) \longrightarrow ClO_2^-(aq) + O_2(g)$$

Find out the elements which undergo a change in O.N.

O. N. of Cl decreases by 4 per Cl-atom

$$\overset{+7}{Cl_2}\overset{-7}{O_7}(g) + \overset{+1}{H_2}\overset{-1}{O_2}(aq) \longrightarrow \overset{+3}{Cl}\overset{-2}{O_2^-}(aq) + O_2(g)$$

O.N. of O increases by 1per O-atom

Divide the given skeleton equation into two half equations.

Reduction half equation : $Cl_2O_7 \longrightarrow ClO_2^-$

Oxidation half equation : $H_2O_2 \longrightarrow O_2$

To balance the reduction half equation

$$Cl_2O_7(g) + 6H^+(aq) + 8e^- \longrightarrow 2ClO_2^-(aq) + 3H_2O(l)$$

To balance the oxidation half equation

$$H_2O_2(aq) \longrightarrow O_2(g) + 2H^+ + 2e^-$$

To balance the complete reaction

$$Cl_2O_7(g) + 6H^+(aq) + 8e^- \longrightarrow 2ClO_2^-(aq) + 3H_2O(l)$$
$$4H_2O_2(aq) \longrightarrow 4O_2(g) + 8H^+(aq) + 8e^-$$

$$Cl_2O_7(g) + 4H_2O_2(aq) \longrightarrow 2ClO_2^-(aq) + 3H_2O(l) + 4O_2(g) + 2H^+ + (aq)$$

This represents the balanced redox reaction. (1½)

25. (i) Oxidation of toluene to benzoic acid in acidic medium.

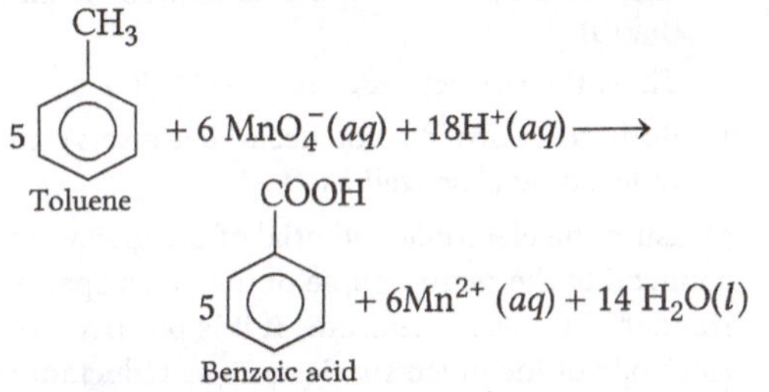

Oxidation of toluene to benzoic acid in basic and neutral medium.

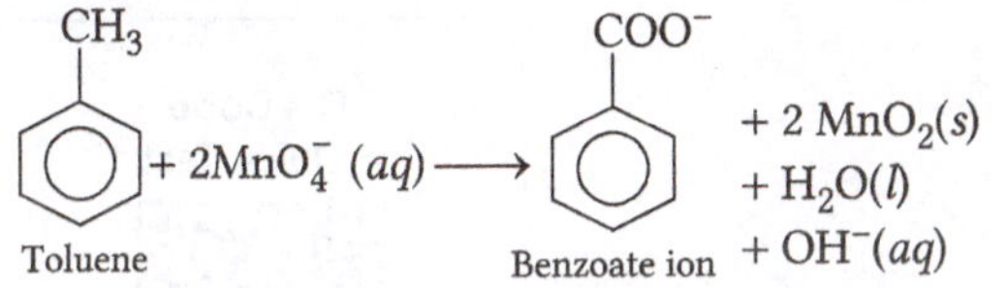

On industrial scale, alcoholic potassium permanganate is preferred to acidic or alkaline because in the presence of alcohol, both the reactants $KMnO_4$ and $C_6H_5CH_3$ are mixed very well and form homogeneous solution.

In homogeneous medium, reaction takes place faster than in heterogeneous medium. Further more in neutral medium, OH^- ions are produced in the reaction itself. (2½)

(ii)
$$\underset{\text{(from inorganic mixture)}}{\underset{\text{Sodium chloride}}{2NaCl}} + 2H_2SO_4 \longrightarrow 2NaHSO_4 + 2HCl$$

HCl is a weak reducing agent. It cannot reduce H_2SO_4 to SO_2, that's why pungent smelling gas HCl is obtained.

$$\underset{\text{(from inorganic mixture)}}{\underset{\text{Sodium bromide}}{2NaBr}} + 2H_2SO_4 \longrightarrow 2NaHSO_4 + 2HBr$$

$$2HBr + H_2SO_4 \longrightarrow \underset{\text{Red vapours}}{Br_2\uparrow} + SO_2\uparrow + 2H_2O$$

HBr is a strong reducing agent, it reduces H_2SO_4 to SO_2 and is itself oxidised to Br_2. That's why we get red vapours of bromine when conc. H_2SO_4 reacts with inorganic mixture containing bromide salt. (2½)

26. (i) The electrochemical series or redox activity is based on the decreasing order of reduction potentials. This means that the species which gets reduced is higher in the electrochemical series as compared to the other which is to be oxidised (lose electrons).

In reaction (a), B^+ gets reduced by A and therefore B is higher than A in electrochemical series.

In reaction (b), D^+ gets reduced by B and therefore, D is higher in the electrochemical series than B.

In reaction (c), C^+ does not get reduced by D, therefore, C is lower than D in electrochemical series. But according to reaction (d), C^+ gets reduced by B and therefore, C is higher in electrochemical series than B.

Thus, the correct order is $D > C > B > A$. (3)

(ii) Both reactions do not occur because A cannot be reduced by C as well as D. (2)

27. Measure the electrode potential of the given species by connecting the redox couple of the given species with standard hydrogen electrode. If it is positive, the electrode of the given species acts as reductant and if it is negative, it acts as an oxidant.

Find the electrode potentials of the other given species in the same way, compare the values and determine their comparative strength as an reductant or oxidant.

e.g. Measurement of standard electrode potential of Zn^{2+}/Zn electrode using SHE as a reference electrode.

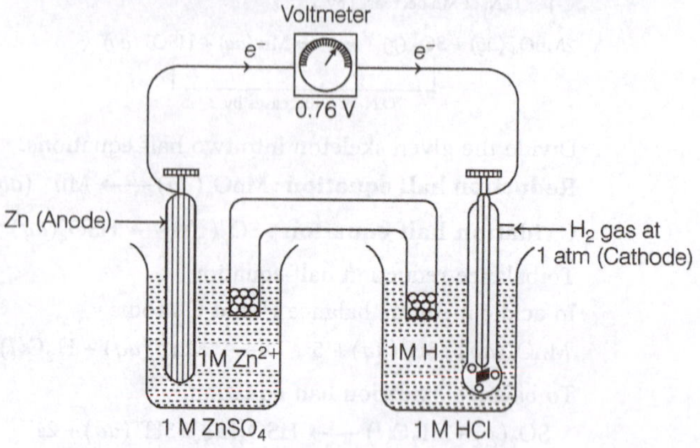

The EMF of the cell comes out to be 0.76 V. (reading of voltmeter is 0.76 V). Zn^{2+}/Zn couple acts as anode and SHE acts as cathode.

$$\therefore \quad E^\circ_{cell} = 0.76 = E^\circ_{cathode} - E^\circ_{anode}$$

$$0.76 = 0 - E^\circ_{anode}$$

$$E^\circ_{anode} = -0.76\text{ V}$$

$$E^\circ_{Zn^{2+}/Zn} = -0.76\text{V}.$$

(5)

QR Code for Quick Test 1

QR Code for Quick Test 2

QR Code for Quick Test 3

SELF ASSESSMENT TEST

Objective Type Questions [1 Mark]

1. Which of the following element undergoes oxidation in the reaction given?

$$SnCl_2 + 2FeCl_2 \longrightarrow SnCl_4 + 2FeCl_2$$

(a) iron (b) tin (c) chlorine (d) ferrous

2. Out of the given processes, which does not involve either oxidation or reduction.
(a) Formation of slaked lime from quick lime.
(b) Heating mercuric oxide
(c) Formation of manganese chloride from manganese oxide.
(d) Formation of zinc from zinc blende.

3. Match Column I with Column II for the oxidation states of central atoms.

Column I		Column II	
A.	$Cr_2O_7^{2-}$	1.	+3
B.	MnO_4^-	2.	+7
C.	VO_3^-	3.	+5
D.	FeF_6^{3-}	4.	+6

Codes

	A	B	C	D		A	B	C	D
(a)	2	1	4	3	(b)	4	3	1	2
(c)	4	2	3	1	(d)	4	3	2	1

4. A standard reduction electrode potentials of four metals are given as $A = -0.25$ V, $B = -0.14$ V, $C = -0.126$, $D = -0.402$ V. Name the metal that displaces A from its aqueous solution is

(a) A (b) B (c) C (d) D

5. For the redox reaction,
$MnO_4^- + C_2O_4^{2-} + H^+ \longrightarrow$
$Mn^{2+} + CO_2 + H_2O$ the correct coefficients of the given species for the balanced reaction are

	MnO_4^-	$C_2O_4^{2-}$	CO_2
(a)	2	10	5
(b)	10	5	2
(c)	5	10	2
(d)	2	5	10

Assertion-Reason [1 Mark]

■ **Directions** (Q. Nos. 6-8) In the following questions, an Assertion (A) is followed by a corresponding Reason (R). Use the following keys to choose the appropriate answer.

(a) Both (A) and (R) are correct and (R) is the correct explanation of (A).
(b) Both (A) and (R) are correct but (R) is not the correct explanation of (A).
(c) (A) is correct and (R) is incorrect.
(d) (A) is incorrect and (R) is correct.

6. **Assertion** (A) The decomposition of hydrogen peroxide to form water and oxygen is an example of disproportionation reaction.

Reason (R) The oxygen of peroxide is in −1 oxidation state and it is converted to zero oxidation state in O_2 and −2 oxidation state in H_2O.

7. **Assertion** (A) In the species, Br_3O_8 each of two extreme bromine exhibits oxidation state of +6 and the middle bromine of +4.

Reason (R) The average of three oxidation numbers of bromine of the Br_3O_8 is 16/3.

8. **Assertion** (A) In the reaction between potassium permanganate and potassium iodide, permanganate ions act as oxidising agent.

Reason (R) Oxidation state of manganese changes from +2 to +7 during the reaction.

Short Answer Type I Questions [2 Marks]

9. Nitric acid acts only as an oxidising agent while nitrous acid acts both as an oxidising as well as reducing agent. Explain.

10. Find the value of n in

$$4MnO_4^- + 8H^+ + ne^- \longrightarrow Mn^{2+} + 4H_2O$$

11. Can Fe^{3+} oxidise Br^- to Br_2 at 1 M concentrations?

$$E^\circ_{(Fe^{3+}/Fe^{2+})} = 0.77 \text{ V and } E^\circ_{(Br/Br^-)} = 1.09 \text{ V}$$

Short Answer Type II Questions [3 Marks]

12. Two half-cells are $Al^{3+}(aq)/Al$ and $Mg^{2+}(aq)/Mg$. The reduction potentials of these half-cells are -1.66 V and -2.36 V respectively. Calculate the cell potential. Write the cell reaction also.

13. How many millimoles of potassium dichromate is required to oxidise 24 mL of 0.5 M Mohr's salt solution in acidic medium?

14. Does the oxidation number of an element in any molecule or any polyatomic ion represent the actual charge on it ?

Also write the oxidation and reduction half reactions from the following redox reaction.

$$2Fe + 2H_2 + O_2 \longrightarrow 2Fe(OH)_2$$

Case-Study [4 Marks]

15. The concept of electron transfer is found unable to explain the redox changes or electron shift in case of covalent compounds. To explain these changes a new concept, called oxidation number is introduced. Oxidation number is defined as the charge that an atom of the element has in its ion or appear to have when present in the combined state with other atoms.

Each atom that participates in an oxidation-reduction is assigned an oxidation number that reflects its ability to acquire, donate or share electrons. Certain elements assume the same oxidation number in different compounds. Other notably the non-metals and the transition elements, can assume a variety of oxidation numbers. In the nomenclature of inorganic chemistry, the oxidation number of an element that may exist is more than one oxidation state is indicated by a roman numeral in parenthesis after the name of the element.

(i) What is the oxidation number of underlined element in $K\underline{O}_2$?

(ii) What is the oxidation state of iron in brown ring complex compound, $[Fe(H_2O)_5NO]SO_4$?

Or

What is the change in oxidation number of Mn when $KMnO_4$ is reduced with oxalic acid in acidic medium?

(iii) What is the oxidation state of sulphur in sodium tetrathionate, $[Na_2S_4O_6]$?

Long Answer Type Questions [5 Marks]

16. (a) All decomposition reactions are not redox reactions. Give justification.

(b) Explain why

$3Fe_3O_4(s) + 8Al(s) \longrightarrow 9Fe(s) + 4Al_2O_3(s)$ is an oxidation reaction?

(c) Fluorine reacts with ice and results in the change.

$$H_2O(s) + F_2(g) \longrightarrow HF(g) + HOF(g)$$

Justify that this reaction is a redox reaction.

17. (a) Calculate the oxidation number of phosphorus in the following species.

(i) HPO_3^{2-}

(ii) PO_4^{3-}

(b) What sorts of information can you draw from the following reaction ?

$$(CN)_2(g) + 2OH^-(aq) \longrightarrow CN^-(aq) + CNO^-(aq) + H_2O(l)$$

Answers

1. (b) **2.** (a) **3.** (c) **4.** (d) **5.** (d) **6.** (a) **7.** (a) **8.** (c) **10.** $n = -5$

12. $+0.70$ V **13.** 2 millimoles

08 CHAPTER

Organic Chemistry : Some Basic Principles and Techniques

Carbon is capable to form millions of compounds with other heteroatoms (like H, O, N, S, P and halogens). These compounds are called **organic compounds** and studied separately in a branch called **organic chemistry**. In this chapter, we shall study about some basic principles and properties of organic

YOUR STUDY GOALS

8.1 Vital Force Theory of Organic Compounds
8.2 Tetravalence of Carbon : Shapes of Organic Compounds
8.3 Structural Representations of Organic Compounds
8.4 Classification of Organic Compounds
8.5 Nomenclature of Organic Compounds
8.6 Isomerism
8.7 Fundamental Concepts in Organic Reaction Mechanism
8.8 Fission of a Covalent Bond
8.9 Resonance
8.10 Methods of Purification of Organic Compounds
8.11 Qualitative Analysis of Organic Compounds
8.12 Detection of Other Elements : Lassaigne's Test
8.13 Quantitative Analysis

YOUR PRACTICE GOAL

- Objective Type Questions (32 Qs ; 21 MCQs, 9 A-R, 2 Case-Study)
- Subjective Type Questions (30 Qs; 10 SA-I, 15 SA-II, 5LA)

8.1 Vital Force Theory of Organic Compounds

Organic chemistry deals with the study of such compounds (hydrocarbons) and their derivatives.

Organic compounds are vital for sustaining life on earth and include complex molecules like genetic information DNA and proteins that constitute essential compounds of our blood, muscles and skin.

In 1815, a Swedish chemist Berzilius proposed that the organic compound could be obtained only from living organisms in the presence of a mysterious force. This mysterious force was known as **vital force**. The theory was called **vital force theory**.

This theory was not questioned until 1828, when Friedrich Wohler synthesised an **organic compound urea** by heating an inorganic compound ammonium cyanate.

$$\underset{\text{Ammonium cyanate}}{NH_4CNO} \xrightarrow{\text{Heat}} \underset{\text{Urea}}{NH_2—CO—NH_2}$$

The preparation of urea gave a new direction to the chemist who started working for the preparation of other organic compounds. Later after the synthesis of acetic acid and methane vital force theory was found incorrect.

Further, the development of electronic theory of covalent bonding directed organic chemistry into its modern shape.

8.2 Tetravalence of Carbon : Shapes of Organic Compounds

The electronic configuration of carbon is $1s^2 2s^2 2p^2$. In all of its known stable compounds, carbon is tetravalent. The tetravalency of carbon can be explained by exciting one of the paired $2s$ electrons to empty $2p$-orbital by absorbing energy from the system (according to classical concept of bonding). However, 4 equivalent C—H bonds in CH_4 is explained on the basis of concept of **hybridisation** (according to modern concept of bonding).

Carbon shares these electrons with other elements to form covalent compounds. The effect of hybridisation on different bond characteristics is tabulated below.

Hybridisation and Bond Characteristics

Bond	Hybridisation	Number of σ-bonds formed by hybrid orbital	Geometry	*s*-character, *p*-character	C—C bond length (pm)	C—H bond length (pm)
Single (—)	sp^3	4	Tetrahedral	25%, 75%	154	111
Double (=)	sp^2	3	Trigonal planar	33.3%, 66.7%	134	110
Triple (≡)	sp	2	Linear	50%, 50%	120	108

From the table, it can be concluded that

- sp-hybrid orbitals have maximum s-character, so it is closer to the nucleus. Therefore, it forms shorter and stronger bond as compared to both sp^2 and sp^3-hybrid orbitals which has more p-character that result in the formation of longer and weaker bonds.
- The sp^2-hybrid orbital is intermediate in s-character between sp and sp^3. Therefore, the length and enthalpy of the bond formed by sp^2-orbitals are also intermediate between them.

  The hybridisation also afffects the electronegativity of carbon. The s-character is directly proportional to the electronegativity.

  Thus, order of electronegativity of hybrid orbitals is

  $$sp > sp^2 > sp^3.$$

  This relative electronegativity is reflected in several physical and chemical properties of the molecules concerned.

σ- and π-Bonding in Organic Compounds

Carbon has a unique property that it can form both types of covalent bonds, i.e. the σ (called sigma, the bond formed by the linear or axial or end to end overlapping of orbitals) and the π (pi, the bond formed by the parallel or sidewise overlapping of orbitals) bonds.

- Single bonds are sigma bonds (σ).
- Double bond contains one σ and one π-bond.
- Triple bond contains one σ and two π-bonds.

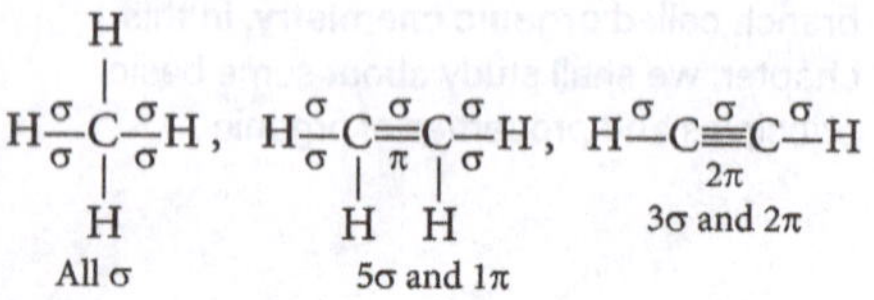

Some Characteristic Features of π-Bonds

- **Side-by side overlap** Forms from lateral overlap of p-orbitals.
- **Weaker than sigma bond** Less effective overlap makes pi bonds weaker which results from direct overlap along the bond axis.
- **Restricts rotation** Pi bonds prevents the free rotation of bonded atoms because rotating would break the side-to side overlap of the orbitals.
- **Existence in double and triple bonds** Double bonds have one pi bond, triple bonds have two.
- **Electron density above and below the bond axis** In a pi bond, the electron density is concentrated above and below the axis of the bonded atoms rather than along the axis itself, as seen in sigma bonds.
- **Shortens bond length** Pi bonds shorten the overall bond length in compounds because additional bonds pull the atom closer.

TEACHER'S TIP

σ-bonds formed by axial or linear overlapping so, it is strong in nature. π-bonds are weaker than σ-bonds.

8.3 Structural Representations of Organic Compounds

Structures of organic compounds are represented in the following way

Two-Dimensional Representation [Complete, Condensed and Bond-Line Structural Formulae]

There are several ways to represent the organic compounds. The following three ways are used for 2-D structural representation of organic compounds.

(i) Dash Structure or Complete Structure

If in the Lewis structure or dot structure of an organic compound, all the bond pairs are replaced by a dash (—) and omitting the unshared electron pairs, then the obtained structure is called **dash structure** or **complete structure.** (Here, a single dash shows single bond, double dash shows double bond and triple dash shows triple bond).

e.g. The Lewis dot structure and dash structure of ethane are

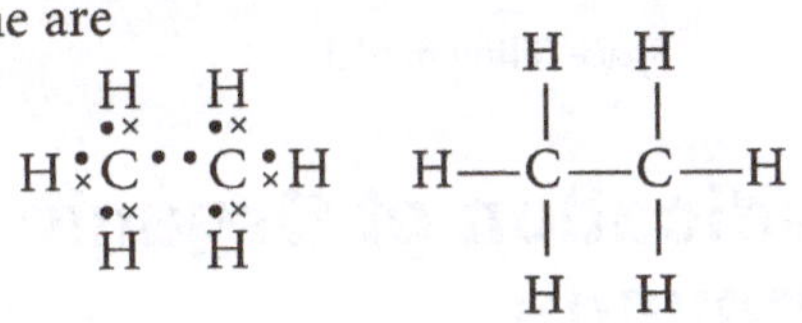

Similarly, we can write dash structures of ethene, ethyne and methanol that are as follows

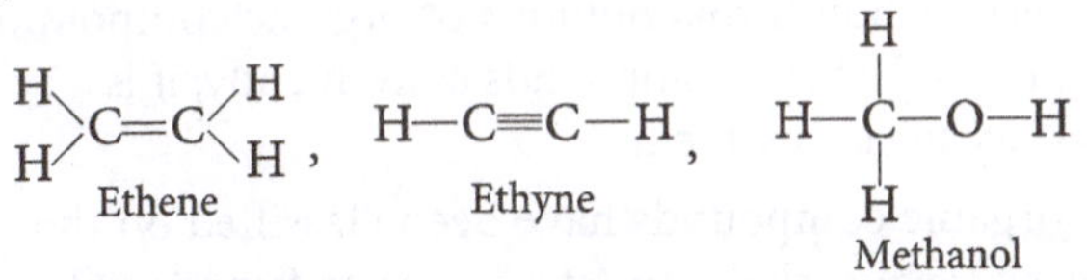

(ii) Condensed Structure

When all the bonds (except double and triple bonds) are omitted and the number of identical groups attached to an atom is represented by a subscript, the obtained structure is called **condensed structure** or **condensed structural formula.**

Thus, ethane, ethene, ethyne and methanol in their condensed form can be written as

CH_3CH_3;	$H_2C{=}CH_2$;	$HC{\equiv}CH$;	CH_3OH
Ethane	Ethene	Ethyne	Methanol

Similarly, $CH_3CH_2CH_2CH_2CH_2CH_3$ can be further condensed to $CH_3(CH_2)_4CH_3$.

(iii) Bond Line Structure

In these structures, the carbon-carbon bonds are represented by *zig-zag* lines.

In this structure a single, double and triple bonds are represented by single, double and triple lines.

The intersection and the endings represents carbon atoms carrying appropriate number of hydrogen atoms requires to satisfy the valency of carbon atoms. Moreover, the hetero atoms (O, Cl, N etc) and the hydrogen atoms attached to them are clearly written as such.

e.g. The bond line and condensed structures of 3-methyloctane are

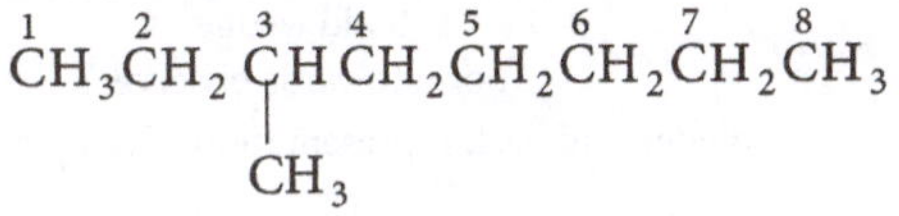

So, draw 7 lines in *zig-zag* manner.

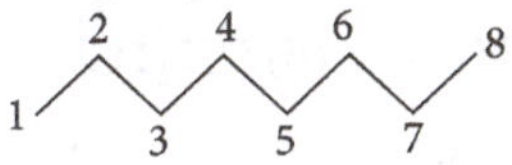

Attach 1 vertical line at carbon-3.

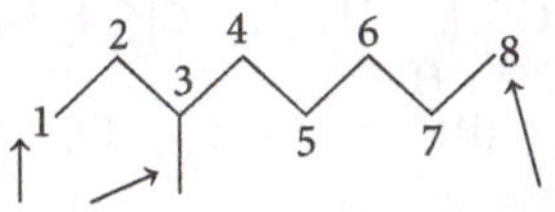

Terminals represent methyl group (CH_3).

In cyclic compounds, the bond line formulas can be represented as

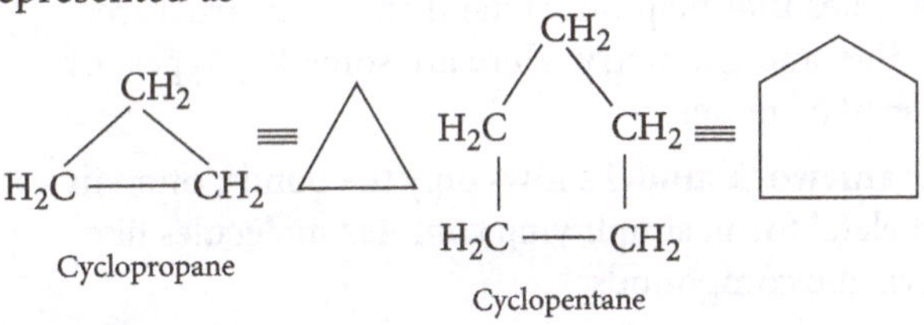

Three-Dimensional Representation of Organic Molecules

To represent a two dimensional structure of organic molecule three-dimensionally on paper (3-D), following conventions should be kept in mind.

- Normal lines (—) always shows the groups lying in the plane of the paper.

- Solid-wedge (—) shows the bond projecting out of the plane of paper and towards the observer.
- Dashed-wedge (┈) also, shows the bond projecting out of the plane of paper but it is away from the observer.
- The broad end of the wedge (both solid-wedge and dashed-wedge) is towards the observer.

Keeping the above conventions in mind, the 3-D structure (wedge and dash representation) of methane (CH_4) molecule on paper can be represented as

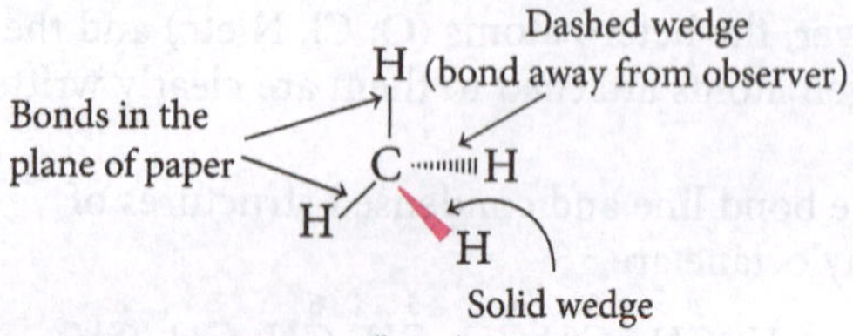

Wedge and dash representation of CH_4

Example 1 **Write three-dimensional (wedge-dashed wedge-line) representations for the following.**

(i) CH_3CH_2OH (ii) CH_2FCl

Sol.

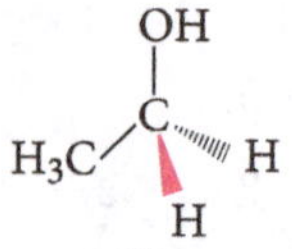

(i)

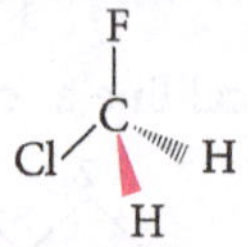

(ii)

Molecular Models

Molecular models are visual representation of molecules that help understand their 3D structure, bonding and geometry. Here are some key types of molecular model.

- **Framework model** shows only the bonds, often in skeletal form, simplifying complex molecules like organic compounds.

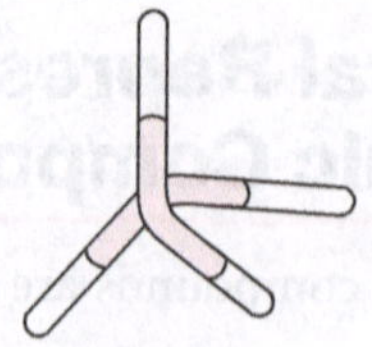

Framework model

- **Ball and stick model** shows atoms as balls and bonds as sticks, clarifying bond angles.

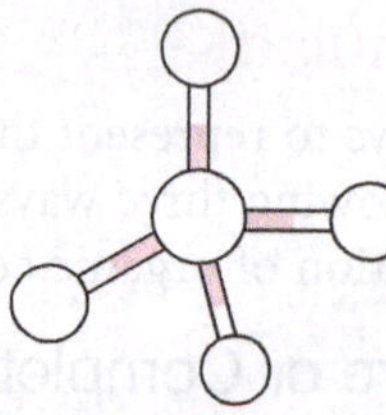

Ball and stick model

- **Space filling model** uses overlapping spheres to represent actual atomic sizes and molecular shape.

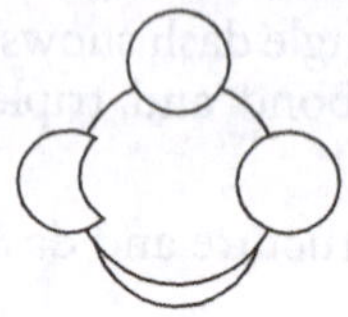

Space filling model

8.4 Classification of Organic Compounds

Due to its unique catenation power (power of self linking), carbon forms millions of organic compounds thus, to study these compounds conveniently, it is necessary to classify them.

The organic compounds have been classified on the basis of **carbon skeleton** (structure) or **functional groups with the concept of homology.**

Classification Based on Carbon Skeleton

On the basis of carbon skeleton, organic compounds are classified into different classes as shown in the chart.

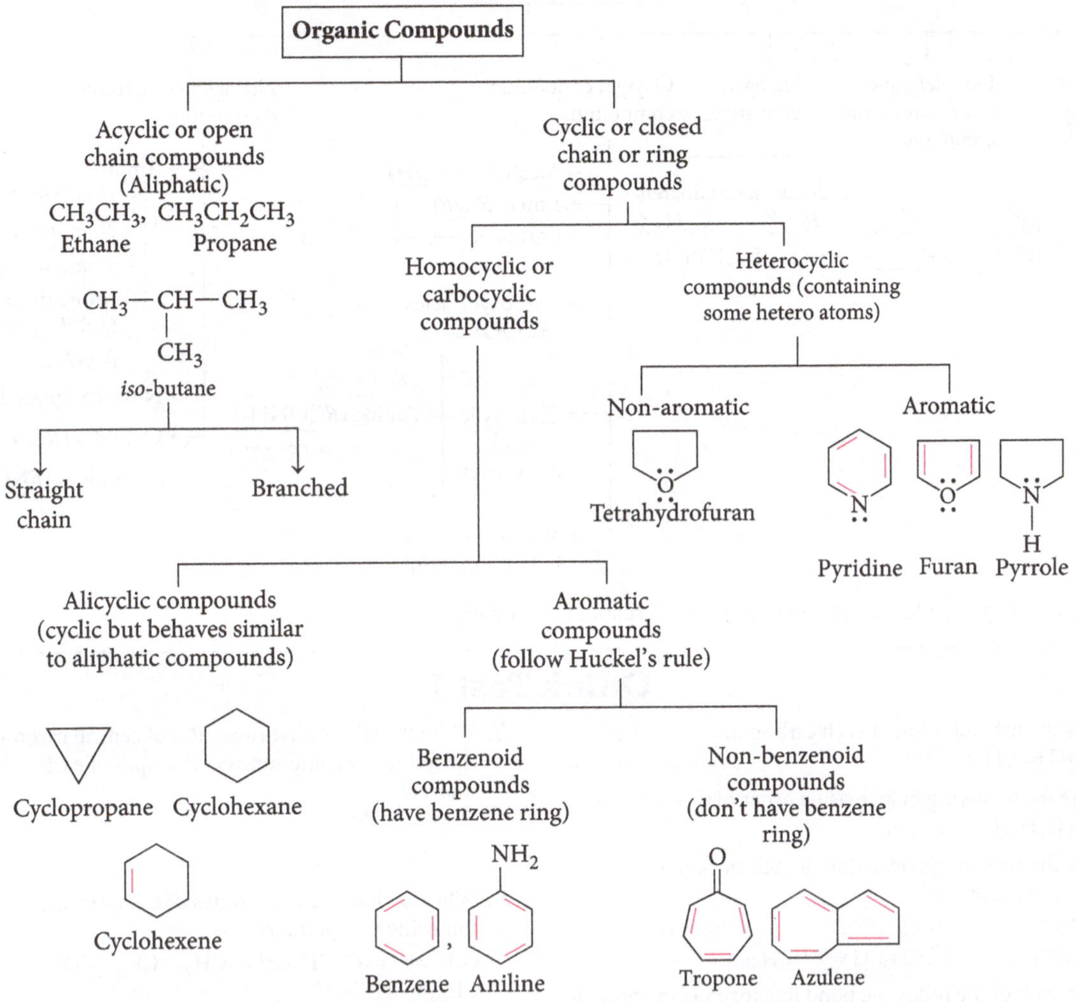

Classification Based on Functional Groups

Before discussing this type of classification, it is important to know about the **functional group** and **homologous series.**

Functional Group

An atom or a group of atom present in an organic compound, which is responsible for the chemical properties of the compound is called the **functional group**. e.g. Hydroxyl group (—OH) etc.

Homologous Series

The group or series of compounds having characteristic functional group is called the **homologous series** and the members of the series are called **homologous.**

e.g. The homologous series of alkanes is

CH_4 (Methane), C_2H_6 (Ethane)

The general characteristics of a homologous series are

- All the members of a series contain same elements and the functional group.
- All the members can be represented by a single general formula. e.g. C_nH_{2n+2} is the general formula for alkanes.
- The molecular formula of each homologue (member) differs from its previous and successive member by $—CH_2$ unit, i.e. their molecular mass differs by 14 units.

On the basis of functional groups, organic compounds are classified into following families or homologous series.

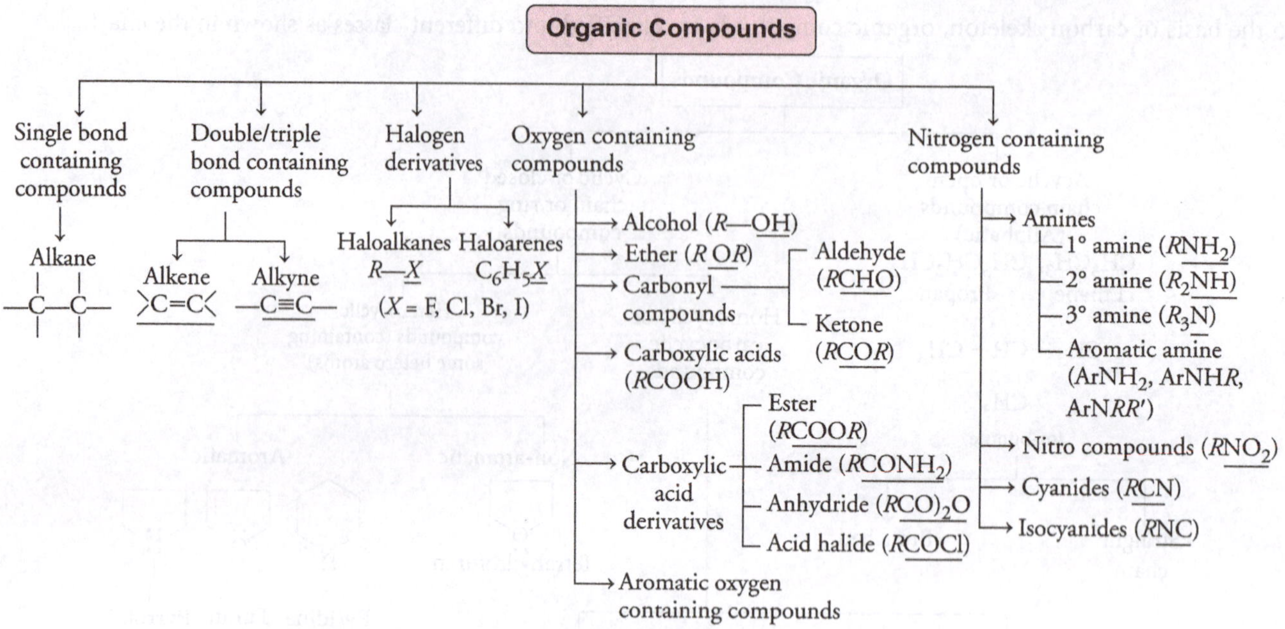

(Underlined groups are the functional groups of respective series).

Quick Test 1

1. What is the hybridisation of each carbon in $H_2C=C=CH_2$? *NCERT Exemplar*

2. Arrange the following in increasing order of C—C bond length : C_2H_6, C_2H_4, C_2H_2.

3. What is the type of hybridisation of each carbon in the following compounds?

(i) CH_3Cl (ii) $(CH_3)_2CO$ (iii) CH_3CN
(iv) $HCONH_2$ (v) $CH_3CH=CHCN$

4. Expand each of the following bond line formula to show all the atoms including carbon and hydrogen.

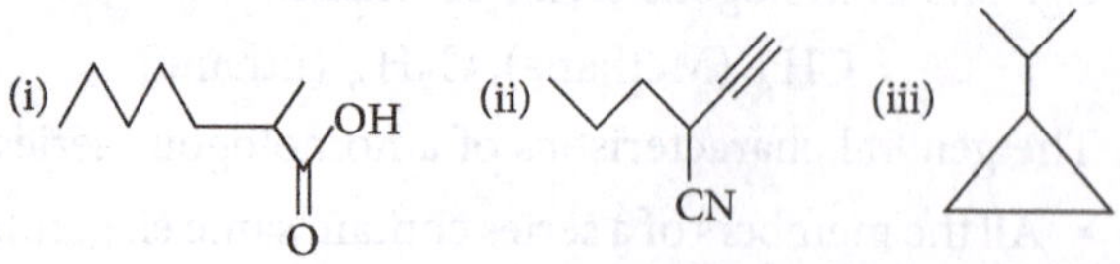

5. For each of the following compounds, write a condensed formula and also their bond-line formula.

(i) $HOCH_2CH_2CH_2CH(CH_3)CH(CH_3)CH_3$

(ii) $N\equiv C—CH(OH)—C\equiv N$ *NCERT*

6. Indicate the σ- and π-bonds in the following molecules.

C_6H_6, C_6H_{12}, CH_2Cl_2, $CH_2=C=CH_2$, CH_3NO_2, $HCONHCH_3$ *NCERT*

7. Write the state of hybridisation of central carbon atom in the following compounds and shapes of each of the molecules.

(i) $CH_3—C(=O)—CH_3$ (ii) $(CH_3)_3CCl$ (iii) $HC\equiv N$

8. What are hybridisation states of each carbon atom in the following compounds?

$CH_2=C=O$, $CH_3CH=CH_2$, $(CH_3)_2CO$, $CH_2=CHCN$, C_6H_6 *NCERT*

9. Draw all polygon formula for the molecular formula C_5H_{10}.

10. Identify the functional groups in the following compounds.

(i)
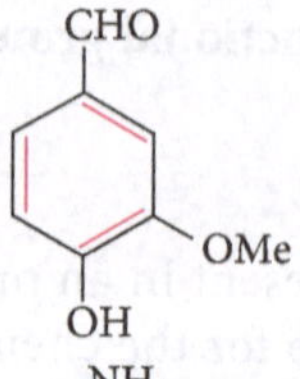

(ii)
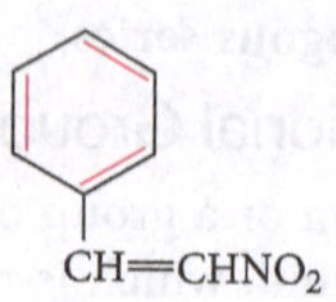

(iii)
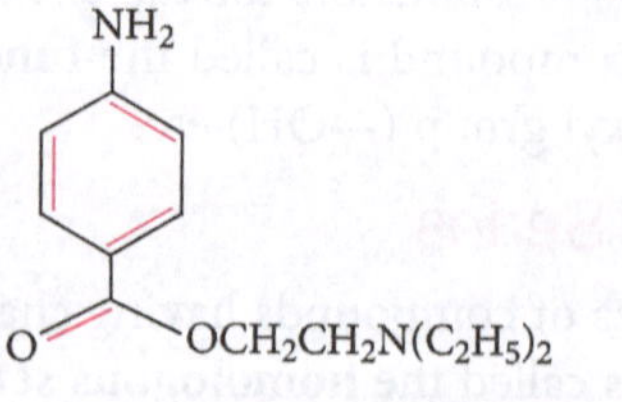

For Solutions, See QR Code on Pg. 341

8.5 Nomenclature of Organic Compounds

Out of several systems, the most advanced and systematic is the **IUPAC system of nomenclature,** which was proposed by IUPAC (International Union of Pure and Applied Chemistry).

Before going in detail of IUPAC system, we discuss the oldest system of nomenclature, called the **trivial system**.

Trivial System of Nomenclature

It is the oldest system of nomenclature also called **common names** in which the names of organic compounds were assigned on the basis of their source or some properties. e.g.

- Acetic acid is named so because it is the chief constituent of vinegar (Latin Acetum).
- Similarly, citric acid got its name from citrus fruits and formic acid from red ants (Latin name for which is formica).
- Butyric acid got its name from butter (butyrum).
- Also, Buckminster fullerene is a common name of C_{60} cluster as its structure is similar to the geodesic domes, desinged by the famous architect R. Buckminster fuller.

Trivial names of some other organic compounds are tabulated below.

Common or Trivial Names of Some Organic Compounds

Compound	Common name	Compound	Common name
CH_4	Methane	$CHCl_3$	Chloroform
$H_3CCH_2CH_2CH_3$	*n*-butane	C_6H_6	Benzene
$(H_3C)_2CHCH_3$	*Iso*-butane	$C_6H_5OCH_3$	Anisole
$(H_3C)_4C$	*Neo*-pentane	$C_6H_5COCH_3$	Acetophenone
$H_3CCH_2CH_2OH$	*n*-propyl alcohol	$CH_3OCH_2CH_3$	Ethyl methyl ether
HCHO	Formaldehyde	$(H_3C)_2CO$	Acetone

The IUPAC System of Nomenclature

A systematic name of an organic compound is generally derived by identifying the parent hydrocarbon (or alkane) and the functional groups attached to it.

After that, the name of parent hydrocarbon is modified by using suitable prefixes and suffixes to get the actual name of the compound.

An example of a molecule showing parent chain and functional group is given below.

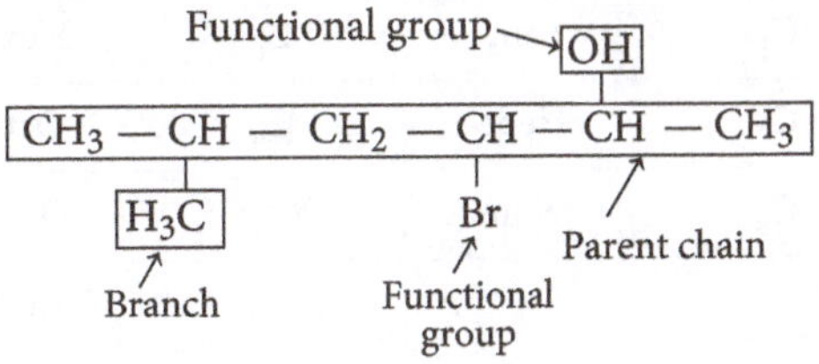

The speciality of this system is that one organic compound can have only one IUPAC name. It mainly consists of following parts.

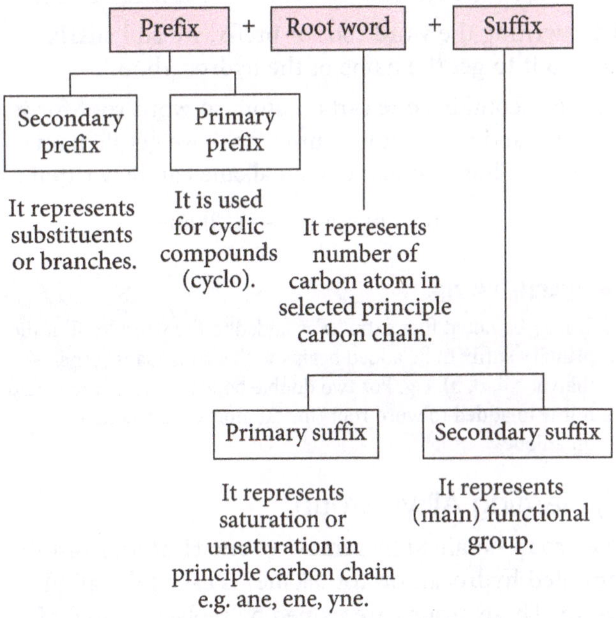

IUPAC Nomenclature of Alkanes or Saturated Hydrocarbons

(i) Nomenclature of Straight Chain Hydrocarbons (or Parent Hydrocarbon)

To write the name of straight chain hydrocarbon, first we write the '**word root**' or '**prefix**' that indicates the number of carbon atoms present in that chain (except from CH_4 to C_4H_{10}, where the prefixes are derived from trivial names) with the help of following table.

Word Root Representing C-atoms

Chain length	Word root	Chain length	Word root
C_1	Meth–	C_2	Eth–
C_3	Prop–	C_4	But–
C_5	Pent–	C_6	Hex–
C_7	Hept–	C_8	Oct–
C_9	Non–	C_{10}	Dec–
		C_{11}	Undec–
		C_{20}	Icos–
		C_{21}	Henicos–
		C_{30}	Triacont–

After writing the word root or prefix, we add **suffix** 'ane' to it to get the name of the hydrocarbon.

e.g. CH_4 contains one carbon atom so word root for it is 'meth' and after adding suffix 'ane', we get its name methane. Thus, the name of an alkane can be written as

word root + ane ⟶ alkane

TEACHER'S TIP

It may be noted that extra '*a*' is added to the word 'root' if the primary suffix to be added begins with a consonant (other than a, e, i, o, u). e.g. For two double bonds, suffix is diene and if it is to added to word root (for 4C atoms), it becomes butadiene.

(ii) Naming Alkyl Group

The group obtained by removing one H-atom from the saturated hydrocarbon (or alkane) is called the **alkyl group**. These groups are named by replacing 'ane' of alkane by 'yl'.

e.g. Alkane – ane + yl ⟶ alkyl

$$\underset{\text{Methane}}{CH_4} \xrightarrow{-H} \underset{\text{Methyl group}}{—CH_3}$$

Some alkyl groups are listed in the table given below.

Alkane		Alkyl group	
Molecular formula	Name of alkane	Structural formula	Name of alkyl group
CH_4	Methane	$—CH_3$	Methyl
C_2H_6	Ethane	$—CH_2CH_3$	Ethyl
C_3H_8	Propane	$—CH_2CH_2CH_3$	Propyl
C_4H_{10}	Butane	$—CH_2CH_2CH_2CH_3$	Butyl
$C_{10}H_{22}$	Decane	$—CH_2(CH_2)_8CH_3$	Decyl

Some alkyl groups can also be represented by their abbreviation. For example methyl ($—CH_3$) is abbreviated as Me, ethyl ($—C_2H_5$) as Et, propyl ($—C_3H_7$) as Pr and butyl ($—C_4H_9$) as Bu.

Some alkyl groups are found in branched form.

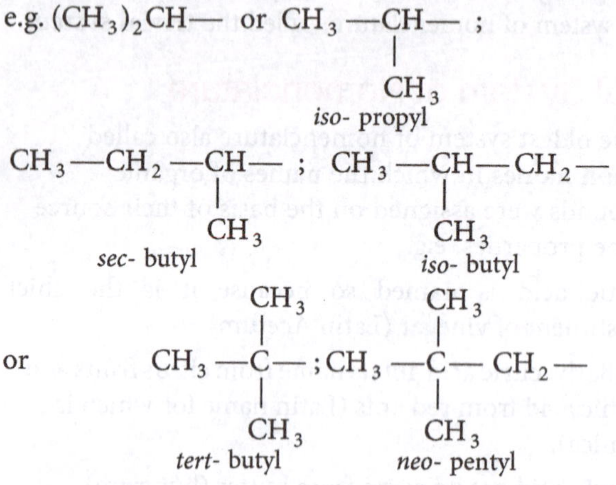

or $(CH_3)_3C—CH_2—$

(iii) Nomenclature of Branched Chain Alkanes or Hydrocarbons

The hydrocarbons in which small chains of carbon atoms are attached at one or more carbon atoms of the parent chain are called the branched chain hydrocarbons. The small chains (or branches) represent the alkyl group.

e.g.

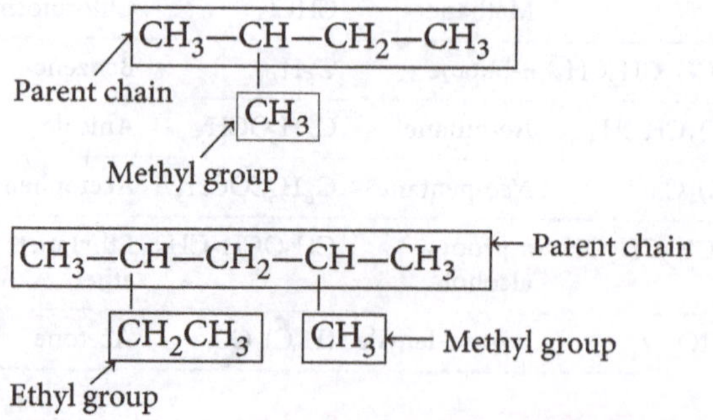

To write the name of such compound, the following rules have to be followed.

TEACHER'S TIP

If two different chains of equal length are possible, the chain with maximum number of side chains or alkyl groups is selected.

Nomenclature of Acyclic Hydrocarbons

Rule	Explanation	Example
Longest chain rule	Select the longest chain of carbon atoms and consider it as parent or root chain and other chains attached to it are known as side chain (substituents).	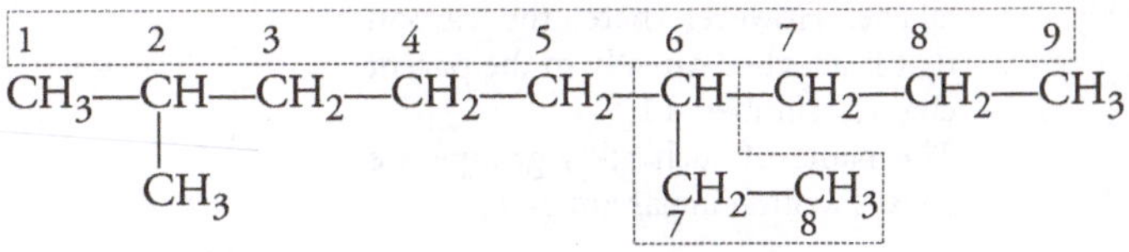 ✓ (correct way, as longest chain has 9C atoms) ⊗ (Incorrect way, as the longest chain has only 8C atoms)
Position of the substituent	• Number the longest possible chain to give an identification number to each C-atom of the longest chain in such a way that the branched carbon atoms (or alkyl groups) get the lowest possible numbers. • The branches (or small chains) are named by adding the prefix of the alkyl group to the parent chain and their location is indicated by appropriate numbers. • However, if the hydrocarbon have several branches (or alkyl groups) they are named alphabetically.	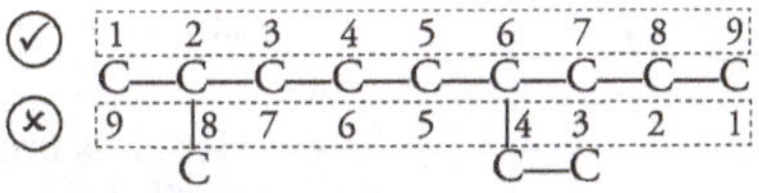 (∵ Position of branch = 2 and 6) (∵ Position of branch = 4 and 8) **Note** Numbering is done in the parent chain to identify the parent alkane and to locate the position of branch. 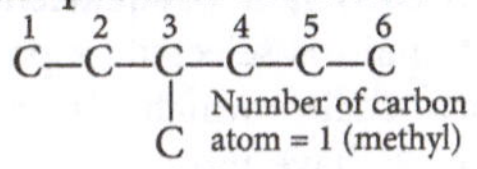 3-methylhexane 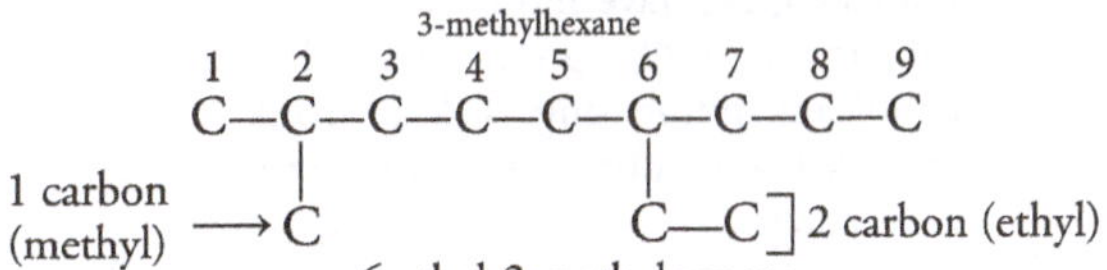 6-ethyl-2-methylnonane
Presence of more than one same substituent	• If the parent chain contains two or more identical branches or alkyl groups (or substituents), they are named by adding prefixes like di (for 2), tri (for 3), tetra (for 4), penta (for 5), hexa (for 6), hepta (for 7) etc., alongwith their locations separated by comma before their names. • However, while writing the names of alkyl groups (or substituents) alphabetically, these prefixes are not considered.	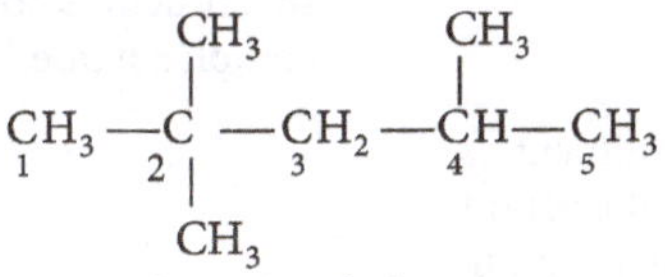 2,2,4-trimethylpentane (∵ Three methyl groups are present at 2, 2 and 4 positions) 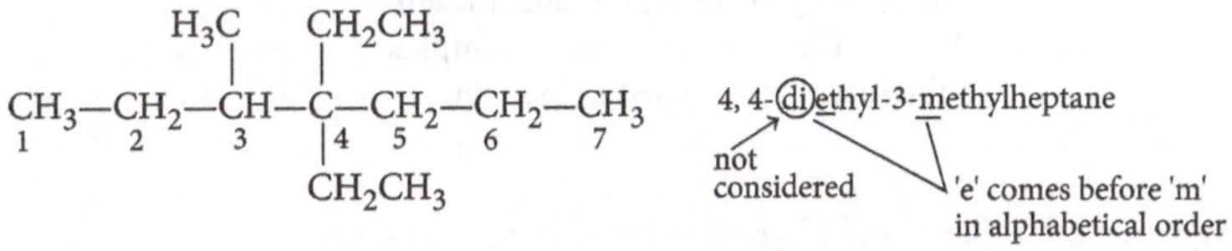
Numbering of different substituents at equivalent position	• If two different alkyl groups occupy equivalent positions in the parent chain then numbering is done from the side which gives lower number to the group coming first in alphabetical order.	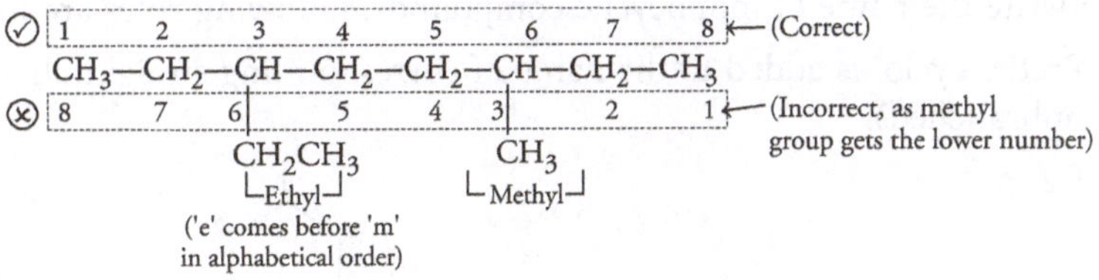

TEACHER'S TIP

If two different chains of equal length are possible, the chain with maximum number of side chains or alkyl groups is selected.

Naming the compound with complex substituents

- If the alkyl substituent is complex (i.e. further branched) then its name is given in the similar manner as of alkane. However, here, the carbon that is attached directly to the parent chain is numbered 1.
The name of such alkyl groups are always written in parenthesis ( ).

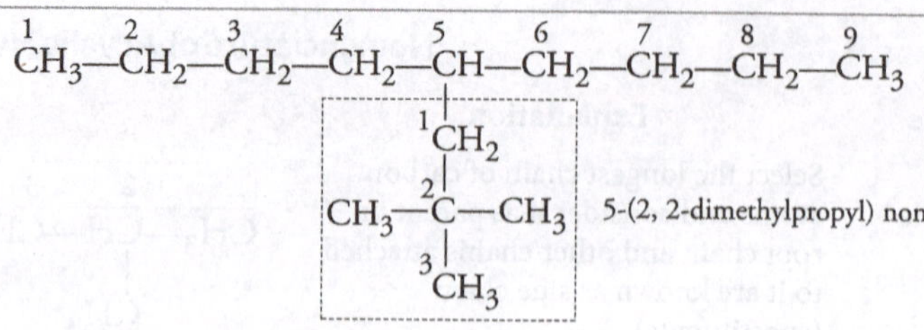

5-(2, 2-dimethylpropyl) nonane

- If the branched alkyl groups like *iso*-, *neo*-, *sec*-, *tert*- are not further branched (or substituted) then they can also be written in IUPAC nomenclature.

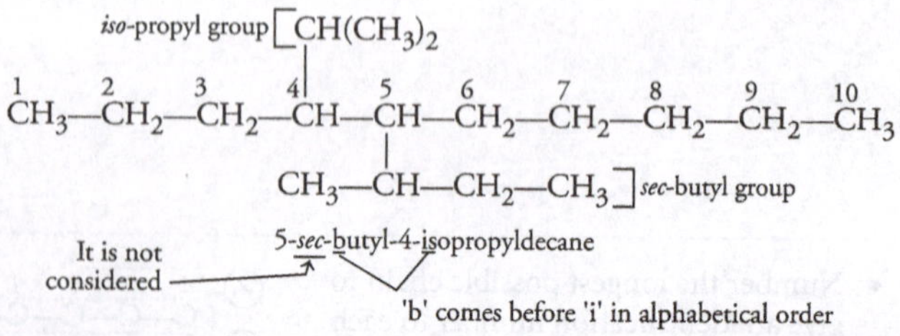

5-*sec*-butyl-4-isopropyldecane

It is not considered

'b' comes before 'i' in alphabetical order

Note Here it is important to note that while naming alphabetically, the prefix *iso* and *neo* are considered but *sec*- and *tert*- are not.

- If there are two chains of equal length, then that chain is selected as parent (or root) chain which is more branched, i.e. have more number of substituent or alkyl groups. In such a condition, numbering is done from the side that is closer to substituent or alkyl chain.

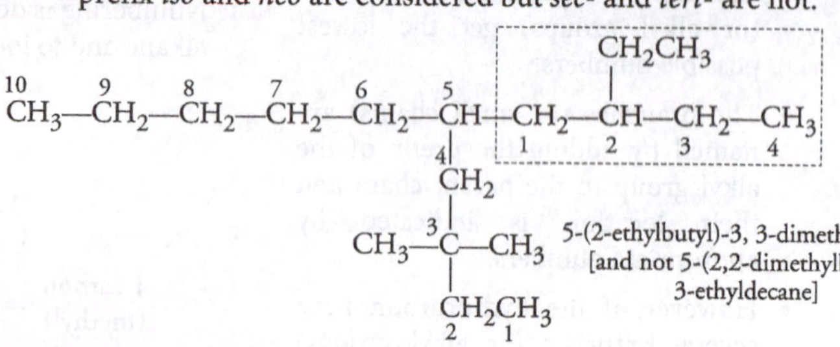

5-(2-ethylbutyl)-3, 3-dimethyldecane [and not 5-(2,2-dimethylbutyl)-3-ethyldecane]

Note While deciding the alphabetic order the name of complex substituent is considered to begin with the first letter of its complex name.

- If the same complex substituent is present more than once on the parent chain at same or different position, then prefix like *bis*; *tris*, *tetrakis*, *pentakis* are used to indicate the multiplicity of complex substituent. Also, this name of complex substituent is enclosed in bracket.

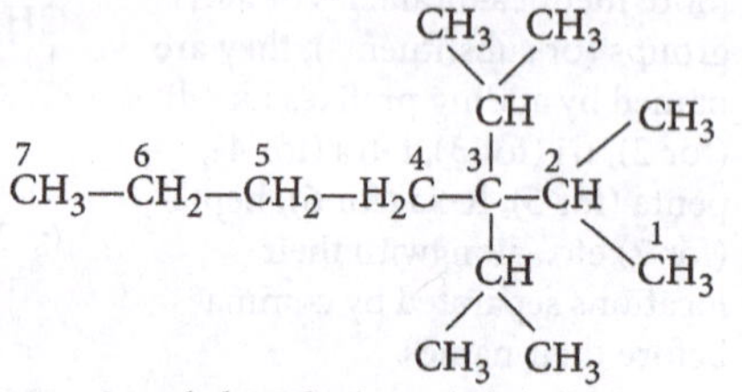

2-methyl-3-3 *bis* (1-methylethyl) heptane

Nomenclature of Cyclic Hydrocarbons

To write the name of monocyclic compounds, following rules are followed.

- Prefix 'cyclo' is added to the name of corresponding straight chain alkane, if the hydrocarbon is unsubstituted (or unbranched).
e.g.

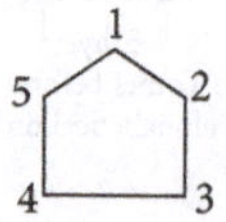

Cyclopentane

Name of corresponding open chain alkanes

Prefix

- If the cyclic hydrocarbon is substituted.

(a) Number the chain in such a manner that lower number is given to the group that comes first in alphabetical order.

e.g.

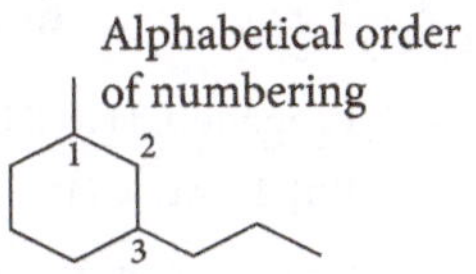

1-methyl-3-propylcyclohexane

(b) Number the chain in such a manner that more branched carbon gets the lower number

e.g.

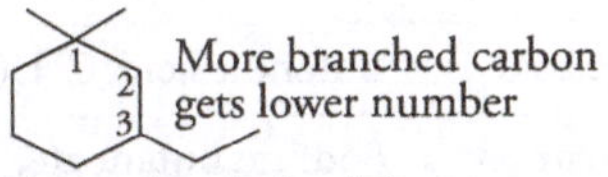

3-ethyl-1, 1-dimethylcyclohexane
(not 1-ethyl-3, 3-dimethylcyclohexane)

- If the side chain have more number of carbon atoms than that present in the ring, then the ring or cycle is treated as substituent and discussed rules will be followed.

e.g.

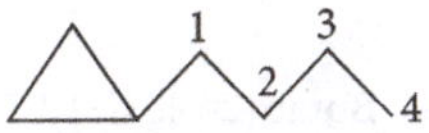

(1-cyclopropyl) butane

Example 2 **Structures and IUPAC names of some hydrocarbons are given below. Explain why the names given in the parentheses are incorrect?**

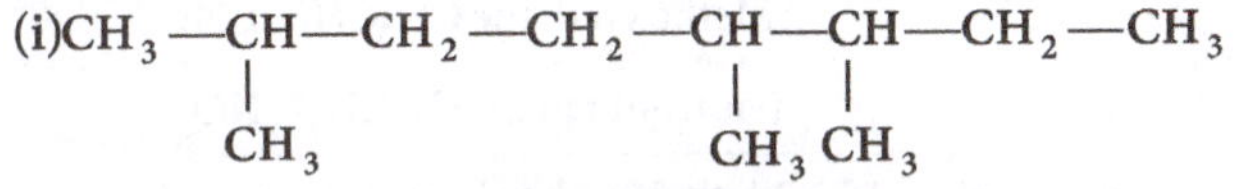

2,5,6-trimethyloctane
[and not 3,4,7-trimethyloctane]

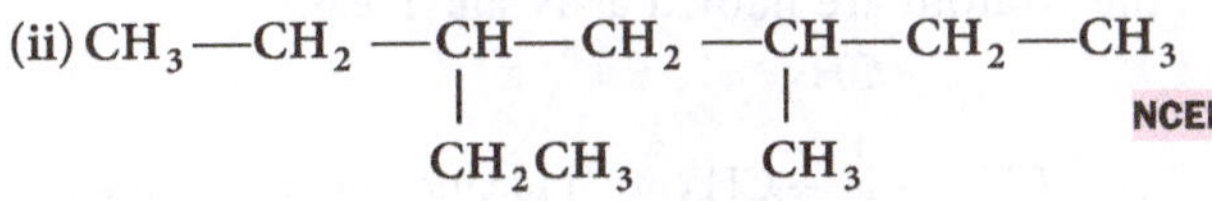

NCERT

3-ethyl-5-methylheptane
[and not 5-ethyl-3-methylheptane]

Sol. (i) Because locant number, 2, 5, 6 is lower than 3, 4, 7,

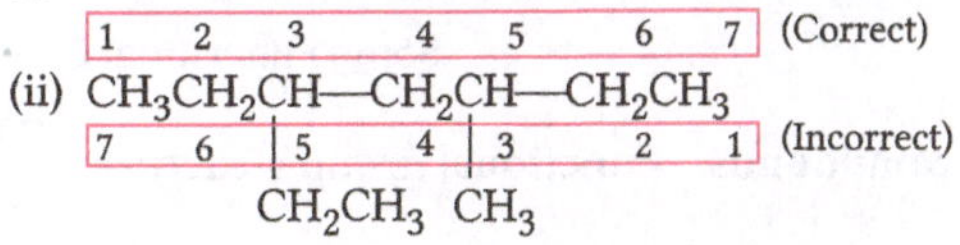

Since, substituents are in equivalent position so lower number is given to ethyl which comes first in the name according to alphabetical order.

IUPAC Nomenclature of Organic Compounds having Functional Groups

IUPAC nomenclature of organic compounds having functional groups are shown by following ways.

(i) Nomenclature of Monofunctional Compounds

The compounds having only one functional group are called **monofunctional compounds.** To write name of such compounds, following rules have to be followed.

- Choose the longest carbon chain that contains functional group.

e.g.

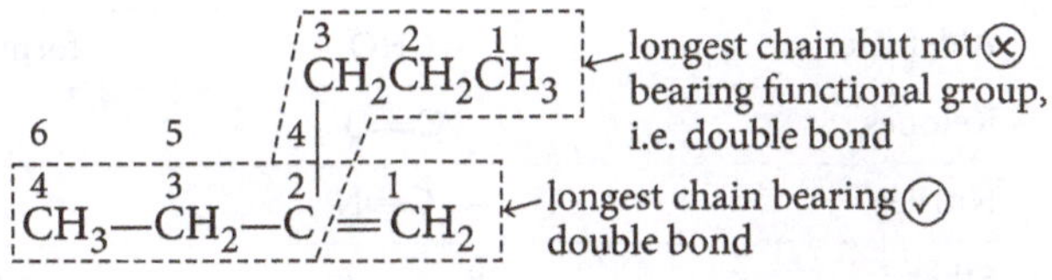

- Number the chain in such a way that the required functional group gets the lowest possible number in the chain.
- Write the suffix of the main functional group after the name of the parent hydrocarbon by omitting its 'e'.
- In order to write the primary suffix, the presence of carbon-carbon multiple bond in the main chain is observed.

The suffix of various functional groups along with their examples are tabulated below.

Some Functional Groups and Classes of Organic Compounds

Class of compounds	Functional group structure	IUPAC group prefix	IUPAC group suffix	Example
Alkanes	—	—	-ane	Propane, $CH_3(CH_2)\,CH_3$
Alkenes	$>C{=}C<$	—	-ene	But-1-ene, $CH_2{=}CHCH_2CH_3$
Alkynes	$—C{\equiv}C—$	—	-yne	But-1-yne, $CH{\equiv}CCH_2CH_3$
Arenes	—	phenyl	—	Benzene, 
Halides	$-X$ (X = F, Cl, Br, I)	halo-	—	1-bromobutane, $CH_3(CH_2)_2CH_2Br$
Carboxylic acids	—COOH	carboxy	-oic acid	Butanoic acid, $CH_3(CH_2)_2COOH$
Carboxylate ions	$—COO^-$	—	-oate	Sodium butanoate, $CH_3(CH_2)_2COO^-\,Na^+$
Esters	—COOR	alkoxycarbonyl	-oate	Methyl propanoate, $CH_3CH_2COOCH_3$
Acyl halides	—COX (X = F, Cl, Br, I)	halocarbonyl	-oyl halide	Butanoyl chloride, $CH_3(CH_2)_2COCl$
Amines	$—NH_2$, $>NH$, $>N—$	amino–	-amine	Butan-2-amine, $CH_3CHNH_2CH_2CH_3$
Amides	$—CONH_2$, —CONHR, $—CONR_2$	-carbamoyl	-amide	Butanamide, $CH_3(CH_2)_2CONH_2$
Alcohols	—OH	hydroxy-	-ol	Butan-2-ol, $CH_2CH_2CHOHCH_3$
Aldehydes	—CHO	formyl or oxo	-al	Butanal, $CH_3(CH_2)_2CHO$
Ketones	$>C{=}O$	oxo–	-one	Butan-2-one, $CH_3CH_2COCH_3$
Nitriles	$—C{\equiv}N$	cyano	nitrile	Butanenitrile, $CH_3CH_2CH_2CN$
Ethers	R—O—R	alkoxy–	—	Methoxyethane $CH_3CH_2OCH_3$
Nitro compounds	$—NO_2$	nitro	—	1-nitrobutane, $CH_3(CH_2)_3NO_2$
Sulphonic acids	$—SO_3H$	sulpho	sulphonic acid	Methylsulphonic acid CH_3SO_3H

* While naming 2° or 3° amines, the groups directly attached to the N-atom are named as N-alkyl. e.g.

$(CH_3)_2NH$ or $CH_3—NH—CH_3$; N- methylmethanamine

$CH_3—N(C_3H_7)—C_2H_5$ [C_3H_7] longest] ; N- ethyl, N- methylpropanamine

$CH_3—N(CH_3)—CH_3$] identical groups are present. N, N- dimethylmethanamine

(ii) Nomenclature of Polyfunctional Compounds

The compounds having more than one functional group are called **polyfunctional compounds.**

- The first step to write the name of such compound is the selection of principal functional group on the basis of priority order. The order of decreasing priority for some functional groups is

  $—COOH$, $—SO_3H$, —COOR (R = alkyl group), —COCl, $—CONH_2$, —CN, —HC=O, $>C{=}O$, —OH, $—NH_2$, $>C{=}C<$, $—C{\equiv}C—$.

  e.g. If in a compound —OH and —CHO both groups are present then —CHO is the principal functional group. The —R, C_6H_5—, halogens (—F, —Cl, —Br, —I), $—NO_2$, alkoxy (—OR) etc., are always consider as prefix substituents.

- Choose the longest chain that have principal functional group as well as double or triple bond. e.g.

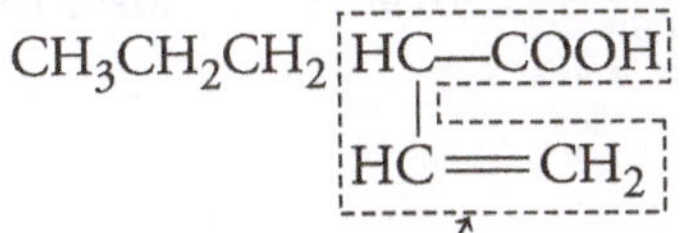

Longest chain bearing functional group as well as double bond

- Number the chain in such a manner that the principal functional group gets the lowest possible number.
- Now, write the prefix for functional groups other than the principal functional group before the name of the parent alkane and add suffix for the principal functional group by omitting 'e' of the alkane.

e.g. $HO\overset{7}{C}H_2(\overset{4,5,6}{CH_2})_3\overset{3}{C}H_2\overset{2}{C}O\overset{1}{C}H_3$

∵ Priority order $>CO > —OH$

Prefix for $—OH^-$ is 'hydroxy', suffix for $>C{=}O$ is 'one'. There are 7 carbon atoms, so alkane is heptane. Therefore, its IUPAC name is 7-hydroxyheptan-2-one.

Similarly, $Br\overset{3}{C}H_2\overset{2}{C}H{=}\overset{1}{C}H_2$

3-bromoprop-1-ene

- If more than one functional group of the same type are present, their number is indicated by adding di, tri, etc. before the class suffix. In such cases, the full name of the parent alkane is written before the class suffix. e.g.

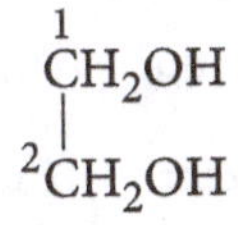

Ethane-1, 2-diol

'e' of alkane is not omitted.

$CH_2{=}CH—CH{=}CH_2$

Buta-1, 3-diene

Example 3 **Write the IUPAC names of the compounds (i)-(iv) from their structures.**

(i) 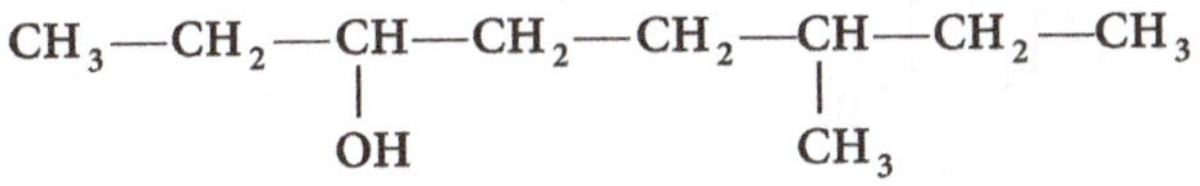

(ii) 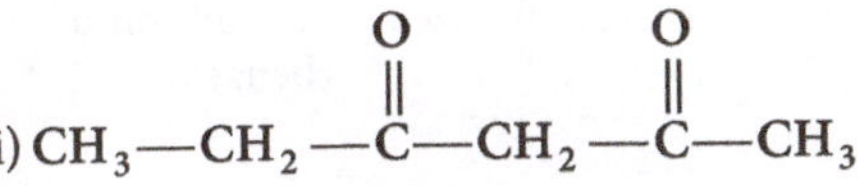

(iii) 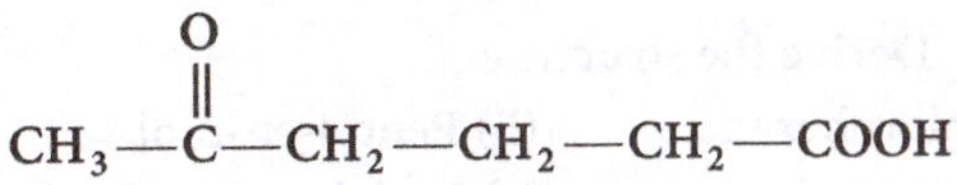

(iv) $CH{\equiv}C—CH{=}CH—CH{=}CH_2$ **NCERT**

Sol. Follow the given steps to solve out such problems.

Step I Predicting the principal functional group and suffix for the functional group

$—OH$ (ol), $>C{=}O$ (–one), $—COOH$ (oic acid), $>C{=}C<$ (ene)

Step II Predicing substituent and their prefix

$—CH_3$ (methyl), $>C{=}O$ (oxo), $\equiv$ (suffix-yne as it has no prefix).

Step III Number of C-atoms and parent alkane

8 carbon (octane), 6 carbon (hexane), 6 carbon (hexane), 6 carbon (hexane)

Step IV Substituent location in all cases.

Step V **IUPAC name**

(i) 6-methyloctan-3-ol

(ii) Hexane-2,4-dione

(iii) 5-oxohexanoic acid

(iv) Hexa-1, 3-dien-5-yne

Writing Structural Formula from the Name of the Compound

To write the structure of an organic compound from its name, the following steps are involved.

- Write a straight chain of carbon atoms according to the number of carbon atoms in the parent compound. At this stage, do not attach any hydrogen atoms to the carbon.

C—C—C—C—C—C

- Number the chain of carbon atoms from any end.

$\overset{1}{C}—\overset{2}{C}—\overset{3}{C}—\overset{4}{C}—\overset{5}{C}—\overset{6}{C}$

- In case, the name of the compound contains -ene or -yne, then draw double or triple bond at indicated locations.
- Attach substituents and functional groups at the given location.
- Make each carbon tetravalent by attaching a suitable number of hydrogen atoms.

Example 4 Derive the structure
(i) 2-chlorohexane, (ii) Pent-4-en-2-ol,
(iii) 3-nitrocyclohexene, (iv) Cyclohex-2-en-1-ol,
(v) 6-hydroxy-heptanal. **NCERT**

Sol. (i) 'Hexane' indicates the presence of 6 carbon atoms in the chain. The functional group chloro is present at carbon 2. Hence, the structure of the compound is $CH_3CH_2CH_2CH_2CH(Cl)CH_3$.

(ii) 'Pent' indicates that parent hydrocarbon contains 5 carbon atoms in the chain. 'en' and 'ol' correspond to the functional groups C=C and OH at carbon atoms 4 and 2 respectively. Thus, the structure is $CH_2{=}CHCH_2CH(OH)CH_3$.

(iii) As the name indicates, the compound is cyclic with a double bond.

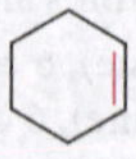

The prefix 3-nitro means that a nitro group is present on C-3. Numbering is done from the carbon atom bearing double bond.

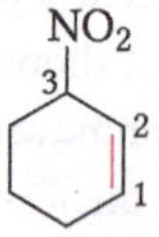

(iv) Again the compound is cyclic with a double bond. Here '1— ol' means that —OH group bears 1-position because it comes before double bond in priority order series of functional group.

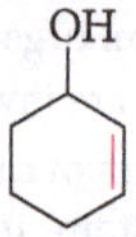

(v) "Heptanal" indicates the compound to be an aldehyde containing 7 carbon atoms in the parent chain. '6-hydroxy' indicates that — OH group is present at carbon 6.

Thus, $\overset{7}{C}H_3\overset{\overset{OH}{|}}{\overset{6}{C}}H\overset{5}{C}H_2\overset{4}{C}H_2\overset{3}{C}H_2\overset{2}{C}H_2\overset{1}{C}HO$

Remember that carbon atom of — CHO group is included while numbering the carbon chain.

Nomenclature of Substituted Benzene Compounds

(i) Nomenclature of Monosubstituted Benzene Ring

Such compounds are named by adding prefix of the substituent before the name benzene.

S.No.	Structural representation	Common name	IUPAC name
1.	CH_3 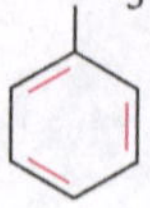	Toluene	Methyl benzene
2.	OCH_3 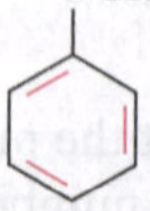	Anisole	Methoxy benzene
3.	NH_2 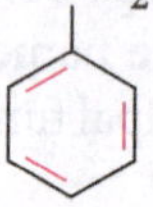	Aniline	Amino benzene

(ii) Nomenclature of Disubstituted Benzene Ring

***Step* 1** Numbering of the carbon atoms of the ring in such a manner that the substituents get the lowest possible numbers.

***Step* 2** Substituent of the base compound is assigned number 1 and then the direction of numbering is choosen such that the next substituent get the lowest number.

***Step* 3** Now write the name as in the previous case but with locations of the substituents. If both the substituents are same, add the prefix 'di' before the name of the substituents.

S.No.	Structural representation	Common name	IUPAC name
1.	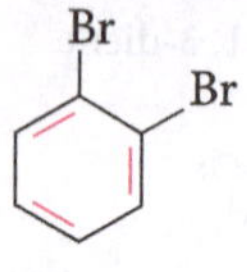	*o*-bromobenzene	1,2-dibromo benzene
2.	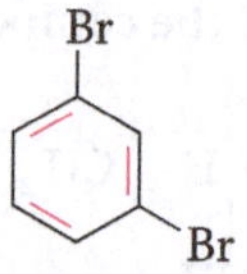	*m*-bromobenzene	1,3-dibromo benzene
3.		*p*-bromobenzene	1,4-dibromo benzene

In trivial system of nomenclature the position 1,2; 1,3; 1,4; are also called *ortho* (*o*), *meta* (*m*) and *para* (*p*) positions.

(iii) Nomenclature of Tri-or Higher Substituted Benzene

For naming these compounds, following rules have to be followed.

- Number the carbon atoms of the ring in such a manner that the higher priority group gets the lowest possible number.
- Write the prefix of the substituents in alphabetical order alongwith the locations before the benzene or trivial name of substituted benzene.

S.No.	Structural representation	Correct IUPAC name	Incorrect IUPAC name
1.	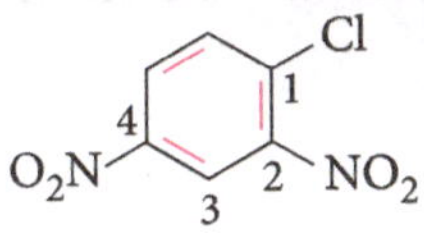	1-chloro-2,4-dinitrobenzene	4-bromo-1,3-dinitrobenzene
2.	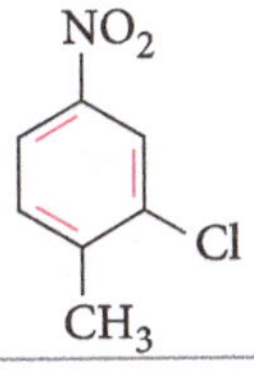	2-chloro-1-methyl-4-nitrobenzene	4-methyl-5-chloro-nitro benzene

Note If benzene ring is attached to a chain that contains functional group, then it is considered as the substituent and named as phenyl (Ph).

Example 5 **Write the structural formula of**

(i) *o*-ethylanisole,
(ii) *p*-nitroaniline,
(iii) 2, 3-dibromo-1-phenylpentane,
(iv) 4-ethyl-1-fluoro-2-nitrobenzene. **NCERT**

Sol.

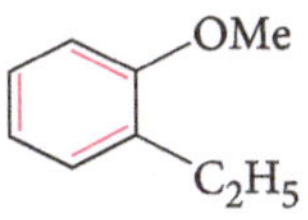

(i)

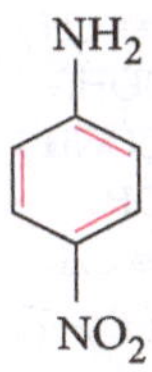

(ii)

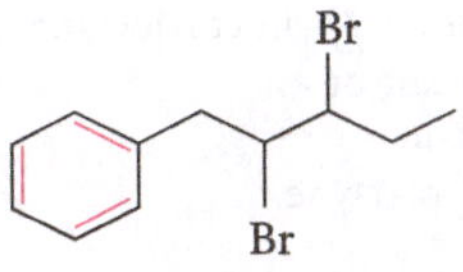

(iii)

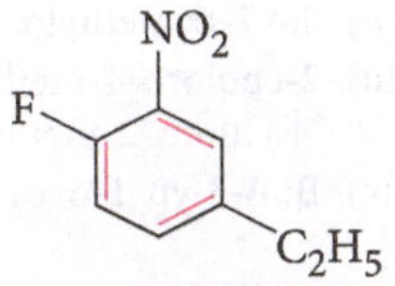

(iv)

8.6 Isomerism

The phenomenon of existence of two or more compounds having the same molecular formula but different structural formula, properties such as physical and chemical properties or spatial arrangement is called **isomerism**. Such compounds are called **isomers.**

Types of Isomerism

The different types of isomerism are shown in the following flow chart.

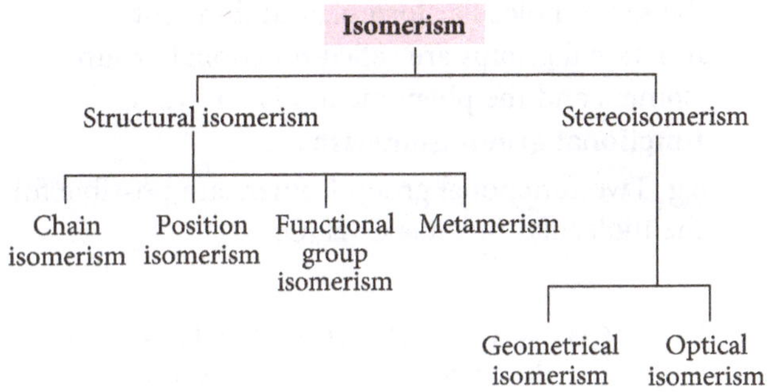

1. Structural Isomerism

Compounds having same molecular formula but different structural formula (i.e. way of linking) are called structural isomers and this phenomenon is called **structural isomerism**. It is also called **constitutional isomerism**. These are further classified into following sub-types.

(i) **Chain isomerism** Two or more compounds that have same molecular formula but different carbon skeletons are called **chain or nuclear isomers** and this phenomenon is called **chain isomerism.**

e.g. The chain isomers for C_5H_{12} are as follows

$CH_3CH_2CH_2CH_2CH_3$
Pentane

$$\begin{array}{c} \quad CH_3 \\ \quad | \\ CH_3—CHCH_2CH_3 \end{array}$$
Iso- pentane
(2- methylbutane)

$$\begin{array}{c} CH_3 \\ | \\ CH_3—C—CH_3 \\ | \\ CH_3 \end{array}$$
Neo-pentane
(2,2- dimethylpropane)

TEACHER'S TIP
Only alkanes having atleast 4 carbon atoms can exhibit chain isomerism.

(ii) **Position isomerism** It arises due to difference in the position of substituent atom or functional group on the carbon skeleton.
Such compounds are called position isomers and the phenomenon is known as **position isomerism.** e.g. The two isomers are possible for the molecular formula C_4H_8.

$$\underset{\text{But-1-ene}}{CH_3—CH_2—CH{=}CH_2} \; ; \quad \underset{\text{But-2-ene}}{CH_3—CH{=}CH—CH_3}$$

(iii) **Functional group isomerism** Compounds having the same molecular formula but different functional groups are called functional group isomers and the phenomenon is known as **functional group isomerism.**

e.g. Two functional group isomers are possible for the molecular formula C_3H_6O.

$$\underset{\text{Propanone}}{CH_3—\overset{\overset{\displaystyle O}{\|}}{C}—CH_3} \; ; \; \underset{\text{Propanal}}{CH_3—CH_2—\overset{\overset{\displaystyle H}{|}}{C}{=}O}$$

Note Generally, compounds having the same general formula exhibit functional isomerism.

General Formula for Different Functional Groups

S. No.	General formula	Functional isomers
1.	C_nH_{2n}	Alkene and cycloalkane
2.	C_nH_{2n-2}	Alkyne, cycloalkene and alkadiene
3.	$C_nH_{2n+2}O$	Alcohol and ether
4.	$C_nH_{2n}O$	Aldehydes, ketones and epoxides
5.	$C_nH_{2n}O_2$	Acids, ester, hydroxy aldehyde and hydroxy ketone.

(iv) **Metamerism** If two or more compounds have the same functional group but the alkyl group attached to the same functional group is different then the phenomenon is called **metamerism** and the compounds are called **metamers.** e.g. $C_4H_{10}O$ can be represented by following two formula $CH_3OC_3H_7$ (methoxypropane) and $C_2H_5OC_2H_5$ (ethoxyethane).

2. Stereoisomerism

Compounds having the same molecular formula (constitution) and the same connectivity of atoms in their molecules, but different 3-dimensional orientation of their atoms in space are called **stereoisomers** and this phenomenon is called **stereoisomerism.** It is further classified into **optical** and **geometrical isomerism.** (Geometrical isomerism will be discussed in the next chapter and about optical isomerism you will read in class XII).

Quick Test 2

1. Give the IUPAC name of the following compound.

$$CH_3—\underset{\underset{\displaystyle Br}{|}}{CH}—\underset{\underset{\displaystyle O}{\|}}{C}—\underset{\underset{\displaystyle CH_3}{|}}{CH}—CH_3$$

2. Give condensed and bond line structural formulae and identify the functional group(s) present, if any, for
(i) 2,2,4-trimethylpentane
(ii) 2-hydroxy-1,2,3-propanetricarboxylic acid
(iii) hexanedial. NCERT

3. Identify the functional groups present in the following compounds.
(i)

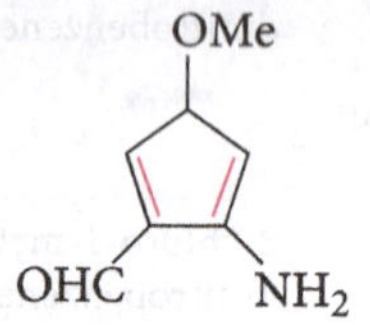

(ii)

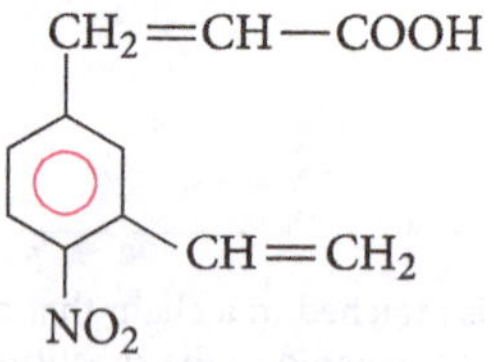

(iii) $CH_3—CH_2—CO—\underset{\underset{\displaystyle CH_2—COCl}{|}}{CH_2}$

(iv) $CH_2{=}CH—CH_2—\overset{\overset{\displaystyle O}{\|}}{C}—NH_2$

4. Write down the formulae of the first four members of each homologous series beginning with the following compounds.
(i) $CH_2{=}CH_2$
(ii) HCOOH
(iii) CH_3COCH_3
(iv) CH_3OH
(v) $HC{\equiv}CH$

5. Which of the following represents the correct IUPAC name for the compounds concerned?
(i) 2,2-dimethylpentane or 2-dimethylpentane
(ii) 2,4,7-trimethyloctane or 2,5,7-trimethyloctane
(iii) 2-choloro-4-methylpentane or 4-chloro-2-methylpentane
(iv) But -3-yn-1-ol or But-4-ol-1-yne NCERT

6. The following organic compounds are popularly known by their common names. Write the structural formulas and IUPAC names.

(i) *neo*-pentane (ii) Acetone
(iii) Vinyl chloride (iv) *tert*-amyl alcohol

7. Give IUPAC names of the following structures.

(i) 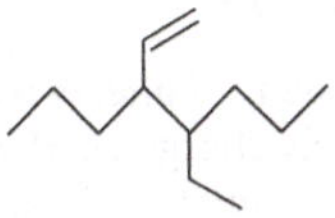

(ii) 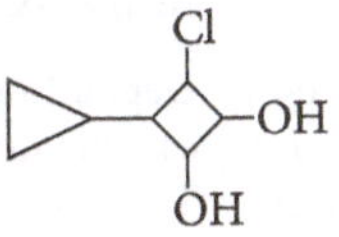

(iii) 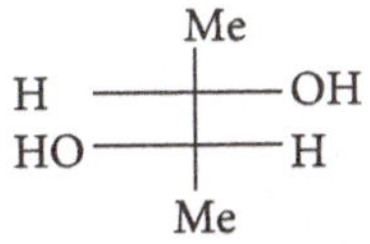

8. Write structural formulae for compounds named as
(i) 1-bromoheptane
(ii) 5-bromoheptanoic acid

9. Compounds with same molecular formula but differing in their structures are said to be structural isomers. What type of structural isomerism is shown by
$CH_3—S—CH_2—CH_2—CH_3$
and $CH_3—S—CH(CH_3)_2$?

10. An alkane has a molecular mass of 72. Draw all its possible chain isomers and write their IUPAC names.

For Solutions, See QR Code on Pg. 341

8.7 Fundamental Concepts in Organic Reaction Mechanism

In organic reactions, the attacking reagent reacts with the organic molecule or substrate to give the required product. The reactions involve the formation of one or more intermediate(s) and finally the product(s).

Thus, a general organic reaction can be represented as

$$\text{Organic molecule (Substrate)} \xrightarrow{\text{Attacking reagent}} \text{(Intermediate)} \longrightarrow \text{Product(s)}$$
$$\text{(Intermediate)} \longrightarrow \text{Byproducts}$$

A sequential account of each step, describing details of electron movement, energetics during bond cleavage and bond formation, and the rates of transformation of reactants into products (kinetics) is called the organic reaction mechanism. It helps in predicting the reaction of different organic compounds.

In the following sections, we shall learn some of the principles that explain how these reactions take place.

8.8 Fission of a Covalent Bond

There are two possible ways through which a covalent bond can get cleaved. These are **homolytic cleavage** and **heterolytic cleavage.**

1. Heterolytic Cleavage or Heterolysis

If a covalent bond breaks in such a way that both the electrons of shared pair are taken away by one of the bonded atoms, the bond fission is called **heterolytic fission.** For hypothetical compounds heterolytic fission can be shown as

$$X—Y \xrightarrow{\text{Heterolysis}} X^+ + Y^-$$

(when X is less electronegative than Y)

$$X—Y \xrightarrow{\text{Heterolysis}} X^- + Y^+$$

(when Y is less electronegative than X)

Note The bond breaking in this cleavage is shown by a full-headed arrows.

In the obtained species, one is positively charged and has a sextet (6) of electrons (carbocation) and the other is negatively charged with octet of electrons and atleast one lone pair (carbanion).

Because of the generation of charged species, reactions involving such cleavage (heterolytic cleavage) are also called **ionic** or **heteropolar** or just **polar reactions.**

e.g. The heterolysis of methyl bromide can be represented as

$$H_3C—Br \longrightarrow H_3C^+ + Br^-$$

Differences between Carbocation and Carbanion

	Carbocation (Carbonium ion)	Carbanion
Definition	The carbon which has sextet of electrons in valence shell and bear a positive charge, then the species is called **carbocation** (earlier called carbonium ion). e.g. CH_3^+ (methyl carbonium ion).	The heterolytic cleavage can also give a species in which the carbon atom bears a formal negative charge. It has octet of electrons in its valence shell such a species is called **carbanion.**
Classification	Depending upon the attachment of one, two or three carbon atoms to the positively charged carbon, the carbocations are categorised as **primary, secondary** or **tertiary carbocations respectively.** e.g. $CH_3\overset{+}{C}H_2$ Ethyl carbocation 1° ; $(CH_3)_2\overset{+}{C}H$ *iso*- propyl carbocation 2° ; $(CH_3)_3\overset{+}{C}$ *tert*- butyl carbocation 3°	Depending upon the attachment of one, two or three carbon atoms to the negatively charged carbon. These are also categorised as primary (1°), secondary (2°) and tertiary (3°).
Stability	Carbocations are highly reactive and unstable species. As the number of alkyl group attached to positively charged carbon increases, the stability of carbocations increases due to inductive and hyperconjugative effects. Thus, the order of stability of carbocation is $\overset{+}{C}H_3 < CH_3\overset{+}{C}H_2 < (CH_3)_2\overset{+}{C}H < (CH_3)_3\overset{+}{C}$ or methyl carbocation < 1° < 2° < 3°.	These are also unstable and reactive species. The order of stability of carbanions is given as $(C_6H_5)_3C > (C_6H_5)_2\bar{C}H > C_6H_5\bar{C}H_2 >$ allyl $> \bar{C}H_3 >$ (1°> 2°> 3° carbanions)
Structure	In $\overset{+}{C}H_3$, the carbon atom hybridise to give three sp^2-hybrid orbitals, each of which overlaps with the 1*s* orbital of hydrogen atom to give a (C) sp^2 — H(1*s*) σ bond. Thus, there are in all three σ bonds that are directed towards the corners of a triangle. Thus, its shape is trigonal planar. The remaining orbital (unhybridised orbital) is perpendicular to the molecular plane and is empty. 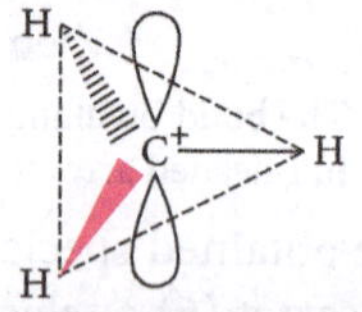 Shape of methyl cation	The structure of simple carbanions is usually pyramidal with C-atom carrying the negative charge in sp^3-hybrid state and can be seen as 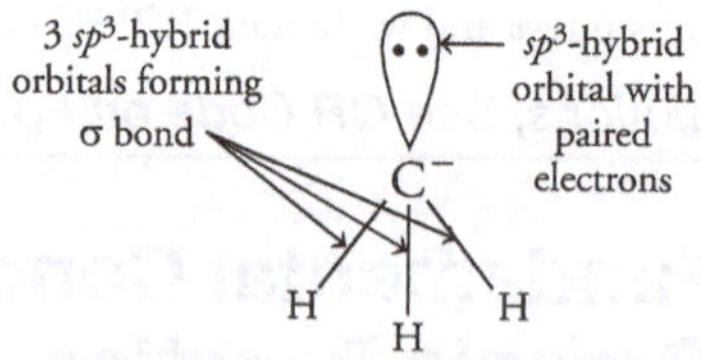

Example 6 **Write structures of various carbocations that can be obtained from 2-methylbutane. Arrange these carbocations in order of increasing stability.**

Sol. 2-methyl butane has four different sets of equivalent H-atoms.

$$CH_3—\underset{\underset{CH_3}{|}}{CH}—CH_2—CH_3$$

Removal of H-atom from any of C-atom gives four different carbocations.

$$CH_3 \rightarrow \underset{\underset{CH_3}{|}}{\overset{\beta}{CH}} \rightarrow \overset{\alpha}{CH_2} \rightarrow \overset{+}{C}H_2 \quad \text{(I) (1°)}$$

$$CH_3 \rightarrow \underset{\underset{CH_3}{|}}{CH} \rightarrow \overset{+}{C}H \leftarrow CH_3 \quad \text{(II) (2°)}$$

$$CH_3 \rightarrow \underset{\underset{CH_3}{|}}{\overset{+}{C}} \leftarrow CH_2 — CH_3 \quad \text{(III) (3°)}$$

$$\overset{+}{C}H_2 \leftarrow \underset{\underset{CH_3}{|}}{CH} \leftarrow CH_2 — CH_3 \quad \text{(IV) (1°)}$$

Stability of carbocation decreases in the order 3°> 2°> 1°. So, III (3° carbocation) is most stable followed by II (2° carbocation). Out of I and IV (both are 1° carbocation), I has a CH_3 group at β-carbon while II has a CH_3 group at α-carbon. As +*I*-effect decreases with distance, hence IV is more stable than I. Therefore, the overall stability of these four carbocations increases in the order.

$$I < IV < II < III$$

2. Homolytic Cleavage or Homolysis

If a covalent bond breaks in such a way that each atom takes away one electron of shared pair, the fission is called **homolysis** or **homolytic cleavage**. This cleavage involves movement of only one electron, which is represented by **half headed (fish hook :⌒)** curved arrow.

e.g. $R-X \xrightarrow[\text{Light}]{\text{Heat or}} \underset{\text{Alkyl free radical}}{R^{\bullet}} + X^{\bullet}$

Free Radicals

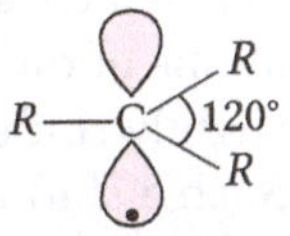

The neutral chemical species, formed by the homolytic cleavage are called the **free radicals.** It is a planar species in which the C-atom bearing the odd electron is sp^2-hybridised. The carbon atom lies in the center of the triangle and the three bonds are directed towards the three corners of planar trigonal geometry. The odd electron lies in the unhybridised *p*-orbital perpendicular to the plane.

Classification

Alkyl free radicals are also classified as primary, secondary or tertiary.

The relative stability of alkyl free radicals follows the order.

$$\underset{\textit{Tert}\text{-butyl free radical}}{(CH_3)_3\dot{C}} > \underset{\textit{Iso}\text{-propyl free radical}}{(CH_3)_2\dot{C}H} > \underset{\text{Ethyl free radical}}{CH_3-\dot{C}H_2} > \underset{\text{Methyl free radical}}{\dot{C}H_3} > \text{Vinyl}$$

Structure

These species carry a high energy unpaired electron, called the **odd electron**, which makes them highly reactive towards other similar reagents and other non-polar covalent bond. The organic reactions involving homolytic cleavage are called **free radical** or **homopolar** or **non-polar reactions.**

Substrates and Reagents

Ions are generally not formed in the reactions of organic compounds. Instead, molecules as such participate in the reaction. It is convenient to name one as substrate and other as reagent.

- Generally, a molecules whose carbon is involved in new bond formation is called **substrate.**
- The species or compounds which attack on a substrate molecule and bring about a chemical change is called **reagent.**
- When carbon-carbon bond is formed, the choice of naming the reactants as **substrate** and reagent is arbitrary and depends on molecules under **observation.**

Organic Reagent

Organic reagents can be classified into following two categories

1. Nucleophiles or Nucleophilic Reagents

An electron rich species having a lone pair of electrons is called a nucleophile ($Nu^{:}$), i.e. nucleus loving species.

It can be classified into two categories.

(i) **Charged electrophiles**
e.g. Negatively charged species like, H^-, Cl^-, Br^-, I^-, carbanions, $-\bar{O}H$, $-\bar{O}R$, $-\bar{S}R$, $-CN^-$. Nucleophiles can also be seen in the form of neutral molecules.

(ii) **Neutral Nucleophiles** It can be clasified into two categories

- Neutral covalent compounds in which central atom has complete octet, has at least one lone pair of electrons and all atoms present on the central atom are not electronegative are called **neutral nucleophile.**

  e.g. $H_2\ddot{\underset{\cdot\cdot}{O}}$, $\ddot{N}H_3$, $R\ddot{N}H_2$, $R\ddot{\underset{\cdot\cdot}{O}}H$, $R\ddot{\underset{\cdot\cdot}{S}}H$, etc.

- Organic compounds containing carbon-carbon multiple bonds also behave as the nucleophile, e.g. alkene, alkyne, benzene, $CH_2{=}CH-CH{=}CH_2$, $CH_2{=}CH-C{\equiv}CH$, etc.

2. Electrophiles or Electrophilic Reagents

An electrophile (E^+) is defined as electron deficient species which attacks on electron rich centre, i.e. nucleophilic centre.

It can be divided into two categories.

(i) **Charged electrophiles** Positively charged species in which central atom has incomplete octet is called charged electrophile.
e.g. H^+, Cl^+, Br^+, I^+, NO_2^+, SO_3 and carbocations (because of the presence of sextet of electrons).

(ii) **Neutral electrophiles** The electrophiles can also be seen in the form of neutral molecules, e.g. carbenes ($\ddot{C}R_2$), nitrenes ($\ddot{N}R$), BF_3 etc.

- All neutral covalent compounds in which central atom has incomplete octet, e.g. $BeCl_2$, BH_3, $ZnCl_2$, AlX_3, FeX_3, $\ddot{C}H_3$, $\ddot{C}X_2$ etc.
- Compounds having functional group like carbonyl group ($\rangle C{=}O$) or alkyl halides (because of the polarity of $C—X$ bond).
- All those compounds in which central atom is bonded by two or more than two electronegative atoms, e.g. BX_3, AlX_3, FeX_3, PCl_3, PCl_5, etc.

Electron Movement in Organic Reactions

In a polar organic chemical reaction the electrophiles receive electron pair from nucleophile interaction.

Curved arrows are used to show the movement of electrons in organic reactions. The tail of the arrow shows the point from where the electron pair is shifted and the head of the arrow indicates the point to which the electron pair may move.

The shifting of electron pairs in some chemical reactions is shown below.

(i) $=Y— \leftrightarrow —Y=$ from π-bond to adjacent bond position.

(ii) $=Y— \leftrightarrow —\ddot{Y}—$ from π-bond to adjacent atom

(iii) $—\ddot{Y}— \leftrightarrow —Y=$ from atom to adjacent bond position.

e.g. $H\ddot{O}:^- + CH_3—Br: \longrightarrow CH_3OH + :Br:^-$

Electron Displacement Effects in Covalent Bonds

The bonding pairs of the covalent bond in organic compounds undergo electronic displacements on their own or under the influence of an attacking agent. These electronic displacements is because of the presence of atom or substituents group in the molecule, it causes permanent polarisation of the bond. Inductive effect and resonance effect involve such type of electron displacements.

If electronic displacement is due to the presence of attacking reagent, it generates temporary polarisation. Such type of displacement is called **electromeric** or **polarisability effects**. Now we will discuss about the above mentioned effects one by one.

Inductive Effect

When a covalent bond is formed between two unlike atoms of different electronegativities, electron density is slightly shifted towards the more electronegative atom. Such a shift of electron density results in a polar covalent bond. This causes a permanent dipole to arise in the molecule and is referred as **inductive effect.**

e.g. In a chain of carbon atoms having C—Cl bond, the C attached directly to the Cl atom because of its less electronegativity and acquires some positive charge (δ^+).

The carbon that is bonded directly to the $C^{\delta+}$ also lose some of its electron density due to more polar $C^{\delta+}$ and hence, acquires somewhat less positive charge (δ^{++}). Similarly, the next carbon (C_3) also acquires some positive charge but less than (δ^{++}) as shown below.

$$\overset{\delta\delta\delta^+}{\underset{3}{CH_3}}—\overset{\delta\delta^+}{\underset{2}{CH_2}} \rightarrow —\overset{\delta^+}{\underset{1}{CH_2}} \rightarrow —\overset{\delta^-}{Cl}$$

This induction of polarity, due to the presence of polar bond in an organic molecule, is called inductive effect.

Features of Inductive Effect

Special features of inductive effect are

- it is a permanent effect.
- it operates through σ-bonds.
- it decreases in magnitude as we move away from the cause of polarity (i.e. polar bond).
- it is generally observed in saturated compounds.

TEACHER'S TIP

This effect is passed on to the subsequent bonds also but the effect decreases rapidly as the number of intervening bonds increases and becomes vanishingly small after three bonds.

Difference Between Positive and Negative Inductive Effects

Negative Inductive Effects	Positive Inductive Effects
The electron withdrawing atom or group of atoms have tendency to attract electron pair toward itself, due to which carbon attached with these groups, attain positive charge. This effect is called as **negative inductive effect.**	The electron donating atoms or groups having smaller electron affinity than hydrogen are said to have **positive inductive effect.**
These electron withdrawing groups which cause this effect are called as **−*I* groups.**	The groups which cause such effect are called **+*I* groups.**
Some of the −*I*-effect producing groups in decreasing order with respect to H are $R_3\overset{+}{N} > \overset{+}{N}H_3 > NO_2 > CN > SO_3H > CHO > CO > COOH > COCl > COOR > CONH_2 > F > Cl > Br > I > OH > OR > NH_2 > C_6H_5 > H$	The order of +*I* effect of some groups is as follows $3°$ or $(CH_3)_3C— > 2°$ or $(CH_3)_2CH— > 1°$ or $CH_3CH_2— > CH_3$

Applications of Inductive Effect

The various applications of inductive effect are as follows

(i) **Relative stability of carbocation, free radical and carbanion** It helps in determining the stability of free radicals, carbocations and carbanions. Following relationship are considered.

(a) Stability of carbocation or free radical

$$\propto +I \text{ power of the group} \propto \frac{1}{-I \text{ power of the group}}$$

Thus, the stability order for carbocations and free radicals is $1° < 2° < 3°$.

(b) Stability of carbanions $\propto -I$ power of the group

$$\propto \frac{1}{+I \text{ power of the group}}$$

and the stability order for carbanions is

$$1° > 2° > 3°.$$

(ii) **Acidic and basic strength** It helps in **determining the strength of acids and bases.** Following relationships are considered.

(a) Strength of an acid $\propto K_a \propto \frac{1}{pK_a} \propto$ stability of acid anion.

As stability of acid anion (or conjugate base) $\propto -I$ power of group present

$$\propto \frac{I}{+I \text{ power of group present}}$$

Thus, strength of acid increases with the attachment of group showing −*I*-effect and decreases with the attachment of group showing +*I*-effect.

Note Although Ph group is −*I*-effect showing group, HCOOH (formic acid) is more acidic than benzoic acid (PhCOOH). This is because of +*R* (resonance effect) of phenyl (Ph or C_6H_5) group.

(b) Similarly, **strength of a base** $\propto +I$ power of group present in the base $\propto K_b \propto \frac{1}{pK_b}$

$$\propto \frac{1}{-I \text{ power of group present in the base}}$$

However, this relation is not true for amines in their aqueous solutions as here the basicity is decided by combined effect of inductive effect, solvation effect and steric hindrance.

The order of some of the amines are as

R of amine	Relative basic strength
$CH_3—$	$2° > 1° > 3° > NH_3$
$C_2H_5—$	$R_2NH > R_3N > RNH_2 > NH_3$
$Me_2CH—$	$RNH_2 > NH_3 > R_2NH > R_3N$
$Me_3C—$	$NH_3 > RNH_2 > R_2NH > R_3N$

The above two relations can be summarised as

Acid/Base	Group with + *I*-effect	Group with − *I*-effect
Acidic strength of acid	Decreases with this group	Increases with this group
Basic strength of base	Increases with this group	Decreases with this group

Example 7 Arrange the following compounds in increasing order of acidity.

I. $CH_3CH(Br)CH_2COOH$

II. $CH_3CH_2CH(Br)COOH$

III. $CH_3CH_2C(Br)_2COOH$

IV. $CH_2BrCH_2CH_2COOH$

Sol. As we know inductive effect decreases as we move away from the cause of polarity. Here, Br is the cause of polarity, so as the distance between Br and COOH increases, inductive effect as well as acidity decreases. Thus, the order of acidity is

$$III > II > I > IV$$

8.9 Resonance

When a single Lewis dot structure is unable to explain all the properties of a compound, two or more structures, called the **canonical forms** or **resonating structures or contributing structures** are drawn to explain all the properties of that compound, then the actual structure of the compound is in between these canonical forms and is called the **resonance hybrid** of these canonical forms. This phenomenon is called **resonance.** e.g. Benzene is a resonance hybrid of following two canonical forms.

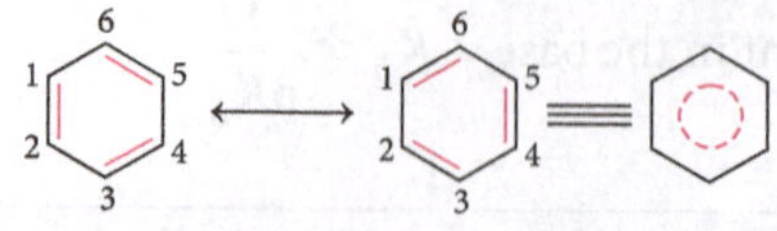

I II Resonance hybrid

Canonical forms

The resonating structures are hypothetical, i.e. have no real existence.

Resonance Energy

The energy of actual structure (or resonance hybrid) is lower than that of any of the canonical forms. The difference between hybrid and the energy of most stable (lowest energy) canonical form is called the **resonance stabilisation energy** or **resonance energy.** The more the number of important canonical forms more is the resonance energy. In case of resonating structures of equivalent energy, resonance is of great importance.

Conditions For Resonance

While writing resonance structures, the following conditions or rules are considered.

- The arrangement of atoms must be identical or almost same in every resonance structure.
- The energy content of all the canonical forms must be nearly the same.
- Each canonical form must have the same number of unpaired electrons.
- All the atoms in a molecule taking part in resonance should be present in same plane.

Stability of Canonical Forms

Among the canonical forms the most stable canonical form can be judged by following rules.

- Among all the canonical forms, the form without charges will be the most stable one.
- Among the charged forms
  - The structure in which maximum number of covalent bonds are present and octet of all the atoms (except hydrogen which has a duplet) are complete is most stable one.
  - The structure with less charge separation of opposite charge and more dispersal of charge, is more stable than the others.

Example 8 Draw the resonance structures of the following compounds.

(i) $CH_2{=}CH-\ddot{C}l:$

(ii) $CH_2{=}CH-CH{=}CH_2$

(iii) $CH_2{=}CH-\underset{|}{C}{=}O$ (with H on C)

Sol.

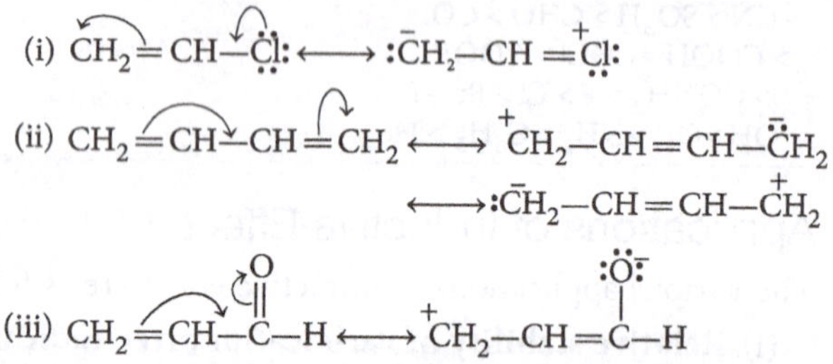

Example 9 Explain why the following two structures, I and II cannot be the major contributors to the real structure of CH_3COOCH_3. **NCERT**

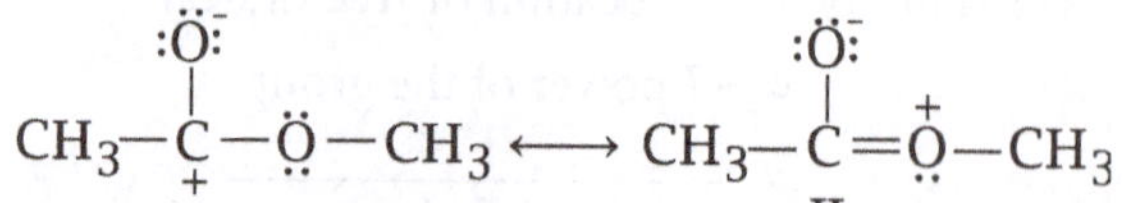

I II

Sol. In both the structures, there is charge separation and in structure I, the octet of one of the carbon is incomplete. That's why these two structures are less important contributors.

Example 10 Which of the following ions is more stable? Use resonance to explain your answer.

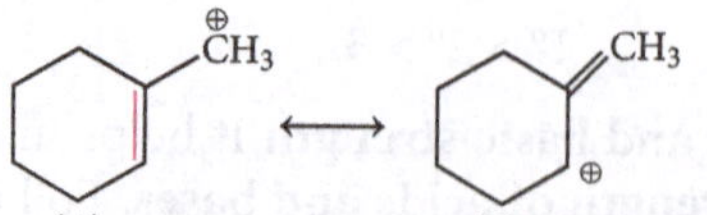

(A) (B)

Sol. Carbocation (A) is more stable than carbocation (B). Carbocation (A) is more planar and hence is stabilised by resonance while carbocation (B) is non-planar and hence it does not undergo resonance.

Further, double bond is more stable within the ring in comparison to outside the ring.

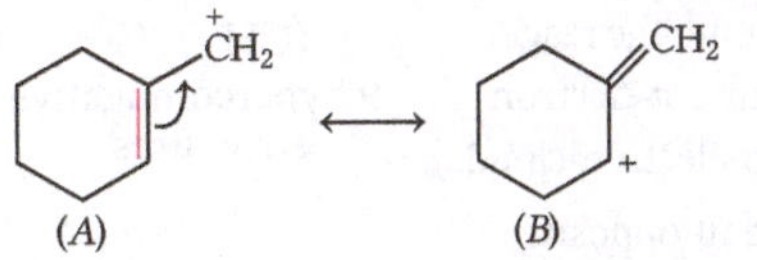

(A) (B)

Resonance Effect

The polarity developed within a molecule due to the interaction of two π-bonds or of a π-bond with the lone pair of electrons present on the adjacent atom is called the **resonance effect** (*R*). It is transmitted through the chain. It is also a permanent effect.

Depending upon the direction of transfer of electrons, this effect can be of following two types

Positive Resonance Effect (+*R* effect)	Negative Resonance Effect (–*R* effect)
When the electrons move away from the atom or substituent group attached to the conjugated system, the effect is called **positive resonance effect.**	When the electrons are transferred towards the atom or substituent group attached to the conjugated system, the effect is called **negative resonance effect.**
In this effect, electron densities increase at certain places, e.g. groups like halogen, —OH, —O*R*, —OCO*R*, —NH_2, —NH*R*, — NR_2 show + *R*-effect.	It results in decrease in density at certain places, i.e. at 2 and 4 or at *o*-and *p*-positions. Thus, now the *meta* (or 3) position becomes electron rich as compared to *o*-and *p*-positions and is generally attacked by the electrophile. — COOH, —CHO, C=O , —CN and —NO_2 are —*R* showing groups.
The + *R*-effect of NH_2 group in aniline is shown as 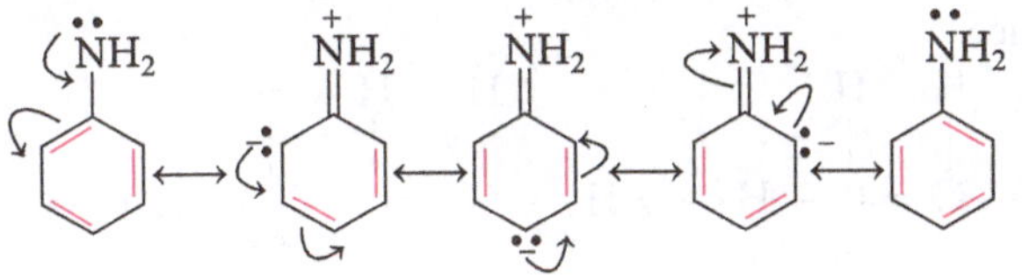	The –*R*-effect of—NO_2 in nitrobenzene can be represented in the following manner. 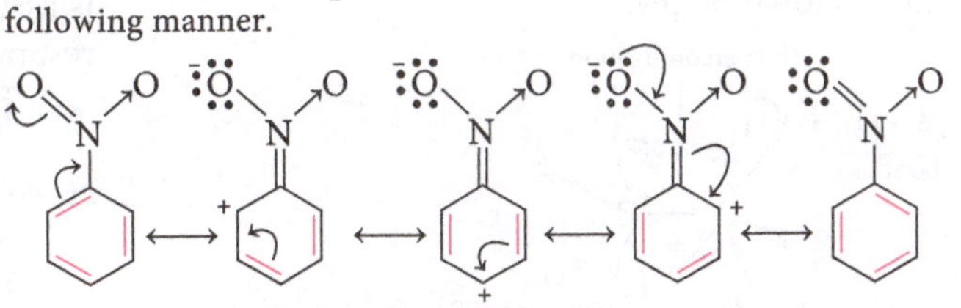

Note When single and double bonds are present alternately either in open chain or in cyclic system, the system is called conjugated system and such system often exhibit abnormal behaviour. In these systems, the π-bonds are delocalised and hence, polarity is developed.

Electromeric Effect (*E*-effect)

The polarity developed due to complete transfer of a shared pair of π-electrons to any of the atoms linked directly to the multiple bond in the presence of an attacking reagent is called the **electromeric effect.** It is a **temporary effect** and operates only in the presence of attacking reagent. It is a strong effect because of the involvement of weak π-bonds.

The electromeric effect is represented by means of a curved arrow beginning at original position of the electron pair and terminating where the pair has migrated. This effect may also be of + *E* type or of – *E* type.

Positive Electromeric Effect (+ *E*-effect)	Negative Electromeric Effect (– *E*-effect)
If the electrons of the π-bond are transferred to that atom of the double bond to which the reagent gets finally attached, it is known as + ***E*-effect.**	If the electrons of the double bond are transferred to an atom of the double bond other than the one to which the reagent gets finally attached, the effect is known as – ***E* effect.**
$CH_3—CH{=}CH_2 + \underset{\text{(Attacking reagent)}}{H^+} \longrightarrow CH_3—\overset{+}{C}H—CH_3$	$>C{=}O + \underset{\text{(Attacking reagent)}}{CN^-} \longrightarrow >C(CN)—O^-$

TEACHER'S TIP

- If π- and σ-bond both are present in a compound, the reagent always attacks the π-electron cloud first because π-electron cloud is always much more exposed than a σ-electron cloud.
- If inductive and electromeric effects operate in opposite directions, the electromeric effect predominates over the inductive effect.

Hyperconjugation

It is the considered as **special case of resonance**. The stabilising interaction that involves delocalisation of σ-electrons of C—H bond of an alkyl group linked directly to an atom of unsaturated system or to an atom having unshared *p*-orbital, is called **hyperconjugation**. It is a **permanent effect** and during this, partial conjugation is developed between the σ-electrons of C—H bond and the unsaturated system or the unshared *p*-orbital e.g. The positively charged carbon of ethyl cation ($CH_3CH_2^+$) has empty *p*-orbital, with which one of the C—H bonds of the methyl group align in its plane and thus, the electrons of the C—H bonds can be delocalised into the empty *p*-orbital as shown below.

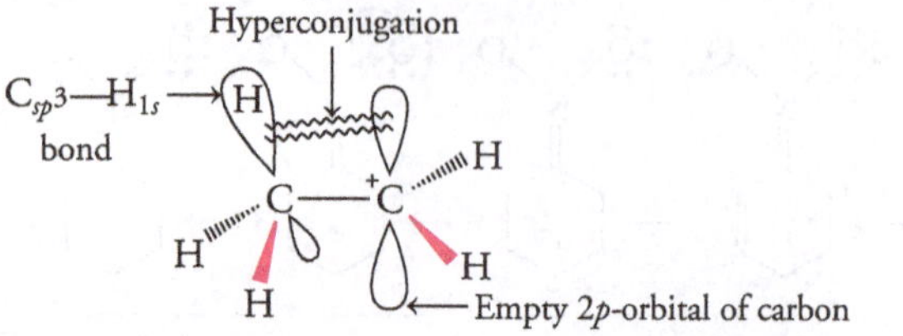

Orbital diagram showing hyperconjugation in ethyl cation

Such type of overlap makes the carbocation more stable because electron density from the adjacent σ-bond helps in dispersing the positive charge.

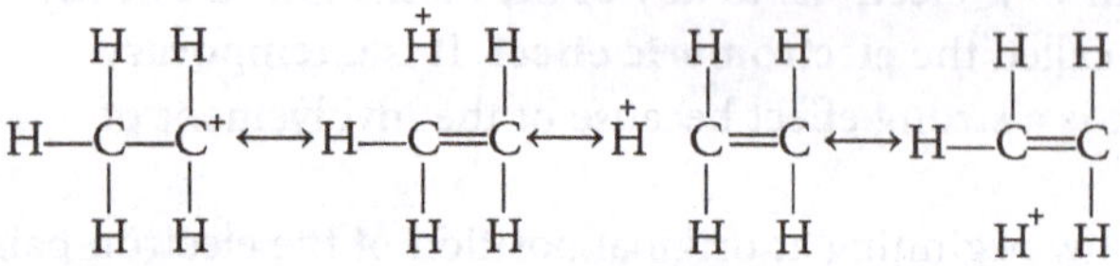

Hyperconjugation of Alkyl Carbocation

In general, as the number of alkyl groups attached to a positively charged carbon increases, the number of hyperconjugative structures increases and hence, the stability of cation increases.

Thus, the order of relative stabilities of carbocation is

$(CH_3)_3C^+$	>	$(CH_3)_2CH^+$	>	$CH_3CH_2^+$	> CH_3^+
9 hyperconjugative structures		6 hyperconjugative structures		3 hyperconjugative structures	

TEACHER'S TIP

Hyperconjugation involves both σ and π-orbitals whereas resonance only involves π-orbitals.

Hyperconjugation in Alkenes and Alkyl Arenes

Delocalisation of electrons due to hyperconjugation in case of alkenes is shown in below.

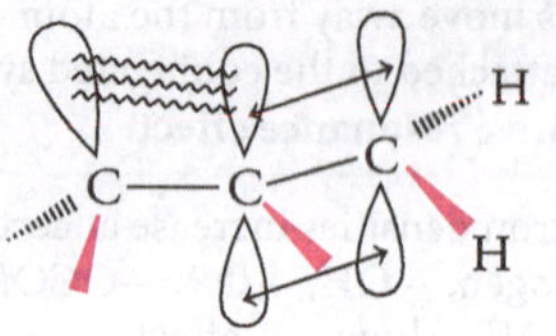

Orbital diagram showing hyperconjugation in propene

There are several ways to visualise hyperconjugative effect. An important of which is that in which C—H bond is assumed to have partial ionic character because of resonance.

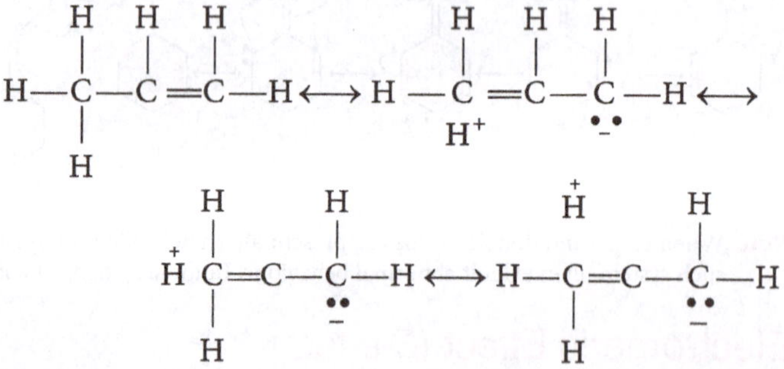

In such a condition, term 'no bond resonance' is used for hyperconjugation.

Conditions For Hyperconjugation

These are as follows

- Compound should have at least one sp^2-hybrid carbon of either alkene, alkyl carbocation or alkyl free radical.
- α-carbon with respect to sp^2-hybrid carbon should have atleast one hydrogen. More the number of H—C bonds attached to the unsaturated system, more stable will be the alkene.

Example 11 **Explain why $(CH_3)_3\overset{+}{C}$ is more stable than $CH_3\overset{+}{C}H_2$ and $\overset{+}{C}H_3$ is the least stable cation.** **NCERT**

Sol. $(CH_3)_3C^+$ has 9 hyperconjugative structures due to the presence of 9 C—H bonds but $CH_3CH_2^+$ possess only 6 hyperconjugative structures due to the presence of only 6 C—H bonds in conjugation with *p* orbital. Thus, $(CH_3)_3C^+$ is more stable than $CH_3CH_2^+$.

In CH_3^+, the C—H bonds are perpendicular to the plane of vacant *p*-orbital, so there is no overlapping between the electron of C—H bond and hence, CH_3^+ have no hyperconjugative stability. Thus, it is least stable among the given species.

Types of Organic Reactions and Mechanisms

The organic reactions can be categorised into following four categories.

1. Substitution Reactions

A substitution reaction is that which involves the direct replacement (displacement or substitution) of an atom or a group of atoms in an organic molecule by another atom or group of atoms without any change in the remaining part of the molecule.

e.g.

$$R\text{—}CH_3 + X_2 \xrightarrow[520\text{-}670\text{ K}]{h\nu \text{ or}} \underbrace{R\text{—}CH_2X}_{\text{Substitution product}} + HX$$

(Substituent: X)

On the basis of intermediate species, substitution reactions can further be classified into three categories. These are as follows

	Category	Definition	Example
(i)	**Free radical substitution reactions**	Substitution reaction brought about by free radicals.	Halogenation of alkanes $CH_4 + Cl_2 \xrightarrow[-HCl]{h\nu} CH_3Cl$ Chloromethane
(ii)	**Electrophilic substitution reactions**	Substitution reaction initiated by electrophiles.	Friedal Craft's Alkylation 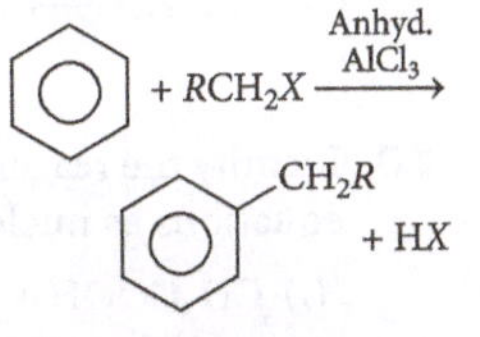 These reactions are characteristic of aromatic compounds.
(iii)	**Nucleophilic substitution reactions**	Substitution reactions which begins with attack of nucleophile.	These are usually written as S_N (S-substitution, N = nucleophile) and are of two types, i.e. unimolecular (shown as S_N1) and bimolecular (shown as S_N2). These reactions are generally seen in alkyl halides and alcohols. e.g. $RX + KOH(aq) \longrightarrow ROH + KX$

2. Elimination Reactions

An elimination reaction is one that involves the loss of two atoms or groups of atoms from the same or adjacent atoms of a substance in one or more step, leading to the formation of a multiple (double or triple) bond. Elimination reaction is given by those compounds which have a nucleophile as leaving group, i.e.

$$\bar{X},\ O\bar{H},\ \overset{\ominus}{O}R,\ \overset{\oplus}{N_2},\ N_3,\ \overset{\oplus}{N}R_3,\ \overset{\oplus}{S}R_2$$

Generally in these reactions, there is loss of two σ-bonds and gain of one π-bond, consequently, the product of such reactions is usually less stable than the reactant.

Elimination reactions are of two types

α-elimination Reactions or 1,1-elimination Reactions	β-elimination Reactions
• In these reactions, the loss of two atoms or groups occur from the same atom of the substrate molecule.	• In these reactions, the loss of two atoms or groups occur from the adjacent atoms of the substrate molecule.
• e.g. Base-catalysed dehydrohalogenation of chloroform to form dichlorocarbene. $CHCl_3 \xrightarrow{H^+} :\bar{C}Cl_3 \xrightarrow{-Cl^-} :CCl_2$ Dichlorocarbene	• e.g. Acid-catalysed dehydration of alcohols. $H\text{—}\overset{\beta}{C}H(OH)\text{—}\overset{\alpha}{C}H_2\text{—}H$ Ethane $\xrightarrow{\text{Conc. } H_2SO_4} CH_2{=}CH_2 + H_2O$ Ethene

3. Addition Reactions

Reactions which involve combination between two reacting molecules to give a single molecule of the product are called **addition reactions**. Generally, in these reactions one π-bond is cleaved and two σ-bonds are formed.

Such reactions are of typical compounds containing multiple (double and triple) bonds.

e.g. $R-CH=CH_2 + HX \longrightarrow R-\underset{\displaystyle X}{\underset{|}{C}H}-CH_3$

On the basis of the intermediate species, addition reactions can be further classified into following two categories.

Electrophilic Addition Reactions	Nucleophilic Addition Reactions
In these reactions, the electrophilic part of reagents initiates the reaction.	In these reactions, the nucleophilic part of reagent initiates the reaction.
Often involve unsaturated compounds like alkenes and alkynes.	These additions are seen in those compound which have unevenly distributed electron cloud, i.e. have a π-bond between two atoms of different electronegativity.
e.g. $\underset{CH_2}{\overset{CH_2}{\parallel}} + Br_2 \longrightarrow \underset{CH_2Br}{\overset{CH_2Br}{\mid}}$	e.g. π-electrone cloud in aldehydes and ketones. $HCN + H_3C-\overset{\overset{O}{\parallel}}{C}-CH_3 \longrightarrow H_3C-\overset{\overset{OH}{\mid}}{\underset{\underset{CN}{\mid}}{C}}-CH_3$

4. Rearrangement Reactions

Reactions involving the migration of an atom or a group from one site to another within the same molecule are called rearrangement reactions.

In this reaction nothing is added from outside and nothing is eliminated.

e.g. 1-bromobutane rearranges to 2-bromobutane in the presence of anhydrous $AlCl_3$ at 575 K.

$$\underset{\text{1-bromobutane}}{CH_3-CH_2-CH_2-CH_2-Br} \xrightarrow[575\ K]{\text{Anhyd. } AlCl_3} \underset{\text{2-bromobutane}}{CH_3-CH_2-\overset{\overset{Br}{|}}{C}H-CH_3}$$

(You will study about the above mentioned reactions in more details in next chapter and later in class XII).

Quick Test 3

1. Write the correct stability order for the following carbocations.

$(CH_3)_3C\overset{+}{C}H_2, (CH_3)_3\overset{+}{C}, CH_3CH_2\overset{+}{C}H_2$

2. Identify the most stable species in the following set of ions giving reasons. *NCERT Exemplar*

(i) $\overset{+}{C}H_3, \overset{+}{C}H_2Br, \overset{+}{C}HBr_2, \overset{+}{C}Br_3$ (ii) $\overset{-}{C}H_3, \overset{-}{C}H_2Cl, \overset{-}{C}HCl_2, \overset{-}{C}Cl_3$

3. Show the polarisation of carbon-magnesium bond in the following structure. *NCERT Exemplar*

$CH_3-CH_2-CH_2-CH_2-Mg-X$

4. Which bond is more polar in the following pair of molecules?

(i) H_3C-H or H_3C-Br (ii) H_3C-NH_2 or H_3C-OH
(iii) H_3C-OH or H_3C-SH *NCERT*

5. Which of the following compounds will not exist as resonance hybrid. Give reason for your answer. *NCERT Exemplar*

(i) CH_3OH (ii) $R-CONH_2$
(iii) $CH_3CH=CHCH_2NH_2$

6. Explain why alkyl groups act as electron donors when attached to a π-system? *NCERT Exemplar*

7. Which of the two structures A and B given below is more stabilised by resonance. Explain.

$\underset{A}{CH_3COOH}$ and $\underset{B}{CH_3CO\overset{\ominus}{O}}$

8. What is the relationship between the members of following pairs of structures? Are they structural or geometrical isomers or resonance contributors? *NCERT*

(i) 

(ii) $\underset{H}{\overset{D}{}}\rangle C=C\langle\underset{D}{\overset{H}{}}$ $\underset{H}{\overset{D}{}}\rangle C=C\langle\underset{H}{\overset{D}{}}$

(iii) $H-\overset{\overset{\overset{+}{O}H}{\parallel}}{C}-OH$ $H-\overset{\overset{OH}{|}}{C^+}-OH$

9. Classify the following reactions in one of the reaction type studied in this unit.

(i) $CH_3CH_2Br + HS^- \longrightarrow CH_3CH_2SH + Br^-$
(ii) $(CH_3)_2C=CH_2 + HCl \longrightarrow (CH_3)_2CCl-CH_3$
(iii) $CH_3CH_2Br + HO^- \longrightarrow CH_2=CH_2 + H_2O + Br^-$
(iv) $(CH_3)_3C-CH_2OH + HBr \longrightarrow (CH_3)_2CBrCH_2CH_3 + H_2O$ *NCERT*

10. Identify the reagents shown in bold in the following equations as nucleophiles or electrophiles.

(i) $CH_3COOH + \underline{HO^-} \longrightarrow CH_3COO^- + H_2O$
(ii) $CH_3COCH_3 + \underline{^-CN} \longrightarrow (CH_3)_2C(CN)(OH)$
(iii) $C_6H_6 + \underline{CH_3\overset{+}{C}O} \longrightarrow C_6H_5COCH_3$ *NCERT*

For Solutions, See QR Code on Pg. 341

8.10 Methods of Purification of Organic Compounds

As organic compounds have some impurities associated with them, i.e. these are not pure. Hence, it is essential to remove these impurities from them. The process of removal of impurities is called **purification**. A number of methods are available for the purification. The choice of a particular technique or method depends upon the nature of the compound whether solid or liquid and also on nature of impurities.

The purity of an organic compound can be ascertained by determining its physical constants like m.p., b.p., specific gravity, refractive index and viscosity.

Following techniques are used to purify an organic compound

Sublimation

(i) **Principle** This process is employed to separate non-sublimate impurities from a sublimate compound can be separated by this method.

(ii) **Process** In this process, the impure solid is taken in china dish and on heating solids which convert directly into vapours without converting into liquid phase and the vapours upon cooling give back the solid.

$$\text{Solid} \underset{\text{Cool}}{\overset{\text{Heat}}{\rightleftharpoons}} \text{Vapours}$$

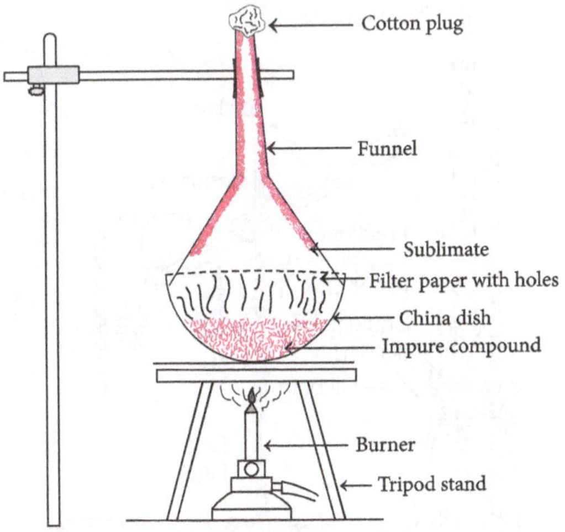

Ordinary sublimation

(iii) **Applications** Impure samples of naphthalene, anthracene, camphor, benzoic acid, NH_4Cl, $HgCl_2$, dry ice, salicylic acid, iodine etc., can be purified by this method provided that impurities are non-volatile.

TEACHER'S TIP

A mixture of two or more sublimates cannot be separated by **sublimation**. Such mixtures are separated by chemical methods.

Crystallisation

(i) **Principle** This process involves solidification of a pure substance from its dissolved state. It is based on the difference in the solubilities of the compound and the impurities in a suitable solvent.

(ii) **Process** The process of crystallisation involves the following steps

Selection of the solvent
↓
Preparation of the solution
↓
Filteration
↓
Crystallisation
↓
Separation and drying of crystals

In this method, the impure compound is dissolved in such a solvent in which it is sparingly soluble at room temperature but highly soluble at higher temperature.

- The solution is then concentrated upto the saturation point when the saturated solution is cooled slowly, the crystals of the pure compound separate out which are removed by filtration. The filtrate is called the **mother liquor**.
- When, a compound is highly soluble in one solvent and very less soluble in the other, a mixture of these two can be used for the crystallisation of the compound.
- If impurities give colour to the solution, then these are removed by adsorbing over activated charcoal.
- Similarly, if there is very less difference between the solubilities of the compound and the impurities, **repeated crystallisation** is necessary.

(iii) **Applications** Sugar having common salt as impurity can be crystallised through hot ethanol as it is soluble in hot ethanol but common salt does not.

Distillation

(i) **Principle** This process is based upon the difference in the boiling points of two liquids or two components. Thus, it is used to separate

- a volatile liquid from a non-volatile impurity.
- two liquids having large difference in their boiling points.

(ii) **Process** In this method, when the mixture of the liquids (having large difference in their boiling point) is heated by taking in a round bottom flask, the vapours of the lower boiling liquid are formed first.

- These vapours are condensed by the condenser and collected in a receiver.
- The vapours of higher boiling liquid are formed later and thus, collected separately. The apparatus used for simple distillation is shown in the following figure.

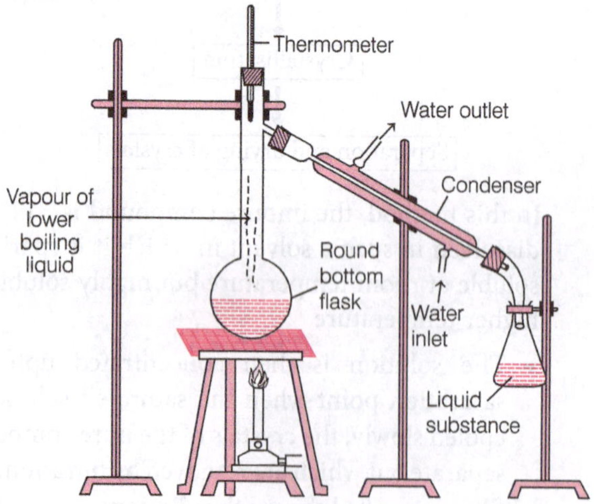

Simple distillation

(iii) **Applications** The mixtures of chloroform and aniline, ether and toluene, benzene, aniline, etc. are separated by this technique.

Fractional Distillation

(i) **Principle** It is used to separate the liquids, boiling points of which are nearly equal, i.e. within the limit of 10 K to 15 K. The vapours of higher boiling liquid condense before the vapours of lower boiling liquids.

(ii) **Process** In this method, a fractionating column is fitted over the mouth of the round bottom flask.

- As the vapours rise in the fractionating column, it becomes rich in the vapours of more volatile component.
- Fractionating column provides many surfaces for heat change between the ascending vapours and the descending condensed liquid.
- Some of the condensing liquid also get heat from the ascending vapours and revaporises.
- Thus, the vapours become rich in the low boiling component. The vapours of low boiling component move upward and reach at the top which contains mainly vapours of pure low boiling liquids.
- The vapours are collected in a receiver by passing through a condenser.
- After a series of successive distillations, the remaining liquid in the distillation flask gets enriched in high boiling component. Each successive condensation and vaporisation unit in the fractionating column is called a **theoretical plate.** Commercially columns with hundreds of plates are available.

(iii) **Applications** This method is used to separate different fractions of crude oil in petroleum industry.

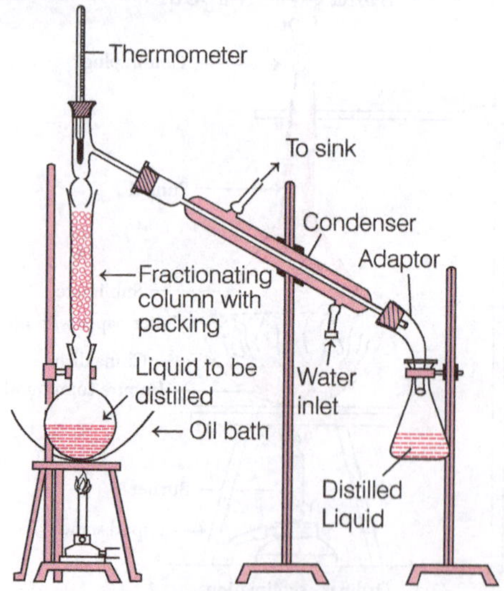

Fractional distillation

Distillation Under Reduced Pressure

(i) **Principle** It is used for those liquids which have a tendency to decompose at a temperature below their boiling point. At boiling point, vapour pressure of liquid is equal to its atmospheric pressure.

(ii) **Process** Under reduced pressure the liquid will boil at low temperature. Thus, temperature for decomposition is not reached. The reduced pressure is achieved by using a water pump or vacuum pump.

(iii) **Applications** Boiling point of glycerol is 563 K but it decomposes much before its boiling temperature.

However, at 12 mm of Hg pressure, glycerol boils at 453 K without decomposition, so glycerol is separated from spent lye in soap industry by using this method.

Other examples include H_2O_2, concentration of sugar cane juice in sugar industry.

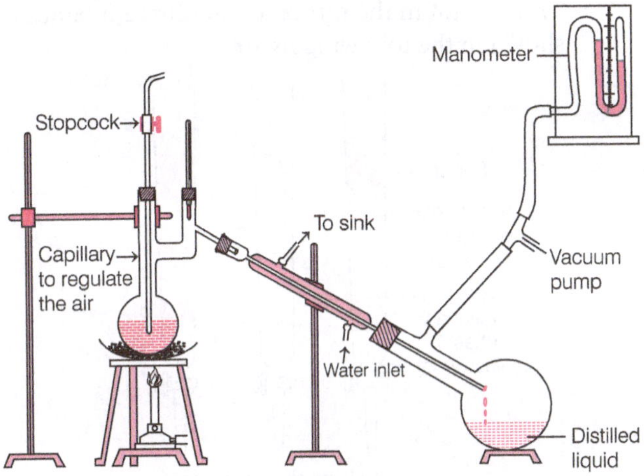

Distillation under reduced pressure

Steam Distillation

(i) **Principle** This technique is used for purifying steam volatile compounds that are immiscible with water.

(ii) **Process** In this method, the impure liquid is taken in a heated flask and steam is passed over it with the help of a steam generator.

- The mixture of steam and the volatile organic compound is condensed and collected in a receiver. From this mixture, water is removed by using separating funnel.
- During steam distillation, a liquid boils only when the sum of vapour pressure of the liquid (p_1) and of water (p_2) becomes equal to the atmospheric pressure (p), i.e. $p = p_1 + p_2$.
- Since, $p_1 < p$, so the liquid will vapourise at a temperature much below than its boiling point. e.g. A mixture of water and a steam volatile insoluble substance will vapourise close but below 373 K.

(iii) **Applications** The technique is used for separating aniline from aniline-water mixture.

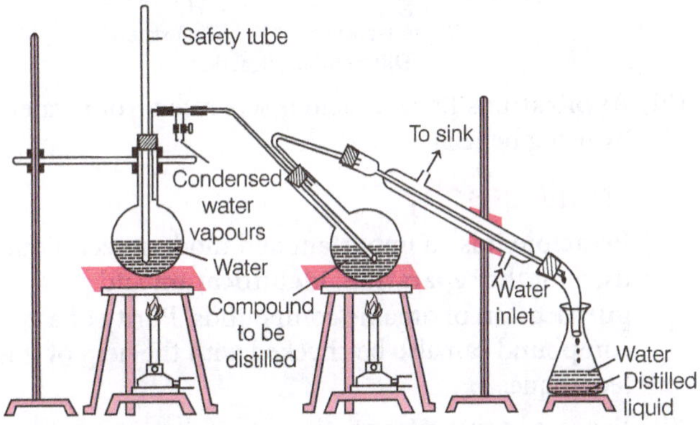

Steam distillation

Differential Extraction

(i) **Principle** This process is based on the more solubility of solute in a suitable organic solvent (or compound) as compared to water and is used to separate a given organic compound present in an aqueous solution from the water.

(ii) **Process** The process involves shaking of solution with a suitable organic solvent in which the compound is more soluble as compared to water such as ether, chloroform or benzene, in a separating funnel (which is shown below in the figure).

- While performing such an act one point should be kept in mind that solvent and water must form two distinct layers that can be separated by using separating funnel.
- The organic solvent from the compound can be removed by either distillation or evaporation.

- If the solubility of organic compound is very less in the organic solvent then a very large quantity of the solvent is required to extract even a very minute amount of the compound.
- In such a condition, **continuous extraction** is used, which involves the repeated use of same solvent for the extraction of the compound.

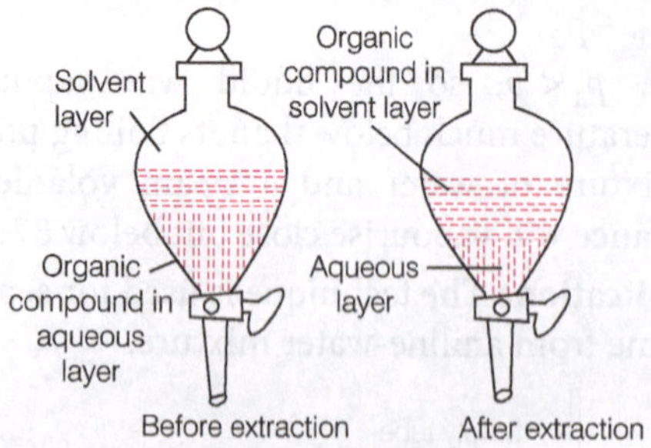

Differential extraction

(iii) **Applications** Benzoic acid is separated from water by using benzene.

Chromatography

(i) **Principle** It is an important and modern technique used for the **separation, identification** and **purification** of organic compounds. Purity of a compound can also be checked with the help of this technique.

(ii) **Process** In this method, there are following two phases.

- The mixture of substances to be tested which may be in solid or liquid state act as the **stationary phase.**
- The pure solvent or mixture of solvents or a gas which is allowed to pass over the stationary phase is called the **mobile phase.**
- The components of the mixture get gradually separated from one another.

Depending upon the principle involved, the chromatography is classified into different categories, two important of which are as follows

I. Adsorption Chromatography

(i) **Principle** This method is based upon the different rates of adsorption of different compounds by an adsorbent.

(ii) **Process** When the mobile phase is passed over the stationary phase (adsorbent), the components of the mixture move by different distance over the stationary phase and thus, they can be separated or identified.

(iii) **Applications** Silica gel and alumina are generally used as adsorbent during this process.

Two main chromatographic methods working on the principle of differential adsorption are as follows

1. Column Chromatography

(i) **Principle** The mixture is passed through adsorbent packed in glass tube.

(ii) **Process**

- A glass tube containing adsorbent (stationary phase) and is fitted with a stopcock at its lower end is called the **column.**
- The mixture of substance to be separated is placed at the top portion of the column over the adsorbent.
- When the suitable solvent or mixture of solvent, called the **eluant** is allowed to pass through the column, different components due to their different rate of adsorption move different distances.
- Thus, result in the formation of different bands as shown in the following figure.

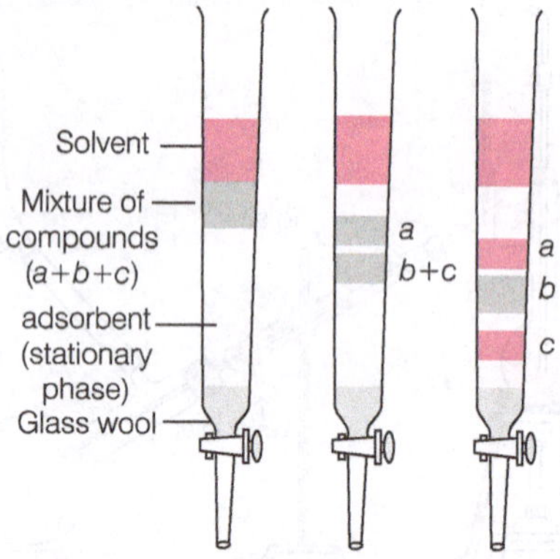

Column chromatography

- The most readily adsorbed component is retained at the top and the less readily adsorbed components form separate band below it at various distances.

(iii) **Applications** Mixture of naphthalene and benzophenone.

2. Thin Layer Chromatography (TLC)

(i) **Principle** In this method, a glass plate of suitable size is coated with a thin layer (about 0.2 mm) of adsorbent. (Silica gel or alumina). This plate is called the **thin layer chromatography plate** or **chromaplate.**

(ii) **Process**

- On chromaplate, the solution of mixture to be separated is applied in the form of a small spot, about 2 cm above the one end.
- The plate is then placed in a closed jar having eluant.
- As the eluant rises up the plate, the components of the mixture move with it upto different distances depending upon their different rates of adsorption and get separated from one another as shown below.

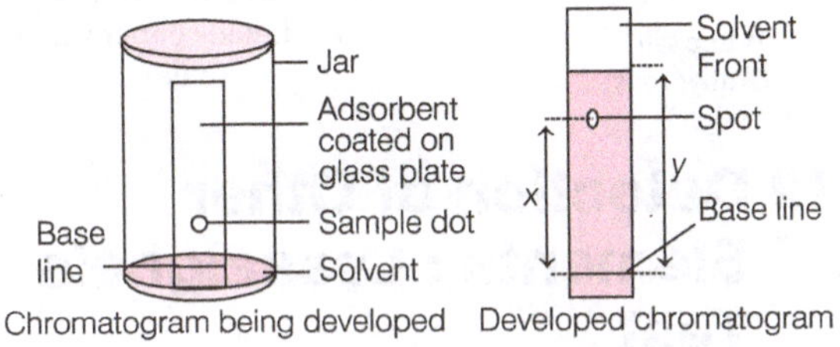

Thin layer chromatography

(iii) **Applications** The relative adsorption of different components is expressed in terms of retardation factor (R_f values) which is given as

$$R_f = \frac{\text{Distance moved by the substance from base line } (x)}{\text{Distance moved by the solvent from base line } (y)}$$

The spot of the coloured components are visible on the TLC plate due to their own colour. However, the spots of colourless substance are made visible by placing the plate

- under UV light.
- in a covered jar having few crystals of iodine. (component that adsorb iodine appear in the form of brown spots).
- an appropriate reagent may be spread on the plate, e.g. ninhydrin solution is sprayed to detect the presence of amino acids.

TEACHER'S TIP

Column chromatography is the simplest among all the chromatographic techniques. It is named so because in column chromatography the entire process is carried out in a long glass tube known as column.

II. Partition Chromatography

(i) **Principle** This method is based on the continuous differential partitioning of components of a mixture between stationary and mobile phases.

(ii) **Process**

- **Paper chromatography** is a type that works on this principle. In this method, a special type of paper, called the **chromatography paper** is used.
- This paper contains water trapped in it and act as the **stationary phase.**
- The mixture of the components to be separated is placed in the form of small spot about 2 cm above from the lower end (at the base line).
- When this strip is suspended in a suitable solvent or a mixture of solvents which act as the **mobile phase**, the solvent start rising up the paper due to capillary action and flows over the spot.
- The paper selectively retains different components on the basis of their different partition in the two phases.
- The paper strip so obtained is called the **chromatogram.**
- The spots of separated coloured components are visible at different heights from the original spot of the mixture on the chromatogram.
- However, the spots of colourless substances are observed by using the same methods as done in thin layer chromatography.

(iii) **Application**

- For separating of sugars and amino acids.
- For separating a coloured ink.

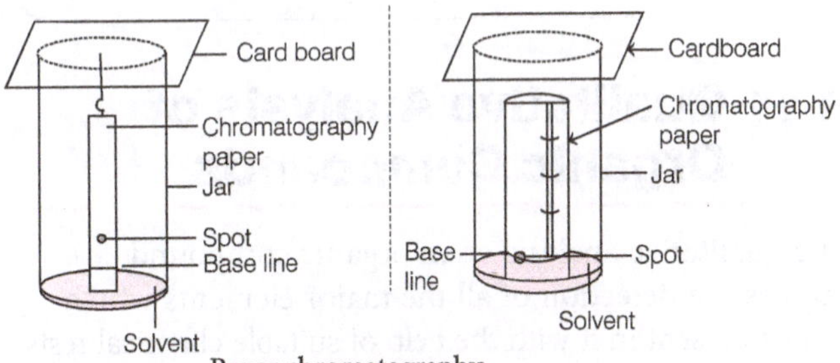

Paper chromatography

TEACHER'S TIP

Generally, sharp m.p. (in case of solids) and b.p. (in case of liquids) are used as a criteria for purity because their determination is feasible in the laboratory.

Quick Test 4

1. What type of solvent should be chosen for crystallisation ? DIKSHA
2. Name a suitable technique of separation of the components from a mixture of calcium sulphate and camphor. NCERT
3. If a liquid compound decomposes at its boiling point, which method(s) can you choose for its purification. It is known that the compound is stable at low pressure, steam volatile and insoluble in water. NCERT Exemplar
4. Describe the method, which can be used to separate two compounds with different solubilities in a solvent S. NCERT
5. Benzoic acid is an organic compound. Its crude sample can be purified by crystallisation from hot water. What characteristic differences in the properties of benzoic acid and the impurity make this process of purification suitable?
6. Suggest a method to purify
   (i) camphor containing traces of common salt.
   (ii) kerosene oil containing water.
   (iii) a liquid which decomposes at its boiling point.
7. Two liquids *A* and *B* can be separated by the method of fractional distillation. The boiling point of liquid *A* is less than boiling point of liquid *B*. Which of the liquids do you expect to come out first in the distillate? Explain. NCERT Exemplar
8. What type of solvent should be chosen for the differential extraction of an organic compound? DIKSHA
9. Suggest methods for the separation of the following mixtures
   (i) a mixture of liquid *A* (bp 365K) and liquid *B* (bp 355 K)
   (ii) a mixture of liquid *C* (bp 348 K) and liquid *D* (bp 478 K).
10. What is the principle of paper chromatography? DIKSHA

For Solutions, See QR Code on Pg. 341

8.11 Qualitative Analysis of Organic Compounds

The qualitative analysis of an organic compound implies the detection of all the major elements which can be present in it with the help of suitable chemical tests.

Detection of Carbon and Hydrogen

To detect the presence of carbon and hydrogen, the compound is heated with dry copper (II) oxide. By this, carbon is oxidised to CO_2 and hydrogen to water. H_2O is detected by anhydrous $CuSO_4$ (white) which turns it blue and CO_2 is detected by lime water which turns milky that confirms the presence of hydrogen and copper. This method is known as **copper oxide test.**

$$C + 2CuO \xrightarrow{\Delta} 2Cu + CO_2$$

(Turns lime water milky)

$$\underset{\text{Lime water}}{Ca(OH)_2} + CO_2 \longrightarrow \underset{\text{Milky}}{CaCO_3\downarrow} + H_2O$$

$$CuO + 2H \xrightarrow{\Delta} Cu + H_2O$$

(From organic compound)

(Water drops turns anhydrous $CuSO_4$ to blue)

$$\underset{\substack{\text{White salt}\\\text{(Anhydrous)}}}{CuSO_4} + 5H_2O \longrightarrow \underset{\substack{\text{Hydrated copper sulphate}\\\text{(blue)}}}{CuSO_4 \cdot 5H_2O}$$

8.12 Detection of Other Elements : Lassaigne's Test

The elements other than C and H (like N, S, *X*, P) present in organic compound are detected with the help of **Lassaigne's test.** In this test, the compound is fused with small quantity of Na metal in a fusion tube to convert the elements present in covalent form into their ionic forms. Following reactions take place.

$$Na + C + N \xrightarrow[\Delta]{\text{Fusion}} \underset{\text{Sodium cyanide}}{NaCN}$$

$$2Na + S \xrightarrow[\Delta]{\text{Fusion}} \underset{\text{Sodium sulphide}}{Na_2S}$$

$$Na + C + N + S \xrightarrow{\Delta} \underset{\text{Sodium sulphocyanide}}{NaSCN}$$

(when N and S both are present)

$$Na + \underset{\text{Halogen}}{X} \xrightarrow{\Delta} \underset{\text{Sodium halide}}{NaX}$$

Cyanide, sulphide, sulphocyanide and halide of sodium so formed on sodium fusion are extracted from the fused mass by boiling it with distilled water. This extract is known as **sodium fusion extract** or Lassaigne's extract.

TEACHER'S TIP

- Organic compounds being covalents normally do not have ionisable groups, hence direct test is not possible for them.
- Lassaigne's test fails in case of diazo compounds.

Test	Confirmatory Test	Reactions Involved
Test for Nitrogen	A part of the sodium fusion extract is boiled with freshly prepared solution of iron (II) sulphate and then the solution is acidified with concentrated H_2SO_4 (which oxidise Fe^{2+} into Fe^{3+}). Formation of Prussian blue colour shows the presence of nitrogen. **Lassaigne's test** is positive for nitrogen only when the compound contains carbon alongwith nitrogen. $NH_2NH_2 \cdot HCl$ contains nitrogen but does not contain carbon, thus, NaCN is not formed and hence, test of N is negative.	$6CN^- + Fe^{2+} \longrightarrow \underset{\text{Hexacyanidoferrate}}{[Fe(CN)_6]^{4-}}$ $[Fe(CN)_6]^{4-} + 4Fe^{3+} \xrightarrow{xH_2O} \underset{\text{Prussian blue}}{Fe_4[Fe(CN)_6]_3 \cdot xH_2O}$
Test for Sulphur	(i) The sodium fusion extract is acidified with acetic acid and lead acetate is added to it. A black precipitate of lead sulphide indicates the presence of sulphur. (ii) On treating sodium fusion extract with sodium nitroprusside, appearance of a violet colour further indicates the presence of sulphur.	$Na_2S + \underset{\text{Lead acetate}}{(CH_3COO)_2Pb} \longrightarrow \underset{\text{Black ppt.}}{PbS\downarrow} + 2CH_3COO^-Na^+$ $\underset{\text{From sodium extract}}{Na_2S} + \underset{\text{Sodium nitroprusside}}{Na_2[Fe(CN)_5NO]} \longrightarrow \underset{\text{Violet colour}}{Na_4[Fe(CN)_5NOS]}$
Test for Nitrogen and Sulphur	If the compound contains sulphur and nitrogen both, sodium sulphocyanide is formed in Lassaigne's extract which gives blood red colour of $Fe[(SCN)]^{2+}$ on reaction with $FeCl_3$. **Caution** If sodium fusion is carried out with excess of sodium, the thiocyanate decomposes to yield cyanide and sulphide. These ions give their usual tests. $NaSCN + 2Na \longrightarrow NaCN + Na_2S$	$\underbrace{Na + C + N + S}_{\text{From organic compound}} \longrightarrow \underset{\text{Sodium sulphocyanide}}{NaSCN}$ $\underset{\text{(Pale yellow)}}{Fe^{3+}} + SCN^-(aq) \longrightarrow \underset{\text{(Blood red)}}{Fe[(SCN)]^{2+}(aq)}$
Test for Halogens	The sodium fusion extract is acidified with dil. HNO_3 and then treated with $AgNO_3$ if a participate is formed, it indicates the **presence of a halogen.** The colour of precipitate, in turn, indicates the nature of halogen, *viz.* • white colour ppt. soluble in NH_4OH indicates chlorine. • pale yellow colour ppt. sparingly soluble in NH_4OH indicates bromine and • yellow colour ppt. insoluble in NH_4OH indicates iodine.	$NaCN + HNO_3 \longrightarrow NaNO_3 + HCN\uparrow$ $Na_2S + 2HNO_3 \longrightarrow 2NaNO_3 + H_2S\uparrow$ $Na + X \longrightarrow \underset{\text{Lassaigne's extract}}{NaX}$ $(X = Cl, Br, I)$ $NaCl + AgNO_3 \longrightarrow \underset{\text{White ppt.}}{AgCl} + NaNO_3$ $NaBr + AgNO_3 \longrightarrow \underset{\text{Dull yellow ppt.}}{AgBr\downarrow} + NaNO_3$ $AgNO_3 + NaI \longrightarrow \underset{\text{Yellow ppt.}}{AgI\downarrow} + NaNO_3$
Test for Phosphorus	For the detection of phosphorus, organic compound is fused with sodium peroxide (oxidising agent) hence, phosphorus is converted into sodium phosphate. The fused mass is extracted with water and the water extract is boiled with conc. HNO_3. Upon cooling, a few drops of ammonium molybdate solution are added, a yellow ppt. confirms the presence of phosphorus in the organic compound.	$5Na_2O_2 + \underset{\text{Compound}}{2P} \xrightarrow{\text{Fuse}} \underset{\text{Sodium phosphate}}{2Na_3PO_4} + 2Na_2O$ $Na_3PO_4 + 3HNO_3 \longrightarrow H_3PO_4 + 3NaNO_3$ $H_3PO_4 + \underset{\text{Ammonium molybdate}}{12(NH_4)_2MoO_4} + 21HNO_3 \longrightarrow$ $\underset{\text{(Yellow ppt.) Ammonium phosphomolybdate}}{(NH_4)_3PO_4 \cdot 12MoO_3\downarrow} + 21NH_4NO_3 + 12H_2O$

8.13 Quantitative Analysis

This type of analysis of compounds is very useful in organic chemistry as it helps in the determining the mass percentage of different elements present in a given organic compound. In Chapter-1, we have already studied the mass percentage of elements and use it in the determination of empirical and molecular formula.

The percentage of different elements present in an organic compound can be determined with the help of following methods.

Estimation of Carbon and Hydrogen

(i) **Method and its principle** The C and H in an organic compound are estimated by **Liebig method**. In this method, the organic compound is heated with dry cupric oxide in an atmosphere of dry oxygen (or air) free from CO_2. Thus, the C and H present in the organic compound are oxidised to CO_2 and water vapours, respectively.

$$C_xH_y + (x + y/4)O_2 \longrightarrow xCO_2 + (y/2)H_2O$$

- CO_2 vapours are passed through weighed potassium hydroxide containing in another U-tube which absorbs CO_2 completely. The increase in the weight of potassium hydroxide corresponds to the weight of CO_2 produced.

$$2KOH + CO_2 \longrightarrow K_2CO_3 + H_2O$$

- Water vapours are passed through weighed anhydrous calcium chloride containing in tube (U-shaped). Increase in the weight of $CaCl_2$ corresponds to the weight of H_2O formed.

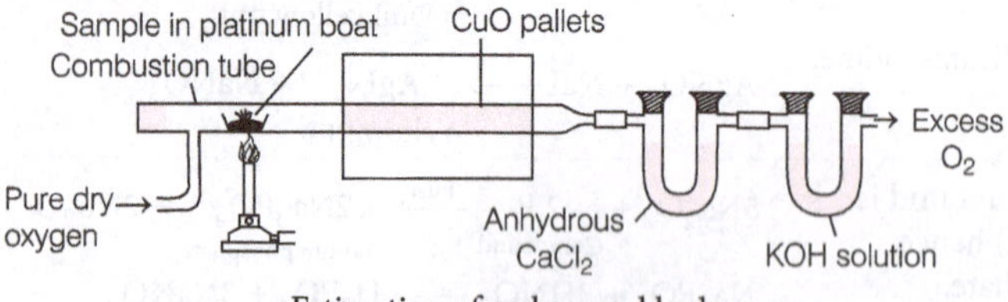

Estimation of carbon and hydrogen

(ii) **Formula** From the respective weights, the percentage of C and H can be determined as

$$\% \text{ of carbon} = \frac{12 \times \text{mass of } CO_2 \times 100}{44 \times \text{mass of organic compound}}$$

$$\% \text{ of hydrogen} = \frac{2 \times \text{mass of } H_2O \times 100}{18 \times \text{mass of organic compound}}$$

Example 12 **On complete combustion, 0.246 g of an organic compound gave 0.198% of carbon dioxide and 0.1014 g of water. Determine the percentage composition of carbon and hydrogen in the compound.** **NCERT**

Sol. Percentage of carbon $= \frac{12 \times 0.198 \times 100}{44 \times 0.246} = 21.95\%$

Percentage of hydrogen $= \frac{2 \times 0.1014 \times 100}{18 \times 0.246} = 4.58\%$

Estimation of Nitrogen

Following two methods are used to estimate the percentage of nitrogen in an organic compound.

A. Dumas Method

(i) **Method and Principle** In this method, organic compound is heated with dry cupric oxide in a combustion tube in the atmosphere of CO_2. Upon heating, C and H present are oxidised to CO_2 and water vapours respectively, while N_2 is set free.

$$C_xH_yN_z + (2x + y/2)CuO \longrightarrow xCO_2 + y/2\,H_2O + \frac{z}{2}N_2 + (2x + y/2)Cu$$

A small amount of N_2 might be oxidised to its oxides but they are reduced back to N_2 with the help of Cu placed at the end of the combustion tube. The mixture of gases so produced is collected over an aqueous solution of potassium hydroxide which absorbs carbon dioxide. Nitrogen is collected in the upper part of the graduated tube.

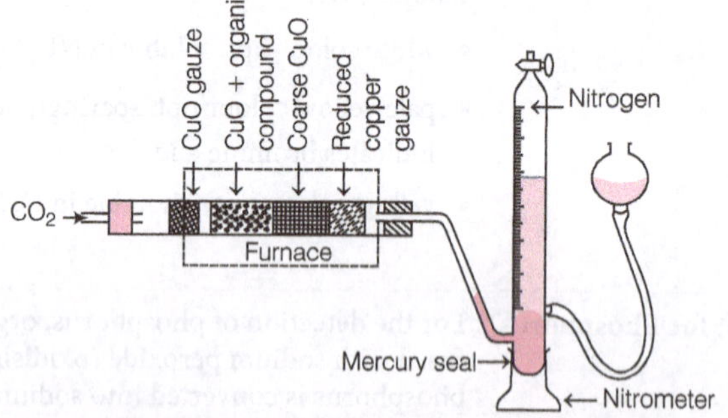

Dumas method for the estimation of nitrogen

(ii) **Formula** Let the mass of organic compound $= m$ g;

Volume of nitrogen collected $= V_1$ mL;

Room temperature $= T_1$K

Volume of nitrogen at STP $= \frac{p_1V_1 \times 273}{760 \times T_1}$

(let it be V mL)

where, p_1 and V_1 are the pressure and volume of nitrogen.

p_1 = Atmospheric pressure − Aqueous tension

$\because$ 22400 mL N_2 at STP weight 28 g

$\therefore$ V mL N_2 at STP weights $= \dfrac{28 \times V}{22400}$ g

$$\therefore \text{Percentage of nitrogen} = \frac{28 \times V \times 100}{22400 \times m}$$

Example 13 In Dumas method for estimation of nitrogen, 0.3 g of an organic compound gave 50 mL of nitrogen collected at 300 K temperature and 715 mm pressure. Calculate the percentage composition of nitrogen in the compound.
(Aqueous tension at 300 K = 15 mm). **NCERT**

Sol. Volume of nitrogen collected at 300 K and 715 mm pressure = 50 mL

Actual pressure = 715 − 15 = 700 mm;

Volume of nitrogen at STP $= \dfrac{273 \times 700 \times 50}{300 \times 760} = 41.9$ mL

$\because$ 22,400 mL of N_2 at STP weights = 28 g

$\therefore$ 41.9 mL of nitrogen weights $= \dfrac{28 \times 41.9}{22400}$ g

$\therefore$ Percentage of nitrogen $= \dfrac{28 \times 41.9 \times 100}{22400 \times 0.3} = 17.46\%$

B. Kjeldahl's Method

(i) **Method and Principle** This method is based on the principle that when the nitrogenous compound is heated with conc. H_2SO_4 in the presence of potassium sulphate, (which raises the boiling point of H_2SO_4) and $CuSO_4$ (catalyst), the nitrogen present in the compound is converted to ammonium sulphate. The ammonium sulphate, so formed is decomposed with excess of alkali (NaOH) and NH_3 get evolved that is estimated volumetrically, using the titration of an acid.

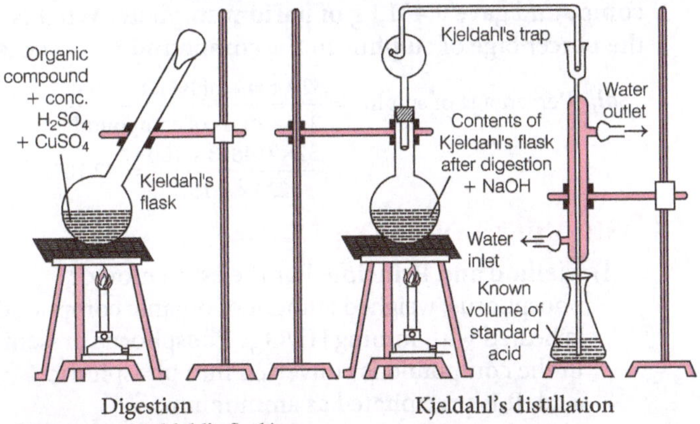

Kjeldahl's method for estimating nitrogen

It is done by estimating unreacted sulphuric acid left after the absorption of ammonia by titrating it with standard alkali solution.

The difference between the initial amount of acid taken and that left after the reaction gives the amount of acid reacted with ammonia.

$$\text{Organic compound} + H_2SO_4 \longrightarrow (NH_4)_2SO_4 \xrightarrow{2\,NaOH} Na_2SO_4 + 2NH_3 + 2H_2O$$

$$2NH_3 + H_2SO_4 \longrightarrow (NH_4)_2SO_4$$

(ii) **Formula**

Let the mass of organic compound taken = m g

Volume of H_2SO_4 of molarity, M taken = V mL

Volume of NaOH of molarity, M, used for titration of excess of $H_2SO_4 = V_1$ mL

V_1 mL of NaOH of molarity $M = \dfrac{V_1}{2}$ mL of H_2SO_4 of molarity M

Volume of H_2SO_4 of molarity M unused $= (V - V_1/2)$ mL

$(V - V_1/2)$ mL of H_2SO_4 of molarity M $= 2(V - V_1/2)$ mL of NH_3 solution of molarity M.

1000 mL of 1 M NH_3 solution contains = 17 g NH_3 or 14 g of N

$2(V - V_1/2)$ mL of NH_3 solution of molarity M contains

$$= \frac{14 \times M \times 2\,(V - V_1/2)}{1000} \text{ g N}$$

$$\text{Percentage of N} = \frac{14 \times M \times 2\,(V - V_1/2)}{1000} \times \frac{100}{m} = \frac{1.4 \times M \times 2(V - V_1/2)}{m}$$

TEACHER'S TIP

Kjeldahl's method is not applicable to compounds containing nitrogen in nitro and azo groups and nitrogen present in the ring, as nitrogen of these compounds is not quantitatively converted into ammonium sulphate.

Example 14 During estimation of nitrogen present in an organic compound by Kjeldahl's method, the ammonia evolved from 0.5 g of the compound in Kjeldahl's estimation of nitrogen, neutralized 10 mL of 1 M H_2SO_4. Find out the percentage of nitrogen in the compound. **NCERT**

Sol. 1 M of 10 mL H_2SO_4 = 1 M of 20 mL NH_3

$\because$ 1000 mL of 1 M ammonia contains nitrogen = 14 g

$\therefore$ 20 mL of 1 M ammonia will contain nitrogen $= \frac{14 \times 20}{1000}$ g

$\therefore$ Percentage of nitrogen $= \frac{14 \times 20 \times 100}{1000 \times 0.5}$

$= 56.0\%$

Estimation of Halogens

(i) **Method and Principle** In the case of halogens, estimation is done with **Carius method.**

Here, the weighed amount of organic compound is heated in a sealed tube called the **Carius tube,** with fuming HNO_3 in the presence of $AgNO_3$. Carbon and hydrogen present in the compound are oxidised to CO_2 and H_2O.

As a result, halogen present in the organic compound is converted into AgX which is filtered, washed, dried and weighed.

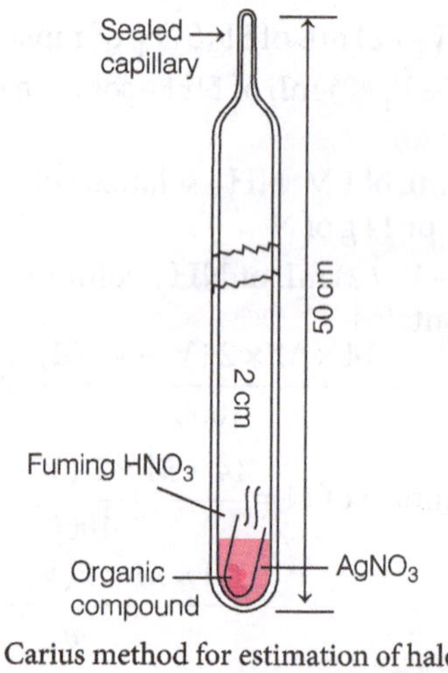

Carius method for estimation of halogen

(ii) **Formula** Let the mass of organic compound taken = m g

Mass of AgX formed = m_1 g

1 mol of AgX contains 1 mol of X

Mass of halogen is m_1 g of AgX

$$= \frac{\text{atomic mass of } X \times m_1 \text{g}}{\text{molecular mass of AgX}}$$

$$\text{Percentage of halogen} = \frac{\text{atomic mass of } X \times m_1 \times 100}{\text{molecular mass of AgX} \times m}$$

Thus,

$$\% \text{ of chlorine} = \frac{35.5}{143.5} \times \frac{\text{mass of AgCl} \times 100}{\text{mass of compound}}$$

$$\% \text{ of bromine} = \frac{80}{188} \times \frac{\text{mass of AgBr} \times 100}{\text{mass of compound}}$$

$$\% \text{ of iodine} = \frac{127}{235} \times \frac{\text{mass of AgI} \times 100}{\text{mass of compound}}$$

Example 15 **In carius method of estimation of halogen, 0.15 g of an organic compound gave 0.12 of AgBr. Find out the percentage of bromine in the compound.** **NCERT**

Sol. Percentage of bromine $= \frac{80}{188} \times \frac{\text{mass of AgBr} \times 100}{\text{mass of compound}}$

$= \frac{80 \times 0.12 \times 100}{188 \times 0.15} = 34.04\%$

Estimation of Sulphur

(i) **Method and Principle** It is also estimated by **Carius method.** In this case, the compound is heated with sodium peroxide or fuming HNO_3, resulting to oxidation of its sulphur to H_2SO_4 which is collected as $BaSO_4$ by using excess of barium chloride solution. The precipitate of $BaSO_4$ is filtered, washed, dried and weighed.

(ii) **Formula** Let the mass of organic compound taken = m g and the mass of barium sulphate formed = m_1 g

1 mole of $BaSO_4$ = 233 g $BaSO_4$ = 32 g sulphur

m_1 g $BaSO_4$ contains $= \frac{32 \times m_1}{233}$ g sulphur

$$\text{Percentage of sulphur} = \frac{32 \times m_1 \times 100}{233 \times m}$$

Example 16 **In sulphur estimation, 0.157 g of an organic compound gave 0.4813 g of barium sulphate. What is the percentage of sulphur in the compound ?** **NCERT**

Sol. Percentage of sulphur $= \frac{32 \times \text{mass of } BaSO_4 \times 100}{233 \times \text{mass of compound}}$

$= \frac{32 \times 0.4813 \times 100}{233 \times 0.157} = 42.10\%$

Estimation of Phosphorus

(i) **Method and Principle** For the estimation of phosphorus, weighed amount of organic compound is heated with fuming HNO_3. Phosphorus present in the compound is converted into phosphoric acid. It is precipitated as ammonium phosphomolybdate, $(NH_4)_3PO_4 \cdot 12MoO_3$, by adding ammonia and ammonium molybdate.

(ii) **Formula**

Let the mass of organic compound taken $= m$ g and mass of ammonium phosphomolybdate $= m_1$ g

Molar mass of $(NH_4)_3PO_4 \cdot 12MoO_3 = 1877$ g

$$\text{Percentage of phosphorus} = \frac{31 \times m_1 \times 100}{1877 \times m} \%$$

Alternative Method and Method and Principle

Alternatively, the contents of the tube are heated with $MgCl_2$ solution in the presence of NH_4Cl and NH_4OH (magnesia mixture), the $MgNH_4PO_4$ so formed is collected, washed, dried and ignited to get magnesium pyrophosphate $(Mg_2P_2O_7)$ which is weighed and the percentage of P is calculated.

Formula

$$\text{Percentage of P} = \frac{62 \times \text{mass of } Mg_2P_2O_7 \text{ formed}}{222 \times \text{mass of the compound}} \times 100\%$$

Where, 222 u is the molar mass of $Mg_2P_2O_7$ and 62 is the mass of two P-atom present in $Mg_2P_2O_7$.

Estimation of Oxygen

If sum of percentage of all other elements present in a compound is less than 100, then % of oxygen =100 – sum of % of all other elements.

Direct Method for Estimation of Oxygen

(i) **Method and Principle** In this method, a calculated quantity of the organic compound is heated in a stream of nitrogen gas and the obtained oxygen is converted into CO by passing the gaseous mixture over red hot coke. The CO is warmed with I_2O_5 (iodine pentoxide), which oxidises CO to CO_2 and itself gets reduced to I_2.

$$\text{Compound} \xrightarrow{\text{Heat}} O_2 + \text{other gaseous products}$$

$$2C + O_2 \xrightarrow{1373\text{ K}} 2CO\ ] \times 5 \quad \ldots \text{(A)}$$

$$I_2O_5 + 5CO \longrightarrow I_2 + 5CO_2\ ] \times 2 \quad \ldots \text{(B)}$$

From the equation; 1 mol $O_2 \equiv 2$ mol $CO \equiv 2$ mol CO_2. It means 32 g O_2 liberated = 88 g CO_2 obtained.

(ii) **Formula**

Let the mass of organic compound taken = m g

Mass of carbon dioxide produced = m_1 g

$\therefore$ m_1 g carbon dioxide is obtained from

$$= \frac{32 \times m_1}{88} \text{ g } O_2$$

$$\therefore \text{ Percentage of oxygen} = \frac{32 \times m_1 \times 100}{88 \times m} \%$$

The percentage of oxygen can also be derived from the amount of iodine produced.

TEACHER'S TIP

Now days, the detection of elements in an organic compound is done by using only microquantities of substances and automatic experimental tenchiques. An apparatus, known as **CHN elemental analyser**, is used for the determination of elements likes carbon, hydrogen and nitrogen. This apparatus required a very small quantity of the organic compund (1-3 mg). Moreover, it displays the values on a screen in a very short time.

Quick Test 5

Conceptual Questions

1. Will CCl_4 give white precipitate of AgCl on heating it with silver nitrate? Give reason for your answer. *NCERT*
2. Why is nitric acid added to sodium extract before adding silver nitrate for testing halogens? *NCERT Exemplar*
3. Why is necessary to use acetic acid and not sulphuric acid for acidification of sodium extract for testing sulphur by lead acetate test? *NCERT*
4. For testing halogens in an organic compound with $AgNO_3$ solution, sodium extract (Lassaigne's test) is acidified with dilute HNO_3. What will happen if a student acidifies the extract with dilute H_2SO_4 in place of dilute HNO_3? *NCERT Exemplar*
5. Why is a solution of potassium hydroxide used to absorb carbon dioxide evolved during the estimation of carbon present in an organic compound? *NCERT*
6. In DNA and RNA, nitrogen atom is present in the ring system. Can Kjeldahl's method be used for the estimation of nitrogen present in these? Give reason. *NCERT Exemplar*

Numerical Questions

7. A sample of 0.50 g of an organic compound was treated according to Kjeldahl's method. The ammonia evolved was absorbed in 50 mL of 0.5 M H_2SO_4. The residual acid required 60 mL of 0.5 M solution of NaOH for neutralisation. Find the percentage composition of nitrogen in the compound. *NCERT*
8. 0.3780 g of an organic chloro compound gave 0.5740 g of silver chloride in Carius estimation. Calculate the percentage of chlorine present in the compound. *NCERT*
9. In the estimation of sulphur by Carius method, 0.468 g of an organic sulphur compound afforded 0.668 g of barium sulphate. Find the percentage of sulphur in the given compound. *NCERT*
10. An organic compound contains 69% carbon and 4.8% hydrogen, the remainder being oxygen. Calculate the masses of carbon dioxide and water produced when 0.20 g of this substance is subjected to complete combustion. *NCERT*

Answers

7. 56.0 8. 37.566 % 9. 19.60 % 10. 0.506 g, 0.0864 g

For Solutions, See QR Code on Pg. 341

Mind Map

Organic Chemistry : Some Basic Principles and Techniques

Organic Compounds Carbon containing chemical compounds.

Classification

1. Acyclic or open chain. e.g., CH_4, CH_3CHO
2. Cyclic or closed chain
   - Homocyclic
     - Alicyclic, e.g., cyclopropane
     - Aromatic, e.g., benzene
   - Heterocyclic e.g., furan

Functional Group

These are atom or group of atoms responsible for their chemical behaviour. e.g., alcohol group (—OH).

Homologous Series

It is a series of compounds differing from its previous and successive members by —CH_2. e.g., alkane (CH_4, C_2H_6).

Isomerism

This phenomenon arises when compounds have same molecular formula but differ in structures, atoms or spatial arrangement.

- **Structural Isomerism**
  This phenomenon arises when compounds have similar molecular formula but differ in way of bonding.
  - **Chain** having different carbon skeleton.
  - **Position** differ in position of bond or functional group etc.
  - **Functional group** possessing different functional groups.
  - **Metamerism** having different alkyl groups with same functional group.
- **Stereo Isomerism**
  This phenomenon arises when compounds having similar molecular and structural formula but differ in their spatial arrangement.
  - Optical
  - Geometrical

Fission/Cleavage of Bond

Breaking of covalent bond.

- **Homolytic** Each atom takes its shared electrons and produces free radicals.
- **Heterolytic** One atom takes shared electrons and produces ions (carbocation and carbanion).
- **Nucleophiles** Electron rich species having a lone pair of electrons e.g., Cl^-, Br^-, H_2O, NH_3, etc.
- **Electrophiles** Electron deficient species.e.g., H^+, BF_3, $BeCl_2$, PCl_3, etc.

Electron Displacement Effects in Covalent Bond

Inductive Effect (I)
It is induction of polarity due to the presence of polar bond. It is a permanent effect. Atoms or groups having greater/lesser electrons affinity than H, shows $+I$ or $-I$ effect.

Resonance Effect (R)
It is polarity developed due to the interaction of two π–bonds or π bonds with lone pair of electrons present on the adjacent atoms.
- It is a permanent effect.
- When the electrons move away/towards the atom or group attached to the conjugated system, $+R$ or $-R$ effect is produced.

Electrometric Effect (E)
Polarity developed due to complete transfer of a shared pair of π electrons to atom linked with multiple bond.
If electron of the π-bond are transferred to atoms/ neighbouring atom of the double bond to which reagent is attached, it produces $+E$ or $-E$ effect.

Hyperconjugation
Delocalisation of σ electrons of C—H bond.

Purification

Sublimation
It is used to separate sublimable compounds from non-sublimable impurities.

Crystallisation
Used for purifying solid organic compounds and based on the difference in solubilities of compound and impurities in a solvent.

Distillation
Used to separate a volatile liquid from a non-volatile impurity or two liquids having large difference in their boiling point, e.g., chloroform and aniline.
- When difference in boiling point is very low (10-15 K), fractional distillation is used.
- When liquid have a tendency to decompose before its boiling point, distillation under reduced pressure is used. e.g., glycerol.
- When compound or impurity is steam volatile, steam distillation is used. e.g., aniline.

Differential extraction
It is used to extract an organic compound from its aqueous solution by shaking it with an organic solvent in which it is more soluble than water.

Chromatography
It is based on the difference in the rates at which the components of a mixture are adsorbed on a suitable adsorbent.
- Adsorption
  - Column
  - Thin layer
- Partition
  - Paper

Qualitative and Quantitative Analysis

Qualitative Analysis

Used to detect elements present in a sample.

Test for C and H H_2O turns anhyd. $CuSO_4$ blue, CO_2 turns lime water milky.

Test for N Sodium extract $+FeSO_4$ + conc. $H_2SO_4 \rightarrow$ Prussian blue colour.

Test for S Sodium extract + acetic acid + lead acetate $\rightarrow$ Black ppt.
Sodium extract + sodium nitroprusside $\rightarrow$ Purple colour

Test for X (Cl, Br, I) Sodium extract $+X_2$ + $AgNO_3$ White ppt. $\Rightarrow$ Cl, Dull yellow ppt.$\Rightarrow$ Br, Yellow ppt. $\Rightarrow$ I

Test for P Fused sample with Na_2O_2 + H_2O + conc. HNO_3 + Δ, cooling, ammonium molybdate $\rightarrow$ yellow ppt.

Quantitative Analysis

It is used to detect percentage of elements present in organic compound.

$$\%\text{ of C} = \frac{12 \times \text{mass of } CO_2 \times 100}{44 \times \text{mass of O.C.}}$$

$$\%\text{ of H} = \frac{2 \times \text{mass of } H_2O \times 100}{18 \times \text{mass of O.C.}}$$

$$\%\text{ of N} = \frac{28 \times V \times 100}{22400 \times m} \text{ (Duma's method)}$$

$$= \frac{1.4 \times M \times 2\left(V - \frac{V_1}{2}\right)}{m} \text{ (Kjeldahl's method)}$$

$$\%\text{ of } X = \frac{\text{atomic mass of } X \times \text{mass of Ag } X \text{ formed} \times 100}{\text{molecular mass of Ag}X \times \text{mass of O.C.}}$$

$$\%\text{ of S} = \frac{32 \times \text{mass of } BaSO_4 \times 100}{233 \times \text{mass of O.C.}} \text{ (Carius method)}$$

$$\%\text{ of P} = \frac{62 \times \text{mass of } Mg_2P_2O_7 \times 100}{222 \times \text{mass of O.C.}}$$

EXAM PATTERN QUESTIONS

Objective Type Questions

Multiple Choice Questions (MCQs)

[1 Mark]

1. Which type of bond is formed between carbon atom and nitrogen atom in $CH_3CH_2NO_2$?

(a) Covalent bond (b) Ionic bond
(c) Dative bond (d) None of these

2. Choose the correct bond-line formula for

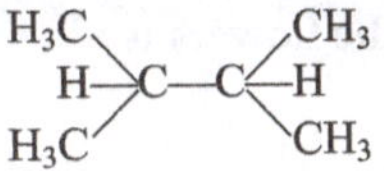

(a)  (b) 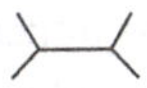

(c) 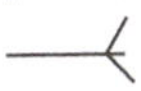 (d) 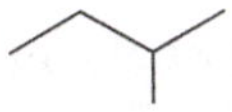

3. Which of the following is a homocyclic alicyclic compound?

(a) 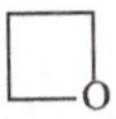 (b)  (c) 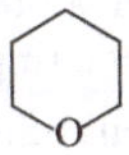 (d) 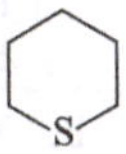

4. Which of the following is the correct IUPAC name? **NCERT Exemplar**

(a) 3-ethyl-4, 4-dimethylheptane
(b) 4,4-dimethyl-3-ethylheptane
(c) 5-ethyl-4, 4-dimethylheptane
(d) 4,4-*bis*(methyl)-3-ethylheptane

5. Correct IUPAC name for $H_3C—\underset{\displaystyle C_2H_5}{\underset{|}{CH}}—\underset{\displaystyle C_2H_5}{\underset{|}{CH}}—CH_3$ is .... **NCERT Exemplar**

(a) 2-ethyl-3-methylpentane
(b) 3, 4-dimethylhexane
(c) 2-*sec*-butylbutane
(d) 2, 3-dimethylbutane

6. The IUPAC name for $CH_3—\overset{\displaystyle O}{\overset{\|}{C}}—CH_2—CH_2—\overset{\displaystyle O}{\overset{\|}{C}}—OH$ is **NCERT Exemplar**

(a) 1-hydroxypentane-1,4-dione
(b) 1,4-dioxopentanol
(c) 1-carboxybutan-3-one
(d) 4-oxopentanoic acid

7. The IUPAC name for **NCERT Exemplar**

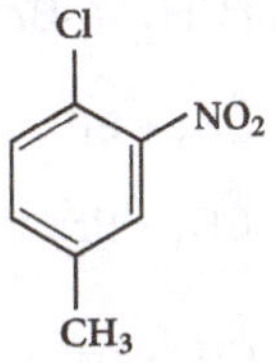

(a) 1-chloro-2-nitro-4-methylbenzene
(b) 1-chloro-4-methyl-2-nitrobenzene
(c) 2-chloro-1-nitro-5-methylbenzene
(d) *m*-nitro-*p*-chlorotoluene

8. In which of the following, functional group isomerism is not possible? **NCERT Exemplar**

(a) Alcohols (b) Aldehydes
(c) Alkyl halides (d) Cyanides

9. The number of structural isomers possible for the molecular formula C_3H_9N is

(a) 4 (b) 5
(c) 2 (d) 3

10. Study the structures given below carefully and choose the type of isomerism they represent.

$$CH_3—\underset{\displaystyle CH_3}{\underset{|}{\overset{\displaystyle CH_3}{\overset{|}{C}}}}—CH_3 \text{ and } CH_3—\overset{\displaystyle CH_3}{\overset{|}{CH}}—CH_2—CH_3$$

(a) chain isomerism
(b) position isomerism
(c) functional isomerism
(d) metamerism

11. What is the correct order of decreasing stability of the following cations? **NCERT Exemplar**

$$\underset{\text{I}}{CH_3—\overset{\oplus}{C}H—CH_3}\ ; \quad \underset{\text{II}}{CH_3—\overset{\oplus}{C}H—OCH_3}\ ;$$

$$\underset{\text{III}}{CH_3—\overset{\oplus}{C}H—CH_2—OCH_3}$$

(a) II > I > III (b) II > III > I
(c) III > I > II (d) I > II > III

12. **Electrophilic addition reactions proceed in two steps. The first step involves the addition of an electrophile. Name the type of intermediate formed in the first step of the following addition reaction.** **NCERT Exemplar**

$$H_3C{-}HC{=}CH_2 + H^+ \longrightarrow ?$$

(a) 2° carbanion (b) 1° carbocation
(c) 2° carbocation (d) 1° carbanion

13. **Covalent bond can undergo fission in two different ways. The correct representation involving a heterolytic fission of CH_3—Br is** **NCERT Exemplar**

(a) 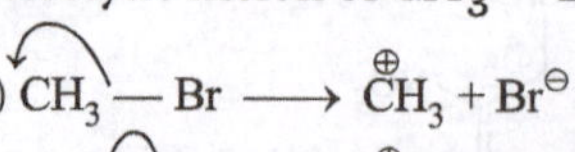

(b) 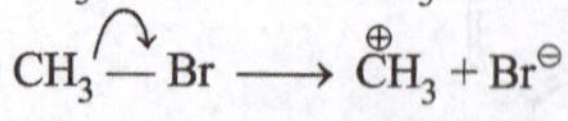

(c) 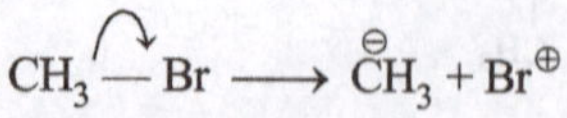

(d) 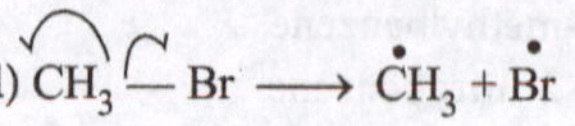

14. **In which of the following compounds the carbon marked with asterisk is expected to have greatest positive charge?** **NCERT Exemplar**

(a) $^*CH_3{-}CH_2{-}Cl$
(b) $^*CH_3{-}CH_2{-}Mg^+Cl^-$
(c) $^*CH_3{-}CH_2{-}Br$
(d) $^*CH_3{-}CH_2{-}CH_3$

15. **The addition of HCl to an alkene proceeds in two steps. The first step is the attack of H^+ ion to >C=C< portion which can be shown as** **NCERT Exemplar**

(a) 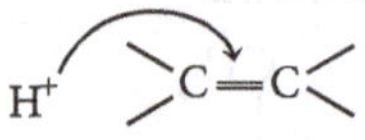 (b) 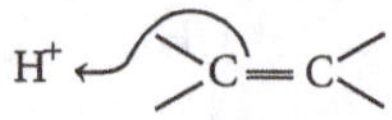

(c) 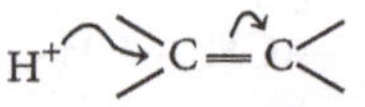 (d) All of these are possible

16. **Ionic species are stabilised by the dispersal of charge. Which of the following carboxylate ion is the most stable?** **NCERT Exemplar**

(a) $CH_3{-}\overset{O}{\overset{\|}{C}}{-}O^-$ (b) $Cl{-}CH_2{-}\overset{O}{\overset{\|}{C}}{-}O^-$

(c) $F{-}CH_2{-}\overset{O}{\overset{\|}{C}}{-}O^-$ (d) $F_2CH{-}\overset{O}{\overset{\|}{C}}{-}O^-$

17. **Which of the following method is used to purify liquids having very high boiling points and those which decompose at or below their boiling points?**

(a) Simple distillation
(b) Fractional distillation
(c) Distillation under reduced pressure
(d) None of the above

18. **During hearing of a court case, the judge suspected that some changes in the documents had been carried out. He asked the forensic department to check the ink used at two different places. According to you which technique can give the best results?** **NCERT Exemplar**

(a) Column chromatography
(b) Solvent extraction
(c) Distillation
(d) Thin layer chromatography

19. **The principle involved in paper chromatography is** **NCERT Exemplar**

(a) adsorption (b) partition
(c) solubility (d) volatility

20. **The fragrance of flowers is due to the presence of some steam volatile organic compounds called essential oils. These are generally insoluble in water at room temperature but are miscible with water vapour in vapour phase. A suitable method for the extraction of these oils from the flowers is** **NCERT Exemplar**

(a) distillation
(b) crystallisation
(c) distillation under reduced pressure
(d) steam distillation

21. **Match the Column I with Column II.**

	Column I		Column II
A.	Compounds containing only one type of atoms joined in the form of a ring.	(i)	Homocyclic compounds
B.	When atoms other than carbon atoms are present in the ring.	(ii)	Non-benzenoid compounds
C.	Benzene and other related ring compounds.	(iii)	Heterocyclic compounds
D.	Compounds which do not contain benzene ring but aromatic in nature.	(iv)	Benzenoid compounds

Choose the correct option among the options given below

(a) A-(i), B-(iii), C-(iv), D-(ii)
(b) A-(i), B-(ii), C-(iii), D-(iv)
(c) A-(iv), B-(iii), C-(ii), D-(i)
(d) A-(iii), B-(i), C-(ii), D-(iv)

Assertion-Reason [1 Mark]

■ **Directions** (Q. Nos. 22-30) In the following questions. An Assertion (A) is followed by a corresponding Reason (R). Use the following keys to choose the appropriate answer.

(a) Both (A) and (R) are correct and (R) is the correct explanation of (A).
(b) Both (A) and (R) are correct but (R) is not the correct explanation of (A).
(c) (A) is correct and (R) is incorrect.
(d) (A) is incorrect and (R) is correct.

22. **Assertion** (A) Acyclic compounds consist of straight or branched chain compounds.

Reason (R) Acyclic compounds have aromatic character.

23. **Assertion** (A) All the carbon atoms in $H_2C{=}C{=}C{=}CH_2$ are sp^2-hybridised.

Reason (R) In this molecule, all the carbon atoms are attached to each other by double bonds.

24. **Assertion** (A) 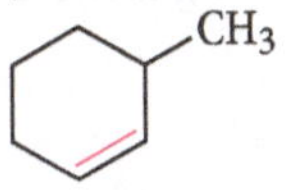 is 3-methylcyclohexene.

Reason (R) In numbering, double bonded carbon atoms get preference to the alkyl group in cycloalkenes.

25. **Assertion** (A) In bond-line structural representations, only atoms specifically written are oxygen, chlorine, nitrogen etc.

Reason (R) In bond-line structural representations, line junctions denote carbon atoms bonded to appropriate number of hydrogens required to satisfy the valency of the carbon atoms.

26. **Assertion** (A) Heterolytic fission involves the breaking of a covalent bond in such a way that both the electrons of the shared pair are carried away by one of the atoms.

Reason (R) Heterolytic fission occurs readily in polar covalent bonds.

27. **Assertion** (A) A covalent bond may be cleaved either by heterolytic cleavage or by homolytic cleavage.

Reason (R) Heterolytic cleavage of CH_3Br will give $\overset{+}{C}H_3$ and Br^-.

28. **Assertion** (A) Free radicals are short lived and highly reactive.

Reason (R) Free radicals are highly unstable.

29. **Assertion** (A) Inductive effect and resonance effect cause permanent polarisation of bond.

Reason (R) These involve electron displacements due to the influence of an atom or a substituted group present in the molecule.

30. **Assertion** (A) Conjugated system show abnormal behaviour, it contains alternate single and double bonds in an open chain or cyclic system.

Reason (R) In conjugated system, π-electrons are delocalised and the system develops polarity.

Competency Based Que.

Case-Study [4 Marks]

31. Read the given case and answer the following questions.

An intermediate is a molecular entity, that is formed from the reactants and reacts further to give the directly observed products of a chemical reaction. Most chemical reactions are stepwise, that is they take more than one elementary step to complete.

An intermediate is the reaction product of each of these steps, except for the last one, which forms the final very isolated. Also, owing to the short lifetime, they do not remain in the product mixture.

In certain cases, they are separated and stored. For example matrix isolation and low temperature.

Matrix isolation is a technique that is used experimentally in physics and chemistry that included a material that has been trapped with in an unreactive material. Host matrix generally embedded. Guest particles can be molecules, atoms and ions. The guest is isolated within the host matric. Competency Based Que.

(i) What happen when CH_3CH_2Cl undergoes homolytic fission?

(ii) Which of the following is most stable free radical?

(a) $CH_3\dot{C}HCH_3$ (b) 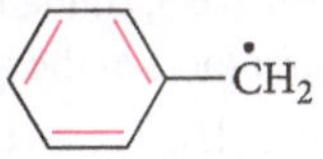

(c) $\dot{C}H_2{-}CH(CH_3)_2$ (d) $\dot{C}H_2{-}CH_3$

Or

What is the common name of the simplest aromatic amine?

(a) Benzylamine (b) Benzamine

(c) Aniline (d) Aminobenzene

(iii) Which of the following represents the correct order of the relative stabilities of the carbocations?

(a) $\overset{\oplus}{C}H_3 < CH_3\overset{\oplus}{C}H_2 < \overset{\oplus}{C}H_2OCH_3$

(b) $\overset{\oplus}{C}H_2OCH_3 > \overset{\oplus}{C}H_3 > CH_3\overset{\oplus}{C}H_2$

(c) $\overset{\oplus}{C}H_3 < \overset{\oplus}{C}H_2OCH_3 < CH_3\overset{\oplus}{C}H_2$

(d) $CH_3\overset{\oplus}{C}H_2 > \overset{\oplus}{C}H_3 > \overset{\oplus}{C}H_2OCH_3$

32. Read the given case and answer the following questions.

When a single Lewis dot structure is unable to explain all the properties of a compound, two or more structures, called the canonical forms or resonating structures, are drawn to explain all the properties of that compound, them the actual structure of the compound is in between these canonical form and is called the resonance hybrid of these canonical forms. This phenomenon is called resonance.

The resonating structure are hypothetical, i.e. have no real existence. The energy of actual structure or resonance hybrid is lower than, that of any of the canonical forms. The difference between hybrid and the energy of most stable (lowest energy) canonical

form is called the resonance stabilisation energy or resonance energy.

The more the number of important canonical forms more is the resonance energy. In case of resonating structures of equivalent energy, resonance is of great important. **Competency Based Que.**

(i) In the given pair of resonating structure which is more stable?

$$\underset{(a)}{R-\overset{\oplus}{C}=\ddot{O}:} \longleftrightarrow \underset{(b)}{R-C\equiv\overset{\oplus}{O}:}$$

(ii) Write the correct relation between resonance and bond order.

Or Write the difference between positive resonance and negative resonance effect.

(iii) Write all the resonating structures of phenoxide ion.

Subjective Type Questions

Short Answer Type I Questions [2 Marks]

1. Draw the formulae for the first three members of each homologous series starting with formic acid and methanol.

2. Write dash, condensed and bond line structural formulae for the isomers of the molecular formulae.

(i) C_8H_{10} (ii) C_3H_6O

3. What is homologous series? Write its important characteristics.

4. Give the structure of each of the following compounds:

(i) 2-3-dibromo-3-ethylheptane

(ii) 1-bromo-2-iodocyclobutene

5. Which family of hydrocarbon is represented by the general formula, C_nH_{2n-2}? Write the IUPAC and common names of the first three members of this family.

6. Classify the following pairs as position, chain, functional isomers or stereoisomers. **Competency Based Que.**

(i) Diethylamine and methylpropyl amine

(ii) Ethanol and dimethyl ether

7. Giving justification, categorise the following molecules/ions as nucleophiles or electrophiles

$NO_2^+, HS^-, BF_3, C_2H_5O^-, (CH_3)_3N, Cl^+, (CH_3)_3C^+=O, NH_2^-$

8. By mistake, an alcohol (b.p. 97°C) was mixed with a ketone (b.p. 68°C). Suggest a suitable method to separate the two compounds. Explain the reason for your choice. **DIKSHA**

9. Draw all possible isomers of a compound with molecular formula, $C_4H_{10}O$. Classify them as chain and position isomers.

10. What is the basic principle of distillation under reduced pressure? **DIKSHA**

Short Answer Type II Questions [3 Marks]

11. Name the compounds whose line formulae are given below. **NCERT Exemplar**

(a) 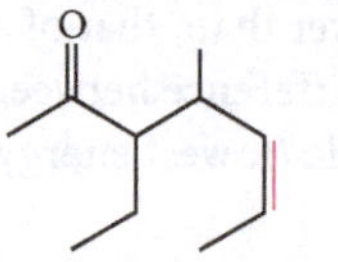

(b) 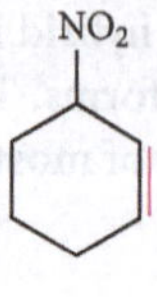

12. What are reactive intermediates? How are they generated by bond fission?

13. The structure of triphenylmethyl cation is given below. This is very stable and some of its salts can be stored for months. Explain the cause of high stability of this cation. **NCERT Exemplar**

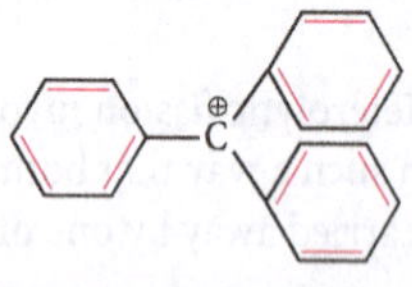

14. Compounds with same molecular formula but differing in their structures are said to be structural isomers. What type of structural isomerism is shown by **NCERT Exemplar**

$$CH_3-S-CH_2-CH_2-CH_3 \text{ and } CH_3-S-CH\begin{matrix} CH_3 \\ CH_3 \end{matrix}$$

15. The order of basicity of amines expected on the basis of inductive effect is $NH_3 < RNH_2 < R_3N$. However, the observed order of basicity is $NH_3 < RNH_2 < R_2NH > R_3N$. How will you account for the difference?

16. Draw the resonance structures of the following compounds. **NCERT Exemplar**

(i) $CH_2=CH-\ddot{\underset{..}{Cl}}:$

(ii) $CH_2=CH-CH=CH_2$

(iii) $CH_2=CH-\underset{\underset{H}{|}}{C}=O$

17. Identify electrophilic centre in the following compounds $CH_3CH=O, CH_3CN, CH_3I$.

18. Resonance structures of propenal are given below. Which of these resonating structures is more stable? Give reason for your answer.

$$\underset{I}{CH_2=CH-CH=O} \longleftrightarrow \underset{II}{\overset{\oplus}{C}H_2-CH=CH-\overset{\ominus}{O}}$$

Competency Based Que.

19. Which of the following ions is more stable? Use resonance to explain your answer. **NCERT Exemplar**

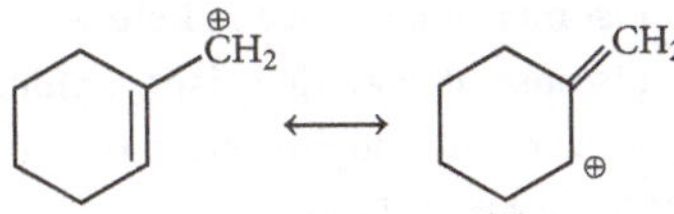

(A) (B)

20. Write structures of various carbocations that can be obtained from 2-methylbutane. Arrange these carbocations in order of increasing stability. **NCERT Exemplar**

21. Arrange the following.

(i) $C_6H_5\overset{+}{C}HCH_3$, $C_6H_5\overset{+}{C}HCH=CH_2$, $C_6H_5CH_2\overset{+}{C}H_2$, $C_6H_5\overset{+}{C}(CH_3)_2$ in order of increasing stability.

(ii) $CH_3\overset{+}{C}H_2$, $C_6H_5\overset{+}{C}H_2$, $(CH_3)_3C^+$, $CH_2=CH\overset{+}{C}H_2$ in order of decreasing stability.

(iii) $HC\equiv C^-$, $CH_2=CH^-$, $CH_3\bar{C}H_2$, $\bar{C}H_3$, $(CH_3)_2CH^-$, $C_6H_5\bar{C}H_2$ in order of increasing stability.

Competency Based Que.

22. What is the principle of steam distillation for the purification of organic compounds? With the help of diagrams describe the method of steam distillation.

23. A liquid with the high boiling point decomposes on simple distillation but it can be steam distilled for its purification. Explain how is it possible?

24. Write the chemical equations involved in the Lassaigne's test for nitrogen in an organic compound.

25. Discuss the reactions and the principle underlying the estimation of the following: **Competency Based Que.**

(i) Duma's method for estimation of nitrogen.

(ii) Carius method for the estimation of halogens and sulphur.

(iii) Phosphorus

Long Answer Type Questions [5 Marks]

26. Draw a diagram of bubble plate type fractionating column. When do we require such type of a column for separating two liquids. Explain the principle involved in the separation of components of a mixture of liquids by using fractionating column. What industrial applications does this process have? **NCERT**

27. For the following bond cleavages, use curved- arrows to show the electron flow and classify each as homolysis or heterolysis. Identify reactive intermediate produced as free radical, carbocation and carbanion. **NCERT**

(i) $CH_3O{-}OCH_3 \longrightarrow CH_3\dot{O} + \dot{O}CH_3$

(ii) 

(iii) 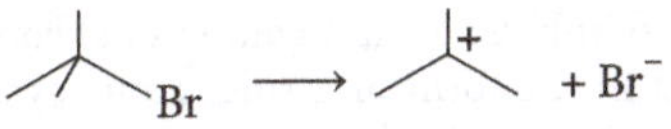

(iv) 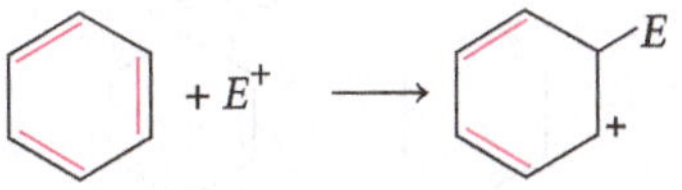

Hint: Free radicals are the result of homolysis while ions (carbanion or carbocation) are formed when reactant undergoes heterolysis.

28. Explain the terms inductive and electromeric effects. Which electron displacement effect explains the following correct orders of acidity of the carboxylic acids? **NCERT**

(i) $Cl_3CCOOH > Cl_2CHCOOH > ClCH_2COOH$

(ii) $CH_3CH_2COOH > (CH_3)_2CHCOOH > (CH_3)_3C{\cdot}COOH$

29. (i) Write the formula of prussian blue colour formed in Lassaigne's test for nitrogen detection.

(ii) Write the formula for estimation of nitrogen by Kjeldahl's method.

(iii) Name the method used to separate

(a) glycerol from spent lye in soap industry.

(b) aniline from aniline water mixture.

Competency Based Que.

30. Draw all possible carboxylic acids and esters for a compound with molecular formula $C_4H_8O_2$. Write the IUPAC name also.

Hints & Solutions

Objective Type Questions

1. (a) A covalent bond is formed between carbon and nitrogen atom. If duplet (2) or octet (8) is completed by sharing of electrons between two electronegative elements, the bond formed is called covalent bond.

2. (b) The correct bond-line formula for

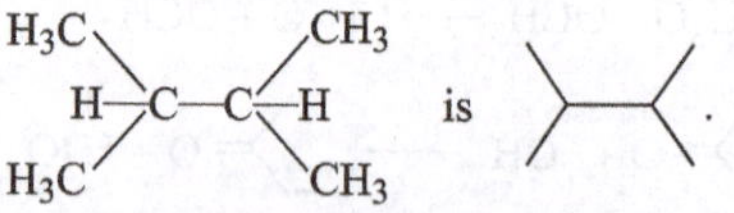

3. (b) Alicyclic (aliphatic cyclic) compounds contain carbon atoms joined in the form of a ring. Homocyclic means it contains only C-atoms in the ring, e.g.

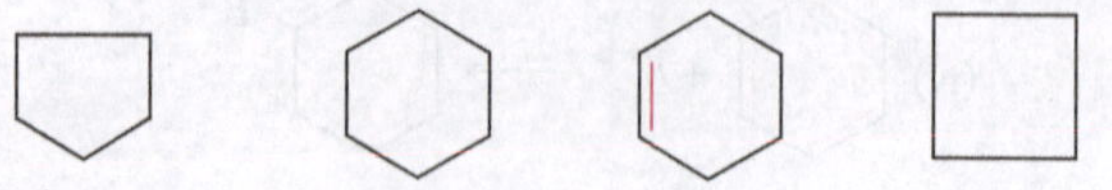

Cyclopentane Cyclohexane Cyclohexene Cyclobutane

4. (a) 3-ethyl-4, 4-dimethylheptane is the correct IUPAC name having structure.

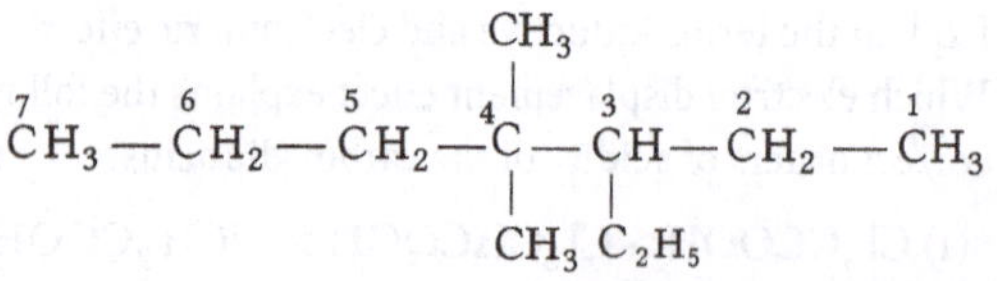

5. (b)

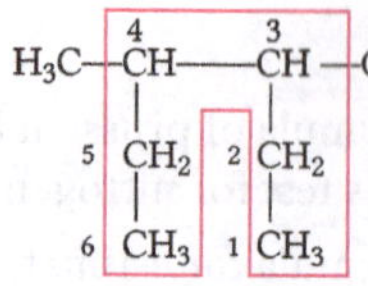

3, 4-dimethylhexane

6. (d) When more than one functional group lie in the main chain, nomenclature is done according to that functional group which has higher priority.

Carboxylic acid (—COOH) has higher priority than ketone ($\rangle$C=O). Thus, the correct IUPAC name for given structure is 4-oxopentanoic acid.

7. (b) The IUPAC name of given compound is

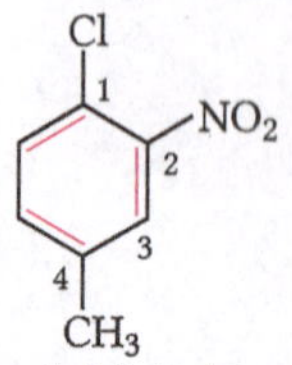

1-chloro-4-methyl-2-nitrobenzene

8. (c) Two or more compounds having the same molecular formula but different functional groups are called functional isomers.

Functional isomer of alcohol is ether.

Functional isomer of aldehyde is ketone.

Functional isomer of cyanide is isocyanide.

However, alkyl halides do not show functional isomerism.

Hence, option (c) is correct.

9. (a) Structural isomers of C_3H_9N are

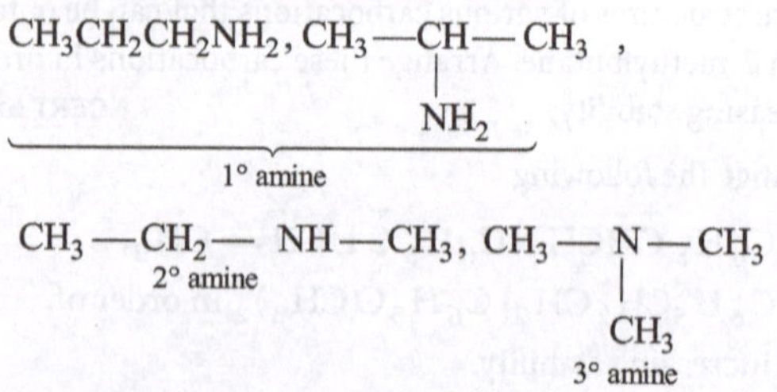

10. (a)

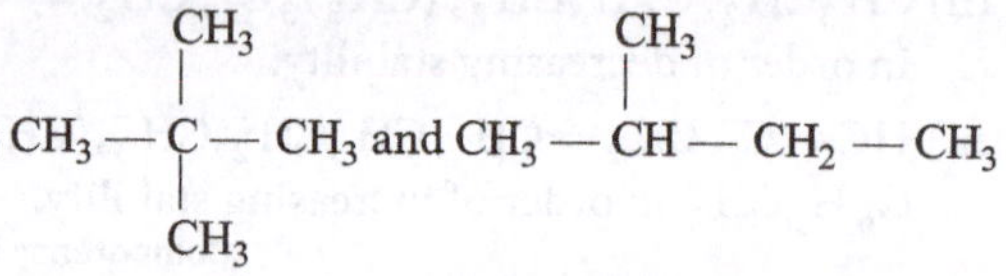

are chain isomers as they have different carbon chains.

11. (a) Stability of the given cations can be understood by the following structures.

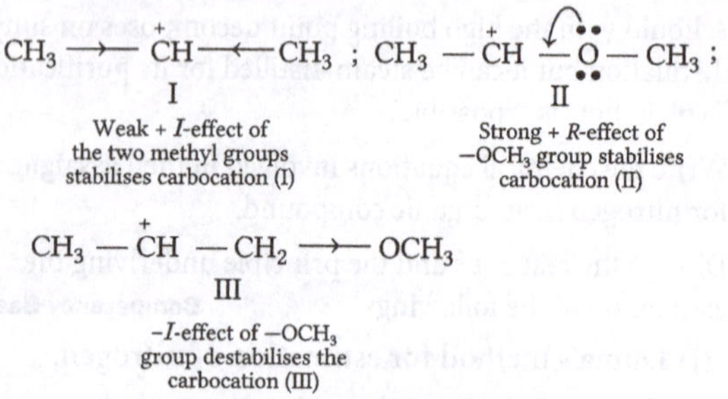

Hence, the stability of carbocation decreases

II > I > III.

12. (c) When electrophile attacks $CH_3—CH=CH_2$ delocalisation of electrons can take place, in two possible ways.

$$CH_3—CH=CH_2 + H^+ \longrightarrow CH_3—\overset{\oplus}{C}H—CH_3$$

(2° carbocation)

$$CH_3—CH_2—\overset{\oplus}{C}H_2$$

(1° carbocation)

As 2° carbocation is more stable than 1° carbocation thus first addition is more feasible.

13. (b) Arrow denotes the direction of movement of electrons

$$CH_3—Br \longrightarrow \overset{\oplus}{C}H_3 + Br^{\ominus}.$$

Since, Br is more electronegative than carbon, hence heterolytic fission occurs in such a way that $—CH_3$ gets the positive charge and Br gets the negative charge. Thus, option (b) is correct.

14. (*a*) Electronegativity of Cl, Br, C and Mg follows the order Cl > Br > C > Mg.

$*CH_3 \rightarrow CH_2 \rightarrow Cl$ $(-I\text{-effect})$

$*CH_3 \leftarrow CH_2 \leftarrow Mg^{+}Cl^{-}$

$*CH_3 \rightarrow CH_2 \rightarrow Br$ $(-I\text{-effect})$

$*CH_3—CH_2—CH_3$ $(+I\text{-effect})$

$-I$-effect of Cl > Br.

Hence, $CH_3—CH_2—Cl$ has the greatest positive charge.

15. (*b*)

***Step* I** π-bonds create an electron cloud, electrophile ($H^{+}Cl^{\ominus}$) from H — Cl attacks the electron cloud, delocalise the electrons and form a carbocation.

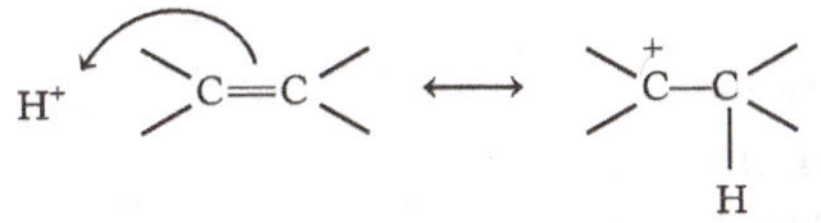

***Step* II** The chloride anion attacks the carbocation.

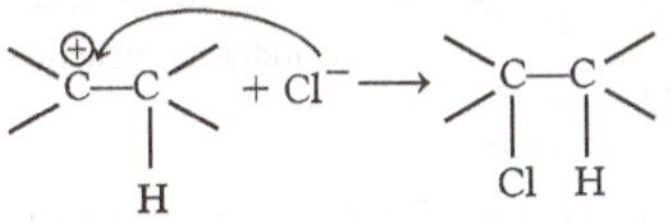

16. (*d*) In all the given carbocations, the negative charge is dispersed which stabilises these carbocations.

Here, the negative charge is dispersed by two factors, i.e. +*R*-effect of the carboxylate ion (conjugation) and *I*-effect of the halogens. These effects are shown in the carbocations

(a)

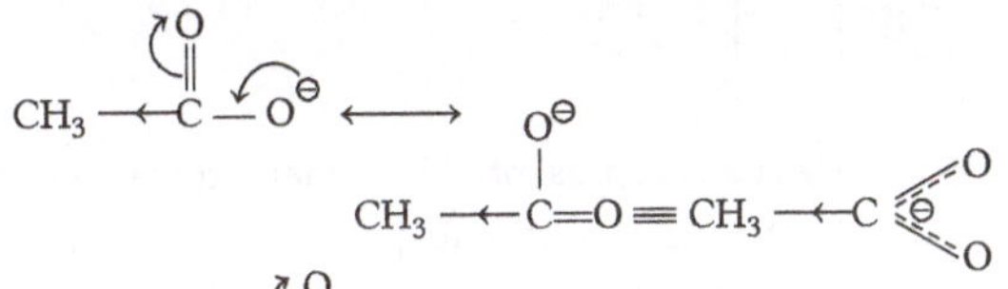

(b)

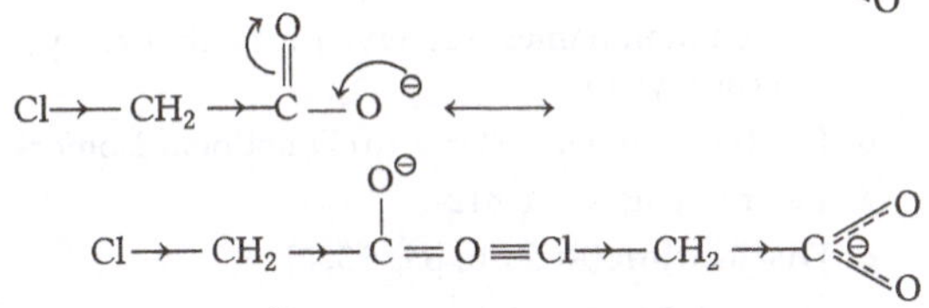

(c)

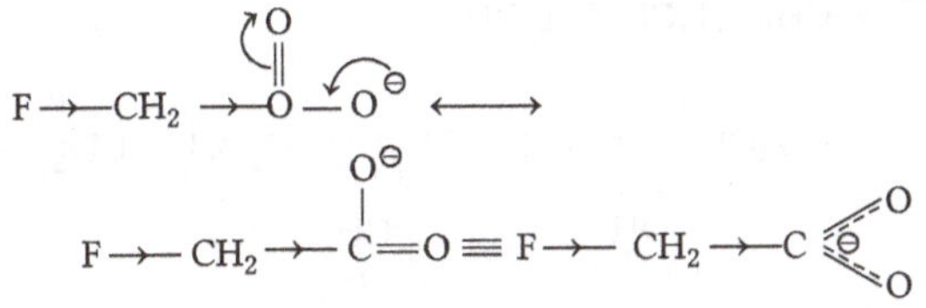

(d)

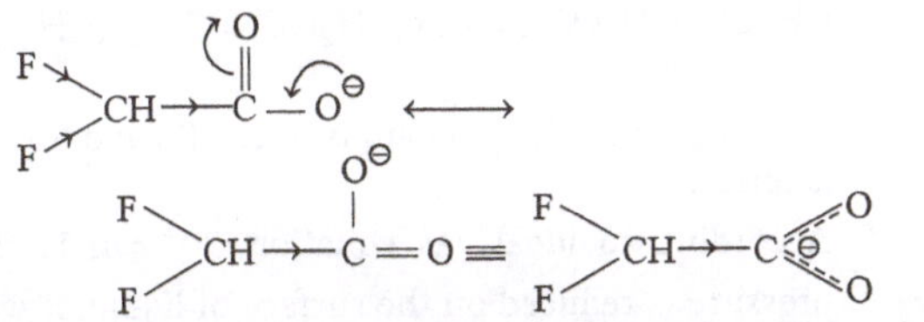

As it is clearly evident from the above structures, that +*R*-effect is common in all the four structures, therefore, overall dispersal of negative charge depends upon the number of halogen atoms and electronegativity. Since, F has the highest electronegativity and two F-atoms are present in option (d), thus, dispersal of negative charge is maximum in option (d).

17. (*c*) Distillation under reduced pressure method is used to purify liquids having very high boiling points and those, which decompose at or below their boiling points. Such, liquids are made to boil at a temperature lower than their normal boiling points by reducing the pressure on their surface. A liquid boils at a temperature at which its vapour pressure is equal to the external pressure. The pressure is reduced with the help of a water pump or vacuum pump.

18. (*d*) Thin Layer Chromatography (TLC) is type of adsorption chromatography which involves separation of substances of a mixture over a thin layer of an adsorbent coated on a glass plate.

19. (*b*) Partition chromatography is based on continuous differential partitioning of components of a mixture between stationary and mobile phases. Paper chromatography is a type of partition chromatography.

20. (*d*) As we know, essential oils are insoluble in water and have high vapour pressure at 373K but are miscible with water-vapour in vapour phase, it means these are steam volatile. Hence, steam distillation technique is used for the extraction of essential oils.

21. (*a*) The correct match is A-(i), B-(iii), C-(iv), D-(ii).

22. (A) is correct and (R) is incorrect.

Correct Reason Acyclic compounds does not have aromatic character.

23. (*d*) (A) is incorrect and (R) is correct.

Correct Assertion Hybridisation of C can be find out by counting σ-bonds and π bonds present on C-atom.

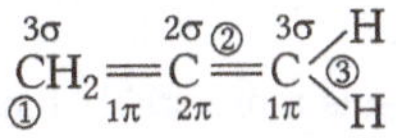

C_1 and C_3 carbon are sp^2-hybridised while C_2-carbon is *sp*-hybridised.

24. (*a*) Both (A) and (R) are correct and (R) is the correct explanation of (A).

25. (*a*) Both (A) and (R) are correct and (R) is the correct explanation of (A).

26. (*b*) Both (A) and (R) correct but (R) is not the correct explanation of (A).

Correct Explanation In heterolytic fission, the two atoms are differ considerably in their electronegativities and hence shared pair of electrons is carried by more electronegative atom.

27. (*b*) Both (A) and (R) are correct but (R) is not the correct explanation of (A).

28. (*b*) Both (A) and (R) are correct but (R) is not the correct explanation of (A).

Correct Explanation Free radicals contains odd electrons, so they are short lived and they readily try to pair up the odd electrons to become a neutral molecule.

29. (*a*) Both (A) and (R) are correct and (R) is the correct explanation of (A).

30. (*a*) Both (A) and (R) are correct and (R) is the correct explanation of (A).

31. (i) When CH_3CH_2Cl undergoes homolytic cleavage results in the formation of free radical.

$$CH_3CH_2—Cl \xrightarrow[\text{Fission}]{\text{Homolytic}} CH_3\dot{C}H_2 + \dot{C}l$$ **(1)**

(ii) (*b*) Among the given free radicals 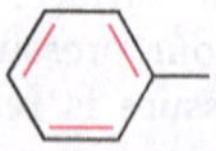 $\dot{C}H_2$ is most stable due to resonance. **(1)**

In the remaining free radicals, more the alkyl groups bonded to the electron deficient carbon, more stable in the radical.

This the correct order of stability of given free radicals.

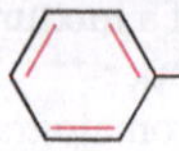 $\dot{C}H_2 > CH_3\dot{C}HCH_3 > \dot{C}H_2—CH_3 > \dot{C}H_2—CH(CH_3)_2$

Or

(*c*) The simplest amine is $C_6H_5NH_2$ and is known as aniline. This name is also accepted as the IUPAC name. **(1)**

(iii) (*a*) The dispersal of the charge stabilises the carbocation more the number of alkyl groups, the greater in dispersal of positive charge and therefore, more in the stability of carbocation.

Thus, the correct order of relative stability is

$$\overset{\oplus}{C}H_2OCH_3 > CH_3\overset{\oplus}{C}H_2 > \overset{\oplus}{C}H_3$$
(*C*) (*B*) (*A*) **(2)**

32. (i) Structure (a) is more stable than structure (b) because the positive charge is present on the highly electronegative oxygen. **(1)**

(ii) The correct relation between the resonance and bond order formula is $B.O = \frac{\text{No. of bonds}}{\text{No. of resonating structures}}$ **(1)**

Or Refer to text on page 315. **(1)**

(iii) The phenoxide ion has 5 resonating structures. These are

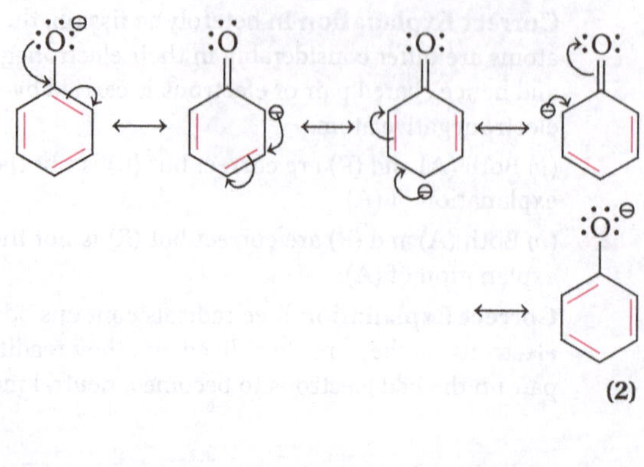

(2)

Subjective Type Questions

1. HCOOH, CH_3COOH, C_2H_5COOH **(1)**
CH_3OH, C_2H_5OH, C_3H_5OH **(1)**

2. (i) C_8H_{10}

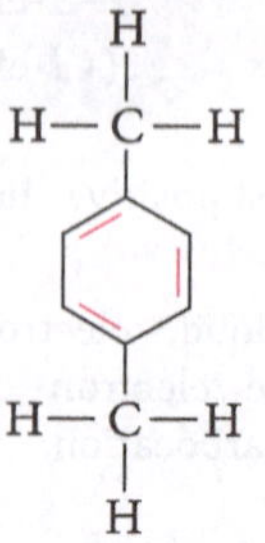

(Dash structure)

$CH_3—C_6H_4—CH_3$ (Condensed structure)

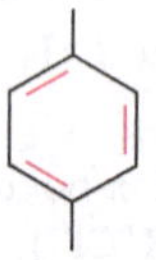

Bond line structure **(1)**

(ii) C_3H_6O

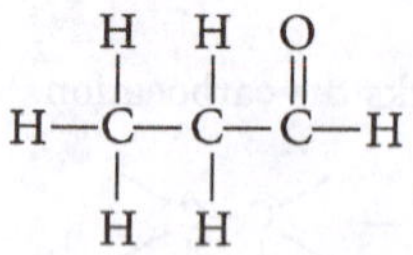

(Dash structure)

CH_3CH_2CHO (Condensed structure)

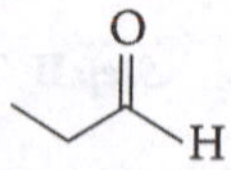

(Bondline structure) **(1)**

3. Refer to page 297 (Topic-1 : Homologous series) **(2)**

4. (i) $\overset{7}{C}H_3—\overset{6}{C}H_2—\overset{5}{C}H_2—\overset{4}{C}H_2—\overset{3}{C}(Br)(C_2H_5)—\overset{2}{C}H(Br)—\overset{1}{C}H_3$ **(1)**

(ii) 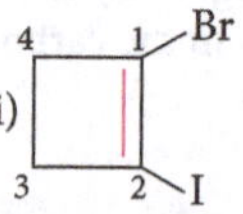 **(1)**

5. • Alkyne is represented by general formula C_nH_{2n-2}. **(1)**
• IUPAC name – Ethyne, propyne, 2-butyne.
• Common names – Acetylene, methyl acetylene, crotonylene. **(1)**

6. (i) Stereoisomers **(1)** (ii) Functional isomers **(1)**

7. Refer to pages 311-312. **(2)**

8. **Distillation** (Refer to page 320). **(2)**

9. $CH_3CH_2CH_2CH_2OH$, (1)

$CH_3CH_2CH(OH)CH_3$, (2) $CH_3CH(CH_3)CH_2OH$, (3) $CH_3—C(CH_3)(OH)—CH_3$, (4)

$CH_3CH_2CH_2OCH_3$, (5) $CH_3CH_2OCH_2CH_3$, (6) $(CH_3)_2CHOCH_3$ (7) **(1)**

Isomer (1) and (2) are chain isomers, (3) and (6) are position isomers. **(1)**

10. According to ideal gas equation, $pV = nRT$, thus, if the pressure is reduced on the surface of liquid, it will boil at a lower temperature as compared to its original boiling point. In the technique of distillation under reduced pressure, the pressure is reduced with the help of a vacuum pump. **(2)**

11. (a) 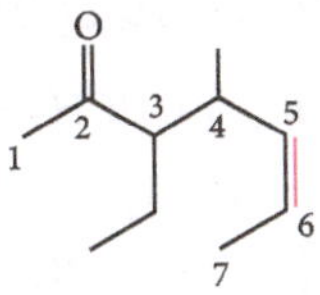

3-ethyl-4-methylhept-5-en-2-one (C-atoms of the longest possible chain are numbered in such a way that the functional group, $>C{=}O$, gets the lowest possible locant) (1½)

(b) 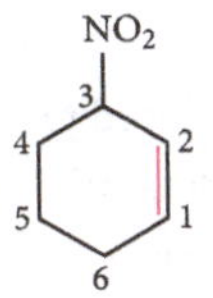

3-nitrocyclohex-1-ene (C-atoms of the ring are numbered in such a manner that double bond gets the lowest possible locant followed by the $—NO_2$ group) (1½)

12. The reactive intermediates are those chemical species which are produced during the course of the reaction. There are many reactive intermediate, three of which are carbocation, carbanion and the free radical. (1)

Carbocation and carbanion are generated by the heterolytic bond fission while free radicals are generated by homolytic bond fission. (1)

$$CH_3—Cl \longrightarrow \overset{+}{C}H_3 + Cl^-$$

$$(CH_3)_2—Zn \longrightarrow 2\,CH_3^- + Zn^{2+}$$

(Heterolytic bond fission)

$$CH_3—CH_3 \longrightarrow 2\dot{C}H_3$$

(Homolytic bond fission) (1)

13. In triphenylmethyl cation, due to resonance, the positive charge can move at both the *o*- and *p*-position of each benzene ring. This is illustrated below. (1)

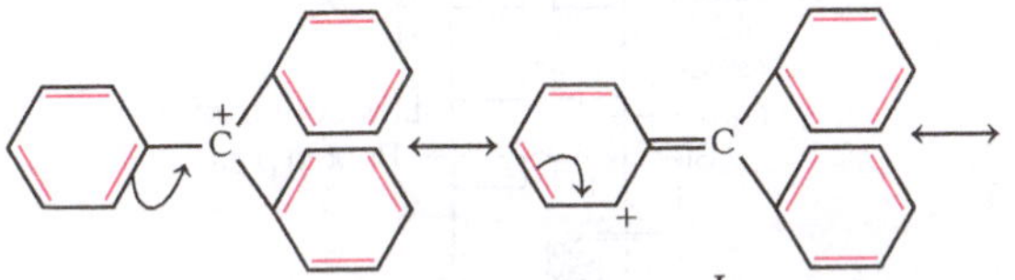

I

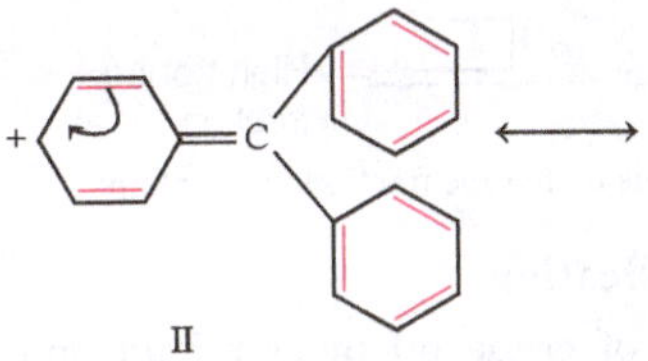

II

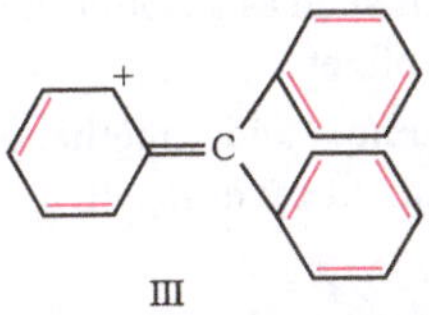

+ Six more such structures are possible due to other two benzene rings.

III (2)

14. The two isomers which differ in the position of the functional group on the carbon skeleton are called position isomers and this phenomenon as position isomerism. (1)

Thus, (A) and (B) may be regarded as position isomers and further they cannot be regarded as metamers since metamers are those isomers which have different number of carbon atoms on either side of the functional group. (1)

But here, the number of carbon atoms on either side of sulphur atom (functional group) is the same, *i.e.*, 1 and 3.

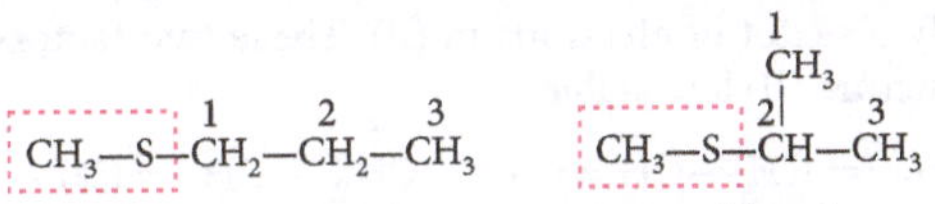

Methyl *n*-propylthio ether (*A*)

Isopropylthio ether (*B*) (1)

15. This order of basicity is observed in case of solvent phase as the energy of hydration also becomes important here. The following important factors can be considered.

(i) **Effect of electron releasing groups** More the number of electron-releasing groups present in a molecule, more is the increase in its electron density and more is the basic character.

So, according to this effect, the order should be $NH_3 < RNH_2 < R_2NH < R_3N$. (1)

(ii) **Hydration enthalpy** The more hydrogen bonds a molecule (ammonium ion) can form with water, the more will be its basic character. So, the order should be $NH_3 > RNH_2 < R_2NH < R_3N$

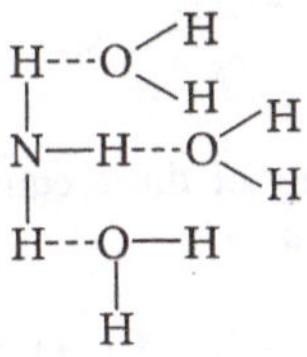

Ammonia

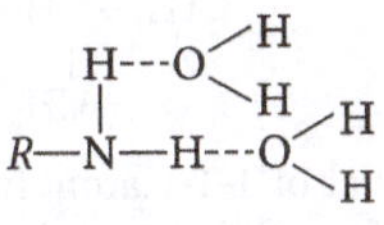

1° amine (Most stable)

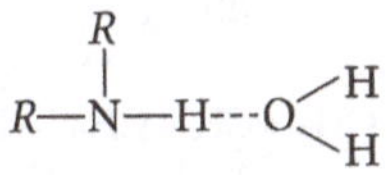

2° amine

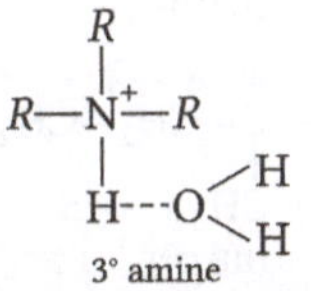

3° amine (1)

(iii) **Inductive effect** The more is the crowding of groups in a molecule, the lesser will be its basicity. So, the order should be $NH_3 > RNH_2 > R_2NH > R_3N$.

Combining all the factors, we get the order of basicity as $NH_3 > RNH_2 > R_3N$. (1)

16.

(i) $CH_2{=}CH—\ddot{\underset{..}{Cl}}: \longleftrightarrow :\bar{C}H_2—CH{=}\overset{+}{\underset{..}{Cl}}:$ (1)

(ii) $CH_2{=}CH—CH{=}CH_2 \longleftrightarrow \overset{+}{C}H_2—CH{=}CH—\bar{C}H_2 \longleftrightarrow :\bar{C}H_2—CH{=}CH—\overset{+}{C}H_2$ (1)

(iii) $CH_2{=}CH—\overset{O}{\overset{\|}{C}}—H \longleftrightarrow \overset{+}{C}H_2—CH{=}\overset{:\ddot{O}:^-}{\overset{|}{C}}—H$ (1)

17. $CH_3\underline{C}H{=}O$, $H_3C\underline{C}{\equiv}N$, and $H_3\underline{C}-I$, the underlined carbon atoms are electrophilic centres as they will have partial positive charge due to polarity of the C—O or C—N or C—I bonds. **(3)**

18. The structure having more covalent bonds in a resonating structure, has more stability. Further, there is charge separation in structure (II) and the terminal carbon has only a sextet of electrons in (II). These two factors makes structure (II) less stable.

$$\underset{\text{I}}{CH_2{=}CH{-}CH{=}O} \leftrightarrow \underset{\text{II}}{\overset{\oplus}{C}H_2{-}CH{=}CH{-}\overset{\ominus}{O}}$$

Hence, I > II in terms of stability. **(3)**

19. Carbocation (A) is more stable than carbocation (B). Carbocation (A) is more planar and hence is stabilised by resonance while carbocation (B) is non-planar and hence it does not undergo resonance.

Further, double bond is more stable within the ring in comparison to outside the ring.

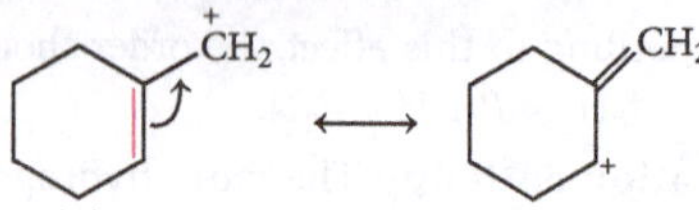

(A) (B) **(3)**

20. 2-methylbutane has four different sets of equivalent H-atoms.

$$CH_3-\underset{\underset{CH_3}{|}}{CH}-CH_2-CH_3$$

Removal of 1-1-1 atom from any of these equivalent sets gives four different carbocations.

$$CH_3{\to}\overset{\beta}{\underset{\underset{CH_3}{\uparrow}}{CH}}{\to}\overset{\alpha}{C}H_2{\to}\overset{+}{C}H_2 \quad (I)\ (1°) \qquad CH_3{\to}\underset{\underset{CH_3}{\uparrow}}{CH}{\to}\overset{+}{C}H{\leftarrow}CH_3 \quad (II)\ (2°)$$

$$CH_3{\to}\underset{\underset{CH_3}{\uparrow}}{\overset{+}{C}}{\leftarrow}CH_2{-}CH_3 \quad (III)\ (3°) \qquad \overset{+}{C}H_2{\leftarrow}\underset{\underset{CH_3}{\uparrow}}{CH}{\leftarrow}CH_2{-}CH_3 \quad (IV)\ (1°)$$

(1½)

Stability of carbocation decreases in the order 3°> 2°>1°. So, III (3° carbocation) is most stable followed by II (2°carbocation). Out of I and IV (both are 1° carbocation) I has a CH_3 group at β-carbon while II has a CH_3 group at α-carbon. As +*I*-effect decreases with distance, hence IV is more stable than I.

Therefore, the overall stability of these four carbocations increases in the order.

I < IV < II < III **(1½)**

21. (i) $C_6H_5CH_2\overset{+}{C}H_2 < C_6H_5\overset{+}{C}HCH_3 < C_6H_5\overset{+}{C}(CH_3)_2 < C_6H_5\overset{+}{C}HCH{=}CH_2$ **(1)**

(ii) $(CH_3)_3C^+ > C_6H_5\overset{+}{C}H_2 > CH_2{=}CH\overset{+}{C}H_2 > CH_3\overset{+}{C}H_2$ **(1)**

(iii) $(CH_3)_2CH^- < CH_3CH_2^- < CH_3^- < CH_2{=}CH^- < C_6H_5CH_2^- < HC{\equiv}C^-$ **(1)**

22. Refer to page 321 [Steam distillation] **(3)**

23. Refer to page 321 [Distillation under reduced pressure] **(3)**

24. Refer to page 325. [Topic 5 : Test for nitrogen] **(3)**

25. (i) Refer to page 326-3327 [Duma's method] **(1)**

(ii) Refer to page 328 [Carius method] **(1)**

(iii) Refer to page 328-329 [Estimation of phosphorus] **(1)**

26. The bubble plate type fractionating column is shown in the figure. The tower is divided into number of compartments by mean of shelves having openings. **(1)**

The openings are covered with caps called **bubble caps.** Each shelf is provided with an overflow pipe which keeps the liquid to a certain level and then allows the rest to trickle down to the lower shelf.

Such type of column is used for continuous separation of bulk quantities of liquids.

e.g. Distillation of fermented liquid for manufacture of rectified spirit. **(1½)**

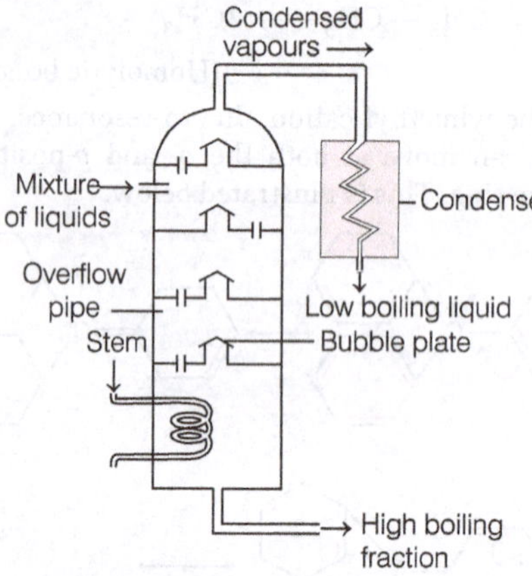

Bubble plate type fractionating column

(1½)

Industrial application

(i) Separation of crude oil in petroleum industry into various useful fractions such as gasoline, kerosene oil, diesel oil, lubricating oil, etc.

(ii) Separation of acetone and methanol from *pyroligneous acid* obtained by destructive distillation of wood. **(1)**

27. 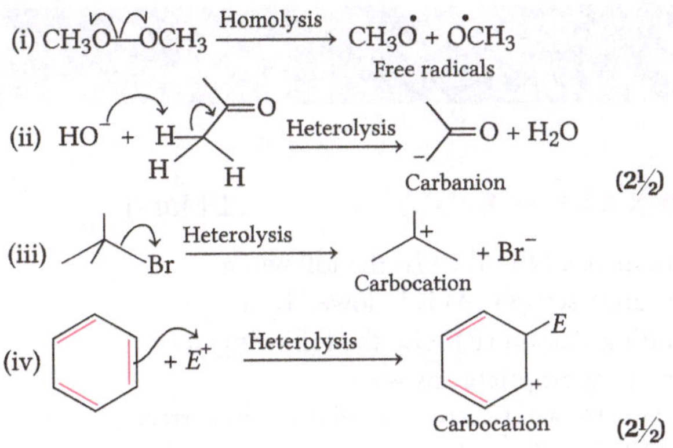

(2½)

(2½)

28. Refer to text on pages 312 and 313. (2)

(i) 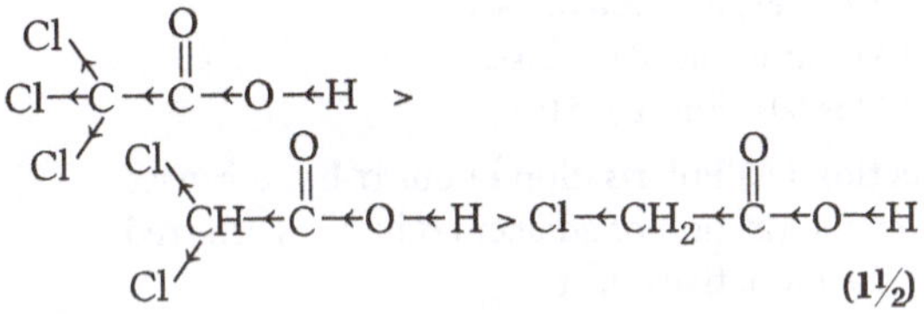

(1½)

$-I$**-effect** As the number of halogen atoms decreases, the overall $-I$-effect decreases and the acidic strength of carboxylic acids decreases accordingly.

(ii) 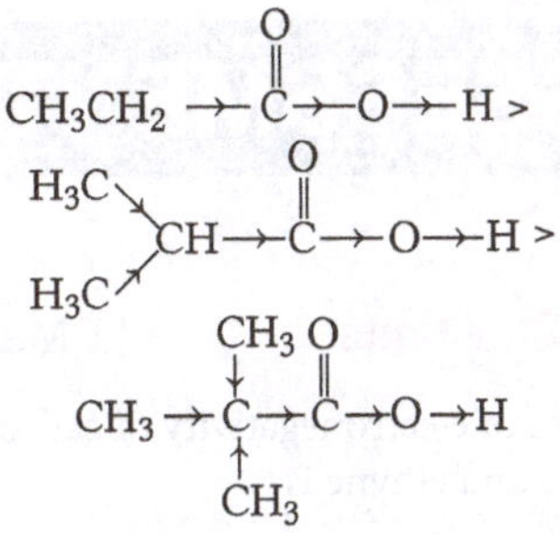

(1½)

$+I$**-effect** As the number of alkyl groups increases, the $+I$-effect increases and the acidic strength of carboxylic acids decreases accordingly.

29. (i) $Fe_4[Fe(CN)_6]_3 \cdot xH_2O$ (1)

(ii) $\% \text{ of N} = \dfrac{1.4 \times M \times 2(V - V_1/2)}{m}$ (2)

(iii) (a) Distillation under reduced pressure (1)

(b) Steam distillation. (1)

30. $CH_3CH_2COOCH_3$, $CH_3COOCH_2CH_3$
Ethyl propanoate, Ethyl ethanoate

$HCOOCH_2CH_2CH_3$; $HCOO—CH—(CH_3)_2$
Propyl methanoate; 2-methylethyl methanoate

$CH_3CH_2CH_2COOH$; CH_3CHCH_3 (with COOH on the middle carbon)
Butanoic acid; 2-methyl propanoic acid (5)

QR Code for Quick Test 1	QR Code for Quick Test 2	QR Code for Quick Test 3	QR Code for Quick Test 4	QR Code for Quick Test 5

SELF ASSESSMENT TEST

Objective Type Questions [1 Mark]

1. The correct order of electronegativity of carbon in ethane, ethene and ethyne is
   (a) ethane < ethene < ethyne
   (b) ethyne < ethene < ethane
   (c) ethene < ethyne < ethane
   (d) ethene < ethane < ethyne

2. In which of the following molecules, the resonance effect is not present?

   (a) 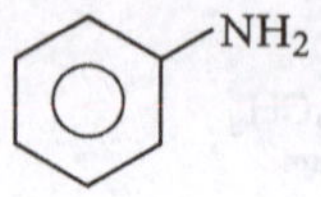 (b) 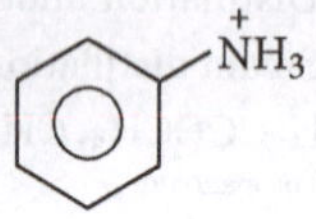

   (c) 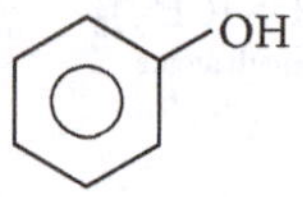 (d) 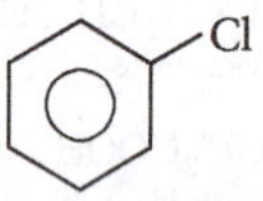

3. There are how many resonance structure of phenoxide ion?
   (a) 4 (b) 5 (c) 6 (d) 3

4. Among the following, the least stable resonance structure is

   (a) 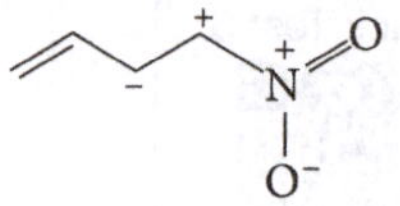 (b) 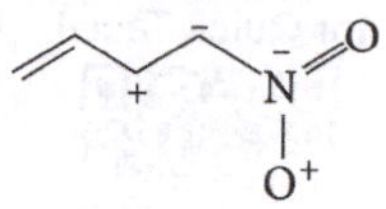

   (c) 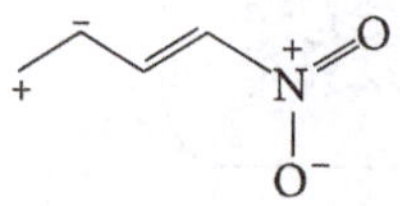 (d) 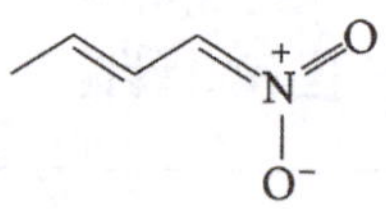

5. One of the stable resonating forms of methyl vinyl ketone is

   (a) $\overset{+}{C}H_2—\overset{-}{C}H—\overset{\overset{O}{||}}{C}—CH_3$

   (b) $\overset{+}{C}H_2—CH—\overset{\overset{O^-}{|}}{C}—CH_3$

   (c) $\overset{-}{C}H_2=CH—\overset{\overset{O}{||}}{C}—CH_3$

   (d) $CH_2=CH—\overset{\overset{O^-}{|}}{C}—CH_3$

Assertion Reason [1 Mark]

Directions (Q. Nos. 6-8) In the following questions, an Assertion (A) is followed by a corresponding Reason (R). Use the following keys to choose the appropriate answer.
(a) Both (A) and (R) are true and (R) is the correct explanation of (A).
(b) Both (A) and (R) are true and (R) is not the correct explanation of (A).
(c) (A) is true but (R) is false.
(d) (A) is false but (R) is true.

6. **Assertion** (A) Polarisation of one σ-bond caused by the polarisation of adjacent σ bond is referred to as the inductive effect.
   Reason (R) The substituents can be classified as electron withdrawing of electron donating groups relative to hydrogen.

7. **Assertion** (A) Allyl and benzyl carbonium ions are stable than propyl carbonium ions.
   Reason (R) Electron releasing groups stabilise carbonium ions.

8. **Assertion** (A) Inductive effect and resonance effect cause permanent polarisation of bond.
   Reason (R) These involve electron displacements due to the influence of an atom or a substituted group present in the molecule.

Short Answer Type I Questions [2 Marks]

9. Draw all position isomers of an alcohol with molecular formula, C_3H_8O.

10. (i) $CH_2=\bar{C}H$ is more basic than $HC\equiv C^-$. Explain why?
    (ii) Which of the two : $O_2NCH_2CH_2O^-$ or $CH_3CH_2O^-$ is expected to be more stable and why?

11. Lassaigne's test is not shown by diazonium salts, though they contain nitrogen. Why?

Short Answer Type II Questions [3 Marks]

12. (i) How many σ-bonds and π-bonds are present in the second member of the alkene series?

(ii) How many σ- and π-bonds are present in each of the following molecules?

(a) $CH_3CH_2C{\equiv}N$

(b) $CH_3—CH{=}CH—CH_2—C{\equiv}CH$

(c) $CH_2{=}C{=}CH_2$

13. (i) What are primary and secondary suffixes as applied to IUPAC nomenclature?

(ii) Name the compounds whose line formulae are given below.

(a) 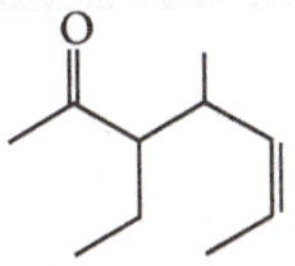

(b) 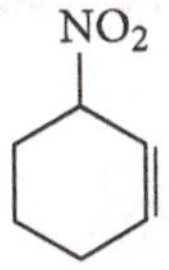

14. Explain the reason for the fusion of an organic compound with metallic sodium for testing nitrogen, sulphur and halogens. **NCERT**

Case-Study [4 Marks]

15. In a polar covalent bond, the electrons are shifted to the more electronegative atom and hence, a polarity is developed in the bond.

e.g. In a chain of carbon atoms having C—Cl bond, the C attached directly to the Cl-atom because of its less electronegativity acquires some positive charge (δ^+).

The carbon (C_2) that is bonded directly to the $C^{\delta+}$ also loose some of its electron density due to more polar $C^{\delta+}$ and hence, acquires somewhat less positive charge (δ^{++}).

Similarly, the next carbon (C_3) also acquires some positive charge but less than (δ^{++}) as shown below.

$$\underset{3}{\overset{\delta\delta\delta^+}{CH_3}}—\underset{2}{\overset{\delta\delta^+}{CH_2}}\rightarrow\underset{1}{\overset{\delta^+}{CH_2}}\rightarrow\overset{\delta^-}{Cl}$$

This induction of polarity, due to the presence of polar bond in an organic molecule, is called inductive effect.

(i) Among the following molecules/ions are the *I*-effect, resonance effect and hyperconjugation all operating simultaneously?

$(CH_3)_3C^+$, $(CH_3)_3C—\overset{+}{C}H_2$, $CH_3CH{=}CH—CH{=}O$

(ii) Arrange the following in the increasing order of stability

$F—CH_2—COO^-$, $ClCH_2COO^-$, $BrCH_2COO^-$, ICH_2COO^-

Or

Give the difference between inductive and resonance effect.

(iii) Write the application of *I*-effect.

Long Answer Type Questions [5 Marks]

16. (i) Suggest a method to purify

(a) camphor containing traces of common salt.

(b) kerosene oil containing water.

(c) a liquid which decomposes at its boiling point.

(ii) Which of the two structures *A* and *B* given below is more stabilised by resonance.

Explain $\underset{(A)}{CH_3COOH}$ and $\underset{(B)}{CH_3COO^-}$

17. (i) How does (a) an Electron Withdrawing Group (EWG) and (b) an Electron Donating Group (EDG) influence the acid strength of carboxylic end?

(ii) Explain, why an organic liquid vapourises at a temperature below its boiling point in its steam distillation?

Answers

1. (a)	2. (b)	3. (b)	4. (b)
5. (b)	6. (b)	7. (b)	8. (a)

09

CHAPTER

Hydrocarbons are the compounds of carbon and hydrogen only. The main sources of these compounds are coal and petroleum. These are used for synthesising many important substances such as polymers (e.g. polyethene, polystyrene, etc.), dyes and drugs. In short, these play a key role in making our lives more convenient.

▼ YOUR STUDY GOALS

9.1 Classification of Hydrocarbons
9.2 Alkanes
9.3 Alkenes
9.4 Alkynes
9.5 Aromatic Hydrocarbons

▼ YOUR PRACTICE GOAL

- Objective Type Questions (40 Qs ; 25 MCQs, 13 A-R, 2 Case-study)
- Subjective Type Questions (32 Qs; 10 SA-I, 15 SA-II, 7 LA)

Hydrocarbons

9.1 Classification of Hydrocarbons

Any two carbon atoms of a hydrocarbon may combine through single (—), double (=) or triple (≡) bonds. Depending upon the manner of attachment of carbon atoms, hydrocarbons can be classified in three major classes that are shown as follows

Hydrocarbons (Compounds of C and H only)

- **Saturated hydrocarbons** (Carbon atoms are joined together through single bonds only).
  - Alkanes: Open chain e.g. $CH_3—CH_3$ (ethane)
  - Cycloalkanes: Closed chain e.g.

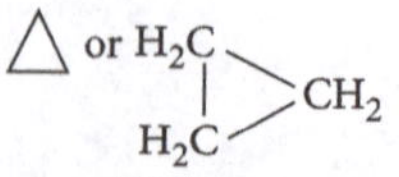

(Cyclopropane)

- **Unsaturated hydrocarbons** (One or more multiple bond(s) are present between the carbon atom).
  - Alkenes: have atleast one double bond between carbon atoms. e.g. $CH_2=CH_2$ (ethene), $CH_3—CH=CH_2$ (propene) etc.
  - Alkynes: have atleast one triple bond between carbon atoms. e.g. $CH\equiv CH$ (acetylene), $CH_3—C\equiv CH$ (propyne) etc.
- **Aromatic hydrocarbons** (Alternate single and double bond and $(4n+2)\pi$ electrons are present).

e.g.  (Benzene)

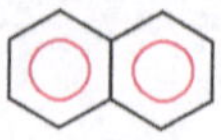
(Naphthalene)

9.2 Alkanes

These are the open chain saturated hydrocarbons, in which carbon atoms are joined together only through single bonds.

These are the simplest hydrocarbons and were earlier called **'paraffins'** (*Latin : parum*, little ; affinis, affinity) because of their inert (non-reactive) nature towards many acids, bases and other reagents.

General molecular formula for these compounds is C_nH_{2n+2} (where, $n=1, 2, 3, \ldots$). If $n=1$, we get CH_4 (methane), the first member of alkane series. By replacing the hydrogen(s) of CH_4 by —CH_3 or other alkyl groups, we get the complete series of members of this group.

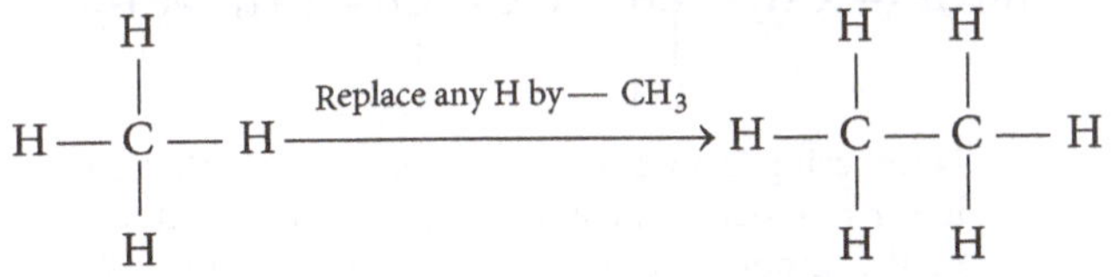

Note Groups having one H-atom less than the alkanes are called **alkyl groups**. General molecular formula for these groups is C_nH_{2n+1}.
e.g. —CH_3 is the alkyl group (methyl group) derived from methane by replacing its one hydrogen atom.

Structure of Alkanes

In alkanes, the central C-atom is sp^3-hybridised and have four half-filled sp^3-hybridised orbitals. These four orbitals form four σ-bonds either with four H-atoms using their 1*s*-orbitals (sp^3—s bonding) or with other carbon atoms (sp^3—sp^3 linkage) or both.

e.g. Consider the structure of methane.

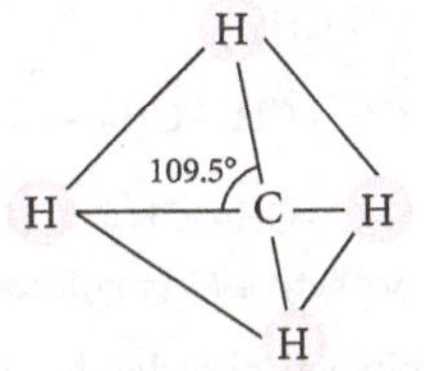

Structure of methane

The four σ-bonds are directed toward the corners of a regular tetrahedron, i.e. they are multiplanar (not in one plane). The average C—C and C—H bond lengths are approximately 154 pm and 112 pm respectively.

Thus, methane have four sp^3-*s*-σ bonds formed between sp^3-orbitals of C and 1*s*-orbital of H.

Nomenclature of Alkanes

The nomenclature of hydrocarbons has been discussed below

1. Writing IUPAC Name from a Given Structure

In the previous chapter, you have read that alkanes are named by adding the suffix 'ane' to the 'root word', IUPAC names of some simple alkanes are given below.

Name	Molecular Formula	Name	Molecular Formula
Methane	CH_4	Decane	$C_{10}H_{22}$
Ethane	C_2H_6	Icosane	$C_{20}H_{42}$
Propane	C_3H_8	Triacontane	$C_{30}H_{62}$

However, in complex structures, naming can be done as follows

Structure	IUPAC name	Remarks
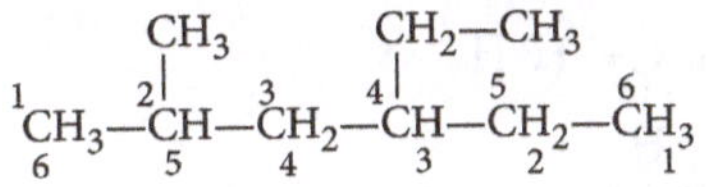	4-ethyl-2-methylhexane ('e' comes first in the alphabetical order)	The numbering is done from the end which gives the lowest sum and in accordance with alphabetical order of the name of substituent.
If the substituent group is also complex then separate numbering is also done in it. 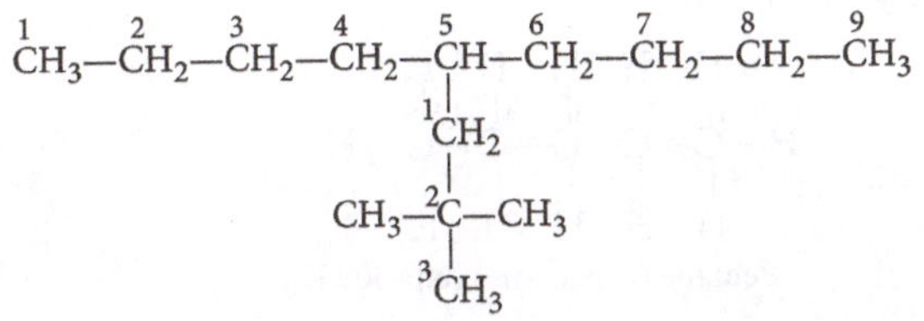	5-(2,2-dimethylpropyl nonane)	Substituent numbering starts with carbon that is linked with the principal chain.

Structure	IUPAC name	Remarks
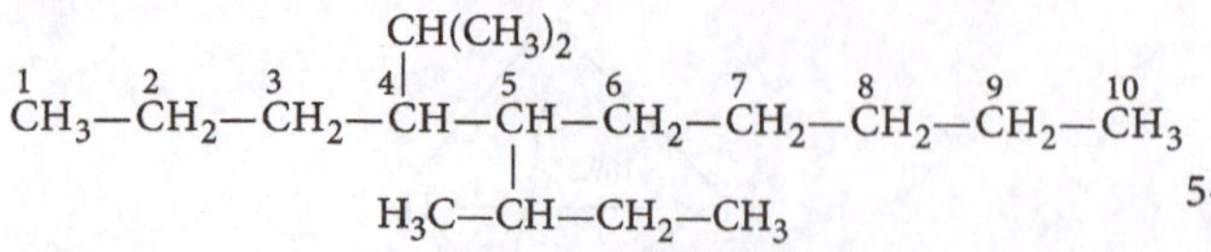 5-*sec*-butyl-4-*iso* propyldecane ('b' comes first in alphabetical order, here 's' of *sec* is not considered.)	5-*sec*-butyl-4-*iso*-propyldecane	(i) The prefix *sec*, di, tri, etc., are not considered in alphabetical order while writing the IUPAC name. (ii) Only the first letter of root word is considered, if arranged in alphabetical order.

2. Writing Correct Structure From the Given IUPAC Name

To write the structure of a compound from its name, first draw the longest chain of carbon atoms (according to root word) and then number it.

Now attach the different substituent at the mentioned places and satisfy the valencies of all the C-atoms by putting required number of hydrogen atoms.

e.g. The structure of 3-ethyl-2, 2- dimethylpentane can be written as

Step I Here 'pent' is the root word, so the principal chain have five C-atoms. Thus, draw five C-atoms in a straight chain.

$$C—C—C—C—C$$

Step II Give number to the carbon atoms (you can give number from either sides).

$$C^1—C^2—C^3—C^4—C^5$$

Step III Attach ethyl group at third carbon and methyl groups at second carbon.

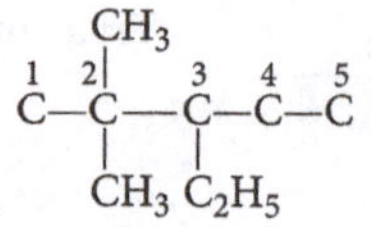

Step IV Satisfy the valency of each carbon atom by adding the required number of hydrogen atoms.

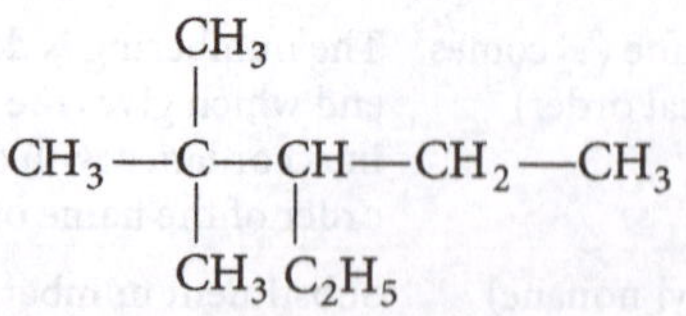

Example 1 Write structures for each of the following compounds. Why are the given names incorrect? Write correct IUPAC names.

(i) 2-ethylpentane

(ii) 5-ethyl-3-methylheptane **NCERT**

Sol. (i)

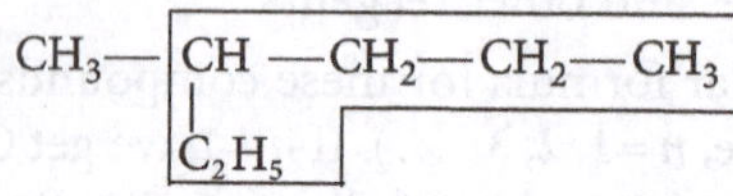

Longest chain is of six carbon atoms and not of five. Hence, the correct name of the compound is 3-methylhexane.

(ii)

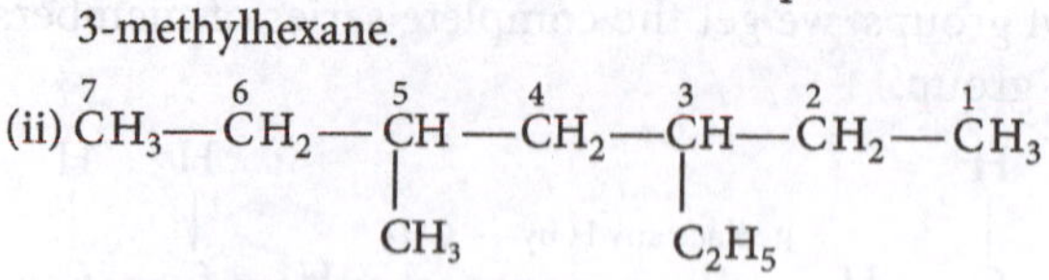

Numbering is always started from the end that gives lower number to the ethyl group as compared to methyl group (because in alphabets 'e' comes first than 'm').

Isomerism of Alkanes

First three members of alkane family, i.e. methane, ethane and propane have only one structure but higher alkanes can have more than one structure.

e.g. Four carbon atoms can be joined in the following two different ways with molecular formula, C_4H_{10}.

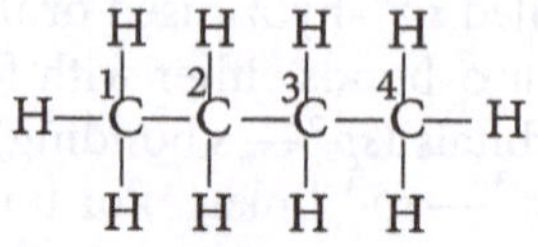

Butane (*n*-butane) (b.p. 273 K)

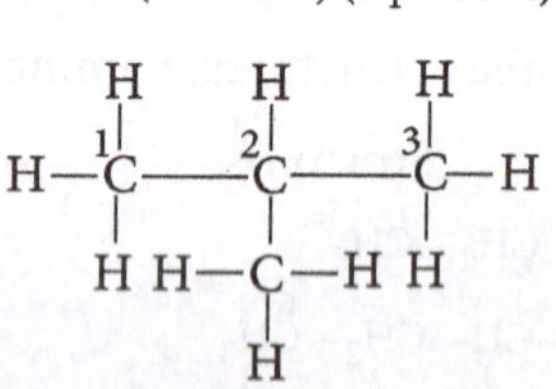

2-methylpropane (*iso*-butane) (b.p. 261 K)

Similarly, C_5H_{12} can have three different structures which are given below.

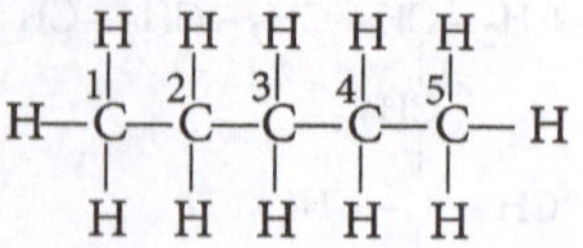

Pentane (*n*-pentane) (b.p. 309 K)

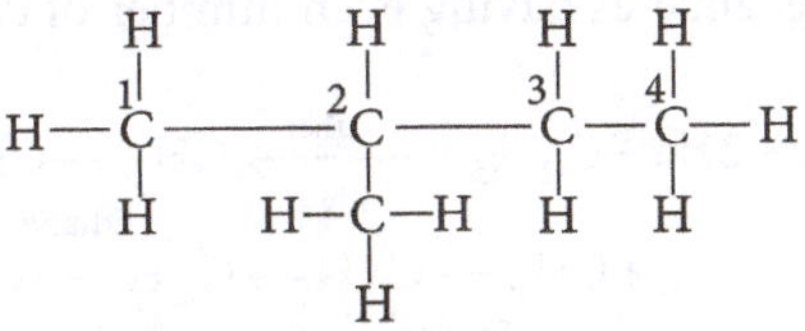

2-methylbutane (*iso*-pentane) (b.p. 301 K)

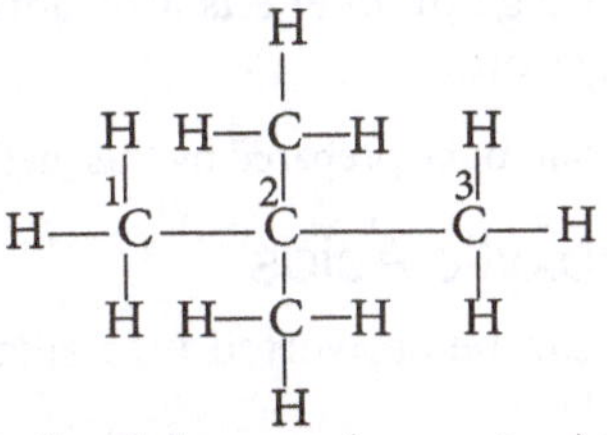

2, 2-dimethylpropane (*neo*-pentane) (b.p. 282.5 K)

We see, that the two structures derived from the molecular formula C_4H_{10} and three structures derived from the molecular formula C_5H_{12} have different properties (boiling point).
Such structures which have different properties due to the difference in their structures are called **structural isomers.** Also the structural isomers which differ in chain of carbon atoms are known as **chain isomers.**

Note The number of possible isomers for C_6H_{14} and C_7H_{16} are respectively 9 and 75.

Example 2 Write structures of different chain isomers of alkanes corresponding to the molecular formula C_6H_{14}. Also write their IUPAC names. NCERT

Sol. (i) $CH_3—CH_2—CH_2—CH_2—CH_2—CH_3$

n-hexane

(ii) 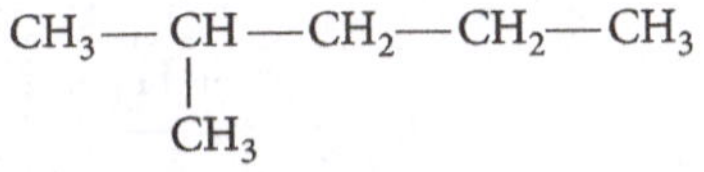

2-methylpentane

(iii) 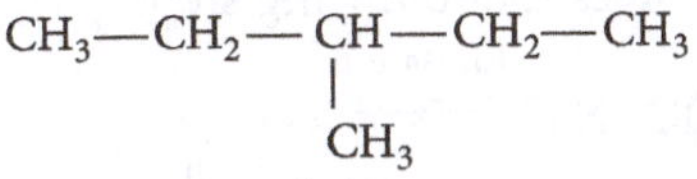

3-methylpentane

(iv) 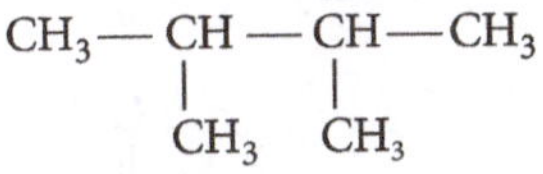

2,3- dimethylbutane

(v) 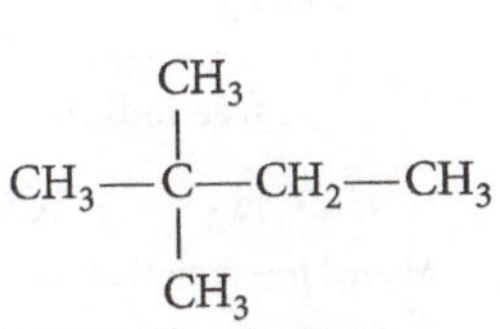

2,2-dimethylbutane

Types of Carbon and Hydrogen Atoms

Depending upon the number of carbon atoms or any other element (except hydrogen) attached to a given carbon atom, the hydrogen atoms and carbon atoms are classified into following classes.

	Type	Examples
(i)	**1° or Primary** The carbon to which no other carbon or only one carbon atom is attached is called **1°** or **primary carbon atom.** The hydrogen atoms attached to this carbon atom are called 1° hydrogen.	1° carbon CH_4 4 primary (1)° hydrogens; 1° carbon 1° carbon $CH_3—CH_3$ 6 primary (1)° hydrogens **Note** Terminal carbon atoms are always primary.
(ii)	**2° or Secondary** The carbon which is bonded to two other carbon atoms, is called **2°** or **secondary carbon atom** and hydrogen atoms attached to it are called secondary or 2° hydrogens.	1° carbon 2° carbon 1°carbon $CH_3—CH_2—CH_3$ (This compound contains 6 primary and 2 secondary hydrogen atoms).
(iii)	**3° or Tertiary** The carbon linked with three other carbon atoms, is called **3°** or **tertiary carbon atom** and the hydrogen atoms attached to it, is called **3°** or **tertiary hydrogen atom.**	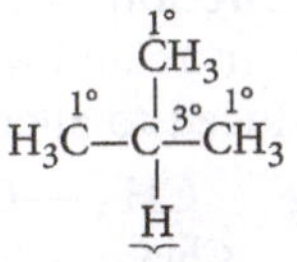 3° hydrogen Only 1 tertiary hydrogen atom is present in this compound.
(iv)	**4° or Quaternary** The carbon which is bonded to four other carbon atoms is called **quaternary carbon atom** or ***neo*-carbon.**	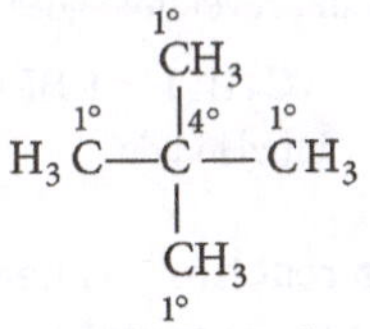 1 quaternary carbon **Note** The nature of hydrogen atoms in quaternary carbon atom is never quaternary. Mostly they are primary hydrogen.

Methods of Preparation of Alkanes

The main sources of alkanes are petroleum and natural gas. However, they can also be synthesised by the following methods.

1. From Unsaturated Hydrocarbons

When unsaturated compounds, i.e. alkenes or alkynes, are treated with dihydrogen in the presence of finely divided catalysts (i.e. Pt, Pd or Ni), alkanes are obtained and the reaction is called **hydrogenation reaction.**

e.g. $$\underset{\text{Ethene}}{CH_2{=}CH_2} + H_2 \xrightarrow{Pt/Pd/Ni} \underset{\text{Ethane}}{CH_3{-}CH_3}$$

$$\underset{\text{Propyne}}{CH_3{-}C{\equiv}C{-}H} + 2H_2 \xrightarrow{Pt/Pd/Ni} \underset{\text{Propane}}{CH_3{-}CH_2{-}CH_3}$$

In these reactions, metal adsorb the dihydrogen and provides surface for activating H—H bonds. Platinum (Pt) and palladium (Pd) catalyse the reaction at room temperature but in case of nickel (Ni), high temperature and pressure is required.

Note If unsaturated compounds are reduced by using Ni as catalyst at a temperature of 200°-300° C, the reaction is called **Sabatier Senderen's reaction.**

2. From Alkyl Halides

The following methods are used to convert alkyl halides into alkanes. They are as follows.

(i) **Reduction** All the alkyl halides, except fluorides, when treated with zinc and dilute HCl, get reduced to alkanes.

e.g. $$\underset{\text{Chloromethane}}{CH_3{-}Cl} + H_2 \xrightarrow{Zn,\,H^+} \underset{\text{Methane}}{CH_4} + HCl$$

TEACHER'S TIP

Alkyl iodide can also be reduced by using red P and HI. Here, red P is used to remove iodine as volatile PI_3, otherwise the reaction being reversible goes in backward direction.

$$\underset{\text{Ethyl iodide}}{C_2H_5I} + HI \xrightarrow{\text{Red P}} \underset{\text{Ethane}}{C_2H_6} + I_2$$

(ii) **Wurtz reaction** When alkyl halides are treated with sodium metal in the presence of dry ether (free from moisture) it results in the formation of an alkane having double number of carbons as that are present in parent halide. This reaction is called **Wurtz reaction.**

$$\underset{\text{Bromoethane}}{C_2H_5Br} + 2Na + BrC_2H_5 \xrightarrow{\text{Dry ether}} \underset{n\text{-butane}}{C_2H_5{-}C_2H_5} + 2NaBr$$

If different alkyl halides are used, the product is non-separable mixture of alkanes, so this method is more suitable for the synthesis of symmetrical alkanes, i.e. alkanes having even number of carbon atoms.

e.g. $$CH_3X + 2Na + C_2H_5X \xrightarrow[-NaX]{\text{Ether}} \underset{\text{Ethane}}{CH_3{-}CH_3} + \underset{\text{Propane}}{CH_3{-}C_2H_5} + \underset{\text{Butane}}{C_2H_5{-}C_2H_5}$$

(A small percentage of alkene is also obtained during this reaction).

Note Methane cannot be prepared by this method.

3. From Carboxylic Acids

Carboxylic acids can be converted into alkanes by following methods

(i) **Decarboxylation** (removal of —CO_2) When sodium salts of carboxylic acids are heated with sodalime (a mixture of NaOH and CaO) CO_2 is eliminated and alkanes having one carbon atom less than the parent compound is obtained. Thus, sodalime acts as the decarboxylating agent.

$$\underset{\text{Sodium ethanoate}}{CH_3COO^-Na^+} + NaOH \xrightarrow[\Delta]{CaO} \underset{\text{Methane}}{CH_4} + Na_2CO_3$$

(ii) **Kolbe's electrolytic method** When aqueous solution of sodium or potassium salt of a carboxylic acid is subjected to electrolysis, it gives an alkane having even number of carbon atoms at the anode. In this method, a new C—C linkage is developed.

$$\begin{matrix} CH_3COO^-Na^+ \\ + \\ CH_3COO^-Na^+ \end{matrix} + 2H_2O \xrightleftharpoons{\text{Electrolysis}} \underbrace{\begin{matrix} CH_3 \\ | \\ CH_3 \end{matrix} + 2CO_2\uparrow}_{\text{At anode}} + \underbrace{H_2\uparrow + 2Na^+OH^-}_{\text{At cathode}}$$

Mechanism It involves the following steps

Step I $$2CH_3COO^-Na^+ \xrightleftharpoons{\text{Ionisation}} 2\,CH_3{-}\overset{\overset{\displaystyle O}{\|}}{C}{-}O^- + 2Na^+$$

Step II At anode,

$$\underset{\text{Acetate ion}}{2\,CH_3{-}\overset{\overset{\displaystyle O}{\|}}{C}{-}O^-} \xrightarrow{-2e^-} \underset{\text{Acetate free radical}}{2\,CH_3{-}\overset{\overset{\displaystyle O}{\|}}{C}{-}\ddot{\underset{\cdot\cdot}{O}}\,\bullet} \longrightarrow \underset{\text{Methyl free radical}}{2\dot{C}H_3} + 2CO_2\uparrow$$

Step III $H_3\dot{C} + \dot{C}H_3 \longrightarrow H_3C—CH_3$

Step IV At cathode,

$$H_2O + e^- \longrightarrow OH^- + \dot{H}$$

$$2\dot{H} \longrightarrow H_2\uparrow$$

Because of the generation of OH^- ions, the solution becomes alkaline.

TEACHER'S TIP

CH_4 cannot be prepared by this method. This method is not suitable for alkanes having odd number of carbon atoms, as in such case a mixture of hydrocarbons is formed which is difficult to separate.

Flowchart of Alkane Synthesis

Reaction involved in synthesis of alkanes

- Hydrogenation: $\underset{\text{Ethene}}{CH_2{=}CH_2} + H_2 \xrightarrow{Pt/Pd/Ni} \underset{\text{Ethane}}{CH_3—CH_3}$
- Reduction: $\underset{\text{Chloromethane}}{CH_3—Cl} + H_2 \xrightarrow{Zn, H^+} \underset{\text{Methane}}{CH_4} + HCl$
- Wurtz reaction: $\underset{\text{Bromoethane}}{C_2H_5Br} + 2Na + BrC_2H_5 \xrightarrow{\text{Dry ether}} \underset{n\text{-butane}}{C_2H_5—C_2H_5} + 2NaBr$
- Decarboxylation: $\underset{\text{Sodium ethanoate}}{CH_3COO^-Na^+} + NaOH \xrightarrow[\Delta]{CaO} \underset{\text{Methane}}{CH_4} + Na_2CO_3$
- Kolbe's electrolytic method: $2CH_3COO^-Na^+ + H_2O \xrightarrow{\text{Electrolysis}} CH_3—CH_3 + CO_2\uparrow + H_2\uparrow + 2Na^{\oplus}OH^{\ominus}$

Physical Properties of Alkanes

Alkanes exhibit following physical properties.

1. Physical State

Alkanes possess weak van der Waals' forces. Due to which, their first four members (C_1 to C_4) are gases, C_5 to C_{17} are liquids and all other higher ones (i.e. $>C_{18}$) are waxy solids. They are colourless and odourless.

2. Dipole Moment

Due to the presence of only covalent C—C and C—H bonds and very less difference between the electronegativites of carbon and hydrogen, alkanes are almost non-polar and have zero dipole moment.

3. Solubility

Being non-polar, these are insoluble in water but soluble in alcohol, ether, benzene etc. The solubility diminishes with increase in molecular weight.

4. Boiling Point

As the number of carbon atoms or molecular mass increases, the boiling point of alkane increases because van der Waals' forces increase due to increased surface area. However, branching results in decrease in boiling point due to decreased surface area which results in weaker van der Waals' forces.

e.g. Order of boiling point of alkanes is 2, 2-dimethyl propane (282.5) < 2-methylbutane (300.9) < pentane (309.1).

5. Melting Point

Melting point also increases with increase in molecular weights but alkanes with even number of carbon atoms have higher melting point than the preceding and succeeding members, due to their well packed structures.

6. Density

Alkanes are lighter than water and their density also increases with increase in molecular mass.

Chemical Properties of Alkanes

Although alkanes are almost inert towards most of the reagents, but they show following reactions under suitable conditions of temperature and pressure.

1. Substitution Reactions

The reactions in which hydrogen atom(s) of a hydrocarbon is (are) substituted by other group(s) are called **substitution reactions.**

Alkanes undergo several substitution reactions like halogenation, nitration and sulphonation.

Halogenation

When an alkane is treated with a halogen at higher temperature (573-773 K) or in the presence of diffused sunlight or ultraviolet light, the hydrogen atoms of alkanes are successively replaced by halogen atoms. This reaction is known as halogenation.

e.g. $CH_4 + Cl_2 \xrightarrow{h\nu} \underset{\text{Chloromethane}}{CH_3Cl} + HCl$

$$CH_3Cl + Cl_2 \xrightarrow{h\nu} \underset{\text{Dichloromethane}}{CH_2Cl_2} + HCl$$

$$CH_2Cl_2 + Cl_2 \xrightarrow{h\nu} \underset{\text{Trichloromethane}}{CHCl_3} + HCl$$

$$CHCl_3 + Cl_2 \xrightarrow{h\nu} \underset{\text{Tetrachloromethane}}{CCl_4} + HCl$$

Towards this reaction, the order of reactivity of halogens is $F_2 > Cl_2 > Br_2 > I_2$ and the order of rate of replacement of hydrogens from alkanes is 3° > 2° > 1°.

Thus, **fluorination** is a violent process which is difficult to control so carried out in dark whereas during **iodination** presence of oxidising agent such as HIO_3 or HNO_3 is necessary as the reaction is very slow and reversible.

$$CH_4 + I_2 \rightleftharpoons CH_3I + HI$$

$$\text{and } HIO_3 + 5HI \longrightarrow 3I_2 \uparrow + 3H_2O$$

Mechanism Halogenation process proceeds through free radical mechanism which involves following three steps

Step I **Initiation** (Generation of free radical)

$$Cl—Cl \xrightarrow[\text{Homolysis}]{h\nu} \underset{\text{Chlorine free radical}}{\dot{C}l + \dot{C}l}$$

Step II **Propagation** (Chain reactions)

$$CH_4 + \dot{C}l \xrightarrow{h\nu} \dot{C}H_3 + H—Cl$$

$$\dot{C}H_3 + Cl—Cl \xrightarrow{h\nu} CH_3—Cl + \underset{\text{Chlorine free radical}}{\dot{C}l}$$

The above reaction gives the required products but many other side reactions also occur during the process. Two such reactions are as follows

$$CH_3Cl + \dot{C}l \longrightarrow \dot{C}H_2Cl + HCl$$

$$\dot{C}H_2Cl + Cl—Cl \longrightarrow CH_2Cl_2 + \dot{C}l$$

Step III **Termination** Either by complete consumption of reactants or due to reaction of two free radicals

$$\dot{C}l + \dot{C}l \longrightarrow Cl—Cl$$

$$H_3\dot{C} + \dot{C}H_3 \longrightarrow H_3C—CH_3$$

$$H_3\dot{C} + \dot{C}l \longrightarrow H_3C—Cl$$

Thus, ethane is also produced as by product during the free radical chlorination of methane.

Like in halogenation process, the hydrogen in alkane is replaced by a halogen. When the hydrogen atom of alkane is replaced by a nitro group ($—NO_2$) or sulphonic group ($—SO_3H$). It is known as nitration or sulphonation respectively.

2. Combustion

When alkanes are heated in excess of air or dioxygen, they are oxidised to give carbon dioxide and water. A large amount of heat is evolved during this reaction. Thus, alkanes are used as fuels.

The general combustion equation for any alkane is

$$C_nH_{2n+2} + \left(\frac{3n+1}{2}\right)O_2 \longrightarrow nCO_2 + (n+1)H_2O$$

$$CH_4(g) + 2O_2(g) \longrightarrow CO_2(g) + 2H_2O(l); \quad \Delta_c H^\ominus = -890 \text{ kJ mol}^{-1}$$

$$C_4H_{10}(g) + \frac{13}{2}O_2(g) \longrightarrow 4CO_2(g) + 5H_2O(l); \quad \Delta_c H^\ominus = -2875.84 \text{ kJ mol}^{-1}$$

If air or dioxygen is insufficient, incomplete combustion of alkanes takes place and carbon black is formed as product.

Carbon black is used for making ink, printer ink, black pigments and as filters.

$$CH_4(g) + O_2(g) \xrightarrow[\text{combustion}]{\text{Incomplete}} C(s) + 2H_2O(l)$$

3. Controlled Oxidation

If alkanes are heated in controlled supply of dioxygen or air and in the presence of suitable catalysts, a variety of oxidation products are obtained as follows

$$2CH_4 + O_2 \xrightarrow{\text{Cu/523 K/100 atm}} \underset{\text{Methanol}}{2CH_3OH}$$

$$CH_4 + O_2 \xrightarrow[\Delta]{Mo_2O_3} \underset{\text{Methanal}}{HCHO} + H_2O$$

$$2CH_3CH_3 + 3O_2 \xrightarrow[\Delta]{(CH_3COO)_2Mn} \underset{\text{Ethanoic acid}}{2CH_3COOH} + 2H_2O$$

Generally, alkanes do not undergo oxidation but alkanes having tertiary H-atom undergo oxidation to corresponding alcohols by treating them with potassium permanganate.

$$\underset{\text{2- methylpropane}}{(CH_3)_3CH} \xrightarrow[\text{Oxidation}]{KMnO_4} \underset{\text{2- methylpropan- 2- ol}}{(CH_3)_3COH}$$

4. Isomerisation

When *n*-alkanes are heated with anhydrous $AlCl_3$ and HCl gas, they isomerise to give branched chain alkanes as the major product which are given below

$$CH_3(CH_2)_4CH_3 \xrightarrow{\text{Anhyd. } AlCl_3/HCl} CH_3CH(CH_3)\text{—}(CH_2)_2\text{—}CH_3 + CH_3CH_2\text{—}CH(CH_3)\text{—}CH_2\text{—}CH_3$$

n- hexane → 2- methylpentane + 3- methylpentane

5. Aromatisation

Straight chain alkanes having six or more C-atoms when heated to 773 K at 10-20 atm pressure in the presence of Cr_2O_3, V_2O_5 or Mo_2O_3 supported over alumina gel, get dehydrogenated (i.e. loss hydrogen) and cyclised to give benzene and its homologoues.

This reaction is known as **aromatisation** or **reforming.**

e.g.

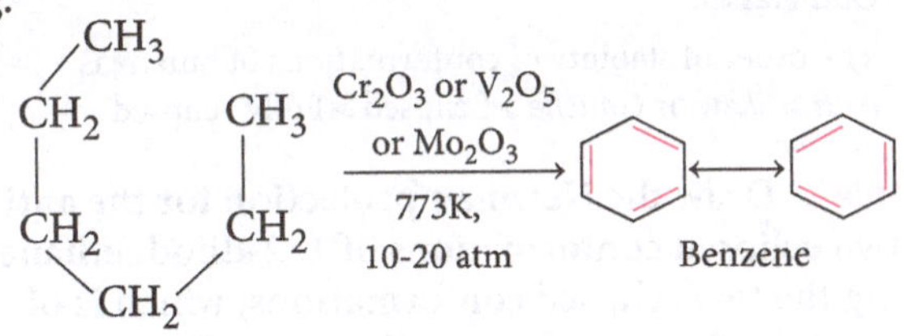

If *n*-heptane is used in place of *n*-hexane, toluene, $(C_6H_5CH_3)$ is obtained as the product.

6. Pyrolysis or Cracking

Higher alkanes when heated at a higher temperature get decompose to give smaller fragments like lower alkanes, alkenes etc. This reaction is called **pyrolysis.**

e.g. $\underset{\text{Dodecane}}{C_{12}H_{26}} \xrightarrow[973\text{ K}]{Pt/Pd/Ni} \underset{\text{Heptane}}{C_7H_{16}} + \underset{\text{Pentene}}{C_5H_{10}}$ + Other products

This reaction takes place by free radical mechanism and used to prepare oil gas or petrol gas from kerosene oil.

7. Reaction with Steam

When methane is treated with steam at 1273 K and in the presence of nickel as catalyst, it gives carbon monoxide and dihydrogen gas.

$$CH_4 + H_2O \xrightarrow[\Delta]{Ni} CO + 3H_2$$

The above reaction is an industrial process for the synthesis of dihydrogen.

Conformations

The rotation of carbon-carbon single bond (σ-bond), due to cylindrical symmetry of σ-MOs (molecular orbitals) along internuclear axis, in alkanes results into different spatial arrangements of atoms in space, that are interconvertible.

These arrangements are called **conformations, conformers** or **rotamers**. In general, alkanes possess infinite number of conformations.

However, weak repulsive interaction are present between the adjacent bonds in alkanes so, the rotation of C—C single bond is not completely free and is hindered by a small energy barriers of 1-20 kJ mol^{-1}.

The repulsive interaction between the adjacent bond is called **torsional strain.**

Conformations of Ethane

Considering the ball and stick model of ethane, one carbon atom is kept stationary and the other carbon atom is rotated around the C—C axis.

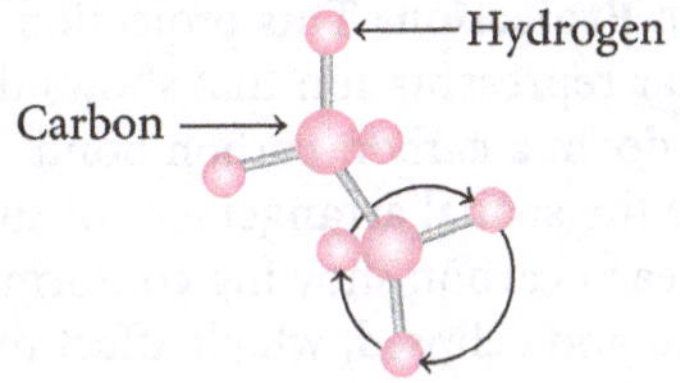

The rotation results in an infinite number of arrangements of the hydrogen atom attached to one carbon atom with respect to the hydrogen atom of the second carbon atom.

These infinite number of different arrangements are called **conformation.** However, there are two extreme cases discussed below.

1. Staggered Conformation

The conformation in which the hydrogen atoms attached to the two carbon atoms are as far apart as possible is called the **staggered conformation.**

2. Eclipsed Conformation

The conformation in which the hydrogen atoms attached to the two carbon atoms are as close together as possible is called **eclipsed conformation.**

Any intermediate conformation between the above two is called ***skew*** or ***gauche*** **conformation.**

In all the conformations, the bond angles as well as bond lengths remain the same.

TEACHER'S TIP

Isomers can be resolved and separated by chemical methods while conformers cannot be separated.

The staggered and eclipsed conformations of ethane in three dimensions can be represented by following two projections.

(i) **Sawhorse Projections** In this projections, molecules are shown in 3D along a bond, highlighting atom positions to reveal staggered or eclipsed conformation.
Sawhorse projections for eclipsed and staggered conformation of ethane are as follows

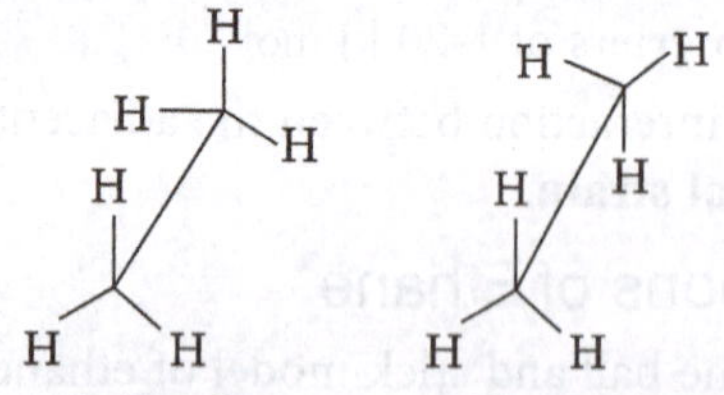

(a) Eclipsed (b) Staggered

Sawhorse projections of ethane

(ii) **Newman Projections** This projection is a 3D molecular representation that shows the view directly down a carbon-carbon bond. This helps visualize the spatial arrangement of substituents around each carbon showing conformations like staggered and eclipsed, which affect molecular stability.
The Newman's projections for staggered, eclipsed *skew* conformations of ethane are shown below.

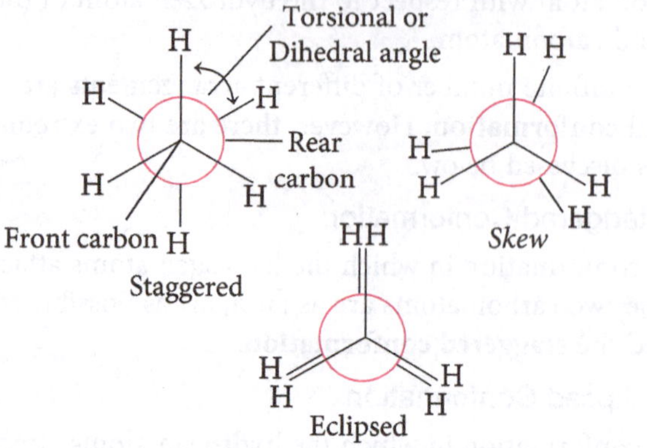

Newman's projections of ethane

Relative Stability of Conformations

In staggered conformation, since the electron clouds of carbon-hydrogen bonds are as far apart as possible, so it has minimum repulsive forces, minimum energy and maximum stability.

On the other hand, eclipsed conformation has maximum repulsive forces, maximum energy and minimum stability because in it the electron clouds of carbon hydrogen bonds are too close to each other. The angle of rotation about C—C bond is called the **dihedral angle** or **torsional angle** and is maximum, i.e. 180° in staggered conformation and minimum (0°) in eclipsed conformation.

Thus, torsional strain is minimum in staggered conformation and maximum in eclipsed form. Hence, staggered conformation is more stable than the eclipsed conformation.

The two forms differ in energy by 12.5 kJ mol^{-1}. This energy barrier is so small that small thermal or kinetic energy is sufficient to overcome it by intermolecular collisions, hence the different conformations of ethane can not be separated and isolated.

Note The field of conformation analysis was developed by the brilliant research carried out by Derek H Barton and Odd Hassel.

The order of stability of conformations of butane is *Anti* > *Skew* or *Gauche* > Eclipsed > Fully eclipsed.

Example 3 Draw the Newman projection for the anti and two eclipsed conformations of 1, 2-diiodoethane. Among the two eclipsed conformations, which is of higher energy?

Sol. I—CH_2—CH_2—I (III) is of higher energy than (II) because in (III), the bulky iodine atoms are very close to each other. Therefore, repulsion between them is maximum.

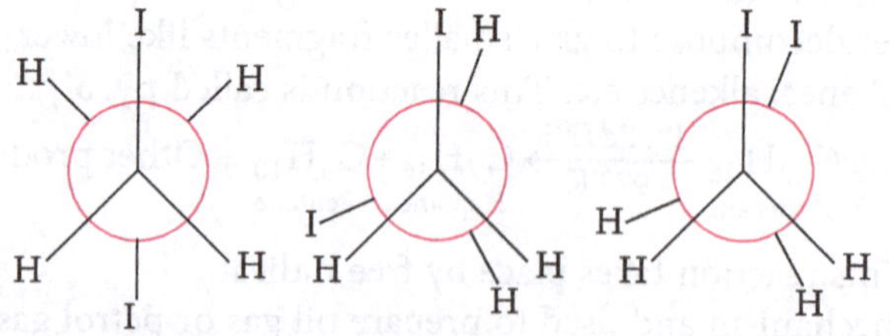

Anti (I) Eclipsed (II) Eclipsed (III)

Quick Test 1

1. Sodium salt of which acid will be needed for the preparation of propane? Write chemical equation for the reaction. NCERT
2. What effect does branching of an alkane chain has on its boiling point? NCERT
3. Identify the structure of *A* and *B*;
CH_3—$CH_2COOH \xrightarrow{KOH} A \xrightarrow{\text{Kolbe's electrolysis}} B$
4. *n*-propylmagnesium bromide on hydrolysis gives propane. Is there any other Grignard reagent which also gives propane? If so, give its name, structure and equation for the reaction.

5. Write structural formulas of the following compounds.
   (i) 3, 4, 4, 5-tetramethylheptane
   (ii) 2, 5-dimethylhexane *NCERT*
6. Why is Wurtz reaction not preferred for the preparation of alkanes containing odd number of carbon atoms? Illustrate your answer by taking one example. *NCERT*
7. Write hydrocarbon radicals that can be formed as intermediates during monochlorination of 2-methylpropane. Which of them is more stable? Give reasons. *NCERT Exemplar*
8. In the alkane $H_3C\ CH_2—C(CH_3)_2—CH_2CH(CH_3)_2$, identify 1°, 2°, 3° carbon atoms and give the number of H-atoms bonded to each one of these. *NCERT*
9. Suggest a route to prepare ethyl hydrogensulphate ($CH_3—CH_2—OSO_2—OH$) starting from ethanol (C_2H_5OH). *NCERT Exemplar*
10. The relative reactivity of 1°, 2°, 3° hydrogens towards chlorination is 1 : 3.8 : 5.
    Calculate the percentages of all monochlorinated products obtained from 2-methylbutane. *NCERT Exemplar*

For Solutions, See QR Code on Pg. 383

9.3 Alkenes

The unsaturated hydrocarbons having atleast one double bond are called alkenes. Their general formula is C_nH_{2n} (where, $n = 2, 3, 4 \ldots$) as they have two carbon atoms less than the alkanes. These are also named as **olefins** (oil forming) as the first member of this class, i.e. ethene (C_2H_4) forms oily liquid when treated with chlorine.

Structure of Double Bond

In alkenes, each double bonded carbon atom contains three sp^2-hybrid orbitals, out of which two are used to form sp^2-s σ-bonds with two hydrogens and the remaining one overlaps axially with sp^2-orbital of other carbon atom to form a strong σ-bond.

The unhybridised 2p-orbitals of both the carbon atoms overlap laterally or sideways to give a weak pi (π) bond.

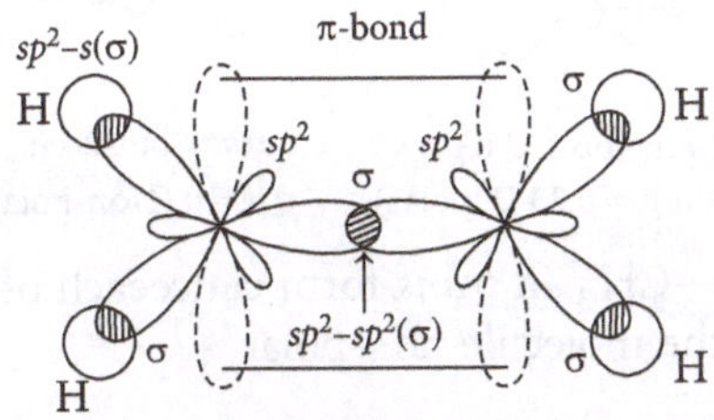

Orbital picture of ethene

The bond length of double bond (134 pm) is shorter than that of single bond (154 pm).

Because of the presence of pi (π) bonds, alkenes act as a source of loosely bound mobile electrons and thus, readily attacked by the reagents that are in search of electrons, i.e. electrophilic reagents, to give more stable single bonded compounds.

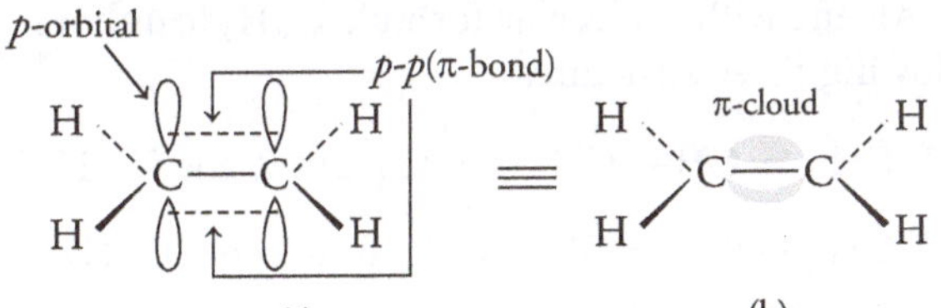

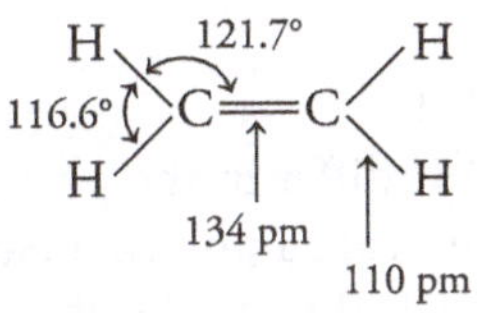

Orbital picture of ethene showing formation of (a) π-bond, (b) π-cloud and (c) bond angles and bond lengths

The strength of double bond is much greater than that of single bond in ethane.

Nomenclature of Alkenes

While naming alkenes, follow the following rules (according to IUPAC system).

- Choose the longest chain bearing double bond.
- Number the chain from the end that is closer to the double bond.
- Write the root word and add suffix 'ene'.
- If any substituent is present, write its name before the root word.

IUPAC names of other alkenes are as follows

IUPAC Names of some Alkenes

Structure	IUPAC name
$CH_3—CH{=}CH_2$	Propene
$CH_3—CH_2—CH{=}CH_2$	But-1-ene
$CH_3—CH{=}CH—CH_3$	But-2-ene
$CH_2{=}CH—CH{=}CH_2$	Buta-1, 3-diene
$CH_2{=}C(CH_3)—CH_3$	2-methylprop-1-ene
$CH_2{=}CH—CH(CH_3)—CH_3$	3-methylbut-1-ene

Isomerism in Alkenes

Alkenes can exhibit structural as well as stereoisomerism.

1. Structural Isomerism

Because of the possibility of several structures for a single molecular formula, alkenes having atleast 4 C-atoms are able to exhibit structural isomerism. e.g. Alkene with molecular formula C_4H_8 can have following three structures.

I. $\overset{1}{CH_2}=\overset{2}{CH}—\overset{3}{CH_2}—\overset{4}{CH_3}$ But-2-ene (C_4H_8)

II. $\overset{1}{CH_3}—\overset{2}{CH}=\overset{3}{CH}—\overset{4}{CH_3}$ But-2-ene (C_4H_8)

III. $\overset{1}{CH_2}=\overset{2}{C}—\overset{3}{CH_3}$ 2-methylprop-1-ene (C_4H_8)
$\quad\quad\quad\;|$
$\quad\quad\;\;CH_3$

Structures I and II differ in the position of double bond, so these are called **position isomers.** But structures I and III, II and III differ in the chain of carbon atoms, so these are called **chain isomers.**

Thus, it is obvious that alkenes generally exhibit chain and position isomerism.

Example 4 **Write structures and IUPAC names of different structural isomers of alkenes coresponding to C_6H_{12}.**

Sol.

	Structure	IUPAC name
(a)	$CH_2=CH—CH_2CH_2CH_2CH_3$	Hex-1-ene
(b)	$CH_3—CH=CH—CH_2CH_2CH_3$	Hex-2-ene
(c)	$CH_3—CH_2—CH=CH—CH_2CH_3$	Hex-3-ene
(d)	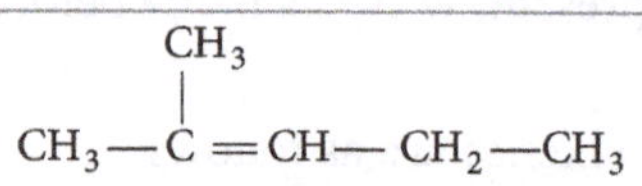	2-methylpent-2-ene
(e)	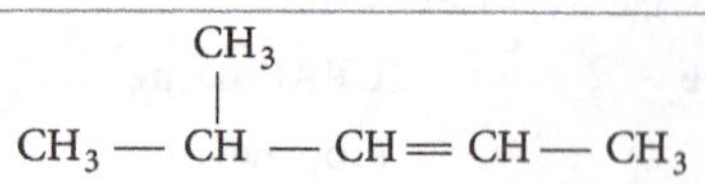	4-methylpent-2-ene
(f)	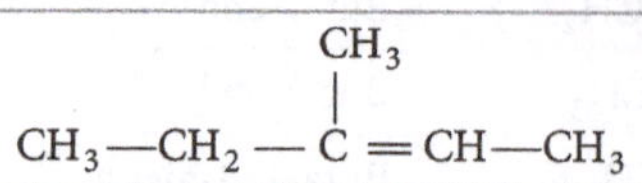	3-methylpent-2-ene
(g)	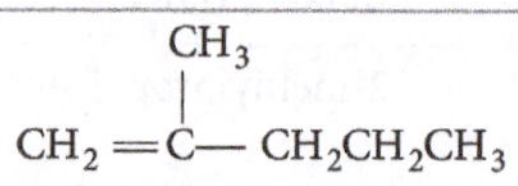	2-methylpent-1-ene
(h)	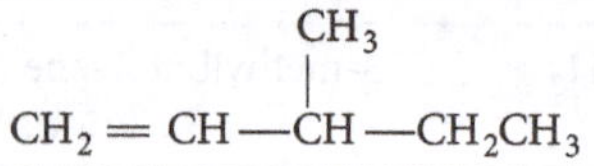	3-methylpent-1-ene
(i)	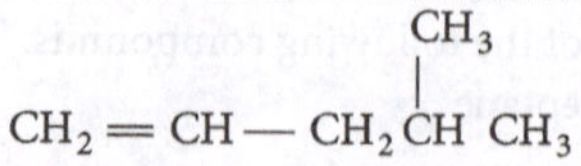	4-methylpent-1-ene
(j)	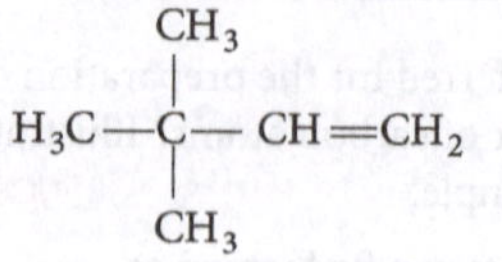	3,3-dimethylbut-1-ene
(k)	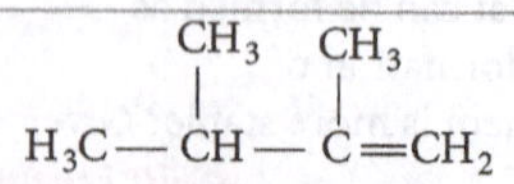	2,3-dimethylbut-1-ene
(l)	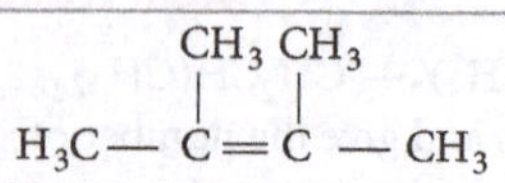	2,3-dimethylbut-2-ene

2. Stereoisomerism

Alkenes also exhibit geometrical isomerism (a type of stereoisomerism) due to the possibility of different geometrical arrangements in space, as rotation around the double bond is restricted, not free. Thus, alkenes having the general formula $YXC=CXY$ or $XYC=CXZ$ or $XYC=CZW$ generally exist in following geometrical arrangements.

(i) ***cis*-form** If the identical atoms or groups lie on the same side of the double bond, the isomer is called *cis*-form.

e.g.

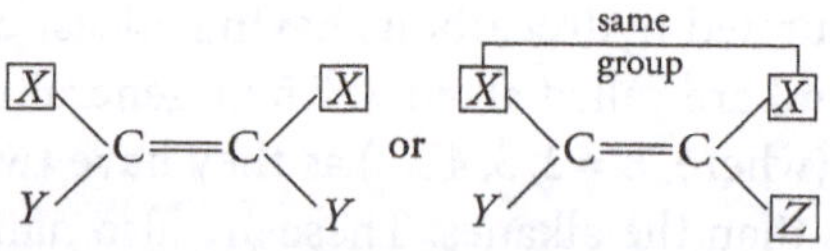

(ii) ***trans*-form** If the identical atoms or groups lie on the opposite side of the double bond, the isomer is called *trans*-form.

e.g.

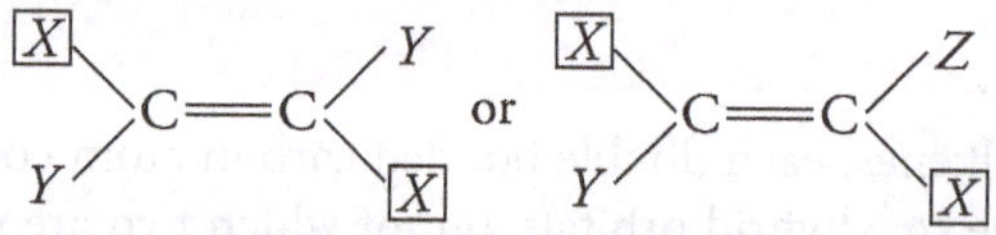

Due to different geometrical arrangement in space, the *cis* and *trans*-isomers differ in their properties like boiling and melting points, solubility, dipole moment etc. e.g. The *cis*, *trans*-isomers of but-2-ene have the following structures.

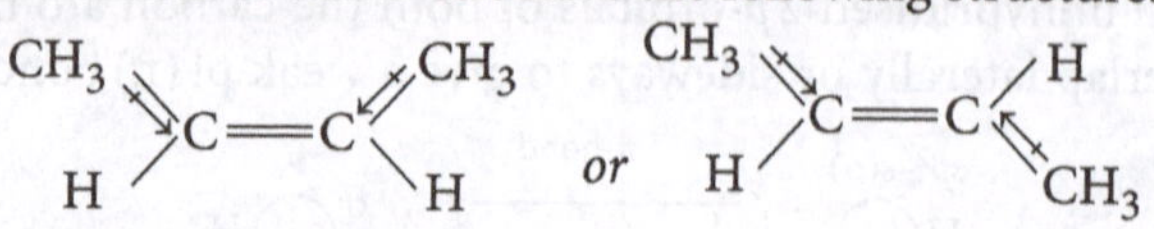

cis-but-2-ene (bp 277 K) (dipole moment μ = 0.33 D, polar) *trans*-but-2-ene (bp 274 K) μ = 0 (Non-polar)

dipoles of C—CH_3 in *trans*-form canceeach other and thus, makes the molecule non-polar.

However, melting point of *trans*-form is higher than that of *cis*-form.

(For more details about the nomenclature and isomerism of alkenes, also see the previous chapter.)

Example 5 **Which of the following compounds will show *cis-trans* isomerism?** **NCERT**

(i) $(CH_3)_2C{=}CH{-}C_2H_5$ (ii) $CH_2{=}CBr_2$
(iii) $C_6H_5CH{=}CH{-}CH_3$ (iv) $CH_3CH{=}CClCH_3$

Sol. For exhibiting *cis-trans* (or geometrical isomerism, a molecule must fulfill the following conditions).

(i) It must have atleast one double bond.

(ii) The groups attached to each double bonded carbon atom must be different.

(iii) Atleast one same group is present on the two double bonded carbon. Structure (iii) and (iv) fulfill all the above conditions, so both will exhibit *cis-trans* isomerism.

Example 6 **Draw *cis* and *trans*-isomers of the following compounds. Also write their IUPAC names.**

(i) $ClHC{=}CHCl$

(ii) $C_2H_5CCH_3{=}CCH_3C_2H_5$ **NCERT**

Sol.

(i)

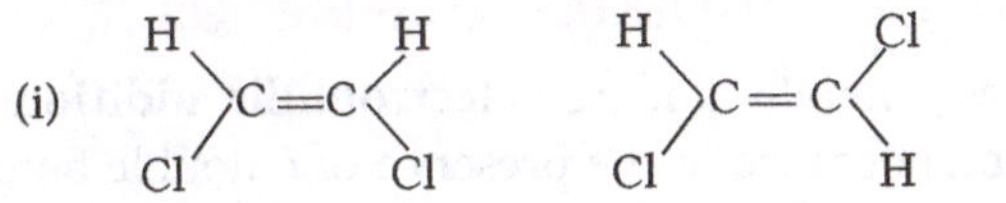

cis-1, 2-dichloroethene *trans*-1, 2-dichloroethene

(ii)

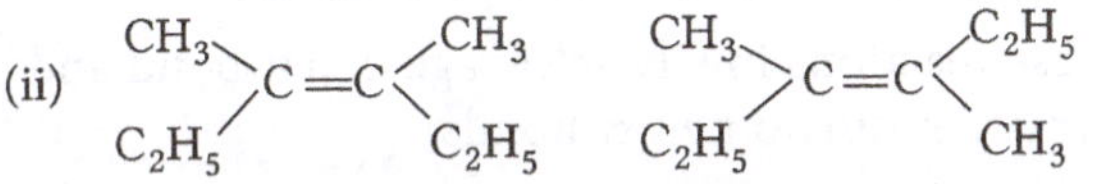

cis-3, 4-dimethylhex-3-ene *trans*-3,4-dimethylhex 3-ene

Methods of Preparation of Alkenes

Following methods can be used to prepare alkenes from different substances.

1. From Alkynes

When alkynes are treated with calculated quantity of dihydrogen in the presence of palladised charcoal partially deactivated with poisons such as sulphur compounds, quinoline etc.

They get reduced to *cis*-alkenes, i.e. hydrogens are added to the same side of the double bond. Partially deactivated palladised charcoal is known as **Lindlar's catalyst.**

However, if Na in liquid ammonia is used in place of Pd/C, *trans*-alkenes are the major product.

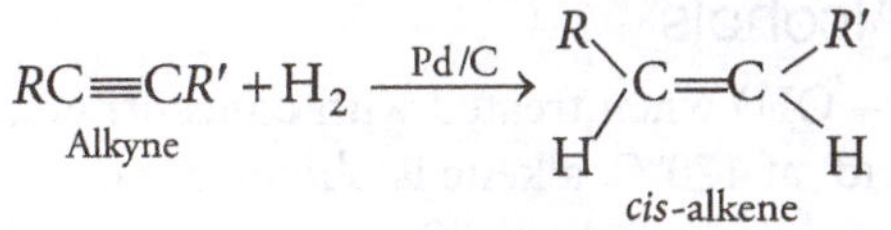

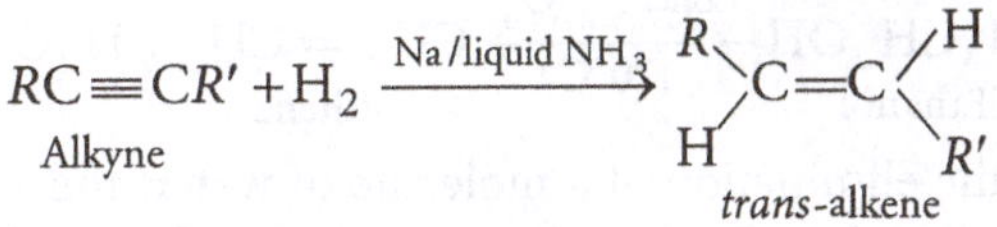

2. From Alkyl Halides

When alkyl halides are heated with alcoholic potash (KOH in alcohol or ethanol), a HX (halogen acid) molecule is eliminated to give alkene.

Due to the elimination of H as well as halogen, the reaction is called **dehydrohalogenation.**

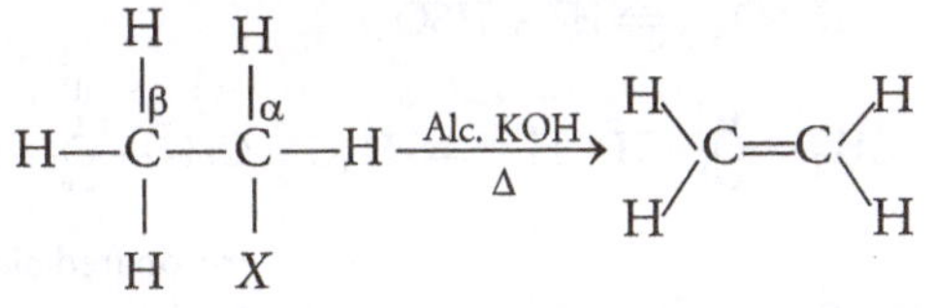

$(X = Cl, Br, I)$

This reaction is also known as **β-elimination reaction,** since hydrogen atom is eliminated from the β-carbon atom (carbon atom next to the carbon to which halogen is attached).

The order of reactivity of halogens towards this reaction is

$$I_2 > Br_2 > Cl_2$$

This is because as the size of halogen increases, C—X bond strength decreases, i.e. it becomes weaker.

Further, the order of reactivity of alkyl group is

$$3° > 2° > 1°.$$

TEACHER'S TIP

The above elimination is governed by Saytzeff rule, according to which, more substituted (or more stable, i.e. symmetrical) alkenes are the major product of an elimination reaction.

3. From *Vicinal* Dihalides

Dihalides having two halogen atoms at adjacent carbon atoms are called ***vicinal* dihalides.** When such halides are treated with zinc metal, both the halogen atoms are taken up by Zn to give an alkene. Due to the removal of halogen atoms, the reaction is called **dehalogenation.**

e.g. $CH_2Br{-}CH_2Br + Zn \longrightarrow CH_2{=}CH_2 + ZnBr_2$

$CH_3CHBr{-}CH_2Br + Zn \longrightarrow CH_3CH{=}CH_2 + ZnBr_2$

4. From Alcohols

Alcohols ($R—OH$) when treated with concentrated sulphuric acid at 170°C, alkene is obtained, i.e.

$$\underset{\text{Ethanol}}{CH_3CH_2OH} \xrightarrow[170°C]{\text{Conc. } H_2SO_4} \underset{\text{Ethene}}{CH_2=CH_2} + H_2O$$

Because of the elimination of a molecule of water, the reaction is called **dehydration.** Since, presence of an acid is essential for the dehydration process, so the reaction is also known as **acidic dehydration of alcohols.** It is also an example of β-elimination reaction, because of the removal of H from β-carbon atom.

Mechanism of acidic dehydration of alcohol

Step I Generation of protonated alcohol.

$$H_2SO_4 \rightleftharpoons H^+ + HSO_4^-$$

$$H_3CCH_2—\ddot{O}—H + H^+ \rightleftharpoons \underset{\text{Protonated alcohol}}{H_3C—CH_2—\overset{H}{\underset{\oplus}{\ddot{O}}}—H}$$

Step II Generation of carbonium ion

$$H_3C—CH_2—\overset{H}{\underset{\oplus}{\ddot{O}}}—H \longrightarrow \underset{\text{Carbonium ion}}{H_3C—\overset{\oplus}{C}H_2} + H_2O$$

Step III Removal of proton

$$H_2\underset{H}{C}—\overset{\oplus}{C}H_2 \rightleftharpoons H_2C=CH_2 + H^+$$

Note
- Ease of dehydration is in the order of 3° > 2° > 1° because of the involvement of reactive intermediate, i.e. carbocation.
- In some cases, rearrangement also occurs to give more stable carbocation, if possible.

Flowchart of Alkene Synthesis

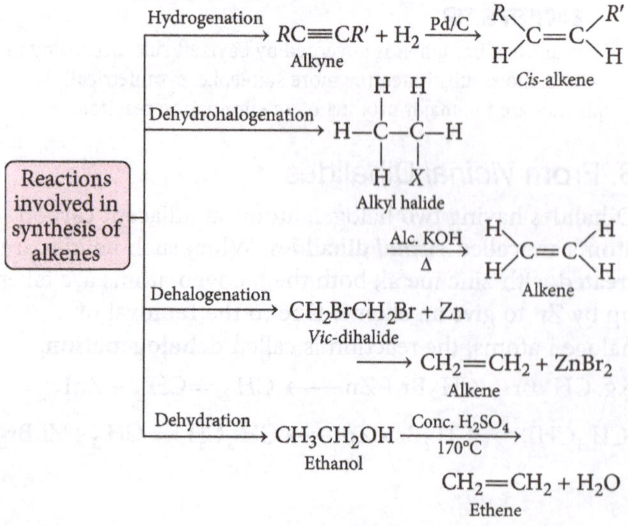

Physical Properties of Alkenes

1. Physical State, Colour and Odour

First three alkenes are gases, next 14 are liquids and rest are solids. Alkenes are colourless and odourless except ethene which has faint sweet odour.

2. Solubility

Alkenes are insoluble in water but soluble in non-polar solvents like benzene, ether, CCl_4 etc.

3. Boiling and Melting Points

These also show same trend of boiling and melting points as alkanes (i.e. increases with increase in molecular mass but decreases with branching) but geometrical isomers behave differently. *cis*-alkenes have higher boiling point as compared to their *trans*-isomers. However, melting point is higher in case of *trans*-isomers.

4. Polarity and Density

In general, *trans*-form has almost zero dipole moment and thus, exhibits weaker intermolecular attractions. These are lighter than water and the density gradually increases with rise in molecular mass.

Chemical Properties of Alkenes

Alkenes generally undergo **electrophilic addition reactions** because of the presence of a double bond (a strong σ and a weaker π-bond), π electrons of which being loosely held are easily polarisable.

These reactions involve cleavage of a π-bond and formation of two new σ-bonds.

$$>C=C< + E—Nu \longrightarrow >\underset{E}{C}—\underset{Nu}{C}<$$

In polar solvents, addition proceed by ionic mechanism (at low temperature), whereas in the presence of light or non-polar solvents, the addition occurs by free radical mechanism (at high temperature).

1. Addition of Dihydrogen

Alkenes when treated with H_2 in the presence of finely divided Ni, Pd or Pt, give alkane as the product.

$$\underset{40\text{ kcal}}{—C=C—} + \underset{104\text{ kcal}}{H—H} \longrightarrow \underset{2\times 87\text{ kcal}}{—\underset{H}{C}—\underset{H}{C}—}$$

$$\Delta H = -30 \text{ kcal mol}^{-1}$$

The evolved heat is called **heat of hydrogenation**.

2. Addition of Halogens

Alkenes give addition product, i.e. *vicinal* dihalides, when treated with halogens like Cl_2 or Br_2. I_2 does not give this reaction under normal conditions of temperature and pressure.

$$\underset{\text{Ethene}}{CH_2{=}CH_2} + Br{-}Br \xrightarrow{CCl_4} \underset{\text{1, 2-dibromoethane}}{\underset{Br\qquad Br}{CH_2{-}CH_2}}$$

The solution of bromine in CCl_4 is reddish orange in colour. When any unsaturated compound is added to this solution, its colour gets discharged due to the addition of bromine at the unsaturation site (=bond). This reaction is used as a test for unsaturation.

3. Addition of Hydrogen Halides

When alkenes react with hydrogen halides (HCl, HBr, HI), alkyl halides are obtained.

The order of reactivity of hydrogen halides towards this reaction is HI > HBr > HCl

- If the alkene is symmetrical, only one product is formed.

  e.g. $CH_2{=}CH_2 + H{-}Br \longrightarrow CH_3{-}CH_2{-}Br$

  $$CH_3{-}CH{=}CH{-}CH_3 + HBr \longrightarrow CH_3{-}CH_2{-}\underset{Br}{CHCH_3}$$

- If the alkene is unsymmetrical, several products are obtained and the nature of major product depends upon the reaction conditions.

  e.g. If HBr is added to an unsymmetrical alkene, say propene, the following products are possible.

$$CH_3{-}CH{=}CH_2 + H{-}Br \longrightarrow \begin{cases} CH_3{-}\underset{Br}{CH}{-}CH_3 & \text{2-bromopropane (I)} \\ CH_3{-}CH_2{-}CH_2{-}Br & \text{1-bromopropane (II)} \end{cases}$$

However, I is the major product in accordance with **Markovnikov's rule**. It states that negative part of the addendum (adding molecule) gets attached to that carbon atom which possesses lesser number of hydrogen atom. This can also be understood by considering the mechanism of the reaction.

Mechanism It involves following steps

Step I Generation of electrophile

$$HBr \longrightarrow H^+ + Br^-$$

Step II Attack of electrophile on double bond (generation of carbocation)

$$\overset{3}{H_3C}{-}\overset{2}{CH}{=}\overset{1}{CH_2} + H{-}Br \xrightarrow{H^+}$$

$$H_3C{-}CH_2{-}\overset{+}{CH_2} + Br^- \qquad H_3C{-}\overset{+}{CH}{-}CH_3 + Br^-$$

(a) Less stable primary carbocation

(b) More stable secondary carbocation (so readily attacked by Nu^-)

Step III Attack of nucleophile (here Br^-) on the more stable carbocation.

$$H_3C{-}\overset{+}{CH}{-}CH_3 \xrightarrow{Br^-} \underset{\text{2-bromopropane (major product)}}{H_3C{-}\underset{Br}{CH}{-}CH_3}$$

Anti-Markovnikov's Addition or Peroxide Effect or Kharash Effect

If HBr is added to an unsymmetrical alkene say propene, in the presence of peroxide 1-bromopropane is the major product in accordance with anti Markonikov's or Kharash rule. (It states that the negative part of the addendum goes to that carbon atom which has more number of hydrogen atoms). This is also called **peroxide effect** or **Kharash effect** (first observed by M S Kharash and F R Mao in 1933)

$$CH_3{-}CH{=}CH_2 + HBr \xrightarrow{(C_6H_5CO)_2O_2} \underset{\text{1-bromopropane}}{CH_3{-}\underset{CH_2Br}{CH_2}}$$

Mechanism This reaction takes place by free radical mechanism and involves the following steps.

Step I Initiation Generation of free radical ($\dot{Br}$)

$$\underset{\text{Benzoyl peroxide}}{C_6H_5{-}\overset{O}{\overset{\|}{C}}{-}O{-}O{-}\overset{O}{\overset{\|}{C}}{-}C_6H_5} \xrightarrow{\text{Homolysis}}$$

$$2C_6H_5{-}\overset{O}{\overset{\|}{C}}{-}\ddot{\underset{\cdot\cdot}{O}}{:} \longrightarrow 2\dot{C}_6H_5 + 2CO_2$$

$$\dot{C}_6H_5 + H{-}Br \xrightarrow{\text{Homolysis}} C_6H_6 + \dot{Br}$$

Step II **Propagation** Attack of $Br^{\bullet}$ at double bond

(i)

$$CH_3-CH=CH_2 + \dot{Br} \xrightarrow{\text{Homolysis}} \underset{\substack{(a)\\ \text{(Less stable primary free radical)}}}{CH_3-\underset{Br}{\underset{|}{CH}}-\dot{C}H_2} \quad \underset{\substack{(b)\\ \text{(More stable secondary free radical)}}}{CH_3-\dot{C}H-CH_2-Br}$$

(ii) $$CH_3-\dot{C}H-CH_2Br + H-Br \xrightarrow{\text{Homolysis}} \underset{\text{(Major product)}}{CH_3-CH_2-CH_2Br} + \dot{Br}$$

(iii) $$CH_3-\underset{Br}{\underset{|}{CH}}-\dot{C}H_2 + H-Br \xrightarrow{\text{Homolysis}} \underset{\text{(Minor product)}}{CH_3-\underset{Br}{\underset{|}{CH}}-CH_3} + \dot{Br}$$

Step III **Termination** $\dot{Br} + \dot{Br} \longrightarrow Br_2$

In case of HF, HCl and HI, the major product remain the same whether the alkene is symmetrical or unsymmetrical in case of anti-Markonikov's addition. This is because The bonds between halogen and hydrogen is very strong in HF and HCl that's why $RO^{\bullet}$, free radical is unable to break them homolytically. Thus, mechanism of reaction is not modified.

In the case of HI, although $RO^{\bullet}$ free radical produces homolytic cleavage but $I^{\bullet}$, free radical formed has more tendency to form I_2 as compared to form free radical of carbon.

EXAMPLE 7. Write IUPAC names of the products obtained by addition reactions of HBr to hex-1-ene. **NCERT**

(i) In the absence of peroxide.

(ii) In the presence of peroxide.

Sol. (i) $$\underset{\text{Hex-1-ene}}{CH_2=CH-CH_2-CH_2-CH_2-CH_3} + H-Br \xrightarrow[\text{No peroxide}]{} CH_3-\underset{Br}{\underset{|}{CH}}-CH_2-CH_2-CH_2-CH_3$$

2-bromohexane (according to Markovnikov's rule)

(ii) $$CH_2=CH-CH_2-CH_2-CH_2-CH_3 + H-Br \xrightarrow[\text{Peroxide}]{} Br-CH_2-CH_2-CH_2-CH_2-CH_2-CH_3$$

1-bromohexane (according to anti- Markovnikov's rule)

4. Addition of Sulphuric Acid

Alkenes react with cold concentrated sulphuric acid to give an addition product in accordance with Markovnikov's rule.

$$H_3C-CH=CH_2 + H-O-\overset{\overset{O}{\|}}{\underset{\underset{O}{\|}}{S}}-O-H \longrightarrow \underset{\text{Ethyl hydrogen sulphate}}{CH_3-\overset{\overset{OSO_2OH}{|}}{CH}-CH_3} \quad \text{or } C_3H_7HSO_4$$

5. Addition of Water (Hydration)

When alkenes are treated with a few drops of concentrated sulphuric acid, addition of water takes place in accordance with Markovnikov's rule and alcohols are obtained as the product.

$$\underset{\text{2-methylpropene}}{CH_3-\underset{CH_3}{\underset{|}{C}}=CH_2} + \overset{+}{H}\overset{-}{OH} \xrightarrow{H^+} \underset{\text{2-methylpropan-2-ol}}{(H_3C)_2\underset{OH}{\underset{|}{C}}-CH_3}$$

6. Oxidation

- When alkenes are treated with cold, dilute (1%) alkaline solution of $KMnO_4$ (Baeyer's reagent), they produce vicinal glycols.

  The alkaline potassium permanganate solution is bright pink in colour and upon reaction with alkene the solution becomes colourless.

  Hence, the reaction is also used as a **test for unsaturation.**

$$CH_3-CH=CH_2 + H_2O + O \xrightarrow[273\text{ K}]{\text{Dil. } KMnO_4} \underset{\text{Propane-1, 2-diol}}{CH_3-\underset{OH}{\underset{|}{CH}}-\underset{OH}{\underset{|}{CH_2}}}$$

- However, ketones and/or acids are the major products if acidic $KMnO_4$ or acidic $K_2Cr_2O_7$ are used as oxidising reagent (depending upon the nature of alkene and experimental conditions).

$$\underset{\text{But-2-ene}}{CH_3{-}CH{=}CH{-}CH_3} \xrightarrow{KMnO_4/H^+} \underset{\text{Ethanoic acid}}{2CH_3COOH}$$

$$(CH_3)_2C{=}CH_2 \xrightarrow{KMnO_4/H^+} \underset{\text{Propan-2-one}}{(CH_3)_2C{=}O} + CO_2 + H_2O$$

7. Ozonolysis

Alkenes react with O_3 to give ozonide which on reduction with $Zn{-}H_2O$ cleaved to give smaller molecule.

e.g.

$$\underset{\text{Propene}}{CH_3CH{=}CH_2} + O_3 \longrightarrow$$

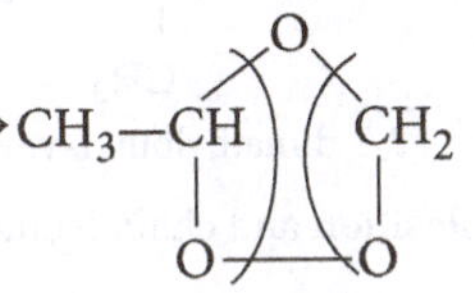

Propene ozonide

$$\xrightarrow{Zn + H_2O} \underset{\text{Ethanal}}{CH_3CHO} + \underset{\text{Methanal}}{HCHO}$$

This reaction is also **helpful for deciding the structure of alkene and location of double bond**. To decide the structure of alkene from ozonolysis products, bring the products together in such a way that their O-atoms are face to face, replace O by C=C bond.

Thus,

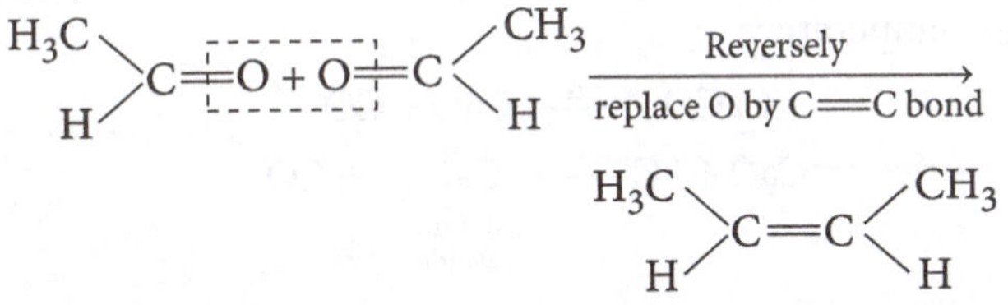

8. Polymerisation

When a large number of **monomers** (small molecules) combine to give a molecule bearing high molecular mass, called the **polymer**, the process is called **polymerisation**.

The polymerisation reactions can be seen as

$$\underset{\text{Ethene}}{n(CH_2{=}CH_2)} \xrightarrow[\text{Catalyst}]{\text{High temperature/pressure}} \underset{\text{Polythene}}{-\!\!(CH_2{-}CH_2)_n\!\!-}$$

$$\underset{\text{Propene}}{n(CH_3{-}CH{=}CH_2)} \xrightarrow[\text{Catalyst}]{\text{High temperature/pressure}} \underset{\text{Polypropene}}{-\!\!(\underset{|\atop CH_3}{CH}{-}CH_2)_n\!\!-}$$

9.4 Alkynes

The compounds containing atleast one triple bond are called **alkynes**. It is an another class of unsaturated compounds, having 4C-atoms less than the alkanes, so general formula of these compounds is C_nH_{2n-2} (where $n = 2, 3, 4$).

The first stable member of this series is **ethyne** (or **acetylene**) which is commonly used for arc welding in the form of oxyacetylene flame obtained by mixing acetylene and oxygen gas.

Structure of Triple Bond

In ethyne (the first member of alkyne series), both the carbon atoms has two *sp*-hybridised orbitals. Out of which one form *sp-s* σ bond with 1*s* orbital of H-atom.

The other *sp*-hybridised orbital of one carbon atom overlaps axially with the *sp*-hybridised orbital of other to form a C—C σ bond.

The H—C—C bond angle is 180°. Each carbon atom also contain two unhybridised *p*-orbitals that are perpendicular to each other and also to the plane of C—C σ bond, but the 2*p*-orbitals of one carbon atom are parallel to the 2*p*-orbitals of other C-atom.

These two 2*p*-orbitals overlap laterally or sideways to give two pi (π) bonds between two carbon atoms as shown below.

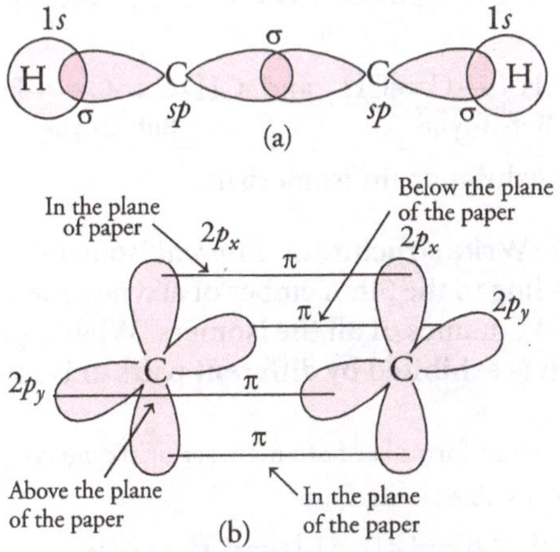

Orbital picture of ethyne showing
(a) sigma overlaps (b) pi overlaps

Thus, in ethyne molecule, there are one C—C σ bond, two C—H σ bonds and two C—C π bonds. The C≡C bond is stronger and shorter (120 pm) than the C=C and C—C.

Electron cloud between two C-atoms of ethyne is cylindrically symmetrical about the internuclear axis, so ethyne is a linear molecule.

TEACHER'S TIP

Alkynes are linear molecules that have an angle of 180°. Therefore, alkynes does not show geometrical and stereo-isomerism.

Nomenclature of Alkynes

Alkynes are named by adding suffix (yne) to the root word. Common and IUPAC names of a few members of alkyne series are given below

Common and IUPAC Names of Alkynes (C_nH_{2n-2})

Value of n	Formula	Structure	Common name	IUPAC name
2	C_2H_2	$H—C\equiv CH$	Acetylene	Ethyne
3	C_3H_4	$CH_3—C\equiv CH$	Methylacetylene	Propyne
4	C_4H_6	$CH_3CH_2—C\equiv CH$	Ethylacetylene	But-1-yne
4	C_4H_6	$CH_3—C\equiv C—CH_3$	Dimethyl-acetylene	But-2-yne

Isomerism of Alkynes

Alkynes having 4 or more carbon atoms exhibit position isomerism, due to difference in the position of triple bond in different compounds.

e.g. Following two position isomers are possible for butyne.

$$\underset{\text{But- 1- yne}}{CH_3CH_2—C\equiv CH} \quad \text{and} \quad \underset{\text{But- 2- yne}}{CH_3C\equiv C—CH_3}$$

They also exhibit chain isomerism.

Example 8 **Write structure of different isomers corresponding to the 5th member of alkyne series. Also write IUPAC names of all the isomers. What type of isomerism is exhibited by different pairs of isomers?** **NCERT**

Sol. Molecular formula of 5th member of alkyne is C_6H_{10}.

The possible isomers are

(a) $HC\equiv C—CH_2—CH_2—CH_2—CH_3$
Hex-1-yne

(b) $CH_3—C\equiv C—CH_2—CH_2—CH_3$
Hex-2-yne

(c) $CH_3—CH_2—C\equiv C—CH_2—CH_3$
Hex - 3 - yne

(d) $HC\equiv C—\underset{\underset{CH_3}{|}}{CH}—CH_2—CH_3$
3-methylpent-1-yne

(e) $HC\equiv C—CH_2—\underset{\underset{CH_3}{|}}{CH}—CH_3$
4-methylpent-1-yne

(f) $CH_3—C\equiv C—\underset{\underset{CH_3}{|}}{CH}—CH_3$
4-methylpent-2-yne

(g) $HC\equiv C—\overset{\overset{CH_3}{|}}{\underset{\underset{CH_3}{|}}{C}}—CH_3$
3,3-dimethylbut-1-yne

Position and chain isomerism is shown by different pairs.

Methods of Preparation of Alkynes

Following methods are used to prepare alkynes.

1. From Calcium Carbide

When calcium carbide is treated with water, ethyne is obtained.

$$CaC_2 + 2H_2O \longrightarrow Ca(OH)_2 + C_2H_2$$

Calcium carbide is prepared by heating the lime stone and then treating the obtained quicklime with coke at high temperature.

$$CaCO_3 \xrightarrow{\Delta} CaO + CO_2\uparrow$$

$$CaO + 3C \longrightarrow \underset{\text{Calcium carbide}}{CaC_2} + CO$$

Note Other metallic carbide of group II (alkaline earth metals) also give the similar reaction with water.

2. From *Vicinal* Dihalides

Vicinal dihalides when treated with alcoholic KOH and $NaNH_2$ undergo dehydrohalogenation to give respective alkynes.

e.g.

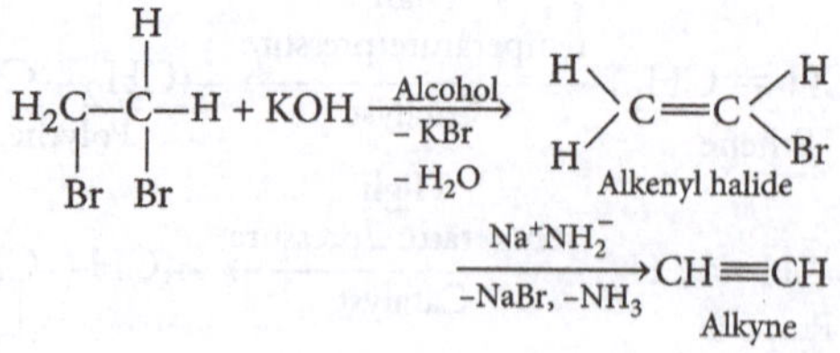

Flowchart for Alkyne Synthesis

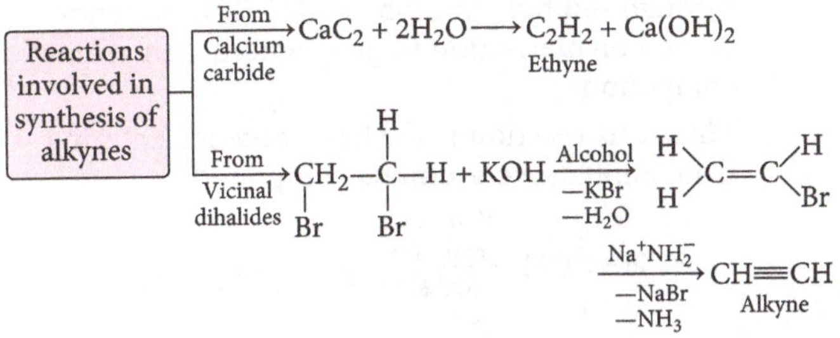

Physical Properties of Alkynes

- First three members of alkynes are gases, next eight are liquids and higher alkynes are solids.
- All alkynes are colourless and odourless except acetylene which has garlic odour.
- Melting and boiling points and densities of alkynes are slightly higher than that of corresponding alkenes and alkanes. These properties generally increases with increase in molecular mass.
- These are lighter than water and also insoluble in it. However, they are soluble in non-polar solvents like benzene, ether, etc. Alkynes are weakly polar in nature.

Chemical Properties of Alkynes

Alkynes exhibit the following characteristic reactions.

1. Acidic Character of Alkyne

In ethyne (or alkynes) the *sp*-hybridised carbon atom possesses maximum *s*-character and hence, maximum electronegativity.

Due to which, it attracts the shared electron pair of C—H bond to a greater extent and makes removal of proton easier. That's why the hydrogen(s) attached with the triply bonded carbon atoms are acidic in nature and gives the following reactions.

Type of Reaction	Reaction Involved
Reaction with Na in liq. NH_3 or $NaNH_2$ with Na metal Alkynes form monosodium ethynide and disodium ethynide.	$CH_3—C\equiv C—H + Na^+NH_2^- \longrightarrow CH_3—C\equiv C^-Na^+ + NH_3$ (Sodium propynide)
Reaction with Tollen's reagent With Tollen's reagent (ammoniacal $AgNO_3$), a white precipitate of silver salt is obtained.	$H—C\equiv C—H + 2AgNO_3 + 2NH_4OH \longrightarrow Ag—C\equiv C—Ag$ (Silver acetylide (white ppt.)) $+ 2NH_4NO_3 + 2H_2O$

These reactions are not shown by alkenes and alkanes, hence used for distinction between alkynes, alkenes and alkanes. The order of acidity of different compounds is

- $HC\equiv CH > H_2C=CH_2 > CH_3—CH_3$
- $HC\equiv CH > CH_3—C\equiv CH >> CH_3—C\equiv C—CH_3$

2. Addition Reactions

Alkynes also undergo electrophilic addition reactions. Because of the presence of a triple bond, two moles of the reagent are added to it.

Mechanism It involves the formation of vinylic cation and then addition product.

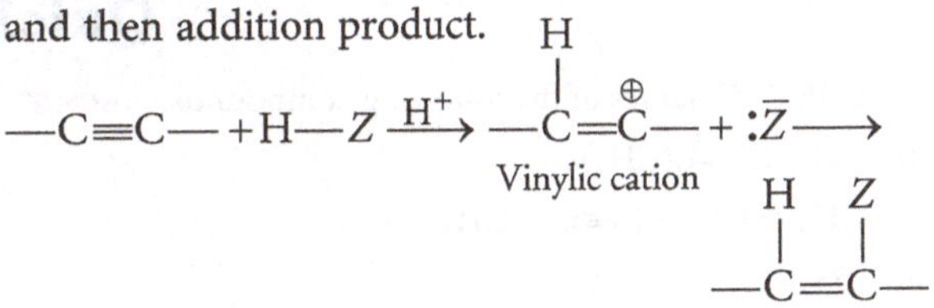

The addition product obtained depends upon the stability of vinylic cation.

The addition of reagent takes place in accordance to Markovnikov's rule.

Type of Reactions	Reactions Involved
Addition of dihydrogen This process is known as catalytic hydrogenation	$HC\equiv CH + H_2 \xrightarrow{Pt/Pd/Ni} [H_2C=CH_2] \xrightarrow{H_2} CH_3—CH_3$ (Alkene) (Alkane)
Addition of halogens	$CH_3—C\equiv CH \xrightarrow{Br_2} [CH_3CBr=CHBr]$ (1, 2-dibromopropene) $\xrightarrow{Br_2} CH_3CBr_2CHBr_2$ (1,1,2,2-tetrabromopropane) **Note** Alkynes also decolourise the red brown colour of bromine water (in CCl_4). This is used as a test for unsaturation.
Addition of hydrogen halide	$CH_3—C\equiv CH + H—Br \longrightarrow [CH_3—C(Br)=CH_2]$ (2 - bromopropene) $\longrightarrow CH_3—C(Br_2)—CH_3$ (2,2 - dibromopropane)
Addition of water It occurs in the presence of mercuric sulphate and dilute sulphuric acid at 333 K. Carbonyl compounds are the product of this reaction.	$CH\equiv CH + H—OH \xrightarrow[333\,K]{Hg^{2+}/H^+} CH_2=C(OH)—H \xrightarrow{Isomerisation} CH_3—C(=O)—H$ (Ethyne) (Ethanal)

3. Polymerisation

(i) **Linear polymerisation** Under suitable conditions, ethyne molecules undergo linear polymerisation to give a high molecular weight polyene, called polyacetylene +CH=CH—CH=CH+_n, which is a conductor of electricity under special conditions.

Thin film of polyacetylene is good conductor, lighter and cheaper than the metal conductors, so it is used as electrode in batteries.

(ii) **Cyclic polymerisation** When ethyne is passed through red hot iron tube at 873 K, it undergoes cyclic polymerisation to give benzene, an aromatic compound.

Thus, this reaction is the best route for entering from aliphatic to aromatic compounds.

$$3CH\equiv CH \xrightarrow[873\ K]{\text{Red hot iron tube}}$$ 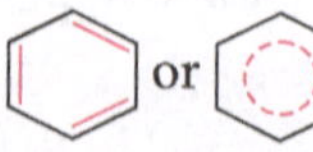

Quick Test 2

1. Write IUPAC names of the following compounds. NCERT

(i) $CH_3CH=C(CH_3)_2$

(ii) $CH_2=CH—C\equiv C—CH_3$

(iii) 

(iv) $CH_3CH=CH—CH_2—CH=CH—CH(C_2H_5)—CH_2—CH=CH_2$

2. How would you distinguish between

(i) But-1-yne and but-2-yne (ii) Propene and propyne

3. Alkynes on reduction with sodium in liquid ammonia form *trans*-alkenes. Will the butene thus formed on reduction of 2-butyne show geometrical isomerism? NCERT Exemplar

4. Draw the *cis*- and *trans*- structures of hex-2-ene. Which isomer will have higher boiling point and why? NCERT

5. Propanal and pentan-3-one are the ozonolysis products of an alkene. What is the structural formula of the alkene? NCERT

6. Complete the following reactions.

(i) Iso-propyl bromide $\xrightarrow[\text{Heat}]{\text{Alc. KOH}} A \xrightarrow[\text{Peroxide}]{\text{HBr}} B$

(ii) *n*-propyl alcohol $\xrightarrow[443\ K]{\text{Conc. } H_2SO_4} A \xrightarrow[\text{Heat}]{O_2,\ Ag} B$

7. An alkene *A* contains three C—C σ-bonds, eight C—H σ-bonds and one C—C π-bond. *A* on ozonolysis gives two moles of an aldehyde of molar mass 44 u. Write IUPAC name of *A*. NCERT

8. Write IUPAC name of the products obtained by the ozonolysis of the following compounds : NCERT

(i) Pent-2-ene

(ii) 3,4-dimethylhept-3-ene

(iii) 2-ethylbut-1-ene

(iv) 1-phenylbut-1-ene

9. An alkyl halide (*X*) of formula $C_6H_{13}Cl$ on treatment with alcoholic KOH or potassium *tert*-butoxide gives two isomeric alkenes *Y* and $Z(C_6H_{12})$. Both alkenes on hydrogenation give 2, 3-dimethylbutane. Predict the structure of *X*, *Y* and *Z*.

10. In the presence of peroxide, addition of HBr to propene takes place according to anti-Markovnikov's rule but peroxide effect is not seen in the case of HCl and HI. Explain. NCERT Exemplar

For Solutions, See QR Code on Pg. 383

9.5 Aromatic Hydrocarbons

Aromatic hydrocarbons are specialised cyclic compounds which are known for their characteristic unique smell. (Greek : Aroma = fragrance). The group is also called **arenes.**

Most of the aromatic compounds were found to contain benzene ring. Benzene ring is highly unsaturated and is involved in most of the reactions of aromatic hydrocarbon. The unsaturation of benzene ring is retained.

Benzene and its derivatives are called the **benzenoid compounds.** However, there are many aromatic hydrocarbons also that do not have benzene ring. Such compounds are called **non-benzenoid compounds.**

e.g.

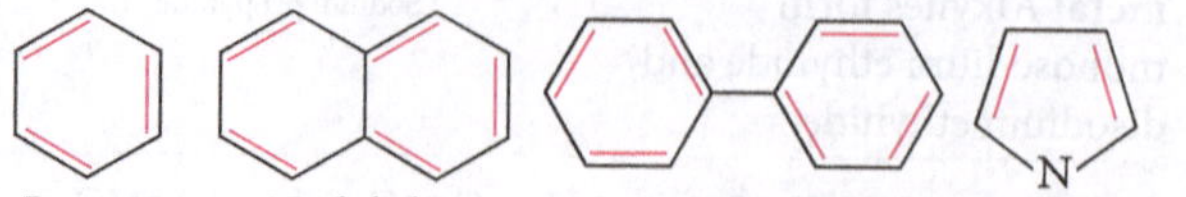

Benzene (benzenoid) | Naphthalene (benzenoid) | Biphenyl (benzenoid) | Pyrrole (non-benzenoid)

Nomenclature and Isomerism of Benzenoid Compounds

(For nomenclature and isomerism of aromatic compounds see chapter 12). Since, all the six hydrogen atoms of benzene are equivalent, so it gives only one type of product on monosubstitution.

However, disubstitution gives three products *viz*., 1,2 or 1,6 (or *ortho*), 1,3 or 1,5 (or *meta*) and 1,4 (or *para*).

e.g.

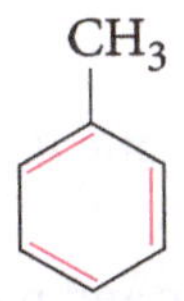

Methylbenzene (toluene)

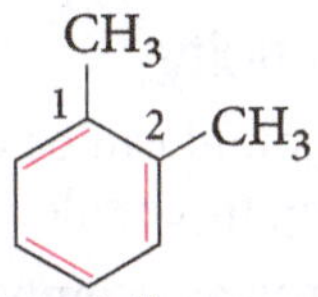

1, 2-dimethylbenzene (*o*-xylene)

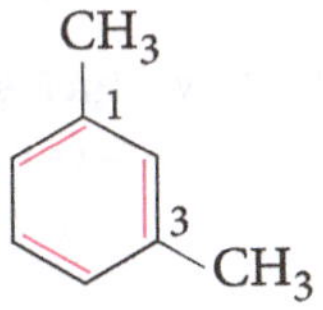

1, 3-dimethylbenzene (*m*-xylene)

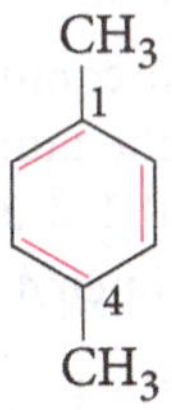

1, 4-dimethylbenzene (*p*-xylene)

Structure of Benzene

Based on the following facts, structure of benzene was formulated.

- Benzene was first time isolated by Michael Faraday in 1825. Its molecular formula is C_6H_6 which shows the presence of high degree of unsaturation into it. It is highly stable molecule.
- It forms a triozonide with O_3, which shows the presence of three double bonds.
- Further, on substitution, it gives only one monosubstituted product, which shows that all the six carbon and six hydrogen atoms of benzene are identical.

Cyclic Structure of Benzene : Kekule's Hypothesis

On the basis of above observations, August Kekule's in 1865 proposed the following structure for benzene having cyclic arrangement of six carbon atoms with alternate single and double bond and one hydrogen atom attached to each carbon.

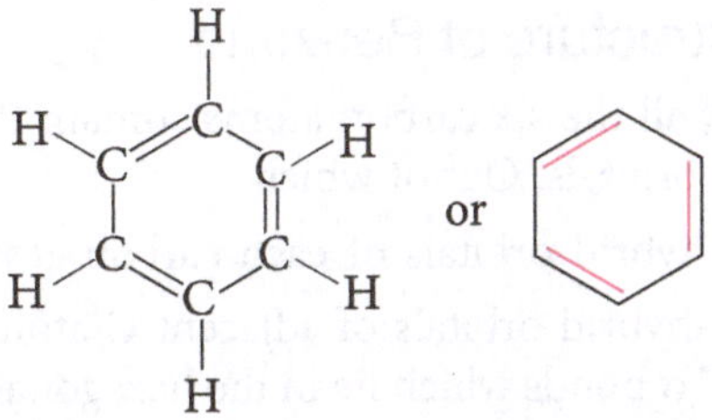

However, the above structure indicates the possibility of formation of two isomeric 1, 2-dibromobenzene, in one isomer of this, Br-atom is attached to the double bonded C-atoms whereas in other it is attached to single bonded C-atoms.

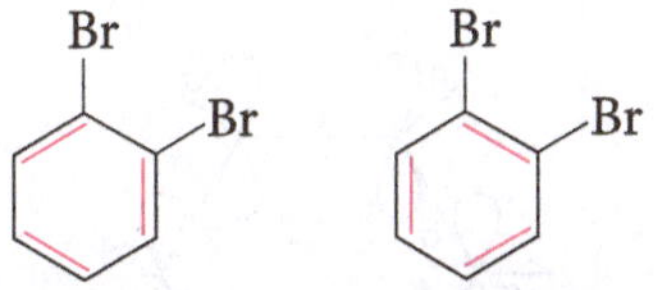

However, in actual practice only one *ortho* substituted product is obtained. Thus, Kekule's solved this problem by suggesting the concept of oscillating nature of double bond in benzene.

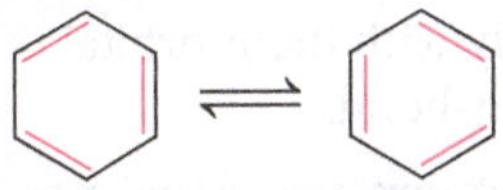

However, he remained unable to explain the unusual stability and preference for substitution rather than addition reaction in benzene. To give answer of these questions, concept of resonance were introduced.

Resonance and Stability of Benzene

The stability of benzene can be explained on the basis of concept of resonance. According to Kekule's, benzene is a resonance hybrid of the two structures (*A*) and (*B*) and the hybrid structure may be represented by inserting a circle or a dotted circle in the hexagon as shown in (*C*). The circle represent the six electrons which are delocalised between the six carbon atoms of the benzene ring.

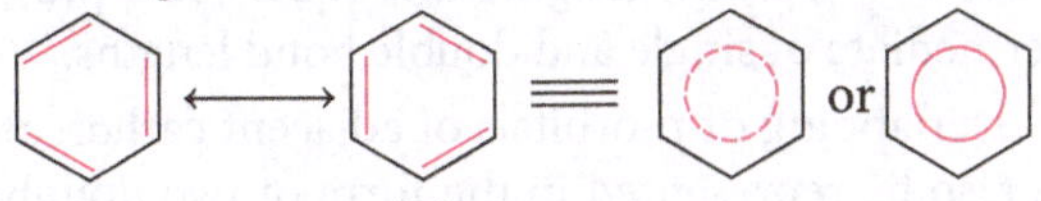

(*A*) (*B*) (*C*)

TEACHER'S TIP

The extra stability that a compound gets as a result of having delocalised electrons is called delocalisation energy or resonance energy.

Orbital Structure of Benzene

In benzene, all the six carbon atoms contain three sp^2-hybrid orbitals. Out of which

- two sp^2-hybrid orbitals of each carbon atom overlap with sp^2-hybrid orbitals of adjacent C-atoms to form six C—C σ bonds which lie in the hexagonal plane.
- the remaining sp^2-hybrid orbital of each carbon atom overlaps with the 1*s*-orbital of a hydrogen atom to give six C—H σ bonds.
- each C atom also has one unhybridised *p*-orbital which is perpendicular to the plane of the ring as shown in the figure.

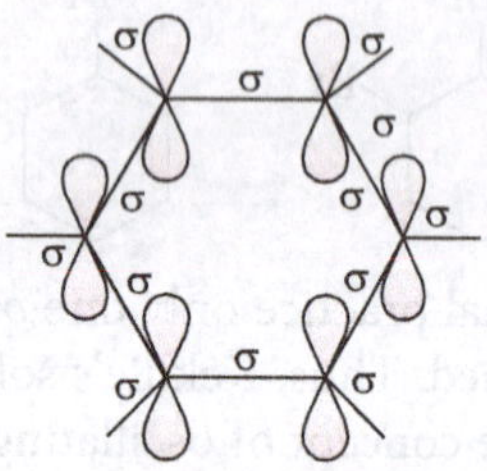

- The unhybridised *p*-orbital of each carbon atom overlaps laterally with the *p*-orbital of adjacent carbon atom to form a π-bond.
- In general, there are two equal possibilities of three π-bonds by the overlap of *p*-orbitals of C_1—C_2, C_3—C_4, C_5—C_6 in Fig. (a) and C_2—C_3, C_4—C_5, C_6—C_1 in Fig.(b) respectively as shown in the following figures.

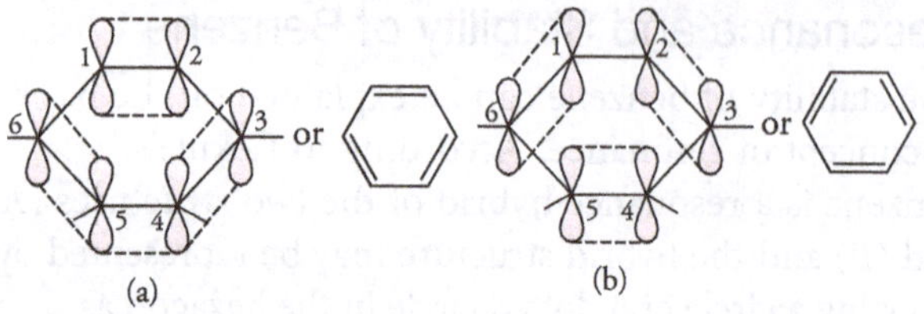

(a) (b)

The above fact is also supported by X-ray diffraction which showed that

- all the C—C bond lengths are equal (139 pm) and intermediate of single and double bond lengths.
- the overlapping of *p*-orbitals of adjacent carbon atoms can also be represented in the form of two doughnuts (rings) of electron clouds, one above and one below the plane of the hexagonal ring as shown below.

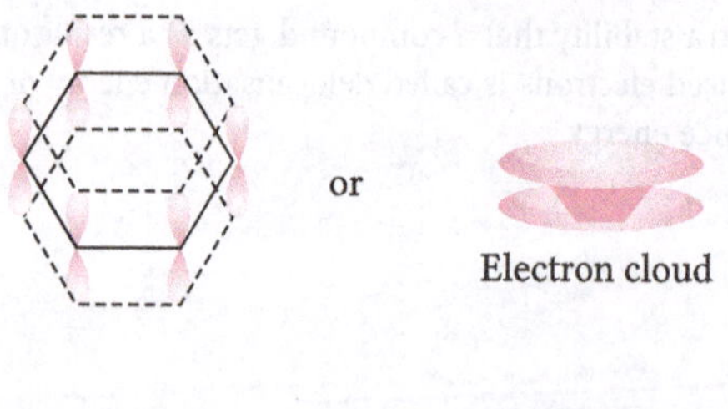

Electron cloud

- The six π-electrons are, thus, delocalised and can move freely about the six carbon nuclei. This delocalised π-electron cloud is attracted more strongly by the nuclei of the carbon atoms than the electron cloud localised between two carbon atoms and makes the benzene ring more stable.

  Further, absence of pure double bond shows the non-reactivity of benzene towards usual reactions of alkenes and also explains its unusual behaviour.

Aromaticity

A compound can be considered as aromatic if it follows following three rules.

- An aromatic compound must be cyclic and planar.
- An aromatic compound must have the conjugated system in it.
- An aromatic compound must follow **Huckel rule** which states that the number of π-electrons $= (4n + 2)$; where n = integer 0, 1, 2, 3 etc. e.g.

(a) Cyclopropenyl cation

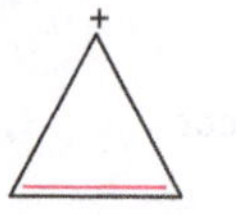

Number of π-electrons = 2

$(4n + 2) = 2$ for $n = 0$ thus, Huckel's rule is followed.

(b)

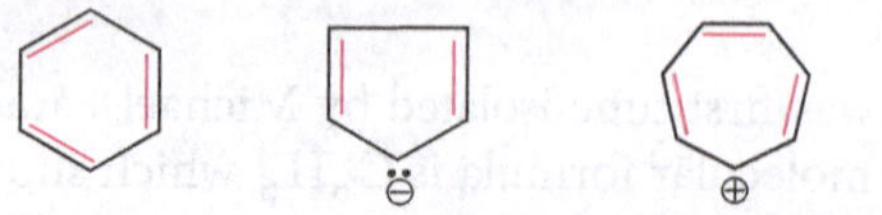

Benzene Cyclopentadienyl anion Cycloheptatrienyl cation

Number of π-electron = 6

$(4n + 2) = 6$ for $n = 1$ thus, Huckel's rule is followed.

(c) Naphthalene

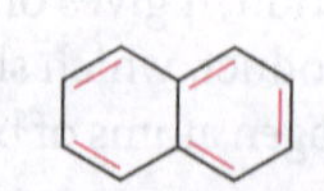

Number of π-electrons = 10

$4n + 2 = 10$ for $n = 2$ thus, Huckel's rule is followed

(d)

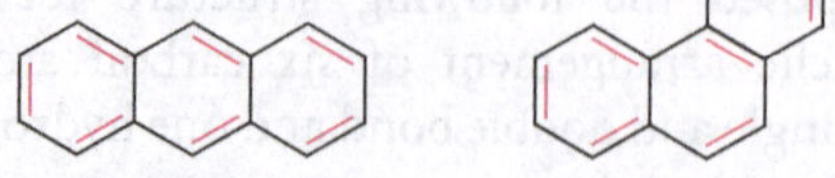

Anthracene Phenanthrene

Number of π-electrons = 14.

$4n + 2 = 14$ for $n = 3$ thus, Huckel's rule is followed.

Those compounds which does not follow the above 3 rules are called **non-aromatic.**

These non-aromatic compounds may be cyclic with conjugated system.

e.g. 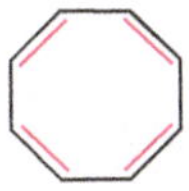 (cyclooctatetraene) is cyclic with conjugated system but it does not follow Huckel rule and its plane is also distorted that's why it is non-aromatic.

Preparation of Benzene

Benzene is commercially obtained from coal tar. However, in laboratory, it is prepared by following processes.

1. Cyclic Polymerisation of Ethyne

When acetylene is passed through a red hot metallic tube, cyclic polymerisation takes place and benzene is formed.

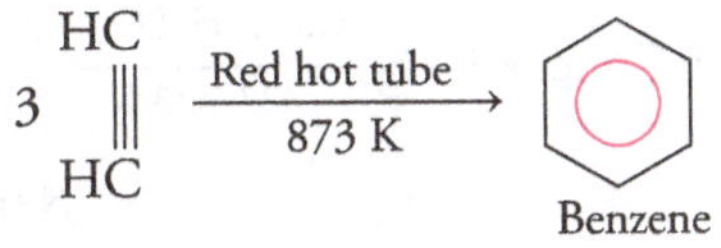

2. Decarboxylation of Aromatic Acids

When sodium salt of benzoic acid is heated with sodalime (NaOH + CaO), it gives benzene.

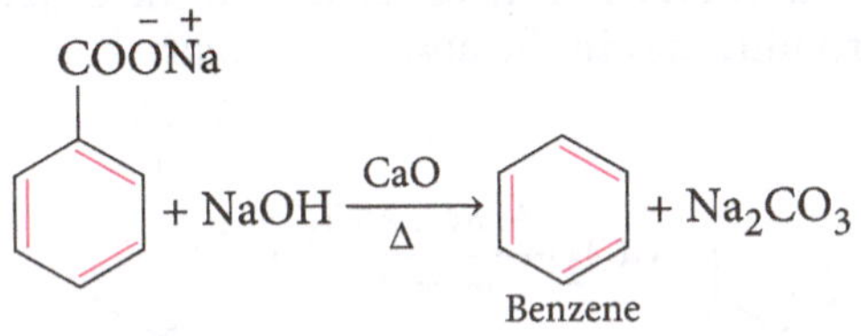

3. Reduction of Phenol

When vapours of phenol are passed over heated zinc dust, benzene is obtained.

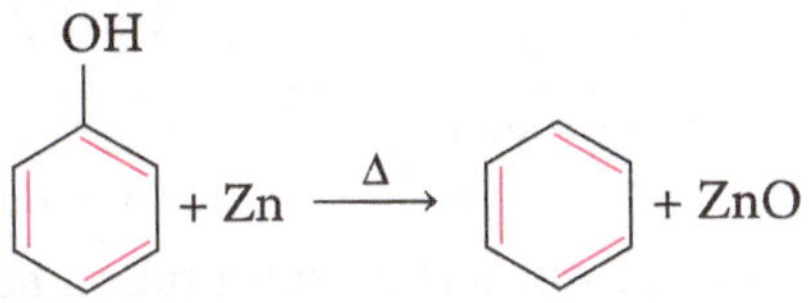

Flowchart of Benzene Synthesis

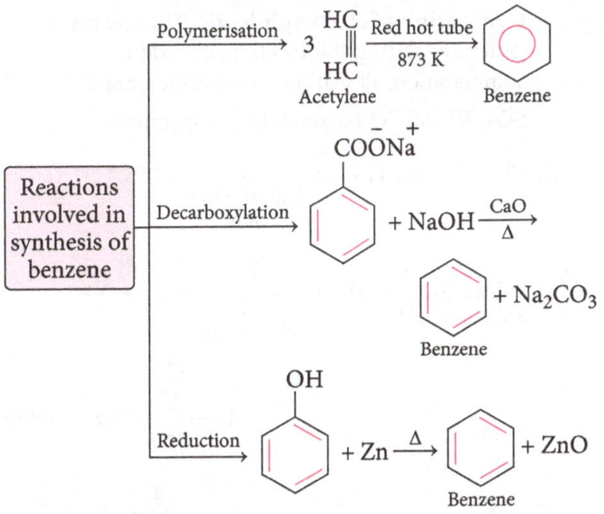

Physical Properties

- Aromatic hydrocarbons being non-polar molecules are insoluble in water but are readily miscible with organic solvents.
- They are colourless liquids or solids that have characteristic aroma, e.g. naphthalene balls.
- They burn with sooty flame.
- The melting point and boiling point of aromatic hydrocarbons increase with increasing molecular mass.

> **TEACHER'S TIP**
> Amongst isomeric arenes, the *para*-isomer has highest melting point because it is most symmetrical.

Chemical Properties

Arenes are characterised by electrophilic substitution reactions. However, under special conditions they can also undergo addition and oxidation reactions.

1. Electrophilic Substitution Reactions

The reactions in which an electrophile substitutes the hydrogen atom of the benzene ring, are called **electrophilic substitution reactions.**

Mechanism It involves following steps

Step I **Generation of electrophile, E^+** The electrophile generated during chlorination, nitration, sulphonation, alkylation and acylation are Cl^+, NO_2^+, SO_3, R^+, RC^+O (acylium ion) respectively.

(i) $Cl—Cl + AlCl_3 \longrightarrow \underset{\text{Chloronium ion}}{Cl^+} + [AlCl_4]^-$

(ii) $\underset{\text{Sulphuric acid}}{HO_3SO—H} + \underset{\text{Nitric acid}}{H—\ddot{O}—NO_2} \rightleftharpoons H—\overset{H}{\overset{|+}{O}}—NO_2 + HSO_4^-$

$\underset{\text{Protonated nitric acid}}{H—\overset{H}{\overset{|+}{O}}—NO_2} \rightleftharpoons H_2O + \underset{\text{Nitronium ion}}{\overset{\oplus}{NO_2}}$

(iii) $2H_2SO_4 \rightleftharpoons SO_3 + HSO_4^- + H_3O^+$

(iv) $CH_3—Cl + AlCl_3 \longrightarrow \overset{+}{C}H_3 + [AlCl_4]^-$

(v) $CH_3—\underset{\underset{O}{||}}{C}—Cl + AlCl_3 \longrightarrow CH_3—\underset{\underset{O}{||}}{\overset{+}{C}} + [AlCl_4]^-$

Step II Formation of carbocation (arenium ion)

E^+ attacks on the benzene ring to give σ-complex or arenium ion, in which one of the carbon is sp^3-hybridised.

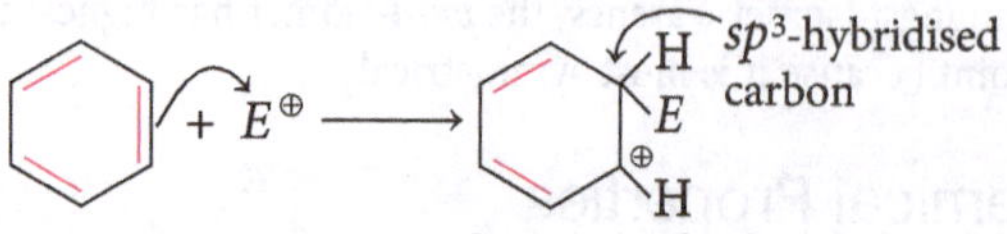

Sigma complex (arenium ion)

The arenium ion gets stabilised by resonance

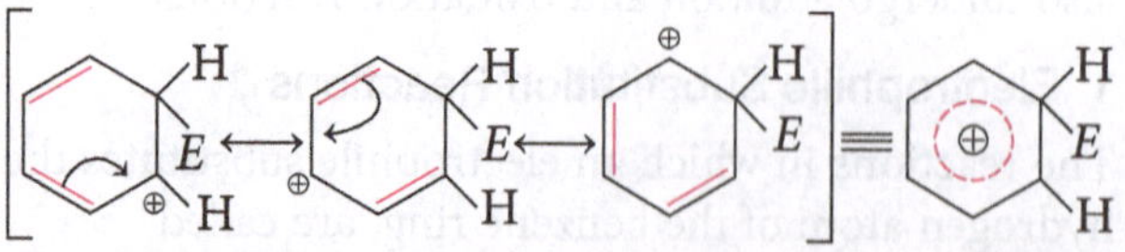

Step III **Removal of proton** To regain aromatic character, the σ-complex lose one proton to $AlCl_4^-$ or HSO_4^- as shown below.

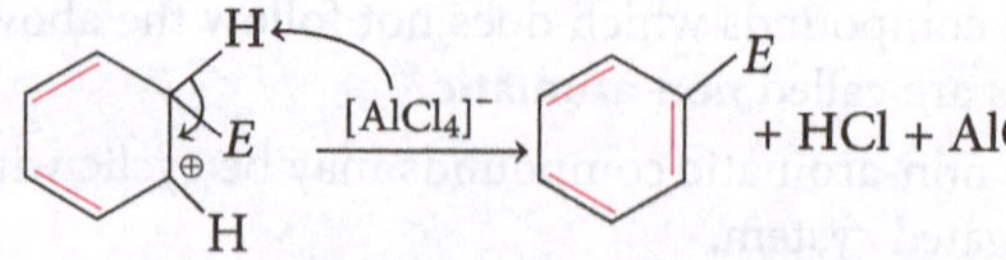

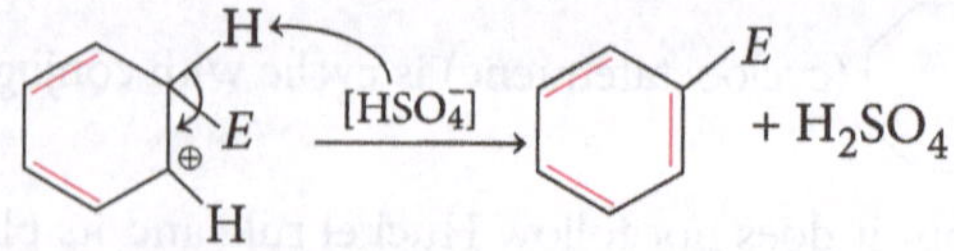

Various reactions include in electrophilic substitution reactions are

(i) **Nitration** Benzene undergoes nitration when treated with conc. HNO_3 in the presence of conc. sulphuric acid.

As we have seen, the electrophile nitronium ion NO_2^+ was produced by transfer of a proton from sulphuric acid to nitric acid.

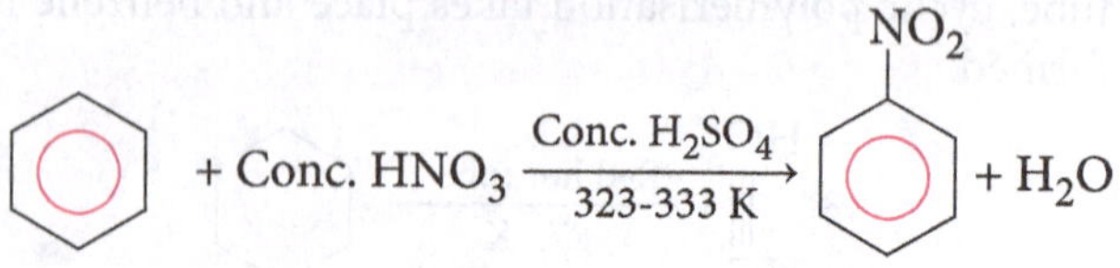

Nitrobenzene

(ii) **Halogenation** Benzene undergoes chlorination or bromination when it is treated with chlorine or bromine in the presence of Lewis acid catalyst, aluminium chloride or ferric chloride or ferric bromide and in the absence of light.

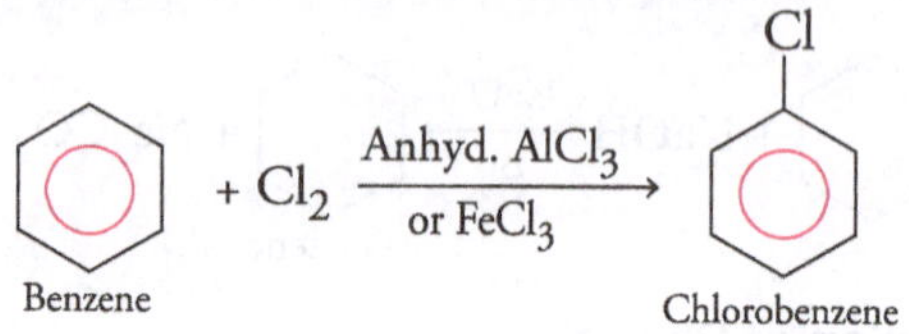

Benzene — Chlorobenzene

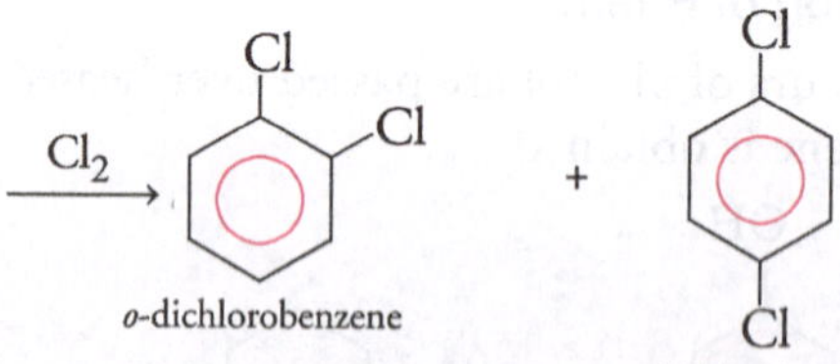

o-dichlorobenzene + *p*-dichlorobenzene

If E^+ is in excess, further substitution takes place, e.g. benzene on treatment with excess of chlorine in the presence of anhydrous $AlCl_3$ can be chlorinated to hexachlorobenzene (C_6Cl_6).

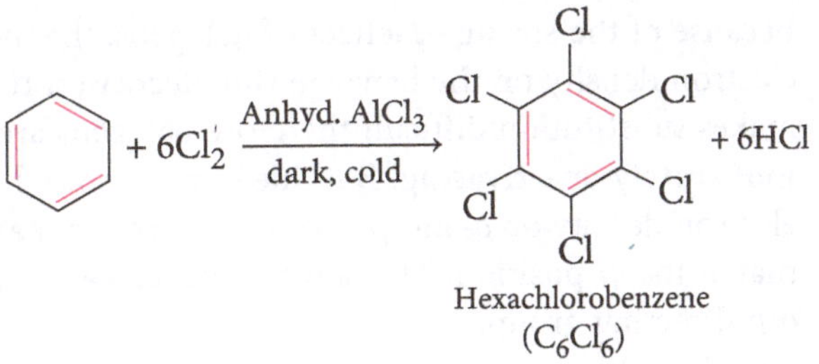

(iii) **Sulphonation** It is done by heating benzene with fuming sulphuric acid (oleum).

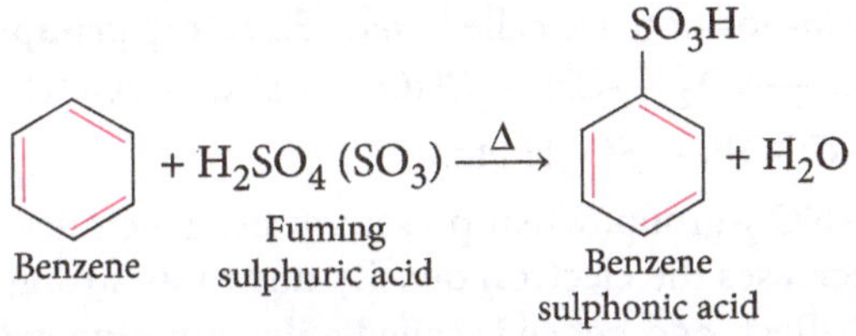

(iv) **Friedel-Crafts alkylation** When benzene is treated with alkyl halide in the presence of anhyd. $AlCl_3$, it gives alkyl benzene. This reaction is called Friedel-Crafts alkylation.

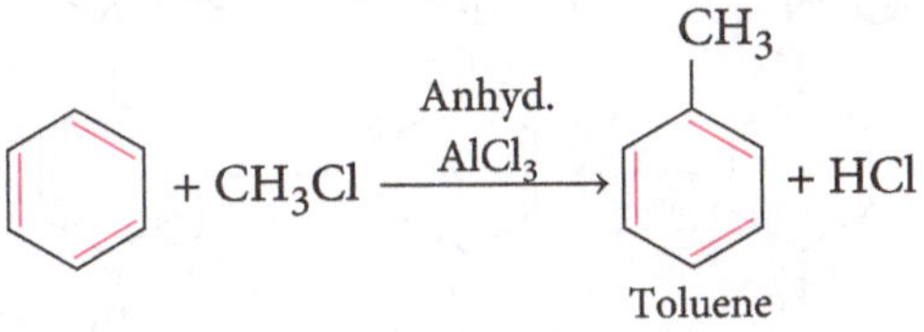

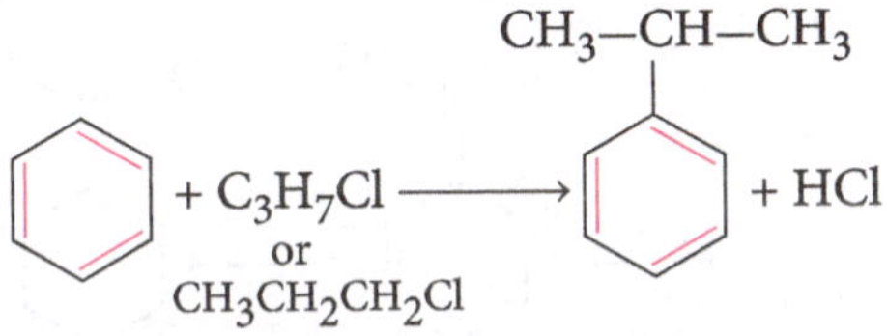

$$[\because CH_3CH_2CH_2Cl + AlCl_3 \xrightarrow[AlCl_4^-]{} \underset{1°\text{(less stable)}}{CH_3CH_2\overset{+}{C}H_2}$$

$$\xrightarrow{\text{Rearrangement}} \underset{2°\text{(more stable)}}{CH_3\overset{+}{C}HCH_3}]$$

(v) **Friedel-Crafts acylation** When benzene is treated with alkyl halide or acid anhydride in the presence of a Lewis acid (like $AlCl_3$), acyl benzene is obtained as a product.

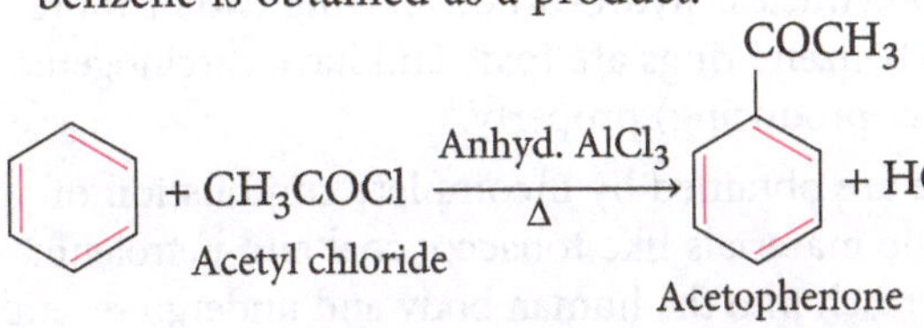

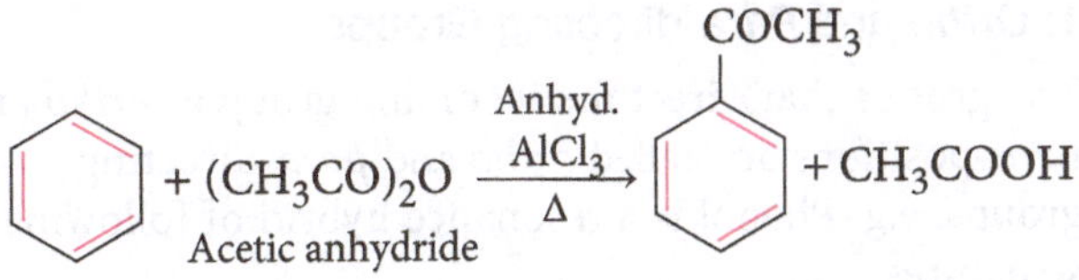

2. Addition Reactions

- When benzene is treated with hydrogen in the presence of nickel catalyst, under vigorous conditions, i.e. at high temperature and/or pressure, it gets reduced to cyclohexane.

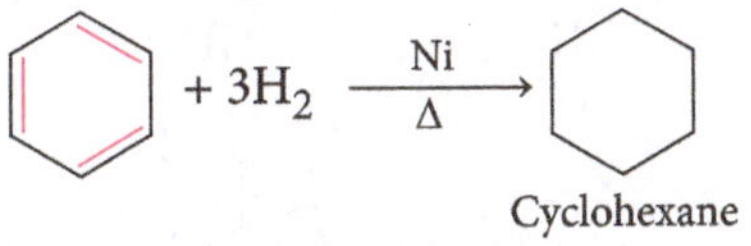

- When benzene is treated with chlorine molecules in the presence of UV light, addition of Cl takes place and benzene hexachloride, $C_6H_6Cl_6$ or **gammaxane** is obtained.

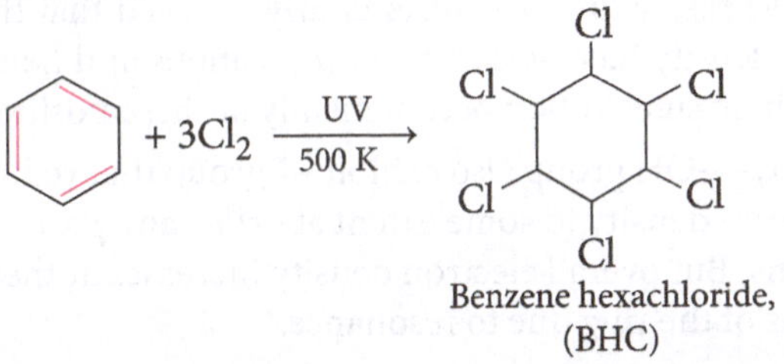

3. Combustion

When benzene is burnt in excess of air, it burns with sooty flame to give CO_2 and H_2O.

$$C_6H_6 + \frac{15}{2}O_2 \longrightarrow 6CO_2 + 3H_2O$$

The general reaction for the combustion of aromatic hydrocarbons is

$$C_xH_y + \left(x + \frac{y}{4}\right)O_2 \longrightarrow xCO_2 + \frac{y}{2}H_2O$$

Directive Influence of a Functional Group in Monosubstituted Benzene

When monosubstituted benzene is subjected to further substitution, it may give three disubstituted products, however, not in equal amounts.

In general, two types of behaviour are observed. Either *o*/*p* or *m* product is obtained predominantly. This behaviour depends upon the nature of the group already present in the benzene ring and is called the **directive influence of substituents.**

1. *Ortho* and *Para*-directing Groups

The groups that direct the incoming group at *ortho* and *para*-positions are called *ortho* and *para*-directing groups. e.g. Phenol is a resonance hybrid of following structures

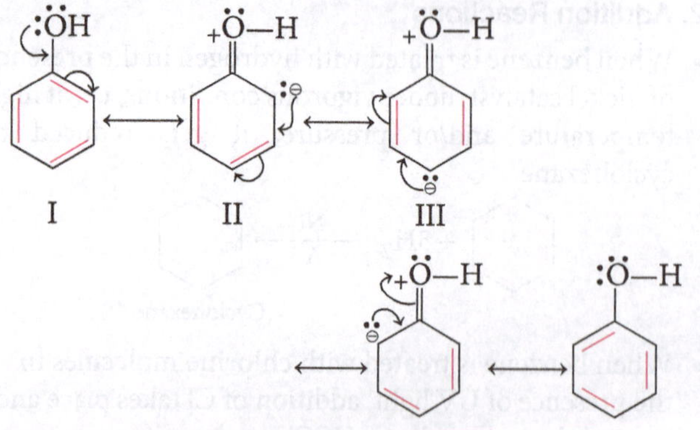

I II III IV V

The above resonating structures clearly revealed that the electron density increases at *o* and *p*-positions and hence, electrophilic substitution occurs mainly at these positions.

However, —OH group also exhibit $-I$ group that reduces the electron density to some extent at *ortho* and *para* -positions. But overall electron density increases at these positions of the ring due to resonance.

Other groups that direct the incoming groups at *o* and *p*-positions, i.e. **activating groups** are $—NH_2$, —NH*R*, $—NHCOCH_3$, $—OCH_3$, $—CH_3$, $—C_2H_5$ etc.

TEACHER'S TIP

Halogens are exceptionally different due to their ring deactivating properties. In simpler words, halogens are those *o*-and *p*-directing group which deactivate benzene nucleus for further electrophilic substitution. It is because of their high electronegativity value.

Resonating Structures of Chlorobenzene

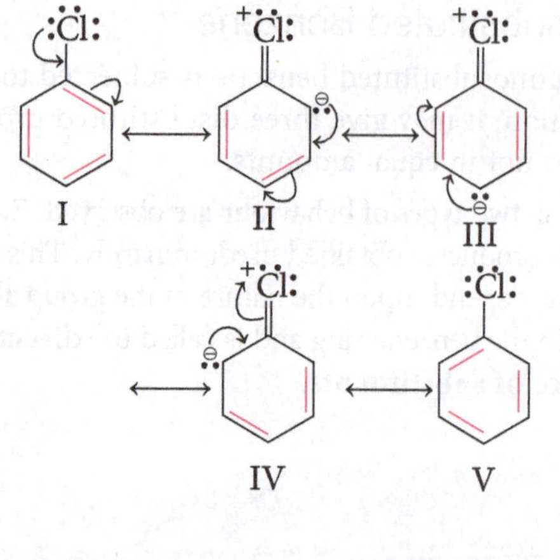

I II III IV V

Because of the strong $-I$-effect of halogens, the overall electron density on the benzene ring decreases. It makes substitution difficult therefore halogens are **moderately deactivating.** But due to resonance the electron density on *o*-and *p*-position is greater than that at the *m*-position. That's why halogens are *o*/*p*-directing group.

2. *Meta*-directing Group

The groups that direct the incoming group to *meta*-position are called ***meta*-directing groups.** e.g. $—NO_2$, —CN, —CHO, —CO*R*, —COOH, —COO*R*, $—SO_3H$ etc.

$—NO_2$ group, when present at benzene nucleus, decreases the electron density due to its strong $-I$-effect and hence is called a **deactivating group.**

Further nitrobenzene is a resonating hybrid of following structures

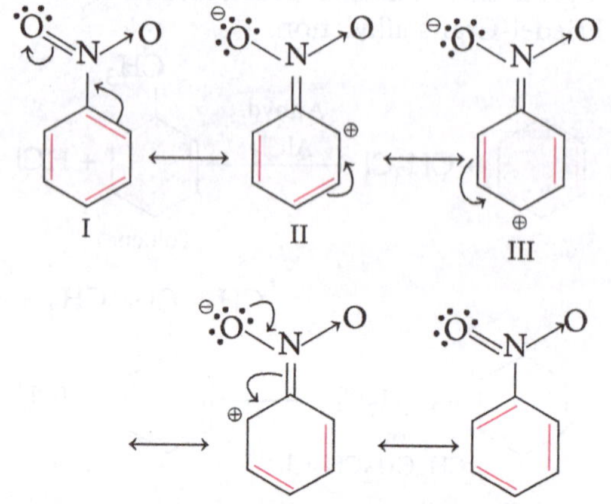

I II III IV V

The given structures show that the overall electron density on the benzene ring decreases and thus, the electrophilic substitution becomes difficult. The electron density on *o*-and *p*-position is comparatively lesser than that at *m*-position. So, electrophile attacks at *meta*-position, i.e. substitution occurs at *meta*-position.

Carcinogenicity and Toxicity

The polynuclear hydrocarbons having two or more fused benzene rings are toxic and have carcinogenic (cancer producing) property.

These are obtained by incomplete combustion of organic materials like tobacco, coal and petroleum. They reach into the human body and undergo several biochemical reactions. They damage DNA and cause cancer. Some examples of carcinogenic hydrocarbons are as follows

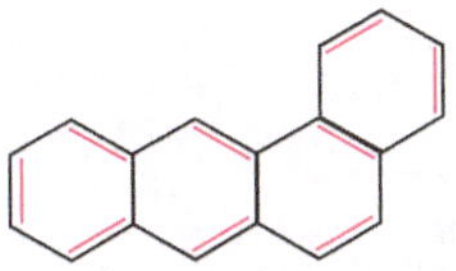

1, 2-benzanthracene

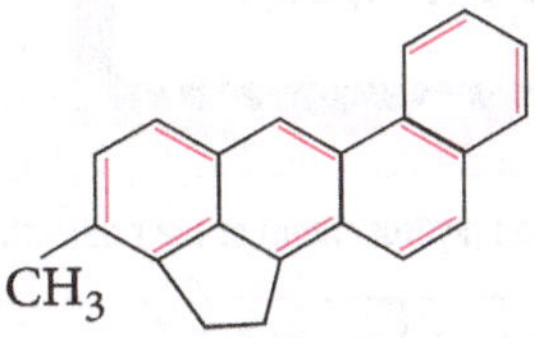

3-methylcholanthrene

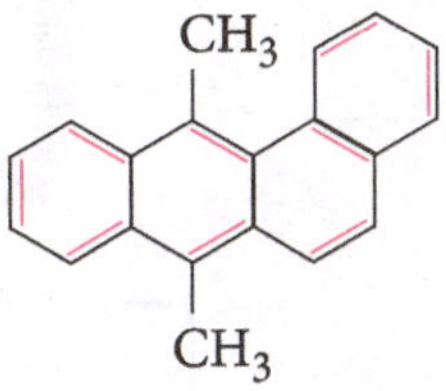

9, 10-dimethyl-1,2-benzanthracene

Quick Test 3

1. Suggest the name of a Lewis acid other than anhydrous aluminium chloride which can be used during ethylation of benzene. *NCERT*

2. Why does benzene undergo electrophilic substitution reactions easily and nucleophilic substitutions with difficulty? *NCERT*

3. Suggest a route for the preparation of nitrobenzene starting from acetylene? *NCERT Exemplar*

4. Why iodination of benzene is carried out in the presence of nitric acid or iodic acid?

5. What will be the product obtained as a result of the following reaction and why? *NCERT Exemplar*

 $+ CH_3-CH_2-CH_2Cl \xrightarrow{AlCl_3}$

6. Complete the following

(i) H_3C-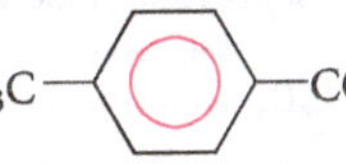$-\overset{-}{C}OO\overset{+}{N}a \xrightarrow[\text{Heat}]{\text{Sodalime}}$

(ii) 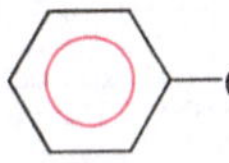$-OH \xrightarrow{\text{Zn dust}}$

7. Why do alkenes prefer to undergo electrophilic addition reaction while arenes prefer electrophilic substitution reactions? Explain *NCERT Exemplar*

8. Explain why the following systems are not aromatic ? *NCERT*

(i) 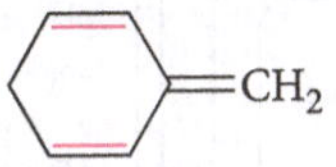

Non-aromatic

(ii) 

Non-aromatic

(iii) 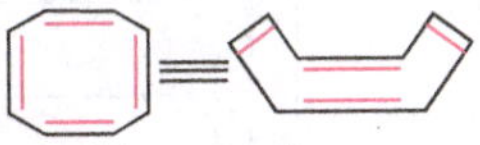

Non-aromatic

9. Write down the products of ozonolysis of 1, 2-dimethyl benzene (*o*-xylene). How does the result support Kekule structure of benzene? *NCERT*

10. Arrange the following set of compounds in order of their decreasing relative reactivity with an electrophile, E^+. *NCERT*

(i) Chlorobenzene, 2, 4-dinitrochlorobenzene, *p*-nitrochlorobenzene

(ii) Toluene, *p*-$H_3C-C_6H_4-NO_2$, *p*-$O_2N-C_6H_4-NO_2$

Also explain your answer.

For Solutions, See QR Code on Pg. 383

Mind Map

Hydrocarbons

Hydrides of carbon (hydrocarbon) or their derivatives.

Saturated Hydrocarbons (Alkanes)

- Also called **paraffins.**
- Contains only single bond between carbon atoms.
- Have general formula C_nH_{2n+2}.
  e.g. methane (CH_4), ethane (C_2H_6), etc.
- They have tetrahedral geometry with sp^3 hybridisation and 109°28' bond angle.
- Root word + ane = alkane name

Isomerism

Exhibit only chain isomerism if have 4 or more C atoms.

Preparation Methods

(i) $CH_2{=}CH_2 + H_2 \xrightarrow{Ni} CH_3CH_3$ (ethane)

(ii) $R{-}Cl + H_2 \xrightarrow{Zn,\,H^+} R{-}H + HCl$

(iii) $2RCl \xrightarrow[\text{Dry ether}]{2\,Na} R{-}R + 2\,NaCl$ (Wurtz reaction)

[Not used for alkanes having odd number of C atoms]

(iv) $RCOONa \xrightarrow[\Delta,\,CaO]{NaOH} R{-}H$

(v) $RCOONa \xrightarrow[\text{Kolbe's electrolytic method}]{\text{Electrolysis}} R{-}R$ (at anode)

Properties

(i) Their BP and MP increases with molar mass. BP decreases with branching.

(ii) $CH_4 \xrightarrow[h\nu]{Cl_2} CH_3Cl + HCl$ (Halogenation)

(iii) $C_nH_{2n+2} + \left(\frac{3n+1}{2}\right)O_2 \xrightarrow{\text{Combustion}} nCO_2 + (n+1)\,H_2O$

(iv) $CH_4 + O_2 \xrightarrow{Cu} CH_3OH \xrightarrow{Mo_2O_3} HCHO$

(v) n-alkane $\xrightarrow[AlCl_3]{\text{Anhy.}}$ Branched alkane

(vi) n-alkane $\xrightarrow[\text{Or } V_2O_3]{Cr_2O_3}$ Aromatic hydrocarbon

(vii) Higher alkane $\xrightarrow[973\,K]{Pd,\,Pt}$ Aromatic hydrocarbon

(viii) $CH_4 + H_2O \xrightarrow[\Delta]{Ni} CO + 3H_2$

Conformations

These are different arrangements due to rotation around C—C bond.

Staggered

The most stable form in which groups are as far apart as possible.

Eclipsed

The least stable form in which groups are as close as possible.

Skew or Gauche

Intermediate conformation between staggered and eclipsed.

Unsaturated Hydrocarbons

They have atleast one (=) or (≡) bond

Alkenes

- Also called **olefins.**
- General formula is C_nH_{2n}.
- Double bonded C are sp^2 hybridised with trigonal planar shape and 120° angle.
- Root word + ene = Alkene name

Isomerism

They exhibit position, chain and geometrical isomerism.

Preparation Methods

(i) $RC{\equiv}CR' \xrightarrow[H_2]{Pd/C}$ *cis*-alkene

(ii) Alkyne $\xrightarrow[\text{Liq. } NH_3]{Na}$ *trans*-alkene

(iii) $CH_3CH_2X \xrightarrow[-HX]{\text{Alc. } KOH} CH_2{=}CH_2$

(iv) $CH_2Br{-}CH_2Br \xrightarrow{Zn} CH_2{=}CH_2$

(v) $CH_3CH_2OH \xrightarrow[170°C,\,-H_2O]{H_2SO_4} CH_2{=}CH_2$

Properties

(i) Their BP and MP increases with increase in molar mass. BP of *cis* form is higher but MP is higher for *trans* form.

(ii) $CH_2{=}CH_2 + HBr \rightarrow CH_3CH_2Br$

(–ve part goes to that C atom which has less H atom but in the presence of peroxide opposite is true).

(iii) Alkene + $H_2O \rightarrow$ Alcohol

(iv) $CH_2{=}CH_2 + H_2O + O \xrightarrow{KMnO_4} CH_2(OH){-}CH_2(OH)$

(v) $RCH{=}CHR + O_3 \xrightarrow{Zn/H_2O} 2RCHO$

(vi) Polymerisation

n-alkene $\xrightarrow[\text{and P}]{\text{High T}}$ Polyene

Alkynes

- General formula C_nH_{2n-2}.
- Triple bonded C are sp hybridised with linear shape and 180° bond angle.
- Root word + yne = Alkyne name

Isomerism

Exhibit chain and position isomerism.

Preparation Methods

(i) $CaC_2 + 2H_2O \longrightarrow Ca(OH)_2 + C_2H_2$

(ii) $CH_2BrCH_2Br \xrightarrow[NaNH_2]{KOH,\,\text{Alcohol}} CH{\equiv}CH$

Properties

(i) Their MP and BP increases with increase in molecular mass.

(ii) These are lighter than water.

(iii) These are acidic due to the presence of H atoms at triple bonded C atoms.

$CH_3C{\equiv}CH \xrightarrow[\text{or } NaNH_2]{\text{Na in liq } NH_3} CH_3C{\equiv}C^-Na^+$

(iv) $-C{\equiv}C- \xrightarrow{Br_2} -CBr_2{-}CBr_2-$

(v) $-C{\equiv}C- + H_2O \xrightarrow{Hg^{2+}/H^+} -CH{=}C(OH)- \xrightarrow{\text{Isomerisation}} -CH_2{-}C(=O)-$

(vi) Polymerisation

n-acetylene $\rightarrow$ polyacetylene

Acetylene $\xrightarrow[\text{red hot tube}]{873K}$ Benzene

Aromatic Hydrocarbons

Cyclic compounds having benzene nucleus.

Aromaticity

For a compound to be aromatic it must be cyclic, planar, have conjugate system and $(4n+2)\,\pi\,e^-$ (Huckel's rule)

Benzene

- Its formula is C_6H_6.
- Due to resonance in it all the C–C bond lengths are equal.
- All C are sp^2 hybridised.

Preparation Methods

(i) $CH{\equiv}CH \xrightarrow[\text{red hot tube}]{1500°C}$ Benzene

(ii) 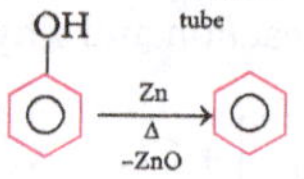

Properties

(i) They burn with sooty flame.

(ii) $C_6H_6 \xrightarrow{\text{Conc.}HNO_3 + H_2SO_4} C_6H_5NO_2$

(iii) $C_6H_6 + Cl_2 \xrightarrow{\text{Anhy. } AlCl_3} C_6H_5Cl$

(iv) $C_6H_6 + CH_3Cl \xrightarrow[\text{Friedal Crafts Alkylation}]{\text{Anhy. } AlCl_3} C_6H_5CH_3$ (Toluene)

(v) $C_6H_6 + CH_3COCl \xrightarrow[\text{Friedel crafts acylation}]{\text{Anhy. } AlCl_3} C_6H_5COCH_3$ (Acetophenone)

(vi) $C_6H_6 + 3H_2 \xrightarrow{Ni} C_6H_{12}$

(vii) $C_6H_6 + 3Cl_2 \xrightarrow{UV\ 500K} C_6H_6Cl_6$ (BHC)

Directive Influence of Functional Groups

Towards electrophilic substitution

(i) $-NH_2$, $-NHR$, $-NHCOCH_3$, $-OH$, $-CH_3$, $-C_2H_5$, etc., are o/p directing activating groups.

(ii) Halogens are o/p directing but deactivating.

(iii) $-NO_2$, $-CN$, $-CHO$, $-CO_2$, $-COOH$, $-SO_3H$, etc., are meta directing and deactivating groups.

EXAM PATTERN QUESTIONS

Objective Type Questions

Multiple Choice Questions [1 Mark]

1. The given reaction,

$CH_3—Cl + H_2 \xrightarrow{Zn,\ H^+} CH_4 + HCl$ **is an example of**

(a) hydration (b) dehydrogenation
(c) carbocation (d) reduction process

2. Which of the following is the general formula for alkanes?

(a) C_nH_{2n} (b) C_nH_{2n+2} (c) C_nH_{2n-2} (d) C_nH_n

3. Which of the following is true for alkanes?

(a) They are unsaturated hydrocarbons
(b) They have atleast one double bond
(c) They are saturated hydrocarbons
(d) They have atleast one triple bond

4. Which products are formed when alkanes undergo complete combustion? Competency Based Que.

(a) Carbon monoxide and water.
(b) Carbondioxide and water.
(c) Carbon and water.
(d) Methane and water.

5. The reaction of $C_6H_5CH{=}CHCH_3$ with HBr produces

(a) $C_6H_5\underset{\underset{Br}{|}}{C}HCH_2CH_3$ (b) $C_6H_5CH_2\underset{\underset{Br}{|}}{C}HCH_3$
(c) $C_6H_5CH_2CH_2CH_2Br$ (d)

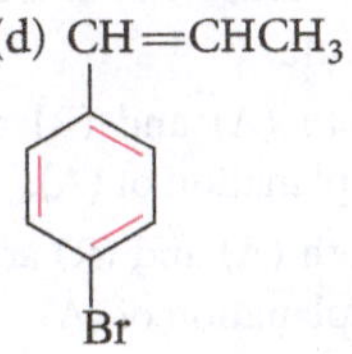

6. The addition of HBr to 1-butene gives a mixture of products *A*, *B* and *C*.

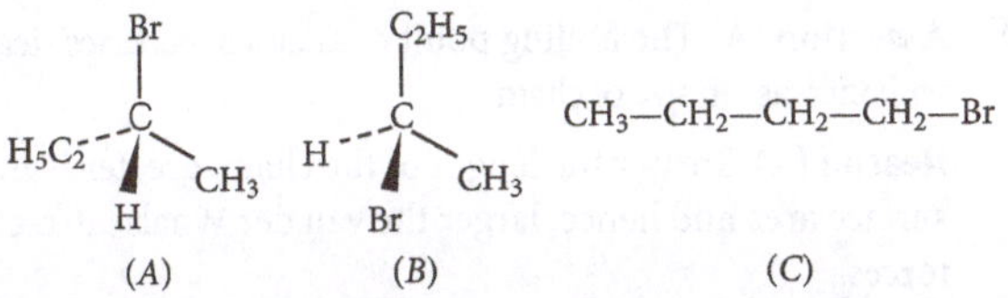

(A) (B) (C)

The mixture consists of

(a) *A* and *B* as major and *C* as minor products
(b) *B* as major, *A* and *C* as minor products
(c) *B* as minor, *A* and *C* as major products
(d) *A* and *B* as minor and *C* as major products

7. Addition of cold conc. H_2SO_4 with alkenes is an example of

(a) electrophilic substitution reaction
(b) nucleophilic substitution reaction
(c) electrophilic addition reaction
(d) nucleophilic addition reaction

8. Which type of bond is present in alkenes?

(a) Single bond only
(b) Double bond only
(c) At least one double bond
(d) At least one triple bond

9. The increasing order of reduction of alkyl halides with zinc and dilute HCl is NCERT Exemplar

(a) $R—Cl < R—I < R—Br$ (b) $R—Cl < R—Br < R—I$
(c) $R—I < R—Br < R—Cl$ (d) $R—Br < R—I < R—Cl$

10. Arrange the following hydrogen halides in order of their decreasing reactivity with propene. NCERT Exemplar

(a) HCl > HBr > HI (b) HBr > HI > HCl
(c) HI > HBr > HCl (d) HCl > HI > HBr

11. Which functional group is present in alkynes?

(a) C=C (Double bond)
(b) C≡C (Triple bond)
(c) OH (Hydroxyl group)
(d) C=O (Carbonyl group)

12. Alkynes on reduction with sodium in liquid ammonia forms

(a) *cis*-alkene (b) alkane
(c) *trans*-alkene (d) Both (a) and (c)

13. On passing vapours of phenol over heated zinc dust it gets reduced to

(a) toluene (b) aniline
(c) benzene (d) C_6H_5OH

14. Which of the following deactivates the benzene ring towards electrophilic substitution and is *o*/*p*-directing?

(a) $—Cl^{\ominus}$ (b) $—OCH_3$
(c) —CHO (d) All of these

15. Arrange the following in decreasing order of their boiling points. **NCERT Exemplar**

A. *n*-butane
B. 2-methylbutane
C. *n*-pentane
D. 2, 2-dimethylpropane

(a) $A > B > C > D$
(b) $B > C > D > A$
(c) $D > C > B > A$
(d) $C > B > D > A$

16. Arrange the halogens F_2, Cl_2, Br_2, I_2, in order of their increasing reactivity with alkanes. **NCERT Exemplar**

(a) $I_2 < Br_2 < Cl_2 < F_2$
(b) $Br_2 < Cl_2 < F_2 < I_2$
(c) $F_2 < Cl_2 < Br_2 < I_2$
(d) $Br_2 < I_2 < Cl_2 < F_2$

17. Which of the following reactions of methane is incomplete combustion? **NCERT Exemplar**

(a) $2CH_4 + O_2 \xrightarrow{Cu/523\,K/100\,atm} 2CH_3OH$
(b) $CH_4 + O_2 \xrightarrow{Mo_2O_3} HCHO + H_2O$
(c) $CH_4 + O_2 \longrightarrow C(s) + 2H_2O(l)$
(d) $CH_4 + 2O_2 \longrightarrow CO_2(g) + 2H_2O(l)$

18. Conformations of ethane in which hydrogen atoms attached to two carbon atoms are closest to each other are known as

(a) eclipsed
(b) *skew* boat
(c) staggered
(d) partially eclipsed

19. Which of the following will not show geometrical isomerism?

(a) 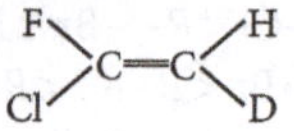
(b) 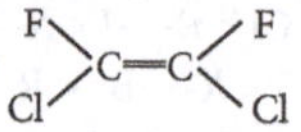
(c) 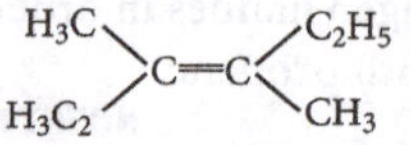
(d) 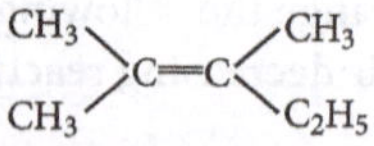

20. Which of the following has higher dipole moment; *cis*-2-butene and *trans*-2-butene?

(a) *Cis*-but-2-ene
(b) *Trans*-but-2-ene
(c) Both have same dipole moment
(d) None of the above

21. Arrange the following alkyl halides in decreasing order of the rate of β-elimination reaction with alcoholic KOH. **NCERT Exemplar**

A. 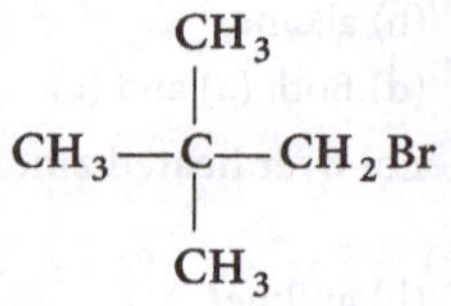
B. CH_3-CH_2-Br
C. $CH_3-CH_2-CH_2-Br$

(a) $A > B > C$
(b) $C > B > A$
(c) $B > C > A$
(d) $A > C > B$

22. $CH_2{=}CHBr \xrightarrow{NaNH_2} A \xrightarrow[\text{tube, 873 K}]{\text{Red hot iron}}$ 

Here, A refers to **Competency Based Que.**

(a) $CH{\equiv}CH$
(b) $CH_3-C{\equiv}CH$
(c) CH_3-CH_3
(d) $CH{\equiv}C-NH_2$

23. Arrange the following carbanions in order of their decreasing stability.

A. $H_3C-C{\equiv}C^-$
B. $H-C{\equiv}C^-$
C. $H_3C-CH_2^-$

(a) $A > B > C$
(b) $B > A > C$
(c) $C > B > A$
(d) $C > A > B$

24. The aromatic compound among the following is

(a) 
(b) 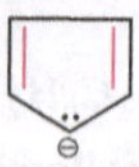
(c) 
(d) All of these

25. In the reaction, Y is

 + H_2SO_4 (Fuming sulphuric acid) $\xrightarrow{\Delta} Y$,

(a) $C_6H_5SO_3H$
(b) C_6H_5OH **Competency Based Que.**
(c) $C_6H_5SO_2$
(d) C_6H_5CHO

Assertion-Reason [1 Mark]

Directions (Q. Nos. 26-38) In the following questions, a statement of assertion is followed by a corresponding statements of reason of the following statements, choose the correct one.

(a) Both (A) and (R) are correct and (R) is the correct explanation of (A).
(b) Both (A) and (R) are correct but (R) is not the correct explanation of (A).
(c) (A) is correct but (R) is incorrect.
(d) (A) is incorrect but (R) is correct.

26. **Assertion** (A) The boiling point of alkanes increases steadily with increase in size of chain.

Reason (R) Greater the length of the chain, greater is the surface area and hence, larger the van der Waals' attractive forces.

27. **Assertion** (A) Melting point of alkanes with even number of carbon atoms are higher than those of alkanes with odd number of carbon atoms.

Reason (R) Alkanes with even number of carbon atoms fit together better in a crystal lattice.

28. **Assertion** (A) Alkanes are also called paraffins.

Reason (R) Alkanes are highly reactive compounds.

29. **Assertion** (A) Cyclopropane is easily reduced to propane.

Reason (R) There is cleavage of C—C bond due to strain in cyclopropane.

30. **Assertion** (A) Among isomeric pentanes, 2, 2-dimethylpentane has the lower boiling point.

Reason (R) Branching in hydrocarbon does not affect the boiling point.

31. **Assertion** (A) 1-butene on reaction with HBr in the presence of a peroxide, produces 1-bromobutane.

Reason (R) It involves the formation of a 1° free radical.

32. **Assertion** (A) Alkenes undergo addition reactions.

Reason (R) Alkenes contains at least one double bond.

33. **Assertion** (A) Methane burns with a blue flame in the presence of sufficient oxygen.

Reason (R) Complete combustion of methane produces carbon dioxide and water.

34. **Assertion** (A) Propene reacts with HBr to give isopropyl bromide as major product but *n*-propyl bromide as minor product.

Reason (R) *Iso*-propyl carbonium ion is more stable than *n*-propyl carbonium ion.

35. **Assertion** (A) Ethene on treating with Br_2 in presence of NaCl forms CH_2ClCH_2Br and CH_2BrCH_2Br.

Reason (R) This addition involves the formation of free radicals.

36. **Assertion** (A) Alkynes are more reactive than alkanes.

Reason (R) Alkynes have a triple bond that is weaker than a single bond.

37. **Assertion** (A) 1-hexyne is converted to *cis*-1-hexene by Lindlar's catalyst.

Reason (R) 1-hexyne is converted to *n*-hexene by the reduction with hydrogen gas in the presence of Pd/Ni.

38. **Assertion** (A) CH_4 does not react with Cl_2 in dark.

Reason (R) Chlorination of CH_4 takes place in sunlight.

Case-Study [4 Marks]

39. Read the given case and answer the following questions.

In alkane, the distribution of electrons in a sigma molecular orbital is symmetrical around the internuclear axis of the C—C bond. Thus, it permits the possibility of free rotation about the C—C single bond. Due to this rotation, different spatial arrangements of carbon atoms in space are observed which can change into one another. Such spatial arrangement of carbon and hydrogen atoms which can be converted into one another by rotation around a C—C single bond is called conformation or conformer or rotamer. Alkanes can thus have an infinite number of conformations by rotation around C—C single bonds.

Competency Based Que.

(i) Which is most stable conformation of ethane? Explain.

(ii) The different conformations of ethane can not be separated and isolated. Why?

(iii) Give reason for the more stability of chair form of cyclohexane than boat form.

Or

Which is the most stable conformation of ethylene glycol?

40. Read the given case and answer the following questions.

Aromaticity is defined as a property of the conjugated cycloalkenes which enhances the stability of a molecule due to the delocalisation of electrons present in the π-π orbitals.

Aromatic molecules are said to be very stable and they do not break so easily and also reacts with other types of substances. The organic compounds which are not said to be aromatic are known as aliphatic compounds. These might be in cyclic form, but only the aromatic rings have a special kind of stability.

We encounter aromaticity in our day-to-day lives. Even our bodies function with the help of certain aromatic compounds.

Aromatic compounds are essential in the industry and around 35 million tonnes of these compounds are known to be produced worldwide every year in the form of polymers and chemicals, such as the nylon and polyester. These compounds are important even in the field of the biochemistry of all the living things.

Aromatic compounds are less stable compounds and they have many kinds of chemicals as well as synthetic uses.

In fact, the nucleic acids and the amino acids that make up our cell structure make use of these aromatic compounds. But, the main thing is what makes aromatic compounds? The aromatic compounds are said to exhibit some special characteristics or called as rules which are given below.

- **The aromatic compounds are always cyclic structures.**
- **Each element of the ring within the structure must and should have a *p*-orbital ring which is in perpendicular form to the ring and this makes it a planar molecule.**

- **All the compounds obey the Huckel's rule, i.e. all the aromatic compounds should have the $(4n+2)\pi$ number of electrons.**
- **The last one is that the organic compound has to be flat.**

Competency Based Que.

(i) Compound X forms a white ppt. on reacting with $AgNO_3$ however Y does not. Give reaction.

X-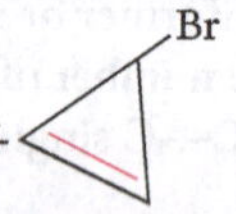

Y-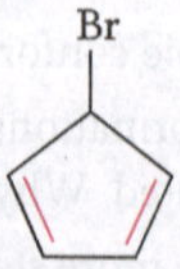

(ii) In the Friedal-crafts acetylation of an aromatic ring the role of the $AlCl_3$ is to

(a) withdraw electrons from the aromatic ring

(b) function as a Lewis base

(c) chlorinate the aromatic ring

(d) form a $CH_3-\overset{+}{C}(=O)$ ion

Or

Which of the following obeys Huckel's rule?

(a) 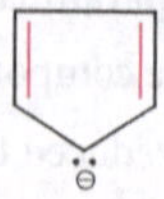 (b) 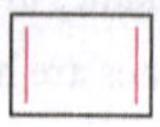

(c) 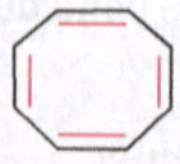 (d) 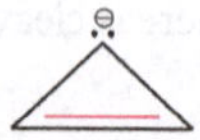

(iii) Which is a non-aromatic compound?

(a) 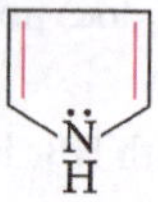 (b) 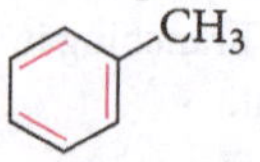

(c)  (d) 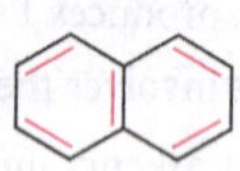

Subjective Type Questions

Short Answer Type I Questions [2 Marks]

1. Write the structures and names of products obtained in the reactions of sodium with a mixture of 1-iodo-2-methylpropane and 2-iodopropane. **NCERT Exemplar**

2. Among Newman and Sawhorse projections for the eclipsed and staggered conformations of ethane. Which is more stable and why? **NCERT Exemplar**

3. Give the IUPAC names of each of the following.

(i) 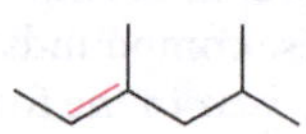 (ii) 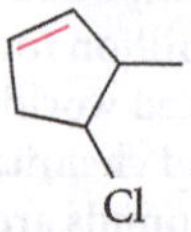

(iii) 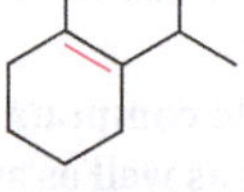 (iv) 

4. Write structures of all the alkenes which on hydrogenation give 2-methylbutane. **NCERT**

5. The intermediate carbocation formed in the reactions of HI, HBr and HCl with propene is the same and the bond energy of HCl, HBr and HI is 430.5 kJ mol^{-1}, 363.7 kJ mol^{-1} and 296.8 kJ mol^{-1} respectively. What will be the order of reactivity of these halogen acids? **NCERT Exemplar**

6. Give the structures of A and B.

$$C + D \xleftarrow{\text{Hot } KMnO_4} \underset{\substack{(C_6H_{12})}}{A} \xrightarrow[\text{(ii) Zn, } H_2O]{\text{(i) } O_3} B + C$$

(Isomers of formula C_3H_6O) (Isomers of formula C_3H_6O)

7. Complete the following reactions and predict the name of the products. **Competency Based Que.**

(a) $CH_3-CH=CH_2 + HBr \longrightarrow$

(b) $CH_3-C\equiv C-CH_3 + Na \xrightarrow{\text{Aqueous } NH_3}$

8. Write chemical equation for combustion reaction of toluene. **NCERT**

9. Despite their $-I$ effect, halogens are o-and p-directing in haloarenes. Explain **NCERT Exemplar**

10. Out of benzene, m-dinitrobenzene and toluene which will undergo nitration most easily and why? **NCERT**

Short Answer Type II Questions [3 Marks]

11. Write the reaction for the preparation of butane by

(i) Wurtz reaction (ii) Kolbe's reaction

12. Rotation around carbon-carbon single bond of ethane is not completely free. Justify the statement. **NCERT Exemplar**

13. Write IUPAC names of the following compounds

(i) $(CH_3)_3CCH_2C(CH_3)_3$ (ii) $(CH_3)_2C(C_2H_5)_2$

(iii) Tetra-*tert*-butylmethane **NCERT**

14. In the alkane $H_3C\ CH_2—C(CH_3)_2—CH_2CH(CH_3)_2$, identify 1°, 2°, 3° carbon atoms and give the number of H-atoms bonded to each one of these. **NCERT**

15. How do you account for the formation of ethane during chlorination of methane? **NCERT**

16. A hydrocarbon containing two double bonds on reductive ozonolysis produces glyoxal, ethanal and propanone. Predict the structure of the hydrocarbon and also give its IUPAC name.

17. List the following alkenes in decreasing order of reactivity towards electrophilic addition.

(i) $ClCH_2CH{=}CH_2$ (ii) $(CH_3)_2C{=}CH_2$

(iii) $CH_3CH{=}CH_2$ (iv) $CH_2{=}CHCl$

Explain your order. **Competency Based Que.**

18. An alkene *A* on ozonolysis gives a mixture of ethanal and pentan-3-one. Write structure and IUPAC name of *A*. **NCERT**

19. For the following compounds, write structural formulae and IUPAC names for all possible isomers having the number of double or triple bonds as indicated

(i) C_4H_8 (one double bond)

(ii) C_5H_8 (one triple bond) **NCERT**

20. Predict the major product(s) of the following reactions and explain their formation. **NCERT Exemplar**

$$H_3C—CH{=}CH_2 \xrightarrow[\text{HBr}]{(Ph—CO—O)_2}$$

$$H_3C—CH{=}CH_2 \xrightarrow{\text{HBr}}$$

21. Addition of HBr to propene yields 2-bromopropane, while in the presence of benzoyl peroxide. The same reaction yields 1-bromopropane. Explain and give mechanism. **NCERT Exemplar**

22. Name the organic products of the reaction of but-2-ene with each of the following reagents and write a balanced equation for each reaction.

(i) Hydrogen bromide

(ii) Bromine dissolved in tetrachloromethane

23. Why is benzene extraordinarily stable though it contains three double bonds? **NCERT**

24. Arrange benzene, *n*-hexane and ethyne in decreasing order of acidic behaviour. Also give reason for this behaviour. **NCERT**

25. An alkene (molecular weight = 56) on reaction with trioxygen followed by zinc/CH_3COOH gave only ethanal. Identify the structure of the alkene.

Long Answer Type Questions [5 Marks]

26. Write structures of different isomeric alkyl groups corresponding to the molecular formula C_5H_{11}. Write IUPAC names of alcohols obtained by attachment of —OH groups at different carbons of the chain. **NCERT**

27. Write IUPAC names of the products obtained by the ozonolysis of the following compounds.

(i) Pent-2-ene

(ii) 3,4-dimethylhept-3-ene

(iii) 2-ethylbut-1-ene

(iv) 1-phenylbut-1-ene **NCERT**

28. Write the IUPAC names of the following compounds. **NCERT**

(i) $\begin{array}{l}(CH_3)_2CH—CH{=}CHCH_2CH{=}CH—\underset{\displaystyle C_2H_5}{\underset{|}{C}}HCH_3\end{array}$

(ii) 

(iii) $CH_2{=}C(CH_2CH_2CH_3)_2$

(iv) $\begin{array}{l}CH_3—CH_2CH_2CH_2 \qquad\quad CH_2CH_3\ CH_3\\ \qquad\qquad\qquad |\qquad\qquad\qquad\quad |\qquad\quad |\\ \qquad\qquad CH_3—CH—CH{=}CCH_2—CH—CH_3\end{array}$

Also calculate the number of σ and π-bonds.

29. An alkyl halide $C_5H_{11}Br(A)$ reacts with ethanolic KOH to give an alkene '*B*', which reacts with Br_2 to give a compound '*C*', which on dehydrobromination gives an alkyne '*D*'. On treatment with sodium metal in liquid ammonia, one mole of '*D*' gives one mole of the sodium salt of '*D*' and half a mole of hydrogen gas. Complete hydrogenation of '*D*' yields a straight chain alkane. Identify *A*, *B*, *C* and *D*. Give the reactions involved. **NCERT Exemplar**

30. How will you convert benzene into **NCERT**

(i) *p*-nitrobromobenzene

(ii) *m*-nitrochlorobenzene

(iii) *p*-nitrotoluene

(iv) acetophenone

31. Assign structures to the following. **Competency Based Que.**

(i) An alkyne (X) has molecular formula C_5H_8. It reacts neither with sodamide nor with ammoniacal cuprous chloride.

(ii) A hydrocarbon 'Y' decolourises bromine water. On ozonolysis it gives 3-methyl butanal and formaldehyde. Give the name of the compound.

(iii) A hydrocarbon (Z) has molecular formula C_8H_{10}. It does not decolourise bromine water and is oxidised to benzoic acid on heating with $K_2Cr_2O_7$. It can also have three other isomers A, B and C. Write the structures of Z, A, B and C.

32. The ring systems having following characteristics are aromatic.

(i) Planar ring containing conjugated π-bonds.

(ii) Complete delocalisation of the π-electrons in ring system, i.e. Each atom in the ring has unhybridised p-orbital, and

(iii) Presence of $(4n + 2)$ π- electrons in the ring where n is an integer ($n = 0, 1, 2, \ldots\ldots$) [Huckel's rule].

Using this information classify the following compounds as aromatic/non-aromatic. **NCERT Exemplar**

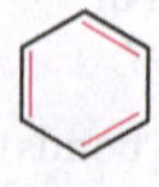
(A)

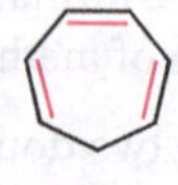
(B)

(C)

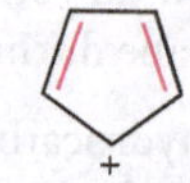
(D)

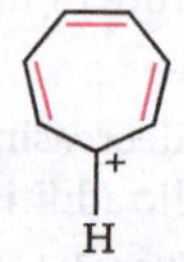
(E)

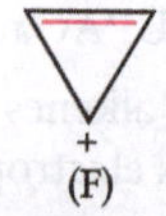
(F)

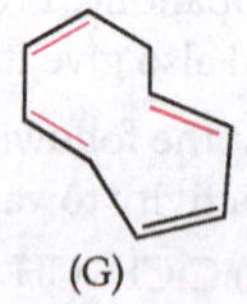
(G)

Hints & Solutions

Objective Type Questions

1. (*d*) It is an example of reduction process. Reduction means the addition of hydrogen to a molecule or the removal of oxygen from a molecule.
2. (*b*) The general formula of alkane is C_nH_{2n+2}.
3. (*c*) Alkanes are saturated hydrocarbons because they only have single bonds between carbon atoms.
4. (*b*) In complete combustion, alkanes reacts with oxygen to form carbon dioxide and water.
5. (*a*) The reaction of prop-l-enyl benzene with HBr gives an electrophilic addition reaction.

$$\underset{\text{Prop-1-enylbenzene}}{C_6H_5CH=CHCH_3} + H^+Br^- \longrightarrow \underset{\text{1-bromopropyl benzene}}{C_6H_5\underset{\substack{|\\ Br}}{C}HCH_2CH_3}$$

6. (*a*) The alkene is unsymmetrical, hence will follow Markovnikov's rule to give major product.

$$\underset{\text{Butene-1}}{CH_3-CH_2-CH=CH_2} + H-Br \longrightarrow$$

$$CH_3-CH_2-CHBr-CH_3 \text{ or } C_2H_5-\underset{\substack{|\\ H}}{\overset{\substack{Br\\ |}}{C^*}}-CH_3 \quad (I)$$

$$+ \underset{\text{(minor product)}}{CH_3-CH_2-CH_2-CH_2Br}$$

Since, I contains, a chiral carbon, it exists in two enantiomers (*A* and *B*) which are mirror images of each other.

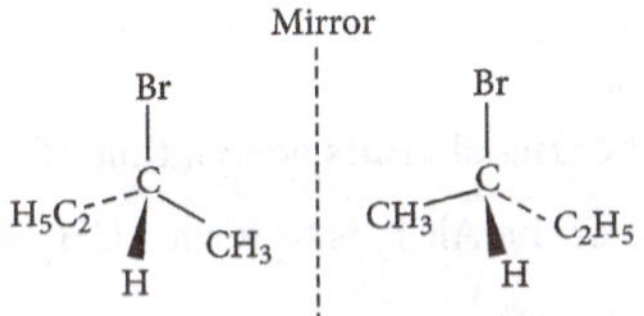

(*A*) (*B*)

7. (*c*) When cold concentrated sulphuric acid adds to alkenes in accordance with Markovnikov's rule to form alkyl halogen sulphate by electrophilic addition reaction.
8. (*c*) Alkenes contain atleast one double bond between carbon atoms.
9. (*c*) The reactivity of halogens with alkane is $F_2 > Cl_2 > Br_2 > I_2$ Hence, reduction of alkyl halide with Zn and dilute HCl follows reverse order i.e., $R—I > R—Br > R—Cl$. Further, the reactivity of this reduction increases as the strength of C—*X* bond decreases.
10. (*c*) When the size of the halogen increases, the strength of H—*X* bond decreases and hence, reactivity increases. The order of reactivity of hydrogen halides is HI > HBr > HCl.
11. (*b*) Alkynes are characterised by the presence of atleast one triple bond ($C \equiv C$).
12. (*c*) Alkynes on reduction with sodium in liquid ammonia produce *trans*-alkenes.
13. (*c*) On passing vapours of phenol over zinc duct it gets reduced to benzene. In this reaction, proton and phenoxide ion are produced. This proton accepts an electron from zinc dust and forms zinc oxide and phenoxide ion gets converted to benzene.
14. (*a*) Chloride ion is electron withdrawing group due to its electronegative nature it deactivates the benzene ring for electrophilic substitution and is *o*/*p*-directing.
15. (*d*)

	Compound	Boiling point
A.	*n*-butane	272.6 K
B.	2-methyl butane	301 K
C.	*n*-pentane	309.2 K
D.	2, 2-dimethyl propane	282.6 K

Order of boiling point is $C > B > D > A$.

16. (*a*) Rate of reaction of alkanes with halogens is

$$F_2 > Cl_2 > Br_2 > I_2.$$

17. (*c*) During incomplete combustion of alkanes with insufficient amount of air or dioxygen carbon black is formed which is used in the manufacture of ink, printer ink, black pigments and as filters. Thus,

$$CH_4(g) + O_2(g) \xrightarrow[\text{combustion}]{\text{Incomplete}} C(s) + 2H_2O\,(l)$$

18 (*a*) Conformation in which hydrogen atoms attached to two carbons are as closed together as possible is called eclipsed conformation.

19. (*d*) In option (d), a carbon with double bond has two same functional groups (CH_3) attached. The rotation around carbon will not produce a new compound. Hence, geometrical isomerism is not possible.
20. (*a*) *Cis*-form of alkene is found to be more polar than the *trans* form. e.g. Dipole moment of *cis*-but-2-ene is 0.33 Debye, whereas, dipole moment of the *trans* form is almost zero or it can be said that *trans*-but-2-ene is non-polar.

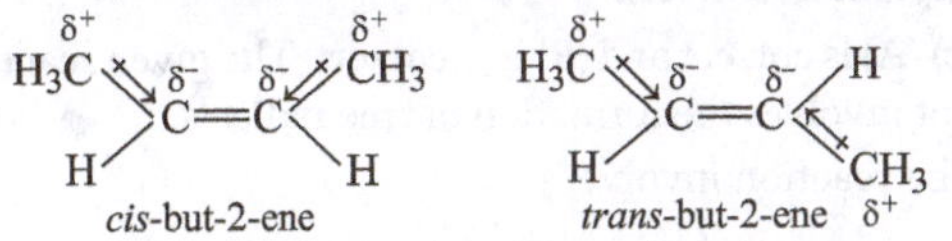

cis-but-2-ene (μ = 0.33 D) *trans*-but-2-ene (μ = 0)

21. (*d*) Alkyl halides on heating with alcoholic potash eliminates one molecule of halogen acid to form alkene. Hydrogen is eliminated from β-carbon atom. Nature of alkyl group determines rate of reaction.

i.e. $3° > 2° > 1°$ or $A > C > B$.

22. (*a*)

$$CH_2=CHBr \xrightarrow{NaNH_2} \underset{(A)}{H-C\equiv CH} + NaBr + NH_3$$

$$\downarrow \text{Red hot iron tube, 873 K}$$

Benzene

23. (*b*) + *I*-effect decreases the stability of carbon anion. Since, (CH_3) group has + *I*-effect, therefore, it intensifies the negative charge and hence destabilises (A) relative to (B).

sp-hybridised carbanion is more stabilised than sp^3.

$$\underset{sp\,(B)}{CH\equiv C^-} > \underset{(A)^{sp}}{CH_3 - C\equiv C^-} > \underset{(C)\quad sp^3}{CH_3 - CH_2}$$

Hence, B > A > C

24. (*d*) A planar cyclic molecule having $(4n+2)$ electrons is generally aromatic. Thus, all given options because of the presence of 6π electrons are aromatic.

25. (*a*)

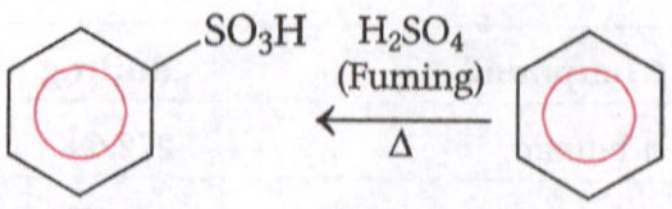

Y

26. (*a*) Both (A) and (R) are correct and (R) is the correct explanation of (A).

27. (*a*) Both (A) and (R) are correct and (R) is the correct explanation of (A).

28. (*c*) Alkanes are called paraffins because they are less reactive due to the presence of single bonds only. Thus, the reason is incorrect.

29. (*a*) Both (A) and (R) are correct and (R) is the correct explanation of (A).

30. (*c*) (A) is correct and (R) is incorrect.

On branching in hydrocarbon, boiling point decreases.

31. (*c*) (A) is correct and (R) is incorrect.

Addition of hydrogen bromide on alkene in the presence of peroxide takes place *via* free radicals.

Two free radicals are formed. Second degree (2°) free radical is more stable, governs the product.

32. (*a*) Alkenes undergo addition reaction due to the presence of a double bond, which is reactive.

33. (*c*) Both (A) and (R) are correct and (R) is the correct explanation of (A).

34. (*a*) Both (A) and (R) are correct and (R) is the correct explanation of (A).

35. (*c*) (A) is correct and (R) is incorrect. The given reaction does not involves the formation of free radicals.

The reaction involve,

$$CH_2{=}CH_2 \xrightarrow[NaCl]{CH_2} H_2\overset{+}{C}{=}\overset{-}{C}H_2 \xrightarrow{+Br^+} H_2\overset{+}{C}{=}\overset{-}{C}H_2Br$$

$+Br^+$ → $BrCH_2—CH_2Br$ (1,2-dibromoethane); $+Cl^-$ → $ClCH_2CH_2Br$ (1-bromo-2-chloroethane)

36. (*c*) Alkynes are more reactive due to the high electron density in the triple bond, but a triple bond is not weaker than a single bond.

37. (*c*) (A) is correct but (R) is incorrect.

The 1-hexyne is converted to *cis*-1-hexene by the reduction with hydrogen gas in the presence of Pd /$BaSO_4$ (Lindlar's catalyst).

$$\text{1-hexyne} \xrightarrow{Pd/BaSO_4} \textit{cis}\text{-1-hexene (addition reaction)}$$

38. (*b*) Both (A) and (R) are correct but (R) is not the correct explanation of (A).

Chlorination of CH_4 does not take place in dark, free radicals can be generated only in the presence of sunlight as this reaction follows free radical mechanism and which is necessary for the reaction to proceed further.

39. (i) The most stable conformation of ethane is staggered since the electron clouds of carbon-hydrogen bonds are as for apart as possible, so it has minimum repulsive forces minimum energy and maximum stability.

(ii) The different conformations of ethane can not be separated and isolated because of small energy barrier.

(iii) The reason of more stability of chair form of cyclohexane than boat form is free of torsional chain and free of angle strain.

Or

Gauches

40. (i) *X* forms an aromatic species on loosing Br which forms a white precipitate with Ag^+ ion of $AgNO_3$.

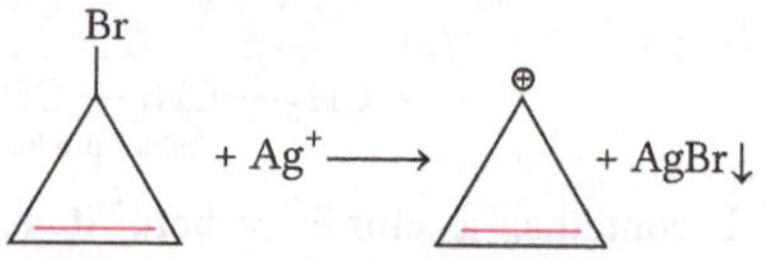

Y cannot loose Br because resulting compound is not aromatic and hence not stable. Therefore, it does not form ppt.

(ii) (*d*) In the friedel-crafts acetylation of an aromatic ring, the role of the $AlCl_3$ is to form a $CH_3—\overset{+}{C}(=O)$ ion.

Or (*a*) As $(4n+2)\pi$ electrons are present in the ring (a) thus, this compound obey Huckel's rule.

(iii) (*c*) Cyclooctatetrane has 8π-electrons. It does not follow Huckel's rule and is also not planar (has tube shaped structure) therefore, it is non-aromatic.

Subjective Type Questions

1. (i) $\underset{\text{1-iodo-2-methylpropane}}{CH_3\underset{|}{\overset{}{C}H}(CH_3)CH_2I} + 2Na + ICH_2—\underset{\underset{CH_3}{|}}{CH}—CH_3 \xrightarrow{\Delta}$

$$CH_3—\underset{\underset{CH_3}{|}}{CH}—(CH_2)_2—\underset{\underset{CH_3}{|}}{CH}—CH_3 + 2NaI$$

2, 5-dimethyl hexane **(1/2)**

(ii) $CH_3-CH(CH_3)-I + 2Na + I-CH(CH_3)-CH_3 \xrightarrow[\text{Dry ether}]{\Delta}$

2-iodopropane

$CH_3-CH(CH_3)-CH(CH_3)-CH_3 + 2NaI$

2, 3-dimethyl butane **(1/2)**

(iii) $CH_3-CH(CH_3)-CH_2-I + 2Na + I-CH(CH_3)-CH_3 \xrightarrow[\text{Dry ether}]{\Delta}$

1-iodo-2-methyl propane 2-iodopropane

$CH_3-CH(CH_3)-CH_2-CH(CH_3)-CH_3 + 2NaI$

2, 4-dimethyl pentane **(1)**

2. Staggered form of ethane is more stable than the eclipsed conformation by about 12.5 kJ mol^{-1}. This is because any two hydrogen atoms on adjacent carbon atoms of staggered conformation are maximum apart while in eclipsed conformation, they cover or eclipse each other in space. Thus, in staggered form, there is minimum repulsive forces, minimum energy and maximum stability of the molecule. **(2)**

3. (i) 3, 5-dimethyl-2-hexene or 3,5-dimethylhex-2-ene **(1/2)**

(ii) 4-chloro-3-methylcyclopentene **(1/2)**

(iii) 1-*sec*-butyl-2-methylcyclohexene or 1-methyl-2-(1-methylpropyl) cyclohexene **(1/2)**

(iv) 2-pentyl-1-heptene or 2-pentylhept-1-ene **(1/2)**

4. Structure of 2-methylbutane is

$\overset{1}{C}H_3-\overset{2}{C}H(CH_3)-\overset{3}{C}H_2-\overset{4}{C}H_3$

2-methylbutane **(1)**

Put the double bonds at different positions and also satisfy the tetravalency of each carbon atom in the molecule.

$CH_2=C(CH_3)-CH_2-CH_3$, $CH_3-C(CH_3)=CH-CH_3$,

2-methylbut-1-ene, 2-methylbut-2-ene

$CH_3-CH(CH_3)-CH=CH_2$

3-methylbut-1-ene **(1)**

5. Addition of halogen acids to an alkene is an electrophilic addition reaction.

$CH_3-CH=CH_2 + H^+ \xrightarrow[\text{Ist step}]{\text{Slow}} CH_3-\overset{+}{C}H-CH_3$

$\xrightarrow[\text{IInd step}]{X^-,\ \text{fast}} CH_3-CH(X)-CH_3$

First step is slow so, it is rate determining step. The rate of this step depends on the availability of proton. This in turn depends upon the bond dissociation enthalpy of the H—X molecule. Lower the bond dissociation enthalpy of H—X molecule, greater the reactivity of halogen halide.

Since, the bond dissociation energy decreases in the order; HI (296.8 kJ mol^{-1}) < HBr (363.7 kJ mol^{-1}) < HCl (430.5 kJ mol^{-1}). Therefore, the reactivity of the halogen acids decreases from HI to HCl, i.e. HI > HBr > HCl. **(2)**

6. (*B*) and (*C*) are CH_3CH_2CHO (propanal) and CH_3COCH_3 (propanone). Hence, *A* is

$CH_3CH_2-C(H)=O + O=C(CH_3)-CH_3 \longrightarrow CH_3CH_2CH=C(CH_3)-CH_3$ (*A*)

$\xrightarrow{\text{Ozonolysis}} CH_3CH_2CHO\ (B) + CH_3COCH_3\ (C)$ **(1)**

$CH_3CH_2CH=C(CH_3)-CH_3\ (A) \xrightarrow{\text{Hot } KMnO_4} CH_3CH_2COOH\ (D) + CH_3-C(CH_3)=O\ (C)$ **(1)**

7. (a) $CH_3-CH=CH_2 + HBr \longrightarrow CH_3-CH(Br)-CH_3$

Prop-1-ene; 2-bromopropane **(1)**

(b) $CH_3-C\equiv C-CH_3 + Na \xrightarrow{aq.\ NH_3}$ (CH₃)(H)C=C(H)(CH₃)

2-butyne; *trans*-2-butene **(1)**

8. The combustion reaction of toluene is -

$C_7H_8(g) + 9O_2(g) \xrightarrow{\Delta} 7CO_2 + 4H_2O(g)$ **(2)**

9. Halogens are moderately deactivating group. Because of their strong –*I* effect, overall electron density on benzene ring decreases. However, due to resonance the electron density on *o* and *p*-positions is greater than that at *m*-position. Hence, they are also *o* and *p*-directing groups. **(1)**

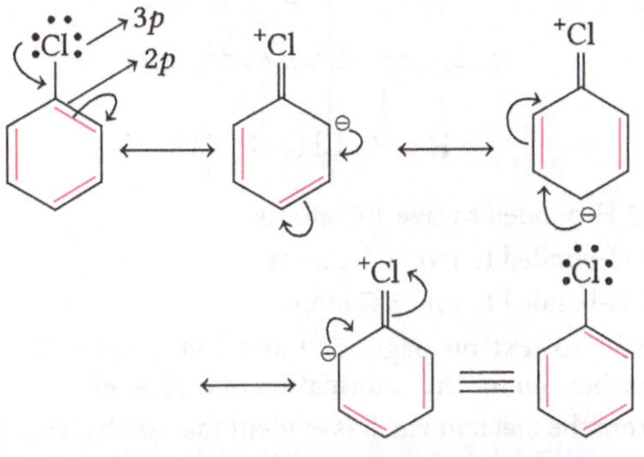

(1)

10. Nitration of benzene is an electrophilic substitution reaction. Presence of electron releasing group such as $-CH_3$ activates the benzene nucleus towards electrophilic substitution while presence of electron withdrawing group such as $—NO_2$ deactivates the benzene nucleus towards electrophilic substitution. **(1)**

Therefore, the ease of nitration decreases in the order

toluene > benzene > *m*-dinitrobenzene.

Thus, toluene will undergo nitration most easily. **(1)**

11. (i) Ethyl bromide on reaction with sodium in the presence of dry ether yields butane. **(0.5)**

$$2C_2H_5Br + 2\,Na \xrightarrow{\text{Dry ether}} \underset{\text{Butane}}{CH_3CH_2CH_2CH_3} + 2NaBr$$ **(1)**

(ii) An aqueous concentrated solution of sodium propanoate on electrolysis yields butane at anode. **(0.5)**

$$2CH_3CH_2COONa\,(aq) + 2H_2O\,(l) \xrightarrow{\text{Electrolysis}} CH_3CH_2CH_2CH_3 + 2CO_2 + H_2 + 2NaOH$$ **(1)**

12. Rotation around C—C single bond is not completely free and it is restricted due to repulsions between the electron clouds of C—H bonds in the adjacent carbon atoms.

Therefore, ethane exists in infinite number of conformations.

Out of these, two extreme conformations are staggered and eclipsed, refer to text on page 351. **(3)**

13. The expanded structures of these alkanes are

(i) 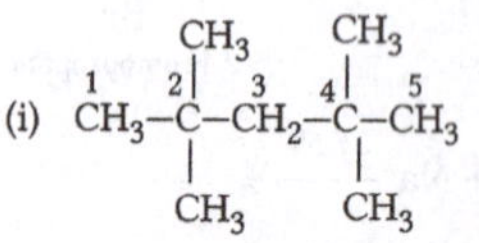

2,2,4, 4-tetramethylpentane **(1)**

(ii) 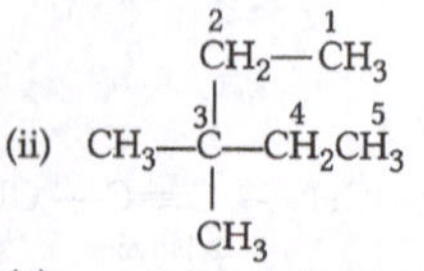

3, 3-dimethylpentane **(1)**

(iii) 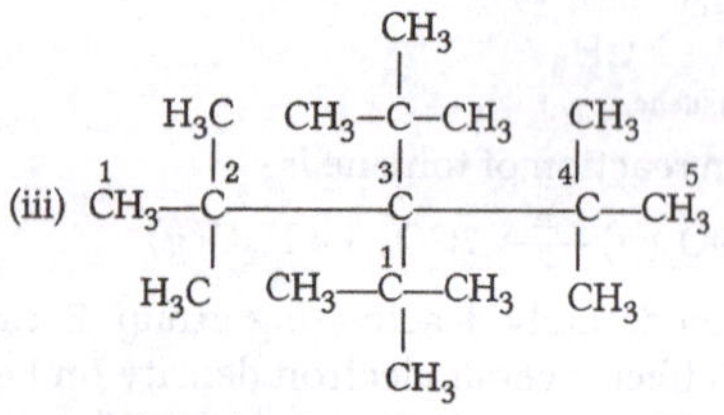

3, 3-di-*tert*-butyl-2,2,4,4-tetramethylpentane or 3,3-*bis* (1, 1-dimethylethyl)-2,2,4,4-tetramethylpentane **(1)**

14. 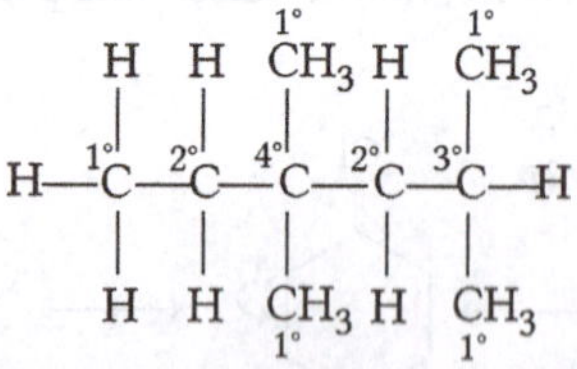

15 H-bonded to five 1°C-atoms **(1)**

4 H-bonded to two 2°C-atoms **(1)**

1 H-bonded to one 3°C-atom **(1)**

15. Refer to text on pages 349 and 350. (Free radical chain mechanism for the chlorination of methane).

From the mechanism, it is evident that methyl free radicals are produced during propagation step. If two methyl free radicals combine with each other a molecule of ethane is formed. **(3)**

16. ***Step* I** Write the structures of the products with their carbonyl group facing one another.

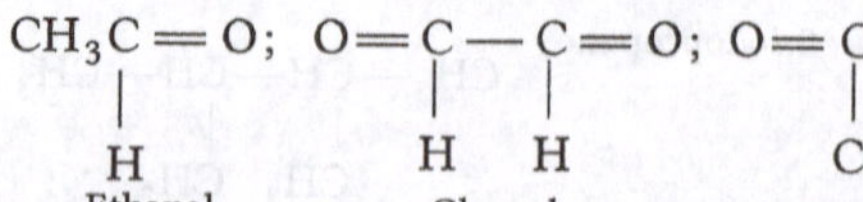

Ethanal   Glyoxal   Propanone **(1.5)**

***Step* II** Remove oxygen and put double bonds between the carbonyl carbons.

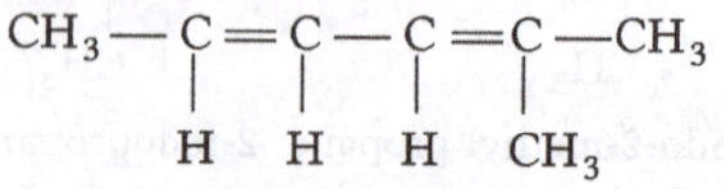

(1.5)

Thus, the compound is **2-methyl-2, 4-hexadiene.**

17. Electron donating alkyl groups make the π-bond more electron rich and more reactive. Conversely, electron withdrawing groups such as Cl make the π-bond more electron deficient and less reactive. The order is **(2)**

$$\underset{\text{(two } CH_3 \text{ groups)}}{CH_3—C(CH_3)=CH_2} > \underset{\text{(one } CH_3 \text{ group)}}{CH_3—CH=CH_2}$$

$$> \underset{\text{(one alkyl group with Cl atom)}}{Cl—CH_2CH=CH_2} > \underset{\text{(Cl is directly bonded to double bonded carbon)}}{CH_2=CH—Cl}$$ **(1)**

18. 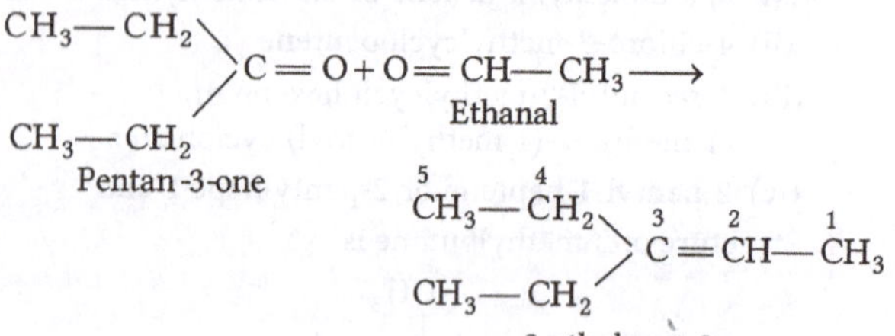

Pentan-3-one   Ethanal

3-ethylpent-2-ene

(*A*) **(3)**

19. (i) Isomers of C_4H_8 having one double bond are

(a) $\overset{4}{C}H_3\overset{3}{C}H_2—\overset{2}{C}H=\overset{1}{C}H_2$

But-1-ene

(b) 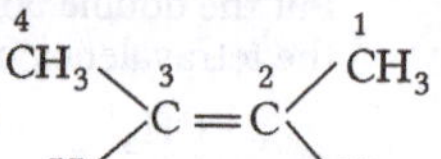

cis-but-2-ene

(c) 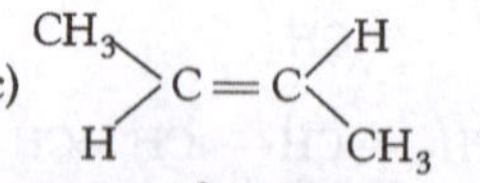

trans-but-2-ene

(d) $CH_3—C(CH_3)=CH_2$

2-methylprop-1-ene **(2)**

(ii) (a) $\overset{5}{C}H_3\,\overset{4}{C}H_2\overset{3}{C}H_2\overset{2}{C}\equiv\overset{1}{C}H$

Pent-1-yne

(b) $\overset{5}{C}H_3\,\overset{4}{C}H_2—\overset{3}{C}\equiv\overset{2}{C}—\overset{1}{C}H_3$

Pent-2-yne

(c) $\overset{4}{C}H_3—\overset{3}{C}H(CH_3)—\overset{2}{C}\equiv\overset{1}{C}H$

3-methylbut-1-yne **(1)**

20. In presence of organic peroxides, the addition of HBr to propene follows anti-Markovnikov's rule (or peroxide effect) to form 1-bromopropane (*n*-propyl bromide)

$$Ph-\overset{O}{\overset{\parallel}{C}}-O-O-\overset{O}{\overset{\parallel}{C}}-Ph \xrightarrow[\text{fission}]{\text{Homolytic}}$$

$$2Ph-\overset{O}{\overset{\parallel}{C}}-\dot{O} \longrightarrow 2Ph^{\bullet} + 2CO_2 \quad \textbf{(1)}$$

$$Ph^{\bullet} + HBr \longrightarrow C_6H_6 + Br^{\bullet}$$

$$H_3C-CH=CH_2 + Br^{\bullet} \xrightarrow{\text{Slow}} \underset{\text{2° Free radical (more stable)}}{H_3C-\dot{C}H-CH_2Br}$$

$$\xrightarrow{\text{H-Br}} \underset{\text{1-bromopropane}}{H_3C-CH_2-CH_2Br} + \dot{B}r \quad \textbf{(1)}$$

However, in absence of peroxides, addition of HBr to propene follows Markovnikov's rule and gives 2-bromopropane as major product.

$$\underset{\text{Propene}}{CH_3-CH=CH_2} + H^+ \xrightarrow{\text{Slow}} \underset{\text{More stable 2° carbocation}}{CH_3-C^+H-CH_3}$$

$$\xrightarrow[\text{Fast}]{Br^-} \underset{\text{2-bromopropane}}{CH_3-\underset{Br}{\underset{|}{CH}}-CH_3} \quad \textbf{(1)}$$

21. Refer to text on page 357 and 358. **(3)**

22. (i) $CH_3-CH=CH-CH_3 + HBr \longrightarrow$

$$\underset{\text{2-bromobutane}}{CH_3-\underset{Br}{\underset{|}{CH}}-CH_2-CH_3} \quad \textbf{(1/2)}$$

(ii) $CH_3-CH=CH-CH_3 + Br_2 \xrightarrow{CCl_4}$

$$\underset{\text{2,3-dibromobutane}}{CH_3-\underset{Br}{\underset{|}{CH}}-\underset{Br}{\underset{|}{CH}}-CH_3} \quad \textbf{(1/2)}$$

23. Resonance and delocalisation of electrons generally lead to the stability of benzene molecule.

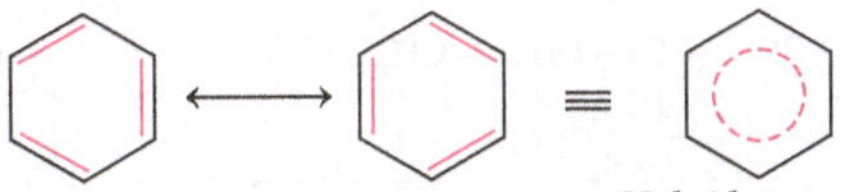

Hybrid structure **(1)**

The dotted circle in the hybrid structure represents the six electrons which are delocalised between the six carbon atoms of the benzene ring. Therefore, presence of delocalised π-electrons in benzene makes it more stable than the hypothetical cyclohexatriene. **(2)**

24. The hybridisation state of carbon in the given compounds is

Benzene ; $\underset{n\text{-hexane}}{CH_3-(CH_2)_4-CH_3}$; $\underset{\text{Ethyne}}{H-C\equiv C-H}$ **(1)**

Type of hybridisation	sp^2	sp^3	sp
s-character	33.33%	25%	50%

(1)

Acidic character increases with increase in *s*-character of the orbital. Hence, decreasing order of acidic behaviour is ethyne > benzene > hexane **(1)**

25. First of all we will derive the molecular formula of alkene, C_nH_{2n}; $12n + 2n = 56$ or $14n = 56$

$\therefore$ $n = 4$ **(1)**

Thus, the molecular formula of alkene is C_4H_8. **(1)**

As it is giving only ethanal on reaction with O_3 followed by reduction, the alkene is symmetrical and its structure is

$$\underset{\text{But-2-ene}}{H-\overset{H}{\underset{H}{C}}-\underset{H}{C}=\underset{H}{C}-\overset{H}{\underset{H}{C}}-H} \quad \textbf{(1)}$$

26.

Structures of $-C_5H_{11}$ group	Corresponding alcohols	Name of alcohol
(i) $CH_3-CH_2-CH_2-CH_2-CH_2-$	$CH_3-CH_2-CH_2-CH_2-CH_2-OH$	Pentan-1-ol
(ii) $CH_3-\underset{\mid}{CH}-CH_2-CH_2-CH_3$	$CH_3-\underset{OH}{\underset{\mid}{CH}}-CH_2-CH_2-CH_3$	Pentan-2-ol
(iii) $CH_3-CH_2-\underset{\mid}{CH}-CH_2-CH_3$	$CH_3-CH_2-\underset{OH}{\underset{\mid}{CH}}-CH_2-CH_3$	Pentan-3-ol
(iv) $CH_3-\overset{CH_3}{\overset{\mid}{CH}}-CH_2-CH_2-$	$CH_3-\overset{CH_3}{\overset{\mid}{CH}}-CH_2-CH_2-OH$	3-methylbutan-1-ol
(v) $CH_3-CH_2-\overset{CH_3}{\overset{\mid}{CH}}-CH_2-$	$CH_3-CH_2-\overset{CH_3}{\overset{\mid}{CH}}-CH_2-OH$	2-methylbutan-1-ol

Structures of $-C_5H_{11}$ group	Corresponding alcohols	Name of alcohol
(vi) $CH_3-\overset{CH_3}{\underset{\vert}{\overset{\vert}{C}}}-CH_2-CH_3$	$CH_3-\overset{CH_3}{\underset{OH}{\overset{\vert}{C}}}-CH_2-CH_3$	2-methylbutan-2-ol
(vii) $CH_3-\overset{CH_3}{\underset{CH_3}{\overset{\vert}{C}}}-CH_2-$	$CH_3-\overset{CH_3}{\underset{CH_3}{\overset{\vert}{C}}}-CH_2OH$	2,2-dimethyl propan-1-ol
(viii) $CH_3-\overset{CH_3}{\overset{\vert}{CH}}-\overset{\vert}{C}H-CH_3$	$CH_3-\overset{CH_3}{\overset{\vert}{CH}}-\overset{OH}{\overset{\vert}{CH}}-CH_3$	3-methylbutan-2-ol

(5)

27. Solve as in question 18 of SA (3 marks). (1)

(i) propanal + ethanal (1)

(ii) pentan-2-one + butan-2-one (1)

(iii) pentan-2-one + methanal (1)

(iv) propanal + benzaldehyde (1)

28. (i) 2, 8-dimethyldeca-3, 6-diene

σ-bonds $= 33$, π-bonds $= 2$ (2)

(ii) Octa-1, 3, 5, 7-tetraene

σ-bonds $= 17$, π-bonds $= 4$ (1)

(iii) 2-propylpent-1-ene

σ-bonds $= 23$, π-bonds $= 1$ (1)

(iv) 4-ethyl-2, 6-dimethyldec-4-ene

σ-bonds $= 41$, π-bonds $= 1$ (1)

29. 1 mole of alkyne *D* gives 1 mole of sodium alkynide and 1 / 2 mole of H_2. Furthermore, *D* gives straight chain alkane on hydrogenation, and is obtained from five membered compound therefore, *D* must be five membered straight chain terminal alkyne, i.e. 1-pentyne. Since, alkene *B* on reaction with Br_2 forms a compound '*C*' which on dehydrohalogenation, gives 1-pentyne, therefore, '*C*' must be 1,2-dibromopentane and alkene '*B*' must be 1-pentene. Since, alkene '*B*' is obtained by dehydrohalogenation of alkyl halide, therefore, alkyl halide *A* must be 1-bromopentane. Reactions are as follows (3)

$$\underset{\text{1-pentene }(B)}{CH_3CH_2CH_2CH=CH_2} \xrightarrow{Br_2 \text{ in } CS_2}$$

$$\underset{\text{1, 2-dibromopentane }(C)}{CH_3CH_2CH_2-\overset{2}{C}HBr-\overset{1}{C}H_2Br} \xrightarrow[-\,2HBr]{\text{Alc. KOH,}} \underset{\text{1-pentyne }(D)}{CH_3CH_2CH_2C\equiv CH}$$

$$\xrightarrow{\text{Na in liq. } NH_3} \underset{\text{Sodium 1-pentynide}}{CH_3CH_2CH_2C\equiv C^-Na^+} + \frac{1}{2}H_2$$

(2)

30. (i) Since, the two substituents in the benzene ring are present at *p*-position, therefore, the first substituent in the benzene ring should be an *o*, *p*-directing group.

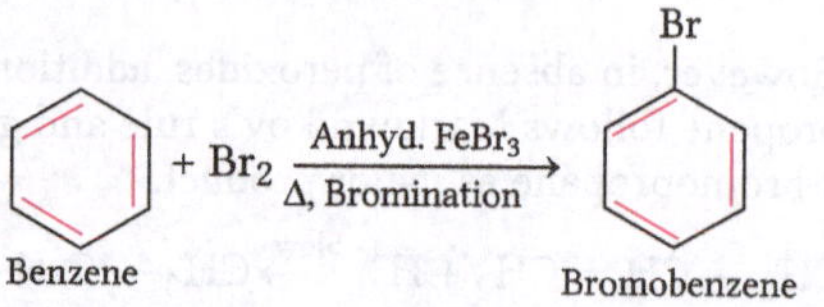

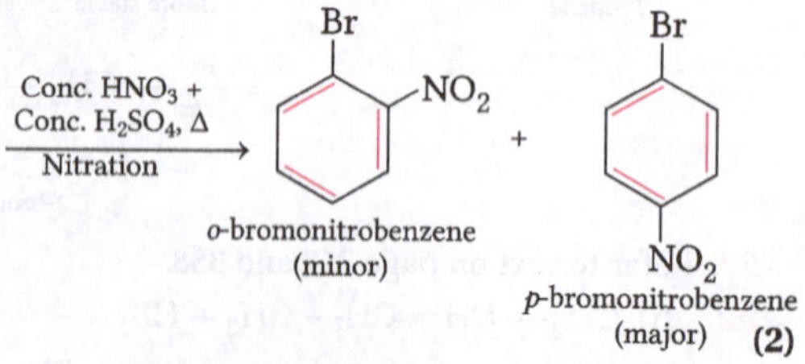

(2)

(ii) Since, the two substituents in the benzene ring are present at *m*-positions, therefore, the first substituent in the benzene ring should be *m*-directing.

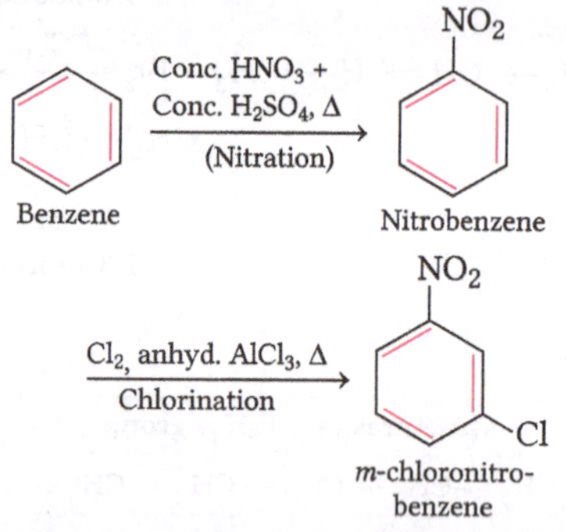

(1)

(iii)

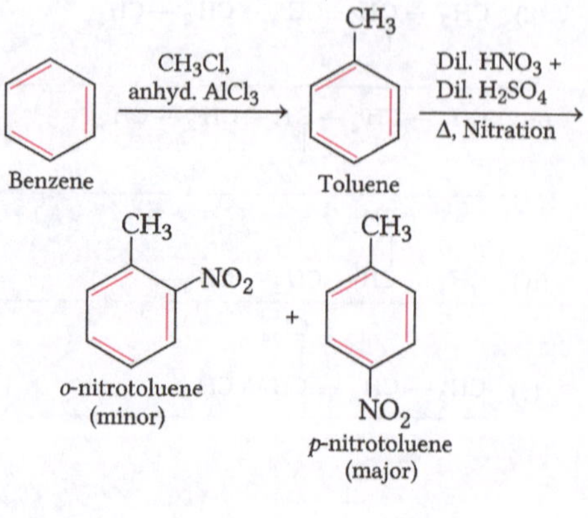

(1)

(iv) Acetophenone can be prepared by Friedel Crafts acylation.

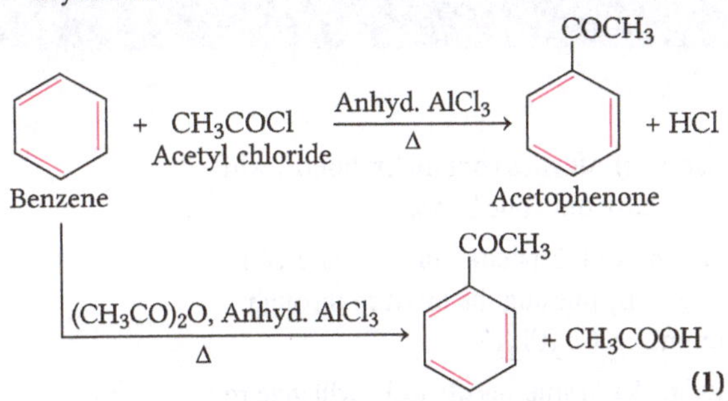

(1)

31. (i) Alkyne X is C_5H_8. Since, it does not react with sodamide or ammoniacal, cuprous chloride, the triple bond cannot be terminal. **(1)**

$\therefore$ X is $CH_3CH_2C \equiv CCH_3$ (Pent-2-yne)

(ii) Hydrocarbon 'Y' is alkene because it decolourises bromine water. From the products of ozonolysis, the structure of alkene can be predicted.

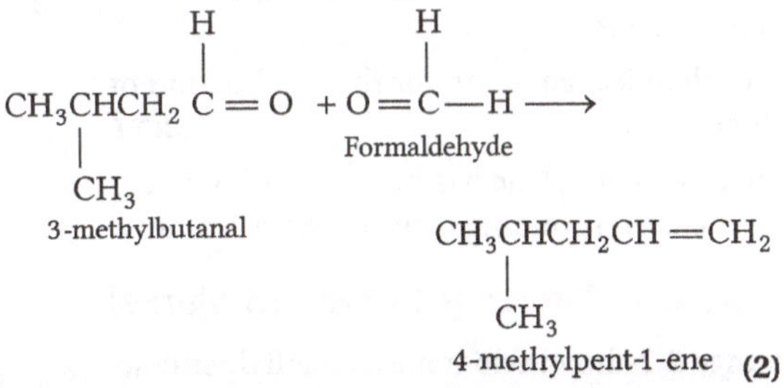

(2)

(iii) Since, it does not decolourise bromine water, it is arene. Its formula is

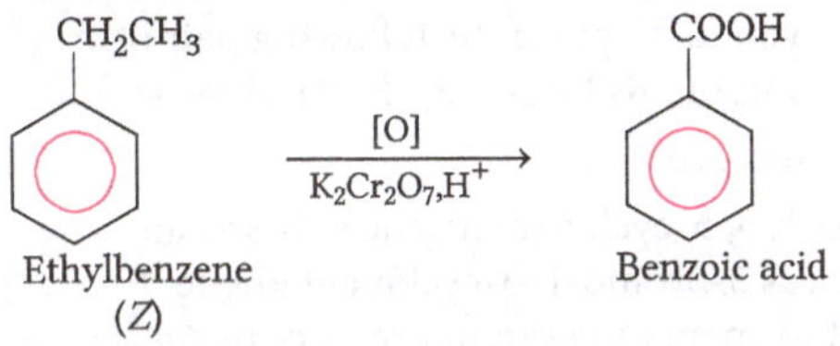

The other three isomers are

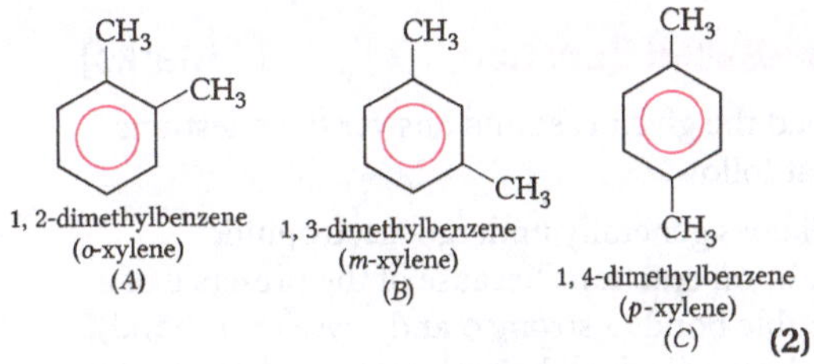

(2)

32.

	Compound	Planar ring	Complete delocalisation of π-electron	Huckel's rule $(4n + 2)\ \pi$ electron	Aromatic or non-aromatic
A.		✓	✓	$6\pi\ e^-$ Huckel's rule obeyed	Aromatic
B.		×	× Incomplete (sp^3-hybrid carbon)	$6\pi e^-$	Non-aromatic
C.		✓	✓	$6\pi e^-$ ($4n$ + 2+lone pair e^-) Huckel's rule verified	Aromatic
D.	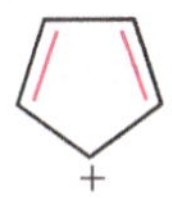	✓	×	$4\pi e^-$	Anti-aromatic
E.	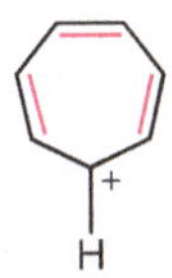	✓	✓	Huckel's rule obeyed	Aromatic
F.		✓	✓	$2\pi e^-$ Huckel's rule verified $n = 0$	Aromatic
G.	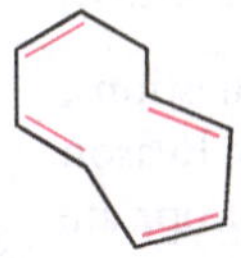	✓	×	$8\pi e^-$ Huckel's rule not verified	Non-aromatic

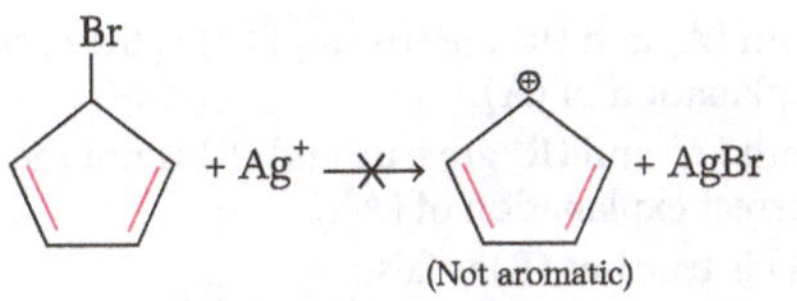

(5)

QR Code for Quick Test 1

QR Code for Quick Test 2

QR Code for Quick Test 3

SELF ASSESSMENT TEST

Objective Type Questions [1 Mark]

1. The possible rotamers of ethane is/are
(a) 2 (b) 3 (c) 4 (d) ∞

2. When $CH_3—C\equiv CH$ reacts with one mole of HBr, then the product obtained is
(a) bromoethene (b) dibromopropane
(c) 2-bromopropene (d) 1-bromopropane

3. Which of the following set of functional groups is *meta*-directing group?
(a) $—NO_2$, $—NH_2$, —COOH, —COOR
(b) $—NO_2$, —CHO, $—SO_3H$, —COR
(c) —CN, —CHO, $—NHCOCH_3$, —COOR
(d) —CN, $—NH_2$, —NHR, $—OCH_3$

4. Which of the following reaction is used to increase the length of the carbon chain?
(a) Wolff Kishner's reaction
(b) Clemmensen reduction
(c) Kolbe's electrolysis
(d) Wurtz reaction

5. Which of the following is not a process of halogenation of alkanes?
(a) Acylation (b) Chlorination
(c) Bromination (d) Iodination

Assertion-Reason [1 Mark]

Directions (Q. Nos. 6-8) In the following questions. an Assertion (A) is followed by a corresponding Reason (R). Use the following keys to choose the appropriate answer.

(a) Both (A) and (R) are true and (R) is the correct explanation of (A).
(b) Both (A) and (R) are true and (R) is not the correct explanation of (A).
(c) (A) is true but (R) is false.
(d) (A) is false but (R) is true.

6. **Assertion** (A) Addition of HBr on 2-butene does not give isomeric products.

Reason (R) Addition of HBr on 2-butene follows Markovnikov's rule.

7. **Assertion** (A) Alkynes are more reactive towards nucleophilic addition reaction as compared to alkenes.

Reason (R) Alkynes contain 2π-bonds, while alkenes have only one bond.

8. **Assertion** (A) Ethylene can be separated from acetylene by pussing the mixture through ammoniacal Cu_2Cl_2.

Reason (R) Ammoniacal $CuCl_2$ will give red copper acetylide ppt. with C_2H_2, whereas C_2H_4 will be neutral to ammoniacal Cu_2Cl_2.

Short Answer Type I Questions [2 Marks]

9. Why do hydrocarbon molecules with an odd number of carbon atoms have lower melting points than those with an even number of carbon atoms?

10. Write chemical equation for the combustion of hexyne. **NCERT**

11. Explain why *p*-xylene has higher melting point than the corresponding *ortho* or *meta*-isomers.

Short Answer Type II Questions [3 Marks]

12. Arrange 2,2-dimethylbutane, 3-methylpentane and *n*-hexane in increasing order of their boiling point.

13. How will you distinguish the following pair of organic compounds by giving chemical tests?
Propane and propene

14. 7-bromo-1, 3, 5-cycloheptatriene exists as an ion whereas 5-bromo-1, 3-cyclopentadiene does not form an ion even in presence of Ag^+. Explain.

Case-Based Question [4 Marks]

15. Read the given case and answer the questions that follow.

Alkenes generally undergo electrophilic addition reactions because of the presence of a double bond (a strong σ and a weaker π-bond), π-electrons which being loosely held are easily polarised. These reactions involve cleavage of a π-bond and formation of two new σ-bonds.

In polar solvents, addition proceed by ionic mechanism (at low temperature), whereas in the presence of light or non-polar solvents, the addition occurs by free radical mechanism (at high temperature).

Apart from addition reactions alkenes also participate in the oxidation, ozonolysis and polymerisation reaction.

(i) Give the reaction of 1-butene with HBr in the presence of a peroxide.

(ii) Name the organic products of the reaction of but -2-ene with bromine dissolved in tetrachloromethane

(iii) Addition of unsymmetrical reagent to unsymmetrical alkene takes place according to which rule?

(iv) Write the reaction of polymerisation of ethylene.

Or

An alkene *A* on ozonolysis gives a mixture of ethanal and pentan-3-one. Write structure and IUPAC name of *A*.

Long Answer Type Questions [5 Marks]

16. (i) Arrange the three isomeric pentanes in order of increasing stability at room temperature.

(ii) Give a method of preparation of propane from (a) an alkene (b) an alkyl halide.

(iii) Write the structure of all the alkenes that can be hydrogenated to form 2-methyl butane.

(iv) Why is light or heat necessary to initiate the chlorination reaction?

17. (i) Write the name of the products and also explain mechanism of the reaction between phenol with concentrated sulphuric acid.

(ii) What happens when chlorine is passed through the boiling toluene?

(iii) Convert the following :

(a) Toluene to benzoic acid

(b) Toluene to benzaldehyde

Answers

1. (d) **2.** (c) **3.** (b) **4.** (d) **5.** (a)
6. (c) **7.** (a) **8.** (a)

10 CHAPTER

To be Assessed Formatively

The s-Block Elements

Elements in which valence or outermost electron enters in the *s*-orbital are called **s-block elements**. This block lies on the extreme left of the periodic table. As *s*-orbital can accommodate a maximum of two electrons, so only two blocks *viz* group 1 (alkali metals) and group 2 (alkaline earth metals) are included in this block. The last member of each group i.e. francium in case of group 1 and radium in case of group 2, being radioactive in nature, occur only in trace quantities.

YOUR STUDY GOALS

YOUR PRACTICE GOAL

- Objective Type Questions
  (23 Qs ; 20 MCQs, 2 A-R & 1 Case Study)
- Subjective Type Questions
  (12 Qs; 7 SA-I, 3 SA-II & 2 LA)

10.1 Group 1 Elements: Alkali Metals

This group include lithium (Li), sodium (Na), potassium(K), rubidium (Rb), caesium (Cs) and francium (Fr). They are collectively called **alkali metals** as they form hydroxides on reaction with water which are strongly alkaline in nature.

Occurrence

The alkali metals occur in nature only in the form of their compounds, i.e. these are never found in free state as these are highly reactive.

Sodium and potassium are the seventh and eighth most abundant elements in the earth's crust. While other elements i.e. lithium, rubidium and caesium are much less abundant. Francium, the longest lived isotope with half-life of 21 minutes occurs only in traces.

10.2 General Characteristics of Group 1 Elements

Atomic Properties of Alkali Metals

The important atomic properties of alkali metals and their trends are as follows

(i) Electronic Configuration

The general electronic configuration of these elements is[inert gas] ns^1 as their penultimate quantum level have stable noble gas electronic configuration.

Electronic Configuration of Alkali Metals

Element	Electronic configuration	
	with inert gas core	Complete
Li (3)	[He] $2s^1$	$1s^2\,2s^1$
Na (11)	[Ne] $3s^1$	$1s^2\,2s^2\,2p^6\,3s^1$
K (19)	[Ar] $4s^1$	$1s^2\,2s^2\,2p^6\,3s^2\,3p^6\,4s^1$
Rb (37)	[Kr] $5s^1$	$1s^2\,2s^2\,2p^6\,3s^2\,3p^6\,3d^{10}\,4s^2\,4p^6\,5s^1$
Cs (55)	[Xe] $6s^1$	$1s^2\,2s^2\,2p^6\,3s^2\,3p^6\,3d^{10}\,4s^2\,4p^6\,4d^{10}\,5s^2\,5p^6\,6s^1$
Fr (87)	[Rn] $7s^1$	$1s^2\,2s^2\,2p^6\,3s^2\,3p^6\,3d^{10}\,4s^2\,4p^6\,4d^{10}\,4f^{14}\,5s^2\,5p^6\,5d^{10}\,6s^2\,6p^6\,7s^1$

Due to the presence of only one electron in the valence shell, they are **paramagnetic** and exhibit only +1 oxidation state, i.e. readily form monovalent M^+ ions by losing this electron. Thus, they never exist in free state in nature.

The alkali metal cations, Li^+, Na^+, K^+, Rb^+ and Cs^+ are **diamagnetic** because of the absence of unpaired electrons. All these cations have stable noble gas configuration.

(ii) Atomic and Ionic Radii

The atomic and ionic radii of alkali metals are largest in the corresponding period. This is because as the atomic number increases along a period, nuclear charge also increases which results in decreased size.

On moving **down the group**, as the atomic number of alkali metals **increases**, their radii also increases because shielding effect predominates over nuclear charge.

The size of monovalent alkali metal ion (M^+), however, is always smaller than its parent atom due to increase in nuclear charge.

(iii) Ionisation Enthalpy

The **first ionisation enthalpy** of alkali metals is **lowest** among corresponding period because atoms of alkali metals are largest in their respective period, therefore outermost electrons that are far away from the nucleus experience a less force of attraction from the nucleus and hence, can be easily removed. However, their **second ionisation enthalpy is very high** (because of inert gas configuration).

On **moving down** the group, ionisation enthalpies **decrease** progressively. This is because the effect of increasing size outweighs the increasing nuclear charge and the outermost electron is very well screened from the nuclear charge.

The ionisation energies of K, Rb and Cs are so less that they exhibit photoelectric effect, i.e. these can emit electrons even with the falling of light on them.

(iv) Hydration Enthalpy

The amount of energy released when one mole of gaseous ions combine with water to form hydrated ions is called the **hydration enthalpy**.

It **decreases** as the size of alkali metal ions **increases**, i.e. the order of hydration enthalpy is

$$Li^+ > Na^+ > K^+ > Rb^+ > Cs^+$$

Thus, Li^+ possesses the maximum degree of hydration and hence most of its salts are hydrated.

e.g. $LiCl \cdot 2H_2O$, $Li_2CO_3 \cdot 3H_2O$, etc.

As a consequence of hydration enthalpy, the ionic size of these ions in aqueous solution follows the order

$$Li^+ > Na^+ > K^+ > Rb^+ > Cs^+$$

Hence, among alkali metal ions, **Cs^+ has the highest and Li^+ has the lowest mobility in aqueous solution.**

(v) Electropositive or Metallic Character

Alkali metals are the **most electropositive** elements in the periodic table and their metallic character **increases** on moving **down the group** as the tendency to lose the valence electron increases.

These all are metals and thus, are good conductors of heat and electricity.

They exhibit metallic lustre due to the oscillation of free electrons.

Physical Properties of Alkali Metals

The physical properties of alkali metals are as follows

(i) Physical Appearance

They are all silvery white, soft and malleable metals. They are so soft that they can easily be cut with a knife. The reason for softness of alkali metals is the presence of weak metallic bonding because of the presence of only one valence electron in them. This softness increases down the group.

(ii) Density

Because of their large size, alkali metals have low densities. Li, Na and K are even lighter than water. The density of these elements increases on moving down the group from Li to Cs but **potassium is lighter than sodium** due to increase in its atomic volume. Li is the lightest metal known.

(iii) Melting and Boiling Point

Since, the metallic bonding between these elements is weak, so these elements have low melting and boiling points. The melting and boiling point decreases on moving down the group due to decrease in the extent of metallic bonding.

(iv) Flame Colouration

Alkali metals and their salts (mainly chlorides) give characteristic colour to the oxidising flame as their losely bound valence electron gets excited to the higher energy level by the heat energy of flame.

When it comes to its original state (ground state), it emit radiations in the visible region, which gives characteristic colours to the flame e.g.

Metal	Li	Na	K	Rb	Cs
Colour	Crimson red	Yellow	Violet	Red violet	Blue
λ/nm	670.8	589.2	766.5	780.0	455.5

Because of their tendency of giving characteristic colours to the flame, these can be detected by the respective flame tests and can be determined by flame photometry or atomic absorption spectroscopy.

Due to this property, caesium and potassium act as electrodes in photoelectric cells.

Atomic and Physical Properties of the Alkali Metals

Property	Lithium (Li)	Sodium (Na)	Potassium (K)	Rubidium (Rb)	Caesium (Cs)	Francium (Fr)
Occurrence in lithosphere*	18 ppm	2.27 (% by wt)	1.84 (% by wt)	78-12 ppm	2-6 ppm	$\sim 10^{-18}$ ppm
Atomic number	3	11	19	37	55	87
Atomic mass (g mol^{-1})	6.94	22.99	39.10	85.47	132.91	(223)
Ionisation enthalpy /kJ mol^{-1}	520	496	419	403	376	~ 375
Hydration enthalpy /kJ mol^{-1}	– 506	– 406	– 330	– 310	– 276	–
Metallic radius / pm	152	186	227	248	265	–
Ionic radius M^+/pm	76	102	138	152	167	(180)
Density/g cm^{-3}	0.53	0.97	0.86	1.53	1.90	–
mp/K	454	371	336	312	302	–
bp/K	1615	1156	1032	961	944	–
Standard potentials $E°$/V for (M^+/M)	– 3.04	– 2.714	– 2.925	– 2.930	– 2.927	–

* Lithosphere : The earth's outer layer; its crust and part of the upper mantle.

Chemical Properties of Alkali Metals

The alkali metals are highly reactive due to larger size and low ionisation enthalpy therefore they never occur in free state. The reactivity of metals increases down the group.

(i) Reactivity towards Air

Alkali metals get tarnished when exposed to dry or moist air due to formation of oxide in dry air which gets converted into hydroxides and carbonates in presence of moist air.

$$4M(s) + O_2(g) \longrightarrow 2M_2O(s)$$
$$M_2O(s) + H_2O(l) \longrightarrow 2MOH(aq)$$
$$2MOH(aq) + CO_2(g) \longrightarrow M_2CO_3(aq) + H_2O(l)$$
$$(M = \text{alkali metal})$$

Thus, in order to protect these metals from exposure to air, these must be stored at a place where air is not present. When these metals are heated in excess of air or oxygen, they burn vigorously to form different oxides depending upon the nature of metal.

e.g. Lithium forms monoxide, sodium forms mainly peroxide, the other metals form superoxides. The superoxide O_2^- ion is stable only in the presence of large cations such as K, Rb, Cs.

$$4\,Li + O_2 \longrightarrow 2\,Li_2O \text{ (oxide)}$$
$$2\,Na + O_2 \longrightarrow Na_2O_2 \text{ (peroxide)}$$
$$M + O_2 \longrightarrow MO_2 \text{ (superoxide)}$$
$$\text{(where, } M = \text{K, Rb, Cs)}$$

In all these reactions alkali metals are oxidised from their 0 to +1 oxidation state. Lithium, however, also reacts with nitrogen of air forming lithium nitride Li_3N.

$$6\,Li + N_2 \longrightarrow \underset{\text{Lithium nitride}}{2\,Li_3N}$$

(ii) Reactivity towards Water or Other Proton Releasing Substance

Alkali metals react with water to give metal hydroxide and dihydrogen (hydrogen gas).

$$2M + 2H_2O \longrightarrow 2M^+ + 2OH^- + H_2\uparrow$$

They also react with other **protonic substances** like alcohol, gaseous ammonia and alkynes to give metal compound and hydrogen gas. e.g.

$$2C_2H_5OH + 2Na \longrightarrow \underset{\text{Sodium ethoxide}}{2C_2H_5\overset{-}{O}\overset{+}{N}a} + H_2(g)$$
$$2Na(s) + 2NH_3(g) \longrightarrow \underset{\text{Sodamide}}{2NaNH_2(s)} + H_2(g)$$
$$HC\equiv CH(g) + 2\,Na(s) \longrightarrow \underset{\text{Disodium acetylide}}{\overset{+}{N}a\overset{-}{C}\equiv \overset{-}{C}\overset{+}{N}a(s)} + H_2(g)$$

Lithium because of its small size and very high hydration energy is less reactive than sodium towards the reaction with alkyne, however, its $E°$ value is more negative than sodium. Other elements of the group react explosively with water.

This is because the generated heat often ignites dihydrogen produced.

TEACHER'S TIP

In order to protect alkali metals from direct contact with air and water, they are stored in hydrocarbon solvents like kerosene oil, petroleum, ether, hexane, etc. Lithium because of its low density, floats over these solvents and usually comes in contact with air, that's why it is kept wrapped in paraffin wax.

(iii) Reactivity towards Dihydrogen

Alkali metals react directly with hydrogen gas at about 673 K (Li at 1073 K) to form their ionic hydrides, melting points of which is very high because of the presence of intercolumbic forces of attraction between the metal atom and hydride ion.

$$2M(s) + H_2(g) \longrightarrow 2M^+H^-(s)$$

(iv) Reactivity towards Halogens

Alkali metals react vigorously with halogens (elements of group 17, i.e. fluorine, chlorine, bromine and iodine) to give alkali metal halides of the type M^+X^-. These compounds are ionic in nature with the exception of halides of lithium as polarisation power of lithium is highest because of its small size.Thus, halides of lithium are generally covalent and among them, LiI is the most covalent because of high polarisability of I^- ion. [Recall from chapter 4, according to Fajans' rule, covalent character varies inversely with size of cation and directly with size of anion.]

(v) Reducing Nature

It depends upon the value of standard electrode potential or standard reduction electrode potential ($E°$ or $E°_{red}$).

Higher the negative value of $E°$, more will be the reducing nature. Electrode potential is a measure of the tendency of an element to lose electrons in the aqueous solution. It mainly depends upon the following three factors, i.e.

(a) $Li(s) \longrightarrow Li(g)$; Sublimation enthalpy

(b) $Li(g) \longrightarrow Li^+(g) + e^-$; Ionisation enthalpy

(c) $Li^+(g) + H_2O \longrightarrow Li^+(aq)$; Enthalpy of hydration

With the small size of its ion, lithium has the highest hydration enthalpy. However, ionisation enthalpy of Li is highest among alkali metals but hydration enthalpy predominates over ionisation enthalpy. Therefore, lithium is the strongest reducing agent in aqueous solution. Among other elements of the group, $E°$ is least negative for sodium and hence, sodium has the least reducing tendency.

Example **The $E°$ for Cl_2/Cl^- is + 1.36, for I_2/I^- is + 0.53, for Ag^+/Ag is + 0.79, Na^+/Na is – 2.71 and for Li^+/Li is – 3.04. Arrange the following ionic species in decreasing order of reducing strength : I^-, Ag, Cl^-, Li, Na.** **NCERT**

Sol. The decreasing order of $E°$ values is

$$\underset{(1.36)}{Cl_2/Cl^-} > \underset{(0.79)}{Ag^+/Ag} > \underset{(0.53)}{I_2/I^-} > \underset{(-2.71)}{Na^+/Na} > \underset{(-3.04)}{Li^+/Li}$$

As we know, more is the negative value of $E°$, higher is the reducing strength. Thus, the correct order of reducing strength is : $Li > Na > I^- > Ag > Cl^-$.

(vi) Solution in Liquid Ammonia

Alkali metals when dissolved in liquid ammonia gives deep blue solution, which is paramagnetic and conducting in nature. This solution also behaves as a good reducing agent.

$$M + (x+y)NH_3 \longrightarrow \underset{\text{Ammoniated cations}}{[M(NH_3)_x]^+} + 2\underset{\text{Ammoniated electrons}}{[e(NH_3)_y]^-}$$

The ammoniated electrons are responsible for the blue colour of the solution as they absorb the energy from visible region of light and thus, imparts blue colour to the solution. Under anhydrous conditions or in the presence of impurities, the blue solution gets decomposed to give metal amide and dihydrogen. However, in the absence of these conditions, the solution can be stored for several days.

$$M^+_{(am)} + e^- + NH_3\,(l) \longrightarrow MNH_{2(am)} + \frac{1}{2}H_2(g)$$

$$Na^+_{(am)} + e^- + NH_3(l) \longrightarrow \underset{\text{Sodium amide}}{NaNH_{2(am)}} + \frac{1}{2}H_2(g)$$

(here, *am* indicates the solution in ammonia).

If the solution of alkali metal in liquid ammonia is concentrated, following changes are observed.

- Its colour becomes copper bronze and the solution acquires metallic lustre because of the formation of metal ion clusters.
- The solution becomes diamagnetic because of the grouping of ammoniated electrons of opposite spins, together.
- The conductivity and reducing tendency of the solution decreases as free electrons are bounded with ammoniated metal cations, which are now called **expanded metals.**

Uses of Alkali Metals

Alkali metals are very important for us in several field. Some of their important applications are given below.

Uses of Lithium

The applications of lithium are as follows

- Lithium is used for making alloys, e.g. its alloy with lead is called 'white metal' and is used to make bearings for motor engines and sheets for cables.
  Its alloy with aluminium, because of high tensile strength and elasticity, is used for making aircraft parts. Its alloys with magnesium (14% Li) being extremely tough and corrosion resistant, is used for making armour plates.
- It is used in thermonuclear reactions and electro-chemical cell (i.e., batteries).
- It is also used for the synthesis of compounds that are very useful for us e.g. Li_2CO_3 is used for making a variety of tough waterproof glass. $Li(OH)_2$ is used for absorbing CO_2, $LiHCO_3$ and lithium salicylate are used for treating rheumatism as the lithium urate formed is soluble in water.
  $LiAlH_4$ is a good reducing agent and is widely used in organic synthesis.

Uses of Sodium

The important uses of sodium are as follows.

- It is alloyed with lead (Na/Pb alloy) to make $PbEt_4$ and $PbMe_4$, which were earlier used as anti-knock additives to petrol.
- Liquid sodium metal or its alloy with potassium is used as a coolant in fast breeder nuclear reactors.
- Sodium metal is also used in sodium vapour lamp.

- It being a good reductant is used in the extraction of boron and silicon.

  It also catalysed some important organic synthesis reactions like synthesis of fats from oils, Wurtz reaction, etc.

Uses of Potassium

Important uses of potassium are as follows

- It plays a key role in biological systems.
- It is used in the synthesis of many important compounds e.g. potassium chloride is used as a fertilizer; potassium hydroxide in the manufacture of soft soap, it is also used as an excellent absorbent for CO_2; potassium nitrate in ceramics, colour TV tubes and fluorescent light tubes.

Uses of Caesium

It is used in devising photoelectric cells.

10.3 Anomalous Properties of Lithium

Lithium because of its very small atomic and ionic radii, high polarising power (i.e. charge/radius ratio) and non-availability of *d*-orbitals differs from rest of the members of the group in several respects, however, it shows resemblance in some of its properties with magnesium which is placed diagonally opposite to it (diagonal relationship).

Points of Difference between Lithium and other Alkali Metals

Lithium differs from other alkali metals in the following respects.

- Lithium is the hardest of all the alkali metals.
- The melting and boiling points of lithium are highest among the group.
- Lithium form monoxide, with oxygen while sodium forms peroxide Na_2O_2 and other alkali metal form superoxide, MO_2.
- Lithium is less reactive and on combustion, unlike other alkali metals, it forms nitride along with monoxide (Li_2O).

$$6\,Li + N_2 \longrightarrow 2\,Li_3N$$

- Lithium is the strongest reducing agent among the group.
- Lithium hydroxide on heating decomposes to form lithium oxide while other alkali metal hydroxides do not.

$$2\,LiOH \longrightarrow Li_2O + H_2O$$

Further, lithium carbonate on heating decomposes to give CO_2 while other alkali metal carbonates do not

$$Li_2CO_3 \longrightarrow Li_2O + CO_2$$

- Lithium does not react with ethyne (acetylene) to form lithium ethynide (acetylide) while all other alkali metals react to form the corresponding alkynides.

$$\underset{\text{Acetylene}}{2Na + HC{\equiv}CH} \xrightarrow[196\text{ K}]{\text{Liquid NH3}} \underset{\substack{\text{Disodium}\\\text{acetylide}}}{Na^+C^-{\equiv}C^-Na^+} + H_2$$

- $LiHCO_3$ is known in solution but not in solid state while the bicarbonates of other alkali metals are known in solid state.
- Fluorides, oxides, phosphates, oxalate and carbonates of Li are sparingly soluble while that of other metals are freely soluble.
- $LiNO_3$ on heating gives a mixture of Li_2O, NO_2 and O_2 while nitrates of rest of alkali metals yield nitrite and oxygen.

$$4\,LiNO_3 \xrightarrow{\Delta} 2\,Li_2O + 4\,NO_2\uparrow + O_2\uparrow$$

$$2NaNO_3 \longrightarrow NaNO_2 + O_2\uparrow \text{ (thermally stable)}$$

- Li_2SO_4 is the only alkali metal sulphate which does not form double salts, e.g. alum.
- LiCl is highly deliquescent and soluble in alcohol and pyridine. LiCl separates out from aqueous solution as hydrated crystals of $LiCl\cdot 2H_2O$ whereas chlorides of other alkali metals are insoluble in organic solvents and do not form hydrated crystals under ordinary temperature.
- Only lithium combines with carbon and forms carbide whereas other alkali metals do not react with carbon directly.

$$2\,Li + 2C \xrightarrow{\text{Heat}} \underset{\substack{\text{Dilithium}\\\text{acetylide}}}{Li^+C^-{\equiv}C^-Li^+}$$

Quick Test 1

1. Why are alkali metals not found in nature? NCERT
2. Explain, why is sodium less reactive than potassium? NCERT
3. Which colours are imparted to flame when the following elements are introduced in the flame one by one?
   (i) Strontium (ii) Barium (iii) Calcium
4. Why are potassium and caesium, rather than lithium used in photoelectric cells? NCERT
5. What is the oxidation state of K in KO_2? NCERT
6. Sodium fire in the laboratory should not be extinguished by pouring water. Why?
7. How would you explain LiI is more soluble than KI in ethanol?
8. Why is LiF almost insoluble in water whereas LiCl is soluble not only in water but also in acetone? NCERT
9. Lithium is the only alkali metal that forms nitride directly on reaction with air. Explain.

For Solutions, See QR Code on Pg. 401

10.4 Group 2 Elements : Alkaline Earth Metals

In this group, the elements present are beryllium (Be), magnesium (Mg), calcium (Ca), strontium (Sr), barium (Ba) and radium (Ra).

Except beryllium, all are collectively called **alkaline earth metals** because of the alkaline nature of their oxides and hydroxides and the occurrence of their oxides in the earth's crust (the thin rocky outer layer of the earth).

The first element beryllium differs from the rest of the members and shows diagonal relationship with aluminium.

Occurrence

These elements occur in the form of silicates, sulphates, carbonates and phosphates. Calcium and magnesium are the fifth and sixth most abundant elements in the earth's crust.

Strontium and barium, however, occur in lesser quantities. Beryllium exists in small quantities as silicate minerals like beryl $Be_3Al_2Si_6O_{18}$ and phenacite Be_2SiO_4.

Radium being radioactive, is the extremely scrare and comprises only 10^{-10}% of igneous rocks [the rocks formed from magma (molten rock) that has cooled and hardened].

10.5 General Characteristics of Group 2 Elements

Atomic Properties of Alkaline Earth Metals

(i) Electronic Configuration

The general electronic configuration of these elements is [inert gas] ns^2.

Some of the examples are tabulated below

Electronic Configuration of Alkaline Earth Metals

Element with their atomic number	Electronic configuration with inert gas core	Complete electronic configuration
Be (4)	[He] $2s^2$	$1s^2\,2s^2$
Mg (12)	[Ne] $3s^2$	$1s^2\,2s^2\,2p^6\,3s^2$
Ca (20)	[Ar] $4s^2$	$1s^2\,2s^2\,2p^6\,3s^2\,3p^6\,4s^2$
Sr (38)	[Kr] $5s^2$	$1s^2\,2s^2\,2p^6\,3s^2\,3p^6\,3d^{10}\,4s^2\,4p^6\,5s^2$
Ba (56)	[Xe] $6s^2$	$1s^2\,2s^2\,2p^6\,3s^2\,3p^6\,3d^{10}\,4s^2\,4p^6\,4d^{10}\,5s^2\,5p^6\,6s^2$
Ra (88)	[Rn] $7s^2$	$1s^2\,2s^2\,2p^6\,3s^2\,3p^6\,3d^{10}\,4s^2\,4p^6\,4d^{10}\,4f^{14}\,5s^2\,5p^6\,5d^{10}\,6s^2\,6p^6\,7s^2$

Because of the presence of two electrons in the valence shell, they are diamagnetic and exhibit only +2 oxidation state, i.e. form divalent M^{2+} ions by losing these two valence electrons. After losing these valence electrons, they acquire the configuration of nearest noble gas. The compounds of these elements are predominantly ionic.

(ii) Atomic and Ionic Radii

Along the period, atomic and ionic radii of these elements are smaller than the corresponding alkali metals because of the increased nuclear charge. On moving down the group, the atomic and ionic radii increases because of the addition of an extra shell of electrons in the succeeding element and the increasing screening effect.

(iii) Ionisation Enthalpy

The ionisation enthalpy of alkaline earth metals are low because of their fairly large size in the respective period. But these are higher than the ionisation enthalpies of alkali metals as alkali metals are larger in size and have less nuclear charge as compared to alkaline earth metals. On moving down the group, ionisation enthalpy decreases due to increase in screening or shielding effect.

However, in case of second ionisation enthalpy, the value is more for alkali metals as compared to corresponding alkaline earth metal. This is because after losing one electron, the alkali metals acquire stable electronic configuration, from which removal of another electron is difficult but in case of alkaline earth metal, the loss of one electron gives ns^1 configuration, from which electron can be removed comparatively easily.

TEACHER'S TIP
Remember that the second ionisation enthalpy of an element is always larger than its first ionisation enthalpy because of the increased nuclear charge.

(iv) Hydration Enthalpy

Like alkali metal, their hydration enthalpy also decreases as the size of alkaline earth metal ion increases, i.e. $Be^{2+} > Mg^{2+} > Ca^{2+} > Sr^{2+} > Ba^{2+}$

However, the hydration enthalpy of alkaline earth metal ions are higher than those of alkali metal ions as alkaline earth metal ions are smaller in size as compared to alkali metal ions. Thus, the compounds of alkaline earth metals are more extensively hydrated as compared to those of alkali metals. e.g. $MgCl_2$ and $CaCl_2$ exist in the form of $MgCl_2 \cdot 6H_2O$ and $CaCl_2 \cdot 6H_2O$ but such hydrates are not known for the compounds of alkali metals like NaCl and KCl.

(v) Dipositive oxidation state (M^{2+})

The alkaline earth metals have two electrons more than the nearest gas configuration therefore they can easily lose these two electrons to form divalent cations, thus alkaline earth metals uniformly show an oxidation state of +2.

Physical Properties of Alkaline Earth Metals

Alkaline earth metals exhibit the following physical properties.

(i) Physical State

These are silvery white metals that have metallic lustre. But beryllium and magnesium are greyish. These are soft metals (i.e. can be cut by knife) but comparatively harder than the alkali metals due to the stronger metallic bonding (because of the presence of more electrons) as compared to the alkali metals.

(ii) Melting and Boiling Points

The melting and boiling points are not regular in the group, mainly due to different crystal structures of the metals. However, these are higher than those of alkali metals due to their smaller sizes.

(iii) Density

Their density does not show any regular trend but in general, these are more denser than alkali metals because of the greater strength of metallic bond and more closely packed crystal structure. Their density generally decreases from Be to Ca and then increases from Ca to Ba.

(iv) Flame Colouration

Like alkali metals, these elements also impart characteristic colours to the flame. This is because their valence electron get excited to the higher energy level by the energy of flame.

When they drop back to their original state, they emit energy in the form of visible light. The colour imparted by calcium, strontium and barium are respectively red, crimson and apple green. However, Mg and Be, being smaller in size and because of their high ionisation enthalpy, do not impart colour as electrons are very tightly bound and a large amount of energy is required to excite them.

(v) Electrical and Thermal Conductivities

Being metallic in nature, these elements are good conductor of heat and electricity. The general and atomic properties of alkaline earth metals are summarised in the following table.

Atomic and Physical Properties of the Alkaline Earth Metals

Property	Beryllium (Be)	Magnesium (Mg)	Calcium (Ca)	Strontium (Sr)	Barium (Ba)	Radium (Ra)
Occurrence in lithosphere	2 ppm	2.76% by wt	4.6% by wt	384 ppm	390 ppm	10^{-6} ppm
Atomic number	4	12	20	38	56	88
Atomic mass (g mol^{-1})	9.01	24.31	40.08	87.62	137.33	226.03
Metallic radius/pm	111	160	197	215	222	—
Ionic radius M^{2+}/pm	31	72	100	118	135	148
Ionisation enthalpy (I)/kJ mol^{-1}	899	737	590	549	503	509
Ionisation enthalpy (II)/kJ mol^{-1}	1757	1450	1145	1064	965	979
Hydration enthalpy (kJ/mol)	− 2494	− 1921	− 1577	− 1443	− 1305	—
mp/K	1560	924	1124	1062	1002	973
bp/K	2745	1363	1767	1655	2078	(1973)
Density/g cm^{-3}	1.84	1.74	1.55	2.63	3.59	(5.5)
Standard reduction potential $E°/V$ for (M^{2+}/M)	− 1.97	− 2.36	− 2.84	−2.89	− 2.92	− 2.92
Flame colour	—	—	Brick red	Crimson	Apple green	Crimson

(vi) Nature of Bonds Formed

Like alkali metals, alkaline earth metals predominantly form ionic compounds which are however, less ionic than the corresponding alkali metal compounds. The tendency to form ionic compounds increases down the group. The first member form covalent compounds. Mg also show some tendency for covalency. All other elements form ionic compound.

Chemical Properties of Alkaline Earth Metals

The strong tendency to lose their valence electrons makes, alkaline earth metals highly reactive and the reactivity increases on moving down the group due to increase in size and decrease in ionisation enthalpy.

Further, the ionisation enthalpies of alkaline earth metals are higher than that of alkali metals, so these are less reactive as compared to alkali metals in their chemical reactions.

Some important chemical reactions given by alkali earth metals are as follows

(i) Reactivity towards Air

The first two members of the family, i.e. beryllium and magnesium are kinetically inert towards oxygen because of the formation of a layer of their oxide on their surface. The other members of the group, however, are reactive towards air and give their oxides and nitrides.

On heating in excess of air, beryllium burns brilliantly to give beryllium oxide (BeO) and beryllium nitride (Be_3N_2). Magnesium being more electropositive burns with dazzling brilliance to give its oxide and nitride (i.e. MgO and Mg_3N_2). Calcium, strontium and barium are readily attacked by air to form the oxide and nitride.

(ii) Reactivity towards Water

As compared to alkali metals, alkaline earth metals have less tendency to react with water.

Be shows no reaction with water (cold as well as hot in the form of steam); Mg does not react with cold water, i.e. it reacts with hot water (steam) only to give its hydroxide while rest of the members react with cold water to give their hydroxide and hydrogen gas.

$$Ca + 2H_2O \longrightarrow Ca(OH)_2 + H_2 \uparrow$$

Like, alkali metal hydroxides, these hydroxides are basic in nature.

(iii) Reactivity towards Halogen

Alkaline earth metals combine with halogen at elevated temperature to give halides of the type MX_2 (where, M = alkaline earth metal and X = halogen).

$$M + X_2 \longrightarrow MX_2$$

(iv) Reactivity towards Hydrogen

Alkaline earth metals except beryllium when heated with hydrogen form hydride of the type MH_2.

$$M + H_2 \xrightarrow{\Delta} \underset{\text{Alkaline earth metal hydride}}{MH_2} \quad (M = \text{Mg, Ca, Sr, Ba})$$

BeH_2, however, is obtained by treating beryllium chloride with $LiAlH_4$ (which is a stronger reductant).

$$2\,BeCl_2 + LiAlH_4 \longrightarrow 2\,BeH_2 + LiCl + AlCl_3$$

All the hydrides of alkaline earth metals react with water to give dihydrogen.

$$MH_2 + 2\,H_2O \longrightarrow M(OH)_2 + 2\,H_2$$

This reaction shows that these compounds have reducing nature.

(v) Reactivity towards Acids

Being highly reactive, these elements displace hydrogen from mineral acids like HCl, H_2SO_4, etc.

$$M + 2HCl \longrightarrow MCl_2 + H_2$$

$$Mg + 2HNO_3(5\%) \longrightarrow Mg(NO_3)_2 + H_2$$

Except Mg, other members of the group do not give H_2 with HNO_3.

(vi) Reducing Nature

The standard reduction potential ($E°$) for these elements are highly negative and the negative value increases on moving down the group. Thus, these elements are good reductants and their reducing power increases on moving down the group from Be to Ba. Therefore, $E°$ is least negative for Be.

However, its reducing behaviour is because of the large hydration energy associated with the small Be^{2+} ion and relatively large value of the atomisation enthalpy of the metal.

Further because of their higher ionisation enthalpies and less negative electrode potentials than the corresponding alkali metals, the alkaline earth metals are weaker reducing agents than alkali metals.

(vii) Solutions in Liquid Ammonia

Like alkali metals, these elements also dissolve in liquid ammonia to give deep blue black solutions because of the formation of ammoniated ions, which can be recoverd from the solutions.

$$M + (x + 2y)NH_3 \longrightarrow [M(NH_3)_x]^{2+} + 2\,[e(NH_3)_y]^-$$

In concentrated form, the colour of these solutions become bronze because of the formation of metal clusters. These solutions decompose very slowly forming amides and evolving H_2, but the reaction is accelerated by many transition metals and their compounds.

$$e^-(NH_3)_y \longrightarrow NH_2^- + \frac{1}{2}H_2 + (y-1)NH_3$$

If ammonia is evaporated from the solution, hexammoniates of the formula $[M(NH_3)_6]^{2+}$ are obtained which slowly decomposed to give corresponding metal amides.

$$[M(NH_3)_6]^{2+} + 2e^- \longrightarrow M(NH_2)_2 + 4NH_3 + H_2$$

(viii) Tendency of Complex Formation

Among alkaline earth elements, Be and Mg have the maximum tendency to form complexes because of their small size and higher charge density. e.g. BeF_2 combines with F^- ions to form the tetrahedral complex, $[BeF_4]^{2-}$.

$$BeF_2 + F_2 \longrightarrow [BeF_4]^{2-}$$

Chlorophyll is an important complex of magnesium.

Uses of Alkaline Earth Metals

Alkaline earth metals are used in several fields. Some of these applications are listed below.

Uses of Beryllium

The important uses of beryllium are as follows.

- Beryllium is used in making alloys. An alloy of beryllium with copper is used for making high strength springs.
- Metallic beryllium is used for making windows of X-ray tubes.

Uses of Magnesium

Some of the important uses of magnesium are as follows

- It is an important alloying metal, i.e. alloyed with aluminium, zinc, manganese and tin. Its alloy with aluminium being lighter is used for making parts of aircraft.

- Its powder or ribbon form is used in flash powders and bulbs, incendiary bombs and signals.
- It is used for cathodic protection of other metals as oxygen scavenger.
- A suspension of magnesium hydroxide in water, also called **milk of magnesia**, is used as an antacid drug, i.e. neutralises the excess acid of stomach.
- Compounds of magnesium like magnesium carbonate and magnesium hydroxide are used in making toothpastes.
- Magnesium is used as a deoxidiser for removing last traces of oxygen from copper, steel, etc.
- Magnesium is also used to prepare Grignard reagent, an industrially important compound in organic synthesis.
- It is used for the ignition of thermite charge in aluminothermy.

Uses of Calcium, Barium and Radium

Important uses of these elements are as follows.

- Calcium is used as a reductant in metallurgical processes for the metal oxide that cannot be reduced by carbon.
- It is used for making several important compounds like calcium carbonate, plaster of Paris, gypsum.
- Calcium and barium are used to create vacuum (i.e. remove air) in vacuum tubes because of their ability to react with oxygen and nitrogen at elevated temperature.
- Compounds of radium are used in radiotherapy, e.g. for treating cancer.

10.6 Anomalous Behaviour of Beryllium

Beryllium because of its exceptionally small atomic and ionic size, high ionisation enthalpy and non-availability of *d*-orbital in its valance shell differ from rest of the members of group 2 in several properties. However, it resembles in some of its properties with aluminium placed diagonally opposite to it. Beryllium differs from rest of the members of the group in following respects.

- Beryllium is harder than other members of its group.
- It has higher melting and boiling points than other members.
- Beryllium forms covalent compounds because of high charge density and greater polarising power.

  Because of covalent character, salts of beryllium are easily hydrolysed. e.g.

  $$BeCO_3 + 4H_2O \longrightarrow [Be(H_2O)_4]^{2+} + CO_3^{2-}$$

- Beryllium oxide and hydroxide are amphoteric in nature, whereas oxides of other alkaline earth metals are basic in nature.
- Beryllium carbide reacts with water to give methane gas whereas carbides of other alkaline earth metals give acetylene gas.

  $$Be_2C + 4H_2O \longrightarrow 2Be(OH)_2 + CH_4$$
  $$CaC_2 + 2H_2O \longrightarrow Ca(OH)_2 + HC \equiv CH$$

- Beryllium does not extend its coordination number beyond four since its valence shell ($n = 2$) contains only four (one *s* and three *p*) orbitals. The remaining elements of this group can show a coordination number of six by making use of *d*-orbitals alongwith *s* and *p*-orbitals.

Quick Test 2

1. Beryllium and magnesium do not give colour to flame whereas other alkaline earth metals do so. Why? *NCERT*

2. Explain $E°$ for $M^{2+}(aq) + 2e^- \longrightarrow M(s)$ (where, $M = Ca$, Sr or Ba) is nearly constant. *NCERT*

3. Which member of the alkaline earth metals family has
(i) least reactivity (ii) lowest density
(iii) highest boiling point
(iv) maximum reduction potential?

4. Compare the alkali metals and alkaline earth metals with respect to
(i) ionisation enthalpy.
(ii) basicity of oxides. *NCERT*

For Solutions, See QR Code on Pg. 401

EXAM PATTERN QUESTIONS

Objective Type Questions

Multiple Choice Questions (MCQs) [1 Mark]

1. **Alkali metals show regular trend in their physical and chemical properties with the**
(a) increasing atomic number
(b) increasing *s*-electrons
(c) decreasing atomic number
(d) None of the above

2. **All the alkali metals have electronic configuration, ns^1 outside the noble gas core. They readily lose electron to give**
(a) monovalent ions (b) divalent ions
(c) trivalent ions (d) Both (a) and (b)

3. **The alkali metals have low melting point. Which of the following alkali metal is expected to melt if the room temperature rises to 30°C?** **NCERT Exemplar**
(a) Na (b) K (c) Rb (d) Cs

4. **The low melting point of alkali metals is due to**
(a) weak metallic bonding
(b) presence of only one valence electron
(c) lower density
(d) Both (a) and (b)

5. **The order of decreasing ionisation enthalpy in alkali metals is**
(a) Na > Li > K > Rb (b) Rb < Na < K < Li
(c) Li > Na > K > Rb (d) K < Li < Na < Rb

6. **The alkali metals and their salts show characteristic colour to**
(a) an oxidising flame
(b) a reducing flame
(c) they don't show any colour to any flame
(d) Both (a) and (b)

7. **Alkali metals are kept in kerosene oil. Which of the following reason(s) is/are correct regarding this statement?**
(a) Due to high reactivity of alkali metal
(b) Due to high ionisation enthalpy of alkali metals
(c) Due to large size of alkali metals
(d) Both (a) and (b)

8. **The reducing power of a metal depends on various factors. Suggest the factor which makes Li the strongest reducing agent in aqueous solution.** **NCERT Exemplar**
(a) Sublimation enthalpy (b) Ionisation enthalpy
(c) Hydration enthalpy (d) Electron-gain enthalpy

9. **When sodium is dissolved in liquid ammonia, a solution of deep blue colour is obtained. The colour of the solution is due to**
(a) ammoniated electron (b) sodium ion
(c) sodium amide (d) ammoniated sodium ion

10. **Which of the following element(s) is used as electrode(s) in photoelectric cells?**
(a) Sodium (b) Caesium
(c) Potassium (d) Both (b) and (c)

11. **The alkaline earth metals have smaller size than those of corresponding alkali metals. This is due to**
(a) increase in ionisation enthalpy
(b) decrease in nuclear charge
(c) increase in nuclear charge
(d) increase in number of shells

12. **Along the group, size and ionisation enthalpy of the group II elements respectively,**
(a) increases and decreases (b) decreases and increases
(c) increases and increases (d) decreases and decreases

13. **Which of the following order is correct regarding electropositive character of alkaline earth metals?**
(a) Be < Mg > Ca < Sr < Ra (b) Be > Mg > Ca > Sr > Ba
(c) Be < Mg < Ca < Sr < Ba (d) None of the above

14. **Alkali metals are generally silvery white but beryllium and magnesium appears to be**
(a) reddish (b) greyish
(c) yellowish (d) None of these

15. **A substance which gives brick red flame and breaks down on heating to give oxygen and a brown gas is** **NCERT Exemplar**
(a) magnesium nitrate (b) calcium nitrate
(c) barium nitrate (d) strontium nitrate

16. Powder of beryllium burns in air frequently to produce
(a) BeO (b) Be_3N_2
(c) Be_2O (d) Both (a) and (b)

17. Colour of solution prepared by dissolution of alkaline earth metal in ammonia solution, is
(a) blue (b) deep blue black
(c) bronze (d) brown

18. Which of the following is used as antacid in medicine?
(a) Suspension of magnesium carbonate in water
(b) Suspension of hydroxide of magnesium in water
(c) Suspension of hydroxide of calcium in water
(d) Suspension of calcium carbonate in water

19. Which of the following is used in radiotherapy?
(a) Barium salt (b) Calcium salt
(c) Radium salt (d) Strontium salt

20. The oxides and hydroxides of Be are .... are nature.
(a) acidic (b) basic
(c) amphoteric (d) neutral

Assertion-Reason [1 Mark]

Directions (Q. Nos. 21 and 22) In the following questions, a statement of Assertion is followed by a corresponding statements of Reason of the following statements, choose the correct one.
(a) Both (A) and (R) are correct and (R) is the correct explanation of (A).
(b) Both (A) and (R) are correct but (R) is not the correct explanation of (A).
(c) (A) is correct but (R) is incorrect.
(d) (A) is incorrect but (R) is correct.

21. Assertion (A) Lithium shows a diagonal relationship with magnesium.
Reason (R) Lithium and magnesium have similar ionic radii and charge densities.

22. Assertion (A) Alkali metals act as strong reducing agents.
Reason (R) They have a high tendency to lose their valence electron due to low.

Case-Study [4 Marks]

23. Ready the given case and answer the following questions :
The alkali metals (Group 1) and alkaline earth metals (Group 2) are highly reactive due to their low ionisation enthalpies. Alkali metals are soft and have low melting points, while alkaline earth metals are harder and have higher melting points. The reactivity of alkali metals increases down the group, and they readily react with water to form hydroxides and hydrogen gas. Alkaline earth metals also react with water, but less vigorously. Some important compounds of these elements, such as sodium carbonate (Na_2CO_3) and calcium hydroxide ($Ca(OH)_2$), are widely used in industry.

(i) (a) Why does alkali metals and their salts give characteristic colour to the flame?
(b) Give a reaction of alkali metal with a protonic substance.

(ii) Which of the following explains why alkali metals are more reactive than alkaline earth metals?
(a) Alkali metals have lower atomic radii than alkaline earth metals.
(b) Alkali metals have lower ionisation enthalpy than alkaline earth metals.
(c) Alkaline earth metals form stronger metallic bonds than alkali metals.
(d) Alkaline earth metals have higher hydration enthalpy than alkali metals.

(iii) Which of the following statements is correct regarding the reaction of alkali metals with water?
(a) The reaction is endothermic and forms metal oxides.
(b) The reaction is highly exothermic and produces hydrogen gas.
(c) Alkali metals react with water to form metal peroxides and oxygen gas.
(d) The reaction of alkali metals with water is slower than that of alkaline earth metals.

Or

Why is lithium less reactive with water compared to other alkali metals?
(a) Lithium has a lower atomic size and stronger metallic bonding.
(b) Lithium has a very high density compared to other alkali metals.
(c) Lithium has the highest hydration enthalpy among alkali metals, stabilising its ions in solution.
(d) Lithium reacts with water to form a protective oxide layer, preventing further reaction.

Subjective Type Questions

Short Answer Type I Questions [2 Marks]

1. Find out the oxidation state of sodium in Na_2O_2. **NCERT**

2. (i) Predict giving reason, the outcome of the reaction

$$LiI + KF \longrightarrow KI + LiF$$

(ii) The reaction $-\overset{|}{\underset{|}{C}}-Cl + MF \longrightarrow -\overset{|}{\underset{|}{C}}-F + MCl$

proceed better with KF than with NaF.

3. Why the ionisation enthalpies of alkali metals decrease as the atomic number increases down the group?

4. All compounds of alkali metals are easily soluble in water but lithium compounds are more soluble in organic solvents. Explain. **NCERT Exemplar**

5. Comment on each of the following observations.

(i) The mobilities of the alkali metal ions in aqueous solution are $Li^+ < Na^+ < K^+ < Rb^+ < Cs^+$.

(ii) Lithium is the only alkali metal which forms nitride directly. **NCERT**

6. How do you account for the strong reducing power of lithium in aqueous solution? **NCERT Exemplar**

7. When an alkali metal dissolves in liquid ammonia the solution can acquire different colours. Explain the reasons for this type of colour change. **NCERT**

Or

When a metal of group 1 was dissolved in liquid ammonia, the following observations were obtained.

(i) Blue solution was obtained initially.

(ii) On concentrating the solution, blue colour changed to bronze colour. How do you account for the blue colour of the solution? Give the name of the product formed on keeping the solution for sometime. **NCERT Exemplar**

Short Answer Type II Questions [3 Marks]

8. When heated in air, the alkali metals form various oxides.

Mention the oxides formed by Li, Na and K. **NCERT Exemplar**

9. (i) Which colour is imparted to flame by sodium?

(ii) Why are lithium salts commonly hydrated and those of the other alkali metal ions usually anhydrous?

(iii) Out of KOH and NaOH, which is a stronger base and why? **NCERT**

10. Arrange the following in the order of property.

(i) $BaCl_2$, $MgCl_2$, $BeCl_2$, $CaCl_2$ increasing ionic character.

(ii) $Mg(OH)_2$, $Sr(OH)_2$, $Ba(OH)_2$, $Ca(OH)_2$ increasing solubility in water.

(iii) BeO, MgO, BaO, CaO increasing basic character.

Long Answer Type Questions [5 Marks]

11. (i) Name the groups which constitute s-block elements.

(ii) Why cannot sodium and potassium be prepared by the electrolysis of their aqueous solutions?

(iii) Why is the density of potassium less than sodium?

(iv) Why are alkali metals soft and have low melting points?

(v) What happens when K burns in air? Give chemical equation.

12. Answer the following.

(i) What is hydrolith?

(ii) Which elements of alkaline earth metals family do not give characteristic flame colouration?

(iii) Out of NaOH or $Mg(OH)_2$, which is a stronger base?

(iv) Which element in the group 2 is radioactive?

(v) Which out of Mg^{2+}, Ba^{2+}, Ca^{2+} has maximum ionic mobility in water?

Hints & Solutions

Objective Type Questions

1. (a) The alkali metals show regular trend in their physical and chemical properties with the increasing atomic number.

2. (a) Alkali metals have one valence electron ns^1 outside the noble gas core. So, they readily lose this electron to produce monovalent cation.

$$M \longrightarrow M^+ + e^-$$

3. (d) The energy binding the atoms in the crystal lattice of the alkali metals is low due to their large atomic radii and especially due to the presence of one valence electron per metal atom as compared to large number of available vacant orbitals.
Hence, alkali metals have low melting and boiling points. The melting point of alkali metals decreases from Li to Cs as cohesive force decreases with increase in atomic size. Melting point of Cs = 302 K *i.e.*, 29°C.

4. (d) Alkali metals have low melting point because the metallic bonding between these elements is weak due to presence of only valence electron.

5. (c) In alkali metals, the ionisation enthalpy decreases on moving down the group. Thus, the correct order of decreasing ionisation enthalpy is Li > Na > K > Rb.

6. (a) Alkali metals and their salts impart characteristic colour to an oxidising flame. This is because heat from the flame excites the outermost electron to a higher energy level.

7. (a) Because of their high reactivity towards air and water, alkali metals are kept in kerosene oil.

8. (c) Standard reduction potential ($\overset{\circ}{E}_{RP}$) is a measure of tendency of an element to lose electron in aqueous solution. Higher the negative $\overset{\circ}{E}_{RP}$, greater is the ability to lose electrons.
Due to small size of Li, it has highest hydration energy, which accounts for highest $E°$ value.

9. (a) The blue colour of the solution of alkali metals in liquid ammonia is due to the ammoniated electron which absorbs energy in the visible region of light and thus imparts blue colour to the solution.

10. (d) When Cs and K are irradiated with light, the light energy absorbed may be sufficient to make the metal atom lose an electron. This property makes Cs and K useful as electrodes in photoelectric cell.

11. (c) Smaller size of alkaline earth metal is due to high value of nuclear charge, which increases along a period from left to right.

12. (a) Along the group, size of the group II elements increases while ionisation enthalpy decreases.

13. (c) The electropositive character increases on moving down the group in alkaline earth metals as the tendency to lose the valence electrons increases. Thus, the correct order of electropositive character of alkaline earth metals is Be < Mg < Ca < Sr < Ba.

14. (b) Alkaline earth metals are generally silvery white but Be and Mg appears to be greyish in colour.

15. (b) Calcium gives brick red coloured flame. Hence, calcium nitrate on heating decomposes into calcium oxide, with evolution of a mixture of NO_2 and O_2.

$$2Ca(NO_3)_2 \longrightarrow 2CaO + NO_2 + O_2$$

NO_2 is brown coloured gas.

16. (d) Powdered beryllium burns brilliantly in air to give BeO and Be_3N_2.

17. (b) $M + (x + y)\,NH_3 \longrightarrow [M(NH_3)_x]^{2+} + 2[e\,(NH_3)_y]^-$
Alkaline earth metals dissolve in liquid ammonia to give deep blue black coloured solution.

18. (b) Magnesium hydroxide dissolved in water is known as milk of magnesia. It is used as an antacid in medicine.

19. (c) Radium salts are radioactive in nature hence they are used in radiotherapy.

20. (c) The oxides and hydroxides of Be are amphoteric in nature, as it reacts with both acids and bases.

21. (a) Both (A) and (R) are correct, and (R) is the correct explanation of (A).
Due to the diagonal relationship, lithium and magnesium have similar properties such as hardness, solubility and electorde potentials.

22. (c) Alkali metals act as strong reducing agents because they readily lose their single valence electron to achieve a stable noble gas configuration, thus undergoing oxidation and causing reduction in other substances. Therefore, (A) is correct but (R) is incorrect.

23. (i) (a) Refer to text on page 388.
(b) Refer to text on page 389. **[2]**

(ii) (b) Alkali metals lose their valence electron more easily due to their lower ionisation enthalpy, marking them more reactive. **[1]**

(iii) (b) The reaction is highly exothermic and produces hydrogen gas. Alkali metals react vigorously with water, forming hydroxides and releasing hydrogen gas with a lot of heat. **[1]**

Or (c) Lithium has the highest hydration enthalpy among alkali metals, stabilising its ions in solution. Due to its small size, Li^+ has strong hydration enthalpy, which reduces its overall reactivity with water compared to other alkali metals.

Subjective Type Questions

1. Let x be the oxidation state of Na in Na_2O_2.

   Na_2O_2 contains a peroxide linkage in which O has an oxidation state of -1.

   $$\overset{x}{Na_2}\overset{-1}{O_2}$$

   or $2x + 2(-1) = 0$ or $x = +1$. [2]

   Thus, the oxidation state of sodium in Na_2O_2 is $+1$.

2. (i) Large cation (K^+) can stabilise large anion (I^-).

   (ii) This is because the larger cation (K^+) can stabilise larger anion (Cl^-). [1]

3. Refer to page 387.

4. Exceptionally small size of Li^+ ion and high polarising power, these are the two factors which develops covalent character in the lithium compounds (Fajan's rule).

   Compounds of other alkali metals are ionic in nature. So, they are soluble in water, while lithium compounds being relatively covalent are soluble in alcohol and other organic solvents. [2]

5. (i) Smaller the size of the ion, more highly it is hydrated and greater the hydration of the ion, lower is its ionic mobility.

   Since, the extent of hydration decreases in the order

   $$Li^+ > Na^+ > K^+ > Rb^+ > Cs^+$$

   Therefore, ionic mobility increases in the reverse order $Li^+ < Na^+ < K^+ < Rb^+ < Cs^+$ [1]

   (ii) Because of its smaller size, lithium like magnesium forms a nitride while other alkali metals do not.

   $$6\,Li(s) + N_2(g) \xrightarrow{\Delta} 2\,Li_3N\,(s)$$ [1]

6. Refer text on page 389. [2]

7. Refer text on page 389 and 390. [2]

8. Refer to page 390. [3]

9. (i) Sodium imparts a golden yellow colour to the flame. [1]

   (ii) Because of its smallest size among alkali metals. Li^+ has the maximum degree of hydration. That's why lithium salts are commonly hydrated and those of other alkali metal ions usually anhydrous.

   $$\underset{\Delta H_{\text{hydration}} \text{ in decreasing order}}{\overrightarrow{Li^+ > Na^+ > K^+ > Rb^+ > Cs^+}}$$ [1]

   (iii) KOH is a stronger base than NaOH. Due to large size of K, K—O bond is weaker than Na—O bond. KOH has more concentration of ^-OH than NaOH, hence, is a stronger base than NaOH. [1]

10. (i) Order : $BeCl_2 < MgCl_2 < CaCl_2 < BaCl_2$

    Ionic character increases down the group as the size of the cation increases, reducing its polarising power. [1]

    (ii) Order : $Mg(OH)_2 < Ca(OH)_2 < Sr(OH)_2 < Ba(OH)_2$

    Solubility of hydroxides increases down the group because lattice energy decreases more rapidly than hydration energy. [1]

    (iii) Order : $BeO < MgO < CaO < BaO$

    Basicity increases down the group as the metallic character increases, making the oxides more ionic. [1]

11. (i) *s*-block contains only two groups; group 1 (alkali metals) and group 2 (alkaline earth metals). [1]

    (ii) The electrode potential, i.e. reduction potential of Na (-2.71 V) or K (-2.92) is much lower than that of H_2O (-0.83V), therefore, upon electrolysis, water gets reduced in preference to Na^+ or K^+ ions. In other words, sodium and potassium cannot be obtained by electrolytic reduction of Na^+ and K^+ ions in aqueous solution. [1]

    (iii) This is due to abnormal increase in the atomic size of potassium. [1]

    (iv) Alkali metals have only one valence electron per metal atom. As a result, the binding energy of alkali metal ions in the close-packed metal lattices are weak. Therefore these are soft and have low melting points[1]

    (v) $K + O_2 \rightarrow KO_2$, potassium superoxide will be formed. [1]

12. (i) Hydrolith is calcium hydride (CaH_2), a compound that reacts with water to release hydrogen gas. [1]

    (ii) Beryllium (Be) and Magnesium (Mg) do not give a characteristic flame colour because their small atomic size and high ionisation energy prevent easy excitation of electrons. [1]

    (iii) NaOH (Sodium hydroxide) is a stronger base than $Mg(OH)_2$ because it is highly soluble in water and completely dissociates, whereas $Mg(OH)_2$ is only slightly soluble. [1]

    (iv) Radium (Ra) is the radioactive element in Group 2.

    (v) Ba^{2+} (Barium ion) has the highest ionic mobility in water because it has the largest ionic radius and the weakest hydration energy, allowing it to move more freely. [1]

QR Code for Quick Test 1

QR Code for Quick Test 2

11

CHAPTER

To be Assessed Formatively

The *p*-Block Elements

Elements in which the last electron enters in *p*-orbital of outermost shell are called ***p*-block elements.**

Since, *p*-orbitals can accommodate a maximum of 6 electrons, so a total of 6 groups, *viz.* group 13 (III A), group 14 (IV A), group 15 (V A), group 16 (VI A), group 17 (VII A or halogens) and group 18 (zero or noble gases) belong to this block. All these elements are placed at extreme right of the periodic table.

Most of the elements of this block are non-metals. However, it also contains metals as well as **metalloids.**

YOUR STUDY GOALS

11.1 General Characteristics of *p*-Block Elements
11.2 Group 13 Elements : The Boron Family
11.3 Group 14 Elements : The Carbon Family
11.4 Group 15 Elements : The Nitrogen Family
11.5 Group 16 Elements : The Oxygen Family
11.6 Group 17 Elements : The Halogen Family
11.7 Group 18 Elements : The Noble Gases

YOUR PRACTICE GOAL

- Objective Type Questions (24 Qs ; 18 MCQs, 5 A-R & 1 Case Study)
- Subjective Type Questions (21 Qs; 12 SA-I, 6 SA-II & 3 LA)

11.1 General Characteristics of *p*-Block Elements

Some common features exhibited by the elements of *p*-block are as follows

General Electronic Configuration

The general valence shell configuration of these elements is $ns^2np^{1\text{-}6}$ (where, $n = 1, 2, 3 \ldots$) with the exception of helium, in which the last electron enters in *s*-orbital but it is placed with noble gases because of the similarities in properties.

Oxidation States

Elements of *p*-block exhibit following two types of oxidation states.

(i) Group Oxidation State

The group oxidation state or maximum oxidation state exhibited by a *p*-block element is equal to the total number of valence electrons, i.e. maximum oxidation state = *ns*-electrons + *np*-electrons (where, n = outermost shell).

e.g. The electronic configuration of $C(6) = 1s^2\ \underbrace{2s^2\ 2p^2}_{\text{Outermost shell}}$ thus, its maximum oxidation state = 2 + 2 = 4.

The group oxidation state generally increases across a period from left to right.

(ii) Other Oxidation State

Heavier members of each group also exhibit an oxidation state which is two units less than the group oxidation state. This oxidation state is more stable as compared to their group oxidation states. The reason for the existence of this oxidation state is the reluctance of *ns*-electrons to take part in bonding, which is also called **inert pair effect**. This effect arises because the energy required to unpair the electrons, in case of heavier members, is more than the energy released in the formation of two additional bonds.

General Electronic Configuration and Oxidation States of p-Block Elements

Group	13	14	15	16	17	18
General electronic configuration	ns^2np^1	ns^2np^2	ns^2np^3	ns^2np^4	ns^2np^5	ns^2np^6 ($1s^2$ for He)
First member of the group	B	C	N	O	F	He
Group oxidation state	+3	+4	+5	+6	+7	+8 (+2 for He)
Other oxidation states	+1	+2, −4	+3, −3	+4, +2, −2	+5, +3, +1, −1	+6, +4, +2

Nature of Elements

In this block non-metals, metals and metalloids all are present. The non-metallic character decreases on moving down a group. Thus, the heaviest element of each group, infact is more metallic in nature. The metalloids present in this block are B, Si, Ge, As, Sb, Te, At etc.

Nature of Oxides

The oxides of non-metals are acidic or neutral in nature and that of metals are generally basic in nature. Thus, acidic nature of oxides decreases but basic nature of oxides increases on moving down a group of the block.

Formation of Anion

Non-metals possess higher ionisation enthalpies and higher electronegativities as compared to metals and hence, they have higher tendency to form anions.

Nature of Compounds

When a highly reactive non-metal combines with a highly reactive metal, **ionic compound** is formed. This is because, there is large difference in the electronegativities of combining elements. Further, when a highly reactive non-metal combines with another highly reactive non-metal, **covalent compound** is formed because of the small differences in the electronegativities of the combining elements.

Anomalous Behaviours of First Member of Each Family

The first member of each group of *p*-block differs from rest of the members of its corresponding group due to its very small size and unavailability of *d*-orbitals.

Few of such anomalies are as follows

(i) Maximum Covalency

Because of the absence of *d*-orbitals, the elements of second period (i.e. first member of each group) cannot expand its covalency beyond four, i.e. their maximum covalency is four (because of the availability of one $2s$ and three $2p$ orbitals).

Other members of the groups because of the presence of *d*-orbitals can expand their covalence above four. That's why boron, the first member of group 13, can form only $[BF_4^-]$ but not $[BF_6]^{3-}$, but aluminium, which also belongs to the same group, can form $[AlF_6]^{3-}$ ion.

(ii) Formation of $p\pi$-$p\pi$ Bonds

The first member of each group because of its small size and non-availability of *d*-orbitals have a unique tendency to form $p\pi$-$p\pi$ multiple bonds with itself [e.g. C=C, C≡C, N≡N] or with the other elements of second period (e.g. C=O, C=N, C≡N, N=O).

In case of heavier members, since *d*-orbitals are available, so they form $p\pi$-$d\pi$ bond or $d\pi$-$d\pi$ bond instead of $p\pi$-$p\pi$ bond.

Since, the energy of d-orbitals is higher as compared to p-orbitals, the $p\pi$-$d\pi$ or $d\pi$-$d\pi$ bonding contribute less towards the overall stability of the molecules as compared to $p\pi$-$p\pi$ bonding.

e.g. NO_3^- in which the coordination number of N is 3, involves $p\pi$-$p\pi$ bonding, whereas PO_4^{3-} in which coordination number of P is 4, involves $p\pi$-$d\pi$ bonding (because of the availability of d-orbitals in case of P).

11.2 Group 13 Elements : The Boron Family

The elements present in this group are **Boron** (B), **Aluminium** (Al), **Gallium** (Ga), **Indium** (In), **Thallium** (Tl) and **Nihonium** (Nh). Nh is a synthetically prepared radioactive element. Boron is typically a non-metal but other members of the family show metallic properties.

The non-metallic nature of B is probably because of its small size, high ionisation enthalpy and comparatively high electronegativity. Aluminium is a metal but shows many chemical similarities to boron.

Occurrence

Boron is a rare element and constitutes 0.0001% by mass of the earth crust. It exists in two isotopic forms *viz* B^{10} (19%) and B^{11} (81%). Its chief minerals are as follows

(i) Borax or tincal : $Na_2B_4O_7 \cdot 10H_2O$ [*In India, it is found is Puga valley (Ladakh) and Sambhar lake (Rajasthan)*]

(ii) Kernite : $Na_2B_4O_7 \cdot 4H_2O$

(iii) Colemanite : $Ca_2[B_3O_4(OH)_3]_2 \cdot 2H_2O$

(iv) Orthoboric acid : H_3BO_3

Aluminium, the second member of the group, is the **most abundant metal** and the **third most abundant element** in the earth's crust (8.3% by mass) after oxygen and silicon.

Its important minerals are

(i) Bauxite : $Al_2O_3 \cdot 2H_2O$

(ii) Cryolite : Na_3AlF_6

(iii) Mica : $K_2O{\cdot}3Al_2O_3 \cdot 6SiO_2 \cdot 2H_2O$

or $KAl_2(Si_3AlO_{10})(F, OH)_2$.

In India, mica is found in Madhya Pradesh, Karnataka, Odisha and Jammu.

(iv) Corundum, Al_2O_3

Gallium, indium and thallium are less abundant elements in nature.

General Properties of Group 13 Elements

1. Atomic Properties of Boron Family

Important atomic properties of elements of group 13 and their trends are as follows

(a) **Electronic configuration** The general valence shell configuration of these elements is ns^2np^1 (where, $n = 1, 2, 3\ldots$) as shown in the following table.

Electronic Configuration of Elements of Group 13

Element	Atomic number	Electronic configuration	
		Complete	With inert gas core
Boron (B)	5	$1s^2\,2s^2\,2p^1$	$[He]\,2s^2\,2p^1$
Aluminium (Al)	13	$1s^2\,2s^2\,2p^6\,3s^2\,3p^1$	$[He]\,3s^2\,3p^1$
Gallium (Ga)	31	$1s^2\,2s^2\,2p^6\,3s^2\,3p^6\,3d^{10}\,4s^2\,4p^1$	$[Ar]\,3d^{10}\,4s^2\,4p^1$
Indium (In)	49	$1s^2\,2s^2\,2p^6\,3s^2\,3p^6\,3d^{10}\,4s^2\,4p^6\,4d^{10}\,5s^2\,5p^1$	$[Kr]\,4d^{10}\,5s^2\,5p^1$
Thallium (Tl)	81	$1s^2\,2s^2\,2p^6\,3s^2\,3p^6\,3d^{10}\,4s^2\,4p^6\,4d^{10}\,4f^{14}\,5s^2\,5p^6\,5d^{10}\,6s^2\,6p^1$	$[Xe]\,4f^{14}\,5d^{10}\,6s^2\,6p^1$
Nihonium (Nh)	113	$1s^2\,2s^2\,2p^6\,3s^2\,3p^6\,3d^{10}\,4s^2\,4p^6\,4d^{10}\,4f^{14}\,5s^2\,5p^6\,5d^{10}\,5f^{14}\,6s^2\,6p^6\,6d^{10}\,7s^2\,7p^1$	$[Rn]\,5f^{14}\,6d^{10}\,7s^2\,7p^1$s

The above table clearly shows that the first two members, i.e. boron and aluminium, have noble gas core, the next two members, i.e. gallium and indium have noble gas plus 10*d*-electrons core and the remaining element, i.e. thallium, has noble gas plus 14 *f* and 10*d*-electron cores. These inner cores make the chemistry of these elements more complex than the elements of *s*-block.

(b) **Atomic radii** The atomic and ionic radii of elements of group 13 are smaller as compared to that of the elements of group 2 due to the increase in effective nuclear charge. On moving down the group, the atomic radii increases because of the successive addition of one extra shell of electrons, however there is an anomaly at gallium.

Atomic radii of Ga (135 pm) is less than that of Al (143 pm). This is because the extra 10 *d*-electrons present in Ga atom do not screen the nucleus effectively. Consequently, electrons of Ga are attracted more by the nucleus and results in decreased radii.

(c) **Ionisation enthalpy** The ionisation enthalpy first decreases from B to Al, then increases from Al to Ga, again decreases from Ga to In and again increases from In to Tl.

Thus, the ionisation energy of boron is highest in the group since its atomic size is the smallest and the shielding effect is lowest. The sharp decrease from B to Al is due to appreciable increase in atomic size and the shielding effect of *s* and *p*-electrons of the penultimate energy shell.

In case of Ga, there are 10*d*-electrons in the penultimate energy shell which shield the nuclear charge less effectively, so that the outer electron is held firmly by the nucleus. As a result, the ionisation energy remains nearly the same as that of aluminium inspite of the fact that atomic size increases. In case of indium, the number of *d*-electrons and their shielding effect remains the same as in gallium. The ionisation energy, however, decreases in indium due to increase in atomic size from Ga to In.

The increase in ionisation energy from In to Tl is because the nuclear charge increases considerably by 32 units which outweighs the shielding effect all the electrons of the inner shells including of 14 *f* and 5 *d* electrons.

The first three ionisation enthalpies of these elements have the order $\Delta_i H_1 < \Delta_i H_2 < \Delta_i H_3$. Since, the total of three successive ionisation energies is very high, these elements have very little tendency to form trivalent ion, i.e. ions of the type M^{3+}.

B does not form M^{3+} ion because of the fact that the sum of three ionization energies in the case of B is so large that small atom of B is not able to accommodate that energy even if given artificially from outside.

In case of Al, the sum of first three ionisation energies decrease considerably and hence, it is able to form Al^{3+} ion.

(d) **Electronegativity** On moving down the group, the electronegativity first decreases from B to Al and then increases marginally because of the discrepancies in atomic size of the elements.

2. Physical Properties

The important physical properties of elements of group 13 and their trends are as follows

(a) **Physical state** Boron is a non-metal. It is extremely hard, black coloured solid which exists in several allotropic forms (^{10}B and ^{11}B). Rest of the members of the family are soft metals with high electrical conductivity. The electropositive or metallic character of these elements increases on moving down the group.

(b) **Melting and boiling points** The melting point of boron is unusually high because of its very strong crystalline lattice. After B, the melting point first decreases upto Ga and then increases again upto Tl. The melting point of Ga is so low (303 K) that it could exist in liquid state during summer.

Boiling points of these elements show a more regular trend. It decreases regularly on moving down the group. This is an indication of the fact that atoms of the elements are held less and less closely as we move down the group.

(c) **Density** It increases on moving down the group from B to Tl. This is because of the fact that the increase in atomic mass of the elements outweighs the effect of increased atomic size.

3. Chemical Properties

The chemical properties exhibited by elements of group 13 are as follows

(a) **Oxidation state and chemical reactivity** Boron shows consistently +3 oxidation state in its compounds, while rest of the elements show +1 as well as +3 oxidation states. The +1 oxidation state becomes more and more stable as we move down the group i.e. Al< Ga< In< Tl. This is because of the presence of intervening *d* and *f*-orbitals which do not shield the nucleus effectively. Consequently effective nuclear charge increases, that holds the *ns* electrons tightly so that they do not participate in bonding (inert pair effect).

Thus, in Tl, +1 oxidation state is more predominant whereas the +3 oxidation state is strongly oxidising in nature. Further, compounds in +1 oxidation state are more ionic as compared to that in +3 oxidation state.

The compounds of Tl(I) show close resemblance with alkali metals, e.g. TlOH is highly soluble and a strong base, like NaOH; similarly Tl_2CO_3 shows resemblance with Na_2CO_3 and K_2CO_3.

(b) **Reactivity towards air** The crystalline form of boron is inert towards air but its amorphous form when heated in air, forms boron oxide, B_2O_3.

$$4B(s)+3O_2(g)\xrightarrow{\Delta}2B_2O_3(s)$$

Aluminium, being reactive, readily forms aluminium oxide, Al_2O_3 with air which covers the surface of the metal and thus, protects it from further attack. However, when Al is heated in air, Al_2O_3 is obtained. Other members of the family also form oxides of the type M_2O_3 when heated in air.

$$4E(s)+3O_2(g)\xrightarrow{\Delta}2E_2O_3(s)$$

(where, E = B, Al, Ga, In, Tl)

These elements also form nitride when treated with dinitrogen at high temperature.

$$2B+N_2\xrightarrow{\Delta}\underset{\text{Boron nitride}}{2BN}$$

The acidic nature of oxides decreases and the basic nature of oxides increases on moving from B to Tl.This is because as we move down the group, the atomic size of elements goes on increasing whereas the ionisation energy decreases, due to which, the strength of *MO* bond goes on decreasing in similar way.

Thus, boron trioxide or boron oxide is acidic and reacts with basic (metallic) oxides to give metals borates. Aluminium and gallium oxides are amphoteric while oxides of indium and thallium are basic in nature.

(c) **Reactivity towards acids and alkalies** Boron neither reacts with acids nor with alkalies even at moderate temperature. Aluminium, being amphoteric, reacts with acids as well as alkalies and liberates dihydrogen.

e.g. $$2Al(s)+\underset{\text{Acid}}{6HCl(aq)}\longrightarrow 2Al^{3+}(aq)+6Cl^-(aq)+3H_2(g)$$

$$2Al(s)+2NaOH(aq)+6H_2O(l)\longrightarrow \underset{\text{Sodium tetrahydroxo aluminate (III)}}{2Na^+[Al(OH)_4]^-(aq)}+3H_2(g)$$

If instead of HCl conc. HNO_3 (nitric acid) is used, Al becomes passive because of the formation of a protective oxide layer over its surface.

$$2Al+6HNO_3(\text{conc.})\longrightarrow Al_2O_3+6NO_2+3H_2O$$

(d) **Reactivity towards halogens** These elements react with halogens to form trihalides with the exception of TlI_3.

$$2E(s)+3X_2(g)\longrightarrow 2EX_3(s)\,(X=F, Cl, Br, I)$$

- **Monomeric and dimeric forms** The trihalides of B exist as discrete molecules (monomeric) while the trihalides of other elements exist as dimers both in vapour state and in non-polar solvent, e.g.

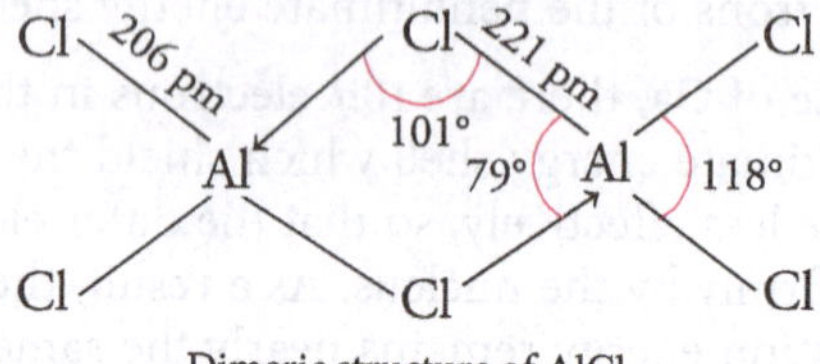

Dimeric structure of $AlCl_3$

Dimer structure disappears when the halides are dissolved in water. This is due to high hydration energy when $[M(H_2O)_6]^{3+}$ and $6X^-$ ions are formed making the solution a good conductor of electricity. The solution becomes acidic owing to hydrolysis.

$$Al_2Cl_6+12H_2O\rightleftharpoons 2[Al(H_2O)_6]^{3+}+6Cl^-+\text{Energy}$$

However, B atom owing to its small size, cannot coordinate with four larger halide ions and hence, cannot form the dimeric molecules. That is why boron trihalides always exist in monomeric forms.

- **Lewis acid character of trihalides of group 13** The trihalides of all the elements of this group act as **Lewis acids, i.e. they are electron deficient** and have the tendency to accept the electron pair.

  The electron accepting tendency of trihalides follow the order.

  $$B > Al > Ga > In$$

  The relative strengths of trihalides of B as Lewis acids have been determined by measuring their heats of formation as well as by studying their infrared spectra. The result of these studies is

  $$BF_3 < BCl_3 < BBr_3$$

  This order is just the reverse of what should be expected normally from the electronegativities of halogens.

Explanation of Lewis Acid Character of Trihalides of Group 13

This anomalous behaviour can be explained on the basis of tendency of halogen atom to back donate its one pair of electrons to the boron atom, which can be shown as

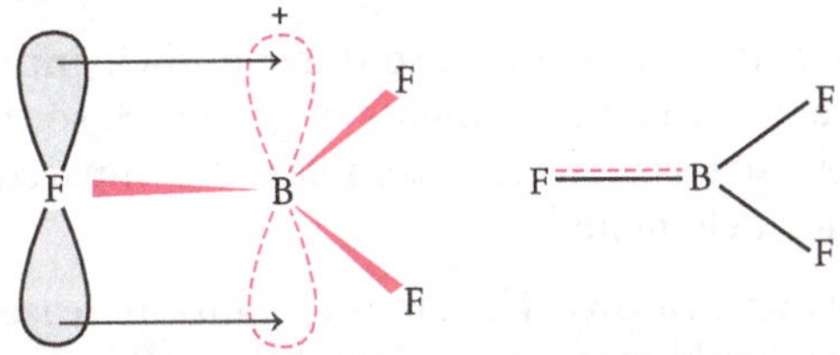

Phenomenon of back bonding in BF_3 molecule

Infact in BF_3 molecule, where the $2p$-orbitals of each F atom are fully-filled, one of the $2p$-orbitals of B is vacant. Therefore, an additional $p\pi$-$p\pi$ bond is established between these $2p$-orbitals of same energy due to partial transference of electronic character from fully-filled orbital to vacant as shown in the above figure. Thus, the B—F bond acquires some double bond character. This type of bond formation is called **back bonding**. Similar structure for other two B—F bonds are equally probable as

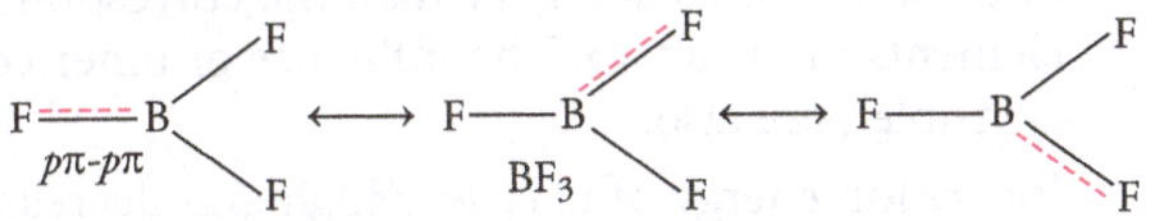

As a result of back donation of electrons from F to B, the electron deficiency of B atom get compensated resulting in decrease in Lewis acid character. This tendency to form back bonds is maximum in case of BF_3 and falls rapidly as we move to BCl_3 and BBr_3 due to the fact that the energy difference between fully-filled orbital of halogen ($Cl-3p$; $Br-4p$) and vacant orbitals of B ($2p$) increases.

Anomalous Behaviour of Boron

Owing to its extremely small size, high electron density, high electronegativity and non-availability of d-electrons, boron exhibits following anomalous properties.

- Boron is a typical non-metal, while other members of the group are metals.
- Its melting and boiling points are higher than the other members of the group.
- It forms only covalent compounds while other members can form covalent as well as ionic compounds. The maximum covalency of B is four.
- Only boron exhibits allotropy and exists in crystalline as well as amorphous forms.
- Except boron all other halides of the group elements are hydrolysed in water and exist as tetrahedral species $[M(OH)_4]^-$ and octahedral species $[M(H_2O)_6]^{3+}$, in aqueous medium.
- The monomeric trihalides are electron deficient and act as strong Lewis acids. Boron trifluoxide easily reacts with Lewis bases such as NH_3 to complete its octet around boron

$$F_3B + :NH_3 \longrightarrow F_3B \longleftarrow NH_3$$

Quick Test 1

1. What is inert pair effect?
2. Why the elements of the second row (first short period) show a number of differences in properties from other members of their respective families?
3. What is the formula of kernite, an ore of boron?
4. Atomic radius of gallium (135 pm) is less than that of aluminium (143 pm). Give reason.

   Or How would you justify the lower atomic radius of Ga as compared to Al?
5. $Tl(NO_3)_3$ acts as an oxidising agent. Explain.
6. White fumes appear around the bottle of anhydrous aluminium chloride. Give reason. *NCERT*
7. Why does boron trifluoride behave as a Lewis acid? *NCERT*
8. Boron is unable to form BF_6^{3-} ion. Explain. *NCERT*
9. Why is B—X bond distance in BX_3 shorter than the theoretically expected value?
10. How can you explain higher stability of BCl_3 as compared to $TlCl_3$? *NCERT*

For Solutions, See QR Code on Pg. 429

11.3 Group 14 Elements : The Carbon Family

The group 14 (IVA) contains 6 elements namely **Carbon** (C), **Silicon** (Si), **Germanium** (Ge), **Tin** (Sn), **Lead** (Pb) and **Flerovium** (Fl). Carbon is an essential constituent of all organic matter while silicon is an important constituent of inorganic matter.

Occurrence

All the members of this family are well known. Silicon is the second and carbon is the seventeenth most abundant element (by mass) in the earth's crust. The percentage abundance of these elements in the earth's crust is shown below.

Element	C	Si	Ge	Sn	Pb
Abundance (mass%)	0.02	27.7	1.5×10^{-4}	2.1×10^{-4}	13×10^{-4}

Carbon can exist in free as well as in combined state. In elemental state, it exists in the form of coal, diamond, graphite and fullerene whereas in combined state, it exists in the form of metal carbonates, hydrocarbons and carbon dioxide gas (which is only 0.03% in the air).

Thus, carbon is a versatile element in the world and essential constituent of all living organisms.

Naturally occurring carbon contains two stable isoopes: ^{12}C and ^{13}C. In addition to these, third isotope, ^{14}C is also present. It is a radioactive isotope with half-life 5770 years and use for radiocarbon dating.

Silicon generally exists in the form of silica and silicates. It is an important constituent of ceramics, glass and cement. Germanium (Ge), tin (Sn) and lead (Pb) are present in trace amounts. Sn mainly exists in the form of cassiterite, SnO_2 and Pb mainly exists as galena, PbS. Its other forms are anglesite ($PbSO_4$) and cerrussite ($PbCO_3$). Flerovium is synthethically prepared radioactive element.

TEACHER'S TIP

Ultrapure form of Ge and Si are used to make transistors and semi-conductor devices.

General Properties of Group 14 Elements

1. Atomic Properties

Important atomic properties of elements of group 14 and their trends are as follows

(a) **Electronic configuration** The general valence shell electronic configurations of these elements is $ns^2\ np^2$ (where, $n=1, 2, 3, \ldots$) as shown below.

Electronic Configuration of Elements of Group 14

Element	Atomic number	Complete electronic configuration	Electronic configuration with inert gas core
Carbon (C)	6	$1s^2 2s^2 2p^2$	[He] $2s^2 2p^2$
Silicon (Si)	14	$1s^2 2s^2 2p^6 3s^2 3p^2$	[Ne] $3s^2 3p^2$
Germanium (Ge)	32	$1s^2 2s^2 2p^6 3s^2 3p^6 3d^{10} 4s^2 4p^2$	[Ar] $3d^{10} 4s^2 4p^2$
Tin (Sn)	50	$1s^2 2s^2 2p^6 3s^2 3p^6 3d^{10} 4s^2 4p^6 4d^{10} 5s^2 5p^2$	[Kr] $4d^{10} 5s^2 5p^2$
Lead (Pb)	82	$1s^2 2s^2 2p^6 3s^2 3p^6 3d^{10} 4s^2 4p^6 4d^{10} 4f^{14} 5s^2 5p^6 5d^{10} 6s^2 6p^2$	[Xe] $4f^{14} 5d^{10} 6s^2 6p^2$

Since, these elements also differ in their inner core, just like the elements of group 13, so their chemistry is also more complex as compared to *s*-block elements.

(b) **Covalent radius** The atomic radius increases considerably from C to Si and thereafter from Si to Pb, there is only a small increase. This is because of the poor shielding effect of intervening *d* and *f*-orbitals in case of Ge, Sn and Pb. Due to which, the effective nuclear charge increases and nucleus holds the outer shell more tightly. This results in decrease in radii.
The atomic radius of these elements, however, is smaller than the corresponding elements of group 13 due to increased nuclear charge.

(c) **Ionisation enthalpy** The first ionisation enthalpy of these elements is higher than the corresponding elements of group 13. The influence of inner core is visible here also.

Ionisation energy of C is very high and decreases sharply as we move from carbon to silicon. It is because there is an presence increase in the size of Si-atom.

After Si, the decrease in IE is regular but not so much and not very sharp from Si to Sn due to presence of *d*-electrons in them.

However, a marginal increase is seen between Sn and Pb. This is because of the consequence of poor shielding effect of intervening *d* and *f*-orbitals in Pb due to which, there is a marginal decrease in atomic radius, which increases the ionisation energy marginally.

(d) **Electronegativity** These elements are somewhat more electronegative as compared to the elements of group 13 because of their smaller size. C is the most electronegative element of the group. While on moving down the group electronegativity decreases upto Si and then becomes constant. Such a different trend in electronegativity is because of the fact that *d*-orbitals are filled up in the case of Ge and Sn while in the case of Pb, *d* and *f*-orbitals are filled up.

2. Physical Properties

All the elements of this group are solids. The trends of physical properties of these elements are as follows

(a) **Metallic or electropositive character** First two members of this group are non-metals (C and Si); the middle one is metalloid (Ge), while Sn and Pb are metals. The metallic or electropositive character increases down the group.

$$\underbrace{\text{C} \quad \text{Si}}_{\text{Non-metals}} \qquad \underbrace{\text{Ge}}_{\text{Metalloid}} \qquad \underbrace{\text{Sn} \quad \text{Pb}}_{\text{Metals}}$$

The change from non-metallic to metallic character is due to less effective nuclear charge and increased number of available orbitals with increase in the size of the atom.

(b) **Melting and boiling points** The melting and boiling points of first member i.e. carbon are exceedingly high. The values decrease as we move from carbon to lead. The melting point of Sn and Pb are relatively low because the *M*—*M* bonds are weaker.

They do not use all the four outer electrons for metallic bonding. Melting and boiling points of group 14 elements are much higher than those of corresponding of group 13.

Example 1 Among group 14 elements name

(i) the most electronegative element.

(ii) most metallic element.

(iii) the elements having tendency to form $p\pi$- $p\pi$ bonds.

Sol (i) Among group 14 elements carbon is the most electronegative element.

(ii) Lead is the most metallic element (as down the group metallic character increases).

(iii) Carbon have the tendency to form $p\pi$-$p\pi$ bonds.

3. Chemical Properties

The trends of various chemical properties exhibited by elements of group 14 are as follows

(a) **Oxidation state** Because of the presence of four valence electrons, the maximum or group valency or maximum oxidation state of these elements is + 4. They also exhibit +2 oxidation state. Some negative oxidation states of carbon are also known.

The compounds of these elements in +4 oxidation state are generally covalent. This is because, the sum of first four ionisation enthalpies of these elements is very high.

The stability of +2 oxidation state increases down the group due to inert pair effect (i.e. because of inability of ns^2 electrons of valence shell to participate in bonding).

Thus, Pb^{2+} exists as stable ion and is much more stable and common that Pb^{4+} ions.

The order of stability of ions of this group are as follows

$$Ge^{2+} < Sn^{2+} < Pb^{2+} ; Ge^{4+} > Sn^{4+} > Pb^{4+}$$

From the above it is also clear that the compounds of Ge^{2+} are unstable while compounds of Ge^{4+} are stable. Thus, the compounds of Ge^{2+} get oxidised into Ge^{4+} easily and act as a reducing agent.

$$\underset{\substack{\text{Less stable} \\ \text{(Reducing agent)}}}{Ge^{2+}} \xrightarrow{-2e^-} \underset{\text{More stable}}{Ge^{4+}}$$

The compounds of Sn^{2+} are less stable than Sn^{4+}. Thus, Sn^{2+} compounds also act as reducing agents. In the case of lead, Pb^{2+} compounds are more stable than Pb^{4+} compounds. The Pb^{4+} compounds, thus, act as oxidising agents.

$$\underset{\substack{\text{Less stable} \\ \text{(Oxidising agent)}}}{Pb^{4+}} + 2e^- \longrightarrow \underset{\text{More stable}}{Pb^{2+}}$$

Further in tetravalent state, the octet of element of group 14 is complete, i.e. their compounds act as electron precise molecules and hence, in general, they neither accept nor lose electrons.

Example 2 Out of $PbCl_2$, $SnCl_2$, $SnCl_4$ and $PbCl_4$, which one is most commonly used as a reducing agent and why?

Sol Sn^{4+} is more stable than Sn^{2+} thus Sn^{2+} have a great tendency to get converted into Sn^{4+} by losing two electrons hence, from the given compounds, $SnCl_2$ is used as reducing agent.

(b) **Reactivity Towards Oxygen** When heated in oxygen, these elements form two types of oxides *viz.* monoxides and dioxides.

(i) **Monoxides** Elements of this group form monoxides of general formula *MO*, e.g. CO, SiO, GeO, SnO and PbO. The SiO exists only at high temperature. Oxides in higher oxidation states of the elements are generally more acidic than those in lower oxidation states. Among monoxides CO is neutral, GeO is distinctly acidic, SnO and PbO are amphoteric.

(ii) **Dioxides** Elements of this group form dioxides, of the general formula MO_2, e.g. CO_2, SiO_2, GeO_2, SnO_2 and PbO_2. The dioxides —CO_2, SiO_2 and GeO_2 are acidic whereas, SnO_2 and PbO_2 are amphoteric in nature.

(c) **Reactivity towards water** C, Si and Ge do not react with water while Sn reacts with steam and forms SnO_2 and H_2.

$$Sn(s) + 2H_2O(g) \xrightarrow{\Delta} SnO_2(s) + 2H_2(g)$$

Lead also remains unaffected due to the formation of a protective film of lead oxide over its surface.

(d) **Reactivity towards halogen** Elements of this group form halides of the type MX_4 and MX_2 (where X = F, Cl, Br, I). Except C, all these combine directly with halogen under suitable conditions. Most of the tetrahalides (i.e. MX_4) are covalent in nature and sp^3 hybridised with tetrahedral geometary. SnF_4 and PbF_4 are ionic halides.

The thermal stability of halides of different elements with a common halogen decreases with increasing atomic number. Whereas the thermal stability of tetrahalides of the same element decreases with increase in molecular mass of the tetrahalide,

i.e. $CX_4 > SiX_4 > GeX_4 > SnX_4 > PbX_4$
$CF_4 > CCl_4 > CBr_4 > Cl_4$

Heavier members Ge to Pb are able to make halides of formula MX_2. The stability of dihalides increases down the group.

On considering the thermal and chemical stability PbX_2 is more stable than PbX_4 on the other hand GeX_4 is more stable than GeX_2.

The tetrahalides of C are not hydrolysed by water under normal conditions (due to the absence of *d*-orbitals) while the tetrahalides of other elements are readily hydrolysed due to the availability of empty *d*-orbitals in them.

$SiCl_4$ undergoes hydrolysis by initially accepting lone pair of electrons from oxygen of water molecule in *d*-orbitals of Si, finally leading to the formation of $Si(OH)_4$ as shown below.

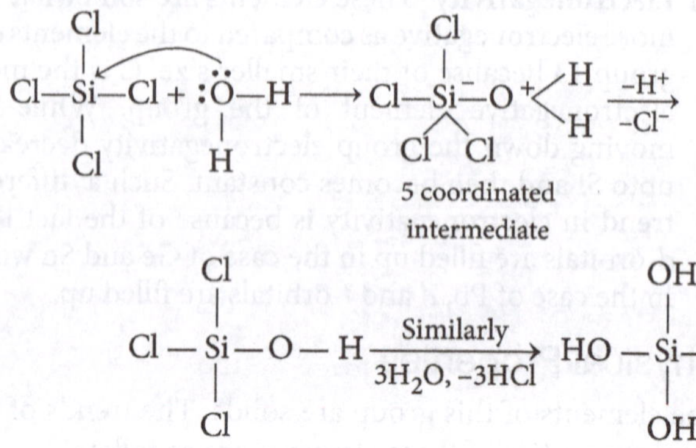

Silicic acid

Heavier members of this family (i.e. from Ge to Pb) also form dihalides, stability of which increases on moving down the group.

Note PbI_4 does not exist because Pb—I bond initially formed during he reaction does not release enough energy to unpaired $6s^2$ electrons and excite one of them to higher orbital to have four unpaired electrons around lead atom.

Important Trends and Anomalous Behaviour of Carbon

The size of carbon is smallest among the group but it has high electronegativity and ionisation enthalpy. Moreover, in it *d*-orbitals are also not present. Due to these reasons, its properties are quite different from other members of the group. Few of such properties are

Covalency

Carbon, due to the absence of *d*-orbitals, cannot expand its valence shell and thus, its maximum covalency is four.

Other members, however, have vacant *d*-orbital and thus, can expand their covalency beyond four. They form pentacoordinated and hexacoordinated complex. e.g. SiF_4 can combine with $2F^-$ ions.

$$SiF_4 + 2F^- \longrightarrow [SiF_6]^{2-}$$

but $[CF_6]^{2-}$ does not exist. Similarly, $[GeCl_6]^{2-}$, $[Sn(OH)_6]^{2-}$ also exist. In these species hybridisation of central atom is sp^3d^2.

$p\pi$-$p\pi$ Multiple Bonding

It has a high tendency of formation of $p\pi$-$p\pi$ multiple bonds either with its own atoms (e.g. C=C, C≡C) or with other atoms such as O, N, S (e.g. C=O, C≡N, C=S, etc.) While other members do not have this tendency as their atomic orbitals are too large. (Other members have a tendency of $d\pi$-$p\pi$ bonding).

Catenation

The ability of like atoms to link together, through covalent bond is called **catenation**. Carbon exhibits the remarkable property of catenation.

The tendency of catenation depends upon the strength of element-element bond which is described in terms of bond energy. The bond energy values for different elements of this group are given as

Bond Energies of Elements of Carbon Family

Bond	Bond energy (kJ/mol)
C—C	348
Si—Si	297
Ge—Ge	260
Sn—Sn	240

Due to property of catenation and $p\pi$ - $p\pi$ bond formation, carbon is able to show allotropic forms.

TEACHER'S TIP

Down the group, the size increases and electronegativity decreases, thus tendency to show cation decreases. The order of catenation is C >> Si > Ge ≈ Sn. Lead does not show catenation.

Quick Test 2

1. Arrange the hydrides of group 14 in increasing order of reducing power.
2. Why does silicon show a higher covalency than carbon?
3. Select the member(s) of group 14 that
   (i) forms the most acidic dioxide.
   (ii) is commonly found in +2 oxidation state.
   (iii) used as semi-conductor. *NCERT*
4. PbO_2 is a stronger oxidising agent than SnO_2. *NCERT Exemplar*
5. Why does C differ from rest of elements?

For Solutions, See QR Code on Pg. 429

11.4 Group 15 Elements : The Nitrogen Family

Group 15 elements are called **pnicogens** and their compounds are known as **pniconides**. The name is derived from the Greek word *pnicomigs* which means suffocation as group 15 elements form suffocative gases.

Group 15 elements include nitrogen, phosphorus, arsenic, antimony and bismuth. Nitrogen and phosphorus are non-metals, arsenic and antimony are metalloids and bismuth is a typical metal. So, down the group, metallic character increases.

Occurrence

Molecular nitrogen (N_2) comprises about 78% by volume of earth's atmosphere. It occurs as sodium nitrate, $NaNO_3$ (chile saltpetre) and potassium nitrate, KNO_3 (Indian saltpetre) in the earth's crust. Since, nitrates are readily soluble in water, so these are not widely spread on the earth's crust. Nitrogen is also an important constituent of amino acids, proteins and nucleic acids in living beings.

Major amounts of phosphorus occur in a mineral family known as apatites of general formula, $3Ca_3(PO_4)_2 \cdot CaX_2$ or $Ca_9(PO_4)_6 \cdot CaX_2$ (where, X = F, Cl or OH), e.g. fluorapatite, $[Ca_9(PO_4)_6 \cdot CaF_2]$, which are the major components of phosphate rocks. Phosphorus is essential constituent of animal and plant materials. It is present in bones as well as in living cells. Nearly, 60% bones and teeth are made up of $Ca_3(PO_4)_2$ or $[3\{Ca_3(PO_4)_2\} \cdot CaF_2]$. It is also present in various biomolecules like DNA, RNA, ATP, ADP and phosphoproteins (found in eggs and milk).

Arsenic, antimony and bismuth are found mainly as sulphide minerals, e.g. arsenopyrites (FeAsS), stibnite (Sb_2S_3), bismuth glance (Bi_2S_3).

General Properties of Group 15 Elements

1. Atomic Properties of Group 15 Elements

Different atomic properties of group 15 elements and their trends are discussed below:

(a) **Electronic configuration** The valence shell electronic configuration of these elements is ns^2np^3 (where, n = number of shells), i.e. s-orbital is fully filled while p-orbital is half-filled in order to make it extra stable.

Electronic Configuration of Group 15 Elements

Element	Atomic number	Atomic mass	Electronic configuration
Nitrogen (N)	7	14	$[He] 2s^2 2p^3$
Phosphorus (P)	15	31	$[Ne] 3s^2 3p^3$
Arsenic (As)	33	75	$[Ar] 3d^{10} 4s^2 4p^3$
Antimony (Sb)	51	122	$[Kr] 4d^{10} 5s^2 5p^3$
Bismuth (Bi)	83	209	$[Xe] 4f^{14} 5d^{10} 6s^2 6p^3$

(b) **Atomic and ionic radii** On moving down the group as the atomic number increases, the atomic and ionic radii (in a particular oxidation state) of the elements increases due to increase in number of shells. There is considerable increase in covalent radius from N to P.

However, from As to Bi, only small increase in covalent radius is observed. It is due to the presence of completely filled *d*- or *f*-orbitals in heavier members which poorly shields the valence electrons of these elements. As a result, the effective nuclear charge increases which reduces the effect of addition of a new energy shell to some extent.

(c) **Ionisation enthalpy** Ionisation enthalpy of group 15 elements is much more than that of group 14 elements in the respective period due to smaller atomic radii and extra stable electronic configuration of half-filled *p*-orbitals. Thus, the valence electrons are strongly attracted by the nucleus and hence, they have less tendency to lose electrons.

The order of successive ionisation enthalpies as expected is $\Delta_i H_1 < \Delta_i H_2 < \Delta_i H_3$.

On moving down the group, ionisation enthalpy decreases from N to Bi due to the gradual increase in atomic radii and shielding effect which reduces the force of attraction on the valence electrons by the nucleus.

(d) **Electronegativity** On moving down the group from N to Bi, electronegativity decreases due to the gradual increase in atomic size.

Electronegativity of N is the fourth highest in the periodic table. Such high electronegativity enables N-atoms to form H-bonds.

2. Physical Properties

Different physical properties of group 15 elements and their trends are given below:

(a) **Atomicity** All the elements of this group are polyatomic. Nitrogen (dinitrogen) is a diatomic gas while other members are solids of different atomicity.

(b) **Metallic character** Metallic character increases down the group due to increase in the atomic size and decrease in ionisation enthalpy. Nitrogen and phosphorus are non-metals, arsenic and antimony are metalloids and bismuth is a metal.

(c) **Melting point** On moving down the group, the melting point first increases from N to As (because of the increase in atomic size) and then decreases upto Bi because of their tendency to form three covalent bonds instead of five covalent bonds due to inert pair effect. This results in weakening of the attraction among their atoms thereby lowering their melting points.

(d) **Boiling point** Boiling point in general increases from top to bottom due to increase in their atomic size. But NH_3, exceptionally, has more boiling point than PH_3.

(e) **Allotropy** All elements tend to show allotropy except nitrogen.

3. Chemical Properties

Chemical properties of group 15 elements are discussed below

(a) **Oxidation states** The common oxidation states of group 15 elements are -3, $+3$ and $+5$. The tendency to show -3 oxidation state decreases down the group due to increase in atomic size and metallic character.

However, Bi does not form any compound in -3 oxidation state. The stability of $+5$ oxidation state decreases down the group. Bi forms only one compound in $+5$ oxidation state, i.e. BiF_5 whereas, the stability of $+3$ oxidation state increases down the group due to **inert pair effect**. However, elements of this group form both ionic (i.e. BiF_3, SbF_3) and covalent compounds (i.e. NCl_3, PCl_3, $AsCl_3$, $SbCl_3$) in $+3$ oxidation state.

The covalent character decreases in the order: $N > P > As > Sb > Bi$.

(b) **Disproportionation** Nitrogen shows $+1$, $+2$ and $+4$ oxidation states also when it reacts with oxygen. Phosphorus also shows $+1$ and $+4$ oxidation states in some oxoacids.

In the case of nitrogen, all oxidation states from $+1$ to $+4$ tend to disproportionate in acid solution, e.g. HNO_2 undergoes disproportionation reaction in acidic medium.

$$3HNO_2 \longrightarrow HNO_3 + 2NO + H_2O$$

Similarly, in case of phosphorus, nearly all intermediate oxidation states disproportionate into +5 and −3 in both acid and alkali. In case of arsenic, antimony and bismuth, +3 oxidation state becomes increasingly stable with respect to disproportionation.

TEACHER'S TIP

Those redox reactions in which the same element undergoes oxidation and reduction, are called **disproportionation reaction.**

e.g $$3H\overset{+3}{N}O_2 \longrightarrow H\overset{+5}{N}O_3 + 2\overset{+2}{N}O + H_2O$$

(c) **Maximum covalency** The maximum covalency of nitrogen is 4 because only four orbitals (one *s* and three *p*) are available for bonding. It does not form compounds in +5 oxidation state such as NCl_5, NF_5, etc., due to the absence of *d*-orbitals in its valence shell.

Heavier members (e.g. phosphorus) can expand their covalency as in etc., due to the availability of vacant *d*-orbitals in the outermost shell.

(d) **Catenation** The elements of group 15 have a tendency to form bonds with itself (self-linking of atoms), which is known as catenation. The tendency towards catenation decreases on moving down the group due to decrease in bond enthalpy. Nitrogen has little tendency for catenation due to repulsion between non-bonded electron pairs.

The N—N bond is weaker than the single P — P bond due to high interelectronic repulsion of the non-bonding electrons in N_2 owing to small bond length. Therefore, the catenation property is weaker in nitrogen as compared to phosphorus.

(e) **Reactivity towards hydrogen** These elements form volatile hydrides with the formula EH_3 (where, $E = N$, P, As, Sb, Bi). The important properties of these hydrides are discussed below :

Stability of Hydrides

On moving down the group, thermal stability decreases from NH_3 to BiH_3 due to increase in the atomic size of the central atom which tends to decrease the bond strength of M—H bond, thereby leading to decrease in bond dissociation energy of M—H bond.

The thermal stability order of the hydrides is as follows

$$NH_3 > PH_3 > AsH_3 > SbH_3 > BiH_3$$

Reducing Character

The reducing character of hydrides of group 15 elements increases down the group in the order:

$$NH_3 < PH_3 < AsH_3 < SbH_3 < BiH_3$$

This order is due to decrease in the thermal stability of hydrides down the group and thus, their tendency to liberate hydrogen increases and hence, their reducing character increases from NH_3 to BiH_3. Therefore, NH_3 is a mild reducing agent while BiH_3 is the strongest reducing agent amongst all the hydrides.

Basic Character

These hydrides are Lewis bases due to the presence of lone pair of electrons on the central atom. Their basic character decreases down the group and thus, the order of basic character is as follows

$$NH_3 > PH_3 > AsH_3 > SbH_3 \geq BiH_3$$

The decrease in basic character down the group is due to increase in the size of central atom thereby leading to decrease in the electron density on the central atom as lone pair of electrons occupy a larger volume. Therefore, the tendency to donate a lone pair of electrons decreases consequently and hence basic strength decreases.

Bond Angle

It gradually decreases down the group as bond pair-lone pair repulsion decreases. All hydrides are pyramidal in shape (sp^3-hybridisation) with a lone pair of electrons.

Boiling Point

The boiling point of NH_3 is more than that of PH_3 due to H-bonding. The boiling point increases down the group from PH_3 to BiH_3 due to increase in the magnitude of van der Waals' forces.

Example 3 The HNH angle value is higher than HPH, HAsH and HSbH angles. Why? NCERT

Sol. In all the hydrides of group 15 elements, the central atom is sp^3 hybridised and three of the four sp^3 orbitals form three E—H σ-bonds while the fourth orbital contains lone pair of electrons. As the lone pair-bond pair repulsions are stronger than the bond pair-bond pair repulsions, therefore, in NH_3, the bond angle decreases from 109° 28′ to 107.8°.

On moving from N to Sb, the electronegativity of the central atom decreases. As a result, the bond pairs of electrons lie away from the central atom and therefore, the force of repulsion between the adjacent bond pairs decreases and consequently, the bond angles decreases from NH_3 to SbH_3.

(f) **Reactivity towards oxygen** The elements of group 15 form two types of oxides E_2O_3 and E_2O_5. The oxide in the higher oxidation state is more acidic than that in the lower oxidation state.

Their acidic character decreases down the group. E_2O_3 type oxides of N and P are purely acidic, while oxides of As and Sb are amphoteric and oxides of Bi are basic.

Trends in acidic character of different oxides of group 15 elements

(i) $N_2O < NO < N_2O_3 < N_2O_4 < N_2O_5$ (Neutral: N_2O, NO)

(ii) $N_2O_3 > P_4O_6 > As_4O_6 > Sb_4O_6 > Bi_2O_3$ (Amphoteric: As_4O_6, Sb_4O_6; Basic: Bi_2O_3)

(iii) $N_2O_5 > P_4O_{10} > As_4O_{10} > Sb_4O_{10}$

(g) **Reactivity towards halogens** These elements directly combine with halogen to form trihalides (EX_3) and pentahalides (EX_5). All trihalides are stable (except those of nitrogen i.e. NBr_3 and NI_3) and have pyramidal shape. In case of nitrogen, only NF_3 is known to be stable. They are easily hydrolysed by water.

Trihalides except BiF_3 are predominantly covalent in nature. N does not form pentahalides due to the absence of *d*-orbital in its valence shell, however P, As and Sb form pentahalides. Bi does not form pentahalides due to the inert pair effect.

Pentahalides involve sp^3d-hybridisation and have trigonal bipyramidal shape. All the pentahalides act as Lewis acids. It is because the central atom can easily accept the halide ions due to the presence of vacant *d*-orbital and it can extend their coordination number. Pentahalides are more covalent than trihalides.

(h) **Reactivity towards metals** These elements react with metals to form their binary compounds exhibiting –3 oxidation state, e.g. Ca_3N_2, Ca_3P_2, Na_3As, Zn_3Sb_2 and Mg_3Bi_2.

Anomalous Properties of Nitrogen

Behaviour of nitrogen is different from rest of the elements because of the following reasons:

(i) Smaller size, high ionisation enthalpy, high electronegativity and the absence of *d*-orbital.

(ii) It has a unique ability to form $p\pi$-$p\pi$ multiple bonds with itself and with other atoms like C and O having small size and high electronegativity. Heavier elements of this group do not form $p\pi$-$p\pi$ bonds as their atomic orbitals are so large and diffused that they cannot have effective overlapping.

The anomalous properties shown by nitrogen, due to the above reasons are as follows:

- Nitrogen is a gas, while other members are found in solid state.
- Nitrogen (N_2) exists as a diatomic molecule with a triple bond ($N\equiv N$). Consequently, its bond enthalpy (941.4 kJ mol^{-1}) is very high. In contrast to nitrogen, P, As and Sb form single bond as P—P, As—As and Sb—Sb while bismuth forms metallic bonds in elemental state.
- Nitrogen forms trinegative ion, i.e. N^{3-} while other members do not.
- Nitrogen is chemically inert under ordinary conditions due to high bond dissociation energy, while other members are quite reactive because of the presence of single bond in their molecules.
- Nitrogen cannot form $d\pi$-$p\pi$ bond due to the absence of *d*-orbitals so, it cannot expand its covalency beyond four as the heavier members of this group can, e.g. $R_3P{=}O$ or $R_3P{=}CH_2$ (R = alkyl group).

  Phosphorus and arsenic can form $d\pi$-$d\pi$ bond with transition metals when their compounds like $P(C_2H_5)_3$ and $As(C_6H_5)_3$ act as ligands.
- The hydride of nitrogen (NH_3) is highly basic in nature while the hydrides of other elements are slightly basic. Moreover, only hydrides of nitrogen shows H-bonding while those of other members do not.
- Nitrogen forms five oxides (i.e. N_2O, NO, N_2O_3, N_2O_4 and N_2O_5) while other members of the family form only two oxide (i.e. tri and pentoxides).
- Except NF_3, other halides of nitrogen, i.e. NCl_3 NBr_3 and NI_3 are unstable while the halides of other elements are fairly stable.
- Nitrogen does not form complexes due to the non-availability of *d*-orbitals while other members have a tendency of complex formation, e.g. $[PCl_6]^-$, $[AsCl_6]^-$, etc.

Quick Test 3

1. Though nitrogen exhibits +5 oxidation state, it does not form pentahalide. Give reason. NCERT
2. PH_3 has lower boiling point than NH_3. Why?
3. Why is BiH_3, the strongest reducing agent amongst all the hydrides of group 15 elements?
4. Why is N_2 less reactive at room temperature? NCERT
5. Explain why NH_3 is basic while BiH_3 is only feebly basic? NCERT

For Solutions, See QR Code on Pg. 429

11.5 Group 16 Elements : The Oxygen Family

Oxygen, sulphur, selenium, tellurium and polonium belongs to group 16 of the periodic table and are collectively known as **chalcogens**.

The name is derived from the Greek word cholcos, meaning ore formers, since they all are be found in copper ores. Most copper minerals contain either oxygen or sulphur and frequently the other members of the group.

All these elements except polonium are non-metallic. Selenium and tellurium show some metallic character, hence are also called as metalloids. Polonium has metallic character and is radioactive.

Occurrence

Oxygen is the most abundant of all the elements on earth. It forms about 46.6% by mass of earth's crust. It is the major constituent of silicate minerals. As water, it comprises 89% by weight of the water present in rivers, seas and oceans. It occurs as ozone (O_3) in the upper atmosphere.

Oxygen occurs in the free form as O_2 and makes 20.95% by volume of the atmosphere. Sulphur is the sixteenth most abundant element and constitutes 0.03-0.1% by mass of the earth's crust. It occurs in the combined form as sulphide ores such as galena (PbS), zinc blende (ZnS), copper pyrites $(CuFeS_2)$ and sulphates such as gypsum $(CaSO_4 \cdot 2H_2O)$, epsom salt $(MgSO_4 \cdot 7H_2O)$, barite $(BaSO_4)$.

It is also present as H_2S in natural gas and crude oil and as organosulphur compounds in coal. Some organic materials such as eggs, proteins, garlic, onion, mustard, hair and wool also contain sulphur. Other elements such as selenium and tellurium occur as metal selenides and tellurides in sulphide ores. Polonium occurs in nature as a decay product of thorium and uranium minerals.

General Properties of Group-16 Elements

1. Atomic Properties

Different atomic properties of group 16 elements are discussed below :

(a) **Electronic configuration** The electronic configuration of outermost shell of group 16 elements is ns^2np^4 (where, n = number of shells).

Electronic Configuration of Group 16 Elements

Element	Atomic number	Atomic mass	Electronic configuration
Oxygen (O)	8	16	$[He]\,2s^2 2p^4$
Sulphur (S)	16	32	$[Ne]3s^2 3p^4$
Selenium (Se)	34	79	$[Ar]3d^{10}4s^2 4p^4$
Tellurium (Te)	52	128	$[Kr]\,4d^{10}5s^2 5p^4$
Polonium (Po)	84	210	$[Xe]4f^{14}5d^{10}6s^2 6p^4$

(b) **Atomic and ionic radii** Due to increase in the number of shells, atomic and ionic radii increases on moving down the group.

Atomic radii of group 16 elements are smaller than the radii of group 15 elements in the respective periods. Size of oxygen atom is exceptionally small in comparison with other group 16 elements.

(c) **Ionization enthalpy** It decreases from O to Po due to increase in atomic size. However, ionization enthalpy of the elements of this group is lower than those of group 15 elements in the corresponding periods. Because group 15 elements have extra stable half-filled p-orbitals electronic configurations.

(d) **Electron gain enthalpy** Electron gain enthalpy of oxygen is less negative than sulphur owing to compact size of oxygen atom due to which inter-electronic repulsions are larger in O. From sulphur onwards, enthalpy again becomes less negative upto Po.

(e) **Electronegativity** Oxygen has the highest electronegativity value after fluorine. Electronegativity decreases down the group with an increase in atomic number. This indicates that metallic character increases from O to Po.

(f) **Multiple bond formation** The tendency of these elements to form multiple bonds to C and N decreases as we go down the group from sulphur to tellurium.

(g) **Catenation** In group 16, only sulphur has a strong tendency of catenation. Oxygen shows catenation behaviour less than sulphur. Due to its smaller size, oxygen experiences repulsions between their lone pair of electrons present on oxygen atom and bond pair of O—O bond hence, O—O bonds are weaker than S—S bonds.

2. Physical Properties

Different physical properties of group 16 elements are given below:

(a) **Physical state** Oxygen is a diatomic gas while other elements are polyatomic solids.

(b) **Metallic character** Oxygen and sulphur are non-metals. Selenium and tellurium are metalloids while polonium is short lived radioactive metal (half-life is about 13.8 days).

(c) **Allotroy** All the elements of this group show allotropy. The prominent allotropes of oxygen are dioxygen and ozone while those of sulphur are rhombic and monoclinic sulphur.

(d) **Melting and boiling points** Melting and boiling points increase down the group with the increase in atomic number upto Te. Po has lower melting and boiling points than those of Te. Oxygen is diatomic CO_2 and sulphur is polyatomic, therefore, there is a large difference in melting and boiling points of O_2 and S_8.

3. Chemical Properties

Chemical properties of group 16 elements are given below:

(a) **Oxidation states** The elements of group 16 exhibit a number of oxidation states. The stability of –2 oxidation state of these elements decreases down the group. Polonium hardly shows –2 oxidation state. Since, electronegativity of oxygen is very high, it shows only negative oxidation state as -2 except in case of OF_2 and O_2F_2 where oxidation state are $+2$ and $+1$ respectively. In H_2O_2, oxygen exists in –1 state. Sulphur, selenium, tellurium and polonium show $+2$, $+4$ and $+6$ oxidation states and $+4$ oxidation state is shown in their compounds with oxygen and $+6$ with fluorine. The stability of $+6$ oxidation state decreases down the group and the stability of $+4$ oxidation state increases due to inert pair effect. Bonding in $+4$ and $+6$ oxidation states is primarily covalent.

(b) **Reactivity towards hydrogen** All the elements of group 16 form stable, volatile and bivalent hydrides of EH_2 or H_2E type (where, E = O, S, Se, Te or Po).

Acidic character Their acidic character increases from H_2O to H_2Te. The increase in acidic character can be explained in terms of decrease in bond enthalpy for the dissociation of H—E bond down the group.

As the atomic size increases down the group, the bond length increases and hence, the bond strength decreases, thereby leading to the decrease in bond enthalpy down the group.

Consequently, the cleavage of E—H bond becomes easier. As a result, the tendency to release hydrogen as proton increases, i.e. acidic strength increases down the group. Therefore, H_2O is least acidic while H_2Po is most acidic.

The overall order of increasing acidic strength is as follows

$$H_2O < H_2S < H_2Se < H_2Te$$

Thermal stability The thermal stability of hydrides decreases from H_2O to H_2Te because as the size of central atom in H_2E increases, the H—E bond becomes weaker and hence, can be broken easily on heating.

Melting and boiling points of hydrides of oxygen, i.e. H_2O is exceptionally very high due to strong H-bonding. Other elements of this group do not form H-bonding as they are less electronegative and their hydrides exist as gases.

However, the melting and boiling points of hydrides of S, Se and Te gradually increase due to increase in magnitude of van der Waals' forces of attraction with increase in the size of the atom.

Thus, the overall order of melting and boiling points of hydrides are

$$H_2S < H_2Se < H_2Te < H_2O.$$

(c) **Reactivity towards oxygen** The elements of this group form dioxides and trioxides of EO_2 and EO_3 type (where, E = S, Se, Te or Po). O_3 and SO_2 are gases while SeO_2 is solid. On moving down the group, acidic character decreases (in the same oxidation state). So, SO_2 and SeO_2 are acidic, whereas TeO_2 and PoO_2 are amphoteric.

Reducing property of dioxides decreases from SO_2 to TeO_2. SO_2 is reducing agent, as +6 oxidation state of S is more stable than +4, while TeO_2 is an oxidising agent. Since the stability of +6 decreases down the group, i.e. from S to Te.

Hence, the reducing character of dioxides decreases while their oxidising character increases. Besides EO_2 type, sulphur, selenium and tellurium also form EO_3 type oxides (SO_3, SeO_3, TeO_3).

Acidic character of the oxide of a particular element increases with the increase in oxidation state of the element. Thus, SO_2 is less acidic than SO_3.

(d) **Reactivity towards halogens** Group 16 elements form number of halides of the type EX_2, EX_4 and EX_6 (where, E = S, Se, Te and X = halogen). The stability of the halides decreases in the order:

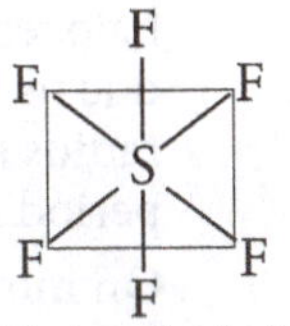

SF_6 (octahedral)

$$F^- > Cl^- > Br^- > I^-$$

Amongst hexahalides, hexafluorides are only stable halides which are gaseous in nature and have sp^3d^2 -hybridisation and octahedral structure. The relative stability decreases in the order:

$$SF_6 > SeF_6 > TeF_6$$

SF_6 is thermally stable and chemically inert. Its chemical inertness is due to the fact that all the six F atoms sterically protect the sulphur atom from the attack by the reagents to such an extent that even thermodynamically most favourable reactions like hydrolysis do not occur. However, as the size of the central atom increases, steric hindrance decreases and hence, the hydrolysis becomes easy.

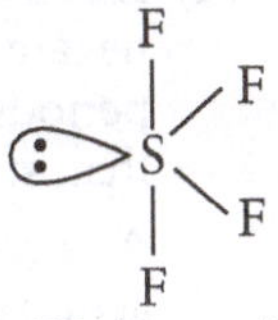

SF_4 (*See-saw*)

Monohalides like S_2F_2, S_2Cl_2, S_2Br_2, Se_2Cl_2, etc., are dimeric in nature and undergo disproportionation.

e.g. $2Se_2Cl_2 \longrightarrow SeCl_4 + 3Se$

All elements except oxygen form dichlorides and dibromides possessing sp^3 -hybridisation and they thus have tetrahedral shape.

Among tetrafluorides, SF_4 is gas, SeF_4 is liquid, TeF_4 is solid with sp^3d-hybridisation and have trigonal bipyramidal structure and *see saw* geometry due to the presence of lone pair of electrons in equatorial position, which repel bond pair of electrons (of axial S—F bonds). That's why, all the bonds in SF_4 are not equal.

Anomalous Properties of Oxygen

Owing to its small size, high charge density and non-availability to *d*-orbitals, oxygen differs from rest of the members in the following respects.

- Oxygen is a diatomic gas while all other members are solid with eight membered puckered ring structure.
- Most of the compounds of oxygen are ionic and polar covalent due to its high electronegativity.
- Oxygen usually exhibits −2 oxidation state. However, it also exhibits +2 and −1 oxidation states. Other members usually does not show these oxidation states.
- Due to the absence of *d*-orbitals, oxygen shows a maximum covalency of 4 and in general, it rarely exceeds two while the other group members can show a maximum covalency of six.
- Oxygen forms $p\pi$ - $p\pi$ multiple bond while, S form $d\pi$ - $p\pi$ bonds.
- Only the hydride of oxygen, i.e. H_2O is non-poisonous and is a liquid while, the hydrides of other members are poisonous gases.
- Oxygen is paramagnetic while, rest are not.
- Due to small size and high electronegativity, compounds of oxygen form hydrogen bonds. e.g. H_2O forms intermolecular hydrogen bonding but H_2S does not.

Quick Test 4

1. Elements of group 16 generally show lower value of first ionisation enthalpy compared to the corresponding periods of group 15. Why? NCERT
2. How would you account for the following? The electron gain enthalpy with negative sign is less for oxygen than that of sulphur.
3. There is a large difference between the melting and boiling points of oxygen and sulphur. Why?
4. H_2S is less acidic than H_2Te. Why? NCERT
5. Write the order of thermal stability of the hydrides of group 16 elements. NCERT
6. Out of H_2O and H_2S, which one has higher bond angle and why? NCERT Exemplar

For Solutions, See QR Code on Pg. 429

11.6 Group 17 Elements : The Halogen Family

Fluorine, chlorine, bromine, iodine and astatine belong to group 17 and are collectively known as **halogens.** Greek word '*halo*' means 'salt' and '*genes*' means 'born', i.e. salt producers.

The elements of group 17 show great similarity amongst themselves like groups 1 and 2 elements. That much similarity is not found in the elements of other groups and also there is a regular gradation in their physical and chemical properties. These are highly reactive non-metallic elements.

Note Astatine is a radioactive element and rare in nature hence, its reactivity and non-metallic properties are little known.

Occurrence

Fluorine and chlorine are fairly abundant while bromine and iodine are less abundant. Fluorine is present mainly as insoluble fluorides [fluorspar (CaF_2), cryolite (Na_3AlF_6) and fluoroapatite [$3Ca_3(PO_4)_2 \cdot CaF_2$]. It is present in small quantities in soil, river water plants and bones and teeth of animals. Sea water contains chlorides, bromides and iodides of sodium, potassium, magnesium and calcium but it mainly contain sodium chloride solution (2.5% by mass).

The deposits of dried up seas and beds of inland lakes contain sodium chloride and carnallite, ($KCl \cdot MgCl_2 \cdot 6H_2O$) and calcium chloride ($CaCl_2$). Bromine occurs in sea water and salt lakes as bromides of alkali and alkaline earth metals,

i.e. NaBr, KBr, $MgBr_2$, etc. Iodine is present in various sea weeds (upto 0.5% by mass) and in chile saltpetre [upto 0.2% as sodium iodate ($NaIO_3$)].

General Properties of Group 17 Elements

1. Atomic Properties

Different atomic properties of group 17 elements are discussed below:

(a) **Electronic configuration** All the elements of this group have seven electrons in their outermost shell (ns^2np^5) which is one electron short of electronic configuration of the next noble gas in their respective periods.

Electronic Configuration of Halogens

Element	Atomic number	Atomic mass	Electronic configuration
Fluorine	9	19	[He] $2s^22p^5$
Chlorine	17	35	[Ne] $3s^23p^5$
Bromine	35	80	[Ar] $3d^{10}4s^24p^5$
Iodine	53	127	[Kr] $4d^{10}5s^25p^5$
Astatine	85	210	[Xe] $4f^{14}5d^{10}6s^26p^5$

(b) **Atomic and ionic radii** Atomic and ionic radii of halogens are the smallest in their respective periods due to maximum effective nuclear charge. Atomic radius of fluorine like the elements of second period is extremely small.

On moving down the group, atomic and ionic radii increases from F to I due to increase in the number of quantum shells.

(c) **Ionisation enthalpy** Halogens have little tendency to lose electron. Thus, they have very high ionization enthalpy next to inert gas. On moving down the group, ionisation enthalpy decreases due to increase in atomic size.

(d) **Electron gain enthalpy** Halogens have highest negative electron gain enthalpy in their respective periods because they have only one electron less than stable noble gas configurations.

As a result, they readily accept one electron to acquire the noble gas configuration. Electron gain enthalpy becomes less negative on moving from chlorine to iodine.

However, negative electron gain enthalpy of fluorine is less than that of chlorine due to small size of fluorine atom. It has very high inter-electronic repulsions in the relatively small 2*p*-orbitals.

Hence, incoming electron experiences less attraction from the nucleus. Despite, lower value of its electron gain enthalpy with negative sign, fluorine (F_2) is a stronger oxidising agent than Cl_2. It is due to

(i) low enthalpy of dissociation of F—F bond.

(ii) high hydration enthalpy of F^- ion.

(e) **Electronegativity** Halogens have very high electronegativity. On moving down the group, electronegativity decreases. Fluorine is the most electronegative element in the periodic table.

2. Physical Properties

Halogens display gradual variations in their physical properties.

Different physical properties of halogens are given below:

(a) **Physical state** Fluorine and chlorine are gases, bromine is a liquid and iodine is a solid.

Note Bromine is the only non-metal which is liquid at STP.

(b) **Melting and boiling points** Their melting and boiling points steadily increase with atomic size due to increase in van der Waals' forces of attraction as these molecules are held together by these forces of attraction.

(c) **Colour** All halogens are coloured due to absorption of radiations in visible region which results in the excitation of outer electrons to higher energy level. By adsorbing different quanta of radiation, they display different colours. e.g. F_2 has yellow, Cl_2 has greenish-yellow, Br_2 has red and I_2 has violet colour.

(d) **Solubility** Fluorine and chlorine react with water. Bromine and iodine are sparingly soluble in water but highly soluble in organic solvents like chloroform, carbon disulphide and hydrocarbons to give coloured solutions.

(e) **Enthalpy of dissociation** Fluorine has smaller bond dissociation enthalpy than chlorine and bromine, while X—X bond dissociation enthalpies from Cl onwards show the expected trend Cl—Cl > Br—Br > I—I. This is due to the small size of F atom and large electron-electron repulsion among the lone pairs of fluorine. The bond dissociation enthalpy follows the order:

$$\text{Cl—Cl} > \text{Br—Br} > \text{F—F} > \text{I—I}$$
$$242.6 > 192.8 > 158.8 > 151.1$$

3. Chemical Properties

Chemical properties of group 17 elements are as follows

(a) Oxidation States

All the halogens show –1 oxidation state. Other halogens excluding fluorine show +1, +3, +5 and +7 oxidation states because of gradual promotion of *np*-electrons to *nd*-electrons.

	ns	*np*	*nd*	
Halogen atom in ground state (other than fluorine)	⥮	⥮ ⥮ 1	□ □ □ □ □	1 unpaired electron accounts for –1 or +1 oxidation states
First excited state	⥮	⥮ 1 1	1 □ □ □ □	3 unpaired electrons account for +3 oxidation state
Second excited state	⥮	1 1 1	1 1 □ □ □	5 unpaired electrons account for +5 oxidation state
Third excited state	1	1 1 1	1 1 1 □ □	7 unpaired electrons account for +7 oxidation state

Fluorine atom has no *d*-orbital in its valence shell and therefore cannot expand its octet, and being the most electronegative element, it shows only –1 oxidation state. The higher oxidation states of chlorine, bromine and iodine are found mainly when the halogens are in combination with the small and highly electronegative fluorine and oxygen atoms. e.g. In interhalogens (when a halogen is in combination with a different halogen atom) like ClF, IF, ICl, oxides and oxoacids. The oxidation states of + 4 and + 6 occur in the oxides and oxoacids of chlorine and bromine.

(b) Trends in Chemical Reactivity

All the halogens are highly reactive. Their reactivity decreases down the group. They reacts with metals and non-metals to form halides.

Some important trends in the chemical reactivity and their compounds are discussed below:

Oxidising Power

The acceptance of an electron readily is due to the strong oxidising nature of halogens.

F_2 is the strongest oxidising halogen and it oxidises other halide ions in solution or even in the solid phase. In general, a halogen oxidises halide ions of higher atomic number.

Fluorine oxidises all the halides.

$$F_2 + 2X^- \longrightarrow 2F^- + X_2 \qquad [X = \text{Cl, Br, I}]$$

Chlorine oxidises only bromide and iodide ions.

$$Cl_2 + 2X^- \longrightarrow 2Cl^- + X_2 \qquad [X = \text{Br, I}]$$

Bromine oxidises only iodide ion.

$$Br_2 + 2I^- \longrightarrow 2Br^- + I_2$$

Hence, the oxidising ability of halogens decreases from fluorine to iodine as:

$$F_2 > Cl_2 > Br_2 > I_2$$

The decreasing oxidising ability of halogens in the aqueous solution down the group can be illustrated by their standard electrode potential ($E°$) values.

X_2	F_2	Cl_2	Br_2	I_2
$E°$ (volts)	2.87 V	1.36 V	1.09 V	0.54 V

$$\frac{1}{2}X_2(g) \xrightarrow{\frac{1}{2}\Delta_{diss}H°} X(g) \xrightarrow{\Delta_{eg}H°} X^-(g) \xrightarrow{\Delta_{hyd}H°} X^-(aq)$$

The relative oxidising power of halogens can be further illustrated by their reactions with water.

Fluorine oxidises water to oxygen.

$$2F_2(g) + 2H_2O(l) \longrightarrow 4HF(aq) + O_2(g)$$

Chlorine and bromine undergoes disproportionation on reaction with water and gives corresponding hydrohalic and hypohalous acids.

$$X_2(g) + H_2O(l) \longrightarrow HX(aq) + HOX; [X = Cl \text{ or } Br]$$

The reaction of iodine with water is non-spontaneous. Iodide ion can be oxidised by oxygen in acidic medium.

$$4I^-(aq) + 4H^+(g) + O_2(aq) \longrightarrow 2I_2(s) + 2H_2O(l)$$

Reactivity towards Hydrogen

All halogens react with hydrogen to give hydrogen halides but affinity towards hydrogen decreases down the group. Hydrogen halides dissolve in water to produce hydrohalic acids. The acidic strength of these acids increases from HF to HI. This is because the stability of these halides decreases down the group due to decrease in bond (H—X) dissociation enthalpy in the order.

$$H—F > H—Cl > H—Br > H—I$$

Reactivity towards Oxygen

Halogens form many oxides with oxygen but most of the oxides are unstable. Fluorine forms two oxides, i.e. OF_2 and O_2F_2. However, only OF_2 is thermally stable at 298 K. The compounds OF_2 and O_2F_2 are called **oxygen fluorides** and both are strong fluorinating agents because of the higher electronegativity of fluorine. O_2F_2 oxidises plutonium to PuF_6, this helps to remove Pu as PuF_6 from spent nuclear fuel. Chlorine, bromine and iodine form oxides in +1 to +7 oxidation states. A combination of kinetic and thermodynamic factors lead to generally by decreasing order of stability of oxides formed by halogens.

Iodine > Chlorine > Bromine

The oxides of higher oxidation state are more stable than that of lower oxidation state. Chlorine form oxides like Cl_2O, ClO_2, Cl_2O_6 and Cl_2O_7. These oxides are very reactive and strong oxidising agent and tend to explode.

Note ClO_2 is used as a bleaching agent in paper pulp industry, in textile and in water treatment.

The bromine oxides Br_2O, BrO_2, BrO_3 are the least stable halogen oxides which exist only at low temperatures. These are powerful oxidising agents. Iodine forms oxides such as I_2O_4, I_2O_5, I_2O_7, which are insoluble solids and decompose on heating.

Note I_2O_5 is a very good oxidising agent and is used in the estimation of carbon monoxide (CO).

Reactivity towards Metals

Halogens react with metals to give metallic halides, e.g. bromine reacts with magnesium to give magnesium bromide.

$$Mg(s) + Br_2(l) \longrightarrow MgBr_2(s)$$

The ionic character of the halides decreases down the group. If a metal exhibits more than one oxidation state, the halides in higher oxidation state will be more covalent than that in lower oxidation state, e.g. $SnCl_4$, $PbCl_4$, $SbCl_5$ and UF_6 are more covalent than $SnCl_2$, $PbCl_2$, $SbCl_3$ and UF_4, respectively.

Reactivity of Halogens towards Other Halogens

Halogens combine amongst themselves to form a number of compounds called **interhalogen compounds** of the type XX', XX'_3, XX'_5, XX'_7, where, X is a halogen of larger size and X' is a halogen of smaller size.

Anomalous Behaviour of Fluorine

Ionisation enthalpy, electronegativity and electrode potential are all higher for fluorine than expected from the trends set by other halogens. The ionic and covalent radii, melting and boiling points, enthalpy of bond dissociation and electron gain enthalpy are quite lower than expected. This is due to the small size, highest electronegativity, low F—F bond dissociation enthalpy and non-availability of d-orbitals in valence shell. Most of the reactions of fluorine are exothermic because it forms small and strong bonds with other elements. Fluorine tends to form only one oxoacids while other halogens form a number of oxoacids. Due to the strong hydrogen bonding, hydrogen fluoride is a liquid while other hydrogen halides are gases.

Quick Test 5

1. Halogens have maximum negative electron gain enthalpy in the respective periods of the periodic table. Why? *NCERT Textbook*
2. Although electron gain enthalpy of fluorine is less negative as compared to chlorine, fluorine is a stronger oxidising agent than chlorine. Why? *NCERT Textbook*
3. F_2 has lower bond dissociation enthalpy than Cl_2. Why? *Delhi 2015; All India 2015*
4. Fluorine exhibits only −1 oxidation state whereas other halogens exhibit +1, +3, +5 and +7 oxidation states also. Explain. *NCERT Textbook*
5. Acidic character increases from HF to HI. Account for this. *Delhi 2015; All India 2015*

For Solutions, See QR Code on Pg. 429

11.7 Group 18 Elements : The Noble Gases

Group 18 consists of six elements helium, neon, argon, krypton, xenon and radon. All these are gases, which are almost chemically inert hence, the elements of this group are called **inert gases**. They form very few compounds, that's why, these are termed as **noble gases**. Helium is a *s*-block element but has been placed in group 18, at the top, as its chemical inertness is similar to the rest of the members of group 18.

Occurrence

All the noble gases except radon occur in the atmosphere. Their atmospheric abundance in dry air is nearly 1% by volume, of which argon (0.93%) is the major constituent. Helium is also present in natural gas to the extent of 2 to 7%. He and sometimes Ne are found in minerals of radioactive origin, e.g. pitch blende, monazite, cleveite. Xenon and radon are the rarest elements of this group. Radon is radioactive. It is obtained as a decay product of radium (Ra-226).

$$^{226}_{88}Ra \longrightarrow ^{222}_{86}Rn + ^{4}_{2}He + Q$$

General Properties of Group 13 Elements

1. Atomic Properties

Different atomic properties of group 18 elements are discussed below:

(a) **Electronic configuration** Electronic configuration of their outermost shell is ns^2np^6 except helium which has $1s^2$ electronic configuration. Atomic number and atomic mass of group 18 elements with their electronic configuration are given in the following table.

Electronic Configuration of Group 18 Elements

Element	Atomic number	Atomic mass	Electronic configuration
Helium	2	4	$1s^2$
Neon	10	20	$[He]2s^22p^6$
Argon	18	40	$[Ne]3s^23p^6$
Krypton	36	84	$[Ar]3d^{10}4s^24p^6$
Xenon	54	131	$[Kr]4d^{10}5s^25p^6$
Radon	86	222	$[Xe]4f^{14}5d^{10}6s^26p^6$

(b) **Ionisation enthalpy** All inert gases have very high ionisation enthalpy due to stable electronic configuration. However, it decreases down the group with increase in atomic size.

(c) **Atomic radius** Atomic radii of inert gases are larger than expected because electron cloud is slightly expanded due to van der Waals' radii. Atomic radii increase down the group.

(d) **Electron gain enthalpy** These elements have large positive values of electron gain enthalpy because they have stable electronic configuration and have no tendency to accept the electron.

2. Physical Properties

Different physical properties of group 18 elements are given below:

(i) **Atomicity** All gases are monoatomic due to the unavailability of unpaired electron.

(ii) **Physical state** They are colourless, odourless and tasteless gases. They are sparingly soluble in water.

(iii) **Melting and boiling points** The melting and boiling points of noble gases are quite low in comparison to other elements of comparable masses because they have no interatomic forces except weak dispersion forces.

However, melting and boiling points are increased down the group due to increase in the magnitude of van der Waals' forces.

Helium has the lowest boiling point (4.2 K) of any known substance. It has an unusual property of diffusion through rubber, glass or plastics.

3. Chemical Properties

Noble gases are least reactive elements due to the following reasons:

- The noble gases except He ($1s^2$) have completely filled (ns^2np^6) electronic configuration in their valence shell.
- They have high ionisation enthalpy and more positive electron gain enthalpy.

Discovery of Compounds of Inert Gases

The first compound of Xe was $Xe^+PtF_6^-$ which was discovered by **Neil Bartlett**. When oxygen is treated with PtF_6, a red compound $O_2^+PtF_6^-$ was formed.

In this compound, the ionisation enthalpy of molecular oxygen was identical with that of Xe. This idea led to the discovery of compounds of Xe, when mixing of xenon and PtF_6 resulted in the formation of a red compound $Xe^+PtF_6^-$. The compounds of Kr are fewer.

Only the difluorides of Kr (KrF_2) has been studied. No compounds of Rn have been isolated but only RnF_2 has been identified by radio-tracer technique. No true compounds of Ar, Ne or He are known yet.

Quick Test 6

1. Why are the elements of group 18 known as noble gases? *NCERT Textbook*
2. Why do noble gases have comparatively large atomic sizes? *NCERT Textbook*
3. Noble gases have very low boiling points. Why? *NCERT Textbook*
4. Give reason.
   Boiling points of noble gases increase from helium to radon. *NCERT Textbook*
5. What inspired N Bartlett for carrying out reaction between Xe and PtF_6? *NCERT*

For Solutions, See QR Code on Pg. 429

EXAM PATTERN QUESTIONS

Objective Type Questions

Multiple Choice Questions (MCQs) [1 Mark]

1. The second period elements of *p*-block starting from boron, are restricted to a maximum covalency of

(a) four (using 1*s*, 2*s* and two 2*p* orbitals)
(b) six (using 1*s* and 2*s* -orbitals)
(c) four (using 2*s* and three 2*p* orbitals)
(d) six (using 1*s* and three 2*p* orbitals)

2. First ionisation enthalpy ($\Delta_i H$ kJ mol^{-1}) for the elements of group 13 follows the order **NCERT Exemplar**

(a) B > Al > Ga > In > Tl
(b) B < Al < Ga < In < Tl
(c) B < Al > Ga < In > Tl
(d) B > Al < Ga > In < Tl

3. The relationship between first second and third ionisation enthalpies of each group-13 element is

(a) $\Delta_i H_1 > \Delta_i H_2 > \Delta_i H_3$
(b) $\Delta_i H_1 < \Delta_i H_2 < \Delta_i H_3$
(c) $\Delta_i H_1 = \Delta_i H_2 = \Delta_i H_3$
(d) $\Delta_i H_3 < \Delta_i H_1 < \Delta_i H_2$

4. The element which exists in liquid state for a wide range of temperature and can be used for measuring high temperature is **NCERT Exemplar**

(a) B (b) Al (c) Ga (d) In

5. Which of the following oxides is acidic in nature? **NCERT Exemplar**

(a) B_2O_3 (b) Al_2O_3 (c) Ga_2O_3 (d) In_2O_3

6. $AlCl_3$ achieves stability by forming a dimer. Structure of this dimer is

(a) 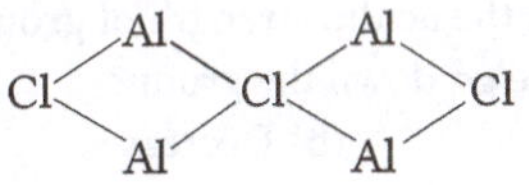

(b) 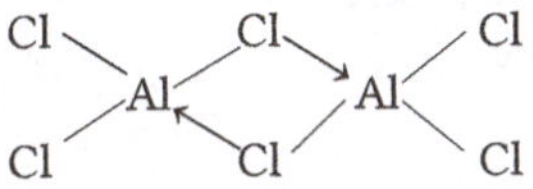

(c) 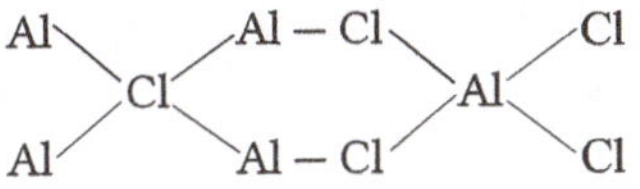

(d) None of the above

7. The tendency to behave as Lewis acid decreases as the size

(a) increases (b) decreases
(c) remains same
(d) first increases then decreases

8. The tendency of Ge, Sn and Pb to show +2 oxidation state increases in the sequence

(a) Ge = Sn < Pb (b) Ge < Sn < Pb
(c) Ge > Sn > Pb (d) Ge > Sn = Pb

9. Catenation, i.e. linking of similar atoms depends on size and electronic configuration of atoms. The tendency of catenation in group 14 elements follows the order **NCERT Exemplar**

(a) C > Si > Ge > Sn (b) C >> Si > Ge ≈ Sn
(c) Si > C > Sn > Ge (d) Ge > Sn > Si > C

10. All group-14 members when heated in oxygen form

(a) monoxide (b) dioxide
(c) trioxide
(d) monoxide and dioxide both

11. As we move down group 15 in the periodic table, the elements transition from

(a) metallic to non metallic character
(b) non-metallic to metallic character
(c) gaseous to solid state
(d) solid to gaseous state

12. What is the general valence shell electronic configuration of group 15 elements?

(a) ns^2np^2 (b) ns^2np^3
(c) ns^2np^4 (d) ns^1np^4

13. Which of the following elements has the highest ionisation enthalpy?

(a) Phosphorus (b) Arsenic
(c) Nitrogen (d) Bismuth

14. Which group 15 element has the highest density?

(a) Phosphorus (b) Arsenic
(c) Antimony (d) Bismuth

15. Which of the following hydrides of group 16 has the highest thermal stability?

(a) H_2S (b) H_2Se
(c) H_2O (d) H_2Te

16. When group 16 elements react with halogens, they form a variety of halides. Which of the following hexahalides (EX_6) is the most stable?

(a) SF_6 (b) SeF_6
(c) TeF_6 (d) PoF_6

17. **Which of the following trends is observed in group 17 elements?**
(a) The boiling points decrease down the group.
(b) The oxidising power increases down the group.
(c) The bond dissociation energy decreases from Cl_2 to I_2.
(d) The electron affinity of fluorine is the highest among all elements.

18. **Which of the following noble gases forms the most stable compounds?**
(a) He (b) Ne
(c) Ar (d) Xe

Assertion-Reason [1 Mark]

Directions (Q. Nos. 19-23) In the following questions, a statement of Assertion is followed by a corresponding statements of Reason of the following statements, choose the correct one.
(a) Both (A) and (R) are correct and (R) is the correct explanation of (A).
(b) Both (A) and (R) are correct but (R) is not the correct explanation of (A).
(c) (A) is correct but (R) is incorrect.
(d) (A) is incorrect but (R) is correct.

19. **Assertion** (A) The tendency to exhibit –3 oxidation state decreases down the group in group 18 elements.
Reason (R) Metallic character increases down the group.

20. **Assertion** (A) The stability of the +5 oxidation state decreases down the group.
Reason (R) The electronegativity of elements increases down the group.

21. **Assertion** (A) Nitrogen shows anomalous behavior compared to other group 15 elements.
Reason (R) Nitrogen has vacant *d*-orbitals, which allow it to expand its covalency.

22. **Assertion** (A) Nitrogen does not form $p\pi$-$d\pi$ bonds like phosphorus and arsenic.
Reason (R) Nitrogen lacks vacant d-orbitals in its valence shell.

23. **Assertion** (A) The boiling points of noble gases increase the group.
Reason (R) The strength of van der Waals' forces increases down the group.

Case-Study [4 Marks]

24. **Read the given case and answer the following questions.**
The elements of group 16, also known as the chalcogens, include oxygen (O), sulphur (S). selenium (Se), tellurium (Te), and polonium (Po). These elements exhibit a general trend in their atomic, physical and chemical properties. Oxygen, being the smallest and most electronegative, is a gas at room temperature, while others exist as solids. Oxygen and sulphur are non-metals, selenium and tellurium are metalloids, while polonium is a metal.

(i) (a) Give the general electronic configuration of group-16 elements.
(b) Which one has more negative electron gain enthalpy, O or S?

(ii) Which of the following statements is incorrect regarding group 16 elements?
(a) Oxygen has the highest electronegativity in the group.
(b) Ionisation enthalpy increases down the group.
(c) The metallic character increases down the group.
(d) Oxygen exists as a diatomic gas, whereas sulphur exista as S_8 solid.

(iii) Why does oxygen not show +6 oxidation state like sulphur and selenium?
(a) Oxygen has a strong inert pair effect.
(b) Oxygen lacks vacant *d*-orbitals.
(c) Oxygen is a metal, so it does not show +6 state.
(d) Oxygen prefers forming ionic bonds over covalent bonds.

Or

What is the trend in the acidio strength of group 16 hydrides (H_2E) as we go down the group?
(a) Increases (b) Decreases
(c) First increases, then decreases
(d) Remains the same

Subjective Type Questions

Short Answer Type I Questions [2 Marks]

1. Discuss the pattern of variation in the oxidation states of B to Tl. NCERT

2. Why does gallium undergo disproportionation reactions?

3. How does electron deficient compound BF_3 achieve electronic saturation, i.e. fully occupied outer electron shells ?

4. Standard electrode potential values, $E^{\ominus}$ for Al^{3+}/Al is –1.66 V and that of Tl^{3+} / Tl is + 1.26 V.

Predict about the formation of M^{3+} ion in solution and compare the electropositive character of the two metals. **NCERT**

5. BCl_3 is trigonal planar while $AlCl_3$ is tetrahedral in dimeric state. Explain.

Or

BCl_3 exists as monomer whereas $AlCl_3$ is dimerised through halogen bridging. Given reason. Explain the structure of the dimer of $AlCl_3$ also.

6. Explain why is there a phenomenal decrease in ionisation enthalpy from carbon to silicon? **NCERT**

7. $[SiF_6]^{2-}$ is known whereas $[SiCl_6]^{2-}$ not. Give possible reasons. **NCERT**

8. Rationalise the given statements and give chemical reactions. **NCERT**
(i) Lead (II) chloride reacts with Cl_2 to give $PbCl_4$.
(ii) Lead (IV) chloride is highly unstable towards heat.
(iii) Lead is known not to form an iodide, PbI_4.

9. Give reasons for the following.
(i) CCl_4 is immiscible in water, whereas $SiCl_4$ is easily hydrolysed.
(ii) Carbon has a strong tendency for catenation as compared to silicon. **NCERT Exemplar**

10. Consider the compounds, BCl_3 and CCl_4. How will they behave with water? Justify. **NCERT**

11. (i) Why are pentahalides more covalent than trihalides?
(ii) Why is BiH_3 the strongest reducing agent amongst all the hydrides of group 15 elements ? **NCERT**

12. Considering the parameters such as bond dissociation enthalpy, electron gain enthalpy and hydration enthalpy, compare the oxidising power of F_2 and Cl_2. **NCERT**

Short Answer Type II Questions [3 Marks]

13. In some of the reactions, thallium resembles aluminium, whereas in others it resembles with group I metals. Support this statement by giving some evidences. **NCERT**

14. Explain the following.
(i) Gallium has higher ionisation enthalpy than aluminium.
(ii) Boron does not exist as B^{3+} ion.
(iii) Aluminium forms $[AlF_6]^{3-}$ ion but boron does not form $[BF_6]^{3-}$ ion. **NCERT Exemplar**

15. Three pairs of compounds are given below. Identify that compound in each of the pairs which has group 13 element in more stable oxidation state. Give reason for your choice. State the nature of bonding also.
(i) $TlCl_3$, $TlCl$ (ii) $AlCl_3$, $AlCl$
(iii) $InCl_3$, $InCl$ **NCERT Exemplar**

16. A non-metallic element of group 13, used in making bullet proof vests is extremely hard solid of black colour. It can exist in many allotropic forms and has unusually high melting point. Its trifluoride acts as Lewis acid towards ammonia. The element exhibits maximum covalency of four. Identify the element and write the reaction of its trifluoride with ammonia. Explain, why does the trifluoride act as a Lewis acid? **NCERT Exemplar**

17. (i) List the important sources of sulphur.
(ii) Write the order of thermal stability of the hydrides of group 16 elements.
(iii) Why is H_2O a liquid and H_2S a gas? **NCERT**

18. (i) Give two examples to show the anomalous behaviour of fluorine.
(ii) Sea is the greatest source of some halogens. Comment. **NCERT**

Long Answer Type Questions [5 Marks]

19. (i) Write the reactions to justify amphoteric nature of aluminium. **NCERT**
(ii) Anhydrous $AlCl_3$ is covalent. From the data given below, predict whether it would remain covalent or become ionic in aqueous solution (ionisation enthalpy for Al $=5137$ kJ mol^{-1}. $\Delta H_{hydration}$ of $Al^{3+} = -4655$ kJ mol^{-1}) and $\Delta H_{hydration}$ of $Cl^- = 381$ kJ mol^{-1}.
(iii) Account for the following observations.
(a) $AlCl_3$ is a Lewis acid.
(b) Though fluorine is more electronegative than chlorine yet BF_3 is weaker Lewis acid than BCl_3.

20. Give reason.
(i) SF_6 is known but SCl_6 is not.
(ii) SF_6 is inert towards hydrolysis.
(iii) H_2O is liquid while H_2S is a gas.
(iv) Oxygen shows catenation behaviour less than sulphur.
(v) Melting point of H_2Se is greater than H_2S.

21. Explain the following by giving a reason.
(i) ClF_3 exists but FCl_3 does not exist.
(ii) Electron gain enthalpies of halogens are largely negative.
(iii) Fluoride ion has higher hydration enthalpy than chloride ion.
(iv) SO_2 is reducing while TeO_2 is an oxidising agent.
(v) ICl is more reactive than I_2.

Hints & Solutions

Objective Type Questions

1. (c) The second period elements of *p*-block starting from boron are restricted to a maximum covalency of four (using one 2*s* and three 2*p* orbitals).

2. (d) On moving from B to Al, the ionisation enthalpies decreases as expected and this decrease is due to an increase in atomic size and shielding effect.
On moving from Al to Ga, the ionisation enthalpy increases slightly due to increase in effective nuclear charge (caused by poor shielding of 3*d*-electrons).
On moving from Ga to In, again there is slight decrease in ionisation enthalpies due to increased shielding effect.
On moving from In to Tl, ionisation enthalpies show the increase again because 4*f* electrons shield valence electron poorly and so effective nuclear charge increases.

3. (b) $\Delta_i H_1 < \Delta_i H_2 < \Delta_i H_3$

4. (c) Ga exists as liquid from 30°C upto 2000°C and hence, it is used in high temperature thermometry.

5. (a) The nature of oxides changes from acidic to basic through amphoteric on moving down the group.

B_2O_3 (More acidic less basic), Al_2O_3 and Ga_2O_3 (Amphoteric), In_2O_3 and Tl_2O_3 (Basic)

6. (b) Dimeric structure of $AlCl_3$ is stable in nature and can be represented as

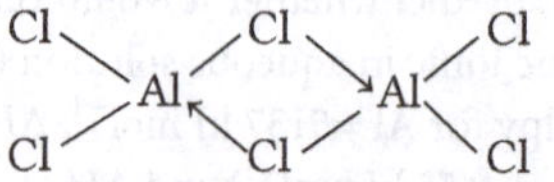

7. (a) The tendency to behave as a Lewis acid decreases with the increase in the size on moving down the group.

8. (b) The tendency of Ge, Sn, Pb to show +2 oxidation state increases on moving from Ge to Pb. Thus, the correct sequence is Ge < Sn < Pb.

9. (b) The tendency to form long open or closed atom chains by combination of some similar atoms is known as catenation. The catenation is maximum in carbon and decreases down the group.

$$C >> Si > Ge \approx Sn$$

This is due to high bond energy of C—C bonds. Down the group, size increases and electronegativity decreases, thereby, tendency to show catenation decreases.

10. (d) Both monoxide and dioxide.

11. (b) Nitrogen and phosphorus are non-metals, arsenic and antimony are metalloids, and bismuth is a metal.

12. (b) ns^2np^3

13. (c) Due to its small size and stable half-filled *p*-orbitals, nitrogen has the highest ionisation enthalpy.

14. (d) The density of group 15 elements increases down the group, with bismuth having the highest density (9.808 g/cm^3).

15. (c) The thermal stability of hydrides decreases down the group due to increasing bond length and decreasing bond dissociation energy. H_2O has the highest stability because of strong hydrogen bonding and high bond enthalpy.

16. (a) SF_6 is the most stable due to strong S—F bonds and steric protection by fluorine atoms, which prevents hydrolysis. Heavier hexahalides are more reactive and less stable.

17. (c) The bond dissociation energy decreases from Cl_2 to I_2 because the bond length increases, weakening the bond. Fluorine has lower electron affinity than chlorine due to high interelectronic repulsion in its small 2*p* orbital.

18. (d) Xenon has relatively low ionisation enthalpy compared to other noble gases, allowing it to form compounds like XeF_2, XeF_4, and XeO_3 with highly electronegative elements like fluorine and oxygen.

19. (a) (A) and (R) are both correct, and (R) is the correct explanation of (A).
As we go down group 15, elements become more metallic making it harder for them to gain electrons and show a −3 oxidation state.

20. (c) (A) is correct, but (R) is incorrect.
Electronegativity decreases down the group, not increases. The inert pair effect causes the +5 state to become less stable.

21. (c) (A) is correct, but (R) is incorrect.
Nitrogen does not have *d*-orbitals, so it cannot expand its covalency beyond four.

22. (a) (A) and (R) are both correct, and (R) is the correct explanation of (A).
$p\pi$-$d\pi$ bonding occurs when a *p*-orbital overlaps with an empty *d*-orbital. Heavier elements like phosphorus and arsenic have vacant *d*-orbitals, allowing them to form such bonds. However, nitrogen, being a second-period element, does not have *d*-orbitals, restricting its bonding to $p\pi$-$p\pi$ interactions instead.

23. (a) (A) and (R) are both correct, and (R) is the correct explanation of (A).
As the atomic size of noble gases increases, the van der Waals' forces between atoms become stronger, leading to higher boiling points.

24. (i) (a) ns^2np^4
(b) S (as O has smaller size, thus electron- electron repulsion will take place).
(ii) (b) Ionisation enthalpy decreases down the group due to increasing atomic size.
(iii) (b) Oxygen does not have *d* orbitals, so it cannot expand its oxidation state to +6, unlike sulphur and selenium
Or (a) The acidic strength increases from H_2O to H_2Te because the *E*–H bond weakens down the group, making it easier to release H^+ ions.

Subjective Type Questions

1.

Element	B	Al	Ga	In	Tl
Oxidation state	+3	+3	+3, +1	+3, +1	+1

Boron and aluminium show an oxidation state of +3 only because they do not exhibit inert pair effect due to the absence of *d* or *f*-electrons. Elements from Ga to Tl show two oxidation states, i.e. +1 and +3. The tendency to show +1 oxidation state increases down the group due to the inability of ns^2 electrons of valence shell to participate in bonding which is called inert pair effect.

Therefore, Tl^+ is more stable than Tl^{3+}.

2. Gallium shows both +1 and +3 oxidation states due to inert pair effect. However, its +3 oxidation state is more stable than +1 oxidation state, hence undergoes disproportionation to form gallium and more stable +3 gallium ions in aqueous solution as shown below.

Reduced

$$\overset{+1}{3GaX(s)} \longrightarrow \overset{0}{2Ga(s)} + \overset{+3}{Ga(aq)} + 3X^-(aq)$$

Oxidised

or $\quad 3Ga^+(aq) \longrightarrow 2Ga(s) + Ga^{3+}(aq)$

3. BF_3 achieve it by the following ways.
   (i) Multiple bonding or $p\pi$-$p\pi$ back bonding, e.g. BF_3 in which a lone pair of electrons present in 2*p*-orbital of one of the fluorine atoms may be transferred to the vacant *p*-orbital on the boron atom. **(1)**
   (ii) Formation of complexes in which electrons are received from a donor molecule, e.g. $F_3B \leftarrow NH_3$. Boron compounds, thus, behave as Lewis acids. **(1)**
4. Since, $E°$ values are more negative in case of Al, so it has higher tendency to form $Al^{3+}(aq)$ ions, whereas Tl^{3+} is highly unstable in aqueous solution and acts as a good oxidising agent. It readily reduces to more stable Tl^+ ion. Al^{3+} being stable, exists in this form and hence, Al is more electropositive as compared to Tl. **(2)**
5. Both BCl_3 and $AlCl_3$ are electron deficient molecules having six electrons in the valence shell of their respective central atoms. To complete their octets, the central atom in each case can accept a pair of electrons from the chlorine atom of another molecule forming dimeric structures.
   However, because of small size of B, it cannot accommodate four big sized Cl atoms around it. Therefore, BCl_3 prefers to exist as a monomeric planar molecule in which B atom is sp^2-hybridised.

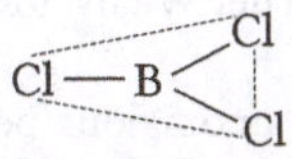

(1)

On the other hand, Al because of its bigger size can easily accommodate four Cl atoms around it.

As a result, $AlCl_3$ exists as a dimer. In this dimer, since the covalency of Al has increased to 4.

Therefore, Al is sp^3-hybridised and the four Cl atoms are held tetrahedrally around it.

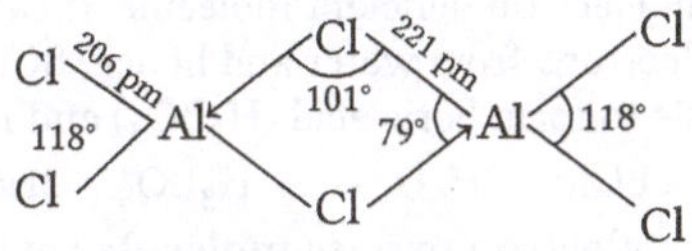

6. As we move from carbon to silicon atomic size increases, i.e. the distance between the outermost electron and nucleus increases. Thus, this electron experience very small attraction from the nucleus and hence, easy to remove. Since, the size of Si-atom is larger, the outer electron experience lesser attraction and hence, its ionisation enthalpy (energy required to remove an electron) is smaller. **([2)**
7. The main reasons for the existence of $[SiF_6]^{2-}$ and non-existence of $[SiCl_6]^{2-}$ are as follows
   (i) Six large chloride ions connot be accommodated around Si^{4+} due to limitation of its size. **(1)**
   (ii) Interaction between lone pair of chloride ion and Si^{4+} is not very strong. **(1)**
8. (i) Due to inert pair effect, Pb is more stable in + 2 state than in +4 oxidation state. Therefore, lead (II) chloride does not react with Cl_2 to give lead (IV) chloride. **(1)**
   (ii) Lead (IV) chloride on heating decomposes to give lead (II) chloride and Cl_2 because lead in + 2 oxidation state is more stable than in + 4 oxidation state.
   $$PbCl_4(l) \longrightarrow PbCl_2(s) + Cl_2(g)$$
   (iii) Due to strong oxidising power of Pb^{4+} ion and reducing power of I^- ion, PbI_4 does not exist. **(1)**
9. (i) CCl_4 does not hydrolysed by water because of the absence of *d*-orbitals in carbon. While $SiCl_4$ is readily hydrolysed by water.
   $$SiCl_4 + 4H_2O \longrightarrow \underset{\text{Silicic acid}}{Si(OH)_4} + 4HCl$$
   The hydrolysis of $SiCl_4$ occurs due to coordination of OH^- with empty 3*d*-orbitals in silicon atom of $SiCl_4$ molecule.

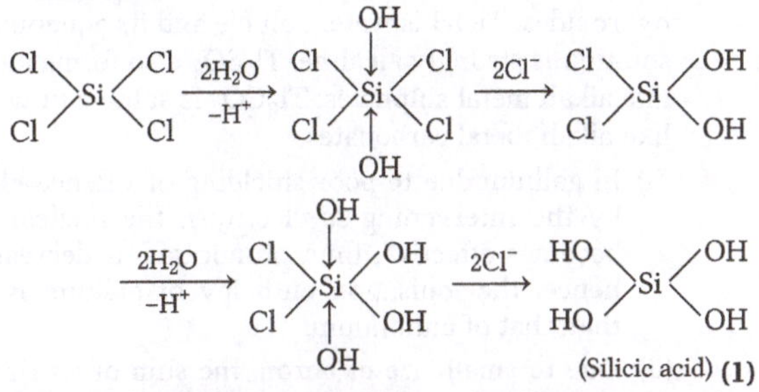

(Silicic acid) **(1)**

   (ii) The catenation is maximum in carbon and decreases down the group. With increase in atomic size, electronegativity decreases and due to this, tendency to show catenation decreases.

C—C bond enthalpy (348 kJ mol^{-1}) is greater than Si—Si bond enthalpy (297 kJ mol^{-1}). Therefore, C—C bond is stronger than Si—Si bond. That's why carbon has much higher tendency for catenation than silicon. **(1)**

10. BCl_3 is an electron deficient molecule. It easily accepts a pair of electrons from water and hence, BCl_3 undergoes hydrolysis to form boric acid (H_3BO_3) and HCl.

$$BCl_3 + 3H_2O \longrightarrow H_3BO_3 + 3HCl \quad \textbf{(1)}$$

CCl_4 is an **electron precise molecule** having absence of *d*-orbitals in C atom and hence, it neither accepts nor donates a pair of electrons. Thus, CCl_4 does not undergo hydrolysis in water. **(1)**

11. (i) In pentahalides, the oxidation state is +5 and in trihalides, the oxidation state is +3. Since, the metal ion with a high charge has more polarising power, therefore, pentahalides are more covalent than trihalides. **(1)**

(ii) As we move down the group the size of the element increases and therefore, the length of the *E*—H bond increases and its strength decreases. In other words, as we move down the group, the *E*—H bond can break more easily to evolve H_2 gas, and it acts as the reducing agent. Thus, Bi—H bond is the weakest amongst the hydrides of elements of group 15 and hence BiH_3 the strongest reducing agent. **(1)**

12. Fluorine is a stronger oxidising agent than chlorine due to its lower bond dissociation enthalpy, higher electron gain enthalpy, and higher hydration enthalpy. The F—F bond is weaker due to strong interelectronic repulsions, making fluorine more reactive. Fluoride ions are also highly hydrated, further stabilising them in solution and enhancing the oxidising power of fluorine compared to chlorine. **(2)**

13. Thallium and aluminium both the elements belong to group 13. Their general electronic configuration for the valence shell is ns^2np^1. Aluminium shows only +3 oxidation state. Like Al, thallium also shows +3 oxidation state in some compounds like Tl_2O_3, $TlCl_3$, etc. Like aluminium, thallium also forms octahedral ions like $[AlF_6]^{3-}$ and $[TlF_6]^{3-}$. Like group-I alkali metals, thallium shows +1 oxidation state due to inert pair effect in some compounds like TlCl, Tl_2O etc. Like alkali metal hydroxides, TiOH is water soluble and its aqueous solution is strongly alkaline. Tl_2SO_4 also forms alums like alkali metal sulphates. Tl_2CO_3 is soluble in water like alkali metal carbonates. **(3)**

14. (i) In gallium due to poor shielding of valence electrons by the intervening 3*d*-electrons, the nuclear charge becomes effective, thus, atomic radius decreases and hence, the ionisation enthalpy of gallium is higher than that of aluminium. **(1)**

(ii) Due to small size of boron, the sum of its first three ionization enthalpies is very high. This prevents it to form +3 ions and forces it to form only covalent compound. That's why boron does not exist as B^{3+} ion. **(1)**

(iii) Aluminium forms $[AlF_6]^{3-}$ ion because of the presence of vacant *d*-orbitals due to which it can expand its coordination number from 4 to 6. In this complex Al undergoes sp^3d^2 hybridisation. On the other hand, boron does not form $[BF_6]^{3-}$ ion, because of the unavailability of *d*-orbitals as it cannot expand its coordination number beyond four. Hence, it can form $[BF_4]^-$ ion (boron in $[BF_4]^-$ ion is sp^3 hybridised). **(1)**

15. (i) Due to strong inert pair effect, +1 oxidation state of Tl is more stable than +3. Since, compounds in lower oxidation state are ionic but covalent in higher oxidation state, therefore, $TlCl_3$ is less stable and covalent in nature but TlCl is more stable and is ionic in nature. **(1)**

(ii) Due to absence of *d*-orbitals, Al does not show inert pair effect. Therefore, its most stable oxidation state is +3. Thus, $AlCl_3$ is much more stable than AlCl. Further, in the solid or the vapour state, $AlCl_3$ is covalent in nature but in aqueous solutions, it ionises to form $Al^{3+}(aq)$ and $Cl^-(aq)$ ions. **(1)**

(iii) Due to inert pair effect, indium exists in both +1 and +3 oxidation states, out of which +3 oxidation state is more stable than +1 oxidation state. In other words, $InCl_3$ is more stable than InCl. Being unstable, InCl undergoes disproportionation reaction.

$$3\,InCl\,(aq) \longrightarrow 2\,In(s) + In^{3+}(aq) + 3Cl^-(aq) \quad \textbf{(1)}$$

16. The only non-metallic element of group 13 is boron. It is an extremely hard black substance and is used in making bullet proof vests. It exists in many allotropic forms and has usually high melting point. Since, B has only *s* and *p*-orbitals but no *d*-orbitals, therefore, at the maximum it can exhibit a covalency of four.

$$H_3\ddot{N} + BF_3 \longrightarrow H_3N \rightarrow BF_3$$

Since, B in BF_3 has only six electrons in its valence shell, therefore, it needs two more electrons to complete its octet. Thus, BF_3 acts as a Lewis acid. **(3)**

17. (i) The important sources of sulphur are

Sulphides : Galena (PbS), zinc blende (ZnS), copper pyrites ($CuFeS_2$), iron pyrites (FeS_2).

Traces of sulphur occur as H_2S.

Organic materials : Eggs, garlic, onion, mustard, hair and wool. **(1)**

Sulphates : Gypsum, epsom salt.

(ii) $H_2O > H_2S > H_2Se > H_2Te > H_2Po$

The thermal stability of the hydrides of group 16 elements decreases down the group because the *M*—H bond dissociation energy decreases with the increase in the size of the central atom. **(1)**

(iii) H_2O forms strong hydrogen bonds, leading to a higher boiling point, making it a liquid at room temperature. H_2S has weak van der Waals' forces, causing it to exist as a gas. **(1)**

18. (i) Fluorine exhibits anomalous behavior due to ita small size, high electronegativity and lack of *d*-orbitals. Unlike other halogens, fluorine does not exhibit variable

oxidation states because it has no vacant *d*-orbitals. Additionally, hydrogen fluoride forms strong hydrogen bonds, making it a liquid, whereas other hydrogen halides like HCl, HBr and HI exist as gases. **(2)**

(ii) The sea is the largest source of chlorine, bromine and iodine. It contains chlorides, bromides and iodides of sodium, potassium, magnesium and calcium, but it mainly contains sodium chloride solution (2.5% by mass). The deposits of dried up seas contain these compounds, e.g. sodium chloride and carnallite, $KCl \cdot MgCl_2 \cdot 6H_2O$. Certain forms of marine life contain iodine in their systems, for example, various seaweeds contain upto 0.5% of iodine. **(1)**

19. (i) Al dissolves both in acids and alkalies evolving dihydrogen and thus, shows amphoteric nature.

$$2Al\,(s) + 3\,H_2SO_4(aq) \longrightarrow Al_2(SO_4)_3(aq) + 3\,H_2(g)$$

$$2Al\,(s) + 2\,NaOH\,(aq) + 6\,H_2O\,(l) \longrightarrow \underset{\text{Sodium tetrahydroxoaluminate (III)}}{2Na^+[Al(OH)_4]^-(aq)} + 3\,H_2(g)$$ **(1)**

(ii) The energy released during hydration of Al^{3+} and $3\,Cl^-$ ions $= -4655 + 3\,(-381) = -5798$ kJ mol^{-1}.

The energy released during hydration is greater than the ionisation enthalpy for Al (5137 kJ mol^{-1}). **(1)**

Hence, $AlCl_3$ will be ionic in solution.

(iii) (a) In $AlCl_3$, Al has only six electrons in its valence shell. It is an electron deficient species. Therefore, it acts as a Lewis acid (electron acceptor).

(b) In BF_3, boron has a vacant 2*p*-orbital and fluorine has one 2*p* completely filled unutilised orbital. Both of these orbitals belong to same energy level therefore, they can overlap effectively and form *p*π-*p*π bond.

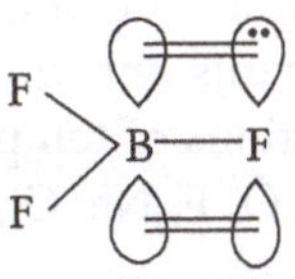

2*p* (vacant) 2*p* (completely filled)

This type of bond formation is known as back bonding. While back bonding to such an extent is not possible in BCl_3 because there is no effective overlapping between the 2*p*-orbital of boron and 3*p*-orbital of chlorine. Therefore, electron deficiency of B is higher in BCl_3 than that of BF_3. That's why BF_3 is a weaker Lewis acid than BCl_3. **(3)**

20. (i) Fluorine atom is smaller in size, so six F^- ions can surround a sulphur atom. The case is not so with chlorine atom due to its large size. So, SF_6 is known but SCl_6 is not known due to interionic repulsion between larger Cl^- ions.

(ii) In SF_6 the six F atoms sterically protect the sulphur atom from attack by water due to steric hindrance. Further, F does not have *d*-orbitals to accept the electrons donated by H_2O molecules. As a result of these two reasons, SF_6 not undergo hydrolysis.

(iii) H_2O undergoes extensive H-bonding due to high electronegativity of O-atom and hence exists as an associated molecule. Therefore, H_2O is a liquid. On the other hand, H_2S does not undergo H-bonding and hence exists as a discrete molecules and as a gas.

(iv) Oxygen shows catenation behaviour less than sulphur because oxygen is smaller in size, so it experiences repulsions between their lone pair of electrons present on oxygen atom and bond pair of O—O bond, hence O—O bonds are weaker than S—S bonds.

(v) Melting point of H_2Se is greater than H_2S because Se is greater in size then S. Due to the increase in size, there is increase in van der Waals' forces of attraction and thus, the melting and boiling points increases. **(1 × 5 = 5)**

21. (i) ClF_3 exists but FCl_3 does not because

(a) Cl has vacant *d*-orbitals and hence, can show an oxidation state of +3 but F has no *d*-orbitals, therefore. it cannot show positive oxidation states. Further, since F can show only −1 oxidation state therefore, it forms only ClF not FCl_3.

(b) Due to larger size, Cl can accommodate three small F-atoms around it while F being smaller cannot accommodate three bigger sized Cl atoms around it.

(ii) Halogens have the smallest size in their respective periods and therefore, have high effective nuclear charge. As a result, they readily accept one electron to acquire the stable electronic configuration of the nearest noble gas. In other words, large amount of energy is released when a halogen atom accepts an electron to form the corresponding halide ion and thus, halogens have maximum negative electron gain enthalpies.

(iii) Hydration enthalpy is a measure of energy released when attractions are set-up between positive or negative ions and water molecules. These attractions are stronger when the ion is smaller.

As we know that F^- is smaller than Cl^- ion. So, F^- ion possess higher hydration enthalpy than Cl^- ion.

(iv) In SO_2, S exists in +4 oxidation state which is less stable than its +6 oxidation state, therefore, it can easily oxidises from +4 to +6 state, hence SO_2 acts as a reducing agent whereas in TeO_2, Te exists in +4 oxidation state which is its most stable state and it cannot oxidise further to +6 state, but can reduce casily to +2 or −2 state. Hence, TeO_2 acts as an oxidising agent.

(v) ICl is more reactive than I_2 because I—Cl bond is weaker than I—I bond. Consequently, ICl bond breaks easily to form halogen atoms (I and Cl) which readily bring about the reactions.

QR Code for Quick Test 1	QR Code for Quick Test 2	QR Code for Quick Test 3	QR Code for Quick Test 4	QR Code for Quick Test 5	QR Code for Quick Test 6

12 CHAPTER

To be Assessed Formatively

The Gaseous State

Matter generally exists in three states i.e. solid, liquid and gaseous state. In these states, the chemical properties of a substance remains the same but rate of a chemical reaction is different. In this chapter, we will focus our discussion mainly on the factors deciding states of matter, characterisation of gaseous and liquid states and laws governing them.

YOUR STUDY GOALS

12.1 Gas Laws
12.2 Ideal Gas and Ideal Gas Equation
12.3 Dalton's Law of Partial Pressures
12.4 Kinetic Molecular Theory of Gases
12.5 Behaviour of Real Gases : Deviation From Ideal Gas Behaviour

YOUR PRACTICE GOAL

- Objective Type Questions (20 Qs ; 11 MCQs, 8 A-R & 1 Case Study)
- Subjective Type Questions (26 Qs; 11 SA-I, 13 SA-II & 2 LA)

It is the simplest state of matter. Only eleven elements, out of the total 118 elements known today, exist in gaseous state under normal conditions of temperature and pressure. These elements are H, He, N, O, F, Ne, Cl, Ar, Kr, Xe, Rn.

Characteristics of Gases

The general characteristics exhibited by gases are as follows

- Gases have neither definite shape nor definite volume. They take the shape and volume of the container in which these are kept.
- They have lower density as compared to liquids and solids.
- They are highly compressible and exert pressure equally in all directions.
- They have high diffusibility, i.e. readily intermix in all proportions without any mechanical aid.
- On heating, they expand appreciably.

12.1 The Gas Laws

Measurable properties of gases like pressure, volume, temperature, mass etc., interdependent on each other and their interdependence leads to the formulation of gas laws. Thus, gas laws are actually the relationships between measurable properties of gases.

These relationships are of great importance as these describe the state of the gas and give quantitative relationships between any two variables when others are kept constant.

Let's discuss the various gas laws in detail.

Boyle's Law
(Pressure-Volume Relationship)

This law was given by **Robert Boyle** in 1662 and states that **at constant temperature, the pressure of a fixed amount** (i.e. number of moles, n) **of a gas varies inversely with its volume.**

Mathematically, $p \propto 1/V$ (at constant T and n)

or $$p = k_1 \frac{1}{V}$$

On rearranging, $pV = k_1$

Here, k_1 = proportionality constant, value of which depends upon the amount of the gas, temperature of the gas and units of pressure and volume.

Thus, the law can also be given as, **at constant temperature, the product of pressure and volume of a fixed amount of a gas is constant.**

Let V_1 be the volume of a given mass of gas at pressure p_1 and at a given temperature T. When the pressure is changed to p_2 at the same temperature, so that volume becomes V_2. Then, according to Boyle's law,

$$p_1V_1 = p_2V_2 = \text{constant (at constant temperature)}$$

or $$\frac{p_1}{p_2} = \frac{V_2}{V_1}$$

Graphical Representation of Boyle's Law

There are three conventional ways of presenting Boyle's law graphically.

(i) **Pressure *vs* Volume graph** When volume of a given mass of a gas is plotted against pressure at different constant temperature, the equilateral **hyperbola** is obtained for each temperature as shown in figure.

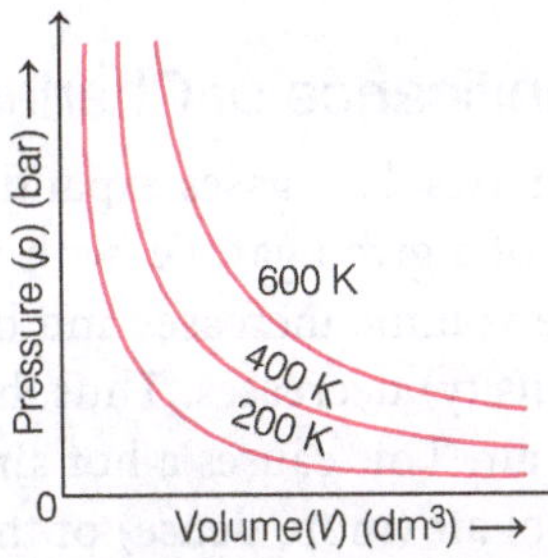

Graph of pressure, p vs, V volume of a gas at different temperatures

The curves in the figure are called **isotherms** (constant temperature plots) as each curve corresponds to a different constant temperature. Since k, depends only on temperature for a given mass of gas, so its value is different for each curve. Here a noticeable point is that as the temperature increases, the position of curve becomes higher.

(ii) **Pressure *vs* 1/Volume graph** On plotting reciprocal of volumes of a fixed mass of a gas against pressures, we get straight lines passing through the origin. The slope of plot increases with rise in temperature of the isotherm as shown in the graph.

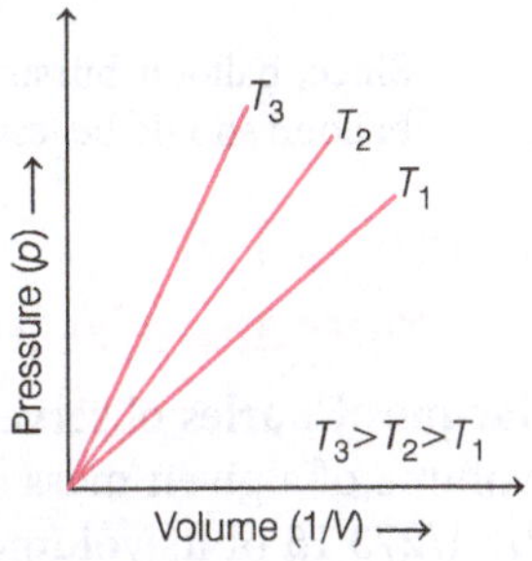

Pressure *vs* 1/Volume plot

Note If pressures are very high, the gases deviate from Boyle's law and thus, in such condition, the graphs of p vs $1/V$ is not a straight line.

(iii) **pV *vs* p graph** When the product of pressure and volume (i.e. pV) is plotted against pressure, at different fixed temperatures, the straight line parallel to pressure axis (X-axis) are obtained.

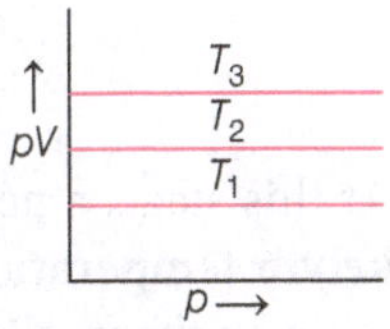

$$T_3 > T_2 > T_1$$

Relationship between Pressure (p) and Density (d)

$$\because \quad \text{Volume}(V) = \frac{\text{Mass}(m)}{\text{Density}(d)}$$

On putting the value of V in Boyle's law expression ($pV = k_1$), we get

$$\therefore \quad p \cdot \frac{m}{d} = k_1$$

or $$d = \left(\frac{m}{k_1}\right) p = k' p$$

Thus, it can be stated that **"at a constant temperature, pressure is directly proportional to the density of a fixed mass of the gas".**

An important example of it is that air at the sea level is denser as it is compressed by the mass of air above it.

Example 1 **A balloon is filled with hydrogen at room temperature. It will burst if pressure exceeds 0.2 bar. If at 1 bar pressure the gas occupies 2.27 L volume, upto what volume can the balloon be expanded?** NCERT

Sol. According to Boyle's law, $p_1V_1 = p_2V_2$

$$1\,\text{bar} \times 2.27\,\text{L} = 0.2\,\text{bar} \times V_2$$

or $$V_2 = \frac{1\,\text{bar} \times 2.27\,\text{L}}{0.2\,\text{bar}} = 11.35\,\text{L}$$

Since, balloon bursts at 0.2 bar pressure, the volume of balloon should be less than 11.35 L.

Charles' Law (Temperature-Volume Relationship)

Jacques Charles observed that at a fixed pressure, the volume of a given mass of a gas increases or decreases by 1/273.15 of its volume at 0°C for each one degree rise or fall in temperature.

If at 0°C the volume of a gas is V_0 and at t°C, it becomes V_t then according to Charles'

$$V_t = V_0\left[1 + \frac{t}{273.15}\right]$$

or $$V_t = V_0\left(\frac{273.15 + t}{273.15}\right) \quad \text{...(i)}$$

At this stage, a new scale of temperature, called the **kelvin temperature scale** or **absolute temperature scale** or **thermodynamic scale** is used. On this scale $273.15 + t = T$.

Thus, if temperature is 0°C, then $T_0 = 273.15$ K. This means that 0°C on the celsius scale is equal to 273.15 K at the kelvin scale and if temperature on the celsius scale is t°C, then, $T = 273.15 + t°\text{C} = T_t\,(\text{K})$

On replacing $273.15 + t$ and 273.15 in the equation (i) by T_t and T_0, we get $V_t = V_0\left(\frac{T_t}{T_0}\right)$

or $$\boxed{\frac{V_t}{V_0} = \frac{T_t}{T_0}}$$

Thus, the general form of the reaction can be written as

$$\frac{V_2}{V_1} = \frac{T_2}{T_1} \quad \text{or} \quad \frac{V_1}{T_1} = \frac{V_2}{T_2} \quad \text{or} \quad \frac{V}{T} = \text{constant} = k_2$$

Thus, $$V = k_2T \quad \text{...(ii)}$$

Here, k_2 is a constant value which depends upon the pressure of the gas, its amount and the units in which volume V is expressed. The above equation [eq. (ii)] is the mathematical expression for Charles' law, according to which **at a constant pressure, the volume of a given mass of a gas is directly proportional to its absolute temperature.** At very low pressures and high temperatures, this law is obeyed by all gases.

Graphical Representation of Charles' Law

The plot of volume *vs* temperature at constant pressure are called **isobars** or **isoplestics.** When volume of fixed mass of a gas is plotted with temperature at different constant pressures, we get **straight line** in each case. On extending these lines to zero volume, all these intercept the temperature axis at – 273.15°C, however, these all have different slopes at different pressures as shown below.

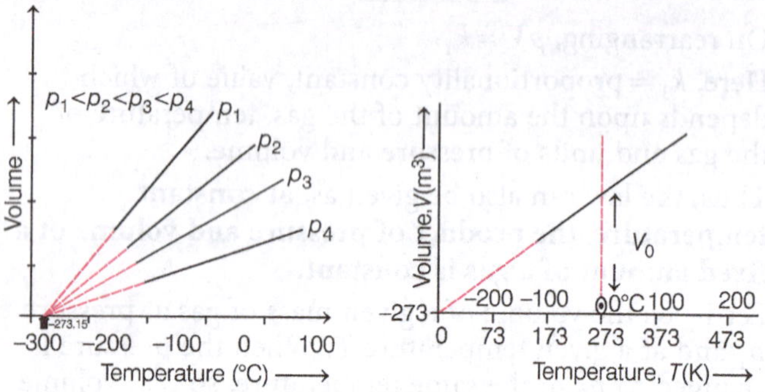

(a) At different constant pressures (b) Only at a fixed (constant) pressure

Volume *vs* temperature plots

When we substitute the temperature – 273.15°C in eq. (i) (as given by Charles'), we get $V = 0$, i.e. the gas will not exist. This is because before reaching this temperature all molecular motions are ceased and thus, the gases are liquified. This temperature (– 273.15°C) is called absolute zero. Thus, the lowest hypothetical temperature at which the gases are supposed to occupy zero volume is called **absolute zero.**

Note Temperature below – 273.15°C is not possible because it corresponds to negative volume which is meaningless.

Practical Significance of Charles' Law

According to Charles' law, gases expand on heating for a constant mass of a given gas, i.e. with increase in temperature, the volume increases and hence, mass per unit volume (density) decreases. Thus, hot air is less dense than cool air. This causes a hot air balloon to rise by displacing cool air (more dense) of the atmosphere.

Example 2 **At what temperature centigrade will the volume of a gas at 0°C double itself, pressure remaining constant?**

Sol. Let the volume of the gas at 0°C = V mL

Thus, we have $V_1 = V$ mL, $V_2 = 2V$ mL

$T_1 = 0 + 273 = 273$ K

T_2 = to be calculated

By Charles' law $\frac{V_1}{T_1} = \frac{V_2}{T_2}$

Substituting the corresponding values, we have

$$\frac{V}{273} = \frac{2V}{T_2} \Rightarrow T_2 = \frac{2V \times 273}{V}$$

$$= 546 \text{ K}$$

$$\therefore \quad T_2 = 546 - 273 = 273°\text{C}$$

Example 3 **On a ship sailing in pacific ocean where temperature is 23.4°C, a balloon is filled with 2 L air. What will be the volume of the balloon when the ship reaches Indian ocean, where temperature is 26.1°C?** NCERT

Sol. Given, $V_1 = 2$ L; $V_2 = ?$

$T_2 = (26.1 + 273)$ K = 299.1 K

$T_1 = (23.4 + 273)$ K = 296.4 K

According to Charles' law,

$$\frac{V_1}{T_1} = \frac{V_2}{T_2} \text{ or } V_2 = \frac{V_1 T_2}{T_1}$$

On substituting the corresponding values, we get

$$\Rightarrow \quad V_2 = \frac{2\text{L} \times 299.1 \text{ K}}{296.4 \text{ K}} = 2.018 \text{ L}$$

Gay-Lussac's Law (Pressure-Temperature Relationship)

According to this law, at constant volume, pressure of a fixed amount of a gas varies directly with the temperature.

This mathematical relationship between pressure and temperature was given by Gay-Lussac's law.

Mathematically, $p \propto T$

or $p/T = \text{constant} = k_3$

The above relationship is derived from Boyle's and Charles' law.

Graphical Representation of Gay-Lussac's Law

The plots of pressure *vs* temperature (K) at constant molar volumes are called **isochore**.

Such plots are shown below.

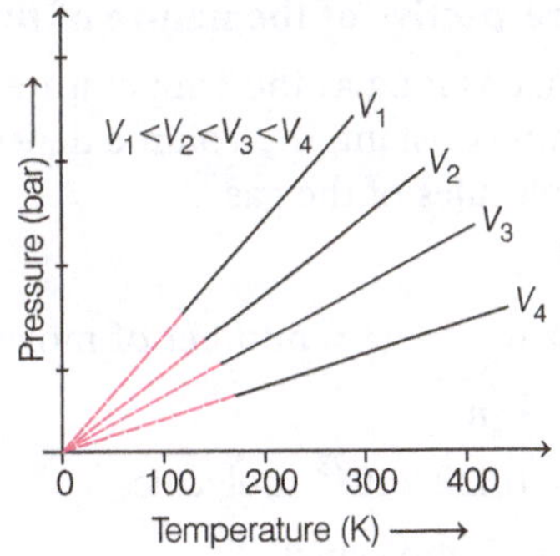

Pressure *vs* temperature (K) graph (Isochores) of a gas

When $\frac{p}{T}$ is plotted against temperature, a straight line parallel to X-axis is obtained as shown below.

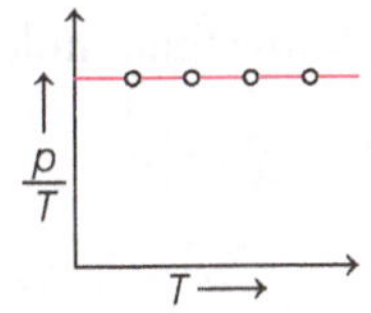

p/T *vs* T plot at constant V

Applications of Gay-Lussac's Law

An important application of this law is the increase or decrease of air pressure in the tyres of automobiles in summers and winters.

In a well inflated tyre, the pressure (air pressure) is almost constant but on a hot summer day it may increase (due to increase in temperature) and hence, the tyre may burst if the pressure is not adjusted properly. Further, in winters due to lowering of temperature, the pressure inside the tyre may reduce.

Example 4 **An iron cylinder contains helium at a pressure of 250 kPa at 300 K. The cylinder can withstand a pressure of 1×10^6 Pa. The room in which cylinder is placed catches fire. Predict whether the cylinder will blow up before it melts or not (mp of the cylinder = 1800 K).**

Sol. According to Gay-Lussac's law, $\frac{p_1}{T_1} = \frac{p_2}{T_2}$

$$\frac{250}{300} = \frac{p_2}{1800} \text{ or } p_2 = 1500 \text{ kPa}$$

As the cylinder can withstand a pressure of 10^6 Pa = 10^3 kPa = 1000 kPa, hence, it will blow up.

Avogadro Law (Volume-Amount Relationship)

This law was given by Italian scientist **Amedeo Avogadro** in 1811. According to this law, **"under the same conditions of temperature and pressure, equal**

volumes of all gases contain equal number of molecules, irrespective of the nature of the gas."

This means that as long as the temperature and pressure remain constant, the volume depends on the number of molecules of the gas.

Mathematically,

$$V \propto n \quad (n = \text{number of moles of the gas})$$

or $$V = k_4 n$$

Since, 1 mol $= 6.022 \times 10^{23}$ molecules

$= N_A$ molecules

(where, N_A = Avogadro's number)

We know that, moles, $n = \dfrac{\text{mass, } (m)}{\text{molar mass, } (M)}$

$$\therefore \quad V = k_4 \frac{m}{M}$$

or $$M = k_4 \frac{m}{V} = k_4 d$$

(Here, d = density of the gas)

Thus, from the above equation, it is also concluded that **"density of a gas is directly proportional to its molar mass".**

Example 5 **If 1 g of each of the following gases are taken at STP, which of the gases will occupy (a) greatest volume and (b) smallest volume?**

$$CO, H_2O, CH_4, NO$$

NCERT Exemplar

Sol. From Avogadro's law, we know that

Volume of 1 mole of the gas

= Gram molecular mass = 22.4 L at STP

Volume occupied by 28 g CO (1 mol CO) = 22.4 L at STP

[$\because$ Molar mass of CO = 12 + 16 = 28 g mol^{-1}]

$\therefore$ Volume occupied by 1 g CO $= \dfrac{22.4}{28}$ L at STP

= 0.8 L at STP

Similarly, volume occupied by 1 g $H_2O = \dfrac{22.4}{18}$ L at STP

[$\because$ Molar mass of H_2O = (2× 1) + 16 = 18 g mol^{-1}]

= 1.24 L at STP

Volume occupied by 1g $CH_4 = \dfrac{22.4}{16}$ L at STP

[$\because$ Molar mass of CH_4 = 12 + (4× 1) = 16 g mol^{-1}]

= 1.4 L at STP

Volume occupied by 1g NO $= \dfrac{22.4}{30}$ L at STP

[$\because$ Molar mass of NO = 14 + 16 = 30 g mol^{-1}]

= 0.75 L at STP

Thus, 1 g CH_4 will occupy maximum volume while 1 g of NO will occupy minimum volume at STP.

Quick Test 1

1. Boyle's law states that at constant temperature, if pressure is increased on a gas, volume decreases and *vice-versa*. But when we fill air in a balloon, volume as well as pressure increases. Why?
2. What will be the minimum pressure required to compress 500 dm^3 of air at 1 bar to 200 dm^3 at 30°C? NCERT
3. A human adult breathes in approximately 0.50 L of air at 1 atm with each breath. If an air tank holds 10 L of air at 200 atm, how many breaths the tank will supply?
4. In terms of Charles' law explain why −273°C is the lowest possible temperature?
5. How does Charles' law explain why hot air balloons rise?
6. Give reasons for the following.
   (i) The size of weather balloon becomes larger and larger as it ascends into higher altitudes.
   (ii) Tyres of automobiles are inflated to lesser pressure in summer than in winter.
7. (i) How does increasing the number of moles of a gas affect its volume of constant temperature and pressure?
   (ii) What would happen to the volume of a gas if the number of molecuels is halved?
8. Calculate the total number of electrons present in 1.4 g of dinitrogen gas. NCERT

For Solutions, See QR Code on Pg. 449

12.2 Ideal Gas and Ideal Gas Equation

A gas which follows Boyle's law, Charles' law and Avogadro's law at all conditions of temperatures and pressures is called an **ideal gas**. In actual practice such a gas is only hypothetical.

Ideal Gas Equation

On combining Boyle's, Charles' and Avogadro's law, we get a single equation, which is called **ideal gas equation.** This equation gives the simultaneous effect of pressure and temperature on the volume of a gas.

We know that,

At constant T and n; $V \propto 1/p$ (Boyle's law)

At constant p and n; $V \propto T$ (Charles' law)

At constant p and T; $V \propto n$ (Avogadro's law)

On combining the above three, we get

$$V \propto \frac{nT}{p} \text{ or } V = R\frac{nT}{p} \quad \ldots\text{(i)}$$

(Here, R = proportionality constant or gas constant)

On rearranging the equation (i), we get

$$\boxed{pV = nRT}$$

This equation is called **ideal gas equation** and is applicable for all gases that behave ideally. It describes the state of any gas, so it is also called **equation of state.** If in this equation, we know any three variable, we can calculate the value of remaining fourth variable.

Let the volume of a certain mass of a gas changes from V_1 to V_2 when the pressure is changed from p_1 to p_2 and temperature from T_1 to T_2. Then, for initial condition, ideal gas equation is

$$p_1V_1 = nRT_1 \text{ or } \frac{p_1V_1}{T_1} = nR \quad \ldots\text{(i)}$$

For final condition, ideal gas equation is

$$p_2V_2 = nRT_2$$

or

$$\frac{p_2V_2}{T_2} = nR \quad \ldots\text{(ii)}$$

From equation (i) and (ii), we get

$$\boxed{\frac{p_1V_1}{T_1} = \frac{p_2V_2}{T_2}}$$

This equation is called **combined gas law.** In this relation, if out of six, the values of five variable are known, the value of remaining variable can be calculated.

Nature and Value of R (Gas Constant)

Gas constant, R is also called **universal gas constant** as its value is same for all the gases.

From the gas equation,

$$R = \frac{pV}{nT} = \frac{\text{pressure} \times \text{volume}}{\text{number of moles} \times \text{temperature}}$$

Values of R in different units are tabulated below.

Units of p	**Units of V**	**Value of R**
Atmosphere	litres or dm^3	0.0821 L atm K^{-1} mol^{-1} or 0.0821 dm^3 atm K^{-1} mol^{-1}
Atmosphere	cm^3	82.1 cm^3 atm K^{-1} mol^{-1}
dyne cm^{-2}	cm^3	8.31×10^7 erg K^{-1} mol^{-1} $= 1.987$ cal K^{-1} mol^{-1}
N m^{-2} or Pa	m^3	8.314 JK^{-1} mol^{-1}
bar	dm^3	0.083 bar dm^3 K^{-1} mol^{-1}

Example 6 **At 25°C and 760 mm of Hg pressure, a gas occupies 600 mL volume. What will be its pressure at a height where temperature is 10°C and volume of the gas is 640 mL?** NCERT

Sol. Given, $p_1 = 760$ mm Hg, $V_1 = 600$ mL

$T_1 = 25 + 273 = 298$ K

$V_2 = 640$ mL

and $T_2 = 10 + 273 = 283$ K

According to combined gas law,

or $$\frac{p_1V_1}{T_1} = \frac{p_2V_2}{T_2}$$

or $$p_2 = \frac{p_1V_1T_2}{T_1V_2}$$

On substituting the corresponding values, we get

$$p_2 = \frac{(760 \text{ mm Hg}) \times (600 \text{ mL}) \times (283 \text{ K})}{(640 \text{ mL}) \times (298 \text{ K})}$$

$$= 676.6 \text{ mm Hg}$$

Relation Between Density and Molar Mass of a Gaseous Substance

We know, ideal gas equation is

$$pV = nRT$$

On rearranging the equation, we get $\dfrac{n}{V} = \dfrac{p}{RT}$

$\because$ Number of moles, $n = \dfrac{\text{mass, } m}{\text{molar mass, } M}$

On substituting the value of n in the above equation, we get,

$$\frac{m}{MV} = \frac{p}{RT}$$

$$\frac{d}{M} = \frac{p}{RT} \quad \text{(where, } d = \text{density)}$$

On further rearranging the equation, we get

$$M \text{ (molecular mass)} = \frac{dRT}{p}$$

Example 7 **Density of a gas is found to be 6.46 g dm^{-3} at 25°C and 5 bar pressure. What will be its density at STP?**

Sol. From ideal gas equation we have,

$$pV = nRT \text{ or } p = \frac{m}{V} \times \frac{RT}{M} = \frac{dRT}{M}$$

$$\therefore \quad d = \frac{pM}{RT}$$

$$\text{or} \quad d \propto \frac{p}{T} \quad [R \text{ and } M \text{ constant for a given gas}]$$

$$\text{or} \quad \frac{d_1}{d_2} = \frac{p_1}{p_2} \times \frac{T_2}{T_1}$$

$$\text{or} \quad d_2 = \frac{d_1 \times p_2 \times T_1}{p_1 \times T_2}$$

$d_1 = 6.46 \text{ g dm}^{-3}, p_1 = 5 \text{ bar},$

$T_1 = 273 + 25 = 298 \text{ K}$

$d_2 = ?, p_2 = 1 \text{ bar}, T_2 = 27 \text{ K}$

$$d_2 = \frac{6.46 \text{ g dm}^{-3} \times 1 \text{ bar} \times 298\text{K}}{5 \text{ bar} \times 273\text{K}}$$

$$= 1.41 \text{ g dm}^{-3}$$

12.3 Dalton's Law of Partial Pressures

This law was formulated by **John Dalton** in 1801. According to this law, "the total pressure exerted by the mixture of non-reactive gases is equal to the sum of the partial pressures of individual gases if they were enclosed separately in the same volume and under the same conditions of temperature."

If $p_1, p_2, p_3 \ldots$ are individual pressures of gases and p_{total} is the total pressure of the mixture of gases at the same temperature then according to Dalton's law of partial pressures $p_{total} = p_1 + p_2 + p_3 + \ldots$ (at constant T, V)

In a mixture of gases, the pressure exerted by an individual gas is called its **partial pressure.**

Applications of Dalton's Law

This law is used to determine the following

(i) Calculation of Partial Pressure of a Gas

Suppose three non-reacting gases A, B and C are taken in a vessel of volume V at temperature T. The partial pressure exerted by these gases are p_1, p_2 and p_3 respectively.

$$\text{Then, } p_1 = \frac{n_1RT}{V}; \; p_2 = \frac{n_2RT}{V}; \; p_3 = \frac{n_3RT}{V}$$

where n_1, n_2 and n_3 are number of moles of gases A, B and C respectively.

Thus, expression for total pressure will be

$$p_{total} = p_1 + p_2 + p_3$$

$$p_{total} = n_1\frac{RT}{V} + n_2\frac{RT}{V} + n_3\frac{RT}{V}$$

$$= (n_1 + n_2 + n_3)\frac{RT}{V}$$

On dividing p_1 by p_{total}, we get

$$\frac{p_1}{p_{total}} = \left(\frac{n_1}{n_1 + n_2 + n_3}\right)\frac{RTV}{RTV} = \frac{n_1}{n_1 + n_2 + n_3} = \frac{n_1}{n} = \chi_1$$

(where, $n = n_1 + n_2 + n_3$)

and χ_1 = mole fraction of first gas.

Thus, $p_1 = \chi_1 p_{total}$ = mole fraction of A × total pressure.

Similarly, for other two gases we can write

$$p_2 = \chi_2 p_{total} \text{ and } p_3 = \chi_3 p_{total}$$

Thus, a general equation can be written as

$$p_i = \chi_i \, p_{total}$$

i.e. partial pressure of a gas = mole fraction of the gas × total pressure

Thus, if we know the total pressure of the mixture of gases. We can calculate the partial pressure of each gas by using the above equation.

(ii) Calculation of Pressure of a Dry Gas

Most of the gases are collected over water, so they are generally moist, i.e. are saturated with water vapours that exert their own pressure. The pressure exerted by these water vapours is called **aqueous tension.** Thus, the pressure of dry gas is calculated by subtracting aqueous tension from the total pressure of the moist gas. i.e.

Pressure of dry gas = Total pressure − aqueous tension

or $\quad p_{dry\ gas} = p_{total}$ − aqueous tension

Example 8 **1500 mL flask contains 400 mg O_2 and 60 mg H_2 at 100°C. What is the total pressure in the flask?**

Sol. ***Step*** I Number of moles of O_2

$$= \frac{w}{m} = \frac{400 \times 10^{-3}}{32}$$

$$= 0.0125$$

$$\text{Number of moles of } H_2 = \frac{w}{m} = \frac{60 \times 10^{-3}}{2} = 0.03$$

$$\text{From } pV = nRT, \ p = \frac{nRT}{V}$$

$$\text{Partial pressure of } O_2 = \frac{0.0125 \times 0.0821 \times 373}{1500 \times 10^{-3}}$$

$$= 0.255 \text{ atm}$$

$$\text{Partial pressure of } H_2 = \frac{0.03 \times 0.0821 \times 373}{1500 \times 10^{-3}}$$

$$= 0.612 \text{ atm}$$

Step II Total pressure = 0.255 + 0.612 = 0.867 atm

Quick Test 2

1. Calculate the temperature of 4.0 moles of a gas occupying 5 dm^3 at 3.32 bar. ($R = 0.083$ bar dm^3 K^{-1} mol^{-1}). NCERT
2. 35 mL of oxygen were collected at 6°C and 758 mm pressure. Calculate its volume at NTP.
3. Value of universal gas constant (R) is same for all gases. What is its physical significance? NCERT Exemplar
4. Write the SI unit of the universal gas constant (R) when pressure is expressed in atm and volume in litres.
5. 34.05 mL of phosphorus vapour weighs 0.0625 g at 546°C and 0.1 bar pressure. What is the molar mass of phosphorus? NCERT
6. State Dalton's law of partial pressures.
7. Pressure exerted by saturated water vapour is called aqueous tension. What correction term will you apply to the total pressure to obtain pressure of dry gas? NCERT Exemplar

For Solutions, See QR Code on Pg. 449

12.4 Kinetic Molecular Theory of Gases

The molecular details about the gases can be visualised with the help of a theory, called the **kinetic molecular theory of gases.** This theory attempts to elucidate the behaviour of gases and also provides a microscopic model of gases.

The main assumptions of this theory are as follows.

(i) Gases are made up of large number of identical tiny particles (i.e. atoms or molecules), which are so far apart that their actual volume is almost negligible as compared to empty space present between them. That's why they are considered as point masses. This assumption explains **the compressible nature of the gases.**

(ii) The intermolecular forces of attraction between the particles of a gas at ordinary temperature and pressure are negligible. That's why **gases expand and occupy all the available space.**

(iii) Particles of the gases are always in a state of constant and random motion. That's why **shape of gases is not definite.**

(iv) The particles of a gas move in all possible directions in straight lines and collide with each other and also with the walls of the container. Thus, they exert some pressure on the wall of the container. Pressure, $p \propto$ number of collision per unit time per unit area by the molecules on the wall of the container.

(v) Collisions of the gas molecules are perfectly elastic i.e. there is no loss of energy or the total energy of the molecules before and after the collision remains the same.

(vi) At a given temperature, the speeds of different particles in a gas are different. However, at a given temperature the distribution of speeds remains constant.

(vii) As the gas molecules has variable speeds, it also have a variable kinetic energy. In this case, we take average kinetic energy. It is directly proportional to the absolute temperature i.e. kinetic energy $\propto$ absolute temperature.

$$\boxed{E = \frac{3}{2} k_b T}$$

where, $k_b = \dfrac{R}{N_A}$ and is called **Boltzmann constant.**

At absolute zero ($T = 0$), kinetic energy of the gas becomes zero. Thus, the thermal motion of the molecules is expected to cease at this temperature. Above relation shows that KE of gas is independent of its nature, pressure and volume of the gas, but depends only on the temperature. This is known as **Maxwell generalisation.**

12.5 Behaviour of Real Gases : Deviation from Ideal Gas Behaviour

Real Gases

Gases that do not obey gas laws under all conditions of temperatures and pressures are called **real gases.** Most of the gases are real in nature i.e. they follow gas laws only at very low pressures and high temperatures (as under such conditions the gas molecules are far apart i.e. not in the influence of each other and hence, intermolecular forces of attraction are negligible).

It is also noticed that easily liquefiable gases such as CO_2, SO_2, NH_3 exhibit larger deviation as compared to gases such as H_2, O_2, N_2 etc., that liquify with difficulty.

To study the deviation of real gases from ideal behaviour, we plot the pV *vs* p and p *vs* V graph for different gases.

This analysis helps to conclude how far the relation $pV = nRT$ reproduce actual p-V-T relationship of gases.

(i) *pV vs p* Plot

We know that, pV *vs* p plots are straight lines parallel to x (or pressure) axis for ideal gases. If we plot pV *vs* p for different real gases at constant temperatures, we find that the plots are not straight lines, which clearly reveals that these gases show deviation from ideal behaviour. Such plots for different real gases are shown in the following figure.

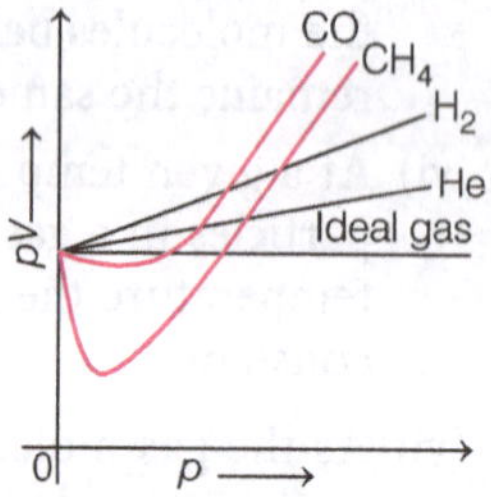

Plot of pV *vs* p for real gas and ideal gas

(b) Pressure *vs* Volume Plot

If we plot experimental values of pressure and volume at constant temperature for real gases and their theoretically calculated values (as obtained by Boyle's law), the two plots do not coincide as shown in the following figure.

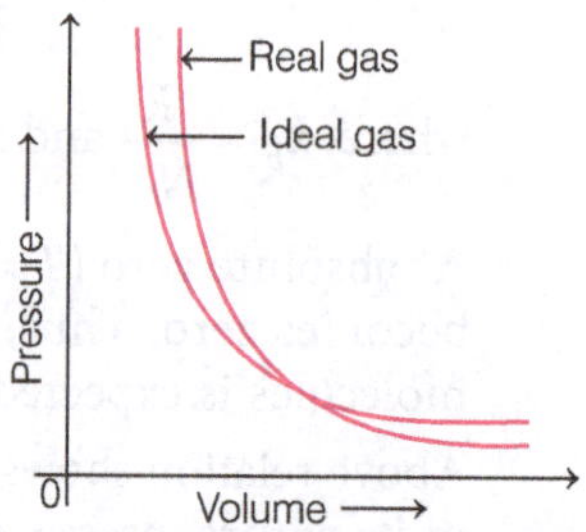

Plot of pressure *vs* volume for real and ideal gases

Thus, from the above discussion it is concluded that real gases deviate from ideal behaviour, i.e. they do not obey the gas laws under all conditions of temperatures and pressures.

Causes of Deviations from Ideal Behaviour

The ideal gas equation was derived on the basis of certain assumptions of kinetic theory of gases. But when studied carefully, it was found that two of these assumptions are not true at high pressure or low temperature. These two assumptions are

(i) the intermolecular forces of attraction between the particles of a gas at ordinary temperature and pressure are negligible.

(ii) volume of the molecules of a gas is negligibly small in comparison to the space occupied by the gas.

The correct assumption at the conditions of high pressure and low temperature are

(i) the forces of attraction or repulsion between the molecules may not be negligible.

(ii) the volume occupied by the gas may be so small that the volume occupied by the molecules may not be negligible.

Corrections of Deviations

In 1983, van der Waals' modified the ideal gas equation by introducing corrections in it for the failure of the two assumptions described above.

(i) Pressure Correction

There exist a very weak intermolecular forces of attraction in between the molecules of real gases. When high pressure is applied to such gases, their molecules become very close to each other and hence, molecular interaction start operating between molecules.

As a result, they do not strike the walls of the container with full impact because these are dragged back by other molecules due to molecular attractive forces. Hence, the pressure exerted by the real gas is lower than that expected for an ideal gas.

$$p_{\text{ideal}} = p_{\text{real}} + \Delta p$$

$\Delta p \propto$ (Number of particles per unit volume)^2

or $\Delta p \propto (n/V)^2$ where, n is the number of mole of the gas, V is the volume of gas.

$$\Delta p = a\frac{n^2}{V^2} \qquad \text{(where, } a = \text{constant)}$$

The corrected pressure then is given by,

$$p_{\text{ideal}} = p_{\text{red observed pressure}} + \underbrace{an^2/V^2}_{\text{Correction term}}$$

(ii) Volume Correction

At high pressure, when gas molecules are in close contact, there exist some repulsive forces. Due to these forces, the molecules of gas behave as small but impenetrable spheres. In such a condition, the volume occupied by these molecules also become significant and hence, the volume available for compression of the gas will be less than the observed volume. If V is the volume of the gas, then

Volume available for compression

$$= \text{total volume of the gas} - \text{volume of the molecules}$$

Then, $V_{\text{corrected}} = V - nb$

where b is the volume occupied by one mole of the molecules and n is the number of moles of the molecules (or gas).

van der Waals' Equation

On putting the values of corrected pressure and volume in ideal gas equation, we get the equation

$$\left(p + \frac{an^2}{V^2}\right)(V - nb) = nRT$$

where, a and b = van der Waals' constants, value of which depend upon the nature of the gas. This equation is known as **van der Waals' equation.**

Significance of van der Waals' Constants

(i) **van der Waals' constant 'a'** It is a measure of the magnitude of the attractive forces among the molecules of the gas. Greater the value of 'a', larger are the intermolecular forces of attraction. It does not depend upon temperature and pressure.

(ii) **van der Waals' constant 'b'** It is a measure of the effective size of the gas molecules and is equal to four times the actual volume of the gas molecules. It is also called **excluded volume** or **co-volume.**

Units of van der Waals' Constants

(i) **Units of 'a'** As $p = \frac{an^2}{V^2}$,

$$\therefore a = \frac{p \times V^2}{n^2} = \text{atm L}^2\ \text{mol}^{-2} \text{ or bar dm}^6\ \text{mol}^{-2}$$

(ii) **Units of 'b'** As volume correction $V = nb$,

$$\therefore b = \frac{V}{n} = \text{L mol}^{-1} \text{ or dm}^3\text{mol}^{-1}$$

Example 9 Calculate the pressure exerted by 10.2 g of ammonia (NH_3) contained in 0.5 L vessel at 315 K. For ammonia $a = 5$ atm L^2 mol^{-2}, $b = 0.036$ L mol^{-1}. Compare the value with the calculated value if the gas were considered as ideal.

Sol. Number of moles of ammonia $n = \frac{10.2}{17} = 0.6$ mole

According to van der Waal's equation,

$$\left(p + \frac{an^2}{V^2}\right)(V - nb) = nRT$$

$$p = \frac{nRT}{(V - nb)} - \frac{an^2}{V^2}$$

$$= \frac{0.6 \times 0.082 \times 315}{(0.5 - 0.6 \times 0.036)} - \frac{5(0.6)}{(0.5)^2}$$

$$= 20.395 \text{ atm}$$

If the gas were considered ideal, then the value of pressure (p) can be obtained by using ideal gas equation as

$$p = \frac{nRT}{V} = \frac{0.6 \times 0.082 \times 315}{0.5}$$

$$= 30.996 \text{ atm}$$

Measurement of Deviation : Compressibility Factor

The extent of deviation shown by real gases from ideal behaviour is measured in terms of **compressibility factor (Z)** which is defined as the ratio of product of pV and nRT. Mathematically,

$$Z = \frac{pV}{nRT}$$

For ideal gases, $Z = 1$ (as for them $pV = nRT$ at all temperatures and pressures).

For ideal gases, if Z is plotted against pressure, a straight line parallel to pressure axis is obtained but in case of real gases, it shows deviation from ideal behaviour as shown in the following graph.

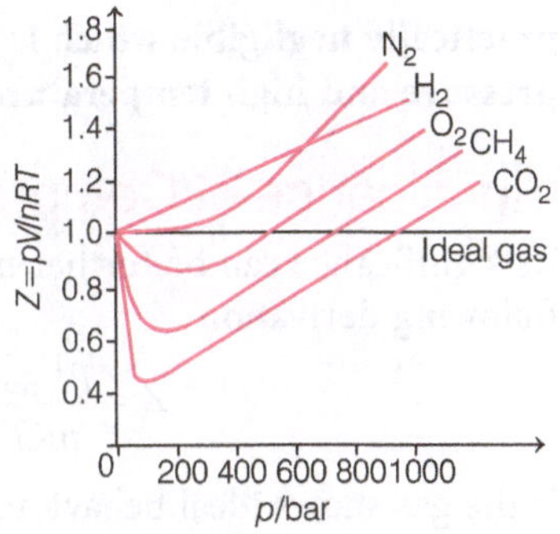

Variation of compressibility factor for some gases

Why Gases Behave Ideally at Low Pressure and High Temperature?

It is found that $Z = 1$ at very low pressure, i.e. in such a condition real gases behave ideally. At high pressure all the gases have $Z > 1$. These are difficult to compress. At intermediate pressures, value of $Z < 1$ for most of the gases. Thus, it is obvious that if the gases occupy large volume or have low or zero pressure then they behave ideally.

This is because in such a condition, the volume of the molecules can be neglected in comparison to the volume of gas. The temperature at which the real gases behave ideally over a wide range of pressure is called **Boyle temperature** or **Boyle point**, T_b. It depends upon the nature of the gas and is specific for a particular gas.

If temperature of a gas is greater than its Boyle point, it shows positive deviation from ideal behaviour and have $Z > 1$. In such a condition, the force of attraction between the molecules are very feeble.

If temperature of a gas is less than its Boyle point, the value of Z first decreases, reaches to minimum value and then further increases on increasing the pressure continuously.

Further, hydrogen and helium have very low Boyle's temperature, i.e. $-165°C$ and $-240°C$ respectively.

So, when measurements are made at near room temperature, the gases are at temperatures much above their Boyle's temperatures. Consequently **Z vs p plots for hydrogen and helium show positive deviations at all pressures.**

The above explanation clearly shows that **real gases behave ideally when intermolecular forces are practically negligible which is the condition at low pressure and high temperature.**

Significance of Compressibility Factor

Its significance can be further understood from the following derivation

$$Z = \frac{pV_{real}}{nRT} \quad \text{...(i)}$$

If the gas shows ideal behaviour, then

$$pV_{ideal} = nRT$$

i.e.

$$V_{ideal} = \frac{nRT}{p} \quad \text{...(ii)}$$

Substituting this value of nRT/p in Eq. (i), we get

$$Z = \frac{V_{real}}{V_{ideal}}$$

Thus, compressibility factor is the ratio of the actual molar volume of the gas (i.e. experimentally observed value of the real gas) to the calculated molar volume (if we consider it as an ideal gas) at the same temperature and pressure.

Note
- For H_2 and He, the compressibility factor Z is always greater than 1 and increases with increase of pressure. This is because H_2 and He are very small molecules, thus the intermolecular forces of attraction in between them are negligible, i.e. 'a' is very very small so that a/V^2 is negligible.

  The van der Waals' equation, therefore, becomes

  $$p(V-b) = RT$$

  or $$pV = RT + pb \text{ or } \frac{pV}{RT} = 1 + \frac{pb}{RT}$$

- Thus, pV/RT i.e. $Z > 1$ and increases as the value of p increases at a fixed temperature.

Quick Test 3

1. Name the energy which arises due to motion of atoms or molecules in a body. How is this energy affected when the temperature is increased?
2. One of the assumptions of kinetic theory of gases states that "there is no force of attraction between the molecules of a gas." How far is this statement correct? Is it possible to liquefy an ideal gas? Explain. *NCERT Exemplar*
3. What would have happened to the gas if the molecular collisions were not elastic?
4. A gas that follows Boyle's law, Charles' law and Avogadro's law is called an ideal gas. Under what conditions a real gas would behave ideally? *NCERT Exemplar*
5. Explain the physical significance of van der Waals' parameters.
6. The van der Waals' constants for two gases are as follows

Gas	a (atm L^2 mol^{-2})	b (L mol^{-1})
X	1.39	0.0391
Y	3.59	0.0427

   Which of them is more easily liquefiable and which has greater molecular size?

7. 1 mole of sulphur dioxide occupies a volume of 350 mL at 27°C and 5×10^6 Pa pressure. Calculate the compressibility factor of the gas.
   Is it less or more compressible than an ideal gas?

For Solutions, See QR Code on Pg. 449

EXAM PATTERN QUESTIONS

Objective Type Questions

Multiple Choice Questions (MCQs) [1 Mark]

1. All gases obey Charles' law at

(a) low temperature and high pressure
(b) low temperature and low pressure
(c) high temperature and high pressure
(d) high temperature and low pressure

2. What would be the effect of increase of temperature on pressure, provided the volume is constant ? NCERT Exemplar

(a) Increases (b) Decreases
(c) Remains same (d) Becomes half

3. Which of the following expression is true for an ideal gas?

(a) $\frac{p_1V_1}{p_2V_2} = \frac{T_1}{T_2}$ (b) $\frac{V_1V_2}{p_1p_2} = T_1T_2$
(c) $\frac{p_1T_1}{p_2T_2} = \frac{V_1}{V_2}$ (d) $p_1V_1T_1 = p_2V_2T_2$

4. The pressure of a 1 : 4 mixture of dihydrogen and dioxygen enclosed in a vessel is one atmosphere. What would be the partial pressure of dioxygen? NCERT Exemplar

(a) 0.8×10^5 atm (b) $0.008\ Nm^{-2}$
(c) $8 \times 10^4\ Nm^{-2}$ (d) 0.25 atm

5. The pressure exerted by the gaseous molecules is due to

(a) the repulsion between gaseous molecules
(b) the attraction between gaseous molecules
(c) collision of the particles with the walls of the container
(d) Both (a) and (b)

6. In kinetic molecular theory, it is assumed that average kinetic energy of the gaseous molecules is directly proportional to the

(a) absolute pressure
(b) absolute volume
(c) absolute temperature
(d) None of these

7. Which curve in figure represents the curve of ideal gas? NCERT Exemplar

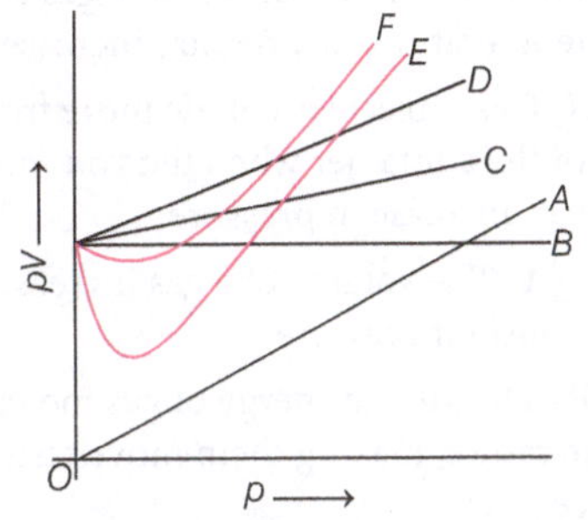

(a) Only B (b) C and D (c) E and F (d) A and B

8. The negative deviation from ideal behaviour means that the

(a) value of pV decreases with decrease in pressure
(b) value of pV decreases with increase in pressure
(c) value of pV increases with increase in pressure
(d) value of pV remains constant with increase in pressure

9. In van der Waals' equation of the gas law, the constant 'a' is a measure of

(a) intermolecular repulsion
(b) intermolecular attraction
(c) volume occupied by the molecules
(d) relative velocity of gaseous molecules

10. The value of Z for real gases below Boyle's temperature initially

(a) increases (b) decreases
(c) remain same (d) increases then decreases

11. Dominance of strong repulsive forces among the molecules of the gas

(a) depends on Z and indicated by $Z = 1$
(b) depends on Z and indicated by $Z > 1$
(c) depends on Z and indicated by $Z < 1$
(d) is independent of Z

Assertion-Reason [1 Mark]

Directions (Q. Nos. 12-19) In the following questions, a statement of Assertion is followed by a corresponding statements of Reason of the following statements, choose the correct one.

(a) Both (A) and (R) are correct and (R) is the correct explanation of (A).
(b) Both (A) and (R) are correct but (R) is not the correct explanation of (A).
(c) (A) is correct but (R) is incorrect.
(d) (A) is incorrect but (R) is correct.

12. **Assertion** (A) When the volume of a gas is decreased at constant temperature, its pressure increases.
Reason (R) Gas molecules collide more frequently with the walls of the container when the volume is reduced, leading to an increase in pressure.

13. **Assertion** (A) The volume of a gas increases when it is heated at constant pressure.
Reason (R) The kinetic energy of gas molecules increases with temperature, making them move faster and occupy more space.

14. **Assertion** (A) Equal volumes of all gases at the same temperature and pressure contain an equal number of molecules.
Reason (R) The volume of a gas is directly proportional to the number of moles at constant temperature and pressure.

15. **Assertion** (A) The total pressure exeted by a mixture of non-reacting gases is equal to the sum of the partial pressures of individual gases.
Reason (R) In a gas mixture, each gas behaves independently and exerts pressure as if it were alkong in the container.

16. **Assertion** (A) Real gas always obey the ideal gas equation $pV = nRT$.
Reason (R) Real gases have negligible intermolecular forces and molecular volume under all conditions.

17. **Assertion** (A) Real gas deviate from ideal behaviour at high pressure and low temperature.
Reason (R) At high pressure, intermolecular forces and the finite size of molecules become significant.

18. **Assertion** (A) The van der Waals equation is the same as the ideal gas equation, with no correction factors.
Reason (R) The van der Waals equation introduces correction terms for intermolecular forces and finite molecualr volume to describe real gases.

19. **Assertion** (A) The compressibility factor (Z) is used to measure the deviation of a real gas from ideal behaviour.
Reason (R) The compressibility factor is defiend as

$$Z = \frac{pV}{nRT}$$

Case-Study [4 Marks]

20. Read the passage carefully and answer the following questions

Gases generally obey the ideal gas equation, $pV = nRT$ but at high pressure and low temperature, real gases show deviations from ideal bahaviour due to intermolecular forces and finite molecualr volume. The van der Waals' equation modifies the ideal gas equation as follows:

$$\left(p + \frac{a}{V^2}\right)(V - b) = nRT$$

Another important parameter is the compressibility factor (Z), defined as

$$Z = \frac{pV}{nRT}$$

(i) (a) Explain why real gases deviate from ideal gas behaviour at high pressure and low temperature?
(b) How do the van der Waals' constants a and b correct these deviations?

(ii) Which of the following statements about the van der Waals equation is correct?
(a) The term $\frac{a}{V^2}$ accounrs for molecular volume.
(b) The term b accounts for intermolecular forces.
(c) The term $\frac{a}{V^2}$ accounts for intermolecualar attractions.
(d) The van der Waals' equation is valid only for ideal gases.

(iii) A gas is found to have a compressibility factor (Z) greater than 1 at very high pressure. This suggests that
(a) the gas behaves ideally.
(b) intermolecular forces are attractive.
(c) repulsive forces dominate.
(d) the gas occupies less volume than expected.

Or

For an ideal gas, the value of Z is always
(a) greater than 1
(b) less than 1
(c) equal to 1
(d) zero

Subjective Type Questions

Short Answer Type I Questions [2 Marks]

1. A gas occupies a volume of 250 mL at 745 mm of Hg and 25°C. What additional pressure is required to reduce the gas volume to 200 mL at the same temperature?

2. A balloon filled with an ideal gas is taken from the surface of the sea deep to a depth of 100 m. What will be its volume in terms of its original volume?

3. For an ideal gas, how does the plot of log p *vs* log V differ from that of log V *vs* log T? Explain.

4. Using the equation of state $pV = nRT$; show that at a given temperature, density of a gas is proportional to gas pressure, p. **NCERT**

5. Calculate the volume occupied by 8.8 g of CO_2 at 31.1°C and 1 bar pressure.
($R = 0.083$ bar L K^{-1} mol^{-1})

6. At 0°C, the density of a certain oxide of a gas at 2 bar is same as that of dinitrogen at 5 bar. What is the molecular mass of the oxide? **NCERT**

7. A mixture of dihydrogen and dioxygen at one bar pressure contains 20% by weight of dihydrogen. Calculate the partial pressure of dihydrogen. **NCERT**

Hints :

- To calculate the partial pressure, total pressure and mole fraction of hydrogen is required, so first calculate number of moles of H_2 and O_2 in the given mixture and mole fraction of hydrogen.
- Then, calculate p_{H_2} by using the formula
$$p_A = p_{total} \times \chi_A$$

8. The relation between pressure exerted by an ideal gas (p_{ideal}) and observed pressure (p_{real}) is given by the equation, $p_{ideal} = p_{real} + \frac{an^2}{V^2}$

(i) If pressure is taken in Nm^{-2}, number of moles in mol and volume in m^3, calculate the unit of '*a*'.

(ii) What will be the unit of '*a*' when pressure is in atmosphere and volume in dm^3?

9. For real gases the relation between p, V and T is given by van der Waals' equation
$$\left(p + \frac{an^2}{V^2}\right)(V - nb) = nRT$$
where, '*a*' and '*b*' are van der Waals' constants, '*nb*' is approximately equal to the total volume of the molecules of a gas. '*a*' is the measure of magnitude of intermolecular attraction.

(i) Arrange the following gases in the increasing order of '*b*'. Give reason.
$$O_2, CO_2, H_2, He$$

(ii) Arrange the following gases in the decreasing order of magnitude of '*a*'. Give reason.
$$CH_4, O_2, H_2$$

10. Two moles of a real gas confined in a 5 L flask exerts a pressure 9.1 atm at a temperature of 27°C. Calculate the value of '*a*'. Given the value of b is 0.052 L mol^{-1}.

11. 1 mole of sulphur dioxide occupies a volume of 350 mL at 27°C and 5×10^6 Pa pressure.
Calculate the compressibility factor of the gas. Is it less or more compressible than an ideal gas?

Short Answer Type II Questions [3 Marks]

12. The variation of pressure with volume of the gas at different temperatures can be graphically represented as shown in figure. On the basis of this graph answer the following questions.

(i) How will the volume of a gas change if its pressure is increased at constant temperature?

(ii) At a constant pressure, how will the volume of a gas change if the temperature is increased from 200 K to 400 K? **NCERT Exemplar**

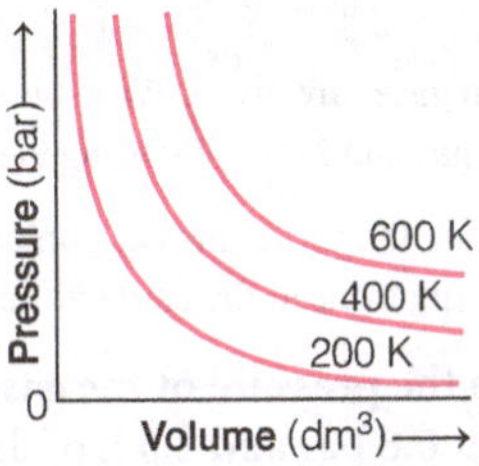

13. A student forgot to add the reaction mixture to the round bottom flask at 27°C but instead he/she placed the flask on the flame. After a lapse of time, he realised his mistake and using a pyrometer he found the temperature of the flask was 477°C. What fraction of air would have been expelled out? **NCERT**

14. A gas is enclosed in room. The temperature, pressure, density and number of moles respectively are t°C, p atm, g cm^{-3} and n moles.

(i) What will be the pressure, temperature, density and number of moles in each compartment, if room is partitioned into four equal compartments?

(ii) What will be the values of pressure, temperature, density and number of moles in each compartment if the walls between the two compartments (say 1 and 2) are removed?

(iii) What will be the values of pressure, temperature, density and number of moles, if an equal volume of gas at pressure (p) and temperature (t) is let inside the same room?

15. A 2.0 L container at 25°C contain 1.25 moles of O_2 and 3.2 moles of C.

(i) What is the initial pressure in the flask?

(ii) If the carbon and oxygen react as completely as possible to form CO, what will be the final pressure in the container?

16. A 5 L vessel contains 1.4 g of nitrogen. When heated to 1800 K, 30% of molecules are dissociated into atoms. Calculate the pressure of the gas at 1800 K.

17. Calculate the total pressure in a mixture of 8 g of dioxygen and 4 g of dihydrogen confined in a vessel of 1 dm^3 at 27°C. ($R = 0.083$ bar dm^3 K^{-1} mol^{-1}). **NCERT**

Hint : To calculate the total pressure exerted by a mixture of gases first find total number of moles of gas and then apply the relation, $pV = nRT$.

18. What will be the pressure exerted by a mixture of 3.2 g of methane and 4.4 g of carbon dioxide contained in a 9 dm^3 flask at 27°C? **NCERT**

19. 2.9 g of a gas at 95°C occupied the same volume as 0.184 g of dihydrogen at 17°C, at the same pressure. What is the molar mass of the gas? **NCERT**

Hints :

- Since, two gases are given. Write two separate equations (for unknown gas and for H_2) by using the relation, $pV = \frac{m}{M}RT$.
- To calculate the molar mass of unknown gas compare both the equations at the same volume and pressure.

20. What will be the pressure of the gaseous mixture when 0.5 L of H_2 at 0.8 bar and 2.0 L of dioxygen at 0.7 bar are introduced in a 1 L vessel at 27°C? **NCERT**

21. Pressure of 1 g of an ideal gas A at 27°C is found to be 2 bar. When 2 g of another ideal gas B is introduced in the same flask at same temperature, the pressure becomes 3 bar. Find a relationship between their molecular masses. **NCERT**

22. The compression factor (compressibility factor) for one mole of a van der Waals gas at 0°C and 100 atm pressure is found to be 0.5. Assuming that the volume of a gas molecule is negligible, calculate the van der Waals' constant a.

23. Calculate the critical constants of a gas whose van der Waals' constants are $a = 0.751\ L^2\ atm\ mol^{-2}$ and $b = 0.0226\ L\ mol^{-1}$.

24. Pressure *versus* volume graph for a real gas and an ideal gas are shown in figure. Answer the following questions on the basis of this graph.

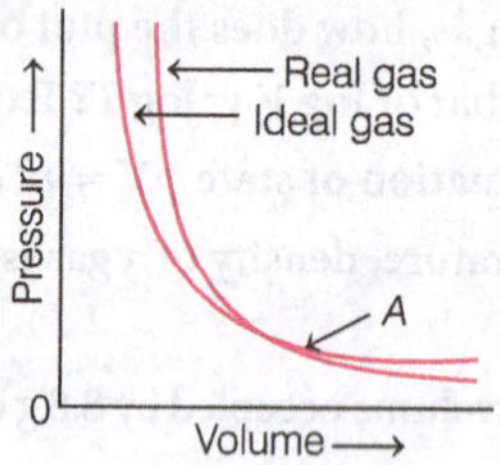

(i) Interpret the behaviour of real gas with respect to ideal gas at low pressure.

(ii) Interpret the behaviour of real gas with respect to ideal gas at high pressure.

(iii) Mark the pressure and volume by drawing a line at the point where real gas behaves as an ideal gas. **NCERT Exemplar**

Long Answer Type Questions [5 Marks]

25. A liquefied petroleum gas (LPG) cylinder weighs 14.8 kg when empty. When full it weighs 29.0 kg and shows a pressure of 2.5 atm. In the course of use at 27°C, the mass of the full cylinder is reduced to 23.2 kg. Find out the volume of the gas in cubic metres used up at the normal usage conditions and the final pressure inside the cylinder. Assume LPG to be n-butane with normal boiling point of 0°C.

26. 135 mL of a gas is collected over water at 25°C and 0.993 bar. If the gas weighs 0.160 g and the aqueous tension at 25°C is 0.0317, calculate the molar mass of the gas.

Hints & Solutions

Objective Type Questions

1. (*d*) All gases obey Charles' law at very low pressures and high temperatures.
2. (*a*) As the temperature increases, average kinetic energy of molecules increases. From Gay-Lussac's law, at constant volume, as the temperature is increased, pressure increases.
3. (*a*) $pV = nRT$ (ideal gas equation)

   If n is constant, then $\frac{p_1V_1}{T_1} = \frac{p_2V_2}{T_2} \Rightarrow \frac{p_1V_1}{p_2V_2} = \frac{T_1}{T_2}$
4. (c) $\because$ Partial pressure of O_2 = Mole fraction of O_2 × total pressure of mixture

   $$= \frac{4}{1+4} \times 1 = \frac{4}{5} \times 1 \text{ atm}$$

   $$= 0.8 \text{ atm} = 0.8 \times 10^5 \text{ N m}^{-2} = 8 \times 10^4 \text{ N m}^{-2}$$
5. (*c*) Particles of gas move in all possible directions in straight line. During their random motion, they collide with each other and with the walls of the container.
6. (*c*) In kinetic molecular theory, it is assumed that average kinetic energy of the gaseous molecules is directly proportional to the absolute temperature.
7. (*a*) For ideal gas pV = constant at all pressures. Therefore, only B represents ideal gas.
8. (*b*) The negative deviation from an ideal behaviour means that the value of pV decreases with increase in pressure.
9. (*b*) The value of 'a' is a measure of magnitude of intermolecular attractive forces within the gas and is independent of temperature and pressure.
10. (*b*) Below Boyle's temperature, real gases first show decrease in Z value with increasing pressure, which reaches a minimum value.
11. (*b*) At high pressure, all the gases have $Z > 1$. These are most difficult to compress, i.e. dominance of strong repulsive forces among the molecules of the gas.
12. (*a*) Both (A) and (R) are correct and (R) is the correct explanation of (A).

    According of Boyle's law, pressure and volume are inversely proportional $\left(p \propto \frac{1}{V}\right)$ is the correct explanation of (A). When volume decreases, molecular collisions increase, causing pressure to rise.
13. (*a*) Both (A) and (R) are correct and (R) is the correct explanation of (A).

    Charle's Law state that volume is directly proportional to temperature $(V \propto T)$ at constant pressure. As molecules gain energy, they spread out, increasing volume.
14. (*a*) Both (A) and (R) are correct and (R) is the correct explanation of (A).

    Avagadro's Law states that $(V \propto n)$ meaning gases with equal volumes at the same conditions have equal molecules.
15. (*a*) Both (A) and (R) are correct and (R) is the correct explanation of (A).

    Dalton's Law states $p_{\text{total}} = p_1 + p_2 + p_3 + \ldots$, as gases exert independent pressure without interacting.
16. (c) (A) is correct but (R) is incorrect.

    Real gases deviate from ideal behaviour at high pressure and low temperature due to molecular interactions.
17. (*a*) Both (A) and (R) are correct and (R) is the correct explanation of (A).

    At **high pressures**, molecules are forced closer, increasing intermolecular forces and making volume corrections necessary.
18. (*d*) (A) is incorrect but (R) is correct.

    The **van der Waals equation** modifies that ideal gas equation to include *a* (for attraction) and *b* (for volume correction).
19. (*a*) Both (A) and (R) are correct and (R) is the correct explanation of (A).

    $Z = 1$ for ideal gases, and $Z \neq 1$ indicates deviations due to intermolecular forces and volume effects.
20. (i) (a) At high pressure, gas molecules are forced close together, and intermolecular attractions becomes significant, reducing the actual pressure exerted on the container walls. At low tempeature, the kinetic energy of molecules decreases, and attractive forces dominate, causing the gas to occupy less volume than expected.

    (b) Real gases deviate from ideal behaviour at high pressure and low temperature due to intermolecular forces and finite molecular volume. The van der Waals equation corrects this by introducing: *a* (accounts for attractive forces, reducing effective pressure) and *b* (accounts for finite molecular volume, preventing infinite compression).

    (ii) (c) The term $\frac{a}{V^2}$ accounts for intermolecular attracitons.

    (iii) (c) Repulsive forces dominate.

    Or

    (c) Equal to 1.

Subjective Type Questions

1. Given, Volume $(V_1) = 250$ mL

Pressure $(p_1) = 745$ mm of Hg

Volume $(V_2) = 200$ mL

Pressure $(p_2) = ?$

Additional $p = ?$

According to Boyle's law, $p_1V_1 = p_2V_2$

745 mg Hg $\times 250$ mL $= p_2 \times 200$ mL

$$p_2 = \frac{745 \text{ mm Hg} \times 250 \text{ mL}}{200 \text{ mL}}$$

$= 931.25$ mm Hg **[1]**

Additional pressure $= p_2 - p_1$

$= 931.25 - 745 = 186.25$ mm Hg **[1]**

Always write the units alongwith the value in calculations as the remaining units help us to find out the correctness of our results.

2. Pressure at the surface $= 76$ cm $= 76 \times 13.6$ cm Hg

$= 1033.6$ cm of Hg $= 10.3$ m of Hg

$\therefore$ Pressure at 100 m depth $= 100 + 10.3$ m $= 110.3$ m

Applying $p_1V_{1,\text{(at surface)}} = p_2V_{2,\text{(at 100 m depth)}}$ **[2]**

$10.3 \times V = 110.3 \times V_2$ or $V_2 = 0.093\,V = 9.3\%$ of V

3. The plot of $\log p$ vs $\log V$ is based on Boyle's law, whereas that of $\log V$ vs $\log T$ is based on Charles' law.

Boyle's law	**Charles' law**
$pV = k$	$\frac{V}{T} = k$
$\log p + \log V = \log k$	$\log V - \log T = \log k$
$\log p = -\log V + \log k$	$\log V = \log T + \log k$ **[1]**

Both equations (i) and (ii) are comparable to $y = mx + C$ and therefore, they represent straight lines. Their plots are as under.

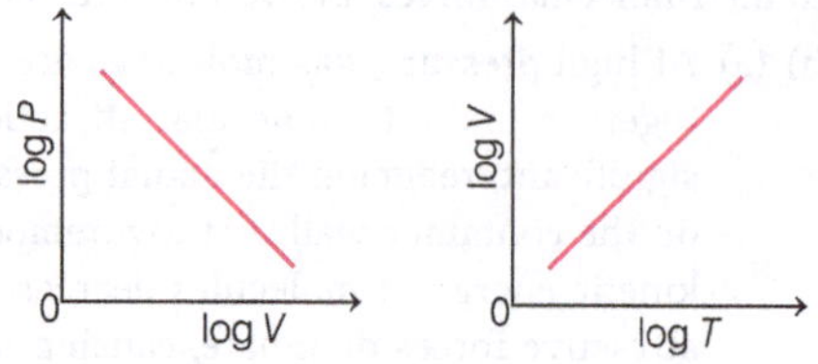

[1]

4. $pV = nRT$

$$pV = \frac{m}{M}RT \qquad \left\{ n = \frac{m}{M} = \frac{\text{mass of gas (g)}}{\text{molar mass of gas}} \right\}$$

or $$p = \frac{mRT}{VM} \text{ or } p = \frac{dRT}{M} \qquad \left(\because \text{Density, } d = \frac{m}{V} \right)$$

or $$d = \frac{pM}{RT};$$

If T = constant, $d \propto p$ **[2]**

5. $pV = nRT$

or $$pV = \frac{m}{M}RT$$

Volume occupied by 8.8 g of CO_2,

$$V = \frac{mRT}{pM}$$

$$= \frac{8.8 \text{ g} \times 0.083 \text{ bar L K}^{-1} \text{ mol}^{-1} \times 304.1 \text{ K}}{1 \text{ bar} \times 44 \text{ g mol}^{-1}}$$

$V = 5.048$ L **[2]**

6. Density, $d = \frac{Mp}{RT}$

When T and d are same and R is constant, then p_1M_1 (gaseous oxide) $= p_2M_2$ (nitrogen).

2 bar $\times M_1 = 5$ bar $\times$ 28 u (molar mass of $N_2 = 28$ u)

Molecular mass of unknown oxide,

$$M_1 = \frac{5 \text{ bar} \times 28}{2 \text{ bar}} = 70 \text{ u}$$ **[2]**

7. A mixture of H_2 and O_2 contains 20% by weight of H_2 means $H_2 = 20$ g and $O_2 = 80$ g

Moles of hydrogen, $n_{H_2} = \frac{20}{2} = 10$ mol

Moles of oxygen, $n_{O_2} = \frac{80}{32} = 2.5$ mol

Mole fraction of hydrogen, $\chi_2 = \frac{n_{H_2}}{n_{H_2} + n_{O_2}} = \frac{10}{10 + 2.5} = 0.8$ **[1]**

Partial pressure of H_2, $p_{H_2} = p_{\text{total}} \times \chi_2$

$p_{H_2} = 1 \text{ bar} \times 0.8 = 0.8$ bar **[1]**

8. Given that, $p_{\text{ideal}} = p_{\text{real}} + \frac{an^2}{V^2}$

(i) $a = \frac{pV^2}{n^2}$ If units of $p = \text{Nm}^{-2}$,

units of $V = \text{m}^3$, units of n = mol

then, units of $a = \frac{\text{Nm}^{-2}\,(\text{m}^3)^2}{(\text{mol})^2} = \text{Nm}^4\ \text{mol}^{-2}$ **[1]**

(ii) If units of p = atm, units of $V = \text{dm}^3$, units of n = mol

then, units of

$$a = \frac{pV^2}{n^2} = \frac{\text{atm.}(\text{dm}^3)^2}{(\text{mol})^2} = \text{atm dm}^6\ \text{mol}^{-2}$$ **[1]**

9. (i) Molar volume occupied by the gas molecules $\propto$ size of the molecules and van der Waals' constant 'b' represents molar volume of the gas molecules. Hence, value of 'b' increases in the following order

$$H_2 < He < O_2 < CO_2$$ **[1]**

(ii) van der Waals' constant 'a' is the measure of magnitude of intermolecular attraction. The magnitude of intermolecular attractions increases with increase in size of electron cloud in a molecule. Hence, for the given gases magnitude of 'a' decreases in the following order

$$CH_4 > O_2 > H_2$$

Greater the size of electron cloud, greater is the polarisability of the molecule and greater are the dispersion forces or London forces. **[1]**

10. $\left(p + \frac{an^2}{V^2}\right)(V - nb) = nRT$

or $a = \left(\frac{nRT}{V - nb} - p\right) \times \frac{V^2}{n^2}$ [1]

$n = 2$ mol, $V = 5$ L, $p = 9.1$ atm, $T = 273 + 27 = 300$ K

$R = 0.082$ L atm mol^{-1}K^{-1}

$$a = \left(\frac{2 \times 0.082 \times 300}{(5 - 2 \times 0.052)} - 9.1\right) \times \frac{(5)^2}{(2)^2}$$

$$= \frac{49.2}{4.896} - 91 \times \frac{25}{4} = (10.05 - 9.1) \times \frac{25}{4}$$

$= 5.94$ atm L^{2}mol^{-2} [1]

11. Compressibility factor, $Z = \frac{pV}{nRT}$

$n = 1$ mol, $p = 5 \times 10^6$ Pa, $V = 350$ mL $= 0.350 \times 10^{-3}$ m^3

$R = 8.314$ Nm K^{-1}, $T = 27 + 273 = 300$ K

$$\therefore X = \frac{5 \times 10^6 \times 0.350 \times 10^{-3}}{1.0 \times 8.314 \times 300} = 0.702$$

Thus, SO_2 is more compressible than an ideal gas (which has $Z = 1$).

12. (i) In accordance with Boyle's law, pressure of a gas is inversely proportional to its volume if temperature is kept constant. Thus, the volume of a gas will decrease if the pressure on the gas is increased keeping the temperature constant. e.g. At 200 K when pressure increases from p_1 to p_2, volume of the gas decreases, $V_2 < V_1$. [1]

(ii) In accordance to Charles' law, volume of a gas is directly proportional to its temperature if pressure is kept constant.

Thus, on increasing temperature, the volume of a gas will increase when pressure is kept constant.

At constant p when we increase the temperature from 200 K to 400 K, the volume of the gas increases, $V_4 > V_3$.

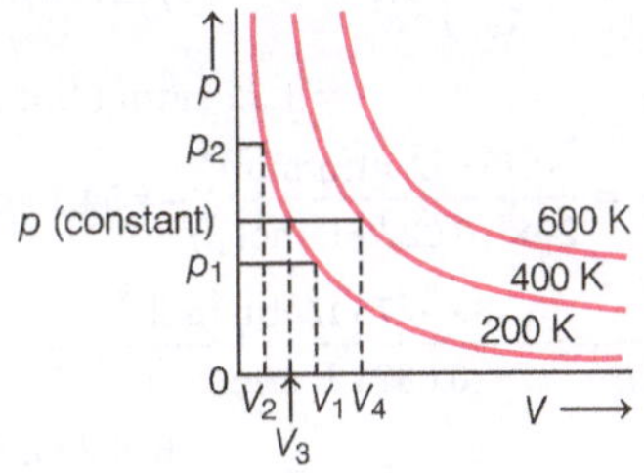

[2]

13. Suppose volume of the air in flask $= V$ cm^3 at 27°C (300 K).

$V_1 = V$ cm^3, $V_2 = ?$, $T_1 = 300$ K, $T_2 = 750$ K

$$\frac{V_1}{T_1} = \frac{V_2}{T_2}$$ [1]

or $\frac{V}{300} = \frac{V_2}{750}$

or $300\ V_2 = 750\ V$ [1]

or $V_2 = 2.5\ V$ (final volume)

Volume expelled $= 2.5\ V - V = 1.5\ V$

Fraction of air expelled $= \frac{1.5\ V}{2.5\ V} = 0.6$ [1]

14. (i) (a) Pressure in each compartment is same, p.

(b) Temperature will remain same (t °C).

(c) Density will remain same (d g cm^{-3}).

(d) Because of partition, volume of each compartment becomes 1/4 and the number of molecules also become 1/4. The number of moles in each compartment will be $n/4$. [1]

(ii) (a) Pressure will remain same (p atm).

(b) Temperature will remain same (t °C).

(c) Density will remain same (d g cm^{-3}).

(d) The number of moles in each compartment will be $n/2$. [1]

(iii) (a) Pressure will be doubled ($2p$ atm).

(b) Temperature will remain same.

(c) Density will remain same (d g cm^{-3})

(d) Number of moles will be doubled, i.e. $2n$. [1]

15. (i) The container contains 1.25 moles of O_2 and 3.2 moles of C. Since, only oxygen is gaseous and carbon will not exert any pressure.

$n = 1.25$ mol, $V = 2.0$ L,

$T = 273 + 25 = 298$ K

$$\therefore p = \frac{nRT}{V}$$

$$= \frac{(1.25 \text{ mol}) \times (0.0821 \text{ L atm mol}^{-1}\text{K}^{-1})(298 \text{ K})}{(2.0 \text{ L})}$$

$= 15.3$ atm [2]

(ii) The reaction is $C + \frac{1}{2}O_2 \longrightarrow CO$

According to the equation, 1 mole of CO will be produced for every 1/2 mole of O_2 used.

$\frac{1}{2}$ mole of O_2 gives $= 1$ mole of CO

1.25 moles of O_2 will give CO $= 1 \times 2 \times 1.25 = 2.50$ mol

$\therefore$ Final pressure

$$p = \frac{(2.50 \text{ mol}) \times (0.0821 \text{ L atm K}^{-1}\text{mol}^{-1}) \times (298 \text{ K})}{2.0 \text{ L}}$$

$= 30.6$ atm [1]

16.

	N_2	$\rightleftharpoons$ 2N
Initial moles	$\frac{1.4}{28} = 0.05$	0
Final moles	$0.05 - \frac{30}{100} \times 0.05$	2×0.015

Dissociation $= 0.05 - 0.015 = 0.035 = 0.030$

$\therefore$ Total number of moles $= 0.035 + 0.030 = 0.065$

i.e. $n = 0.065$ mol, $V = 5$ L, $T = 1800$ K, $p = ?$

From $pV = nRT$, we get

$$p = \frac{nRT}{V}$$

$$= \frac{0.065 \text{ mol} \times 0.0821 \text{ L atm K}^{-1}\text{mol}^{-1} \times 1800 \text{ K}}{5 \text{ L}}$$ **[2]**

$= 1.92$ atm **[1]**

17. Moles of O_2, $n_{O_2} = \frac{\text{mass}}{\text{mol. wt.}} = \frac{8}{32} = 0.25$ mol

[mol. wt. of $O_2 = 16 \times 2 = 32$]

Moles of H_2, $n_{H_2} = \frac{4}{2} = 2.0$ mol

[mol. wt. of $H_2 = 1 \times 2 = 2$]

Total number of moles $= 0.25 + 2.0 = 2.25$ mol **[1]**

Pressure, $p = \frac{nRT}{V}$

$$= \frac{2.25 \text{ mol} \times 0.083 \text{ bar dm}^3 \text{ K}^{-1}\text{mol}^{-1} \times 300 \text{ K}}{1 \text{ dm}^3}$$

$p = 56.025$ bar **[2]**

18. Moles of CH_4, $n_{CH_4} = \frac{\text{Mass of } CH_4}{\text{Molar mass of } CH_4}$

$= \frac{3.2}{16} = 0.2$ mol

Similarly, moles of CO_2, $n_{CO_2} = \frac{4.4}{44} = 0.1$ mol **[1]**

Total moles $= 0.2 + 0.1 = 0.3$ mol **[1]**

$pV = nRT$

Pressure, $p = \frac{nRT}{V}$

$$= \frac{0.3 \text{ mol} \times 0.0821 \text{ dm}^3\text{atm K}^{-1}\text{mol}^{-1} \times 300 \text{ K}}{9 \text{ dm}^3}$$

$= 0.821$ atm $= 8.314 \times 10^4$ Pa **[1]**

19. Unknown gas; H_2 gas

$p_1V_1 = \frac{m_1RT_1}{M_1}$; $p_2V_2 = \frac{m_2RT_2}{M_2}$

$\because$ $p_1V_1 = p_2V_2$

$\therefore$ $\frac{m_1RT_1}{M_1} = \frac{m_2RT_2}{M_2}$ **[1]**

$$\frac{2.9 \text{ g} \times R \times 368 \text{ K}}{M_1} = \frac{0.184 \text{ g} \times R \times 290 \text{ K}}{2 \text{ g mol}^{-1}}$$

Molar mass of unknown gas,

$$M_1 = \frac{2.9 \text{ g} \times 368 \text{ K} \times 2 \text{ g mol}^{-1}}{0.184 \text{ g} \times 290 \text{ K}} = 40 \text{ g mol}^{-1}$$ **[2]**

20. $pV = nRT$

Moles of H_2, $n_{H_2} = \frac{pV}{RT} = \frac{0.8 \times 0.5}{RT} = \frac{0.40}{RT}$

Similarly, moles of O_2, $n_{O_2} = \frac{pV}{RT} = \frac{0.7 \times 2}{RT} = \frac{1.4}{RT}$ **[1]**

Total number of moles $= \frac{0.40}{RT} + \frac{1.4}{RT} = \frac{1.8}{RT}$ **[1]**

Total pressure, $p_{\text{total}} = \frac{nRT}{V} = \frac{1.8 \times RT}{RT \times 1} = 1.8$ atm **[1]**

21. $pV = nRT$

For gas A, $p_AV = n_ART$ ...(i)

Similarly for gas B, $p_BV = n_BRT$ ...(ii)

Number of moles of gas A; $n_A = \frac{1}{M_A}$

(M_A = molar mass of gas A)

Number of moles of gas B; $n_B = \frac{2}{M_B}$

(M_B = molar mass of gas B)

Pressure of gas A, $p_A = 2$ bar

Total pressure, $p_{\text{total}} = p_A + p_B = 3$ bar

Pressure of gas, $p_B = p_{\text{total}} - p_A = 3 - 2 = 1$ bar **[1]**

V, R and T are same for both the gases.

Hence, from Eqs. (i) and (ii),

$$\frac{p_A}{p_B} = \frac{n_A}{n_B} = \frac{1 \times M_B}{M_A \times 2}$$

or $\frac{M_B}{M_A} = \frac{2p_A}{p_B} = \frac{2 \times 2}{1}$

or $M_B = 4\, M_A$ **[2]**

22. $Z = \frac{pV}{nRT}$, i.e. $0.5 = \frac{100 \times V}{1 \times 0.082 \times 273}$

or $V = 0.1119$ L

$$\left(p + \frac{a}{V^2}\right)(V - b) = RT \text{ for 1 mol}$$ **[1]**

Neglecting b, $\left(p + \frac{a}{V^2}\right)V = RT$

or $pV + \frac{a}{V} = RT$

or $\frac{pV}{RT} + \frac{a}{VRT} = 1$

or $a = \left(1 - \frac{pV}{RT}\right)VRT = (1 - 0.5)0.1119 \times 0.082 \times 273$

$= 1.252$ atm L^2mol^{-2} **[2]**

23. $p_c = \frac{a}{27b^2} = \frac{0.751 \text{ L}^2 \text{ atm mol}^{-2}}{27 \times (0.0226 \text{ L mol}^{-1})^2} = 54.5$ atm **[1]**

$T_c = \frac{8a}{27Rb} = \frac{8 \times 0.75 \text{ L}^2\text{atm mol}^{-2}}{27 \times 0.0821 \text{ L atm K}^{-1}\text{mol}^{-1}}$ **[1]**

$\times 0.0226 \text{ L mol}^{-1} = 120$ K

$V_c = 3b = 3 \times 0.0226 \text{ L mol}^{-1} = 0.0678 \text{ L mol}^{-1}$ **[1]**

24. (i) At low pressure, the real gas shows very small deviation from ideal behaviour because the two curves almost coincide at low pressure. **[1]**

(ii) At high pressure, the real gas shows large deviations from ideal behaviour as the curves are far apart. **[1]**

(iii) At point 'A', both the curves intersect each other. At this point real gas behaves as an ideal gas. p_1 and V_1 are the pressure and volume which corresponds to this point A. **[1]**

25. Weight of LPG originally present = 29.0 − 14.8 = 14.2 kg

Pressure = 2.5 atm

Weight of LPG present after use = 23.2 − 14.8 = 8.4 kg

Since volume of the cylinder is constant, applying

$$pV = nRT$$

$$\Rightarrow \frac{p_1}{p_2} = \frac{n_1}{n_2} = \frac{w_1/m}{w_2/m} = \frac{w_1}{w_2}$$

$$\Rightarrow \frac{2.5}{p_2} = \frac{14.2}{8.4}$$

or $$p_2 = \frac{2.5 \times 8.4}{14.2} = 1.48 \text{ atm}$$ **[1]**

$\because$ Weight of used gas = 14.2 − 8.4 = 5.8 kg

$$\text{Moles of gas} = \frac{5.8 \times 10^3}{58} = 100 \text{ mol}$$

Normal conditions $p = 1$ atm;

$$T = 273 + 27 = 300 \text{ K}$$ **[2]**

Volume of 100 mL of LPG at 1 atm and 300 K

$$V = \frac{nRT}{p} = \frac{100 \times 0.082 \times 300}{1}$$

$$= 2460 \text{ L} = 2.460 \text{ m}^3$$ **[2]**

26. $$p_{gas} = p_{total} - p_{H_2O}$$

$$p_{total} = 0.993 \text{ bar}, pH_2O = 0.0317 \text{ bar}$$

$\therefore$ $$p_{gas} = 0.993 - 0.0317 = 0.9613 \text{ bar}$$

Now $$pV = nRT$$

But $$n = \frac{m}{M}, pV = \frac{m}{M}RT$$

or $$M = \frac{mRT}{pV}$$

and $$m = 0.160 \text{ g}, \ V = 135 \text{ mL} = \frac{135}{1000}$$

$$= 0.135 \text{ dm}^3$$

$$T = 25 + 273 = 298 \text{ K}, \ p = 0.9613 \text{ bar}$$

$$R = 0.083 \text{ bar dm}^3 \text{mol}^{-1}\text{K}^{-1}$$

Substituting the values,

$$M = \frac{(0.160 \text{ g}) \times (0.083 \text{ bar mol}^{-1}\text{K}^{-1}) \times (298 \text{ K})}{(0.9613 \text{ bar}) \times (0.135 \text{ dm}^3)}$$

$$= 30.49 \text{ g mol}^{-1}$$ **[5]**

QR Code for Quick Test 1

QR Code for Quick Test 2

QR Code for Quick Test 3

SAMPLE QUESTION PAPER 1

A Highly Simulated Sample Question Paper for CBSE Class XI Examination

CHEMISTRY [Fully Solved]

Time : 3 Hours **Max. Marks : 70**

General Instructions

Read the following instructions carefully.

1. This question paper contains **33 questions**. All questions are **compulsory**.
2. This question paper is divided into **FIVE** sections - **Section A, B, C, D and E.**
3. **SECTION-A** questions number 1 to 16 are multiple choice type questions. Each question carries 1 mark.
4. **SECTION-B** questions number 17 to 21 are very short answer type questions. Each question carries 2 marks.
5. **SECTION-C** questions number 22 to 28 are short answer type questions. Each question carries 3 marks.
6. **SECTION-D** questions number 29 and 30 are case-based questions. Each question carries 4 marks.
7. **SECTION-E** questions number 31 to 33 are long answer type questions. Each question carries 5 marks.
8. There is no overall choice given in the question paper. However, an internal choice has been provided in few questions in all the sections except section A.
9. Kindly note that there is a separate question paper for visually impaired candidates.
10. Use of calculator is NOT allowed.

Section-A

The following questions are multiple choice questions with one correct answer. Each question carries 1 mark. There is no internal choice in this section.

1. What will be the K_p for the reaction

$2NOCl(g) \rightleftharpoons 2NO(g) + Cl_2(g)$ at 1000 K?

Given, that K_C at 1000 K is 3.75×10^{-6}.

(a) 3.11×10^{-4}
(b) 0.311×10^{-4}
(c) 31.1×10^{-4}
(d) 0.0311×10^{-4}

2. Why do the deviations occur from idealised shape of H_2O and NH_3 molecules?

(a) Same hybridisation
(b) Different hybridisation
(c) Repulsive effect
(d) None of the above

3. At 363 K, pure water has $[H_3O^+] = 10^{-6}$ M. The value of K_w at this temperature will be

(a) 10^{-6}
(b) 10^{-12}
(c) 10^{-13}
(d) 10^{-14}

4. Two students performed the same experiment separately and each one of them recorded two readings of mass which are given below. Correct reading of mass is 3.0 g.

Students	Readings (i)	Readings (ii)
A	3.01	2.99
B	3.05	2.95

On the basis of given data, mark the correct option out of the following statements.

(a) Results of both the students are neither accurate nor precise.
(b) Results of student *A* are both precise and accurate.
(c) Results of student *B* are neither precise nor accurate.
(d) Results of student *B* are both precise and accurate.

5. Which of the following represents correct increasing order of the boiling point of the given compounds?

(a) $HF < H_2O < NH_3$
(b) $H_2O < HF < NH_3$
(c) $NH_3 < HF < H_2O$
(d) $NH_3 < H_2O < HF$

6. The structures of a few compounds are given below.

Compounds	Structures
Butan-1-ol	$CH_3CH_2CH_2CH_2OH$
Butan-2-ol	$CH_3—CH_2—CH(OH)—CH_3$
Diethylether	$CH_3—CH_2—O—CH_2—CH_3$
Methoxypropane	$CH_3—O—CH_2—CH_2—CH_3$
Tert-butyl alcohol	$CH_3—C(CH_3)(OH)—CH_3$

Which of the above compounds form a pair of metamers?

(a) Diethylether and methoxypropane
(b) Butan-1-ol and butan-2-ol
(c) Butan-2-ol and diethylether
(d) Methoxypropane and *tert*-butyl alcohol

7. If the concentration of glucose ($C_6H_{12}O_6$) in blood is 0.9 g/L. What will be the molarity of glucose in blood?

(a) 5 M (b) 50 M (c) 0.005 M (d) 0.5 M

8. Consider the following table

General formula	Structure	IUPAC name
X	$CH_2=CH—CH(CH_3)—CH_3$	Y
C_nH_{2n-2}	Z	But-2-yne

Here, X, Y and Z are

(a) $X = C_nH_{2n}$, Y = 3-methylbutene, $Z = CH_3C\equiv C—CH_3$
(b) $X = C_nH_{2n+2}$, Y = 2-methylbut-3-ene, $Z = CH_3CH_2C\equiv CH_3$
(c) $X = C_nH_{2n+2}$, Y = 3-methylbutene, $Z = CH_3C\equiv C—CH_3$
(d) $X = C_nH_{2n}$, Y = 2-methylbut-3-ene, $Z = CH_3CH_2C\equiv CH_3$

9. The reversible expansion of an ideal gas under adiabatic and isothermal is shown in the figure.

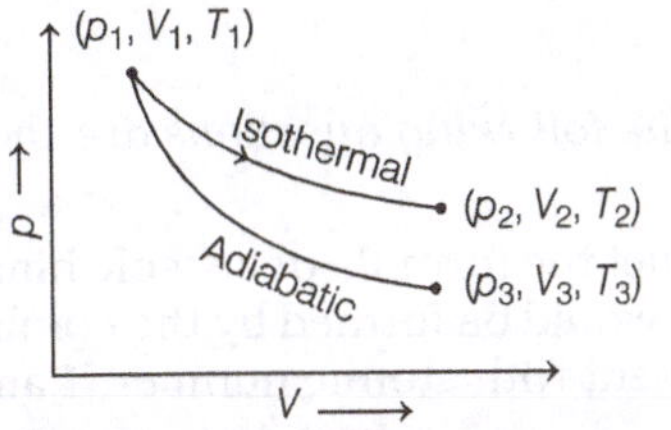

Which of the following(s) is incorrect?

(a) $T_1 = T_2$ (b) $T_3 > T_1$
(c) $W_{isothermal} > W_{adiabatic}$ (d) $\Delta S_{isothermal} > \Delta S_{adiabatic}$

10. The name of the following compound is

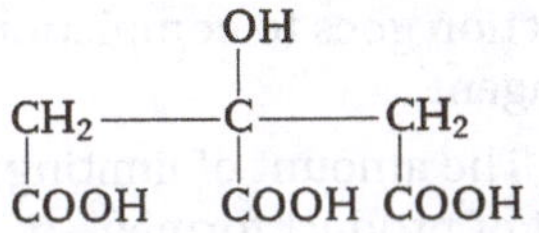

(a) 2-hydroxypropane-1,2,3-tricarboxylic acid
(b) 3-carboxy-3-hydroxy-1,5-pentanedioic acid
(c) citric acid
(d) All of the above

11. Dipole moment is usually designated by a Greek letter 'μ'

$$\mu = Q \times r$$

Here, Q and r represents

(a) Q = charge, r = distance of separation
(b) Q = heat, r = radius of cations
(c) Q = charge, r = radius of cations
(d) Q = charge, r = radius of anions

12. Match the Column I and Column II and pick out correct match codes from the given choices.

	Column I		Column II
A.	Molecule having sp^3d hybridisation of central atom with one lone pair of electrons	1.	SF_4
B.	Molecule having sp^3 hybridisation of central atom with no lone pair of electrons.	2.	XeF_4
C.	Molecule having sp^3d^2 hybridisation of central atom with two lone pair of electrons.	3.	CF_4

Codes

(a) A → (1); B → (3); C → (2)
(b) A → (2); B → (1); C → (3)
(c) A → (3); B → (1); C → (2)
(d) A → (2); B → (3); C → (1)

Assertion-Reason

In the following questions (Q.No. 13-16), a statement of Assertion followed by a statement of Reason is given. Choose the correct answer out of the following choices.

(a) Both (A) and (R) are correct and (R) is the correct explanation of (A).
(b) Both (A) and (R) are correct but (R) is not the correct explanation of (A).
(c) (A) is correct and (R) is incorrect.
(d) (A) is incorrect and (R) is correct.

13. **Assertion** (A) A reactant that is entirely consumed when a reaction goes to completion is known as limiting reagent.

Reason (R) The amount of limiting reagent limits the amount of product formed.

14. **Assertion** (A) *s*-Block elements are highly reactive metals.

Reason (R) They exhibit low ionisation enthalpy.

15. **Assertion** (A) The compound cyclooctatetraene has the following structural formula,

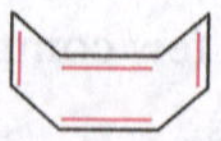

It is cyclic and has conjugated 8π-electron system but it is not an aromatic compound.

Reason (R) Huckel rule does not hold good and ring is not planar.

16. **Assertion** (A) Butane and 2-methyl butane are homologues.

Reason (R) Butane is a straight chain alkane, while 2-methylbutane is a branched chain alkane.

Section-B

This section contains 5 questions with internal choice in one question. The following questions are short answer type and carry 2 marks each.

17. Give reason for the following.

(i) Electron gain enthalpy of O^- is positive, while that of S is negative and electron gain enthalpy S^- is positive, while that of O is negative.

(ii) Why the increasing order of reactivity among group 17 elements is $F > Cl > Br > I$?

18. But-1-yne gives its sodium salt with $NaNH_2$, which on reaction with ethylbromide gives hex-3-yne. Hex-3-yne on reduction with H_2 / Pd - $BaSO_4$ gives *cis* hex-3-ene which on hydrolysis using alk. $KMnO_4$ gives hexane-3, 4-diol.

Write the related chemical equations.

19. (i) The density of 3 M solution of NaCl is 1.25 g mL^{-1}. Calculate molality of the solution.

(ii) What is the concentration of sugar ($C_{12}H_{22}O_{11}$) in mol L^{-1} if its 20 g are dissolved in enough water to make a final volume up to 2 L?

Or Dinitrogen and dihydrogen react with each other to produce ammonia according to the following equation.

$$N_2(g) + 3H_2(g) \longrightarrow 2NH_3(g)$$

(i) Calculate the mass of ammonia produced if 2.00×10^3 g dinitrogen reacts with 1.00×10^3 g of dihydrogen.

(ii) Will any of the two reactants remain unreacted. If, yes which one and what would be its mass?

20. (i) Astronauts observe that the signals from the distant stars are weak, if a photon detector receives a total of 3.15×10^{-18} J from the radiations of 600 nm. Find the number of photons received by the detector.

(ii) What physical mean is attributed to the square of the absolute value of wave function, (ψ^2)?

21. (i) Give the IUPAC name for the following compound.

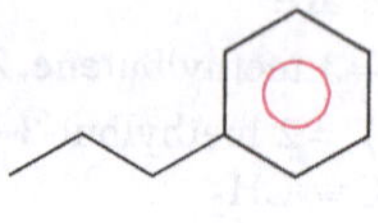

(ii) What is the hybridisation of each carbon in $CH_2{=}C{=}CH_2$?

Section-C

This section contains 7 questions with internal choice in one question. The following questions are short answer type and carry 3 marks each.

22. Answer the following.

(i) The first ionisation enthalpy ($\Delta_i H$) values of the third period elements, Na, Mg and Si are respectively 496, 737 and 786 kJ mol^{-1}. Predict the $\Delta_i H_1$ value for Al.

(ii) Predict the formula of a stable binary compound that would be formed by the combination of element with atomic number 71 and fluorine.

(iii) Electron affinity is positive when O^- changes into O^{2-}. Explain.

23. Explain extensive and intensive properties with examples. Show that mole fraction and molarity are intensive properties.

24. Find out the number of wave made by a Bohr's electron in one complete revolution in its 3rd orbit.

Or

(i) Which has higher energy a photon of red light with a wavelength of 7500 Å or a photon of green light with a wavelength of 5250 Å?

(ii) What is the number of unpaired electrons in Fe^{3+}?

(iii) Calculate the energy of radiation when $\bar{\nu}$ (wave number) $= 4 \times 10^5\ m^{-1}$.

25. (i) Out of σ and π-bonds, which one is stronger and why?

(ii) What type of hybridisation is involved in SF_6?

(iii) Out of *p*-orbital and *sp*-hybrid orbital which has greater directional character and why?

26. (i) Identify the substance that get reduced in the following reaction.

$$Fe_2O_3(s) + 3CO(g) \longrightarrow 2Fe(s) + 3CO_2(g)$$

(ii) The compound AgF_2 is unstable compound. However, if formed, the compound acts as a very strong oxidising agent. Why?

(iii) Zn rod is immersed in $CuSO_4$ solution. What will you observe after an hour? Explain your observation in terms of redox reaction.

27. Two oxides of a metal contain 27.6% and 30.0% of oxygen respectively. If the formula of the first oxide is M_3O_4, find that of the second.

28. (i) Write the structural formula of

(a) *o*-ethylanisole

(b) *p*-nitroaniline

(ii) Write the correct stability order of the following.

$$(CH_3)_3C\overset{+}{C}H_2;\ (CH_3)_3\overset{+}{C},\ CH_3CH_2\overset{+}{C}H_2$$

Section-D

The following questions are case-based questions. Each question has an internal choice and carries 4 (2 + 1 + 1) marks each. Read the passage carefully and answer the questions that follow.

29. An oxidation-reduction (redox) reaction is a type of chemical reaction that involves a transfer of electrons between two species. An oxidation-reduction reaction is any chemical reaction in which the oxidation number of a molecule, atom or ion changes by gaining or losing an electron. Redox reactions are common and vital to some of the basic functions of life, including photosynthesis, respiration, combustion, and corrosion or rusting. The oxidation state of an element corresponds to the number of electrons (e^-) that an atom loses, gains, or appears to use when joining with other atoms in compounds.

The oxidation state of an individual atom is 0. The total oxidation state of all atoms in a neutral species is 0 and in an ion is equal to the ion charge. Group 1 metals have an oxidation state of +1 and group 2 an oxidation state of +2.

The oxidation state of fluorine is −1 in compounds. Hydrogen generally has an oxidation state of +1 in compounds. Oxygen generally has an oxidation state of −2 in compounds. In binary metal compounds, group 17 elements have an oxidation state of −1, group 16 elements of −2 and group 15 elements of −3. The sum of the oxidation states is equal to zero for neutral compounds and equal to the charge for polyatomic ion species.

Redox reactions are comprised of two parts, a reduced half and an oxidised half, that always occur together.

Answer the following questions.

(i) Why does the following reaction occur?

$$XeO_6^{4-}(aq) + 2F^-(aq) + 6H^+(aq) \longrightarrow XeO_3(g) + F_2(g) + 3H_2O\ (l)$$

What conclusion about the compound Na_4XeO_6 (of which XeO_6^{4-} is a part) can be drawn from the reaction?

(ii) 1 mole of acidified $K_2Cr_2O_7$ on reaction with excess KI will liberate *n* moles of I_2, then calculate the value of *n*.

Or

In alkaline medium, ClO_2 oxidises H_2O_2 to O_2 and itself gets reduced to Cl. How many mole of H_2O_2 are oxidised by 1 mole of ClO_2?

(iii) Write the half-reactions for the redox reaction.

$$Al(s) + 3Ag^+(aq) \longrightarrow Al^{3+}(aq) + 3Ag(s)$$

30. A total of four quantum numbers are used to describe completely the movement and trajectories of each electron within an atom. Each electron in an atom has a unique set of quantum numbers; according to the Pauli exclusion principle, no two electrons can share the same combination of four quantum numbers. Quantum numbers are important because they can be used to determine the electron configuration of an atom and the probable location of the atom's electrons.

In atoms, there are a total of four quantum numbers: the principal quantum number (n), the orbital angular momentum quantum number (l), the magnetic quantum number (m_l) and the electron spin quantum number (m_s). The principal quantum number (n), describes the energy of an electron and the most probable distance of the electron from the nucleus. In other words, it refers to the size of the orbital and the energy level an electron is placed in.

The size of the atom and its atomic radius increases. Because the atomic radius increases, the electrons are farther from the nucleus. Thus, it is easier for the atom to expel an electron because the nucleus does not have as strong a pull on it and the ionisation energy decreases. We can designate a principal quantum number (n) and a certain subshell by combining the value of n and the name of the subshell which can be found using (l).

The s orbital, because the value of m_l can only be 0, can only exist in one plane. The p-orbital, however, has three possible because the value of m_l and so, it has three possible orientations of the orbitals, shown by p_x, p_y and p_z. The pattern continues, with the d-orbital containing 5 possible orbital orientations and f has 7.

Answer the following questions.

(i) The unpaired electrons in Al and Si are present in $3p$-orbital. Which electron will experience more effective nuclear charge from the nucleus?

(ii) The correct order of increasing energy of atomic orbitals is

(a) $5p < 4f < 6s < 5d$ (b) $5p < 6s < 4f < 5d$
(c) $4f < 5p < 5d < 6s$ (d) $5p < 5d < 4f < 6s$

Or

A p-orbital can accommodate upto

(a) four electrons
(b) six electrons
(c) two electrons with parallel spins
(d) two electrons with opposite spins

(iii) The number of radial nodes for $3p$-orbital is

(a) 3 (b) 4 (c) 2 (d) 1

Section-E

The following questions are long answer type and carry 5 marks each. All questions have an internal choice.

31. An alkyl halide $C_5H_{11}Br$ (A) reacts with ethanolic KOH to give an alkene 'B', which reacts with Br_2 to give a compound 'C', which on dehydrobromination gives an alkyne 'D'. On treatment with sodium metal in liquid ammonia, one mole of 'D' gives one mole of the sodium salt of 'D' and half a mole of hydrogen gas. Complete hydrogenation of 'D' yields a straight chain alkane. Identify A, B, C and D. Give the reactions involved.

Or

(i) What happens when
(a) bromoethane is heated with zinc and hydrochloric acid?
(b) hydrogen is passed into 2-bromopropane in the presence of palladium?

(ii) Account for the following.
(a) Hydrocarbon molecules with an odd number of carbon atoms have lower melting points than those with an even number of carbon atoms.
(b) The C—C bonds rather than C—H bonds break during cracking of alkanes?
(c) Iodination of benzene is carried out in the presence of nitric acid or iodic acid.

32. Answer the following questions.

(i) Two moles of an ideal gas initially at 27°C and one atmospheric pressure are compressed isothermally and reversibly till the final pressure of the gas is 10 atm. Calculate W for the process.

(ii) The enthalpy of vaporisation of an organic compound at its boiling point (35.0°C) is 26×10^3 J mol^{-1}. Calculate standard enthalpy change for the conversion of liquid to vapour.

(iii) At low temperature, enthalpy change dominates the value of ΔG and at high temperature, it is the entropy which dominates the value of ΔG in Gibbs Helmholtz equation. Why?

Or

(i) Predict the sign of $\Delta S°$ for the following reactions.
(a) $2H_2S(g) + 3O_2(g) \longrightarrow 2H_2O(g) + 2SO_2(g)$
(b) $N_2(g) + 3H_2(g) \longrightarrow 2NH_3(g)$

(ii) Give mathematical relation between
(a) Free energy change and equilibrium constant.
(b) Free energy change, enthalpy change and entropy change.

(iii) Write an expression for work done in an isothermal and irreversible expansion of a gas.

33. (i) The ionisation constant of propanoic acid is 1.32×10^{-5}. Calculate the degree of ionisation of the acid in its 0.05 M solution and also its pH. What will be its degree of ionisation if the solution is 0.01 M in HCl also?

(ii) Calculate the pH of 1 mL of 13.6 M HCl is diluted with water to give 1 L of solution.

(iii) What is the effect of reducing volume on the following system ?

$$2C(s)+O_2(g) \rightleftharpoons 2CO(g)$$

Or

(i) At 700 K, equilibrium constant for the reaction, $H_2(g) + I_2(g) \rightleftharpoons 2HI(g)$ is 54.8. If 0.5 mol L^{-1} of HI(g) is present in equilibrium at 700 K, what are the concentrations of $H_2(g)$ and $I_2(g)$, assuming that we initially started with HI(g) and allowed it to reach equilibrium at 700 K?

(ii) For the following equilibrium, $K_C = 6.3 \times 10^{14}$ at 1000 K

$$NO(g)+O_3(g) \rightleftharpoons NO_2(g)+O_2(g)$$

Both the forward and reverse reactions in the equilibrium are elementary bimolecular reactions. What is K_c for the reverse reaction?

(iii) Explain, why pure liquids and solids can be ignored while writing the equilibrium constant expression?

Solutions

1. (a) Given $K_C = 3.75 \times 10^{-6}$, $T = 1000$ K

For the reaction, $2NOCl(g) \rightleftharpoons 2NO(g) + Cl_2(g)$

$\Rightarrow \quad K_p = K_C(RT)^{\Delta n_g} \quad [\because \Delta n_g = 3-2 = 1]$

$\therefore \quad K_p = K_C(RT)$

$\Rightarrow \quad K_p = 3.75 \times 10^{-6} \times 0.0831 \times 1000 = 3.11 \times 10^{-4}$

2. (c) Greater repulsion between lone pairs of electrons as compared to the lone pair-bond pair and bond pair-bond pair repulsions. These repulsive effects result in deviations from idealised shapes and alterations in bond angles in the molecules.

3. (b) $[H_3O^+] = [OH^-] = 10^{-6}$ M

$$K_w = [H_3O^+][OH^-] = 10^{-6} \times 10^{-6} = 10^{-12} \text{ M}$$

4. (b) Average readings of student, $A = \dfrac{3.01 + 2.99}{2} = 3.00$

Average readings of student, $B = \dfrac{3.05 + 2.95}{2} = 3.00$

Correct reading = 3.00

Average reading of both students are same and equal to the correct reading. Actual readings of student '*A*' are more preise becuase both readings are close to the correct reading [3.00] and has a difference of 0.02 only. Whereas, readings of students '*B*' has difference of 0.1 and hence is less precise.

5. (c) Strength of H-bond is in the order

$$H—N < H—O < H—F$$

but each H_2O molecule is linked to four other H_2O molecules through H-bonds, whereas each HF molecule is linked only to two other HF molecules.

Hence, b.p. of NH_3 < b.p. of HF < b.p. of H_2O

6. (a) Diethylether and methoxypropane form a pair of metamers because they differ only in the number of carbon atoms on either side of ether functional group.

7. (c) Molecular mass of glucose
$= 12 \times 6 + 12 \times 1 + 6 \times 16 = 180$ g
Number of moles in 0.9 g glucose

$$= \frac{0.9}{180} = 5 \times 10^{-3} \text{ moles}$$

$$\text{Molarity} = \frac{\text{No. of moles of glucose}}{\text{Volume of solution (L)}} = \frac{0.005 \text{ mol}}{1 \text{ (L)}} = 0.005 \text{ M}$$

8. (a) For, the organic compound $\overset{1}{C}H_2{=}\overset{2}{C}H{-}\overset{3}{C}H(CH_3){-}\overset{4}{C}H_3$,

IUPAC name (*Y*) is 3-methylbutene. Since, it is an alkene thus, general formula (*X*) is C_nH_{2n}.

The structure of but-2-yne is $\overset{4}{C}H_3{-}\overset{3}{C}{\equiv}\overset{2}{C}{-}\overset{1}{C}H_3$.
(*Z*)

9. (*b*) From first law of thermodynamics, $\Delta U = q + W$

In adibatic expansion, $q = 0$

$\therefore \quad \Delta U = W$

During expansion of a gas, $w = 0$ or $\Delta U < 0$

we know that, $\Delta U = n C_V \Delta T$

$\therefore \quad \Delta T < 0$

or $\quad T_3 < T_1$

Thus, only option (b) is incorrect.

10. (*d*)

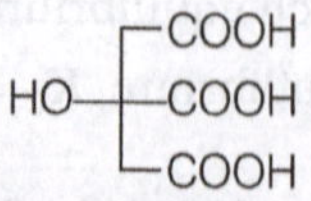

2-hydroxypropane-1,2,3-tricarboxylic acid or 3-carboxy-3-hydroxy-1,5-pentanedioic acid

It is commonly called as citric acid.

11. (*a*) Dipole moment = Charge × Distance of separation
(μ) (Q) (r)

Dipole moment is the product of charge (Q) and distance (r) between the charges.

12. (*a*) A→ 1; B→ 3; C→ 2.

13. (*a*) Both (A) and (R) are correct and (R) is the correct explanation for (A).

14. (*a*) Both (A) and (R) are correct and (R) is the correct explanation of (A).

15. (*a*)  is cyclic and has conjugated 8π-electron system but it is not an aromatic compound because here $(4n+2)\pi$-electrons, i.e. Huckel's rule does not hold in right manner and ring is not planar.

Both (A) and (R) are correct and (R) is the correct explanation of (A).

16. (*b*) Both (A) and (R) are correct but (R) is not the correct explanation of (A). The correct explanation for Assertion is that, butane and 2-methylbutane differ by a —CH_2 unit and molecular mass 14u.

17. (i) Due to small size of O, there is repulsions between the electrons on oxygen and some amount of energy has to be provided to incoming electron. Thus, the electron gain enthalpy of O^- is positive, while that of S is negative.

Similarly, the electron gain enthalpy of S^- is positive, while that of O is negative. **(1)**

(ii) Chemical reactivity of halogens is shown by the gain of an electron leading to the formation of anion. The tendency to gain an electron depends upon their electrode potentials. Their electrode potentials decrease down the group (F>Cl>Br>I). Furthermore, the tendency to gain an electron is also related to electron gain enthalpy.

Electron gain enthalpy becomes less and less negative as we move from chlorine to iodine.

Hence, reactivity decreases from chlorine to iodine. Fluorine has less electron gain enthalpy due to its small size which leads to electron-electron repulsions, but it is the most reactive due to its low bond dissociation enthalpy. **(1)**

18. I. $CH_3CH_2—C{\equiv}CH \xrightarrow[-NH_3]{NaNH_2} CH_3CH_2—C{\equiv}\overset{-\,+}{CNa}$
(But-1-yne) (Sodium salt) **(1/2)**

II. $CH_3CH_2C{\equiv}\overset{+}{C}Na \xrightarrow[-NaBr]{CH_3CH_2Br}$

$CH_3CH_2C{\equiv}C—CH_2CH_3$ **(1/2)**
(Hex-3-yne)

III. $CH_3CH_2C{\equiv}C—CH_2CH_3 \xrightarrow{H_2/Pd\text{-}BaSO_4}$

$CH_3CH_2CH{=}CHCH_2CH_3$ **(1/2)**
(*cis*-hex-3-ene)

IV. $CH_3CH_2CH{=}CHCH_2CH_3 \xrightarrow[\text{Alkaline } KMnO_4]{H_2O}$

$CH_3CH_2\underset{OH}{CH}—\underset{OH}{CH}CH_2—CH_3$ **(1/2)**
(Hexane-3, 4-diol)

19. (i) Given,

Molarity = 3 M

Density = 1.25 g mL^{-1}

Mass of NaCl in 1 L solution = 3 moles × 58.5 g/mol
= 175.5 g

Mass of 1 L solution = 1000 mL × 1.25 g/mL = 1250 g

Mass of water solution = 1250 g − 175.5 g
= 1074.5 g
= 1.0745 kg

$$\text{Molality } (m) = \frac{\text{No. of moles of solute}}{\text{Mass of solvent in kg}}$$

$$= \frac{3\text{ moles}}{1.0745\text{ kg}} = 2.79\text{ m}$$ **(1)**

(ii) Molecular weight of the sugar, $C_{12}H_{22}O_{11}$,

$$m = (12 \times 12.01) + (22 \times 1.0079) + (11 \times 16.00)$$
$$= 342.2938 \text{ g mol}^{-1} \approx 342 \text{ g/mol}$$

Given, $w = 20$ g, $V = 2$ L

$$\text{Molarity} = \frac{w}{m \times V\text{ (L)}} = \frac{20\text{ g}}{342\text{ g/mol} \times 2\text{ L}} = 0.0292 \text{ mol L}^{-1}$$

$= 0.0292$ M **(1)**

Or

(i) $N_2(g) + 3H_2(g) \longrightarrow 2NH_3(g)$

1 mol	3 mol	2 mol
28 g	6 g	34 g

28 g of N_2 reacts with 6 g H_2

$\therefore$ 1 g N_2 will react with $\frac{6}{28}$ g of H_2

$\therefore$ 2000 g N_2 will react with $\frac{2000 \times 6}{28} = 428.57$ g H_2

Hence, N_2 is the limiting reagent and H_2 is in excess. N_2 limits the amount of ammonia produced.

28 g N_2 produces 34 g NH_3

$\because$ 2000 g N_2 produces $\frac{34}{28} \times 2000 = 2428.57$ g NH_3 **(1)**

(ii) Yes, H_2 is in excess, so it will remain unreacted. Amount of H_2 remain unreacted $= 1000$ g $- 428.57$ g $= 571.43$ g **(1)**

20. (i) Total energy received $= 3.15 \times 10^{-18}$ J

Wavelength $(\lambda) = 600$ nm $= 6 \times 10^{-7}$ m

$$\text{Energy } (E) = \frac{hc}{\lambda}$$

$$= \frac{6.626 \times 10^{-34} \text{ kg m}^2 \text{ s}^{-1} \times 3 \times 10^8 \text{m/s}}{6 \times 10^{-7} \text{ m}}$$

$$E = 3.31 \times 10^{-19} \text{ J}$$

Thus, number of photons $= \frac{3.15 \times 10^{-18} \text{ J}}{3.31 \times 10^{-19} \text{ J}} = 9.5 \sim 10$ **(1)**

(ii) $|\psi|^2$ shows the probability of finding the electron at a point with coordinates (x, y, z). **(1)**

21. (i) Propylbenzene **(1)**

(ii)

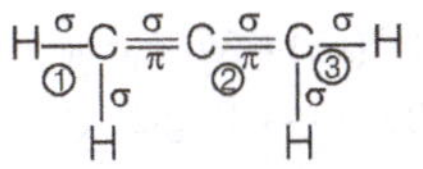

The hybridisation of C_1 carbon is sp^2, for C_2 is sp and for C_3 is sp^2. **(1)**

22. (i) The arrangement of elements, Na, Mg, Al and Si into different groups in order of their increasing atomic numbers is,

Group	11	12	13	14
	Na	Mg	Al	Si

In case of Al, a 3p-electron is to be lost, while in Mg, a 2s-electron is to be lost.

Therefore, $\Delta_i H_1$ of Al will be lower than that of Mg due to the effective shielding of the 3p-electron from the nucleus by 3s-electrons. Therefore, $\Delta_i H_1$ for Al will be lower than 737 kJ/mol. **(1)**

(ii) Element with atomic number 71 is lutetium (Lu) which is a lanthanoid. Its most common valency is 3. Further, fluorine has a valency equal to 1. Thus, formula of the compound would be LuF_3. **(1)**

(iii) When O^- changes into O^{2-}, the change is endothermic. The reason is that O^- repels the incoming electron due to electron repulsion, thus, it needs energy to accept the electron. Hence, electron affinity is positive. **(1)**

23. The properties whose values depend on the quantity or size of matter present in the system are known as **extensive properties**, e.g. mass, internal energy, heat capacity. **(1)**

On the other hand, those properties which do not depend on the quantity or size of matter present are known as **intensive properties**, e.g. temperature, pressure, density.

The ratio of two extensive properties is intensive.

e.g. Mole fraction $= \frac{\text{No. of moles of component}}{\text{Total number of moles}}$ **(1)**

$$= \frac{\text{Extensive}}{\text{Extensive}} = \text{Intensive}$$

Molarity $= \frac{\text{Number of moles}}{\text{Volume}} = \frac{\text{Extensive}}{\text{Extensive}} = \text{Intensive}$ **(1)**

Thus, mole fraction and molarity are intensive properties.

24. In general, number of waves in any orbit is

$$\text{Number of waves} = \frac{\text{Circumference of orbit}}{\text{Wavelength}} = \frac{2\pi r}{\lambda}$$

But $\lambda = \frac{h}{mv}$

$$\text{Number of waves} = \frac{2\pi r}{h/mv} = \frac{2\pi r \cdot mv}{h} = \frac{2\pi(mvr)}{h}$$

The angular momentum of Bohr's 3rd orbit is $mvr = \frac{3h}{2\pi}$

$\therefore$ Number of waves $= \frac{2\pi}{h} \times \frac{3h}{2\pi} = 3$

Number of waves in Bohr's 3rd orbit = 3 **(3)**

Or

(i) A photon of green light with a wavelength of 5250 Å has a higher energy because energy is inversely proportional to the wavelength i.e., $E = \frac{hc}{\lambda}$. **(1)**

(ii) E.C. of $_{26}Fe$: $1s^2 2s^2 2p^6 3s^2 3p^6 3d^6 4s^2$

Fe^{3+} : $[Ar]3d^5$

3d				
1	1	1	1	1

So, there are 5 unpaired electrons are present in Fe^{3+}. **(1)**

(iii) Given : $\bar{\nu} = 4 \times 10^5$ m^{-1}

$$\because \quad E = h\nu = \frac{hc}{\lambda} = hc\bar{\nu}$$

$$\therefore \ E = 6.626 \times 10^{-34} \text{kg m}^2\text{s}^{-1} \times 3 \times 10^8 \text{m/s} \times 4 \times 10^5 \text{m}^{-1}$$

$$= 7.9 \times 10^{-20} \text{ J}$$ **(1)**

25. (i) σ-bond is stronger. This is because σ-bond is formed by head-on overlapping of atomic orbitals and therefore, the overlapping occurs with large extent. Whereas, π-bond is formed by sideways overlapping which occurs with small extent. **(1)**

(ii) SF_6, S is the central atom with six valence electrons.

$\therefore$ Number of hybrid orbitals $= \frac{1}{2}[6 + 6 - 0 + 0] = 6$ **(1)**

Hence, the hybridisation involved in sp^3d^2.

(iii) *sp*-orbital has greater directional character than *p*-orbital. This is because *p*-orbital has equal sized lobes, with equal electron density in both the lobes whereas, *sp*-hybrid orbital has greater electron density on one side. **(1)**

26. (i) In the reaction, Fe_2O_3 loses oxygen and is reduced to Fe. **(1)**

(ii) In AgF_2, Ag is in +2 oxidation state. It is highly unstable so it readily accepts an electron to attain +1 oxidation state which is more stable.

$$Ag^{2+} + e^- \longrightarrow Ag^+$$ **(1)**

That's why AgF_2 acts as a strong oxidising agent.

(iii) The blue colour of $CuSO_4$ solution will get discharged and reddish brown copper metal will be deposited on Zn rod. This is because blue colour Cu^{2+} (in $CuSO_4$) gets reduced to Cu by accepting two electrons from Zn, which gets oxidised to colourless $ZnSO_4$ solution.

$$\overset{0}{Zn}(s) + \overset{2+}{Cu}SO_4\,(aq) \longrightarrow \overset{2+\ 2-}{ZnSO_4}\,(aq) + \overset{0}{Cu}\,(s)$$

(Reduction: $Cu^{2+} \to Cu$; Oxidation: $Zn \to Zn^{2+}$) **(1)**

27. In the first oxide, oxygen = 27.6

Metal = 100 − 27.6 = 72.4 parts by mass.

As the formula of the oxide is M_3O_4, it means

72.4 parts by mass of metal = 3 atoms of metal and

4 atoms of oxygen = 27.6 parts by mass.

In the second oxide, oxygen = 30.0 parts by mass and

metal = 100 − 30 = 70 parts by mass.

But 72.4 parts by mass of metal = 3 atoms of metal.

$\therefore$ 70 parts by mass of metal $= \dfrac{3}{72.4} \times 70$ atoms of metal

= 2.90 atoms of metal

Also, 27.6 part by mass of oxygen = 4 atoms of oxygen.

$\therefore$ 30 part by mass of oxygen $= \dfrac{4}{27.6} \times 30$ atoms of oxygen

= 4.35 atoms of oxygen.

Hence, ratio of $M : O$ in the second oxide

= 2.90 : 4.35 = 1 : 1.5 or 2 : 3

$\therefore$ Formula of the other metal oxide is M_2O_3. **(3)**

28. (i)

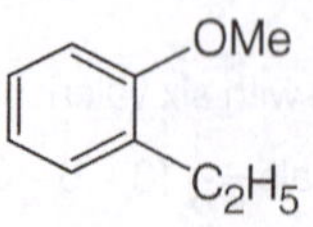

(a)

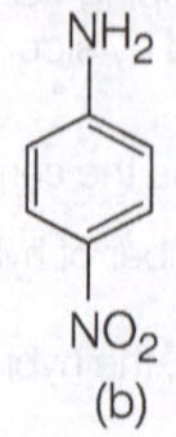

(b) **(2)**

(ii) The stability order is

$$(CH_3)_3\overset{+}{C} > (CH_3)_3C\overset{+}{C}H_2 > CH_3CH_2\overset{+}{C}H_2.$$ **(1)**

29. (i) $\overset{+8}{Xe}O_6^{4-}\,(aq) + 2\overset{-1}{F^-}(aq) + 6H^+(aq) \longrightarrow \overset{+6}{Xe}O_3(g) + \overset{0}{F_2} + 3H_2O\,(l)$

In the above reaction, oxidation number of Xe decreases from +8 (in XeO_6^{4-}) to +6 (in XeO_3) and oxidation number of F increases from −1 (in F^-) to zero (in F_2). Hence, XeO_6^{4-} or Na_4XeO_6 is reduced and F^- is oxidised. **(2)**

(ii) $K_2Cr_2O_7 + \text{Excess KI} \longrightarrow Cr^{3+} + H_2O + nI_2$

$$\overset{6+}{Cr} \xrightarrow{+3e^-} \overset{3+}{Cr}$$

Cr^{6+} accepts $3e^-$, so moles of I_2 = 3. **(1)**

Or

In alkaline medium, the balanced equation is,

$$2ClO_2 + 5H_2O_2 + 2OH^- \longrightarrow 2Cl^- + 5O_2 + 6H_2O$$

2 moles of ClO_2 oxidises 5 moles of H_2O_2

$\therefore$ 1 mole of ClO_2 oxidises $= \dfrac{5}{2} \times 1 = 2.5$ moles of H_2O_2. **(1)**

(iii) $Al(s) \longrightarrow Al^{3+}(aq) + 3e^-$ (oxidation half reaction)

$3Ag^+(aq) + 3e^- \longrightarrow 3Ag(s)$ (reduction half reaction) **(1)**

30. (i) ${}_{13}Al = 1s^2 2s^2 2p^6 3s^2 3p^1$

${}_{14}Si = 1s^2 2s^2 2p^6 3s^2 3p^2$

Si (+4) has greater nuclear charge than aluminium (+3). Hence, 3*p* unpaired electrons of Si experience greater effective nuclear charge than Al. **(2)**

(ii) (*b*) According to Aufbau principle, in the group state of the atoms, electrons are filled in various atomic orbital in the increasing order of energy

$1s < 2s < 2p < 3s < 3p < 4s < 3d < 4p < 5s < 4d < 5p < 6s < 4f < 5d < 6p < 7s$

Thus, correct order is $5p < 6s < 4f < 5d$. **(1)**

Or

A *p*-orbital can accommodate up to two electrons with opposite spins. This is due to Pauli's exclusion principle, which states that any orbital can only accommodate a maximum of two electrons with opposite spins. **(1)**

(iii) (*d*) The number of radial nodes in an orbital is calculated as $n - 1 - l$, where n is the principal quantum number and l is the azimuthal quantum number. For a 3*p* orbital $n = 3$ and $l = 1$, so the number of radial nodes is $3 - 1 - 1 = 1$. **(1)**

31. 1 mole of alkyne *D* gives 1 mole of sodium alkynide and 1/2 mole of H_2. Furthermore, *D* gives straight chain alkane on hydrogenation, and is obtained from five membered compound therefore, *D* must be five membered straight chain terminal alkyne, i.e. 1-pentyne.

Since, alkene *B* on reaction with Br_2 forms a compound '*C*' which on dehydrohalogenation, gives 1-pentyne, therefore, '*C*' must be 1,2-dibromopentane and alkene '*B*' must be 1-pentene.

Since, alkene '*B*' is obtained by dehydrohalogenation of alkyl halide, therefore, alkyl halide *A* must be 1-bromopentane.

Reactions are as follows **(3)**

$$\underset{\text{1-bromopentane }(A)}{CH_3CH_2CH_2CH_2CH_2Br} \xrightarrow[-\,HBr]{\text{Alc. KOH, }\Delta} \underset{\text{1-pentene }(B)}{CH_3CH_2CH_2CH{=}CH_2} \xrightarrow{Br_2 \text{ in } CS_2}$$

$$\underset{\text{1, 2-dibromopentane }(C)}{CH_3CH_2CH_2\text{—}\overset{2}{C}HBr\text{—}\overset{1}{C}H_2Br} \xrightarrow[-\,2HBr]{\text{Alc. KOH}} \underset{\text{1-pentyne }(D)}{CH_3CH_2CH_2C{\equiv}CH}$$

$$\xrightarrow{\text{Na in liq. } NH_3} \underset{\text{Sodium 1-pentynide}}{CH_3CH_2CH_2C{\equiv}C^-Na^+} + \frac{1}{2}H_2$$ **(2)**

Or

(i) (a) Ethane is formed.

$$\underset{\text{Bromoethane}}{CH_3CH_2\text{—}Br} + 2[H] \xrightarrow[\text{Reduction}]{Zn/HCl} CH_3CH_3 + HBr$$ **(1)**

(b) Propane is obtained.

$$\underset{\text{2-bromopropane}}{CH_3\text{—}\underset{\displaystyle CH_3}{\underset{|}{C}H}\text{—}Br} + H_2 \xrightarrow[\text{(Reduction)}]{Pd} \underset{\text{Propane}}{CH_3\text{—}\underset{\displaystyle CH_3}{\underset{|}{C}H_2}} + Br$$ **(1)**

(ii) (a) Molecules with odd number of carbon atoms have lower melting points because they do not fit into crystal lattice easily whereas, hydrocarbons with even number of carbon atoms can fit into crystal lattice easily. **(1)**

(b) Since, the bond dissociation energy of C—C bonds (348 kJ mol^{-1}) is lower than bond dissociation energy of C—H bonds (414 kJ mol^{-1}), therefore, during cracking of alkanes, C—C bonds break more easily C—H bonds. **(1)**

(c) The iodination of benzene is usually brought about by refluxing with iodine and conc. HNO_3 or HIO_3 as they oxidises HI to I_2 and prevents the backward reaction to occur. **(1)**

32. (i) Given, $n = 2$ moles,

$T = 27°C = 300$ K, $p_1 = 1$ atm, $p_2 = 10$ atm

Work done during isothermal reversible compression is given as

$$W = 2.303nRT\log\frac{p_2}{p_1}$$

$$= 2.303 \times 2 \text{ moles} \times 8.314 \text{ JK}^{-1}\text{mol}^{-1} \times 300 \text{ K} \log\frac{10}{1}$$

$$= 11488.28 \text{ J}$$ **(2)**

(ii) The conversion of liquid into vapours is called vaporisation.

For vaporisation of an organic compound

$$\therefore \Delta_{vap}S° = \frac{\Delta_{vap}H°}{T}$$

$$\Delta_{vap}H° = 26.0 \times 10^3 \text{ J mol}^{-1}$$

$$T = 273 + 35 = 308 \text{ K}$$

$$\Delta_{vap}S° = \frac{26.0 \times 10^3 \text{ J mol}^{-1}}{308 \text{ K}} = 84.4 \text{ JK}^{-1} \text{ mol}^{-1}$$ **(2)**

(iii) From Gibbs-Helmholtz equation, we have

$$\Delta G = \Delta H - T\Delta S$$

At low temperature, $T\Delta S$ is small, hence, ΔH dominates. At high temperature, $T\Delta S$ is large, i.e. ΔS dominates the value of ΔG. **(1)**

Or

(i) (a) $2H_2S(g) + 3O_2(g) \longrightarrow 2H_2O(g) + 2SO_2(g)$

Total moles of reactant $= 2 + 3 = 5$ moles

Total moles of product $= 2 + 2 = 4$ moles

Since, the number of gas molecules decreases, the disorder of the system decreases. So, $\Delta S° < 0$. **(1)**

(b) $N_2(g) + 3H_2(g) \longrightarrow 2NH_3(g)$

Total moles of reactant $= 3 + 1 = 4$ moles

Total moles of product $= 2$ moles

The number of gas molecules decreases, leading to a decrease in randomness. So, $\Delta S° < 0$. **(1)**

(ii) (a) The relationship between free energy (ΔG) change and equilibrium constant (K) is given by

$$\Delta G = -RT\ln K$$

[where, R = universal gas constant, T = temperature]

(b) The free energy change (ΔG) is related to enthalpy (ΔH) and entropy (ΔS) as

$$\Delta G = \Delta H - T\Delta S$$ **(1)**

(iii) The expression for work done in an isothermal and irreversible expansion of a gas

$$W = -p_{ex}(V_f - V_i)$$

[where, W = work done by the gas

p_{ex} = work done by gas

$V_f - V_i$ = the change in volume] **(1)**

33. (i) $\underset{\underset{(0.05 - C\alpha)}{\text{Propanoic acid}}}{CH_3CH_2COOH} \rightleftharpoons \underset{C\alpha}{CH_3CH_2COO^-} + \underset{C\alpha}{H_3O^+}$

From Ostwald's dilution law,

$$\alpha = \sqrt{K_a/C} = \sqrt{\frac{1.32 \times 10^{-5}}{0.05}} = 0.016248$$ **(1/2)**

$$[H_3O^+] = C\alpha = 0.05 \text{ M} \times 0.016248$$

$$= 0.0008124$$

$$= 8.124 \times 10^{-4} \text{ M}$$

From, $pH = -\log[H_3O^+]$

$= -\log(8.124 \times 10^{-4}) = 3.0902 \approx 3.09$ **[1/2]**

When the solution contains 0.01 M HCl

$$K_a = \frac{[CH_3CH_2COO^-][H_3O^+]}{[CH_3CH_2COOH]}$$

$$1.32 \times 10^{-5} = \frac{C\alpha \times 0.01}{(0.05 - C\alpha)}$$ **(1)**

($[H_3O^+] = 0.01$ M from HCl. In the presence of 0.01 M HCl, the dissociation of propanoic acid decreases).

$$C\alpha = \frac{1.32 \times 10^{-5} \times (0.05 - C\alpha)}{0.01}$$

$$= \frac{1.32 \times 10^{-5} \times 0.05}{0.01} \quad [\text{as } (0.05 - C\alpha) \approx 0.05]$$

or $0.05 \times \alpha = 6.60 \times 10^{-5}$

$$\alpha = \frac{6.60 \times 10^{-5}}{0.05} = 1.32 \times 10^{-3}$$ **(1)**

(ii) In case of dilution,

$$M_1V_1 = M_2V_2$$

$$13.6\,M \times 1\,L = M_2 \times 1000\,L$$

$$M_2 = \frac{13.6 \times 1}{1000} = 1.36 \times 10^{-2}\,M$$

Now, $pH = -\log[1.36 \times 10^{-2}] = -0.1335 + 2 = 1.8665$

$\Rightarrow pH = 1.87$ **(1)**

(iii) On reducing volume, pressure will increase. According to Le-Chatelier's principle, equilibrium will shift to the side where number of moles of gas decreases. Therefore, in the given reaction, equilibrium will shift in backward direction. **(1)**

Or

(i) As we started the reaction with HI, so equilibrium constant for the dissociation of HI, $[2HI(g) \rightleftharpoons H_2(g) + I_2(g)]$ is required. Thus, calculate the equilibrium constant for backward reaction,

i.e. $K_C \left(K'_C = \frac{1}{K_C} \right)$

and then, calculate $[H_2]$ and $[I_2]$.

For the reaction,

$$H_2(g) + I_2(g) \rightleftharpoons 2HI(g)$$

$$K_C = 54.8$$

$$2HI(g) \rightleftharpoons H_2(g) + I_2(g)$$

$$\therefore \quad K'_C = \frac{1}{K_C} = \frac{1}{54.8}$$

Now, $$K'_C = \frac{[H_2][I_2]}{[HI]^2} = \frac{1}{54.8}$$ **(1)**

Given, $[HI] = 0.5$ mol L^{-1}

Let the concentration of H_2 and $I_2 = x$

$$\therefore \quad \frac{x \cdot x}{[0.5]^2} = \frac{1}{54.8}$$

$$\Rightarrow \quad x^2 = \frac{[0.5]^2}{54.8} = 0.00456$$

$$x = 0.0675\,M$$

$\Rightarrow [H_2] = [I_2] = x = 0.0675$ M **(1)**

(ii) For the reaction,

$$NO(g) + O_3(g) \rightleftharpoons NO_2(g) + O_2(g)$$

$$K_C = 6.3 \times 10^{14} \text{ (at 1000 K)}$$

$$K_C = \frac{[NO_2][O_2]}{[NO][O_3]} = 6.3 \times 10^{14} \quad \ldots(i)$$

For reverse reaction,

$$NO_2(g) + O_2(g) \rightleftharpoons NO(g) + O_3(g)$$

$$K'_C = \frac{[NO][O_3]}{[NO_2][O_2]} \quad \ldots(ii)$$ **(1)**

From Eqs. (i) and (ii), we get

$$K'_C = \frac{1}{K_C}$$

$$= \frac{1}{6.3 \times 10^{14}} = 1.587 \times 10^{-15}$$ **(1)**

(iii) Molar concentration of a pure solid or liquid (if in excess) is constant (i.e. independent of the amount present). That's why pure liquids and solids can be ignored while writing the equilibrium constant expression. **(1)**

SAMPLE QUESTION PAPER 2

A Highly Simulated Sample Question Paper for CBSE Class XI Examination

CHEMISTRY [Unsolved]

Time : 3 Hours **Max. Marks : 70**

Note : *Refer to Instruction S.Q.P. 1*

Section-A

The following questions are multiple-choice questions with one correct answer. Each question carries 1 mark. There is no internal choice in this section.

1. Number of σ-bonds and π-bonds present in

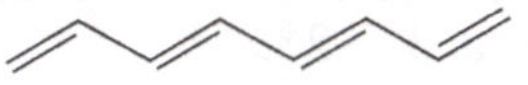 is

σ-bond	π-bond
(a) 17	4
(b) 14	3
(c) 18	4
(d) 15	3

2. Enthalpy change for the reaction,

$4H(g) \longrightarrow 2H_2(g)$ is –869.6 kJ.

The dissociation energy of H—H bond is

(a) –869.6 kJ (b) +434.8 kJ
(c) +217.4 kJ (d) –434.8 kJ

3. A student while performing a test for sulphur, acidified Lassaigne extract with acetic acid and added lead acetate solution to it. He observed that a black precipitate (X) is formed. Identify 'X'

(a) $PbSO_4$ (b) PbS
(c) $Pb(NO_3)_2$ (d) AgI

4. In the chemical reaction,

$$N_2 + 3H_2 \rightleftharpoons 2NH_3$$

at equilibrium point,

(a) equal volumes of N_2 and H_2 are reacting.
(b) equal masses of N_2 and H_2 are reacting.
(c) the reaction will stop.
(d) the same amount of ammonia is formed, as it is decomposed into N_2 and H_2.

5. If the density of a solution is 3.12 g mL^{-1}, the mass of 1.5 mL solution in significant figures is ……… .

(a) 4.7 g (b) 4680×10^{-3} g
(c) 4.680 g (d) 46.80 g

6. The electronic transition from $n = 2$ to $n = 1$ will produce the shortest wavelength in (where, n = principal quantum number)

(a) He^+ (b) H
(c) H^+ (d) Li^{2+}

7. In the graph given below, the one which represents an alkali metal with the higher atomic number is

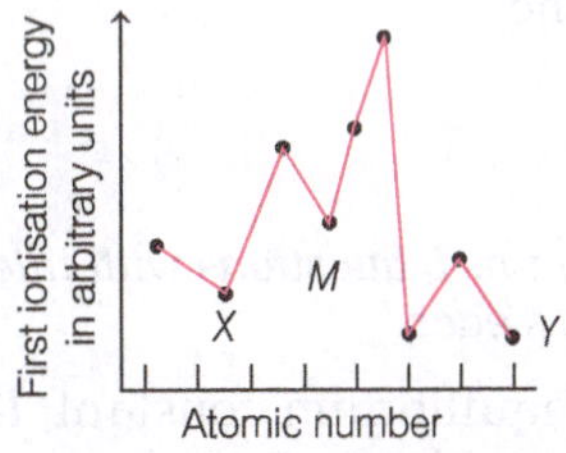

(a) X (b) M (c) Z (d) Y

8. Which of the following will not show geometrical isomerism?

(a) 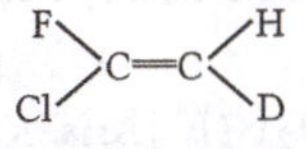 (b) 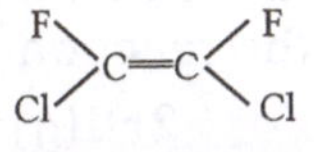

(c) 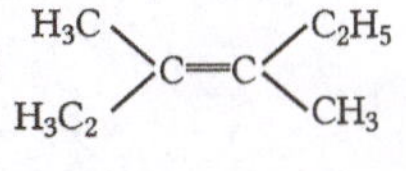 (d) 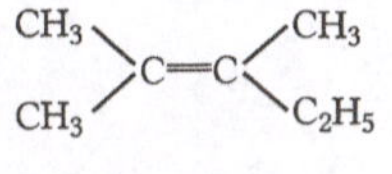

9. Match the compounds given in Column I with the given shape in olumn II and match the correct option.

Column I	Column II
A. XeF_6	1. Distorted octahedral
B. XeO_3	2. Square pyramidal
C. $XeOF_4$	3. Pyramidal

Codes

	A	B	C		A	B	C
(a)	1	2	3	(b)	2	3	1
(c)	3	1	2	(d)	1	3	2

10. The correct order of decreasing electronegativity value among the element *A*-bengllium, *B*-oxygen, *C*-nitrogen and *D*-magnesium is

(a) $B > C > A > D$
(b) $C > D > B > A$
(c) $A > B > C > D$
(d) $A > B > D > C$

11 Which of the following has higher dipole moment; *cis*-but-2-ene or *trans*-but-2-ene?

(a) *cis*-but-2-ene
(b) *trans*-but-2-ene
(c) Both have same dipole moment
(d) None of the above

12 The compound which form only acetaldehyde upon ozonolysis is

(a) ethene
(b) propyne
(c) but-1-ene
(d) but-2-ene

Assertion-Reason

In the following questions (Q.No. 13-16) a statement of Assertion followed by a statement of Reason is given. Choose the correct answer out of the following choices.

(a) Both (A) and (R) are correct and (R) is the correct explanation of (A).
(b) Both (A) and (R) are correct but (R) is not the correct explanation of (A).
(c) (A) is correct and (R) is incorrect.
(d) (A) is incorrect and (R) is correct.

13. Assertion (A) Equal moles of different substances contain 6.022×10^{23} particles.

Reason (R) Equal weights of different substances do not contain the same number of constituent particles.

14. Assertion (A) Energy of radiation is large if its wavelength is large.

Reason (R) Energy of radiation is equal to $h\nu$.

15. Assertion (A) The order of stability of carbocations is $3° > 2° > 1°$.

Reason (R) Carbon atom in carbocations is sp^3-hybridised.

16. Assertion (A) Both toluene and *iso*-propyl benzene give the same product on oxidation with $KMnO_4$.

Reason (R) $KMnO_4$ oxidises aliphatic side chain of arenes to — COOH group.

Answers

1. (a)	**2.** (b)	**3.** (b)	**4.** (d)	**5.** (a)	**6.** (d)
7. (d)	**8.** (d)	**9.** (d)	**10.** (a)	**11.** (a)	**12.** (d)
13. (b)	**14.** (d)	**15.** (c)	**16.** (a)		

Section-B

This section contains 5 questions with internal choice in one question. The following questions are short answer type and carry 2 marks each.

17. At 500 K, equilibrium constant, K_C for the following reaction is 5.

$$\frac{1}{2}H_2(g) + \frac{1}{2}I_2(g) \rightleftharpoons HI(g)$$

What would be the equilibrium constant, K_C for the reaction ?

$$2HI(g) \rightleftharpoons H_2(g) + I_2(g)$$ **[Ans.** $K_C' = 0.04$**]**

18. Give reason :

(i) Can the reaction :

$$Cr_2O_7^{2-} + H_2O \longrightarrow 2CrO_4^{2-} + 2H^+$$

be regarded as a redox reaction?

(ii) MnO_4^{2-} undergoes disproportionation reaction in acidic medium but MnO_4^- does not.

19. (i) A compound on analysis was found to contain C =34.6%, H=3.85% and O=61.55%. Calculate its empirical formula.
(ii) Why diamond is considered as an element not as a compound?

Or Complete the following reactions

(i) $CH_2{=}CH_2 \xrightarrow[H_2O\text{ warm}]{\text{Dil. }H_2SO_4}$

(ii) $CH_3CH{=}CH{-}CH_3 \xrightarrow[(b)\ H_2O/Zn]{(a)\ O_3}$

20. Complete the following reactions.

(i) $HC{\equiv}CH \xrightarrow{NaNH_2} A \xrightarrow{CH_3Br} B$

(ii) $CH_3CH{=}CH_2 \xrightarrow{HBr} A \xrightarrow[\text{Dry ether}]{Na} B$

21. (i) Is there any change in the hybridisation of B and N-atoms as a result of the reaction?

$$BF_3 + NH_3 \longrightarrow F_3B{\cdot}NH_3$$

(ii) What is valence bond approach of covalent bond? Give an examples to illustrate it.

Section-C

This section contains 7 questions with internal choice in one question. The following questions are short answer type and carry 3 marks each.

22. Calculate the oxidation number of the underlined elements in $H_4\underline{P_2}O_7$, $K_2\underline{Mn}O_4$ and $H_2\underline{S_2}O_7$ [**Ans.** 5, 6, 6]

Or

Balance the following equations by the oxidation number method.

(i) $Fe^{2+} + H^+ + Cr_2O_7^{2-} \longrightarrow Cr^{3+} + Fe^{3+} + H_2O$

(ii) $I_2 + S_2O_3^{2-} \longrightarrow I^- + S_4O_6^{2-}$

(iii) $MnO_2 + C_2O_4^{2-} \longrightarrow Mn^{2+} + CO_2$

23. Give reasons for the following.
(i) The first ionisation enthalpy of carbon is more than that of boron but the reverse is true for the second ionisation enthalpy.
(ii) The ionic size of Cl^- is greater than that of K^+ though the two ions are isoelectronic.

24. Explain the following.
(i) SO_3 acts as an electrophile.
(ii) Benzylic free radical is more stable than allylic free radical.
(iii) $O_2NCH_2CH_2O^-$ is more stable than $CH_3CH_2O^-$.

25. (i) Enthalpy of combustion of carbon to CO_2 is -393.5 kJ mol^{-1}. Calculate the heat released upon formation of 35.2 g of CO_2 from carbon and dioxygen gas. [**Ans.** 314.8 kJ mol^{-1}]

(ii) The enthalpy of vaporisation of CCl_4 is 30.5 kJ mol^{-1}. Calculate the heat required for the vaporisation of 284 g of CCl_4 at constant pressure. (Molar mass of CCl_4 = 154 g mol^{-1}) [**Ans.** 56.25 kJ mol^{-1}]

(iii) Carbon monoxide is allowed from to expand isothermally and reversibly form 10 m^3 to 20 m^3 at 300 K and work obtained is 4.754 kJ. Calculate the number of moles of carbon monoxide. [**Ans.** n = 2.75 mol]

26. An organic compound '*A*' of molecular formula C_6H_{12} upon oxidation yields a mixture of '*B*' and '*C*'.
'*A*' absorbs one mole of bromine to give '*D*', while on reduction it gives a saturated hydrocarbon. Identify *A*, *B* and *C*. Also, give all the relevant chemical equations.

27. Explain the following on the basis of valence bond theory.
(i) BF_3 is planar but NH_3 is not.
(ii) CCl_4 and $SiCl_4$ are tetrahedral.
(iii) The HSH bond angle in H_2S is closer to 90° than HOH bond angle in H_2O.

28. 45.4 L of dinitrogen reacted with 22.7 L of dioxygen and 45.4 L nitrous oxide was formed.

The reaction is given below.

$$2N_2(g) + O_2(g) \longrightarrow 2N_2O(g)$$

Which law is being obeyed in this experiment? Write the statement of the law.

Section-D

The following questions are case-based questions. Each question has an internal choice and carries 4 (2 +1+1) marks each. Read the passage carefully and answer the questions that follow.

29. The dissolution of acid in water is different in case of strong and weak acids. In case of strong acids, it fully dissociates when dissolved in water and the pH of the resulting solution can be found by taking the negative log of the strong acid concentration.

$$pH = -\log (\text{strong acid}) \quad \ldots(i)$$

In case of weak acids, the determination of the pH is not as simple because the acid does not dissociate completely when added to water. To find the pH of a weak acid in water, the $[H_3O^+]$ must first be determined from the weak acid equilibrium.

$$HA(aq) \rightleftharpoons H^+(aq) + A^-(aq)$$

	HA	H^+	A^-
Initial :	$[HA]_{initial}$	10^{-7}	0
Dissociation :	$-y$	$+y$	$+y$
Equilibrium :	$[HA]_{initial} - y$	$y + 10^{-7}$	y

10^{-7} is assumed to be negligible compared to y and y is assumed to be negligible compared to $[HA]_{initial}$.

The $[H_3O^+]$ can be determined from the K_a value. Equation (ii) derived below can be used to determine the pH for an aqueous solution of a weak acid.

$$K_a = \frac{[H_3O^+][A^-]}{[HA]} = \frac{[H_3O^+]^2}{[HA]}$$

$$\therefore \quad K_a \times [HA] = [H_3O^+]^2$$

$$[H_3O^-] = \sqrt{K_a \times [HA]}$$

$$pH = -\log [H_3O^+] = -\log \sqrt{K_a \times [HA]}$$

$$-\log \sqrt{K_a \times [HA]} = -\log \sqrt{K_a} - \log \sqrt{[HA]}$$

$$= -\frac{1}{2} \log K_a - \frac{1}{2} [HA]$$

$$= \frac{1}{2} pK_a - \frac{1}{2} \log [HA]$$

$$pH = \frac{1}{2} pK_a - \frac{1}{2} \log [HA] \quad \ldots(ii)$$

Equation (ii) works only when the value of K_a is less then [HA] and when pK_a is between 2 and 12.

(i) The dissociation constant of acetic acid at a given temperature is 1.69×10^{-5}. Calculate the degree of dissociation of 0.01 M acetic acid in the presence of 0.01 M HCl. **[Ans.** 0.169×10^{-3}**]**

(ii) The concentration of hydrogen ion in a sample of soft drink is 3.8×10^{-3} M. Calculate the value of its pH. **[Ans.** 2.42**]**

(a) 1.21 (b) 2.42
(c) 4.84 (d) 3.0

Or

If the ionisation constant of acetic acid is 1.8×10^{-5}, at what concentration will it be dissociated to 2%? **[Ans.** 0.045 M**]**

(a) 0.4 M (b) 0.3 M
(c) 0.15 M (d) 0.045 M

(iii) Calculate the pH of a salt solution of weak acid ($pK_a = 4$) and weak base ($pK_b = 5$) at 25°C. **[Ans.** 6.5**]**

(a) 1.5 (b) 6.5 (c) 3.25 (d) 4.5

30. Compounds having the same molecular formula but different structural formula properties such as physical and chemical properties or spatial arrangement are called isomers and the phenomenon is called isomerism. It is of two types, structural and stereoisomerism. Compounds having same molecular formula but different structural formula are called structural isomers and the phenomenon is called structural isomerism.

In stereoisomerism, the atoms making up the isomers are joined up in the same order but still manage to have a different spatial arrangement. Geometric isomerism is one form of stereoisomerism. Geometric isomers are the isomers occur where you have restricted rotation somewhere in a molecule.

At an introductory level in organic chemistry, examples usually just involve the carbon-carbon double bond and that's what this passage will concentrate on. Think about what happens in molecules where there is unrestricted rotation about carbon bonds, in other words where the carbon-carbon bonds are all single? The next diagram shows two possible configurations of 1,2-dichloroethane.

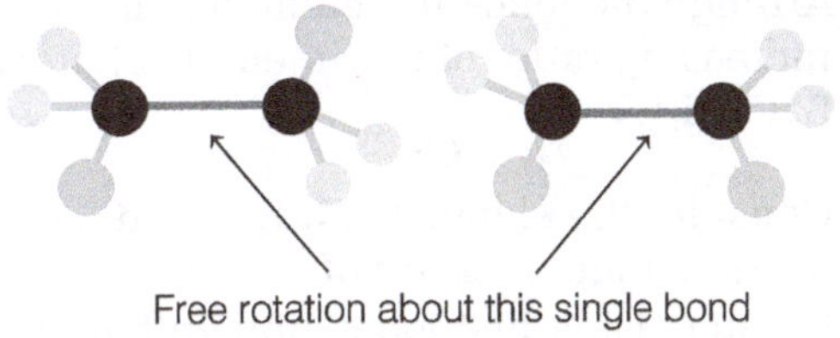

These two models represent exactly the same molecule. You can get from one to the other just by twisting around the carbon-carbon single bond.

These molecules are **not isomers**. If you draw a structural formula instead of using models, you have to bear in mind the possibility of this free rotation about single bonds. You must accept that these two structures represent the same molecule:

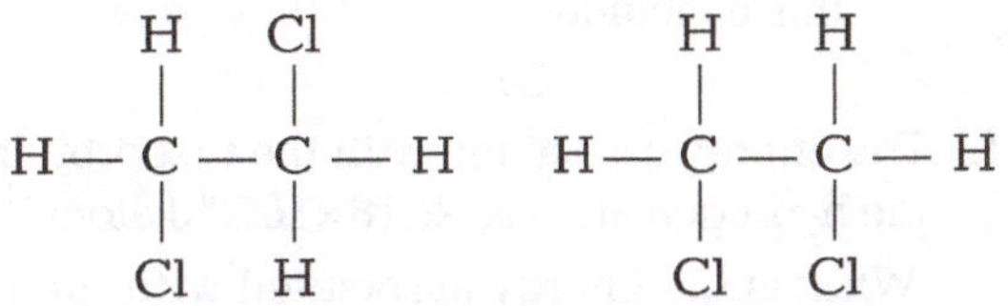

Geometric isomerism (also known as *cis-trans* isomerism or *E-Z* isomerism) is a form of stereoisomerism. This passage explains what stereoisomers are and how you recognise the possibility of geometric isomers in a molecule.

(i) Why *trans*-isomers are more stable than *cis*-isomers?

(ii) How many number of structural isomers possible for the molecular formula C_3H_9N?

Or

Why generally boiling point of *cis*-isomers are higher than *trans*-isomers?

(iii) Write the structural formulae for all the isomers having molecular formula $C_4H_{10}O$.

Section-E

The following questions are long answer type and carry 5 marks each. All questions have an internal choice.

31. State the law of thermodynamics that was first formulated by Nernst in 1906. What is the utility of this law? The equilibrium constant for the reaction $A \rightleftharpoons B$ is 1.8×10^{-7} at 298 K. Calculate the value of $\Delta G°$ for the reaction [$R = 8.314 JK^{-1} mol^{-1}$] and predict the feasibility of the reaction under standard states.

[**Ans.** $\Delta_r G° = 38484.39$ J or 38.48 kJ]

Or (i) Briefly explain the following.

(a) Heat of formation

(b) Heat of combustion

(ii) Write expression for the work done by 1 mole of the gas in each of the following case.

(a) For irreversible expansion of the gas from volume V_1 to V_2.

(b) For reversible isothermal expansion of the gas from volume V_1 to V_2.

(c) For the expansion of the gas into an evacuated vessel.

32. (i) Calculate the wavelength for the emission transition if it starts from the orbit having radius 1.3225 nm and ends at 211.6 pm.

[**Ans.** $\lambda = 434$ nm]

(ii) Observe the figure given below showing Rutherford's scattering experiment and answer the questions that follow :

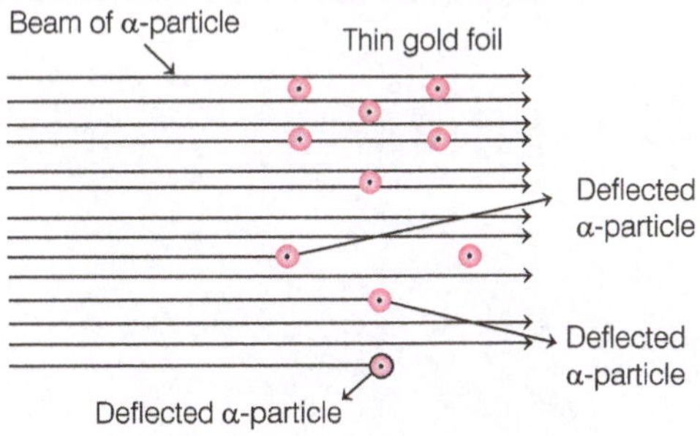

(a) Why a few positively charged α-particles were deflected?

(b) Write any one limitation of Rutherford's model.

(c) The most of the α-particles passed through the foil undeflected. What does this conclude?

Or

(i) The energy associated with the first orbit in the hydrogen atom is -2.18×10^{-18} J atom^{-1}. What is the energy associated with the fifth orbit? **[Ans.** -8.72×10^{-20} J]

(ii) Calculate the radius of Bohr's fifth orbit for hydrogen atom. **[Ans.** 1.3225 nm]

(iii) What is the energy in joules, required to shift the electron of the hydrogen atom from the first Bohr orbit to the fifth Bohr orbit and what is the wavelength of the light emitted when the electron returns to the ground state? The ground state electron energy is -2.18×10^{-11} erg.

[Ans. (i) 2.09×10^{-18} J (ii) 949.8 Å]

33. (i) Would you expect the first ionisation enthalpies for two isotopes of the same element to be the same or different? Justify your answer.

(ii) Give example of three cations and three anions which are isoelectronic with neon.

(iii) Arrange the following elements in the increasing order of non-metallic character B, C, Si, N, F.

Or

(i) Consider the elements N, P, O and S and arrange them in order of

(a) increasing first ionisation enthalpy

(b) increasing negative electron gain enthalpy

(ii) State any two limitations of Newlands' law of octaves.

(iii) Which of the following pairs of atoms/ions is smaller in size and why?

(a) Na and Mg (b) Mg^{2+} and Al^{3+}

SAMPLE QUESTION PAPER 3

A Highly Simulated Sample Question Paper for CBSE Class XI Examination

CHEMISTRY [Unsolved]

Time : 3 Hours **Max. Marks : 70**

Note : *Refer to Instruction S.Q.P. 1*

Section-A

The following questions are multiple-choice questions with one correct answer. Each question carries 1 mark. There is no internal choice in this section.

1. Which of the following ions has larger size although they have the same number of electrons?
 (a) F^-
 (b) Na^+
 (c) Mg^{2+}
 (d) O^{2-}

2. Which of the following exhibit geometrical isomerism?
 (a) 2-methylpropene
 (b) But-1-ene
 (c) But-2-ene
 (d) 2, 3-dibromo-but-2-ene

3. For the reaction, $x + 2y \longrightarrow z$
 5 moles of x and 9 moles of y will produce
 (a) 5 moles of z
 (b) 8 moles of z
 (c) 14 moles of z
 (d) 4.5 moles of z

4. Out of the following, which change will shift the reaction towards the product at equilibrium?
 $I_2(g) \rightleftharpoons 2I(g)$; $\Delta H^\circ(298\text{ K}) = 150\text{ kJ}$
 (a) Increase in total pressure.
 (b) Increase in temperature.
 (c) Decrease in concentration of I_2.
 (d) Increase in concentration of I.

5. The graph between $|\psi|^2$ (radial probability density) and r (radial distance) is shown below.
 This represents

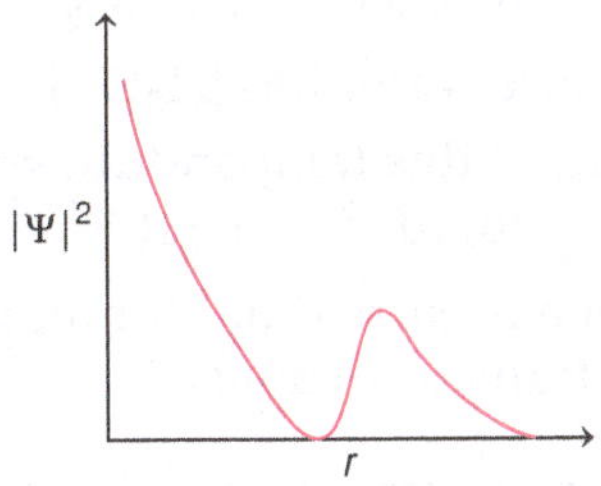

 (a) 3s orbital (b) 2p orbital
 (c) 2s orbital (d) 1s orbital

6. The IUPAC name for the compound,
 $$CH_3-\overset{\overset{\displaystyle O}{\|}}{C}-CH_2CH_2-\overset{\overset{\displaystyle O}{\|}}{C}-OH$$ is
 (a) 1-hydroxypentane-1, 4-dione
 (b) 1, 4-dioxypentanol
 (c) 1-carboxybutan-3-one
 (d) 4-oxopentanoic acid

7. When 1L of CO_2 is heated with graphite, the volume of the gases collected is 1.5 L. Calculate the number of moles of CO produced at STP.
 (a) $\frac{1}{11.2}$ moles (b) $\frac{28}{22.4}$ moles
 (c) $\frac{1}{22.4}$ moles (d) $\frac{14}{22.4}$ moles

8. The increasing order of the atomic radii of the following elements is
(A) C (B) O (C) F (D) Cl (E) Br
(a) (A) < (B) < (C) < (D) < (E)
(b) (C) < (B) < (A) < (D) < (E)
(c) (D) < (C) < (B) < (A) < (E)
(d) (B) < (C) < (D) < (A) < (E)

9. Match the following.

Column I	Column II
A. He	1. High electron affinity
B. Cl	2. Highest ionisation energy
C. Ca	3. Most electropositive element

Codes

	A	B	C		A	B	C
(a)	2	3	1	(b)	1	2	3
(c)	1	3	2	(d)	2	1	3

10. In which of the following, oxidation number of chlorine is +5?
(a) Cl^- (b) ClO^- (c) ClO_2^- (d) ClO_3^-

11. At 363K, pure water has $[H_3O^+] = 10^{-6}$ M. The value of K_w at this temperature will be
(a) 10^{-6} (b) 10^{-12} (c) 10^{-13} (d) 10^{-14}

12. A substance is carried out through the following transformations.

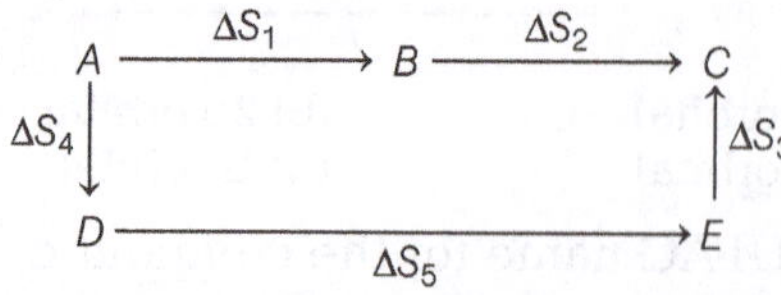

The equation $\Delta S_1 + \Delta S_2 = \Delta S_3 + \Delta S_4 + \Delta S_5$
(a) is true only if the steps are carried out reversibly.
(b) is always true because entropy is a state function.
(c) may be true but need more informations on the process.
(d) is incorrect.

Assertion-Reason

In the following questions (Q.No. 13-16), a statement of Assertion (A) followed by a statement of Reason (R) is given. Choose the correct answer out of the following choices.

(a) Both (A) and (R) are correct and (R) is the correct explanation of (A).
(b) Both (A) and (R) are correct but (R) is not the correct explanation of (A).
(c) (A) is correct and (R) is incorrect.
(d) (A) is incorrect and (R) is correct.

13. **Assertion** (A) Formal charges do not indicate real charge separation within the molecule.
Reason (R) Formal charges help in the selection of the lowest energy structure from a number of possible Lewis structures for a given species.

14. **Assertion** (A) Combustion of 16 g of methane gives 18 g of water.
Reason (R) In the combustion of methane, water is one of the product.

15. **Assertion** (A) The third period in the periodic table contains 18 electrons and not 8 like 2nd period.
Reason (R) In third period, filling of electron starts from $3s^1$ and complete at $3p^6$.

16. **Assertion** (A) Energy of resonance hybrid is equal to the average of energies of all canonical forms.
Reason (R) Resonance hybrid cannot be presented by a single structure.

Answers

1. (d) 2. (c) 3. (d) 4. (b) 5. (c) 6. (d) 7. (c) 8. (b) 9. (d) 10. (d) 11. (b) 12. (b) 13. (b) 14. (d) 15. (d) 16. (d)

Section-B

This section contains 5 questions with internal choice in one question. The following questions are short answer type and carry 2 marks each.

17. A system at equilibrium is described by the equation.

$$SO_2Cl_2 + Heat \rightleftharpoons SO_2 + Cl_2$$

Why does the temperature of the system increase when Cl_2 is added to the equilibrium mixture at constant volume?

18. (i) Draw the two geometrical isomers of but-2-en-1,4 dioic acid.

(ii) Which of the above isomers will have higher dipole moment ?

19. How will you convert benzene into

(i) *p*-nitrobromobenzene?

(ii) *m*-nitrochlorobenzene?

20. In the following redox reactions, identify oxidising agent and the reducing agent.

(i) $H_3PO_2(aq) + 2HgCl_2\ (aq) + 2H_2O(aq) \longrightarrow H_3PO_4(aq) + 2Hg(l) + 4HCl\ (aq)$

(ii) $O_2(g) + PtF_6\ (g) \longrightarrow O_2^+[Pt\ F_6]^-(s)$

Or

Calculate the oxidation number of the underlined element in

(i) $\underline{V}O_2^+$ (ii) $\underline{U}O_2^{2+}$

21. (i) Which properties of the elements depend on the electronic configuration of the atoms and which do not?

(ii) Write the number designation of a group that has 2 electrons beyond a noble gas configuration.

Section-C

This section contains 7 questions with internal choice in one question. The following questions are short answer type and carry 3 marks each.

22. The enthalpy of vaporisation of an organic compound at its boiling point (35.0°C) is 26.0 kJ mol^{-1}. Calculate standard enthalpy change for the conversion of

(i) liquid to vapour. [**Ans.** 84.4 $JK^{-1}\ mol^{-1}$]

(ii) vapour to liquid at 35°C. [**Ans.** –84.4 $JK^{-1}\ mol^{-1}$]

23. Answer the following.

(i) Write the structure of 3-ethyl-4-methylhept-5-en-2-one.

(ii) Draw the possible resonance structure for $CH_3\ddot{\underset{\cdot\cdot}{O}}\overset{+}{C}H_2$ and predict, which of the structure is more stable.

(iii) What type of structural isomerism is shown below?

$$CH_3 — S—CH_2—CH_2—CH_3$$

(*A*)

and $CH_3—S—CH(CH_3)_2$ (*B*)

Or

Give major product in the following reactions :

(i) $CH_3—C(CH_3)(CH_3OH)—CH(OH)—CH_3 \xrightarrow{Conc.\ H_2SO_4}$

(ii) $CH_3—CH_2—CH_2—CH_2—OH \xrightarrow{Conc.\ H_2SO_4}$

(iii) 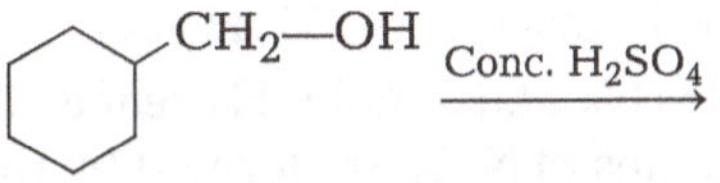

24. Answer the following questions.

(i) Among the molecules, NO^+, N_2, $SnCl_2$ and NO_2^-, identify the species which is isoelectronic with CO.

(ii) What type of atomic orbitals can overlap to form molecular orbitals?

(iii) On the basis of VSEPR theory, draw the structure of XeF_4 molecule.

25. The ionisation constant of propanoic acid is 1.32×10^{-5}. Calculate the degree of ionisation of the acid in its 0.05 M solution and also its pH.

[**Ans.** $\alpha = 1.63 \times 10^{-2}$, pH = 3.09]

26. (i) Why are electron gain enthalpies of Be and Mg positive?

(ii) Arrange the ions Li^{2+}, He^+ and Be^{3+} in the increasing order of their ionic radii.

(iii) Elements in the same group have equal valency.

27. Which of the following species have same shape/same bond order? N_3^-, NO_2^-, CO_2, O_3. Also, draw their structures.

28. What is meant by the term average bond enthalpy?

Why is there difference in bond enthalpy of O—H bond in ethanal and water?

Section-D

The following questions are case-based questions. Each question has an internal choice and carries 4(1+1+2) marks each. Read the passage carefully and answer the questions that follow.

29. The reactant which is present in lesser amount and gets consumed after sometime, i.e. which limits the amount of product formed is called limiting reagent.

The reactant other than the limiting reagent, which is in somewhat excess is called excess reagent. The remaining amount of excess reagent is calculated by subtracting the available amount of limiting reagent from the amount of the excess reagent taken initially. Remember that in stoichiometric reagent as it decides the amount of product obtained.

(i) Consider the following equation.

$$N_2(g)+3H_2(g) \longrightarrow 2NH_3(g)$$

If 2 moles N_2 and 3 moles H_2 reacts, then how many moles of NH_3 are formed by them?

(ii) In the reaction $2A+4B \longrightarrow 3C+4D$, when 5 moles of A reacts with 6 moles of B, then, which one is the limiting reagent?

Or

What would be the limiting reagent if 75 g $C_2H_3Br_3$ reacted with 50.0 g of O_2 in the reaction :

$$4C_2H_3Br_3+11O_2 \longrightarrow 8CO_2+6H_2O+6Br_2$$

(iii) Calculate the amount of $Ca(OH)_2$ formed when 56 g of CaO reacts with 10 g of H_2O.

30. The molecular orbitals obtained by the subtraction of atomic orbitals are called **antibonding molecular** orbitals (AMOs) and are represented by σ^* and π^*. In the formation of AMOs, the electron waves cancel each other due to destructive interference.

In these orbitals, most of the electron density is located away from the space in between the nuclei. Infact, they have a nodal plane (on which the electron density is zero) in between the nuclei and hence, the repulsion between the nuclei is high.

In contrast to the bonding molecular orbital, the electrons placed in these orbital destabilise the molecule because of more mutual repulsion of the electrons in this orbital as compared to the attraction between the electrons and the nuclei which causes a net increase in energy.

(i) Write the condition for the combination of atomic orbtials to form molecular orbitals.

(ii) Which of the following diatomic molecular species has only σ bonds according to MOT?

(a) C_2 (b) Be_2
(c) O_2 (d) N_2

Or

Which one of the following pairs of species have the same bond order?

(a) N_2, O_2^- (b) CO, NO
(c) O_2, NO^+ (d) CN^-, CO

(iii) Which of the following oxides is paramagnetic?

(a) H_2O (b) NO
(c) CO_2 (d) SO_2

Section-E

The following questions are long answer type and carry 5 marks each. All questions have an internal choice.

31. (i) Find energy of each of the photons which correspond to light of frequency 3×10^5 Hz.

(ii) Why did Heisenberg replace the concept of define orbits by the concept of probability?

(iii) Give an important application of de-Broglie concept.

Or

(i) An atomic orbital has $n=3$. What are the possible values of l and m_l?

(ii) Calculate the wavelength of the radiation which would cause photochemical dissociation of a chlorine molecule. The bond dissociation energy of Cl—Cl bond is 245 kJ/mol. **[Ans.** $\lambda = 4.89 \times 10^{-7}$ M]

(iii) Which of the following orbitals are possible?

$1p$, $2s$, $2p$ and $3f$

32. (i) Define entropy and free energy of a system.

(ii) Predict the feasibility of reaction when

(a) both ΔH and ΔS increase.

(b) both ΔS and ΔH decrease.

(c) ΔH decrease but ΔS increase.

Or (i) Show that the pressure volume work,

$$W = -p\Delta V.$$

(ii) What would be the work done on or by the system if the internal energy of the system falls by 100 J even when 200J of heat is supplied to it?

[Ans. = −300 J of work (by the system)]

(iii) State and explain the first law of thermodynamics. Derive its mathematical form.

33. (i) Discuss the structure of double bond.

(ii) What happens when ethyl alcohol is heated in the presence of H_2SO_4 at 443 K?

(iii) An unknown alkene *A* on reductive ozonolysis gives two isomeric carbonyl compounds *B* and *C* having molecular formula C_3H_6O, write the structure of *A*, *B* and *C*.

Or

(i) 7-bromo-1, 3, 5-cycloheptatriene exists as an ion whereas 5 –bromo –1, 3-cyclopentadiene does not form an ion in presence of Ag^+. Explain .

(ii) Explain the term polymerisation with two examples.

(iii) Explain the mechanism of electrophilic addition reactions of alkenes.

SAMPLE QUESTION PAPER 4

A Highly Simulated Sample Question Paper for CBSE Class XI Examination

CHEMISTRY [Unsolved]

Time : 3 Hours **Max. Marks : 70**

Note : *Refer to Instruction S.Q.P. 1*

Section-A

The following questions are multiple-choice questions with one correct answer. Each question carries 1 mark. There is no internal choice in this section.

1. **When zinc reacts with dilute nitric acid, nitrous oxide is produced. What mass of the gas is evolved by treating 325 g zinc with excess of nitric acid?**

(a) 44 g (b) 66 g (c) 55 g (d) 33 g

2. **Which of the following order is correct regarding electropositive character of alkaline earth metals?**

(a) Be < Mg > Ca < Sr < Ra

(b) Be > Mg > Ca > Sr > Ba

(c) Be < Mg < Ca < Sr < Ba

(d) None of the above

3. **Select the incorrect statement from the following.**

(a) A compound with delocalised electrons are more stable than the compound would be if all its electrons were localised.

(b) Six π-electrons delocalised in benzene are referred to the aromatic sextet.

(c) When a compound attains aromaticity, potential energy is decreased.

(d) The compound phenanthrene is a non-aromatic compound.

4. **Which of the molecule has trigonal bipyramidal geometry with bond angles 120° and 90°?**

(a) SF_6

(b) PCl_5

(c) CH_4

(d) BF_3

5. **Which value is closest to the wavelength (in nm) of a quantum of light with frequency of $6 \times 10^{15} s^{-1}$?**

(a) 10 (b) 25 (c) 50 (d) 75

6. **The compounds formed by the highly reactive non-metals with highly reactive metals and the non-metals are respectively**

(a) covalent and ionic

(b) ionic and covalent

(c) metallic and ionic

(d) metallic and covalent

7. **Isomeric pentanes have different value of boiling point. This is due to**

(a) no branching

(b) weak intermolecular force of attraction

(c) large area of contact

(d) None of the above

8. **Match the following columns.**

Column I	Column II
A. 2*s*-orbital	1. Two nodal planes
B. 2*p*-orbital	2. One radial node
C. $3d_{yz}$	3. Zero radial node

Codes

	A	B	C
(a)	2	1	3
(b)	2	3	1
(c)	1	3	2
(d)	3	2	1

9. Five moles of a gas is put through a series of changes as shown graphically in a cyclic process. The process during $A \rightarrow B$, $B \rightarrow C$ and $C \rightarrow A$ respectively are

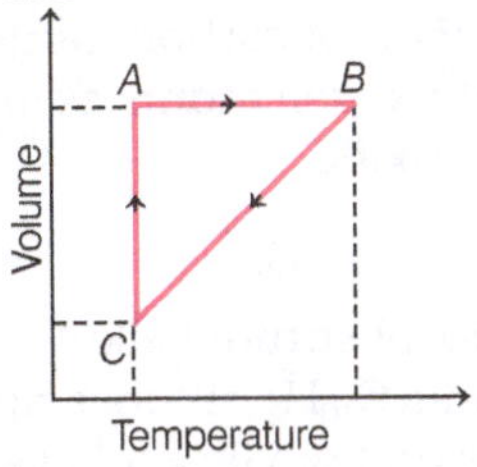

(a) isochoric, isobaric, isothermal
(b) isobaric, isochoric, isothermal
(c) isothermal, isobaric, isochoric
(d) isochoric, isothermal, isobaric

10. For the reaction, $H_2(g) + I_2(g) \rightleftharpoons 2HI(g)$, the standard free energy is $\Delta G° > 0$. The equilibrium constant (K) would be

(a) $k = 0$ (b) $k > 1$ (c) $k = 1$ (d) $k < 1$

11. A buffer solution is a solution whose pH value on keeping in the air

(a) increases rapidly
(b) decreases rapidly
(c) may increase or decrease
(d) does not change

12. Which of the following elements shown as pairs with their atomic numbers belong to the same period is correct?

(a) $Z = 19$ and $Z = 38$ (b) $Z = 12$ and $Z = 17$
(c) $Z = 11$ and $Z = 21$ (d) $Z = 16$ and $Z = 33$

Assertion-Reason

In the following questions (Q.No. 13-16), a statement of Assertion followed by a statement of Reason is given. Choose the correct answer out of the following choices.

(a) Both (A) and (R) are correct and (R) is the correct explanation of (A).
(b) Both (A) and (R) are correct but (R) is not the correct explanation of (A).
(c) (A) is correct and (R) is incorrect.
(d) (A) is incorrect and (R) is correct.

13. **Assertion** (A) In the reaction between potassium permanganate and potassium iodide, permanganate ions act as oxidising agent.
Reason (R) Oxidation state of manganese changes from +2 to +7 during the reaction.

14. **Assertion** (A) A mixture of the solution of a weak acid and its sodium salt acts as a good buffer.
Reason (R) The ratio of the salt to the acid in the mixture does not change substantially when small amount of acid and base is added to the buffer.

15. **Assertion** (A) For a given principal quantum number, *s, p, d, f* ...., subshells, all have different energies.
Reason (R) Mutual repulsion exists among the electrons in a multielectron atoms.

16. **Assertion** (A) The variables like p, V, T are called state functions.
Reason (R) Their values depend only on the state of the system.

Answers

1\. (c) 2. (c) 3. (d) 4. (b) 5. (c) 6. (b) 7. (c) 8. (b)
9\. (a) 10. (d) 11. (d) 12. (b) 13. (c) 14. (a) 15. (b) 16. (a)

Section-B

This section contains 5 questions with internal choice in one question. The following questions are short answer type and carry 2 marks each.

17. The ejection of the photoelectron from the silver metal in the photoelectric effect experiment can be stopped by applying the voltage of 0.35 V when the radiation of 256.7 nm is used. Calculate the work function for silver metal. [Ans. 4.48 eV]

18. (i) What is the value of change in entropy at equilibrium?
(ii) Which quantity out of $\Delta_r G$ or $\Delta_r G°$ will be zero at equilibrium?

19. (i) Why does the dissociation of PCl_5 decrease in the presence of Cl_2?
(ii) Explain the effect of temperature on the endothermic reaction

$$N_2(g) + O_2(g) \rightleftharpoons 2NO(g)$$

20. (i) Why are molecular reactions slow?
(ii) Why is the covalent bond considered as directional?

21. What happens when
(i) hexene is treated with HBr in the presence of peroxide.
(ii) ethyl bromide is heated with alcoholic KOH?

Or Complete the following.
(i) $CH_3—CH_2—CH_2Cl + Alc.KOH \xrightarrow{Heat}$
(ii) $CH_3CH_2OH + Conc.\ H_2SO_4 \xrightarrow{170°C}$

Section-C

This section contains 7 questions with internal choice in one question. The following questions are short answer type and carry 3 marks each.

22. (i) Arrange the following elements in the order of their chemical reactivity in terms of decreasing oxidising property.

F, Cl, O, N

(ii) Arrange the following species in decreasing order of size.

I^-, I^+, I

(iii) Name two species that can have the following electronic configuration.

$1s^2 2s^2 2p^6 3s^2 3p^6 3d^5 4s^1$

23. Give the appropriate reason :

(i) It is preferable to determine the change in enthalpy rather than the change in internal energy.

(ii) It is necessary to define the 'standard state'.

(iii) It is necessary to specify the phase of the reactants and products in a thermochemical equation.

24. (i) On the basis of VSEPR theory, explain the shape of ClF_5.

(ii) Write the formal of sulphuric acid and calculate the formal charge on each oxygen atom.

(iii) Explain, whether BH_4^- and H_3O^+ will have same or different shape.

25. Calculate the weight of carbon monoxide having same number of oxygen atoms as are present in 88 g of carbon dioxide. [**Ans.** 112 g]

Or

Amit has a monosubstituted alkyl benzene with molecular formula $C_{10}H_{14}$. It does not undergo oxidation to any carboxylic acid even under a very drastic condition.

(i) Name the compound that Amit has.

(ii) Write the structures of its monosubstituted isomers.

26. An equilibrium mixture at 300 K contains N_2O_4 and NO_2 at 0.28 and 1.1 atm respectively. If the volume of the container is doubled, calculate the new equilibrium pressures of the two gases.

[**Ans.** $p_{N_2O_4}(aq) = 0.095$ atm, $p_{NO_2}(aq) = 0.64$ atm]

27. A proton is accelerated to one-tenth of the velocity of light. If its velocity can be measured with a precision of ±1%, what must be its uncertainty in position? [**Ans.** 1.05×10^{-13} m]

28. (i) What are the possible structures for a carboxylic acid with a molecular formula $C_4H_8O_2$ and label each C atom as sp^1, sp^2 and sp^3.

(ii) How many σ-bonds and π-bonds are present in the second member of the alkene series?

Section-D

The following questions are case-based questions. Each question has an internal choice and carries 4 (2 + 1 + 1) marks each. Read the passage carefully and answer the questions that follow.

29. When an electron is added to a gaseous atom in its ground state to convert it into a negative ions, the enthalpy change accompanying the process is called the electron gain enthalpy ($\Delta_{eg}H$). It is a direct measure of the ease with which an atom attracts an electron to form anion.

$$X(g) + e^- \longrightarrow X^-(g); \Delta H = \Delta_{eg} H$$

The most stable state of an atom is the ground state. If an isolated gaseous atom is in excited state, comparatively lesser energy will be released on adding an electron. So, electron gain enthalpies of gaseous atoms must be determined in their ground states. Therefore, the terms ground state and isolated gaseous atom has been also included in the definition of electron gain enthalpy is measure either, in electron volts per atom or kJ per mole.

Units The values of electron gain enthalpy are expressed either in electron volt per atom or kilo joules per mole of atoms, e.g. electron affinity of chlorine is -348 kJ mol^{-1}.

(i) Arrange the following elements in order of decreasing electron gain enthalpy.

(a) B, C, N, O (b) F, Cl, Br, I

(ii) Why do noble gases have positive electron gain enthalpy?

Or Why is the electron gain enthalpy of O or F is less than that of S or Cl?

(iii) Write one difference between electron gain enthalpy and electronegativity.

30. The concept of electron transfer is found unable to explain the redox changes or electron shift in case of covalent compounds. To explain these changes a new concept, called oxidation number is introduced. Oxidation number is defined as the charge that an atom of the element has in its ion or appear to have when present in the combined state with other atoms.

In other words, it is also defined as the charge that an atom appear to have in a compound when all other atoms are removed as ions from the compound.

(i) Using electron transfer concept, identify the oxidant and reductant in the redox reactions.

(a) $Zn(s) + 2H^+(aq) \longrightarrow Zn^{2+}(aq) + H_2(g)$

(b) $BrO_3^-(aq) + F_2(g) + 2OH^-(aq) \longrightarrow BrO_4^-(aq) + 2F^-(aq) + H_2O(l)$

(ii) Determine the oxidation number of underlined element in $K[Co(C_2O_4)_2(NH_3)_2]$. **[Ans.** (b)]

(a) 2 (b) 3 (c) −2 (d) −3

Or

State the element which never has positive oxidation number in any of its compound. **[Ans.** (a)]

(a) F (b) Cl

(c) Br (d) I

(iii) If three electron are lost by a metal ion Mn^{3+}, then calculate the final oxidation state of metal.

(a) + 2 (b) +3

(c) +4 (d) +6

Section-E

The following questions are long answer type and carry 5 marks each. All questions have an internal choice.

31. (i) Draw all position isomers of an alcohol with molecular formula C_3H_8O?

(ii) What are free radicals? What is the order of stability of the free radicals?

(iii) Indicate the number of σ and π-bonds in $HCONHCH_3$.

Or

(i) Arrange the following in the order of increasing stability.

(a) $HC{\equiv}C^-, CH_2{=}CH^-, CH_3CH_2^-, CH_3^-, (CH_3)_2CH^-, C_6H_5CH_2^-$

(b) $C_6H_5\overset{+}{C}HCH_3, C_6H_5\overset{+}{C}HCH{=}CH_2, C_6H_5CH_2\overset{+}{C}H_2, C_6H_5\overset{+}{C}(CH_3)_2$

(ii) Discuss the qualitative analysis for halogens.

32. (i) 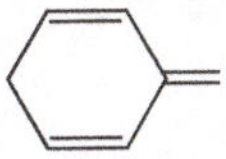 $=CH_2$ is not aromatic. Explain.

(ii) How will you distinguish between but-1-ene and butane?

(iii) Write chemical equation for combustion reaction of the hydrocarbon pentene.

Or (i) Arrange HCl, HBr, HI and HF in order of decreasing reactivity towards alkene.

(ii) Arrange the alkenes 2-methylbut-1-ene (I), 2-methylbut-2-ene (II) and 3-methyl (III) but-1-ene in order of decreasing reactivity towards bromine.

(iii) Give a chemical test to distinguish between ethane and ethyne.

33. A compound on analysis gave the following percentage composition Na = 14.31%, S = 9.97%, H = 6.22% and O = 69.50%. Find the molecular formula of the compound assuming that all the hydrogen in the compound is present in combination with oxygen as water of crystallisation. The molecular mass of the compound is 322. **[Ans.** $Na_2SH_{20}O_{14}$]

Or

(i) (a) Calculate the number of gram of oxygen in 0.10 mole of $Na_2CO_3 \cdot 10H_2O$ **[Ans** 20.8 g]

(b) What volume of 0.34 M KOH is sufficient to react with 20 mL of 0.15 M H_2SO_4 solution? **[Ans.** 17.65 mL]

(ii)(a) What do you mean by mole fraction?

(b) Calculate the mass of a molecule of CO_2? **[Ans.** 7.304×10^{-23} g]

(c) What do you understand by stoichiometric coefficients in a chemical equation?

SAMPLE QUESTION PAPER 5

A Highly Simulated Sample Question Paper for CBSE Class XI Examination

CHEMISTRY [Unsolved]

Time : 3 Hours **Max. Marks : 70**

Note : *Refer to Instruction S.Q.P. 1*

Section-A

The following questions are multiple-choice questions with one correct answer. Each question carries 1 mark. There is no internal choice in this section.

1. A solution is prepared by adding 2g of a substance *A* to 18g of water. Calculate the mass percent of the solute.
(a) 8% (b) 9% (c) 10% (d) 11%

2. A ray of white light is spread out into a series of coloured bands of visible light called
(a) visible band
(b) spectrum
(c) electronic spectrum
(d) None of the above

3. The IUPAC name of the element which is placed in 7th period with 112 atomic number in periodic table is
(a) ununbium
(b) unnilquadium
(c) unnilbium
(d) ununillium

4. The correct way of representing 2-bromobutane is/are
(a) $CH_3CHBrCH_2CH_3$
(b) 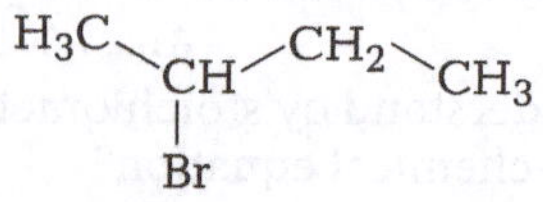
(c) 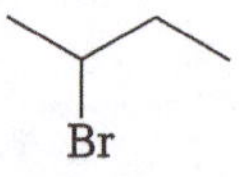
(d) All of the above

5. Which of the following process takes place in oxidation?
(a) Addition of oxygen (b) Addition of hydrogen
(c) Removal of oxygen (d) Removal of chlorine

6. The empirical formula of a compound is CH_2. One mole of this compound has a mass of 42g. Its molecular formula is
(a) C_3H_6 (b) C_3H_8
(b) CH_2 (d) C_2H_2

7. Match the type of the series given in Column I with the wavelength range given in Column II and choose the correct option.

Column I	Column II
A. Lyman	1. Ultraviolet
B. Paschen	2. Near infrared
C. Balmer	3. Visible

Codes

	A	B	C
(a)	1	2	3
(b)	2	3	1
(c)	3	1	2
(d)	1	3	2

8. For the reaction

$$H_2(g) + I_2(g) \rightleftharpoons 2HI(g), \Delta G° < 0$$

then, *K* would be
(a) $K > 1$ (b) $K < 1$
(c) $K = 1$ (d) $K \leq 1$

9. Which of the following radii reflect an increase in size of an atom?

(a) van der Waals' radius
(b) Metallic radius
(c) Covalent (non-metallic) radius
(d) Both (b) and (c)

10. Which graph shows how the energy E of a photon of light is related to its wavelength(λ)?

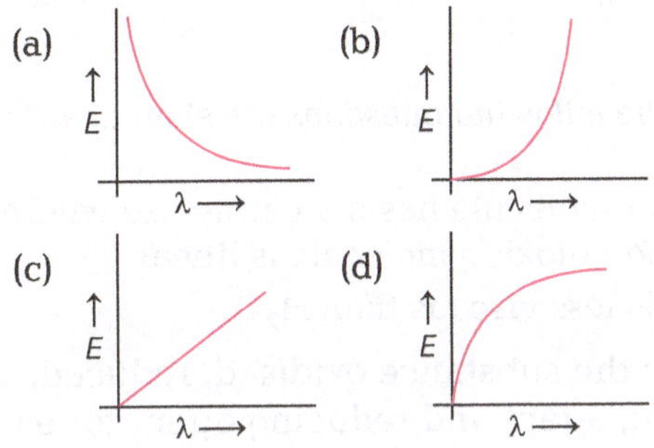

11. $A + B \rightleftharpoons C + D$. If the concentration of A and B are equal at equilibrium and concentration of D will be twice that of A, then what will be the equilibrium constant of the reaction?

(a) 4 (b) 6 (c) $\frac{4}{5}$ (d) $\frac{6}{7}$

12. Which of the following orders of ionic radius is correctly represented?

(a) $H^- > H > H^+$ (b) $Na^+ > F^- > O^{2-}$
(b) $F^- > O^{2-} > Na^+$ (d) $Al^{3+} > Mg^{2+} > N^{3-}$

Assertion-Reason

In the following questions (Q.No. 13-16), a statement of Assertion (A) followed by a statement of Reason (R) is given. Choose the correct answer out of the following choices.

(a) Both (A) and (R) are correct and (R) is the correct explanation of (A).
(b) Both (A) and (R) are correct but (R) is not the correct explanation of (A).
(c) (A) is correct and (R) is incorrect.
(d) (A) is incorrect and (R) is correct.

13. Assertion (A) The atomic and ionic radii generally decreases toward right in a period.

Reason (R) The ionisation enthalpy increases on moving towards left in a period.

14. Assertion (A) The empirical mass of ethene is half of its molecular mass.

Reason (R) The empirical formula represent the simplest whole number ratio of various atoms present in a compound.

15. Assertion (A) In $H_2C{=}CH_2$ molecule, the rotation about carbon-carbon double bond ($C{=}C$) is restricted.

Reason (R) Rotation of one CH_2 fragment with respect to other interferes with maximum overlap of p-orbitals.

16. Assertion (A) NO^+ and CN^- both have same bond order and magnetism.

Reason (R) NO^+ and CN^- are isoelectronic species.

Answers

1. (c) **2.** (b) **3.** (a) **4.** (d) **5.** (a) **6.** (a)
7. (a) **8.** (a) **9.** (a) **10.** (a) **11.** (a) **12.** (a)
13. (c) **14.** (a) **15.** (a) **16.** (a)

Section-B

This section contains 5 questions with internal choice in one question. The following questions are short answer type and carry 2 marks each.

17. (i) How many elements can be accommodated in the present set up of the long form of the periodic table?
(ii) How metals and non-metals differs in their electronic configuration?

18. Nitric acid acts only as an oxidising agent while nitrous acid acts both as an oxidising agent as well as reducing agent. Explain.

19. Give the structure of each of the following compounds.
(i) 2,3-dibromo-3-ethylheptane
(ii) 1-bromo-2-iodocyclobutane

20. Write the reaction for the preparation of butane by
(i) Wurtz reaction
(ii) Kolbe's reaction

21. (i) State and explain the law of chemical equilibrium.

(ii) The equilibrium constant of the reaction.
$A_2(g) + B_2(g) \rightleftharpoons 2AB(g)$ at 100°C is 50. If a one litre flask containing one mole of A_2 is connected to a two-litre flask containing two moles of B_2, how many moles of AB will be formed at 373 K? **[Ans.** 1.86 mol]

Or Using Le-Chatelier's principle, predict the effect of

(i) decreasing the temperature and

(ii) increasing the pressure on each of the following equilibria.

(a) $H_2O(g) + \text{Heat} \rightleftharpoons H_2(g) + \frac{1}{2}O_2(g)$

(b) $2CO(g) + O_2(g) \rightleftharpoons 2CO_2(g) + \text{Heat}$

Section-C

This section contains 7 questions with internal choice in one question. The following questions are short answer type and carry 3 marks each.

22. (i) Electron gain enthalpy value of inert gases are zero. Give reasons.

(ii) Arrange the following in increasing order of first ionisation potential.
Na, Al, Mg and Si

(iii) Among the following oxides, which is most acidic. MgO, Al_2O_3, P_2O_5 and SiO_2

23. 250 mL of 0.5 M sodium sulphate (Na_2SO_4) solution are added to an aqueous solution containing 10.0 g of $BaCl_2$ resulting in the formation of white precipitate of $BaSO_4$. How many moles and how many grams of Barium sulphate will be obtained ? **[Ans.** 0.048 mol and 11.18 g]

24. Give the appropriate reason.

(i) It is preferable to determine the change in enthalpy rather than the change in internal energy.

(ii) It is necessary to define the standard state.

(iii) It is necessary to specify the phase of the reactants and products in a thermochemical equation.

25. An organic compound *A* of molecular formula C_6H_{12} absorbs one mole of bromine to give *B*. On reduction, it gives '*C*', while on oxidation yields a mixture of '*D*' and '*E*'. Deduce the structures of *A*, *B*, *C*. Also, give the relevant chemical equations.

26. Give reason for the following.

(i) Covalent bonds are directional bond while ionic bonds are non-directional.

(ii) Water molecule has bent structure whereas carbon dioxide molecule is linear.

(iii) HF is less viscous than H_2O.

27. Identify the substance oxidised, reduced, oxidising agent and reducing agent for each of the following reactions.

(i) $2AgBr(s) + C_6H_6O_2(aq) \longrightarrow 2Ag(s) + 2HBr(aq) + C_6H_4O_2(aq)$

(ii) $HCHO(l) + 2[Ag(NH_3)_2]^+(aq) + 3OH^-(aq) \longrightarrow 2Ag(s) + HCOO^-(aq) + 4NH_3(aq) + 2H_2O(l)$

(iii) $HCHO(l) + 2Cu^{2+}(aq) + 5OH^-(aq) \longrightarrow Cu_2O(s) + HCOO^-(aq) + 3H_2O(l)$

28. In an atom, an electron is moving with a speed of 600 m/s with an accuracy of 0.005%. Find the certainty with which the position of electron can be located.
$[h = 6.6 \times 10^{-34}\ \text{kg m}^2\text{s}^{-1},\ m_e = 9.1 \times 10^{-31}\ \text{kg}]$
[Ans. 1.92×10^{-3} m]

Or

Calculate

(i) the wavelength of radiation when $\nu = 1568$ kHz **[Ans.** 191.3 m]

(ii) the wave number of radiation when $\lambda = 230$ nm **[Ans.** $4.34 \times 10^6\ \text{m}^{-1}$]

(iii) the frequency of radiation when $\lambda = 500$ nm **[Ans.** $6 \times 10^{14}\ \text{s}^{-1}$]

Section-D

The following questions are case-based questions. Each question has an internal choice and carries 4 (2 + 1 + 1) marks each. Read the passage carefully and answer the questions that follow.

29. On passing electric discharge through gaseous hydrogen, the H_2 molecules get dissociated to produce energetically excited hydrogen atoms that emit electromagnetic radiation of discrete frequencies.

The hydrogen spectrum consists of several series of lines named after their discovers on the basis of experiments.

The Swedish spectroscopist, Johannes Rydberg, told that all series of lines in the hydrogen spectrum could be described by the following expression.

$$\bar{v} = 109{,}677\left(\frac{1}{n_1^2} - \frac{1}{n_2^2}\right)\text{cm}^{-1}$$

(i) An electron in excited hydrogen atom falls from fifth energy level to second energy level. In which region, the spectrum line will be observed and is part of which series of the atomic spectrum.

(ii) Which spectral series in hydrogen atomic spectrum appears in the visible region?

(a) Lyman series
(b) Balmer series
(c) Paschen series
(d) Brackett series [Ans. (b)]

Or

What is the maximum number of emission lines are obtained when the excited electron of a H atom in $n = 5$ drops to the ground state?

(a) 10 (b) 5
(c) 12 (d) 15 [Ans. (a)]

(iii) The maximum number of lines when an excited electron drops from $n = 6$ to the ground state in case of a H-atom.

(a) 14 (b) 15
(c) 16 (d) 12 [Ans. (b)]

30. The concentration of a substance in a saturated solution is defined as its solubility (S). Its value depends upon the nature of solvent and the temperature.

Consider saturated solution of sparingly soluble electrolyte, AB.

$$\underset{\text{Solid}}{AB} \rightleftharpoons \underset{\substack{\text{Unionised}\\\text{molecules}}}{AB} \rightleftharpoons \underbrace{A^+ + B^-}_{\text{Ions}}$$

Applying the law of mass action, $K = \dfrac{[A^+][B^-]}{[AB]}$.

Since, the solution is saturated, the concentration of unionised molecules of the electrolyte will be constant at a particular temperature, i.e. $[AB] = \text{constant} = K'$ (say).

Hence, $[A^+][B^-] = KK' = K_{sp}$ (constant)

This new constant K_{sp} is called solubility product and is defined as the product of the concentration of ions in a saturated solution of an electrolyte at a given temperature.

(i) Write some example of sparingly soluble salts.

(ii) Write the factor on which solubility product depends.

(iii) What happens when ionic product is more than solubility product?

Or

What is the solubility product of $[Zr_3(PO_4)_4]$?

Section-E

The following questions are long answer type and carry 5 marks each. All questions have an internal choice.

31. (i) PCl_5 is trigonal bipyramidal, whereas IF_5 is square pyramidal. Why?

(ii) Water molecule has bent structure whereas carbon dioxide molecule is linear. Explain.

(iii) Draw the Lewis dot structure of O_2^{2-}.

Or

(i) What are the main postulates of valence shell electron pair repulsion (VSEPR) theory?

(ii) Arrange the following species in order of increasing stability.

Li_2, Li_2^+ and Li_2^-.

Explain your answer with the help of molecular orbital theory.

32. (i) What alkanes would be expected from the reaction of sodium with 50:50 mixture of 1-chloropropane and α-chloropropane?

(ii) Write the structure for the compounds having the IUPAC name.

(a) 2-ethyl-2-methylpentane

(b) 2,3,5-trimethylhexane

(iii) Why propane has only one eclipsed conformation while butane has three? Explain.

Or (i) Arrange HCl, HBr, HI and HF in order of decreasing reactivity towards alkene.

(ii) Arrange the alkenes 2-methyl but-1-ene (I), 2-methyl but-2-ene (II) and 3-methyl but-1-ene (III) in order of decreasing reactivity towards bromine.

(iii) Give a chemical test to distinguish between ethane and ethyne.

33. Sodium carbonate, Na_2CO_3 can be obtained by heating sodium hydrogen carbonate, $NaHCO_3$ as

$$2NaHCO_3(s) \rightarrow Na_2CO_3(s) + H_2O(g) + CO_2(g)$$

The essential data are

	$NaHCO_3(s)$	$Na_2CO_3(s)$	$CO_2(g)$	$H_2O(g)$
$\Delta_f H^\circ$ (kJ mol^{-1})	−947.7	−1130.9	−393.51	−241.82
S_m° (J mol^{-1})	102.1	136	188.83	213.74

Calculate the temperature above which $NaHCO_3$ decomposes to give products at 1 bar. **[Ans.** 386.3 K]

Or (i) Explain the state of the chemical reaction when (a) $\Delta G > 0$ (b) $\Delta G < 0$

(ii) The standard Gibbs energy change for the reaction

$N_2(g) + 3H_2(g) \rightleftharpoons 2NH_3(g)$ is -33.2 kJ mol^{-1} at 298 K.

(a) Calculate the equilibrium constant for the above reaction. **[Ans.** 6.6×10^5]

(b) What would be the equilibrium constant if the reaction is written as

$$\frac{1}{2}N_2(g) + \frac{3}{2}H_2(g) \rightleftharpoons NH_3(g)$$

[Ans. 8.1×10^2]

(c) What will be the equilibrium constant if the reaction is

$$NH_3(g) \rightleftharpoons \frac{1}{2}N_2(g) + \frac{3}{2}H_2(g)$$

[Ans. 1.23×10^{-3}]